Systems Management Server 1.2

Updates coverage of SMS from version 1.1 to 1.2.

 Microsoft Management Console

Gives you a first look at MMC, the framework for Windows NT 5.0 Server and Workstation management.

 Distributed Component Object Model

Gets you up to speed with DCOM, the DCOM ((Dcomcnfg.exe), and installing DCOM on Win

 Enterprise Edition Features

Prepares you take advantage of the enterprise-scale networking services offered by Microsoft Cluster Server (MSCS), Microsoft Transaction Server (MTS), and Microsoft Message Queue Server (MSMQ).

 Routing and Remote Access Service

Shows you how to set up on-demand, dial-up routing and enhance your server's RAS capabilities with Microsoft's free Routing and RAS add-in.

 Distributed File System

Delivers step-by-step instructions for creating location-independent Dfs hierarchical shares from existing shares on multiple servers.

 Active Directory Service interfaces

Brings you up-to-date on Microsoft's Windows NT 5.0 directory service architecture, ADSI, which you can use with version 4.0.

 Zero-Administration Windows

Gives you a preview of the ZAW initiative, the Zero-Administration Kit (ZAK), and the Microsoft/Intel NetPC, all which are designed to reduce your network management costs.

Using
Windows NT®
Server 4

Special Edition Using

Second Edition

que®

Special Edition Using

Using Windows NT® Server 4

Second Edition

Written by Roger Jennings with

Donald B. Benage, Steve Crandall, Kate Gregory, Darren Mar-Elia, Kevin Nikkhoo, Michael Regelski, J. Brad Rhoades, Alan Simkins, Robert Bruce Thompson, Paul Thomsen, Stephen Wynkoop

Special Edition Using Windows NT Server 4, Second Edition

Contents at a Glance

I | **Networking with Windows NT Server 4.0**

1 Placing Windows NT Server in Perspective 19
2 Planning Your Windows NT Network Installation 55
3 Understanding the Windows NT Operating System 83
4 Choosing Network Protocols 101
5 Purchasing Networking Hardware 123

II | **Deploying Windows NT Server 4.0**

6 Making the Initial Server Installation 173
7 Setting Up Redundant Arrays of Inexpensive Disks (RAID) 215
8 Installing File Backup Systems 257
9 Understanding the Windows NT Registry 291
10 Using TCP/IP, WINS, and DHCP 321
11 Configuring Windows 95 Clients for Networking 351
12 Connecting Other PC Clients to the Network 399

III | **Administering a Secure Network**

13 Managing User and Group Accounts 441
14 Sharing and Securing Network Resources 483
15 Optimizing Network Server Performance 529
16 Troubleshooting Network Problems 559

IV | **Wide Area Networking and the Internet**

17 Distributing Network Services with Domains 605
18 Integrating Windows NT with NetWare and UNIX 635
19 Managing Remote Access Service 687
20 Setting Up Internet Information Server 4.0 723
21 Administering Intranet and World Wide Web Sites 765

V | **Windows NT Server and Microsoft BackOffice**

22 Taking Advantage of BackOffice Integration 811
23 Running Microsoft SQL Server 6.5 833
24 Messaging with Microsoft Exchange Server 5.0 871
25 Administering Clients with Systems Management Server 1.2 929

VI | **The Trail to Windows NT 5.0**

26 Scaling Windows NT Server 4.0 to the Enterprise   967
27 Distributing File and Directory Services   987

Windows NT Glossary   1003

Index   1031

Table of Contents

Introduction   1

Networking with Windows NT Server 4.0   3

Windows NT Server 4.0, the Internet, and Intranets   4

The Future of Windows NT   5

Who Should Read This Book?   6

How this Book Is Organized   7

How this Book Is Designed   10

Typographic Conventions Used in this Book   11

Bibliography   12

I | Networking with Windows NT Server 4.0

1 Placing Windows NT Server in Perspective   19

Exploring What's New in Windows NT Server 4.0   20
  Server Usability   21
  Client-Side Features   25
  Network Performance and Scalability Features   27
  TCP/IP and NetWare Integration Features   29
  Troubleshooting Tools   31
  Internet, Intranet, and Remote Access Service   36
  Distributed Component Object Model (DCOM)   39
  Telephony API (TAPI) 2.x   41

Using the Windows NT 4.0 Resource Kits   42

Embracing and Extending the Internet   43
  Intranetworking and Internet Information Server   44
  Managing Internet Information Server   46
  Upgrading to Site Server 2.0   47

Scaling Up to Windows NT Server 4.0 Enterprise Edition   49

Coming Attractions in Windows NT 5.0   51

From Here...   53

2 Planning Your Windows NT Network Installation   55

Developing the Network Implementation Plan   56
  Meeting Business Objectives   56
  Determining User and Workgroup Needs   57
  Establishing Security   59
  Determining Fault-Tolerance Requirements   63
  Incorporating Existing Infrastructure   66
  Connecting to the Outside World   68
  Developing an Implementation Schedule   69
  Considering Network Management Needs   69
  Providing for Future Growth   71
  Working Within a Budget   72
  Training Users   74

Managing the Project   74
  Using Project-Management Software to Manage Resources
  and Schedules   75
  Getting Outside Help   77

Balancing Resources and Requirements   79
  Establishing a Minimum Configuration   79
  Allocating Remaining Funds   79

Dealing with Vendors   80

From Here…   81

3 Understanding the Windows NT Operating System   83

Summarizing Windows NT Operating System Features   84
  The Windows NT Executive   86
  Clients and Protected Subsystem Servers   89

Handling Files with NTFS   90
  Understanding the Master File Table   92
  Implementing Recoverability with Transactions   94

Calling Remote Procedures   96

Networking with Windows NT   98

From Here…   99

4 Choosing Network Protocols   101

    Understanding the OSI Seven-Layer Model   102
        The Physical Layer   102
        The Data-Link Layer   103
        The Network Layer   103
        The Transport Layer   104
        The Session Layer   104
        The Presentation Layer   104
        The Application Layer   105
        Comparing Windows NT and OSI Network Layers   105

    Networking with Windows NT's Protocols   106
        NetBEUI and NetBEUI Frame   107
        TCP/IP   108
        NWLink (IPX/SPX)   111
        Data Link Control (DLC)   111
        AppleTalk   112
        Remote Access Service (RAS)   112
        Streams   113

    Supporting a Variety of PC Clients   113
        Windows NT Workstations   114
        Windows 95   114
        Windows for Workgroups 3.1x   115
        Windows 3.1   115
        DOS-Only PCs   115
        OS/2 Clients   116
        Apple Macintosh Computers   116
        UNIX Workstations   116

    Supporting Multiple Servers   116
        Other Windows NT Servers   117
        Novell NetWare Servers   117
        UNIX Servers   117
        Local Intranet Servers   117
        The Internet   118
        Mainframes   118

    Planning for Network Interoperability   118

    Making the Final Protocol Choice   120

    From Here...   121

5 Purchasing Networking Hardware   123

Selecting a Media-Access Method   124
   ARCnet   124
   Token Ring   124
   Ethernet   126
   High-Speed Ethernet Variants   128
   Other High-Speed Media-Access Methods   130
   Media-Access Recommendations   131

Designing a Network Cabling System   132
   Network Topologies   133
   Cable Types   135
   Structured Cabling Systems   139
   Cabling System Recommendations   140
   Expandability and Ease of Maintenance Recommendations   141

Selecting Active Network Components   141
   Network Interface Cards   141
   Repeaters   144
   Simple Hubs   145
   Bridges   147
   Routers   148
   Routing vs. Bridging   149
   Gateways   149
   Enterprise Hubs, Collapsed Backbones, Ethernet Switches, and Virtual LANs   150
   Recommendation Summary for Active Network Components   154

Specifying Server Hardware   155
   General Server Types   155
   Conformance to the Microsoft Windows NT Hardware Compatibility List   156
   Warranties, Maintainability, and Local Service   157
   Choosing the Server Components   157

From Here...   169

II | Deploying Windows NT Server 4.0

6 Making the Initial Server Installation 173

Gathering Information and Making Decisions 174

Preparing to Upgrade from Another Version of Windows 174

Knowing Your Hardware 175

Providing Names and Identification 180

Choosing to Install as a Domain Controller 181

Backing Up Data on an Existing Computer 181

Starting the Basic Installation 182

Running the Setup Program 183

Choosing to Install or Repair 186

Detecting Mass Storage 186

Choosing to Upgrade or Install from Scratch 187

Confirming Basic System Information 187

Setting Up Your Fixed-Disk Drives 188

Watching the Copying Process 189

Identifying the User, Company Name, Licensing Terms, and Computer Name 190

Choosing the Type of Domain Controller 191

Setting the Administrator Password 191

Dealing with the Pentium Floating-Point Division Bug 191

Specifying Creation of an Emergency Repair Disk 191

Fine-Tuning the Installation 192

Joining the Network 192

Finishing Server Setup 198

Creating the Emergency Repair Disk 200

Restarting the Server for the Last Time 201

Creating Software RAID Subsystems 201

Backing Up the Master Boot Record and Partition Boot Sector 201

Saving Fixed-Disk Configuration Data 205

Preparing the Server for Use 206

Installing Service Packs 206

Repairing the Windows NT Server Operating System Installation 209

Recovering from Fixed-Disk Failures   210
    System Drive Boot Failure   211
    Multiple Drive Partition Table Corruption   212
    RAID Subsystem, Volume Set, and Stripe Set Recovery   212
Automating Workstation and Server Installation   212
From Here...   213

7 Setting Up Redundant Arrays of Inexpensive Disks (RAID)   215

Understanding RAID Levels   216
    The RAID Advisory Board   217
    RAID 0   217
    RAID 1   220
    RAID 2   222
    RAID 3   223
    RAID 4   224
    RAID 5   225
    Stacked RAID   227
    Array Sizing   228
Specifying a RAID Implementation   229
    Picking the Best RAID Level for Your Needs   229
    Understanding RAID Product Features   230
    Implementing RAID in Hardware   233
Understanding Windows NT Server 4.0
Software RAID   236
    Windows NT Server RAID Options   237
    Configuration Considerations: Volume Sets,
    Extensibility, and Booting   238
Creating Windows NT Server Stripe and Mirror Sets   239
    Creating RAID 0 Stripe Sets   239
    Creating Drive Configuration and Emergency Repair Disks   242
    Creating RAID 1 Mirror Sets   244
    Creating RAID 5 Stripe Sets with Parity   248
    Saving the Master Boot Record and Partition Table   251
Recovering a Software RAID 1 or RAID 5 Set   251
    Restoring a Mirror Set   252
    Restoring a Stripe Set with Parity   252
Summarizing RAID Recommendations   253

Failure Resistant Disk System Criteria   254

Failure Resistant Disk System Plus Criteria   254

Failure Tolerant Disk System Criteria   254

Disaster Tolerant Disk System Criteria   255

From Here...   255

8   Installing File Backup Systems   257

Understanding Backup Types   258

The Archive Bit   258

Normal Backups   259

Copy Backups   260

Incremental Backups   260

Differential Backups   261

Daily Copy Backups   262

Backup Type Selection   262

Developing a Backup Strategy   264

Organizing Disk Storage   264

Ensuring Backup Integrity   265

Backing Up Open Files   266

Matching Backup Media Capacity to Disk Size   267

Organizing Rotation Methods   267

Using Hierarchical Storage Management (HSM)   272

Considering Enterprise Backup Solutions   273

Storing Data Off Site   273

Developing a Restore Plan   274

Choosing Backup Hardware   275

Tape Drives and Formats   275

Writable Optical Drives   277

WORM Drives   278

Using the Windows NT Server 4.0 Backup Application   278

Setting Up NTBACKUP for Use with Your Tape Drive   279

Backing Up with NTBACKUP   281

Restoring with NTBACKUP   287

Looking Beyond NTBACKUP   289

From Here...   290

9 Understanding the Windows NT Registry   291

Tracking Configuration Settings in the Registry   292
  Types of Registry Information   292
  Windows 3.1+ Configuration Files   292
  Centralized Configuration Management with the Registry   293
  Registry Organization   294
  The Danger of Changing Registry Values   294
  How the Windows NT and Windows 95 Registries Vary   296

Viewing the Registry's Organization   296
  Registry Hives and Files   297
  Keys and Subkeys   299
  Value Entries   300

Understanding Some Important Hives and Keys   301
  The HKEY_LOCAL_MACHINE Hive   301
  HKEY_CURRENT_CONFIG   305
  HKEY_CLASSES_ROOT   305
  HKEY_CURRENT_USER   306
  HKEY_USERS   307

Using the Windows NT Diagnostics Utility   307

Backing Up the Registry   308

Using the Registry Editor   310

Inspecting Another Computer's Registry   311
  Preparing for Remote Registry Editing   311
  Opening the Remote Registry   312

Maintaining Registry Security   313
  Restricting Access to Registry Keys   313
  Viewing an Audit Log   315

Understanding the Interaction of .INI and CONFIG.SYS Files with the Registry   317

Using the Resource Kit's Registry Entry Help File   318

From Here...   319

10 Using TCP/IP, WINS, and DHCP   321

Understanding the Role of TCP/IP   322
  Why Use TCP/IP?   323
  IP Addresses, Host Names, Domain Names, and NetBIOS Names   323

The Problem: Resolving Names and Addresses   325
Some Solutions to the Problem   326

Installing and Configuring TCP/IP for Windows NT Server   328

Implementing Dynamic Host Configuration Protocol   332
The Advantages of DHCP   333
How DHCP Leases IP Addresses to Clients   333
DHCP Server Configuration   334

Implementing Windows Internet Name Service   342
The Advantages of WINS   342
How WINS Registers and Resolves NetBIOS Names   342
WINS Configuration   344

Integrating WINS and DNS   349

From Here...   349

11   Configuring Windows 95 Clients for Networking   351

Understanding Windows 95 Networking Features   352

Installing Network Support   354
Installing Network Interface Cards   354
Changing NIC Settings   356
Installing and Removing Network Clients   358
Completing the Identification Page   361
Completing the Access Control Page   362

Configuring Network Clients   363
Configuring the Client for Microsoft Networks   363
Configuring the Client for NetWare Networks   364
Setting the Primary Network Logon   366

Configuring Network Protocols   366
Configuring NetBEUI   367
Configuring NWLink   369
Configuring TCP/IP   371

Installing File and Printer Sharing   376
File and Printer Sharing for Microsoft Networks   377
File and Printer Sharing for NetWare Networks   378

Managing Windows 95 on the Network   379
Installing Windows 95 from the Network   380
Setting Up User Profiles on the Server   386
Using System Policies   388

Managing Windows 95 Clients Remotely   390
Enabling Remote Management   391
Using Remote Management   392

Browsing Issues with Windows 95 Clients   396

From Here...   397

12 Connecting Other PC Clients to the Network   399

Connecting Windows 3.1 Clients   400
Creating Client Installation Disks   400
Installing the MS-DOS and Windows Client   402
Viewing Changes Made to Windows 3.1 Configuration
and Initialization Files   406
Setting Up Windows to Use the Network Drivers   408
Connecting to Windows NT File and Printer Resources   408
Troubleshooting Connection Problems   410

Connecting Windows for Workgroups 3.11 Clients   410
Installing the 32-Bit TCP/IP Network Protocol   410
Viewing Changes Made to WfWg 3.1+ Configuration
and Initialization Files   414
Logging On and Connecting to Windows NT Server 4.0
Resources   416
Troubleshooting Network Resource Problems   417

Connecting Windows NT Workstation 4.0 Clients   418
Installing the Network Software   418
Attaching to Domain Resources   421
Troubleshooting Connectivity Problems   423
Previewing the Zero Administration Kit for Windows NT
Workstation 4.0 and Windows 95   423

Connecting Macintosh Clients   425
Adding Services for Macintosh on Windows NT Server   425
Setting Up Macintosh Clients   427
Accessing Windows NT Server Resources from the
Macintosh   429
Troubleshooting Services for Macintosh   436

From Here...   437

III | **Administering a Secure Network**

13 Managing User and Group Accounts   441

Defining Account and Group Terminology   442

Working with User Manager for Domains   442

Starting User Manager for Domains   443

Starting Multiple Instances of User Manager   444

Selecting a New Domain with User Manager   445

Using a Low-Speed Connection to Connect to a Domain   446

Managing User Accounts   447

Managing the Built-In User Accounts   447

Adding New User Accounts   449

Modifying User Accounts   451

Managing User Account Properties   454

Assigning Group Membership to a User Account   454

Defining and Managing User Profiles   455

Managing Logon Hours   458

Restricting Logon Privileges to Assigned Workstations   460

Managing Account Information   461

Setting User Dial-In Permissions   462

Using the Add User Account Wizard   463

Administering the Domain Account Policy   467

Setting the Account Policy for Passwords   468

Setting the Account Lockout Policy   469

Managing User Groups   469

Examining Windows NT Server 4.0's Built-In Groups   470

Adding Local Groups   471

Adding Global Groups   473

Copying a Group   473

Deleting Groups from the Domain   474

Deciding When to Use Local Groups or Global Groups   474

Providing Users in Trusted Domains Access to Resources in Trusting Domains   474

Using the Group Management Wizard   475

Managing User Rights Policy   478

Determining User Rights   478

Assigning New User Rights   479

Exploring the Resource Kit's User Administration Utilities   480

From Here...   482

14   Sharing and Securing Network Resources   483

Sharing and Securing Folders and Files   484
    Choosing a Windows NT Server File System   484
    Understanding Folder Shares   485
    Using the Managing Folder and File Access Wizard   490
    Understanding NTFS Permissions   493

Replicating Folders   502
    Creating a Replication User   503
    Starting the Replication Service   503
    Configuring Folder Replication   504

Compressing NTFS Files and Folders   507
    Using Windows NT Explorer's or My Computer's
    Compression Features   507
    Moving and Copying Compressed Files   509

Using Compact.exe at the Command Prompt   510

Taking Advantage of the Resource Kit's Diruse.exe Utility   511

Sharing and Securing Network Printers   512
    Configuring Locally Attached Server Printers as Shared
    Resources   512
    Configuring Network Printer Servers as Shared Resources   517
    Configuring Printer Properties   520

From Here...   527

15   Optimizing Network Server Performance   529

Using Performance Monitor   530
    Using Objects and Counters in Performance Monitor   531
    Charting Performance Characteristics   534
    Using Performance Monitor to Set Alerts   537
    Using Performance Monitor Log Files   539

Optimizing Windows NT 4.0 File and Print Servers   543
    Minimizing Disk Bottlenecks   543
    Eliminating Unneeded Network Protocols   546
    Changing the Binding Order of Multiple Protocols   547

Overcoming Network Media Limitations 548
Reducing File Fragmentation 549

Optimizing Windows NT 4.0 as an Application Server 549
Examining an Application Server's CPU Usage 550
Examining Memory Usage in an Application Server 551

Taking Advantage of Resource Kit Optimization Utilities 554

From Here... 558

16 Troubleshooting Network Problems 559

Relating Network Protocols and Troubleshooting Issues 560
NetBEUI Broadcasting 560
IPX/SPX 561
TCP/IP 562

Using Protocol Analyzers 566
Hardware Protocol Analyzers 566
Software Protocol Analyzers 566
Protocol Analyzer Connection 567

Using Windows NT Server 4.0's Primary Troubleshooting
Tools 568
Using Event Viewer 568
Using Network Monitor 570
Using Performance Monitor as a Network Troubleshooting
Tool 576
Using Windows NT's Network-Related Command-Line
Tools 580

Using the *Windows NT Server Resource Kit* Network Utilities 584
Browser Monitor 585
Browser Status 586
Domain Monitor 587
GetMac 589
Net Watch 589
NSLookup 590
SMBTrace 591
WNTIPcfg 591

Taking Advantage of Other Troubleshooting Resources 591

Solving Windows NT Server Network Problems   592
Understanding and Solving Connectivity Problems   592
Browsing   594
Routing   595
Troubleshooting Trusts   596
Understanding WINS and DNS Name Resolution   599
From Here...   601

IV | Wide Area Networking and the Internet

17   Distributing Network Services with Domains   605
Understanding Domain Architecture and Security   606
Understanding Windows NT Security Identifiers   607
Understanding the Roles of Domain Controllers   608
Understanding the Domain Synchronization Process   611
Adding Backup Domain Controllers to a New Domain   614
Adding Windows NT Clients to the Domain   614
Moving Machines Between Domains and Renaming
Domains   616
Implementing Domains and Trusts Between Domains   618
Distributing Authentication Services   619
Understanding Trust Relationships   623
Understanding Windows NT's Domain Models   626
The Single Domain Model   626
The Single Master Model   627
The Multiple Master Model   628
The Complete Trust Model   629
Hybrid Domain Models   630
Deciding on the Right Domain Design   630
Implementing Resource Sharing   632
Browsing Multiple-Domain Resources   633
From Here...   633

18   Integrating Windows NT with NetWare and UNIX   635
Spanning Multiple Network Protocols   636
Integrating Windows NT Server with Novell NetWare   637

Accessing Novell NetWare Servers with Microsoft Clients 639

Accessing Microsoft Windows NT Servers with NetWare Clients 651

Using Other Windows NT Server Integration Tools for NetWare 660

Integrating Windows NT Server with UNIX 668

Using the Microsoft DNS Server 671

Sharing Windows NT Files with UNIX 677

Building Universal Clients for Microsoft Windows NT, Novell NetWare, and UNIX 679

Configuring Windows for Workgroups 3.11 as a Universal Client 680

Using Windows 95 as a Universal Client 683

Migrating from Novell NetWare to Windows NT Server 683

From Here... 685

19 Managing Remote Access Service 687

Touring the New Communications Features of Windows NT Server 4.0 688

Deciding on a Dial-Up Networking Architecture 689

Understanding TAPI 2.0 692

Setting Up Windows NT Server 4.0 Remote Access Service 694

Installing Internal or External Modems 694

Configuring Dial-Up Networking 699

Granting Client Access with the Remote Access Admin Application 702

Installing and Testing Dial-Up Networking on Clients 704

Windows 95 Clients 704

Windows NT Clients 710

Monitoring Connections with Remote Access Admin 717

Using the Point-to-Point Tunneling Protocol 719

Adding Microsoft Routing and Remote Access Service 720

Using the Resource Kit's RAS Tools 721

From Here... 722

20 Setting Up Internet Information Server 4.0   723

Viewing Microsoft's Internet Product Line   724

Planning Your Site   725

Connecting to the Internet   726
Choosing an Internet Service Provider   727
Understanding Connection Types   727
Resolving Names with the Domain Name Service   734

Understanding IIS and Its Components   736
Understanding World Wide Web Service   736
Understanding the File Transfer Protocol Service   738
Understanding Gopher   740

Understanding How IIS Interacts with the Windows NT Domain Model   741

Installing Internet Information Server 4.0   741
Making an Initial Installation or Upgrading a Prior Version of IIS   742
Using Microsoft Management Console to Administer IIS 4.0   747
Testing the Default IIS 4.0 Installation   748

Setting IIS 4.0 Options   750
Configuring Web Site Options   750
Setting Logging Options   751
Configuring the Security Accounts   753
Configuring Performance Options   754
Configuring Folder Security   754
Configuring the Folders   758
Setting HTTP Header Options   760

Setting FTP Server Options   760

From Here...   764

21 Administering Intranet and World Wide Web Sites   765

Logging to an ODBC Data Source   766
Creating the Logging Database   766
Adding the Logging Table   767
Setting Up ODBC 3.x System Data Sources   771
Specifying the ODBC System Data Source for Logging   779
Writing Sample Queries for Reviewing Logs   780

Using SQL Server Web Assistant to Distribute Activity
Reports   782

Using Crystal Reports with IIS Logs   786
Installing Crystal Reports for IIS   787
Testing Crystal Reports   788

Using Performance Monitor   790

Activating Web Pages with ASP, ADO, and OLE DB   794
The ExAir Sample Active Server Pages   794
ActiveX Data Objects and OLE DB   797

Managing the Content of Your Web Site with Microsoft
FrontPage 97   800
Installing FrontPage 97 and the IIS 3.0 Server Extensions   800
Experimenting with FrontPage Explorer and Editor   802

From Here...   806

V | Windows NT Server and Microsoft BackOffice

22 Taking Advantage of BackOffice Integration   811
Aiming at a Moving BackOffice Server Target   812

Filling Out the BackOffice Family   814
Internet and Intranet Servers   814
Enterprise Middleware   815

Licensing BackOffice Components   816
Per-Seat vs. Per-Server Licensing   816
BackOffice Server 2.5 and Client Access Licenses   818
Windows NT 4.0 License Packages and Cost   819
SQL Server 6.5 Licensing   820
Exchange Server 5.0 Licensing   820
Systems Management Server 1.2 Licensing   821
SNA Server 3.0 Licensing   822
Licensing Costs for All BackOffice Components   822
The Annuity Model for BackOffice Upgrades   824

Using Windows NT Server 4.0's License Manager   825
Control Panel's License Tool   825
License Manager   827

From Here...   832

23 Running Microsoft SQL Server 6.5 833

Positioning SQL Server in the RDBMS Market 834

Installing SQL Server 6.5 835
Installing Files from the Distribution CD-ROM 836
Starting SQL Server and SQL Executive 842
Installing Service Packs 842

Using SQL Enterprise Manager 843
Installing SQL Enterprise Manager on a 32-Bit Client 843
Registering Servers 844
Specifying and Testing Backup Tape Devices 847

Creating and Managing Database Devices 850
Creating a New Database Device 850
Importing Table Structures and Data 852
Working with SQL Tables, Indexes, Tasks, and Triggers 857
Viewing Triggers 860
Viewing Standard Stored Procedures 861
Executing Queries 861
Setting Up Transaction Logging 862

Establishing Database Permissions 865
Using SQL Security Manager to Assign Group Accounts 865
Viewing Logins and Setting Permissions in
SQL Enterprise Manager 868

From Here... 870

24 Messaging with Microsoft Exchange Server 5.0 871

Understanding Exchange Server 872

Surveying Exchange Server's Features 873
Using Exchange for Electronic Mail 874
Sharing Information with Public Folders 875
Using Custom Forms to Build Applications 875
Using Group Scheduling 876
Integrating Exchange with Other Systems 877
Exploring New Features in Exchange Server 5.0 877

Understanding Exchange Server's Server Components 878
Understanding Exchange Administrator 878
Examining the Directory 879

Understanding the Message Transfer Agent 880
Understanding the Information Store 881
Understanding the System Attendant 882
Understanding Recipients 882
Understanding Mailboxes 883
Using a Personal Folder File 884
Using the Offline Folder File 884
Using Public Folders 884
Understanding Distribution Lists 885
Using Connectors 885

Understanding Client Components 887
Examining Microsoft Outlook 887
Understanding the Exchange Client and Schedule+ 891
Understanding the Exchange Forms Designer 894

Understanding Organizations, Sites, and Domains 894

Organizing Your Enterprise 895
Planning Your Site 896
Reviewing Geographic Considerations 896
Considering Functional Considerations 897

Sizing Your Server 897

Running Exchange Setup 900
Running the Setup Program 900
Using Performance Optimizer 903

Configuring Your Site with Exchange Administrator 906
Granting Administrative Permissions to Other Windows
NT Accounts 908
Configuring Information Store Options 909
Setting Up Site Addressing 912

Configuring Your Servers with Exchange Administrator 915

Setting Up Recipients 917
Creating an Administrator's Mailbox 919
Creating User Mailboxes with Exchange Administrator 921
Creating Mailboxes with User Manager for Domains 923
Creating a Recipient Template for Use with Directory
Import 924

Using Directory Import to Create Mailboxes   924

Creating Distribution Lists   926

From Here...   927

25 Administering Clients with Systems Management Server 1.2   929

Introducing Systems Management Server   930

Remote Control and Troubleshooting   931

Hardware and Software Inventory   931

Software Distribution and Installation   931

Network Protocol Analysis   931

Remote Performance Monitoring   932

Customized Data Analysis, Transfer, and Reporting   932

Differences Between SMS and Network Management Applications   932

Server Requirements   933

Supported Networks   934

Wide Area Network Options   934

Clients Supported   934

Planning for Systems Management Server   934

Enterprise Site Topology   935

Component Terminology and Concepts   936

Installing Systems Management Server   937

Creating a Service Account   937

Setting Up SQL Server   939

Installing Systems Management Server on the Primary Site Server   939

Using SMS Administrator   943

Sites Window   945

Packages Window   948

Jobs Window   950

Queries Window   951

Alerts Window   954

Machine Groups Window   954

Site Groups Window   954

Program Groups Window   954

Events Window   954

Installing and Configuring the SMS Client Software   954
   Manual Client Software Installation   954
   Automatic Installation   955
   Client Inventory Management   957
   Remote Control   957
   Network Monitor   960

Building Sites for Enterprise Networks   961
   Communication Between Sites with Senders   962
   Coexistence with NetWare Environments   962

From Here...   963

VI | The Trail to Windows NT 5.0

26 Scaling Windows NT Server 4.0 to the Enterprise   967

Understanding Microsoft's Incremental Approach to Scalability   968

Clustering for Availability Now and Scalability Later   970

Managing the Middle Tier with Transaction Server   973
   Brokering Business Objects   974
   Spanning Transactions over Multiple Components and
   Databases   977

Using Messages to Enable Wide-Area Transactions   979

Using Routing and Remote Access Service   980

Upgrading BackOffice Members for the Enterprise Edition   981

Reducing Client PC Management Costs   982
   The Network PC   982
   Zero Administration Windows   983
   Hydra and the Windows NT Terminal   983

From Here...   984

27 Distributing File and Directory Services   987

Distributing Server Shares with Dfs   988
   Understanding Dfs Roots and Leaves   988
   Installing Dfs on Servers   989
   Installing the Windows 95 Dfs Client   991
   Administering Dfs   993

Activating Directory Services   997
Directory Service Providers   998
Directory Search and Replication   1000
Distributed Security   1000
ADSI Management   1001
From Here...   1002

Glossary   1003

Index   1031

Credits

PRESIDENT
Roland Elgey

SENIOR VICE PRESIDENT/PUBLISHING
Don Fowley

GENERAL MANAGER
Joe Muldoon

MANAGER OF PUBLISHING OPERATIONS
Linda H. Buehler

PUBLISHING MANAGER
Fred Slone

TITLE MANAGER
Al Valvano

EDITORIAL SERVICES DIRECTOR
Carla Hall

MANAGING EDITOR
Caroline Roop

DIRECTOR OF ACQUISITIONS
Cheryl D. Willoughby

ACQUISITIONS EDITOR
Jeff Riley

PRODUCT DIRECTOR
Rob Tidrow

PRODUCTION EDITOR
Susan Shaw Dunn

EDITORS
Sherri Fugit
Kate Givens
Kristen Ivanetich
Patricia Kinyon

COORDINATOR OF EDITORIAL SERVICES
Maureen A. McDaniel

WEBMASTER
Thomas H. Bennett

PRODUCT MARKETING MANAGER
Kourtnaye Sturgeon

ASSISTANT PRODUCT MARKETING MANAGER
Gretchen Schlesinger

TECHNICAL EDITORS
Joel Goodling
Tom Krause
John J. Piraino Sr.

SOFTWARE SPECIALIST
Brandon K. Penticuff

ACQUISITIONS COORDINATOR
Carmen Krikorian

SOFTWARE REALATIONS COORDINATOR
Susan D. Gallagher

SOFTWARE COORDINATOR
Andrea Duvall

EDITORIAL ASSISTANTS
Travis Bartlett
Jennifer L. Chisholm

BOOK DESIGNERS
Ruth Harvey
Kim Scott

COVER DESIGNER
Sandra Schroeder

PRODUCTION TEAM
Marcia Deboy
Jenny Earhart
Tim Neville
Julie Searls
Lisa Stumpf

INDEXER
Chris Wilcox

Composed in *Century Old Style* and *ITC Franklin Gothic* by Que Corporation.

This book is dedicated to Aaron Weule, who's on his way to becoming a Microsoft Certified Systems Engineer specializing in Microsoft BackOffice integration.

About the Author

Roger Jennings is a principal of OakLeaf Systems, a northern California consulting firm specializing in Windows client/server database and digital video applications. Roger is the author of Que Publishing's *Using Access 2 for Windows*, Special Edition; *Special Edition Using Access 95; Special Edition Using Access 97; Unveiling Windows 95; Access Hot Tips*; and *Discover Windows 3.1 Multimedia*. He was a contributing author for Que's *Killer Windows Utilities; Using Windows 3.11*, Special Edition; *Special Edition Using Windows 95*; and *Excel Professional Techniques*. He has also written two books for Windows database developers, is the series editor for a set of books on database technology, and has contributed to the Microsoft Developer Network CD-ROM and Microsoft Developer Network News.

Roger was a member of the beta test team for Microsoft Windows 3.1 and 95; Windows NT 3.1, 3.5, 3.51, and 4.0 (Workstation and Server); Exchange Server; SQL Server 6.0 and 6.5; Proxy Server (code-named *Catapult*); ActiveMovie; Media Server (code-named *Cougar*) and every release of Access and Visual Basic. Roger's also a contributing editor for Fawcette Technical Publication, Inc.'s *Visual Basic Programmer's Journal*. You can reach him on CompuServe at **70233,2161** or via the Internet at **70233.2161@compuserve.com**.

Acknowledgments

Donald M. Benage (Chapters 10 and 24) is an acknowledged information systems professional and Microsoft Certified Systems Engineer with more than 17 years of experience applying leading technologies to complex business solutions. He is the author of Que's *Special Edition Using Microsoft BackOffice, BackOffice Electronic Resource Kit*, and *Special Edition Using Microsoft BackOffice,* Volumes I and II. Don is a frequent speaker at industry seminars and forums dedicated to understanding software development strategies and tools. Specific Microsoft product expertise was further enhanced by his employment with Microsoft Corporation for more than four years, leaving their ranks as a senior systems engineer to pursue other challenges. As a director with G.A. Sullivan, he manages the day-to-day operations of the Technology Center, G.A. Sullivan's research and development facility.

Steve Crandall (Chapters 20 and 21) has more than 18 years of experience in the telecommunications and computer industries. He is now manager of Consulting Services for a large systems and network integrator. A contributor to *Special Edition Using Microsoft Internet Information Server 2*, he is also a Microsoft Certified Systems Engineer.

Kate Gregory (Chapters 4, 6, and 9) is a freelance writer, trainer, and programmer, and is a partner in Gregory Consulting, founded in 1986. Based in rural Ontario, Canada, Gregory Consulting provides clients throughout North America, including Microsoft and IBM, with programming, training, and Web development services. Kate programs exclusively in Visual C++ with an emphasis on Internet projects, and has developed and taught courses on UNIX, C++, the Internet, and HTML. She holds a doctorate in chemical engineering from the University of Toronto, but finds programming and the Internet a lot more fun than modeling blood coagulation. Kate was lead author on Que's *Using Usenet Newsgroups* and *Building Internet*

Applications with Visual C++, and she contributed to Que's *The Official Visual Basic Programmer's Journal Guide to Visual Basic 4*, *Designing Windows 95 Help Systems*, and *Special Edition Using Visual C++ 4*. She is lead author on a complete rewrite of Que's *Special Edition Using Visual C++*, scheduled for release in the fall of 1996. Kate can be reached at **kate@gregcons.com**, and her main Web site is at **http://www.gregcons.com**.

Darren Mar-Elia (Chapters 12, 16, and 17) is a Windows NT and Networking specialist for a large financial services firm in San Francisco. He has more than 10 years of experience in systems and network administration, and was a member of a design team that rolled out 7,000 Windows NT workstations and servers nationwide. A graduate in organizational behavior from the University of California at Berkeley, Darren is certified by Novell as a CNE and is currently working on his Microsoft CSE. He was a contributing author of Que's *Upgrading and Repairing Networks*. You can reach him at **dmarelia@earthlink.net**.

Kevin Nikkhoo (Chapter 25) has more than 15 years of experience in the computer industry and has held positions of senior manager, systems administrator, software developer, and network manager for Fortune 500 firms and smaller companies. He earned an MBA from the University of Southern California and a master's in computer engineering from California State University, Los Angeles, as well as a BSCE from McGill University. Kevin is president of Vertex Systems, Inc., a Microsoft Solution Provider and one of the leading computer technology consulting firms in California. He's a frequent speaker at computer industry conferences and serves on Microsoft's Solution Provider Advisory Council. You can e-mail Kevin at **KevinN@VertexSystems.com** or contact Vertex Systems, Inc. at (310) 571-2222 (voice).

Michael Regelski (Chapters 13 and 15) is the director of software development at Lenel Systems International in Fairport, New York. Lenel Systems is one of the leading suppliers of industrial security products, including photo ID management and access control. Michael has an MS in software development and management and a BS in computer engineering from Rochester Institute of Technology. He has contributed to several other Que books, including *Special Edition Using Visual Basic 4* and *Building Multimedia Applications with Visual Basic 4*.

J. Brad Rhodes (Chapter 10) is an experienced developer of client/server systems with an emphasis on systems architecture. He has spent the past nine years designing and implementing client/server systems with special emphasis on open systems technology. Brad is vice president of technology at Hamilton and Sullivan, a leading provider of client/server solutions to the banking and financial industry. At Hamilton and Sullivan, he oversees the development of next-generation retail and commercial banking solutions. Brad is a Microsoft Certified System Engineer and holds a bachelor of electrical engineering from Southern Illinois University at Edwardsville; he has nearly completed a master's of electrical engineering from Washington University.

Alan Simkins (Chapter 20) is director of systems at Online System Services, Inc., a Denver-based Internet service and content provider and Microsoft Solutions Provider. He has been involved with personal computers since 1984 and holds a BS and MS in computer systems engineering from the University of Arkansas. Alan is a Microsoft Certified Systems Engineer and has held positions as network administrator, network engineer, client/server systems team leader, and database administrator. His current responsibilities include Web administration, database design, and interactive Web development. You can reach Alan via the Internet at **asimkins@ossinc.net** or by telephone at (303) 296-9200.

Robert Bruce Thompson (Chapters 2, 5, 7, 8, 11, 14, and 18) is president of Triad Technology Group, Inc., a network consulting firm in Winston-Salem, North Carolina. He has 24 years of experience in programming, systems analysis, microcomputers, data communications, and network administration. Bob is certified by Novell as a Master CNE, by IBM in Advanced Connectivity, and by AT&T in Network Systems Design, and is now working on his Microsoft CSE. He holds an MBA from Wake Forest University. Bob specializes in network systems design, branch office networking, and the application of technology to the needs of small businesses. He's the lead author of Que's *Windows NT Workstation 4.0 Internet and Networking Handbook* and a contributing author for Que's *Upgrading and Repairing Networks*. You can reach him via Internet mail at **rbt@ttgnet.com**. Triad Technology Group, Inc. may be contacted at (910) 748-9867 (voice) or (910) 748-8714 (fax).

Paul Thomsen (Chapter 25), MCSE, MCT, is the Systems Management Server columnist for *BackOffice Magazine* and a frequent contributor of SMS-related articles. When not writing, Paul is a Personal Computing Integration Specialist for a large governmental organization in Ontario, Canada, and teaches Microsoft and DEC courses in Southeast Asia for Global Consulting Networks. Previously, Paul was a technical specialist and programmer for 15 years, 10 of those in large end-user organizations in government and the health industry. Paul lives at his home fronting Chemong Lake in Peterborough, Ontario. He can be contacted at **pthomsen@sympatico.ca**, or check out his Web page at **http://www3.sympatico.ca/pthomsen**.

Stephen Wynkoop (Chapters 20 and 23, and additions to Chapter 19) is an author and lecturer working almost exclusively with Microsoft-based products and technologies, with emphasis on the Internet and client-server systems. Stephen has been developing applications and consulting in the computer industry for more than 14 years. He's the author of Que's *The BackOffice Intranet Kit* and is a co-author of *Special Edition Using Microsoft SQL Server 6.5*, as well as a contributing author for other Que titles on Internet technologies. Stephen is a regular speaker at Microsoft's Tech*Ed conferences and has written books on Microsoft Access and Office 95 integration. Stephen also is a Microsoft Certified Professional (MCP) for both Windows for Workgroups and Windows NT technologies. You can reach Stephen via the Internet at **swynk@pobox.com**.

Thanks to all the **Microsoft product support personnel** who manned the Windows NT 4.0 beta forum on CompuServe. Their prompt response to issues uncovered during the beta test program for Windows NT 4.0 is greatly appreciated.

Fred Slone, publishing manager, and **Jeff Riley**, acquisitions editor, made sure that I didn't fall too far behind the manuscript submission schedule. **Al Valvano**, title manager, provided helpful guidance for the second edition of this book. **Robert Tidrow**, development editor, provided valuable insight and suggestions for this book's content and organization. **Susan Dunn**, production editor, put in long hours to add last-minute updates to newly released Windows NT Server 4.0 Enterprise Edition features. Thanks also to technical editors **Joel Goodling**, **Tom Krause**, and **John Piraino** for double-checking the content of this book for accuracy. The responsibility for any errors or omissions, however, rests solely on my shoulders.

We'd Like to Hear from You!

As part of our continuing effort to produce books of the highest possible quality, Que would like to hear your comments. To stay competitive, we *really* want you to let us know what you like or dislike most about this book or other Que products.

Please send your comments, ideas, and suggestions for improvement to:

> The Expert User Team
> E-mail: **euteam@que.mcp.com**
> CompuServe: 105527,745
> Fax: (317) 581-4663

Our mailing address is:

> Expert User Team
> Que Corporation
> 201 West 103rd Street
> Indianapolis, IN 46290-1097

You can also visit our team's home page on the World Wide Web at:

> **http://www.mcp.com/que/developer_expert**

Thank you in advance. Your comments will help us to continue publishing the best books available in today's market.

Thank you,

The Expert User Team

Introduction

Microsoft Corporation introduced Windows NT 3.1 in July 1993. Windows NT version 3.5, the first major upgrade to the Windows NT operating system, appeared September 21, 1994. During the second half of 1994, the computer press was devoting much of its coverage of operating systems to the yet-to-be-released Microsoft Windows 95 (then code-named Chicago) and, to a lesser degree, IBM OS/2 Warp. Thus, the release of Windows NT 3.5 was eclipsed by stories about products which, at the time, were best categorized as "projectorware." A point up-grade, Windows NT 3.51, which was intended to provide compatibility with the forthcoming Windows 95 and Object Linking and Embedding (OLE) 2+, appeared with even less fanfare in May 1995.

N O T E This book uses the term *Windows NT* without a type (Server or Workstation) or version number when referring to the basic architecture and attributes of the operating system. The *Workstation* or *Server* identifier is added when discussing features that are applicable to or are most often used by only one version or the other. When comparing features of Windows NT Server 4.0 to features of preceding versions of Windows NT, the version number is included. *Windows NT 3.x* is used when the discussion applies to earlier versions 3.1, 3.5, and 3.51. The term *Windows 3.1+* includes Windows 3.1 and 3.11, and *Windows for Workgroups (WfWg) 3.1+* includes versions 3.1 and 3.11. ■

Windows NT Server is a remarkable network operating system, but it's just now beginning to meet with remarkable commercial success. Windows NT 3.1 didn't live up to Microsoft's initial sales projections primarily because of what was considered at the time to be big-time resource requirements (a minimum of 16M of RAM and about 70M of fixed-disk space, substantially more for the Server version). The lack of 32-bit Windows applications and a reputation for running 16-bit Windows applications somewhat slower than Windows 3.1+ also acted as a throttle on acceptance of the Workstation version. Further, Microsoft's marketing program targeted Windows NT Server to *enterprise computing*, a term that, with *mission-critical*, has become a cliché.

Large corporations and other sizable institutions rarely adopt a network operating system that doesn't have a proven track record for production use. Relatively few buyers of Windows NT 3.1 Advanced Server installed the product in a production environment, because corporate network and PC administrators considered Windows NT 3.1 to be an "immature" operating system, compared with UNIX and NetWare. Those who took the Windows NT 3.1 plunge, however, quickly found Windows NT 3.1 Advanced Server lived up to most, if not all, of Microsoft's claims for its new network operating system.

Windows NT 4.0 is the fourth iteration of Windows NT and now qualifies as a "mature" operating system, although Windows NT has been on the market less than six years. Unlike other Microsoft operating systems, Windows NT began life as a cross-platform product; identical versions were available for Intel X86, DEC Alpha, Silicon Graphics MIPS, and Apple/IBM/Motorola PowerPC computers. Major hardware manufacturers such as Hewlett-Packard, IBM, DEC, Tandem, Amdahl, and Unisys offer high-end servers designed specifically to run Windows NT. The endorsement of Windows NT by these firms, which market proprietary operating systems or their own flavors of UNIX, adds substantial credibility to Windows NT Server in the large-scale networking arena.

N O T E Windows NT Server and 32-bit applications must be individually compiled to executable code for each processor. Microsoft announced in late 1996 that future versions of Windows NT and Microsoft BackOffice components won't support MIPS and PowerPC processors. ■

The most obvious change between Windows NT 3.5+ and Windows NT 4.0 is the adoption of Windows 95's user interface (UI) and operating system shell. The primary visible change to the shell, aside from the taskbar and desktop, is the substitution of Windows Explorer for File Manager. Microsoft originally called Windows NT 4.0 the *Shell Update Release* (SUR) because the company planned in late 1995 to provide the Windows 95 UI and shell in the form of a Service Pack update, rather than as a full version upgrade to Windows NT. The Windows 95 facelift to Windows NT 3.5+ primarily benefits users of Windows NT Workstation 4.0, eliminating the need to train users for and support the legacy UI of Windows 3.1+ used by Windows NT 3.5+ and the new UI of Windows 95.

Beneath the cosmetic improvements, Windows NT Server 4.0 provides several new networking features, the most important of which for networking are the Distributed Common Object Model (DCOM, formerly called NetworkOLE) and a substantial improvement in the Domain Name Service (DNS) for TCP/IP networks. Microsoft needs DCOM to fully implement three-tier client/server computing by using Automation (formerly OLE Automation) components, Microsoft Transaction Server (MTS, code-named Viper), and Microsoft Message Queue Server (MSMQ). MTS and MSMQ are included with Windows NT Server 4.0's Enterprise Edition. DNS is the key to integrating Windows NT with UNIX networks, including the Internet.

Other new networking features of Windows NT Server 4.0 include an improved print spooler, as well as Point-to-Point Tunneling Protocol (PPTP) and the Telephony API (TAPI) 1 to provide secure communication and ease support of mobile users of Windows NT Server 4.0's Remote Access Service (RAS). Microsoft also has enhanced the scalability of Windows NT 4.0's symmetrical multiprocessing (SMP). Each new feature of Windows NT Server 4.0 receives detailed coverage in this book. ■

Networking with Windows NT Server 4.0

Networking, the primary subject of this book, is where Microsoft has made the greatest improvement in Windows NT 4.0. Microsoft claims that Windows NT Server 4.0's file services are more than twice as fast as the original version, and printing has been speeded up, too. Windows NT 4.0 includes Microsoft's new IPX/SPX stack, which appears to offer equal or better performance than Novell's own NetWare drivers. What's more important, however, is that Microsoft has adopted the Internet's venerable TCP/IP (Transport Control Protocol/ Internet Protocol) as the network protocol of choice, making Windows NT Server 4.0 more attractive to Microsoft's target market—Fortune 1000 firms. UNIX servers running TCP/IP over 10BaseT (10 Mbps unshielded twisted-pair) Ethernet cabling now dominate enterprise-wide corporate local area networks. Although 60 percent or more of today's networked PCs may "speak" NetWare's IPX/SPX, by the end of the 1990s TCP/IP is likely to displace the standard Novell protocol in all but the smallest-scale networks.

N O T E   10BaseT Ethernet is the most common network transport medium today, but 100 Mbps 100BaseT rapidly is gaining ground in new network installations and upgrades. 100BaseT network interface cards (NICs), which also are compatible with 10BaseT, now cost about the same as the 10BaseT variety. Windows NT 4.0 transparently supports 100BaseT NICs. 100BaseT hubs are available at a cost of about $80 per port and probably will decline to the $50 per port range by mid-1998. ■

Windows NT 4.0 also thrives in heterogeneous networks by using a combination of TCP/IP, IPX/SPX, and NetBEUI protocols. What's more, you don't pay extra for Windows NT Server 4.0's capability to run simultaneous multiple network protocols.

Windows NT 3.1 Advanced Server established a new standard for ease of installation of a network operating system, and the setup program of Windows NT Server 4.0 is even more streamlined. You can install Windows NT Server 4.0 from CD-ROM in about 30 minutes, and upgrade a Windows 95 or Windows for Workgroups 3.1+ peer-to-peer network with 20 to 30 clients in a day or so. On average, it takes about 15 minutes to reconnect each client to a Windows NT Server 4.0 domain, including reconnecting clients to a relocated Microsoft Mail postoffice. You need a few more minutes per client if you use TCP/IP or IPX/SPX, rather than the Windows Network's simpler NetBEUI protocol.

Ease of installation—especially in a workgroup environment that might connect 20 to 100 clients—isn't the only benefit of using Windows NT Server 4.0. Since its inception, Windows NT Server has required substantially fewer administrative and support resources than its NetWare and UNIX competitors. Windows NT 4.0 offers various administrative tools, notably User Manager for Domains and Server Manager, with improved graphical user interfaces that simplify the life of network administrators. In the longer term, it's not the license fee and installation time that determines the economics of a network operating system—it's the annual administrative and support costs that make or break information system budgets.

Windows NT Server 4.0, the Internet, and Intranets

The remarkable growth of the Internet, brought about primarily by the proliferation of World Wide Web servers, is one of the principal contributors to increased adoption rate of Windows NT Server by organizations of all sizes. Today, most Internet servers run UNIX, but Windows NT Server rapidly is gaining ground as the network operating system of choice for delivering Web pages. Windows NT's advantages cost less for the hardware and software needed to set up a Windows NT Web site, combined with easier administration and reduced support requirements than for UNIX "boxes."

Microsoft arrived late at the Internet table, having waited until December 7, 1995, to elucidate its "Embrace and Extend" Internet strategy. A flurry of press releases and white papers announced Microsoft's intent to become a major player in the Internet server and browser markets. Subsequently, Microsoft released a torrent of free pre-beta (alpha or preview) and beta versions of Internet-related applications, programming tools, and add-ons. To gain market presence, Microsoft lets you download the latest versions of its Internet Information Server (IIS) and Internet Explorer (IE) browser from **http://www.microsoft.com** for only the cost of connect time. Microsoft's objective in giving away these two products obviously is to increase the size of the market for Windows NT Server and Windows 95, respectively. Whether this strategy succeeds in displacing Netscape Navigator as the undisputed leader of the browser business remains to be seen. It's clear, however, that much of the very rapid increase in sales of Windows NT Server during the first half of 1996 derived from the free IIS offer. You no longer need to download IIS and IE from Microsoft's Web site; IIS and IE are included on the Windows NT Server 4.0 CD-ROM.

N O T E The Windows NT Server 4.0 CD-ROM includes version 2.0 of IIS. You must download the Active Server Pages (ASP) add-on to IIS 2.0 from the Microsoft Web site to upgrade to IIS 3.0. ▨

The "real money" on the server side of the Internet business comes from setting up private *intranets*, not creating Internet sites. Intranets offer the convenience of allowing users to browse for information on a corporate local area network (LAN) or wide area network (WAN) by using a conventional Internet browser. Navigating hyperlinks to related HTML-encoded documents with connections to server-resident applications is demonstrably easier for average PC users than running special-purpose, often complex client-side applications. Conventional database query tools and dedicated database front ends often require a substantial amount of user training. Inexperienced users quickly gain a knack for finding the information they need by clicking text and iconic hyperlinks of Web pages. Thus, organizations setting up intranets minimize training costs and, because simple Web-based applications are relatively easy to code, save programming expense. Microsoft sells a license for Windows NT Server with each free copy of IIS and gains the opportunity to sell a copy of Proxy Server (originally code-named Catapult) to provide security for clients connecting to the Internet.

Microsoft announced its Site Server 2.0 and Site Server 2.0 Enterprise Edition in May 1997. (There was no version 1.0.) Site Server 2.0 is a $1,499 integrated package for deploying and managing Internet and intranet Web sites, which includes the Personalization System, Content Replication System, Web Publishing Wizard, Posting Acceptor, Usage Analyst, and Site Analyst. Microsoft also includes "as a promotion" a copy of Visual InterDev for creating dynamic, database-related Web content. The $4,999 Enterprise Edition, designed for conducting electronic commerce on the Web, adds a new version of Microsoft Commerce Server and upgraded versions of Usage Analyst and Site Analyst. The Enterprise Edition supports Microsoft Wallet, a payment system for Web-based purchases.

The Future of Windows NT

Windows NT remains a constantly moving target, with new features added by Service Packs and, less frequently, point or full-version releases at various intervals. Rather than make the leap to a major overhaul of Windows NT (originally code-named Cairo), Microsoft is taking an incremental approach for the next version, Windows NT 5.0. Windows NT 5.0 will provide the Distributed File System (DFS) based on the client/server model of Microsoft Exchange Server, instead of the originally planned Object File System (OFS) of Cairo. Microsoft now intends to incorporate the content-related query features of OFS as an element of the existing Windows NT File System (NTFS). Using the Exchange approach, directory services can use DNS and Internet domain names, as well as the Internet's Lightweight Directory Access Protocol (LDAP) to provide improved integration with the Internet and intranets. Active Directory Service Interface (ADSI, formerly OLE Directory Services or OLE DS) provides plug-in support for LDAP and NetWare Directory Services (NDS) namespaces to provide a uniform method of administering user accounts and network resources in very large networks. Windows NT Server 5.0 also will include or provide for clustering of Windows NT servers to offer the reliability, accessibility, and scalability (RAS) that characterize high-end UNIX systems.

Two-way (failover) clustering is one of the features of Windows NT Server 4.0's Enterprise Edition.

Microsoft's piecemeal delivery of Windows NT 5.0 components as add-ons for Windows NT 4.0 is uncharacteristic of a firm that historically has relied on confidential beta testing of forthcoming products under non-disclosure agreements (NDAs). As an example, Microsoft provided attendees at its November 1996 Professional Developer Conference (PDC) alpha versions of DFS, Distributed Security (Kerberos and X.509 public key encryption), ADSI, MTS, and Microsoft Management Console (MMC). Microsoft released DFS, MTS, and a pre-alpha version of MMC in December 1996, and version 1 of ADSI in February 1997. Each component, available for downloading from **http://www.microsoft.com**, will be included in or available for Windows NT 5.0.

Who Should Read This Book?

Special Edition Using Windows NT Server 4, Second Edition, is intended for an eclectic audience—from networking neophytes to network designers and administrators responsible for setting up and maintaining large networks with Windows NT Server 4.0, either alone or with other network operating systems. This book isn't designed as an introduction to the client-side features of Windows NT, such as the user interface.

Folks for whom *Special Edition Using Windows NT Server 4*, Second Edition, offers the most usefulness fall into the following general categories:

- Network architects designing local area or wide area networks that incorporate Windows NT servers, either in a Microsoft-only or in a heterogeneous networking environment
- Network administrators handling the day-to-day chores necessary to assure network availability, security, and reliability
- Database administrators seeking to provide networked users with expedited access to corporate "information warehouses" with traditional client/server front ends or Web-based data retrieval
- Information systems (IS) managers responsible for planning and administering downsizing (or upsizing) corporate data distribution systems over a private intranet or the Internet
- Human resources directors responsible for overseeing remote-access telecommuting services for their firm's employees
- Network support personnel keeping Windows Networking clients online and helping users gain the maximum benefit from the Windows NT 4.0 domain(s) to which they connect
- Microsoft Solution Providers who provide network management and database consulting services
- Value-added resellers (VARs) of complete networking solutions, which include Windows NT servers

■ Manufacturers and marketers of hubs, bridges, routers, and other networking paraphernalia who need insight into the networking systems management features of Windows NT and Systems Management Server (SMS)

■ Educational institutions and training firms needing an advanced-level text on Windows NT networking for their students

■ Line-management personnel who are members of re-engineering committees charged with integrating information management into the re-engineering process

■ Television broadcast/cable executives and technical personnel involved in evaluating or deploying Internet or intranet connectivity with cable modems or other data-related services, such as InterCast

■ Users of various UNIX flavors who find Windows NT encroaching on the sacred ground of their erstwhile "open system"

The preceding list includes only the most obvious classifications of the potential audience for this book. Even if you're just curious about Microsoft's future operating system and client-server strategies, you'll find this book useful.

How This Book Is Organized

Special Edition Using Windows NT Server 4, Second Edition, consists of 27 chapters divided into six parts of progressively increasing technical complexity. The organization of the book follows the process of establishing a new Windows NT network, either as a self-contained entity or connected into a heterogeneous WAN. The following sections describe the content of each part and chapter of this book.

Part I: Networking with Windows NT Server 4.0

Part I contains chapters that describe Microsoft's design strategy for the Windows NT operating system and its networking features, plus planning and budgeting for a network based on Windows NT Server 4.0.

■ Chapter 1, "Placing Windows NT Server in Perspective," supplies a brief history of the development of Windows NT, explains the new features Microsoft added to Windows NT Server 4.0, describes how Windows NT fits into the PC server markets of the late 1990s, and compares the features of Windows NT Server 4.0 with those of its primary competitors, Novell NetWare and UNIX.

■ Chapter 2, "Planning Your Windows NT Network Installation," details the steps required to plan and budget for networks ranging in size from small workgroup LANs to company-wide, multisite WANs.

■ Chapter 3, "Understanding the Windows NT Operating System," introduces you to the technical foundation of Windows NT and the Windows NT File System (NTFS).

■ Chapter 4, "Choosing Network Protocols," explains how to select one or more of the three principal networking protocols supported by Windows NT based on your network configuration.

■ Chapter 5, "Purchasing Networking Hardware," provides guidance in the selection of the adapter cards, cabling, hubs, routers, and related equipment required to complete the physical network installation.

Part II: Deploying Windows NT Server 4.0

Part II covers the basics of installing and starting up Windows NT Server, along with fixed-disk arrays and backup tape drives, and connecting various client PCs to your server.

■ Chapter 6, "Making the Initial Server Installation," guides you through Windows NT Server 4.0's Setup application, with emphasis on preparing you to answer the questions posed in the Setup dialogs.

■ Chapter 7, "Setting Up Redundant Arrays of Inexpensive Disks (RAID)," describes how to choose between software and hardware RAID implementation and how to take best advantage of Windows NT Server 4.0's software RAID capabilities.

■ Chapter 8, "Installing File Backup Systems," explains the tradeoffs between different types and formats of backup systems, and how to manage server backup operations to ensure against lost data in case of a fixed-disk failure.

■ Chapter 9, "Understanding the Windows NT Registry," introduces you to Windows NT Server 4.0's registration database, which is similar but not identical to the Windows 95 Registry.

■ Chapter 10, "Using TCP/IP, WINS, and DHCP," shows you how to plan for and implement TCP/IP networking, including use of the Windows Internet Name Service and Dynamic Host Configuration Protocol.

■ Chapter 11, "Configuring Windows 95 Clients for Networking," shows you how to set up PCs running Windows 95 to take maximum advantage of Windows NT 4.0 networks, including the use of server-based desktop configurations and policies.

■ Chapter 12, "Connecting Other PC Clients to the Network," provides the details on setting up Windows 3.1+, Windows for Workgroups 3.1+, Windows NT Workstation 4.0, and Macintosh clients to communicate with Windows NT 4.0 servers.

Part III: Administering a Secure Network

Part III encompasses the administrative side of network management with chapters covering user and group accounts, sharing file and printer resources, tuning Windows NT servers, and solving the inevitable problems that arise in homogeneous and heterogeneous networks.

■ Chapter 13, "Managing User and Group Accounts," describes how to use Windows NT Server 4.0's User Manager for Domains, take advantage of the new Add User Accounts and Group Management wizards, and utilize the built-in user groups of Windows NT.

■ Chapter 14, "Sharing and Securing Network Resources," explains Windows NT Server's security system for shared file, folder, and printer resources and how to use the new Managing File and Folder Access Wizard and the Add Printer Wizard to simplify sharing Windows NT Server 4.0's resources.

- Chapter 15, "Optimizing Network Server Performance," describes the Windows NT Server 4.0 Performance Monitor and explains tuning methodology to help you maintain optimum network throughput as your network usage grows.

- Chapter 16, "Troubleshooting Network Problems," provides solutions for typical problems encountered when running multiple network protocols, and how to use the command-line tools included with Windows NT 4.0 and the *Windows NT Resource Kit* to isolate network problems. A brief description of the use of Systems Management Server's Network Monitor also is included.

Part IV: Wide Area Networking and the Internet

Part IV is devoted to the general topic of WANs, including networks with multiple domains, heterogeneous networks, remote access services, and establishing and managing an Internet or intranet site.

- Chapter 17, "Distributing Network Services with Domains," covers Windows NT Server's trusted domains and other distributed networking features that allow a single-user logon for multiple network servers and server-based applications running on LANs and WANs.

- Chapter 18, "Integrating Windows NT with NetWare and UNIX," shows you how to set up and administer Windows NT Server within a Novell NetWare or UNIX networking environment. This chapter also describes the new features of Windows NT 4.0's Domain Name Service (DNS).

- Chapter 19, "Managing Remote Access Service," explains how to configure Windows NT Server 4.0's RAS component to support dial-in access to network resources shared by mobile users.

- Chapter 20, "Setting Up Internet Information Server 4.0," describes the step-by-step process of establishing an Internet or intranet server with Microsoft's IIS 2.0, which is included with Windows NT Server 4.0; IIS 3.0, which adds Active Server Pages; and the newest upgrade, IIS 4.0.

- Chapter 21, "Administering Intranet and World Wide Web Sites," describes key elements of maintaining a Web site that reliably distributes the content of HTML-encoded documents, outlines a Webmaster's duties, and briefly describes the integration of popular HTML authoring tools with an intranet or Internet server.

Part V: Windows NT Server and Microsoft BackOffice

Part V covers the three primary components of BackOffice that run as services under Windows NT Server 4.0: Microsoft SQL Server 6.5, Exchange Server 4.0, and Systems Management Server 1.2. (SNA Server, used to connect to mainframes and IBM AS/400 minicomputers, is beyond the scope of this book.)

- Chapter 22, "Taking Advantage of BackOffice Integration," explains Microsoft's approach to developing client/server business solutions with members of the recently extended BackOffice family. This chapter also covers licensing issues applicable to the BackOffice Server suite and how to use Windows NT 4.0's Licensing service.

■ Chapter 23, "Running Microsoft SQL Server 6.5," describes the basic features of Microsoft's most recent update to SQL Server that includes new database replication features and a SQL Web Page Wizard.

■ Chapter 24, "Messaging with Microsoft Exchange Server 5.0," introduces you to installation and management of Microsoft Exchange Server 5.0, Microsoft's new client/server replacement for file-oriented Microsoft Mail 3+.

■ Chapter 25, "Administering Clients with Systems Management Server 1.2," covers the basics of planning, administration, and management for Microsoft SMS 1.2.

Part VI: The Trail to Windows NT 5.0

Part VI describes the Enterprise Edition of Windows NT Server (Windows NT Server/E), announced on May 20, 1997, and the new Windows NT extensions released—or in beta testing—when this edition was written. These extensions will be included in Windows NT Server 5.0.

■ Chapter 26, "Scaling Windows NT Server 4.0 to the Enterprise," describes the new components of Windows NT Server/E, including failover clustering, Microsoft Transaction Server (MTS), and Microsoft Message Queue Server.

■ Chapter 27, "Distributing File and Directory Services," explains the new Distributed File Service (DFS), Kerberos security, Lightweight Directory Access Protocol (LDAP), and Active Directory Service Interface (ADSI).

Glossary

At the end of this book, the Windows NT Glossary supplies definitions of many of the new buzzwords and technical terms used to describe 32-bit Windows operating systems and applications.

How this Book Is Designed

The following special features are included in this book to assist you as you read:

■ This icon appears next to sections that describe features in Windows NT Server 4.0 that weren't implemented in version 3.x or were added to version 3.5 through a Service Pack.

■ The Internet icon appears next to sections that describe features in Windows NT Server 4.0 that are of importance in setting up and maintaining an Internet or intranet server.

■ Cross-references, like the following, include the names of sections elsewhere in this book that contain information related to the associated text and the page on which you'll find the sections.

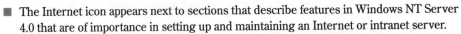

▶ **See** "Section That Appears Elsewhere in the Book," **p. xxx**

N O T E Notes offer suggestions and comments related to the text that precedes the note. ■

ON THE WEB

Some notes provide references to Web sites that provide content related to the subject matter of the preceding text.

TIP Tips describe shortcuts and alternative approaches to gaining an objective. Many of these tips are based on the experience the authors gained during months of testing successive beta versions of Windows NT Server 4.0.

CAUTION

Cautions appear where an action might lead to an unexpected or unpredictable result, including possible loss of data or other serious consequences. The text provides an explanation of how you can avoid such a result.

Typographic Conventions Used in this Book

This book uses various typesetting styles to distinguish between explanatory and instructional text, text you enter in dialogs, and text you enter in code-editing windows.

Typefaces and Fonts

The following type attributes are applied to the text of this book to make reading easier:

- A special `monospaced` font is used for on-screen prompts, code, and SQL statements.

- The **boldface** attribute is used for World Wide Web URLs, other Internet addresses, and FTP sites.

- The text you type at the command prompt or into text boxes is `boldface monospace`.

- When you must substitute a name of your own making for an entry, the `lowercase monospace bold italic` attribute is used for the substitutable portion, as in the example `filename.mdb`. Here, you substitute the name of your file for `filename`, but the .mdb extension is required because it's not italic.

- The *italic* attribute is used for definitions (instead of double quotation marks) and to set off initial items in bulleted lists, where appropriate. The *italic* attribute also is used for emphasis.

Keystrokes and Menu Choices

Keystrokes that you use to perform Windows operations are indicated with the keys joined by a plus sign; Alt+F4, for example, indicates that you press and hold the Alt key while pressing the function key F4. In the rare cases when you must press and release a control key and *then* enter another key, the keys are separated by a comma—Alt, F4, for example.

N O T E Key combinations that perform menu operations requiring more than one keystroke are called *shortcut keys*. An example of such a shortcut is the combination Ctrl+C, which substitutes for the Edit menu's Copy command in most Windows applications.

Accelerator keys (Alt+*key*) for menu choices are indicated by the underscore attribute, as in "Choose Open from the File menu," duplicating the appearance of Windows NT Server 4.0's menu text.

Successive entries in dialogs follow the *tab order* of the dialog—the sequence in which the focus (selection) moves when you press Tab to move from one entry or control option to another. Command buttons, option buttons, and check box selections are treated similarly to menu choices, but their access key letters don't have the underscore attribute.

File names of 32-bit applications and documents created by 32-bit applications appear in mixed case, regardless of the use of long file names (LFNs) or the conventional DOS 8.3 (8-character maximum file name and 3-character extension). This style conforms to the file name display of Windows NT 4.0's Explorer. File names of 16-bit applications and related document files are set in all uppercase.

Bibliography

Publishing limitations preclude a full bibliography for Windows NT and its related BackOffice components. The following sections show you where to obtain additional information in the form of books, CD-ROMs, and online product support for Windows NT Workstation and Server, plus the individual members of the BackOffice suite that were released when this book was written.

Print and CD-ROM Publications

Windows NT has spawned various Microsoft and third-party publications in printed and CD-ROM formats. Most books available on Windows NT have been directed primarily to developers (programmers) of 32-bit applications for Windows NT and now Windows 95. Following is a list of books from Que Corporation and other publishers, plus specialized CD-ROM titles, that are particularly useful for administrators of Microsoft Windows NT Server networks and the BackOffice server suite:

- *Windows NT Workstation 4.0 Internet & Networking Handbook* by Robert Bruce Thompson (Que, ISBN 0-7897-0817-5) is an indispensable aid for linking Windows NT Workstation 4.0 users with Windows NT Server 4.0 over a wide variety of communications channels, including POTS, ISDN, Switched-56, and frame-relay services. This book is the companion volume to Chapter 19, "Managing Remote Access Service." Thompson, a principal of Triad Technology Group, Inc. in Winston-Salem, North Carolina, is the primary contributing author for *Special Edition Using Windows NT Server 4*, having written chapters 2, 5, 7, 8, 11, 14, and 18.

- *The BackOffice Intranet Kit* by Stephen Wynkoop (Que, ISBN 0-7897-0848-5) describes how to take advantage of the BackOffice components, such as SQL Server 6.5, to develop an effective intranet site that provides Web-page access to databases and mainframes. Wynkoop is a contributing author of this book's Chapter 21, "Administering Intranet and World Wide Web Sites."

- *Special Edition Using Windows NT Workstation 4.0* by Paul Sanna, et al. (Que, ISBN 0-7897-0673-3) provides coverage of the client-side features of Windows NT 4.0 that are beyond the scope of this book.

- *Windows 95 and NT 4.0 Registry & Customization Handbook* by Jerry Honeycutt (Que, ISBN 0-7897-0842-6) provides thorough coverage of Windows NT 4.0's Registry, complementing Chapter 9, "Understanding the Windows NT Registry."

- *Special Edition Using Microsoft Internet Information Server 4* (Que, ISBN 0-7897-1263-6) supplies detailed instructions for setting up an Internet or intranet Web site with IIS 4.0. This book extends the coverage of IIS in Chapter 20, "Setting Up Internet Information Server 4.0," and Chapter 21, "Administering Intranet and World Wide Web Sites."

- *Special Edition Using Microsoft FrontPage 97* by Neil Randall and Dennis Jones (Que, ISBN 0-7897-1036-6) supplements the meager written documentation accompanying FrontPage 97 with detailed instructions for designing and implementing Web pages for intranets.

- G.A. Sullivan's *Special Edition Using Microsoft BackOffice*, Volume I (Que, ISBN 0-7897-1142-7) and Volume II (Que, 0-7897-1130-3), provide nearly 1,800 pages of coverage of all the components of Microsoft BackOffice.

- *Special Edition Using Microsoft SQL Server 6.5*, Second Edition, by Stephen Wynkoop (Que, ISBN 0-7897-1117-6) is designed to bring system and database administrators, as well as developers, up-to-date on the latest version of Microsoft SQL Server.

- *Special Edition Using Microsoft Exchange Server 5* by Software Spectrum (Que, ISBN 0-7897-1116-8) is a detailed tutorial and reference for Exchange Server 5.0.

- *Special Edition Using Microsoft Systems Management Server 1.2* by Tim Darby, Lee Hadfield, and Neolani Rodriguez (Que, ISBN 0-7897-0820-5) shows you how to get the most out of SMS 1.2 when managing Windows 3.1+, Windows 95, and Windows NT 4.0 clients.

- *Platinum Edition Using Windows 95* by Ron Person, et al. (Que, ISBN 0-7897-0797-7) is a 1,432-page book that covers all aspects of Windows 95 in detail and is especially useful as a reference for Windows 95 client networking and user/policy management.

ON THE WEB

Additional information on Que's series of books on Microsoft Windows NT, Internet Information Server, and BackOffice and its components is available from the Macmillan Superlibrary at **http://www.mcp.com/que/**.

- *Inside Windows NT* by Helen Custer (Microsoft Press, ISBN 1-55615-481-X) describes the development history and design philosophy of Windows NT, and delves more deeply into details of the operating system than this book.

- *Inside the Windows NT File System* by Helen Custer (Microsoft Press, ISBN 1-55615-660-X) is a monograph that adds a detailed description of Windows NT's NTFS (New Technology File System) to Custer's original book. A brief discussion of the compression system for NTFS files also is included.

- *Windows NT Server Resource Kit* for version 4.0 (Microsoft Press, ISBN 1-57231-344-7) is an indispensable source of technical information about Windows NT Server 4. The Resource Kit consists of three books—*Microsoft Windows NT Networking Guide*, *Server Resource Guide*, and *Server Internet Guide* (for IIS 2.0)—plus the Server Resource Kit CD-ROM. Most of the information in the *Windows NT Resource Kit* for version 3.5 with the *Version 3.51 Update* also is applicable to Windows NT 4.0.

- *Windows NT Server Resource Kit, Supplement One* (Microsoft Press, ISBN 1-57231-344-7), provides additional coverage for IIS 2.0, DNS, ISDN, and Windows NT 4.0 performance tuning.

- *Windows NT Workstation Resource Kit* for version 4.0 (Microsoft Press, ISBN 1-57231-343-9) supplements the *Windows NT Server Resource Kit* with information that's applicable to both the Server and Workstation versions, such as the Registry.

- *Showstopper! The Breakneck Race to Create Windows NT and the Next Generation at Microsoft* by G. Pascal Zachary (The Free Press, ISBN 0-02-935671-7) uses a battlefield metaphor to depict the behind-the-scenes strategy and tactics of Microsoft's development program for Windows NT.

- *Windows NT Magazine* is a monthly publication of Duke Communications International, Inc., designed to help power users and network administrators get the most out of Windows NT. For subscription information, check out **http://www.winntmag.com**, or call (800) 621-1544 or (970) 663-4700.

- *Microsoft Interactive Developer,* published by Fawcette Technical Publications, Inc., covers Internet- and intranet-related topics, with emphasis on Internet Information Server. You can subscribe from Fawcette's Development Exchange Web site, **http://www.windx.com/**, from **http://www.microsoft.com/mind**, or by calling (800) 848-5523 or (415) 833-7100.

- *Microsoft TechNet* is a CD-ROM subscription service designed to aid those responsible for supporting Microsoft productivity applications and systems, including Windows NT and BackOffice. For further information, check out **http://www.microsoft.com/technet/**.

- *Microsoft Developers Network* (MSDN) is a tiered CD-ROM subscription service directed primarily to developers of 32-bit Windows applications. The MSDN CD-ROMs also include white papers on Windows NT and application development strategies for 32-bit Windows. MSDN Library Subscription (formerly Level I) is the basic service, with quarterly updates. MSDN Professional Subscription (formerly Level II) adds copies of Microsoft client operating systems and environments. The Enterprise Subscription (formerly Level III) supplements the preceding versions with developer copies of Windows NT Server and the BackOffice components. A new Universal Subscription adds Microsoft productivity applications to the Enterprise Subscription. For more information on subscribing to MSDN, see **http://www.microsoft.com/support/**.

Online Sources of Windows NT Server Information

The Internet is rapidly becoming the source of product knowledge and support for all PC-oriented products. The following sections list the most important Web sites and newsgroups that pertain to Windows NT Server 4.0 and BackOffice. Windows NT-related support forums on CompuServe also are listed.

Internet Web Sites   As Microsoft continues to "embrace and extend" the Internet and the World Wide Web, much of the information about and support for Microsoft products formerly found on commercial online services—such as CompuServe, America Online, and The Microsoft Network—is moving to the Internet. Following are Web sites devoted to Windows NT, BackOffice, and Internet Information Server:

- The *Microsoft BackOffice Live* home page at **http://backoffice.microsoft.com/** leads to sources of information on Windows NT Server 4.0 and the components of BackOffice 2.5.

- The *Windows NT Home Pages* site at **http://www.ptgs.com/links/serious/nt.htm** provides links to various sites with useful information on and utilities for Windows NT.

- *Windows NT Magazine*'s Professional Support Forums for Windows NT Server and Workstation are located at **http://www.winntmag.com/Forums/index.html**.

- Beverly Hills Software's *NT Advantage* Web site at **http://www.ntadvantage.com/** uses a magazine metaphor to deliver a variety of useful information on Windows NT 4.0 Workstation and Server.

- The NT Internals Web site at **http://www.ntinternals.com/** provides shareware utilities for Windows NT, plus information on operating system topics such as SMP scheduling, system calls, and NTFS defragmentation.

- *Avatar Magazine*, an online service of Fawcette Technical Publications, Inc., complements *Microsoft Interactive Developer* as "an interactive publication for creators of interactive media...from Web sites to digital video." Check out the Avatar site at **http://www.avatarmag.com/**.

- *DevX*, Fawcette Technical Publications' Web site for Windows developers at **http://www.windx.com/**, offers a wide range of news, features, and product reviews of interest to Windows NT Server administrators and programmers.

- Microsoft's *AnswerPoint* home page, **http://www.microsoft.com/supportnet/answerpoint/**, provides information about Microsoft's no-fee and low-fee support services for all its products. For other support options, go to **http://www.microsoft.com/Support/**.

Internet Newsgroups   Microsoft established its own Network News Transport Protocol (NNTP) news server, **msnews.microsoft.com**, in the spring of 1996. You must configure Internet Explorer 2.0 to read newsgroups by choosing Options from the View menu to open the Internet Properties sheet and making the appropriate settings on the News page. Alternatively, you can download the Internet Mail and News readers from **http://www.microsoft.com/ie/imn/**. Following are Microsoft-sponsored and Usenet newsgroups with Windows NT Server 4.0 content:

- A list of the Microsoft-sponsored newsgroups for Windows NT appears at **http://www.microsoft.com/support/news/winnt.htm**. These newsgroups don't provide support by Microsoft employees, but instead rely on user-to-user support. The newsgroups carry the prefix **microsoft.public.windowsnt**.

- Lists of similar Microsoft-sponsored newsgroups for Internet Information Server and each BackOffice component, with links to the newsgroups, are available through the Microsoft Newsgroup drop-down list of the **http://www.microsoft.com/support/** home page.

- Windows NT Usenet newsgroups are found at **comp.os.ms-windows.nt**. Subcategories are **admin, advocacy, misc, pre-release, setup,** and **software**. You can expect to find the greatest initial traffic on Windows NT 4.0 in the **comp.os.ms-windows.nt.pre-release** newsgroup.

CompuServe Forums   In early 1996, Microsoft abandoned direct support of its products on CompuServe by its Product Support Specialists (PSS) in favor of user-to-user support under the auspices of the Windows User Group Network (WUGNet) and other independent organizations. (Unlike its newsgroups and MSN offerings, Microsoft doesn't sponsor the CompuServe support forums, with the exception of MSKB and MSL.) Following are the CompuServe forums that are of primary interest to users of Windows NT:

- The Windows NT Forum (GO WINNT), run by WUGNet, is a source of support for both Windows NT Workstation and Server. You can access the Fixes & Updates library to obtain new Service Packs, drivers, and patches for Windows NT.

- The Windows NT Server (GO NTSERVER) and Windows NT Workstation (GO NTWORK) forums, run by WUGNet, also provide user-to-user support but have less message traffic than WINNT.

- The Microsoft Networks Forum (GO MSNET), run by Stream (a major software reseller), primarily addresses Systems Management Server (SMS) topics.

- The SQL Server Forum (GO MSSQL), run by Stream, is devoted to support for Microsoft SQL Server versions 4.21a and higher.

- The Windows NT SNA Server Forum (GO MSSNA), also run by Stream, provides support for IBM mainframe and AS/400 connectivity.

- The Microsoft Knowledge Base (GO MSKB) is a Microsoft forum with a searchable database of bug fixes, workarounds, technical papers, and press releases for all Microsoft products. The Microsoft Software Library (GO MSL) provides downloadable updates and patches for Microsoft products.

- The Windows Connectivity Forum (GO WINCON), run by WUGNet, covers a wide range of networking and other connectivity issues related to Windows 3.1+, Windows 95, and Windows NT.

- The Windows Users Group Forum (GO WUGNET) offers broad-spectrum coverage of Windows topics from the user's perspective.

Networking with Windows NT Server 4.0

1 Placing Windows NT Server in Perspective   19

2 Plannning Your Windows NT Network Installation   55

3 Understanding the Windows NT Operating System   83

4 Choosing Network Protocols   101

5 Purchasing Networking Hardware   123

CHAPTER 1

Placing Windows NT Server in Perspective

Windows NT Server is on a roll. According to International Data Corporation (IDC), a major market research organization, sales of Windows NT Server increased by more than 370 percent in 1995. IDC reported that Microsoft sold 725,000 licenses for Windows NT Server in 1996, up from 363,000 in 1995. Microsoft reported the sale of its 1 millionth Windows NT Server license in May 1997. In less than four years, Windows NT Server has emerged from niche status as an application server to become a major contender in the mainstream PC file- and printer-sharing server market now dominated by NetWare and, to a lesser extent, UNIX servers.

Microsoft's determination to make Windows NT the primary player in the Internet server market is sure to fuel a substantial proportion of the increase in sales of Windows NT Server 4.0 and its successors, including the Enterprise Edition scheduled for release in late 1997. Although the Internet's public World Wide Web garners most of the publicity, private intranets represent the market with the greatest growth potential for Windows NT Server.

Intranets, which run over existing local area networks (LANs) and wide area networks (WANs), deliver documents coded with the Web's Hypertext Markup Language (HTML) to clients equipped with low-cost or no-cost Web browsing applications. Just as Internet Information

New features of Windows NT Server 4.0

Beyond the Windows 95-style user interface, Windows NT Server 4.0 adds several new components and enhances overall performance.

Windows NT Server 4.0 and the Internet

Windows NT Server 4.0 initially shipped with Internet Information Server 2.0. New features in the IIS 3.0 upgrade to IIS 2.0 and IIS 4.0 offer improved interactivity and better Web-server performance.

Enterprise Edition components

The Enterprise Edition adds clustering, object brokering, transaction processing, prioritized messaging, and increased multiprocessor scaling to Windows NT Server 4.0.

Features promised for Windows NT 5.0

Windows NT 5.0 adds the Distributed File System, Kerberos security, LDAP-based directory services, and other high-end features to make Windows NT a more formidable competitor to UNIX systems.

Server is fully integrated with Windows NT Server 4.0, Microsoft's 32-bit Internet Explorer 4.0 is scheduled to become an integrated component of the Windows NT 5.0 and Windows 9x operating systems by early 1998.

This chapter introduces the fourth iteration of Windows NT Server, which Microsoft originally called the Shell Update Release (SUR). ■

The Mysterious Disappearance of Cairo

The first official use of "Version 4.0" with Windows NT appeared in the boot window of an alpha test release in late 1995 of the Windows 95 user-interface upgrade to Windows NT 3.51. At that time, Microsoft insisted that the SUR would be distributed as a maintenance release (Service Pack) for Windows NT 3.51, not as a new version.

Microsoft's plan was to reserve the official "4.0" designation for the repeatedly delayed Cairo operating system, then scheduled to begin beta testing in 1996. (Microsoft then called Cairo the "next major version of Windows NT.") Microsoft explained that "4.0" was required to notify Windows 95-compliant applications that the upgraded Windows NT operating system supported Windows 95's shell functions.

As the projected release date for Cairo extended into 1997 and then 1998, Microsoft acquiesced to the inevitable and made Windows NT 4.0 an "official" version. In early 1997, Microsoft dropped all references to Cairo and adopted "Windows NT 5.0" as the official name of the next major version. The next version of Windows 95, code-named Memphis and originally expected to be Windows 97, is called *Windows 9x* in this book.

Exploring What's New in Windows NT Server 4.0

Special Edition Using Windows NT Server 4, Second Edition, is devoted to a new release of an existing operating system, making a list of newly added features obligatory. The following sections briefly describe the new features of Windows NT Server 4.0, many of which also apply to Windows NT Workstation 4.0.

 Brief descriptions of new features are most significant to readers now using or at least familiar with prior versions of Windows NT Server. Detailed descriptions of each new Windows NT Server 4.0 feature that appear in the remaining chapters of this book are indicated by the version icon next to this paragraph.

The new features of the standard release of Windows NT Server 4.0 described in the following sections are grouped in the following categories:

- Server usability
- Client-side features
- Network performance and scalability
- TCP/IP and NetWare integration

- Troubleshooting tools
- Internet, intranet, and remote access services
- Distributed Component Object Model (DCOM)

Server Usability

Microsoft's usability improvements for Windows NT Server 4.0 arise primarily from features inherited from Windows 95 (such as the Windows 95 user interface, Explorer, and taskbar) and from the wizards of the Microsoft Office productivity software suite. The following sections describe the most important new features that affect Windows NT Server 4.0's usability from the perspective of a network administrator.

> **N O T E** Unfortunately, Windows NT Server 4.0 didn't inherit all of Windows 95's usability improvements. Windows NT 4.0 doesn't fully support Plug and Play installation of ISA adapter cards, printers, monitors, and other Plug and Play-compliant devices. Windows NT 4.0 also lacks Windows 95's Device Manager page of the System tool. These features are expected to be included in the Windows NT 5.0 release.

Windows 95 User Interface Microsoft's initial objective for the SUR was simply to graft the Windows 95 user interface (UI) to Windows NT to give the high-end operating system the "modern look and feel" before the release of Cairo. There's little controversy that the Windows 95 UI is a substantial improvement over that of Windows 3.1+. Although Windows 95 didn't achieve Microsoft's sales objectives for corporate desktops, it has enjoyed great success in the consumer and small-office/home-office (SOHO) markets. According to IDC, Microsoft shipped more than 60 million copies of Windows 95 since its introduction in August 1995, and sold 2.2 million copies of Windows NT Workstation in 1996.

Unfortunately, Microsoft elected to retain in Windows NT Server 4.0 the consumer-oriented My Computer and Network Neighborhood icons, whose names are believed to have originated with the ill-fated Microsoft Bob shell for Windows 3.1+. Fortunately, you can rename these two icons with more appropriate captions, such as the server name and Network Browser, respectively, as shown in Figure 1.1.

Windows Explorer Windows Explorer (shown in Figure 1.1) substitutes for Windows NT 3.x's File Manager, which in turn was derived from the original File Manager tool of Windows 3.0. From Explorer's File menu, members of groups with the required rights can

- Share drives and folders (but not individual files) in the Sharing page of the *Foldername* Properties sheet
- Establish share permissions, audit access, and take ownership of files and folders in the Security page of the *Foldername* Properties sheet (see Figure 1.2)
- Compress and decompress drives and files or folders (optionally including subfolders) of Windows NT File System (NTFS) volumes

FIG. 1.1

A Windows NT Server 4.0 desktop with Windows Explorer open.

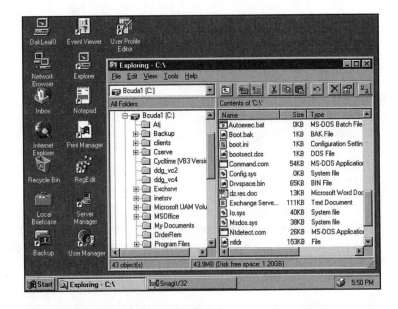

FIG. 1.2

The Security page of the *Foldername* Properties sheet for the Shared folder.

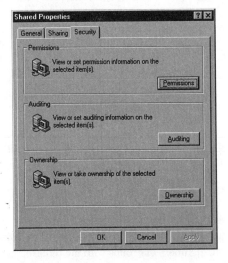

The *Foldername* Properties sheet is identical to that of Windows 95 except for the Security page, which isn't available in Windows 95. Windows NT compression isn't available for volumes formatted for the file allocation table (FAT) system used by DOS, Windows 3.x, and Windows 95. You can establish permissions, auditing, and ownership for a selected file—shared or not—in the *Filename* Properties sheet.

N O T E   This book uses the term *property sheet* when referring to dialogs used to set property values of a Windows NT object, such as a folder, file, user, or group. Property sheets originated with ActiveX controls (formerly OLE Controls, or OCXs), first introduced with Access 2.0.

Most Windows NT property sheets are tabbed dialogs that use the Windows 95 common dialog design. For consistency with ActiveX terminology, the term *property page* describes the view for the tab you click. ■

Task Manager   The Windows NT 4.0 Task Manager provides a substantial extension to the Task Manager tool of Windows NT 3.x. To open Task Manager, right-click the taskbar and choose Task Manager from the pop-up menu. The Task Manager window includes the following tabbed pages:

■ *Applications* lists the applications launched and the status of each (see Figure 1.3). Right-clicking an application entry displays the pop-up menu that provides such choices as jumping to a process or terminating a task.

FIG. 1.3
The Applications page of Windows NT Server 4.0's improved Task Manager.

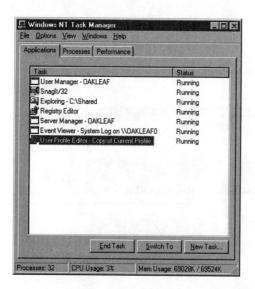

■ *Processes* lists all running executable files and allows you to check the percentage of processor time consumed by each process as well as a variety of other information about the process. Choosing Select Columns from the View menu allows you to customize the Processes display (see Figure 1.4).

■ *Performance* provides graphical displays of current and historical memory and CPU usage (see Figure 1.5).

Administrative Wizards   Microsoft wizards, which originated with Access 1.0, provide step-by-step guidance in the execution of administrative operations that involve an ordered sequence of tasks. All the components of Microsoft Office and Windows 95 have adopted wizards to assist users in performing sequential operations or to streamline single-step tasks. Windows NT Server 4.0 provides the following wizards:

■ The *Add User Account Wizard* guides you through the process of adding new user accounts to a Windows NT Server 4.0 network (see Figure 1.6).

FIG. 1.4

Customizing the display of Task Manager's Processes page.

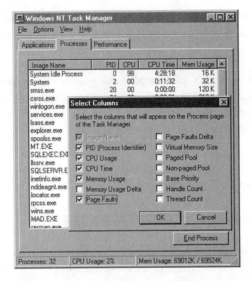

FIG. 1.5

Task Manager's graphical display of server memory and CPU usage.

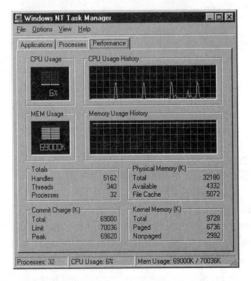

- The *Group Management Wizard* allows you to create and manage groups of users to minimize the effort needed to assign rights to individual user accounts.

- The *Managing File and Folder Access Wizard* provides a five-step method for sharing and securing drives or folders with Microsoft Networking, Apple Macintosh, and Novell NetWare clients (see Figure 1.7).

- The *Add Printer Wizard* sets up local or network printers for printer sharing. The wizard also installs the necessary printer drivers on the server that are automatically downloaded to Windows NT clients when printing to a shared printer.

FIG. 1.6
The second step in adding a new user account with the Add User Account Wizard.

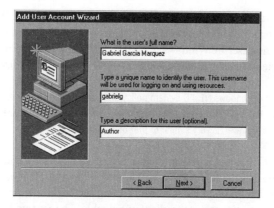

FIG. 1.7
The third step in sharing a server folder with the Managing File and Folder Access Wizard.

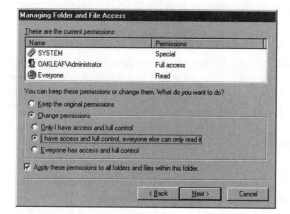

- The *Network Client Administrator Wizard* automates the installation and updating of client software on networked PCs.
- The *License Wizard* lets administrators track software licenses for servers and clients to ensure compliance with licensing agreements.
- The *Add/Remove Programs Wizard* provides a shortcut to Control Panel's Add/Remove Programs tool for installing or removing applications and their associated libraries and Registry keys.
- The *Install New Modem Wizard* detects and sets up modems connected to the server.

The first three wizards in this list are especially useful for administrators new to Windows NT Server. The Network Client Administrator Wizard and License Wizard aid new and experienced network administrators. The last two wizards primarily are of interest to users of Windows NT Workstation 4.0.

Client-Side Features

Windows 95 introduced the concept of server-stored *system policies* and *user profiles* for centralized management of Windows 95 clients and to provide each networked user with his or her own custom desktop when logging on to the network from any location. Windows NT Server 4.0 extends system policies and user profiles to clients running Windows NT Workstation 4.0. The following sections describe Windows NT Server 4.0's new System Policy Editor for establishing system policies and user profiles, and support for diskless Windows 95 clients.

N O T E   The structure of Windows NT 4.0 system policy and user profile files varies from that of Windows 95. Windows NT Server 4.0's methodology for creating and managing system policies and user profiles, however, is very similar to that of Windows 95. ■

System Policy Editor   System administrators use system policies to enforce standardization of client desktops, as well as to limit users' capability to modify the client environment. As an example, you might want to restrict users from editing the client's Registry because making an incorrect Registry entry can render the client unbootable. The System Policy Editor forms the underpinnings of the Zero Administration Kit (ZAK) for clients running Windows NT Workstation 4.0 that Microsoft announced in March 1997.

Windows NT Server 4.0's new System Policy Editor is based on the PolEdit.exe application of Windows 95 (see Figure 1.8). You can create specific system policies for each user group or for individual users. Policy files are stored in the virtual netlogon share (the physical \Winnt\System32\Repl\Import\Scripts folder) and accessed by clients during startup of Windows NT Workstation 4.0. Information stored in the System Policy file modifies the HKEY_CURRENT_USER and HKEY_LOCAL_MACHINE keys of the client's Registry. For more information about the Registry, see Chapter 9, "Understanding the Windows NT Registry."

User Profiles   User profiles contain values of the user-definable settings that control the operating environment of client (and server) PCs running Windows NT 4.0. You create and edit Windows NT 4.0 user profiles for user groups and individual user accounts with Upedit.exe (see Figure 1.9).

N O T E   The Windows NT Server 4.0 Setup program doesn't install the User Profile Editor. You install Upedit.exe and its associated help file from the d:\Clients\SvrTools\WinNT\i386\ folder of the distribution CD-ROM. ■

Remote Server Administration from Windows 95 Clients   The Windows NT Server 4.0 distribution CD-ROM includes separate sets of remote server administration utilities for networked PCs running Windows 95 and Windows NT Workstation 4.0. The Windows 95 version installs the following tools in the Start menu's Programs, Windows NT Tools group:

- *Event Viewer* lets you read the System, Security, and Application logs of any Windows NT computer on the network. Figure 1.10 shows the Windows 95 Event Viewer displaying System events from a Windows NT 4.0 server.

- *Server Manager* lets you manage user connections, shared folders, open resources, replications, and alerts on Windows NT servers.

- *User Manager for Domains* lets you manage groups and users in any domain for which you have Administrator privileges.

FIG. 1.8

Restricting user options for Windows NT 4.0 PCs with the System Policy Editor.

FIG. 1.9

Setting a user group profile for account operators with the User Profile Editor.

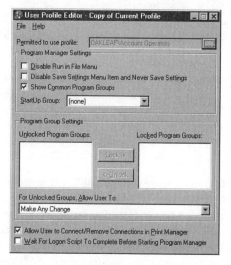

Windows 95 Remote Program Load   Windows 95's *Remote Program Load (RPL)* lets diskless Windows 95 clients boot from Windows NT Server 4.0. Diskless Windows 95 clients are very uncommon, perhaps non-existent; running Windows 95 from a server creates very heavy network traffic. It's likely that Microsoft provided RPL in an effort to counter the Network Computer (NC) proposed by Oracle Corp. The acceptance of NCs in the business and consumer markets of 1997 and beyond remains to be proven.

Network Performance and Scalability Features

Ever-increasing network traffic and expansion of LANs and WANs to accommodate a larger number of domains requires commensurate enhancement of server capabilities, especially the performance of servers used as domain controllers. The following sections discuss the new features of Windows NT Server 4.0 that provide faster access by clients to shared server resources.

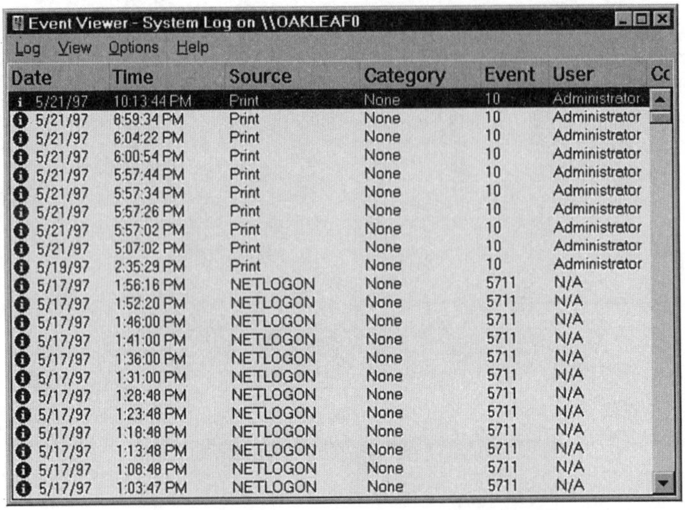

FIG. 1.10

Displaying server system events remotely with the Windows 95 version of Event Viewer.

Date	Time	Source	Category	Event	User	Co
i 5/21/97	10:13:44 PM	Print	None	10	Administrator	
5/21/97	8:59:34 PM	Print	None	10	Administrator	
5/21/97	6:04:22 PM	Print	None	10	Administrator	
5/21/97	6:00:54 PM	Print	None	10	Administrator	
5/21/97	5:57:44 PM	Print	None	10	Administrator	
5/21/97	5:57:34 PM	Print	None	10	Administrator	
5/21/97	5:57:26 PM	Print	None	10	Administrator	
5/21/97	5:57:02 PM	Print	None	10	Administrator	
5/21/97	5:07:02 PM	Print	None	10	Administrator	
5/19/97	2:35:29 PM	Print	None	10	Administrator	
5/17/97	1:56:16 PM	NETLOGON	None	5711	N/A	
5/17/97	1:52:20 PM	NETLOGON	None	5711	N/A	
5/17/97	1:46:00 PM	NETLOGON	None	5711	N/A	
5/17/97	1:41:00 PM	NETLOGON	None	5711	N/A	
5/17/97	1:36:00 PM	NETLOGON	None	5711	N/A	
5/17/97	1:31:00 PM	NETLOGON	None	5711	N/A	
5/17/97	1:28:48 PM	NETLOGON	None	5711	N/A	
5/17/97	1:23:48 PM	NETLOGON	None	5711	N/A	
5/17/97	1:18:48 PM	NETLOGON	None	5711	N/A	
5/17/97	1:13:48 PM	NETLOGON	None	5711	N/A	
5/17/97	1:08:48 PM	NETLOGON	None	5711	N/A	
5/17/97	1:03:47 PM	NETLOGON	None	5711	N/A	

Faster File Sharing on High-Speed LANs   The rapidly declining cost of 100 Mbps adapter cards and switchable hubs is making implementation of Fast Ethernet cost-effective for LANs with heavy traffic, such as that generated by videoconferencing or delivery of full-screen, full-motion video to clients. Microsoft claims up to double the throughput over 100BaseT networks compared with Windows NT Server 3.51, based on tests conducted by National Software Testing Laboratories (NTSL).

Server Scalability   *Scalability* is a measure of the capability of multiprocessing operating systems to provide increased performance by adding processors. A perfectly scalable system delivers four times the performance when you install three additional processors to a conventional single-processor system. High-end UNIX operating systems traditionally have offered better scalability than PC-based network operating systems such as Windows NT and NetWare. Microsoft claims that the *symmetrical multiprocessing* (SMP) of Windows NT Server 4.0 delivers improved performance scalability with high-end server hardware, compared to Windows NT Server 3.5+, especially systems with more than four processors.

N O T E   Scalability with SMP requires that such services as relational database management systems (RDBMSes) and Web servers be written to take maximum advantage of multi-threading in high-load environments. (SMP assigns an application thread for execution by the processor with the lightest workload.) There is overhead in the thread assignment process, so achieving 100 percent (perfect) scalability is impossible. The architecture of the system motherboard and the operating system have a pronounced influence on scalability. NCR reports that Windows NT Server 4.0 can achieve 90 percent scalability with four processors. ■

According to the Aberdeen Group, servers with four processors or fewer comprise 90 percent of the entire server market. 200MHz+ Pentium Pro processors have become the choice for most off-the-shelf, high-performance Windows NT servers. Recent price reductions for DEC's Alpha processor make it a contender for prebuilt commodity servers with one to four processors. When a four-processor server runs out of steam, server clustering technology is likely to be a better choice than adding more processors. Microsoft and third-party approaches to Windows NT Server 4.0 clustering is one subject of the "Scaling Up to Windows NT Server 4.0 Enterprise Edition" section near the end of this chapter.

ON THE WEB

You can review the Aberdeen Group's white paper, "Debunking the NT/SMP Scalability Myth," at **http://
/www.microsoft.com/ntserver/info/aberdeen.htm**.

Expanded Directory Services   The Windows NT Directory Service accommodates a larger number of entries (objects), depending on the amount of RAM installed in the server. (There's no limit to the number of trusting domains.) Windows NT Server 4.0 expands the recommended number of trusted domains from a maximum of 128 in version 3.51 to 140 for 32M, 250 for 64M, and 500 for 128M of RAM. The administrator can override the recommendations and, for example, increase the size of the non-paged pool (NPP) to accommodate 500 trusted domains with a server having 64M of RAM. Doing so, however, isn't a recommended practice, because it results in a dramatic performance hit.

Printing Enhancements   Windows NT 4.0 uses *server-based* rendering of print jobs for printers that don't use the Adobe PostScript page description language. Server-based rendering minimizes the time spent by clients processing complex print jobs generated by desktop publishing, image editing, and similar applications. The file-sharing enhancements of Windows NT Server 4.0 for 100BaseT networks, noted earlier in the section "Faster File Sharing on High-Speed LANs," also speed the processing of print jobs.

Application Server APIs and Fibers for Developers   New APIs for writing server-based applications provide improved performance by updated services, such as SQL Server 6.5. Lightweight threads, which Microsoft calls *fibers*, make it easier for developers to optimize scheduling within multithreaded applications. Microsoft says that Windows NT 4.0 uses "[l]onger quantums to reduce context switches and cache churning" and has "[c]onditional critical section acquire." It's hoped that application programmers will take full advantage of such arcane (but important) new features of Windows NT Server 4.0 when writing 32-bit server applications. (Developer features of Windows NT Server 4.0 are beyond the scope of this book.)

TCP/IP and NetWare Integration Features

Each release of Windows NT Server has improved integration with TCP/IP and NetWare networks. (Built-in support for the TCP/IP protocol was introduced with Windows NT Server 3.5.) The following sections describe the new features of Windows NT Server 4.0 for heterogeneous networks.

Graphical Domain Name Service Tool   Windows NT Server 4.0 now offers a dynamic Domain Name Service (DNS) derived from Microsoft's proprietary Windows Internet Name Service (WINS) protocol. DNS is an Internet-standard service that translates character-based addresses (host names), such as **www.msn.com**, to numeric IP addresses, such as 204.255.247.121. You also can use DNS compound names, such as \\oakleaf1.oakleaf.com\ *whatever*, to access a server share. Using WINS is covered in Chapter 10, "Using TCP/IP, WINS, and DHCP"; DNS is one of the subjects of Chapter 18, "Integrating Windows NT with NetWare and UNIX."

Combining DNS with WINS simplifies the integration of Windows NT Server 4.0 with TCP/IP networks of all types, not just the Internet. Previously, Windows NT Server's DNS was static and required network administrators to create a text-based list of host names and their corresponding IP addresses. Windows NT Server 4.0 allows DNS to query WINS for name resolution. The new graphical Domain Name Service Manager tool of Windows NT Server 4.0 speeds the mapping of DNS server names (see Figure 1.11).

FIG. 1.11

Displaying addresses for a DNS server in the Domain Name Service Manager.

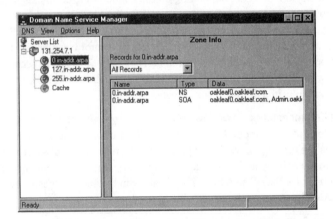

Novell NetWare Interoperability   Windows NT 4.0's Client for NetWare and Gateway Service for NetWare (GSNW) now support NetWare Directory Services (NDS), enabling browsing of NDS resources (by using NetWare 3.1x bindery emulation mode), NDS authentication, and NDS printing. (Gateway Services for NetWare lets a Windows NT 4.0 server process dial-in connections to resources located on NetWare servers.) Figure 1.12 illustrates GSNW's Configure Gateway dialog with a NetWare share added. Windows NT Server 4.0 also supports authentication to multiple NDS trees and can process NetWare logon scripts.

File, Print, and Directory Services for NetWare

File and Print Services for NetWare (FPNW) is a utility that allows Windows NT Server 4.0 to emulate a NetWare 3.12-compatible file and print server. The objective is to allow networked PCs with only Novell client software to access file and print services on a Windows NT 4.0 server. Clients also can run the Windows NT versions of applications now installed as NetWare Loadable Modules (NLMs).

Directory Services Manager for NetWare (DSMN) lets network administrators manage their Windows NT Server and NetWare account information centrally. Only one user account and associated password need be maintained for each user on the network.

FPNW and DSMN aren't included with Windows NT Server 4.0, and individual server licenses must be purchased from Microsoft. FPNW and DSMN now are included in a single product, Microsoft Services for NetWare, which is covered in Chapter 18, "Integrating Windows NT with NetWare and UNIX." The purpose of FPNW and DSMN is to simplify the transition from NetWare to Windows NT servers by eliminating the need to substitute Microsoft for Novell network drivers on the clients.

FIG. 1.12
A NetWare share added to a Windows NT 4.0 server with the Gateway Service for NetWare feature.

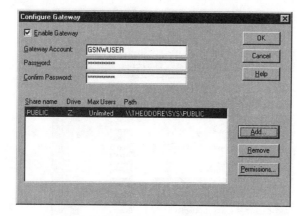

ON THE WEB

More information of Microsoft Services for NetWare is available at **http://www.microsoft.com/windows/common/a2248.htm**.

Multi-Protocol Router (MPR)   The *Multi-Protocol Router* (*MPR*) allows Windows NT Server to route packets and dynamically exchange routing data for TCP/IP, Novell IPX, and AppleTalk protocols by using the *Routing Internet Protocol* (*RIP*) with other routers that use RIP. You need two network cards in the server PC to take advantage of MPR for LAN-to-LAN routing. MPR consists of RIP for TCP/IP, RIP for NWLink IPX/SPX, and BOOTP (Boot Protocol) for Windows NT Server's Dynamic Host Configuration Protocol (DHCP).

N O T E   MPR first appeared in the Service Pack 2 update to Windows NT 3.51; technically, MPR isn't a new feature of Windows NT Server 4.0. ▪

Troubleshooting Tools

As the complexity of server hardware, software, and networks increases, network administrators require sophisticated diagnostic tools to aid in troubleshooting networking problems. The following sections describe Windows NT Server 4.0's improvement to version 3.51's diagnostics program and the new Network Monitor included with Windows NT Server 4.0.

Improved Diagnostics Tool   Windows NT Server 4.0 includes a new Windows NT Diagnostics tool, which centralizes the display of Windows NT system properties in a single window with nine tabbed pages. The pages display only system property values; you must use Control Panel tools or administrative applications to make changes to these values where possible. Following is a list of the tool's pages and the function of each page:

- *Services* (see Figure 1.13) lists all applications and tools that run as Windows NT services and their current status, such as Running or Stopped, plus the devices in use. You use Control Panel's Services tool to change the status of individual services.

FIG. 1.13

The Services page of the Windows NT Diagnostics tool.

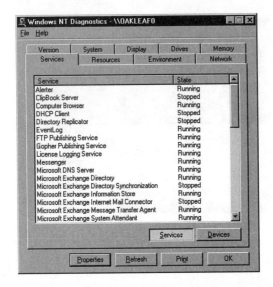

N O T E   A *service* is an application—such as Alerter, DHCP Client, or SQL Server—that can be executed during the Windows NT startup process. Windows NT services are similar in concept to terminate-and-stay-resident (TSR) DOS applications. ■

- *Resources* selectively shows the interrupts (IRQ), I/O ports, DMA channels, and upper memory blocks used by installed hardware, plus a list of hardware devices in use.
- *Environment* displays the values of environmental variables for the system (the server PC) and the location of the local user's temporary files.
- *Network* provides information about logged-on users, the transports in use, network settings, and networking statistics (see Figure 1.14).
- *Version* shows the current version of Windows NT Server 4.0 in use and registration information.
- *System* displays the identifier (AT/AT COMPATIBLE for Intel PCs), the Hardware Abstraction Layer (HAL) in use, information on the server's BIOS, and a list of the installed processors.

FIG. 1.14
Networking statistics displayed by the Network page of the Windows NT Diagnostics tool.

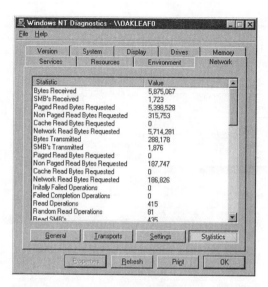

- *Display* shows information about your graphics adapter card and the Windows NT drivers that support the card.

- *Drives* supplies details about the server's removable, fixed, CD-ROM, and network-connected drives.

- *Memory* provides statistics on the available and consumed RAM, with the size and usage of the paging file.

Network Monitor   Windows NT Server 4.0's new Network Monitor tool allows you to capture a snapshot of network traffic that you can analyze later to uncover network performance bottlenecks or to perform other troubleshooting tasks. Network Monitor—derived from the SMS Network Monitor of Microsoft Systems Management Server (SMS) 1.2—provides many of the features of dedicated network analysis systems, such as Network General's Sniffers. The built-in Network Monitor tool captures only traffic to and from the server; the SMS Network Monitor captures all network traffic on the network segment.

Figure 1.15 shows the default arrangement of Network Monitor's window. The following list describes the information presented in the window's four panes:

- *Graphs* displays five bar graphs in the upper-left pane that show the percentage of network usage, plus the number of frames, bytes, broadcasts, and multicasts per second. (Only the first three bar graphs appear in Figure 1.15.)

- Below the bar graphs, *Session Stats* displays detailed information on conversations between nodes defined by Network Address 1 and Network Address 2.

- At the bottom of the window, *Station Stats* presents a columnar list of all network nodes visible to the server, with individual frame and byte counts for each node.

- *Total Stats*, at the upper-right of the window, displays Network Statistics, Capture Statistics, Per Second Statistics, Network Card (MAC) Statistics, and Network Card (MAC) Error Statistics in a scrolling list.

FIG. 1.15
Network Monitor's
default window.

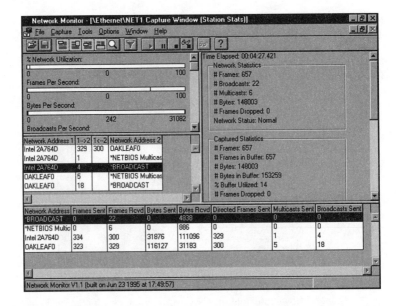

After you install the Network Monitor tools and Agent Service from Control Panel's Network tool, you click the toolbar's Start Capture button (with the VCR play symbol) to begin the logging process. Then click the Stop Capture and View button (with the VCR stop symbol and glasses) when you've captured the desired number of frames. During the capture process, the bar graphs display network activity. The Capture Summary pane takes over Network Monitor's window, as shown in Figure 1.16.

FIG. 1.16
Displaying information
for all frames captured
in the Capture Summary
pane.

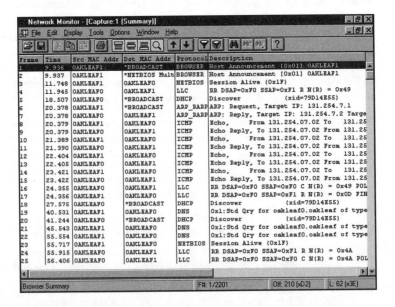

Double-clicking an entry in the Capture Summary pane displays the two additional panes (see Figure 1.17). The middle Capture Detail pane displays the frame data by OSI component layers. The bottom Capture Hex pane displays a hex and ASCII dump of the content of the selected frame.

FIG. 1.17

Displaying information for a specific frame in the Capture Detail and Capture Hex panes.

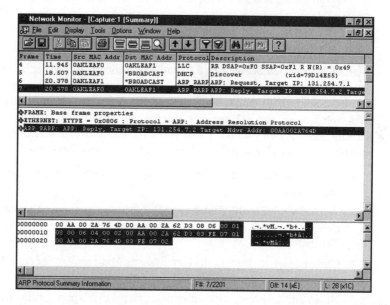

You can apply Network Monitor's Display Filter by clicking the Edit Display Filter toolbar button (with the funnel symbol) to display the Display Filter dialog (see Figure 1.18). You can use Boolean logic to create a custom filter with the AND, OR, and NOT buttons that open the Expression dialog. Creating custom filters is useful in isolating network problems, such as cross-router traffic, that degrade overall network performance.

FIG. 1.18

Designing a capture filter with Display Filter's Expression dialog.

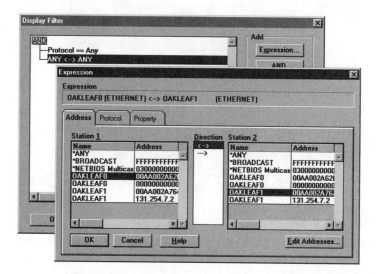

Internet, Intranet, and Remote Access Service

A substantial percentage of the new installations of Windows NT Server 4.0 are likely to be devoted to delivering Web pages via the Internet or, more likely, a private intranet. Later, the section "Embracing and Extending the Internet" discusses Microsoft's Internet and intranet strategy. Meanwhile, the following sections describe the new features of Windows NT Server 4.0 specific to Internet and intranet services, plus a related topic—Remote Access Service (RAS), also called Dial-Up Networking (DUN).

Internet Information Server 2.0, 3.0, and 4.0 Microsoft Internet Information Server 2.0, which is included with the standard retail distribution version of Windows NT Server 4.0, is fully integrated with Windows NT Server 4.0's security and administrative features. IIS supplies Web, Gopher, and FTP services, and uses the Secure Sockets Layer (SSL) to provide the security necessary for communication privacy and simple implementations of online Internet shopping services. New features of IIS version 2.0 are as follows:

- Installation of IIS 2.0 now is incorporated into the Windows NT Server 4.0 Setup application.

- You can administer IIS 2.0 with any Web browser running either on the server or from a client. Microsoft Internet Explorer 2.0 is included on the Windows NT Server 4.0 distribution CD-ROM.

- Other administrative tools include Systems Management Server 1.2 and Simple Network Management Protocol (SNMP).

- NCSA- and CERN-style map files help you port Web pages from UNIX systems to IIS 2.0.

- The Create New Key and Certificate Request dialog of the new Key Manager tool (see Figure 1.19) generates the key pair required to obtain an SSL certificate from VeriSign.

FIG. 1.19

Generating a key pair to obtain a Secure Sockets Layer certificate from VeriSign.

ON THE WEB

For more information on SSL certificates for IIS 2.0, visit **http://www.verisign.com**.

Part

I

Ch

1

- Improvements to IIS 2.0 and Windows NT Server 4.0 increase performance by more than 40 percent, compared with IIS 1.0 running on Windows NT Server 3.51.

- IIS 2.0 offers the Point-to-Point Tunneling Protocol (PPTP) built in to Windows NT Server 4.0 to create secure private intranets that users can access via public data networks, including the Internet.

- The Internet Database Connector (IDC) now can send multiple queries from a single HTML page and correctly format the query result sets.

- Internet Services Application Programming Interface (ISAPI) programming is improved by exposing several server variables to IF %*variable*% statements in template (.HTX) files and by supporting nested IF statements.

- IIS 2.0+ supports Microsoft Proxy Server (originally codenamed *Catapult*) for creating software-based security firewalls with Windows NT 4.0 servers. Proxy Server isn't included with Windows NT Server 4.0; a separate license is required for each installation.

- You can add the Microsoft Index Server (originally codenamed *Tivoli*) to Windows NT Server 4.0 for content indexing and full-text searching of HTML and Microsoft Office documents. Index Server isn't included on the Windows NT Server 4.0 distribution CD-ROM, but it's a component of IIS 3.0.

ON THE WEB

You can download a 60-day trial version of Proxy Server, which requires Windows NT 4.0 Service Pack 2, from **http://www.microsoft.com/proxy/common/eval.htm**. You can download the required files for Index Server from **http://www.microsoft.com/msdownload/iis_is.htm**.

Internet Information Server 3.0 adds Active Server Pages (ASP), OLE DB, and ActiveX Data Objects (ADO) to IIS 2.0. OLE DB and ADO are new database access technologies destined to replace Microsoft's Open Database Connectivity (ODBC) API and the Data Access Object (DAO) of Microsoft Office and Visual Basic. IIS 3.0 requires Windows NT 4.0 Service Pack 2 and is included on the Service Pack 2 CD-ROM. IIS 4.0, in the beta-testing stage when this book was written, adds more features to IIS 3.0, such as HTTP 1.1 compliance, integration with Microsoft Transaction Server, Microsoft Management Console administration, customizable logging, and overall performance improvements. IIS 4.0 is the subject of Chapter 20, "Setting Up Internet Information Server 4.0," and Chapter 21, "Administering Intranet and World Wide Web Sites." A brief description of the new management features of IIS 4.0 appears later in the section "Managing Internet Information Server."

ON THE WEB

You can download the IIS 3.0 ASP extensions from **http://www.microsoft.com/iis/default.asp**.

N O T E Depending on the source of your Windows NT Server 4.0 CD-ROM, IIS 3.0, IE 3.01+, Index Server, and other updated products may be included. If you plan to install IIS 4.0, don't install IIS 2.0 from the CD-ROM or add the IIS 3.0 Active Server Pages upgrade to IIS 2.0. You must remove previous versions of IIS before you can install IIS 4.0. ■

Point-to-Point Tunneling Protocol (PPTP)   PPTP provides data security when you're connecting clients to servers via public data networks, such as the Internet, by using dial-up connections. You can use PPTP to create a virtual private network (VPN) at a very low cost if you're willing to live with the data rates provided by Integrated Services Digital Network (ISDN) or 28.8 kbps modems.

N O T E   Your Internet service provider must have PPTP installed for remote clients to connect by using PPTP. ▆

PPTP uses protocol encapsulation to support multiple protocols via TCP/IP connections and encrypts data to assure privacy. Although PPTP isn't as secure as the protocols under development for Internet commerce that involve bank cards and other credit instruments for payments, it's more secure than today's face-to-face transactions during which a merchant or waiter has temporary possession of your credit card.

RAS Multilink Channel Aggregation   RAS Multilink Channel Aggregation allows dial-in clients to combine multiple modem or ISDN lines to gain faster communication with Windows NT 4.0 servers. This feature is primarily of interest for fixed sites with the need for periodic connections, not to mobile users who seldom have access to multiple lines. Most of today's low-cost digital ISDN modems for the Basic Rate Interface (BRI) automatically bridge two ISDN B (bearer) channels to achieve data rates of 112 kbps or 128 kbps. You can aggregate one or more conventional modems with ISDN modems, but this is unlikely to become a conventional practice. Multilink Channel Aggregation is most useful to bridge from 2 to all 23 B channels of the ISDN Primary Rate Interface to achieve a data rate close to that of a North American T-1 trunk (1.544 Mbps). Multilink Channel Aggregation is one of the subjects of Chapter 19, "Managing Remote Access Service."

FrontPage   Windows NT Server 4.0's distribution CD-ROM includes a copy of FrontPage 1.1, Microsoft's first integrated Web page authoring and management tool. FrontPage 1.1's Web server management component, FrontPage Explorer, provides outline and link views of individual Internet or intranet sites (see Figure 1.20). FrontPage 1.1 also includes an integrated HTML editor for creating Web pages (see Figure 1.21). The bundled FrontPage 1.1 comes with single-server and single-client licenses. You must buy the retail version if you want to support additional servers or clients.

ON THE WEB

In late 1996, Microsoft upgraded FrontPage 1.1 to FrontPage 97 with Bonus Pack, also a retail product. If you've installed an early version of FrontPage 97 on your server, be sure to download the updated server extensions from **http://www.microsoft.com/frontpage/softlib/agreement.htm**. The update fixes a bug that lets unauthorized persons add content to a FrontPage 97 Web site.

FIG. 1.20

The Outline View and Link View panes of the FrontPage 1.1 Explorer application.

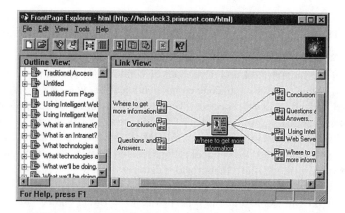

FIG. 1.21

FrontPage 1.1's WYSIWYG Web page editing application.

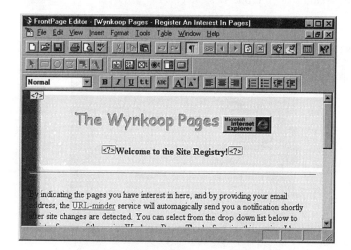

Distributed Component Object Model (DCOM)

The Component Object Model (COM) is Microsoft's specification for creating reusable application components that developers can combine into custom applications to fulfill specific objectives. Microsoft's Object Linking and Embedding (OLE) specification 2+, which includes OLE Automation (now called simply Automation), is an extension to COM. Automation is the foundation on which three-tier client/server applications are built. Three-tier applications consist of the following components:

- *User services* run on the client and provide the user interface to the application. User services communicate with business services.

- *Business services*, also called *business rules*, communicate with data services. Business services are implemented by Automation servers.

- *Data services* provided by relational database management systems (RDBMSes) run on an application server, such as Windows NT Server.

Original OLE Controls (OCXs) and the new, lightweight ActiveX controls also are built on COM. The original implementation of COM required that Automation clients and servers run on the same PC.

Both the Server and Workstation versions of Windows NT 4.0 support Distributed COM (DCOM), which allows stand-alone components (called *out-of-process OLE* or *Automation servers*) and ActiveX DLLs (in-process servers) written to the DCOM specification to communicate across networks. Microsoft provides a DCOM upgrade for Windows 95 and promises to add DCOM support for Macintosh clients. DCOM allows developers to implement three-tier architecture with Automation server applications located on a server, which don't need to be the server running the RDBMS that provides data services. Registered local and remote Automation servers (also called *Remote Automation Objects*) appear in the Applications page of the Distributed COM Configuration Properties sheet shown in Figure 1.22. Two other pages let you set default DCOM properties and security features.

FIG. 1.22

Automation servers registered as DCOM objects in the Applications page of the Distributed COM Configuration Properties sheet.

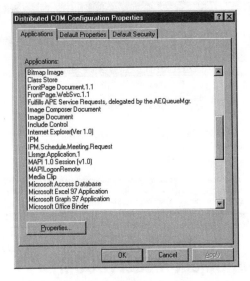

> **N O T E** During its development, Microsoft referred to Distributed COM as *NetworkOLE*, and you may continue to see references to NetworkOLE even by Microsoft employees. The Enterprise Edition of Visual Basic 4.0 implemented what Microsoft called "NetworkOLE 0.9" to support Remote Automation Objects created with Visual Basic running under Windows NT Server 3.51. If you now run Visual Basic 4.0 Remote Automation Objects on a Windows NT 3.51 server, you should upgrade from NetworkOLE 0.9 to DCOM—both the server and the clients—when migrating to Windows NT Server 4.0. VBA 5.0, used by Visual Basic 5.0 and Office 97, includes built-in programming support for DCOM. ■

DCOM is enabled by default, but the Distributed COM Configuration Properties sheet (Dcomcnfg.exe) isn't installed as a Start menu option when you install Windows NT Server 4.0. You can run Dcomcnfg.exe from the \Winnt\System32 folder, or add a shortcut to Dcomcnfg.exe to the Start menu's Programs, Administrative Tools (Common) menu or on the desktop. DCOM is required to use Microsoft Transaction Server (MTS, originally Viper), Microsoft Messaging Queue Server (MSMQ, formerly Falcon), and other new "enterprise extensions" to Windows NT Server 4.0. Chapter 26, "Scaling Windows NT Server 4.0 to the Enterprise," describes how Microsoft plans to use DCOM to implement multitier client/server applications.

▶ **See** "Brokering Business Objects," **p. 974**

Telephony API (TAPI) 2.x

TAPI 2.0 is an updated Win32 service that provides in Windows NT 4.0 the basic functionality of Windows 95's TAPI 1.4. TAPI uses Microsoft and third-party Telephony Service Provider (TSP) products to implement communication services. Windows NT 4.0 includes Microsoft's 32-bit Unimodem (Universal Modem) driver, which first appeared in Windows 95, as a built-in TSP.

TAPI 2.0 is backwardly compatible with TSPs and other TAPI 1.4 telephony applications that run on Windows 95. TAPI 2.0 supports 16-bit TAPI applications through a thunking layer (Tapi.dll) that supplies 32-bit addresses to Windows NT 4.0's Tapi32.dll. Tapi32.dll provides the marshaling layer, using lightweight remote procedure calls (LRPCs), to transfer function requests to Tapisrv.exe and to load and invoke required TSP DLLs.

Windows NT 4.0's TAPI 2.0 components support symmetrical multiprocessing, multithreaded applications, and preemptive multitasking on Intel and RISC processors. According to Microsoft, TAPI 2.0 enhances call-center management with modeling of predictive dialing ports and queues, provides call and data association, and offers music-on-hold features. Applications can negotiate and renegotiate quality-of-service (QoS) parameters to request a specific bandwidth. You must purchase TAPI 2.0-enabled third-party TSPs and application software to take advantage of these new TAPI features.

The Unimodem TSP of Windows NT 4.0 provides substantially improved performance compared with the relatively limited telecommunications features of Windows NT 3.5+. Windows NT 4.0 provides much better support for large modem banks used by RAS (Remote Access Service) servers, and comes with many more modem-definition files. The RAS features of TAPI 2.0 are one of the subjects of Chapter 19, "Managing Remote Access Service."

In March 1997, Microsoft announced the beta version of TAPI 2.1. According to the Microsoft press release, TAPI 2.1 includes a new TAPI remote service provider, a client management tool, and extensible client management APIs. The primary objective of TAPI 2.1, the final version of which is expected to be available in 1997, is to simplify the process of creating client/server telephony applications.

ON THE WEB

You can download the beta version of the TAPI 2.1 Software Developer Kit (SDK) from **http://www.microsoft.com/ntserver/info/tapiannounce21.htm**.

Using the Windows NT 4.0 Resource Kits

Special Edition Using Windows NT Server 4, Second Edition, is a comprehensive tutorial and reference for Windows NT Server 4.0, but publishing limitations preclude detailed coverage of the more arcane features of Windows NT 4.0. Unlike the *Windows NT Resource Kit* for version 3.5, Microsoft broke version 4.0's kit into *Workstation* and *Server* versions, and dropped the very useful *Windows NT Messages* volume of the Windows NT 3.5 version. The Windows NT 4.0 Resource Kits, briefly described in the introduction to this book, comprise the following volumes:

- *Windows NT Server Resource Kit* for version 4.0 contains information specific to Windows NT Server 4.0, with emphasis on networking issues. The Resource Kit consists of three books—*Microsoft Windows NT Networking Guide*, *Server Resource Guide*, and *Server Internet Guide* (for IIS 2.0)—plus the Server Resource Kit CD-ROM. The most important of the tools on the CD-ROM are the DiskProbe and DiskSave utilities discussed in Chapter 6, "Making the Initial Server Installation," and Chapter 7, "Setting Up Redundant Arrays of Inexpensive Disks (RAID)."

- *Windows NT Server Resource Kit Supplement One* provides additional coverage for IIS 2.0, DNS, ISDN, and Windows NT 4.0 performance tuning. Supplement One's CD-ROM adds the Network Connections tool (for mapped network connections), LinkCheck tool (for testing the validity of HTML links), and Web Capacity Analysis Tool, as well as a Microsoft Desktops wizard, an improved Telnet Server, the CACLS tool for command-line Access Control List (ACL) manipulation, a TAPI Heartbeat Monitor, Index Server, and an updated Windows NT Registry Entry Help file. The Supplement One CD-ROM also includes IIS 3.0 and Service Pack 2.

- *Windows NT Workstation Resource Kit* for version 4.0 supplements the *Windows NT Server Resource Kit* with information that's applicable to both the Server and Workstation versions, such as the Registry. The Workstation volume provides detailed information on fixed-disk drive formats, file systems and formats, and the Windows NT software RAID subsystem. The content of the Workstation CD-ROM is essentially identical to that supplied with the *Windows NT Server Resource Kit*.

When you install the Resource Kit(s), Setup adds a new group, Resource Kit 4.0, to the Start menu's Programs menu. Program categories are Configuration, Desktop Tools, Diagnostics, Disk Tools, File Tools, Internet Utils, Online Docs, and Setup. You also get Resource Kit Documentation and Resource Kit Tools Overview menu choices.

ON THE WEB

Microsoft Press announced in March 1997 the Microsoft Windows NT Resource Kits Web site. Information on the site, which initially is free but ultimately will require a subscription payment, is available at **http://mspress.microsoft.com/mspress/articles/ntrk/**. Microsoft says the site will include searchable versions of the Resource Kits, plus "up-to-the-minute" updates.

T I P Don't throw away your *Windows NT 3.5 Resource Kit* or the *Version 3.51 Update*. Most of the information in these two books also is applicable to Windows NT 4.0. The total list price of all three *Windows NT 4.0 Resource Kits* is $260 in the United States.

Embracing and Extending the Internet

 In early 1995, while Microsoft was readying Windows 95 for its long-delayed release and enticing content providers to augment The Microsoft Network online service, other firms were making a beeline to the Internet. Prodigy—then owned by IBM and Sears, Roebuck and Co.— was the first commercial online service to offer access to the World Wide Web, soon to be followed by CompuServe and America Online. Although several software startups offered Web browsers, Netscape's Navigator quickly gathered the lion's share of the browser market. Sun Microsystems was the initial favorite in the UNIX-based Web server category, and Apple gained a substantial share (estimated at as much as 30 percent) of the Web server business for its PowerMacs. Netscape and O'Reilly Associates were among the leaders in supplying commercial Web server software for Windows NT 3.5+. Microsoft, it appeared, was asleep at the Internet switch.

On December 7, 1995, the "sleeping giant" woke up. Microsoft announced that it would "embrace and extend" the Internet. In a flurry of press releases, Microsoft announced the availability of a beta version of Internet Explorer (IE), which is based on technology developed by Spyglass; a stripped-down version of Visual Basic for Applications, Visual Basic Script, for programming interactive Web pages; ActiveVRML for adding virtual reality features; and agreements with several other firms to foster use of Microsoft's new Web browser, including negotiations with Sun Microsystems to license the Java programming language for inclusion within IE.

On June 13, 1996, Microsoft held its Intranet Strategy Day at the San Jose (California) Convention Center, accompanied by a media blitz of gargantuan proportion. Bill Gates and two Microsoft vice presidents, Paul Maritz and Pete Higgins, described how Microsoft intended to divert the lion's share of the lucrative intranet server business from industry-leader Netscape. (Despite the Internet hype, corporate intranets are what's generating real income today for most software vendors.) In July 1996, Microsoft launched its SiteBuilder Workshop at **http://www.microsoft.com/sitebuilder/default.htm**, which received a major facelift in March 1997. Although primarily directed to authors and designers of Web pages that use ActiveX technologies, one section of the Workshop is devoted to site administration, availability, security, and other network administrator duties.

The November 1996 Microsoft Professional Developer Conference offered users of Windows NT Server 4.0 pre-alpha versions of technologies expected to be included in Windows NT Server 5.0 and in IIS 4.0, then code-named K-2. New Windows NT Server 5.0 features are the subject of Part VI of this book, "The Trail to Windows NT 5.0," and are briefly described in the "Coming Attractions in Windows NT 5.0" section at the end of this chapter. The Tech*Ed 97 conference, held in Orlando during May 1997, devoted virtually all its sessions to Internet and intranet application development with Office 97 and the new Visual Studio development tools suite.

One of Microsoft's more remarkable transformations, aside from giving away extraordinary quantities of "free" software, is the candor with which the company now discusses forthcoming Internet- and intranet-related products, as well as the features to be included in future versions of its operating systems. The vast majority of Microsoft's alpha- and beta-testing programs historically have required individuals and firms to sign non-disclosure agreements (NDAs) to participate in the testing process, thereby getting an early look at forthcoming new products or upgraded versions of existing products. With a few exceptions, alpha and beta versions of most Internet-related products are open to all comers.

From the start, the Shell Update Release for Windows NT was an open, public beta program without an NDA requirement. Microsoft distributed more than 200,000 free copies of the second beta version of Windows NT 4.0. Microsoft's new openness in disclosing the technical details behind its Internet strategy is a welcome change for users and developers alike.

N O T E The term *open* or *open systems*, when used by Microsoft's competitors, means *doesn't require Windows*. In the Internet browser business, the term means *not from Microsoft* because it's likely that 90 percent of all browsers run under some version of Microsoft Windows. By no stretch of the imagination does *open* mean *non-proprietary*.

The competition is intense between Microsoft and Netscape to create proprietary extensions to HTML and their respective browsers that become *de facto* Internet standards by virtue of market dominance. So far, Netscape (with an estimated 60 percent to 70 percent of the browser market) has been the hands-down winner of market share. Whether Microsoft can overcome Netscape's lead in the browser market remains to be seen, but Internet Explorer now appears to be gaining ground on Navigator's installed base. █

Intranetworking and Internet Information Server

The conventional definition of an *intranet* is any private network running TCP/IP. This book uses the term *intranet* to mean a private TCP/IP network with an Internet server that can distribute HTML-encoded documents. Intranets mesh well with current organizational buzzwords, such as downsizing, re-engineering, horizontal management, empowering employees, workgroup collaboration, and real-time information distribution.

Many organizations now are using intranets to distribute human resources policy manuals, hortatory messages from upper management, white papers, and other information that would ordinarily require printing and physical distribution. HTML conversion features for word processing applications, such as the Save As HTML choice of Microsoft Word 97's File menu, ease the process of moving from the printed page to a "*Company* Wide Web." Figure 1.23 shows a 12-page Word 97 document converted to a single HTML-encoded Web page.

Intranets also offer a foundation on which to build workflow and project-management applications and, when well implemented, foster collaboration, cooperation, and information sharing among employees. You can connect a private intranet to the Internet through a firewall that lets mobile employees dial in to the intranet through an Internet service provider (ISP) without compromising confidential information. Thus, telecommuters and field sales personnel can communicate with the home office at very low hourly cost, compared with toll-free telephone lines. You can distribute slide shows or full-motion video versions of presentations and computer-based training (CBT) programs by using Microsoft NetShow 2.0 (see Figure 1.24).

FIG. 1.23
A Word 97 document converted to HTML and displayed in Internet Explorer 3.0.

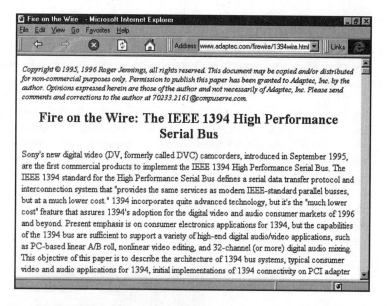

FIG. 1.24
NetShow 2.0 displaying Bill Gates' presentation from a live slide show of the March 19, 1997, Microsoft Developer Days over a 28.8 kbps connection.

One major application for intranets is distributing, in real time, information stored in various corporate databases. Microsoft's Internet Database Connector (IDC), included with IIS 2.0, lets you quickly create dynamic Web pages that return to an HTML table the result set of a user-specified query against a Microsoft SQL Server or Access database, or any other RDBMS that supports ODBC. The SQL Server 6.5 Web Assistant creates entire Web pages from database query result sets with minimum effort. IIS 3.0's Active Server Pages support Microsoft's newly developed OLE DB, Active Data Objects, and the Advanced Data Control for enhanced database connectivity. Access 97 lets you publish database content with the IDC or by automatically converting Access forms to Active Server Pages. Microsoft's Visual InterDev, the successor to the ill-fated Blackbird tools intended to create content for the once-proprietary Microsoft Network, is specifically designed to ease database-to-Web development.

ON THE WEB

You can download Microsoft's "Internet Deployment Guide" for SQL Server 6.5 from **http://www.microsoft.com/sql/inet/SQLInetDeploy.htm**. The self-extracting archive file includes sample code for both IDC and ASP applications.

Another primary drawing card of intranets is the ease with which users can connect to and navigate a well-designed private Web site. When you install IIS 2.0 and its successors, the Setup program installs a temporary home page (see Figure 1.25) at \inetsrv\wwwroot\default.htm (IIS 2.0) or \InetPub\wwwroot\default.htm (IIS 3.0+). Launching IE 3.0+ on any client with a TCP/IP connection to the server and simply typing the DNS server name, the NetBEUI name, or the TCP/IP address of the server in the Address text box displays Default.htm. (You simply replace Default.htm with your own version of that file with hyperlinks to your other HTML pages.) IIS, together with members of Office 97, makes it a quick-and-easy process to create a demonstration intranet site for review and testing by your organization's management.

FIG. 1.25

Displaying the default Web page included with IIS in Internet Explorer 3.0.

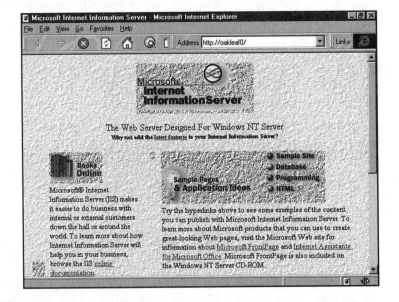

Managing Internet Information Server

IIS 2.0 and 3.0 include the Internet Service Manager for setup and maintenance of World Wide Web (WWW), Gopher, and FTP sites, which the Windows NT Server 4.0 Setup program installs by default in separate subfolders—\inetsrv\wwwroot, \inetsrv\gophroot, and \inetsrv\ftproot, respectively. (IIS 3.0 and 4.0 substitute \InetPub for \inetsrv.) IIS 4.0 uses Microsoft Management Console (MMC) and an MMC snap-in to manage one or more virtual Web and FTP servers. *Snap-ins* are custom-written MMC components for managing Windows NT services. Figure 1.26 shows the MMC's window with the IIS 4.0 Web and FTP services installed and running.

FIG. 1.26
Microsoft Management
Console's window when
running the snap-in for
IIS 4.0.

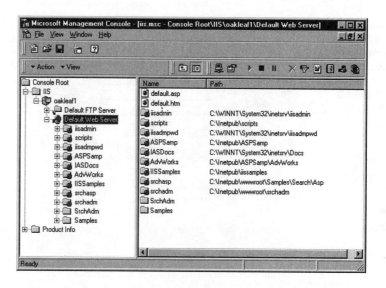

N O T E The Internet Peer Server included with Windows NT Workstation 4.0 includes a copy of
Internet Service Manager for remote administration of Internet Information Server 2.0 and
3.0. You must upgrade to the IIS 4.0 version of the Internet Peer Server to administer IIS 4.0 servers
remotely. The Internet Peer Server lets you test newly created Web pages locally, and then transfer the
pages to the desired location within the \inetsvr or \InetPub folder for distribution. You also can use
the Workstation version to host a Web site by using several third-party Web server applications. ▪

Right-clicking the Default Web Server entry, created when you install IIS 4.0, and choosing
Properties from the pop-up menu displays the default Virtual Server page of the WWW Service
Properties for Virtual Server 1 on *servername* properties sheet (see Figure 1.27). You set identification, connection, and performance-tuning properties for IIS 4.0 on this page. You can set
up multiple virtual servers on a single Windows NT 4.0 server, each with its own home folder.
Setting up and managing IIS 4.0 are the subjects of Chapter 20, "Setting Up Internet Information Server 4.0," and Chapter 21, "Administering Intranet and World Wide Web Sites."

Upgrading to Site Server 2.0

Microsoft Site Server 2.0, standard and Enterprise Edition, were the latest additions to the
BackOffice family when this book was written. Site Server, an add-on to IIS 3.0+, takes advan-
tage of ASP, OLE DB, and ADO. Site Server includes the following three products, which
Microsoft purchased from their original developers in 1996 and 1997:

■ *eShop Technology,* one of the first tools for setting up Web shopping malls. Microsoft
acquired eShop, Inc., in June 1996, rewrote eShop's UNIX code to run it as an ISAPI
(Internet Services API) under IIS 2.0, and released the product as Merchant Server
1.0. A license for Merchant Server costs $18,000, a much lower price in late 1996 than
competing products. Microsoft Commerce Server is an upgrade to Merchant Server that
substitutes ASP and VBScript or JavaScript for Merchant Server's proprietary scripting
language.

FIG. 1.27

The Virtual Server page of the WWW Service Properties for Virtual Server on *servername* sheet of the IIS 4.0 snap-in for MMC.

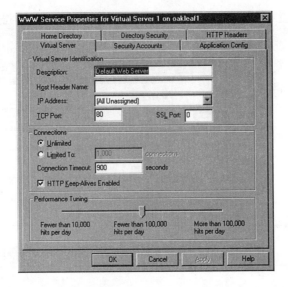

- *Intersé market focus 3,* a leading activity reporting system for intranet and Internet Web sites. Microsoft absorbed Intersé Corp. in March 1997 and rechristened market focus 3 as Usage Analyst in May 1997.

- *NetCarta WebMapper,* a tool for Web-site management, including site diagramming, content analysis, link verification, and reporting. Microsoft acquired NetCarta in December 1996, and renamed WebMapper to Site Analyst in May 1997.

ON THE WEB

You can read or download Microsoft's Internet commerce white paper, "A Foundation for Doing Business on the Internet," from **http://www.microsoft.com/commerce/whitepaper.htm**.

The $1,499-per-server standard version of Site Server, which is designed primarily for Web-site development and management, includes the following components:

- *Personalization System,* which uses ASP to generate Web pages based on the preferences of registered users

- *Visual InterDev* for designing and coding ASP-based Web pages that interact with databases

- *Content Replication System* for staging new Web content and to create mirror sites to improve site response

- *Web Publishing Wizard* for posting to a Web server pages created on networked clients

- *Posting Acceptor* for enabling IIS to accept Web pages via HTTP Post and to automate multiple-site posting with the Content Replication System

- *Site Analyst* and *Usage Analyst* (standard versions) for site management and activity reporting

ON THE WEB

Microsoft has posted product and technical overviews, as well as other detailed information, on the standard version of Site Server at **http://backoffice.microsoft.com/products/SiteServer/**. You can download a trial version of the standard version from **http://backoffice.microsoft.com/downtrial/**.

Site Server Enterprise Edition, designed for establishing Internet shopping sites and carrying a $4,999 per-server license fee, includes all the components of the basic version plus the following:

- *Commerce Server,* which includes the StoreBuilder Wizard, Order Processing Pipeline for implementing business rules, BuyNow for spontaneous purchases, and Commerce Host Administrator for remote site management.

- *Microsoft Wallet* for secure use of credit and debit cards in conducting transactions over the Internet. The default credit-card payment system uses SSL (Secure Sockets Layer); Wallet will support the SET (Secure Electronic Transaction) system when VISA and MasterCard put SET in operation.

- *Usage Analyst Enterprise Edition,* which extends the basic version of Usage Analyst to multihomed and distributed Web servers, each of which must have a Site Server Enterprise Edition license.

The $4,999 license fee for the Enterprise Edition is a dramatic reduction from Merchant Server's $18,000 price, disregarding the added new components. Lowering the license fee lets Microsoft entice smaller businesses into retailing on the Internet. The development cost of content for an effective Internet shopping experience, however, is at least an order of magnitude greater than the software licensing cost.

ON THE WEB

Links to pages with the details of Site Server Enterprise Edition are at **http:// backoffice.microsoft.com/products/SiteServerE/**. Information on Microsoft Wallet and a downloadable implementation **is at http://www.microsoft.com/commerce/wallet/**. The Enterprise Edition also is available on trial from **http://backoffice.microsoft.com/downtrial/**.

N O T E Site Server 2.0 is Microsoft's first release of this product; there was no version 1.0. One explanation of Site Server's version numbering is the computer-industry adage, "Don't buy version 1.0 of any software." A more likely reason is that the primary components of Site Server have gone through least one upgrade after Microsoft's acquisition of the products. ■

Scaling Up to Windows NT Server 4.0 Enterprise Edition

Most information technology (IT) managers haven't considered Microsoft a major player in the enterprise server and networking business. Microsoft traditionally has concentrated on client operating systems, typified by Windows 95, and desktop productivity applications, such as Office 97, to deliver most of its revenues. IBM, DEC, HP, Tandem, Computer Associates, and other heavy-hitters in the mainframe and minicomputer business are the names that come to mind when discussing "enterprise computing" vendors. Most IT managers view Windows NT Server as a product designed for workgroup or small department deployment, or as an intranet/Internet server.

Microsoft is attempting to cast off the workgroup-departmental cloak of Windows NT Server by establishing "strategic relationships" with firms having *bona fide* enterprise credentials for systems management and hardware products. Microsoft's May 20, 1997, Scalability Day press conference in New York City included demonstrations of very large-scale Windows NT-based systems by DEC, HP, Tandem, Data General, and Compaq. The most significant Scalability Day event, however, was the formal announcement of Enterprise Editions of Windows NT Server 4.0, SQL Server 6.5, and BackOffice.

The Enterprise Edition, called Windows NT Server/E and expected by the end of 1997, adds the following new features to Windows NT Server 4.0:

- *Microsoft Cluster Server* (MSCS, formerly code-named Wolfpack) increases server availability by enabling two servers to share a single set of RAID drives. If one server fails, the other server automatically takes over all processing duties. Applications such as SQL Server must be modified to take advantage of MSCS.

- *Microsoft Transaction Server* (MTS, formerly Viper) is a combination object request broker (ORB) and transaction processor (TP) for creating multiple-tier client/server database applications. MTS makes it easier to program and deploy middle-tier components to enforce business rules that maintain database integrity.

- *Microsoft Message Queue Server* (MSMQ, formerly Falcon) provides reliable, prioritized delivery of data over unreliable networks. Typical applications for MSMQ are credit-card verification and security brokerage operations conducted over wide area networks. IIS 4.0 includes a limited version of MSMQ; Windows NT Server/E delivers the full version.

- *Microsoft Routing and Remote Access Service* (Routing and RAS, formerly Steelhead) replaces the multiprotocol router (MPR) and RAS components of Windows NT Server 4.0 to add features such as server-to-server Point-to-Point Tunneling Protocol (PPTP) and demand-dial routing over dial-up connections.

- *Increased SMP scalability* lets the Enterprise Edition take advantage of up to eight processors in a single "super-server" system. The standard edition of Windows NT Server 4.0 reaches an effective scalability limit at four processors.

- *4G RAM Tuning (4GT)* lets you devote 3G of RAM in a 4G system to applications by reducing the amount of RAM allocated to the kernel from 2G to 1G. 4GT improves the performance of large database servers in applications such as data warehousing.

ON THE WEB

Microsoft's initial description of the new features of Windows NT Server/E is available at **http:// www.microsoft.com/ntserver/Info/ntseetb.htm.**

N O T E Microsoft says Windows NT Server/E requires a minimum of a 90MHz Pentium processor and 64M of RAM, but a more practical starting point is dual 233MHz Pentium II processors and 256M or more of RAM. You must install SQL Server 6.5 to use MSMQ and to take full advantage of MTS. ▦

The Enterprise Edition of SQL Server 6.5 includes modifications to accommodate Windows NT Server/E's eight-processor SMP and the changes needed for failover clustering with MSCS. You'll have to wait for SQL Server 7.0 (now code-named Sphinx) to support the multiterabyte (T) databases Microsoft and its partners demonstrated at Scalability Day. The Enterprise Edition of Exchange Server 5.0 increases the size limit of folders from 16G to 16T and adds a few other Internet-related messaging features. Chapter 26, "Scaling Windows NT Server 4.0 to the Enterprise," gives you in-depth coverage of the Enterprise Edition components.

Coming Attractions in Windows NT 5.0

Windows NT 5.0 will deliver most, but not all, of the features promised by the original specification for Cairo. On the other hand, you'll get several new Internet-related features that Microsoft didn't have on the burner during the Cairo definition and early development phase. Windows NT 5.0 will include all the Enterprise Edition add-ons described in the preceding section. Following are the most important publicly announced features of Windows 5.0:

- *Distributed File System* (Dfs) relies on a modified Jet database, similar to that of Microsoft Exchange Server, to store file and folder information. Dfs lets you assign aliases to server shares so that shares of multiple servers appear to clients as having a single server name (see Figure 1.28). Dfs also lets developers write "directory-enabled" applications that can manipulate records in the Dfs databases. Dfs is one of the subjects of Chapter 27, "Distributing File and Directory Services."

FIG. 1.28

Aliasing a server share to a Dfs share with the pre-release version of the Stand Alone Dfs Administrator.

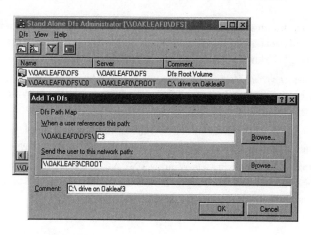

■ *Kerberos 5.0* security uses session tickets to authenticate users, a process that's faster than server authentication with Windows NT's NTLM protocol. When you log on to Windows NT 4.0 with the pre-release version of Dfs installed, you have the option to use Kerberos security instead of Windows NT security. Kerberos security also is covered in Chapter 27.

■ *Active Directory Services* (ADSI) uses the Internet-standard Lightweight Directory Access Protocol (LDAP), derived from the ITU's X.500 directory and messaging standard. ADSI overcomes IT managers' objections to Windows NT 4.0's domain-based directory system. Installing ADS under Windows NT 4.0 adds a Directories shortcut to your desktop that offers you the choice between viewing the conventional WinNT or more detailed LDAP directory structure (see Figure 1.29). You use ASP with Internet Explorer 3+ to view and set the properties of directory entries (see Figure 1.30). Chapter 27 shows you how ADSI and LDAP will change the way you manage large Windows NT networks.

FIG. 1.29

Windows NT 4.0 Explorer displaying LDAP Common Names (CN=) for directory entries in the OAKLEAF Organizational Unit (OU=).

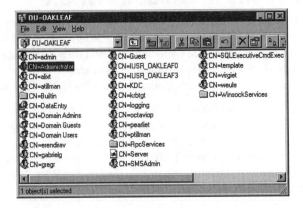

■ *Microsoft Management Console* (MMC) is a new system management tool container that houses Microsoft and third-party "Snap-Ins" to administer network components, including Windows NT servers.

■ *Windows Scripting Host* (WSH) lets you execute batch files written in Visual Basic Script (VBScript or VBS) or JavaScript from Windows NT, either in Windows mode or from the command prompt.

■ *Win32 Driver Model* (WDM) is a new driver architecture that lets hardware developers use the same 32-bit device drivers for Windows 9x and Windows NT 5.0.

■ *64-bit memory addressing* lets Windows NT 5.0 take full advantage of 64-bit RISC processors, such as DEC's Alpha series and the forthcoming 64-bit Intel RISC processor, code-named Merced, which is expected to arrive in 1999.

FIG. 1.30
Entering detailed information for the LDAP record of the Administrator account of the OAKLEAF Organizational Unit (Domain).

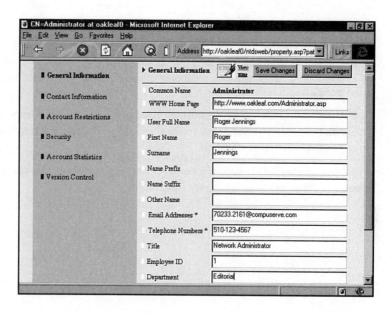

ON THE WEB

An overview of the architecture of MMC is available at **http://www.microsoft.com/management/overview.htm**. You can read more about WSH at **http://www.microsoft.com/management/scrpthost.htm**. Details on WDM are available from **http://www.microsoft.com/hwdev/pcfuture/wdm.htm**.

With the exception of WDM drivers and 64-bit memory addressing, the Windows NT Server 5.0 features in this list are available as beta or final versions for use with version 4.0.

From Here...

The objective of this chapter was to provide an overview of Windows NT Server 4.0 with emphasis on the new features Microsoft added to version 4.0. Microsoft's marketing strategy for Windows NT Server and establishing Internet and intranet servers with Microsoft Internet Information Server 2.0 (included with Windows NT Server 4.0) and IIS 3.0+ also were covered. The chapter concluded with a brief description of the Enterprise Edition of Windows NT Server and the new features expected in Windows NT 5.0.

The balance of Part I of this book, "Networking with Windows NT Server 4.0," is organized in the sequence typical of a new network server installation. The following chapters provide the background you need before you install Windows NT Server 4.0:

■ Chapter 2, "Planning Your Windows NT Network Installation," details the steps required to plan and budget for the hardware and software needed to establish your Windows NT Server 4.0 network.

- Chapter 3, "Understanding the Windows NT Operating System," introduces the technical foundation of Windows NT and the Windows NT File System (NTFS).

- Chapter 4, "Choosing Network Protocols," explains how to select one or more of the three principal networking protocols supported by Windows NT based on your network configuration.

- Chapter 5, "Purchasing Networking Hardware," provides guidance in the selection of the adapter cards, cabling, hubs, routers, and related equipment required to complete the physical network installation.

If you're upgrading an existing Windows NT Server installation, you might want to skip to Chapter 6, "Making the Initial Server Installation."

CHAPTER 2

Planning Your Windows NT Network Installation

Understand the network planning process

Use the 11 key network planning issues described in this chapter to develop a network that meets user, maintainability, and manageability needs.

Prepare a networking budget

Establish a working budget and use it as a tool to manage purchases and to get the most network for your money.

Stay on budget and on time

Use project-management software for managing personnel resources and deadlines.

Take advantage of third-party expertise

Use outside help from vendors and consultants to plan and design your network, and how to choose those sources.

The most important element of a successful PC network installation is thorough planning. A successful network is one that's efficient and effective. *Efficient* means that the network is technically elegant, is installed within budget, and is maintainable and expandable with minimum staff time. *Effective* means that the network fully serves the needs of its users.

This chapter presents the 11 key issues you must consider to plan your network properly. Depending on your particular environment and the scale of your network, some of these issues take precedence over others. Regardless of priority, each issue is important and deserves consideration in the planning process. Considering each planning issue in turn helps you develop a framework for your network, prevents you from overlooking important needs, and avoids common stumbling blocks along the way to implementation. ■

Developing the Network Implementation Plan

Traditionally, most Windows NT Server installations occur within a corporate or institutional environment. Windows NT Server is particularly appealing to small to mid-sized organizations because of its relatively low acquisition cost, moderately priced client licenses, ease of installation, and simplicity of maintenance. Although Microsoft proudly points to "buys" of hundreds of Windows NT Server installations, plus thousands of Windows NT Workstation licenses from well-known Fortune 500 firms, single-server installations with 10 to 100 clients fuel much of the momentum of the Windows NT market.

ON THE WEB

You can download the current version of Microsoft's six-chapter *Microsoft Windows NT Server Deployment Guide: NetWare Integration* from **http://www.microsoft.com/ntserver/info/ entplan.htm**. When this book was written, this Guide had not been updated to Windows NT Server 4.0 (despite Microsoft's promise of a fall 1996 update). The basic concepts outlined in these two publications, however, apply equally to versions 3.51 and 4.0 of Windows NT Server.

Regardless of the size of the organization adopting a Windows NT 4.0 network, the following 11 topics are critical to the planning process:

- Meeting business objectives
- Determining user and workgroup needs
- Establishing security
- Determining fault-tolerance requirements
- Incorporating existing infrastructure
- Connecting to the outside world
- Developing an implementation schedule
- Considering network management needs
- Providing for future growth
- Working within a budget
- Training users

The sections that follow describe these planning elements in detail.

Meeting Business Objectives

It's easy to focus so much attention on the technical issues of planning a network that you lose sight of the primary goal, which is to meet your organization's strategic and tactical business objectives. These objectives may be stated broadly—for instance, "To improve corporate-wide communications among all employees." The objectives may be stated more narrowly: "To provide access to Internet mail and the World Wide Web for executive and administrative staff members." In many cases, the objectives may not be explicitly stated. Whatever the case, you can be sure that before management approves the funds to implement your network installation or upgrade, management must see that the plan will meet a perceived objective or solve a problem.

Talk to upper management to discover the rationale for the project, keeping in mind that the stated reasons aren't always the real reasons why such a project has been initiated. Find out what results upper management foresees. Ask what management expects to be accomplished when the project is complete, or what should be done more quickly, inexpensively, or efficiently as a result of the project.

Part
I
Ch
2

The planning stage also is the time to consider proposing that the scope of the project be expanded beyond that originally requested. Upper management focuses on the big picture and, as a result, is typically unaware of all the implications and possibilities inherent in networking technology. It often happens that planning a network project to solve stated needs also offers you the opportunity to address other pressing computer-related problems with minimum additional money and effort. Upper management may not even realize that the organization is missing such an opportunity, unless you describe the opportunity.

Determining User and Workgroup Needs

You want to keep upper management happy, because it controls the size of your paycheck. But you also want to keep users happy, because unhappy users can make your life miserable. Take the time early in the planning process to find out what users expect from the network; then modify your plan, as needed, to give them as much as possible of what they asked for. If management requirements determine the strategic thrust of the network, user needs determine the tactical direction.

The core unit of network planning, a workgroup, comprises a group of people who share related job functions. Workgroups are typically—although by no means always—formally defined units of the organization. Members of a workgroup often not only use specialized software not used elsewhere in the organization, but they also have a common need to access the same data. A workgroup can range in size from one or two people in a small firm's accounting department to hundreds or even thousands of people in the outbound telemarketing group of a large firm. Figure 2.1 illustrates a network comprising three workgroups—Personnel, Engineering, and Finance—each of which has at least one workgroup server, connected in a switched Ethernet network. The key to determining what comprises a workgroup is to discover shared job functions, plus similarities in the software used and the data accessed.

After you analyze the workgroup structures within your organization and determine which workgroup will be affected by the project, the next step is to talk to workgroup leaders to find out their views on the project. Depending on the workgroup's size and how much time you have available, you may find it worthwhile to talk to each staff member in the group, either individually or in a group meeting. It's during this process that you discover the detailed information about user needs that will allow you to make the network more useful to the people who actually use it.

FIG. 2.1

Personnel, Engineering, and Finance workgroups connected by switched Ethernet.

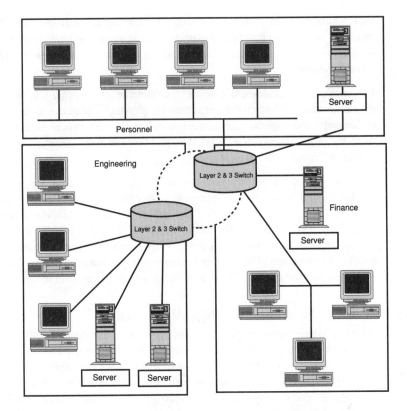

 TIP Ask specific questions, such as "Where would be the best place to locate the network laser printer for your workgroup?" as well as more general questions, such as "What two or three things would make your job easier?" After you go through this process with each workgroup, you have a much better idea of how to configure your network and what minor changes and additions you can make that have a big payoff. You also become a hero to the users simply by asking the questions.

Now is also the time to consider whether workgroups not a part of the original plan can be added at little or no additional cost. For example, the original project might cover connecting the accounting workgroup to a server that shares an accounting database. During the planning phase, you might discover that the human resource management (HRM) group located on the other side of the wall could also be connected within budget and run its HRM application on the same server. Often, all that stands in the way of providing a major benefit to an overlooked workgroup are a few Ethernet cards and an additional hundred feet or so of cable.

N O T E   Workgroups often are provided with a server dedicated to specific workgroup activities, such as accounting, purchasing, production, and marketing. The constantly decreasing cost of server hardware makes distributing the server workload among workgroups economically feasible.

The workgroup servers are organized as members of a common domain serving a single geographic site.

▶ **See** "Implementing Domains and Trusts Between Domains," **p. 618** ■

ON THE WEB

You can download a copy of the Microsoft white paper "Managing Windows NT Domains" from **http://www.microsoft.com/ntserver/info/domainplanwp.htm**.

Establishing Security

Security means protecting your hardware, software, and data. The time to start thinking about security is during the network planning process. Security is made up of the following four elements:

- *Server security* consists of assigning passwords, granting access rights to server volumes and directories, and granting other explicit permissions to use shared data. This aspect of security is covered fully in Chapter 13, "Managing User and Group Accounts," and Chapter 14, "Sharing and Securing Network Resources."

- *Backup security*, discussed in Chapter 8, "Installing File Backup Systems," is absolutely necessary to ensure that data stored on a server or servers isn't lost due to operating system or hardware failures.

- *Physical security* means protecting your servers, hubs, and other active network components by placing them behind locked doors.

- *Data communication security* means protecting your data while it's *on the wire* (in transit between two locations), as well as protecting data resident on local hosts from hackers attempting to gain access from outside your network. Data communication security is especially important if you plan to provide client access to the Internet through your server(s).

ON THE WEB

A detailed analysis of the internal security features of the Windows NT Server operating system is available at **http://www.microsoft.com/ntserver/info/securitysummary.htm** and **http://www.microsoft.com/ntserver/info/itsec.htm**.

Physical Security   Although your environment may make it difficult or impossible to physically secure all your components, strive to put all server-related hardware behind locked doors. Physical security for network servers is especially important today because of the recent trend toward burglary of server-grade PCs. Servers have the latest Pentium or Pentium Pro chips, large amounts of memory, high-speed disk drives, and other costly components bringing top dollar from PC fences.

Part
I
Ch
2

Even more important for most organizations is the possibility of data being stolen. This is a two-edged sword:

- Catastrophic loss of company data is one of the major causes of business failures. Even with a good backup strategy in place, you may find it difficult or impossible to reconstruct all your data in a timely manner.

- You must consider where your stolen data may end up. Your data may be sold to an unscrupulous competitor, providing that company with your customer lists, accounting information, and other confidential company data. Secure your server well.

If you secure your equipment rooms, also be sure to establish a key-control policy to ensure that those on the approved list can always gain access when necessary. Designate backup staff, and make sure that each backup person is provided with a key or with access to the key box. Otherwise, if the primary person is sick, on vacation, or simply unreachable, the backup person may be unable to effect repairs simply because he can't get through a locked door.

In addition to securing access to your active network components, one step you can take to avoid such problems is to establish and post clear policies concerning how and to whom problems should be reported. Be sure to post this information where it's readily accessible to users, and not locked up in the server room. Put them instead over the coffee machine, where users may actually notice them.

Data Communication Security   Unlike physical security, which is primarily concerned with protecting your network hardware from unintentional abuse by employees, data communications security focuses primarily on protecting your data from being compromised by outside intruders. Managers of most local area networks (LANs), which are self-contained within a building or campus, don't need to be too concerned about over-the-wire data communications security. If your LAN is connected to the outside world in any fashion, however, you must take steps to prevent unauthorized access to your data by outside parties.

One important aspect of security is protecting your data from viruses. Most of today's viruses propagate via online data communication, usually as a result of downloading infected files from the Internet or bulletin-board services. Windows NT 4.0 virus-scanning programs are available now from several vendors (including McAfee, Intel, and Symantec), and more are on the way. Figure 2.2 shows the main window of McAfee VirusScan for Windows NT after finding no infected files on the server drive. Any of these scanning products will detect any virus you're at all likely to see in the real world. Don't be too impressed by how many viruses each claims to detect or pay too much attention to the comparative claims. All of them are good; none of them are perfect.

The burgeoning of wide area networks (WANs) and the use of the Internet to carry corporate traffic brings the data communications security issue to the forefront. Banks and other financial institutions long ago established private secure data communications networks to avoid the danger of their data being intercepted or otherwise compromised. Even private, secure networks have been compromised by determined hackers. If your environment requires you to establish links between networks at multiple locations, or if you plan to provide remote access services to mobile users, you should plan to provide at least some data communications security.

FIG. 2.2

The main window of McAfee Virus Scan for Windows NT, with no viruses detected.

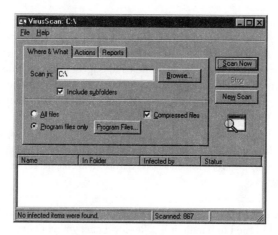

If your security needs are modest, you have only two or three locations in close proximity to link, and you don't need dial-up network access, leased lines from the telephone company (*telco*) may be the solution. Because leased lines provide a hard-wired dedicated link from one location to another rather than go through a telco switch, leased lines are inherently secure. This security stems not from any special efforts made to secure the link, but simply from the link being inaccessible to would-be eavesdroppers.

If, on the other hand, you need to link many widely geographically dispersed locations, you may have a greater problem. The cost of leased lines—especially lines providing high link speeds—mounts very quickly, and even leased lines may not provide an adequately high level of security for your needs. Because you pay for the dedicated bandwidth of a leased line 24 hours a day, 365 days a year, whether you're using the line or not, most companies use packet-switching networks, which charge on a usage basis. Packet switching has brought the cost of providing high bandwidth links to multiple locations within reason.

Until a few years ago, using packet switching usually meant contracting with AT&T, MCI, H&R Block, or a similar provider of specialized data delivery services. Many organizations are turning to the Internet to provide low-cost packet-switched data delivery. In theory, the Internet is an insecure means of data delivery. In practice, the Internet is probably at least as secure as your telephone. Just as your voice telephone conversations can be intercepted by anyone with a reasonable degree of technical competence and the motivation to do so, your Internet traffic can also be intercepted.

You can avoid having your data compromised by using data encryption, either at the application level or at the packet level. Encryption doesn't prevent your data from being intercepted—it simply garbles the data, making it useless to eavesdroppers. How you implement encryption determines what level of security encryption provides for your data.

Application-level encryption depends on the software you're running to perform the encryption. This method can be workable as long as it occurs without requiring user intervention. For example, a client/server database application may be designed so that the client- and server-side software both encrypt outgoing traffic and decrypt incoming traffic transparently to users, leaving would-be eavesdroppers watching a stream of random garbage characters.

Application-level encryption that depends on user intervention can't be considered a reliable means of protecting data. For example, although your e-mail package may allow you to encrypt outgoing messages on demand by taking certain manual steps, the likelihood that individual e-mail users will remember how to encrypt their message—not to mention the likelihood that they'll go to this extra trouble—is small. Depend on application-level encryption only in specialized circumstances, and even then only when the encryption is invisible to users.

N O T E Microsoft's Internet Information Server 2.0, included with Windows NT Server 4.0, provides Point-to-Point Tunneling Protocol (PPTP) for secure communication over the Internet. PPTP is discussed in Chapter 19, "Managing Remote Access Service," and Chapter 20, "Setting Up Internet Information Server 4.0." ▪

Packet-level encryption occurs at the hardware level, typically in the boundary router or in a specialized device designed to handle it. Packet-level encryption encrypts the data portion of each outbound packet, but leaves unchanged the packet and frame header and trailer data, including the source and destination addresses. This means that the encrypted packets can be handled by standard devices along the way to the destination. At the destination, a similar device strips the packet and frame header and trailer information, decrypts the data portion of the packet, and delivers the decrypted data to the addressee.

Packet-level encryption devices can be configured to allow you to designate that only specific networks require that packets sent to them be encrypted, allowing data destined for other networks to go out unencrypted. Thus, for example, you can designate each company network site as requiring encrypted data while allowing users to access other sites normally. This is particularly useful if you plan to use the Internet to deliver your data securely. Figure 2.3 illustrates the use of encrypting routers to assure privacy of communication over the Internet.

Firewalls are another tool in the datacomm security arsenal. Unlike encryption, which is concerned with protecting data in transit, a firewall is designed to control access to your network. Firewalls filter out inbound traffic unless that traffic originates from an approved source. Likewise, you can configure firewalls to filter outbound traffic, thereby allowing internal users to access only approved external hosts.

Like any technology, firewalls aren't a complete guarantee. A technically knowledgeable person can possibly spoof an authorized host and get past your firewall. Still, firewalls are becoming extremely popular as a means to isolate secure internal networks from the anarchy of the Internet. Microsoft's Proxy Server is an example of a firewall that you can implement at moderate cost. Proxy Server is one of the subjects of Chapter 22, "Taking Advantage of BackOffice Integration."

Security Summary Everything has its price, and security is no exception. Assigning long, randomly generated passwords makes guessing a password much more difficult for a hacker, but at the same time makes life more difficult for authorized users. Securing all your equipment behind locked doors limits the chance that the equipment will be damaged accidentally or maliciously, but it also makes it more difficult for your staff to maintain the equipment. Installing over-the-wire encryption hardware and firewalls minimizes the likelihood that your data will be compromised in transit, but it also requires expensive equipment and scarce staff time to install and maintain.

FIG. 2.3
Using router-based encryption to ensure communication privacy on the Internet.

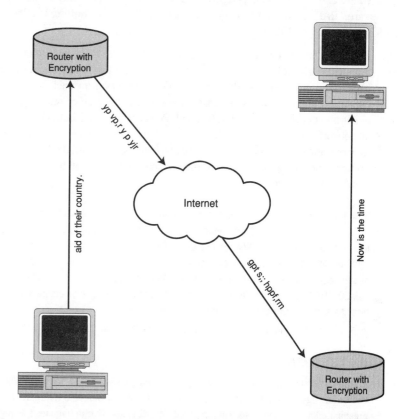

Too much security can be counterproductive—not only in terms of time, money, and effort, but in terms of compromising the security itself. For example, many organizations mandating long, random, frequently changed passwords simply did it because it seemed to be a "good idea at the time." They've been surprised to find a blizzard of yellow sticky notes posted on each monitor with users' passwords written on them. Don't attempt to establish security features that require extraordinary user effort. Instead, determine what data must be protected, and at what level of security. Plan for as much security as you really need, where you need it, and no more.

Determining Fault-Tolerance Requirements

Fault tolerance is a system's capability to continue to function after the failure of one or more critical components. The key to fault tolerance is the use of redundancy to eliminate single points of failure. Most networks provide at least some fault tolerance, although it may be limited to installing an uninterruptible power supply (UPS) to protect against power failures, and perhaps a RAID (redundant array of inexpensive disks) subsystem to guard against fixed-disk failures. Some networks are fully fault tolerant, achieved by providing online backup spares for each device on the network.

UPSes and RAID systems are briefly discussed in Chapter 5, "Purchasing Networking Hardware." RAID systems are covered in detail in Chapter 7, "Setting Up Redundant Arrays of Inexpensive Disks (RAID)."

Building a fault-tolerant network is expensive, and the more fault tolerance you build in, the more expensive it becomes. The cost of providing a backup bridge for each working bridge, a backup router for each working router, a backup server for each working server, and so on escalates quickly. As a result, most networks use redundancy only at those points that are either most critical or most likely to fail. Power failures are both common and critical, so nearly all networks use UPSes to protect against them. Disk failures are less common, but because they're critical, many network servers are equipped with RAID disk subsystems. Hubs, bridges, and routers fail very infrequently, so it's uncommon to see full redundancy implemented for these components.

N O T E   One means of providing server fault tolerance is to implement a *failover system*, in which duplicate servers are connected to a single RAID system by a SCSI adapter in each server. Microsoft announced at the Windows Hardware Engineering Conference (WinHEC) in the spring of 1996 the intention to support failover redundancy as the first step in the company's plan to implement clustering technology for Windows NT servers. Microsoft held a "Scalability Day" press conference on May 20, 1997, in New York City to promote its Wolfpack clustering architecture, which was in the beta-testing stage when this book was written.

▶ **See** "Understanding Microsoft's Incremental Approach to Scalability," **p. 968** ■

ON THE WEB

To learn more about the future of clustering, download the white paper "Microsoft Windows NT Server Cluster Strategy: High Availability and Scalability with Industry-Standard Hardware" from **http://premium.microsoft.com/msdn/library/conf/f4f/d51/s9d32.htm** (requires free registration).

▶ **See** "Clustering for Availability Now and Scalability Later," **p. 970**

To determine fault-tolerance requirements, you must determine the answers to the following questions about each component of the network:

- ■ What happens if a component fails, in terms of immediate effects and in lasting damage?
- ■ How likely is that component to fail?
- ■ If the component fails, is there an alternative method—less expensive than duplicating the component—that will acceptably substitute for the failed component until it can be repaired or replaced?
- ■ What does it cost to provide full, or partial, redundancy for that component? Is the tradeoff of additional cost versus increased reliability justified?

When most people think about fault tolerance, they think only about hardware. A commonly overlooked fault-tolerance issue is data communications reliability. If your network is connected to remote branch offices, vendor and customer sites, or to the Internet, you must consider the reliability of each such link and determine the criticality of the data carried on the link. If the data is high-volume, real-time, and critical to your organization's operations, you may need to duplicate the high-speed links to each remote site. If the data is lower volume or less critical, you may be able to get by with a dial-up link as a backup to the main high-speed link (see Figure 2.4). In the case of batch-mode data transfer, you may be able to dispense with a backup link completely.

Part
I

Ch
2

FIG. 2.4

Substituting analog modem connections over the switched telephone network for a failed T1 leased line.

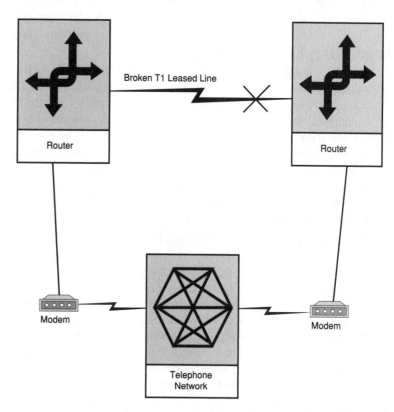

Another issue to consider is designing for fault tolerance by location. For example, your internetwork may comprise a main office in Chicago, plants in Pittsburgh and Winston-Salem, N.C., and national and international sales offices. Consider designing your networks and siting your data storage so that, in case of a data communications link failure, each site is self-supporting to the greatest extent possible. That way, when the link from the Cleveland sales office to corporate headquarters goes down, Cleveland can continue to sell and service accounts, albeit perhaps without real-time inventory data or delivery schedules. Similar results can be achieved on the local level by loading software locally on workstations rather than centrally on the server, replicating databases to multiple servers, having at least some locally attached printers, and so forth. Replication of information stored in relational databases is one of the subjects of Chapter 23, "Running Microsoft SQL Server 6.5."

The key, as usual, is to balance cost versus performance. Install just as much fault tolerance as you really need. If you can't afford even that much, install as much as you can afford, focusing your efforts on the items most likely to break and on those that will cause the most trouble when they do break. If this means that all you can afford is to install a UPS on the server, do so. Don't worry about what you haven't been able to do. Doing anything to increase fault tolerance is better than doing nothing. You might be better off putting some of the fault-tolerance money into a faster server or a network management application package.

Incorporating Existing Infrastructure

In the best of all worlds, you can plan your new network from the ground up, choosing the best components to fit each requirement and integrating the whole into a smoothly functioning system. In the real world, however, you seldom have this luxury. The year-old server in accounting can't be thrown away. The folks in marketing are running NetBEUI on a peer LAN and would rather fight than switch networking protocols. Administration is running IPX/SPX on a Novell NetWare 3.12 server, using a critical application that runs only as a NetWare loadable module (NLM). Engineering is running TCP/IP on UNIX workstations. The graphic designers in the publications department have Macintoshes connected by an AppleTalk network. Office politics alone prevent you from changing any of this, even if you had the budget to replace everything (which you don't).

Software-Related and Protocol-Related Planning Issues   Fortunately, Windows NT Server gives you most of the tools needed to resolve software- and protocol-related problems. Unlike server software from Novell, IBM, and other vendors, Windows NT Server was designed from the ground up to work in a heterogeneous environment. Windows NT Server provides native support for IPX/SPX, NetBEUI, and TCP/IP, thereby eliminating many of the problems of dealing with a mixed-protocol environment. Various add-on products are also available from Microsoft and third parties to provide extended functionality for TCP/IP and NetWare integration, making your job just that much easier. See Chapter 10, "Using TCP/IP, WINS, and DHCP," and Chapter 18, "Integrating Windows NT with NetWare and UNIX," for a complete discussion of these software- and protocol-related issues.

If your network will be connected to the Internet, the network must provide TCP/IP support at the server and the workstations. Now is the time to begin planning for the Internet connection. Consider these three main points:

- *Reserving your domain name and address blocks.* If you don't plan to connect to the Internet immediately, you should contact the InterNIC to obtain legal network addresses and, optionally, a domain name. The advantage to reserving your domain name as soon as possible is to increase the possibility of obtaining a desirable name that's not already in use (domain names are allocated on a first-come, first-served basis).

There isn't much of an advantage in obtaining a legal block of addresses anymore, because most ISPs require that their customers use addresses allocated to the ISP. In fact, many people who change ISPs must deal with the often difficult task of renumbering their network.

■ *Planning Internet address allocations.* Unless you work for a huge multilocation enterprise, the chance of obtaining anything larger than a block of Class C addresses is slim to none. With the "shortage" of IP addresses, the InterNIC and your service provider will require that you subnet your network to take full advantage of the IP address space. Although subnetting isn't rocket science, it requires a solid background in mathematics—primarily in binary logic operations.

■ *Planning for DHCP, WINS, and DNS.* The DHCP server that's bundled with Windows NT Server is a very good tool for managing IP addresses on client machines. DHCP "leases" an IP address to a client for a predetermined amount of time (from one minute to infinity), and is an excellent way to handle situations such as a notebook computer moving from location to location. If your network is composed of multiple LANs, you must have either a DHCP server on each LAN or use a router that forwards DHCP requests to a DHCP server.

▶ **See** "Implementing Dynamic Host Configuration Protocol," **p. 332**

WINS is Microsoft's preferred method for Windows NT Server clients to resolve machine (NetBIOS) names to IP addresses. WINS servers require very little maintenance and, unlike DHCP servers, can be configured to replicate with each other for automatic fail-over. WINS also can be configured to work with the Windows NT DNS server to update the DNS server automatically when a new host IP host is added to the network.

▶ **See** "Implementing Windows Internet Name Service," **p. 342**

DNS is the Internet Protocol's standard method for mapping IP host names with IP addresses, and mapping an IP address to a host name. Windows NT Server clients can be configured to use DNS to resolve the machine name, but Windows NT's DNS has some limitations—most notably, the hosts must be in the same DNS domain. The Windows NT DNS server, new to Windows NT 4.0, can be configured to automatically and dynamically import host names and addresses from a WINS server into a DNS subdomain, greatly reducing IP address management.

▶ **See** "Using the Microsoft DNS Server," **p. 671**

Hardware-Related Planning Issues   Hardware-related integration issues can be thornier than software issues, especially because candidates for replacement are usually hubs, routers, and similar active network components. These hardware devices seldom are seen by upper management, who almost never understand their function. Deciding what legacy networking hardware to keep and work around versus what hardware to replace may be easily accomplished in isolation, but explaining to upper management why it makes sense to replace a recently purchased and expensive piece of networking equipment can be a tough sell. Sometimes you can successfully explain matters to management and convince them of the necessity; sometimes the "Trust-me-we-just-have-to-do-this" method works; and sometimes you must buy the replacement hardware quietly, put the older component on the shelf as a "spare," and hope that no one ever inquires too pointedly about it.

You typically replace existing networking hardware for at least one of these reasons:

- *Compatibility* is usually the easiest sell. If you absolutely need to route TCP/IP and IPX/SPX but your existing router supports only TCP/IP and can't be upgraded to support both, it's easy to make clear to everyone that the old router must be replaced.

- *Capacity* is another easy sell. If you have an existing 12-port dumb hub but your new network requires more than 12 ports at a particular location, it's easy to point out that you can't plug a workstation into a port you don't have.

- *Reliability* is a tougher point to make. Everyone wants the network to be operational 24 hours per day, 7 days per week, and everyone understands that sometimes the network will be down. No one outside your department, however, understands exactly why the network goes down. Replacing older and less reliable components can greatly increase the reliability and uptime of the network as a whole, and it's certainly a valid issue to consider in your network design.

  Getting this point across to upper management can be difficult, particularly if you have been doing your job well and, as a result, haven't had any major network outages recently. Still, it's you (the network administrator) who takes the heat when things fail, and it's you who gets the calls at 4 a.m. to come fix the problem.

- *Manageability* is usually the hardest sell of all. For all but the smallest networks, using manageable active network components can make the difference between having a reliable network run by a productive, proactive network staff, and spending all your time putting out network fires and killing router snakes. *Manageability* means the capability to remotely monitor and control components such as bridges and routers, usually by a standard protocol such as SNMP (Simple Network Management Protocol). Manageability is discussed later in the section "Considering Network Management Needs."

N O T E   A network built with fully managed components can often operate with half the network staff required to operate an unmanaged network, and can do so more efficiently and more effectively. Still, upper management often doesn't fully appreciate the efficiencies of using managed components. You can tell management all day long that managed network components make the difference between making a five-minute change from your desk and having someone spend four hours driving out to a site and making the change manually. Management often still sees only the direct additional costs involved in installing managed components, and ignores the indirect costs associated with using your staff inefficiently. If your network will be medium-size or larger—particularly if you'll have equipment installed at multiple sites—fight for managed components. ■

Connecting to the Outside World

Few networks these days are pure LANs. The proliferation of remote access servers, fax servers, branch office connectivity, and connections to the Internet give a WAN aspect to most so-called LANs. Unless your network has no connections to the outside world, you must understand wide-area connectivity issues in order to plan your network installation properly. The days when the "phone people" and "data people" were separate groups reporting to separate department heads are long gone. If you don't know what a hunt group is or how a BRI ISDN line varies from a T1 connection, find out before you plan your network infrastructure, not afterward. Data communications line charges are becoming an increasingly large portion of monthly IS costs as more and more LANs are extended into WANs. Competition between common data communication carriers has resulted in a bewildering array of alternative services with a wide range of installation, monthly, and usage charges.

The best place to start learning about data communication is your local telco. Ask to talk to the telco's data communications group and set up a meeting. After you understand the basic issues, you're in a much better position to compare the alternatives available for data communications, along with the telco's installation costs and monthly service charges. Understanding the basics also lets you make informed decisions regarding competitive services available from various sources, including your local telco, AT&T, MCI, Sprint, and other common-carrier service providers. After you understand the fundamentals of packet switching, for example, you're in a much better position to judge whether frame relay or ATM makes sense for your WAN.

Developing an Implementation Schedule

Is the most frequent question you hear, "How much is this going to cost?" If so, bringing up a strong second place has to be, "How long is this going to take?" Although some elements of timing are within your control, in many cases you're at the mercy of outside parties, over whom you have little or no control. Purchasing delays, hardware vendor lead times, and data communications line installation delays conspire to prolong the process.

Develop a detailed implementation schedule, and then do your best to stick to it if you want to have your network installed in a timely fashion. The best way to do this is to purchase and use a project-management software package, discussed in more detail later in the section "Using Project-Management Software to Manage Resources and Schedules."

Considering Network Management Needs

Network management protocols have been developed to allow the network administrator to manage connected devices, track resource usage and trends, and detect and correct critical errors and problems, all from a central management workstation. For all but the smallest networks, having remote management installed can mean the difference between a network easily maintained with minimum staff time, and a network occupying your staff full time just to make routine changes and repairs.

Utilities at the network operating system level that are intended to ease user administration, track disk space allocations, administer password policies, and so forth provide useful functions, and certainly fall under the umbrella of network management. So, too, do application metering programs, backup utilities, and LAN hardware inventory programs. Packet-level analysis tools such as sniffers, protocol analyzers, and cable meters are invaluable in tracking down physical problems on the cable, misbehaving components, and the like.

More important by far to the task of keeping the network up and running efficiently on a day-to-day basis, however, are the standards-based applications designed to monitor and manage your active network components remotely by using protocols such as SNMP and Management Information Base (MIB). These applications function by using a central management station to query and control management agents installed on various critical system components, such as hubs and routers. Proxy agents installed on managed components also can be used to monitor components that aren't themselves manageable. For example, a proxy agent running on a managed router can be used to monitor a dumb hub, which otherwise wouldn't be manageable.

These applications monitor your network by allowing you to set threshold levels, referred to as *traps*, for various criteria on the management agent for critical system components. When one threshold level is exceeded, the management agent informs the software running on the central management station, allowing you to take action to correct the problem. Another function of network management applications is remote management. A managed component can be controlled from the central management workstation, eliminating the need to make an on-site visit to make programming changes.

Although the underlying network management protocols used by these applications are standards-based, the implementations aren't. Although the standards-based protocols offer all the basic tools needed for network management, they pay little heed to interface requirements and ease of use. Also, standards-based protocols, by their nature, must use the least-common denominator, making no provision for managing extended features and enhanced functions specific to a particular brand and model of component. As a result, major vendors have developed proprietary network management software that's specific to their own components. These products, many of which are Windows-based, provide graphic representations of the installed components, allowing monitoring and management simply with a mouse click.

Installing network management isn't inexpensive. In addition to the cost of the components themselves, a central management station and management software must be purchased. Management software normally starts around $5,000 for element managers, and escalates rapidly to $20,000 and above for full-function enterprise managers. The cost of the management station itself isn't insignificant, because most of these products specify a minimum of a high-end Pentium with 32M or 64M of RAM and a 21-inch monitor. Some of them require a $30,000 Sun or Hewlett-Packard workstation. Still, all these costs pale in comparison to the usual alternative—hiring additional skilled staff to maintain the network as it expands and extends to remote sites.

N O T E Hewlett-Packard announced in March 1997 its OpenView Network Node Manager for Windows NT. Network Node Manager runs under Windows NT Workstation 4.0 (or Server) and, according to HP, provides "the ability to evaluate network performance, preempt network disruption, and anticipate network growth or realignment." HP has scheduled a mid-1997 release for the Windows NT version of OpenView PerfView for resource and performance analysis, monitoring and planning, and OpenView MeasureWare resource and performance agent software. ■

ON THE WEB

You can read a Network Node Manager product briefing at **http://hpcc997.external.hp.com/nsmd/ ov/main.html**.

For most medium-size and larger networks—particularly those that support multiple sites— the cost of installing network management is quickly repaid in increased productivity and in a reduced need to expand staff as the network grows and extends to other sites. At the same time, given the relatively high cost of purchasing the central management workstation and software, you certainly don't want to duplicate these costs to provide additional stations. Be- cause network management software is proprietary, the only way to avoid doing so is to make sure that all your managed components are provided by the same manufacturer.

N O T E Microsoft's Systems Management Server (SMS), a component of the BackOffice server suite, provides many of the features of large-scale network management systems at moderate cost. The primary advantage of SMS is that it's fully integrated with Windows NT Server 4.0 and is designed specifically for managing Windows clients, as well as providing automated installation of application software for client workstations. A dedicated SMS server usually serves a single domain. Installing SMS is the subject of Chapter 25, "Administering Clients with Systems Management Server 1.2." ■

Providing for Future Growth

All organizations have short-term tactical goals and long-term strategic objectives, all of which must be supported by the network if they're to be successful. As you plan and design your network and internetwork, keep constantly in mind that you're aiming at a moving target. Storage requirements increase as time passes. The total number of employees and worksta- tions served by the network are likely to increase, as well as the number of sites to be con- nected. Newer technologies, such as client/server applications and document imaging, may be implemented in the future, placing increased demands on your servers and on network band- width. A properly planned and designed network must have the scalability needed to support future growth, both that of a predictable nature and that due to unforeseeable changes in the technology and the way your organization does business.

Begin planning for future growth by examining trends for the past few years. Have employee counts been increasing, decreasing, or remaining stable? Has the number of installed PCs increased, or are most newly purchased PCs simply replacing older models? Have all depart- ments and sites been fully computerized, both in terms of hardware and applications, or is computerization an ongoing process? Have some functions of your organization been outsourced? If so, is this outsourcing likely to occur for other functions? Examine each such historical trend and discover whether it will likely continue or change over time.

Turn next to examining expected changes for the near future. What projects are in the plan- ning stage that could affect network resource requirements? Perhaps your paper archives are due to be converted to magneto-optical storage. Your organization may plan to establish a major Web site on the Internet. A new branch office may be in the cards a year or so down the road.

After you consider all these issues and come up with your best guess for what your network will need to support a year, two years, or further in the future, design your network around components that will support its expected future size. Following are four keys to designing your network for future growth:

- *Design your network to comply with industry standards.* The networking landscape is littered with failed attempts by various vendors to propose proprietary components and protocols as industry standards. By sticking with mature and broadly supported standards such as Ethernet, TCP/IP, and SNMP, you ensure that your network will be easily expandable down the road.

- *Provide the network management capabilities needed to monitor traffic and loading, and develop trend analyses.* You need to know where the bottlenecks are now and where they likely will develop in the future, if you're to take action to eliminate them.

- *Design for modularity.* A properly planned and designed network or internetwork can be expanded by incremental additions and upgrades over the years. A poorly designed network may require wholesale replacement of components as needs change. Break down the project into subprojects, treating each site, workgroup, or major department group as an individual element of the network as a whole. Choose components for that group that will support its current size and expected future growth. That way, if unforeseen increases in demand occur, you make changes only to those components that directly support the affected group.

- *Build in overcapacity.* For example, if a particular workgroup currently requires 11 network ports, don't buy a 12-port dumb hub to service that workgroup. If you do, you'll find yourself replacing it two months later when the workgroup adds an employee and decides that it needs to convert one of its stand-alone laser printers to a network printer. Don't even buy the 16-port stand-alone hub. Instead, choose the 24-port stackable hub.

  If you can't afford to buy the managed version now, make sure that the version you do buy is upgradable to include management. You'll pay somewhat more for your hubs and end up with a lot of unused ports. You'll find that as the network grows, however, this small additional cost will be more than offset by the money you don't have to spend to tear out the original component and replace it with what you should have purchased in the first place. A year from now, when you finally convince your boss that you can't live without network management, you'll find it an easier sell if it involves only inexpensive incremental upgrades to existing components rather than a wholesale replacement of all your existing hubs.

Working Within a Budget

The key to working within a budget is to plan exactly what to buy before you spend a cent. Buying networking products on a piecemeal basis is a great temptation but is almost always a mistake. When the project is approved and the budgeted funds are transferred to your account, there's often an impetus to show progress quickly. Vendors encourage this behavior by offering limited-duration specials and promotions. The inevitable result of falling into the trap of piecemeal purchasing is that you either overbuy on the early items and find yourself scrambling later on—perhaps settling for much less than you really need on the later items—or that you take a more conservative approach to spending early and later find that you spent less than you should have on the items purchased first. In either case, you haven't optimized the allocation of funding for the project.

A good way to go about the process is to create a master purchasing spreadsheet with one line item for each individual item to be purchased. If designed properly, this spreadsheet can be an invaluable tool not only for establishing the initial budget, but for tracking receipt of components as they arrive and flagging overdue items.

The following list provides a good starting point for the columns of a purchasing spreadsheet:

- *Item description.* A brief name or description of the item.
- *Estimated cost.* Approximate cost for the line item, used for preliminary budgeting and pulled from *Computer Shopper* or a similar publication.
- *Purchase requisition number.* Useful information to have ready when you follow up with the purchasing department.
- *Purchase requisition date.* Used to flag purchase orders that are slow in arriving.
- *Purchase order number.* Again, useful information to have easily available when you need to follow up with purchasing or with vendors. This also provides an easy visual clue to the status of your orders. If this column is blank, it hasn't been ordered yet.
- *Purchase order date.* The date the purchase order was issued—again, useful when following up with purchasing or vendors.
- *Purchase order amount.* The real dollar amount you'll pay for this line item.
- *Cost differential.* The difference between your estimated cost and the cost on the purchase order. This number tells you how well you budgeted costs initially and how closely you're keeping to budget, allowing you to make adjustments to later purchases to keep to budget.
- *Delivery date.* The requested or promised delivery date for each item. A quick scan of this column will tell you which items are late in arriving and allow you to quickly take follow-up action to resolve the problem.
- *Received.* A simple check-off column that allows you to mark which items have arrived. Again, this provides a quick visual clue to developing delivery problems.
- *Vendor name, contact person, and phone.* Useful information to have readily at hand.
- *Notes.* Miscellaneous information that doesn't fit elsewhere.

N O T E The columns in this spreadsheet will vary, depending on your purchasing policies and procedures. If you have the luxury of being able to do your own purchasing directly rather than work through a purchasing department, for example, many of the columns listed aren't needed.

In addition to this master budgeting spreadsheet, you're likely to find that it's useful to develop supporting spreadsheets for various purposes. Some line items on the master spreadsheet may require more detail than is appropriate, such as server configurations and options. Other related items, such as configuration planning by site or department, can have a separate spreadsheet, with summary totals linked to the master budgeting spreadsheet. This methodology keeps the master to a manageable level of detail.

 One final item that's often overlooked in setting up a project budget is establishing a contingency reserve to cover unexpected requirements. If your budgeted amount seems likely to be adequate to complete the project, or if this is your first such project, 10 percent of the total budgeted amount is a reasonable contingency reserve.

Training Users

The importance of user training and its impact on your planning and budgeting vary widely, depending on your particular situation. If your networking project is simply an upgrade or a replacement of an existing network, and your users continue to use the same applications, training may have a negligible impact on planning and budgeting. If your network is a completely new installation intended to serve users who aren't currently computerized, you may have major planning and budgeting issues to consider, perhaps including a computer training classroom with equipment and instructors. If your network links users who previously used stand-alone PCs, at the very least you must make provision for training these users to use e-mail and other network-specific applications.

You must balance the need for user training against the funds, space, and other resources available, keeping in mind that users being trained can't to do their usual jobs simultaneously. If you decide to provide training, you must decide whether to conduct the training in-house, conduct it at a commercial training center, or pay an independent trainer to give classes at your site. Unless you live in a major metropolitan area or decide to train only on the most common Windows productivity applications, you're likely to find that there's no alternative but to train in-house, because no one offers classes on the software you're using. Many organizations compromise by providing a "train the trainer" program, where one or more chosen individuals from each department or location undergo training and then return to their groups where they, in turn, train the other users.

Managing the Project

After the basic planning and budgeting issues are resolved, you must initiate and manage the installation of the network. The following sections describe how to use commercial project-management software to determine the schedule of the work and to allocate the resources required to complete the installation and startup of the network, including acquiring the services of vendors, value-added resellers, and independent network consultants.

Using Project-Management Software to Manage Resources and Schedules

In the course of planning, purchasing, and implementing your network, you accumulate vast amounts of information: scores of specific user requests, hundreds of to-do items, dozens or hundreds of individual items to be purchased, vendor lead times to be coordinated, and data communications line installation schedules. Throughout the course of the project, many changes occur. Item prices actually quoted may be higher or lower than you initially estimated. Key components may be backordered. Managers suddenly discover a desperate need for something they didn't bother to mention during your initial interviews, and upper management backs up the new requests. Winter storms result in delayed deliveries. All this information must be recorded, updated as changes occur, and kept organized if you're to have any hope of staying on schedule and within budget.

Installation of a PC network is, in fact, a construction project and deserves to be treated as such. Project-management software, which is critical to construction projects, runs the gamut in features and functionality from Schedule+'s to-do lists to mid-range project-management software such as Microsoft Project. Figures 2.5 and 2.6 illustrate Gantt and PERT (Program Evaluation and Review Technique) charts, respectively, for NetWare to Windows NT network migration with a Microsoft Project template included in the *Windows NT Resource Kit* for version 3.51. Simple to-do lists lack the capability to handle a project of this scale. High-end project-management applications, such as Primavera, are intended for people who manage multimillion-dollar construction projects for a living. High-end packages are very expensive, quite difficult to learn, and are overkill for this type of project.

Buy Microsoft Project (or one of the competing mid-range project-management applications) and spend a half day or so learning the basics. You don't need to master every feature of the software to obtain useful results. After you learn to enter and edit tasks and resources, set milestones, track critical paths, and print Gantt charts, you have most of the tools you need to manage your resources and schedules successfully.

In most situations, the major resource you must manage is your own time and that of your staff. The availability of resources affects schedules, because completing any given task requires commitment of a certain time period by a staff member with a particular skill. While that staff member is occupied with a particular task, he's unavailable to work on another task requiring similar skills. You'll likely find that one or two key people form a bottleneck, with more demand for their services than can be fulfilled. As a result, the time line stretches out, even though other resources may be standing idle. Following are three keys to maintaining a schedule from a resource point of view:

■ *Estimate, as accurately as possible, the time needed to complete each task.* This step is critical. If you greatly underestimate the time needed for too many steps, your entire schedule will collapse. Everyone is an optimist when it comes to estimating how long an activity will take, so make your best guess and then double it. As the project proceeds, update these estimates based on your experience to date. You may be surprised to see the effect of a minor change in one aspect of your schedule on the project as a whole.

FIG. 2.5

A Gantt chart created by the Network Planning template for Microsoft Project.

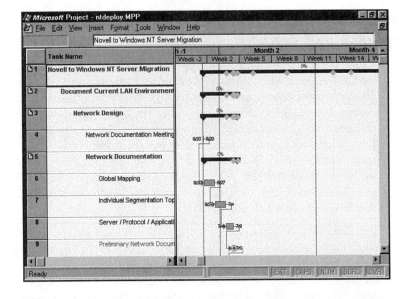

FIG. 2.6

A PERT chart created by the Network Planning template for Microsoft Project.

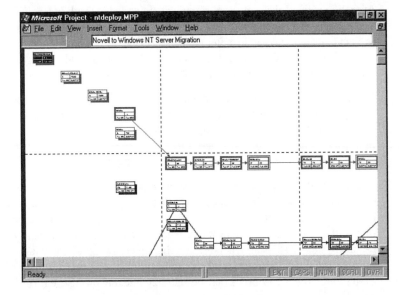

■ *Marshal your resources carefully.* Most organizations have a diverse information systems staff, with each member having a mix of skills. One person may be able to fill in for another in one area, but not in another. Determine which one or two key staff members are likely, because of their special skills, to be in great demand; then schedule other staff members to do as many of the tasks as they possibly can, freeing up the time of the persons with critical skills.

■ *Don't try to manage activities that you don't control.* This seems obvious, but it doesn't always work out the way it should. People can't be two places at the same time, nor can they effectively serve two masters simultaneously. If you're the head of your information systems department, you have no problem in directing your staff to do what needs to be done when it needs to be done. If, on the other hand, you're somewhere lower in the organizational hierarchy, you may find yourself pleading for help from other staff members that have conflicting demands on their time, because you don't have the authority to direct their activities. Managing a project properly requires that you have control of participants' schedules, or at least that you have a solid commitment of a certain percentage of their time over the course of the project. You must be provided with vacation schedules for each staff member. If you don't have the authority to schedule staff resources, your schedule will collapse.

One of the many benefits of using project-management software is the reports it provides. These reports can tip you off early to potential budget overruns, resource conflicts, and deadlines unlikely to be met. These reports, in summary or consolidated form, are also useful for keeping management informed of progress, one often-overlooked aspect of successful project management. Giving management weekly or even daily updates—depending on the size and scope of the project—allows managers to become active participants in the project.

Getting Outside Help

Few organizations have all the in-house skills needed to plan and implement a major networking project, particularly a project that involves internetworking. Even those organizations with such staff often find that other demands on staff time make it impractical to take on a major project while continuing to meet day-to-day obligations for existing networks. As a result, it's often necessary to look outside the organization for help in implementing such a project. Such outside help falls into two categories: manufacturers and value added resellers (VARs) of networking components, and consultants.

Using Vendors and Resellers   Vendors and VARs can be very useful sources of advice in configuring your network. They are obviously intimately familiar with the capabilities of their equipment and have probably installed many similar networks for organizations much like your own.

Balanced against these advantages is the obvious conflict of interest. The vendor or VAR wants to sell specific brands of equipment, so more than likely that person won't recommend competing gear that may be a better or more cost-effective solution for your particular needs. Another negative factor is that the vendor or VAR focuses on just one part of the total picture, leaving you to worry about integrating the system as a whole. On balance, although vendors and VARs often provide a surprisingly high level of commitment to helping you plan and implement your network, you're usually better off to first select a vendor or VAR, and then later use whatever services are available from the vendor or VAR to help you implement your chosen design.

Using Consultants   The second source of outside help is an independent consultant. True consultants bill you only for their time and expenses and, therefore, are an unbiased source of

Part
I

Ch
2

advice—at least in theory. In practice, many individuals and companies who represent themselves as consultants are, in fact, thinly disguised VARs who make some or most of their income from reselling hardware and software. A properly qualified independent consultant can help you with all aspects of your project, from the initial planning through the implementation phase.

Consultants have two drawbacks:

- They can be very expensive. Depending on your location, a good networking consultant will probably charge at least $125 per hour, with specialists in internetworking often getting two to three times that amount. Hours can mount very quickly, unless you keep a tight rein on what the consultant is and isn't expected to do.

  Hiring consultants is often worthwhile, if only in an advisory role. Because consultants have "seen it all before," one hour of their time may save you a day or even a week of your own time. Even more important, recommendations by consultants may save you from making a multithousand-dollar mistake. After you plan and design your network, it's almost always worthwhile to hire a good consultant for a half day or day to sit down with you and go over your plan. He often can point out alternative methods you may not have considered, or better or less expensive sources for components.

- Even a consultant with wide experience has personal preferences for particular manufacturers and specific ways of doing things. A consultant who is, for example, an expert on Cisco routers seldom has as much depth of experience in working with competing routers from DEC or HP. It's human nature to stick with what you know works, and consultants are no exception to this rule. There are many right ways of addressing a problem, although there are many more wrong ways of solving the problem. What you care about is that the route you choose is one of the right ways, and a consultant can help make sure that this happens.

Choosing a consultant can be difficult. There are no state licensing boards for computer consultants; as a result, anyone can call himself a computer consultant, regardless of his qualifications (or lack thereof). To make matters worse, even a consultant who has done good work for you in the past or is highly recommended to you by your peers may not be qualified for your particular project. Even worse, the consultant may not be aware that he isn't qualified for your project and, thus, not disclose this fact.

When you speak to someone for whom the candidate consultant has done work, ask that person whether the project was completed successfully, on time, and under budget. Ask what problems have developed since that time and if the consultant was responsive to the problem. Focus not on personalities, but on results.

A more objective method of assessing a consultant's qualifications is to find what industry certifications he holds and what those certifications imply. Networking hardware and software vendors long ago realized that, in the absence of formal state licensing boards for consultants, it was up to them, the vendors, to provide some mechanism for assuring would-be clients that consultants had achieved at least some minimum level of competence with their products.

N O T E Microsoft has developed a certification program for Windows NT Server called the Microsoft Certified System Engineer, or MCSE. The youth of this program and the still relatively small market share of Windows NT Server, compared with Novell NetWare, means that relatively few people have completed the requirements for the MCSE. (As of early 1997, there were about 10,000 MCSEs in North America.) This situation likely will change, as many Novell Certified NetWare Engineers (CNEs) are adding MCSE certifications to their resumes. Unless the consultant you plan to hire is a specialist in a particular product area, such as data communications, make sure that the consultant you employ holds an MCSE certification. ■

Part

I

Ch

2

Balancing Resources and Requirements

Before you purchase the components to build your network, balance the resources you have available with your requirements. Unless you are in the enviable and unlikely position of being given an unlimited budget, you must make compromises in some areas to get what you need in other areas. It does little good to have the best server on the market if purchasing the server leaves you without enough money to buy network cards for your workstations. Chapter 5, "Purchasing Networking Hardware," is devoted to the hardware acquisition process, but planning is required to assure that you can complete the network installation without exceeding your budget.

Establishing a Minimum Configuration

Begin the purchase planning process by establishing a minimum acceptable configuration for each component. Don't compromise in terms of quality, but rather in terms of features and function. Stick to brand names, but work from the low end of the product line rather than the high end. Determine the minimum server configuration in terms of processor, disk storage, RAM, and other features that will do the job. Install 100BaseT/10BaseT compatible network cards in servers and client PCs, because there's no price penalty for the higher speed cards. Even if you would prefer to install 100 Mbps 100BaseT hubs, instead determine the cost for 10 Mbps 10BaseT hubs to start. Calculate the cost of installing a cabling system with only enough horizontal runs to meet your immediate needs. Plan on unmanaged hubs and other active components rather than the latest and greatest in managed equipment.

If you're lucky, you'll find at the end of this process that you have money left in your budget. If you're very lucky, it may be a significant amount. If you're already over budget, it's time to go to management and state that the job can't be done with the funds available. Don't make the mistake of trying to install a network with inadequate funding.

Allocating Remaining Funds

After you establish a baseline via the process described in the preceding section, carefully consider how the remaining funds, if any, can best be spent.

Server memory can always be upgraded easily later, but Category 3 wire in the wall remains Category 3 wire in the wall forever. Category 5 wiring substantially reduces the cost of upgrading from a 10BaseT to a 100BaseT network. If you must choose between an expensive managed hub, an inexpensive dumb hub that isn't upgradable, or a moderately priced hub that's configured initially as dumb but later can be upgraded to managed, pick the moderately priced hub. You're likely to find the money to upgrade the moderately priced hub in the future, but if you buy the non-upgradable hub, you probably will be stuck with it into the next century.

Maximize the number of free PCI adapter card slots, free drive bays, and memory sockets in the server. There is little, if any, reason to install legacy ISA adapter cards in a Windows NT 4.0 server. For example, if you choose to equip your server with 64M of RAM, specify two 32M SIMMs (single in-line memory modules) in preference to four 16M SIMMs. Later, you won't have to replace all your memory to upgrade the server because it has no free SIMM sockets. Although, in principle, your server may be better off having as many drive spindles running as possible, in practice you're better served by buying fewer larger disks in preference to more smaller ones, leaving drive bays available for future expansion. Substantial improvement in the reliability of large (9G and bigger) fixed-disk drives has occurred in the past two years.

Favor a few expensive items rather than many inexpensive ones. It's always easier to obtain subsequent approval for inexpensive upgrades to many small items than it is to acquire funding for a single expensive upgrade. Upgrading all your workstation NICs from 10 Mbps to 100 Mbps is a much harder sell than is a request to add another 32M of RAM or a few more gigabytes of disk space to the server.

Buy now what you may not be able to buy later. If expanding the memory on your server requires an expansion card, and that card doesn't come with the server, buy the card now. You may not be able to obtain the card when you're ready to add memory.

Similarly, pay close attention to the type of fixed-disk drives supported by your RAID controller. Many RAID controllers support only a few specific drive models. Some controllers require that all drives be identical. You don't want to find in a year or two that your only alternative is to replace all your drives just because the matching drive you need no longer is available.

Dealing with Vendors

A good vendor is a godsend and can be very helpful in the initial planning process. A bad supplier can make your life miserable. Good vendors deliver what you ordered at the price they quoted, and do so on time. Bad vendors are usually a day late and a dollar short. Good vendors have the expertise and take the time to advise you on your purchases. Although you obviously must take into account suppliers' vested economic interest, their close relationship with manufacturers benefits you in terms of timely information and advice.

Unfortunately, good vendors are seldom the lowest bidder. Depending on your environment, you may be forced to buy only from low bidders, or you may have the luxury of choosing vendors based on factors other than simply lowest price. Do everything you can to select a good vendor and direct purchases his way. You'll find that the small additional cost is more than made up for by the services that the vendor provides, not only in terms of good advice, but also in delivery preference for items in short supply, generous interpretation of warranty terms, or provision of equipment on loan. Don't hesitate to use lower prices quoted by other vendors as a bargaining tool, but realize that good vendors incur additional costs to provide additional services and thus are entitled to a moderate price premium.

Decide first what you consider to be commodity items. This decision is determined by the level of in-house expertise and by where you choose to focus your efforts. All shrink-wrapped Fast EtherLink XL PCI or Intel EtherExpress PRO/100 PCI Ethernet cards are the same, so you can safely treat this type of item as a commodity and simply shop for the best price. On the other hand, a Hewlett-Packard NetServer LM2 network server isn't a commodity item. If you have a dozen other NetServers installed and have a network staff to configure them to your way of doing things, adding one more LM2 should be easy, and you can probably safely shop for the lowest price.

From Here...

This chapter outlined the overall process of planning a network installation, with emphasis on establishing a new network or upgrading an existing PC network to Windows NT Server 4.0. Much of the content of this chapter is applicable to planning the installation of any network operating system and isn't specific to Windows NT Server 4.0. The intent of this chapter is to provide you with a planning framework before you delve into the details of Windows NT networking architecture. The remaining three chapters in Part I are devoted to Windows NT 4.0:

- Chapter 3, "Understanding the Windows NT Operating System," describes the architecture of Windows NT with emphasis on Windows NT 4.0 networking features.

- Chapter 4, "Choosing Network Protocols," discusses Windows NT Server 4.0's support for multiple protocols and how to determine the protocol(s) to use for your network.

- Chapter 5, "Purchasing Networking Hardware," describes the process of acquiring the hardware you need to set up or upgrade your Windows NT 4.0 network.

Part
I

Ch
2

Understanding the Windows NT Operating System

Windows NT is, first and foremost, a general-purpose computer operating system for business use. Although this book concentrates on Windows NT Server 4.0 networking features, Windows NT is equally at home running heavy-duty workstation applications, such as computer-aided design of aircraft components or non-linear video editors and animated graphics applications for producing broadcast television programs.

The Workstation and Server versions of Windows NT 4.0 share a common source code base; the network management and application server features of Windows NT Server 4.0 are modular components added to the basic operating system modules of Windows NT Workstation 4.0 or enabled by Registry entries. Thus, the underlying architecture of Windows NT varies markedly from dedicated network operating systems, such as Novell NetWare and Banyan VINES, that concentrate on file and printer sharing.

Windows NT was designed from the ground up as an application server for 32-bit Windows programs; this contrasts with NetWare, which initially gained application services in the form of an add-in to support

Windows NT architecture

The architecture of Windows NT provides a robust operating environment for networked application servers, as well as file and printer sharing.

Objects, subsystems, and virtual memory

Windows NT takes an object-oriented component approach to symmetrical multiprocessing and memory management. The Component Object Model (COM) will play an increasingly important role in future versions of Windows NT.

The New Technology File System (NTFS)

NTFS overcomes FAT16's 2G partition size limit, minimizes unused space in fixed-disk clusters, supports file compression, and provides a very secure file access control system.

Remote procedure calls

RPCs let you distribute application components over multiple servers to create *n*-tier client/server systems. Distributed COM (DCOM) simplifies programming of distributed applications.

Windows NT networking

Windows NT Server 4.0 includes high-performance drivers for TCP/IP, IPX/SPX, NetBEUI, and AppleTalk protocols.

custom-programmed NetWare Loadable Modules (NLMs). The architecture of Windows NT closely resembles that of UNIX, with some added features derived from DEC's VMS operating system.

Unlike other versions of Windows (including Windows 95), Windows NT isn't encumbered with the baggage of backward-compatibility obligations to the installed base of low-end PCs designed to run 16-bit Windows and DOS applications. Windows NT 4.0 doesn't accommodate 16-bit device drivers for adapter cards and other hardware accessories, nor does it support dynamic reconfiguration of ISA adapters in accordance with the Plug and Play hardware standard of Windows 95.

Windows NT 4.0 also isn't optimized for mobile PCs and isn't designed to run computer games; Microsoft has positioned Windows 95 as the operating system of choice for laptop and note-book PCs, as well as personal entertainment applications. Microsoft explicitly designed Windows NT from the ground up for use in corporate and institutional computing environments ranging from small-business LANs to global WANs.

An understanding of the internal complexities underpinning the Windows NT operating system isn't an absolute necessity to plan, budget, set up, and administer a Windows NT network. For example, Windows NT's server-related application programming interfaces primarily are of interest to programmers writing specialized server-based applications, such as tape backup utilities. On the other hand, gaining a working knowledge of Windows NT architecture is quite useful when evaluating tradeoffs between software and hardware implementations of Windows NT Server functions, such as RAID subsystems, Remote Access Service, and multiprotocol routing. If you're familiar with Windows NT architecture and terminology, you're also better prepared to discern between facts and propaganda in vendor specifications and consultant recommendations. Thus, this chapter appears immediately before the chapters related to choosing network protocols and buying networking hardware. ■

Summarizing Windows NT Operating System Features

Microsoft's Windows NT development team set the following objectives for Windows NT:

- *Reliability* by protecting the core operating system from malfunctioning applications and by isolating the operating system and applications from direct operations on hardware. Structured exception handling takes care of application processing and low-level errors. NTFS provides increased reliability for file operations by a built-in transaction logging system.

- *Extensibility* by adopting a client/server model that uses a base operating system (kernel, the client) extended by application programming interfaces (APIs, the servers). In this case, the term *client/server* is used in its single-computer UNIX context, not that of the client/server model applied to networked database and Internet/intranet applications.

- *Portability* across different processor platforms, including RISC systems, through the use of a processor-specific hardware abstraction layer (HAL) that provides the isolation layer between the operating system and hardware. Portability of Windows NT is provided by writing the source code for the operating system, with a few exceptions, in an ANSI-standard C programming language.

- *Security* by compliance with at least the U.S. Department of Defense C2 standard, which provides "need-to-know" protection and auditing capability. Security in Windows NT primarily is implemented through ACLs (Access Control Lists).

- *Compatibility* with existing 16-bit DOS and Windows applications, plus the most common PC hardware devices and peripherals. Windows NT also provides the capability to execute applications written to the POSIX.1 standard, a requirement of the federal government's software procurement policies. Early versions of Windows NT supported NTFS, HPFS (OS/2's High-Performance File System), and FAT file systems. Windows NT 4.0 no longer handles HPFS volumes.

NOTE POSIX is a specification for an interface to an operating system, which need not be (but usually is) UNIX. Microsoft has contracted with a third-party developer, Softway Systems, Inc., to develop a POSIX.2 shell and utilities, which Softway markets as OpenNT. OpenNT replaces the POSIX.1 subsystem of Windows NT and provides case-sensitive file naming (files named File1 and file1 can coexist), file links (a single file can have multiple names), background processing, job control, file user and group access, and file ownership. ■

Part

I

Ch

3

ON THE WEB

Additional information on OpenNT is available at **http://www.softway.com/OpenNT/datasht.htm**.

- *Scalability* for better performance through the use of multiple CPUs with a symmetrical multiprocessing (SMP) architecture. To take advantage of SMP, 32-bit Windows applications must be written to use multiple threads of execution.

Windows NT universally receives high marks for reliability, extensibility, portability, and security. However, many DOS and 16-bit Windows applications—particularly those that write directly to hardware—don't run under Windows NT, and Windows NT requires specially written 32-bit device drivers for adapter cards and peripherals. Windows NT's scalability has limitations; although Windows NT 4.0 claims to support up to 32 processors, you begin to receive diminishing returns when you install more than four to six processors in a single server. Market research in early 1997 indicates that the vast majority of world-wide server PC purchases fall in the one- to four-processor category.

▶ **See** "Network Performance and Scalability Features," **p. 27**
▶ **See** "Deciding on a Multiprocessor System," **p. 160**

NOTE You have little or no reason to run 16-bit Windows or any DOS applications on a Windows NT 4.0 server. Furthermore, the vast majority of the hardware devices that you need to

continues

continued

implement servers are supported by 32-bit Windows NT drivers, either built into Windows NT 4.0 or available from the hardware manufacturer. Software and hardware incompatibilities—especially with sound cards, digital video capture boards, and other multimedia equipment—are barriers to use of Windows NT Workstation 4.0, not the Server version. ■

The following sections describe the basic elements of the Windows NT operating system from a bottom-up perspective.

The Windows NT Executive

The Windows NT executive consists of a collection of system (also called *native*) services, the kernel, and a hardware abstraction layer (HAL), organized as shown in Figure 3.1. Operations that run entirely within the Windows NT executive are called *kernel mode* services. The HAL, code in the kernel, and the Virtual Memory Manager are specific to the category of processor used; Windows NT 4.0 has HALs for Intel 80486 and higher CISC (Complex Instruction Set Computing) processors, and for three RISC processors: MIPS, Alpha AXP, and PowerPC. A replacement HAL is supplied by a computer manufacturer whose design departs from the reference design for a particular processor. In addition to creating a new HAL for each processor family and implementation, Windows NT and 32-bit Windows applications must be recompiled for each processor family. Thus, for example, there are separate versions of the 32-bit Microsoft Office applications for Intel, MIPS, Alpha, and PowerPC systems. Existing 16-bit Windows and DOS applications run on an 80x86 emulator unique to each RISC processor.

FIG. 3.1

The components making up the Windows NT executive.

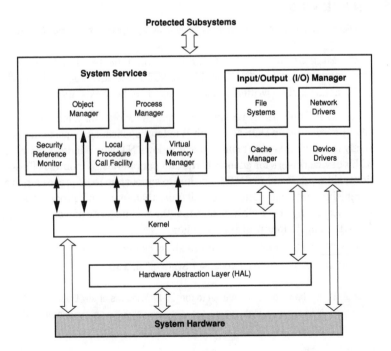

N O T E Microsoft announced in early 1997 that future versions of Windows NT will support only Intel and Alpha processors. MIPS and PowerPC systems running Windows NT haven't gained a significant market share. ■

The Windows NT executive consists of the following components:

- The *Security Reference Monitor (SRM)* provides basic security features, such as tracking user account privileges, managing ACLs, auditing, protecting objects, and limiting access to system resources. User logon is directed to the SRM, which creates an access token for each authenticated user. An *access token* is an object whose properties include users' Security IDs (SID), the SIDs of groups to which each user belongs, and special user privileges.

- *Object Manager (OM)* is responsible for creating objects to represent (abstract) system resources, such as files, hardware devices, and shared memory. Objects expose to the operating system a consistent interface to properties (data) and methods (behavior) of the particular resource. OM manages objects during their lifetime and destroys an object when it's no longer needed.

- The *Local Procedure Call (LPC) Facility*, which provides communication between applications (clients) and protected subsystems (servers), is a localized version of Windows NT's remote procedure call (RPC) feature. RPCs are the subject of the later section "Calling Remote Procedures."

- *Process Manager (PM)* is responsible for managing processes (executable applications) and threads (executable subcomponents of applications). PM handles the allocation of threads to processors when Symmetric Multiprocessing is in use.

- *Virtual Memory Manager (VMM)* allocates protected memory to each process. When memory requirements exceed the amount of available RAM, VMM stores part of the RAM contents to the fixed-disk paging file, and then retrieves the contents when needed (a process also called *swapping*). Paging is very slow compared to direct RAM operations; servers ordinarily have large amounts of RAM (64M or more) to minimize paging operations. Some vital operating system objects and data structures are held in a *non-paged pool* that's never swapped to disk.

- *Input/Output Manager (IOM)* acts on files and devices that manipulate files, including networking components. A description of each IOM component follows this list.

- The *kernel* is a low-level component responsible for handling processor interrupts and software exceptions, synchronizing multiple processors, and scheduling threads for execution. The system services of the executive rely on various low-level objects supplied by the kernel.

- The *hardware abstraction layer (HAL)* consists of a layer of code between the processor and the kernel that translates processor-specific features—such as stack operations, input/output handling, and interrupt controller functions—to a uniform set of interfaces for kernel functions. The HAL (Hal.dll) is relatively small; for example, Windows NT 4.0's HAL for Intel processors is 52K in size.

The Windows NT executive is a self-contained, low-level operating system, lacking only a user interface. The UI for the executive is provided by the Win32 subsystem that's discussed in the next section.

For Windows NT network administrators, the Input/Output Manager is the most important component of the executive, because most network operations occur within the IOM. IOM implements device-independent input/output services for all hardware components except the processor(s). The I/O system of Windows NT is *asynchronous*—that is, when an I/O request is issued, the operating system continues with other tasks until the device involved completes the requested operation. (Protected subsystems also can request synchronous I/O but usually pay a performance penalty for doing so.) The IOM is unique among the executive components because it communicates with the kernel, with the HAL, and directly with hardware components through device drivers (refer to Figure 3.1).

The IOM is comprised of these elements:

- *File systems* support multiple file architectures through layered drivers—thus, new or improved file systems can be added to Windows NT. Windows NT 4.0 supports 16-bit FAT and NTFS file systems; OS/2's HPFS, which was supported in prior versions of Windows NT, can't be used with Windows NT 4.0. For servers, the FAT file system is used only for accessing disks and CD-ROMs. (You can use the FAT file system for a Windows NT server, but doing so is strongly discouraged.) Windows NT 4.0 does *not* support the 32-bit FAT file system included with Service Pack 2 for the OEM (original equipment manufacturer) version of Windows 95 that computer assemblers preinstall on their PCs. NTFS is the subject of the later section "Handling Files with NTFS."

- *Cache Manager* stores the most recently accessed fixed-disk data in system memory to improve the performance of sequential reads. Cache Manager supplements the built-in cache of high-performance SCSI fixed-disk and CD-ROM/WORM drives. Cache Manager also improves write performance by using VMM to perform asynchronous writes in the background.

- *Network drivers* consist of the network server and network redirector. The server receives network I/O requests, and the redirector transmits network requests. The term *redirector*, which originated in the early days of MS-NET and PC-NET, is derived from the process of intercepting file operation requests on the local PC (interrupt int13h for Intel processors) and rerouting (redirecting) the operations over the network to the server.

- *Device drivers* consist of a 32-bit code layer between the preceding three elements and hardware, such as SCSI host adapters for drives, network interface cards (NICs), keyboards, mice, and graphic adapter cards. Windows NT treats network drivers as device drivers.

N O T E   As noted earlier in this chapter and elsewhere, the lack of device drivers for the wide variety of hardware devices used with 16-bit Windows and Windows 95 has hampered the acceptance of Windows NT Workstation. All of today's hardware devices that are designed for use with production servers have Windows NT drivers. These devices are listed in the current version of the

Windows NT Hardware Compatibility List (HCL) that's included with the Windows NT 4.0 documentation and periodically updated by Microsoft. ▦

ON THE WEB

You can obtain the current HCL from **http://backoffice.microsoft.com/**.

Clients and Protected Subsystem Servers

The layers above the Windows NT executive provide *user-mode* services. These layers consist of the environmental subsystems (servers) for 32-bit and 16-bit Windows applications, DOS, OS/2, and POSIX applications, plus client applications in each of these five categories. The Win32 subsystem provides the user interface (graphic display, mouse, and keyboard handlers) for all servers and for those system services of the executive that involve interaction with users via, for instance, User Manager for Domains, Server Manager, and the Virtual Memory settings on the Performance page of the System Properties sheet. Thus, the Win32 subsystem is the only component of Windows NT that's visible to users.

N O T E There's a distinction between the user-mode and kernel-mode services that are components of Windows NT and the term *services* used elsewhere in this book. Unless otherwise noted, *services* refer to executable applications that are startable when Windows NT boots. These services appear in the Service list of Control Panel's Services tool, and may be started automatically or manually or be disabled. The members of Microsoft BackOffice, for example, run as services under Windows NT, as do the Server and Workstation services. (Microsoft implemented Windows NT's Server services as a device driver for various reasons, a description of which is beyond the scope of this book.) ▦

Figure 3.2 shows the relationship of the environmental subsystems and client applications. Local procedure calls (solid lines) provide all communication between subsystems and between clients and subsystems. Subsystems also can request native services by a system trap, shown as a dotted line in Figure 3.2. Each subsystem has its own protected memory space.

N O T E Messages between client applications and environmental subsystems pass through the Windows NT executive, which establishes a separate message queue for each instance of a client application or virtual DOS machine (VDM). For clarity, the trip to and from the executive doesn't appear in Figure 3.2. ▦

Figure 3.2 shows these environmental subsystems:

■ *Virtual DOS machines* provide a protected environment for individual 16-bit DOS applications. The Win32 subsystem provides a character-based window (called a *console*) for user interaction. One VDM is created for each instance of a DOS application.

Part

I

Ch

3

■ *Windows on Win32 (WOW)* runs all 16-bit Windows 3.1+ applications in a single instance of a VDM with common protected memory. Thus, if one unruly Windows 3.1+ application crashes the VDM, all other running 16-bit Windows applications crash with it. Each 16-bit Windows application is assigned its own thread of execution to provide multitasking capability.

■ *The OS/2 subsystem* runs character-based OS/2 applications in a console. The paucity of character-based OS/2 applications that don't have Windows NT equivalents means that system and network administrators seldom need be concerned with using the OS/2 subsystem.

■ *The POSIX.1 subsystem* can run POSIX-compliant applications, which is required for government purchase of "open systems." Windows NT survived a recent appeal by UNIX bidders of an award of a Coast Guard workstation contract to Unisys that proposed to use Windows NT as the operating system. Microsoft's funding of development of the POSIX.2 shell and utilities of OpenNT, mentioned earlier in this chapter, is related to one of the Coast Guard contract requirements. It's likely that Cairo will substitute POSIX.2 for the POSIX.1 subsystem.

FIG. 3.2

The environmental subsystems and client applications that provide user-mode services.

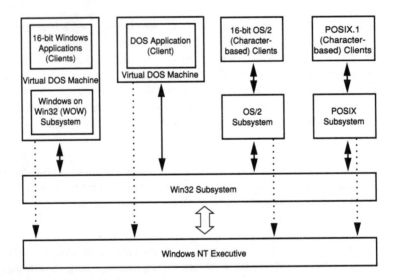

Handling Files with NTFS

One of the most important new features of Windows NT 3.1 was NTFS, an outgrowth of HPFS that Microsoft and IBM developed for OS/2. Following are Microsoft's design objectives for NTFS, with a brief description of how the objectives were achieved:

■ *Support for large fixed-disk drives.* The original version of HPFS had a maximum volume size of 4G. Windows 95's 16-bit FAT file system is limited to 2G volumes with 64K clusters; the large cluster size makes storing small files very inefficient because each file requires a minimum of one cluster. Windows NT uses 64-bit addresses for clusters of physical storage sectors that range from 512 bytes to 4K, depending on the size of the disk and its sector size. (Most fixed disks have a sector size of 512 bytes.) The maximum volume size for NTFS is 2^{64} bytes (16,777,216 terabytes), and files can be up to 2^{64} bytes long. Large volume and file sizes are especially important for storing full-screen, full-motion video for editing and broadcast applications.

- *Recoverability.* NTFS stores two copies of its equivalent of DOS's file allocation table (FAT), called the *master file table (MFT)*. Thus, if the original version of the disk's system data becomes corrupted due to a hardware failure (typically, a bad disk sector), the copy automatically is used on bootup, and the operating system creates a new original from the copy. NTFS uses a transaction log to maintain file consistency in the event of a hardware problem (such as a power failure) or system failure during the write process. NTFS uses the transaction log to return the disk to a consistent state during the next disk access.

- *Fault-tolerance through redundancy.* Windows NT Server can create a software RAID (Redundant Array of Inexpensive Disks) for NTFS volumes. If you choose RAID 1 (*disk mirroring* or *duplexing*) or RAID 5 (*disk striping with parity*), you store two copies of all server files. In case of disk hardware failure, NTFS uses the file copies. If the system detects a bad disk sector, NTFS marks the sector as bad, and then creates a replacement sector from data stored on the other disk. Chapter 7, "Setting Up Redundant Arrays of Inexpensive Disks (RAID)," describes RAID levels and the tradeoffs between implementing RAID arrays in hardware or by software.

- *Security.* Windows NT treats disk files, like processes, as objects. An NTFS file object has properties (also called *attributes*) such as name, creation date, date last updated, archive status, and a security descriptor. A file object also has a set of methods, including open, read, write, and close. Users, including networked users, can't invoke a method of a file object until the Security Reference Monitor determines that they have permission for a particular method.

- *Data compression.* Selective data compression made its first appearance in Windows NT 3.51. Data compression saves disk space at the expense of somewhat slower file access. Unlike the DriveSpace compression utility of DOS 6+ and Windows 95, NTFS lets you selectively compress a folder (and its subfolders) or individual files. On servers, compression usually is reserved for infrequently accessed files or very large files, such as large Windows bitmap (.BMP) files, that aren't already compressed. Compressing and decompressing frequently accessed files reduces server performance by a significant margin.

- *Multiple data streams in a single file.* NTFS permits subdividing the data in a file into individual streams of data. The most common application of multistream files is for storing Macintosh files on Windows NT servers. Macintosh files have two streams (called *forks*): the data fork and the application fork. The application fork contains information on the program that created or can edit the file. (In Windows NT and Windows 95, the Registry associates applications with file extensions, serving a purpose similar to that of the Macintosh's application fork.) The default data stream has no name; additional streams have names. Developers address a particular stream in a file by a suffix preceded by a colon, as in *Filename.ext:streamname.*

■ *Localization with Unicode.* NTFS supports Unicode file names. Unicode uses 16 bits to specify a particular character or symbol, rather than the 7 or 8 bits of ASCII and ANSI characters. 16 bits accommodate 64K characters and symbols, so Unicode doesn't depend on changing code pages for national language support (NLS).

N O T E One recurrent theme in this book is, "Use NTFS, not FAT, for servers." In the early days of Windows NT, some network administrators were reluctant to abandon FAT in favor of NTFS because they wanted to be able to boot a server with a DOS disk and gain access to files in case of a problem booting Windows NT. The emergency repair disk you create when you install Windows NT and the Windows NT Setup program's Repair facility is much more effective than booting from DOS to recover from a system failure. Whether or not you use NTFS or FAT for the operating system files, it's a good practice to store server shares and data files logical volumes or physical drives other than the operating system volume.

▶ **See** "Repairing the Windows NT Server Operating System Installation," **p. 209** ■

The next two sections describe the features of NTFS that are of the most significance to Windows NT Server 4.0 network administrators.

Understanding the Master File Table

The structure of DOS's FAT is relatively simple—FAT stores the DOS 8.3 file or folder name, a set of standard attributes (read-only, hidden, system, and archive bits), size of the file in bytes, and a pointer to (physical location of) the cluster that holds the first byte of file data. NTFS's master file table (MFT) is much larger and more complex than the FAT for a drive having the same directory structure and file complement. The MFT (and its mirror-image redundant copy) is similar in structure to a database table, with fixed-length and variable-length records. (The boot sector contains pointers to the location of the MFT and its mirror copy; file control blocks, or FCBs, point to a particular record in the MFT.)

The MFT of a volume that contained only directories and very small files would comprise the volume's entire contents. Storing the data of small files within an MFT record makes access much faster and minimizes unused cluster space (slack). If the data won't fit in the MFT record, the NTFS driver creates pointer(s) to non-resident data stored in *runs*. A run, also called an *extent*, is a contiguous block of disk space; non-resident data may be stored in one or more runs, which are a maximum of 16 disk clusters.

Microsoft provides only a small amount of "official" information on the MFT in the *Windows NT Resource Kit* and in Helen Custer's *Inside the Windows NT File System* monograph. Figure 3.3 is a simplified diagram of the MFT record structures for files and folders. (Figure 3.3 doesn't show the HPFS Extended Attributes field because Windows NT 4.0 doesn't support HPFS volumes.) The first 16 records of the MFT contain what Microsoft calls "special information," also called *metadata*.

▶ **See** "Print and CD-ROM Publications," **p. 12**

FIG. 3.3

The simplified structure of the file and directory records of the master file table for an NTFS volume.

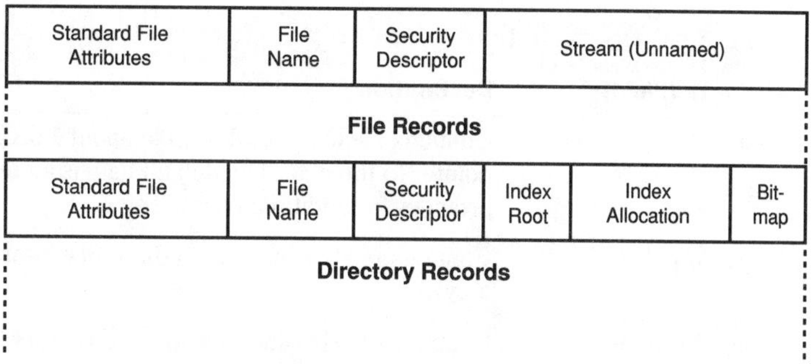

Standard File Attributes	File Name	Security Descriptor	Stream (Unnamed)		

File Records

Standard File Attributes	File Name	Security Descriptor	Index Root	Index Allocation	Bit-map

Directory Records

> **N O T E** Custer's monograph states that MFT is a relational database, apparently because it consists of records with attributes in columns. Normalization rules for relational databases, however, require that all records in a table represent a single entity set and have a consistent set of attributes (columns). Mixing of records for files and directories isn't, in itself, a serious violation of relational database theory because NTFS treats directories as files. However, the Index Root, Index Allocation, and Bitmap attributes of directory records aren't consistent with the Data attribute of file records. Further, the first 16 records contain metadata in fields that vary from the file and index records. Relational database theorists wouldn't consider MFT a properly normalized relational table. ▪

Table 3.1 describes the content of each MFT attribute (field or column), including three attributes that don't appear in Figure 3.3. The terms *attribute*, *property*, *field*, and *column* are interchangeable in discussions of database tables. Similarly, *row* and *record* refer to the same element of a table. A *volume* is a collection of fixed-disk clusters that's identified by a single logical drive letter; an NTFS volume may consist of contiguous clusters on two or more drives, which need not be elements of a RAID array. NTFS lets you combine contiguous free space on two or more disks into a single volume.

Table 3.1   Attributes of the NTFS Master File Table (MFT)

Attribute (Field)	Description
Standard Attributes (Standard Information)	Contains standard file attributes, such as time stamps, archive status, and linkage data, plus an attribute list for large files.
Filename	Contains the Unicode file name (up to 255 characters) and a DOS 8.3 file name created from the Unicode file name. For POSIX, contains additional names for the same file (called *links* or *hard links*).
Security Descriptor	Contains information on ownership, access rights, and other security-related information used by the Security Reference Monitor.

continues

Table 3.1 Continued

Attribute (Field)	Description
Data	Contains file data for files up to about 1.5K in size; otherwise, a pointer to the data. The default data is an unnamed stream; NTFS provides for additional named streams.
Index Root	Contains relative location of directory information (index records only).
Index Allocation	Contains the size and location of directory index (index records only).
Bitmap	Contains a bitmapped image of the directory structure (index records only).
Volume Information	Contains the version number and name of a volume (volume system record only, not shown in Figure 3.3).
Extended Attributes	Previously used for HPFS files, which are no longer supported in Windows NT 4.0 (not shown in Figure 3.3).
User-Defined Attributes	Will contain special attributes for custom searches (not shown in Figure 3.3); reserved for implementation in future versions of Windows NT and NTFS, presumably Cairo.

ON THE WEB

For additional details of the low-level organization of MFT records, check out **http://www.c2.org/ hackmsoft/ntfs/doc/**.

N O T E Bitmaps are a very efficient way to index records in tables, especially where indexes on multiple fields are required. An index dramatically speeds the location of an individual record in a table with a large number of records. Bitmapped indexing, not to be confused with bitmapped graphics, speeds access to the index itself. FoxPro was the first desktop database to take full advantage of bitmapped indexing in its Rushmore technology. After acquiring FoxPro, Microsoft adapted the Rushmore indexing method to Access .mdb files (starting with Access 2.0). The Windows NT 4.0 version of NTFS indexes only the file name field. Cairo is expected to include the capability to create indexes on user-defined attributes for faster searching. ■

Implementing Recoverability with Transactions

Relational database management systems, such as Microsoft SQL Server and Access, use transactions when adding, updating, or deleting records from tables. A transaction assures that *all* operations affecting records of related tables take place; if a problem prevents completion of the entire transaction, the database tables are restored to their original status before the transaction. For example, if an orders database contains Orders and LineItems tables, adding or deleting an Orders record requires simultaneous addition or deletion of the related LineItems record(s). LineItems records without a corresponding Orders record are called *orphan records,* which you don't want in a database. SQL Server uses the reserved words COMMIT TRANS[ACTION] and ROLLBACK TRANS[ACTION] to attempt and reverse a transaction, respectively. Records in a temporary transaction log record the progress of the transaction; information in these records is used to roll back the transaction, if necessary.

> **N O T E** A temporary transaction log, such as that used by Microsoft Access, varies from the persistent transaction log maintained by client/server RDBMSes, such as Microsoft SQL Server. The persistent transaction log records all successful database transactions since the last backup of the database. After restoring the backup copy of a damaged database, the transaction log is executed to bring the restored copy of the tables back to the status of the instant when the damage occurred, less any transactions in progress at that point.
>
> ▶ **See** "Setting Up Transaction Logging," **p. 862** ■

NTFS uses a similar transaction logging process to recover from a system failure during a disk write operation. Following is a brief description of the process of recoverable writing to an NTFS file:

1. The NTFS file I/O driver initiates the write process, including an instruction to the Log File Service to log the transactions involved.
2. The data is written to cache memory under control of Cache Manager.
3. Cache Manager sends the data to the Virtual Memory Manager for background writing to the disk file, a process called *lazy writes,* achieved by periodic flushing of the cache to the disk drive.
4. The VMM sends the data back to the NTFS driver, which passes the data through the Fault Tolerant driver (when using a software RAID array) to the disk driver.
5. The disk driver sends the data to the host controller (usually a SCSI host controller for servers), which passes the data to the destination fixed disk(s).
6. If write caching is enabled on the fixed-disk drive(s), the data is written to on-drive memory, and then transferred locally to the disk. Otherwise, the data is written directly to the disk.
7. If the write operation proceeds without an error, the transaction log record is deleted.
8. If an error occurs, the transaction log record remains in the transaction table. On the next disk access, the Log File Service detects the log record and restores the corresponding MFT record to its original condition before the write attempt.

This transaction logging process takes care of problems associated with operations that affect the directory structure—such as creating, copying, and deleting files—to maintain directory consistency. Errors that occur only when altering the data in the file aren't recoverable unless you have a RAID 1 or RAID 5 array. Contents of the self-contained write cache of a disk drive not written to the disk before a power or hardware failure are lost, and the failure may not be reflected in transaction log records. For this reason, most SCSI drives with read/write caches are shipped with write caching turned off.

Part

Ch

3

Calling Remote Procedures

Remote procedure calls (RPCs) permit applications to be executed by individual components that reside on other networked PCs, a process often called *distributed computing*. The RPC facility of Windows NT conforms to the Open Software Foundation's RPC standards incorporated in its Distributed Computing Environment (DCE) specification, with which virtually all flavors of UNIX comply.

Figure 3.4 is a diagram of a 32-bit Windows application that uses RPCs to connect to functions contained in three Windows DLLs (dynamic link libraries) that reside on three PCs running Windows NT 4.0 Server or Workstation. If the library functions perform very processor-intensive tasks (such as rendering 3-D animated computer graphics for movies), using RPCs for distributed processing rivals the performance of symmetrical multiprocessing (SMP) with two or more processors. Fast network connections, such as 100BaseT or Fiberchannel, are needed if large amounts of data must be passed between the executable program and the library function.

FIG. 3.4

Calling three library functions on remote computers with RPCs.

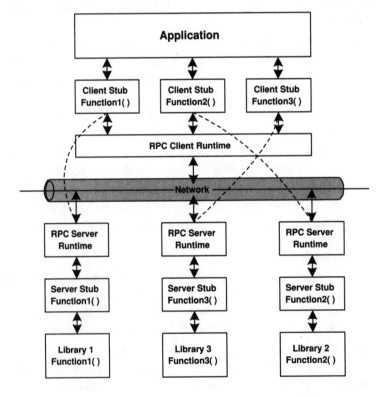

Following is a brief description of each layer shown in Figure 3.4:

- *Application* is the program that calls library functions. Data sent to and returned by the function are implemented as function call arguments, as in RenderFrame(DrawingOut, FrameIn). RenderFrame is the name of the function, DrawingOut is an output parameter, and FrameIn is an input parameter.

- *Client function stubs* have parameters that correspond to the function call arguments. The client stubs marshal the parameter values over the network; *marshaling* processes the parameter values for transmission over the network. Client function stubs take the place of the corresponding functions that ordinarily would be contained in local DLLs.

- *RPC client runtime* is responsible for determining the network location of the called function and the transport protocol required, and connects to the appropriate network driver of the I/O manager.

- *RPC server runtime* receives RPCs and directs each call to the appropriate server function stub. Both the server and client runtime use Windows NT's transport provider interface (TPI) to communicate with the network driver.

- *Server function stubs* unmarshal the function parameters and call the corresponding functions of the local DLL(s).

- *Library functions* contain the code that does the work. Remote DLLs are identical to local versions.

Using conventional RPCs requires developers to create and compile an interface definition language (IDL) file, which creates the client and server stubs for the function. The IDL file also creates header files (function prototypes), which must be added to the calling client application. Thus, C and C++ applications that use RPCs must be recompiled to incorporate the RPC header information.

N O T E RPCs running over NetBEUI networks use the named pipes interface for transferring data. *Named pipes* is an extension to NetBIOS that provides a persistent data conduit between networked processes. Microsoft and IBM first implemented named pipes, which provide a self-contained security mechanism, in LAN Manager. SQL Server, as an example, uses named pipes for receiving SQL statements from clients and returning query result sets and other database information to clients. Named pipes, implemented as a file I/O device, primarily are used for streaming data transport. In addition to named pipes over NetBEUI, Windows NT provides built-in RPC facilities for TCP/IP, IPX/SPX, and DECnet. ■

Distributed COM (DCOM), a new feature of Windows NT 4.0 that previously was called NetworkOLE, adapts the RPC facility to permit communication between Microsoft COM (Component Object Model) objects over networks. DCOM makes distributed computing simpler by eliminating the need to rewrite client applications to accommodate RPCs through the use of (OLE) Automation techniques. (Microsoft's Object Linking and Embedding is built on COM.) DCOM substitutes COM-based client and proxy stubs for client and server function stubs, respectively. For example, a 32-bit Automation client application written in Visual Basic 4.0 or 5.0 easily can be adapted to use Remote Automation Objects (RAOs), which are out-of-process ActiveX servers (executable applications). The Automation Manager supplied with the Enterprise Edition of Visual Basic 4+ took the place of the RPC client and server runtimes and used "Network OLE 0.9" for communication.

▶ **See** "Distributed Component Object Model (DCOM)," **p. 39**

N O T E   In early 1996, with its "Internet incentive," Microsoft began substituting the term *ActiveX* for *OLE* in situations where linking and embedding objects either wasn't involved or was only of minor importance. *OLE Controls*, for instance, became *ActiveX controls*. Now you're likely to see *OLE Automation* replaced by *Automation*. Microsoft didn't change OLE Automation to ActiveX Automation because COM's Automation interface also is used for ActiveX objects, as well as linked and embedded OLE objects. The use of the term *OLE* for linking and embedding documents created with the components of Microsoft Office is expected to continue. ■

Visual Basic 5.0 is designed expressly for creating multithreaded DCOM-compatible ActiveX components. Microsoft Transaction Server (MTS, better known by its code name, Viper), provides a Windows NT process in which to run in-process ActiveX components (DLLs). MTS is one of the subjects of Chapter 26, "Scaling Windows NT Server 4.0 to the Enterprise."

Networking with Windows NT

Windows NT networking processes make extensive use of the RPC facility, which provides a consistent set of methods by which local processes and remote processes communicate. The Server and Workstation versions of Windows NT 4.0 both support RPC networking, allowing users of the Workstation version to share files, printers, and other peripherals. A group of Windows NT Workstation users that share files and peripherals among one another (usually on an ad hoc basis) usually is called a *workgroup*. The workgroup (also called *peer-to-peer*) networking capabilities of Windows NT Workstation 4.0 are quite similar to those of Windows 95, except that there's a limit of 10 simultaneous inbound connections to a PC running Windows NT 4.0. (There's no limit on outbound connections.)

Helen Custer's 1993 book, *Inside Windows NT*, describes NetBEUI as "Windows NT's primary local area network transport protocol." The book contains many references to LAN Manager, which was then Microsoft's only network operating system offering. Microsoft designed Windows NT 3.1 to be fully compatible with LAN Manager servers running OS/2 and LAN Manager clients running on DOS/Windows, Macintosh, and UNIX platforms. LAN Manager compatibility was essential for integrating Windows NT 3.1 into the existing Microsoft networking infrastructure. Historically, NetBEUI has been the most common protocol for workgroup networking with Windows NT, Windows 3.1+, and Windows 95, because it's simple for users to set up and is fast. With the growth of the Internet and increasing use of corporate intranets, TCP/IP has become the protocol of choice for Windows NT Server 4.0 networking.

Peer-to-peer networking isn't limited to NetBEUI; you also can set up workgroups that use TCP/IP or IPX/SPX network transports, or any combination of Windows NT's native or third-party network protocols. You don't need client licenses for Windows NT 4.0 peer-to-peer networking. Peer-to-peer networking receives only cursory coverage in this book because of the limited number of connections permitted to a client running Windows NT Workstation 4.0. You can't use members of the BackOffice server suite on peer-to-peer networks; with the exception of the single-user Workstation (Developer) version of SQL Server, BackOffice applications must be installed on Windows NT Server.

The primary difference between the Server and Workstation versions of Windows NT 4.0 (other than price) is the capability to create and manage network domains. LAN Manger 2.x provided an early version of domain-based networking. (Microsoft originally planned to supply domain networking features to Windows NT as an add-on called LAN Manager for Windows NT.) The most important advantage of the use of domains is the capability to use a single-user logon to multiple servers and services (such as SQL Server and Exchange Server). Network administrators need to create only a single account for each user in his or her primary domain. Trust relationships between domains determine whether secondary domains accept the authentication provided by the user's primary domain. The use of multiple domains in large networks allows distributing management of the network among individual facilities.

▶ **See** "Understanding Domain Architecture and Security," **p. 606**

From Here...

This chapter overviewed the features of Windows NT, with emphasis on the Windows NT file system and networking capabilities. A full description of all the unique features of the Windows NT operating system would require a multivolume set of books, so only brief coverage of the topics of primary interest to network administrators appears in this chapter. The chapter concluded with a discussion of Windows NT's implementation of RPCs, and the differences between the Server and Workstation versions of Windows NT 4.0.

The following chapters provide detailed explanations of the topics discussed in this chapter:

- Chapter 4, "Choosing Network Protocols," explains how to select one or more of the three principal networking protocols supported by Windows NT based on your network configuration.

- Chapter 13, "Managing User and Group Accounts," describes how to use Windows NT Server 4.0's User Manager for Domains, take advantage of the new Add User Accounts and Group Management wizards, and utilize Windows NT's built-in user groups.

- Chapter 17, "Distributing Network Services with Domains," covers Windows NT Server's trusted domains and other distributed networking features that allow single-user logon for multiple network servers and server-based applications running on LANs and WANs.

CHAPTER 4

Choosing Network Protocols

One of the greatest strengths of the Windows NT Server operating system is the variety of networking protocols that it supports. That variety can be a source of confusion, however, when it's time to choose the protocol(s) to use for your network.

This chapter describes the network transport protocols compatible with Windows NT. A *protocol* is a set of rules, implemented in software, that governs communication between two computers. Not all operating systems support all protocols, so you must select the appropriate networking protocols that you set up for Windows NT Server to accommodate all the client computers connected to the network, plus other servers now in use, if any. If your Windows NT servers are to connect to a larger network, such as the Internet or a WAN, you must accommodate this connection in your protocol choice as well.

Chapter 5, "Purchasing Networking Hardware," covers the various physical networks (Ethernet, Token Ring, and others) and provides a detailed discussion of the network cards, cables, and other hardware components that connect the computers. Making these hardware choices doesn't automatically determine the network protocol(s) you use, but your choice of network protocol(s) is likely to determine the network-related peripheral components that you purchase, such as routers. ■

Understand network transport protocols

The Open Systems Interconnect model defines how transport protocols interact with a physical network and with the operating system.

Take advantage of multiple protocols

Windows NT Server 4.0 makes it possible to use more than one network protocol simultaneously.

Choose protocols for client PCs

Windows 95, Windows 3.1+, Macintosh, and UNIX clients can connect simultaneously to Windows NT Server 4.0.

Optimize server performance

Minimizing the number of protocols in use conserves resources and speeds network traffic.

Understanding the OSI Seven-Layer Model

Communication over a network is a complex task. To simplify the task of discussing and building networks, the *OSI (Open Systems Interconnection)* seven-layer network model was developed by the International Standards Organization (ISO), a branch of the United Nations headquartered in Geneva. OSI applies to virtually all computer networking situations. At the heart of OSI is the diagram shown in Figure 4.1. Each layer represents one of the seven different aspects of networking. Layer 1, the physical layer, is the most concrete, consisting of components that actually can be touched. On the other hand, layer 7, the application layer, is the most abstract, consisting of high-level software.

FIG. 4.1

The seven layers of the Open Systems Interconnection (OSI) model.

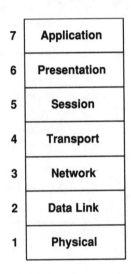

7	Application
6	Presentation
5	Session
4	Transport
3	Network
2	Data Link
1	Physical

The OSI model doesn't correspond precisely to commercial networking software products, some of which span several OSI levels or break an OSI level into several tasks. Instead, the model provides a useful way of discussing the complex task of arranging communication between computers.

The Physical Layer

The physical layer sends bits over the wire or over another connection, such as a fiber-optic cable or wireless connection, between computers. It deals with the electrical signals that represent the 0 (off) or 1 (on) state of a bit traveling over the network cabling. The decision to use a particular type of network interface card or a choice between twisted-pair (10BaseT, 100BaseT) and coaxial cable (10Base2) is a decision about the physical layer, which is implemented in networking hardware.

The Data-Link Layer

The data-link layer deals with *frames*—groups of bits transmitted over the network. It relies on the physical layer to actually send the bits. The data-link layer ensures that frames sent over the network are received and, if necessary, resends them. Ethernet and Token Ring are examples of data-link layers, and each has a different layout for its frames.

> **N O T E** In the official terminology of the OSI model, the group of bits sent by the data-link layer is called a *physical layer service data unit*. In practice, people call it a *frame* or a *data frame*. ▪

The IEEE networking model, established by the IEEE Project 802 committee, divides the data-link layer into two sublayers: Logical Link Control (LLC) and Media Access Control (MAC), as shown in Figure 4.2. The MAC sublayer handles interaction with the physical layer below, and the LLC sublayer handles interaction with the network layer above. The MAC layer provides standard interfaces for Carrier Sense Multiple Access with Collision Detection (CSMA/CD, Ethernet) networks, token-passing bus networks (similar to ARCnet), and Token Ring networks.

FIG. 4.2
The IEEE 802 series standards for Logical Link Control and Media Access Control within the OSI data-link layer.

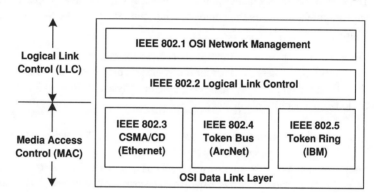

The Network Layer

The network layer deals with *packets*, which may be larger or smaller than frames. If the packets are larger than frames, the network layer breaks the packet into frames to send them, and reassembles them on receipt. If the packets are smaller than frames, the network layer bundles frames into packets to send them and breaks them apart on receipt.

In either case, the network layer relies on the data-link layer to transmit the frames themselves. The network layer also deals with routing packets between computers (*hosts*) on the network, and it knows the addresses of the hosts on the network. Typically, the network layer can adjust the routing of packets to deal with network traffic and congestion. The network layer doesn't keep track of whether packets arrived at their destination or any errors occurred during transmission—that job is handled by the transport layer.

The Transport Layer

The transport layer deals with *messages*, which may be larger or smaller than packets. This layer ensures that messages travel between hosts without data loss and, if necessary, arranges for packets to be re-sent. The transport layer relies on the network layer to transmit the frames.

NetBEUI, TCP/IP, IPX/SPX, and other transport protocols handle the duties of the network layer and the transport layer. It's quite common for the network and transport layers to be combined into a single protocol.

 N O T E   Some people argue that TCP/IP, the Internet's transport protocol, isn't a single protocol, but rather a suite of protocols that includes TCP, IP, UDP, and others. In the future, IP will be changed to accommodate more addresses, but TCP probably won't need to change. Most users and network administrators tend to think of TCP/IP as a single element. ■

The Session Layer

The session layer establishes and maintains a session between applications running on different computers. It knows the names of other computers on the network and handles security issues.

The session layer relies on the transport layer to transmit messages between the two computers. NetBIOS, the session layer for the Windows network, and Sockets, the session layer for TCP/IP, are examples of typical session-layer software. Windows NT uses the 32-bit Windows Sockets (Winsock) session layer.

N O T E   Winsock is the specification developed by more than 20 cooperating vendors that describes implementations of sockets on Windows machines. The first release of the specification was for TCP/IP protocols only, but it was designed to work over other protocols in the future. Several vendors release their own DLLs that implement the Winsock specification; a 32-bit Winsock DLL is included with Windows NT and Windows 95. ■

The Presentation Layer

The presentation layer provides services that a number of different applications use, such as encryption, compression, or character translation (PC ASCII to IBM's EBCDIC, for example, or Intel's little-endian to Macintosh and Motorola's big-endian byte-ordering). The presentation layer relies on the session layer to pass on the encrypted, compressed, or translated material. One implementation of a presentation layer is XDR (External Data Representation) under RPC (Remote Procedure Call).

The Role of Remote Procedure Calls

RPC is a service that allows programmers to create applications consisting of multiple procedures; some procedures run locally, whereas others run on remote computers over a network. RPC is especially useful because it takes a procedural, rather than transport-centered, view of network operations. RPC simplifies the development of distributed or client/server applications. Windows NT 4.0 implements RPC through the PpcSs subsystem, which includes the RPC service and RPC locator. Microsoft RPC is compatible with the Distributed Computing Environment (DCE) standard of the Open Software Foundation (OSFT).

RPC is intended primarily for client/server applications. RPC is used extensively by Microsoft BackOffice applications, such as Microsoft Exchange Server, and for communication between Automation client and Automation server applications. Microsoft's Component Object Model (COM) and Distributed COM (DCOM) are extensions to the basic RPC model that make creating client/server applications simpler for developers.

▶ **See** "Calling Remote Procedures," **p. 96**

▶ **See** "Distributed Component Object Model (DCOM)," **p. 39**

The Application Layer

The application layer handles requests by applications that require network communication, such as accessing a database or delivering e-mail. This layer is directly accessible to applications running on networked computers. It relies on the presentation layer to manipulate and transmit the communication. RPC is an example of an application-layer implementation.

Many important protocols span the presentation and application layers—for example, named pipes and FTP (the File Transfer Protocol, not the application itself). Clients use named pipes, for example, to communicate with Microsoft SQL Server. FTP is familiar to all UNIX and Internet users.

Comparing Windows NT and OSI Network Layers

The networking architecture of Windows NT is built of layers that don't fully correspond to the layers of the OSI model. Figure 4.3 shows Windows NT's layers, as well as the OSI layers for reference.

The keys to Figure 4.3 are Windows NT's two new layers: the Transport Driver Interface (TDI) and the Network Device Interface Specification (NDIS). These layers allow Windows NT to use simultaneously a number of different transport protocols in the layer between TDI and NDIS, and to make the choice of transport protocol transparent to the session and data-link layers.

TDI sits between the transport protocols and the session layer, which may be NetBIOS, Winsock, RPC, or some other session layer, no matter what the transport protocol chosen. TDI isn't so much a program as it is a *specification*—that is, a set of rules for writing the layers above and below it.

The NDIS interface, which sits between network adapter cards and transport protocols, allows any of the transport protocols to run over any of the adapter cards, as long as the protocols are written to the NDIS interface and the adapter card supports NDIS. NDIS also allows multiple protocols to be used at the same time on the same network adapter card.

FIG. 4.3
A comparison of the Windows NT networking model (right) and the OSI model (left).

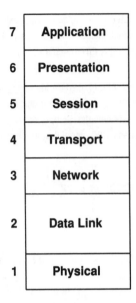

7	Application
6	Presentation
5	Session
4	Transport
3	Network
2	Data Link
1	Physical

Providers

Executive Services

Redirector | Servers

Transport Driver Interface

Transport Protocols

NDIS Interface

Network Card Drivers

Physical

N O T E Windows NT 4.0 uses NDIS 3. 0 Windows NT 5.0 will use NDIS 5.0, which supports Asynchronous Transfer Mode (ATM) with Quality of Service (QoS) features for isochronous transmission of time-sensitive content, such as digital audio and video streams. NDIS 5.0 also will let Windows NT 5.0 support Plug and Play network adapters. ■

ON THE WEB

For more information on NDIS 5.0, go to **http://www.microsoft.com/hwdev/devdes/ndis5.htm**.

Whether you think of the protocols discussed in this chapter as spanning two levels of the OSI model or as the thick central layer of the Windows NT model, the protocols serve the same purpose—they move chunks of information around the network based on the network address of the destination.

Networking with Windows NT's Protocols

Windows NT Server provides built-in support for seven networking protocols:

- NetBEUI and NetBEUI Frame (NBF)
- NWLink (IPX/SPX)
- TCP/IP
- Data Link Control (DLC)
- AppleTalk
- Remote Access Services (RAS)
- Streams

Figure 4.4 shows how each protocol fits into the Windows NT network layer diagram shown earlier in Figure 4.3. The following sections detail each of the seven protocols.

FIG. 4.4
Windows NT's transport protocols between the Transport Driver Interface and the NDIS interface.

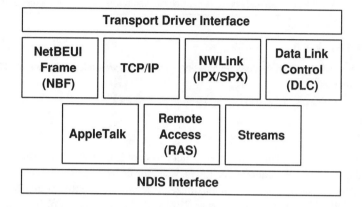

Transport Driver Interface			
NetBEUI Frame (NBF)	**TCP/IP**	**NWLink (IPX/SPX)**	**Data Link Control (DLC)**
	AppleTalk	**Remote Access (RAS)**	**Streams**
NDIS Interface			

NetBEUI and NetBEUI Frame

The NetBIOS Extended User Interface (NetBEUI) protocol, introduced in 1985, is an extension of the NetBIOS data-link layer. IBM developed NetBEUI to handle LANs of 20 to 200 workstations, such as those a company might set up for a single department. IBM's assumption was that gateways between LANs would provide large-scale networking capability.

NetBEUI is a compact, fast protocol, but it's more than 10 years old and doesn't scale well to larger networks. NetBEUI isn't a routable protocol; *routable protocols* let you create a wide area network (WAN) by interconnecting LANs. A routable protocol is vital if your LAN is to be connected to anything but a small cluster of client PCs.

The NetBEUI Frame (NBF) protocol builds on NetBEUI to overcome some of these difficulties. In particular, NBF overcomes the session limit, which is 254 in NetBIOS. This makes it operable for larger networks that must retain compatibility with existing NetBEUI networks.

If you now have a NetBEUI network in operation, the commercial implementation of NetBEUI running on the PCs you plan to connect to your Windows NT server is likely one of the following:

- Microsoft LAN Manager, which uses a server that runs on Microsoft's implementation of OS/2
- IBM LAN Server, which uses a server running under IBM OS/2
- Microsoft MS-Net, an early DOS peer-to-peer networking system similar to IBM's original PC-Net

NetBEUI networks are very simple to implement but are difficult to expand because the NetBEUI protocol isn't routable. To a great extent, NetBEUI's limitations are responsible for Novell NetWare's success in the network operating system market. If you're starting from scratch to build a network around a Windows NT Server machine, plan on using TCP/IP; if you must support NetWare, use IPX/SPX (NWLink).

Part

I

Ch

4

T I P   NetBEUI is a more efficient protocol for network browsing, especially over a Remote Access Service (RAS) modem connection. Running NetBEUI in addition to TCP/IP also is the simplest method of ensuring that Windows 95 and Windows 3.1+ clients can browse network resources efficiently.

ON THE WEB

For technical details on Windows 95 browsing, go to **http://www.microsoft.com/win32dev/netwrk/ browser.htm**.

▶ **See** "Browsing Multiple-Domain Resources," **p. 633**

TCP/IP

Transmission Control Protocol/Internet Protocol (TCP/IP) is the protocol of choice for WANs and is rapidly being adopted for LANs. Used for decades on the Internet and its predecessors, TCP/IP has been fine-tuned to maximize performance in extraordinarily large networks. Unlike NetBEUI, which is a proprietary IBM and Microsoft protocol, TCP/IP is in the public domain. The Internet Engineering Task Force (IETF) is the standards body that coordinates extensions and improvements to TCP/IP through a mechanism known as Requests for Comments (RFCs).

N O T E   A number of Internet standards describe the TCP/IP protocol and related protocols. These are accessible through FTP in the directory **ftp://ftp.merit.edu/documents/std/**. An index to the Internet standards is at **ftp://ftp.merit.edu/documents/std/INDEX.std**. ■

TCP/IP is an incredibly robust and reliable protocol. It was designed to keep the Department of Defense's Advanced Research Projects Agency's network (ARPANET, the precursor to the Internet) functioning, even if many of the cities it connected had been wiped out in a nuclear war. During the early history of ARPANET, only defense contractors and university research facilities were connected. To encourage expansion of the network, commercial users were admitted; today, the vast majority of traffic on the Internet is commercial, not government-related.

N O T E   The term *commercial*, in this case, includes individual users who connect to the Internet through commercial SPs or ISPs. SPs (service providers) lease high-speed connections to the Internet backbone and provide modem banks for individual dial-up access to the Internet. ISPs (Internet service providers) sell dial-up access and other Internet-related services (such as hosting Web pages) to individuals and small companies that don't need an intranet.

▶ **See** "Choosing an Internet Service Provider," **p. 727** ■

TCP/IP is a very flexible protocol that you can deploy in a small-scale LAN and later expand to accommodate hundreds or thousands of users. TCP/IP requires more knowledge to manage than other networks, because each machine must have a unique IP address and subnet mask. Tools such as DHCP and WINS are available in Windows NT Server to simplify these tasks, and experienced TCP/IP administrators are relatively easy to find and hire. If you're setting up a simple TCP/IP LAN with fewer than 100 client PCs, it's a reasonably simple job to administer the LAN after learning how to use Windows NT Server's built-in administrative tools for TCP/IP.

The most important advantage of TCP/IP over NetBEUI is that TCP/IP is *routable*. A *router* is a device that forms a connection between a LAN and a WAN, or between two LANs. The router intercepts network packets and leaves them on the LAN if they're for a machine on the LAN; if not, the router passes the packets to another LAN or WAN. The structure of IP network addresses is designed specifically for efficient routing, and the price of dedicated routing hardware has decreased dramatically over the past few years.

▶ **See** "Routers," **p. 148**

IP Addresses   Every machine on a TCP/IP network has an IP address, such as 205.210.40.3. An IP address—sometimes referred to as a *dotted quad*—consists of four numbers, each in the range of 0–255, separated by dots. When an entire LAN joins the Internet, IP addresses are commonly assigned to the LAN's machines that easily are distinguished from IP addresses on the rest of the Internet. Groups of related addresses are delineated into Class A, B, or C:

- A *Class C address* is actually about 250 IP addresses, each with the same values (for example, 205.210.40) for the first three components. The last component is different for each machine on the LAN. (A LAN with a Class C address can't have 255 machines, because some values for each component are reserved.)

- A *Class B address* is actually about 60,000 IP addresses, each with the same values (for example, 130.105) for the first two components. Each of the last two components can vary. The owners of Class B addresses typically have far fewer than 60,000 machines on their internal networks, but more than 250.

- A *Class A address* is about 15 million IP addresses, all with the same first component (for example, 47) and with three different components at the end.

Only a limited number of these classes are available. For example, first components with values between 1 and 126 are reserved for Class A addresses (in practice, fewer than 50 Class A addresses have been assigned, primarily to Internet builders such as the U.S. military and telecommunications companies). First components between 128 and 191 are available for Class B addresses, and between 191 and 223 for Class C addresses. First components above 223 are reserved; if your installation requires only a single IP address, it's assigned from the Class B or C address of your ISP.

The IP address structure makes routing simple to arrange. If you have a Class C address, for example, traffic destined to an IP address that varies in the first three components from that of your LAN is routed out to the rest of the Internet; traffic with the same first three components as your LAN stays on the LAN. This routing is coded in a value called a *subnet mask*. The subnet mask 255.255.255.0 codes the routing pattern for a Class C address.

You can split a single Class C address into several smaller pieces, each piece on its own LAN. The subnet mask is a bit-by-bit mask of the IP address, with each component representing 8 bits. For example, the subnet mask 255.255.255.224 defines a 31-address subnet with the following properties:

Part
I

Ch
4

■ All traffic for machines with the first three components varying from the routing machine is headed off the LAN.

■ Of the remaining traffic, that for machines where the first 3 bits of the last component match those of the routing machine stays on the LAN. Because only the last 5 bits can vary, 31 (16+8+4+2+1) machines are on this subnet.

■ The remaining traffic is headed off the LAN.

A Class C address could be split into seven such subnets, allowing for great flexibility in combining small LANs. If large LANs are involved, a Class B address can be split in a similar manner.

The job of managing and assigning IP addresses and subnet masks for each client PC can involve substantial effort. The Dynamic Host Configuration Protocol (DHCP) included with Windows NT Server 4.0 reduces this effort significantly. To assign IP addresses by hand, administrators must use Control Panel's Network tool; on the Protocols page, select the TCP/IP protocol and click Properties, choose the IP Address page, and then fill in the IP address and subnet mask as shown in Figure 4.5.

FIG. 4.5

Setting the IP address and subnet mask manually.

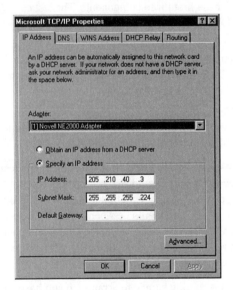

▶ **See** "Implementing Dynamic Host Configuration Protocol," **p. 332**

TCP/IP Printing   TCP/IP provides support for printers connected to the network with an appropriate network interface card. IETF RFC 1179 defines the line printer (LPR) network protocol and utilities for TCP/IP printing. The line printer daemon (LPD) lets clients send print jobs to a spooler on a specified server; the server queues the spooled print job for the designated printer. Unlike TCP and IP, LPR and LPD are not formal Internet standards. Windows NT Server 4.0 provides several low-level enhancements to RFC 1179 TCP/IP printing.

> **N O T E** DLC, the subject of later the "Data Link Control (DLC)" section, now is a more common
> protocol for networked printers such as Hewlett-Packard LaserJets. ■

Commercial TCP/IP Implementations   TCP/IP implementations are available for UNIX systems, the Macintosh, and Windows 3.x, and are included in Windows 95 and Windows NT 4.0 Server and Workstation. A 32-bit TCP/IP protocol stack for Windows 3.1+ is included in the \Clients\Tcp32wfw folder of the Windows NT Server 4.0 distribution CD-ROM. TCP/IP supports many session-layer implementations, including NetBT (NetBIOS over TCP/IP), Sockets (Winsock), Streams, and RPC.

NWLink (IPX/SPX)

The Internetwork Packet Exchange/Sequenced Packet Exchange (IPX/SPX) protocol is the heart of Novell NetWare. Microsoft's implementation of the IPX/SPX protocol is called NWLink. The IPX/SPX protocol is based on the Xerox Network System (XNS) protocol developed by Xerox Corp. XNS, which is no longer in use, had two components: IDP (Internet Datagram Protocol) and SPP (Sequenced Packet Protocol). IPX is based on IDP; SPX is based on SPP.

▶ **See** "Integrating Windows NT Server with Novell NetWare," **p. 637**

Part
I

Ch
4

IPX/SPX is a high-performance protocol for LANs and is easier than TCP/IP to implement and administer. As with TCP/IP, IPX/SPX is a routable protocol, so it can be used to establish a WAN. Because of NetWare's commercial success, IPX/SPX is now the default network protocol installed when you set up Windows 95. Unless you're installing Windows NT Server within an existing NetWare environment, however, TCP/IP is a better protocol choice, especially if you intend to provide Internet or related intranet services to client PCs. To conserve resources, you should uninstall IPX/SPX if you won't be using it. Using Windows NT Server with Novell NetWare servers is one of the primary subjects of Chapter 18, "Integrating Windows NT with NetWare and UNIX."

Data Link Control (DLC)

IBM's Data Link Control (DLC) protocol is used to communicate with mainframes as a component of IBM's System Network Architecture (SNA). Windows NT 4.0 includes a DLC interface device driver. On some LANs, DLC is used to communicate with printers connected directly to the LAN, rather than to a workstation or server. Several high-end Hewlett-Packard LaserJet printers offer DLC interfaces as an option. DLC printers are identified by a 12-byte numerical address for the network card.

> **N O T E** Setup doesn't install Windows NT 4.0's DLC protocol driver by default. You install the DLC
> driver from Control Panel's Network tool by clicking the Add button of the Protocols page,
> and then selecting the DLC Protocol entry in the Network Protocol list. ■

AppleTalk

AppleTalk is the primary network protocol used by Macintosh computers. It's supported by Windows NT Server's Services for Macintosh, which allows Macintosh users to share Mac-format files stored in Windows NT Server folders and use printers connected to a Windows NT server. Shared Windows NT folders appear to Mac users as conventional Mac folders. Mac file names are converted to FAT (8.3) and NTFS standards, including long file names (LFNs), as required. DOS and Windows client applications that support Mac file formats can share the files with Mac users.

Windows NT Server supports the Mac file format, which consists of a resource fork and a data fork. Users can double-click a file stored on a Windows NT server and, by virtue of the signature resource of the resource fork, launch the associated application. The signature resource of the resource fork of a Mac file serves the same purpose as Windows file extension associations. Mac users can drag and drop their files from a Mac folder directly to a Windows NT server folder.

▶ **See** "Setting Up Macintosh Clients," **p. 427**

Remote Access Service (RAS)

Windows NT Server provides Remote Access Service (RAS, also called dial-in networking or Dial-Up Networking) to enable temporary connections to systems that aren't on your LAN—typically, dial-up connections over a conventional telephone line. Windows NT Server includes built-in support for Integrated Services Digital Network (ISDN) modems. A single Windows NT server supports up to 255 simultaneous RAS connections. Chapter 19, "Managing Remote Access Service," covers the subject of dial-up RAS in more detail.

The RAS connection can use SLIP (Serial Line Internet Protocol) or, preferably, PPP (Point-to-Point Protocol) over a dial-up or dedicated phone line, or via the X.25 network communications protocol. When a PPP connection is made, your LAN and the remote site can communicate by using NetBEUI, TCP/IP, or IPX/SPX. PPP with TCP/IP is the most common protocol for connecting mobile users to intranets. The Microsoft Network Client included with Windows 95 uses dial-up PPP with TCP/IP to connect to The Microsoft Network's bank of Windows NT servers and, through MSN, to the Internet.

The new PPTP (Point-to-Point Tunneling Protocol)—announced by Microsoft, 3Com Corp., Ascend Communications, ECI Telematics, and U.S. Robotics in March 1996—allows users to "tunnel" through the Internet to reach their secure networks from a local dial-up connection.

▶ **See** "Using the Point-to-Point Tunneling Protocol," **p. 719**

> **N O T E** RAS clients are available for DOS and Windows 3.1+ and are included with Windows for Workgroups, Windows 95, and Windows NT. Windows 95 supports a single dial-in RAS connection if you buy the Windows 95 Plus! pack to obtain the Windows 95 RAS server upgrade. ■

Streams

Streams is a protocol specification that allows Windows NT to support third-party communications protocols. In effect, the third-party protocol is enclosed by an upper Streams layer and a lower Streams layer (see Figure 4.6). The upper Streams layer talks to the session layer and the third-party protocol; the lower Streams layer talks to the third-party protocol and the data-link layer.

FIG. 4.6
Supporting third-party transport layers with the Streams layer.

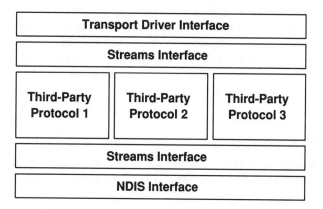

Windows NT 3.1 used a Streams device driver for TCP/IP and IPX/SPX. Streams has a substantial amount of overhead, so Microsoft abandoned the Streams protocol for TCP/IP and IPX/SPX effective with Windows NT 3.5. Windows NT 4.0 supports the Streams protocol for backward compatibility only.

N O T E Streams also is the name of a UNIX session-layer protocol that was developed by AT&T in 1984. AT&T's Streams was intended to serve the same purpose as Sockets, but Sockets and Winsock have been so successful that Streams is no longer implemented in most UNIX systems. It's not at all related to the Windows NT Streams protocol. ■

Part
I
Ch
4

Supporting a Variety of PC Clients

It's possible that you're installing an entire office full of computers, and you can choose the client PCs and operating systems that fit best with Windows NT Server. In this case, Windows NT Workstation 4.0 for desktop PCs and Windows 95 for laptop PCs (and desktop PCs with 16M or less of RAM) are the logical choices. It's more likely, however, that you're integrating a server into an environment that's now running one or more operating systems. The optimum protocol choice allows all your machines to talk to your server without spending large amounts of money or time.

> **N O T E** Theoretically, any protocol can be implemented for any operating system. If you discover an obscure piece of third-party software that lets all the machines in your environment use the same protocol, such a product might seem a likely candidate. In this chapter, the assumption is that you're choosing from the generally available and popular implementations—and that means not every operating system can run every protocol. Integrating obscure third-party software into a network is a chancy proposition, at best. ▓

It's possible for your server to support a number of different protocols at once, but to keep your workload to a minimum, choose your protocol(s) carefully so that you use as few as possible. In addition to making administration more complicated, running several protocols simultaneously consumes more memory on the server and client computers and can have a deleterious effect on system performance. The following sections describe the types of clients commonly connected to Windows NT servers and the networking protocols individual clients support.

Windows NT Workstations

Not surprisingly, using clients running Windows NT Workstation 4.0 allows you to use almost any of the networking protocols supported by Windows NT Server, including the following:

- NetBEUI Frame (NBF)
- NWLink (IPX/SPX)
- TCP/IP

In many cases, your choice of protocol under Windows NT is determined not by your operating system, but by the software your clients run. For example, most Windows Internet software (including Web browsers) runs over TCP/IP with Winsock, but not over NetBEUI or IPX/SPX.

▶ **See** "Connecting Windows NT Workstation 4.0 Clients," **p. 418**

PCs running Windows NT Workstation 4.0 can participate in peer-to-peer (workgroup) networks, which operate independently of the Windows NT server(s) that support the primary (client/server) network. A maximum of 10 workgroup members can connect simultaneously to a Windows NT client that shares the workgroup files. NetBEUI (the Windows network) is the most common method of establishing peer-to-peer workgroups. Most network administrators discourage peer-to-peer file sharing because of security issues, including lack of coordinated access control to sensitive information and centralized backup procedures.

Windows 95

Windows 95 offers the same suite of 32-bit network protocols as Windows NT Workstation. One primary advantage of Windows 95 is the ease in which Plug and Play network adapter cards install. In general, software that runs under Windows NT Workstation also can run under Windows 95; thus, users can choose their operating system without being concerned about networking issues. Another advantage of Windows 95 is that many new PCs are shipping with Windows 95 installed, saving the cost of another operating system. Windows 95 has been designed for less powerful PCs, but you should be aware of limitations (memory or disk space) on the client machines that preclude running Windows 95 efficiently. Chapter 11, "Configuring Windows 95 Clients for Networking," is devoted to optimizing the networking performance of Windows 95 PCs.

Windows for Workgroups 3.1x

Because it's an older product than Windows NT or Windows 95, Windows for Workgroups (WfWg) 3.1x didn't support as many protocols when released. WfWg 3.1x limits the workstation to running only two networks at once. You connect to a Microsoft Windows network with NetBEUI and one other network by running one of the following add-in protocols:

- IPX/SPX
- TCP/IP

Again, the software you're running plays a major part in your choice among these options. Some software runs only over certain network protocols; check your documentation.

▶ **See** "Connecting Windows for Workgroups 3.11 Clients," **p. 410**

Windows 3.1

Windows versions before Windows for Workgroups don't support networking directly; instead, early releases of Windows used DOS-based networking. As with the DOS clients mentioned in the next section, Windows 3.1 clients attached to your Windows NT server can use one of the following protocols:

- NetBEUI
- IPX/SPX
- TCP/IP

It's not possible for one Windows 3.1 client to use more than one network protocol at a time.

▶ **See** "Connecting Windows 3.1 Clients," **p. 400**

N O T E Microsoft supplies with Windows NT Server 4.0 a 16-bit TCP/IP driver for Windows 3.1 and DOS 5.0 and higher—it's a terminate-and-stay-resident (TSR) application. The complete set of 16-bit network drivers are in the \Clients\Msclient folder of the Windows NT Server 4.0 CD-ROM. ▪

DOS-Only PCs

MS-DOS clients have a rather limited set of protocols available but can be connected to your Windows NT server by using one of these protocols:

- NetBEUI
- IPX/SPX
- TCP/IP

It's not possible for one MS-DOS PC to run more than one network protocol simultaneously. You use the drivers from the CD-ROM's \Clients\Msclient folder for DOS-only PCs.

OS/2 Clients

Just as Microsoft has improved PC networking capabilities with each new version of Windows, IBM has increased the networking features of OS/2, generally providing with the operating system access to protocols that in the past could be accessed only with third-party add-ons. OS/2 versions 1.x, 2.x, and Warp all can use any of these protocols:

- NetBEUI
- IPX/SPX
- TCP/IP

Apple Macintosh Computers

You can connect PCs that don't run DOS or Windows to a Windows NT server. The protocols supported for Macs are as follows:

- AppleTalk
- TCP/IP

Choosing AppleTalk will make your life difficult if any non-Macintosh machines (other than your Windows NT server) are on your network, and if you want the Macs to have peer-to-peer access to the files on non-Macintosh workstations. If possible, all Macs connected to a network served by Windows NT should use the TCP/IP protocol.

▶ **See** "Connecting Macintosh Clients," **p. 425**

UNIX Workstations

UNIX systems have even less in common with Windows and DOS systems than Mac systems do. However, TCP/IP is a protocol that was designed for use with various operating systems. Using TCP/IP lets UNIX workstations talk to your Windows NT server without difficulty. Interconnecting with UNIX networks is one of the subjects of Chapter 18, "Integrating Windows NT with NetWare and UNIX."

Supporting Multiple Servers

Arranging for one or more client PCs to be networked to your server may be all you need on a relatively small network. On the other hand, your installation may have other servers that must be connected to your new Windows NT server. Each additional server can communicate by using one or more of the protocols supported by Windows NT.

Other Windows NT Servers

As usual, when the machines to be connected are using the same operating system, you have the most flexibility in choosing a protocol. Interconnected Windows NT servers support the full range of protocols:

- NetBEUI Frame (NBF)
- Data Link Control (DLC)
- NWLink (IPX/SPX)
- TCP/IP
- Streams
- AppleTalk

It wouldn't be wise to choose DLC, Streams, or AppleTalk in this case, because they're limited protocols that might not be supported by other clients on your network, but such a choice is technically possible.

Novell NetWare Servers

To Windows NT Server, talking to a NetWare server isn't very different from talking to a NetWare client—you simply use the IPX/SPX protocol. Novell offers an implementation of TCP/IP for NetWare 3.x and 4.x; if you plan to install the TCP/IP protocol, using TCP/IP to interconnect NetWare and Windows NT servers is preferred.

Part

I

Ch

4

UNIX Servers

UNIX servers, like UNIX clients, should be part of a TCP/IP network. Microsoft's version of TCP/IP is fully compatible with the UNIX implementations of TCP/IP.

Local Intranet Servers

One of the hottest developments in the networking world is *intranetworking*, using Internet software and protocols to communicate within a company. Intranetworking is discussed fully in Chapter 20, "Setting Up Internet Information Server 4.0," and Chapter 21, "Administering Intranet and World Wide Web Sites." People within the company use Internet tools such as e-mail, Web browsers, and FTP file-transfer programs to deliver information over their own internal intranet. TCP/IP is the required protocol to implement an intranet, and all clients connected to the intranet must support TCP/IP. It's a common practice, however, for servers and clients also to support NetBEUI to facilitate network browsing.

Microsoft Internet Information Server (IIS) is a Web server for Windows NT Server 4.0. IIS builds on the strong background of third-party Internet servers previously available for Windows NT, including FTP, Gopher, and Web servers. IIS is fast, secure, and free, thus making it very popular for creating both intranet and Internet sites.

> **N O T E**   Internet Information Server 2.0 is included with Windows NT Server 4.0; IIS 3.0, which
> adds Active Server Pages (ASP) to IIS 2.0, is included on the Windows NT 4.0 Service Pack
> 2+ CD-ROM. IIS 4.0, the subject of Chapter 20, "Setting Up Internet Information Server 4.0," is a major
> upgrade to IIS 3.0 and requires Service Pack 3.

The Internet

Connecting to the Internet can be a very simple or very complex project, as discussed in Chapter 20, "Setting Up Internet Information Server 4.0." Connecting one machine to the Internet through a PPP connection is a very different project from connecting an entire LAN through one server machine. If security issues require that the connection pass through a firewall, the job is even more complex. Chapter 19, "Managing Remote Access Service," addresses some of these issues.

The Internet greatly simplifies the choosing of network protocols. The I in TCP/IP stands for Internet, and TCP/IP is the only protocol that you can use on the Internet.

Mainframes

Many different mainframes exist, but one of the most important players is the IBM AS/400, which uses System Network Architecture (SNA). SNA relies on DLC as its transport protocol. If you use the SNA Server component of Microsoft BackOffice, you can connect to a number of different mainframes, including

- IBM AS/400s
- All IBM mainframes
- IBM plug-compatible mainframes running IBM host software (such as Amdahl, Fujitsu, or Hitachi)
- Tandem
- Fujitsu (using FNA)
- Hitachi (using HNA)
- OS/2 Comm Manager or Extended Services (using APPC)
- UNIX-based SNA gateway products (using APPC)
- IBM RS/6000 RISC computers

Planning for Network Interoperability

If all the workstations you plan to connect to your Windows NT server use the same protocol, life is simple. Assuming that you have a collection of machines to connect to your Windows NT server and that the collection uses two different protocols, the following options are available:

- You can run two or more different protocols on the server.
- You can change the protocol that one set of workstations is using so that all use the same protocol.
- You can replace one set of workstations with a set that runs the same protocol as the others.
- You can gather the workstations into two or more LANs with gateways to handle translation and interconnection.

Setting up Windows NT Server to use one protocol to talk to one set of machines and a different protocol for the rest involves the fewest changes to the workstations, the smallest investment, and the least disruption to your users. This approach has some performance penalties; network processes consume more of your system memory and might even cause paging, which slows your system down. In some cases you'll gladly accept these relatively minor performance penalties to connect previously incompatible workstations.

Changing the protocols the workstations run might allow you to keep the same workstations while running only one protocol. This approach simplifies administration and improves the performance of your server, but it likely will be costly to buy new licenses for the protocol to be implemented on the client workstations. Also, your users may be disrupted as you change the software that joins them together in a network. If some of your workstations are using a specific protocol for significant security or performance reasons, it may not be wise to change the protocol.

You may think it's unlikely that two sets of workstations would use different protocols if it's so simple to make them the same, but it's a matter worth investigating. For example, a wide variety of systems can run TCP/IP, and TCP/IP is a good solution when combining Macintosh and Windows workstations. However, many administrators automatically assume that the protocol is NetBEUI or IPX/SPX for the Windows machines and AppleTalk for the Macs. Another approach for machines that use NetBIOS over NetBEUI is the simple change to running NetBIOS over IPX/SPX.

If none of these solutions seems palatable, perhaps the two sets of workstations should be on two separate LANs. A gateway can transfer traffic between the two LANs while making any necessary translations between the network transport formats.

N O T E There's often some confusion about the name for a device (a combination of hardware and software) that sits between two networks. Chapter 5, "Purchasing Networking Hardware," describes all common network devices in detail. Here are some brief definitions of network device terms used in this chapter:

- *Bridge.* Connects two similar LANs, usually running the same protocol, and passes the data on essentially unchanged.

- *Gateway.* Connects dissimilar networks and translates frame format, byte order for addresses, or similar low-level protocols.

continues

Part

I

Ch

4

continued

- *Router.* Sits between networks and directs traffic to the appropriate network. If the networks are dissimilar, they need a gateway as well as a router.

- *Proxy server.* As part of a firewall, intercepts requests between networks and refuses them or passes them on according to the proxy server's own security rules. ■

Bear in mind that decisions can change with time. For example, you might choose at first to run two protocols (such as TCP/IP and NetBEUI), and then slowly migrate to a single protocol (TCP/IP) as new workstations replace the old ones. Be sure to choose a solution that will work with your future needs as well as your current requirements. These issues, and the mechanics of setting up a network of different workstations, are covered in more detail in Chapter 5 and Chapter 18, "Integrating Windows NT with NetWare and UNIX."

Making the Final Protocol Choice

Perhaps as you've read this chapter, it has become clear that only one protocol fills the bill. You may be combining Macintosh and UNIX workstations and have chosen TCP/IP, so only one protocol is necessary. Or you may have an existing network that uses IPX/SPX and see no reason to change protocols.

If you're building a network from scratch, or need to change the protocol of one of two sets of workstations and aren't sure which one to change, the following are some important issues to consider:

- How big is your LAN? NetBEUI can't handle more than 200 or so workstations. Even NBF isn't the best choice for a large LAN.

- Do you want to connect to WANs or other LANs? A routable protocol (TCP/IP or IPX/SPX) is vital in that case.

- If you're not connected to a WAN, do you plan someday to connect to the Internet? The Internet is becoming vital to many businesses for research, advertising, and customer support, and the Internet or an intranet should be included in your networking plans.

- What software are your users running? What protocols does it support?

The preceding list might cause you to conclude TCP/IP is the one-size-fits-all solution to all your networking needs. Of course, it's not that simple. Managing a TCP/IP server and assigning IP addresses to each machine on the network aren't simple tasks, but Windows NT Server 4.0's upgraded WINS and DHCP features make the task much easier. If your organization has a staff of experienced IPX/SPX administrators, their knowledge and experience are assets that might sway you to choose IPX/SPX for your Windows NT 4.0 servers. Otherwise, choose TCP/IP; it's clear that TCP/IP has become the preferred network protocol for today's PC operating systems.

From Here...

Having chosen a network transport protocol or protocols, you must get the protocol(s) installed and working, and then manage the resulting network. Not surprisingly, a large part of the rest of this book covers these tasks. The following chapters relate directly to networking protocols:

- Chapter 11, "Configuring Windows 95 Clients for Networking," discusses connecting Windows 95 workstations to your server.

- Chapter 12, "Connecting Other PC Clients to the Network," discusses connecting DOS, Windows 3.x, Windows for Workgroups, and Macintosh workstations to your server.

- Chapters 13 through 16 in Part III, "Administering a Secure Network," cover all the details of how to be an effective network system administrator.

- Chapters 17 through 21 in Part IV, "Wide Area Networking and the Internet," cover issues such as connecting to NetWare and UNIX networks, the Internet, and intranets.

- Chapter 25, "Administering Clients with Systems Management Server 1.2," shows you how to make your administration tasks easier.

Part
I

Ch
4

Purchasing Networking Hardware

Windows NT Server 4.0 is a stable and robust network operating system, equally well-suited to environments ranging from small offices to multinational corporations. Choosing the proper hardware to operate it will ensure that your network works reliably and is easy to maintain and expand. Spending some time planning your installation will pay off down the road in fewer problems and easier growth.

Compared with other modern network operating systems, such as Novell NetWare 4.1, Windows NT Server 4.0 makes surprisingly modest hardware demands. Microsoft's specified minimum requirements, however, are unrealistically low for most situations. Fortunately, Windows NT Server scales very well. Whereas Novell NetWare requires adding substantial amounts of memory to support additional disk storage, Windows NT Server 4.0 has no such direct correlation between RAM requirements and the amount of disk storage supported. A Windows NT server that's properly configured initially with adequate processor power and RAM will support substantial growth before requiring replacement or significant upgrading of the server. ■

Maximize network speed and reliability

Choose the best media-access method and cabling topology for your environment.

Improve network throughput with switches and routers

Select appropriate active network components to optimize network performance and to allow for future growth.

Get the most from your server hardware budget

Configure and specify server hardware to meet your immediate and future needs.

Don't let blackouts and brownouts shut you down

Pick the uninterruptible power supply of the correct type and capacity for your server installation.

Selecting a Media-Access Method

The first important decision you must make is which media-access method to use. This decision is comparable in importance to a railroad's choice of which gauge to use (how far apart do you put the tracks?). Everything devolves from this decision, including your choice of active network components, the type of cabling you'll install, and, ultimately, the performance, reliability, and cost of your network.

In Chapter 4, "Choosing Network Protocols," you learn about the OSI Model and the purpose of its various layers. Media-access methods are addressed primarily in the second layer, or data-link layer, with some overlap into the first, or physical, layer. The data-link layer is the subject of an Institute for Electrical and Electronic Engineers (IEEE) standard.

▶ **See** "Understanding the OSI Seven-Layer Model," **p. 102**

ARCnet

One of the oldest media-access methods still in use is ARCnet. Developed in 1977 by DataPoint Corporation, ARCnet (for *Attached Resource Computer Network*) was deservedly popular in the early and mid-1980s. Its combination of simplicity, low cost, and reasonable performance made it a good choice at a time when Ethernet was extremely expensive and Token Ring didn't yet exist.

Thousands of Novell NetWare 2.x networks started with ARCnet, and many of these ARCnet installations are still running today. ARCnet is an obsolete media-access method. If you have a large ARCnet network in place, you might choose to run a Windows NT server on it. Otherwise, don't consider ARCnet.

Token Ring

Introduced by IBM in 1986, Token Ring has a lot going for it, balanced by a few negatives. Token Ring is fast, reliable, and well supported by IBM in both the PC and mainframe environments. Balanced against this are the following factors:

- Token Ring is extremely expensive when compared with Ethernet alternatives. The price of one name-brand Token Ring card can buy between three and five name-brand Ethernet cards. This cost disparity holds true across the range of networking hardware you need, such as hubs, routers, and so forth.

- Token Ring hasn't achieved wide industry acceptance, due initially to IBM's restrictive licensing policies and subsequently to the market dominance of Ethernet. As a result, your choice of network interface cards (NICs) and other active network components is restricted to only a handful of vendors with Token Ring, whereas with Ethernet you can choose among scores of vendors.

Like ARCnet, Token Ring uses a token-passing access method, but with a somewhat different mechanism. In Token Ring, a station with data to be transmitted first waits for an idle token. It changes the status of the token to busy (called a *burdened busy token*), appends a destination address, attaches data to the token, and passes the burdened busy token to the next station in the ring. Each station functions in Token Ring as a unidirectional repeater, receiving data from the downstream station, regenerating it, and passing it to the upstream station. This next station regenerates the burdened busy token and passes it to the next station in sequence. The process continues until the burdened busy token reaches its destination. At the destination, the recipient extracts the data from the token and sends an acknowledgment (ACK) to the originating station. On receipt of this ACK, the originating station generates an idle token and passes it to the next station. Figure 5.1 illustrates a token passing between four computers in the ring.

FIG. 5.1

Passing a token between four computers in a Token Ring network.

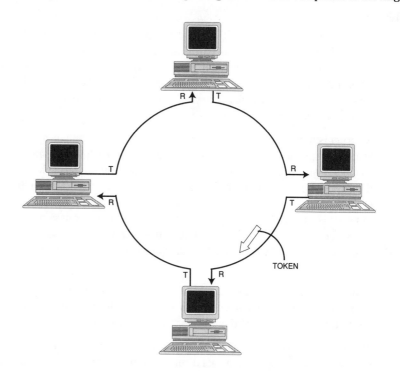

Only one token can exist on the ring at any given time, so one station is designated an *active monitor*. The responsibility of this station is to monitor the ring for out-of-norm conditions, including the absence of a token, a damaged token, or multiple tokens coexisting. When such a condition is found, the active monitor corrects the problem and returns the ring to normal operating conditions.

Token Ring uses a star-wired ring topology in which each station is connected by an individual cable run to a concentrator called a *multistation access unit (MAU)*. Token Ring originally operated on 150-ohm shielded twisted-pair (STP) cable arranged in a star-wired ring with data throughput of 4 Mbps. Newer Token Ring equipment can operate on unshielded twisted-pair (UTP) cable and fiber-optic cable, as well as the original STP cable. The throughput has also been upgraded to 16 Mbps. Many newer Token Ring components can operate at either 4 Mbps or 16 Mbps to ease transition from the older technology to the newer. A ring must be exclusively 4 Mbps or 16 Mbps; the two speeds can't coexist on the same ring.

Part I
Ch 5

Token Ring, including its enhancements, has been adopted as standard 802.5 by the IEEE. Its market share is second only to Ethernet, although the growth of new Token Ring networks has slowed as Ethernet has increased its dominance. Although large numbers of Token Ring networks are installed, Token Ring remains in essence a niche product. It's primarily limited to exclusive IBM shops and to those locations with a need to interconnect their networks to IBM minicomputers and mainframes. Although its commitment to Token Ring remains strong, even IBM has been forced to bow to market realities and begin offering Ethernet as an option.

Ethernet

Invented by Bob Metcalfe in 1973 and developed as a commercial product by DEC, Intel, and Xerox (the union was known as DIX), Ethernet is the media-access method of choice for most new networks being installed today. Ethernet is inexpensive, performs well, is easily extensible, and is supported by every manufacturer of network equipment. Ethernet has become the local-area networking standard by which all others are judged and has a commanding lead in installed base, as well as current sales.

Ethernet is based on a contention scheme for media access known as CSMA/CD, or Carrier Sense Multiple Access with Collision Detection. *Carrier Sense* means that each Ethernet device on the network constantly monitors the carrier present on the cable and can determine when that carrier is idle and when it's in use. *Multiple Access* means that all Ethernet devices on the cable have an equal right to access the carrier signal without obtaining prior permission. Ethernet is called a *baseband system* because only one transmission can be present on the wire at any one time. *Collision Detection* means that if two or more Ethernet devices transmit simultaneously and thereby corrupt all the data, the collision is detected and is subsequently corrected.

Unlike token-based schemes, any Ethernet station is permitted to transmit any time it has data to be sent. When a station needs to transmit, it first listens to make sure that the carrier is free. If the carrier is free, the station begins transmitting the data.

The original Ethernet specification, referred to as 10Base5, operated on 50-ohm thick coaxial cable in a bus topology with a data throughput of 10 Mbps and a maximum segment length of 500 meters. Concerns about the cost and difficulty of working with thick coax cable brought about the 10Base2 specification, which runs the same data rate over thinner and cheaper RG-58 coaxial cable, but limits segment length to only 180 meters. 10Base2, also called *thin Ethernet* or *thinnet*, is very popular in Europe for interconnecting small LANs. Figure 5.2 illustrates 10Base2 cabling to two Ethernet NICs.

With the introduction of the 10BaseT specification, Ethernet was extended from the original physical bus topology to a physical star topology running on inexpensive UTP cable, again with a data rate of 10 Mbps. Unlike 10Base2, 10BaseT requires a hub (described later in the "Simple Hubs" section) to interconnect more than two PCs (see Figure 5.3). You can create a two-PC 10BaseT network with a special cross-connect cable. 10BaseT uses RJ-45 modular connectors (see Figure 5.4), which were originally designed for commercial telephone applications.

FIG. 5.2
Connections between
10Base2 cabling and
Ethernet NICs.

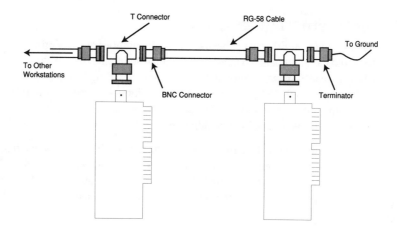

FIG. 5.3
Three PCs connected by
10BaseT to a hub.

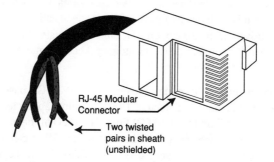

FIG. 5.4
An RJ-45 modular
connector.

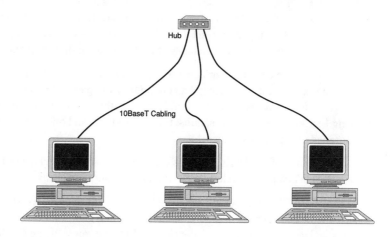

High-Speed Ethernet Variants

As the load on an Ethernet cable increases, the number of collisions increases and the cumulative throughput begins to fall. The traditional solution to this problem has been to divide a heavily loaded network into multiple segments by using bridges (described later in the "Bridges" section). Using bridges to create additional segments essentially breaks the network into multiple neighborhoods. Local traffic within a neighborhood is kept local, and only traffic that needs to cross segment boundaries does so.

To address these perceived Ethernet performance problems, three contending high-speed challengers have arisen. The first, Full Duplex Ethernet, doubles bandwidth to 20 Mbps. The remaining two, 100BaseT and 100VG-AnyLAN, compete at the 100 Mbps level. All these competitors propose to achieve their bandwidth increases by using existing cable in at least one of their variants.

Full Duplex Ethernet   Full Duplex Ethernet (FDE) is a recent scheme for increasing bandwidth beyond the 10 Mbps available with standard Ethernet. An Ethernet device may be transmitting or receiving, but it can't do both simultaneously. FDE devices, on the other hand, transmit and receive data simultaneously, thereby doubling theoretical bandwidth to 20 Mbps.

FDE devices are designed to work on 10BaseT networks with UTP cabling, and achieve their higher data rates simply by placing data on the transmit pair and receive pair simultaneously. Although FDE can coexist with standard 10BaseT Ethernet on the same cabling system, implementing FDE requires that NICs, hubs, bridges, routers, and other active network components be upgraded or replaced to support it.

FDE at 10 Mbps is likely to disappear as superior high-speed alternatives become available to replace it. Don't consider the low-speed version for your network.

100BaseT Fast Ethernet   Of the two competing 100 Mbps proposed standards, 100BaseT (often called Fast Ethernet) was first out of the starting gate. 100BaseT, defined by the IEEE 802.3u standard, remains conceptually close to Ethernet roots, using CSMA/CD media access combined with one of two signaling methods. 100BaseT signaling combines CSMA/CD and FDDI (Fiber Distributed Data Interface) physical-layer specifications and runs on two pairs of a Category 5 cable. 100BaseT can also run on STP (shielded twisted pair) or fiber. The T4 signaling method runs CSMA/CD on four pairs of Category 3 cable. Later, the "Quality Grades" section describes these cable categories.

At the data-link layer, the major change involves timing. CSMA/CD-based systems function on the assumption that all collisions are detected. The maximum cabling length in an Ethernet network is limited by Round Trip Delay (RTD) time. The RTD of the entire network must be small enough that the two devices located farthest from each other can detect a collision in progress. The much higher signaling speed used by 100BaseT means that such collisions are present on the cable and detectable for a much shorter span. As a result, the maximum end-to-end cabling (segment) length for a 100BaseT copper network is 100 meters, the same as that of a 10BaseT network.

Following are the three classes of Fast Ethernet defined by the IEEE 802.3u specification:

- *100BaseTX for Category 5 UTP cabling.* If you have Category 5 cable, or in the unlikely event have installed STP, use 100BaseTX. Later discussions of Fast Ethernet hardware in this chapter assume the use of 100BaseTX.

- *100BaseT4 for Category 3 UTP cabling.* If you have Category 3 cable installed, you must use 100BaseT4. The T4 suffix is derived from the need to use four twisted pairs instead of the two pairs used by 10BaseT and 100BaseTX.

- *100BaseFX for single-mode and multimode fiber-optic cabling.* Depending on the type of connection, 100BaseFX supports segments lengths of up to 2,000 meters on multimode fiber and 10,000 meters on single-mode fiber.

100BaseTX and 100BaseFX support full-duplex operation for even higher effective bandwidth. There is no IEEE standard for full-duplex 100BaseT4.

N O T E The most accessible and detailed source of technical information on 100BaseT alternatives is *Switched and Fast Ethernet: How It Works and How to Use It* (Ziff-Davis Press, 1995, ISBN 1-56276-338-5) by Robert Breyer and Sean Riley, both of whom are engineers in Intel's Fast Ethernet Product Group.

100VG-AnyLAN The second of the 100 Mbps standards is 100VG-AnyLAN, the subject of the IEEE 802.12 committee's standard. Although it's often considered to be an extended version of Ethernet, 100VG-AnyLAN really isn't Ethernet at all, as witnessed by the fact that Hewlett-Packard and AT&T Microelectronics had to organize a new IEEE committee for the standards process. 100VG-AnyLAN replaces Ethernet's CSMA/CD media-access method with a demand-priority method more similar conceptually to that used by Token Ring, although access to the cable is arbitrated by a centralized controller rather than by possession of a token. In fact, the 100VG-AnyLAN specification permits using Token Ring frames as well as Ethernet frames.

100VG-AnyLAN is named for a composite of its 100 Mbps transmission rate, its capability to run on four pairs of Category 3 Voice Grade (VG) cable, and its support for both Ethernet and Token Ring frame types. 100VG-AnyLAN also can be run on two pairs of Category 5 cable, on STP, and on fiber. One advantage cited by 100VG-AnyLAN proponents is its support for *demand priority*, which assigns priority to time-critical data.

The major drawback to 100VG-AnyLAN is that the complexity and processing power required at the hub is similar to that required for a switching hub but doesn't provide the benefits of switching. For the cost of the required 100VG-AnyLAN network cards and hubs, you can instead install switched 100BaseTX Ethernet with much less effort and far superior results. 100VG-AnyLAN is no longer a serious contender for high-speed LANs. Asynchronous Transfer Mode (ATM), which offers quality-of-service (QoS) guarantees, and Gigabit Ethernet are better choices for transporting real-time video and audio data.

Part
I
Ch
5

Gigabit Ethernet   Gigabit Ethernet technology was in the formative stage when this book was written. Gigabit Ethernet, which can deliver 1 Gbps full-duplex bandwidth over short runs of conventional Cat 5 cabling, is primarily intended for server-to-server, server-to-switch, and switch-to-switch backbones that use single-mode and multimode fiber.

The first wave of Gigabit Ethernet NICs, which became available in early 1997, cost from about $1,500 to $3,500 each. The IEEE 802.3z group isn't expected to produce a Gigabit Ethernet standard until mid-1998, but several firms announced pre-standard NICs and switches in late 1996 and early 1997.

Gigabit Ethernet is an alternative to ATM and FDDI that's intended to provide a simple upward migration route from Fast Ethernet. Gigabit Ethernet, however, doesn't provide the robust QoS guarantee of ATM.

Other High-Speed Media-Access Methods

Several other high-speed Ethernet alternatives exist. Each of these has, at one time or another, been proposed as a desktop standard, and each has failed to become such a standard because of the high cost of NICs and hub ports. As a result, each has been largely relegated to use in network backbones.

Fiber Distributed Data Interface (FDDI)   Developed by the ANSI X3T9.5 Committee, the FDDI specification describes a high-speed token-passing network operating on fiber-optic cable (see Figure 5.5). In its original incarnation, FDDI was intended to operate on dual counter-rotating fiber rings with a maximum of 1,000 clients and a transmission rate of 100 Mbps. FDDI can support a large physical network. Stations can be located as far as 2 kilometers apart, and the total network can span 200 kilometers. Like Token Ring, FDDI is deterministic and offers predictable network response, making it suitable for isochronous applications such as real-time video or multimedia.

FIG. 5.5

A fiber-optic cable with a typical FDDI connector.

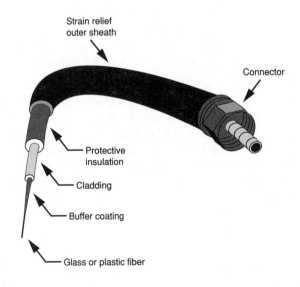

Strain relief outer sheath

Connector

Protective insulation

Cladding

Buffer coating

Glass or plastic fiber

Two classes of FDDI stations exist. Class A stations, also called *dual-attached stations*, attach to both rings by using four fiber strands. This offers full redundancy, because failure of one ring simply causes traffic to shift to the other, allowing communication to continue uninterrupted. Class B stations, also called *singly attached stations*, connect only to the primary ring and do so via a star-wired hub. During a ring failure, only Class A stations participate in the automatic ring reconfiguration process.

FDDI is commonly seen in network equipment rooms, providing the network backbone used to link hubs and other active network components. FDDI to the client is rarely seen, appearing primarily in U.S. government and large corporate locations, where the resistance of fiber-optic cable to electronic eavesdropping outweighs the large additional cost of installing FDDI.

Copper Distributed Data Interface (CDDI)   The FDDI specification actually makes provision for two physical-layer Physical Media Dependencies (PMDs). Traditional FDDI operates on a fiber PMD. CDDI, more properly referred to as Twisted-Pair Physical Media Dependent (TP-PMD), is exactly analogous to FDDI, but runs on Category 5 UTP cable rather than fiber. Gigabit Ethernet provides higher speed at lower cost than CDDI, so CDDI is a very unlikely candidate for new systems.

Asynchronous Transfer Mode (ATM)   ATM competes with FDDI for the network backbone. Although it's usually thought of as running at 155 Mbps on fiber media, ATM hardware is for a wide range of data rates. ATM supports 1.544 Mbps T1 through IBM's 25 Mbps implementation up to the telephone company's OC-48 multigigabit-per-second rates and runs on various media, including fiber-optic cable and unshielded twisted pair. Although ATM to the desktop has from time to time been proposed as a standard, the very high cost of ATM adapters and hub ports has limited ATM to use as a network backbone technology.

ATM is defined at the physical and data-link layers of the OSI Reference Model. It's a high-bandwidth, low-latency transmission and switching methodology similar in concept to traditional packet-switching networks. It combines the high efficiency and bandwidth usage of packet-switching networks with the guaranteed bandwidth availability of circuit-switching networks. ATM uses fixed-length 53-byte cells, each of which contains 48 bytes of data and 5 bytes of header information. Fixed-cell length reduces processing overhead and simplifies the design and construction of the very high-speed switches required for ATM speeds.

The speed and switching capabilities of ATM were major factors in its selection by the ITU (formerly CCITT) as the methodology of choice for broadband Metropolitan Area Networking. ATM is a demand-priority isochronous technology and therefore suitable for real-time applications such as voice, video, and multimedia.

Media-Access Recommendations

If you have an existing ARCnet, Token Ring, or Ethernet network in place that's adequate for your needs, there's no question—use what you have. All these transports are supported by Windows NT Server 4.0 and will provide at least adequate performance within their respective speed limitations.

Part
I

Ch
5

If you're installing a new network or substantially upgrading and expanding an existing one, choose Ethernet and preferably 100BaseTX Fast Ethernet. The performance and expandability constraints of ARCnet make it a candidate to be replaced when your network needs to grow. Most firms replacing ARCnet networks choose Ethernet over the newer high-performance ARCnet variants. Similarly, many firms considering large-scale expansions of an existing Token Ring network, particularly one running at 4 Mbps, find that the limited selection and high cost of 16-Mbps Token Ring NICs and active network components make it possible to replace the entire Token Ring network with 10BaseT or even 100BaseT Ethernet and still spend less than they would simply to upgrade the Token Ring network.

Consider installing 100BaseT if you're planning a large network. 100/10-Mbps NICs are standardized and available now for the same price as 10BaseT 10-Mbps cards. Although 100BaseT hub ports are still expensive, the price per port declined rapidly in early 1997. As of this book's writing, you could buy a dumb eight-port 100BaseTX hub for less than $80 per port. If you can't afford 100BaseTX hubs at present, consider installing 100/10 Mbps-capable cards with the intent of upgrading your hubs and other active network components later as needed. Modern 100BaseT/10BaseT NICs autosense between 100-Mbps and 10-Mbps hubs, so you can replace the 10BaseT hub with a 100BaseTX hub; you don't need to touch the connected PCs.

Designing a Network Cabling System

The importance of cabling to the performance and reliability of your network can't be over-stated. The cabling system is to your network what your circulatory system is to your body. Experienced network managers tell you that the majority of problems in most networks are due to cabling and connector problems. A properly designed, installed, documented, and maintained cabling system lets you avoid these problems and concentrate on running your network. Craftsmanship is the single most important factor in the reliability of a cabling system.

Another issue addressed by a well-designed and properly documented cabling system is that of maintainability. If your cabling system is a rat's nest, adding a station can turn into an all-day affair as you attempt to locate spare pairs, determine in which equipment closet they terminate, and so forth. By contrast, adding a station on a properly structured cabling system takes only a few minutes. If your company is like most, you probably don't have enough skilled network staff to do all that needs to be done. In terms of time saved, the presence of a good cabling system can be just like having one more full-time staff member.

N O T E   When this chapter was written, professionally installed LAN cabling started at about $50 per run. The price can be much greater, depending on the type of cable required, the number of runs to be made, the difficulty of installation, and so forth. Obviously, you can expect to pay more if you live in New York City than if you live in Winston-Salem, N.C. ■

The best approach to make when deciding on a bid to install cable is to focus on those companies that specialize in installing LAN cabling. When making the final decision, use the following guidelines to help you choose the right cabling company for you.

Network Topologies

You can arrange your cabling in many ways, referred to as *topologies*. *Physical topology* describes the way in which the physical components of your cabling are arranged. *Electrical topology* describes the way in which it functions as an electrical circuit. *Logical topology* describes the way in which the system functions as a whole. Physical and logical topologies don't necessarily go hand in hand. It's possible to have a physical topology of one type supporting a logical topology of another. You also can have a hybrid physical topology.

Only three of the many possible physical and logical topologies are commonly used in LAN cabling—the bus, the star, and the ring.

- *Bus* topology (see Figure 5.6) uses a straight piece of cable to which clients are connected along its length, either directly or by means of drop cables. A bus has two ends, each of which is physically terminated with a resistor of the appropriate value, to prevent signal reflection and standing waves.

  The main advantage of a physical bus topology is that it's simple to run and typically uses less cable than any other physical topology. The main disadvantage of a physical bus is that a break anywhere on the cable results in all clients being unable to communicate.

FIG. 5.6
Three PCs connected by a bus, such as 10Base2 Ethernet.

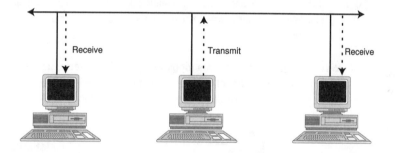

Receive   Transmit   Receive

N O T E Ethernet runs on a bus topology. The older 10Base5 and 10Base2 Ethernet implementations use a logical bus running on a physical coaxial cable bus. The newer 10BaseT Ethernet implementation uses a logical bus running on a physical UTP cable star. ARCnet also runs on a logical bus. Early ARCnet implementations ran a physical bus on RG-62 coaxial cable. Later ones use a logical bus running on a physical UTP star. ∎

- *Star* topology uses a central concentrator, or hub (see Figure 5.7). Each client is connected directly to the hub with a cable to which nothing else is connected. Each end of each cable run in a star is terminated, but this termination is internal at the hub and the client NIC.

  The main advantage of a physical star topology is ease of maintainability and troubleshooting. A cable problem affects only the single device to which that cable is connected; isolation problems are easier than on bus topologies. The only real disadvantage of a physical star is that it typically requires somewhat more cable and labor to install, which is a minor issue in the overall scheme of things. The physical star has become the topology of choice for most new network cabling installations.

Part
I

Ch
5

FIG. 5.7

Six PCs connected to a
hub in a star network.

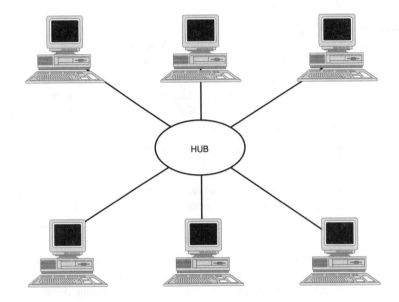

N O T E   10BaseT Ethernet and newer implementations of ARCnet run a logical bus on a physical
star. Token Ring runs a logical ring on a physical star. No common networking method uses
a logical star topology. ▨

■ *Ring* topology is simply a bus topology in which the terminators are eliminated and the
  ends of the cable connect to form a closed ring (see Figure 5.8). In a ring, each device
  connects to exactly two other devices, forming a closed circle.

FIG. 5.8

Four PCs connected in
a ring network.

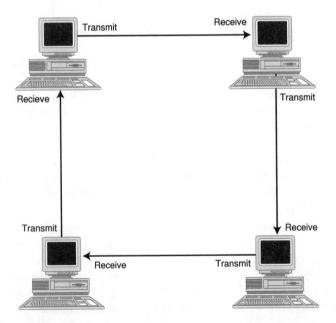

A physical ring topology shares the advantages and disadvantages of a bus. It requires less cable than the star but, like the bus, is difficult to troubleshoot and is subject to complete failure if a break occurs.

N O T E FDDI runs a logical ring on a physical ring. Token Ring runs a logical ring on a physical star. ■

Cable Types

Cable is available in thousands of varieties, but only a few of these are suitable for connecting a LAN. You don't need to know everything about cable to install a LAN successfully, but you should know at least the basics. The following sections describe the main types of cable used for LANs and how to select the cable that's most appropriate for your environment.

Coaxial Cable   Coaxial cable, called *coax* for short, is the oldest type of cable used in network installations. It's still in use and still being installed today. Coax comprises a single central conductor surrounded by a dielectric insulator surrounded by a braided conducting shield (see Figure 5.9). An insulating sheath then covers this assemblage. Anyone with cable television should be familiar with coaxial cable.

FIG. 5.9
Construction of a doubly shielded coaxial cable.

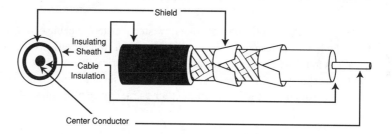

The following three types of coax cable are commonly seen in network installations:

- *Ethernet coax.* The original Ethernet 10Base5 specification uses Ethernet coax. Ethernet coax, usually called *Thick Net*, is a 50-ohm cable about as big around as your thumb. It's inflexible and therefore difficult to run, and is by far the most expensive type of coax treated in this section, typically costing $1 or more per foot. Connections are made to Thick Net by using piercing tap transceivers, whereby an actual hole is drilled through the sheath, shield, and dielectric to reach the center conductor.

  Thick Net is most common now as a network backbone in older installations. The sole advantage of Thick Net is that it allows a maximum cabling run of 500 meters. Almost no Thick Net is being installed today.

- *Ethernet 10Base2 coax.* The difficulty and expense of working with Thick Net resulted in the Ethernet 10Base2 specification, which uses RG-58 coax. RG-58 is a 50-ohm cable that's also called *thinnet* or *Cheapernet*. Thinnet is less than a quarter inch in diameter, is flexible (and therefore easy to install), and typically costs 15 cents per foot.

Thinnet cables terminate in a barrel nut connector (BNC). A thinnet network is run as a daisy chain, with each client using a T-connector to allow connection of one cable coming in to the client and another going out. The end stations have only a single cable with the other connection terminated.

An Ethernet network running on thinnet has all the advantages of Thick Net, except that maximum cable length is limited to 180 meters. Thinnet cabling is still very commonly found connecting Ethernet clients and is still being installed new today, although there are better alternatives. Thinnet is also used at many sites as a backbone media to connect hubs and other active network components.

■ *RG-62 coax.* ARCnet networks were originally installed with RG-62 coax. RG-62 is a 93-ohm cable also used to connect some types of IBM mainframe devices. Except for the different impedance and types of devices it's used to connect, RG-62 is similar to Thick Net and thinnet cable and must be terminated at each end.

 If the network you're building is very small—fewer than 10 clients all located in close physical proximity—you may be tempted to use thinnet coax to avoid the cost of buying a hub. If one client connection fails, all clients on the network fail. If you insist on using 10BaseT, at least buy premade cables in the appropriate lengths to connect each device rather than try to terminate the coax yourself. For any larger network, don't even consider using coax.

Shielded Twisted-Pair Cable   Shielded twisted-pair (STP) cable comprises insulated wires twisted together to form pairs. These pairs are then twisted with each other and enclosed in a sheath. A foil shield protects the cable against electrical interference. Depending on the type of cable, this shield may lie immediately beneath the sheath (protecting the cable as a whole), or individual pairs may be shielded from other pairs. Figure 5.10 shows the construction of a typical STP cable.

FIG. 5.10

Construction of a typical shielded twisted-pair cable.

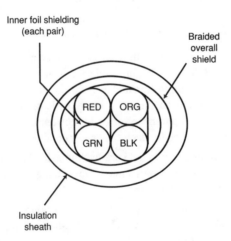

IBM Token Ring was originally designed to run on STP cable, and that's still about the only place where you're likely to see it installed. Most new Token Ring installations are done with unshielded cable. Don't consider using STP cable for your network.

Unshielded Twisted-Pair Cable   Unshielded twisted-pair (UTP) cable dominates network cabling installations today. Like STP cable, UTP cable is constructed from twisted pairs of wire, which are then in turn twisted with each other and enclosed in a sheath (see Figure 5.11). The UTP cable normally used for client cabling includes four such twisted pairs, although UTP cable is available in pair counts ranging from two to more than 1,000. The twist reduces both spurious emissions from the cable and the effects of outside electromagnetic interference on the signal carried by the cable. UTP cable is available in thousands of varieties, differing in pair count, sheath type, signal-carrying capability, and other respects. UTP cable used for network wiring has a nominal impedance of 100 ohms.

FIG. 5.11
A UTP cable with four pairs.

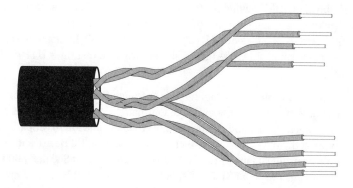

UTP cable is now the *de facto* and *de jure* standard for new network cabling installations. It's inexpensive, easy to install, supports high data rates, and is reasonably resistant to electrical interference, although less so than the other types of cable discussed. Typical four-pair UTP cable ranges in price from 3 cents to 50 cents per foot, depending on the signal-carrying capability of the cable and the type of sheath. Don't consider using anything but UTP cable for your network. Even small networks benefit from the advantages of UTP cable.

Conductor Size   UTP cable is commonly available in 22, 24, and 26 AWG (American Wire Gauge) and uses either solid or stranded conductors. Although 22 AWG cable has some advantage in terms of the distance a signal can travel without degradation, this is primarily of concern in analog phone systems and is outweighed by the additional cost and other factors for data wiring. Data station cabling should use 24 AWG solid conductor cable. Use stranded cable only for patch cords and similar jumpers, in which the flexibility of stranded conductors is needed.

Pair Count   UTP cable is available in pair counts ranging from two to more than a thousand. UTP cable runs made to the client are almost universally four-pair cables. High pair-count cables—25-pair, 50-pair, 100-pair, and greater—are used primarily in voice wiring as riser cables to concentrate station runs and to link floors within a building. Pair count is inextricably linked to the cable's signal-carrying capability, with higher signaling rates being limited to smaller cables.

Part
I

Ch
5

Sheath Material   You can buy UTP cable, designed for inside wiring, with either general-purpose sheathing or plenum-rated sheathing. The sheath of general-purpose cable is usually constructed of polyvinyl chloride (PVC). PVC sheathing is acceptable for wiring that runs inside conduit or in spaces not used to route HVAC source and return. Plenum cable uses sheathing constructed of Teflon or a similar compound. Its use is mandated by law and by the National Electrical Code (NEC) if the cable is exposed within an HVAC (Heating, Ventilation, and Air Conditioning) plenum. When exposed to flame, PVC sheath produces toxic gases, whereas plenum sheath doesn't.

Unfortunately, plenum sheathing is extremely expensive. The same box of Category 5 cable that costs $130 with PVC sheathing may cost nearly $400 with plenum sheathing.

Quality Grades   UTP cable varies widely in terms of how fast a signaling rate it supports and over what distance. The terms Type, Level, and Category are used and often misused interchangeably. The IBM Cabling System defines a variety of cables, each of which is designated a *Type*. Underwriters' Laboratories (UL) runs a LAN cabling certification plan that assigns *Level* ratings to various qualities of UTP cabling. The Electronic Industry Association/Telephone Industry Association (EIA/TIA) has a similar program that rates UTP cables by the following categories:

- *Category 3* cable (Cat 3, for short) is the minimum level for network use. By using the standard two pairs of the available four pairs, Cat 3 cable supports data rates as high as 10 Mbps Ethernet and can be used over short runs for 16 Mbps Token Ring. Cat 3 can support the newer 100 Mbps technologies such as 100BaseT and 100VG-AnyLAN, but only by using all four pairs. Cat 3 typically costs about $60 per 1,000-foot spool in PVC sheathing, and about $125 per spool in plenum sheathing. Cat 3 now is used almost exclusively for voice cabling, with only about 10 percent of new data cabling being done by using Cat 3.

N O T E   Consider very carefully before you decide to install Category 3 cable. Although you can certainly save a few dollars now by installing Cat 3 instead of a higher grade cable, that wire is going to be in your walls for a long time. In 5 or 10 years, you may rue the decision to install Cat 3. Do so only if your budget is such that using Cat 3 is your only option. ■

- *Category 4* (Cat 4) cable is obsolete. Its reason for existing was simply that it was marginally better than Cat 3, allowing 16 Mbps Token Ring networks to operate over greater distances than are supported on Cat 3. It's now stuck in the middle—not much better than Cat 3 and not much cheaper than Cat 5. Don't consider Category 4 cable for your network.
- *Category 5* (Cat 5) cable is the cable of choice for almost every new network installation. Cat 5 cable supports 100 Mbps data rates over only two pairs and offers the potential for carrying data at gigabit rates. Cat 5 typically costs about $130 per 1,000-foot spool in PVC sheathing and about $350 per spool in plenum sheathing. About 80 percent to 85 percent of all new data cabling installed uses Cat 5 cable.

For flexibility, some organizations have gone to the extent of specifying Cat 5 cable for all their cabling, including voice. You should specify Cat 5 cable for your network. Because most of the cost to run cable is in labor, you'll likely pay only a 10 percent to 20 percent overall premium to use Cat 5 rather than Cat 3. Most organizations can easily justify this additional cost because of the additional flexibility Cat 5 offers over the 15- to 25-year life of a typical cabling plant.

Fiber-Optic Cable   Fiber-optic cable (usually called *fiber*) has become increasingly common in network installations. Just a few years ago, fiber was an esoteric and expensive technology. Although fiber-optic cable was initially positioned for use as a network backbone, most networks continued to use coax to carry backbone traffic. Fiber itself was expensive, the active components were costly and in short supply, and even something as simple as putting a connector on a fiber-optic cable was a difficult and expensive process. In recent years, large reductions in the cost of the fiber media itself, improvements in the means used to terminate it, and the widespread availability of inexpensive fiber-based active network components have made fiber-optic cable a realistic alternative for use as a network backbone.

Fiber-optic cable offers the highest bandwidth available of any cable type. It has very low signal attenuation, allowing it to carry signals over long distances. The complete absence of crosstalk allows multiple high-bandwidth links to exist within a single sheath. Fiber-optic cable is completely immune to electromagnetic interference and conversely, because it doesn't radiate, is secure against eavesdropping.

Fiber-optic cable is much smaller in diameter and lighter than copper cables capable of carrying the same bandwidth and is therefore easier to install. Lastly, because many fiber-optic cables have no metallic components, they are electrical insulators and can therefore be used to link buildings without concerns about lightning protection and grounding issues.

Set against all these advantages are a few disadvantages. The installed cost of fiber-optic cable is still somewhat higher than that of copper, and the active network components designed to work with it also cost more. Also, fiber-optic cable is typically more fragile than copper cable, requiring careful attention to bend radius limits and handling requirements during installation.

Structured Cabling Systems

The Electronic Industries Association and Telephone Industries Association (EIA/TIA) recognized the need for a truly standards-based wiring specification. In cooperation with IBM, AT&T, DEC, and other vendors, the EIA/TIA developed the EIA/TIA 568 Commercial Building Telecommunications Wiring Standard. This specification incorporates the best features of each competing standard to develop a composite standard that supports any vendor's equipment. EIA/TIA 568 ensures backward compatibility with existing cabling systems installed by using the propriety cabling standards of each participating vendor.

If you buy an installed cabling system, specify full compliance with both the EIA/TIA 568 Wiring Standard and the EIA/TIA 569 Pathways and Spaces Standard. If you design and install the cabling system yourself, pay close attention to the provisions of both the EIA/TIA 568 and 569 specifications, even if you don't intend for your cabling system to achieve full compliance.

Part
I
Ch
5

Both of these specifications can be purchased from Global Engineering Documents at 800-854-7179. Order these documents if you plan to design and install the cabling system yourself. If you intend to contract the installation, you probably don't need to buy the documents.

Cabling System Recommendations

Whether your cabling system needs to support five clients in a small office or 500 clients in a multibuilding campus, you should adhere to several guidelines to ensure that your cabling system provides the service that you expect:

- Design and install your cabling system in full compliance with the EIA/TIA 568 Commercial Building Telecommunications Wiring Standard by using a star topology running on UTP cable. To the extent that your floor plan allows, adhere closely to the EIA/TIA 569 Pathways and Spaces Standard.

- Pay careful attention to the quality of even the smallest components used. Just as a chain is no stronger than its weakest link, your cabling system is no better than the quality of the worst component that's a part of it. Good installations are often spoiled by using substandard small components. Don't scrimp on patch cords and drop cables.

- Have your cabling installed by LAN cabling specialists. Using the highest quality components means nothing if the craftsmanship of the installer isn't up to par. Use the expertise of your cabling vendor.

- Install new voice cabling at the same time you're cabling for data. It's a great temptation to make do with existing voice cabling, but you may find that the advantages of having a single integrated cabling system more than make up for the small additional cost.

- Install Category 5 cable exclusively for data, and install lots of it. Install at least Cat 3 cables for voice, and carefully consider using Cat 5 for voice as well as data. Make sure that you specify different color cable sheaths for voice and data runs. Consider the EIA/TIA 568 requirement for two runs to each office to be an absolute minimum. Run a voice cable, a data cable, and a spare cable to each wall box, and leave the spare cable unterminated, with sufficient slack on each end to allow you to terminate later as needed. Consider putting three such cable runs into wall boxes on at least two walls of each office. You'll bless your foresight in the coming years.

- Make absolutely certain that your cable installer fully documents the cabling system, from every conductor to every single cable installed. Horizontal cables, riser cables, and punchdown blocks should be numbered and pin assignments provided. You should be able to trace any conductor from the wall jack through punchdown blocks and patch panels to the final termination. If your cabling plant is large, consider buying a cable-management software package to record this information initially and then keep up-to-date with changes and additions to the cabling. Assign one person the responsibility for making changes to the cabling plant, and then make it known that making physical changes to the cabling system without recording them is a serious offense.

Expandability and Ease of Maintenance Recommendations

The first principle here is to overwire your station runs. It costs just a little more to run two cables than it does to run only one. If you have a location that you're absolutely positive never needs more than one cable run, go ahead and run a spare anyway, leaving the spare unterminated with enough slack on both ends for future use. Although you may end up with several $10 pieces of cable left unused in the wall for eternity, the first time you need one of those cable runs will more than pay for every extra run you made.

The second principle is to overwire your backbone and riser runs. If a 25-pair riser does the job now, put in a 50-pair or even a 100-pair riser. If a 6-fiber cable carries your present traffic, install a 12-fiber cable instead. The cable itself is cheap. What costs money is labor, and most of the labor is spent terminating the cable. By installing more pairs than you need and leaving them unterminated, you have the best of both worlds. Having the extra pairs in place costs next to nothing, but they're there and can be terminated if and when you need them.

The third principle is to pay close attention to the physical environment of your wiring closets and equipment rooms. Nothing is more miserable than trying to maintain a cabling system in an overheated or freezing closet while holding a flashlight in your teeth. Make sure that your wiring closets and equipment rooms are well-lighted, properly ventilated, and provided with more electrical receptacles than you think you'll ever need. Your equipment will be much happier, and so will you when you need to change the cabling.

Selecting Active Network Components

If the cabling system is the arteries and veins of your network, the active network components are its heart. By itself, the cabling system is just dead wire. Active network components bring that wire to life, putting data on it and allowing the various parts of your network to communicate with each other.

If you remember only one thing from this section, make it this: The single most important factor in choosing active network components is to *maintain consistency*. After you choose one manufacturer as your supplier, it's easy to be seduced by another manufacturer's component that's a bit cheaper or has a nice feature or better specifications. Don't fall into this trap. You'll pay the price later in dollars, time, and aggravation when you find that you can't solve a problem related to the interaction of the two manufacturers' components because neither will take responsibility, or that you have to buy a second $5,000 network management software package because neither manufacturer's management software works with the other's product.

Network Interface Cards

A network interface card, commonly referred to as a NIC, connects each device on the network to the network cabling system. NICs operate at the physical and data-link layers of the OSI Reference Model. At the physical layer, a NIC provides the physical and electrical connection required to access the network cabling and to use the cabling to convey data as a bit stream.

Part

I

Ch

5

At the data-link layer, the NIC provides the processing that assembles and disassembles the bit stream on the cable into frames suitable for the media-access method in use. Every device connected to the network must be equipped with a network interface, either by means of a peripheral NIC or by means of similar circuitry built directly into the component.

A NIC is media-dependent, media-access-method-dependent, and protocol-independent. *Media-dependent* means that the NIC must have a physical connector appropriate for the cabling system to which it's to be connected. *Media-access-method-dependent* means that even a card that can be connected physically to the cabling system must also be of a type that supports the media-access method in use. For example, an Ethernet card designed for UTP cable can be connected to but doesn't function on a Token Ring network wired with UTP cable.

Protocol-independent means that a particular NIC, assuming that appropriate drivers are available for it, can communicate by using various higher-level protocols, either individually or simultaneously. For example, you can use an Ethernet NIC to connect a client simultaneously to a LAN server running IPX/SPX and to a UNIX host running TCP/IP.

It's common in the industry to differentiate between NICs intended for use in clients and those intended for use in servers. Conventional wisdom says that inexpensive NICs are fine for use in a client where performance is less of an issue, but that you should buy for your server the highest-performance NIC you can afford. In fact, although you can use any NIC in any computer system it fits (client or server), you should pay close attention to selecting NICs for both your clients and your servers. Installing high-performance NICs in your server and using low-performance NICs in your clients is counterproductive. In this situation, because the server NIC can deliver data so much faster than the client NIC can accept it, the network is flooded with retransmissions requested by the client NIC. These constant retransmissions greatly degrade network performance. Balance the performance of the NICs you use in your clients with the performance provided by the server NIC.

The following sections provide guidance on choosing the right NIC for clients and servers.

NIC Bus Types for Client PCs   The first consideration in choosing a client NIC is the client's bus type. There are two schools of thought on this issue:

- Install a NIC that uses the highest performance bus provided by that client. For example, if the client has both ISA and PCI slots, choosing a PCI NIC rather than an ISA NIC will result in better performance. PCI NICs are required to keep up with the data rate of 100BaseT networks.

- The advantages of standardization outweigh the incremental performance benefits of matching the card to the client. Members of this school of thought—faced with a mixed client environment of ISA, PCI, and VLB (Video Local Bus) systems—would choose ISA NICs for all clients.

N O T E   Make sure that the PCI NICs you purchase support PCI busmastering, especially for 100BaseT networks. Some low-cost PCI NICs operate in PCI bus slave mode. Properly designed busmastering NICs greatly increase data throughput and minimize CPU overhead. ■

Standardizing on ISA NICs for 10 Mbps clients usually makes sense. Most client PCI system boards have only three or four PCI slots, so occupying a PCI slot with a 10 Mbps NIC may preclude addition of other PCI cards that can take full advantage of the PCI bus's bandwidth. In a 100BaseT environment, you're likely to need to support a combination of PCI NICs for power users and graphic designers, and 10BaseT ISA NICs for less bandwidth-intensive users.

> **CAUTION**
>
> For clients running Windows NT Workstation 4.0, make sure that your server NIC is listed on the Windows NT Hardware Compatibility List (HCL) described later in the section "Conformance to the Microsoft Windows NT Hardware Compatibility List."

Software-Configurable or Jumper-Configurable NICs A NIC has various settings that usually need adjustment before you can use the card. Nearly all cards are configurable for IRQ. Many require setting DMA, base address, and media type. All ARCnet cards and some Token Ring cards allow users to set the network address. The network (Medium Access Control or MAC) address of Ethernet cards is a globally unique value, similar to a GUID (globally unique ID), preset at the factory.

One important factor that contributes to the usability of a NIC is whether these settings are made by using physical jumpers or by using a software utility. A card that requires setting physical jumpers is inconvenient. Making a change involves disassembling the computer, removing the card, setting the jumpers, and then putting everything back together. It's often necessary to go through this process just to examine how the card is now set. A software-configurable card, on the other hand, can be both examined and set simply by running a program. Buy only software-configurable NICs.

Name-Brand NICs vs. Clone NICs The best reason to pay the premium for a name-brand NIC is that part of that premium goes to pay for better-quality control and reliability. In working with thousands of name-brand and clone NICs over the years, many experienced network administrators seldom see name-brand NICs that were damaged out of the box and almost never experience a failure of a name-brand NIC that wasn't due to some easily explained problem, such as a lightning strike. The choice is yours, but most LAN administrators recognize that the relatively small amount of money saved by buying clone NICs can be rapidly swamped by the costs of just one network failure attributable to using cheap cards.

Full-Duplex vs. Half-Duplex Ethernet Ethernet originated as a half-duplex transmission system; *half-duplex* means that a NIC can't transmit and receive at the same time. A number of vendors supply full-duplex 10 Mbps Ethernet NICs and switching hubs, claiming to double network bandwidth. In reality, full-duplex 10 Mbps Ethernet provides only modest performance improvement over switched 10 Mbps Ethernet but costs considerably more. The current crop of 10/100BaseT auto-sensing NICs provides full-duplex capability out of the box. Don't consider buying 10BaseT (only) full-duplex NICs.

Server NICs All the same factors that apply to choosing client NICs also apply to choosing server NICs, with a few more. Whereas a client NIC is responsible for handling only the traffic of its own client, a server NIC must process traffic from many clients in rapid sequence.

Part

I

Ch

5

Doing so demands a high-speed link to the I/O system of the server. Accordingly, NICs intended for use in servers are universally designed to use a high-speed bus connection.

A factor that's of little concern in client NICs but more important in server NICs is that of processor usage. All NICs require some assistance from the system processor, but a properly designed server NIC should minimize this dependence. This issue is of particular concern with 100BaseT server NICs. In some cases, for instance, one server equipped with four such NICs may lose more than 50 percent of the processor just in handling the overhead for the NICs. High-end server NICs include on-board processors and RAM to reduce processor load. For example, Intel's EtherExpress PRO/100 Smart Adapter has an i960 processor and 2M of RAM. Find out what level of processor usage your proposed server NICs require, and favor those with low usage.

Deciding which NIC to install in your server is straightforward. If you have a PCI server (as recommended in the later section "Choosing a Bus Type"), install a name-brand PCI NIC. In choosing the brand of NIC, simplify global network management issues by giving first preference to a card made by the manufacturer of your other active network components. Alternatively, choose a card made by the server manufacturer to simplify server management.

> **CAUTION**
>
> Make sure that your server NIC is listed on the Windows NT Hardware Compatibility List (HCL), described later in the section "Conformance to the Microsoft Windows NT Hardware Compatibility List." If the NIC isn't on the current HCL, you're likely to find that it won't work with Windows NT Server 4.0.

One of the most valuable pieces of real estate in your network is a server expansion slot. Even though a typical server has many more slots than a client, the competition for these slots is intense. Multiport NICs combine the function of more than one NIC onto a single card. They're available in dual- and quad-NIC versions from various suppliers. If your LAN runs Ethernet and you segment it, consider carefully how many server slots you have available and whether you should buy a dual-port or quad-port NIC.

Repeaters

Repeaters are used to clean up, amplify, and rebroadcast a signal, extending the distance that the signal can be run reliably on a particular type of cable. They function exclusively at the physical layer of the OSI Reference Model. Repeaters are media-dependent and protocol-independent. As purely electrical devices, repeaters are unaware of the content of the signals that they process. They simply regenerate the signal and pass it on. Figure 5.12 illustrates, in the context of the OSI Model, a repeater between two network segments.

Local repeaters are used to extend signaling distance within the confines of a LAN. Remote repeaters are used to extend a LAN segment, often by means of fiber-optic cable, to a remote location without requiring installation of a bridge or router. The clients at the remote site appear logically to be on the same local segment as that to which the remote repeater is attached.

FIG. 5.12
Connecting two network segments with a repeater.

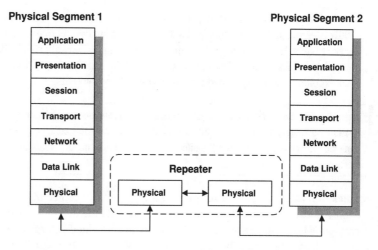

Hubs, bridges, routers, gateways, and all other active network components include basic repeater functionality. Use stand-alone local repeaters as needed to manage cable-length limitations within your network or to extend your LAN to remote locations that don't justify installation of a bridge or router.

Simple Hubs

Hubs are used as concentrators to join multiple clients with a single link to the rest of the LAN. A hub has several ports to which clients are connected directly, and one or more ports that can be used in turn to connect the hub to the backbone or to other active network components.

A hub functions as a multiport repeater. Signals received on any port are immediately retransmitted to all other ports on the hub. Hubs function at the physical layer of the OSI Reference Model. They're media-dependent and protocol-independent. Hubs come in a wide variety of sizes, types, and price ranges.

Stand-Alone Hubs *Stand-alone hubs* are simple and inexpensive devices, intended primarily to serve a self-contained workgroup in which the server is connected to one port and the clients to other ports, and no interconnection to a larger network exists. They range in size from 4 to 24 ports. Depending on port count, stand-alone hubs vary from about the size of a modem to about the size of a pizza box. They normally operate on low voltage supplied by a power brick similar to that used to power external modems, and they consume little power.

Stand-alone hubs offer little or no expandability. This usually isn't a problem because these hubs are inexpensive and can simply be purchased in a size appropriate for your needs. Stand-alone hubs usually offer no provision for management, although high-end stand-alone hubs may have management features standard or as an option. Manageability—the ability to control the hub from a remote management station—normally isn't a major issue in the small workgroup environment for which these hubs are intended.

Part
I

Ch
5

A typical name-brand, eight-port, stand-alone, unmanaged hub has a street price of less than $200, or less than $25 per port. Hubs with higher port counts may cost somewhat more on a per-port basis. Hubs that include management features may approach $100 per port. If your network comprises only a few clients that are all located in close proximity, a stand-alone hub is an excellent and inexpensive way to connect these systems.

 TIP   Make sure that any stand-alone hub you buy has *jabber protection*. This feature monitors each port for constant uncontrolled transmission that will flood the network. If this condition is detected, jabber protection temporarily shuts down the offending port while allowing the rest of the ports to continue functioning.

Stackable Hubs   *Stackable hubs* are a fairly recent development. In the past, you had to choose between a stand-alone hub, which provided little functionality but at a low price, and an enterprise hub—also called a *chassis hub*—which provided enterprise-level functionality but at a very high cost. Stackable hubs do a good job of blending the best characteristics of both hub types. They offer much of the expandability and management capabilities of enterprise hubs at not much greater cost than stand-alone hubs.

What distinguishes a true stackable hub is that it possesses a backplane used to link it directly to a similar hub or hubs, melding the assembled stack into a single hub running a single Ethernet bus. Although stand-alone hubs can be physically stacked and joined simply by connecting a port on one to a port on the next, the result isn't a true stack. To understand why, you need to understand that Ethernet places a limit on the maximum number of repeaters allowed to separate any two stations. A device connected to any port of any hub in a stack of stackable hubs is connected directly to the single bus represented by that stack. As a result, any two devices connected to that stack can communicate while going through only the one repeater represented by that stack. The stack of stand-alone hubs, on the other hand, results in two stations connected to different hubs within that stack going through at least two repeaters to communicate.

Stackable hubs are commonly available in 12- and 24-port versions. Some manufacturers also offer 48-port versions. The street price of stackable hubs ranges from about $75 to $250 per port, depending on port density and what, if any, management options are installed. For most organizations, these hubs offer the best combination of price, features, and expandability available.

Hub Manageability   *Manageability* is another consideration in choosing stand-alone or stackable hubs. Manageability is simply a hub's capability to be configured and monitored from a remote client running specialized software. Although protocols such as Simple Network Management Protocol (SNMP) and Remote Monitoring (RMON) are standardized, their implementations aren't. This means that it's unlikely you can manage one manufacturer's hub with remote software intended for use with another manufacturer's hub. (This is yet another reason to stick with one manufacturer for your active network components.)

Although hub manufacturers attempt to represent *dumb* or unmanaged hubs as a separate category from *smart* or manageable hubs, the reality is that manageability is just one more feature that may be standard, optional, or unavailable on a particular hub. Most low-end stand-alone hubs aren't manageable and can't be upgraded. High-end stand-alone hubs and most stackable hubs either come with management standard or at least offer it as an option. Unless yours is a very small network, you should buy manageable hubs or at least ones that can be upgraded to manageability.

Bridges

Bridges are used to divide a network into mutually isolated segments while maintaining the whole as a single network. Bridges operate at the data-link layer of the ISO Reference Model (see Figure 5.13). They work with *frames*, which are organized assemblages of data, rather than the raw bit stream on which hubs, repeaters, and other physical-layer devices operate.

FIG. 5.13
Connecting two network segments with a bridge.

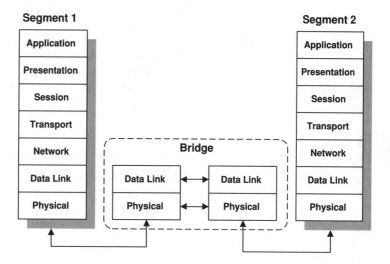

Bridges are media-dependent. A bridge designed to connect to UTP cabling can't connect to a coax cable, and vice versa. Bridges are protocol-independent above the data-link layer. It doesn't matter to an Ethernet frame or to the bridge that directs it whether that frame encapsulates an IP packet, an IPX packet, or some other type of packet at the logical level. A bridge simply sees that the frame originated from a particular hardware address and needs to be sent to another hardware address.

Frames include, in addition to the raw data itself, a header that identifies the address of the source station and the address of the destination station. Frames use physical rather than logical addresses. When a client transmits an Ethernet frame to the server, the source address is the MAC or hardware address of the client's Ethernet card, and the destination address is the MAC address of the Ethernet card in the server.

Part

I

Ch

5

A bridge divides a single network cable into two or more physical and logical segments. The bridge listens to all traffic on all segments and examines the destination hardware address of each frame. If the source and destination hardware addresses are located on the same segment, the bridge simply discards that frame because the destination can hear the source directly. If the source and destination addresses are located on different segments, the bridge repeats the frame onto the segment where the destination address is located. Traffic with both source and destination addresses on the same segment is kept local to that segment and isn't heard by the rest of the network. Only traffic whose source and destination addresses are on different segments is broadcast to the network as a whole.

When used properly, bridges can significantly reduce the total volume of network traffic. This is particularly important on Ethernet networks, because as the network grows and the traffic volume increases, collisions become more frequent and the overall performance of the network degrades.

Another important characteristic of bridges is that they negate the impact of repeaters. Ethernet allows a maximum of four repeaters to intervene between the source and destination stations. By using a bridge, a frame on the source segment may pass through as many as four repeaters (the legal limit) before reaching the bridge. When the bridge places that frame on the destination segment, it may again pass through as many as four repeaters on its way to the destination station. This can be an important design consideration in Ethernet networks, particularly those that are large and physically widespread.

Routers

Routers are used to connect one network to another network. Routers operate at the network layer of the ISO Reference Model (see Figure 5.14). They work with packets, which are composed of an encapsulated frame and added logical addressing information.

FIG. 5.14
Connecting two network segments with a router.

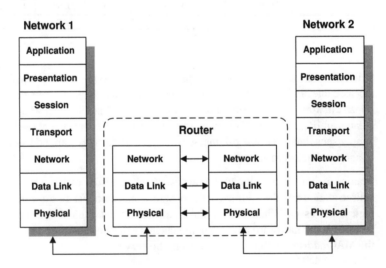

Routers are similar to bridges but are media-independent. A router designed to process IP packets can do so whether it's physically connected to UTP cabling or a coax cable. Routers are protocol-dependent above the data-link layer. A router designed to process IP packets can't process IPX packets and vice versa, although multiprotocol routers designed to process more than one type of network-layer packet do exist.

Packets are encapsulated within a data-link layer frame. They include a header, which identifies the addresses of the source station and the destination station. Packets use logical rather than physical addresses. Unlike bridges, which require the source and destination addresses to be on the same network, router addressing allows the destination address to be on a different network than the source address.

Routers are much more complex than bridges and, accordingly, are more expensive and re-quire more configuration. A bridge makes a simple decision: If the destination address is on the same segment as the source address, it discards the frame; if the two addresses are on different segments, it repeats the frame. A router, on the other hand, must make a complex decision about how to deliver a particular packet to a distant network. It may have to choose the best available route from various alternatives.

Routers work with the logical addressing information contained in network-layer packets, and not all upper-layer protocols provide this information. Windows NT Server includes native support for TCP/IP, IPX/SPX, and NetBEUI. TCP/IP and IPX/SPX packets include the network-layer logical addresses needed by routers and are referred to as *routed* or *routable* protocols. NetBEUI packets don't include this network-layer information and accordingly are referred to as *non-routed* or *non-routable*. This means that if you're using TCP/IP or IPX/SPX transport, you have the choice of designing your network around bridges, routers, or both. If instead you're using NetBEUI, bridging is your only alternative, because routers can't handle NetBEUI packets.

▶ **See** "NetBEUI and NetBEUI Frame," **p. 107**

Part

I

Ch

5

Routing vs. Bridging

The differences between routers and bridges are the differences between a single network and an internetwork. A single network is defined as a group of connected devices that shares a single common network layer address. Bridges are used to join segments within a single network. Routers are used to join separate networks.

Bridges function at the data-link layer and work with hardware addresses, which provide no information about the geographical location of the device. Routers function at the network layer and work with logical addresses, which can be mapped to geographical locations.

Gateways

A *gateway* is used to translate between incompatible protocols and can function at any one layer of the OSI Reference Model or at several layers simultaneously (see Figure 5.15). Gateways are most commonly used at the upper three layers of the OSI Model. For example, if you have some users using the Simple Mail Transfer Protocol (SMTP) for e-mail and others using the Message Handling System (MHS) protocol, a gateway can translate between these two protocols so that all users can exchange e-mail.

FIG. 5.15
Connecting two networks that use dissimilar protocols with a gateway.

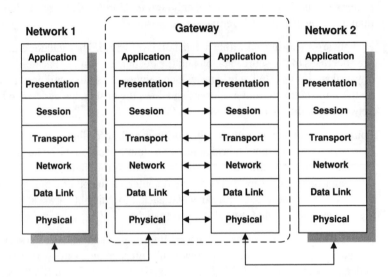

Because of the work they must do to translate between fundamentally incompatible protocols, gateways are usually very processor-intensive and therefore run relatively slowly. In particular, using a gateway to translate transport protocols, such as TCP/IP to and from IPX/SPX, usually creates a bottleneck. Use a gateway only if it's the only solution available, and then only on an interim basis while you migrate to common shared protocols. Gateways typically are difficult to install and maintain, and the translations they provide are often imperfect at best, particularly at the upper ISO layers.

N O T E   The Internet community uses the term *gateway* to refer to a *router*. ■

Enterprise Hubs, Collapsed Backbones, Ethernet Switches, and Virtual LANs

Simple networks use hubs, bridges, and routers as building blocks. As networks become larger and more complex, performance and manageability requirements often make it necessary to make fundamental changes to the network architecture. The following sections describe how to use enterprise hubs, collapsed backbones, Ethernet switches, and virtual LANs to accommodate the demands of large and complex networks.

Enterprise Hubs   Enterprise hubs use a wall-mounted or rack-mounted chassis that provides two or more passive backplanes into which feature cards are inserted to provide the exact functionality needed (see Figure 5.16). Cards are available to provide hubs for Ethernet, Token Ring, FDDI, and ATM networks. Other cards can be installed to provide routing, bridging, gateway, management, and other functions.

FIG. 5.16

A typical enterprise hub with plug-in cards.

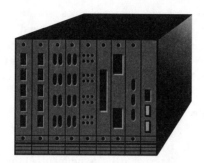

An enterprise hub is something you buy only if you have to. The unpopulated chassis alone can cost more than $10,000. The cards used to populate an enterprise hub also are expensive, both in absolute terms and on a per-port basis. But despite the cost, you would buy an enterprise hub instead of a collection of stackables for three reasons: to establish a collapsed backbone, to implement Ethernet switching, and to build a virtual LAN.

Collapsed Backbones   *Collapsing the backbone* simply means to move all active network components into a single physical cabinet and then link them by using a very high-speed bus. Rather than locate hubs and other active network components in equipment rooms near the clients, these components are reduced to cards contained in a single chassis sited centrally. This scheme has certain perceived advantages both in terms of management and in terms of implementing technologies such as switching and virtual LANs.

Ethernet Switches   Conventional Ethernet networks with hubs are limited to about 37 percent of the theoretical 10 Mbps bandwidth because of the rapidly growing number of collisions and packet retransmissions that occur as traffic increases. Switched Ethernet eliminates collisions by providing a "private pipe" between Ethernet nodes. Today's most common configuration for switched Ethernet is 10BaseT half-duplex connections to clients and 100BaseT full duplex connections to server and other Ethernet switches.

> **N O T E**   The actual data throughput limit of a shared (hub) Ethernet network is about 25 percent of the theoretical speed. For instance, at 37 percent utilization you get 2.5 Mbps (about 300 K/sec) from a 10BaseT network and 25 Mbps (about 3 M/sec) from a shared 100BaseT network. The reduction from 37 percent to 25 percent is a result of Ethernet packet overhead. With standard switched Fast Ethernet, the data throughput limit increases to 70 Mbps (about 9 M/sec). A full-duplex Fast Ethernet connection between switches can deliver up to 140 Mbps. ■

Part

I

Ch

5

To understand Ethernet switches, you need to understand the progression in hub design and functionality from simple stand-alone hubs and stackables to the modern full-featured enterprise hub:

- Stand-alone hubs are simple repeaters. All devices connected to any port on a stand-alone hub are connected to the single segment represented by that hub.

- At the entry level, enterprise hubs and a few stackables provide a backplane that supports multiple segments. Each hub card is, in effect, a stand-alone hub operating on its own segment. A station's segment is determined by which physical hub card it's connected to. Using multiple hub cards segments traffic but does nothing to interconnect the separate segments. Moving traffic between two or more of these segments requires a bridge or router.

- At the next step, an enterprise hub replaces physical assignment of ports to segments with a switched matrix, which allows logical assignment of any port to any segment. This assignment is static rather than dynamic. A port is assigned to a particular segment until the network manager intervenes to change the assignment. At this level, the enterprise hub still provides no interconnectivity between ports located on different segments. The only real difference between this arrangement and the one described in the preceding bullet point is that you can change port assignments programmatically rather than go out and physically move a jumper cord. Adding a management card to the chassis provides the capability to make these changes programmatically. Many installed enterprise hubs are working at this level.

- The next logical step is to provide self-contained bridging and routing functions within the enterprise hub. This is accomplished by adding a card or cards to the chassis to provide these connectivity functions—in effect combining your hubs, bridges, and routers into a single box. Many installed enterprise hubs and nearly all newly purchased ones function at this level.

- The final step in the evolution of the hub is to provide a switching backplane, which can connect any port to any other port dynamically and under control of the hub itself. Rather than link a port to a segment, the hub links a port directly to another port by building up and tearing down (as needed) dedicated logical channels on its high-speed backplane—in effect assigning each port to its own segment. It's at this level that your enterprise hub essentially becomes a switch.

The single characteristic that distinguishes a hub from a switch is that, on the hub, all traffic generated by any port is repeated and heard by all other ports on the hub, whereas a switch establishes virtual circuits that connect the two ports directly (see Figure 5.17). Ports not a part of the virtual circuit can't hear traffic on this virtual circuit. In essence, the hub resembles a CB radio conversation, whereas the switch resembles a telephone conversation. To look at it another way, each device attached to a switch port is to all intents and purposes connected to its own dedicated bridge or router port.

Switches use one or both of two methods to process traffic. *Store-and-forward* processing receives and buffers the entire inbound frame before processing it, whereas *cut-through* begins processing the inbound frame as soon as enough of it has arrived to provide the destination address. A cut-through switch therefore never has possession of the entire frame at any one time. The advantage of cut-through is raw speed and increased throughput. The advantage of store-and-forward is that because the entire frame is available at once, the switch can perform error checking, enhanced filtering, and other processing on the frame. Both methods are used successfully and, in fact, many switches incorporate elements of both types of processing.

FIG. 5.17

Traffic between six PCs with a switched Ethernet hub.

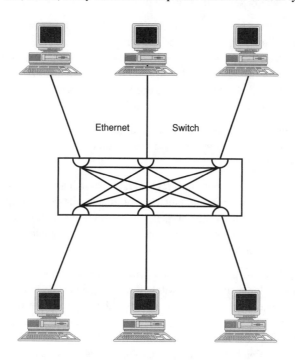

Ethernet   Switch

The first and most common type of switch is the segment switch, which is similar in concept to a bridge or a router. Functioning as a switched learning bridge, the segment switch provides basic filtering and forwarding between multiple segments.

The next step up in switches is the private LAN switch, in which each port can connect to any other port via a dedicated virtual segment built up and torn down as needed by the switch itself. As long as the software is properly written and the backplane has sufficient cumulative bandwidth, every pair of ports can, in theory, communicate with each other at full network bandwidth without contention or collision. In practice, of course, some ports (such as servers) are more popular than others, so the theoretical cumulative throughput of any switch can never be reached. A private LAN switch simply extends the concept of bridging multiple segments to reduce traffic to its ultimate conclusion of providing each device with its own segment.

You also can add routing functionality to a switch. The switches discussed earlier filter and forward frames and otherwise function as bridges at the data-link layer of the OSI Reference Model. Routing switches extend this functionality to working with the network layer of the OSI Model. The level of routing functionality varies by manufacturer and model, from those on the low end (which provide barrier routing) to those on the high end (which essentially provide each device with a dedicated router port). Routing switches are expensive components, and as the level of routing functionality increases, so does the price.

Virtual LANs   Switching is itself the logical conclusion of the use of segmenting to reduce traffic. However, reducing traffic to the extent that a particular frame or packet is received only by the designated port raises a fundamental problem.

Until now, the discussion has focused only on user traffic, those frames and packets containing user data. There is, however, another type of traffic on a LAN. Overhead or administrative traffic comprises frames and packets used by the network to maintain itself. Novell servers generate Service Advertising Protocol (SAP) traffic to inform all devices on the LAN of the services available from that server. Routers use Routing Information Protocol (RIP) and other protocols to communicate routing information to each other.

All this administrative traffic is essential. Without it, the LAN doesn't run. For switching to reach its ultimate utility, you must somehow ensure that this overhead traffic is heard by all devices that need to hear it.

The solution to this problem is a *virtual LAN (VLAN)*, which allows any arbitrary group of ports to be clustered under programmatic control. Just as all the users attached to a traditional Ethernet segment hear all the traffic present on that segment, all the users on a VLAN hear all the traffic on the VLAN. The difference is that VLAN users can be located on different physical networks and scattered broadly geographically.

With a traditional hub, the physical port into which a client is connected determines which network that client belongs to. With a switch, the physical port no longer determines which network the client belongs to, but the client must still belong to a network physically located on that switch. With a VLAN, any client plugged into any port located on any switch can be logically configured to be a member of any network. This feature of VLANs breaks the dependency of physical location to network membership, allowing users to be relocated anywhere within the internetwork and still remain a member of the same network.

Some building blocks of VLAN technology have been around for several years, but the technology as a whole hasn't yet been fully implemented. The high cost of fast data links has also contributed to the slow adoption of VLANs. As the technology continues to mature and the cost of high-speed data links continues to drop, VLANs will become an increasingly common part of the network landscape.

Recommendation Summary for Active Network Components

The following list summarizes the recommendations for active network components discussed in the preceding sections, with additional suggestions for power conditioning and spares:

- Scale the infrastructure to your needs, keeping in mind that most networks grow. In a typical network, installed components should have at least 25 percent of their capacity unused and should be easily expandable to at least 100 percent additional capacity. If your initial configuration puts you at or near capacity on a particular component, install the next level up.

- Choose one manufacturer for your active network components and then buy all the components you can from that one manufacturer. Standardize as much as possible, even to the extent of using the same model within the manufacturer's line when possible.

- Consider buying only manageable components or those that can be upgraded to manageability. If your entire network can run from only one hub and is likely to remain small, you can safely avoid the extra expense of manageability. Otherwise, look to the future.

- Understand fully the differences between bridges and routers and use them appropriately to control network traffic.

- Provide a standby uninterruptible power supply (UPS) in each equipment room and make sure that each active network component is connected to the UPS. UPSes are the subject of the later section "Providing Power Protection."

- Provide full lightning protection to supplement that provided by the UPS. Protect all wires connected to the network, including AC power, telephone lines, and leased lines. Ideally, you should provide such protection for each client as well. If you don't do so, at least protect key active network components such as bridges, routers, and servers by installing data-line protectors.

- Buy standby spares for critical network components. Even if your system is under a maintenance contract, having a spare hub available can make the difference between being down for 15 minutes and being down for a day.

Specifying Server Hardware

The most important computer on your network is the server. The server runs Windows NT Server software to provide shared access to programs, data files, and printers. On many Windows NT Server networks, programs actually run centrally on the server itself. For small networks, the server represents most of the cost of the network. On larger networks, the cost of the server becomes a correspondingly smaller part of the total cost, but the server is no less important for this fact.

Many Windows NT Server installations use a standard PC with upgraded memory and disk storage as their server. Others are designed around a true purpose-built server. Although using an upgraded PC as a server can be viable for a very small network, purpose-built servers have many advantages in architecture, performance, and redundancy features. Using a purpose-built server benefits any network and should be considered mandatory if your network will have more than a handful of users.

General Server Types

For convenience and marketing reasons, true servers are usually classified by the size of network they're intended to support. There's a great deal of overlap in these categories, and a fully configured entry-level server may, in fact, exceed a minimally configured mid-range server in price and capability.

Part
I

Ch
5

Workgroup Servers A *workgroup server* is the entry-level server. It's designed to support up to 25 or so users running primarily file and print sharing, but can function as a light-duty application server as well.

Workgroup servers cost little more than an equivalently configured PC, running from about $3,000 on the low end to perhaps $8,000 or $9,000 when fully expanded. They're usually based on a single Pentium Pro processor and usually can't be upgraded to multiple processors. Disk arrays and Error Checking and Correcting (ECC) memory are optional items, if they're offered at all. Workgroup servers are usually built in a mini- or mid-tower case, although some use a full-tower case.

Departmental Servers Departmental servers are the mid-range servers, supporting from 20 to 150 users. They can do double duty as both file and print servers, and as moderate-duty application servers. The price of departmental servers ranges from about $10,000 on the low end to perhaps $40,000 on the high. At this level, disk arrays, ECC memory, and redundant power supplies are often standard equipment or are at least available as options. Departmental servers are based on 166 MHz or faster Pentium Pro processors.

Although they may be offered at the entry level with a single processor, these servers are designed to support symmetrical multiprocessing (SMP) with at least two processors. Cases are always at least full-tower, and may be double-wide cubes or rack-mountable.

Enterprise Servers Enterprise servers are the high-end products. They can provide file and print sharing services for 100 to 500 users and at the same time support heavy-duty application server functions in a transaction-processing environment. Enterprise servers range in price from perhaps $30,000 to $100,000 and more. At this level, fault tolerance and redundancy elements, such as disk arrays, ECC memory, and duplicate power supplies, are standard.

Enterprise servers available today are based on 166 MHz and faster Pentium Pro processors and offer SMP support for at least two and usually four processors. Enterprise servers include hardware support for RAID systems, often with redundant RAID controllers. Cases are monsters, providing as many as 28 drive bays, redundant power supplies, and other features that increase availability.

Conformance to the Microsoft Windows NT Hardware Compatibility List

Make sure that any server you consider, with all its peripheral components, appears on the Microsoft Windows NT Server Hardware Compatibility List. A printed booklet with this information ships with the Windows NT Server software. However, the list is updated frequently to account for rapid changes within the industry, and you should download the most recent version when you're ready to place the order for your server.

ON THE WEB

You can retrieve the most recent version of the Hardware Compatibility List from **http://www. microsoft.com/ntserver/info/hwcompatibility.htm**. It can also be found in Library 1 of the WINNT forum or Library 17 of the MSWIN32 forum on CompuServe Information Service.

Warranties, Maintainability, and Local Service

Server downtime can cost your company hundreds or even thousands of dollars per hour. More important, it can cost a LAN manager his job. When the LAN is down, employees still draw salaries, queries go unanswered, orders go unfilled, and work backs up. The issues of reliability and service are therefore an important aspect—some would say the *most* important aspect—of choosing a server.

You can configure your server with every fault-tolerant and redundancy feature offered by the manufacturer. Despite every precaution you take, the day will still come when your server goes down. What happens then can make the difference between an unpleasant episode and a disaster. The time to consider this problem is when you buy your server.

Choosing the Server Components

Know what role your server will play and the tasks it will be required to perform. Older-generation network operating systems, such as Novell NetWare, focus almost exclusively on providing shared file and print services, a use that Windows NT Server also supports admirably. However, unlike Novell NetWare, Windows NT Server is also a stable and reliable application server platform.

Providing only file and printer sharing puts a relatively light load on a server. Raw processor speed is much less important than disk subsystem performance and network I/O. Although any server operating system likes memory, a file server has relatively modest RAM requirements.

An application server needs more of everything than a file server, such as the following:

- More processor power by far, because user programs are actually running on the server.
- More memory to support the user programs running on the server.
- Better disk performance, because an application server is usually running disk-intensive database applications. In theory, an application server should require less network I/O performance because most of the data is manipulated internally, and data on the network is limited to requests and queries from the clients and results being sent back to them. In practice, most client/server applications—particularly in-house designs—are written so poorly that network I/O jumps drastically when they're implemented.

There's no hard-and-fast dividing line between file servers and application servers. Any computer that can run Windows NT Server 4.0 can function as an application server. What distinguishes the two server types is what you run on them and what hardware you provide to support what you choose to run. There's a great deal of overlap between configurations appropriate for each. Following are common configurations for file/printer sharing and application servers:

- A typical Windows NT server configured as a file and printer server might have one 166 MHz or faster Pentium or Pentium Pro processor, 48M or 64M of RAM, and a few gigabytes of disk storage.

Part

I

Ch

5

■ A typical Windows NT server configured as an application server might have two or four 166 MHz or faster Pentium Pro processors, 128M or 256M of RAM, and 10G+ of RAID disk storage.

The first system might be a perfectly adequate application server in a small network with light application server demands, whereas the second configuration might not even be an adequate file server in a large location with hundreds of clients using it to share files and printers.

The second factor to consider is how much fault tolerance you need and how much you're willing to pay to get it. If your server supports critical applications, place fault-tolerance, redundancy, and maintenance issues at the top of your list of priorities. Modern purpose-built servers have many fault-tolerance features built in, including RAID disk subsystems, ECC memory, and redundant power supplies. If your application is truly critical, weigh the costs versus the benefits of providing complete redundancy, including one or more hot standby servers, standby power generators, and so forth.

The third factor to consider is whether to buy a new server or to convert an existing machine to run Windows NT Server 4.0. Particularly at smaller locations, the latter choice often seems attractive. Although it may seem that you can save money by just adding some memory and disk to an existing system, the reality is almost always that attempting to do so results in a server that costs nearly as much as a new purpose-built server and is substantially inferior to it.

Deciding on the Processor(s)   The fundamental nature of a server is determined by the type of processor it uses—and how many. Windows NT Server gives you a wide range of flexibility in making this choice. Windows NT Server runs on popular processors from Intel, DEC, IBM, and other manufacturers. The following sections examine the issues involved in selecting the processor that your server will use.

RISC-Based Servers   Windows NT Server 4.0 was designed from the ground up to be a processor-independent operating system. In addition to running on the Intel x86 series of processors, Windows NT Server 4.0 is available for several RISC processors from other manufacturers, including the DEC Alpha, the MIPS, and the PowerPC. Microsoft has stated that future versions of Windows NT will be available only for Intel and Alpha processors. Thus, DEC's Alpha series is your only long-term alternative to Intel processors.

Alpha processors usually outperform Intel processors at similar clock speeds and are available in models with substantially higher clock speeds than Intel's Pentium Pro and Pentium II. Servers built with Alpha processors, however, are substantially more costly than similarly configured Intel servers. Consider an Alpha-based server if performance, not cost, is your primary selection criterion.

N O T E   DEC announced in mid-March 1997 a 533MHz Alpha 21164PC processor priced below Intel's 200MHz Pentium Pro, but with substantially faster performance. Unlike the Pentium Pro, the 21164PC doesn't have an on-chip Level 2 cache, which explains at least a part of the reduced price. DEC's aggressive pricing indicates that Alpha servers are likely to reach price parity with Pentium Pro servers during 1997. ■

Intel Processors The Pentium traditionally has been the mainstream processor for Windows NT Server. It's available in versions running at 75 MHz, 90 MHz, 100 MHz, 120 MHz, 133 MHz, 150 MHz, and 166 MHz. The 90 MHz and 100 MHz versions are closely related, as are the 120 MHz and 133 MHz versions. When Microsoft released Windows NT 4.0, most purpose-built servers used one or two 133 MHz or faster Pentium processors.

The Pentium Pro offers some significant architectural and performance advantages over the Pentium when running 32-bit software, such as Windows NT Server. It shows up to 50 percent greater performance compared with the Pentium of the same clock speed. The Pentium Pro, designed from the ground up to be used in multiple-processor systems, allows the use of up to four processors without the additional complex and expensive multiprocessing circuitry required by the Pentium.

There's little doubt that the Pentium Pro is now the processor of choice for servers. When this book was written, multiprocessor versions of Pentium Pro systems were becoming common. Release of multiprocessor Pentium Pro servers was delayed by problems Intel encountered with support for SMP systems based on the Pentium Pro. Pentium Pro servers with one or two CPUs now are available from a multitude of vendors, large and small. For a new Intel-based server installation, 200 MHz or faster Pentium Pro(s) is the obvious choice.

N O T E Intel announced its Pentium II processor series on May 7, 1996. Pentium II processors, which include Intel's MMX multimedia extensions, mount on a snap-in Single Edge Contact (SEC) printed circuit card and come in 233-MHz, 266-MHz, and 300-MHz versions with 512K of on-card L2 cache. Initially, Pentium II processors are more expensive than Pentium Pro chips, primarily because of their faster clock speeds and new mounting method. By the end of 1997, it's likely that most high-end Intel-based servers will use multiple Pentium II processors. ■

Sizing Processor Cache Memory Processor cache memory (usually just called *cache*) consists of a relatively small amount of very high-speed memory interposed between the processor and the main system memory. Cache buffers the very high-speed demands of the processor against the relatively modest speed of the main system's DRAM.

All Intel Pentium processors have processor cache memory built in. This internal cache is called Level 1 (L1) cache. Pentium processors have 8K of L1 cache. Pentium Pro processors come with 256K or 512K of L1 cache. L1 cache is essential; without it, the processor would spend most of its time waiting for the slower main memory to provide data. 8K of L1 cache isn't enough to provide adequate performance.

The key determinant of a cache's value is its *hit rate*, which is simply a percentage expressing how often the required data is actually present in the cache when it's needed. Hit rate can be increased either by increasing the size of the cache itself or by improving the efficiency of the algorithms used to determine which data is kept in cache and which is discarded.

Increasing the cache hit rate to improve performance must be done by adding a second level of external cache, called Level 2 (L2) cache. Following are the three types of external L2 cache:

Part I
Ch 5

■ *Asynchronous (async) cache* is the least expensive and least desirable of the three. Async cache uses relatively slow and inexpensive cache RAM and provides the least caching benefit. However, everything is relative, and a system equipped with L2 async cache greatly outperforms no L2 cache at all.

■ *Pipeline burst cache* is in the middle. Somewhat more expensive than async cache and considerably more efficient, pipeline burst cache is found most commonly on low-end and mid-range servers. Upgrading from async cache to pipeline burst cache for very little money is often possible. Doing so is worth the expense.

■ *Synchronous (synch) cache* is by far the best-performing technology. Because it requires very high-speed synchronous SRAM chips, synch cache is quite expensive and is likely to be found on mid-range and high-end servers. The Pentium II uses SRAM on a separate cache bus, creating what Intel calls the Dual Independent Bus (DIB).

The question of how much L2 processor cache to get and of what type may be resolved by the server you choose. You may find that the amount and type of cache is fixed, or you may find that you have alternatives as to size and type. In general, prefer quality to quantity. A system with 128K of synchronous cache usually outperforms a system with four times as much asynchronous cache. If you're given the option, consider 128K of pipeline burst cache as a minimum for your single-processor Pentium server, but get 256K or 512K if you can. For Pentium Pro servers, specify 512K of L2 cache—preferably SRAM—despite the price premium.

Deciding on a Multiprocessor System   Windows NT Server 4.0 has native support for up to 32 processors in an SMP arrangement, although commonly available servers usually support only two or four processors, with a few servers offering support for eight. SMP increases the load capacity (most commonly simultaneous users) of server services, such as SQL Server 6+, which are optimized for SMP. Adding processors doesn't scale linearly—that is, a system with two processors isn't twice as fast, nor can it handle twice as many simultaneous database users as the same system with only one. This is because overhead is involved in managing work (threads) assigned to multiple processors and in maintaining cache coherency. In fact, under light load conditions, a multiprocessor server may be slower than a single-processor server because of this overhead. Experience has shown that a system with two processors is perhaps 70 or 80 percent faster than the system with only one processor with a well-written, multithreaded application under full load conditions. Equipping a system with four Pentium processors can be expected to result in a server about three times faster under full load than the same server with only one processor attempting to service the same load.

▶ **See** "Server Scalability," **p. 28**

Dual-processor system boards carry a modest price premium over the single-processor variety. Even if your current requirements are fully met by a single processor server, being able to add a second processor can mean the difference between having to upgrade the server and having to replace it.

Determining Memory Requirements   Servers run on memory. Every time Windows NT Server has to swap data from RAM to disk, you take a big performance hit. A server using a slow processor with lots of memory outperforms a server with a fast processor and less memory every time. Memory makes up a relatively small percentage of the overall cost of a typical server. The drastic price reduction for DRAM that occurred in early 1996 has made additional memory very affordable.

Memory can be designed with one or more extra bits that are used to increase its reliability. Parity memory has one such extra bit. A 30-pin parity SIMM is actually 9 bits wide rather than 8, with the extra bit assigned as a parity check bit. Similarly, a 72-pin parity SIMM is actually 36 bits wide rather than 32 bits, with the extra 4 bits used as a parity check. Parity can detect single-bit errors. When it detects such an error, the result is the infamous `Parity Check Error--System Halted` message.

TIP For clients, the future is no doubt non-parity memory. In fact, the Intel Triton chip set used by most Pentium system boards doesn't even support parity memory; it ignores the 9th bit if it's present. That's a clue, by the way. If the server you're considering for purchase uses the Triton chip set, you can be assured that the system board wasn't intended for use in a server.

Memory reliability is so important in a server that even parity memory isn't a sufficient safeguard. Borrowing from mainframe technology, manufacturers of Intel-based servers have begun using Error Checking and Correcting (ECC) memory. ECC memory usually is 11 bits wide, dedicating 3 error-checking bits for each 8 data bits. ECC memory can detect and correct single-bit errors transparently. Single-bit errors are the vast majority, so ECC memory avoids nearly all the lockups that would otherwise occur with parity memory. Just as important, ECC memory can at least detect multiple-bit errors and, depending on the type of ECC memory, may also be able to correct some of these errors. Although ECC memory may lock the system on some multiple-bit errors, this is far preferable to allowing data to be corrupted, which can occur with simple parity memory.

Although ECC memory is 11 bits wide or wider, its implementations normally use standard SIMMs and simply allocate an extra SIMM to provide the ECC function. This allows the system to use standard SIMM memory rather than proprietary and costly memory designed especially as ECC memory. ECC memory is usually standard on enterprise-level servers, standard or optional on departmental-level servers, and may be optional or not available on workgroup-level servers. You should install ECC memory if possible.

Although Windows NT Server loads in 16M of system memory, you won't have much of a server with only that amount. As with any network operating system, the more memory, the better the performance. Following are recommendations for the initial amount of RAM you need to install for different server environments:

- If you're configuring your Windows NT server to provide only file and print sharing, consider 32M the absolute minimum. 48M is a better starting point, and if your server supports many users, you should probably consider equipping it with 64M to start.

- If your Windows NT server provides application server functions, such as SQL Server or Exchange Server, consider 64M as the bare minimum and realize that some products may not run in this little memory. 128M is usually a safer starting point; specify 256M for SQL Server and Internet Information Server 3+ running on a single Web server with heavy traffic.

Part
I

Ch
5

■ As a general rule of thumb, calculate what you consider to be a proper amount of memory given your particular configuration and the software you plan to run, and then double it as your starting point. Monitor your server's performance, and add more memory as needed.

Consider the availability of SIMM sockets when you're configuring memory. Buy the densest SIMMs available for your server to conserve SIMM sockets. Choose two 32M SIMMs in preference to four 16M SIMMs. Bear in mind that the day may come when you have no more room to add memory without swapping out what you already have installed.

Choosing a Bus Type   All newly designed servers use the PCI bus; make sure that the server you buy uses PCI. All other bus designs for servers are obsolete, including EISA, VLB, and MCA buses. PCI still limits the number of slots available on a single PCI bus, so larger servers use either dual PCI or bridged PCI buses. These systems simply use supporting circuitry to double the bus or to extend a single PCI bus to provide additional PCI slots. Unless you must support a particular legacy ISA device, such as a telephony card, there's no need for ISA slots on a server system board.

Deciding on Intelligent I/O Subsystems   Intel has proposed an intelligent I/O subsystem for high-performance servers named I_2O (pronounced *eye-two-oh*). The objective of I_2O is to offload I/O interrupt processing to a separate CPU, such as Intel's venerable i960 RISC processor, to free the host CPU(s) to handle data processing chores. I_2O is designed to eliminate I/O bottlenecks by splitting device drivers into host and I/O components connected by a messaging layer. I_2O consists of the following components:

■ *Hardware Device Modules (HDMs)* are OS-independent device driver components written by hardware manufacturers to the I_2O standards.

■ The *OS-Specific Module (OSM)* provides an interface between the operating system, such as Windows NT, and HDMs. OS vendors, such as Microsoft, are responsible for writing the OSM.

■ The *Real-Time Operating System (RTOS)* is the firmware that programs the I/O CPU. Intel licenses the runtime version of Wind River's IxWorks RTOS for I_2O with its i960 I/O processors.

More than 100 companies have joined the I_2O Special Interest Group (SIG). Microsoft, Novell, and The Santa Cruz Operation are among the operating system vendors developing OSMs at the writing of this book. SuperMicro was the first manufacturer to incorporate I_2O on a dual Pentium Pro system board. Adoption of I_2O by name-brand server vendors for their high-end product lines is expected by mid-1997.

ON THE WEB

You can get additional technical information on I_2O at **http://developer.intel.com/design/IIO/ response/it/techno.htm**. Details on SuperMicro's initial product are at **http://www.supermicro. com/dhnpres2.htm**.

Specifying Disk Subsystems   The disk subsystem comprises the disk controllers and fixed-disk drives of your server. Choosing a good disk subsystem is a key element in making sure that your server performs up to expectations. The following sections discuss SCSI-2 fixed-disk drives and SCSI-2 host adapter cards. Tape backup systems, which almost always are SCSI-2 devices, are the subject of Chapter 8, "Installing File Backup Systems." EIDE (Enhanced Integrated Drive Electronics) drives are designed for desktop PCs and don't belong in a server.

Small Computer System Interface (SCSI)   Small Computer System Interface (SCSI, pronounced *scuzzy*) is a general-purpose hardware interface that allows the connection of various peripherals—hard-disk drives, tape drives, CD-ROM drives, scanners, printers, and so forth—to a host adapter that occupies only a single expansion slot. You can connect up to seven such devices to a single host adapter and install more than one host adapter in a system, allowing for the connection of a large number of peripheral devices to a system.

SCSI is the dominant drive technology in servers for the following two reasons:

- SCSI supports many devices and device types on a single host adapter. Expansion slots are precious resources in a server. SCSI's capability to conserve these slots by daisy-chaining many devices from a single host adapter is in itself a strong argument for its use in servers.

- SCSI provides request queuing and elevator seeking. Other drive technologies process disk requests in the order in which they're received. SCSI instead queues requests and services them in the order in which the data can be most efficiently accessed from the disk.

N O T E   Request queuing isn't a particular advantage in a single-user, single-tasking environment because requests are being generated one at a time by a single user. In Windows NT Server's multiuser, multitasking environment, however, queuing and elevator seeking offer major performance advantages. Rather than service disk requests in the order in which they're received, SCSI determines the location of each requested item on the disk and then retrieves it as the read head passes that location. This method results in much greater overall disk performance and a shorter average wait for data to be retrieved and delivered to the requester. ■

Part

I

Ch

5

SCSI is a bus technology. In fact, it's convenient to think of SCSI as a small LAN contained within your server. Up to eight devices can be attached to a standard SCSI bus. The SCSI host adapter itself counts as one device, so as many as seven additional devices can be attached to a single host adapter. Any two of these devices can communicate at any one time, either host to peripheral or peripheral to peripheral.

SCSI can transfer data by using one of two methods. Asynchronous SCSI, also referred to as *Slow SCSI*, uses a handshake at each data transfer. Synchronous, or Fast, SCSI reduces this handshaking to effect a doubling in throughput.

SCSI uses various electrical connections, differing in the number of lines used to carry the signal. Single-ended SCSI uses unbalanced transmission, where the voltage on one wire determines the line's state. Differential SCSI uses balanced transmission, where the difference in voltage on a pair of wires determines the line's state. Single-ended SCSI allows a maximum cable length of 3 meters for Fast SCSI and 6 meters for Slow SCSI. Differential SCSI allows cable lengths up to 25 meters. Single-ended SCSI is intended primarily for use within a single cabinet, whereas Differential SCSI allows the use of expansion cabinets for disk farms.

You should be aware of the following terminology used to refer to SCSI subsystems:

- *SCSI-1* uses an 8-bit bus connection and 50-pin D-Ribbon (Centronix) or D-Sub (DB50) external device connectors (25-pin DB25 connectors also are used). SCSI-1 offers a maximum data transfer rate of 2.5 M/sec asynchronous and 5 M/sec synchronous. SCSI-1 is obsolete.

- *SCSI-2* uses an 8-bit, 16-bit, or 32-bit bus connection. The data-transfer rates range from 2.5 M/sec for 8-bit asynchronous connections to 40 M/sec for 32-bit synchronous connection.

- *Fast SCSI* is a SCSI-2 option that uses synchronous transfers to double the data transfer rate compared with systems using Asynchronous SCSI. Fast SCSI requires a 50-pin Micro-D external device connector, which is considerably smaller than the D-Sub connector.

- *Wide SCSI* is a SCSI-2 option that uses a 16-bit or 32-bit wide connection to double or quadruple the data-transfer rate compared with the 8-bit wide connection used by SCSI-1. 16-bit Wide SCSI uses a 68-pin Micro-D connector for external devices. Fast and Wide SCSI-2 was the standard for server fixed-disk drives in 1996.

N O T E Wide SCSI lets you connect 15 SCSI devices to a single host adapter. Dual host adapters, such as the Adaptec AHA-3940UW Ultra Wide adapter, consist of two host adapters on a single PCI card, letting you connect up to 30 devices to two internal and one external SCSI cables. ▪

- *Ultra SCSI* is a subset of the SCSI-3 specification, which was pending approval when this book was written. Ultra is Fast SCSI with a doubled clock rate, which provides twice the potential throughput. Ultra and Ultra Wide SCSI host adapters are readily available, and delivery of large quantities of Ultra and Ultra Wide SCSI drives began in late 1996. Seagate, Quantum, IBM, and other major suppliers of fixed-disk drives supply Ultra Wide SCSI drives with capacities ranging from about 2G to 20+G. To prevent interference from transmission-line reflections, single-ended (standard) Ultra SCSI has a limit of four devices on a 3-meter cable or eight devices on a 1.5-meter cable. Ultra Wide SCSI is the obvious choice for new servers. Many of the newer Pentium Pro system boards include an on-board Ultra Wide SCSI port.

- *Ultra2 SCSI,* scheduled for commercial implementation in 1997, doubles Ultra SCSI's data transfer rate to 40 M/sec (16-bit) or 80 M/sec (32-bit). Ultra2 SCSI uses low-voltage differential (LVD) chip technology to provide the benefits of differential SCSI without requiring expensive discrete driver chips. Ultra2 SCSI's differential mode lets you connect up to 16 devices with a total cable length up to 12 meters. Although Ultra2 SCSI's initial applications will likely be capturing and editing digital video content, the large drive capacity and ability to chain up to 16 drives on a cable is attractive for creating very-high-performance RAID arrays.

SCSI Bus Termination and Cables Proper bus termination is essential for successful data transfer from SCSI devices to the SCSI host adapter card. You must terminate both the internal (ribbon cable) and external SCSI buses. If you're using only internal or only external devices, the adapter card's built-in termination circuitry must be enabled. Internal termination must be disabled if you connect a combination of internal and external devices. In most cases, you determine whether on-card termination is enabled by setting the adapter's BIOS parameters during the hardware boot process. Figure 5.18 illustrates SCSI termination for internal devices; Figure 5.19 shows termination of a combination of typical internal and external SCSI devices.

N O T E Internal devices include termination circuitry, which usually is enabled or disabled with a jumper. Drives that conform to the SCAM (SCSI Configured AutoMagically) specification don't require setting a jumper. You terminate external devices with a connector that contains the termination circuitry. Active (rather than passive) termination is necessary for Fast, Wide, and Ultra SCSI devices. ▪

FIG. 5.18
SCSI termination for internal devices.

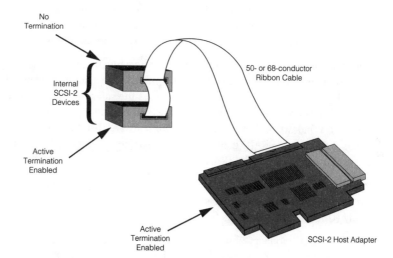

FIG. 5.19
SCSI termination for a combination of internal and external devices.

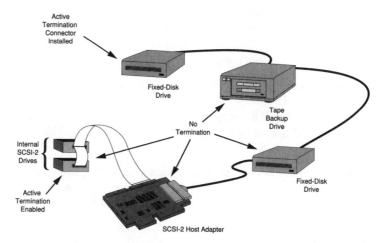

Part
I

Ch
5

Use of the highest quality SCSI cables—both internal and external—is almost as critical as proper termination, especially with Fast and Ultra SCSI. SCSI cables act as transmission lines, so a constant impedance is necessary to minimize reflection and attenuation of SCSI signals, especially at high data rates. Granite Digital is one of the few manufacturers of high-performance SCSI cables, terminators, cable testers, repeaters, and active switch boxes.

ON THE WEB

To find out more about Granite Digital's products, see **http://www.scsipro.com/**.

Disk Controllers   If you buy a purpose-built server, the choice of host adapter is straight-forward. Low-end servers normally are equipped with a standard SCSI-2 host adapter and offer few options, except perhaps the amount of cache RAM on the adapter. High-end servers normally ship with a host adapter, which provides various hardware RAID options. Mid-range servers usually offer a choice between a standard host adapter and an upgraded adapter with hardware RAID support. In each case, your options are limited to those host controllers offered by the server manufacturer. This is really no limitation at all, because server manu-facturers carefully balance their systems to optimize throughput with the chosen adapter.

When you choose a disk subsystem, consider how much disk redundancy you want to provide. At the simplest level, a Windows NT server might have a single host adapter connected to one or more disk drives. Disk redundancy increases the safety and performance of your disk sub-system at the cost of requiring additional disk drives and more complex host adapters or CPU overhead. Windows NT's built-in support for software RAID (Redundant Array of Inexpensive Disks) and hardware RAID controllers is the subject of Chapter 7, "Setting Up Redundant Arrays of Inexpensive Disks (RAID)."

Providing Power Protection   All this expensive hardware does you no good whatsoever un-less you keep it supplied with clean, reliable AC power provided by an uninterruptible power supply (UPS). A UPS performs the following two functions:

- It supplies auxiliary power to keep your network components running when the mains power fails. UPSes vary in how much power they supply, the quality of that power, and for how long they can supply it.

- It conditions the mains power to protect your equipment against spikes, surges, drops, brownouts, and electrical noise, all which can wreak havoc with your servers, clients, and active network components.

Understanding UPS Types   The original UPS designs comprised a battery, charging circuitry, and an inverter. The load—your equipment—is never connected directly to mains power but is instead powered at all times by the inverter, driven by battery power. The battery is charged constantly as long as there is mains power (see Figure 5.20). This type of UPS is called a *true UPS*, or an *online UPS*.

An online UPS has several advantages. First, because the load is driven directly by battery power at all times rather than switched to battery when mains power fails, there's no switch-over time. Second, because there's no switch, the switch can't fail. Third, full-time battery operation allows the equipment to be completely isolated from the AC mains power, thereby guaranteeing clean power.

FIG. 5.20

Power flow in an online UPS.

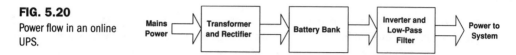

Balanced against these advantages are a few drawbacks. First, an online UPS is expensive, often costing 50 to 100 percent more than alternatives. Second, because an online UPS constantly converts mains AC voltage to DC voltage for battery charging and then back to AC to power the equipment, efficiencies are often 70 percent or lower, compared to near 100 percent for other methods. In large installations, this may noticeably increase your power bill. Third, battery maintenance becomes a more important issue with a true UPS, because the battery is in use constantly.

The high cost of online UPS technology led to the development of a less expensive alternative that was originally called a *standby power supply (SPS)*. Like an online UPS, an SPS includes a battery, charging circuitry, and an inverter to convert battery power to 120-volt AC. Unlike the online UPS, the SPS also includes a switch. In ordinary conditions, this switch routes mains power directly to the equipment being powered (see Figure 5.21, top). When the mains power fails, the switch quickly transfers the load to the battery-powered inverter, thus maintaining power to the equipment (see Figure 5.21, bottom).

FIG. 5.21

A standby power supply with mains power (top) and powering the server during a power outage (bottom).

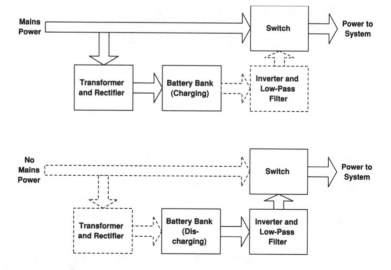

A simple SPS functions in only two modes. When mains power is at or above the minimum threshold voltage required, it's passed directly to the computer. When mains power voltage falls below the threshold, the SPS switches to battery power. This means that each time a sag or brownout occurs, your systems are running on battery power. A typical simple SPS may switch to battery if the incoming voltage drops below 102 volts—a relatively common occurrence.

A line-interactive SPS adds power-conditioning functions to monitor and correct the voltage of the incoming mains power. When a sag or brownout occurs, the line-interactive SPS draws more current at the lower voltage in order to continue providing standard voltage to your equipment without using battery power. A typical line-interactive SPS may continue to provide standard AC voltage to your equipment without using battery power when mains power voltage drops as low as 85 volts, thereby reserving its battery for a true blackout situation.

Understanding UPS Specifications   The three critical elements of a UPS are how much power it can provide, of what quality, and for how long. The first two are determined by the size and quality of the inverter circuitry. The third is determined by the size of the battery connected to the UPS.

The VA (volt-ampere) rating of a UPS determines the maximum amount of power that the UPS can supply and is determined by the rating of the components used in the inverter circuitry of the unit. For example, an SPS rated at 600 VA can supply at most 5 amps of current at 120 volts. Trying to draw more than 5 amps overloads and eventually destroys the inverter circuitry.

The second essential issue in choosing a UPS is the quality of power it provides, which is determined by the design of the inverter circuitry. Nearly all online UPSes and the better-grade SPSes provide true sine-wave output from their inverters. Less expensive units with lower-quality inverters provide only an approximation of sine-wave output, using square wave, modified square wave, or sawtooth waveforms. Any of these departures from true sine-wave output puts an additional burden on the power supply of connected components, causing overheating of the component power supply and making its failure more likely. Don't settle for less than true sine-wave output in your UPS.

The third essential issue in choosing a UPS is how long it can continue to provide backup power for a given load. This is determined by the type and amp-hour rating of the battery. The amp-hour rating is simply the product of how many amps of current the battery is rated to provide times the number of hours it can provide that current.

Sizing a UPS   Calculating UPS loads and runtimes is imprecise at best. Servers and other components, even when fully configured, usually draw considerably less power than the rating of their power supplies, which are rated for the maximum load the system can support. Even nominally identical components can vary significantly in their power draw. Loads vary dynamically as tape drives, Energy Star compliant monitors, and other components come on- and offline.

Although you can use commercially available ammeters in an attempt to determine exactly what each of your components really draws and size your UPS accordingly, few system managers do so. Most elect to simply sum the component wattages (applying the power factor correction for components with switching power supplies), add a fudge factor for safety, and then buy the next size up.

Managing UPS Systems Manageability is another issue you need to consider when choosing a UPS. There are two aspects to UPS manageability, as follows:

- Any but the most inexpensive UPS makes provision for interaction with the network operating system, allowing the UPS to signal the server to shut down gracefully when backup power is about to run out, and thereby avoiding disk corruption and other problems that result from a sudden unexpected loss of power.

  Windows NT Server provides this function directly, but only for supported UPS models. Check the latest version of the Hardware Compatibility List to verify that your UPS is supported. Even if it isn't, the UPS manufacturer may provide software that runs on Windows NT Server 4.0 to add this functionality.

- True remote management is provided by an SNMP agent included with the UPS. This allows the UPS to be monitored, tested, and controlled from a remote-management client. If you're running such a remote-management package to control other aspects of your network, make sure that the UPS model you choose is supported by your management software package.

From Here...

This long chapter covered the three primary categories of hardware required to set up a Windows NT network: network cabling, active network components, and server systems. Ethernet was recommended as the media-access method, 10BaseT or 100BaseT for cabling, ISA NICs for 10BaseT clients, and PCI NICs for 100BaseT clients and servers running either 10BaseT or 100BaseT. Guidelines for choosing Pentium- and Pentium Pro-based servers, along with recommendations for SCSI-2 drives and host adapter cards, were included. The chapter concluded with a description of the two basic types of uninterruptible power supplies.

The following chapters provide further information on the topics discussed in this chapter:

- Chapter 6, "Making the Initial Server Installation," guides you through Windows NT Server 4.0's setup application, with emphasis on preparing you to answer the questions posed in the setup dialogs.

- Chapter 7, "Setting Up Redundant Arrays of Inexpensive Disks (RAID)," describes how to choose between software and hardware RAID implementation and how best to take advantage of Windows NT Server 4.0's software RAID capabilities.

- Chapter 8, "Installing File Backup Systems," explains the tradeoffs between different types and formats of backup systems and how to manage server backup operations to ensure against lost data in case of a fixed-disk failure.

- Chapter 19, "Managing Remote Access Service," explains how to select and install modems, as well as configure Windows NT Server 4.0's RAS component to support dial-in access to shared network resources by mobile users.

Part

I

Ch

5

Deploying Windows NT Server 4.0

6   Making the Initial Server Installation   173

7   Setting Up Redundant Arrays of Inexpensive Disks (RAID)   215

8   Installing File Backup Systems   257

9   Understanding the Windows NT Registry   291

10   Using TCP/IP, WINS, and DHCP   321

11   Configuring Windows 95 Clients for Networking   351

12   Connecting Other PC Clients to the Network   399

CHAPTER 6

Making the Initial Server Installation

One primary selling point of Windows NT Server 4.0 is its ease of installation. A "standard" installation, using default values, on a new server computer takes less than 30 minutes. But Windows NT Server 4.0 is such a powerful and flexible operating system that a one-size-fits-all "standard" installation procedure is sure to shortchange some users or, in the worst case, deprive all users of the potential capabilities of Windows NT Server 4.0.

The process of installing a network operating system starts long before you put the distribution CD-ROM into the drive. This is especially true for Windows NT Server 4.0, because you have several decisions that shouldn't be made while staring at an installation question in a dialog on-screen. If your server is now running another operating system, you have many more decisions to make than if you're installing Windows NT on a brand-new computer. If you're installing Windows NT Server 4.0 for the first time, you should read this chapter thoroughly before touching the door of the CD-ROM drive. ■

Pre-installation planning

Windows NT Server 4.0 provides many installation options. Advance planning is the key to efficient use of the Setup program.

The basic installation process

You can install Windows NT Server 4.0 from the CD-ROM in less than 30 minutes, if you know the pitfalls to avoid.

Operations after installation

After you complete the basic Setup operation, you can add additional services, alter drive partition properties, and create RAID mirror sets or stripe sets.

Service Pack updates

Microsoft periodically issues Service Packs (SPs) to update Windows NT. Installing the latest SP improves server security and assures compatibility with new and upgraded services.

Fixed-disk failure recovery

The files generated by the Windows NT 4.0 Resource Kit's DiskProbe and DiskMap utilities are essential to recover from a boot sector or catastrophic fixed-disk failure.

Gathering Information and Making Decisions

You must consider several major issues before you start to install Windows NT Server 4.0. Are you installing Windows NT Server over another operating system? Are you familiar with all the hardware contained in or attached to your server? Is your computer already connected to a network (perhaps in a peer-to-peer configuration), or are you installing Windows NT Server 4.0 and a new network at the same time? The following sections cover each issue.

N O T E If you're upgrading Windows NT Server 3.5+ to version 4.0, the installation process is very close to automatic. All your existing settings—including Registry entries, users, groups, and services—are preserved. Thus, much of the advice in the following sections doesn't apply to a Windows NT upgrade. The most important change involves the new hardware device drivers required for version 4.0. Be sure to review the "Knowing Your Hardware" section before upgrading. ■

Preparing to Upgrade from Another Version of Windows

If you're running Windows 3.1, Windows for Workgroups 3.11, or Windows 95 on your server, it's a reasonably good bet that you plan to continue to use existing files (and possibly applications) after you install Windows NT. For example, you may be sharing database files that you plan to share from Windows NT Server 4.0. In this case, you must tread very carefully during the installation procedure.

N O T E It's an uncommon practice to run conventional end-user Windows applications on a production Windows NT server. If you're upgrading a PC used as a peer-to-peer server in a Windows 95 or Windows for Workgroups 3.1+ environment, it's recommended that you devote the server PC entirely to Windows NT Server. Uninstall Windows 95 applications, such as Microsoft Office 95 or 97, before installing Windows NT to conserve disk space. (You must reinstall Office 95 or 97 applications to run them under Windows NT Server or Workstation.)

If you're upgrading from 16-bit Windows or Windows 95, install Windows NT in its own folder (\Winnt), not your existing \WINDOWS directory or \Windows folder. By doing so, you can easily delete the old operating system files after completing the Windows NT Server installation. ■

In addition to accessing existing files, do you want to be able to continue to use the existing operating system? As a rule, running two operating systems on a server (called *dual-booting*) is very dangerous. You don't want people to be able to boot the server into DOS/Windows or some other operating system, bypassing all the security procedures you've instituted under Windows NT Server. If someone with access to the room that holds the server can boot it into another operating system, that person can access (read and change) any file that operating system can read. Further, dual-booting precludes the use of NTFS (NT File System) for volumes that other Windows versions must be able to access.

Assuming that you want to keep all the old files but not use the old operating system, do you want your old settings preserved and used in Windows NT Server? You need to know the answers to these questions before you begin the installation procedure.

N O T E Some decisions you make during installation, such as deciding whether the computer will be a domain controller or a server, can't be undone without completely reinstalling Windows NT Server. If you're installing Windows NT Server 4.0 in an existing Windows domain, you must know the role that the new server plays in the domain—Primary Domain Controller (PDC), Backup Domain Controller (BDC), or plain server. If you're installing Windows NT Server over an existing version, the server role is predefined. If you install over Windows NT Workstation, you're limited to a plain server installation if you want to preserve your existing settings. Before you start an upgrade, make sure that the server is connected to the network and the network connection is active. Later, the section "Choosing to Install as a Domain Controller" explains these roles. ■

Before proceeding with the Windows NT Server installation on a PC that shares folders, back up at least the shared folders to tape or to another PC with adequate disk space. Backing up to tape and to another PC is the best insurance against tape drive or media failure. Backing up to another PC is particularly important if you have a backup tape drive that isn't supported with a new Windows NT 4.0 driver. Later, the section "Backing Up Data on an Existing Computer" discusses backup operations in greater detail.

Knowing Your Hardware

The Setup program that installs Windows NT Server provides automatic hardware detection, but you need to answer questions about your hardware and make decisions before you start the installation process. The most important question about any hardware component you plan to use is this: Is the hardware component supported by Windows NT Server? If it isn't supported, you may have to install custom Windows NT drivers provided by your hardware manufacturer.

The product documentation that accompanies the retail version of Windows NT Server 4.0 includes the Hardware Compatibility List (HCL) booklet. Updates to the HCL are provided at regular intervals at the following locations:

- On the Web at **http://www.microsoft.com/ntserver/info/hwcompatibility.htm**
- By FTP, on **ftp.microsoft.com**, in the directory /bussys/winnt/winnt-docs/hcl
- On CompuServe, in the **WINNT** forum, Library 1
- On CompuServe, in the **MSWIN32** forum, Library 17

ON THE WEB

A Microsoft white paper for Windows NT Server 3.51 that explains HCL terminology and how to use the HCL is available at **http://www.microsoft.com/syspro/technet/boes/bo/winntas/technote/mscompt.htm**. Most of the content of the white paper is applicable to Windows NT Server 4.0.

Be sure to check all the hardware in your system against this list before you begin to install Windows NT Server. If a hardware component you plan to use isn't on the list, you must obtain a 32-bit Windows NT driver. If such a driver isn't supplied with the hardware, contact the vendor or manufacturer to obtain an updated Windows NT 4.0 driver.

Part
II
Ch
6

CAUTION

Don't assume that because your current hardware is supported by an earlier version of Windows NT that it's supported by Windows NT 4.0. The device driver architecture has been substantially changed in version 4.0. Check the Hardware Compatibility List and obtain a driver, if you need one, before you begin the installation process.

 T I P Microsoft offers Ntcomp.exe, a hardware compatibility testing tool that you can use to verify whether your hardware can run Windows NT Server 4.0. Ntcomp.exe creates two floppy disks; you boot from the first disk, and then insert the second disk when requested. You get a green light indicator if your PC can run Windows NT 4.0, a yellow light if Ntcomp.exe can't determine its compatibility, and a red light if you can't install Windows NT 4.0 on the machine. Ntcomp.exe runs in 8M of RAM and doesn't test for the required amount of RAM to run Windows NT 4.0.

 ON THE WEB

You can download Ntcomp.exe from **http://www.microsoft.com/KB/ARTICLES/Q163/0/03.HTM**.

Drivers for Legacy SCSI Host Adapters   Some less common hardware that was fully supported in earlier versions of Windows NT is now slightly less supported. You need a driver disk for older SCSI host adapters, but you can build the driver disk from files supplied on the Windows NT Server 4.0 CD-ROM. The following SCSI host adapters require you to create a driver disk:

- Always IN-2000
- Data Technology Corporation 3290
- Maynard 16-bit SCSI Adapter
- MediaVision Pro Audio Spectrum-16
- Trantor T-128 and T-130B
- UltraStor 124f EISA Disk Array Controller

To create the driver disk, format a floppy disk and copy all the files from the driver folder to this disk. The CD-ROM driver folder is one of the following:

- \drvlib\storage\retired\X86 for 486, Pentium, or Pentium Pro machines
- \drvlib\storage\retired\MIPS for machines with a MIPS RISC processor
- \drvlib\storage\retired\ALPHA for machines with a DEC Alpha processor
- \drvlib\storage\retired\PPC for IBM/Motorola PowerPCs

Label the disk as the driver disk for retired storage drivers for Windows NT Server 4.0, and keep it ready to use during the installation.

Fixed-Disk Drive(s)   Windows NT Server supports SCSI and IDE devices (primarily fixed-disk drives, CD drives, and tape drives), as well as other mass-storage devices, including the SCSI RAID drive arrays discussed in Chapter 7, "Setting Up Redundant Arrays of Inexpensive Disks (RAID)." Windows NT Server automatically detects mass storage devices during the installation processes and assigns these devices logical drive letters, beginning with C:.

As part of the installation process, you can partition your fixed-disk drives or ask Windows NT Server to respect the existing partitions. After the drives are partitioned, you install a file system on each partition. When you partition a drive, it appears to the operating system as two or more smaller drives, usually called *volumes*. The first partition of each physical fixed disk is assigned a drive letter in sequence; the remaining partitions are then assigned drive letters.

The two main reasons for partitioning a drive are that it's to be accessed by more than one operating system, or that you want to use drive letters as a convenient way to organize the drive. Partitioning a server drive for dual-boot operation is uncommon, because dual-booting production servers isn't a recommended practice.

Some examples of partitioning for organizational reasons include the following:

- *Network access permissions.* Rather than assign these on a folder-by-folder basis, you might find it more convenient to partition the drive to permit access to all the folders of one partition and deny access to others.
- *Backups.* Different partitions, each accessed by its own drive letter, might be on a different backup schedule.
- *Controlling disk space use.* Put a folder or group of folders that should be restricted to a limited size on a relatively small partition. Disk full messages automatically limit users' ability to store additional files. Windows NT Server 4.0 doesn't include a quota system for allocating disk space to users; several third-party tools, such as QuotaAdvisor and Quota Server, provide user and group disk space quotas.

ON THE WEB

You can get more information on QuotaAdvisor from **http://www.wquinn.com** and on Quota Server from **http://www.argent-nt.com/qs.html**.

Part

II

Ch

6

If your drive is already partitioned and you plan to use the files that are kept on it, maintain the existing partitions. You can't repartition a drive without losing the information stored in the partition. If the first partition is smaller than 150M or the volume is compressed, you won't be able to maintain the existing partitions and will have to back up the files, repartition the disk, and then restore the files into the new partitions. You should have at least 150M of available uncompressed disk space to install Windows NT Server 4.0.

Each partition has an assigned *file system*, a method of storing and organizing files. You can use the following two file systems with Windows NT Server 4.0:

- *NTFS*, the Windows NT File System, allows long file names and handles security well. The files are accessible to DOS, 16-bit Windows, or Windows 95 programs if they're run under Windows NT, but aren't accessible to such programs if the machine is running DOS, Windows 3.x, or Windows 95.

Your server shouldn't be running two operating systems, so NTFS is your file system of choice. There's no practical limit to the size of an NTFS partition. NTFS minimizes the amount of slack (unusable space due to the use of large clusters to store small files) and lets you compress drives, folders, or individual files to conserve disk space.

■ *FAT*, the 16-bit File Allocation Table, works with various operating systems (primarily DOS) but isn't as robust or secure as NTFS. 16-bit FAT partitions are limited to a size of 2G. If, for example, you use a Seagate ST15150W 4.3G Barracuda drive with the FAT file system, you must create a minimum of three partitions to gain access to all the drive's capacity. You would use a FAT file system on a dual-boot system, which isn't recommended for servers.

N O T E   OEM Service Release (OSR) 2 of Windows 95 offers the option of using a 32-bit version of the FAT file system, called FAT32. The retail version of Windows 95 doesn't include the FAT32 option and OSR 2 is officially offered only to computer assemblers for preinstalling Windows 95 on their PCs. The primary reason for providing FAT32 is to overcome the 2G partition size barrier of DOS and to allow the use of a smaller cluster size in order to reduce the percentage of slack on large fixed-disk drives. NTFS has neither the 2G partition limit nor the slack problem.

Windows NT 4.0 doesn't support FAT32 and won't recognize volumes formatted as FAT32. If you're upgrading a Windows 95 PC that uses FAT32 to Windows NT 4.0, you must FDISK and reformat at least the C: partition to an active DOS FAT16 boot partition when installing Windows NT 4.0. To make the disk space in other FAT32 partitions accessible to Windows NT, you delete and re-create the partitions, and then format the partitions to FAT16 or NTFS. ■

The C: volume—the active system partition on the first internal hard disk of all RISC systems and most x86 systems—is the Windows NT system partition. The system partition contains a specific set of files, such as Ntdetect.com, Ntldr, and Boot.ini, used to start Windows NT Server and can't be compressed. The system partition can't be part of a volume set or a stripe set during installation. If this restriction poses a problem for you, set aside a 300M (minimum 150M) system partition; the rest of the drive can be partitioned more flexibly. Alternatively, you can install on a different partition the \Winnt folder, which contains the Windows NT 4.0 system files not required for the boot process. Most Windows NT Server users install all the system files on the C: partition.

N O T E   Microsoft recommends at least a 300M FAT system partition for systems that don't require full operating system security. This space is used for Windows NT installation, pagefile, and (if desired) DOS or Windows 95 installation. Microsoft says that the advantage of this configuration is that you can copy over drivers or boot files in the event of virus, file corruption, or upgrade problems. If you provide physical security for your server, you can follow Microsoft's advice. Otherwise, use NTFS to preclude unauthorized persons from booting the server from a DOS disk and gaining covert access to its files. ■

If you won't be using any other operating system and don't have any organizational reasons for partitioning a single drive, you can make each drive one partition that uses NTFS. It's much more common, however, to share files from a partition other than that which contains the system files and paging file. If your drive contains files that you want to use after the installation, don't change the partitioning or the file system; instead, convert the file system to NTFS after the installation.

N O T E It's possible to convert the file system to NTFS as part of Setup and preserve all your existing files. However, if you quit Setup without completing all the steps, the conversion won't be done. It's less confusing—and usually quicker—to leave the file system alone until Setup is complete, and then convert it to NTFS.

To convert a FAT (DOS, Windows 3.x) or HPFS (OS/2) partition to NTFS and preserve all the files on it, open a Command Prompt window (sometimes called a *DOS box*) from the Start menu by choosing Programs and MS-DOS Prompt. Type **convert *d*: /fs:ntfs** (where *d*: is the drive you want to convert) in the text box and press Enter. If you try to convert the system partition (typically C:), you'll be warned that the Convert program can't get exclusive access, but that the conversion can be scheduled as part of the next restart. Choose Yes, and then restart Windows NT Server to proceed with the conversion. Several additional restarts are required before the conversion completes. ■

CD-ROM Drive   Installing Windows NT Server 4.0 requires access to a CD-ROM drive, preferably with a SCSI interface. You don't need one of the high-speed 12X or 16X drives designed for multimedia applications; a 2X drive is quite adequate for installing server software, including Microsoft BackOffice components. It's possible to install Windows NT Server 4.0 over the network from a CD-ROM drive of another machine, but such a process is cumbersome.

Network Adapter   The Setup software detects most ISA and PCI network adapter cards (NICs) automatically, but asks you to confirm the IRQ number, I/O base port address, memory buffer address, and other network card settings. PCI NICs configure themselves during the PC's startup process, similar to Windows 95's Plug and Play feature for newer ISA adapters. If you installed the ISA NIC yourself, you have the required information that you need to accept the proposed values or enter new values. If you didn't install the NIC, be sure to obtain the required network card settings from your computer vendor or the technician who installed the card.

N O T E Windows NT 4.0 doesn't support Windows 95's Plug and Play (PnP) features of ISA adapters, so it might not recognize PnP ISA NICs that configure properly under Windows 95. Most PnP ISA NICs have a jumper setting that lets you disable PnP and software- or jumper-configure the adapter to a specific IRQ and I/O base address. Most internal PnP modems also provide manual settings. Manually configuring your ISA PnP cards is the safest approach for a server. If you're upgrading from Windows 95 to Windows NT Server 4.0 and have PnP ISA adapters installed, you can install the Pnpisa.drv driver from the \Drvlib\Pnpisa\X86 folder of the Windows NT Server 4.0 CD-ROM after you make the initial server installation. Pnpisa.drv doesn't provide dynamic resource management, but it does let you specify I/O addresses and IRQ levels to avoid conflicts. For more information on installing and using Pnpisa.drv, refer to the Readme.wri file in \Winnt\System32. ■

Part
II

Ch
6

If the PC has a network card, you can use Control Panel's Network tool or Windows Setup to display the current IRQ and I/O address range settings for your network card. Figure 6.1 shows the Resources page of the property sheet for an Intel EtherExpress 16/16TP ISA network card. Click the Advanced tab to display additional settings for the network adapter. Windows 3.1+'s Network Setup dialog leads to dialogs that display similar information.

FIG. 6.1

The Resources page of the property sheet for a typical network adapter displaying the current IRQ and I/O address range.

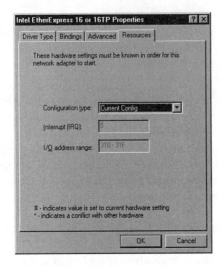

Providing Names and Identification

During the installation process, you must provide the following names and numbers:

- Your name, or the name of the corporate contact responsible for this copy of Windows NT Server 4.0
- The name of the organization
- The product ID from the inside back cover of the Windows NT Server Installation Guide or from a sticker on the case of the CD-ROM
- The computer name assigned to the server

The computer name must be unique on your network—it must not match a group or domain name on your network. The computer name also can't be longer than 15 characters. Make sure that you know the names of the computers, domains, and groups on your network, and the way that names are assigned. In some environments, computers are named for the person or department using them, for the function they serve, or according to a more whimsical pattern, such as names of flowers or precious stones. Make sure that the name for this server makes sense in your environment. If you aren't sure about it, contact the person who named the other machines to confirm your choice of a server name. If your entire network is new, take a moment to think of a logical scheme for naming machines on the network.

Choosing to Install as a Domain Controller

A *domain* is a group of computers that have the same administrative rules—for example, all the computers that belong to one department. There may be several domains on a network. Using domains makes administration much easier, because you don't need to set up an account for each user on each server. One machine, the *Primary Domain Controller (PDC)*, maintains the domain account database. Other machines on the network that don't have copies of the account database are *domain servers*, also called *plain servers*. Computers with copies of the account database are called *Backup Domain Controllers (BDCs)*. Chapter 17, "Distributing Network Services with Domains," discusses in detail the architecture of Windows NT Server domains.

If you plan to set up multiple Windows NT servers, you must decide which server acts as the PDC, which server(s) act as the BDC(s), and which server(s) act as the domain servers. (This decision isn't easily reversible—in fact, making some changes of domain status requires a full reinstallation of Windows NT Server.) For new installations, you install Windows NT Server 4.0 as the PDC first, and then add BDCs and domain servers while the PDC is operating and connected to the network.

When you install Windows NT Server on the first server of a domain, you must create a PDC and name the domain. Choose a simple name that isn't being used by an existing domain, if any. Avoid punctuation and spaces in the domain name, but an underscore may be used to improve readability. The OAKLEAF domain, used by many of the examples of this book, includes two servers (OAKLEAF0 and OAKLEAF3) and three workstations (OAKLEAF1, OAKLEAF2, and OAKLEAF4). Users of all client computers connected to the network must know the name of the domain controller(s) to which each client connects.

Backing Up Data on an Existing Computer

Before you undertake a step as significant as changing the operating system (or reinstalling your current operating system), you must back up the data on your system. Chapter 8, "Installing File Backup Systems," shows you how to organize backups and use the Windows NT backup system with tape drives. If the machine stores vital data, the safest approach is to make two backups, each on different media. For example, back up to tape, and then copy the crucial files over the network to a different hard drive in case the tape is unreadable. In many instances, backup tapes are found to be unreadable, either due to a defect in the tape or tape drive, or because the format of the tape is specific to the prior operating system.

Another problem, mentioned earlier in the chapter, is the current lack of Windows NT 4.0 drivers for many low-end backup tape drives. If your computer is already running Windows NT and is a Primary Domain Controller, make sure that the Backup Domain Controller has an up-to-date copy of the domain account database.

After the backup, if the drive is compressed, you must decompress it. Whether the drive is compressed with Stacker, DoubleSpace for DOS 6, or DriveSpace for Windows 95, you must undo the compression before you try to install Windows NT Server 4.0 on the drive. Don't try

Part

II

Ch

6

to decompress before the backup; one disaster the backup ensures against is data loss during decompression. After you decompress the drive, however, back up the decompressed files that you want to preserve.

If the drive is compressed, it's because not all the files fit without compression. Thus, it's likely that the first step in the decompression process is to remove some files temporarily, preferably by moving them to another server. Moving files without inconveniencing users of vital data isn't a simple task and requires planning. For example, users must be warned to save and close files by a certain time, and the files must be unavailable for a short time after that. Don't forget to clear at least 148M (preferably 200M) of free drive space to install Windows NT Server 4.0.

In addition to the 148M of free drive space, you need a blank 3 1/2-inch disk that's labeled *Windows NT Server Emergency Repair Disk* and is further identified with the name of the Windows NT server. You don't need to format the disk; the Setup program formats the disk for you. If your A: drive accommodates 2.88M disks, use an unformatted disk or a disk formatted to 1.44M (don't use a disk preformatted at 2.88M).

Starting the Basic Installation

After you make your decisions, gather the necessary information, and prepare your computer, you're ready to run Setup. The setup process involves many steps and a substantial number of `Press Enter to Continue` prompts. Most decisions don't need detailed explanations, but some steps are critical for a satisfactory installation.

Following is a summary of steps that comprise the installation process:

1. Create boot disks, if necessary.
2. Start Setup from the boot disks, a network share, or from an existing operating system.
3. Choose to install or repair.
4. Detect mass storage.
5. Choose to upgrade or install from scratch.
6. Confirm basic system information.
7. Set up your fixed-disk drive(s).
8. Watch the copying process.
9. Identify the user, company name, and licensing terms.
10. Choose the type of domain controller.
11. Select the locale.
12. Set the administrator password.
13. Check for the Pentium floating-point division bug.
14. Fine-tune the installation.
15. Join the network.

16. Finish Setup.

17. Configure virtual memory.

18. Install IIS.

19. Set the time and date.

20. Configure your display.

21. Create the emergency repair disk.

22. Restart the computer for the last time.

The following sections describe each step in detail.

Running the Setup Program

If you're installing Windows NT Server 4.0 on a computer with a CD-ROM drive supported by Windows NT Server, insert the first Setup disk, labeled *Setup Boot Disk*, in the A: drive. Then insert the Windows NT Server CD-ROM in the CD-ROM drive, reboot the computer, and skip to the section "Choosing to Install or Repair." Setup uses disks for the first part of the installation procedure, and then automatically detects and uses the CD-ROM drive for the rest of the installation.

The following sections pertain to installing Windows NT Server over the network from another server or from a CD-ROM drive that isn't supported by Windows NT Server but is supported by DOS or Windows 95.

Creating Setup Boot Disks   The Windows NT Server 4.0 distribution CD-ROM claims to be bootable, but relatively few CD-ROM drives or system BIOSes support bootable CD-ROMs. In most cases, you receive a `Can't Find NTLDR` message if you try to boot from the CD-ROM. To install Windows NT Server 4.0 on most PCs with a supported CD-ROM but no operating system installed, you must use Setup boot disks to install a minimal version of Windows NT on the PC. If you have the distribution CD-ROM but no boot disks, have three formatted, blank 3 1/2-inch disks ready and follow these steps to create the required boot disks:

1. Insert the distribution CD-ROM in the CD-ROM drive of a PC running DOS, Windows NT, or Windows 95. If the Setup splash screen appears, close it.

2. At the command prompt, log on to the CD-ROM drive and change to the \I386 folder (or the folder for the appropriate platform).

3. Type `winnt /ox` (DOS or Windows 95) or `winnt32 /ox` (Windows NT) and press Enter to start the Setup program.

4. Accept or correct the path to the CD-ROM files, and then press Enter or click Continue. Windows NT displays the dialog shown in Figure 6.2.

5. Insert a disk labeled *Windows NT 4.0 Server Setup Disk #3* in the A: drive and click OK to continue.

6. When prompted, insert the remaining two disks, *Windows NT 4.0 Server Setup Disk #2* and *Windows NT 4.0 Server Setup Boot Disk*, and press Enter or click OK.

Part
II

Ch
6

FIG. 6.2

The Windows NT 4.00 Server Installation/ Upgrade dialog for creating Setup boot disks.

Windows NT 4.00 Server Installation/Upgrade

Setup requires you to provide three formatted, blank high-density floppy disks. Setup will refer to these disks as "Windows NT Server Setup Boot Disk," "Windows NT Server Setup Disk #2," and "Windows NT Server Setup Disk #3."

Please insert one of these disks into drive A:. This disk will become "Windows NT Server Setup Disk #3."

Click OK when the disk is in the drive, or click Cancel to exit Setup.

OK   Cancel

The disks are necessary if your Windows NT installation becomes corrupt, requiring use of the emergency repair disk created later in the installation process. Leave the Setup boot disk in the A: drive and restart your computer, booting from the A: drive. Skip to the "Choosing to Install or Repair" section to continue with the description of the setup process.

TIP If you receive a Non-System or Disk Error message when attempting to start from the Setup boot disk, check the system BIOS to make sure that drive A: is listed as a boot drive. You also receive this error if the boot disk is defective; in this case, make a new set of boot disks.

Installing from a Network Server Installing over the network is more common for workstations, which may not all have CD-ROM drives, than for servers. You must have an operating system installed and a functional network connection to install Windows NT Server from a network server. To install Windows NT Server 4.0 over the network, you need another machine on the network with either the Windows NT Server CD-ROM in a shared CD-ROM drive, or a prepared Windows NT Server installation folder with a copy of one of the three folders from the CD-ROM.

- ■ \I386 contains all the files needed to install to computers that use Intel 80486 and Pentium processors. These processors are members of the Intel I386 family.
- ■ \Mips is for RISC machines using Silicon Graphics MIPS processor(s).
- ■ \Alpha is for RISC machines using DEC's Alpha processor family.
- ■ \Ppc is for PowerPCs from Apple, IBM, and others that use the PowerPC RISC processor.

To prepare an installation folder for network setup of Windows NT Server, follow these steps:

1. Create a folder on the server with an appropriate name, such as Installnt.
2. Share the folder, giving the Administrator group at least Read access.
3. Create a subfolder with the same name as the one you copy from the CD-ROM—for example, \I386.
4. Copy the installation files from the CD-ROM's subfolder to the new installation subfolder.

To start Setup from the new computer after the Windows NT installation folder is created, or to run from an unsupported CD-ROM drive, you follow almost identical steps:

1. Label four blank 3 1/2-inch disks as *Setup boot disk, Setup disk 2, Setup disk 3,* and *Windows NT Server Emergency Repair Disk.* Add the name of the computer to the emergency repair disk. You can use the other three disks for installation on other computers; the emergency repair disk is specific to the computer on which the installation is made.

2. Start the machine where Windows NT Server is to be installed by using the existing operating system, which must either support an attached CD-ROM drive or have a network connection.

3. If the machine is using DOS, change to the network drive and directory or to the CD-ROM drive and directory that holds the installation files. If the machine is using Windows 95, open an Explorer window for the network or CD drive. If the machine is using a previous version of Windows NT, open a File Manager window for the network or CD drive. (If the machine runs Windows 3.1x, exit Windows, if necessary, and perform the installation from DOS.)

4. From DOS, run WINNT.EXE by typing `winnt` and pressing Enter. From earlier versions of Windows NT, run Winnt32.exe by double-clicking the file in File Manager. From Windows 95, run Winnt.exe by choosing Run from the Start menu, typing `winnt`, and then pressing Enter.

5. When requested, provide the drive and directory name for the location of the installation files.

6. Insert each formatted setup disk when prompted. The WINNT or WINNT32 program copies the required setup files to the disks.

7. Continue the setup process as described later, starting with the section "Choosing to Install or Repair."

Installing from an Existing Operating System   If you have a compatible CD-ROM drive and operating system, you can start the Setup program from DOS or Windows as follows:

■ For Windows NT 3.5+ or DOS/Windows 3.1+, use the method described earlier in the "Creating Setup Boot Disks" section, but omit the `/ox` command-line parameter.

■ For Windows 95, inserting the CD-ROM in the drive uses AutoPlay to display the splash screen shown in Figure 6.3. (This splash screen also appears if you insert the CD-ROM into a PC running Windows NT 4.0, which also supports AutoPlay.)

In either case, you're prompted to confirm the location of the files on the CD-ROM; then Setup copies all the setup files to a temporary folder, requests you to reboot, and begins the installation process. You need approximately 250M of free disk space to store the installation copies and the working copies of the files. When the files are copied, remove the CD-ROM from the drive (and the disk, if any, in your A: drive), and reboot the computer. On restarting, the Boot.ini file automatically starts the Windows NT setup process.

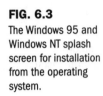

FIG. 6.3
The Windows 95 and
Windows NT splash
screen for installation
from the operating
system.

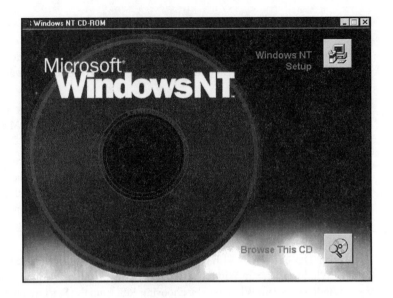

Choosing to Install or Repair

If you use the setup disks, Setup runs from the setup boot disk, requests a second disk, and then displays a blue (DOS) screen titled Windows NT Server 4.0 Setup: Welcome to Setup, which asks whether you want to repair an existing Windows NT Server installation or continue with a full installation.

TIP At any point in the setup process where you're prompted for input, pressing F1 provides Help. Pressing F3 exits Setup. Input options are summarized at the bottom of the screen.

The first part of this chapter covers installing Windows NT Server 4.0 for the first time, so press Enter to continue the installation process. You're requested to insert Setup Disk #2 and press Enter.

N O T E One of the last setup steps is building the emergency repair disk, which you use to repair a damaged or corrupted installation of Windows NT Server. The repair process is described in the section "Repairing the Windows NT Server Operating System Installation" near the end of this chapter. ■

Detecting Mass Storage

The mass-storage devices (SCSI and IDE adapters) on your system ordinarily are detected automatically during the setup process, and Setup automatically installs the required driver(s). You can skip the automatic detection process and select the driver yourself. The automatic detection process is somewhat slow, so if you're installing Windows NT Server on a number of similar machines, you might want to select the mass-storage driver manually.

N O T E   If your device isn't on the supported hardware list, the automatic detection process won't find it. Also, some hardware combinations cause the automatic detection to hang the Setup program. If Setup hangs, reboot the computer, start Setup again, and bypass the automatic detection process. Allow automatic detection at least five minutes before assuming it has hung. ■

Press Enter to proceed or S to skip the automatic detection process. After Setup detects hardware and loads drivers, you're given an opportunity to confirm the hardware that was detected and to add more mass-storage devices, if necessary. If you press S to add devices manually, a list of drivers known to Windows NT appears; choose a driver from the list. If you have a driver disk, choose Other and insert the disk when prompted. When all the drivers are loaded, press Enter to continue.

N O T E   IDE and ESDI drives are detected at this point too, but not shown to you. You set up your fixed-disk drives later in the Setup process. ■

If you receive a `Setup could not find any hard drives` message, you probably have a boot sector virus. See the section "Recovering from Fixed-Disk Failures," near the end of this chapter, for actions to take in case of a Master Boot Record problem. If your boot drive is a SCSI drive, make sure that the SCSI chain is properly terminated and that the SCSI BIOS for the boot drive is enabled.

After selecting mass-storage devices, the Windows NT End-User License Agreement (EULA) appears. To read the license agreement, press Page Down 13 times, and then press F8 to accept the terms of the agreement. If you don't press F8, installation terminates.

You're then requested to insert the distribution CD-ROM into the drive and press Enter.

Choosing to Upgrade or Install from Scratch

If an earlier version of Windows NT is detected on your hard drive, at this point you can choose to upgrade, preserving as many of your old settings as possible. If you choose to upgrade by pressing Enter, skip to the "Watching the Copying Process" section. If you choose to install from scratch by pressing N, or if a previous version wasn't installed on your hard drive, the installation continues as described in the following section.

Confirming Basic System Information

Setup reports the basic computer hardware it has detected and asks for your confirmation of its findings. You may want to change the keyboard layout at this point (if, for example, you're using a Dvorak or other alternative layout), but the balance of the reported information is almost invariably correct. To change an entry, use the up and down arrows to highlight it, and then press Enter. A list of choices appears; choose the one you want with the up and down arrows and the Enter key. When the hardware summary is correct, highlight No Changes and press Enter to continue.

Part

II

Ch

6

Setting Up Your Fixed-Disk Drives

After you watch the detection of mass-storage devices, add more drivers if needed, and then confirm your hardware, you next must make Windows NT Server work with your fixed-disk drive(s). This involves the following basic steps:

1. Partition the drive(s).
2. Format with the right file system.
3. Specify the installation folder.

The following sections describe each of the preceding steps in detail.

 If you receive an Unable to find a valid partition message, use DOS's FDISK to verify that the boot drive has a valid primary DOS partition. If you have more than one SCSI adapter, make sure that the SCSI BIOS of the adapter not connected to your boot drive is disabled. A boot sector virus also can cause this message.

Partitioning the Drive(s)   The first partition is the system partition. On RISC machines, the system partition must be drive C:, which is the preferred location for the system partition of x86 computers. If you have more than one partition, make sure that the first one (C:) has sufficient room for the system files (about 148M). As noted earlier in this chapter, you can elect to install the non-bootable Windows NT system files in another partition, if necessary, to reduce the C: partition disk space requirement.

Setup shows the partitions that already exist on your fixed-disk drive. Use the up and down arrow keys to highlight a partition or the unpartitioned space; then press D to delete it, C to create a partition in unpartitioned space, or Enter to choose it as the system partition.

Formatting with the Right File System   Next, choose a file system and optionally format the partition with that system. You can choose to format the partition with FAT or NTFS; keep in mind, however, that these two options destroy the data stored on the partition. If the partition is already formatted, you can elect to convert it to NTFS or retain the existing format. As noted earlier, unless you have a compelling reason to use the FAT format, choose NTFS.

Use the up and down arrows to highlight your choice (for example, Convert to NTFS) and press Enter to continue.

Specifying the Install Folder   Setup now needs to know where to put the Windows NT and system files. The default suggestion, C:\Winnt, ordinarily is satisfactory. You can, however, install these files in a folder of any name on a partition of the first physical (boot) drive. To change the folder name, press Backspace to remove the suggested name and type your chosen name.

At this point, Setup looks for previous versions of Windows on your machine. (If you formatted your system partition in the previous step, you wiped out any previous versions that were on the machine.) Rather than ask you to choose whether to upgrade or dual boot, Setup determines the answer based on whether you use the same folder. Following are your options when you choose the same or a different installation folder:

- If you have a previous version of Windows NT, installing in the same folder causes your old settings to be used in this new installation and the old version to be removed. Installing in a different folder allows you to dual-boot between the older version and Windows NT Server 4.0.

- If you have Windows 95, you can't migrate your settings and aren't allowed to use the same folder. You can dual-boot between Windows 95 and Windows NT Server 4.0.

- If you have Windows 3.x, you dual-boot regardless of the folder choice you make. If you use the same folder, your settings are migrated; if you use a different folder, you must specify new settings throughout the rest of Setup.

 T I P You don't want to dual-boot a server machine, so be sure to remove Windows 95 or Windows 3.x before reaching this step. If you want to remove an existing operating system at this point, exit Setup, delete Windows 95 or Windows 3.x, and restart the installation process.

Watching the Copying Process

Now that Setup can access your partitioned and formatted drive(s), and has established where the system files are to go, it's time to copy the files to the fixed disk. Before doing so, Setup offers to examine your fixed-disk drive for defects. Press Enter to allow the examination to proceed, or Esc to skip it. (If you're having trouble installing Windows NT Server and find yourself at this point in the install repeatedly, it's not necessary to repeat the examination every time.) After the examination is performed or skipped, Setup copies files to the folder chosen in the previous step. The time required to create the copies depends on the speed of the CD-ROM or network connection, and the performance of your fixed-disk drive.

> **N O T E** An error message during the copying process that indicates a checksum error between the file on the CD-ROM and that of your fixed-disk drive indicates a hardware problem. The most likely source of the problem is a damaged CD-ROM surface, dirt on the CD-ROM drive's optical components, a defective fixed disk, or a defective disk controller. Another less likely source of check-sum errors is improper termination of a chain of SCSI devices. Improper SCSI termination usually results in an installation failure before the copying process starts.
>
> Recovery from such an error depends on what happened and why. You may be able to correct the problem and choose Retry; more than likely you'll have to begin the Setup process again. If the CD is damaged, you must replace it. ■

When the copying process is complete, Windows NT Server is ready to run, but additional configuration information is required to finalize the installation process. At this point, you're prompted to remove a disk still in the A: drive. Also remove the CD-ROM. Press Enter to re-start the system.

Part
II

Ch
6

 T I P If Setup hangs during the file-copying process, your computer may be using reserved memory required by Setup. In your computer's system BIOS, disable 32-bit Enhanced File Throughput and Video Shadow

continues

continued

RAM, if enabled. Another source of the problem might be that Setup has used the wrong Hardware Abstraction Layer (HAL). Restart Setup; when the message Windows NT is examining your hardware configuration appears, press F5 to display the HAL menu. If you're installing Windows NT Server on a single-processor Pentium PC, choose the single processor HAL; if you have a different configuration, select Other and insert the HAL disk provided by the vendor of your system board.

After the computer restarts, the rest of the process proceeds under the operating copy of Windows NT Server. Setup's simple character-based interface is replaced with Windows NT-style dialogs, and you indicate choices by clicking dialog buttons instead of pressing keys. The Help and Exit Setup options remain available but are activated by dialog command buttons. Also, you use the Back and Next buttons to move through the Setup Wizard (as Microsoft calls this next stage of Setup). You're requested to insert the CD-ROM into the drive indicated in the Copy Files From text box, and then click OK to copy the additional files. After the files are copied, click Next to continue.

Identifying the User, Company Name, Licensing Terms, and Computer Name

Provide the full (first and last) name of the main user (usually you) and the company name, as discussed earlier in this chapter, if you aren't upgrading an existing Windows NT installation. Click Next to continue.

You must type the product ID from the inside back cover of the installation guide or from the sticker on the Windows NT Server 4.0 CD-ROM case. Click Next to continue. If you're upgrading an existing Windows NT Server installation, Setup copies files; skip to the "Specifying Creation of an Emergency Repair Disk" section.

The next step asks you to choose your licensing method—Per Server or Per Seat. Per Server licensing requires a client license for every simultaneous connection to this server; Per Seat requires a client license for every client machine in your installation. Which is better for you depends on how many clients and servers you have, and how many servers each client connects to at once. Here are some examples:

- If you have 100 clients that mostly run stand-alone and connect to a server only 10 at a time, you would need 100 client licenses under the Per Seat method, but only 10 under the Per Server method. Choose Per Server.

- If you have 100 clients and four servers, and every machine is connected to at least two servers at all times, you would need 200 or more licenses under the Per Server method but only 100 under the Per Seat method. Choose Per Seat.

After selecting the licensing method, click Next to enter the computer name for the server, which is limited to a maximum of 14 characters. The name you assign at this point appears to all other computers on the network. Press Next to continue.

▶ **See** "Licensing BackOffice Components," **p. 816**

Choosing the Type of Domain Controller

The Server Type dialog offers you three options:

- Primary Domain Controller
- Backup Domain Controller
- Stand-Alone Server

You must install the Primary Domain Controller before any other domain servers; this decision is difficult to reverse. The first Windows NT server you install in a network always is a Primary Domain Controller. Click Next to continue.

If this is the first server on your network, you're creating a new domain, so you name the domain at this point. (You should have already picked out a unique domain name.) If the domain already has a Primary Domain Controller, you can join the domain as a Backup Domain Controller. Make sure that the Primary Domain Controller is operational and that you know the administrator password for the domain. If you choose to install this server as a stand-alone server, the domain name is simply the domain you join.

No matter what server type you choose, Setup searches the network for existing domain names. For a Primary Domain Controller, Setup searches to verify that the new name is unique. For a secondary domain controller or a stand-alone server, Setup ensures that the domain name you supply exists.

Setting the Administrator Password

The Administrator account is used to manage this installation of Windows NT Server. Someone who knows the Administrator password can add and delete users, install and remove applications, and make any other system changes that might be required. When you install a Primary Domain Controller, you set this password. Choose a sensible password that's hard to forget yet difficult to guess. You enter it twice in this dialog; both entries must be the same, to rule out a slip of the fingers as you type it.

Dealing with the Pentium Floating-Point Division Bug

If your machine is an Intel Pentium-based computer, Setup checks for the known floating-point division bug. If you have a faulty chip, you're given the option of turning off the Pentium's floating-point operations and simulating them within Windows NT instead. Although the simulated calculations are much slower, they're always right, so you should choose to disable the hardware floating-point calculations. If your Pentium chip doesn't have a faulty floating-point module, you won't see this screen.

Specifying Creation of an Emergency Repair Disk

At the end of a successful setup, Windows NT Server saves the computer's configuration information to the disk so that if your fixed-disk drive becomes corrupted, you can recover your configuration information. At this point in the Setup process, you're asked whether you want to make an emergency repair disk later. Doing so is *strongly* recommended. Using the emergency repair disk is covered later in the section "Repairing the Windows NT Server Operating System Installation."

Fine-Tuning the Installation

If the computer is to be a dedicated server rather than a workstation, you can save disk space by skipping the installation of accessories such as CD Player, games, screen savers, wallpaper, and so on.

> **N O T E**   If you've installed Windows NT Server 4.0 on another computer, you can eliminate the Readme files from this installation. Before making this election, however, make sure that you have access to the Windows NT Server 4.0 Readme files on at least one computer. ■

Choose the components you want installed or not installed in the Select Components dialog. If you want to install part of a component, such as Multimedia, click the Details button to select individual applications. Click OK on the Details dialog to return to the list of components. When that list has each component selected, deselected, or partially selected as you prefer, click Next to move to the next stage of Setup.

Joining the Network

Now all of Setup is complete, except for setting up the network. Confirm that you want to go on to the network portion of Setup by clicking Next. You can't get back to earlier screens after moving to the network portion. You perform the following general steps for the network installation:

1. Describe your connection to the network.
2. Choose to install Internet Information Server.
3. Choose and configure a network adapter.
4. Choose protocols.
5. Choose services.
6. Confirm network bindings.
7. Start the network and join a domain.

Describing Your Connection to the Network   The first question Setup asks is how you connect to your network. If your machine has a network adapter card (as it almost certainly does), choose Wired to the Network. If you dial up to a network (an unlikely choice for Windows NT Server), choose Remote Access to the Network.

Choosing to Install Internet Information Server   Internet Information Server makes your information available over the Internet or a corporate intranet, and is discussed fully in Chapter 20, "Setting Up Internet Information Server 4.0." At this point in the Setup process, you specify only whether you intend to install it.

Choosing and Configuring a Network Adapter   Assuming that you have one or more network adapters, in the next step Setup detects them automatically. A functioning network adapter card is required for installation of a Primary Domain Controller or a Backup Domain Controller, but the network doesn't need to be operational at this point in the installation process.

Click Start Search to find the first adapter. If a second adapter is to be found, click Find Next to search for it. If you have an adapter that wasn't found, click Select from list to specify the card yourself. Click Next to move on.

Choosing Protocols   Next, choose one or more network protocols: IPX/SPX, TCP/IP, or NetBEUI. (This decision is discussed in detail in Chapter 4, "Choosing Network Protocols.") You can configure multiple protocols by checking more than one box in this dialog. The most common combination is NetBEUI and TCP/IP, unless you have an existing Novell NetWare network, in which case you should select all three protocols. You can add or remove network protocols with Control Panel's Network tool after installing Windows NT Server.

Choosing Services   You can choose to install any of these five network services:

- Internet Information Server
- RPC Configuration
- NetBIOS Interface
- Workstation
- Server

Adding new services after the fact is harder than adding them now, and you can use Control Panel's Services tool later to disable services that you don't want to run. You also can add or remove network services with the Services page of Control Panel's Network tool (see Figure 6.4). For most server installations, it's best to install all the preceding services at this point.

FIG. 6.4

Adding or removing network services in the Services page of the Network property sheet.

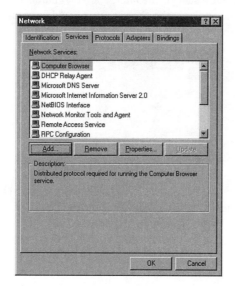

Part

II

Ch

6

Even more services are available if you click Choose From List:

- DHCP Relay Agent
- Gateway (and Client) Services for NetWare
- Microsoft DHCP Server
- Microsoft DNS Server
- Microsoft Internet Information Server
- Microsoft TCP/IP Printing
- Network Monitor Agent
- Network Monitor Tools and Agent
- Remote Access Service
- Remoteboot Service
- RIP for Internet Protocol
- RIP for NWLink IPX/SPX compatible transport
- RPC support for Banyan
- SAP Agent
- Services for Macintosh
- Simple TCP/IP Services
- SNMP Service
- Windows Internet Name Service

Network Settings Setup confirms that you're ready to install the adapters, protocols, and services that were selected over the previous few dialogs. Click Next, and you have the opportunity to confirm adapter settings, such as the interrupt (IRQ) number and I/O port address (see Figure 6.5). As discussed earlier in the chapter, you should know these settings before you start the installation procedure.

FIG. 6.5

Setting the interrupt number, I/O port address, and other properties for your network adapter.

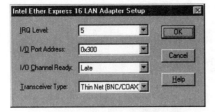

The Network Settings property sheet is next. You can display the same properties by using the Protocols page of Control Panel's Network tool (see Figure 6.6) after you install Windows NT

Server 4.0. To configure a protocol, select it from the list on the Protocols page and click the Properties button. If you're not sure how to use this property sheet, you can leave it for now and bring it up again after Windows NT Server is completely installed.

FIG. 6.6

The Protocols page of the Network property sheet for adding and configuring networking protocols.

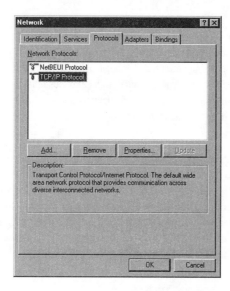

Each network protocol is configured separately. Figure 6.7 shows the configuration dialog for TCP/IP, the Microsoft TCP/IP Properties sheet.

FIG. 6.7

The IP Address page of the Microsoft TCP/IP Properties sheet.

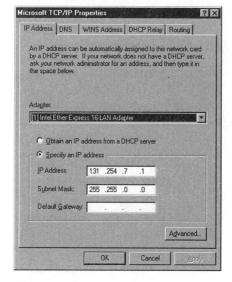

Part

II

Ch

6

On the IP Address page, set the IP address and subnet mask for your machine, or tell Windows NT to use DHCP (Dynamic Host Configuration Protocol) to assign an IP address dynamically. If you didn't establish these settings during your network planning process, get them from the person who did.

N O T E IP addresses uniquely identify machines on TCP/IP networks, such as the Internet, and are specifically assigned. You can't just arbitrarily choose an IP address; you must use an address that makes sense both within your network and, if applicable, on the Internet. The subnet mask is used to distinguish between IP addresses on your network and those that aren't. Like the IP address, the subnet mask is determined during the network planning process. The default gateway, if specified, must also be determined by a network administrator.

▶ **See** "IP Addresses," **p. 109** ∎

The DNS (Domain Name Service) page is used to control the way the server looks up domain names of other computers on a LAN or WAN (see Figure 6.8). You enter the IP addresses of one or more DNS servers accessible to your server. DNS servers translate a fully qualified domain name such as **www.mcp.com** into an IP address. You can get these addresses from the same person who provided your server's IP address. Some networks use multiple DNS servers, checking the local one first and then asking a remote DNS server if the name wasn't found in the local one. To change the priority of an IP address within the list, click the Up↑ or Down↓ buttons.

▶ **See** "Using the Microsoft DNS Server," **p. 671**

FIG. 6.8

The DNS page of the Microsoft TCP/IP Properties sheet.

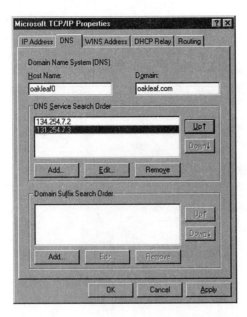

The WINS Address page describes the way that WINS (Windows Internet Name Service) looks up the domain names of other computers (see Figure 6.9). Enter the IP addresses of your primary and secondary WINS servers as provided by the person who told you your own IP address. For machines local to your network, you may want to use DNS and LMHOSTS services; if so, select their check boxes. The Scope ID is usually left blank; provide a Scope ID only if you're told to do so by your network administrator.

▶ **See** "Implementing Windows Internet Name Service," **p. 342**

FIG. 6.9

The WINS Address page of the Microsoft TCP/IP Properties sheet.

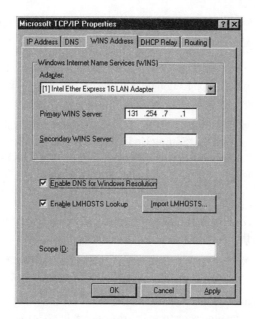

The DHCP Relay page identifies your DHCP servers. These servers manage IP addresses within your internal network, and you get their addresses from the person who told you to use DHCP rather than specify the IP address of your machine. If you need to adjust the other parameters on this page rather than accept the defaults, this person will tell you so.

▶ **See** "Implementing Dynamic Host Configuration Protocol," **p. 332**

The Routing page is relevant only to machines with more than one network adapter, each with its own IP address(es). If you turn on IP forwarding, your server can route traffic between the two networks.

Confirming Network Bindings   Now Setup gives you a chance to adjust your network bindings. If you aren't sure what network bindings are or why you might want to adjust them, leave them alone. The default bindings usually are adequate for installation and network startup.

You can enable and disable communications between services and adapters or protocols by double-clicking the service name, clicking the adapter or protocol, and then clicking the Enable or Disable button.

Part
II

Ch
6

Starting the Network and Joining a Domain   After Windows NT is configured for your network hardware, Setup loads the network software and establishes a connection to the network. Confirm that you've made all the choices by clicking Next, and then wait while the network starts. Setup asks for a domain name. Provide the same domain name you used earlier and wait while Setup searches the network. If you're joining a domain but not installing a Primary Domain Controller, provide the Administrator name and password here.

Finishing Server Setup

Click the Finish button to move to the final Setup steps. Setup creates Program menu groups and desktop icons, if you had an earlier version of Windows installed. Adding groups and icons doesn't install the applications or make any changes to the settings and configurations stored in Windows 3.1+'s .INI or REG.DAT files, or in Windows 95's Registry. You must rerun the application's Setup program if the application must be reconfigured for Windows NT or if you're upgrading from Windows 95.

Installing Internet Information Server   The dialogs and decisions involved in installing IIS are covered in detail in Chapter 20, "Setting Up Internet Information Server 4.0." (Microsoft supplies IIS 2.0 on the Windows NT Server 4.0 retail distribution CD-ROM. Chapter 20 describes how up update IIS 2.0 or 3.0 to 4.0.) To install only World Wide Web services, clear the Gopher Service and FTP Service check boxes. Click OK to continue. Accept the default folders for the service(s) you install, unless you have a specific reason to do otherwise. Click OK twice to continue and then to confirm your choices. Setup copies a number of files to your drive. Click OK when advised that you must establish an Internet domain name for the server.

In the Install Drivers dialog, select SQL Server in the Available ODBC Drivers list, even if you haven't installed SQL Server, and click OK to continue.

Setting the Time and Date   You now get a chance to set the time, date, and time zone. On the Time Zone page, select your time zone from the drop-down list. This list is arranged numerically according to the time difference from Universal Time (UT, formerly known as Greenwich Mean Time, GMT). Zones east of Greenwich, England, appear above it in the list. After you choose your time zone, the map of the world in this dialog scrolls so that your time zone is in the center. Windows NT Server knows the rules for use of Daylight Savings Time; make sure that the Automatically Adjust for Daylight Savings Time box is marked or cleared, as appropriate for your location.

> **N O T E** If your server's BIOS automatically adjusts for daylight savings time, Windows NT and the BIOS double the time change. In this case, clear the Automatically Adjust for Daylight Savings Time check box. Control Panel's Date/Time tool lets you enable or disable Windows NT's automatic daylight time change feature after installation. ■

On the Date & Time page, set the current date and time with the spin controls.

After Setup is complete and Windows NT Server is running, you can bring up this property sheet again with the Control Panel's Date/Time tool (see Figure 6.10).

FIG. 6.10

Using the Date/Time tool to set the time zone, and the current time and date.

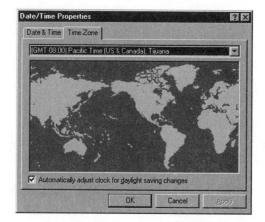

Configuring Your Display   Until now, the setup program has used standard VGA resolution (640¥480 pixels) with 16 colors. Windows NT attempts to detect the type of chip on your graphics adapter card. If you're using an adapter with a popular Windows graphics accelerator chip for which a DirectDraw driver is included with Windows NT, click OK when the Detected Display message box appears. Otherwise, you must install a driver from a disk provided by the graphics card supplier.

The Settings page of the Display Properties sheet (see Figure 6.11) lets you set a resolution and color depth suited to the combination of your graphics adapter card and video display unit (VDU). Some adapter cards provide additional features and controls on the Settings page. For a simple adapter, follow these steps to set your display properties:

1. Click the Display Type button to confirm that the correct graphics adapter card has been detected and change the selection, if necessary.

FIG. 6.11

Configuring the color depth and resolution of your display.

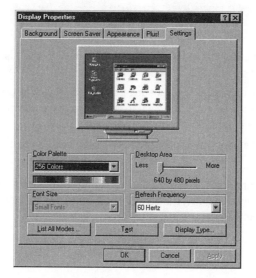

Part

II

Ch

6

2. Adjust the number of colors, resolution, and refresh frequency. For servers, a resolution of 800×600 pixels and a color depth of 256 colors is adequate. If you have a 15-inch or smaller display, the Large Fonts selection improves readability in 800×600 resolution.

3. Click the Test button to examine the results of the settings you choose.

4. Click OK to close the Display Properties sheet.

Creating the Emergency Repair Disk

At this point, Windows NT Server 4.0 is installed, configured, and ready to act as a network server. The final step is to create an emergency repair disk to use in case of a catastrophic failure. Any 3 1/2-inch disk will suffice, because Setup formats the disk before copying the files. Label the emergency repair disk with the server name you assigned and store it in a safe location.

Be sure to update your emergency repair disk frequently to keep the configuration data up-to-date. Your server's configuration is likely to change appreciably during the first few hours of use as you install applications, change users and groups, and so on. The pace of change slackens with time, but you should make a habit of updating your emergency repair disk regularly. To create an updated emergency repair disk, follow these steps:

1. Insert your original emergency repair disk or a new disk in drive A:. From the Start menu choose Run, type **rdisk** in the Open text box, and click OK to open the Repair Disk Utility dialog (see Figure 6.12).

FIG. 6.12
The Repair Disk Utility dialog.

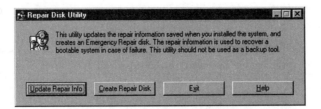

2. Click Update Repair Info to update the disk's content. (If you've lost your emergency repair disk, insert a blank disk and choose Create Repair Disk.)

3. Confirm your intent to update the existing emergency repair disk (see Figure 6.13). Click OK when asked whether you want to create an emergency repair disk, and then click OK to format the disk and create the updated version.

4. After the updated emergency repair disk is created, click Exit to close the Repair Disk Utility dialog.

It's a generally accepted practice to create a duplicate of the emergency repair disk for off-site storage, along with duplicates of driver disks you used during Setup. Driver disks also are needed during the repair process.

FIG. 6.13
Confirming the update
operation.

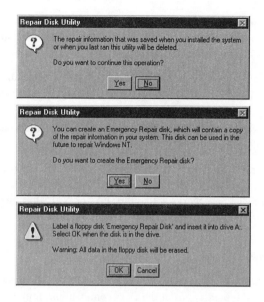

 T I P Add an entry to the Administrative Tools Program menu for Rdisk.exe to make the program easier to run after every significant configuration change.

Restarting the Server for the Last Time

After you make the emergency repair disk, Setup completes all the tasks required to install and configure Windows NT Server 4.0 and automatically restarts the server. Remove the emergency repair disk from the A: drive and remove the CD-ROM to allow the system to boot from the fixed-disk drive. (The boot process takes more time if you converted a FAT partition to NTFS as part of the setup process, because it's at this point that the format conversion occurs.) After Windows NT loads, press Ctrl+Alt+Delete to log on, and use the administrative account name and password you created earlier to log on to Windows NT Server. Your installation is complete.

Creating Software RAID Subsystems

If you intend to use Windows NT 4.0's software RAID implementation to provide fault-tolerant mirror set(s) (RAID 1) or stripe sets with parity (RAID 5), use Disk Administrator to create the RAID subsystem(s) at this point.

▶ **See** "Creating Windows NT Server Stripe and Mirror Sets," **p. 239**

Backing Up the Master Boot Record and Partition Boot Sector

Boot sector viruses and other maladies can render your Windows NT server unbootable. If a partition table, which defines the location(s) of partition(s) on a physical drive, is corrupt, you can't access the partition(s). Backing up the master boot record (MBR) and all partition boot

Part
II

Ch
6

sectors is especially important when you use mirror sets (RAID 1). The Windows NT 4.0 Resource Kits (for Server and Workstation) include the following two disk utilities for backing up and restoring the MBR and partition boot sector:

- *DiskSave* (DISKSAVE.EXE), a 16-bit DOS application that backs up and restores the MBR for disk 0 (usually the C: disk) and the partition boot sector for the system partition of disk 0.

- *DiskProbe* (Dskprobe.exe), a 32-bit Windows application that can back up and restore MBRs for all disks and partition boot sectors for all partitions.

Using DiskSave   You must use DiskSave, the simpler application, to recover from a boot sector virus on drive C: by replacing the MBR and partition boot sector. The binary format of the files created with DiskSave works with either FAT or NTFS formats. (You can't use DiskProbe for recovery of other drive's MBRs and partition boot sectors until you can start Windows NT.)

To use DiskSave, follow these steps:

1. Create a DOS boot disk, preferably with MS-DOS 6.22, by inserting a blank, formatted disk in drive A: and typing **sys a:** at the DOS command prompt. (Creating a boot disk from Windows 95 doesn't work.)

2. Copy DISKSAVE.EXE from your \Ntreskit folder or the Resource Kit distribution CD-ROM to the disk.

3. Boot your server from the disk and run DISKSAVE.EXE.

4. Press F2 to back up the MBR. Type a file name to save the file, such as DSK0MBR.DAT, and press Enter.

5. Press F4 to back up the partition boot sector. Type a file name to save the file, such as DSK0PBS.DAT, and press Enter.

Keep the disk in a safe place, preferably with your emergency repair disk, in case you need to recover your first drive. If you convert from FAT to NTFS or change the partition structure of drive 0, use DiskSave to create new copies of the MBR and the partition boot sector.

Using DiskProbe   Saving the MBR of more than one physical drive and partition boot sectors of more than the system partition of drive 0 requires DiskProbe. Saving MBRs and partition boot sectors of multiple drives is especially important when using RAID 1 or higher disk subsystems. Perform the following operations immediately after you establish the final configuration of your drive(s).

To use DiskProbe to back up the MBR(s) and partition boot sector(s) of your drive(s) and partitions after having installed the Resource Kit, follow these steps:

1. From the Start menu choose Programs, Resource Kit 4.0, Disk Tools, and DiskProbe to launch DiskProbe.

2. From the Drives menu choose Physical Drive to open the Open Physical Drive dialog. Figure 6.14 shows the dialog for a computer (OAKLEAF3) with three physical drives. Don't clear the Read Only check boxes.

FIG. 6.14

DiskProbe's Open Physical Drive dialog for a computer with three physical drives.

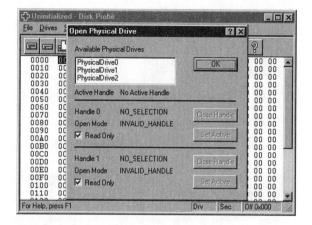

3. Double-click the drive whose MBR you want to copy in the Available Physical Drives list to set Handle 0 to the selected drive.

4. Click the Set Active button to make Handle 0 the active drive handle (see Figure 6.15), and then click OK to display the content of the MBR in DiskProbe's Bytes window.

FIG. 6.15

Activating Handle 0 for the selected physical drive.

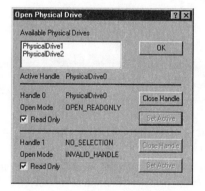

5. From the Sectors menu choose Read to open the Read Sectors dialog (see Figure 6.16). Accept the default values for Starting Sector (0) and Number of Sectors (1), and click the Read button to close the dialog. Data in the 512-byte MBR appears in DiskProbe's window.

6. From the File menu choose Save As to open the Save As dialog. Select the A: drive and type a distinguishing file name with a .dsk extension (see Figure 6.17). Click Save to save the MBR to the disk and close the dialog.

Part

II

Ch

6

FIG. 6.16

Selecting the master boot record (sector 0) to read.

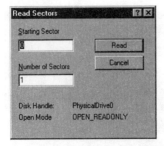

FIG. 6.17

Saving the master boot record to floppy disk.

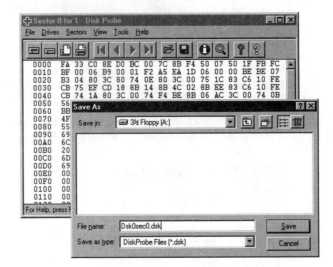

7. Repeat steps 2 through 6 for each physical drive. You must click the Close Handle button of Handle 0 before double-clicking another physical drive.

8. From the Drives menu choose Logical Drive to open the Open Logical Volume dialog. By default, the logical volume is the primary partition of the selected drive and is assigned Handle 1.

9. Click the Set Active button to make the logical volume of Handle 1 active (see Figure 6.18). Click OK to close the dialog.

10. From the Sectors menu choose Read to open the Read Sector dialog. Type 0 for the Starting Sector and accept the default Number of Sectors (1). Click the Read button to close the dialog. Data in the 512-byte partition boot sector appears in DiskProbe's Bytes window.

11. From the File menu choose Save As and save the partition boot sector data in a suitably identified file on a DiskProbe disk. (Use a disk other than the DiskSave disk to prevent inadvertent use of the wrong files when restoring.)

FIG. 6.18
Setting the active handle to Handle 1 for the partition boot sector of the C: drive.

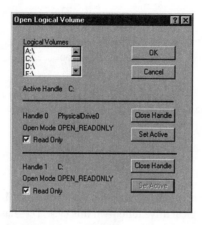

12. Repeat steps 8 through 11 for each of the partitions of your drives. You must click the Close Handle button of Handle 1, double-click the desired partition in the Logical Volumes list, and then click the Set Active button to choose a volume other than the primary partition of the physical drive specified by handle 1.

13. Close DiskProbe.

Store the DiskProbe disk in a safe place with the DiskSave and emergency repair disks.

Saving Fixed-Disk Configuration Data

The DiskMap command-line utility (Diskmap.exe) of the Resource Kit lets you print a record of the configuration of each fixed disk on your server. After you configure your drive(s), run **diskmap /d# > diskmap#.txt** from the command prompt, where **#** is the drive number, beginning with 0 for the first drive. Print the Diskmap#.txt files and keep them for future reference in case you need to recover a drive. Listing 6.1 shows the DiskMap output for the C: and D: volumes of OAKLEAF0, two equal-size NTFS partitions of a 4.3G Seagate Barracuda drive.

Listing 6.1 DiskMap's Output for a 4.3G Drive with Two Partitions

```
Cylinders  HeadsPerCylinder SectorsPerHead BytesPerSector MediaType
     522              255             63            512        12
TrackSize = 32256, CylinderSize = 8225280, DiskSize = 4293596160 (4094MB)

Signature = 0xf8069812
     StartingOffset     PartitionLength StartingSector PartitionNumber
*            32256          2146765824             63               1
       2146830336          2146765824             63               2

MBR:
          Starting                Ending        System    Relative    Total
   Cylinder Head Sector   Cylinder Head Sector     ID     Sector     Sectors
*        0    1    1          260  254   63       0x07         63    4192902
       261    0    1          521  254   63       0x05    4192965    4192965
```

continues

Listing 6.1 Continued

```
     0    0    0          0    0    0     0x00          0               0
     0    0    0          0    0    0     0x00          0               0

EBR: (sector 4192965)
         Starting                Ending       System    Relative    Total
   Cylinder Head Sector   Cylinder Head Sector   ID      Sector      Sectors
      261    1    1           521  254   63     0x07        63        4192902
        0    0    0             0    0    0     0x00          0               0
        0    0    0             0    0    0     0x00          0               0
        0    0    0             0    0    0     0x00          0               0
```

The asterisk (*) in the first entry of the MBR indicates the Windows NT system partition (C:).
Each additional partition with a logical drive letter—in this case, D:—has an extended boot
record (EBR).

Preparing the Server for Use

If you installed Windows NT Server on a machine that was running Windows 3.1x and installed
Windows NT in the same directory as before (typically, \WINDOWS), the Program Manager
settings for a user (other than the administrator) are initialized. In this case, the Programs
menu choices are based on the Windows 3.1+ settings that were present before Windows NT
Server was installed. For example, if there was a program group called Invoices under Windows 3.1+, each new user sees a Programs menu group called Invoices with the same program
items in it. Groups with names such as Main aren't migrated in this manner, because new
Windows NT Server equivalents of these Programs menu groups were created earlier in the
Setup process.

If the machine is to be a dedicated server with no access by ordinary users, running existing
applications is of no consequence. If the server is also used as a workstation (not a recommended practice in a production environment), create local accounts for the workstation users.
Log on to the other users' local accounts to oversee the migration of Windows 3.1+ applications
and fix any problems that appear before releasing the computer for others to use.

▶ **See** "Managing User Accounts," **p. 447**

> **N O T E** Setup doesn't install printers; you set up printers connected to your server (or shared by
> other servers or workstations) by using the Printers tool of My Computer. You must know the
> make and model of your printer, and the port to which it's connected. Check the Hardware Compatibil-
> ity List to verify that Windows NT includes a driver for your printer. ■

Installing Service Packs

When Microsoft releases the retail version of an operating system, such as Windows NT 4.0,
it's unusual (but not unknown) for the content of the distribution CD-ROM to change.

Microsoft handles bug fixes and minor updates to the distribution files with *Service Packs*. When this book was written, Microsoft had released the following three official and one unofficial Service Packs for Windows NT 4.0, plus *Hot Fixes*, all which apply to both the Workstation and Server versions:

- *Service Pack 1 (SP1)*, issued primarily for bug fixes related to intermittent file corruption
- *Service Pack 2 (SP2)* for additional bug fixes and upgrades required for IIS 3.0 and other Internet-related products
- *Service Pack 1A*, an unofficial downgrade of SP2 to accommodate pre-alpha versions of Windows NT 5.0 extensions distributed at the November 1996 Professional Developer's Conference
- *Hot Fixes*, patches for regression bugs introduced by SP2
- *Service Pack 3 (SP3)*, primarily hot fixes to SP2 and patches to remove potential security holes uncovered by hackers

SP3 is a major update to both the Server and Workstation versions of Windows NT 4.0. SP3 includes the following new or updated components for Windows NT Server 4.0:

- *Active Server Pages (ASP) 1.0b*, an update to the ASP components provided with the Internet Information Server (IIS) 3.0 upgrade to IIS 2.0
- *Microsoft Index Server 1.1* for indexing documents on the server, primarily (but not exclusively) for Web servers
- *Microsoft NetShow 1.0* for broadcasting illustrated audio and low bandwidth streaming video over intranets or the Internet
- *Microsoft FrontPage 97 Server Extensions*, an update to the FrontPage 1.1 version included with Windows NT 4.0
- *Crystal Reports for Internet Information Server* to create formatted reports from IIS log files

SP3 also adds the following security features to Windows NT Server:

- *SMB signing* provides increased security for the Server Message Block authentication protocol, better known as the Common Internet File System (CIFS).
- *Password filtering* lets network administrators test user passwords to ensure that they meet established security standards, such as inclusion of upper- and lowercase letters, as well as numbers.
- *Anonymous access restrictions* prevent unauthorized users from viewing lists of users and server share names, as well as the server's Registry.
- *Strongly encrypted user passwords* prevent even system administrators from obtaining access to passwords.
- *CryptoAPI 2.0* supports public-key and symmetric-key encryption, as well as certificate-based functions.

Part II
Ch 6

Microsoft's OEM licensees usually provide the latest available Service Pack when preinstalling Windows NT 4.0 Server or Workstation. Service packs sometimes are slipstreamed into Windows NT retail SKUs (stock-keeping units) without a change in packaging. The blue Windows NT 4.0 startup screen displays the latest Service Pack installed, with the exception of Service Pack 1A (shown as Service Pack 1) and Hot Fixes (not shown).

ON THE WEB

The latest Service Pack for Windows NT 4.0 is available for downloading at **http:// www.microsoft.com/NTServerSupport/Content/ServicePacks/Default.htm**. For links to lists of bugs fixed by current Service Packs, go to **http://www.microsoft.com/NTServerSupport/Content/ ServicePacks/Doineed.htm**. You also can obtain the latest service packs from **ftp:// ftp.microsoft.com/bussys/winnt/winnt-public/fixes/usa/nt40/**.

N O T E   Microsoft says you don't need to download service packs unless you experience a problem that's solved by the Service Pack. You need at least Service Pack 2 to run many newly upgraded members of the Microsoft BackOffice family. Service Pack 3 solves a number of Windows NT security issues and other problems that otherwise require hot fixes to SP2. ■

With the exception of the Service Pack 1A downgrade and Hot Fixes, Service Packs are cumulative. That is, if you install the latest Service Pack, all the fixes from the preceding Service Pack are installed and, presumably, prior regression bugs also are fixed. After bad experiences with regression bugs in Service Pack 2, Microsoft started limited beta testing of its Service Packs for Windows NT 4.0.

N O T E   Because of the very large size of the SP3 files, Microsoft also offers SP3 on a CD-ROM that you can order by telephone, fax, or mail. Ordering details are available on Microsoft's Service Pack Web page. ■

CAUTION

Don't try to install Service Packs directly from the CD-ROM. Instead, copy the contents of the appropriate install folder (i386 for Intel PCs) to a temporary folder on your PC's fixed-disk drive, and then run Setup.exe from this folder. Trying to install from the Service Pack 2 CD-ROM, as an example, caused many systems to fail during the reboot process and corrupted existing Windows NT Server 4.0 installations.

To install a Service Pack, download its .exe file from Microsoft's Web or FTP site, following any instructions provided in an accompanying Readme.txt file.

Repairing the Windows NT Server Operating System Installation

You can ruin your Windows NT Server software in various ways, and in some cases there's no way to recover. Making complete backups frequently is one way to reduce the recovery work involved; having an emergency repair disk is another.

This section assumes that you have a problem that prevents your server from booting successfully. It further assumes that the Last Known Good choice during the boot process is of no assistance, and that you can't edit the Registry remotely from another computer to adjust your settings. The last resort is to reinstall Windows NT Server from scratch—but first try using your emergency repair disk.

Gather (from off-site storage, if necessary) the emergency repair disk, originals or copies of the three Setup disks, any driver disks you used during the original installation, and the original CD-ROM used for installation. If any of these are missing, the repair process may be impossible. Follow these steps to attempt to repair the server:

1. Correct hardware problems, if any, and install replacement hardware as needed.

2. Boot from the Windows NT Server 4.0 boot disk, switch to Setup Disk 2 when prompted, and select Repair at the first prompt. You can select one or more of these choices:

   - Inspect Registry Files
   - Inspect Startup Environment
   - Verify Windows NT System Files
   - Inspect Boot Sector

   Move the highlight up and down through this list with the arrow keys, and press Enter to select or deselect the highlighted item. If you have no idea what's wrong, leave all the items selected. When your list is complete, highlight Continue (perform selected tasks) and press Enter.

3. Repair checks for mass storage devices by using the same process as Setup. The steps and keystrokes involved are identical to those discussed in the earlier section "Detecting Mass Storage."

4. When asked whether you have the emergency repair disk, press Enter if you do and Esc if you don't.

5. You're prompted for the original installation media (the CD-ROM) so that installed files can be compared to the originals.

6. After a partial file examination process, you have a chance to restore Registry files. You should try at least one repair attempt without restoring Registry files. If that doesn't make the system bootable, and no backups are available, repeat the repair process and restore the Registry files. All changes made since the emergency repair disk was created—whether you installed an entire application suite or changed a user's desktop settings—will be lost.

Part

II

Ch

6

7. Repair examines the remaining files on your fixed-disk drive and compares them to files on the installation media. If a file is found that varies from the original, you're given four choices:

- Press Esc to skip this file—that is, leave the version Repair thinks is corrupted on your fixed-disk drive.
- Press Enter to repair this file—that is, copy the original file from the CD-ROM to your fixed-disk drive.
- Press A to repair this file and all additional files Repair thinks are corrupted, with no more prompts.
- Press F3 to stop the repair attempt.

8. When the Repair process is complete, you're prompted to remove any disk still in the drive. Press Enter to restart the computer.

When a reboot is successful, you have the following problems to tackle:

- You must establish the cause of your catastrophic problem and make sure that it has been solved.
- You'll likely need to perform some reconfiguration, because some of your configuration information might be lost or reverted to old values.
- You must restore data from backup tape(s) if data files were lost.
- You must notify users of the problem and let them know whether they need to update their own configurations.

If you can't reboot the system and suspect corruption of your MBR or partition boot sector, use the techniques outlined in the next section.

If the Repair process doesn't work after several tries, you must reinstall Windows NT Server from scratch, and then reinstall applications as needed. In the event of serious corruption, you may lose all the user and group information for your server. A successful Repair operation takes about half as long as an install; always try a Repair first.

TIP If you have another Windows NT server acting as a Backup Domain Controller, you can regain your user and group settings by promoting the BDC to a Primary Domain Controller, reinstalling Windows NT Server as a BDC, and resynchronizing the two domain controllers.

▶ **See** "Promoting a Backup Domain Controller to a Primary Domain Controller," **p. 610**

Recovering from Fixed-Disk Failures

The reliability of fixed-disk drives and controllers has improved markedly during the past five years. Three- and five-year warranties for high-capacity SCSI drives are common, and vendors quote MTBF (mean time between failure) times in the hundreds of thousands of hours. Regardless of vendor promises, drives fail prematurely for various reasons, the most common of which is an excessively high temperature environment. Another cause of temporary (soft) drive failure is a power outage that occurs during a critical write operation. The following sections discuss recovery from soft failures of individual drives, which usually are recoverable, and hard failures of RAID drives, which require drive replacement.

System Drive Boot Failure

The most common cause of boot failure appears to be boot sector viruses introduced by executing files from infected floppy disks, a problem more likely with Windows NT Workstation than Server. It's conceivable, however, that a hacker could infect an Internet server with a boot sector virus. The probability of a boot sector virus infecting a server is small but finite. To recover from a corrupted boot sector, you need the copy of the master boot record for your system drive created with either the DiskSave or DiskProbe utilities, as described earlier in the "Backing Up the Master Boot Record and Partition Boot Sector" section.

> **CAUTION**
>
> Performing low-level binary write operations on fixed-disk drives is a hazardous activity. Using the wrong files with DiskSave or incorrect settings with DiskProbe can render your drive(s) inoperable. Use DiskSave and, especially, DiskProbe for recovery only after you exhaust all other resources.
>
> Drive failure occurs more commonly as a result of hardware problems than MBR corruption. Verify that all drives are powered up and spinning. Make sure that all cables are properly connected to the disk controller and drives, and check the cables for physical damage. Verify that SCSI drives are correctly terminated. Remove all drives but the boot drive from the SCSI chain, making sure that termination is correct, to determine whether another device is causing bus problems.

 TIP A common cause of unexplained disk failures is oxidation of a power or signal cable connector contacts. Before performing low-level write operations, remove and reseat the SCSI host controller (if installed), and remove and reconnect drive cables at each connection point.

To use DiskSave to replace your MBR or partition boot sector, follow these steps:

1. Boot the server from the DOS boot disk and run Disksave.exe from the disk.
2. Press F3 to restore the MBR for the system drive.
3. Type the saved MBR file name and press Enter.
4. Attempt to boot the computer from the system drive.
5. If the boot fails, reboot the server from the DOS boot disk and run Disksave.exe again.
6. Press F5 to restore the partition boot sector for the system drive.
7. Type the saved MBR file name and press Enter.
8. Again, attempt to boot the computer from the system drive.

Part
II

Ch
6

Multiple Drive Partition Table Corruption

You use DiskProbe to rewrite partition table information to multiple drives of a bootable server. A full discussion of reconstructing partition tables is beyond the scope of this book. The *Windows NT Workstation 4.0 Resource Kit* provides lengthy descriptions of disk restoration procedures, including restoring partition tables with DiskProbe.

RAID Subsystem, Volume Set, and Stripe Set Recovery

Theoretically, RAID subsystems with SCSI drives provide built-in, automatic restoration of the content of a failed drive. Recovery methods for hardware RAID subsystems depend on the RAID type and vendor-specific design features. Windows NT Server 4.0's software RAID systems include recovery capability. Recovering a software mirror set (RAID 1) is more complex than restoring a failed drive of a striped set with parity (RAID 5).

▶ **See** "Recovering a Software RAID 1 or RAID 5 Set," **p. 251**

Volume sets and stripe sets (RAID 0) aren't fault tolerant. If one drive fails, the entire volume fails. Thus, volume sets or stripe sets result in reduced reliability and shouldn't be used for production servers. In the event of corruption of the Registry, which contains configuration information for volume sets and stripe sets, you might not be able to gain access to volume sets or stripe sets. The *Windows NT Workstation 4.0 Resource Kit* provides the FTEdit program (Ftedit.exe) that lets you rebuild the Registry entries for volume sets and stripe sets. Because volume sets and stripe sets don't apply to servers, use of FTEdit isn't germane to this book. The Resource Kit includes a complete description of how to use FTEdit, which primarily is applicable to PCs running Windows NT Workstation 4.0.

Automating Workstation and Server Installation

Microsoft has gone to great lengths to provide system administrators with the ability to automate the installation of multiple copies of Windows NT 4.0 Workstation and Server. It's much more common to automate workstation than server installation, but the processes are quite similar and use the same utilities. This section briefly describes resources for automating the Setup process.

Automated setup requires that you create a server share to hold the contents of the appropriate folder of the distribution CD-ROM, typically \i386 for Intel PCs.

You use the following basic tools to automate the installation of Windows NT 4.0 Workstation or Server:

- *Answer files* (Unattend.txt) to provide the answers to questions that Setup asks during installation or upgrade operations
- *Uniqueness database files* (UDFs) that replace standard entries in Unattend.txt with computer- and user-specific information, such as the computer's NetBEUI name, IP address, logon ID, and temporary password

- *OEM* folder and subfolders for installing components that aren't included in the retail version of Windows NT 4.0
- *SysDiff* utility for automatically installing additional applications based on a snapshot (template) from a reference system
- *Network installation startup disks* to provide PCs without an installed operating system the ability to boot and connect to the network for the installation

Computers being upgraded from an earlier version of Windows NT use the `winnt32` command for setup; `winnt` is applicable to all other systems, including computers that start from a network installation startup disk. The typical command-line syntax for initiating an automated setup is

```
{\\server\share\¦d:}winnt[32] /b /u:answer.txt /udf:uniq_id,udf_file.txt
```

The `/b` parameter specifies that the boot files are installed on the fixed disk, not floppy disks. `/u:answer.txt` specifies the answer file; `/udf:uniq_id,udf_file.txt` specifies the Uniqueness ID for the computer and user, plus the name of the UDF. Both answer.txt and *udf_file*.txt must be located in the base folder of the distribution share. If you run Winnt from an AUTOEXEC.BAT file on a network installation startup disk, you must precede the `winnt` command with

```
net use d: \\server\share
cd d:
```

NetBEUI is the preferred transport protocol for installing Windows NT 4.0 from a network share because it's faster than IPX/SPX or TCP/IP. However, NetBEUI isn't routable, so you must use TCP/IP or IPX/SPX to install Windows 4.0 over a routed network.

Authoring Answer.txt files and using SysDiff is beyond the scope of this book. The *Windows NT Workstation 4.0 Resource Kit* provides an introduction to network installation of Windows NT 4.0.

ON THE WEB

A more detailed "Guide to Automating Windows NT Setup" is available as a Word .doc file from **http://www.microsoft.com/ntworkstation/info/Deployment-guide.htm**. Much of the 130-page "Guide" is oriented to pre-installation of Windows NT by assemblers of workstation and server PCs, but the "Guide" provides much more complete information than the Resource Kit on the installation automation process.

Part
II

Ch
6

From Here...

This chapter covered the basic steps for installing Windows NT Server 4.0, repairing an installation, recovering from disk drive failures, and automating installation of Windows NT 4.0 Server and Workstation. After you have your server up and running, more work needs to be done before your server can be considered completely installed. The remaining chapters of this part of the book cover other aspects of setting up your server and the clients that connect to the server:

- Chapter 7, "Setting Up Redundant Arrays of Inexpensive Disks (RAID)," explains how the RAID approach can make your system more reliable.

- Chapter 8, "Installing File Backup Systems," explains how to protect your network users from personal mistakes, as well as from hardware trouble.

- Chapter 9, "Understanding the Windows NT Registry," introduces you to the database that stores all the settings and configuration information you provide.

- Chapter 10, "Using TCP/IP, WINS, and DHCP," shows you how to plan for and implement TCP/IP networking, including use of the Windows Internet Name Service and Dynamic Host Configuration Protocol.

- Chapter 11, "Configuring Windows 95 Clients for Networking," tackles the work involved in connecting Windows 95 workstations to your server.

- Chapter 12, "Connecting Other PC Clients to the Network," describes the process of attaching machines running other operating systems to your server.

Two chapters in Part III, "Administering a Secure Network," and two chapters in Part IV, "Wide Area Networking and the Internet," also are relevant to network administrators performing Windows NT Server 4.0 installations:

- Chapter 13, "Managing User and Group Accounts," covers setting up users and groups on your server to make it usable.

- Chapter 14, "Sharing and Securing Network Resources," describes some of the setting up that a successful network requires.

- Chapter 19, "Managing Remote Access Service," covers the Remote Access Service, including installing it and getting it working.

- Chapter 20, "Setting Up Internet Information Server 4.0," describes the installation process to create a private intranet or to connect your server to the Internet.

CHAPTER 7

Setting Up Redundant Arrays of Inexpensive Disks (RAID)

A *redundant array of inexpensive disks (RAID)* uses multiple fixed-disk drives, high-speed disk controllers, and special software drivers to increase the safety of your data and to improve the performance of your fixed-disk subsystem. All commercial RAID subsystems use the Small Computer System Interface (SCSI, pronounced *scuzzy*), which now is undergoing a transition from SCSI-2 to SCSI-3 (also called *Ultra Wide SCSI*). Virtually all network servers now use narrow (8-bit) or wide (16-bit) SCSI-2 drives and controllers. Ultra-wide SCSI host adapters for the PCI bus can deliver up to 40M per second (40M/sec) of data to and from the PC's RAM.

RAID levels 1 and higher protect your data by spreading it over multiple disk drives and then calculating and storing parity information. This redundancy allows any one drive to fail without causing the array itself to lose any data. A failed drive can be replaced and its contents reconstructed from the information on the remaining drives in the array.

RAID benefits

Use RAID to increase the security of your data and the performance of your server.

RAID levels

Balance the advantages and drawbacks of the various RAID levels and how to choose a RAID level to match your specific data storage requirements.

Hardware vs. software RAID

Decide between hardware-based RAID implementations and the native software RAID support provided by the Windows NT Server operating system.

Windows NT Server 4.0 software RAID

Quickly set up SCSI stripe sets, mirror sets, or stripe sets with parity with Windows NT Server 4.0's Disk Manager.

Software RAID recovery

Use Disk Manager to recover failed drives in a RAID 1 or RAID 5 subsystem.

RAID increases disk subsystem performance by distributing read tasks over several drives, allowing the same data to be retrieved from different locations, depending on which location happens to be closest to the read head(s) when the data is requested. RAID 0 increases read and write performance but doesn't provide data protection.

There are several levels of RAID, each of which is optimized for various types of data handling and storage requirements. You can implement RAID in hardware or in software. Modern network operating systems, such as Windows NT Server, provide native software support for one or more RAID levels.

The various component parts of RAID technology were originally developed for mainframes and minicomputers. Until recently, the deployment of RAID systems was limited by its high cost in those environments. In the past few years, however, RAID has become widely available for PC LANs. The cost of disk drives has plummeted. Hardware RAID controllers have become reasonably priced. For example, Adaptec's new AAA-131 RAID controller has a street price in the $500 range. The cost objections to implement RAID systems are now disappearing. Your server deserves to have a RAID system; don't even consider building a server that doesn't use RAID level 1 or higher.

N O T E   Most chapters in this book use the term *fixed-disk drive* to distinguish these drives from other data-storage devices, such as removable media devices (typified by Iomega's Zip and Jaz products), CD-ROM, magneto-optic, and other storage systems that use the term *drive*. In this chapter, the term *drive* means a fixed-disk (Winchester-type) drive. ■

Understanding RAID Levels

Disk drives do only two things: write data and read data. Depending on the application, the disk subsystem might be called on to do frequent small reads and writes; or the drive might need to do less frequent, but larger, reads and writes. An application server running a client/server database, for example, tends toward frequent small reads and writes, whereas a server providing access to stored images tends toward less frequent, but larger, reads and writes. The RAID levels vary in their optimization for small reads, large reads, small writes, and large writes. Although most servers have a mixed disk access pattern, choosing the RAID level optimized for the predominant environment maximizes the performance of your disk subsystem.

The various RAID levels are optimized for various data storage requirements in terms of redundancy levels and performance issues. Different RAID levels store data bit-wise, byte-wise, or sector-wise over the array of disks. Similarly, parity information might be distributed across the array or contained on a single physical drive.

RAID levels 1 and 5 are very common in PC LAN environments. All hardware and software RAID implementations provide at least these two levels. RAID level 3 is used occasionally in specialized applications and is supported by most hardware and some software RAID implementations. RAID levels 2 and 4 are seldom, if ever, used in PC LAN environments, although some hardware RAID implementations offer these levels.

N O T E Although RAID really has only levels 1 through 5 defined, you'll commonly see references to RAID 0, RAID 0/1, RAID 6, RAID 7, and RAID 10, all of which are de facto extensions of the original RAID specification. These uses have become so common that they're now universally accepted. Because RAID is a model or theoretical framework (rather than a defined protocol or implementation), manufacturers continue to market improved RAID technology with arbitrarily assigned RAID levels. ■

The RAID Advisory Board

The RAID Advisory Board (RAB) is a consortium of manufacturers of RAID equipment and other interested parties. RAB is responsible for developing and maintaining RAID standards and has formal programs covering education, standardization, and certification. Supporting these three programs are six committees: Functional Test, Performance Test, RAID-Ready Drive, Host Interface, RAID Enclosure, and Education.

RAB sells several documents, the most popular of which is *The RAIDbook*, first published in 1993. *The RAIDbook* covers the fundamentals of RAID and defines each RAID level. It's a worthwhile acquisition if you want to learn more about RAID. *Computer Technology Review* magazine hosts a RAB section in each monthly issue.

ON THE WEB

To see the magazine's Web site, point your browser to **http://www.ctreview.com/**.

The RAB Certification Program awards logos to equipment that passes its compatibility- and performance-testing suites. The RAB Conformance Logo certifies that a component so labeled complies with the named RAID level designation as published in *The RAIDbook*. The RAB Gold Certificate Logo certifies that a product meets the functional and performance specifications published by RAB. In mid-1996, 20 firms were authorized to apply the RAB Gold Certificate Logo to their products.

ON THE WEB

For more information about the RAID Advisory Board and its programs, contact Joe Molina, RAB Chairman, at the RAID Advisory Board, affiliated with Technology Forums Ltd., 13 Marie Lane, St. Peter, MN 56082-9423, (507) 931-0967, fax (507) 931-0976, e-mail **0004706032@mcimail.com**. You also can reach the RAID Advisory Board at **http://www.andataco.com/rab/**.

RAID 0

Part

II

Ch

7

RAID 0 is a high-performance, zero-redundancy array option. RAID 0 isn't properly RAID at all. It stripes blocks of data across multiple disk drives to increase the throughput of the disk subsystem (see Figure 7.1) but offers no redundancy. If one drive fails in a RAID 0 array, the data on all drives on the array is inaccessible. RAID 0 is used primarily for applications needing the highest possible reading and writing data rate.

FIG. 7.1

A diagram of RAID 0 (Sector Striping) with two drives.

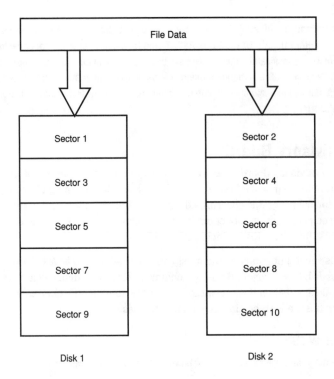

Nevertheless, there's a place for RAID 0. Understanding RAID 0 is important because the same striping mechanism used in RAID 0 is used to increase performance in other RAID levels. RAID 0 is inexpensive to implement for two reasons:

- No disk space is used to store parity information, eliminating the need to buy either larger disk drives or more of them for a given amount of storage.
- The algorithms used by RAID 0 are simple ones that don't add much overhead or require a dedicated processor.

RAID 0 uses striping to store data. *Striping* means that data blocks are alternately written to the different physical disk drives that make up the logical volume represented by the array. For instance, your RAID 0 array might comprise three physical disk drives that are visible to the operating system as one logical volume. Suppose that your block size is 8K and that a 32K file is to be written to disk. With RAID 0, the first 8K block might be written to physical drive 1, the second block to drive 2, the third to drive 3, and the final 8K block again to drive 1. Your single 32K file is thus stored as four separate blocks residing on three separate physical hard disk drives.

This block-wise distribution of data across multiple physical hard disks introduces two parameters used to quantify a RAID 0 array. The size of the block used—in this case, 8K—is referred to as the *chunk size*, which determines how much data is written to a disk drive in each operation. The number of physical hard disk drives comprising the array determines the *stripe width*. Both chunk size and stripe width affect the performance of a RAID 0 array.

When a logical read request is made to the RAID 0 array (fulfillment of which requires that an amount of data larger than the chunk size be retrieved), this request is broken into multiple smaller physical read requests. Each read request is directed to and serviced by the individual physical drives on which the multiple blocks are stored. Although these multiple read requests are generated serially, doing so takes little time. The bulk of the time needed to fulfill the read request is used to transfer the data itself. With sequential reads, which involve little drive head seeking, the bottleneck becomes the internal transfer rate of the drives themselves. Striping lets this transfer activity occur in parallel on the individual disk drives that make up the array, so the elapsed time until the read request is completely fulfilled is greatly reduced.

Striping doesn't come without cost in processing overhead, and this is where chunk size affects performance. Against the benefit of having multiple spindles at work to service a single logical read request, you must weigh the overhead processing cost required to write and then read this data from many disks rather than just one. (*Spindle* is a commonly used synonym for a physical drive.) Each SCSI disk access requires numerous SCSI commands to be generated and then executed, and striping the data across several physical drives multiplies the effort required accordingly.

Reducing the block size too far can cause the performance benefits of using multiple spindles to be swamped by the increased time needed to generate and execute additional SCSI commands. You can actually decrease performance by using too small a block size. The break-even point is determined by your SCSI host adapter and by the characteristics of the SCSI hard disk drives themselves, but, generally speaking, a block size smaller than 8K risks performance degradation. Using block sizes of 16K, 32K, or larger offers correspondingly greater performance benefits.

Sequential reads and writes make up a small percentage of total disk activity on a typical server disk subsystem. Most disk accesses are random; by definition, this means that you'll probably need to move the heads to retrieve a particular block of data. Because head positioning is a physical process, relatively speaking it's very slow. The benefit of striping in allowing parallel data transfer from multiple spindles is much less significant in random access because all the system components are awaiting relatively slow head positioning to occur. Therefore, striping does little to benefit any particular random-access disk transaction, but it does benefit random-access disk throughput as a whole.

N O T E One primary application for RAID 0 is the capture and playback of high-quality digital video and audio data. By adding multiple Ultra Wide SCSI 2 drives, such as the 4.3G Seagate Barracuda ST34371W or the 9G ST19171W, to a chain of devices connected to an Adaptec AHA-3940UW SCSI host adapter, you can obtain sustained data-transfer rates up to almost the 40M/sec rating of the host adapter. Such data rates can support the 270 Mbps (megabits per second) data rate of decompressed, component digital video that conforms to the international ITU-R BT.601 (D-1) standard used for broadcast television. This application for RAID 0 pertains to high-performance Windows NT Workstation 4.0 installations but not to conventional network servers. ■

Part

II

Ch

7

RAID 1

What do you do to make sure that you don't suffer by losing something? The obvious answer is to make a copy of it. RAID 1 works this way, making two complete copies of everything to mirrored or duplexed pairs of disk drives. This 100 percent redundancy means that if you lose a drive in a RAID 1 array, you have another drive with an exact duplicate of the failed drive's contents. RAID 1 offers the greatest level of redundancy, but at the highest cost for disk drives (see Figure 7.2).

FIG. 7.2

A diagram of RAID 1 (mirroring or duplexing) with two drives.

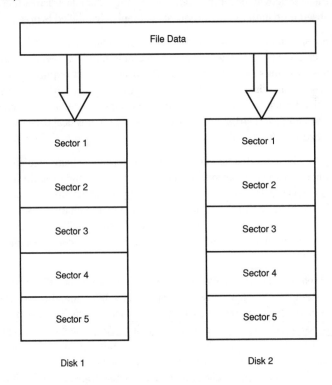

Mirroring means that each disk drive has a twin. Anything written to one drive is also written to the second drive simultaneously. Mirroring is 100 percent duplication of your drives. If one drive fails, its twin can replace it without loss of data.

Mirroring has two disadvantages:

- The most obvious is that you must buy twice as many disk drives to yield a given amount of storage.
- The process of writing to both drives and maintaining coherency of their contents introduces overhead, which slows writes.

Mirroring has two advantages:

- Your data is safely duplicated on two physical devices, making catastrophic data loss much less likely.

■ Read performance is greatly increased because reads can be made by the drive whose heads happen to be closest to the requested data.

Duplexing is similar to mirroring, but it adds a second host adapter to control the second drive or set of drives. The only disadvantage of duplexing, relative to mirroring, is the cost of the second host adapter—although duplex host adapters, such as the Adaptec AHA-3940UW, are less costly than buying two AHA-2940UW single-host adapters. Duplexing with two cards, however, eliminates the host adapter as a single point of failure.

In a large server environment, the cost of duplicating every disk drive quickly adds up, making RAID 1 very expensive. With smaller servers, however, the economics can be very different. If your server has only one SCSI hard disk drive installed, you might find that you can implement RAID 1 for only the relatively small cost of buying another similar disk drive. At this writing, the cost of 1G of high-performance SCSI-2 storage was about $250, based on the $1,150 street price of a 4.3G Seagate ST34371W drive.

RAID 1 Read Performance   RAID 1 reads are usually faster than those of a stand-alone drive. To return to the hardware store analogy, there are now multiple checkout lines, each of which can handle any customer. With RAID 1 reads, any given block of data can be read from either drive, thereby shortening queues, lowering drive usage, and increasing read performance. This increase occurs only with multithreaded reads. Single-threaded reads show no performance difference, just as though all but one of the checkout lines were closed.

Most RAID 1 implementations offer two alternative methods for optimizing read performance. The first is referred to as *circular queue* or *round-robin scheduling*. With this method, read requests are simply alternated between the two physical drives, with each drive serving every second read request. This method equalizes the read workload between the drives and is particularly appropriate for random-access environments, where small amounts of data—record or block sized—are being accessed frequently. It's less appropriate for sequential-access environments, where large amounts of data are being retrieved. Most disk drives have buffers used to provide read-ahead optimization, and the drive hardware itself reads and stores the data immediately following the requested block on the assumption that this data is most likely to be requested next. Alternating small block requests between two physical drives can eliminate the benefit of this read-ahead buffering.

The second method used in RAID 1 to increase read performance is called *geometric, regional*, or *assigned cylinder scheduling*. This method partially overcomes the relatively slow speed of drive head positioning. By giving each of the two drives comprising the RAID 1 array responsibility for covering only half of the physical drive, this head positioning time can be minimized. For example, by using mirrored drives, each having 1,024 cylinders, the first drive might be assigned responsibility for fulfilling all requests for data that's stored on cylinders 0 through 511, with the second drive covering cylinders 512 through 1,023.

Although this method is superficially attractive, it seldom works in practice. Few drives have their data distributed in such a way that any specific cylinder is equally likely to be accessed. Operating system files, swap files, user applications, and other frequently read files are likely to reside near the front of the disk. In this situation, your first disk might be assigned literally 90 percent or more of the read requests. Second, even if the data were to be distributed to

Part

II

Ch

7

equalize access across the portion of the disk occupied by data, few people run their drives at full capacity, so the second drive would have correspondingly less to do. This problem can be addressed by allowing a user-defined split ratio, perhaps assigning disk 1 to cover the first 10 percent or 20 percent of the physical drive area and disk 2 to cover the remainder. In practice, no known RAID 1 systems allow user tuning to this extent.

RAID 1 Write Performance   RAID 1 writes are more problematic. Because all data has to be written to both drives, it appears that there's a situation where customers have to go through one checkout line to complete a transaction. They then have to go to the back of the other checkout line, wait in the queue, and then again complete the same transaction at the other register. RAID 1, therefore, provides a high level of data safety by replicating all data, an increase in read performance by allowing either physical drive to fulfill the read request, and a lower level of write performance due to the necessity of writing the same information to both drives.

Overall RAID 1 Performance   It might seem that RAID 1 would have little overall impact on performance, because the increase in read performance would be balanced by the decrease in write performance. In reality, this is seldom the case.

First, in most server environments, reads greatly outnumber writes. In a database, for example, any particular record might be read 10 times or 100 times for every single time it's written. Similarly, operating system executables, user application program files, and overlays are essentially read-only. Any factor that benefits read performance at the expense of write performance will greatly increase overall performance for most servers most of the time.

Second, although it might seem reasonable to assume that writing to two separate drives would cut write performance in half, in reality the performance hit is usually only 10 percent to 20 percent for mirrored writes. Although both physical writes must be executed before the logical write to the array can be considered complete, and the two write requests themselves are generated serially, the actual physical writes to the two drives occur in parallel. Because it's the head positioning and subsequent writing that occupy the bulk of the time required for the entire transaction, the extra time needed to generate the second write request has just a small impact on the total time required to complete the write.

RAID 2

RAID 2 is a proprietary RAID architecture patented by Thinking Machines Inc. It distributes the data across multiple drives at the bit level. RAID 2 uses multiple dedicated disks to store parity information and, thus, requires that an array contain a relatively large number of individual disk drives. For example, a RAID 2 array with four data drives requires three dedicated parity drives. RAID 2 has the highest redundancy of any of the parity-oriented RAID schemes.

The bit-wise orientation of RAID 2 means that every disk access occurs in parallel. RAID 2 is optimized for applications such as imaging, which requires the transfer of large amounts of contiguous data.

RAID 2 isn't a good choice for random-access applications, which require frequent small reads and writes. The amount of processing overhead needed to fragment and reassemble data makes RAID 2 slow, relative to other RAID levels. The large number of dedicated parity drives required makes RAID 2 expensive. Because nearly all PC LAN environments have heavy random-disk access, RAID 2 has no place in a PC LAN. However, RAID 2 does have some specific advantages for special-purpose digital video servers.

RAID 3

RAID 3 stripes data across drives, usually at the byte level, although bit-level implementations are possible (see Figure 7.3). RAID 3 dedicates one drive in the array to storing parity information.

FIG. 7.3
A diagram of RAID 3 (byte striping with dedicated parity disk) with three drives.

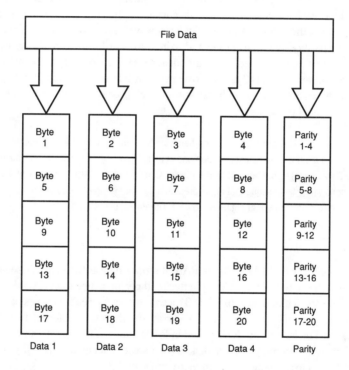

Like RAID 2, RAID 3 is optimized for long sequential disk accesses in applications such as imaging and digital video storage, and is inappropriate for random-access environments such as PC LANs. Any single drive in a RAID 3 array can fail without causing data loss, because the data can be reconstructed from the remaining drives. RAID 3 is sometimes offered as an option on PC-based RAID controllers but is seldom used. One primary application for RAID 3 is digital video and audio data storage for automated commercial insertion, direct-to-home satellite, and other TV broadcast uses.

RAID 3 can be considered an extension of RAID 0 in that it stripes small chunks of data across multiple physical drives. In a RAID 3 array that comprises four physical drives, for example, the

Part
II

Ch
7

first block is written to the first physical drive, the second block to the second drive, and the third block to the third drive. The fourth block isn't written to the fourth drive, however; it's written to the first drive to begin the round-robin again.

The fourth drive isn't used directly to store user data. Instead, the fourth drive stores the results of parity calculations performed on the data written to the first three drives. This small chunk striping provides good performance on large amounts of data, because all three data drives operate in parallel. The fourth, or parity, drive provides the redundancy to ensure that the loss of any one drive doesn't cause the array to lose data.

For sequential data transfers, RAID 3 offers high performance due to striping, and low cost due to its reliance on a single parity drive. It's this single parity drive, however, that's the downfall of RAID 3 for most PC LAN applications. By definition, no read to a RAID 3 array requires that the parity drive be accessed unless data corruption has occurred on one or more of the data drives. Reads, therefore, proceed quickly. However, every write to a RAID 3 array requires that the single parity drive be accessed and written to in order to store the parity information for the data write that just occurred. The random access typical of a PC LAN environment means that the parity drive in a RAID 3 array is overused, with long queues for pending writes, whereas the data drives are underused because they can't proceed until parity information is written to the dedicated parity drive.

N O T E   RAID 3 is a common option on hardware RAID implementations. In practical terms, RAID 5 is a universally available option and is usually preferred over RAID 3 because it offers most of RAID 3's advantages but none of its drawbacks. Consider using RAID 3 only in very specialized applications where large sequential reads predominate—for example, a dedicated imaging server or for distributing (but not capturing) digital video data. Otherwise, use RAID 5. ■

RAID 4

RAID 4 is similar to RAID 3, except RAID 4 stripes data at the block or sector level rather than at the byte level, thereby providing better read performance than RAID 3 for small random reads. The small chunk size of RAID 3 means that every read requires participation from every disk in the array. The disks in a RAID 3 array are, therefore, referred to as being *synchronized* or *coupled*. The larger chunk size used in RAID 4 means that small random reads can be completed by accessing only a single disk drive instead of all data drives. RAID 4 drives are, therefore, referred to as being *unsynchronized* or *decoupled*.

Like RAID 3, RAID 4 suffers from having a single, dedicated parity disk that must be accessed for every write. RAID 4 has all the drawbacks of RAID 3 and doesn't have the performance advantage of RAID 3 on large read transactions. About the only environment for which RAID 4 would make any sense at all is one in which nearly 100 percent of disk activity is small random reads. Because this situation isn't seen in real-world server environments, don't consider using RAID 4 for your PC LAN.

RAID 5

RAID 5 (see Figure 7.4) is the most common RAID level used in PC LAN environments. RAID 5 stripes both user and parity data across all the drives in the array, consuming the equivalent of one drive for parity information.

FIG. 7.4
A diagram of RAID 5 (sector striping with distributed parity) with five drives.

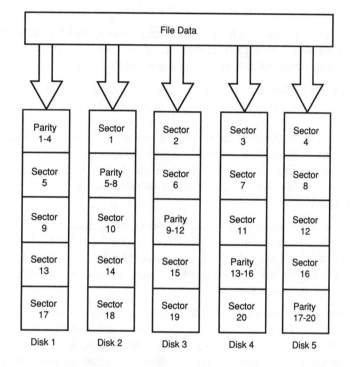

With RAID 5, all drives are the same size, and one drive is unavailable to the operating system. For example, in a RAID 5 array with three 1G drives, the equivalent of one of those drives is used for parity, leaving 2G visible to the operating system. If you add a fourth 1G drive to the array, the equivalent of one drive is still used for parity, leaving 3G visible to the operating system.

RAID 5 is optimized for transaction-processing activity, in which users frequently read and write relatively small amounts of data. It's the best RAID level for nearly any PC LAN environment and is particularly well suited for database servers.

The single most important weakness of RAID levels 2 through 4 is that they dedicate a single physical disk drive to parity information. Reads don't require accessing the parity drive, so they aren't degraded. This parity drive must be accessed for each write to the array, however, so RAID levels 2 through 4 don't allow parallel writes. RAID 5 eliminates this bottleneck by striping the parity data onto all physical drives in the array, thereby allowing both parallel reads and writes.

Part
II

Ch
7

RAID 5 Read Performance   RAID 5 reads, like RAID levels 2 through 4 reads, don't require access to parity information unless one or more of the data stripes is unreadable. Because both data and parity stripes are optimized for sequential read performance where the block size of the requested data is a multiple of the stripe width, RAID 5 offers random read performance similar to that of RAID 3. Because RAID 5 allows parallel reads (unlike RAID 3), RAID 5 offers substantially better performance on random reads.

RAID 5 matches or exceeds RAID 0 performance on sequential reads because RAID 5 stripes the data across one more physical drive than does RAID 0. RAID 5 performance on random reads at least equals RAID 0, and it's usually somewhat better.

RAID 5 Write Performance   RAID 5 writes are more problematic. A RAID 0 single-block write involves only one access to one physical disk to complete the write. With RAID 5, the situation is considerably more complex. In the simplest case, two reads are required—one for the existing data block and the other for the existing parity block. Parity is recalculated for the stripe set based on these reads and the contents of the pending write. Two writes are then required—one for the data block itself and one for the revised parity block. Completing a single write, therefore, requires a minimum of four disk operations, compared with the single operation required by RAID 0.

The situation worsens when you consider what must be done to maintain data integrity. The modified data block is written to disk before the modified parity block. If a system failure occurs, the data block might be written successfully to disk, but the newly calculated parity block might be lost. This leaves new data with old parity and thereby corrupts the disk. Such a situation must be avoided at all costs.

Transaction Processing with RAID 5   RAID 5 addresses the problem of keeping data blocks and parity blocks synchronized by borrowing a concept from database transaction processing. Transaction processing is so named because it treats multiple component parts of a related whole as a single transaction. Either the whole transaction completes successfully, or none of it does.

RAID 5 uses a two-phase commit process to ensure data integrity, further increasing write overhead. It first does a parallel read of every data block belonging to the affected stripe set, calculating a new parity block based on this read and the contents of the new data block to be written. The changed data and newly calculated parity information are written to a log area with pointers to the correct locations. After the log information is written successfully, the changed data and parity information are written in parallel to the stripe set. When the RAID controller verifies that the entire transaction completed successfully, it deletes the log information.

RAID 5 Data Caching   The two-phase commit process obviously introduces considerable overhead to the write process, and in theory slows RAID 5 writes by 50 percent or more relative to RAID 0 writes. In practice, the situation isn't as bad as you might expect. Examining the process shows that the vast majority of extra time involved in these overhead operations is consumed by physical positioning of drive heads. This brings up the obvious question of caching.

On first glance, caching might appear to be of little use for drive arrays. Drive arrays range in size from a few gigabytes to the terabyte range. (A *terabyte* is 1,024 gigabytes.) Most arrays service mainly small random read requests; even frequent large sequential reads can be—in this context, at least—considered random relative to the overall size of the array. Providing enough RAM to do read caching realistically on this amount of disk space would be prohibitive simply on the basis of cost. Even if you were willing to buy this much RAM, the overhead involved in doing cache searches and maintaining cache coherency would swamp any benefits you might otherwise gain.

Write caching, however, is a different story. Existing RAID 5 implementations avoid most of the lost time by relocating operations, where possible, from physical disk to non-volatile or battery-backed RAM. This caching, with deferred writes to frequently updated data, reduces overhead by an order of magnitude or more and allows real-world RAID 5 write performance that approaches that of less-capable RAID versions.

Stacked RAID

One characteristic of all RAID implementations is that the array is seen as a single logical disk drive by the host operating system. This means that it's possible to *stack* arrays, with the host using one RAID level to control an array of arrays, in which individual disk drives are replaced with second-level arrays operating at the same or a different RAID level. Using stacked arrays allows you to gain the individual benefits of more than one RAID level while offsetting the drawbacks of each. In essence, stacking makes the high-performance RAID element visible to the host while concealing the low-performance RAID element used to provide data redundancy.

One common stacked RAID implementation is referred to as *RAID 0/1*, which is also marketed as a proprietary implementation called *RAID 10* (see Figure 7.5). This method combines the performance of RAID 0 striping with the redundancy of RAID 1 mirroring. RAID 0/1 simply replaces each individual disk drive used in a RAID 0 array with a RAID 1 array. The host computer sees the array as a simple RAID 0, so performance is enhanced to RAID 0 levels. Each drive component of the RAID 0 array is actually a RAID 1 mirrored set; thus, data safety is at the same level you would expect from a full mirrored set.

Other stacked RAID implementations are possible. For example, replacing the individual drives in a RAID 5 array with subsidiary RAID 3 arrays results in a RAID 53 configuration.

Another benefit of stacking is in building very large capacity arrays. For reasons described earlier, RAID 5 is the most popular choice for PC LAN arrays. However, for technical reasons described later, a RAID 5 array should normally be limited to five or six disk drives. At this writing, the largest disk drives available in production quantities for PC LANs hold about 9G, placing the upper limit on a simple RAID 5 array at about 50G. Replacing the individual disk drives in a simple RAID 5 array with subsidiary RAID 5 arrays allows extending this maximum to 250G or more. In theory, it's possible to use three tiers of RAID—an array of arrays of arrays—to further extend capacity to the terabyte range.

Part
II

Ch
7

N O T E   Seagate has announced a 23G version of its 5 1/4-inch Elite product line, which increases the practical upper size limit of a simple RAID 5 array to about 150G. ▪

FIG. 7.5

A diagram of RAID 0/1 (sector striping to mirrored target arrays) with four drives.

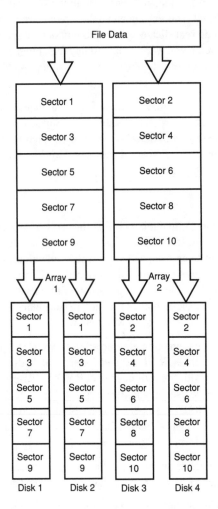

Array Sizing

So far this chapter has discussed redundancy, but it hasn't explained in detail what happens when a drive fails. In the case of RAID 0, the answer is obvious. The failed drive contained half of your data, and the half remaining on the good drive is unusable. With RAID 1, the answer is equally obvious. The failed drive was an exact duplicate of the remaining good drive, all your data is still available, and all your redundancy is gone until you replace the failed drive. With RAID 3 and RAID 5, the issue becomes much more complex. Because RAID 3 and RAID 5 use parity to provide data redundancy rather than physically replicate the data as does RAID 1, the implications of a drive failure aren't as obvious.

In RAID 3, the failure of the parity drive has no effect on reads, because the drive is never accessed for reads. For RAID 3 writes, failure of the parity drive removes all redundancy until the drive is replaced, because all parity information is stored on that single drive. When a data drive fails in a RAID 3 array, the situation becomes more complicated. Reads of data formerly stored on the failed drive must be reconstructed by using the contents of the other data drives and the parity drive. This results in a greatly increased number of read accesses and correspondingly lowered performance.

With RAID 5, the situation is similar to a failed RAID 3 data drive. Because every drive in a RAID 5 array contains data and parity information, the failure of any drive results in the loss of both data and parity. An attempt to read data formerly residing on the failed drive requires that every remaining drive in the array be read and parity used to recalculate the missing data. In a RAID 5 array containing 15 drives, for example, a read and reconstruction of lost data would require 14 separate read operations and a recalculation before a single block of data could be returned to the host. Writes to a RAID 5 array with one failed drive also require numerous disk accesses.

To make matters worse, when the failed drive is replaced, its contents must be reconstructed and stored on the replacement drive. This process, usually referred to as *automatic rebuild*, normally occurs in the background while the array continues to fulfill user requests. Because the automatic rebuild process requires heavy disk access to all the other drives in an already crippled array, performance of the array can degrade unacceptably. The best way to limit this degradation is to use a reasonably small stripe width, limiting the number of physical drives in the array to five or six at most.

Specifying a RAID Implementation

Up to this point, the discussion of RAID levels has been limited to theoretical issues, such as relative performance in read and write mode. The following sections offer concrete recommendations to implement a RAID subsystem for your Windows NT server.

Picking the Best RAID Level for Your Needs

In theory, there are two important considerations in selecting the best RAID implementation for your particular needs:

- *The type of data to be stored on the array.* The various RAID levels are optimized for differing storage requirements. The relative importance in your environment of small random reads versus large sequential reads and of small random writes versus large sequential writes, as well as the overall percentage of reads versus writes, determines—in theory, at least—the best RAID level to use.

- *The relative importance to you of performance versus the safety of your data.* If data safety is paramount, you might choose a lower performing alternative that offers greater redundancy. Conversely, if sheer performance is the primary issue, you might choose a higher performing alternative that offers little or no redundancy. In this case, use backups and other means to ensure the safety of your data.

Part
II

Ch
7

Always lurking in the background is also, of course, the real-world issue of cost.

These issues can be summarized for each RAID level as follows:

■ RAID 0 striping offers high performance, but its complete lack of redundancy and accompanying high risk of data loss makes pure RAID 0 an unrealistic choice for nearly all environments, although it makes sense in applications that generate large transitory temp files. RAID 0 is inexpensive because it's supported by many standard SCSI host adapters and requires no additional disk drives.

■ RAID 1 mirroring provides 100 percent redundancy for excellent data safety and, at the same time, offers reasonably good performance. RAID 1 is often an excellent choice for small LANs, offering decent performance and a high level of safety at a reasonable cost. Because RAID 1 is supported by most standard host adapters and requires that each data drive be duplicated, it's inexpensive to implement in small arrays but very expensive for large arrays.

■ RAID 3 byte striping with dedicated parity offers good data safety and high performance on large sequential reads, but its performance on random reads and writes makes it a poor choice for most LANs. The growth of imaging applications is revitalizing RAID 3 to some extent, because these applications fit well with RAID 3 strengths. If you're doing imaging, consider implementing RAID 3 on the logical volume used to store images.

■ RAID 5 sector striping with distributed parity offers good data safety, good read performance for small random reads and large sequential reads, and reasonable write performance. RAID 5 usually turns out to be the best match for the disk access patterns of small and mid-size LANs. RAID 5 can be inexpensive to implement because it requires only a single additional disk drive and can be implemented in software. Various RAID 5 hardware implementations are also available, offering better performance than software versions but at a correspondingly higher price. If your server has only one array, RAID 5 is almost certainly the way to go.

■ Stacked RAID is useful when performance and data safety are high priorities relative to cost. In particular, RAID 0/1, when properly implemented, can combine the high performance of RAID 0 with the complete redundancy of RAID 1. At the same time, RAID 0/1 eliminates the drawbacks of both—except, of course, the cost. Stacked RAID is also useful if your total array capacity must exceed 50G.

■ Multiple arrays are worth considering if your data storage requirements are large and diverse. Rather than try to shoehorn all your data into a single array running a compromise level of RAID, consider installing multiple arrays, each of which runs the RAID level most appropriate for the type of data being stored and the patterns of access to that data.

Understanding RAID Product Features

You can implement RAID in various ways. The SCSI host adapter in your current server might provide simple RAID functionality. You can replace your current SCSI host adapter with a host adapter that offers full RAID support. Software RAID support is provided natively by most network operating systems, including Windows NT Server 4.0. If you're buying new server hardware, chances are that the vendor provides hardware RAID support standard or as an option. If you need to upgrade your existing server, you can choose among various external RAID arrays that provide features, functionality, and performance similar to that provided by internal server RAID arrays.

Hot Swappable Disks and Hot Spare Disks   Most external RAID subsystems and many servers with internal RAID subsystems allow hard disk drives to be removed and replaced without turning off the server. This feature, known as *hot swapping*, allows a failed disk drive to be replaced without interrupting ongoing server operations.

A similar method, known as *hot sparing*, goes one step further by providing a spare drive that's installed and powered up at all times. This drive can automatically take the place of a failed drive on a moment's notice. Most systems that provide hot sparing also support hot swapping to allow the failed drive to be replaced at your leisure.

Obviously, the drive itself and the system case must be designed to allow hot swapping or hot sparing. Most internal server RAID arrays and nearly all external RAID arrays are designed with front external access to hard drives for this reason. Hot swapping is a necessity for production servers; hot sparing is a very desirable option.

Automatic Rebuild   With hot swapping or hot sparing, the integrity of the array itself is restored by doing a rebuild to reconstruct the data formerly contained on the failed drive and to re-create it on the replacement drive. Because rebuilding is a very resource-intensive process, a well-designed RAID subsystem gives you the choice of taking the array down and doing a static rebuild, or of allowing the rebuild to occur dynamically in the background while the array continues to service user requests. Ideally, the array should also let you specify a priority level for the background rebuild, allowing you to balance users' need for performance against the time needed to re-establish redundancy.

In practice, performance on an array with a failed drive—particularly on a RAID 5 array— might already be degraded to the extent that trying any sort of rebuild while users continue to access the array isn't realistic. The best solution in this case is usually to allow the users to continue to use the array (as is) for the rest of the day and then to do the rebuild overnight. Your choice in this situation is a static rebuild, which is far faster than a dynamic background rebuild.

Disk Drive Issues   External RAID arrays and internal server RAID arrays typically offer the least flexibility in choice of drives. Although these subsystems use industry-standard disk drives, the standard drives are repackaged into different physical form factors to accommodate custom drive bay designs as well as the proprietary power and data connections needed to allow hot swapping. Because these proprietary designs fit only one manufacturer's servers or even just one particular model, they're made and sold in relatively small numbers. This combination of low volume and a single source makes the drives quite expensive.

Another related issue is that of continuing availability of compatible drives. Consider what might happen a year or two from now when you want to upgrade or replace drives. The best designs simply enclose industry-standard drives in a custom chassis that provides the mechanical and electrical connections needed to fit the array. By using these designs, drives can be upgraded or replaced simply by installing a new supported standard drive in the custom chassis. Beware of other designs that make the chassis an integral part of the drive assembly; you'll pay a high price for replacement drives, if you can find them at all.

Software-based RAID offers the most flexibility in selecting drives. Because software-based RAID subsystems are further isolated from the disk drives than are hardware-based RAID implementations, most software-based RAID implementations—both those native to NOSes and those provided by third parties—care little about the specifics of your disk drives. Software RAID depends on a standard SCSI host adapter to communicate with the disk drives. As long as your host adapter is supported by your software and your drives are supported in turn by the host adapter, you're likely to find few compatibility problems with software-based RAID. Typical software-based mirroring, for example, doesn't even require that the second drive in a mirror set be identical to the first, but simply that it's at least as large as the first drive. Windows NT Server's implementation of software-based RAID is described later in the section "Understanding Windows NT Server 4.0 Software RAID."

Power Supplies   Most external and some internal server RAID arrays use dedicated redundant power supplies for the disk drives. The arrangement of these power supplies significantly affects the reliability of the array as a whole. Some systems provide a dedicated power supply for each individual disk drive. Although this seems to increase redundancy superficially, in fact it simply adds more single points of failure to the drive component. Failure of a power supply means failure of the drive that it powers. Whether the failure is the result of a dead drive or a dead power supply, the result is the same.

A better solution is to use dual load-sharing power supplies. In this arrangement, each power supply can power the entire array on its own. The dual power supplies are linked in a harness that allows each to provide half of the power needed by the array. If one power supply fails, the other provides all the power needed by the array until the failed unit can be replaced. Another benefit of this arrangement is that because the power supplies normally run well below their full capacity, their lives are extended and their reliability is enhanced when compared with a single power supply running at or near capacity. Power supplies also can be hot swappable (although this feature is more commonly called *hot pluggable* when referring to power supplies).

Stacked and Multiple-Level Independent RAID Support   Some environments require a stacked array for performance, redundancy, or sizing reasons. Others might require multiple independent arrays, each running a different RAID level or mix of RAID levels. If you find yourself in either situation, the best solution is probably either an external RAID array or a high-end internal server RAID array.

The obvious issue is whether a given RAID implementation offers the functionality needed to provide stacks and multiple independent arrays. The not-so-obvious issue is the sheer number of drives that must be supported.

External RAID arrays support many disk drives in their base chassis, and they usually allow expansion chassis to be daisy-chained, extending the maximum number of disks supported even further. High-end servers support as many as 28 disk drives internally, and again often make provision for extending this number via external chassis. Mid-range servers are typically more limited in the number of drives they physically support and in their provisions for stacking and multiple independent arrays. A typical mid-range server RAID array doesn't support multiple independent arrays, but it might offer simple RAID 0/1 stacking.

Manageability Look for a RAID implementation that provides good management software. In addition to providing automatic static and dynamic rebuild options, a good RAID management package monitors your array for loading, error rates, read and write statistics by type, and other key performance data. The better packages even help you decide how to configure your RAID array for optimum performance.

Implementing RAID in Hardware

Hardware-based RAID implementations usually offer the best performance for a given choice of RAID level and drive performance. Another advantage of hardware RAID is that server resources aren't devoted to calculating parity and determining which drive is to receive which block of data. The following sections offer recommendations for the specification of hardware-based RAID subsystems for your server.

Obtaining RAID as a Server Option If you're buying a new server, by all means consider the RAID options offered by the server manufacturer. Any system seriously positioned for use as a server offers RAID as an option, if not as standard equipment. Low-end servers might offer RAID as an option. Mid-range and high-end servers come standard with RAID and often offer optional external enclosures to expand your disk storage beyond that available in the server chassis alone.

Purchasing RAID as a part of your server has the following advantages, most of which are related to single-source procurement:

- One manufacturer supplies the server and the RAID hardware, so the RAID hardware can be tweaked to optimize performance.

- Internal server RAID offers the best chance to avoid ROM revision-level issues and other nasty compatibility problems. If you have a problem, you can complain to one source and not have to worry about finger-pointing by different vendors.

- Driver updates are available from a single source, relieving you of having to play the systems integrator game the next time you want to upgrade your network operating system or replace disk drives.

- Single-source warranty and maintenance is a definite benefit. If you buy a combination server and RAID array from a major manufacturer, you make only one phone call when your server breaks. Large server manufacturers have trained service personnel located near you and can provide service 24 hours a day, seven days a week.

- Availability of known-compatible disks at upgrade time provides scalability insurance. Server manufacturers realize that you aren't likely to buy their servers unless you can be certain that parts for them will continue to be available for some reasonable time.

Upgrading an Existing Server to Hardware RAID If your current server is otherwise suitable, upgrading the server to hardware RAID might be a viable alternative to buying a new

Part

II

Ch

7

server. This upgrade can range from something as simple and inexpensive as adding another disk drive and enabling mirroring on your SCSI host adapter, to a process as complex—and potentially expensive—as adding an external RAID array cabinet. Somewhere in the middle (in cost and complexity) is replacing your existing SCSI host adapter with a dedicated RAID controller.

Mirroring with Your Current SCSI Host Adapter   The SCSI host adapter in your current server might support RAID 0, RAID 1, or both. Even if it doesn't support simple RAID, replacing the host adapter with one that offers RAID 0 or RAID 1 support is an inexpensive alternative. If your server has only one or two SCSI hard drives, this method allows you to implement mirroring at the cost of simply buying a matching drive for each existing drive.

This approach buys you 100 percent redundancy and decent performance, and does so inexpensively. What it doesn't provide are other features of more expensive hardware RAID implementations, such as hot swappable drives and redundant power supplies. Still, for smaller servers, this is a set-and-forget choice. If your server is small enough that buying the extra disk drives is feasible, and if you don't care that you'll need to take down the server to replace a failed drive, this method might well be the best choice. It gives you about 95 percent of the benefits of a full-blown RAID 5 implementation for a fraction of the cost.

Adding a Dedicated RAID 5 Controller Card   The next step up in hardware RAID—in terms of cost and performance—are dedicated RAID controller cards. These cards replace your existing SCSI host adapter and include a dedicated microprocessor to handle RAID 5 processing. They range in price from about $500 to perhaps $2,500, depending on their feature sets, the number of SCSI channels provided, the amount and type of on-board cache supplied, and other equipment.

All these cards support at least RAID 1 and RAID 5, and most offer a full range of RAID levels, often including various enhanced non-standard RAIDs. The Adaptec AAA-131 host adapter, for example, is a low-cost (about $500 street price) host adapter that supports RAID 0, 1, 5, and 0/1 (10) with hot-swappable drives in the RAID 5 configuration. The AAA-131 is designed for entry-level servers, which Adaptec Inc. defines as serving 60 or fewer clients. The AAA-132 provides two independent SCSI channels on a single adapter, and the AAA-133 gives you three channels. Figure 7.6 shows the high-end Adaptec AAC-330 host adapter designed for mid-range servers. The AAC-330 uses an Intel i960 RISC microprocessor for improved performance when serving a large number of clients.

N O T E   Most RAID controller cards are sold through original equipment manufacturer (OEM) arrangements with server vendors. For instance, the Mylex DAC960—one of the better examples of this type of adapter—is used by Hewlett-Packard to provide RAID support in its NetServer line of servers. HP modifies the BIOS and makes other changes to optimize the DAC960 for use in the company's servers. The Adaptec AAC330 is sold through OEM and VAR (value-added reseller) channels; the Adaptec AAA130 is available from distributors and some computer retailers. ■

If you decide to use one of these cards, budget for two of them. Few organizations accept having their LAN down for an extended period if the RAID controller fails. On-site maintenance is the exception rather than the rule for these cards. Even doing a swap via overnight courier usually means that your LAN will be down for at least a day or two.

FIG. 7.6
The Adaptec AAC-330 RAID*port* host adapter, which uses an Intel i960 RISC processor to provide mid-range server capabilities (courtesy of Adaptec, Inc.).

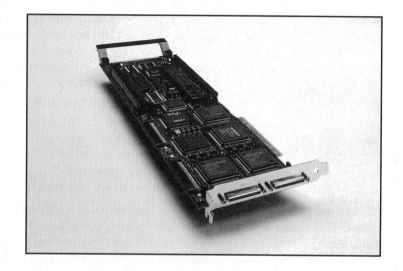

Using an External RAID Enclosure   External RAID enclosures are the high end of hardware RAID, offering all the features of internal server arrays and more. Hot-pluggable, load-balancing dual power supplies are a common feature, as are hot-swappable drives, extensive management capabilities, a full range of RAID options, and provision for stacked RAID. Most of these units support multiple independent RAID arrays, and some allow connection of more than one host. Most units also allow you to add additional slave enclosures to expand your disk capacity. As you might expect, all this functionality substantially increases the acquisition cost.

External RAID subsystems are of two types. The first is based on one of the dedicated RAID controller cards described in the preceding section. In this type of unit, called a *dumb external array*, all the RAID intelligence is contained on the card installed in the server cabinet, and the external enclosure simply provides mounting space and power for the disk drives. The enclosure makes provision for hot-swapping and redundant power supplies, but the actual RAID functionality remains with the server. RAID configuration and management is done at the server. Although such subsystems physically resemble more sophisticated external arrays, in concept these units are really just simple extensions of the dedicated RAID controller card method and accordingly are relatively inexpensive. They're usually priced in the $3,000 to $5,000 range for the enclosure and controller, before being populated with disk drives.

The second type of unit, called a *smart external array*, relocates RAID processing to the external enclosure and provides one or more SCSI connectors by which the host server (or servers) is connected to the array. The host server sees a smart external array as just another standard SCSI disk drive or drives.

With this type of smart array, RAID configuration and management are done at the array itself. Because these arrays are intended for use in diverse environments—including Novell

Part
II

Ch
7

NetWare, Windows NT Server, and UNIX—these arrays usually offer various methods for setup and programming. A typical unit might be programmable in a UNIX environment by connecting a dumb terminal to a serial port on the external array or by using Telnet. In a Windows NT Server 4.0 environment, you use provided client software for the network operating system. These arrays have available full software support—drivers and management utilities— for several operating systems, although they often come standard with support for only one operating system of your choice. Support for additional operating systems and extended functionality with your chosen operating system is often an extra-cost option. Smart external RAID arrays start at around $8,000 or $10,000, without drives, and go up rapidly from there.

Smart external arrays offer everything you might want in a RAID unit, including support for stacked RAID, multiple independent arrays, and multiple host support. Because manufacturers realize that these are critical components, on-site maintenance is available, provided by the manufacturer or by a reputable third-party service organization. Construction of these units resembles minicomputer and mainframe practices rather than typical PC peripherals.

The first major concern when you use smart external arrays is drive support. Some units allow you to add or replace drives with any SCSI drive of the appropriate type that's at least as large as the old drive. Other units require that you use only drives that exactly match the existing drives by make, model, and sometimes even by ROM revision level. Still other units can use only drives supplied by the array manufacturer, because the drives themselves have had their firmware altered. *Firmware* is a synonym for replaceable ROMs or reprogrammable non-volatile RAM (NVRAM). These manufacturers tell you that these firmware changes are required for performance and compatibility reasons, which might be true. However, the net effect is that you can then buy new and replacement drives only from the array manufacturer, which is usually a very expensive alternative.

The second major concern is software support. With smart external arrays, you're at the mercy of the array manufacturer for NOS support, drivers, and management utilities. Make absolutely certain before buying one of these arrays that it has software support available for Windows NT Server 4.0. It does you no good to accept a vendor's assurance that the array supports Windows NT, only to find later that the array supports only versions 3.5 and earlier.

Understanding Windows NT Server 4.0 Software RAID

All the RAID implementations examined so far are implemented by specialized hardware. It's possible, however, to use the server CPU to perform RAID processing, thereby avoiding buying additional hardware. Windows NT Server 4.0 includes as a standard feature RAID 0, RAID 1, and RAID 5 functionality built into the NOS software, allowing you to build a RAID subsystem by using only standard SCSI host adapters and drives. Because Windows NT Server 4.0 provides these RAID options, you might wonder why anyone would buy expensive additional hardware to accomplish the same thing.

The first reason is performance. In theory, at least, using software RAID can have scalability performance advantages. Because software RAID runs as another process on the server, upgrading the server processor or increasing the number of processors simultaneously upgrades RAID processing. In practice, this potential advantage usually turns out to be illusory. Although Microsoft has done a good job of incorporating RAID functionality into Windows NT Server 4.0, a well-designed hardware RAID solution always offers better performance, particularly on larger arrays. Benchmark tests nearly always show software RAID bringing up the rear of the pack in performance relative to hardware RAID, and even Microsoft admits that its software RAID solution is outperformed by a well-designed hardware RAID. Also, although using the server CPU to perform RAID processing can be acceptable on a small or lightly loaded server, doing so on a more heavily loaded server—particularly one running as an application server—steals CPU time from user applications and, therefore, degrades overall server performance.

The second reason that might mandate against using Windows NT Server software RAID is that of flexibility, convenience, and server uptime. In terms of reliability, Windows NT Server software RAID secures your data just as well as hardware RAID does. What it doesn't do, however, is provide redundant power supplies, hot swapping of disks, background rebuild, and other hardware RAID features designed to minimize server downtime. As a result, a server running Windows NT software RAID is no more likely to lose data than a server running hardware RAID, but is considerably more likely to be down for extended periods while failed disk drives are repaired and rebuilt. Unless you're running Windows NT Server on a system equipped with hot swappable drives and other RAID amenities—which would usually be equipped with a hardware RAID controller anyway—this lost ability to hot swap drives and otherwise maintain the array without taking down the server might be unacceptable.

If yours is a small array on a server supporting a limited number of users, the drawbacks of Windows NT Server software RAID might be an acceptable tradeoff for reduced costs. For larger arrays and critical environments, buy the appropriate hardware RAID solution.

Windows NT Server RAID Options

On the reasonable assumption that software RAID is better than no RAID, using Windows NT Server 4.0 to provide RAID functionality makes sense, particularly for small servers that otherwise wouldn't be equipped with RAID functionality. The following RAID options are available with Windows NT Server:

■ RAID 0 is referred to by Microsoft as *Disk Striping*, or the use of stripe sets. Like any RAID 0 arrangement, stripe sets increase disk subsystem performance but do nothing to provide data redundancy. The failure of any disk drive in a stripe set renders the data on the remaining drives in the stripe set inaccessible. Windows NT Server allows a stripe set to comprise from 2 to 32 individual disks. Increasing the number of disks in a stripe set increases the probability of data loss, because failure of a single drive results in a failure of the entire stripe set. If the disks assigned to a stripe set vary in size, the smallest determines the common partition size of the stripe set. The remaining space on other drives in the stripe set might be used individually or assigned to a volume set.

Part
II
Ch
7

■ RAID 1, referred to by Microsoft as *Disk Mirroring*, or the use of mirror sets, is supported directly by Windows NT Server for any hardware configuration with at least two disk drives of similar size. Windows NT Server doesn't require that the mirrored drive be identical to the original drive, but only that the mirrored drive be at least as large. This considerably simplifies replacing failed drives if the original model is no longer available. RAID 1 duplexing is supported directly for any hardware configuration with at least two disk drives of similar size and two disk controllers. As with any duplex arrangement, this removes the disk controller as a single point of failure. As with mirrored drives, Windows NT Server doesn't require duplexed drives to be identical.

■ RAID 5, referred to by Microsoft as *Disk Striping with Parity*, is also supported natively by Windows NT Server for any hardware configuration with at least three disk drives and one or more disk controllers. Windows NT Server allows as many as 32 drives in a striping set, although to maintain acceptable performance when a single drive fails, it's a better idea to limit the RAID 5 array to five or six drives.

 Don't install the paging file on a RAID 5 set unless you have no other choice, because a paging file on a RAID 5 subsystem causes a significant performance hit. The paging file contains only temporary data, so loss of a drive with the paging file doesn't result in data loss. If you must provide fault tolerance for your paging file, create a RAID 1 mirror set for the paging file.

Configuration Considerations: Volume Sets, Extensibility, and Booting

In addition to mirror sets and stripe sets, Windows NT Server provides a similar disk-management function called a *volume set*. Volume sets, although often confused with RAID, provide neither the data safety of RAID 1 or RAID 5, nor the performance benefits of RAID 0. A volume set simply allows a single logical volume to span more than one physical disk drive. With a volume set, data isn't striped to multiple disk drives, but instead is written sequentially to each disk drive in the volume set as the preceding drive is filled. A volume set allows you to combine the capacity of two or more smaller disk drives to provide a single larger volume. Because volume sets are accessed as a single logical unit, the failure of any single drive in a volume set renders the data on the remaining drives inaccessible. Volume sets commonly are called *JABD*—Just a Bunch of Drives.

Because volume sets don't provide data redundancy or performance benefits, and because by their nature they increase the chances of data loss due to drive failure, volume sets are normally a poor choice for configuring your disk storage. If your data storage requirements exceed the capacity of the largest disk drives available to you, a far better choice is to use RAID 5 to provide a single large volume with data redundancy. The chief advantage of volume sets is that, unlike stripe sets and mirror sets, they're dynamically extensible. If a volume set begins to fill up, you can increase its capacity simply by installing another physical disk drive and adding its space to the existing volume set. If, on the other hand, a stripe set or mirror set approaches its total capacity, your only option is to tear down the existing set, add drive capacity, build a new set, and restore your data.

One final issue to consider before you decide to implement Windows NT Server software RAID is that of system booting. Windows NT Server doesn't allow the system to boot from either a stripe set or a stripe set with parity, but does allow the system to boot from a mirror set. This means that to implement a stripe set, your server must have at least three physical disk drives—one boot drive and at least two drives to comprise the stripe set. (Partitioning one drive of a two-drive set to hold the operating system isn't recommended.) Similarly, implementing a stripe set with parity requires at least four drives—one from which the system boots and at least three more drives for the volume of the stripe set with parity. It's therefore common for small Windows NT Server systems to have five disk drives, the first two of which comprise a mirror set from which the system boots and on which applications reside, and the final three of which comprise a stripe set with parity on which most of the data is stored.

Creating Windows NT Server Stripe and Mirror Sets

After you install a sufficient number of drives and ensure that your SCSI host adapter recognizes each drive, you can create one or more of the three levels of RAID supported by Windows NT Server 4.0. The following sections provide the instructions for implementing Windows NT 4.0's software RAID 0, 1, and 5. RAID 0 and 1 require two physical drives; RAID 5 requires three physical drives. Each drive must have unused space in which to create the stripe set or mirror volume.

▶ **See** "Setting Up Your Fixed-Disk Drives," **p. 188**

N O T E The computer used in the following example is OAKLEAF3, a 133MHz Pentium server that dual-boots Windows 95 for digital video editing and Windows NT Server 4.0 for network test purposes. OAKLEAF3 is equipped with two Seagate ST15150W 4.3G Barracuda Wide SCSI drives (Bcuda1, Disk 0, and Bcuda2, Disk 1); a 1G Micropolis narrow SCSI drive (Microp1, Disk 2); and a Toshiba 4X SCSI CD-ROM drive connected to an Adaptec AHA-2940UW host controller. Bcuda1 has five 800K FAT partitions (Bcuda1p1 through Bcuda1p5), and Bcuda2 has two 4G FAT partitions (Bcuda2p1 and Bcuda2p2). Microp1 is divided into 800K (Microp1p1) and 200K (Microp1p2) partitions. The Bcuda1p4, Bcuda2p2, and Microp1p2 partitions were deleted (converted to free space) before performing the steps described in the following sections. ■

Creating RAID 0 Stripe Sets

Creating a RAID 0 stripe set is the simplest of the three processes offered by Windows NT 4.0's Disk Administrator. To create a RAID 0 stripe set, proceed as follows:

1. Log on as administrator and run Disk Administrator by choosing Programs, Administrative Tools, and Disk Administrator from the Start menu.
2. Click to select an unused area on the first disk drive.
3. Ctrl+click to select additional unused areas on other disk drives, up to a total of as many as 32 disk drives. You can select only one area on each disk drive. Figure 7.7 shows 800M and 2G areas of free space selected on Disk 0 and Disk 1, respectively.

FIG. 7.7

Selecting free space areas on two physical drives to create a RAID 0 stripe set.

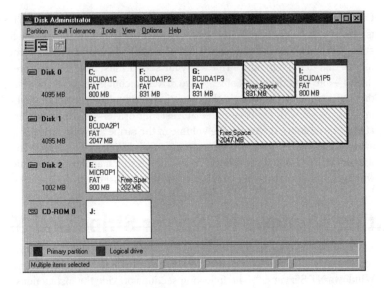

4. From the Partition menu, choose Create Stripe Set to open the Create Stripe Set dialog, which displays in the Create Stripe Set of Total Size box the default total size of the stripe set spanning all selected drives (see Figure 7.8). This total size takes into account the smallest area selected on any disk drive, adjusting (if necessary) the sizes of the areas on the other selected drives to set all to identical size. The total size value is approximately the size of the smallest disk area multiplied by the number of drives in the stripe set.

FIG. 7.8

Setting the total size of the stripe set in the Create Stripe Set dialog.

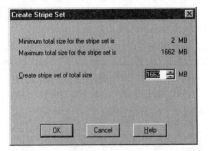

5. Click OK to accept the default size. Windows NT Server prepares to create the stripe set and assigns it a single default drive letter (see Figure 7.9). At this point, no changes have been made to the drives.

6. From the Partition menu, choose Commit Changes Now. A message box informs you that changes have been made to your disk configuration. Click Yes to accept and save the changes.

7. A second message box notifies you that the update was successful, and that you should save the disk configuration information and create a new emergency repair disk. (These steps are performed at the end of this procedure.) Click OK.

FIG. 7.9

The stripe set before
making the changes to
the selected partitions.

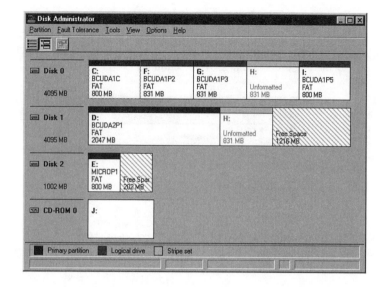

N O T E If another message box tells you that you must restart the computer for the changes to take
effect, click OK to begin system shutdown. After Windows NT Server is restarted, again log
on as administrator and run Disk Administrator. The need to shut down and restart Windows NT
depends on the status of the selected disk regions before beginning this process. ▪

8. Click to select the newly created but unformatted stripe set (see Figure 7.10). From the
   Tools menu, choose Format to open the Format Drive D: dialog.

FIG. 7.10

Selecting the
unformatted
stripe set.

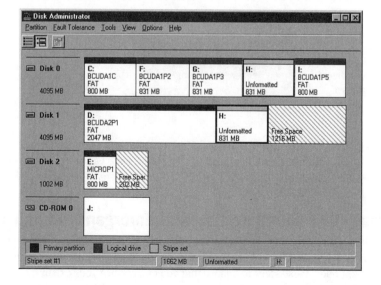

Part

II

Ch

7

9. Type a name for the volume in the Label text box (see Figure 7.11). In the Format Type drop-down list, you can choose an NTFS or FAT file system; select NTFS (the default). Marking the Quick Format check box bypasses drive sector checking during the formatting process. Click OK to continue.

FIG. 7.11

Adding a volume label and selecting the file system type.

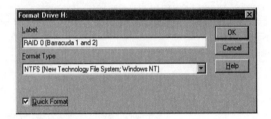

NOTE If you haven't previously formatted the free space used for the stripe set, clear the Quick Format check box. A full format tests for bad sectors during the formatting process and marks bad sectors unusable in the drive's sector map. ◼

10. A confirmation dialog warns you that continuing overwrites the contents of the volume. Click Yes to continue formatting.

11. If you marked the Quick Format check box in the Format Drive *D:* dialog, the Quick Format progress indicator appears only briefly. For a conventional formatting operation, the progress indicator appears for a minute or more, depending on the size of the volume.

12. When formatting is complete, a dialog informs you of the total available disk space on the new volume (see Figure 7.12). Click OK. The new volume is ready for use (see Figure 7.13).

FIG. 7.12

The Format Complete dialog displaying the size of the stripe set volume.

NOTE The status bar at the bottom of Disk Administrator's window isn't updated at the completion of the formatting process. To update the status bar, select another volume, and then reselect the newly created set. ◼

Creating Drive Configuration and Emergency Repair Disks

After making permanent changes to your drive configuration, always save the configuration changes, replace the repair information on the fixed disk, and create a new emergency repair disk. Follow these steps to ensure that you can restore your existing configuration in case of a system failure:

FIG. 7.13

Disk Administrator
displaying the newly
created RAID 0 stripe
set.

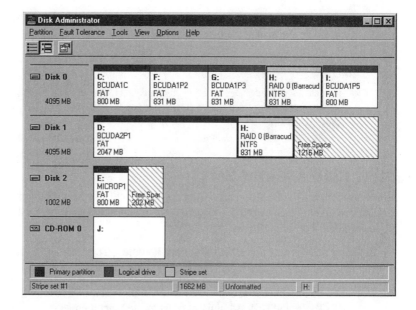

FIG. 7.13

Disk Administrator
displaying the newly
created RAID 0 stripe
set.

1. To save the current drive configuration, choose Configuration and then Save from the Partition menu to display the Insert Disk dialog. Insert a formatted disk and click OK to save the configuration. In case of a major catastrophe, you can use the disk to restore the current drive configuration by choosing Configuration and then Restore from the Partition menu.

2. Choose Run from the Start menu, type `rdisk` in the Open text box, and click OK to open the Repair Disk Utility window (see Figure 7.14).

FIG. 7.14

The opening window of
the Repair Disk Utility.

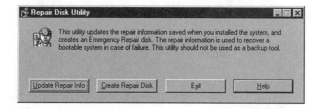

3. Click the Update Repair Info button. The confirmation dialog appears. Click OK to continue the update process. The progress indicator displays the status of the update, which takes a minute or two.

4. After the local repair information is updated, a message box appears, asking whether you want to create an emergency repair disk. After updating local repair information, it's imperative that you create a new emergency repair disk. Insert a disk (which doesn't need to be formatted) in the disk drive and click Yes.

5. Replace your existing emergency repair disk with the new emergency repair disk, which should be stored in a safe location. (Consider making two emergency repair disks,

Part
II

Ch
7

storing one disk off site.) The old disk is unusable with the new repair information stored on the local fixed disk.

> **CAUTION**
>
> If you don't create an emergency repair disk after updating local repair information, the repair disk likely won't work when used in the event of a major system failure. In this case, your only alternative is to reinstall Windows NT Server 4.0.

Creating RAID 1 Mirror Sets

Mirror sets vary from stripe sets; whereas stripe sets may span as many as 32 drives, mirror sets are created on a paired drive basis. You must first create a standard formatted volume, and then create the mirror drive.

Creating and Formatting a New Standard Volume   To create and format a new separate volume from the free space available on a single drive, follow these steps:

1. Log on as administrator and run Disk Administrator by choosing Programs, Administrative Tools, and Disk Administrator from the Start menu.

2. Click to select an unused area on the fixed-disk drive (see Figure 7.15).

FIG. 7.15

Selecting an unused area of a drive in which to create a new standard volume.

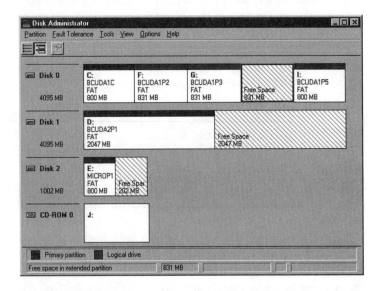

3. From the Partition menu, choose Create to open the Create Logical Drive dialog, which displays in the Create Logical Drive of Size box the default total size of the free space of the selected drive (see Figure 7.16). Accept the default size unless you want to create a volume of a smaller size.

FIG. 7.16

Setting the size of the volume in the Create Logical Drive dialog.

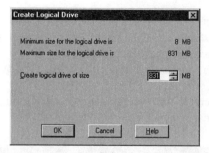

4. Click OK. Windows NT Server prepares to create the stripe set, assigning the volume a single default drive letter. At this point, no changes have been made to the drive and the drive (H in Figure 7.17) is disabled.

FIG. 7.17

The proposed volume before making the changes to the selected partition.

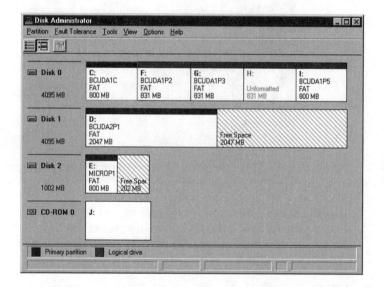

N O T E You can't format the inactive volume shown in Figure 7.17 because the Tools menu's Format option is disabled at that point. You must commit the changes to create the new volume's partition, and then format the partition. ▨

5. From the Partition menu, choose Commit Changes Now. A message box informs you that changes have been made to your disk configuration. Click Yes to accept and save the changes. A second message box notifies you that the update was successful, and that you should save the disk configuration information and create a new emergency repair disk. These two steps are performed after you complete the drive reconfiguration process. Click OK.

Part

II

Ch

7

N O T E   If another message box tells you to restart the computer for the changes to take effect,
click OK to begin system shutdown. After Windows NT Server is restarted, again log on as
administrator and run Disk Administrator. The need to shut down and restart Windows NT depends on
the status of the selected disk regions before the beginning of this process. ■

6. Click to select the newly created but unformatted volume (H in Figure 7.18). From the
   Tools menu, choose Format to open the Format Drive *D*: dialog.

FIG. 7.18

Selecting the active but
unformatted volume.

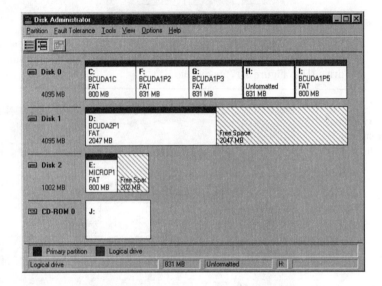

7. Type a name for the volume in the Label text box. From the Format Type drop-down list
   you can choose an NTFS or FAT file system; select NTFS (the default). Marking the
   Quick Format check box bypasses drive sector checking during the formatting process.
   Click OK to continue.

N O T E   As recommended in the earlier section on RAID 0 stripe sets, don't use Quick Format if
you haven't previously formatted the free space used for the new volume. A full format
tests for bad sectors during the formatting process and marks bad sectors as unusable in the drive's
sector map. ■

8. A confirmation dialog warns you that continuing overwrites the contents of the volume.
   Click Yes to continue formatting. If you marked the Quick Format check box, the Quick
   Format progress indicator appears only briefly.

9. When formatting is complete, a dialog informs you of the total available disk space on the
   new volume. Click OK. The new volume is ready for use as an independent volume or as
   a member of a mirror set.

N O T E If your new volume is intended as an independent volume (not a member of a mirror set), update the configuration and repair information as described earlier in the section "Creating Drive Configuration and Emergency Repair Disks." ▄

Creating the Mirror of the Standard Volume Mirroring creates a formatted volume of the same size as the new standard volume, but on another physical drive. To create the mirror partition, follow these steps:

1. From Disk Administrator, select the newly formatted standard volume.

2. Ctrl+click an unused area on another disk drive that's at least as large as the newly created volume (see Figure 7.19).

FIG. 7.19

Selecting the formatted volume and the free space on another physical drive to create the mirror set.

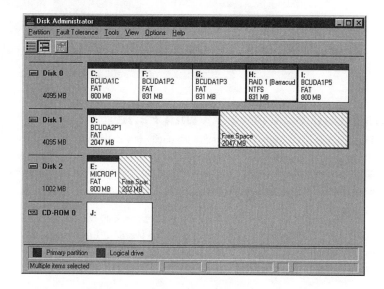

3. From the Fault Tolerance menu, choose Establish Mirror.

4. From the Partition menu, choose Commit Changes Now. Windows NT Server creates the mirror set and assigns the drive letter of the first drive of the set (H in Figure 7.20).

N O T E The mirror set isn't created immediately on completion of step 4. Setting up the mirror partition and formatting the partition occurs as a background task. Disk Administrator's status bar displays INITIALIZING during the process. To determine when the process is complete, periodically select another volume, and then reselect the mirror set. The process is complete when you see HEALTHY on the status bar. ▄

5. Update the configuration and repair information as described earlier in the section "Creating Drive Configuration and Emergency Repair Disks."

Part

II

Ch

7

FIG. 7.20
Disk Administrator
displaying the newly
created mirror set
(drive H).

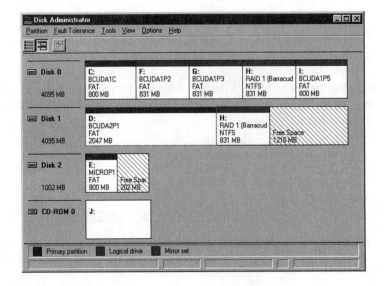

Creating RAID 5 Stripe Sets with Parity

The process of creating a stripe set with parity is very similar to that used to create a RAID 0 stripe set. Whereas a RAID 0 stripe set can be created on only two physical drives, a RAID 5 stripe set with parity requires a minimum of three drives—one for parity information and at least two for data.

> **N O T E** Despite the need for a minimum of three drives, RAID 5 is the best choice for software RAID. In addition to the benefits of RAID 5 over RAID 1 mentioned earlier in this chapter, recovering a RAID 5 system after a disk failure is much easier than recovering a RAID 1 system, especially if the primary disk fails and you must recover from the shadow disk. ■

To create a stripe set with parity, proceed as follows:

1. Log on as administrator and run Disk Administrator by choosing Programs, Administrative Tools, and then Disk Administrator from the Start menu.

2. Click to select an unused area on the first disk drive.

3. Ctrl+click at least two additional unused areas on other disk drives, up to a total of as many as 32 disk drives. You can choose only one area on each disk drive. Figure 7.21 shows three unused areas selected on drives 0, 1, and 2.

4. From the Fault Tolerance menu, choose Create Stripe Set with Parity. The Create Stripe Set with Parity dialog appears, displaying the total size of the stripe set with parity spanning all selected drives. This total size takes into account the smallest area selected on any disk drive, adjusting (if necessary) the sizes of the areas on the other selected drives to set all to identical size.

FIG. 7.21
Selecting a minimum of three areas of free space to create a RAID 5 stripe set with parity.

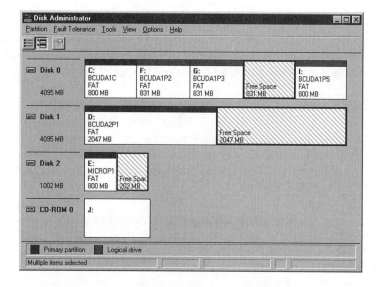

5. Click OK to accept the default. Windows NT Server prepares to create the stripe set with parity and assigns a drive letter (see Figure 7.22). The stripe set with parity must now be prepared for use.

FIG. 7.22
The three partitions proposed for the RAID 5 stripe set.

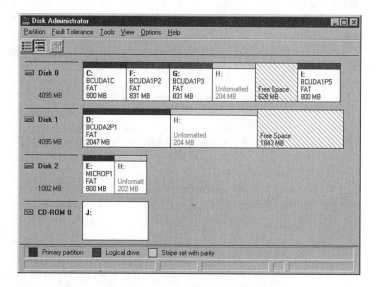

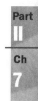
Part
II

Ch
7

6. From the Partition menu, choose Commit Changes Now. A dialog tells you that changes have been made to your disk configuration. Click Yes to accept and save the changes. A message box notifies you that the update was successful. Click OK.

N O T E   If another message box tells you to restart the computer for the changes to take effect,
click OK to begin system shutdown. After Windows NT Server is restarted, again log on as
administrator and run Disk Administrator. The need to shut down and restart Windows NT depends on
the status of the selected disk regions before the beginning of this process. ■

7. Select the newly created but unformatted stripe set with parity. From the Tools menu,
   choose Format to open the Format Drive *D*: dialog.

8. Type a name for the volume in the Label text box (see Figure 7.23). From the Format
   Type drop-down list you can choose an NTFS or FAT file system; select NTFS (the
   default). The Quick Format check box is disabled when you create a RAID 5 stripe set.
   Click OK to continue.

FIG. 7.23

Adding a label to the
RAID 5 volume and
selecting the file
system.

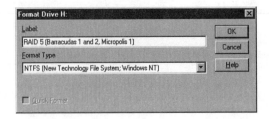

9. When formatting is complete, a dialog informs you of the total available disk space on the
   new volume. Click OK, and the new RAID 5 volume is ready for use (see Figure 7.24).

FIG. 7.24

The formatted RAID 5
volume ready for use.

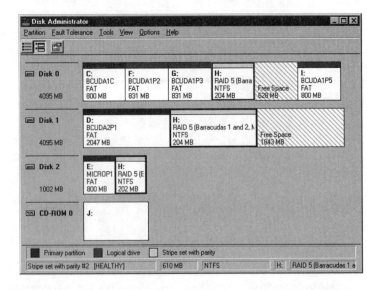

N O T E   As is the case with mirror sets, RAID 5 volumes aren't ready for use until the background
processing to create the additional partitions and format the partitions completes. This

process can take several minutes when creating large RAID 5 volumes. The process is complete and you can use the drive when HEALTHY appears on the status bar, as shown in Figure 7.24. ■

Saving the Master Boot Record and Partition Table

After you finish setting up your software RAID subsystem, use the DiskSave or DiskProbe utilities of the *Windows NT Server Resource Kit* to create a copy of the master boot record (MBR) and partition table on a disk. You might need to use the saved file in the event of your inability to recover from a drive failure, especially with a RAID 1 mirror set.

▶ **See** "Recovering from Fixed-Disk Failures," **p. 210**

Recovering a Software RAID 1 or RAID 5 Set

Failure of a member of a mirror set or stripe set with parity results in the creation of an orphan volume. Windows NT 4.0 detects an orphan volume under either of these two conditions:

■ During a failed write operation, in which case you receive an error message similar to that shown in Figure 7.25

■ During Windows NT startup, in which case a severe error is logged in the event log

FIG. 7.25

The error message that occurs when a drive fails in a software RAID 1 or RAID 5 subsystem.

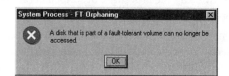

> **N O T E** You can't restore a failed RAID 0 array. Failure of a member of a plain striped set is a catastrophic failure. You must restore your last backup or, if you don't have a full backup, install Windows NT Server 4.0 from scratch and back up whatever data is valid from your last backup tape. ■

In either case, operations continue, taking advantage of Windows NT's RAID 1 or RAID 5 fault-tolerance. Disk Administrator's status line displays *Volume #N* [RECOVERABLE] for the se-lected volume. When a drive fails, create a backup with a fresh tape immediately; your RAID set is no longer fault-tolerant, and failure of another drive will result in loss of all data since the last backup.

CAUTION

Don't shut down Windows NT Server 4.0 when a drive failure occurs—you might not be able to restart your system. Make a full backup immediately, and then proceed restoring your system as soon as possible.

Part

II

Ch

7

Restoring a Mirror Set

To recover a failed RAID 1 mirror set, you must first break the mirror set, and then reconstruct it after installing a new drive, preferably of the same make and model as the failed drive. After making a complete backup of the remaining good drive(s) of the mirror set, follow these steps to recover a mirror set:

1. Launch Disk Administrator and select the mirror set volume.

2. Choose Break Mirror from the Fault Tolerance menu. You must break the mirror set to recover.

3. Click Yes to confirm that you want to break the mirror set. The working partition receives the logical drive letter assigned to the set, and the orphan partition receives the next available drive letter.

4. Choose Commit Changes Now from the Partition menu.

5. Make an independent backup of the working partition.

6. Shut down the system and remove the failed drive. If the failed drive is the shadow drive, set the SCSI device ID of the shadow drive to that of the primary drive. Replace the failed drive with the same make and model set to the appropriate SCSI device ID.

7. Restart the system.

8. Re-create the mirror set by using the procedure described earlier in the section "Creating the Mirror of the Standard Volume."

9. Re-create your emergency repair disk and use the Resource Kit's DiskSave or DiskProbe utility to save the master boot record and partition table to disk.

N O T E If you can't restart the system by using the shadow drive, change the SCSI device ID of the drive to its original setting and install the replacement drive with the SCSI device ID set to that of the failed drive. Run Windows NT 4.0 Setup with the boot disks and install Windows NT Server 4.0 in the same folder as your original installation. Restore the mirror backup, including the Registry, to the replacement drive. Verify that the restoration works, and then use Disk Manager to delete the shadow partition and re-create the mirror set. ■

Restoring a Stripe Set with Parity

Restoring a RAID 5 subsystem is much easier than recovering a RAID 1 mirror set. To recover from failure of a RAID 5 drive, follow these steps:

1. After making a full backup, shut down the system and replace the failed drive.

2. Restart the system, launch Disk Administrator, and select the RAID 5 volume.

3. Select the unpartitioned space on the replacement drive.

4. Choose Regenerate from the Fault Tolerance menu.

5. Close Disk Administrator and restart the system. Regeneration of the failed drive's contents occurs automatically in the background after Windows NT restarts.

6. Re-create your emergency repair disk and use the Resource Kit's DiskSave or DiskProbe utility to save the master boot record and partition table to disk.

NOTE If your system runs application services—such as SQL Server, Exchange, or SMS—and you receive the message `The drive cannot be locked for exclusive use`, stop all unnecessary services and click OK to continue the regeneration process. ■

Summarizing RAID Recommendations

Given the wide diversity of RAID products available and the equally broad range of needs and budgets, making hard-and-fast recommendations for the most appropriate means of implementing RAID is difficult. However, the following observations serve as useful guidelines:

■ If your disk storage requirements are small, consider using your existing SCSI host adapter to implement mirroring. If your host adapter doesn't support hardware mirroring, consider replacing it with one that does. Buy an additional disk drive to mirror to each existing drive. The result will be greatly increased data safety and better performance at minimal cost. Choose this hardware method in preference to the RAID 1 software functions of Windows NT Server on the basis of performance and minimizing load on the server.

■ If your disk storage requirements are moderate—particularly if you need RAID 5— consider using either Windows NT Server software RAID or one of the hardware alternatives. Windows NT Server RAID 5 support appears to be rock solid and performs well on smaller arrays. It's worth considering if the tradeoffs in flexibility, ease of maintenance, and server loading are of minor importance to you. If any or all of these factors concern you, choose a hardware RAID implementation.

■ If you're buying a new server, buy one with built-in hardware RAID support. In addition to the performance benefits of hardware RAID, the presence of hot swappable drives and similar components will contribute to increased uptime for your server.

■ If your storage requirements are large or if you need stacked RAID, multiple independent arrays, or support for multiple hosts, a good external RAID enclosure is the only way to go. Give preference to those units that use industry standard components as widely as possible, rather than those that use proprietary hardware modifications to squeeze out the last ounce of performance.

The best way to assure that a hardware RAID system meets your data-security requirements is to buy a system certified to a particular data availability level by RAB. In 1996, RAB established the following rating system based on the data availability of RAID systems:

■ Failure Resistant Disk System (FRDS)

■ Failure Resistant Disk System Plus (FRDS+)

■ Failure Tolerant Disk System (FTDS)

■ Disaster Tolerant Disk Systems (DTDS)

Part
II

Ch
7

The following sections describe FRDS, FRDS+, FTDS, and DTDS criteria, which are increasingly demanding. The content of the following sections is based on current RAB publications.

Failure Resistant Disk System Criteria

At the minimum, any hardware RAID subsystem should conform to the FRDS criteria. FRDS systems are suitable for small workgroup servers and data marts. A *data mart* is a database server that consolidates data from other servers for online analysis and decision support. Meeting RAB's criteria for FRDS certification requires that a RAID system exhibit the following five properties:

- Protection against data loss and loss of access to data due to disk failures
- Capability to reconstruct a failed disk's contents to a replacement disk while the system is in operation
- Protection against data loss due to a write hole
- Protection against data loss due to the failure of any storage-related component
- Continuous monitoring of replaceable units and indication of failure

A *write hole* occurs when a failure occurs during a disk write operation, placing the array in an inconsistent state. In a mirrored (RAID 1) array, a write hole occurs when the mirrored drive fails momentarily before copying the new data. In this case, the data on the two drives varies. In a parity (RAID 5) array, such a failure may cause regeneration of incorrect data when a drive is replaced.

Failure Resistant Disk System Plus Criteria

Large workgroup and departmental servers, and any database server in heavy online transaction processing service, should meet at least FRDS+ criteria. In addition to FRDS, qualification for FRDS+ requires these features:

- Active, preconfigured replaceable drive(s)
- Automatic swap and hot swap of drives
- Protection against data loss due to cache failure
- Protection against data loss due to external power failure
- Protection against data loss as a result of out-of-range temperature
- Active out-of-range environment notification

The primary operating advantage of FRDS+ over FRDS is that replacing a failed drive doesn't involve a system shutdown. Automatic swap and hot-swap operations occur without loss of data accessibility.

Failure Tolerant Disk System Criteria

The FTDS classification defines systems on which organizations rely to perform their primary business functions. Examples are credit-card verification, Internet service provision, airline reservation, and the like. In addition to FRDS+ properties, receiving FTDS certification requires

- Disk channel (SCSI chip, cable, or backplane) failure
- Controller module failure
- Cache failure
- Power supply failure

FTDS relies on redundant components, such as dual-copy caches and multiple controllers. Thus, FTDS is substantially more costly than FRDS or FRDS+ implementations. FTDS+, which specifies data accessibility in case of a total computer failure, requires a failover clustering system.

Disaster Tolerant Disk System Criteria

To qualify for Disaster Tolerant Disk System (DTDS) certification, a disk subsystem must meet the RAB requirements for FRDS+ and FTDS+, but must also be capable of providing continuous access to data with multiple inoperative components. DTDS products are likely to be available from only a few RAID vendors and are expected to be very expensive, at least for the next few years.

From Here...

Although RAID arrays are found on virtually every production server, many network designers and administrators don't have a firm grasp of the relative advantages and disadvantages of RAID levels and implementation strategies. Thus, this chapter provided a detailed description and comparison of these two subjects of major importance to server performance and reliability.

The remaining chapters in Part II cover the other basic elements of setting up Windows NT Server and connecting Windows 95 and other clients to your network:

- Chapter 8, "Installing File Backup Systems," describes how to choose and set up backup systems for your RAID array. Although server RAID arrays are relatively secure, periodic backup to tape or other storage media is an absolute necessity to ensure against data loss in case of a catastrophe.
- Chapter 9, "Understanding the Windows NT Registry," takes you inside the Registry files used by Windows NT Server 4.0 through the use of the Registry Editor, which you use to inspect Registry values and, under very specific conditions, modify these values.
- Chapter 10, "Using TCP/IP, WINS, and DHCP," shows you how to plan for and implement TCP/IP networking, including use of the Windows Internet Name Service (WINS) and Dynamic Host Configuration Protocol (DHCP).
- Chapter 11, "Configuring Windows 95 Clients for Networking," provides the information you need to optimize the network functions of Windows 95 client PCs.
- Chapter 12, "Connecting Other PC Clients to the Network," describes how to connect computers running Windows 3.1+, DOS, and the Macintosh operating system to your Windows NT Server 4.0 network.

Part
II

Ch
7

CHAPTER 8

Installing File Backup Systems

Disk drives fail, taking critical data with them. People accidentally delete the wrong file. Databases become corrupt, sometimes for no apparent reason. It's your job as network administrator to protect against these and other causes of data loss by maintaining backup copies of your important data.

Backing up your data to tape or other removable storage media serves these purposes:

Windows NT backup types

Understand the types of backup available and how each type of backup can best be used to ensure the safety of your data.

Backup tape rotation

Choose a tape-rotation method that stores multiple copies of your data for safety, while allowing fast and easy retrieval of backup data when needed.

Tape backup hardware

Select the best backup hardware for your server, taking into account cost, speed, reliability, and storage capacity.

The Windows NT backup program

Get started with Windows NT's NTBACKUP program, and then select a third-party backup application with features to suit your server installation.

- You have a copy of your data to protect against the catastrophic data loss that occurs when a disk drive fails and your RAID subsystem can't regenerate the data.

- You get an offline copy of data that you can recover if the working copy of a file is deleted or improperly modified.

- You get a data archive that can be preserved for historical or legal purposes.

- You can maintain a copy of your data, off premises, to protect against fire or other natural disasters.

In addition, proper data backup contributes to your employment security. Many organizations have a policy of immediately terminating any network administrator responsible for an unrecoverable data loss. Even without such a policy, failure to properly back up data might result in the need of the responsible person to seek alternative employment.

The advent of RAID and other redundancy options has made some LAN administrators more casual about backing up critical data. In reality, RAID addresses only the first of the four preceding reasons for backing up. The other three reasons make backing up just as crucial as it was before RAID subsystems became a common feature of servers running Windows NT. ■

Understanding Backup Types

Windows NT Server 4.0 provides built-in support for various backup devices, primarily tape backup drives. The Microsoft Hardware Compatibility List for Windows NT, current when this book was written, identifies 145 individual makes and models of backup devices compatible with Windows NT Server 4.0. Before you choose backup hardware and software for your Windows NT Server 4.0 installation, however, it's important to understand how Windows NT Server 4.0 handles the file backup process. The following sections explain the purpose of the file archive bit and the types of backup operations supported by Windows NT Server 4.0 and third-party device drivers for backup devices.

ON THE WEB

You can obtain the current version of the Hardware Compatibility List for Windows NT from Microsoft's Windows Hardware Quality Labs Web site at **http://www.microsoft.com/isapi/hwtest/ hsearchn4.idc** or by FTP from **ftp://ftp.microsoft.com**, in the /bussys/winnt/winnt-docs/hcl folder.

The Archive Bit

For you to manage a backup strategy, it's essential that your backup software has a way of knowing when a file has been created or modified since the last normal backup. One way to do this is to examine the date/time stamp on each file, and compare it with the time that the last backup was done to determine whether the file has changed. This method, used by the backup applet bundled with Windows 95, is simple in concept but unreliable in use. Using date/time stamps to determine the files to back up is unreliable, because many programs alter the contents of a file but don't change the date/time stamp when doing so. As a result, a better method of determining backup currency is needed. Fortunately, such a method has been available since the early days of MS-DOS.

Like MS-DOS, Windows NT stores with each file an attribute called the *archive bit*. The archive bit is set to on (a value of 1) when a file is created or modified to indicate that the file hasn't been backed up since the last change to it occurred. Because the archive bit is set to on whenever a file has been written to, it provides a completely reliable means of knowing when a file has changed. Windows NT Server 4.0 backup functions, like all modern full-featured backup programs, uses the archive bit to manage backup.

Normal Backups

A *normal backup* copies all selected files, regardless of the state of their archive bits, to the tape drive or other backup media, and then turns off the archive bit on all files that have been copied (see Figure 8.1). Most third-party backup software refers to this process as a *full backup*.

FIG. 8.1

A normal or full backup, which copies all selected files to tape and turns off the archive bit.

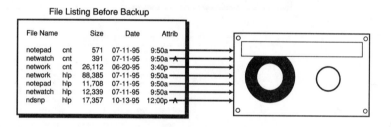

File Listing Before Backup

File Name		Size	Date	Attrib
notepad	cnt	571	07-11-95	9:50a
netwatch	cnt	391	07-11-95	9:50a -A
network	cnt	26,112	06-20-95	3:40p
network	hlp	88,385	07-11-95	9:50a
notepad	hlp	11,708	07-11-95	9:50a
netwatch	hlp	12,339	07-11-95	9:50a
ndsnp	hlp	17,357	10-13-95	12:00p -A

File Listing After Backup

File Name		Size	Date	Attrib
notepad	cnt	571	07-11-95	9:50a
netwatch	cnt	391	07-11-95	9:50a
network	cnt	26,112	06-20-95	3:40p
network	hlp	88,385	07-11-95	9:50a
notepad	hlp	11,708	07-11-95	9:50a
netwatch	hlp	12,339	07-11-95	9:50a
ndsnp	hlp	17,357	10-13-95	12:00p

N O T E A normal backup doesn't necessarily copy all files from a particular volume or disk drive, but it might simply copy a file or set of files from a specified folder or folders on the selected volume or disk drive. What determines a normal backup is that all *selected* files are copied without regard to the state of their archive bit. ■

Re-creating a failed hard drive from a normal backup set of the entire drive is straightforward. If the system drive has failed, you must replace the drive and reinstall Windows NT Server before proceeding. If the system drive is operable, after replacing the data drive, use the Windows NT Server backup application, NTBACKUP, to do a full restore of the tape to the new drive. Partial restores, such as those of accidentally deleted files, are equally straightforward. NTBACKUP is described later in the section "Using the Windows NT Server 4.0 Backup Application."

Copy Backups

A *copy backup* is identical to a normal backup, except that copy backups skip the final step of resetting to off all the archive bits on backed up files (see Figure 8.2). Most third-party backup software refers to this process as a *full copy backup*. The resulting backup tape is identical to what would have been created by a normal backup, but the archive bit status of the files on the disk remains unchanged. The main purpose of a copy backup is to allow you to create an archive or off-site backup set without affecting your main backup set's rotation process.

FIG. 8.2

A copy backup, which copies all selected files to tape but leaves the archive bit unchanged.

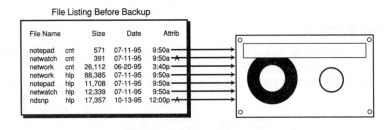

Because the contents of a copy backup set are indistinguishable from those of a normal backup set, restore procedures are identical for these two types of backups.

Incremental Backups

An *incremental backup* copies to the backup media all selected files that have their archive bit turned on, and then turns the archive bit off for the files that have been copied (see Figure 8.3). The tape from the first incremental backup done after a normal backup contains only those files altered since the last normal backup. Subsequent incremental backup tapes contain only those files that changed since the last incremental backup. After each incremental backup is completed, all files have their archive bits turned off as though a normal backup were done.

Re-creating a failed hard drive from incremental backup sets is a bit more involved than using a normal backup set, because each incremental backup tape contains only some of the changed files, and different incremental backup tapes might contain different versions of the same file.

To re-create a failed disk drive, you first restore the most recent normal backup set to the replacement disk. Then you restore all incremental backup sets created after the normal backup set, beginning with the earliest and proceeding sequentially to the latest incremental backup set.

FIG. 8.3

An incremental backup, which copies only changed files to tape and sets the archive bit to off.

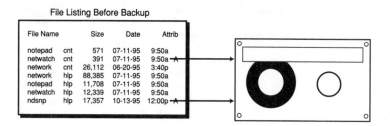

File Listing Before Backup

File Name		Size	Date	Attrib
notepad	cnt	571	07-11-95	9:50a
netwatch	cnt	391	07-11-95	9:50a
network	cnt	26,112	06-20-95	3:40p
network	hlp	88,385	07-11-95	9:50a
notepad	hlp	11,708	07-11-95	9:50a
netwatch	hlp	12,339	07-11-95	9:50a
ndsnp	hlp	17,357	10-13-95	12:00p

File Listing After Backup

File Name		Size	Date	Attrib
notepad	cnt	571	07-11-95	9:50a
netwatch	cnt	391	07-11-95	9:50a
network	cnt	26,112	06-20-95	3:40p
network	hlp	88,385	07-11-95	9:50a
notepad	hlp	11,708	07-11-95	9:50a
netwatch	hlp	12,339	07-11-95	9:50a
ndsnp	hlp	17,357	10-13-95	12:00p

Restoring an accidentally deleted file is a more complex process. To ensure that you get the latest version of the file, you must start by examining the most recent incremental backup set and work backward until you locate the most recent occurrence of the file on an incremental backup set. If the file in question hasn't changed since the last normal backup, you might have to work all the way back to the last normal backup set before you locate the file. Fortunately, most backup software makes this process somewhat easier by allowing you to search backup logs to locate the file so that you can load the proper tape directly.

 T I P The incremental backup is best suited to environments where a relatively large number of different files change each day. Because the incremental backup sets the archive bit to off after each file is backed up, each file is backed up only on the day that it's changed. This might reduce the number of tapes needed for each daily tape set, and also cuts down on the time required for daily partial backups.

Differential Backups

A *differential backup* copies to the backup media all selected files that have their archive bits turned on, but then leaves the archive bits unchanged on the files that have been copied (see Figure 8.4). Each differential backup set contains all files changed since the last normal backup. Each differential backup set also is larger than the preceding set, because later sets contain all the files previously backed up, plus all files changed since that last backup.

FIG. 8.4

A differential backup, which copies only changed files to tape and leaves the archive bit unchanged.

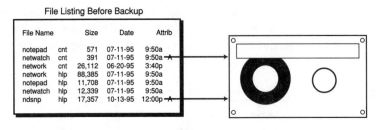

File Listing Before Backup

File Name		Size	Date	Attrib
notepad	cnt	571	07-11-95	9:50a
netwatch	cnt	391	07-11-95	9:50a A
network	cnt	26,112	06-20-95	3:40p
network	hlp	88,385	07-11-95	9:50a
notepad	hlp	11,708	07-11-95	9:50a
netwatch	hlp	12,339	07-11-95	9:50a
ndsnp	hlp	17,357	10-13-95	12:00p A

File Listing After Backup

File Name		Size	Date	Attrib
notepad	cnt	571	07-11-95	9:50a
netwatch	cnt	391	07-11-95	9:50a A
network	cnt	26,112	06-20-95	3:40p
network	hlp	88,385	07-11-95	9:50a
notepad	hlp	11,708	07-11-95	9:50a
netwatch	hlp	12,339	07-11-95	9:50a
ndsnp	hlp	17,357	10-13-95	12:00p A

Re-creating a failed hard drive with a differential backup set is relatively straightforward. As with an incremental backup set, you begin by restoring the last normal backup set. Because each differential backup set contains all files changed since the last normal backup, however, you need to restore only the most recent differential backup set. Restoring an accidentally deleted file is similarly straightforward. If the file is listed on your most recent differential backup log, restore from the latest differential backup set. Otherwise, restore from the last normal backup.

Daily Copy Backups

A *daily copy backup* copies all selected files that have been modified that day, but leaves the archive bits unchanged on the copied files (see Figure 8.5). Like the Windows 95 backup mentioned earlier in the section "The Archive Bit," the daily copy backup uses file date stamps to determine their eligibility for backup, rather than examine the status of the archive bit.

Unlike the incremental backup, which copies all files changed since the last normal backup or incremental backup was done, the daily copy backup must be run at least once each day if it's to be successfully used to archive files changed since the last normal backup. If you fail to run the daily copy backup on one particular day, none of the files changed on that day are written to tape until the next normal, copy, incremental, or differential backup is done. Because it ignores the state of the archive bit, the daily copy backup also fails to back up changed files if the file date stamp wasn't altered at the time the file was changed.

Backup Type Selection

A normal backup has the considerable advantages of thoroughness and simplicity. Each normal backup set contains all the selected files on your hard drive. No tape juggling is required to locate a particular file. If a problem occurs, simply retrieve the last normal backup tape and do a full or partial restore, as appropriate. The primary problem with normal backups is that they consume large numbers of backup tapes and take a long time to complete.

FIG. 8.5

A daily copy backup, which copies only changed files to tape, based on the file date, and leaves the archive bit unchanged.

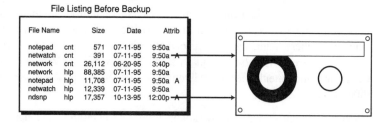

File Listing Before Backup

File Name		Size	Date	Attrib
notepad	cnt	571	07-11-95	9:50a
netwatch	cnt	391	07-11-95	9:50a ◄A
network	cnt	26,112	06-20-95	3:40p
network	hlp	88,385	07-11-95	9:50a
notepad	hlp	11,708	07-11-95	9:50a A
netwatch	hlp	12,339	07-11-95	9:50a
ndsnp	hlp	17,357	10-13-95	12:00p ◄A

File Listing After Backup

File Name		Size	Date	Attrib
notepad	cnt	571	07-11-95	9:50a
netwatch	cnt	391	07-11-95	9:50a A
network	cnt	26,112	06-20-95	3:40p
network	hlp	88,385	07-11-95	9:50a
notepad	hlp	11,708	07-11-95	9:50a A
netwatch	hlp	12,339	07-11-95	9:50a
ndsnp	hlp	17,357	10-13-95	12:00p A

NOTE Doing a proper backup requires that the contents of the server disk be static—that is, that files not be in use and subject to change by users while the backup process proceeds. For many organizations, this means that the best time to do backups is during evening hours and on weekends. Assuming that the server can be taken down for backup at 7 p.m. and must be back in service by 7 a.m., the backup must be completed within 12 hours.

The fastest 4mm DAT tape drives commonly used for Windows NT Server backup can transfer data at a sustained rate of perhaps 30M/minute, or about 1.8G/hour, allowing time to back up a little more than 20G overnight on weekdays. Even the larger 8mm tape drives with automatic tape changers top out at 60M/minute or so, extending the maximum to perhaps 40G or 50G for an overnight backup. If your server disk "farm" is larger than 40G or 50G, if you have multiple servers to back up to a single tape drive, or if your company's hours of operation are longer, you don't have time to complete a normal backup each night. ▉

Another reason that it might not be feasible to use only normal backup sets is tape capacity. Unless your IS department or computer room is staffed 24 hours a day, 7 days a week (24×7), overnight backups require either that the size of the backup set not exceed the capacity of a single tape, or that expensive "jukebox" tape changers are used to do unattended backups.

It's for these reasons that the concepts of incremental and differential partial backups were developed. Using incremental or differential backups with less-frequent normal backups allows only changed files to be backed up routinely, whereas the unchanged bulk of the disk contents are backed up only weekly, or monthly, typically over the course of a weekend. Because only a subset of the full disk is copied to tape each night, the time and tape capacity factors become lesser issues.

The choice between using incremental backup or differential backup for your partial backups depends on how many files are changed, how frequently the files are changed, the size of the files, and how frequently you expect to need to do restores. If most of your files are large and change infrequently, choosing incremental backup minimizes the total amount of data that must be written to tape, because this data is written only once each time the file changes when using incremental backup (instead of each time a backup is done with differential backup). Conversely, if you have many small files that change frequently, the storage economy of incremental backup is likely to be outweighed by the ease of file retrieval with differential backup.

If you're fortunate enough to have a tape drive large enough to do a normal backup on a single tape and have the time each night to complete a normal backup, then do so. Using only normal backups makes it much easier to manage the backup process and much less likely that you might accidentally overwrite the wrong tape or otherwise compromise the integrity of your backup sets. If—as is more common—you must depend on less frequent normal backups and daily partial backups, decide whether using incremental backup or differential backup better suits your data; then use the method that best matches your needs. For typical Windows NT servers, a program that uses normal backups, with differential backups, is the best choice.

Developing a Backup Strategy

Developing a coherent backup strategy that reliably safeguards your data requires more than simply deciding to do a normal backup each weekend and a partial backup every night. You must also consider several other factors, discussed in the following sections, that bear on data integrity and managing the backup process.

Organizing Disk Storage

The first issue to consider when developing a backup strategy is how to arrange the data on your server's fixed-disk drives. If you have only a single disk volume on your server, there's nothing to decide. If, however, you have multiple volumes, you can decide what type of data resides on each volume. Figure 8.6 shows one possible arrangement of data on volumes intended to make backup easier. Making the correct data organization decisions eases the entire backup process; making the wrong decisions can complicate backup operations needlessly.

A satisfactory organization places user home directories and other areas with files that frequently change on one or more volumes but segregates system files and other files that change infrequently in a separate volume of their own. Depending on the number of volumes that you've created and the types of data you must store, you can extend this file segregation process. For example, if you have a large database that's updated infrequently, you might decide to place it on a dedicated volume, thereby minimizing or obviating entirely the need for backup of that volume. Similarly, if you have large imaging files that change frequently, you may allocate a volume to them and then use incremental backup for only that volume, using differential backup for other volumes where its use is more appropriate. Always manage your volumes with backup issues in the back of your mind.

FIG. 8.6
Organizing disk volumes to optimize backup operations.

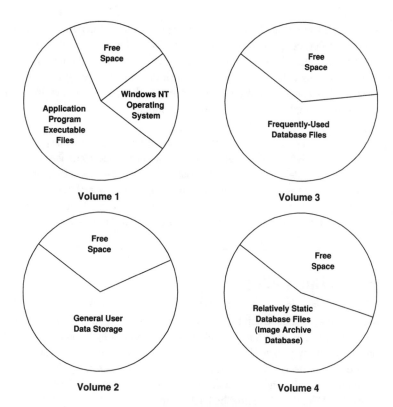

Volume 1

Volume 3

Volume 2

Volume 4

N O T E Client/server relational database management systems (RDBMSes), such as Microsoft SQL Server 6.5, present special difficulties in backing up data because their files remain open whenever the RDBMS is running. Most RDBMSes therefore provide a backup system independent of the backup application supplied with Windows NT Server 4.0.

RDBMS backup procedures use a periodic *database dump*, which is equivalent to a normal backup. Incremental backups save the content of a *transaction log*, which lists all modifications to the database since the last dump. On completion of a database dump, the transaction log file is deleted. RDBMS transaction logs vary from the transitory transaction logs created by Windows NT's Log File Service for NTFS volumes. ∎

Ensuring Backup Integrity

The second issue to consider when developing a backup strategy is how you verify the integrity of your backups. Many LAN administrators have found, to their sorrow, that the backup tape they relied on to restore a failed drive is unreadable. You don't want to find this out when it's too late to recover your data. The way to avoid this problem is to perform a *verify operation* to confirm that the contents of the backup tape correspond to the contents of the disk drive.

Inexpensive tape drives use a single head to perform both read and write operations. Doing a verify with these tape drives requires a second complete pass of the tape through the drive, doubling backup time. More expensive tape drives have separate read and write heads, accommodating a process called *verify-after-write*. With these drives, the write head records to tape the backup data, which is then read immediately by the second read head and compared with the data stream coming from the fixed-disk drive. Read-after-write tape drives definitely are preferred, because such drives can perform both a backup and verify during a single tape pass—assuming that the backup software supports read-after-write.

TIP   Periodically reading backup tapes created by one tape drive on another tape drive that accommodates the same format is a necessity to ensure that you don't have tape interchange problems. If you have an undiscovered interchange problem and your source tape drive fails or is destroyed in a calamity, you can't restore your backup by using another tape drive. Interchange problems usually occur as a result of mechanical changes in the tape path or head alignment that don't affect verify operations on the same drive. Interchange problems are more likely to occur with high-density tape formats, such as 4mm DAT and 8mm.

Backing Up Open Files

The third major issue to consider when developing a backup strategy is how to handle the backup of open files. Open files on the network pose a difficult problem for network administrators who want to make sure that all files are successfully backed up. Most backup programs, including the Windows NT Server 4.0 backup application, let you specify how to handle open files on the network. You can elect to bypass open files during the backup operation, or return to open files at the end of a backup session to determine whether the open files have been closed and can therefore now be backed up.

Backing up an open file also isn't practical because the file might be written to and closed while being written to the tape drive. This results in a corrupted file stored to tape. Consider the result of backing up an open database file that has related index files open. The main database file is successfully written to tape in its current state, and the backup software continues to read other files from the disk. A user saves data, modifying both the main database file and one or more index files. (Separate data and index files are used by desktop database systems such as dBASE, FoxPro, and Paradox.) Because the main database file has already been written but the index files haven't, the resulting backup tape contains an older version of the main database file and newer versions of the index files. If you then restore this database and its associated index files, the index files don't match the database files, and applications can't access the database files.

The only way to handle the open file backup problem is to use a RAID subsystem (described in Chapter 7, "Setting Up Redundant Arrays of Inexpensive Disks (RAID)") to provide built-in redundancy for your disk storage.

Matching Backup Media Capacity to Disk Size

When selecting a tape drive, keep in mind that the disk storage on your server is likely to grow larger as time passes. Remember also that the nominal capacities stated for tape drives assume 2:1 compression of the data being backed up. A tape drive rated at 14G capacity might have only a 7G native capacity, depending on file compression to gain the remaining 7G. If you back up a typical mix of files on a server used primarily for office automation tasks, you might find that the drive achieves the estimated 2:1 compression ratio. If you're backing up a disk drive dedicated to fixed images or video files, which usually are stored in a compressed format, you might find that you achieve compression ratios of 1.1:1 or less.

Organizing Rotation Methods

Tapes should be rotated in an organized manner to satisfy the following five goals:

- The tape containing the most recent backup of that data is quickly available so that the server can be restored to use with minimum delay.

- Older copies of the current data can be archived for the period necessary to ensure that damage or deletion of important data, which isn't noticed immediately, can be retrieved from the most recent archived backup where the data still exists in a usable form.

- A backup copy of critical data can be stored off site to guard against catastrophic damage to the server and on-site backup copies.

- The integrity and usability of the backup sets is preserved if one or more tapes break or are lost.

- Wear on tapes is equalized, avoiding continuous use of some tapes and infrequent use of others.

Some tape-rotation methods use normal backups exclusively; others use less frequent normal backups with daily incremental or differential backups; still others can be used either way. You might be forced to use a rotation that includes partial backups if your tape drive can't store a normal backup set to a single tape, or if time constraints don't allow daily normal backups. If neither condition applies, you're better served by a rotation that uses normal backups exclusively.

Weekly Normal Backup with Daily Differential Backup (Four-Tape Method)   The four-tape rotation method, shown in Figure 8.7, is very commonly used for small servers. The backup tape set comprises at least four tapes, labeled *Weekly A*, *Weekly B*, *Daily A*, and *Daily B*. The rotation begins with a normal backup to Weekly A on Friday of Week 1, followed by a daily differential backup to Daily A on Monday through Thursday of Week 2. On Friday of Week 2, a normal backup is done to Weekly B, followed by daily differential backups to Daily B on Monday through Thursday of Week 3. On Friday of Week 3, a normal backup is done to Weekly A, and the cycle begins again.

FIG. 8.7

A weekly normal backup with daily differential backup that uses four tapes.

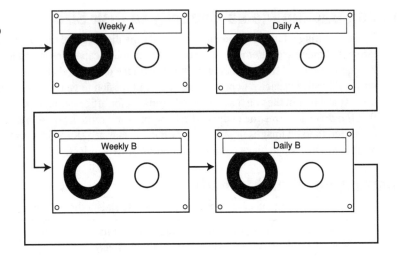

Although the four-tape method is simple to administer and uses a minimum number of tapes, it suffers the following drawbacks:

- Retrieval of historical copies of your data is limited to a two-week span.

- You're faced with the choice of either storing the normal backup off site, where it's not quickly accessible, or having the normal backup readily available for use, but at risk.

- All daily backups are written to a single tape over the course of a week, so you must return to the last weekly tape if the daily tape in use fails.

- Daily tapes are used four times more often than weekly tapes, making the daily tapes much more likely to fail.

You can make the following minor modifications to this rotation scheme to address the preceding problems without substantial complication of the backup administration process:

- A copy backup can be processed monthly to a tape that's then stored off site, addressing the first two problems of the preceding list. Depending on your need for historical data, this set can comprise 12 tapes labeled *January* through *December*, cycled on a yearly basis, or three tapes labeled *Month 1* through *Month 3*, cycled on a quarterly basis.

- By adding two tapes to the set, you can provide two daily differential backups tapes in each set and alternate using them. When using this method, label tapes *Weekly A, Weekly B, Daily A—Odd, Daily A—Even, Daily B—Odd*, and *Daily B—Even*. You make weekly normal backups as discussed earlier but alternate using daily tapes—use the Odd tape if the day of the month is odd, and the Even tape if the day of the month is even. This way, when you run a differential backup, the tape you're writing to is never the one containing the most recent backup set. This eliminates the third problem described earlier. Because it alternates daily backups between two tapes, it also reduces uneven tape wear.

- You can extend the preceding method to use eight tapes labeled *Monday A* through *Thursday A* and *Monday B* through *Thursday B* for daily differential backups. At the small cost of six additional tapes, you eliminate the third and fourth problems of the preceding list. If a daily tape fails, you lose only that day's backup, rather than have to return to the last prior full weekly backup. Each tape is used once every two weeks, equalizing wear, although the daily tapes from later in the week and (in particular) the weekly tapes will still be used somewhat more heavily due to the larger size of the backup sets written to them.

Weekly Normal Backup with Daily Incremental Backup (10-Tape Method) This version of the 10-tape rotation method, shown in Figure 8.8, uses 10 tapes, labeled *Weekly 1*, *Weekly 2*, *Monday 1* through *Thursday 1*, and *Monday 2* through *Thursday 2*. The rotation begins with a normal backup to Weekly 1 on Friday of week 1, followed by a daily incremental backup to the appropriately labeled daily 2 tape on Monday through Thursday of week 2. On Friday of week 2, a normal backup is done to Weekly 2, followed by daily incremental backups to the appropriately labeled daily 1 tape on Monday through Thursday of week 3. On Friday of week 3, a normal backup is done to Weekly 1, and the cycle begins again.

FIG. 8.8

A weekly normal backup with daily incremental backup that uses 10 tapes.

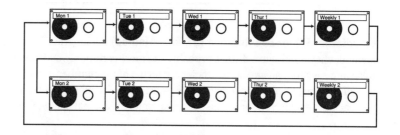

This version of the 10-tape method shares the first two drawbacks of the four-tape method, allowing only two weeks of historical data and making no provision for off-site storage. These problems can be addressed by making a copy backup each month, which is stored off site and rotated on a quarterly or annual basis. The third problem, loss of a daily tape, is more difficult to address. Because a daily incremental backup tape contains only a subset of the files changed during that week, loss of one daily incremental backup tape might require you to return to the last normal backup to retrieve a copy of a particular file. Also, if you need to restore a failed hard drive, loss of one incremental backup tape that happens to contain critical or interdependent files might force you to roll your restore back to the last preceding normal backup. The only way to protect against this problem is to run the incremental backup twice each day to different daily tapes, defeating the purpose of using a partial backup rotation scheme.

Although this version of the 10-tape method is commonly used, it offers the worst of all worlds. This version of the 10-tape method puts your data at risk, uses no fewer tapes than other methods, and saves very little time compared to using differential backups. Don't consider using this version of the 10-tape method.

Daily Full Backups with Two-Set Rotation (an Alternative 10-Tape Method) This alternative 10-tape method (see Figure 8.9) is the simplest tape-rotation system in common use that uses normal backups exclusively. It uses 10 tapes, labeled *Monday 1* through *Friday 1* and *Monday 2* through *Friday 2*. A normal backup is done each day to the appropriate tape, and the full set is cycled every two weeks. The major drawback to this method is that it limits historical data to a two-week span. Again, the historical problem can be addressed simply by doing a biweekly or monthly normal backup to a separate tape and archiving the tape. The archive tapes can be rotated on a quarterly or annual basis.

FIG. 8.9

A daily full backup with two-set rotation that uses 10 tapes.

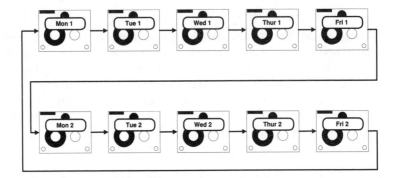

Grandfather-Father-Son Rotation (21-Tape Method)   The grandfather-father-son (or GFS) method, shown in Figure 8.10, is probably the most commonly used tape-rotation method. It's relatively easy to manage, fairly efficient in terms of the number of tapes required, and supported by almost every backup software package on the market. A GFS rotation can use normal backups exclusively, or can use a combination of normal backups and partial backups.

FIG. 8.10

A grandfather-father-son tape rotation that uses 21 tapes (only one set of the Mon through Thu tapes are active).

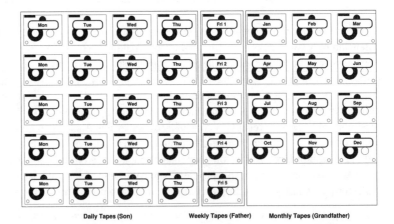

GFS is nearly always an acceptable, if not optimum, choice for a small or medium-size Windows NT server. The two primary drawbacks to GFS are that it uses some tapes more heavily than others and that, in its unmodified form, makes no provision for balancing off-site storage needs with quick retrieval requirements.

A typical GFS rotation scheme requires 21 tapes to be used over the course of a year, although this number can be altered depending on your particular archiving needs. Four daily tapes are

Part
II

Ch
8

labeled *Monday* through *Thursday*. Five weekly tapes are labeled *Friday 1* through *Friday 5* (the fifth Friday tape accommodates months with five Fridays). Twelve monthly tapes are labeled *January* through *December*.

The daily tapes are used on the day corresponding to the tape label and are overwritten every week. Each Friday, the correspondingly numbered Friday tape is used, meaning that Friday tapes are overwritten only once each month. On the last day of each month, a normal backup is done to the corresponding monthly tape, which is therefore overwritten only once per year.

TIP Depending on your needs, you can alter the time span between archival backups. Firms for which archiving is less critical can substitute quarterly tapes for monthly ones. Firms for which archiving is very important may choose to substitute biweekly or even weekly archive tapes for the monthly tapes described here.

Tower of Hanoi Rotation (TOH)   The Tower of Hanoi (TOH) rotation method (see Figure 8.11) is named for a game that uses three posts and several rings of various diameters. The object of the game is to relocate the rings by using a minimum number of moves so that the rings are placed in sequence on a post, with the largest ring on the bottom and the smallest on the top. The TOH backup model introduces new tapes to the backup set periodically, using the newly introduced tape every other rotation. TOH doubles the time before the previous tape comes back into the rotation, consequently doubling the time before earlier tapes are introduced back into the rotation.

FIG. 8.11
The Tower of Hanoi tape rotation.

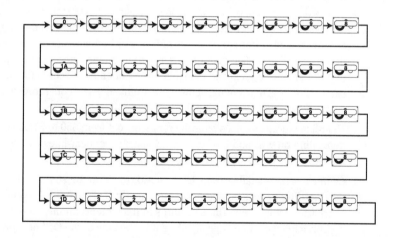

The TOH rotation has many advantages, but at the cost of considerable complexity in terms of managing the tape rotation. Wear on individual tapes is distributed relatively evenly over time with this method, but the real advantage of TOH versus GFS and other methods is that TOH saves many versions of each file, allowing you to selectively retrieve different versions of the file.

> **N O T E**   If the backup software you select supports a Tower of Hanoi rotation, consider using it for
> its many advantages, particularly if yours is a medium or large LAN. If your software doesn't
> provide TOH, don't even consider attempting to implement TOH rotation manually. You will almost
> certainly use the wrong tape at one time or another, destroying the integrity of the rotation. ■

Using Hierarchical Storage Management (HSM)

A concept called *Hierarchical Storage Management* (*HSM*) was originally developed in the mainframe arena and is beginning to migrate to PC LANs. HSM is based on the fact that, although fixed-disk drives offer fast access to data, they are an expensive commodity of finite capacity on real-world LANs. Tapes and other backup media offer much slower access but can be extended to essentially unlimited capacity simply by adding more tapes. HSM uses fast but limited-capacity fixed-disk drives to store backup data that's needed quickly, plus tapes to store an unlimited amount of data that doesn't need to be retrieved as quickly.

HSM categorizes storage devices as online, near-line, and offline:

- *Online* storage devices offer immediate high-speed access to real-time data, with typical access times on the order of 10 ms (milliseconds). Online storage devices offer relatively small storage capacity on the order of 1G to 10G. Online storage is the most expensive type per byte stored, costing from $250 to $2,500 per 1G stored, depending on configuration. Disk drives and RAID arrays are online storage devices.

- *Near-line* storage devices also offer immediate access to data, but with much slower access times and correspondingly lower costs per byte stored. The fastest near-line devices—that is, magneto-optical and WORM (write-once, read-many) drives and arrays—usually offer access times of 50 ms or better, nearly as fast as a standard disk drive, but not quite fast enough to serve as a primary storage medium. Slower near-line devices, such as optical and tape jukeboxes, often have access times measured in seconds or tens of seconds, allowing on-demand access of archived data with short delays acceptable for occasional use.

  Near-line storage devices typically range in cost from $50 to $1,000 per 1G stored, depending on type and total capacity. Capacities of near-line devices, such as jukeboxes, range from 50G to 1,000G (1 terabyte), and more.

- *Offline* storage usually means tape cartridges sit on the shelf. Offline storage is used for data needing to be accessed very infrequently, if at all, but too valuable to be discarded. Retrieving data stored offline requires human intervention—someone has to locate the appropriate tape and physically place it in the tape drive. Offline storage is very inexpensive per byte stored. A $20 tape might hold more than 20G, putting the cost at less than $1 per 1G stored.

The key to HSM systems is that files are automatically migrated from the faster (and more expensive) online storage devices to near-line storage and eventually to offline storage, based on the usage patterns of the particular file. This process is managed by the HSM software itself, without the need for routine intervention by the LAN administrator. Infrequently used files, which must nevertheless remain available, can be designated as near-line.

Considering Enterprise Backup Solutions

Enterprise backup systems combine sophisticated backup software, often including HSM capabilities, with hardware designed to offer an integrated, centralized backup solution for the entire enterprise. Although enterprise backup systems aren't cheap, the alternative is replicated software and hardware on multiple servers.

Palindrome's Backup Director and Legato's Network Archivist products historically have been the leaders in the enterprise backup market, although competing products from Seagate, Cheyenne, Symantec, and others are now beginning to appear. Used with high-capacity tape drives or tape auto-changers, these products automate the backup process for a large multiserver network, allowing administration from a central location.

One unique product deserves mention in the enterprise storage category. The Intel Storage Express system is a turnkey software and hardware solution to enterprise backup. Storage Express handles multiple servers that run different network operating systems, including Windows NT Server and Novell NetWare. Storage Express can back up drives of individual workstations running DOS, Windows 3.x, Windows NT, OS/2, and several flavors of UNIX. It is expandable on a modular basis to provide as much as 144G of tape capacity by using either 4mm DAT or 8mm drives.

Storing Data Off Site

The issue of off-site storage of backup tapes presents a conundrum. Although you want to keep your data stored safely off site to guard against catastrophic damage to your LAN, at the same time you want backup copies of your data to be readily accessible when you need them.

N O T E There are at least two good reasons to maintain an off-site set of backup tapes. Most obviously, doing so protects against catastrophic data loss due to fires and natural disasters, which might claim your on-site backup tapes at the same time they destroy your server.

Less obvious but just as important to many companies is the need to maintain archival sets of backup data for legal or other reasons. It may be necessary to keep several years' worth of data relating to tax issues, personnel files, and so on. Space constraints alone often make it necessary to keep these archives off site. ■

The best available fire-safe storage units can't guarantee that fragile tapes will survive a major fire. Many businesses suffering a catastrophic data loss find themselves out of business shortly thereafter; thus, there's no substitute for off-site storage. It's obviously preferable that the contents of the tapes stored off site be as up-to-date as possible. However, because off-site tapes are a last-ditch defense that are never likely to be used, some currency sacrifice may be acceptable.

The opposite side of the safety issue is the need for backup data to be quickly accessible. If a hard drive fails on a production LAN, you need to restore as soon as possible from the most recent backup. Having the LAN down can cost your company hundreds, thousands, or even tens of thousands of dollars per hour in lost productivity and orders. Having to wait several hours or longer to get your hands on the most recent backup is unacceptable.

Developing a Restore Plan

Most network administrators back up dozens or hundreds of times for each episode requiring a full restore. Network administrators may perform partial restores of accidentally deleted files on a weekly or even daily basis, but full restores are rare, usually occurring only when the server disk storage system is upgraded, the operating system is changed, or a disk drive crashes. You don't get much practice doing full restores. To make matters worse, when you do need to do a full restore, you're often working under the gun, with a crashed hard drive and many upset users waiting for the server to return to life. Accordingly, it's worthwhile to spend some time to develop a plan to make sure that when you do need to do a full restore, you can do so easily and quickly. You need to do the following to assure a successful data-restore process:

- *Maintain the integrity of your backup sets.* There's no worse feeling for LAN administrators than attempting to do a full restore of a crashed drive, only to find that the backup set(s) are corrupted or otherwise unusable. Running a comparison on your backup can help ensure against this happening, but the only real way to make sure that your backup set is usable is to try to restore from it. You obviously don't want to test the integrity of a backup set by restoring to a production server, lest you find that the backup set was corrupt and that by restoring you've also corrupted the live data on the server.

  If you have a test-bed, development, or standby server available, periodically try to restore your production backup to that server. If the spare server doesn't have enough disk space to do a full restore, at least make sure that you can restore to the extent of the available disk space. If your backup sets span multiple tapes, make sure that at least the change from restoring tape 1 to restoring tape 2 succeeds. Otherwise, you might find that you can restore only the first tape from each set.

- *Make sure that spare hardware is available immediately.* Tape drives are relatively reliable devices; they die only when you really need them. Although there's no scientific basis for the preceding statement, a corollary to Murphy's Law is, "When something really bad occurs," such as a disk crash, "other bad happenings are likely to follow in its wake." Whatever tape drive you choose, make sure that you have at least two drives of the same make and model on site. Also, make sure that you have whatever hardware is needed to install to the failed drive from scratch, including a spare SCSI host adapter and cables.

- *Prepare and maintain an emergency repair kit.* If the C drive fails, it does you no good to have a functioning tape drive and a good backup tape if you have no way to boot the server. Your emergency repair kit must contain everything needed to rebuild your server from scratch. You need a boot disk, diagnostic software, the Windows NT Server 4.0 distribution CD, a copy of your backup program, any drivers that you have installed or updated yourself, and so on. The emergency repair kit also should include the tools needed to open the server and replace failed components.

It's also critical that this kit be kept up-to-date. Many network administrators take the first step of building such a kit, but then ignore the fact that every change made to the production server renders this kit increasingly obsolete. You don't want to find that your emergency kit contains version 4.2 of your backup program but that it won't restore the backup you did with version 4.3. Build an emergency restore kit and keep it up-to-date.

■ *Plan to minimize server downtime in the event of a failure.* Even if you have everything you need readily at hand when a drive fails, the process of running the restore can take several hours. Every minute of this time increases the users' level of aggravation and costs your company money in salaries and lost sales.

You can do little to make the restore run faster, but one step guaranteed to save time is having a prebuilt C system disk sitting on the shelf, ready to use. This disk should be bootable and should include a full installation of Windows NT Server 4.0, with all special drivers needed to support the peripherals on your server. It should also include an installed copy of your backup software. If your system drive fails, you can plug this spare drive into the server and avoid wasting an hour or two of tracking down distribution disks, reinstalling Windows NT Server 4.0 and its drivers, and getting your backup software installed and running.

Choosing Backup Hardware

Backup and tape drives traditionally are considered synonymous. Although tape is the overwhelming choice of backup media for most network administrators, various optical storage technologies are beginning to nip at its heels. These technologies are still niche products, insofar as the backup market is concerned, because they're largely proprietary in nature and because their cost per byte stored is still relatively high in most cases. Still, it's worth examining some of these alternatives briefly for their current value in fitting specific needs and their possible future value as an alternative to tape. The following sections describe the relative merits of common tape backup formats and alternative optical storage systems for backup and archiving data.

Tape Drives and Formats

Tape drives are the traditional method for backing up data. In terms of reusability and cost per byte stored, the tape drive is now—and likely will remain—the best choice for backing up Windows NT 4.0 servers. The following sections describe the most common types of tape drives in use today.

Quarter-Inch Cartridge (QIC) Drives
Most tape drives sold today are quarter-inch cartridge or QIC-compatible. These form factors are used for QIC cartridges:

■ Full-size cartridges are about the size of a small paperback book and are commonly referred to as a DC-600, although various versions of this cartridge exist.

■ Smaller cartridges are the familiar 3 1/2-inch minicartridge commonly called a DC-2000, but many versions of this cartridge exist.

QIC-80 minicartridges originally stored 80M on a 205-foot tape, but they have since been expanded. 120M capacity is achieved by the use of 307 1/2-foot tapes, and 250M is achieved by the use of data compression. The newer cartridges with 350M capacity use an even longer tape. QIC-80 drives are controlled by the diskette controller and are too small and too slow for serious consideration as a backup solution for all but the smallest servers.

In response to the rapid growth in the size of disk drives, the Quarter-Inch Cartridge Standards Committee approved the QIC-3010 standard in 1991 and the QIC-3020 standard in 1993. The QIC-3010 standard specifies a 3 1/2-inch minicartridge tape with a native capacity of 340M and a compressed capacity of 680M. The QIC-3020 standard specifies a 3 1/2-inch minicartridge tape with a 680M native capacity and a 1.36G compressed capacity.

The most recent activity on the QIC-80 front has been the introduction of Travan technology by Hewlett-Packard's Colorado Memory Systems subsidiary, which manufactures the drives, and 3M, which produces the tapes. First shipped in the summer of 1995, Travan drives use tapes that look like a lopsided QIC-80 minicartridge. The drives, compatible with QIC-80, QIC-3010, and QIC-3020 media, can read from and write to standard QIC-3010 and QIC-3020 cartridges.

The initial Travan media, designated TR-1, provided 400M native capacity, with compression achieving 800M per tape. Travan levels TR-2 and TR-3 began shipping in the fall of 1995, and TR-4 was released in mid-1996. The TR-2 tape uses a modified QIC-3010 cartridge to provide 800M native capacity, yielding 1.6G with compression. The TR-3 tape provides 1.6G native capacity with a modified QIC-3020 cartridge, yielding a nominal 3.2G of storage by using compression. The TR-4 tape stores 4G natively, or 8G with compression. Several firms, including Colorado and Seagate, supply TR-4 Travan drives.

Some newer QIC-3020 drives use the ATAPI IDE interface, so backup speeds are constrained by the tape-drive mechanism rather than by disk data transfer rate. Given that media capacities are increasing—particularly with Travan TR-2, TR-3, and TR-4—it remains to be seen whether these faster QIC drives will provide adequate performance and capacity for low-end servers. The drives' lack of separate read and write heads precludes read-after-write, requiring a second compare pass for data verification.

Digital Linear Tape (DLT)   The high-end tape backup hardware and media is called Digital Linear Tape (DLT). Because it's very fast, offers large capacities, and is extremely reliable, DLT is beginning to replace DAT and 8mm tape drives in large server environments. Current DLT drives have capacities of 40G compressed, or 20G uncompressed, so even a very large disk subsystem can be backed up to a single tape.

DLT divides the tape into multiple parallel horizontal tracks. While the single write head remains stationary, the DLT drive streams the tape past it, allowing the drive to record information to tape as fast as the server can supply it. This removes the tape drive as the bottleneck restricting backup speed and limits backup performance only by the maximum throughput available from the server.

DLT drives and tapes are also extremely robust. A typical DLT drive is rated at 15,000 in-use hours MTBF (mean time between failures). The tapes themselves are rated at 500,000 hours, so the average tape should outlast the technology itself.

Helical Scan Tapes   Originally developed for use in video recording, helical scanning works by running a tape past a head that rotates at an angle relative to the motion of the tape. The resulting tracks resemble diagonal lines running from one edge of the tape to the other, repeating this pattern from end to end on the tape.

The advantage of helical scanning is that information can be packed more densely on the media. The most common application of helical scan recording is the consumer VCR; both VHS and 8mm VCRs, as well as the new Digital Video (DV) camcorders and VCRs, use helical scanning. Helical scan recording is a mature technology, although it's more expensive to implement than the linear recording used in QIC-80 drives.

The following helical scan tape backup technologies were available when this book was written:

- Digital Audio Tape (DAT) is also called 4mm for the width of its tape. DAT drives comply with standards set by the Digital Data Storage (DDS) Group. The original 1991 DDS specification provided 2G natively and 4G with compression on a 90-meter tape. The DDS-2 standard, released in 1993, doubled this capacity to 4G native and 8G compressed on a 120-meter tape, doubling transfer rates. DDS-3, adopted in late 1994, specifies capacities of 12G native and 24G compressed.

  DAT drives use a minicartridge tape that costs less than $20. The best DAT drives provide data-transfer rates of about 30M per minute, or 10 times that of a standard QIC-80 drive. Internal DAT drives have a street price of less than $1,000 for the 2G/4G DDS versions, and perhaps $200 more for the 4G/8G DDS-2 versions. The 12G/24G DDS-3 versions carry prices in the $2,000 range.

- 8mm, also named for the width of its tape, is derived from the 8mm videotape format and is an alternative to DAT drives. (8mm is commonly called DAT, although properly that term is reserved for the 4mm format.) 8mm drives are available at street prices of about $1,200 for internal drives with capacities of 3.5G native and 7G compressed, and about $1,500 for similar drives with capacities of 7G native and 14G compressed. Jukebox changers are available for applications in which a single 8mm tape isn't large enough. Exabyte offers a typical changer, holding up to 10 14G tapes, for a total capacity of 140G. 8mm drives use minicartridge tapes that cost about $20 each. The drives offer data transfer rates up to twice those of 4mm DAT.

The best backup solution for most Windows NT Server environments with moderate storage capacity (100G or less) is either 4mm or 8mm tape. Both drive types are available only with a SCSI-2 interface. The drives are fast, inexpensive, and reliable; the tapes are small and inexpensive.

Writable Optical Drives

Writable optical drives today are used primarily for archiving data, rather than backup. Various new technologies include erasable CD-ROMs (CD-E) and writable digital video discs (DVDs, also called *digital versatile discs*), which store up to 4.7G. Even farther in the future are exotic writable disc technologies, based on cholesteric liquid crystals (CLCs), which promise up to 280G of storage per side.

The following sections describe currently available drives that use lasers to write to and read from discs that, for the most part, have the same dimensions as conventional audio CDs and CD-ROMs.

CD-Recordable Drives   Recordable CD (CD-R) technology has been around for a few years, but it's just now joining the mainstream. With prices on drives dropping below the magic $500 point, sales of CD-R drives are climbing rapidly. CD-R drives are similar to standard CD-ROM drives, but CD-R drives use a higher powered laser that can write to specially designed CDs. These CDs can then be read in any standard CD-ROM drive.

CD-R's relatively low capacity of 680M, its use of relatively expensive media (about $5 per disc), and its lack of rewritability make CD-R a poor choice for routine backup. The first two issues are likely to be addressed at least incrementally as the technology improves, although revolutionary improvements are unlikely. The read-only nature of a CD-R disc can be an advantage for applications such as data archiving.

Magneto-Optical Drives   Magneto-optical (MO) disks are another technology sometimes considered for use as a backup media. Magneto-optical disks use a combination of a high-power laser and a magnetic head to write to their media. The laser heats the media, allowing the magnetic head to realign the magnetic particles. Because this action is repeatable, MO disks are read-write like a traditional disk drive, rather than write-once like CD-R and WORM drives.

MO drives now have performance more similar to that of hard-disk drives than the performance usually associated with optical drives. However, MO drives have relatively low capacity and high media costs, making them inappropriate as backup devices for most situations.

WORM Drives

Write-once, read-many (WORM) technology has been available longer than either CD-R or MO devices. WORM drives are available in various platter sizes up to 12 inches and in capacities of up to 6G per disc. WORM jukeboxes can provide near online storage capacity in the terabyte range. WORM drives are incrementally rewritable (data can be added incrementally), allowing backup of multiple versions of the same file or folder to a WORM disk.

WORM is an excellent—if expensive—archiving medium. For applications that require storing huge amounts of data, such as document imaging, the nearly online performance of WORM can be considered adequate for online use.

Using the Windows NT Server 4.0 Backup Application

The Windows NT Server 4.0 backup application, NTBACKUP, has two obvious advantages: it's included with Windows NT 4.0 (so it's free), and, as a bundled application, compatibility and reliability problems are less likely to occur. Balanced against these advantages are NTBACKUP's paucity of high-end features and limited options. If your LAN is relatively small, the LAN's architecture is simple, and your backup requirements are modest, NTBACKUP suffices. For single-server environments that use a simple tape-rotation method and have no need to backup workstations from the server, NTBACKUP is more than adequate.

NTBACKUP can back up files stored on a drive that uses either the NTFS or FAT file systems, and it can restore the files backed up from a drive that uses one file system to a drive that uses the other file system. NTBACKUP does only file-by-file backups and makes no provision for doing a disk-image backup. It supports only tape drives as destination devices. You can't, for example, back up from one hard drive to another by using NTBACKUP.

Setting Up NTBACKUP for Use with Your Tape Drive

The NTBACKUP program files are installed when you install Windows NT Server. Before using NTBACKUP, however, you must first install support for your tape drive by following these steps:

1. From Control Panel, double-click the Tape Devices tool to display the Tape Devices property sheet (see Figure 8.12). The Devices page shows installed tape devices. You highlight a displayed tape device and click the Properties button to display the properties for that device. You also can click the Detect button to attempt to automatically detect and install a driver for a physically installed tape device that's not shown in the list.

FIG. 8.12
The Devices page of the Tape Devices property sheet.

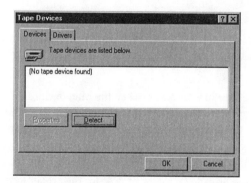

2. To install a new tape device manually, click the Drivers tab. Windows NT builds a driver list for several seconds, and then displays the Drivers page (see Figure 8.13). The Drivers page shows a list of installed tape device drivers.

3. You can click the Remove button to remove a currently installed driver. If no driver is shown for the tape drive you want to install, click the Add button. Windows NT 4.0 again creates a driver list. After a few seconds, the Install Driver dialog appears (see Figure 8.14).

N O T E   Click the Have Disk button of the Install Driver dialog to install a new or updated driver provided by your tape drive's manufacturer. ∎

FIG. 8.13

The Drivers page of the Tape Devices property sheet.

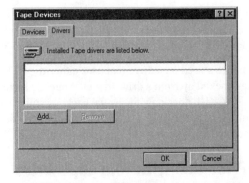

FIG. 8.14

The Install Driver dialog, listing manufacturers and tape device types.

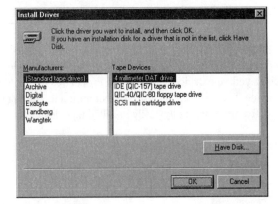

4. Select the manufacturer of your tape drive in the Manufacturers list and then select one of the supported tape devices made by that manufacturer from the Tape Devices list. Click OK to install the driver for that tape drive, or Cancel to abort the process.

5. You're prompted to insert the Windows NT 4.0 distribution CD-ROM disk into your CD-ROM drive (see Figure 8.15). You can type the path where the files are located, select the location from the drop-down list, or browse for the proper location. The distribution files for a server running an Intel processor are located in the \i386 folder of your CD-ROM drive.

FIG. 8.15

The Files Needed dialog for installing tape backup drivers.

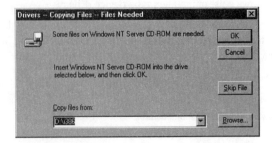

6. After the Copy Files From text box is completed properly, click OK to begin installing the new tape device driver.

7. When the files are copied, you're prompted to restart Windows NT for the changes to take effect.

Backing Up with NTBACKUP

Using NTBACKUP to back up your files requires several steps. You must prepare and label the media; select the volumes, folders, and files to be included in the backup set; choose the appropriate backup options to use; and then run the backup itself. Optionally, you may choose to run a comparison pass after completing the backup to verify the integrity of your backup set.

Preparing and Labeling Media   Depending on the type of tape drive you use, there might be little—or quite a lot—of preparation needed. QIC tape drives require that tapes be formatted before use and that they be periodically retensioned to avoid breakage. The QIC formatting process takes considerable time, but you can avoid such time consumption by purchasing preformatted tapes. Like VCR tapes (the other technology that uses helical scanning), DAT and 8mm tapes require neither formatting before use nor periodic retensioning.

NTBACKUP gives you several tape tools, most of which you'll seldom need to use. NTBACKUP allows you to erase tapes by using either a standard erase (which simply deletes the header information) or a secure erase (which actually overwrites the data on the tape). NTBACKUP allows you to retension tapes that require such maintenance, and allows you to eject a tape if your tape drive supports software-controlled ejection. (Now *there's* a useful feature!)

Labeling Your Backup Tapes

If your labeling habits are poor, now is the time to fix them. The last thing you need is poorly labeled backup tapes. Inadequate tape labels make it much more likely that you'll eventually back up to the wrong tape. Also, poorly labeled backup tapes make it nearly impossible to find the correct tape days or weeks later when you need to do a restore. Make it a standard practice to label your tapes legibly and indelibly. Otherwise, you'll sooner or later regret not doing so.

How you label a tape depends on several factors, including the tape rotation method you use and the practices particular to your site. Make sure that the label is permanently affixed, and includes at least the server name, the volume ID (if appropriate), the set to which the tape belongs, and the tape number. For example, you might label a tape as follows:

    Admin Server

    SYS volume

    Set A

    Tape 1 of 1

This indicates that that tape is number 1 of 1 from Set A, used to back up the SYS volume of the Administration server. Alternatively, if you are of a minimalist bent, something like the following might do as well:

    \\ADMIN\SYS

    A-1

TIP Always maintain a manual backup log, indicating the date that each backup was done, the contents of that backup, the type of backup, and the tape set to which the data was written. That way, if the server crashes, you won't find yourself trying to retrieve the software-generated backup log from a crashed hard disk drive.

Many people record this information on a label attached to the tape itself. A better practice is to keep a spiral-bound notebook nearby and record the details of each backup session in this notebook. This makes it easy to retrieve the information when needed without sorting through a pile of tapes.

Selecting Drives, Folders, and Files to Be Backed Up   After you prepare and label your tapes, the next step is to run NTBACKUP and select the drives, folders, and files to be backed up. Proceed as follows:

N O T E   Before trying to run a backup, make sure that you're logged on as either an Administrator or as a Backup Operator. Otherwise, you might not have the necessary permissions to access all files that need to be backed up, and the resulting backup tape will be incomplete. ■

1. From the Start menu, choose Programs, Administrative Tools (Common), and Backup to open the Backup – [Tapes] window (see Figure 8.16). If a blank formatted tape is in the tape drive, it's shown in the left pane as `Blank Tape`. If the tape contains data, the left pane displays the creation date and other particulars of the tape, and the right pane displays a brief summary of the tape's contents.

FIG. 8.16

The Backup – [Tapes] window, with a blank tape inserted in the tape drive.

 TIP If you have more than one tape drive installed, now is the time to verify that you have the correct tape drive selected. To do so, from the Operations menu choose Hardware Setup. In the Hardware Setup dialog, select the tape drive you want to use from the drop-down list of installed tape devices and click OK.

2. To begin selecting the drives, folders, and files to be backed up, from the Window menu choose Drives. The Backup – [Drives] window appears (see Figure 8.17).

FIG. 8.17
The Backup – [Drives] window, displaying drives accessible to NTBACKUP.

3. To select an entire drive to be backed up, mark the check box to the left of that drive's icon. To back up only some of the folders and files on a particular drive, double-click the icon for that drive to view a folder tree for that drive (see Figure 8.18). The folder tree view is similar to Windows NT Explorer, showing folders in the left pane and the files contained in a selected folder in the right pane. Single-clicking a folder name in the left pane displays the files contained in that folder in the right pane.

FIG. 8.18
NTBACKUP's folder view, displaying folders and files available for backup.

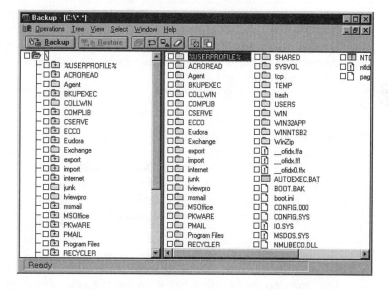

4. Select folders to be backed up by marking the check box to the left of the folder, which selects all files contained in that folder and its subfolders. Alternatively, you select individual files within a folder by marking the check box for that file or files in the right window pane and leaving the folder name in the left pane unmarked (see Figure 8.19).

N O T E The check box for folders that aren't selected for backup are empty. The check box for folders in which all files and subfolders are selected for backup are marked with an × on a white background. The check box for folders in which only some files and subfolders are selected for backup are marked with an × on a gray background. ■

FIG. 8.19

Selecting specific folders and files for backup.

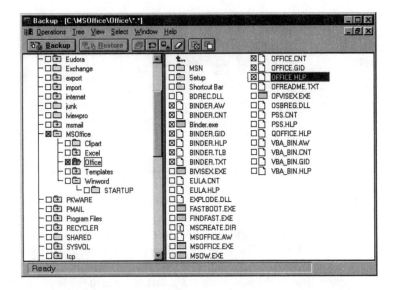

 TIP If you want to back up many, but not all, files on a particular drive, you can select those folders and files individually by marking their check boxes. An easier way, however, is simply to mark the check box for the drive itself, which appears at the extreme top left of the folder tree pane. Doing so marks all folders and files on the drive to be backed up. You can then clear the check boxes for those folders and files that you don't want to back up.

5. Repeat steps 3 and 4 for any other drives to be backed up.

Choosing Options and Running the Backup   After you select the drives, folders, and files to be backed up, the next step is to choose backup options. To do so, click the Backup button in the Backup window to display the Backup Information dialog. The Backup Information dialog is divided into three sections (see Figure 8.20). The first section presents several items about the currently mounted tape, including its name, owner, and creation date. The first section also allows you to specify various options that determine how the backup job is run.

The first set of backup options are as follows:

■ The *Tape Name* text box allows you to enter a descriptive name for this tape.

■ The *Verify After Backup* check box allows you to specify whether you want to do a second comparison pass after the backup is complete. Leaving this option selected ensures that the backup data is written to tape successfully, but nearly doubles the time needed to complete the backup.

■ The *Backup Local Registry* check box lets you specify whether the Registry is backed up. The Registry, described fully in Chapter 9, "Understanding the Windows NT Registry," is a critical component of Windows NT. You should back up the Registry as a matter of course. Don't clear this check box unless you have a very good reason for doing so.

- The *Operation* section lets you choose whether the current backup data is added to the end of the current tape or overwrites the current contents of the tape. Append adds and Replace overwrites.

- The *Restrict Access to Owner or Administrator* check box lets you secure the contents of the tape against unauthorized access. When this check box is marked, the contents of the tape can subsequently be accessed only by the tape's owner or by a member of the Administrators or Backup Operators group. This check box remains disabled (gray) unless you select the Replace option in the Operation section.

- The *Hardware Compression* check box determines whether hardware compression is used on drives that support it. If your drive doesn't provide hardware compression, this check box is disabled.

FIG. 8.20

Setting backup options in the Backup Information dialog.

The second section of the Backup Information dialog, Backup Set Information, lets you specify information about particular backup sets. The scroll bar lets you view one such set at a time (you see the scroll bar only if you have selected more than one drive to be backed up). Each backup set includes the following information:

- *Drive Name* is the drive (for example, C) that you picked during the selection process described earlier.

- *Description* is a free text area in which you can enter a brief meaningful description of the contents of the backup set.

- *Backup Type* is a drop-down list from which you can select Normal, Copy, Incremental, Daily Copy, or Differential to do your backup.

The third section of the Backup Information dialog, Log Information, lets you specify logging information for the backup session, including the log file name and location, and the level of detail you want the log to contain:

- The *Log File* text box allows you to enter the drive, folder, and name of the file to which session information is to be logged as an ASCII text file.

- When selected, the *Full Detail* option button causes all transaction detail to be logged, including the names of all files and folders that are backed up. Although this level of detail can be useful at times, the resulting log files can be huge.

- When selected, the *Summary Only* option button logs only critical exception information, such as tape mounting information, start time of the backup, and files that were selected for backup but couldn't be opened.

- When selected, the *Don't Log* option button disables all logging functions.

After you select the options desired, click OK to begin the backup. The backup then begins, unless you've chosen the Replace option and the target tape already contains data. If so, you'll be prompted to make sure that you really want to overwrite the tape. When the backup completes, a compare pass begins, if you chose that option.

N O T E Regardless of the setting for Log Information, if NTBACKUP encounters corrupted files, it displays the problem in the status area of the Backup Status dialog and records this problem in the file Corrupt.lst. If this happens, you first should determine the reason for it. After you do so to your satisfaction, delete Corrupt.lst before trying to restore from that or any other tape. Failing to delete Corrupt.lst results in error messages informing you of corrupt files each time you try to restore from that or any other tape. ■

As the backup begins, the Backup Status dialog appears, displaying the progress of your backup until it completes (see Figure 8.21).

FIG. 8.21

Displaying backup progress and status messages in the Backup Status dialog.

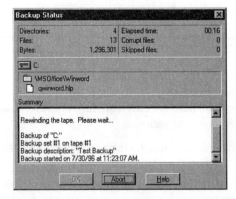

 The backup applet bundled with Windows NT Server 4.0 is a trimmed-down version of Seagate BackupExec for Windows NT. If you like NTBACKUP but would prefer a product with more power and flexibility, consider purchasing BackupExec.

ON THE WEB

For more information on Seagate Software's BackupExec Version 6.11 for Windows NT, see **http://www.smg.seagatesoftware.com/products/window_nt/sbewinntesse.htm**.

N O T E Unlike most third-party backup software, NTBACKUP has weak automation features. The biggest shortfalls are the absence of a comprehensive macro language and built-in support for tape-rotation algorithms. NTBACKUP has no native scheduler, but it can be run from the command line by using the Windows NT scheduler service, AT commands, and batch files.

You can invoke all NTBACKUP options from the command line to build an automated backup scheduling system of sorts, leaving you only with the problem of managing tape rotations manually. For a complete list of available commands and syntax, see the topic "Using Batch Files to Do Backups" in the NTBACKUP help file. If you need scheduling and other automation features, you're far better off buying a commercial backup software package, such as BackupExec, instead of spending a lot of time trying to make NTBACKUP do things it really wasn't designed to do. ▨

Restoring with NTBACKUP

Restoring with NTBACKUP is relatively straightforward. NTBACKUP allows a backup set to be restored to the same system from which it was made, or to a different system. NTBACKUP also allows backup sets made from either supported file system to be restored to a disk that uses NTFS or FAT. The following steps show you how to use NTBACKUP to restore files to your system:

1. Insert the tape that contains the data to be restored into your tape drive.

2. From the Start menu, choose Programs, Administrative Tools (Common), and Backup to run NT Backup. The Backup – [Tapes] window appears (see Figure 8.22). The left pane of this window displays the name and creation date of the tape. The right pane displays the folder backed up to the root level of the tape, the set number, and the number of the tape within that set.

FIG. 8.22

The Backup – [Tapes] window, displaying the tape date and the folder backed up.

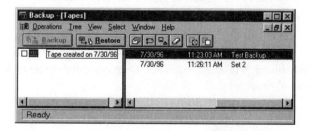

3. Double-click the folder name in the right pane of the window. NTBACKUP loads the catalog from tape and displays the folder tree contained on the tape (see Figure 8.23).

FIG. 8.23

NTBACKUP displaying tape contents in folder tree format.

4. Select the drives, folders, and files to be restored in the same manner as you specified them earlier in the section "Selecting Drives, Folders, and Files to Be Backed Up."

5. After you select all the drives, folders, and files you want to restore, click the Restore button to begin restoring. The Restore Information dialog appears (see Figure 8.24).

FIG. 8.24

Selecting restore options in the Restore Information dialog.

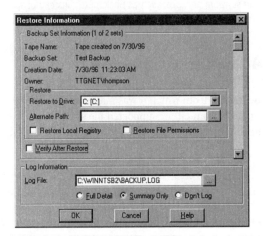

The Restore Information dialog is divided into two sections. The Backup Set Information section displays properties of the mounted tape, including its name, the backup set of which it is a member, its creation date, and its owner. The Backup Set Information section also allows you to set the following options:

- The *Restore to Drive* drop-down list allows you to select the drive to which the backup set is to be restored. NTBACKUP can restore to any drive visible to Windows NT, including those on other servers.

- The *Alternate Path* text box allows you to restore to a path other than that from which the files were originally backed up.

- When selected, the *Restore Local Registry* check box causes NTBACKUP to restore Registry information if it's present on the backup tape.

- The *Restore File Permissions* check box determines whether ACL (Access Control List) information will be restored with the file. If this box is selected, the original ACL information is re-created as the file is restored. If the box is deselected, the restored file instead inherits the ACL information of the directory to which it's restored. If you're restoring to a FAT partition, this check box remains grayed out, because Windows NT Server doesn't support permissions on file systems other than NTFS.

■ When selected, the *Verify After Restore* check box causes NTBACKUP to perform a comparison pass after completing the restore to verify that restored files correspond to those stored on tape. Exceptions are written to the log file.

The second section of the Restore Information dialog, Log Information, allows you to specify logging information for the restore session, including the log file name and location, and the level of detail you want the log to contain:

■ The *Log File* text box allows you to enter the drive, folder, and name of the file to which session information is to be logged as an ASCII text file. Figure 8.25 illustrates a typical log file opened in Windows Notepad.

FIG. 8.25

Windows Notepad
displaying records
created by a typical
backup log.

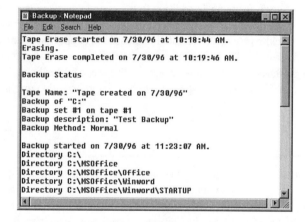

■ The *Full Detail* option button, when selected, causes all transaction detail to be logged.

■ The *Summary Only* option button, when selected, logs only critical exception information—for example, files selected for restore that couldn't be read from tape.

■ The *Don't Log* option button, when selected, disables all logging functions.

After you select the options desired, click OK to begin the restore. The restore then begins and runs to completion, with a message that tells you the process is complete. When the restore completes, a compare pass begins (if you selected that option).

Looking Beyond NTBACKUP

Choosing the right backup software is as important as choosing the right backup hardware. Windows NT Server 4.0's NTBACKUP is a quite competent application, but it's a bit Spartan. NTBACKUP provides fundamental backup features, but you won't find the bells and whistles on it like those provided by third-party backup software.

If you have multiple servers, plan to use Tower of Hanoi or other complex tape-rotation methods, or must back up workstations that run diverse operating systems, you need to consider purchasing one of the commercial backup programs available from numerous third parties. Third-party software is needed if you must back up multiple servers in a heterogeneous network, such as a network that includes both Windows NT and Novell NetWare servers.

The rapid market growth of Windows NT Server 4.0 has backup software vendors scrambling to release enhanced versions of their products for Windows NT. Just a couple of years ago, third-party backup choices for Windows NT were very limited, both in number and in feature sets. That situation has changed for the better and continues to improve with every passing month. Nearly all the big-name backup software publishers that previously concentrated their efforts exclusively on Novell NetWare now have released Windows NT Server versions; in some cases, the Windows NT version appears to have more features than the original version for NetWare.

Most of these software products, in addition to the complete selection of basic backup features you might expect, offer extensive customization options, powerful macro languages to automate the entire backup process, automated databases to support sophisticated tape-rotation algorithms, and the capability to back up workstations running diverse operating systems. Describing these third-party offerings is beyond the scope of this book. Vendor sites and magazine reviews on the Web are the best source of current information on third-party backup software.

From Here...

Backing up critical data and assuring the ability to restore data when required are a network administrator's primary responsibility. Thus, this entire chapter is devoted to backup methodology, hardware, and software. If you're upgrading a network from an earlier version of Windows NT Server or from another network operating system, now is an ideal time to re-examine your data backup and restore practices, and to consider upgrading your backup hardware to greater capacity and faster data-transfer rates.

The following chapters contain material relating to data backup operations:

- Chapter 5, "Purchasing Networking Hardware," discusses the SCSI-2 interface used by the majority of backup drives.
- Chapter 21, "Administering Intranet and World Wide Web Sites," explains the backup issues specific to this growing market for Windows NT Server 4.0.
- Chapter 23, "Running Microsoft SQL Server 6.5," includes sections describing how to use disk dumps and log copies to back up and restore SQL Server databases.

CHAPTER 9

Understanding the Windows NT Registry

f you've used Windows 95 or previous versions of Windows NT, you've already seen the Registry at work. When you double-click a file on your Windows 95 desktop or in Windows NT 3.5+'s File Manager, entries in the Registry enable Windows NT Server to launch the application associated with that file. One category of Registry entries creates associations between file extensions and the application that launches and, in most cases, lets you edit a particular type of file.

But the Registry does much more than launch the appropriate application for a particular document type. The primary duty of the Windows NT 4.0 Registry is to provide a central repository of information about the hardware and software installed on the server, as well as personalized Desktop configuration information for each user account. Registry entries also determine which Windows NT services start automatically during the boot process. The Registry stores almost all the configuration changes you make with the Control panel tools. ■

Purpose of the Registry

The Registry is a hierarchical database containing configuration information for hardware, software, and users.

Registry organization

The Registry is organized into hives, which contain keys. Keys have one or more value entries.

Registry files

The Registry appears to be monolithic, but its information is stored in multiple .dat files. Log files store changes to Registry values until the changes become permanent.

Registry editing tools

Windows NT offers two Registry editors: Windows 95-style Regedit.exe, which offers an extended Find function, and the traditional Windows NT Regedt32.exe.

Remote Registry editing

You can edit the Registries of remote computers that run Windows 95 or Windows NT or edit the Registry of your Windows NT server from a Windows NT or Windows 95 client.

Tracking Configuration Settings in the Registry

The Registry keeps track of all configuration information for a computer, including applications, hardware, device drivers, and network protocols. The Registry is a set of flat-file databases, each having a hierarchical organization. Windows NT uses the Registry during the boot process to determine which device drivers to load and in what sequence to load them. Registry entries store desktop settings for one or more users. Most of the administrative tools you use to configure Windows NT Server and keep it running smoothly alter Registry entries. The following sections briefly describe how Windows NT uses the Registry.

Types of Registry Information

The Registry is the one place that stores virtually everything that Windows NT needs to know about your hardware, software, and the users who may log on to the system. The Registry stores the following types of information:

- Information about your hardware and the device drivers required by the hardware.
- A list of services, such as SQL Server and Exchange Server, to start immediately after the boot process.
- Network information, including details about each network interface card and protocol in use.
- OLE and ActiveX information, such as the file name and location of each OLE server and ActiveX component.
- File association information—what application launches what kind of file, and vice versa.
- The time zone and local language.
- For each user, program folders and other Start menu settings.
- For each user, desktop settings such as colors and wallpaper.
- For each user, all preferences in all user applications, unless the applications are older 16-bit applications that use .INI files. Preferences include the "recent files" list on the File menu.
- All user profiles.
- User and group security information.

Windows 3.1+ Configuration Files

Under Windows 3.1, the settings described in the preceding section were maintained in many different files. System-wide settings were kept in one of the following files:

- AUTOEXEC.BAT
- CONFIG.SYS
- WIN.INI
- SYSTEM.INI
- REG.DAT

If you're an administrator or a power user of a Windows 3.1x machine, you probably use the SysEdit application to open the first four of these files at once. SysEdit provides a convenient editing environment for text-based system configuration files. Many 16-bit Windows applications have their own configuration (also called an *initialization* or *INI*) file. Most applications use *APPNAME*.INI for this purpose, but some applications use alternative file names and extensions.

Windows 3.1+'s REG.DAT provides OLE server information and file extension associations. You use the 16-bit RegEdit application to edit REG.DAT. When you need to change or view the settings for an application, the first task is to guess what file the settings might be in and then to determine what utility to use to edit the file.

Part

II

Ch

9

Centralized Configuration Management with the Registry

Windows NT's Registry keeps everything in one place, eliminating the need for the various types of initialization files of 16-bit Windows. You can view Registry settings by using one tool—the Windows NT 4.0 Registry Editor. Windows NT 4.0 provides two versions of the Registry Editor: Regedit.exe, a Single Document Interface (SDI) Explorer-type tool derived from the Windows 95 RegEdit application (see Figure 9.1); and Regedt32.exe, a Multiple Document Interface (MDI) version that originated in Windows NT 3.1 (see Figure 9.2). Regedit.exe offers the advantage of a more flexible Find feature; Regedt32.exe offers advanced administrative features, such as the ability to set security and audit properties of individual keys. The choice of versions is up to you; Windows 95 users are likely to choose Regedit.exe, and most users experienced with prior versions of Windows NT opt for Regedt32.exe. This chapter uses Regedt32.exe, except as noted.

FIG. 9.1

Regedit.exe's SDI window with two top-level keys expanded.

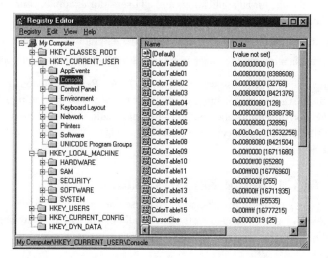

FIG. 9.2
The default cascade arrangement of Regedt32.exe's MDI windows when launched.

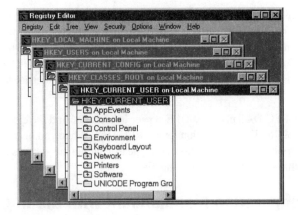

N O T E   Neither version of the Registry Editor appears as a choice in the default Start menu hierarchy. Microsoft deliberately "hides" the Registry Editor to discourage users from manually altering Registry data. Regedit.exe is located in the \Winnt folder; Regedt32.exe is located in \Winnt\System32. Most network and system administrators create a desktop shortcut for one or both of the Registry Editor versions. ■

Registry Organization

The Registry is arranged in a logical and straightforward way that clearly distinguishes among the following three classes of settings:

- System-wide, for all applications and all users (for example, your computer's microprocessor type)
- System-wide, for one user (for example, your Windows Desktop color scheme)
- Per application for each user (for example, the last four files you opened in Excel)

Although you continue to use various tools to change Registry values in Windows NT 4.0, don't underestimate the value of using just one tool to view any of the settings. Navigating such a large collection of settings and configuration information can be a bit intimidating, but understanding the structure and content of the Registry is very important when administering Windows NT Server 4.0.

The Danger of Changing Registry Values

Changing entry values in the Registry can cause your server to be unstartable. Rather than change Registry entry values directly, you should use one of the following tools to change these values:

- Most hardware settings are handled by the hardware recognition process when you start your computer. PCI adapter cards configure themselves automatically during startup. Because Windows NT 4.0 doesn't fully support Plug and Play for ISA cards, legacy ISA adapters usually use jumpers or semi-permanent software configuration methods. Alternatively, you can install the Pnpisa.sys driver, which lets you statically configure PnP ISA adapters. When you install hardware drivers, driver configuration information is stored in the Registry.

▶ **See** "Network Adapter," **p. 179**

■ Many system configuration and application settings are set when you run the appropriate setup program. For this reason, it's important not to relocate applications by simply moving their files. Registry entries aren't updated when you move an application's executable and support files, so you must remove and reinstall most applications to change their location.

■ The Administrative Tools menu (see Figure 9.3) contains User Manager, Disk Administrator, Performance Monitor, Backup, Event Viewer, and Windows NT Diagnostics tools. Using these dedicated tools to interact with the Registry is far safer and more intuitive than using the Registry Editor.

Part
II

Ch
9

FIG. 9.3
Applications in the
Administrative Tools
program group that
manipulate Registry
values.

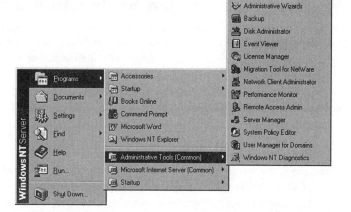

■ Control Panel (see Figure 9.4) contains the Accessibility Options, Add/Remove Programs, Console, Date/Time, Devices, Display, Fonts, Internet, Keyboard, Licensing, Modems, Mouse, Multimedia, Network, ODBC, PC Card (PCMCIA), Ports, Printers, Regional Settings, SCSI Adapters, Server, Services, Sounds, System, Tape Devices, Telephony, and UPS tools, in addition to any tools that are added by applications you install (typically, other servers run as services). Control Panel tools interact with a small part of the Registry—for example, the Keyboard tool changes the user's keyboard settings in the Registry.

■ Using desktop applications changes the Registry. For example, the list of recent files is generated automatically as you open files in the application.

■ Most OLE servers and ActiveX components register themselves when they're installed or run for the first time.

FIG. 9.4
Control Panel tools that make changes to the Registry.

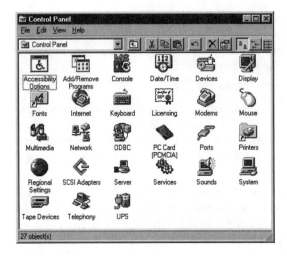

How the Windows NT and Windows 95 Registries Vary

In many important ways, the Windows NT Registry is similar to the Windows 95 Registry. Certainly, the concepts are the same. The same tools and applications read from and write to the Registry, and the Regedit.exe Registry Editor of Windows 95 and Windows NT 4.0 is quite similar. However, the names for specific collections of information stored within the Registry aren't identical. Nonetheless, experience with the Windows 95 Registry is readily transferable to Windows NT Server 4.0's Registry.

N O T E Both Windows NT 4.0 and Windows 95 use Registry files, but the internal (binary) structure of the files varies greatly between the two operating systems. The difference in file structure is the primary reason that Microsoft couldn't provide an automatic upgrade utility from Windows 95 to Windows NT 4.0 when Windows NT 4.0 was released, although upgrading from Windows 3.1+ to Windows NT 4.0 is supported. (Upgrading creates or preserves the Registry information for installed applications.) The capability to upgrade automatically from Windows 95 to Windows NT 4.0 is more important for the Workstation version than the Server version, because production servers seldom run desktop applications. ■

Viewing the Registry's Organization

Understanding the Registry requires you to learn another new vocabulary. The Registry is made up of *keys*, some of which have *subkeys*. Keys have *value entries*, and groups of keys and their value entries are gathered into a *hive*. The Registry is a hierarchical (not a relational) database; keys correspond to records in the database.

Registry Hives and Files

The Registry is arranged in a hierarchy quite similar to a folder tree. At the top of the hierarchy are the following five hives:

- *HKEY_LOCAL_MACHINE* contains system-wide hardware information and configuration details stored in the SAM, Security, Software, and System configuration files.
- *HKEY_CLASSES_ROOT* contains OLE and ActiveX information and file associations.
- *HKEY_CURRENT_CONFIG* contains startup information stored in the System files that's also kept in HKEY_LOCAL_MACHINE.
- *HKEY_CURRENT_USER* contains all the settings specific to the current user, which are stored in the Ntuser.dat file located in the \Winnt\Profiles*Username* folder.
- *HKEY_USERS* contains all settings for all users, stored in Ntuser.dat files, including the current user and a default user, which is stored in the \Winnt\Profiles\Default User folder.

These five hives are permanent Registry components. Figure 9.5 shows Regedt32.exe displaying each hive and its topmost keys in a tiled window. Each hive is discussed in individual sections later in this chapter.

FIG. 9.5

The five top-level Registry hives and their top-level keys.

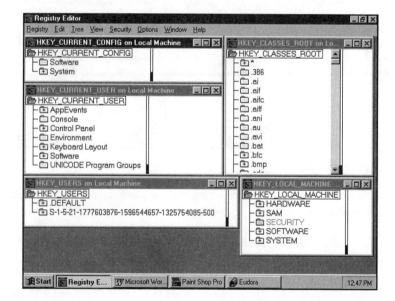

Configuration files associated with Registry hives are stored in the \Winnt\System32\Config folder. Figure 9.6 highlights the four System files that store the contents of the HKEY_LOCAL_MACHINE and HKEY_CURRENT_CONFIG hives. Configuration files use the following extensions:

- Files without an extension hold the current version of the configuration information.

- *.alt* holds a backup copy of the HKEY_LOCAL_MACHINE\System key, which is critical to starting Windows NT. Only the System file (discussed in the next section) has an .alt version.

- *.LOG* contains the transaction log that holds all changes made to the configuration file until the change is made permanent.

- *.dat* contains user information. Only the new Ntuser.dat files use the .dat extension. Ntuser.dat in \Winnt\System32\Config replaces the Username*xxx* and Admin*xxx* files of prior versions of Windows NT. Ntuser.dat in \Winnt\System32\Profiles\DefaultUser replaces the previous Userdef file. Ntuser.dat.log is the log file for Ntuser.dat.

- *.sav* files are created by the text mode part of Windows NT 4.0 Setup and are used in the event that the graphics mode part of Setup fails.

FIG. 9.6

Configuration (Registry hive) files in the \Winnt\System32\Config folder.

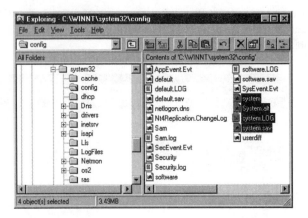

 N O T E   Userdiff and Userdiff.log aren't associated with a Registry hive or key. Windows NT 4.0 employs Userdiff files when updating user profiles created with prior versions of Windows NT.

As mentioned earlier, pairing hive and log files ensures that the Registry can't be corrupted. For example, if the power fails as your change to a value entry is written, the value might be changed, but the date stamp might still contain the old date and time, or the size of the entry might not be correct. The hive and log approach guarantees that these types of errors don't happen.

When it's time to write out changes to a hive file, Windows NT inserts a few extra steps. First, Windows NT writes to the log file the new data and instructions for where the data goes. After this data is safely written to the disk, Windows NT writes a special mark at the beginning of the hive file to indicate that it's being changed. The changes are written to the hive file and, on completion, the mark is removed. If a power failure or other serious problem occurs during the process, Windows NT notices when opening the file that the "being changed" mark exists, re-creates the changes from the log file, and then removes the mark. This process maintains the consistency of the hive file.

N O T E The relationship between the hive and log files is similar to that between SQL Server's device and log files. Log files record all transactions (operations that modify database values) since the last backup. In the event of a failure that requires restoration of the backup copy, the backup copy is loaded and the transaction log is run against the database to add the post-backup entries. In SQL Server, log files are stored on a physical device (disk drive) separated from the device containing the database(s). Windows NT hive and log files are stored on the same disk. ▨

Keys and Subkeys

Just as a folder in a file system can have subfolders, a hive has *keys* and a key can have *subkeys*. Just as a subfolder is itself a folder, a subkey is a key, another named collection of information. Each key can have many subkeys, each of which can have even more subkeys, and the hierarchy can be many levels deep.

The HKEY_LOCAL_MACHINE hive has the following four keys, which commonly are also called hives because they have associated configuration files:

■ *HKEY_LOCAL_MACHINE\SAM* is the directory services database (formerly Security Account Manager) stored in the SAM files.

■ *HKEY_LOCAL_MACHINE\Security* stores local security information, such as specific user permissions, in the Security files.

■ *HKEY_LOCAL_MACHINE\Software* holds configuration information for applications and their components in the Software files.

■ *HKEY_LOCAL_MACHINE\System* stores information that controls startup of Windows NT and loads the necessary device drivers, followed by Windows NT services.

The HKEY_LOCAL_MACHINE\System hive is loaded so early that a simpler process is needed. System.alt is just a copy of the System hive file. The changes to System aren't logged, but the "being changed" mark is still used. After System is written, System.alt is written in the same way. If the power fails while your computer is writing System, Windows NT will notice the "being changed" mark and use System.alt as a safe backup. Of course, the changes being made when the failure occurred are lost.

By convention, hive, key, and subkey names are gathered into full names and separated with backslashes that appear like folder path names. An example is a key called HKEY_LOCAL_MACHINE\HARDWARE\DESCRIPTION\System\MultifunctionAdapter\0\DiskController\0\FloppyDiskPeripheral. The FloppyDiskPeripheral key is a subkey of the 0 key, which is a subkey of the DiskController key, and so on, up to the hive HKEY_LOCAL_MACHINE.

N O T E Key names can contain spaces, just as spaces are permissible in Windows 95 and Windows NT 4.0's long file names (LFNs). Hive names use underscores in place of spaces. ▨

Value Entries

To continue the analogy of a file structure further, a key can contain value entries and subkeys, just as a folder can contain files and subfolders. *Value entries* in keys resemble files in folders. A value entry contains the information to examine or change, just as a file contains the data you display or edit. A key can (and often does) support more than one value entry.

A value entry has three components:

- The name of the value entry
- The type of information it contains (numerical or character data, for instance)
- The value of the information (c:\program.exe or 0, for example)

The following sections describe each of these components.

Value Entry Names   Microsoft chose reasonably comprehensible names for most value entries; you probably can guess what CurrentUser, InstallDate, LogFilePath, and DiskCacheSize contain without any need for documentation. Much of the information is added to the Registry when you install programs on the system, and application vendors may not choose sensible or easy-to-understand names.

When there's only one value entry in a key, it's possible—but not necessarily wise—that the programmer who added the key left the name unassigned. When omitting a single value name, the Registry Editor shows (Default) in place of the missing value entry name. This practice is quite common in the file association entries of the HKEY_CLASSES_ROOT key. Use the name of the key to understand the information in the value entry.

Data Types   The data type must be one of the following five allowable data types:

- *REG_BINARY.* Raw binary data, which is displayed by the Registry Editor in hexadecimal format.
- *REG_DWORD.* Exactly 4 bytes of binary data. The Registry Editor can display these values as binary, decimal, or hexadecimal numbers.
- *REG_SZ.* A string of characters terminated by a NULL character.
- *REG_MULTI_SZ.* Several strings of characters separated by NULL characters and terminated by two NULL characters.
- *REG_EXPAND_SZ.* A string of characters that contains a symbol to be expanded when the value is used. The symbol begins and ends with a % character.

The REG_EXPAND_SZ symbols correspond to environment variables—for example, %PATH% expands to the value of the PATH environment variable. Most environment variables also are stored in the Registry but aren't all under the same key. Some environment variables are in the HKEY_LOCAL_MACHINE\SYSTEM\CurrentControlSet\Control\Session Manager\Environment key, and others appear under HKEY_CURRENT_USER\Environment. Environment settings in AUTOEXEC.BAT aren't stored in the Registry, but some applications modify both AUTOEXEC.BAT and the Registry during installation, so many of your environment variables are accessible from the Registry.

The value entry is a number or a string according to the type. Binary numbers are almost impossible to read in the Registry Editor, but specific tools, such as Windows NT Diagnostics (discussed in its own section later in this chapter), can display these value entries in a more meaningful format.

Understanding Some Important Hives and Keys

Part

II

Ch

9

It's not possible to list all the keys in your Registry, because keys are added every time you install hardware or software. It's not even possible to list all the keys in the Registry of a typical machine running Windows NT Server and no applications; publication limits on page count preclude such a listing. It's also not useful to provide a list of all Registry keys; once you know roughly where to look, it's quicker to use the Registry Editor to search for the exact key or value entry. Thus, this section doesn't attempt to describe all Registry keys, but it suggests appropriate locations to search for particular classes of Registry entries.

The HKEY_LOCAL_MACHINE Hive

As mentioned earlier, HKEY_LOCAL_MACHINE contains system-wide hardware information and configuration details. This key has five important subkeys, four of which are so important that they're located in the standard hive list you've already seen. In addition to SAM, Security, Software, and System (the standard hive keys of HKEY_LOCAL_MACHINE), there's also a Hardware key.

SAM   SAM is an acronym for *Security Account Manager*. This key contains the database of user and group information, as well as security information for the domain. Although SAM is mentioned throughout the documentation and help files for Windows NT 4.0, the new name for SAM is the directory services database. Microsoft is changing the name in preparation for the transition to the Distributed File System (DFS) and Active Directory Services (ADS) that will occur with Windows NT 5.0. These new features are described in Chapter 26, "Scaling Windows NT Server 4.0 to the Enterprise."

SAM has one subkey, again called SAM, which contains two subkeys—Domains and RXACT. RXACT doesn't ordinarily contain anything, but Domains has two subkeys—Account and Builtin.

> **CAUTION**
>
> Don't attempt to change any value in the SAM key or its subkeys with the Registry Editor. You could leave a user's account unusable. Utilize User Manager to make the changes, as described in Chapter 13, "Managing User and Group Accounts."
>
> ▶ **See** "Working with User Manager for Domains," **p. 442**

The entire HKEY_LOCAL_MACHINE\SAM key is also accessible as HKEY_LOCAL_MACHINE\SECURITY\SAM. Changes you make in one key are immediately reflected in the other key.

Security   This key contains policies as well as a link to the directory services (SAM) database. The subkeys are Policy, RXACT, and SAM. This material is discussed in more detail in Chapter 14, "Sharing and Securing Network Resources."

▶ **See** "Understanding NTFS Permissions," **p. 493**

Software   This key is where system-wide configuration information is stored for each software product installed on the computer. For example, if you install Visual C++ 4.0, there's a key called HKEY_LOCAL_MACHINE\Software\Microsoft\Developer\Directories with two value entries. One value entry, Install Dirs, holds the name of the folder into which the program was installed. The other value entry, ProductDir, holds the name of the main directory to be used by the product.

Nothing in the Developer subkey contains any user-specific settings; user-specific entries are stored elsewhere in the Registry, under HKEY_CURRENT_USER\Software (discussed later). For example, user-specific Developer Studio settings would be in the HKEY_CURRENT_USER\Software\Microsoft\Developer key.

As mentioned earlier, the Registry must be updated if you move software from one location to another—for example, between fixed-disk drives in the same machine. Thus, it's usually quicker and easier to uninstall the software, and then reinstall the software in the new location. Depending on the application, many different keys may need to be modified to point to the new drive or folder. Let the uninstall and reinstall software do the work, and heed the general rule: *never change the Registry by hand.*

The Software key is organized by the name of the company that makes the software. Several keys are present, even if you haven't installed any applications. They include the following:

■ *Classes.* Another name for the HKEY_CLASSES_ROOT key, discussed in its own section later in this chapter.

■ *Description.* Names and version numbers of installed software. Don't change these.

■ *Microsoft.* Information related to products from Microsoft, including many that are installed automatically with Windows NT Server.

■ *Program groups.* The information for all the Common Program Groups. Change these only with Program Manager.

■ *Secure.* Just a handy place to keep keys that need more security.

System and the Last Known Good Menu   This key contains information used during startup that can't be fully determined by Windows NT Server until startup is over. All but two of System's subkeys are called *control sets.* The Select and Setup subkeys are not control sets, but rather are used by Windows NT to choose which control set to use on startup.

A control set is all the information needed to start the system. Two to four control sets are kept in System, with names such as ControlSet001 and ControlSet002. There's also a CurrentControlSet, which is linked to one of the other control sets. This allows you to switch back to a control set that works if you (or an application you run, or a system crash) make changes to the Registry that prevent the computer from starting.

Fortunately, during startup you have a chance to press the space bar to use the Last Known Good menu, a specific control set. The subkey that implements the Last Known Good feature, called Select, has four value entries:

- *Default.* The number of the control set (a value of 002 means use ControlSet002) that will be used at the next startup unless the user chooses Last Known Good.
- *Current.* The number of the control set that was used this time at startup.
- *LastKnownGood.* The number of the control set that represents the values that succeeded most recently.
- *Failed.* The number of the control set that was used during a failed startup. When you choose Last Known Good, this control set is no longer current. By storing the number of a bad control set as the Failed value, Windows NT lets you know where to look for the bad setting that caused startup to fail.

You may sometimes see a Clone subkey in the System key. This subkey is used to build that LastKnownGood value. During startup, the current control set is copied into Clone. If the startup succeeds, Clone is copied into LastKnownGood.

If your Registry is corrupted, choosing the Last Known Good menu during startup makes it possible to start Windows NT Server so that you can (or might be able to) correct the problem that caused the corruption. Your Registry might become corrupted for various reasons, but bad sectors on your fixed disk or (far more frequently) user errors usually are the culprits. If you edit your Registry by hand and make a serious mistake, you may leave your server unbootable. Using Last Known Good saves you from a complete reinstall.

N O T E Although every boot problem is different, here's a typical pattern:

1. A power failure or hardware error requires a reboot, or you perform a routine reboot after changing Registry entries with the Registry Editor or some other tool.
2. The system doesn't boot into Windows NT Server.
3. You power down and on powerup watch for the Last Known Good prompt.
4. You press the spacebar to use the Last Known Good control set.
5. You examine both the current control set and the failed one to see what's different. You also figure out what changes you need to make to your current configuration (if any) that will achieve the effect you originally wanted without preventing a successful boot.

CAUTION

If you make changes to any of the control sets discussed in this section (other than CurrentControlSet) within the Registry Editor, you can void the insurance that these keys provide for you. Use Server Manager or Control Panel's Devices, Network, Server, or Services tool. Use the Registry Editor to *look* at entries, not *change* them.

Part
II

Ch
9

Each control set contains two subkeys—Control and Services. The exact subkeys in each key vary, but the typical subkeys in the Control subkey are as follows:

- Use the *BootVerificationProgram* subkey to tell the system how to define "succeeded" if you don't want to use the default definition. *Make sure that you know what you're doing before you alter this key value.*

- *ComputerName* contains the ComputerName and ActiveComputerName subkeys. Change the values of these subkeys only with Control Panel's Network tool.

- *ServiceGroupOrder* lists the order in which groups of services should be started.

- *GroupOrderList* lists the order to start services within a group.

- *HiveList* contains the location of the hive files, usually \Winnt\System32\Config. *Do not change.*

- With its subkeys, the *Keyboard Layout* subkey defines the keyboard language layout. You change it with Control Panel's Regional Settings tool.

- *Lsa* is used by the local security authority. *Do not change.*

- *NetworkProvider* defines the network provider. You change it with Control Panel's Network tool.

- *Nls* defines national language support. Change it with Control Panel's Regional Settings tool.

- *Print*—with its subkeys Environments, Monitors, Printers, and Providers—defines the printers and printing environment for the system. You change it with the Start menu's Printers folder.

- *PriorityControl* defines the priority separation. Change it with Control Panel's System tool.

- *ProductOptions* shows the product type (for example, Winnt). *Do not change.*

- *SessionManager* contains global and environment variables. Its Environment and MemoryManagement subkeys can be changed with Control Panel's System tool; *do not change the others.*

- *Setup* contains hardware choices. Change it with Windows NT Setup.

- *TimeZoneInformation* contains time-zone settings. You change it with Control Panel's Date/Time tool.

- *Virtual device drivers* contains information about virtual device drivers. *Do not change.*

- *Windows* contains various paths needed by the system. *Do not change.*

- *WOW* contains Windows on Windows options for running 16-bit applications. *Do not change.*

The Services subkey of each control set has a hundred or so subkeys, so these subkeys aren't listed here. The Services subkeys describe device drivers, file system drivers, service drivers, and other hardware drivers. Use Windows NT Diagnostics to view the information in these subkeys. Utilize User Manager or Control Panel's Devices, Network, or Services tool to change the information in these subkeys.

Finally, the Setup subkey of HKEY_LOCAL_MACHINE\System is used by Windows NT Setup. Don't change the Setup subkey values.

Hardware   All the information in the HKEY_LOCAL_MACHINE\Hardware key is written into the Registry during startup, disappears when you shut down the machine, and then is recalculated and rewritten during the next startup. That makes it meaningless to change Hardware values in an attempt to solve a system problem, and that's also why the Hardware key isn't stored in hive files. To view Hardware key values in a more readable format, use the Windows NT Diagnostics utility, described later in the section "Using the Windows NT Diagnostics Utility."

Part

II

Ch

9

The Hardware key contains the following standard subkeys:

- *Description*. Describes the hardware recognized automatically by the system.
- *Devicemap*. Points to the location in the Registry where the driver for each device is located. Typically, this is in the Services subkey of one of the control sets.
- *Resourcemap*. Points to the location in the Registry where the driver for each resource is located. Typically, this is in the Services subkey of one of the control sets.

HKEY_CURRENT_CONFIG

Windows NT implements *hardware profiles*, which make it simple for users to switch a number of settings related to hardware at once. For example, a laptop user might have "docked" and "mobile" profiles, with the mobile profile using a lower density screen, different color scheme, and so on. This is unlikely to be of interest on a server, which usually keeps the same hardware configuration at all times. Hardware profiles primarily are of interest to users of Windows NT Workstation 4.0.

To implement this feature, Windows NT no longer assumes that there's only one set of hardware settings; this new key holds the current settings. Behind the scenes, changing your hardware profile from mobile to docked involves copying the docked profile into this HKEY_CURRENT_CONFIG key.

HKEY_CLASSES_ROOT

This key, linked to HKEY_LOCAL_MACHINE\SOFTWARE\Classes, contains file association and OLE and ActiveX server information. The file-association keys all have a name that starts with a period (.) and represents a file extension, such as .BMP or .TXT. Each key has one value entry, typically with no name, that contains the name of a key for the application that will launch files with that extension. To change file association keys, use the File Types page of Explorer's Options property sheet by choosing Options from the View menu (see Figure 9.7).

FIG. 9.7
Associating file types
with applications.

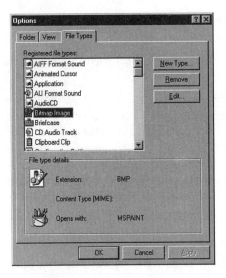

The OLE-related keys have names that don't start with a period. The subkeys vary from application to application but all have a CLSID subkey for the OLE Class ID. A Class ID is a 32-byte identifier, called a *globally unique ID (GUID)*, that's guaranteed to be different each time a developer generates a value. One important value entry is shell\open\command, which contains the command line to be used when a file of this type is opened by double-clicking a file in Explorer. For example, the value item HKEY_CLASSES_ROOT\Word.Document.6\shell\open\command has the value c:\MSOFFICE\WINWORD\WINWORD.EXE /w on those few installations of Windows NT Server that run desktop applications. Other subkeys cover the behavior of the application as an OLE server. For example, HKEY_CLASSES_ROOT\Word.Document.6\protocol\StdFileEditing\Verb\0 has the value Edit, an OLE verb.

> **CAUTION**
> Don't edit these values unless specifically directed to do so by your application vendor or Microsoft. You could leave the application unusable.

HKEY_CURRENT_USER

This key stores all the current profile information for the user who's logged on to the server at the moment. A *user profile* is a collection of keys that contains all the information about one user. The current user profile information overrides prior user profile settings in HKEY_LOCAL_MACHINE. The subkeys of HKEY_CURRENT_USER—none of which you should change with Registry Editor—are as follows:

  ■ *Console.* Defines the base options, window size, and so on for character-based applications such as Telnet.

- *Control Panel.* All user-specific information set by Control Panel (such as colors, wallpaper, and double-click rate).
- *Environment.* Environment variables set with Control Panel's System tool.
- *KeyboardLayout.* This user's keyboard layout. Change with Control Panel's Keyboard tool.
- *Printers.* The printers installed for this user. Change with Print Manager.
- *Software.* All settings (options, preferences, customizations, recently opened files, window sizes, and more) for all the software that this user has access to. The structure of this subkey is the same as the HKEY_LOCAL_MACHINE\Software key, but the names of the keys under the product name and of the value entries are different. These entries are changed by the applications that use them.

When users log on, their profiles are copied from HKEY_USERS into HKEY_CURRENT_USER. If the correct profile for a user isn't found, the default profile (discussed in the next section) is used.

HKEY_USERS

The HKEY_USERS key contains all the active user profiles, each under a key with the same name as the user's Security ID string. HKEY_USERS also contains a .DEFAULT subkey with all the default settings for a new user. The subkeys under each user and under .DEFAULT are the same as those listed in the preceding section for HKEY_CURRENT_USER.

Using the Windows NT Diagnostics Utility

In many of the preceding sections, you read warnings against modifying Registry values. Sometimes, however, you need to know the value of a Registry setting, particularly a hardware setting. One way to look at all your hardware-related Registry settings at once is to use Winmsd, the Windows NT Diagnostics utility.

As its name implies, the Windows NT Diagnostics utility helps you diagnose the behavior of your system by examining various settings at once. To run Winmsd, from the Start menu choose Programs, Administrative Tools, and Windows NT Diagnostics. Winmsd gathers various settings into nine tabbed pages (see Figure 9.8):

- *Version.* Operating system information, including version number, build number, serial number, and registered owner.
- *System.* Processor and BIOS information.
- *Display.* Display type, settings, and drivers.
- *Drives.* All fixed, removable, and remote drives, arranged by type (floppy, local hard drive, CD-ROM, remote hard drive) or drive letter.
- *Memory.* System memory and paging files.
- *Services.* Running or Stopped status for all system services or devices.

- *Resources.* Ports, mouse, floppy drives, and other system resources.
- *Environment.* Environment variables.
- *Network.* Domain, workgroup, access level, and what user is logged on now. Network settings and statistics are also available.

FIG. 9.8
Checking Windows NT version data in the Windows NT Diagnostics utility.

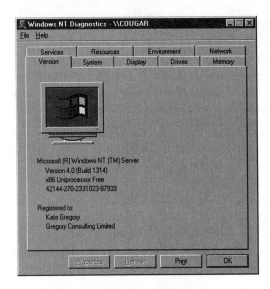

If you aren't sure which Control Panel tool or Registry key to use to check a Registry value, use Winmsd. Winmsd is quick, and you can't accidentally change a value. If you want to keep a record of the settings described in the preceding list, use the printed reports from Winmsd rather than compile a written list from values displayed by the Registry Editor.

Backing Up the Registry

Backing up the Registry often is very important, especially before you change anything to try to fix a problem. Some, but not all, Registry information is saved on the emergency repair disk. The following are four different ways to back up the Registry:

- From within the Regedt32.exe Registry Editor, choose Save Key from the Registry menu and save the key to alternate media, such as tape or a drive elsewhere on the network. (All configurations files won't fit on a 1.44M disk.) To restore from this backup, choose Restore Key from the Registry Editor's Registry menu. You must individually select each hive window and save its associated configuration file.

  In Regedit.exe, choose Export Registry File from the File menu to open the Export Registry File dialog. Select All in the Export Range section to export the contents of the entire Registry to a single text file with a .reg extension (see Figure 9.9). Using Regedit.exe to export Registry files is simpler than using Regedt32.exe. Saving the

OAKLEAF0 Registry resulted in a 5M text file; Figure 9.10 shows the first few lines of the file in Notepad.

FIG. 9.9
Using Regedit.exe to save the entire Registry as a text-format .reg file.

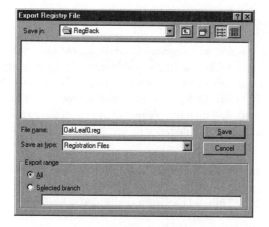

FIG. 9.10
Windows NT 4.0 Notepad displaying the first few lines of a 5M .reg backup file.

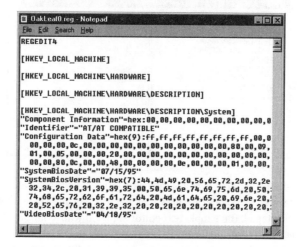

- If you back up to tape by using Windows NT Backup, mark the Backup Local Registry check box in the Backup Information dialog, and the Registry is backed up to tape with regular files. To restore from this backup, use Windows NT Restore.

  ▶ **See** "Using the Windows NT Server 4.0 Backup Application," **p. 278**

- Use the Regback.exe or Repair.exe programs included on the *Windows NT Resource Kit* CD-ROM to back up Registry files. To restore the Registry, use Regrest.exe or Repair.exe.

- From another operating system, copy the files in the \Winnt\System32\Config folder to alternative media. Also copy the user information hives from each

\Winnt\Profiles*Username* folder. To restore the Registry, use the other operating system to copy the backups into those folders again.

Using the Registry Editor

The Registry Editor is the best way to get a feel for the hierarchical nature of the Registry. Experienced users can also utilize the Registry Editor to edit the Registry when there's no other way to accomplish certain changes. As mentioned earlier, neither Regedit.exe or Regedt32.exe are available directly from the Start menu. From the Start menu choose Run (or use the command prompt), and then type **regedt32** or **regedit** to run the Registry Editor. When Regedt32.exe first starts, the Registry Editor displays the five topmost keys, as shown earlier in Figure 9.2.

Earlier in Figure 9.5, the subkeys under each key are collapsed, and each is represented by a single line in the right pane. To expand a collapsed key or to collapse an expanded one, double-click the name of the key. Figure 9.11 shows an expanded subkey.

FIG. 9.11

Expanding a Registry key to display subkeys.

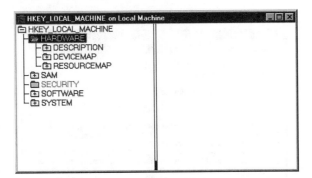

The right pane of each window displays the value entries. For each value entry, three pieces of information, separated by colons, are provided: name, type, and value. Figure 9.12 shows the value entries for Notepad, the simple text editor supplied with Windows NT. Some value entries (such as lfFaceName) are strings, whereas others (such as lfPitchAndFamily) are binary numbers. If the value of a value entry hasn't yet been set, the Registry Editor displays (value not set).

As mentioned earlier in the section "Value Entry Names," an entry of (Default) in the name column means that the value entry doesn't have a name. A (Default) entry is always displayed, so every key appears to have at least one value entry.

To adjust the relative sizes of the panes, click the border between the panes and drag it left or right. To change the value of a value entry, double-click somewhere on its line; this action is the same as choosing Binary, String, DWord, or MultiString (as appropriate) from the Edit menu, described in a later section.

FIG. 9.12
Displaying some
primary settings for
Notepad in the
HKEY_CURRENT_USER\
Software\Microsoft\
Notepad key.

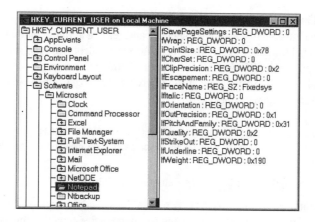

> **CAUTION**
> Be very careful when deleting or editing value entries. There is no undo for these operations.

Inspecting Another Computer's Registry

Occasionally, you may need to view or change a setting on another computer that's not located with your Windows NT Server computer. Fortunately, Windows NT Server can view and edit Registry entries of other computers running Windows NT or Windows 95. You also can edit the Registry of your server from another Windows 95 or Windows NT machine.

Rather than travel to the computer with the problem or tell the user to make the change with another tool, you might choose to edit the Registry remotely from your computer in at least the following situations:

- The user can't tell you what's wrong and can't search through the Registry to report what settings have been changed.

- The user doesn't have the authority or the skill to change a Registry value, even when you can dictate the necessary keystrokes by telephone.

- The problem is so quick to fix, and the remote computer is so far away (in another building or another city) that it's not worth the time for you to go to the computer.

- The problem is one that makes the computer very hard to use. An example is when the background and foreground text colors have been set to the same color so that no one can read the text in dialogs.

Preparing for Remote Registry Editing

Of course, you don't just take over the Registry of any other computer on your network and start changing values. Preparation is involved, especially if the remote computer is running Windows 95 or you want to use Windows 95 to edit the Registry of a machine running Windows NT.

Editing a Windows 95 Registry from Windows NT   If the remote computer is running Windows 95, you must enable user-level security and remote administration from that computer's Control Panel. First, use the Network tool's Access Control page and select User-Level Access Control. Then use the Password tool's Remote Administration page and mark Enable Remote Administration of this Server. Finally, on the Network tool's Configuration page, mark Add the Microsoft Remote Registry Services.

> **N O T E**   The details of this process are covered in Chapter 11, "Configuring Windows 95 Clients for Networking," and in the *Windows 95 Resource Kit* Help, included with the CD-ROM version of Windows 95.

> ▶ **See** "Managing Windows 95 Clients Remotely," **p. 390** ▪

Editing a Windows NT Registry from Windows 95   If you're trying to manipulate a Windows NT Registry from a Windows 95 machine (perhaps to fine-tune the departmental server from your desktop), you must add the Microsoft Remote Registry services and arrange user-level access; however, you don't need to enable remote administration of the Windows 95 machine. No preparation is required on the Windows NT Server machine.

Editing a Windows NT Registry from Windows NT   If you need to manipulate the Registry of one Windows NT machine from another (any combination of Windows NT Server and Windows NT Workstation), no preparation is required.

Opening the Remote Registry

To edit from a Windows NT machine, start Regedt32.exe, and use the Registry menu's Select Computer command to open windows with the HKEY_LOCAL_MACHINE and HKEY_USERS keys of the remote computer. Alternatively, start Regedit.exe and choose Connect Network Registry from the Registry menu. Then inspect or change the keys and value entries of the remote computer. The changes take effect immediately, so use extra care—especially if the remote computer is in use while you're changing the Registry. You might want to save this task for a time when the remote machine isn't in use, or arrange such a time with your users.

From a Windows 95 machine, start Registry Editor and choose Connect Network Registry from the Registry menu to open the remote Registry. You can then inspect or change the keys and value entries of the remote computer. Figure 9.13 shows a Windows 95 client (OAKLEAF1, My Computer) connected to the Registries of OAKLEAF0 (Windows NT Server 4.0) and OAKLEAF3 (Windows95). The HKEY_DYN_DATA hive appears only for Windows 95 Registries.

> **CAUTION**
> As mentioned earlier, take great care, especially when changing settings on a departmental server. A single keystroke could inconvenience a large number of users.

FIG. 9.13
Using Windows 95's
Regedit.exe to connect
to remote Windows NT
Server 4.0 (OAKLEAF0)
and Windows 95
(OAKLEAF3) Registries.

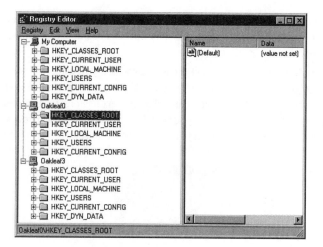

Maintaining Registry Security

You can restrict users' ability to change Registry values in a number of ways. Such restrictions should be part of an overall security plan that allows users to access only those administrative features they need.

First, don't provide Administrator access to non-administrators. You can restrict the access of non-administrator users to the Registry. You also should consider deleting Registry Editor and Policy Editor from client computers. On Windows NT machines, delete Regedit.exe and Poledit.exe from the \Winnt folder, and remove Regedt32.exe from the \Winnt\System32 folder. For PCs running Windows 95, delete Regedit.exe and Poledit.exe from the \Win95 folder. You can administer clients from the server, which usually is in a location with more physical security than the rest of the network, or from your client PC.

To control access to individual keys, you can add or remove names from the Access Control List (ACL) for each key. If you care enough about a particular key's value to restrict access, you should audit access to the key, or audit failed access attempts.

> **CAUTION**
>
> Excessive access restrictions can make applications unusable or the system unbootable. Always make sure that the Administrator has access to all keys. Always back up the Registry before implementing any security restrictions.

Restricting Access to Registry Keys

The process of restricting access involves several different administrative tools. Only Regedt32.exe provides access to the security properties of keys. Follow these steps to set up auditing and security for one or more key values:

1. In User Manager for Domains, choose Policies from the Audit menu, and make sure that Audit These Events is selected. Select Success or Failure, or both, for File or Object Access.

2. Within Registry Editor, select the key for which you want to restrict access, and then choose Owner from the Security menu. Figure 9.14 shows the Owner dialog. If you aren't the owner of a key, you can't change permissions for that key. As administrator, you can change the owner to yourself, but you can't return ownership unless the original owner gives you Full Control permissions on the key.

FIG. 9.14

Displaying the owner of a Registry key with the Owner dialog.

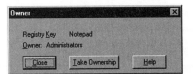

3. After you confirm or take ownership of the key, choose Permissions from the Security menu. The Registry Key Permissions dialog is used to assign permissions to the groups listed (see Figure 9.15). To add another group, click Add; to remove a group, click Remove. When the permissions for this key are correct, click OK.

FIG. 9.15

Setting access permission with the Registry Key Permissions dialog.

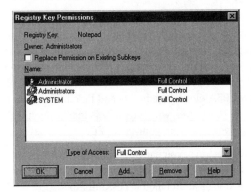

The available permissions are as follows:

- *Full Control.* Users in the group can view, change, take ownership, and change permissions. Administrators and the System group should have Full Control on every key.

- *Special Access.* Users in the group can view and change the key.

- *Read.* Users in the group can only read the key.

4. Choose Auditing from the Security menu to arrange auditing of key access. The Registry Key Auditing dialog appears (see Figure 9.16).

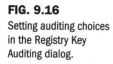

FIG. 9.16
Setting auditing choices
in the Registry Key
Auditing dialog.

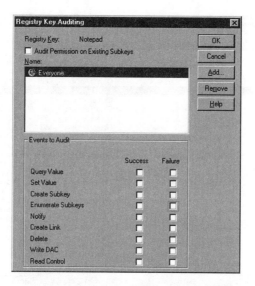

5. Select the types of accesses you want to be logged for each group.

You probably don't want to log successful accesses because there may be a large number of accesses. For example, many keys are updated every time a user runs an application, and each update may generate several log entries. Logging failed accesses allows you to discover applications that are no longer working for users, or users who are trying to change keys for which they have no permission.

The types of access audits are as follows:

- *Query Value.* An attempt to learn the value of the key.
- *Set Value.* An attempt to change the value of the key.
- *Create Subkey.* An attempt to make a subkey within the key.
- *Enumerate Subkeys.* An attempt to list the subkeys of this key.
- *Notify.* Notification events from the key.
- *Create Link.* An attempt to create a link within a key.
- *Delete.* An attempt to delete the key.
- *Write DAC.* An attempt to change the permissions (Discretionary Access Control) on a key.
- *Read Control.* An attempt to learn the permissions on a key.

Viewing an Audit Log

To view the audit logs, from the Start menu choose Programs, Administrative Tools, and Event Viewer. From the Log menu choose Security to see a list of the logged events. Figure 9.17 shows a sample list. These entries aren't very helpful beyond the user name; double-click one to see details like those in Figure 9.18.

FIG. 9.17

Event Viewer's Security log listings for Registry events.

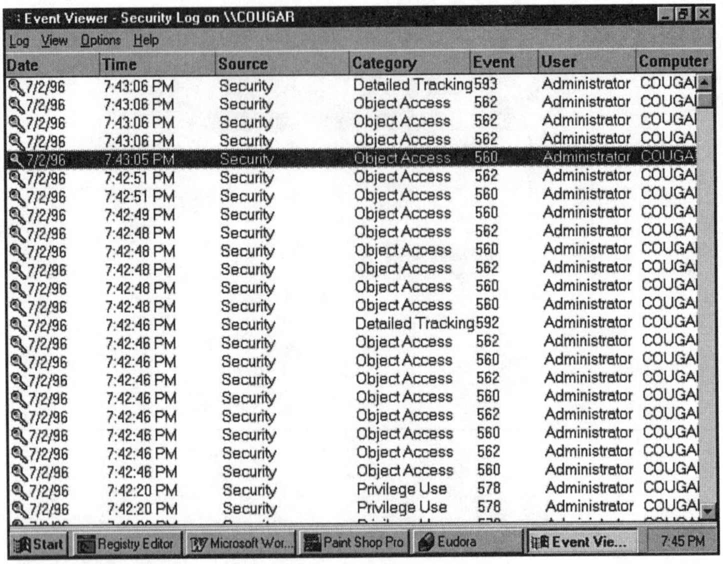

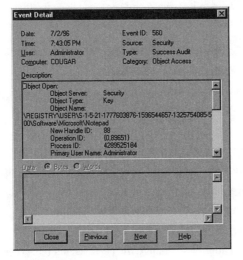

FIG. 9.18

Viewing Security log entry detail for opening a Registry key object.

These entries were generated as follows:

1. Auditing was turned on in User Manager for Domains.

2. In Registry Editor, auditing was turned on for both success and failure for any access to keys under HKEY_USERS*the-SID-of-the-account-in-use-at-the-time*\Software\ Microsoft\Notepad.

3. In Notepad, the font was changed, and then Notepad was closed.

4. In the Event Viewer, the menu item Log Security was chosen.

Even at a cursory glance, Figure 9.18 shows that the Notepad key was changed. Further investigation could narrow down the source of a user's trouble quite easily. For example, if you're logging only failures, you might relax security restrictions so that the operation no longer fails.

Understanding the Interaction of .INI and CONFIG.SYS Files with the Registry

Part

II

Ch

9

At the beginning of this chapter, you learned that the Registry is a place to store the sort of settings and configuration values once contained in CONFIG.SYS, AUTOEXEC.BAT, WIN.INI, SYSTEM.INI, and *APPNAME*.INI files for individual applications. Applications written for Windows NT or Windows 95 use the Registry to determine settings and configuration values.

Sixteen-bit applications written for Windows 3.x run under Windows NT but, obviously, such applications aren't Registry-aware. To run, 16-bit applications need their *APPNAME*.INI files to contain settings and configuration values. The setup programs of Windows 3.x applications often modify WIN.INI and SYSTEM.INI and create an *APPNAME*.INI file for the application. As a result of the Windows NT Setup process, you find WIN.INI and SYSTEM.INI files in \Winnt, the system root directory. These files don't affect the behavior of Registry-aware programs at all, but affect the behavior of older 16-bit applications.

N O T E   As a rule, 16-bit applications don't need to reside on a Windows NT 4.0 server, unless the server shares these applications with client PCs. If you must run 16-bit Windows applications on the server, you need to be aware of the interaction of Registry and .INI file entries. ■

A developer can access the information in an .INI file in two ways. If the programmer has chosen the "brute-force" method of opening the file and reading through it, the application operates completely independently of the Registry. However, Microsoft provides a set of Windows API functions to look up values in an .INI file, and most developers use these Windows API .INI file functions because they simplify programming. Under Windows NT, these .INI file functions have the same name as under Windows 3.x, but for certain specific keys the functions operate on the Registry rather than on an .INI file. This means that 16-bit programs, written by developers before the Registry existed, store their configuration entries in the Registry.

The HKEY_LOCAL_MACHINE\Software\Microsoft\WindowsNT\CurrentVersion\ IniFileMapping key maps .INI file entries to Registry keys. Figure 9.19 shows the win.ini subkey and its value entries. The value for each value entry is the Registry key to which it's mapped (note that each key may have a number of value entries). The strings USR and SYS stand for the keys HKEY_CURRENT_USER and HKEY_LOCAL_MACHINE\Software, respectively.

FIG. 9.19

Displaying the mapping of WIN.INI entries to Registry keys.

Also, three symbols—!, #, and @—may be present as the first character of the value. In all cases, a request to read from or write to the .INI file is translated into a request to read or write a Registry entry, but if one of these characters is present, the connection is made even tighter. The meaning of each of the three symbols is as follows:

- ! means that, as well as write the value to the Registry, the value should be written to the .INI file.

- # means that when a user first logs on to Windows NT, the value should be initialized from the .INI file.

- @ means that if the mapped key doesn't contain the value entry being requested, the request fails rather than goes to the .INI file.

Using the Resource Kit's Registry Entry Help File

The Server and Workstation versions of the *Windows NT Resource Kit* for version 4.0 provide Regentry.hlp, a 32-bit WinHelp file that describes virtually every Registry entry for Windows NT 4.0. An updated version of Regentry.hlp, which adds new Registry entries for Internet Information Server, is included on the CD-ROM of the *Windows NT Server Resource Kit, Supplement One* for version 4.0. When you install the Resource Kit, Setup puts Regentry.hlp in the \Ntreskit folder.

Regentry.hlp's Contents page provides an alphabetic list of Registry entries, as well as access to collections of keys and subkeys grouped by function. If you need to know the purpose or allowable values of a Registry key, Regentry.hlp is a very valuable resource. In addition to the Registry backup and restore utilities (described earlier in the section "Backing Up the

Registry"), the Resource Kit provides a number of other useful command-line utilities for streamlining Registry operations.

From Here...

It's possible to use Windows NT Server 4.0 with only a vague idea of the Registry and the purpose it serves—at least until a Registry-related problem arises. As a network administrator, you must know what information is stored in the Registry and how to change Registry entries when necessary. It's important to understand how dangerous it can be to edit Registry values with the Registry Editor, and why, despite the danger, you occasionally must use the editor to alter values.

Many of the remaining chapters in this book touch on the Registry from time to time, but the following chapters elaborate on Registry entries:

- Chapter 8, "Installing File Backup Systems," explains the tradeoffs between different types and formats of backup systems, and how to manage server backup operations to ensure against lost Registry data in case of a fixed-disk failure.

- Chapter 13, "Managing User and Group Accounts," covers the issues of user administration and security that affect the user-related keys of the Registry.

- Chapter 17, "Distributing Network Services with Domains," covers additional Registry-related security issues.

Part
II

Ch
9

Using TCP/IP, WINS, and DHCP

This chapter describes TCP/IP (Transmission Control Protocol/Internet Protocol) and related applications that have gained wide acceptance and use over the last decade. TCP/IP is the network protocol used on the Internet, which by itself makes the topic worthy of study. It's also very useful in private networks, especially as they grow in size.

The chapter begins with a brief tutorial on TCP/IP. Those familiar with the subject from a background in UNIX networking can skip this section, or at least just skim it. No claims are made of academic rigor—the tutorial is intended to be a practical and accessible overview for those interested in background material. Nothing presented in the tutorial is essential for installing and using TCP/IP, although it may help you understand some of the terminology used by TCP/IP aficionados and *why* things are done the way they are. ■

Understanding the role of TCP/IP

Organizations building intranets and connecting to the Internet use TCP/IP exclusively or with other network protocols. You learn how TCP/IP works, its advantages, its potential problems, and solutions for those problems.

Installing and configuring TCP/IP

Install and configure TCP/IP and related components, such as the SNMP service and the FTP server service. Configure Windows NT Server to use a HOSTS file, a Domain Name System (DNS) server, or both.

Using Dynamic Host Configuration Protocol (DHCP)

Set up and configure the DHCP Server service with DHCP Manager to lease IP addresses to networked clients. Create static addresses for servers and other key network components and manage the IP address pool.

Taking advantage of Windows Internet Name Service (WINS)

Configure a WINS server with WINS Manager to resolve NetBIOS names to dynamically assigned IP addresses.

Understanding the Role of TCP/IP

TCP/IP is a suite of network protocols that describe precisely how information can be transmitted from one computer to one or more additional computers. TCP/IP is designed to operate in environments where the conditions aren't particularly suitable for this task, and therefore has a strong error-detection and correction capability. Most often, the term *TCP/IP* denotes not only the protocol suite itself but also a group of compatible applications and utilities that have been created and used to implement and test the protocols.

Members of the Internet community have developed TCP/IP cooperatively by using a proposal and peer-review process involving documents called *Request for Comments (RFCs)*. A person or group proposes a design and publishes an RFC describing that design. Other members of the community, some of whom may refine the proposal with their own additions again put forth in an RFC, review it. Some of these designs are implemented, tested, and refined even further. Eventually, an RFC that describes a set of standards is developed, and manufacturers design products that conform to one or more of these RFCs.

This process turns out to be quite effective, over time, at discovering and eliminating problems. The RFC process is ongoing, and existing RFCs are available for public review. RFCs primarily are intended for individuals and organizations who design products and services to be used on the Internet. Some RFCs include useful information for Internet users and don't describe standards at all. RFC 1118, "The Hitchhikers Guide to the Internet," is an example of this type of RFC.

ON THE WEB

InterNIC maintains an index to all RFCs at **http://www.internic.net/ds/dspg2intdoc.html**. "The Hitchhikers Guide to the Internet" is at **http://www.internic.net/rfc/rfc1118.txt**.

Some terminology used with TCP/IP may be confusing at first. The term *host* describes a component on a network, such as a computer or router. In some circles, the term *host* has the connotation of a *large* computer system, such as an IBM mainframe computer. In the context of TCP/IP discussions, a host can be a desktop personal computer or laptop, or a multiprocessor supercomputer.

The term *gateway* describes a piece of equipment commonly referred to as a *router*, which is used to create wide area network (WAN) connections to remote locations. Don't confuse *gateway* with its other connotation, which is that of a connection to a computer system having a different operating system or communications protocol. For the purposes of TCP/IP, your *default gateway* is nothing more than the router that connects your local area network (LAN) to the rest of your WAN.

▶ **See** "Routers," **p. 148**

Finally, the term *Internet* itself can be confusing. *Internet*, with a capital I, is generally used to describe the worldwide collection of public and private networks that link educational institutions, research facilities, commercial organizations, government agencies, and military sites. The term *internet*, with a lowercase i, refers to any collection of TCP/IP networks linked with routers. Private internets, or *internetworks*, are increasingly referred to by the term *intranet*. *Extranets* are virtual private networks (VPNs) that provide secure connections to corporate intranets over the Internet. For more extensive coverage of the Internet, see Chapter 20, "Setting Up Internet Information Server 4.0."

Why Use TCP/IP?

The use of TCP/IP is growing for many reasons. During the last decade, many organizations implemented LANs in offices and sites throughout their facilities. Eventually, they wanted to connect these LANs into WANs. Also, a growing number of organizations have started to view the WAN as a strategic resource, critical to the success of their efforts. To implement these views, they need a protocol that can manage large numbers of systems in a routed, WAN environment. This is precisely what TCP/IP was designed to deliver.

TCP/IP is also the protocol used on the Internet and is therefore useful for individuals and organizations who want to attach directly to the Internet or access it through a service provider. Furthermore, TCP/IP allows a high degree of interoperability between dissimilar systems, such as computers running Windows NT and UNIX operating systems. TCP/IP also provides an environment that supports the development of powerful applications having feature-rich programmatic interfaces.

IP Addresses, Host Names, Domain Names, and NetBIOS Names

The central capability provided by TCP/IP, as already mentioned, is a transmission facility—moving information from point A to point B. The transmission of information must be done in a manner that takes into account the involvement of both computers and humans. The computers must be able to send and receive information accurately and quickly, and their human operators must easily be able to specify what actions they want and understand the results.

That computers and humans require different naming schemes for the elements of a network is the source of much of the difficulty surrounding its operation. Computers must have a unique *address* for each component on the network to accurately send information to just those components for which it was intended. Humans also must be able to specify the computer they want to communicate with, and to name their own computer system so that they can describe it to other humans, especially if they're sharing information on the network. But the kind of name appropriate for computer use is much different from what's suitable for humans.

This leads to one central problem that TCP/IP must solve—name and address resolution. Three types of names are designed for humans, and two addresses are designed primarily for computers and their operating systems and applications. Matching a name with its corresponding address is more difficult than it might at first appear. A Windows NT network using TCP/IP uses the following name types:

- *Machine address,* also called *hardware address.* In Ethernet networking, the machine address is a guaranteed unique address that's "hard wired" or manufactured into a computer network product, such as a network adapter for a personal computer. Ethernet network adapters use a Media Access Control (MAC) address, which includes a portion that's specific to a particular manufacturer so that two different manufacturers never create the same address. Within their private *address space*, each manufacturer must make sure that it never creates two devices with the same address. This is usually done by including a ROM chip or similar element with a unique identifier that becomes part of the address. MAC addresses are expressed as 12 hexadecimal digits (for example, 00 04 AC 26 5E 8E), often written with a space between each two digits for human readability. Other hardware networks, such as ATM and token-ring networks, use different schemes to assign machine addresses.

■ *IP address*, used by operating systems and networking software on TCP/IP networks. If you create a private network, you must make sure that no two devices have the same IP address. If you want to attach to the Internet, you must request part of the address space from InterNIC (Network Information Center) for your organization to use and then manage that portion so that no two components use the same address.

ON THE WEB

You can contact InterNIC via e-mail at **info@internic.net**. By phone, you can call 1-800-444-4345 in the United States, or 1-619-455-4600 in Canada or elsewhere. You also can visit InterNIC's Web server at **http://www.internic.net**.

IP addresses are written in a form known as *dotted decimal notation*. For example, 123.45.67.89 is a valid IP address. Each part is called an *octet* and can range from 1 to 254 (0 and 255 are generally reserved for special purposes). This address must be unique for each device on a given network. It's composed of two parts, the *network ID* and the *host ID*. The network ID, the first two octets, must be the same for all devices on a particular network segment or subnetwork and different from all other subnetworks. The host ID, the last two octets, must be unique within a particular network ID.

■ *Host name*, the "human-compatible" name for a computer or device on a TCP/IP network. A host name is also called an *FQDN* (Fully Qualified Domain Name), or simply a *domain name* when specified in full. A host name for a server might be *dataserver*, and its FQDN might be *dataserver.company.com*. Applications using host names are generally case sensitive. You can use this name instead of the IP address when entering many commands for TCP/IP-specific applications and utilities. FQDNs aren't used when entering Windows-based Microsoft networking commands, such as NET USE or NET VIEW, which require a NetBIOS name.

N O T E Using the same name for your host and NetBIOS names eliminates confusion when entering commands. Each name still retains its own role, however, and the applications that use these names are each designed for a particular type of name (either NetBIOS or host name, but rarely both). ■

■ *Domain name*, another name for the host name. The last part of this hierarchical name (*company.com* for example), is referred to as a *first-level* (or *top-level*) *name* and is used to uniquely identify your organization to the Internet community. Often a request for a domain name in an application or operating system utility refers only to the first-level name, not the FQDN.

- *NetBIOS name,* used for Microsoft networking commands, such as NET USE, and automatically used on your behalf when performing networking functions with Windows-based graphical utilities, such as File Manager or the Windows 95 Network Neighborhood. A NetBIOS name can be 15 characters long (for example, DATASERVER). Applications using NetBIOS names aren't generally case sensitive.

The Problem: Resolving Names and Addresses

During the execution of a network command, the application or operating system must eventually discover the machine address of the devices involved. Because users almost never enter the machine address into an application, you must use some means of *resolving* the host name, NetBIOS name, or IP address to machine address. Various mechanisms for this purpose have been developed and are discussed in this section.

Separate mechanisms exist for each type of name, and sometimes more than one process may occur. For example, an application that knows the host name may first resolve the name to an IP address and then to a machine address. The mechanisms for resolving each type are presented in the following list and are discussed in more detail in the next section. Some of these mechanisms are based on standards as defined in RFCs or other standards documents, and others are Microsoft-specific methods. IP addresses are resolved to machine addresses by using the following methods:

- Address Resolution Protocol (ARP), defined in RFC 826
- A search of the corresponding ARP cache in the computer's memory

Host names are resolved to IP addresses by using the methods in the following list. If the computer is configured to use all methods, the methods are tried in the following order:

- HOSTS file
- Domain Name Service (DNS)
- Windows Internet Name Service (WINS)
- A local broadcast
- LMHOSTS file

NetBIOS names are resolved to IP addresses by using the methods presented in the following list. If the computer is configured to use all methods, the methods are tried in the following order:

- A NetBIOS name cache in the computer's memory
- WINS
- A local broadcast
- LMHOSTS file
- HOSTS file
- DNS

Name-resolution mechanisms for host names and NetBIOS names are similar but are carried out in a different order. The mechanisms used can vary, depending on how the computer is configured.

Some Solutions to the Problem

The following sections provide an overview of how the various name- and address-resolution mechanisms function. Some mechanisms include many options and implementation details. This overview presents only the most salient points to help you gain a general understanding of the processes involved. Additional information is provided in the *Windows NT Networking Guide* volume of the *Windows NT Resource Kit*.

ARP   The Address Resolution Protocol is part of the TCP/IP protocol suite. You must use ARP only on a TCP/IP address that's known to reside on the local physical network. An IP address for a host on the same local network is resolved as follows:

1. The computer checks its own ARP cache, a list of IP addresses, and corresponding hardware addresses that it dynamically manages in memory as it operates.

2. If the computer doesn't find the address in the ARP cache, an ARP request is broadcast on the local network (broadcasts aren't generally forwarded through routers). This request includes its own hardware address and IP address and the IP address that needs to be resolved. The ARP request is an IP broadcast message. On an Ethernet network, the IP broadcast message maps to an Ethernet broadcast.

3. Each computer or host on the local network receives the ARP request. If the IP address doesn't match each computer's or host's own address, the computer or host discards and ignores the request. If it does match, the host responds with an ARP reply directly (not broadcast) to the original host with its own hardware address. It also updates its own ARP cache with the hardware address of the original host.

4. The original host receives the reply and updates its own ARP cache for future use. A communications link can now be established.

If a destination machine isn't on the same physical network as the sending machine, there's no need to resolve the machine address of the destination machine. The packet is routed at the IP level trough an intermediate router. The IP portion of TCP/IP needs to resolve the MAC address of the router so that the packet can be forwarded to the router.

Local Broadcasts   The Microsoft implementation of TCP/IP uses an enhanced version of the *b-node* (broadcast method) of NetBIOS name resolution described in RFCs 1001 and 1002. Broadcasts are used only after the computer first checks the NetBIOS name cache and attempts to contact a WINS server, if implemented (see "Implementing Windows Internet Name Service" later in this chapter). Broadcasts use an address that all computers on the local network segment accept and evaluate. Three broadcasts are sent before the next mechanism is attempted.

 T I P   To list the contents of the NetBIOS cache on a computer, type **nbtstat -c**. For other uses of the nbtstat command, type **nbtstat -?**.

LMHOSTS File   The LMHOSTS file is a text file that lists IP addresses and the corresponding NetBIOS name for remote hosts only (because active local hosts are discovered by WINS or broadcast first). It's closely related to the HOSTS file described in the following section. The LMHOSTS file, located by default in the *systemroot*\\SYSTEM32\\DRIVERS\\ETC directory, is specifically designed to resolve NetBIOS names. It's consulted by traditional TCP/IP utilities (if they accept NetBIOS names) only after trying the NetBIOS name cache, WINS, and b-node broadcasts.

TCP/IP utilities search the LMHOSTS file sequentially from top to bottom, so frequently used names (such as servers) should generally be listed near the top. By using the #INCLUDE directive in the file, you can load entries from a centralized copy of the LMHOSTS file from a server. A sample LMHOSTS file included with Windows NT Server provides examples of this and other directives and describes their use. Additional information is provided in the *Windows NT Networking Guide*.

T I P   You can create entries with the #PRE directive in the LMHOSTS file and use the following command to manually preload these entries into your NetBIOS name cache, thereby avoiding the need to perform broadcasts (even without WINS):

nbtstat -R

Be sure to enable LMHOSTS lookup in the TCP/IP configuration dialog if you want to use this technique. See the later section "Installing and Configuring TCP/IP for Windows NT Server" for more information.

HOSTS File   The HOSTS file, like the LMHOSTS file, is a text file that lists IP addresses and the corresponding host name. This file, located by default in the *systemroot*\\SYSTEM32\\DRIVERS\\ETC directory, is designed to resolve TCP/IP host names and FQDNs and is the first mechanism that traditional TCP/IP utilities consult. NetBIOS-based utilities consult it only after trying the NetBIOS name cache, WINS, b-node broadcasts, and the LMHOSTS file. TCP/IP utilities search the HOSTS file sequentially from top to bottom, so frequently used names (such as servers) should generally be listed near the top. The HOSTS file must be located on the local computer.

Domain Name Service (DNS)   DNS is an IP address resolution method frequently used on UNIX systems. One or more DNS servers are implemented and can then be consulted to resolve names not listed in the local HOSTS (or LMHOSTS) file. Desktop computers running Windows NT Workstation can be configured to use DNS. Microsoft has also included a DNS in Windows NT Server 4.0. Configuring Windows NT to use DNS for name resolution is described later in the section "Installing and Configuring TCP/IP for Windows NT Server."

▶ **See** "Using the Microsoft DNS Server," **p. 671**

Dynamic Host Configuration Protocol (DHCP)   Dynamic Host Configuration Protocol (DHCP) is a protocol that allows IP addresses to be assigned automatically from a pool of available IP addresses centrally stored and managed on one or more servers. Other TCP/IP-related information, such as the subnet mask and default gateway, can also be retrieved. DHCP servers don't share information with other DHCP servers or with DNS servers. The IP address pool managed by a DHCP server must be entirely owned by that server. No other server or individual should be able to assign an address from that pool.

DHCP is defined in RFCs 1533, 1534, 1541, and 1542. DHCP is an extension to, and builds on, the BOOTP protocol defined in RFC 951, which automatically assigns IP addresses to diskless workstations. Microsoft has designed a server-based service, an administration utility, and client software that implement the DHCP protocol. The installation and configuration of DHCP on Windows NT Server is covered in detail later in the section "Implementing Dynamic Host Configuration Protocol."

Windows Internet Name Service (WINS)   WINS is a NetBIOS Name Server (NBNS) implemented as a Windows NT service. Also included with Windows NT Server are an administration utility and client software. WINS can be used with or without DHCP to register NetBIOS names and resolve them to IP addresses without using b-node broadcasts, which can be problematic in large networks. Name-resolution requests are resolved by using directed datagrams (network packets) that are routable.

WINS is a dynamic name service that tracks network names as users start and stop client workstations. Multiple WINS servers can be configured to provide redundancy and to improve name-resolution performance. Changes to the names database on one WINS server are replicated to other WINS servers set up as push or pull partners. The installation and configuration of WINS on Windows NT Server 4.0 is covered in detail later in the section "Implementing Windows Internet Name Service."

Installing and Configuring TCP/IP for Windows NT Server

This section shows you how to install TCP/IP on a Windows NT server, including all the TCP/IP options Windows NT Server 4.0 offers. Microsoft's implementation includes various client-based utilities for the TCP/IP suite, such as Finger, `lpr`, `rcp`, `rexec`, `rsh`, Telnet, and `tftp`.

Both client and server support is provided for FTP (File Transfer Protocol). FTP allows a Windows NT server or workstation to interact with UNIX workstations and other platforms supporting TCP/IP. Notably missing from the connectivity utilities is support for NFS, the Network File System that makes files on UNIX servers accessible to PCs running Windows, but NFS is available from third-party software companies for Windows NT servers. A number of diagnostic utilities also are offered: `arp`, `hostname`, `ipconfig`, `lpq`, `nbtstat`, `netstat`, `ping`, `route`, and `tracert`. An SNMP agent, implemented as a Windows NT service, enables use of a remote network management console, such as Sun Net Manager or HP Open View, with your server.

▶ **See** "Using Windows NT's Network-Related Command-Line Tools," **p. 580**

▶ **See** "Installing the SNMP Service," **p. 577**

You can install TCP/IP during the original setup of Windows NT Server or add it later from Control Panel's Network tool. In this section, you add TCP/IP to an existing Windows NT Server 4.0 installation. Adding it during the initial setup is an almost identical process, so the following steps should still be helpful. You simply follow these instructions when you get to the network portion of Setup.

▶ **See** "Joining the Network," **p. 192**

To install TCP/IP and related services, follow these steps:

1. From the Start menu, choose Settings and Control Panel.

2. Double-click the Network icon to open the Network property sheet. On the Protocols page, click the Add button to open the Select Network Protocol dialog (see Figure 10.1). Select the TCP/IP Protocol item in the Network Protocol list and click OK.

Part

II

Ch

10

FIG. 10.1
Selecting the network protocols to install.

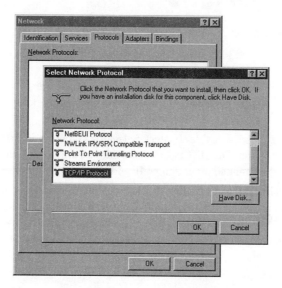

3. A dialog requesting the full path to the distribution files appears. Enter the location by using the drive letter of your local CD-ROM drive with the Windows NT Server 4.0 distribution CD-ROM inserted or the Universal Naming Convention (UNC) name of a shared network resource with the distribution files. (The UNC name option is feasible only if you have another network transport protocol already installed and operational.) Click Continue to copy the required files to your server.

The Microsoft TCP/IP Properties sheet, shown in Figure 10.2, appears on completion of the copy process. (If the Microsoft TCP/IP Properties sheet doesn't appear, double-click the newly added TCP/IP Protocol item in the Network Protocols list.)

FIG. 10.2

The default IP Address page of the Microsoft TCP/IP Properties sheet.

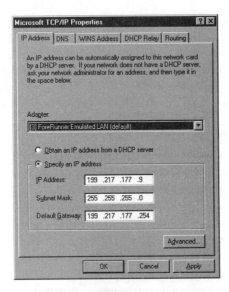

4. Use the IP Address page to set the IP address for this server (refer to Figure 10.2). You can set up an IP address in two ways:

- Obtain the address via DHCP (see "Dynamic Host Configuration Protocol (DHCP)" earlier in this chapter). Select the Obtain an IP Address from a DHCP Server option. The DHCP server provides all the needed information. DHCP is primarily intended for assigning IP addresses to client workstations.

- Statically assign an IP address, which is the most common method for servers. You must obtain a unique dotted decimal IP address from a central authority on your network. This person also can provide the subnet mask. The Default Gateway is the main router used to forward packets to and from other networks, most likely the Internet.

CAUTION

If you're unsure which IP address to use, check with the person who's responsible for managing IP addresses in your organization before you finish this process. If you're the person responsible and you're still unsure, review the earlier section "IP Addresses, Host Names, Domain Names, and NetBIOS Names" for guidance, and spend some time planning your IP addressing scheme.

It's very important that two computers don't have the same IP address. If you assign two computers the same TCP/IP address, one or both of the computers can't use the network. If this machine was an important server, this server would no longer be available.

5. Use the Advanced button to configure additional TCP/IP settings for additional adapters. A computer with more than one network adapter is called a *multihomed* computer.

6. The DNS page lets you enter one or more DNS servers for name resolution (see Figure 10.3). Windows NT has already set your host name to the machine name that you picked for your computer. Enter a valid domain name—for instance, **gasullivan.com**, if your network has a DNS server installed. The domain suffix search order lets you search multiple domain name spaces.

FIG. 10.3
Setting the DNS options for the server.

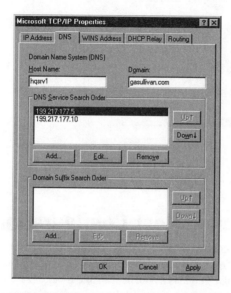

Part
II

Ch
10

7. If WINS is enabled on your network, you can enter the IP addresses of primary and secondary WINS servers on the WINS Address page (see Figure 10.4). If a DNS server is available on the network, marking the Enable DNS for Windows Resolution check box causes the TCP/IP protocol to check the DNS server first for name resolution.

8. The Routing page has one check box, Enable IP Forwarding; marking it enables static routing and, if installed, dynamic routing on this computer.

   ▶ **See** "Using Routing and Remote Access Service," **p. 980**

9. Click OK to commit the changes and close the property sheet. You must reboot the machine so that all the changes take effect.

In addition to the base protocol, you may want to install some of the TCP/IP-specific services. These services include TCP/IP printing (which lets users print to TCP/IP printers), simple TCP/IP, and SNMP. (*SNMP*, or *Simple Network Management Protocol*, lets you configure and monitor network devices.) These services are most useful when you print to existing UNIX host printers. The simple TCP/IP services install an FTP server and a Telnet server. The SNMP services allow this computer to become the source of SNMP events or the destination of SNMP messages.

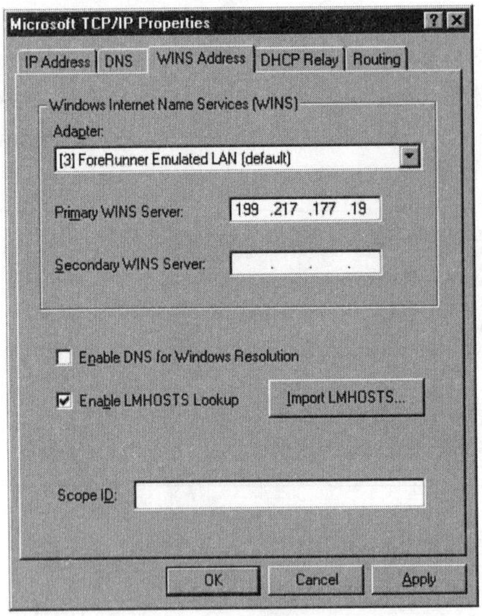

FIG. 10.4

Setting the Windows
Internet Name Services
(WINS) server address.

Implementing Dynamic Host Configuration Protocol

Setting up a DHCP server requires defining a *scope*, configuring client reservations, configuring DHCP clients, testing clients, viewing and managing DHCP client leases, and maintaining your DHCP database. A DHCP scope is a pool of available IP addresses and (optionally) additional addressing information for various shared devices or services. As a DHCP client computer connects to the network, a unique IP address is assigned and, with the addresses of other shared resources (for example, servers), can be transmitted to the client computer.

The IP address is said to be *leased* to the client computer because it can be returned to the pool of available addresses and used by another client later. You can define global options that apply to all scopes defined on a DHCP server. You can also define options that apply to only one scope.

You need several pieces of information before you can complete the configuration of DHCP. You must answer the following questions before configuring DHCP:

■ Will all the computers on your network be DHCP clients? If not, you must be sure to exclude the addresses from the pool of available addresses. In general, servers, routers, and other similar devices should be configured with static IP addresses.

■ What information, in addition to the IP address, do you want to configure automatically? A default gateway? WINS server? DNS server?

■ What options can you configure for all clients on the network? What options do all clients on a particular subnet share? Are any options unique for specific clients?

■ How many DHCP servers do you need? If your network consists of multiple physical subnets connected by routers, your routers must act as BOOTP Relay Agents as specified in RFC 1542, or you must put a DHCP server on each subnet with DHCP clients. If your router doesn't support RFC 1542 (many older routers don't), you may be able to upgrade it to add such support without having to replace the router.

- What range of addresses and other information should you include in the scope defined on each DHCP server? Should you define multiple scopes for any servers? Remember, DHCP servers don't share information with other DHCP servers or DNS servers. Each must have its own set of addresses to offer to the clients it will service. Additional information on defining a scope is provided later in the section "Creating a DHCP Scope."

N O T E   If you're unsure of the answers to some of these questions, read the following sections for additional background on the operation of DHCP and how it's configured. If you're still not clear on the information, remember that you can update the DHCP scope later and force clients to renew their leases, which automatically updates them with new information. ■

The Advantages of DHCP

DHCP offers several advantages over the manual configuration of TCP/IP addresses:

- Network users aren't required to enter an IP address, subnet mask, or any other addressing information. Therefore, they're much less likely to enter a random address or copy an address from a colleague's computer (following the reasoning that if a colleague's address works, an identical configuration also will work on their own computer).

- The process of manually entering an IP address, subnet mask, and other configuration information is prone to error, even with an educated user population that cooperates fully with the process. There are too many numbers and settings to expect a large group of users to set them without error. When users change computers or locations, the settings must be redone.

- A fair amount of administrative overhead is associated with managing the list of valid IP addresses, even with a DNS. This process is also inherently difficult to divide among several individuals unless each is knowledgeable about the technology and cooperates fully with one another.

- DHCP lets users configure their own computers without having to contact an administrator to get valid IP addresses. This eliminates errors, delays, and frustration.

- When users move their computer to a new location or travel with a laptop containing a PCMCIA Ethernet adapter or similar device, they automatically receive a valid address for the new location when they start their computers.

How DHCP Leases IP Addresses to Clients

Before you install the DHCP server, an overview of the DHCP lease address process may help you administer the process more effectively. Following is a basic description of how DHCP leases IP addresses:

1. A client computer starts and initializes an unconfigured version of TCP/IP. Then it broadcasts a request for an IP address. The request contains the computer's hardware address and computer name so that DHCP servers know who sent the request.

2. All DHCP servers with an available lease that's valid for the client send a response by using a broadcast message (because the client doesn't have an IP address yet). The message includes the client's hardware address, the IP address being offered, the subnet mask, the duration of the lease, and the IP address of the server making the offer. The server must reserve the address in case the offer is accepted.

3. The client accepts the first offer it receives. It broadcasts its acceptance to all DHCP servers with a message including the IP address of the server whose offer was accepted. Other servers release the temporary reservation on their offered addresses.

4. The server with the selected address sends an acknowledgment message with the IP address, subnet mask, and possibly other information defined in the scope as described in the next section. The client receives the acknowledgment and initializes a full version of TCP/IP. The client now can communicate with other hosts on the LAN or WAN.

DHCP Server Configuration

You use the DHCP Manager utility to configure a DHCP server. To open DHCP Manager, from the Start menu choose Programs, Administrative Tools, and DHCP Manager. You can start, stop, pause, and continue the DHCP service as you can all services—by using the Services icon in the Control Panel or by using the Windows NT Server Manager. Make sure that the service, formally named Microsoft DHCP Server, is started.

The rest of this section describes the procedures you use to define a DHCP scope, set various options, and configure and test DHCP client workstations. You also can reserve certain manually assigned addresses (for example, for servers and routers) so that they're excluded from the pool of available addresses managed by the DHCP service.

Creating a DHCP Scope   To create a DHCP scope, follow these steps:

1. Start DHCP Manager as explained in the preceding section.

2. From the Scope menu choose Create to display the Scope dialog. Figure 10.5 depicts a completed scope.

3. Enter the range of IP addresses to include in this scope. It's usually a good idea to include the full list of addresses used on this network or subnet and then explicitly exclude those addresses managed by a DNS or other DHCP server. You may also want to set aside a range of addresses for servers, routers, or other network devices so that you can establish addressing conventions that make it easier to identify shared devices by their IP addresses. For example, within a given scope, you might set aside host IDs from .1 to .20 for servers and .250 to .254 for routers and hubs, even if you don't need them all at this time.

FIG. 10.5

Establishing a DHCP scope containing an IP address pool, excluded ranges, and optional characteristics.

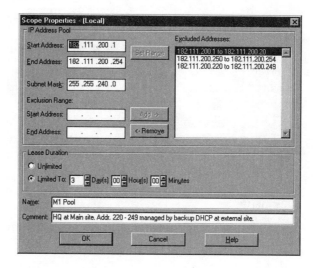

4. Enter a subnet mask. If you aren't subnetting, the *class* of your IP address determines the mask. For example, 255.255.255.0 would be used for class C addresses suitable for small networks with fewer than 255 hosts. The example configuration shown in Figures 10.4 through 10.10 uses the third octet to subnet class B addresses into 14 subnets.

5. Enter a name for the pool and optionally include a descriptive comment. Set the lease duration based on the volatility of your host population. For example, if you have a very stable network, set a long duration. If you have a small range of addresses that an ever-changing group of traveling laptop users must share, set a short duration.

6. Click OK. A dialog informs you that the scope has been defined but not activated. You can activate it now or wait and activate it later by highlighting the scope and choosing Activate from the Scope menu.

Figure 10.6 shows another scope, which would compliment the scope shown in Figure 10.5 on a network with two subnets. A DHCP server would be implemented on each subnet. Each DHCP server can back up the other with a range of addresses from the other scope.

Configuring Global Options   To set options that are provided to all clients from all scopes as they receive an IP address lease, follow these steps:

1. Start DHCP Manager, if necessary.

2. From the DHCP Options menu choose Global to open the DHCP Options: Global dialog.

3. In the DHCP Options: Global dialog, select an option from the Unused Options list. Click Add to move it to the Active Options list.

Part
II

Ch
10

FIG. 10.6

Another scope that compliments the scope in Figure 10.5 for a small network involving two subnets.

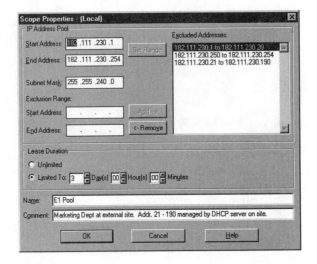

N O T E Options that are good candidates for global definition are DNS servers and WINS servers because they can be accessed across routers and therefore are available to multiple subnets. ▨

4. Select the option in the Active Options list, and click Value to expand the DCHP Options: Global dialog (see Figure 10.7).

5. Click Edit Array to open the IP Address Array Editor dialog (see Figure 10.8).

FIG. 10.7

Configuring options that apply to all scopes that the DHCP server manages.

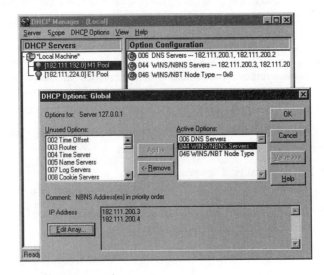

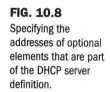

FIG. 10.8
Specifying the addresses of optional elements that are part of the DHCP server definition.

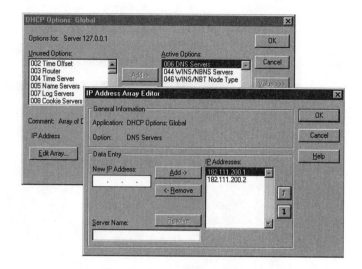

6. Enter the IP addresses of elements that correspond to the option you selected in step 4, which is shown in the General Information section. Click Add.

7. Repeat steps 3 through 6 for each option you want to apply globally to all scopes.

8. Use the arrow buttons in the IP Address Array dialog to arrange the entries from the top down in the order in which you would like them to be used (not all options are consulted in this order, depending on the nature of the option used). Click OK twice to return to the DHCP Manager window.

Configuring Scope Options   To set options that are provided to clients from a particular scope as they receive an IP address lease, follow these steps:

1. Start DHCP Manager, if necessary.

2. Highlight the scope for which you want to set options. From the DHCP Options menu choose Scope to open the DHCP Options: Scope dialog.

3. Select an option from the Unused Options list. Click Add to move it to the Active Options list.

N O T E   An option that's a good candidate for scope-specific definition is the address of the default gateway because many subnets have only one router used to connect to the rest of the network. ■

4. Select the option in the Active Options list, click Value, and then click Edit Array to open the IP Address Array Editor dialog.

5. Enter the addresses of elements that correspond to the option you selected in step 3, which is listed in the General Information section (see Figure 10.9). Click Add.

Part
II

Ch
10

FIG. 10.9

Configuring options that
apply to only one scope
in the IP Address Array
Editor dialog.

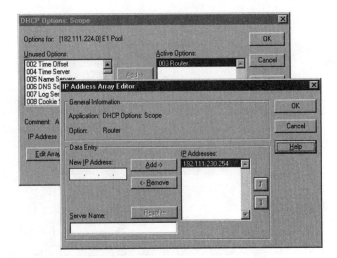

6. Use the arrow buttons to arrange the entries from the top down in the order in which
   you would like them to be used. Click OK to return to the DHCP Options: Scope dialog.

7. After you set any additional options that apply to this scope, click OK to return to the
   DHCP Manager window.

Configuring Client Reservations   Occasionally, a client computer must always have the same
IP address. This can occur based on the needs of a particular application. Also, if you're using a
client workstation as a peer server and sharing resources with many other clients, it may be
useful to reserve its address so that it doesn't change, much as server addresses are best not
to change. To reserve an IP address for a particular client, follow these steps:

1. Start DHCP Manager, if necessary.

2. View any current reservations by choosing Active Leases from the Scope menu.

3. To enter a new reservation, choose Add Reservations from the Scope menu to open the
   Add Reserved Clients dialog (see Figure 10.10).

4. The IP address is partially filled in, based on the scope you're using. You might want to
   change part of the address if you're subnetting. Enter the remainder of the host ID to
   complete the address.

5. In the Unique Identifier text box, enter the hardware address of the network adapter in
   the computer for which you're creating the reservation.

 To find the hardware address for a Windows NT computer, run Winmsd.exe and click the Network
button. You can also find it on most Windows clients (including Windows NT) by typing **net config
wksta** at a command prompt.

FIG. 10.10

Reserving a particular IP address for a specific computer so that its IP address never changes.

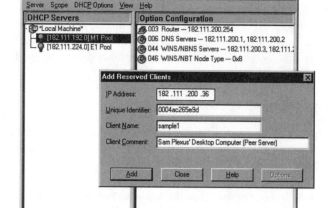

6. Enter a client name for this computer. Usually this name is the NetBIOS name for the computer, although you can enter anything here without affecting the operation of the lease or the computer in question.

7. Enter a comment, if you want, describing the client computer. Click OK to define the reservation.

Configuring DHCP Clients   You configure Windows clients to use DHCP as follows:

■ *Windows NT Workstation 4.0.* Launch Control Panel's Network tool, click the Protocols tab, double-click the TCP/IP Protocol item, and select the Obtain an IP Address from a DHCP Server option on the IP Address page of the Microsoft TCP/IP Properties sheet.

■ *Windows 95.* Launch Control Panel's Network tool, which opens with the Configuration page of the Network property sheet active. Double-click the TCP/IP–> *Network Adapter* item, and select the Obtain an IP Address Automatically option on the IP Address page of the TCP/IP Properties sheet.

N O T E   Windows 95 clients that use dial-up connections to an Internet service provider usually select the Obtain an IP Address Automatically option for the TCP/IP –> Dial-Up Networking item. ■

■ *Windows for Workgroups.* Run Network Setup and mark the Enable Automatic DHCP Configuration check box in the TCP/IP Configuration dialog.

All other settings can be received from the DHCP server if they're defined in the scope used by this client. Any entries made for other parameters (the default gateway, for example) take precedence over values received from the DHCP server.

Part
II

Ch
10

Testing DHCP Clients   In this section, you use the `Ipconfig` diagnostic command-line utility to report the status of your current network configuration. Use `Ipconfig` to view the IP address you've leased from a DHCP server and other information passed to your computer from the defined scope. To verify the operation of DHCP, view your current address, release it, and then renew a lease. This operation is only for testing or other diagnostic and troubleshooting use.

To test the operation of a DHCP client, follow these steps:

1. Start the client computer and log on to the network.

N O T E   If you can't even complete this task, you must reconfigure your client software. Make sure that you've loaded the correct version of TCP/IP, especially for older Windows for Workgroups clients. ▧

2. Open a command prompt. Type the following command:

   `ipconfig /all`

   This command displays a full listing of your IP address and all options that were defined globally, for your scope, or for your individual client workstation.

3. If you've defined options for DNS servers, WINS servers, a default gateway, and so on, try using the `ping` command with their addresses. This command "bounces" a test packet off the other machine and returns it to your computer to test basic network connectivity. For example, by using the address of a WINS server defined in the examples used for the figures, you would enter

   `ping 182.111.200.3`

   You should receive a series of replies with the time it took to make the trip to the remote host and back. Ping other devices configured for your scope or globally on your network.

4. Enter the following command to release your IP address:

   `ipconfig /release`

5. Re-enter the command

   `ipconfig /all`

6. You no longer have an IP address and can't communicate with other hosts on the network. Now enter the following:

   `ipconfig /renew`

   This command renews your lease, probably with the same address (unless another host happened to lease it while it wasn't being used). Check the information you received from the DHCP server by using the `/all` option with `ipconfig` again.

Viewing DHCP Client Leases and Reservations   To view the current status of the leases and reservations supplied by a DHCP server, follow these steps:

1. Start DHCP Manager.

2. Select a scope in the left pane of the window and choose Active Leases from the Scope menu to open the Active Leases dialog (see Figure 10.11).

FIG. 10.11

Displaying active leases and reservations for a defined scope.

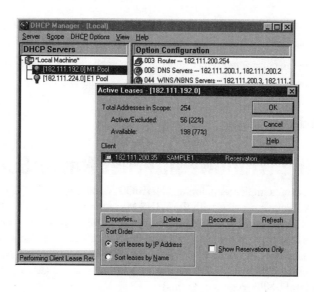

3. Use the Sort Order options to sort the listing by name or by IP address. By marking the check box, you can show only reservations (without leases). Also, you can select any of the listed leases or reservations and then click Properties for additional information.

4. You can also click the Reconcile button to validate the listing after the DHCP database is restored from a backup copy or after a system crash.

Maintaining the DHCP Database   The DHCP database, DHCP.mdb (like the WINS database, WINS.mdb) uses a modified version of the Jet (Access) database file structure. Jet databases increase in size when updated, because replaced or deleted records are *marked* for deletion, not physically deleted. At periodic intervals, you should compact the DHCP database by using a command-line utility provided for that purpose. Jetpack.exe reclaims wasted space in the database left by the update process. For large networks, this maintenance should be performed approximately once a week; for smaller networks, once a month is appropriate. You must stop the Microsoft DHCP Server service before you can perform this operation, so this operation is best done during off-peak times.

To use Jetpack.exe to compact the DHCP database, follow these steps:

1. Use Control Panel's Services tool or Windows NT Server Manager to stop the service. You can also use the following command:

```
net stop dhcpserver
```

2. Open a command prompt and change to the \systemroot\System32\DHCP directory. Make a backup copy of the database, just in case it's needed:

```
copy dhcp.mdb dhcp.bak
```

3. Use Jetpack to compact the DHCP database, creating a new temporary file that replaces the existing database:

```
jetpack dhcp.mdb temp.mdb
```

Part

II

Ch

10

4. Delete the existing database (remember, you have a backup copy):

   `del dhcp.mdb`

5. Rename the compacted temporary database as the in-use database:

   `ren temp.mdb dhcp.mdb`

6. Restart the service:

   `net start dhcpserver`

Implementing Windows Internet Name Service

WINS is Microsoft's implementation of a NetBIOS Name Server (NBNS). It's implemented as a Windows NT Server service, with the WINS Manager administrative utility program and appropriate client software. WINS registers the NetBIOS names used by client and server computers as they start. When a Microsoft networking command, such as NET USE, initiates a networking operation, WINS handles the subsequent need to resolve a NetBIOS name to complete the command. WINS can also resolve TCP/IP host names after the local HOSTS file is checked and the DNS server is consulted.

The Advantages of WINS

WINS dramatically reduces the amount of broadcast traffic on the network. Because name resolution with WINS is handled by direct communication between WINS servers and clients, broadcast name registration requests and name query requests are therefore minimized.

You also don't need to configure all clients to use WINS—you can operate a mixed environment. WINS resolves names from clients across routers and can therefore support multiple subnets.

If a WINS server isn't available, the design of the system still enables clients to use broadcasts so that they're not disabled when a WINS server is down. WINS servers can replicate the names in their databases to other WINS servers so that a single, dynamic names database is represented and managed across the enterprise network.

How WINS Registers and Resolves NetBIOS Names

To use WINS, you must configure a WINS server and start the service, whose formal name is listed in the Services dialog simply as Windows Internet Name Service. The next section covers the steps involved in configuring a WINS server.

After you set up one or more WINS servers and WINS-enabled clients, the process of registering and resolving names involves a number of distinct processes that are carried out in a natural order.

Before you configure a WINS server, it's helpful to understand the configuration of the client and how WINS name resolution happens. The steps involved in WINS name registration follow:

1. A WINS client is configured with the address of the primary and an optional secondary WINS server. The WINS server names can be specified on the client or received with an IP address as one of the optional DHCP parameters passed from a DHCP server. As the client starts, it sends its NetBIOS name directly to the WINS server in a name registration request.

2. If the WINS server is available and the name isn't already registered to another client, the registration is successful, and a message is returned to the client with a positive registration and the amount of time for which the name is registered, known as the *Time to Live (TTL)*.

3. If a duplicate name is found, the server sends a name challenge to the currently registered client. If the client responds and affirms that it's using the name, the new registration is denied by sending a message to the requesting client. If the currently registered client doesn't respond to three queries, the name is released and registered to the new client.

4. If the ARP client can't find the primary WINS server after three attempts, an attempt is made to find the secondary WINS server (if the client has been configured for a secondary WINS server). If the secondary WINS server also can't be found with three ARP requests, the client resorts to a standard b-node broadcast to register its name with the local subnet.

By default, a WINS client uses the h-node (hybrid) implementation of NetBIOS over TCP/IP. The process involved in WINS name resolution follows:

1. When actions in the Windows interface enter or implicitly specify a command, a name resolution is required. The NetBIOS name cache is checked first to see whether the NetBIOS name mapping to an IP address is available.

2. If the mapping isn't in the NetBIOS name cache, a name-resolution query is sent directly to the primary WINS server. If no response is returned, the request is sent three times.

3. If the primary WINS server doesn't respond, the secondary WINS server (if configured) is tried as many as three times. If either the primary or secondary WINS server receives the request, it looks up the name in its database and sends the IP address back to the client or replies with a `Requested name does not exist` message if it's not listed in the database.

4. If the name can't be resolved by a WINS server (because the server is unavailable or the name isn't in the database), a b-node name-resolution query is broadcast as many as three times.

5. If the name still isn't resolved, the LMHOSTS (if configured) and HOSTS files are searched.

6. If the name isn't in LMHOSTS or HOSTS, the DNS (if configured) is consulted.

Part II

Ch 10

WINS Configuration

A single WINS server can resolve names for an entire WAN because the requests are sent as directed datagrams and can be routed. A secondary WINS server provides redundancy and fault tolerance. Additional WINS servers can be provided based on the number of client requests received and performance considerations in large network environments. A rough rule of thumb is that a typical WINS server can handle as many as 1,200 name registrations and 700 name queries per minute. A pair of WINS servers should be able to handle as many as 8,000 WINS clients under typical network conditions. If you implement servers with two or more processors, a pair of WINS servers should handle more than 12,000 clients.

WINS servers don't need to be domain controllers as well. They should be configured with a static IP address, subnet mask, default gateway address, and other TCP/IP options. Using DHCP assigned options is possible but not recommended.

Entering Basic Configuration Information   To configure the basic operation of your WINS server, follow these steps:

1. From the Start menu, choose Programs, Administrative Tools (Common), and WINS Manager to open WINS Manager's window.

2. From the Server menu choose Configuration to open the WINS Server Configuration dialog (see Figure 10.12).

FIG. 10.12

The WINS Server Configuration dialog for controlling the behavior of the WINS server.

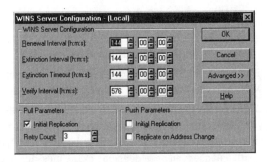

3. The WINS Server Configuration section contains settings for time periods that control the basic behavior of the server: the length of time a name is registered and how often a client must reregister its name. For most installations, the default values are appropriate. Click OK after making any adjustments.

4. From the Options menu choose Preferences to open the Preferences dialog (see Figure 10.13).

5. The settings you make in the Preferences dialog control the address display and refresh rate of the statistics display. Make any changes you want to configure the display to suit your needs. For example, you might want to select an Address Display option that shows both the NetBIOS name and the IP address. Click OK.

FIG. 10.13

The Preferences dialog for controlling the refresh rate of the Statistics display and setting the format of the address display.

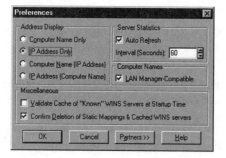

Entering Static Mappings for Non-WINS Clients   If you have non-WINS clients on your network, you should enter static mappings for these computers, especially if they're involved in resource sharing, which is possible with Windows for Workgroups, Windows 95, and Windows NT Workstation. If another computer attempts to use a shared resource on one of these devices, the WINS server can still provide name resolution, even though the original (non-WINS) computer didn't register its name. By entering a static mapping, the non-WINS client appears in the WINS database anyway. To enter a static mapping, follow these steps:

1. Start WINS Manager, if necessary.

2. From the Mappings menu choose Static Mappings. Click the Add Mappings button to display the Add Static Mappings dialog (see Figure 10.14).

FIG. 10.14

Using the Add Static Mappings dialog to map the NetBIOS name of a non-WINS client to an IP address for inclusion in the WINS database.

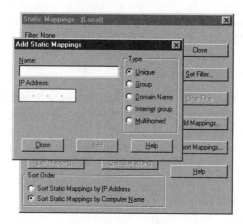

3. Enter the name and IP address you want to register. For normal client workstations, select the Unique option.

4. Click the Close button twice to close the two dialogs.

Configuring WINS Clients   You can configure WINS clients by simply entering the address of a primary WINS server, and optionally a secondary WINS server, into the client's configuration. You can do this manually by using Control Panel's Network tool (run Network Setup for Windows for Workgroups clients) or automatically by using DHCP. If you're using DHCP, you

Part
II
Ch
10

can manually configure individual clients, and those settings take precedence over the DHCP settings. If you use DHCP to configure WINS addresses, you must also configure clients with option 046 WINS/NBT Node type; otherwise, WINS won't work with DHCP. Set option 046 WINS/NBT Node type to 0x8 (h-node or hybrid).

Viewing WINS Name Mappings   To view the NetBIOS name/IP address mappings now registered on a WINS server, follow these steps:

1. Start WINS Manager, if necessary.

2. From the Mappings menu choose Show Database. The Show Database dialog appears (see Figure 10.15).

FIG. 10.15
The WINS database and its NetBIOS name to IP address mappings.

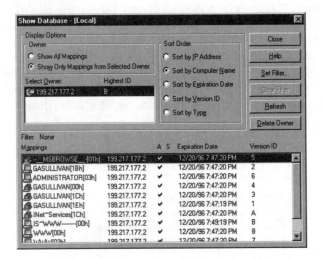

3. Select the option in the Sort Order section that corresponds to the order you prefer. In the Owner section, you can select an option to display all mappings or only those for the server selected in the Select Owner list if you've defined multiple WINS servers. You can also use the Set Filter button to enter name or IP address criteria, using the asterisk (*) as a wild card. A filter displays only matching entries and can be useful for finding a particular entry in a large list.

Configuring WINS Push/Pull Partners   WINS servers can replicate their mappings database to other WINS servers. When you configure a WINS server to replicate with another server, you can configure the server as a push partner with the other server, a pull partner, or both:

■ Designating a WINS server as a *push partner* causes the server to send messages to its partners when its WINS database has received a specified number of changes. When the partners respond, only the *changes* to the database are replicated to the other servers.

■ Configuring a server as a *pull partner* allows you to specify a time when its partner should make requests. This way is recommended to provide replication of a WINS database over slow links because you can schedule the transfer for off-peak time periods. For example, you can configure two servers on either side of a slow link each to pull from the other server at different times during the night. A server can be configured to act in both roles with one or more other WINS servers.

To configure a push or pull partner, follow these steps:

1. Start WINS Manager, if necessary.

2. From the Server menu choose Replication Partners to open the Replication Partners dialog (see Figure 10.16).

FIG. 10.16
Configuring push and pull replication partners to replicate NetBIOS name/IP address database entries.

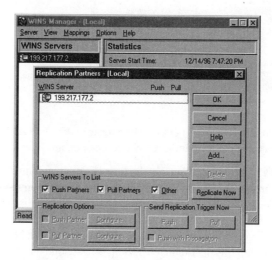

3. Click Add to open the Add WINS Server dialog and enter the name of the server to or from which you want to replicate. Click OK to close the dialog.

4. WINS Manager tries to locate the server on the network. If WINS Manager finds the server, it adds the server's name and IP address to the WINS Server list. If it can't find the server, it asks you to enter the IP address of the server in the Validate WINS Server dialog. Click OK.

5. Highlight the new server or another server in the list, and make a selection in the Replication Options dialog. This example configures both options, but you may want to choose only one. Mark the Push Partner check box and then click Configure to open the Push Partner Properties dialog.

6. Enter the number of changes that can be made to the local database before the changes are pushed to the replication partner. The smallest number you can enter is 20 (see Figure 10.17). Click OK to close the dialog.

FIG. 10.17

Configuring replication of changes between the local server and the selected push partner.

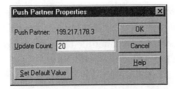

7. Mark the Pull Partner check box and then click Configure to open the Pull Partner Properties dialog.

8. Type a starting time in the Start Time text box by using the *HH*:*MM*:*SS* AM/PM format, and use the spin buttons to set a replication interval (see Figure 10.18).

FIG. 10.18

Configure the replication of changes between the local server and the pull partner.

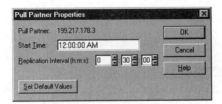

9. Click OK to close the dialog. Check marks appear in the Push and Pull columns of the Replication Partners dialog to indicate which relationships have been established.

Maintaining the WINS Database   You use the Jetpack command-line utility used to compact the DHCP database to compact the WINS database as well. It's recommended that you compact the database if it grows larger than 30M. This maintenance is required for the same reasons you must maintain the DHCP database. See the section "Maintaining the DHCP Database" earlier in this chapter for more information. You must stop the Microsoft WINS Server service before performing this operation, so backup is best done during off-peak times.

To use Jetpack to compact the WINS database, follow these steps:

1. Use Control Panel's Services tool or the Windows NT Server Manager to stop the WINS service. You can also use the following command:

```
net stop wins
```

2. Open a command prompt and change to the *\systemroot*\SYSTEM32\WINS directory. Make a backup copy of the database just in case it's needed, as follows:

```
copy wins.mdb wins.bak
```

3. Use Jetpack to compact the DHCP database, creating a new temporary file that replaces the existing database:

```
jetpack wins.mdb temp.mdb
```

4. Delete the existing database (remember, you have a backup copy):

```
del wins.mdb
```

5. Rename the compacted temporary database as the in-use database:

   `ren temp.mdb wins.mdb`

6. Restart the service with the following command:

   `net start wins`

Integrating WINS and DNS

Windows NT Server supports another method of name resolution, in addition to WINS, called the Domain Name System (DNS). DNS is widely used on computers running UNIX. It's also the primary name-resolution mechanism used by computers on the Internet. The DNS server implemented on Windows NT Server is guaranteed to interoperate with the BIND implementation of DNS on which many of the UNIX systems are based. Microsoft added WINS interoperability to the basic DNS server to ensure tight integration with the Windows NT Server environment. The WINS and DNS servers can now share name spaces.

▶ **See** "Understanding WINS and DNS Name Resolution," **p. 599**

The DNS server has been enhanced so that it can attempt to resolve a host name through a request to the WINS server. You can configure the DNS server with an unlimited number of WINS servers that should be tried for host name-resolution requests. When configured in this fashion, the DNS server attempts to resolve the host name from its database files. If it doesn't find an A record in its local records and the host name is fewer than 15 characters long, the DNS server tries to resolve the name from the WINS servers. Conversely, Microsoft has also extended the WINS naming service to use DNS. The WINS server in a DNS server environment appends the NetBIOS name to a configured domain name and passes the resolution request on to the DNS server.

▶ **See** "Using the Microsoft DNS Server," **p. 671**

DHCP presents a challenge with regard to name resolution. If a client computer on the network is now configured to use DHCP to obtain an IP address, it will have a dynamically assigned IP address. There's no provision in the DNS system to allow for dynamic updates of DNS configuration data. As a result, DNS can't be used to resolve dynamically assigned addresses. WINS provides this capability, but it's useful only in a single corporate LAN environment. Therefore, it's not possible for someone outside the current network to establish a connection to a machine that's getting its IP address dynamically. If you're setting up a machine that people on the Internet need to reach, you should assign that machine a static IP address.

From Here...

This chapter began with a tutorial overview of TCP/IP and related technologies. It described how to install, configure, and use TCP/IP as your primary network protocol. The chapter concluded with the details of setting up and configuring DHCP and WINS to dynamically assign IP addresses and manage NetBIOS names. For more information on these and related topics, see the following chapters:

Part
II

Ch
10

■ Chapter 11, "Configuring Windows 95 Clients for Networking," shows you how to set up PCs running Windows 95 to take maximum advantage of TCP/IP-based networks.

■ Chapter 12, "Connecting Other PC Clients to the Network," provides the details on setting up Windows 3.1+, Windows for Workgroups 3.1+, Windows NT Workstation 4.0, and Macintosh clients to communicate with Windows NT 4.0 servers via TCP/IP and other network protocols.

■ Chapter 18, "Integrating Windows NT with NetWare and UNIX," shows you how to set up and administer Windows NT Server's DNS Server.

■ Chapter 20, "Setting Up Internet Information Server 4.0," describes step by step the process of establishing an Internet or intranet server with Microsoft's IIS 4.0, which replaces version 2.0 that comes with Windows NT Server 4.0.

Configuring Windows 95 Clients for Networking

Network adapters and drivers

You can set up Windows 95 to provide network support, including installing network adapter drivers.

Network client software

Install and configure network client software, including the Client for NetWare Networks.

Multiple protocol support

Install and configure network transport protocols.

Shared client resources

Install and configure shared resources by using file and printer sharing for Microsoft Networks and NetWare Networks.

Client policies and the Registry

Restrict client reconfiguration by users with the Policy Editor and remotely edit Windows 95 Registries with the Registry Editor.

An ideal workstation operating system installs and configures the network client software and interface cards automatically, supports a wide variety of network transport protocols, provides a single unified logon to servers running different network operating systems, and accommodates virtually all existing hardware and software for Intel-based PCs. Microsoft Windows 95 meets all these criteria. Although Windows 95 is not yet perfect, it's the most versatile operating system now available for networked PC clients, especially laptop and notebook PCs, as well as desktop PCs equipped with legacy adapter cards that Windows NT Workstation 4.0 doesn't support. (Microsoft defines *legacy* devices as hardware components that don't support Windows 95's Plug and Play standards.) According to market research sources, Microsoft had sold more than 60 million licenses for Windows 95 by the end of 1996, but only about 4 million licenses for all versions of Windows NT Workstation.

With multisite, multiplatform internetworks becoming common, and user demands for Internet access increasing, network administrators increasingly find that they must deal with multiple network transport protocols. The Internet and most private intranets run over TCP/IP, your legacy NetWare servers understand only IPX/SPX, and the peer-to-peer network down the hall uses NetBEUI. Your NetWare servers run NetWare Core Protocol (NCP), and your Windows NT servers run Server Message Block (SMB). The folks in sales need PPP dial-up networking. Tying all these diverse systems and protocols together requires a client operating system that allows you to support all these protocols simultaneously and still have enough memory left to run applications. Windows 95 fulfills this requirement. ■

Understanding Windows 95 Networking Features

Many network managers eagerly anticipated the retail release of Windows 95 on August 24, 1995. Windows 95 promised to eliminate most of the client-side problems that have plagued LAN administrators for years. Its built-in support for many networks and its extensible architecture provided these important networking features:

■ *Multiple client support.* With earlier-generation client operating systems, installing software for more than one type of network operating system was problematic at best. The client software was provided by the network operating system (NOS) vendor, and conflicts often occurred when installing a second network protocol. Even if you could install and configure support for a second protocol successfully, the additional memory required often made it difficult to run applications on the client. Sane LAN managers didn't even think about trying to install support for a third protocol.

These problems disappeared when Microsoft released Windows 95, with its built-in support for multiple clients. Out of the box, Windows 95 provides native support for Novell NetWare, Artisoft LANtastic, Banyan VINES, DEC PATHWORKS, and SunSoft PC-NFS. Of course, it also fully supports Microsoft networking systems, including LAN Manager, Windows for Workgroups 3.11, Windows NT Workstation, and Windows NT Server.

■ *Multiple protocol support.* Windows 95 has built-in support for TCP/IP, IPX/SPX, and NetBEUI, which collectively are the transport protocols used on the vast majority of networks. Windows 95 handles the two major network core protocols, with full support for Microsoft SMB and nearly full support for Novell NCP. Windows 95 supports both Microsoft Network Driver Interface Specification (NDIS) and Novell Open Datalink Interface (ODI) for NICs (network interface cards, also called network adapters). Windows 95 supports a wide variety of standard communications protocols, such as named pipes and remote procedure calls (RPCs). In short, Windows 95 includes every network protocol you'll likely need. In the unlikely event that a building block you need is missing, the extensible, 32-bit architecture of Windows 95 means that a third-party product may be written to fill the void.

▶ **See** "Calling Remote Procedures," **p. 96**

■ *Simultaneous connection to multiple networks.* Whereas Windows 3.1 allows you to connect to only one network and Windows for Workgroups 3.11 to only two networks simultaneously, Windows 95 imposes no limitation on the number of types of simultaneous network protocols in use.

- *Single network logon.* If your network runs more than one NOS, Windows 95 lets you connect to all servers simultaneously at logon, provided that you establish identical user names and passwords on the various servers. Windows 95 automatically processes logon scripts on Windows NT and NetWare servers.

- *Automatic server reconnection.* When a downed server returns to service, Windows 95 reconnects to that server automatically, remapping drive letter assignments and printer connections as established before the failure.

- *Automatic client setup.* Windows 95 makes installing and configuring network clients easy. During setup, Windows 95 detects the network interface card in the workstation and automatically installs the appropriate 32-bit protected-mode drivers for the NIC. Windows 95 may be installed locally to the client's fixed disk or run as a shared copy on the network server. (Running shared copies of Windows 95, however, isn't a recommended practice.)

  Windows 95 provides full scripting support to allow automated installation and configuration. It automatically detects and configures Plug and Play and PC Card (formerly PCMCIA) devices. Setup and configuration are performed from Control Panel's Network tool, with setup information stored in the Registry, thus eliminating the need for manual maintenance of configuration files. System policies and user profiles may be established to automate installation and to control user access to resources.

- *Peer-to-peer networking.* When Microsoft shipped Windows for Workgroups 3.11 with built-in peer networking, many wondered whether third-party peer networks, such as LANtastic and PowerLAN, could survive. With Windows 95, Microsoft has made life much more difficult for third-party peer-to-peer NOS vendors. Any Windows 95 PC running either the Client for Microsoft Networks or the Client for NetWare Networks can share its disk and printer resources with other Windows 95 PCs on the network. Windows 95 provides user-level security on Windows NT Server and NetWare server-based networks by using the existing server's security system for user verification and authentication. Windows 95 also provides share-level security on Microsoft networks.

- *Dial-up networking.* Windows 95 comes equipped for remote access to networks. The dial-up networking client supports connection to TCP/IP and IPX/SPX networks via Point-to-Point Protocol (PPP), Serial Line Internet Protocol (SLIP), and NetWare Connect. For additional information on dial-up networking with Windows NT Server 4.0, see Chapter 19, "Managing Remote Access Service."

- *Long file-name support.* Windows 95 finally eliminates the antiquated DOS 8.3 file-naming convention. Windows 95 allows a file name to be as long as 255 characters, or 260 characters including the path.

- *Improved network performance.* Windows 95 uses 32-bit protected-mode client software, drivers and protocols implemented as VxDs, and virtual "anything" drivers, offering significantly better performance than that provided by older 16-bit real-mode drivers. Network performance is further enhanced by the use of VCACHE to cache network data, allowing frequently accessed network data to be read from a local cache rather than be transferred repeatedly across the network. In addition to offering faster data access, VCACHE also reduces network congestion by cutting traffic.

Part

II

Ch

11

■ *Minimal conventional (DOS) memory usage.* Windows 95 provides all the preceding networking features with a near-zero conventional memory footprint. Installing multiple 16-bit clients and protocol stacks under DOS and Windows 3.x consumed a substantial amount of the 640K of conventional memory available to DOS. Windows 95 eliminates this conventional memory problem by using Windows (extended) memory to run network client software, drivers, and protocols.

Installing Network Support

If Windows 95 is installed on a client PC that already has a network interface card installed and is connected to an active network, the Setup program recognizes the situation and makes the decisions necessary to automatically install and configure Windows 95 to provide network services. If you need to convert a stand-alone PC running Windows 95 to a network workstation, you can easily modify your existing Windows 95 configuration to provide network services. Adding network support to a Windows 95 client is done from Control Panel's Network tool and requires the following steps:

1. Install a network adapter in the workstation and configure Windows 95 to recognize it. If both the workstation BIOS and the network adapter are Plug and Play compliant, Windows 95 will recognize the newly installed adapter and configure itself and the adapter automatically. Otherwise, you may have to install and configure the appropriate drivers manually.

2. Install the client software for one or more network operating systems.

3. Fill out the information required in the Identification page of the Network property sheet, providing a unique name for the workstation, identifying the workgroup to which it belongs, and providing a description for the workstation.

4. Fill out the information required in the Access Control page of the Network property sheet, if the workstation shares file or print resources on the network.

When you've completed these steps, you've installed basic network support for Windows 95. The following sections describe each step in detail. This chapter later covers customizing the client software, installing and configuring protocols, and enabling other network services.

Installing Network Interface Cards

When you install Windows 95, you can choose to have Setup locate installed network adapter cards. Windows 95 includes a large database of information about hundreds of popular NICs and their default settings. If a NIC is installed in the client, chances are that Windows 95 can automatically locate the NIC and load the proper drivers for it during the installation process.

If automatic identification fails, if you need to change settings for an installed adapter, or if you need to install a new adapter, you can do so from Control Panel's Network tool. Unlike earlier Windows versions, which required that some network settings be changed by manually editing text files in various locations, Windows 95 centralizes all network installation and configuration functions within Control Panel's Network tool.

To install a NIC manually, proceed as follows:

1. Double-click Control Panel's Network tool. The Network property sheet appears with the Configuration page active (see Figure 11.1).

FIG. 11.1

The Configuration page of Control Panel's Network property sheet.

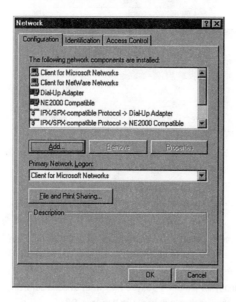

2. Click the Add button. The Select Network Component Type dialog appears, from which you can add a client, an adapter, a protocol, or a service (see Figure 11.2).

FIG. 11.2

Selecting the network adapter in the Select Network Component Type dialog.

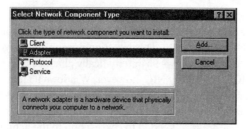

3. Select Adapter and click the Add button to display the Select Network Adapters dialog (see Figure 11.3). From the Manufacturers list on the left, select the manufacturer of the adapter you're installing. A list of supported network adapters from the selected manufacturer appears in the Network Adapters list on the right. Select the appropriate adapter and click OK to install the drivers for the selected adapter.

Part

II

Ch

11

FIG. 11.3

 Installing the drivers for a NIC in the Select Network Adapters dialog.

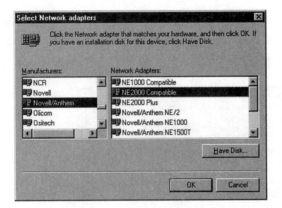

TIP If your network adapter doesn't appear in the list, you have two alternatives:

- Refer to your NIC's documentation to determine whether it can emulate a NIC that does appear on the list. If so, configure the adapter to emulate the supported adapter and try to install it.

- You can install drivers provided by the adapter manufacturer by using the Have Disk button in the Select Network Adapters dialog. Use this method as a last resort if the manufacturer provides only 16-bit real-mode drivers, which occupy conventional memory and are much slower than the 32-bit protected-mode drivers supplied with Windows 95. If the manufacturer supplies a driver specifically for Windows 95, you may want to consider using the manufacturer's driver instead of that supplied with Windows 95.

Changing NIC Settings

If Windows 95 appears to identify your NIC correctly but you still can't communicate with the network, the most likely cause is that the IRQ, DMA, or base address of the adapter doesn't match the settings used by Windows 95. This situation doesn't arise if you're using both a PnP BIOS and a PnP NIC, because Windows 95 automatically changes NIC settings as needed. If you're using an older BIOS or a legacy NIC, however, Windows 95 may install the NIC by using the manufacturer's default settings, which may or may not correspond with the NIC's current settings. You can correct this mismatch by altering the settings from within Windows 95 for IRQ, DMA, or base address as needed to correspond to the actual settings of the adapter.

To view and change settings for your network adapter, proceed as follows:

1. From Control Panel, double-click the System tool to open the System Properties sheet.

2. Click the Device Manager tab to display the Device Manager page.

3. Click the + icon next to the Network Adapters item to show installed network adapters. Highlight the adapter to be viewed or changed (see Figure 11.4).

FIG. 11.4

The Device Manager page of the System Properties sheet, showing a NE-2000 Compatible network adapter installed.

4. Click the Properties button to display the property sheet for that adapter (see Figure 11.5). The General page shows basic information about the adapter, including type, manufacturer, and version.

FIG. 11.5

The network adapter property sheet for an NE2000-compatible NIC.

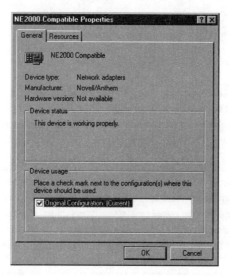

It also shows status information in the Device Status section. This section should always display the message `This device is working properly`. If another message appears here, your network adapter may be inoperable or misconfigured.

If you use multiple hardware configurations, the Device Usage section allows you to mark one or more boxes to indicate for which configuration(s) this device should be used.

5. Click the Resources tab to display information about the IRQ, base memory address, and other resources used by the network adapter (see Figure 11.6). If your network adapter was detected automatically when you installed Windows 95, the Use Automatic Settings check box is marked, and the settings for each resource type are disabled. You must clear this check box before making any changes to the resource settings.

FIG. 11.6

The network adapter resources page for an NE2000-compatible NIC.

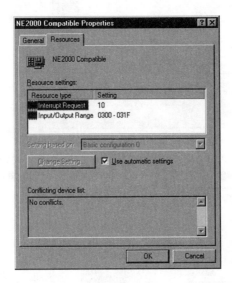

N O T E At the bottom of the adapter's property page is the Conflicting Device List. If there are no conflicts, you may safely leave the settings as they are. If the Conflicting Device List shows one or more devices whose settings conflict with those of your network adapter, you must change settings for either the network adapter or the conflicting device to eliminate the conflict. ▪

  Using the same settings for all network adapters makes it easier to maintain your network. Many network adapter manufacturers and many users have standardized on using IRQ 10 and Base Memory Address 300H for just this reason. On most computer systems, these values aren't already in use by other devices. For this reason, if a conflict arises between a network adapter set to these values and another device, it's usually better to change the settings for the other device and leave the network adapter as is.

Installing and Removing Network Clients

Windows 95 makes several default choices for a NIC, whether the NIC is automatically installed during Windows 95 installation or installed manually later. IPX/SPX (NWLink) and

NetBEUI transport protocols are both installed, allowing the client workstation to operate with Windows NT Server, Novell NetWare, and Microsoft peer-to-peer (workgroup) networks. The Client for Microsoft Networks is installed as the Primary Network Logon. The Client for NetWare Networks is installed as a secondary client. These default choices are designed for the most common network environments.

There are two common reasons to change these default selections:

■ You may need client software that isn't installed by default.

■ For performance reasons, you may want to remove support for an unused client.

The following sections describe how to add and remove network client drivers.

Installing a Network Client   In addition to the Client for Microsoft Networks and the Client for NetWare Networks, Windows 95 provides client drivers for Banyan VINES, FTP Software NFS Client (InterDrive 95), Novell 16-bit ODI NetWare, and SunSoft PC-NFS. Additional client driver packages and updates are also available from third parties. To install one of these additional network clients, follow these steps:

1. From the Network property sheet, click Add to open the Select Network Component Type dialog (see Figure 11.7).

FIG. 11.7
Selecting a network client in the Select Network Component Type dialog.

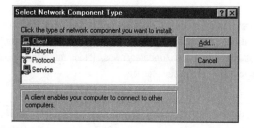

2. Select Client and click Add.

3. In the Select Network Client dialog, highlight the client you want to install and click OK (see Figure 11.8). Alternatively, you can install a third-party network client from disk by clicking Have Disk and following the prompts. In either event, you're returned to the main Network property sheet, where you continue setup and configuration.

The NetWare client software supplied with Windows 95 works well in a Novell NetWare 3.1x environment, but lacks support for NetWare Directory Services (NDS) used with NetWare 4.x servers. Until recently, if you needed NDS support, your only alternative was to run 16-bit real-mode Novell drivers under Windows 95, with additional memory consumption and performance penalties. Better alternatives are now available. Novell supplies a native 32-bit Windows 95 NetWare client that includes NDS support. Microsoft supplies Service for NetWare Directory Services, an update that's installed as a service.

FIG. 11.8

Selecting a network
client to add.

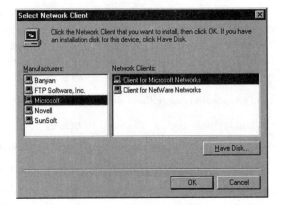

Novell released in mid-February 1996 the NetWare Client 32 for Windows 95. This full-featured client software, available in two versions, was updated in January 1997. The first version, a 10M file named 95enu_n2.exe, is intended for installations from a local or network hard drive. The second version, a 10M file named 95enu_d2.exe, can be used to create a disk installation set. Both files are dated January 17, 1997.

ON THE WEB

You can download either version of the NetWare Client 32 for Windows 95 from CompuServe (GO NWCL32). The two versions also are available on the Web at **http://www.novell.com/**, or via anonymous FTP at **ftp.novell.com** in the /pub/updates/nwos/ folder. You also can purchase the client software on disk for $99 from authorized Novell resellers.

T I P Some users of the Novell NetWare Client 32 for Windows 95 dated February 5, 1996, have reported stability and compatibility problems with this release. The 1997 versions of the NetWare Client 32 for Windows 95 corrects these problems.

ON THE WEB

The Microsoft Service for NetWare Directory Services is installed as a service that enhances the functionality of the original Client for NetWare Networks included with Windows 95. You can download the required files from the Web at **http://www.microsoft.com/windows/software/msnds.htm**.

N O T E   Microsoft's Service Pack 1 for Windows 95 includes an update to Shell32.dll that lets you browse NetWare Directory Service printers from the Add Printer wizard. This update is applicable only if you've installed Microsoft's Service for NetWare Directory Services.

Service Pack 1 also fixes a potential security problem when using Windows 95's file and printer sharing (described later in the "File and Printer Sharing for Microsoft Networks" section). A complete list of the fixes in Service Pack 1 is provided in the "Updating Shared Files with Service Packs" section near the end of this chapter. ■

ON THE WEB

You can download Service Pack 1 from **http://www.microsoft.com/windows/software/servpak1/ sphome.htm**.

Removing a Network Client   You should remove a network client that's not being used, because extra clients consume resources and slow performance. To remove an extra network client in the main Network property sheet, highlight the unused network client and click Remove. The unused network client driver is removed immediately.

Completing the Identification Page

The Identification page of the main Network property sheet contains information about the client and the workgroup to which the client belongs (see Figure 11.9).

FIG. 11.9

The Identification page of the Network property sheet, including the computer name and description, and the workgroup to which it belongs.

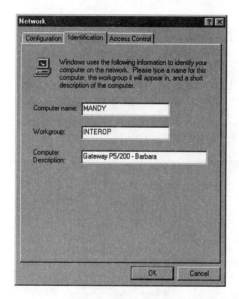

The Identification page consists of these elements:

- The *Computer Name* text box specifies the network name of the computer. It must be unique on the network and can include up to 15 alphanumeric characters. It can't include spaces, but can include the following characters:

    ! @ # $ % ^ & ( ) - _ ' { } . ~

    During installation, Windows 95 generates a default computer name by using the first eight characters of the user name.

- The *Workgroup* text box specifies the workgroup to which the computer belongs. Like the Computer Name, the Workgroup can include up to 15 alphanumeric characters, including the following characters but excluding spaces:

    : ! @ # $ % ^ & ( ) - _ ' { } . ~

Part
II

Ch
11

During installation over Windows 3.1+, Windows 95 by default uses the previously defined workgroup name. If no workgroup has been defined, Windows 95 generates a default workgroup name by using the first 15 characters of the organization name.

■ The *Computer Description* text box is a free-text description of the computer. The text box is used primarily to identify the client to other clients that use peer-based services. The text box may include up to 48 alphanumeric characters but can't include commas. During installation, Windows 95 by default inserts the licensing information user name in this text box.

Completing the Access Control Page

If a client shares its local file and print resources with other workstations on the network, the Access Control page of the Network property sheet is used to specify how permission to access these resources is determined (see Figure 11.10).

FIG. 11.10

The Access Control page of the Network property sheet, which lets you specify share-level or user-level access control.

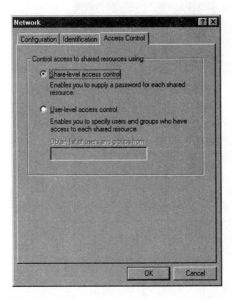

Share-Level Access Control   Share-level access control allows each shared resource on the workstation to be protected by a workgroup password. By using Explorer, you right-click a local folder name and choose Sharing to specify whether that folder is to be shared. If the folder is shared, you may specify the following access security options:

■ *Read-Only access* lets you enter the Read-Only Password for that resource. Another user with this password can view but not alter the contents of the shared folder.

■ *Full access* lets you enter the Full Access Password for that resource. Another user with this password can view and alter the contents of the shared folder.

■ *Depends on Password access* lets you enter a Read-Only Password and a Full Access Password for that resource. Another user with either password can view the contents of the shared folder. Only a user with the Full Access Password can alter the contents.

Access to shared local printers is specified in a similar manner. Share-level access control can be used with file and printer sharing for Microsoft Networks. This feature isn't available if you're using file and printer sharing for NetWare Networks.

User-Level Access Control   User-level access control allows a user seeking access to shared resources to be validated by using the account information stored for that user on a Windows NT domain or on a Novell NetWare server.

When you select User-Level Access Control, the Obtain List of Users and Groups From text box is enabled. If you're using file and printer sharing for Microsoft Networks, enter the name of a Windows NT domain or an individual Windows NT server here. If you're using file and printer sharing for NetWare Networks, enter the name of a NetWare 3.1x server, or the name of a NetWare 4.x server running in bindery emulation mode.

When users attempt to access a shared resource on the local system, Windows 95 first validates them with the specified server. If the users have no account on the specified server, they are refused access to the shared resource. If they have accounts on the server, Windows 95 determines their access rights to the local shared resource.

Granting access with user-level access control is done in similar fashion as the preceding method for share-level access control, but with a further refinement. Share-level access control limits access based solely on a user's possession of the password for that shared resource. User-level access control adds an access control list (ACL), which allows access to a shared resource to be specified by individual user name and groups. Full or read-only access to a particular shared resource can be granted, with the access method determined separately for each user and group. User-level access control also allows you to refine access levels by defining custom access for specific users or groups.

Unlike share-level access control, user-level access control can be used with both file and printer sharing for Microsoft Networks or file and printer sharing for NetWare Networks.

Configuring Network Clients

By default, Windows 95 installs both the Client for Microsoft Networks and the Client for NetWare Networks. For most networks, these clients operate properly when installed with the default settings. Common configuration items can be changed by using Control Panel's Network tool for the client in question. Changes that affect the low-level operation of the client aren't usually needed. When low-level changes are needed, you make the modifications by using the System Policy Editor or by altering values in the Windows 95 Registry.

Configuring the Client for Microsoft Networks

The Client for Microsoft Networks Properties sheet contains a single page with the following sections (see Figure 11.11):

- The *Logon Validation* section allows you to specify whether to log on to a Windows NT domain. To do so, select this check box and type the domain name in the Windows NT Domain text box.

- The buttons in the *Network Logon Options* section let you specify Quick Logon or Logon and Restore Network Connections. The Quick Logon option connects you to the network but doesn't attempt to verify the availability of network resources that you've mapped as logical drives until you try to access the mapped drive. The Logon and Restore Network Connections option verifies that each mapped resource is accessible before completing the logon process.

FIG. 11.11

Configuring the Client
for Microsoft Networks.

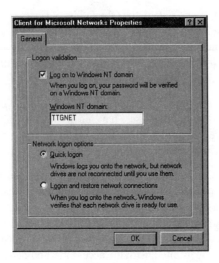

Configuring the Client for NetWare Networks

The Client for NetWare Networks uses the NWLink IPX/SPX compatible transport protocol exclusively, and normally requires little configuration. Compared with using native Novell client software, the biggest change that most users will notice is that the Client for NetWare Networks doesn't support the Novell NWPOPUP utility. Microsoft supplies WINPOPUP as a substitute. Like NWPOPUP, WINPOPUP allows users to send messages to and receive them from each other. Unlike NWPOPUP, WINPOPUP doesn't respond to NetWare system messages, such as new mail notifications, by popping up a message box over the running application.

The General page of the Client for NetWare Networks Properties sheet lets you set logon parameters for the NetWare server (see Figure 11.12).

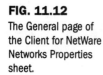

FIG. 11.12

The General page of the Client for NetWare Networks Properties sheet.

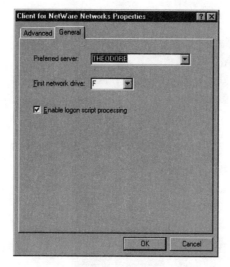

Specify the following items on the General page:

- The *Preferred Server* drop-down list lets you specify which NetWare server the Windows 95 workstation connects to when Windows 95 starts. You also can leave this box empty, in which case Windows 95 at startup connects to the "nearest" NetWare server—that is, the server that responds fastest. If the client PC is running NetWare client software when Windows 95 is installed, Preferred Server defaults to the setting in the Novell NET.CFG file.

- *First Network Drive* lets you specify the lowest drive letter assigned to a network drive. Early versions of DOS reserved drives A through E as local drives, and drive F was assigned as the first network drive. Larger hard drives partitioned into multiple volumes have become common, consuming more local drive letters. CD-ROM drives and other drives that use removable media have also proliferated, consuming still more drive letters.

 To ensure that workstations with various hardware configurations can use consistent network drive letter assignments, you should leave room for additional local drives by setting this parameter to a higher drive letter than F. Many organizations use H as the first network drive letter, assigning it to the user's Home folder as a mnemonic. Using H as the first network drive provides room for three or four local fixed-disk drive volumes, a CD-ROM drive, and a removable disk drive.

- The *Enable Logon Script Processing* check box, if selected, causes Windows 95 to run the NetWare logon script for the user logging on.

The Advanced page of the Client for NetWare Networks Properties sheet lets you select from the Value drop-down list for each Property displayed (see Figure 11.13).

Part

II

Ch

11

FIG. 11.13
The Advanced page of
the Client for NetWare
Networks Properties
sheet.

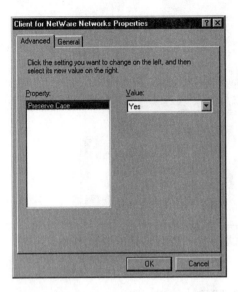

Setting the Primary Network Logon

The Primary Network Logon determines which client software handles startup functions, such as user authentication and running logon scripts. By default, Windows 95 sets the Client for Microsoft Networks as the Primary Network Logon. You can set one of the other installed network clients as your Primary Network Logon if you prefer your startup functions to be performed by that client. You also can select Windows Logon as your Primary Network Logon, if you prefer not to connect automatically to the network each time you start Windows 95.

To specify your preferred Primary Network Logon, select the client in the Primary Network Logon drop-down list of the Network property sheet (see Figure 11.14) and click OK. The Network property sheet closes and the System Settings Change message box appears, informing you that changes don't take effect until the next time you start Windows. Click Yes to restart Windows immediately and put your changes into effect.

Configuring Network Protocols

One of Microsoft's objectives for Windows 95 was to minimize the need for user intervention to configure network protocols. In most cases, Windows 95's default configuration for the protocols you choose are satisfactory. If not, the following sections describe how to configure Windows 95's network protocols manually.

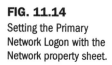

FIG. 11.14
Setting the Primary
Network Logon with the
Network property sheet.

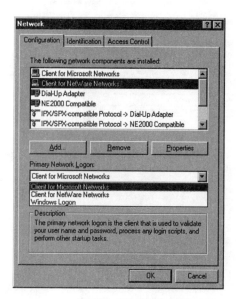

Configuring NetBEUI

NetBIOS Extended User Interface (NetBEUI) is a fast and simple transport protocol used by
Windows for Workgroups 3.1+ and other DOS and Windows peer-to-peer LANs. NetBEUI
packets don't contain network header information, so NetBEUI isn't routable; thus, it's inappropriate for large networks. If Windows 95 detects the presence of NetBEUI on the network
during installation, the Setup program automatically installs NetBEUI support. You normally
don't need to make changes to the NetBEUI configuration.

To display the NetBEUI Properties sheet for the network, select in Control Panel's Network
tool's Configuration page the NetBEUI entry that's bound to your NIC and click the Properties
button. (Alternatively, double-click the NetBEUI entry.) The NetBEUI Properties sheet displays the Bindings page (see Figure 11.15). If you don't plan to share your files or a printer
attached to your computer with other members of your workgroup by using NetBEUI, click the
File and Printer Sharing for Microsoft Networks entry to clear the check box.

The Advanced page of the NetBEUI Properties sheet (see Figure 11.16) lets you specify values
for Maximum Sessions and NCBS for the real-mode NetBEUI driver. These tuning parameters
affect only the real-mode driver, which Windows 95 normally doesn't use. The protected-mode
NetBEUI driver is configured dynamically.

Part
II

Ch
11

FIG. 11.15

The Bindings page of the NetBEUI Properties sheet.

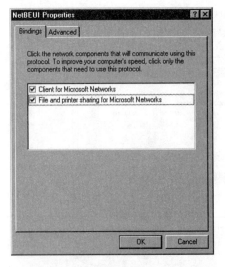

FIG. 11.16

The Advanced page of the NetBEUI Properties sheet.

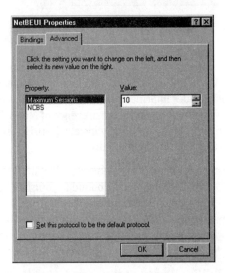

The Set this Protocol to Be the Default Protocol check box, if marked, sets NetBEUI as the default protocol. This option should always be unmarked if your network includes Windows NT Server or NetWare servers. It should be marked only if you're running a peer-to-peer network, and only then if that network includes workstations that aren't running Windows 95.

Configuring NWLink

NWLink is Microsoft's implementation of the IPX/SPX transport protocol originally developed by Novell for NetWare. The default transport protocol used by Windows NT Server, NWLink is fully interoperable with IPX/SPX running on NetWare servers and clients. Windows 95 installs the NWLink protocol automatically when the Client for NetWare Networks is installed, because the Client uses the NWLink protocol exclusively. NWLink can also be used to support other client software, including the Client for Microsoft Networks.

Most client PCs require few or no changes to the default settings for NWLink. If the client is running Novell client software when Windows 95 is installed over an existing Windows 3.x installation, the setup program configures Windows 95 NWLink settings to correspond to the settings specified in the Novell NET.CFG configuration file.

The Bindings page of the IPX/SPX-Compatible Protocol Properties sheet of Control Panel's Network tool lets you specify which clients and services use NWLink transport (see Figure 11.17). For better performance, clear the check boxes for network components that don't need to use NWLink.

FIG. 11.17
The Bindings page of the IPX/SPX-Compatible Protocol Properties sheet.

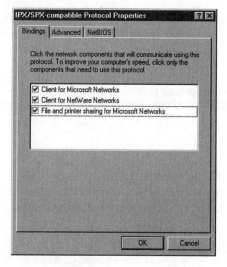

The Advanced page of the IPX/SPX-Compatible Protocol Properties sheet lets you specify parameters that affect the low-level functioning of the NWLink protocol (see Figure 11.18). With one exception (Frame Type), these values are set dynamically and shouldn't be changed.

N O T E If an otherwise functional Windows 95 network workstation can't see a NetWare server on an Ethernet network, the problem is almost certainly a frame type mismatch. NetWare can use any of four Ethernet frame types: Ethernet_802.2, Ethernet_802.3, Ethernet_II, and Ethernet_SNAP. The frame types used by the server and the workstation must be identical for communication to take place. ▪

FIG. 11.18

The Advanced page of the IPX/SPX-Compatible Protocol Properties sheet.

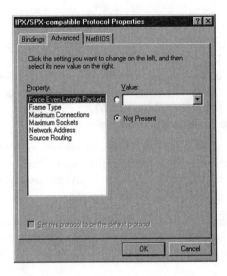

The Windows 95 IPX/SPX protocol defaults to frame type Auto, which usually succeeds in detecting the frame type used by the NetWare server. If auto detection fails, you must explicitly set the frame type in the Advanced page of the IPX/SPX-Compatible Protocol Properties sheet. You can set the frame type to Auto, Ethernet 802.2, Ethernet 802.3, Ethernet II, Token Ring, or Token Ring SNAP.

NetWare 3.11 and earlier servers default to the Ethernet_802.3 frame when using Ethernet. The corresponding Windows 95 frame type is Ethernet 802.3. NetWare 3.12 and higher servers default to Ethernet_802.2 frames, for which the corresponding Windows 95 frame type is Ethernet 802.2.

Choosing the Correct Ethernet Frame Type

For an Ethernet network, Novell recommends using the Ethernet_802.2 frame type, and Microsoft recommends that Windows 95 be set to frame type Auto. Both recommendations are *wrong*.

Ethernet 802.2, the most recent standards-based Ethernet frame, uses the OSI 802.2 LLC specification. Ethernet II is an older specification, which was originally developed by DEC, Intel, and Xerox. Newer isn't always better, however. The majority of Ethernet traffic worldwide still uses Ethernet II frames. All active components understand how to handle Ethernet II frames. On the Internet, Ethernet II always works. The same can't be said for Ethernet 802.2.

If your workstations need Internet access, if your network includes a UNIX host, or if you plan to use SNMP management on your NetWare servers, run Ethernet II. Even if you have no current need for these services, using Ethernet II now makes the transition to these services easier. There are no performance penalties or other drawbacks to using Ethernet II instead of Ethernet 802.2. Set your Windows 95 frame type to Ethernet II and add Ethernet_II frame support to each of your NetWare servers.

The NetBIOS page of the IPX/SPX-Compatible Protocol Properties sheet lets you enable the use of NetBIOS over IPX/SPX (see Figure 11.19). Windows 95 workstations can communicate with each other, and with Windows NT Server and NetWare servers directly, by using only the NWLink protocol. However, some network applications, such as IBM/Lotus Notes, require NetBIOS to communicate. Disable NetBIOS over IPX/SPX support unless you have applications that specifically require NetBIOS.

FIG. 11.19

The NetBIOS page of the IPX/SPX-Compatible Protocol Properties sheet.

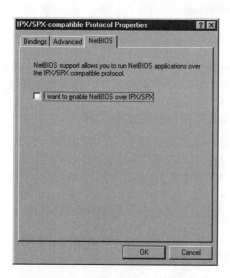

Part

II

Ch

11

Configuring TCP/IP

Windows 95 doesn't install support for the TCP/IP transport protocol by default. If your network includes UNIX hosts or your clients need access to the Internet, you must install TCP/IP support as described earlier in the "Installing a Network Client" section. The basics of TCP/IP networking are covered in Chapter 10, "Using TCP/IP, WINS, and DHCP." After TCP/IP is installed on the Windows 95 client, you must configure the protocol. TCP/IP is designed for use in internetworks and requires that the administrator have both a deeper understanding of the protocol and the willingness to configure and manage the protocol.

The following sections describe how to configure the TCP/IP protocol by using the six pages of the TCP/IP Properties sheet.

Allocating an Internet Protocol Address   The IP Address page of the TCP/IP Properties sheet lets you specify how your workstation is allocated an Internet Protocol (IP) address (see Figure 10.20).

Following are the parameters that you can specify in the IP Address page:

- *Obtain an IP Address Automatically.* If your network includes a Windows NT Server running the Dynamic Host Configuration Protocol (DHCP) service, select this option.

The DHCP server allocates an IP address to the workstation automatically at startup. For more information about DHCP, see Chapter 10, "Using TCP/IP, WINS, and DHCP."

■ *Specify an IP Address.* If your network doesn't include a DHCP server or you simply want to specify the IP address for this workstation manually, select this option. Enter the appropriate IP Address and Subnet Mask in the text boxes provided. Chapter 10, Chapter 18, "Integrating Windows NT with NetWare and UNIX," and Chapter 20, "Setting Up Internet Information Server 4.0," discuss assignment of IP addresses.

CAUTION

Use extreme care when you enter the IP Address and Subnet Mask values. If either value is entered incorrectly, problems ranging from subtle address conflicts to a network crash will result.

FIG. 11.20

The IP Address page of the TCP/IP Properties sheet.

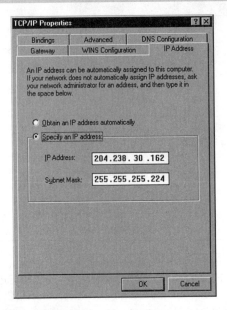

Using the Windows Internet Name Service   The WINS Configuration page of the TCP/IP Properties sheet (see Figure 11.21) lets you specify whether this client uses the Windows Internet Name Service (WINS) and, if so, which server or servers provide WINS.

▶ **See** "Implementing Windows Internet Name Service," **p. 342**

You can set the following parameters on the WINS Configuration page:

■ *Disable WINS Resolution.* Select this option if you don't have a WINS server running on your network or don't want the client to use WINS.

FIG. 11.21

The WINS Configuration page of the TCP/IP Properties sheet.

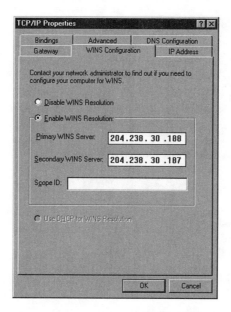

TCP/IP Properties

| Bindings | Advanced | DNS Configuration |
| Gateway | WINS Configuration | IP Address |

Contact your network administrator to find out if you need to configure your computer for WINS.

○ Disable WINS Resolution

◉ Enable WINS Resolution:

Primary WINS Server: `204.238. 30 .188`

Secondary WINS Server: `204.238. 30 .187`

Scope ID:

○ Use DHCP for WINS Resolution

OK   Cancel

Part
II
Ch
11

■ *Enable WINS Resolution.* Select this option if you have a WINS server running on your network and want this client to use the service. If you choose this option, enter the appropriate IP addresses for the primary WINS server and, if applicable, for the secondary WINS server. Enter also the scope ID, if you're using NetBIOS Scope (also called TCP/IP Scope) to identify the client.

N O T E Using NetBIOS Scope is uncommon; don't confuse NetBIOS scope with DHCP scope, which defines the range of TCP/IP addresses available for lease by clients. ■

■ *Use DHCP for WINS Resolution.* Select this item if you have a DHCP server running on your network and have enabled DHCP on this client.

Specifying a TCP/IP Gateway   The Gateway page of the TCP/IP Properties sheet lets you add and remove gateways used by the Windows 95 client (see Figure 11.22). The term *gateway* can be used in two ways: In the OSI Reference Model, *gateway* refers to a device that translates upper-level protocols. In the Internet community, *gateway* refers to a router. Microsoft uses *gateway* to refer only to a router.

▶ **See** "Routers," **p. 148**

Enter the IP address of the gateway and click the Add button to add a gateway to the Installed Gateways list. The first gateway appearing in the Installed Gateways list is the default, which is used when available. If the default gateway is unavailable, Windows 95 attempts to access other installed gateways in the order in which they appear in the Installed Gateways list.

FIG. 11.22

The Gateway page of the TCP/IP Properties sheet.

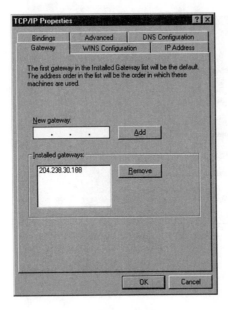

N O T E To remove an installed gateway, highlight the entry and click the Remove button. ▪

Binding the TCP/IP Protocol to Clients and Services The Bindings page of the TCP/IP Properties sheet lets you specify which clients and services use the TCP/IP transport protocol (see Figure 11.23). For better performance, clear the check box next to clients and services that don't need to use TCP/IP transport.

The Client for Microsoft Networks normally should be bound to TCP/IP. File and printer sharing for Microsoft Networks should be bound to TCP/IP only if you plan to use these services across a TCP/IP-based internetwork.

Setting Low-Level TCP/IP Parameters The Advanced page of the TCP/IP Properties sheet lets you alter low-level TCP/IP configuration parameters and specify TCP/IP as your default protocol (see Figure 11.24). Selecting the Set This Protocol to Be the Default Protocol check box causes Windows 95 to use TCP/IP transport as the default. Most installations that support TCP/IP use TCP/IP as the default protocol.

Using the Domain Name Service to Resolve IP Addresses The DNS Configuration page of the TCP/IP Properties sheet (see Figure 11.25) lets you enable or disable the use of Domain Name Service (DNS) to resolve IP addresses and, if DNS is enabled, to provide DNS configuration information to the client. DNS translates character-based addresses, such as server names, to numeric IP addresses.

▶ **See** "Using the Microsoft DNS Server" **p. 671**

FIG. 11.23

The Bindings page of the TCP/IP Properties sheet.

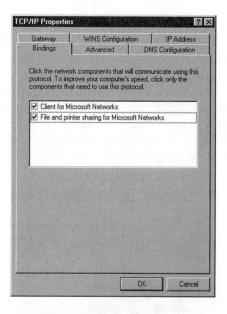

FIG. 11.24

The Advanced page of the TCP/IP Properties sheet.

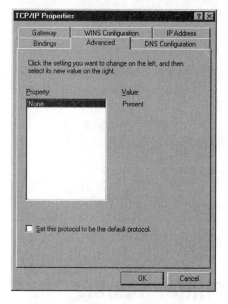

The DNS Configuration page offers the following settings:

- *Disable DNS*, if selected, causes the client not to use DNS to resolve IP addresses.
- *Enable DNS*, if selected, causes the client to use DNS to resolve IP addresses.

- *Host* is the name of the client computer system—for example, kiwi.

- *Domain* is the Internet domain—not to be confused with the Windows NT domain, of which the client is a member. In Figure 11.25, the client is a member of the ttgnet.com Internet domain.

- *The DNS Server Search Order* section lets you add and remove the IP addresses for one or more servers that provide DNS services. The IP address that appears first in this list is the primary DNS and is used whenever the device at the address is available. The IP address that appears second in the list is the secondary DNS and is used only if the primary DNS device is unavailable.

- *The Domain Suffix Search Order* section lets you add and remove Internet domains to be searched. This feature allows partially qualified names to be resolved. For example, if your primary Internet domain is widget.com but you frequently access a host named NTS that belongs to the domain gadget.com, specifying gadget.com as a secondary search domain allows that host to be resolved when specified simply as NTS rather than as NTS.gadget.com.

FIG. 11.25

The DNS Configuration page of the TCP/IP Properties sheet.

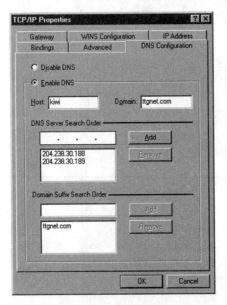

Installing File and Printer Sharing

Windows 95 offers two ways to share your local files and printers with other clients on the network. If the client runs the Client for Microsoft Networks, you can install the Server Message Block (SMB) file and printer sharing for Microsoft Networks. If the client runs the Client for NetWare Networks, you can install the NetWare Core Protocol (NCP) based file and printer sharing for NetWare Networks. Only one of these services can be installed on a client. The following sections describe how to set up file and printer sharing on both types of networks.

File and Printer Sharing for Microsoft Networks

File and printer sharing for Microsoft Networks lets you share the local disk and printer resources of a client with any other computer on the network that supports SMB services, including systems running Windows NT Server and Workstation, Windows for Workgroups 3.11, LAN Manager, and DEC PATHWORKS. Using file and printer sharing for Microsoft Networks requires that the client run the Client for Microsoft Networks service. If you're using user-level security, a Windows NT Server domain controller must be used to provide authentication.

▶ **See** "Understanding Domain Architecture and Security," **p. 606**

To install file and printer sharing for Microsoft Networks, follow these steps:

1. From Control Panel, double-click the Network tool.
2. In the Configuration page of the Network property sheet, click the Add button.
3. In the Select Network Component Type dialog, double-click Service.
4. In the Select Network Service dialog, select Microsoft in the left list. Then select File and Printer Sharing for Microsoft Networks on the right, as shown in Figure 11.26. Click OK to close the open dialogs.

Part
II

Ch
11

FIG. 11.26

Installing file and printer sharing for Microsoft Networks.

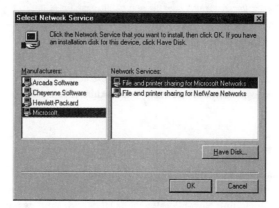

After you install file and printer sharing for Microsoft Networks, you must enable file sharing, printer sharing, or both. To enable one or both of these services, follow these steps:

1. From Control Panel, double-click the Network tool to open the Network property sheet.
2. Click the File and Print Sharing button to open the File and Print Sharing dialog (see Figure 11.27).

3. Select either or both of the check boxes of the File and Print Sharing dialog to enable file sharing, printer sharing, or both.

FIG. 11.27

Enabling file and print sharing services.

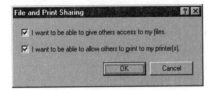

N O T E The preceding process only *enables* the client to provide file and print sharing services. You must determine which files and printers you want to share, if any, and explicitly specify sharable resources as described earlier in the "Share-Level Access Control" section. Shared resources are visible to any Microsoft Networking client that browses the network. ■

CAUTION

In October 1995, Microsoft announced that a potentially serious security problem existed for users running file and printer sharing for Microsoft Networks and NetWare Networks. A fix for this and other problems is included in Windows 95 Service Pack 1, mentioned earlier in the chapter. Before you install and enable file and printer sharing for Microsoft Networks or for NetWare Networks, make sure that you first install Windows 95 Service Pack 1 on the client. A complete list of the fixes in Service Pack 1 is included in the "Updating Shared Files with Service Packs" section near the end of this chapter.

ON THE WEB

Service Pack 1 is now available as a 1.2M file named Setup.exe from Microsoft's Web site at **http://www.microsoft.com/windows/software/servpak1/enduser.htm** or from the Microsoft Download Service BBS.

File and Printer Sharing for NetWare Networks

File and printer sharing for NetWare Networks lets you share the local disk and printer resources of a client with other computers on networks that support Novell NetWare Core Protocol (NCP) services, including Novell NetWare for DOS and Windows-based clients, other clients running Windows 95 that use the Client for NetWare Networks, and systems running Windows NT. Using file and printer sharing for NetWare Networks requires that the client run the Client for NetWare Networks instead of the Novell-supplied client software. Share-level security isn't available with the Microsoft implementation of this service. If you're enabling user-level security, a NetWare server must be used to provide authentication.

To install file and printer sharing for NetWare Networks, follow these steps:

1. From Control Panel, double-click the Network tool to open the Network property sheet.
2. On the Configuration page of the Network property sheet, click the Add button.

3. In the Select Network Component Type dialog, double-click Service.

4. In the Select Network Service dialog, select Microsoft in the left list. Then select File and Printer Sharing for NetWare Networks in the right list and click OK to close the dialogs.

As is the case for file and printer sharing for Microsoft Networks, after you install file and printer sharing for NetWare Networks, you must enable file sharing, printer sharing, or both. To enable one or both of these services, follow these steps:

1. From Control Panel, double-click the Network tool to open the Network property sheet.

2. Click the File and Print Sharing button to open the File and Print Sharing dialog.

3. Select either or both of the check boxes to enable file sharing, print sharing, or both.

A client that's sharing resources by using file and printer sharing for NetWare advertises its availability as a peer-to-peer server and the availability of the shared resources by using either Workgroup Advertising or Novell Service Advertising Protocol (SAP). The visibility of shared resources to other clients browsing the network depends both on what client software the remote computer uses and which of the two advertising methods the peer server uses, in accordance with the following rules:

- Another client running the Client for NetWare Networks sees shared resources provided by a peer server exactly as any other shared resources on the network. If the peer server is using Workgroup Advertising, it appears in a workgroup. A peer server running SAP isn't presented as a member of a workgroup, but instead appears only when you view the entire network.

- Another client running the Novell NETx shell or VLM redirectors sees shared resources on a peer server only if the peer server is running SAP advertising. Shared directories appear as volumes on the server, and shared printers appear as Novell print queues. If the peer server runs Workgroup Advertising, its shared resources aren't visible to clients running Novell-provided clients.

> **CAUTION**
>
> A potentially serious security problem exists for users running file and printer sharing for NetWare Networks. Refer to the caution in the earlier "File and Printer Sharing for Microsoft Networks" section for details.

Managing Windows 95 on the Network

Windows 95's network installation and administration features are a significant improvement over Windows 3.x. Like Windows 3.x, Windows 95 can be installed to a local client fixed-disk drive from distribution files stored on a network drive, or can be installed as a shared copy to run from the network server. (Using a shared copy of Windows 95 isn't a recommended practice due to the amount of network traffic-sharing Windows 95 generates.) Unlike Windows 3.x, Windows 95 provides a wealth of features intended to ease management of client configurations and of the network itself.

Part
II

Ch
11

Installing Windows 95 from the Network

You can install Windows 95 to the network server by using Server-Based Setup. This process copies the Windows 95 distribution files to the network server and allows Windows 95 clients to be installed directly from the server. After the files are installed to the server, Machine Directory Setup allows you to create *machine directories*, which contain files specific to the hardware configurations of particular workstations.

Installing Windows 95 to the Server with Server-Based Setup   In Windows 95, the Server-Based Setup program, Netsetup.exe, prepares the server for installing Windows 95 clients from the network. Netsetup.exe replaces the Administrative Setup procedure (SETUP /A) used in Windows for Workgroups 3.1+. The Server-Based Setup program creates and maintains shared machine directories on the server and creates setup scripts to automate the client installation process. After Netsetup.exe installs and configures the Windows 95 distribution files on the server, clients can run Windows 95 Setup.exe from the server to complete the local installation.

Before beginning this procedure, make sure that you have at least 80M of free disk space on the server volume to which the Windows 95 distribution files are to be installed. ■

NOTE   To install a setup copy of Windows 95 on Windows NT Server 4.0 from a Windows 95 client, follow these steps:

1. From the Start menu, click Run and browse the Windows 95 CD-ROM for the program \win95\admin\NETTOOLS\NETSETUP\Netsetup.exe. Double-click Netsetup.exe and then click OK to run the program. The Server Based Setup window appears (see Figure 11.28).
2. In the Set Server Install Path section, click the Set Path button. Type the path name for the server folder in which to install the Windows 95 setup files. If the specified folder doesn't exist, you're asked whether you want to create the folder.
3. After entering the installation path, the Install button is enabled. Click Install to open the Source Path dialog (see Figure 11.29).
4. Decide where you want shared files to be installed and indicate your choice in the Install Policy section by selecting Server, Local Hard Drive, or User's Choice:
   - If you choose Server, shared files are always run from the server, saving disk space on clients at the expense of creating substantial additional network traffic.
   - Choosing Local Hard Drive means that the shared files are installed to each client's local hard disk, occupying additional drive space but reducing network traffic.
   - Choosing User's Choice lets you decide each time Windows is installed from the network whether to run the shared files from the server or from the local hard disk.

Unless you have a very compelling reason to allow users to run Windows 95 shared files from the server, choose Local Hard Drive.

FIG. 11.28

Setting the server install path, performing machine directory setup, and making setup scripts in the Server Based Setup window.

FIG. 11.29

Selecting the type of network installation and specifying the installation path in the Source Path dialog.

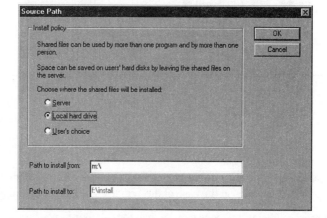

Part

II

Ch

11

5. Verify that the Path to Install From entry is correct, changing it if necessary. The Path to Install To is displayed in a text box but can't be changed at this point. (If you must change the installation path, click Cancel to return to the previous dialog and then click Set Path to respecify the path.) After verifying that all the information is correct, click OK.

6. The Create Default dialog lets you choose to accept a default setting of options that the Server-Based Setup program uses to create batch setup scripts to automate the installation process (see Figure 11.30). Unless you have a specific reason for doing otherwise, click the Create Default button.

FIG. 11.30

Specifying the default settings for Server-Based Setup in the Create Default dialog.

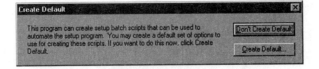

7. If you choose to create defaults, the Server Based Setup Default Properties sheet appears (see Figure 11.31). This sheet displays a hierarchical listing of all policy items that you can edit for use as defaults during automated installation. After you finish editing these items, click OK to close the property sheet.

FIG. 11.31

Editing default setup values in the Server Based Setup Default Properties sheet.

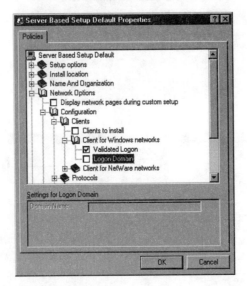

8. A dialog appears with a prompt to enter your product identification number. Enter the number that appears on the case of the Windows 95 CD-ROM and click OK.

The copy process begins and copies more than 80M of files to your server drive, so make sure that you have adequate disk space available before beginning the installation. After all files are copied to the installation directory, the setup program marks the files as read-only. The program then tells you that installation is complete.

Performing a Machine Directory Setup   After the files are installed to the network server, you're returned to the Server Based Setup window. The next step is to create any needed machine directories. Although only a small subset of the Windows 95 files are specific to a particular client, these files are too large to fit on a floppy disk. If a particular client boots from a floppy drive, or is diskless and uses Remote Initial Program Load (RIPL), that client's files can be stored in a specific machine directory on the server. Files stored in a machine directory are specific to an individual client configuration. To install a machine directory, proceed as follows:

1. In the Machine Directory Setup section of the Server Based Setup window, click the Add button to add a machine folder by using the Set Up Machine dialog.

2. In the Set Up Machine dialog, select Set Up One Machine to create a machine directory for a single client (see Figure 11.32). Type the name of the client in the Computer Name text box.

FIG. 11.32
Creating a folder for computer-specific installation in the Set Up Machine dialog.

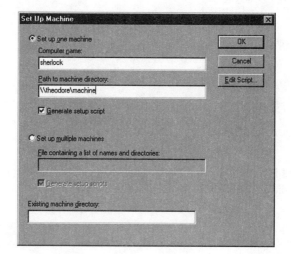

3. Type the path name for the machine directory in the Path to Machine Directory text box.

N O T E   Attempting to use mapped drive letter syntax, such as f:*folder*, causes an error. Use UNC syntax for the directory name: *Servername**Foldername*. ▪

4. If you want to generate a setup script for this client, mark the Generate Setup Script check box.

5. To change default policy values, click Edit Script to display the *Computername* Properties sheet (see Figure 11.33). Edit the policies as needed for this client. When your changes are complete, click OK to return to the Set Up Machine dialog.

6. Click OK to create the machine directory, save the information, and close the Set Up Machine dialog.

You can select Set Up Multiple Machines in the Set Up Machine dialog to create machine directories for several similar clients simultaneously. In this case, type the path and name of a file that contains the names and directories for the group of clients for which machine directories are to be set up. The Set Up Multiple Machines selection is useful primarily for a large number of identically configured clients.

Part

II

Ch

11

FIG. 11.33

Editing computer-specific setup policies in the *Computername* Properties sheet.

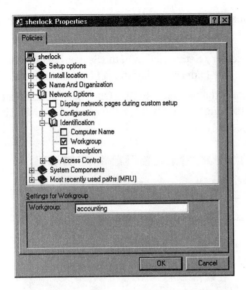

Updating Shared Files with Service Packs   Microsoft has committed to releasing Windows 95 updates periodically. The first such update, Windows 95 Service Pack 1, was released in early 1996.

ON THE WEB

As noted earlier in the chapter, you can download this 1.2M update from **http://www.microsoft.com/ windows/software/servpak1/enduser.htm**. For complete instructions on installing the Service Pack in a network environment, refer to the Admin.doc file included with the distribution file, Setup.exe.

Windows 95 Service Pack 1 includes the following enhancements and fixes:

- *OLE32 Update* fixes a potential security hole with Microsoft Office 95 applications that use OLE. Previously, slack space in the application data files could contain data from deleted files, which could be viewed by using Notepad or another editor.

- *Shell Update* fixes a file-copy problem that could result in zero-length files when copying a file onto itself when using two views of the same network resource. If you've installed the Service for NetWare Directory Services update, the Shell Update also makes it possible to browse NDS printers from the Add Printer wizard.

- *Common Dialog Update for Windows 3.1 Printer Drivers* fixes problems when using 32-bit applications to print with Windows 3.1 drivers.

- *File and Printer Sharing for Microsoft Networks* fixes a security hole that exists when using file and printer sharing for Microsoft Networks on a network that uses Samba SMBCLIENT. It also fixes a security hole when using user-level security.

- *Samba* fixes a situation in which the different file-naming conventions used by Windows 95 and UNIX could cause problems. This update to Vredir traps file names that are legal UNIX file names but not legal Windows 95 file names.

- *File and Printer Sharing for NetWare Networks* fixes a security hole that might have allowed unauthorized users to access restricted data.

- *Password List* fixes a potential security hole that occurred when connecting to a password-protected resource and saving the password. The original distribution used an easily broken encryption method to store the passwords. This update makes the stored encrypted password almost impossible to recover by illicit means.

- *System Agent* fixes Sage.dll to correct problems with floating-point calculations performed while System Agent was running.

- *Exchange* updates the version of the Microsoft Exchange client shipped with Windows 95 to add various enhancements and fixes.

- *Printer Port* adds support for ECP ports used by newer laser printers and fixes some minor timeout problems.

Microsoft issued a major upgrade to Windows 95, called OEM Service Release (OSR) 2, in late 1996. The full version of OSR 2, which adds the optional FAT32 file system to Windows 95, is available only to PC assemblers.

ON THE WEB

Parts of OSR 2 are available for downloading from **http://www.microsoft.com/windows95/ default.asp**. Choose Free Software from the Activity menu, click Product Updates, and then click the OSR 2 Downloadable Components button.

The Downloadable components of OSR 2 fall into the following categories:

- *Internet and Multimedia* includes Internet Explorer 3.0 (not the current 3.01 version), the Internet Connection Wizard, Internet Mail and News, NetMeeting 1.0 (not the current 2.0 version), Personal Web Server, DirectX 2.0, Direct3D, and ActiveMovie 1.0.

- *Networking and Communications* offers Dial-Up Networking (DUN) improvements; VoiceView modem support; an updated NetWare client that fully supports NetWare 4.x, including NetWare Directory Services (NDS); a 32-bit Data Link Control protocol for SNA host connectivity; and Infrared Data Association (IrDA) 2.0 drivers.

ON THE WEB

You also must download the ISDN Accelerator Pack 1.1 from **http://www.microsoft.com/windows/ common/aa2725.htm** to obtain the complete set of DUN improvements.

- *Additional Features* provides Wang Imaging for Windows 95, updated OLE components, enhanced Windows Messaging client, and fixes to Microsoft Fax.

Part

II

Ch

11

Unless you're using Windows 95 clients with NetWare 4.x or need ISDN connectivity, there's no pressing need to upgrade Windows 95 clients with the downloadable components of OSR 2. These components, along with updated hardware drivers not available for download, will be incorporated in the forthcoming Windows 9x.

Setting Up User Profiles on the Server

Many companies need to accommodate roving users—those who can log on at different workstations—by making sure that each user's personal profile is used at whatever workstation he or she uses to log on. This need is accommodated by storing user profile information on the network server, where it's accessible from any connected workstation. After user profiles are enabled, Windows 95 handles this process automatically, synchronizing user profile information between the server and the local hard disk.

If your network server is running Windows NT Server, the only special requirement for handling roving users is that a home directory must exist for each such user on the server. If the server is running Novell NetWare, a mail directory must exist for the user.

When a roving user logs into a Windows 95 client workstation, Windows 95 first examines the local hard drive and that user's home directory on the server to locate a User.dat file for that account. If a User.dat file exists for that user in both places, the most recent copy is used. If it exists in only one place, that copy is used, but is then saved to both the local and network drives. If it exists in neither place, the default is used and is then saved under that logon name to both the local hard drive and to the home directory on the server.

If that same roving user then logs on to a different Windows 95 client workstation, the process is repeated. If User.dat exists on both the local hard drive and the server, the latest version is used and then saved to both the local hard drive and the server.

Because Windows 95 always checks for multiple copies of User.dat in different locations, uses the latest version for the current session, and then saves the latest version to all locations where a User.dat was found for each user, roving users will always be using the latest version of their User.dat. All these processes occur automatically and transparently to the users. It's simply the way Windows 95 is designed to work. The only requirements for it to occur are as follows:

■ Each user has an account and a home directory on the Windows NT server or a mail directory on the NetWare server, and

■ User profiles are enabled on the User Profiles page of the Password Properties sheet (see Figure 11.34), and either

■ Client for Microsoft Networks is the primary network logon if the profiles are to be stored on the NT Server

or

Client for NetWare Networks is the primary logon if the profiles are to be stored on a Novell server.

FIG. 11.34

The Passwords Properties sheet's User Profiles page.

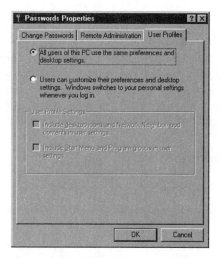

N O T E A user profile is stored in the user's home directory on a Windows NT server. Creating a user account on a Windows NT server doesn't automatically create a home directory for that user, so you must manually create the directory if that user roves.

A user profile is stored in the user's mail directory on a Novell server. This directory is created automatically when the NetWare user is created, so no further action is needed. ■

The Windows 95 Registry comprises two files—User.dat and System.dat. User.dat contains information about user settings and preferences. System.dat contains information about system hardware configuration and settings. Using user profiles allows more than one user to use the same Windows 95 system while maintaining individual settings for each user. Windows 95 updates and maintains user profile information automatically after user profiles are enabled. You can use mandatory user profiles to limit users' ability to alter desktop settings and to provide a consistent interface throughout the network, making training and client-management issues considerably easier to deal with.

User profile information can be stored either locally on the client or on the network server. If the user profile information is stored locally, Windows 95 uses the settings for a specific user when that user logs on to that client, allowing each user of the client to have his or her own desktop settings and other preferences available at logon. If user profile information is instead stored on the network server, users can log on to any Windows 95 client running a 32-bit protected-mode client and still be presented with their preferred settings.

User profiles store only user information and not system information, so various client hardware configurations are each handled by the local System.dat file specific to the individual client. Desktop settings and other user-specific information, on the other hand, are retrieved from the user profile information of User.dat stored on the server's home directory for the user.

Using System Policies

System policies are defined in a policy file stored on the network server. When a user logs on, local Registry values are superseded by those stored in the system policy file. Using system policies lets you enforce mandatory system configurations and control what users are permitted to do and change on the desktop. You can use system policies to standardize such network settings as client and protocol configurations and peer-based resource sharing. System policies form the foundation of Microsoft's and Intel's NetPC specification and the forthcoming Zero Administration Windows (ZAW) initiative.

▶ **See** "Zero Administration Windows," **p. 983**

ON THE WEB

You can read about ZAW and the Zero-Administration Kit (ZAK) at **http://www.microsoft.com/ windows/zak/**.

You can create and change system policies by using the System Policy Editor, Poledit.exe (more commonly called *PolEdit*). You can use PolEdit to change Registry settings on either a local or remote computer. You can create a standardized set of Registry settings, store them in a system policy file, and then use this file to standardize the Registry on many systems. You can apply these system policy settings individually or to groups already defined on a Windows NT server or a NetWare server.

Installing the System Policy Editor   PolEdit isn't installed by default when you install Windows 95. To install PolEdit on a Windows 95 management client, proceed as follows:

1. Double-click Control Panel's Add/Remove Programs tool to open the Add/Remove Programs Properties sheet.

2. Click the Windows Setup tab to show the Windows Setup page (see Figure 11.35).

3. Click the Have Disk button to open the Install From Disk dialog (see Figure 11.36).

4. Click Browse and locate the \admin\apptools\poledit directory of the Windows 95 CD-ROM. Two .INF files appear: grouppol.inf and poledit.inf.

5. Select grouppol.inf and click OK. You're returned to the Install From Disk dialog with \admin\apptools\poledit\grouppol.inf specified as the Copy Manufacturer's Files From location.

6. Click OK to display the Have Disk dialog (see Figure 11.37) and to choose the Components to be installed. Select Group Policies to install group-based support for system policies. Select System Policy Editor to allow setting system policies for your network. Click Install to begin installing the software.

7. When the Add/Remove Programs Properties sheet reappears, click OK to complete the installation. You're prompted to restart your computer for the changes to take effect.

FIG. 11.35

The Windows Setup page of the Add/Remove Programs Properties sheet.

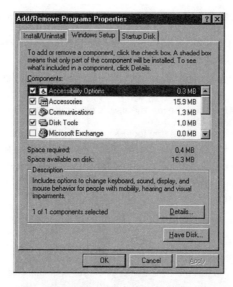

FIG. 11.36

Using the Install From Disk dialog for installing Poledit.exe.

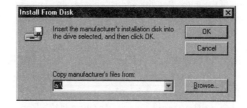

FIG. 11.37

The completed Have Disk dialog with Group Policies and System Policy Editor added.

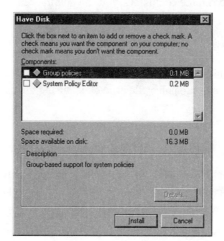

Using the System Policy Editor   You can use PolEdit in the following modes:

- *Registry mode* lets you edit the Registry of a local or remote computer directly. Any changes you make to the Registry take effect immediately.

- *Policy File mode* lets you create and modify .POL system policy files that can subsequently be used on other clients. Changes that you make to a policy file take effect only when the policy file is invoked during the user's next network logon.

To use Registry mode to make changes to a local Registry, run PolEdit. From the File menu choose Open Registry. Two icons appear—Local User and Local Computer. Clicking Local User, which corresponds to data contained in the User.dat portion of the Registry, displays a hierarchical tree showing user items that may be edited. Clicking Local Computer similarly lets you edit items contained in the System.dat part of the Registry.

> **CAUTION**
>
> Configuration changes are stored in the Registry. Using Control Panel tools to make Registry changes is far safer than other methods and conceals the intricacies of the Registry from the person making the changes. PolEdit permits direct editing of a subset of the Registry. The Registry Editor, Regedit.exe (also known as RegEdit), permits direct editing of the entire Registry and is the most powerful—as well as most dangerous—choice. Use the least powerful Registry editing tool that accomplishes your editing objective.

To use Registry mode to make changes to a remote Registry, run PolEdit. From the File menu choose Connect. When prompted, enter the name of the remote computer to open that computer's Registry for editing. If you have administrative privileges on that computer, if user-level access control is enabled on the remote computer, and if the Remote Registry service is enabled on both the local and remote computers, you can edit the remote Registry as though it were local.

To use Policy File mode to create and modify system policy files, run PolEdit. From the File menu, choose New File to create a new system policy file, or Open File to open an existing system policy file. Changes that you make to the system policy file are saved when you exit PolEdit but take effect only when the policy file is invoked during the user's next network logon.

Managing Windows 95 Clients Remotely

Windows 95 provides several tools designed to allow you to manage networked clients running Windows 95 from a central management client rather than make on-site visits to the client. These remote management tools include the following:

- *System Policy Editor,* described in the preceding section, lets you make direct changes to remote clients on an individual basis and to create system policy files that control the behavior of multiple clients on the network.

- *Registry Editor* is another tool that you can use to make direct changes to a remote client's Registry. Unlike Policy Editor, which can change only a subset of Registry entries, Registry Editor has full access to the Registry. You also can use Windows NT 4.0's Regedit.exe or Regedt32.exe to manage Windows 95 Registries remotely.

  ▶ **See** "Using the Registry Editor," **p. 310**

- *System Monitor* reports performance information across the network, using virtual device drivers to monitor many aspects of system performance. System Monitor is a much simpler version of the Simple Network Management Protocol (SNMP).

- *Net Watcher* lets you manage shared resources across the network when you're using the peer-to-peer LAN features of Windows 95.

- *Backup agents* are provided for Cheyenne ARCserve and Arcada Backup Exec to allow you to back up client files from a central server that uses Cheyenne or Arcada backup software, respectively.

The following sections describe how to enable remote management of clients over the network and how to use System Policy Editor, Registry Editor, System Monitor, and Net Watcher with remote clients.

Enabling Remote Management

Before you can use the remote management features provided by Windows 95, you must first enable some functions on the remote clients to be managed and on the central management client. Although the specific requirements vary with the remote management features you want to use, making the following changes on the remote client provides full remote management access:

- *Enable user-level security,* as discussed earlier in this chapter. Although some remote management functions are available with only share-level security enabled on the remote client, enabling user-level security gives you access to all remote management functions.

- *Enable remote administration,* if necessary. If the remote client has user-level security enabled, remote administration is enabled automatically. If the remote client uses share-level security, remote administration must be enabled manually. To do so, double-click Control Panel's Passwords tool and mark the Enable Remote Administration of this Server check box. For share-level security, enter a password to control access to remote administration. For user-level security, add specific users as administrators.

- *Grant remote administration privileges* to the administrator. With user-level security enabled, certain users are automatically granted remote administration privileges, as follows:

  - On a Windows NT Server network, members of the DOMAIN ADMINISTRATORS group
  - On a Novell NetWare 3.1x network, the user SUPERVISOR
  - On a Novell NetWare 4.x network, the user ADMIN

- *Install file and printer sharing,* as detailed earlier in this chapter.

Part
II

Ch
11

■ *Install Microsoft Remote Registry service.* From Control Panel, double-click the Network tool. Click Add and choose Service. Click the Have Disk button and specify the \admin\ nettools\remotreg directory on the Windows 95 distribution CD. Select Microsoft Remote Registry (see Figure 11.38) and click OK to install the remote Registry service.

FIG. 11.38

Installing Microsoft Remote Registry service from the Windows 95 CD-ROM.

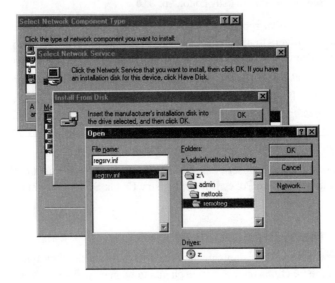

In addition to the preceding items, the following changes are needed on the central management client:

■ Install Remote Registry services, as described earlier.

■ Verify transport protocol support to ensure that the management client has at least one protocol (NWLink, TCP/IP, or NetBEUI) in common with each remote client to be managed.

Using Remote Management

After you enable remote management, you can use System Policy Editor, Registry Editor, and other tools to manage remote clients, as described in the following sections.

Using Policy Editor Remotely   You can use PolEdit to make changes to the Registry on a remote client. Most of these changes take effect immediately, but some require that the remote client be restarted for them to take effect.

To use PolEdit remotely, follow these steps:

1. Run PolEdit and choose Connect from the File menu to open the Connect dialog.

2. Type the name of the remote client with the policy to be edited. If the proper services are installed and enabled on both your client and the remote client, and if you have

the necessary permissions, the remote client's Registry is loaded into PolEdit. PolEdit's title bar shows the name of the remote client whose Registry is being edited (see Figure 11.39).

3. Make the necessary changes and save them.

FIG. 11.39
Policy Editor displaying the Local User and Local Computer icons for a remote Windows 95 computer (OAKLEAF3).

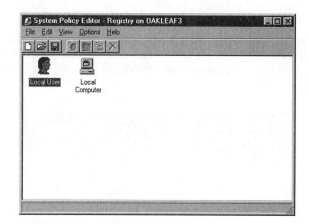

Using Registry Editor Remotely   Like Policy Editor, Registry Editor can be used to make changes to the Registry of a remote client. To use Registry Editor remotely, follow these steps:

1. Run Registry Editor. From the Registry menu, choose Connect Network Registry.
2. In the Connect Network Registry dialog, type the name of the remote client to be edited. If you have the proper services loaded and permissions granted, the Registry of the remote client is loaded into Registry Editor, appearing as a branch below the existing Registry information for the local machine (see Figure 11.40).
3. Make the necessary changes and save them.

FIG. 11.40
Registry Editor displaying the Registry keys of the local (OAKLEAF1, My Computer) and remote (OAKLEAF3) Windows 95 computers.

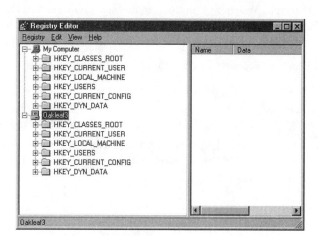

Part
II

Ch
11

Using System Monitor Remotely   You can use System Monitor to view performance statistics of a remote system. Using System Monitor remotely requires that the remote client have the Remote Registry service installed.

To use System Monitor to view performance statistics on a remote system, do the following:

1. Run System Monitor. From the File menu choose Connect.

2. In the Connect dialog, type the name of the remote client to be monitored and click OK. If the necessary services are installed on both computers and you have the appropriate permissions, System Monitor displays parameters for the remote system (see Figure 11.41).

FIG. 11.41

Monitoring processor usage and file system bytes read of a remote Windows 95 computer (OAKLEAF3).

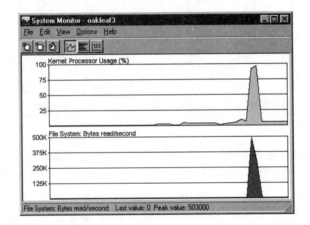

Using Net Watcher Remotely   Net Watcher lets you monitor and control shared resources on the network. By using Net Watcher, you can add and delete shared resources on remote clients, display shared resources and connected users, close files left open by users, and disconnect users. Using Net Watcher to control remote clients requires that the remote clients have file and print sharing enabled, so that a client can share resources with other clients on the network. Such a client is referred to as a *peer-to-peer server*, *peer server*, or simply a *server*.

To use Net Watcher to connect to a remote client, follow these steps:

1. Run Net Watcher and choose Select Server from the Administer menu.

2. In the Select Server dialog, type the name of the remote client (peer server) you want to control. Alternatively, click the Browse button to browse a list of available servers.

3. Type the password for the peer server you select, if necessary. You're connected to the remote client, and Net Watcher displays the default shares for the selected client in the right pane (see Figure 11.42).

FIG. 11.42

Using Net Watcher to display the users sharing folders of a remote Windows 95 computer (OAKLEAF3).

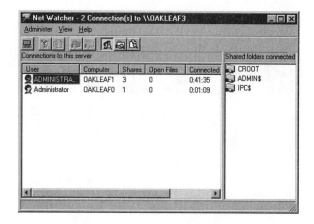

To use Net Watcher to add shared folders on a remote client, do the following:

1. After you connect to the remote client as described in the preceding steps, choose Shared Folders from the View menu to display the Shared Folders dialog.

2. Click Add Shared Folder to display the Enter Path dialog.

3. Type the name of the folder to be shared. Alternatively, click the Browse button to browse for the folder to be shared and select the drive or folder you want to share. When you click OK, the *Sharename* property sheet appears, with the Not Shared option selected.

4. Select the Shared As option, complete the share information (see Figure 11.43), and click OK to close the dialog. The information you supply here depends on whether you're using share-level access or user-level access, as described earlier in this chapter. (Figure 11.43 shows the entries for user-level access.) After you complete this step, the newly shared folder is added to the Shared Folder view and is accessible to other users (see Figure 11.44).

Part
II

Ch

11

FIG. 11.43

Setting up a share on a remote Windows 95 computer (OAKLEAF3) with user-level access.

FIG. 11.44

The additional server share (DROOT) displayed by Net Watcher.

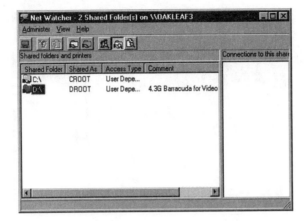

To use Net Watcher to remove shared folders on a remote client, follow these steps:

1. After you connect to the remote client (as described earlier in this section), choose Shared Folders from the View menu to display the Shared Folders dialog.

2. Select the folder that's no longer to be shared, click Stop Sharing Folder, and, when prompted, confirm that you want to stop sharing that folder. The shared folder is removed from the Shared Folder view and is no longer accessible to other users.

Browsing Issues with Windows 95 Clients

Windows 95 clients don't support browsing of Windows NT 4.0 Server (or Workstation) folder and printer shares with names longer than 12 characters. During the browser dialect negotiation, Windows 95 tells Windows NT Server 4.0 that it accepts only 8.3 short file names. Make sure that you maintain all share names within the 12-character limit. The Distributed File System (Dfs), which will be included in Windows NT 5.0, solves this problem. Dfs is the one of the subjects of Chapter 27, "Distributing File and Directory Services."

ON THE WEB

For more information on this browsing issue, see **http://www.microsoft.com/kb/articles/q160/8/ 43.htm**.

Windows 95 clients that are simultaneous members of a peer workgroup and a Windows NT domain often exhibit browsing problems. If the workgroup name and domain name vary, Network Neighborhood shows only members of the workgroup, not domain resources. Double-clicking Entire Network or the domain name entry usually displays the domain servers after a brief delay. To eliminate this inconvenience, change the name of the workgroup in the Properties page for the Client for Windows Networks to the client's domain name.

ON THE WEB

More information on this workgroup browsing issues is available from **http://www.microsoft.com/kb/articles/q140/3/90.htm**.

You can improve the browsing performance of TCP/IP-only DUN clients connecting to Windows NT Server 4.0's Remote Access Service (RAS) by adding the NetBEUI protocol for browsing domain resources within the subnet of the RAS server. (NetBEUI packets aren't routable.) NetBEUI is a simpler and more efficient browsing protocol than TCP/IP.

From Here...

One primary responsibility of Windows NT Server 4.0 network administrators is to assure that Windows 95 clients, whether desktop or portable PCs, gain the maximum possible benefit from Windows NT networking. This chapter described how to set up and administer Windows 95 clients to accommodate NetBEUI, TCP/IP, and IPX/SPX protocols. If you're migrating from Novell NetWare to a Windows NT Server 4.0 environment, Windows 95's capability to run multiple network protocol stacks without consuming conventional DOS memory is an important consideration. Combinations of NetBEUI for high-speed network communication in departmental Windows NT networks and TCP/IP for wide area networking, including access to intranets and the Internet, also is common.

The following chapters contain information related to or complementing the content of this chapter:

- Chapter 12, "Connecting Other PC Clients to the Network," describes how to set up Windows 3.1, Windows for Workgroups 3.1+, Windows NT Workstation 3.5+ and 4.0, and Apple Macintosh clients for networking with Windows NT Server 4.0.

- Chapter 13, "Managing User and Group Accounts," describes how to optimize the structure of and manage client accounts on Windows NT 4.0 servers.

- Chapter 18, "Integrating Windows NT with NetWare and UNIX," discusses how to optimize the use of Windows NT Server 4.0 with Novell NetWare and UNIX networks, with emphasis on TCP/IP connectivity and the Domain Name Service.

Part
II

Ch
11

CHAPTER 12

Connecting Other PC Clients to the Network

One of Windows NT Server's strengths is its capability to provide file, print, and application services to a number of different Windows and Macintosh clients.

Windows 3.1+ is the least functional of the client platforms, from a networking viewpoint. Windows for Workgroups (WfWg) incorporates the network components that Windows 3.1+ lacks, making WfWg 3.1x Windows NT Server-aware and providing additional flexibility in its support of other Windows NT Server 4.0 features, such as multiple networking protocols. For these reasons, WfWg is the most common 16-bit client platform in use by today's Windows NT Server networks.

The prevalence of WfWg clients is beginning to decline, however, as 32-bit Windows 95 and Window NT Workstation become the standard operating systems for mobile and desktop PCs, respectively. Despite the overwhelming dominance of the Windows 95 operating system for consumer PCs, market research firms estimate that only 20 percent to 25 percent of corporate desktop PCs had adopted Windows 95 by mid-1997. Most of the 60+ million copies of Windows 95 that Microsoft has sold since

Windows 3.1+

Windows 3.1+ clients can run only one network protocol at a time.

Windows for Workgroups 3.11

WfWg 3.11 lets you run multiple protocol stacks simultaneously.

Windows NT Workstation 4.0

Windows NT Workstation's client network setup is quite similar to that for Windows 95.

Apple Macintosh System 6.0.7 or higher

Windows NT Server 4.0's Services for Macintosh provides file and printer sharing for networked Mac clients running System 6.0.7 or higher.

September 1995 are installed on new PCs, many of which are sold to individual users. Thus, in a corporate setting, most clients you're likely to connect to Windows NT Server 4.0 today run WfWg 3.1x and, to a lesser extent, Windows 3.1+. Many large organizations decided to bypass Windows 95 and install Windows NT Workstation on their new client PCs.

Windows NT Workstation 4.0 provides the greatest security, functionality, flexibility, and stability of all the Windows clients. Accordingly, Windows NT Workstation requires more PC resources than Windows 3.1+ and WfWg 3.11. Windows NT takes full advantage of the new Intel Pentium Pro processors and provides symmetrical multiprocessing (SMP) for 32-bit threaded applications. An increasing number of organizations are equipping their power users with dual-processor workstations with the 32M or more of RAM required to take advantage of SMP with high-end graphics applications, such as Adobe PhotoShop. Much of the information in Chapter 11, "Configuring Windows 95 Clients for Networking," applies to connecting both Windows 95 and Windows NT 4.0 clients to the network.

Macintosh client support is provided as part of Windows NT Server 4.0. In essence, your Windows NT server becomes an AppleShare server to provide file and print services to your Mac clients. ■

Connecting Windows 3.1 Clients

Microsoft designed Windows 3.1+ as a stand-alone product with networking capability added as an extension to the underlying MS-DOS operating system. The easiest way to provide Windows 3.1+ clients with connectivity to Windows NT 4.0 servers is to upgrade the client PCs from Windows 3.1+ to Windows for Workgroups 3.11. If you have a reason not to upgrade Windows 3.1+ clients to WfWg 3.11, the following sections describe how to install the Microsoft Client for DOS and Windows that's included on the Windows NT Server 4.0 CD-ROM in the \Clients\Msclient folder. The Microsoft Client for DOS and Windows also is useful for network installation of Windows 95 or Windows NT Workstation 4.0 on PCs without a CD-ROM drive.

▶ **See** "Integrating Windows NT Server with Novell NetWare," **p. 637**

N O T E   If your Windows 3.1 clients now connect to one or more Novell NetWare 3.x or 4.x servers, you can avoid the installation of additional network client software by setting up Windows NT Server 4.0 to provide the IPX/SPX transport, in addition to NetBEUI or TCP/IP.

Windows 3.1, unlike WfWg 3.11, requires you to choose a single network protocol. It's possible, but inconvenient, to use a multiboot DOS technique so that Windows 3.1 clients can change network protocols. ■

Creating Client Installation Disks

You need the Windows NT Server 4.0 CD-ROM and two high-density disks to create the DOS setup disks for installing the Network Client v3.0 for MS-DOS and Windows. You install from the disks the DOS-based drivers on each computer running Windows 3.1 that connects to your Windows NT server. Follow these steps to create the installation disks:

1. If you haven't previously copied the client installation files to a \Clients folder of a server drive for server-based installation, insert the Windows NT Server 4.0 CD-ROM into your CD-ROM drive.

2. From the Windows NT Server 4.0 Start menu, choose Programs, Administrative Tools, and then Network Client Administrator to open the Network Client Administrator dialog.

3. Select Make Installation Disk Set (see Figure 12.1) and click Continue to display the Share Network Client Installation Files dialog.

FIG. 12.1

Selecting the Make Installation Disk Set option of the Network Client Administrator dialog.

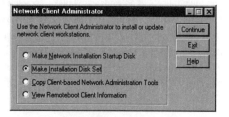

4. In the Path text box of the Share Network Client Installation Files dialog, type the path to the \Clients folder. If you use the CD-ROM, type or browse to the *d*:\Clients folder, where *d*: is the drive letter for your CD-ROM drive. Select the Use Existing Path option (see Figure 12.2) and click OK to open the Make Installation Disk Set dialog.

FIG. 12.2

Setting the path to the Windows NT Server 4.0 distribution CD-ROM.

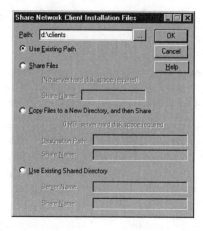

Part

II

Ch

12

5. The Network Client or Service list box of the Make Installation Disk Set dialog lets you choose the client drivers to copy. Select Network Client v3.0 for MS-DOS and Windows (see Figure 12.3). Make sure that the disk destination drive is correct, and click OK to create the two disks. If the disks aren't formatted, mark the Format Disks check box.

FIG. 12.3

Selecting Network Client v3.0 for MS-DOS and Windows in the Make Installation Disk Set dialog.

 T I P If you anticipate the need to create additional sets of network install disks, copy the files from the *d*:\Clients folder to a \Clients folder on your server. Creating a \Clients folder is one of the options of the Share Network Client Installation Files dialog. Be sure to adhere to DOS 8.3 file conventions when establishing share names for Windows 3.1x, WfWg 3.1x, and Windows 95. Restrict share names to eight characters or less; Windows 95 accommodates 12-character share names, but sticking with conventional eight-character share names is the most compatible approach.

Installing the MS-DOS and Windows Client

Now that you've created the installation disks, the next step is to install the network drivers on your Windows 3.1 client. As part of the disk creation, a Setup program is provided to facilitate this process. The following steps describe how to install the Network Client v3.0 for MS-DOS and Windows on a Windows 3.1 client PC:

1. You must install the client software from DOS, so exit Windows to the DOS prompt.

2. Insert client disk #1 and type **a:\setup** at the command line. Press Enter to run the Setup application and display the initial Setup screen.

3. Press Enter to continue to display the screen where you select the path to which to install the network drivers. The default is C:\NET (see Figure 12.4). Choose a different drive or directory, if desired, and press Enter to continue.

4. Setup first prompts you to select a network card driver. Scroll the list and choose the correct driver for your network card. If your card isn't listed, choose the Network Adapter Not Shown on List Below option, which lets you load an adapter driver from disk. The network card manufacturer usually provides a disk with drivers for popular operating systems. In this case, Setup looks for the OEMSETUP.INF file to load the driver for the Microsoft Network Client.

5. Setup next examines your system and proposes to allocate memory to network buffers for best performance (see Figure 12.5). Press Enter to accept the buffer allocation, or press C to continue without optimizing buffer memory.

N O T E You can have the network drivers allocate part of your system's RAM as a packet buffer. This provides for fewer packet drops if your network card can't process packets fast enough but consumes additional system RAM. In most cases, you can accept the default buffer allocation. ■

FIG. 12.4

Specifying the path to the client's network files.

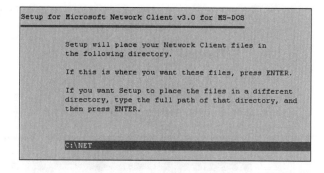

```
Setup for Microsoft Network Client v3.0 for MS-DOS

        Setup will place your Network Client files in
        the following directory.

        If this is where you want these files, press ENTER.

        If you want Setup to place the files in a different
        directory, type the full path of that directory, and
        then press ENTER.


    C:\NET
```

FIG. 12.5

Specifying allocation of network memory buffers to optimize network performance.

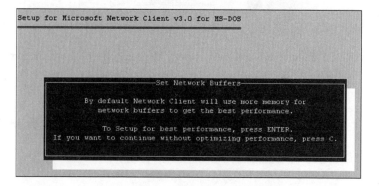

```
Setup for Microsoft Network Client v3.0 for MS-DOS




                        ─Set Network Buffers─

            By default Network Client will use more memory for
               network buffers to get the best performance.

                  To Setup for best performance, press ENTER.
        If you want to continue without optimizing performance, press C.
```

6. Setup prompts you for a user name that identifies the client to the network. This name also becomes your computer name. Type the computer name in the User Name text box (see Figure 12.6), and press Enter to continue.

FIG. 12.6

Specifying the User Name for the client.

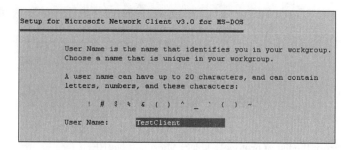

```
Setup for Microsoft Network Client v3.0 for MS-DOS

        User Name is the name that identifies you in your workgroup.
        Choose a name that is unique in your workgroup.

        A user name can have up to 20 characters, and can contain
        letters, numbers, and these characters:

            !  #  $  %  &  ( )  ^  _  `  ( )  ~

        User Name:      TestClient
```

7. The screen displays a list of the default values for Names, Setup Options, and Network Configuration. Use the arrow keys to select Change Network Configuration (see Figure 12.7), and press Enter to continue.

Part
II

Ch
12

FIG. 12.7

Preparing to change the
network configuration.

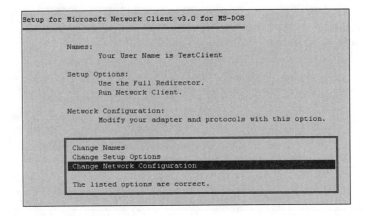

```
Setup for Microsoft Network Client v3.0 for MS-DOS

        Names:
                Your User Name is TestClient

        Setup Options:
                Use the Full Redirector.
                Run Network Client.

        Network Configuration:
                Modify your adapter and protocols with this option.

            ┌──────────────────────────────────────┐
            │  Change Names                          │
            │  Change Setup Options                  │
            │  Change Network Configuration          │
            │                                        │
            │  The listed options are correct.       │
            └──────────────────────────────────────┘
```

8. Assuming that Setup has correctly detected your network adapter, it's identified as the Installed Network Adapter. By default, NWLink IPX is the default network protocol.

   To change to NetBEUI, the most common protocol for small Windows NT networks, press Tab and use the arrow keys to select the NWLink IPX Compatible Transport in the upper box. Press Tab to return to the configuration options, select Remove (see Figure 12.8), and press Enter.

   ▶ **See** "NetBEUI and NetBEUI Frame," **p. 107**

FIG. 12.8

Removing the NWLink
IPX Compatible
Transport.

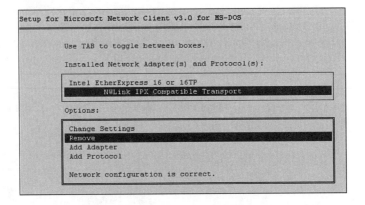

```
Setup for Microsoft Network Client v3.0 for MS-DOS

        Use TAB to toggle between boxes.

        Installed Network Adapter(s) and Protocol(s):
            ┌──────────────────────────────────────┐
            │  Intel EtherExpress 16 or 16TP         │
            │          NWLink IPX Compatible Transport│
            └──────────────────────────────────────┘
        Options:
            ┌──────────────────────────────────────┐
            │  Change Settings                       │
            │  Remove                                │
            │  Add Adapter                           │
            │  Add Protocol                          │
            │                                        │
            │  Network configuration is correct.     │
            └──────────────────────────────────────┘
```

9. From the list of protocols, select Microsoft NetBEUI (see Figure 12.9) and press Enter. Select Network Configuration Is Correct and press Enter again.

FIG. 12.9

Selecting the Microsoft NetBEUI protocol in place of NetWare's IPX.

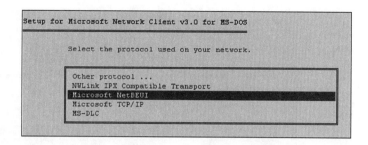

```
Setup for Microsoft Network Client v3.0 for MS-DOS

    Select the protocol used on your network.

    ┌──────────────────────────────────────────┐
    │ Other protocol ...                         │
    │ NWLink IPX Compatible Transport            │
    │ Microsoft NetBEUI                          │
    │ Microsoft TCP/IP                           │
    │ MS-DLC                                     │
    └──────────────────────────────────────────┘
```

N O T E Many large organizations are adopting TCP/IP as the primary or sole network protocol for client/server communication. You can elect to install TCP/IP, instead of or in addition to NetBEUI or IPX, in step 9. The TCP/IP stack requires additional conventional memory. Consumption of conventional memory may be a problem for clients that load several device drivers and TSRs (terminate-and-stay-resident applications). Chapter 10, "Using TCP/IP, WINS, and DHCP," covers Windows NT Server 4.0's basic TCP/IP capabilities.

▶ **See** "TCP/IP," **p. 108** ■

10. Select Setup Options and press Enter to view your Microsoft Client setup options (see Figure 12.10).

FIG. 12.10

Preparing to set up domain logon during the boot process.

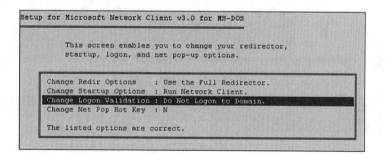

```
Setup for Microsoft Network Client v3.0 for MS-DOS

        This screen enables you to change your redirector,
        startup, logon, and net pop-up options.

    ┌────────────────────────────────────────────────────┐
    │ Change Redir Options     : Use the Full Redirector.  │
    │ Change Startup Options   : Run Network Client.       │
    │ Change Logon Validation : Do Not Logon to Domain.    │
    │ Change Net Pop Hot Key   : N                         │
    │                                                      │
    │ The listed options are correct.                      │
    └────────────────────────────────────────────────────┘
```

Part
II

Ch
12

11. If you want to validate your Windows 3.1x client to your Windows NT Server domain, select Change Logon Validation and press Enter. In the next screen, select Logon to Domain, press Enter, select The Listed Options Are Correct, and press Enter again (see Figure 12.11). If you plan to use Domain Logon Validation, you must make sure to use the Full Redirector (the default).

12. If you plan to log on to a Windows NT domain, highlight the Names option and press Enter. Change the Domain Name text to correspond to your Windows NT Server domain name. After entering the domain name, use the Tab and arrow keys to accept changes.

13. Select The Listed Options Are Correct (see Figure 12.12) and press Enter to complete installation of the files required for the client.

FIG. 12.11

Verifying the Setup options for the client installation.

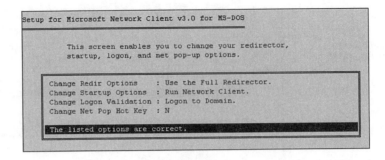

```
Setup for Microsoft Network Client v3.0 for MS-DOS


            This screen enables you to change your redirector,
            startup, logon, and net pop-up options.


    Change Redir Options     : Use the Full Redirector.
    Change Startup Options   : Run Network Client.
    Change Logon Validation  : Logon to Domain.
    Change Net Pop Hot Key   : N

    The listed options are correct.
```

FIG. 12.12

Verifying all your client software installation options in the final installation screen.

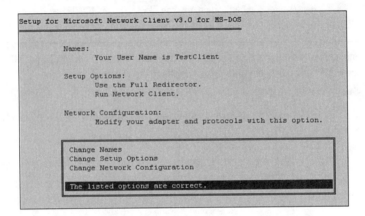

```
Setup for Microsoft Network Client v3.0 for MS-DOS


    Names:
          Your User Name is TestClient

    Setup Options:
          Use the Full Redirector.
          Run Network Client.

    Network Configuration:
          Modify your adapter and protocols with this option.


    Change Names
    Change Setup Options
    Change Network Configuration

    The listed options are correct.
```

Viewing Changes Made to Windows 3.1 Configuration and Initialization Files

The Setup program adds the following line to the client's CONFIG.SYS file:

```
Device=c:\net\ifshelp.sys
```

The client's AUTOEXEC.BAT file is modified to include the following additional instruction:

```
c:\net\net start
```

The Microsoft client software uses the PROTOCOL.INI file to store network adapter and protocol configuration. Following are typical entries in PROTOCOL.INI for NetBEUI with an NE2000-compatible network adapter:

```
[network.setup]

version=0x3110
netcard=ms$ne2clone,1,MS$NE2CLONE,1
transport=ms$ndishlp,MS$NDISHLP
transport=ms$netbeui,MS$NETBEUI
lana0=ms$ne2clone,1,ms$netbeui
lana1=ms$ne2clone,1,ms$ndishlp
[MS$NE2CLONE]
```

```
IOBASE=0x300
INTERRUPT=3
DriverName=MS2000$
[ndishlp$]
DriverName=ndishlp$
Bindings=
[protman$]
DriverName=protman$
[data]
version=v4.00.950
netcards=
[protman]
DriverName=PROTMAN$
PRIORITY=MS$NDISHLP
[MS$NDISHLP]
DriverName=ndishlp$
BINDINGS=MS$NE2CLONE
[MS$NETBEUI]
DriverName=netbeui$
SESSIONS=10
NCBS=12
BINDINGS=MS$NE2CLONE
LANABASE=0
```

The SYSTEM.INI file contains information about your NetBIOS computer name, the default user name, workgroup or domain, and the location of the password file for that user name. The password file (*.PWL) is stored on the local machine in an encrypted format; Windows NT clients use password files stored on the server. The first time users log on to Windows NT, they are prompted to create the password file for the user name specified in the SYSTEM.INI file. The following are typical SYSTEM.INI networking entries:

```
[network]
sizworkbuf=1498
filesharing=no
printsharing=no
autologon=yes
computername=WINDOWS1
lanroot=C:\NET
username=USER1
workgroup=WORKGROUP
reconnect=yes
dospophotkey=N
lmlogon=1
logondomain=MASTER
preferredredir=full
autostart=full
maxconnections=8

[network drivers]
netcard=ne2000.dos
transport=ndishlp.sys,*netbeui
devdir=C:\NET
LoadRMDrivers=yes
[Password Lists]
*Shares=C:\NET\Share001.PWL
```

Part

II

Ch

12

N O T E   The preceding .INI files are created during the client networking setup process. If you need to edit the entries in these files, use DOS's EDIT.EXE, or Windows SYSEDIT.EXE or Notepad. For instance, if you want to change the name of the Windows NT domain to which you log on during client startup, you edit the `logondomain` entry in the SYSTEM.INI file. Changes you make take effect when you reboot the client PC. ■

Setting Up Windows to Use the Network Drivers

After the DOS network drivers are in place, you must tell Windows 3.1 which network drivers you're using. Start Windows, and follow these steps to install the Windows network drivers:

1. From the Main group, double-click the Windows Setup icon to open the Windows Setup window. From the Options menu choose Change System Settings to open the Change System Settings dialog.

2. In the Network list, select Microsoft Network (or 100% Compatible), as shown in Figure 12.13. Click OK to continue.

FIG. 12.13

Installing Microsoft Networking in Windows 3.1.

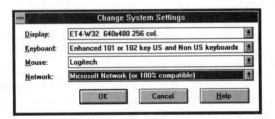

3. You're prompted for your original Windows 3.1 disk 2. Insert the disk in the drive and press Enter. After the drivers are loaded, choose Restart Windows to make the changes effective.

Connecting to Windows NT File and Printer Resources

After installing the client network drivers and setting up Windows 3.1 for networking, you're ready to connect to Windows NT Server 4.0 resources. To connect a Windows 3.1 client to a Windows NT server, follow these steps:

1. Open File Manager.

2. From the Disk menu choose Network Connections to open the Network Connections dialog.

3. By using the standard Universal Naming Convention (UNC) notation, *SERVERNAME**SHARENAME*, type the network path to a Windows NT server share. In the Drive drop-down list, select the drive letter to which you want to map the share (see Figure 12.14).

FIG. 12.14

Setting the path to a Windows NT server share.

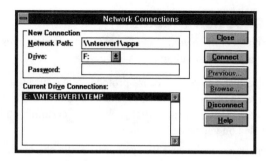

4. Click Connect to map the server share to the selected drive letter. The next time you open the Network Connections dialog, your mapped drive appears in the Current Drive Connections list.

You connect to printers shared by Windows NT servers by following these steps:

1. Open Print Manager from the Main program group.

2. From the Options menu choose Network Connections to open the Printers – Network Connections dialog.

3. Type the network path of the server and printer share to which you want to connect. Select a local LPT port (LPT1 if you don't have a local printer) to redirect to the shared printer (see Figure 12.15). Leave the Password text box empty, unless you want to restrict access to the printer. (Some organizations restrict access to color laser printers because of the high cost per page.)

4. Click the Connect button to connect to the Windows NT server's printer queue.

Part

II

Ch

12

FIG. 12.15

Connecting to a printer shared by a Windows NT server.

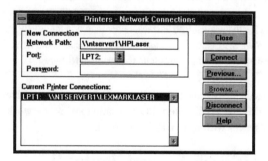

N O T E Unlike Windows NT clients, which download the required printer driver from the server, you must install the appropriate printer driver for your networked printer on the local workstation. In most cases, you need either the Windows 3.1+ installation disks or a Windows 3.1+ printer driver from the printer supplier to make the shared printer operable from the client. ■

Troubleshooting Connection Problems

If you have problems connecting to your Windows NT server's resources, following are a number of potential areas for troubleshooting:

- If you're using NetBEUI as your network protocol, make sure that your Windows NT server is on the same physical network segment as your client, or at least bridged to your client segment. Also make sure that your server is running the network protocol that you've installed on your client.

- When your client boots, make sure that you provide the correct password and receive confirmation of your connection to the Windows NT domain. The Command Completed Successfully message appears if all is well.

- If you receive an Access Denied message when trying to connect to a Windows NT server resource, make sure that the network administrator for the server has given your Windows 3.1 client user account appropriate permissions to the resource.

Connecting Windows for Workgroups 3.11 Clients

Windows for Workgroups 3.11 offers greatly improved networking connectivity compared with Windows 3.1. Because the network drivers for WfWg are Windows-based, you can install multiple network drivers, and the NetWare and NetBEUI drivers don't consume conventional (DOS) memory. The TCP/IP stack for WfWg 3.1 includes TSR drivers that run in conventional memory. WfWg 3.11 includes a TCP/IP protocol stack, which Microsoft developed after the release of the original 3.1 version of WfWg, that runs in extended memory.

 Most, but not all, users of WfWg 3.1 upgraded to WfWg 3.11 when Microsoft released the enhanced version. If you have any clients running WfWg 3.1 and plan to use TCP/IP, it's a better idea to upgrade these clients to WfWg 3.11 with its latest TCP/IP stack, rather than add the TCP/IP stack supplied with Windows NT Server 4.0. WfWg 3.11 also lets you use multiple protocols. If the WfWg 3.11 stack you install isn't the latest version, upgrade the clients from the Windows NT Server 4.0 version.

The following sections describe how to install the TCP/IP network drivers from the Windows NT Server 4.0 CD-ROM on a WfWg client PC, upgrade existing networking files, and connect to a Windows NT 4.0 server with the TCP/IP protocol.

Installing the 32-Bit TCP/IP Network Protocol

Installing or updating the TCP/IP protocol for WfWg 3.1+ requires one high-density disk and the Windows NT Server 4.0 CD-ROM. You'll also likely need the distribution disks for the version of WfWg 3.1+ installed on the client and, if not supported by WfWg 3.1+, a network adapter driver disk.

To create the required installation disk, install the TCP/IP protocol on clients running WfWg 3.1+, and update your WfWg configuration to allow connectivity to Windows NT Server resources, follow these steps:

1. If you haven't previously copied the client installation files to a \Clients folder of a server drive for server-based installation, insert the Windows NT Server 4.0 CD-ROM into your CD-ROM drive.

2. From the Windows NT Server 4.0 Start menu, choose Programs, Administrative Tools, and then Network Client Administrator to open the Network Client Administrator dialog.

3. Select Make Installation Disk Set and click Continue to display the Share Network Client Installation Files dialog.

4. In the Path text box of the Share Network Client Installation Files dialog, type the path to the \Clients folder. If you use the CD-ROM, type or browse to the *d*:\Clients folder, where *d*: is the drive letter for your CD-ROM drive. Select the Use Existing Path option (refer to Figure 12.2) and click OK to open the Make Installation Disk Set dialog.

5. The Network Client or Service list box of the Make Installation Disk Set dialog lets you choose the client drivers to copy. Select TCP/IP 32 for Windows for Workgroups 3.11. Make sure that the disk destination drive is correct, and click OK to create the first of two installation disks. If the disk isn't formatted, mark the Format Disks check box.

6. Create \WIN and \SYSTEM directories on the second formatted, blank disk. By using Explorer, copy NET.EXE and NET.MSG from the \Clients\update.WfW folder of the CD-ROM to the \WIN directory of the disk. Copy all the remaining files in \Clients\ update.WfW to the \SYSTEM directory. The second disk is used to update the WfWg network files after you set up the TCP/IP protocol.

7. Start WfWg 3.1+ and, from the Network program group, click Network Setup to open the Network Setup dialog.

8. Click Networks to open the Networks dialog, select the Install Microsoft Windows Network option (see Figure 12.16), and then click OK to close the Networks dialog and return to the Network Setup dialog.

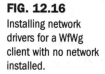
FIG. 12.16
Installing network drivers for a WfWg client with no network installed.

Part
II

Ch
12

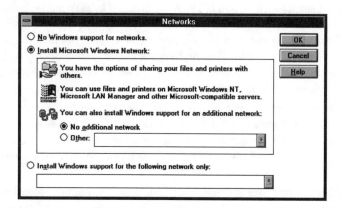

9. Click Drivers in the Network Setup dialog to open the Network Drivers dialog. Click Add Adapter to open the Add Network Adapter dialog, and select the adapter driver installed in the client PC (see Figure 12.17). Click OK to close the Add Network Adapter dialog and return to the Network Drivers dialog.

FIG. 12.17

Selecting the client PC's network adapter card.

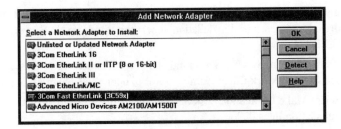

10. Click Add Protocol in the Network Drivers dialog to open the Add Network Protocol dialog. Double-click the Unlisted or Updated Protocol list item to install the updated version of TCP/IP from the disk (see Figure 12.18).

FIG. 12.18

Selecting installation of the client PC's network protocol from a disk.

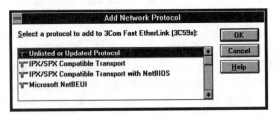

N O T E Although WfWg 3.11 has TCP/IP, NWLink, and NetBEUI, it's a good idea to load the latest driver versions, as noted in the tip of the preceding section. ■

11. At the prompt, insert the disk with the network protocol update and click OK. A message box confirms that you're installing Microsoft TCP/IP-32 3.11b. Click OK to install the protocol files on the client's drive and then return to the Network Drivers dialog.

12. By default, NetBEUI and NWLink are installed by WfWg 3.1+. You can remove these protocols by selecting the unneeded protocol in the Network Drivers list of the Network Drivers dialog and then clicking Remove. After you're done configuring the adapter drivers, click Close to close the Network Drivers dialog, and then click OK in the Network Setup dialog to end the network setup operation and open the Microsoft Windows Network dialog.

13. You're prompted to provide your computer name, workgroup name, and default logon name (see Figure 12.19). For authentication by your Windows NT server, the default logon name is the user name of your server account. The workgroup name is *not* the name of the Windows NT domain to which you connect, and it shouldn't duplicate the name of any domain on the network.

14. After entering user and machine information, you might be asked to supply your network adapter driver disk(s) or some of your original WfWg disks. In some cases, you may have trouble finding the correct driver files on your network adapter driver disk.

Look for a directory such as \NDIS or \WFW, which contains an OEMSETUP.INF file. (On the PC used for this example, which has a 3Com Etherlink III adapter, the correct driver files were located in \NDIS\WFW.) Follow the instructions of the message boxes to add or update the network adapter driver(s).

FIG. 12.19

Providing the user name, workgroup name, and computer name.

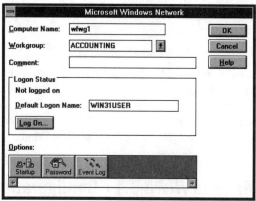

15. After updating network adapter drivers, the Microsoft TCP/IP Configuration dialog prompts you to enter in the TCP/IP information, including IP address, default gateway, and other TCP/IP-specific parameters (see Figure 12.20). Although the appearance of the TCP/IP Properties sheet of Windows 95 varies from the TCP/IP Configuration dialog of WfWg 3.1+, you specify the same values for TCP/IP parameters in both environments.

▶ **See** "Configuring TCP/IP," **p. 371**

See "Configuring TCP/IP," p. 371

Part
II

Ch
12

FIG. 12.20

TCP/IP Configuration options in WfWg.

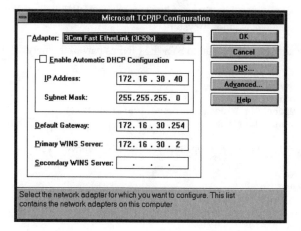

16. After completing the TCP/IP configuration, click OK to exit the network setup operation, and then exit to DOS.

17. Insert the second disk with the \WIN and \SYSTEM directories. Locate the client's existing NET.EXE and NET.MSG files (usually in c:\windows) and overwrite the existing versions with the copies in the disk's \WIN directory. Next, copy the .DLL and .386 files in the disk's \SYSTEM directory to the \WINDOWS\SYSTEM subdirectory, also overwriting the existing versions.

18. Restart WfWg to load the updated network applications and drivers.

When WfWg starts, you're prompted for the logon name that you specified in step 13 and for a password. Enter the password to be used for the Windows NT server account. The first time you log on after setting up networking, a message box asks whether you want to create a password file. As with the Network Client for DOS, the .PWL file is created locally and contains an encrypted version of the password. The .PWL file is used for Windows NT domain account authentication during the logon process.

Viewing Changes Made to WfWg 3.1+ Configuration and Initialization Files

The Setup program adds the line `Device=c:\windows\ifshelp.sys` to the client's CONFIG.SYS file, where `c:\windows` is the directory containing the WfWg system files. The client's AUTOEXEC.BAT file is modified to include the following additional instruction:

```
c:\windows\net start
```

The Microsoft Network Client for DOS/Windows 3.1 stores network protocol information in the PROTOCOL.INI and SYSTEM.INI files, located in the c:\net subdirectory. Most of the network driver components in WfWg load when you start WfWg, so the preceding network installation process puts all its changes into the SYSTEM.INI file in the WfWg system subdirectory, usually c:\windows\system.

The following additions are made to SYSTEM.INI as part of the network installation:

```
[boot]
network.drv=wfwnet.drv
[boot.description]
network.drv=Microsoft Windows Network (version 3.11)
secondnet.drv=No Additional Network Installed
[386Enh]
network=*vnetbios,*vwc,vnetsup.386,vredir.386,vserver.386
[Network]
FileSharing=No
PrintSharing=No
winnet=wfwnet/00025100
multinet=nonet
LogonDisconnected=Yes
EnableSharing=no
```

```
UserName=WIN31USER
Workgroup=ACCOUNTING
ComputerName=wfw1
Comment=wfw workstation
logonvalidated=yes
reconnect=yes
LogonDomain=NEWDOMNT
AutoLogon=Yes
StartMessaging=Yes
LoadNetDDE=Yes
LMLogon=1
DomainLogonMessage=Yes
cachethispassword=yes
[tcm$el59x0]
NameServer1=172.16.30.2
DefaultGateway=172.16.30.254
IPMask=255.255.255.0
IPAddress=172.16.30.40
Description=3Com Fast EtherLink (3C59x)
Binding=tcm$el59x

[MSTCP]
EnableRouting=0
Interfaces=tcm$el59x0
deadgwdetect=1
pmtudiscovery=1

[DNS]
DNSServers=
HostName=wfw1
DomainName=
DNSDomains=

[NBT]
NameServer1=172.16.30.2
LANABASE=0
EnableProxy=0
EnableDNS=0

[Password Lists]
*Shares=C:\WINDOWS\Share000.PWL
WIN31USER=C:\WINDOWS\WIN31USE.PWL
[network drivers]
devdir=C:\WINDOWS
LoadRMDrivers=No
netcard=el59x.dos
transport=ndishlp.sys
```

Part

II

Ch

12

All protocol configuration information, including this client's TCP/IP configuration information, is kept in the SYSTEM.INI file, rather than the PROTOCOL.INI file used by DOS/ Windows 3.1+–based clients. You can use a text editor, such as Notepad or SysEdit, to change your network settings for WfWg in the SYSTEM.INI file. Be sure to restart WfWg after you make changes to SYSTEM.INI.

Logging On and Connecting to Windows NT Server 4.0 Resources

To access Windows NT Server resources, you must set up the domain logon process for the client. Follow these steps:

1. From WfWg's Control Panel, double-click the Network icon to open the Microsoft Windows Network dialog.

2. Click the Startup button to open the Startup Settings dialog. Accept the default settings in the Startup Options group, making sure that the Log On at Startup check box is marked.

3. Mark the Log On to Windows NT or LAN Manager Domain check box and type the name of your Windows NT Server domain in the Domain Name text box (see Figure 12.21). Click OK twice to close the Startup Settings dialog and exit the Microsoft Windows Network dialog.

FIG. 12.21

Setting domain logon options in the Startup Settings dialog.

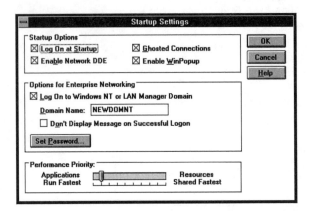

4. Exit and restart WfWg. On startup, the Welcome to Windows for Workgroups dialog opens, requesting entry of the user name for this client and that user's password.

5. You're prompted for a domain logon. If you use the same user name for the domain as for the workgroup, enter the same password as for the workgroup. Make sure that the Create Password File check box is marked.

N O T E The next time you start WfWg, you log on to the workgroup. If the domain user name and password are the same as that for the workgroup, you log on to the Windows NT domain without the additional prompt. ▓

T I P If you don't want to see the workgroup logon prompt at startup, delete the workgroup user name password so that the logon process skips the workgroup logon dialog and proceeds directly to the domain logon.

After you log on to the domain, the WfWg client processes a logon script that you've defined for the client's domain user name in Windows NT Server. You need to create a logon script for WfWg clients only if you want to automate additional logon operations.

After the Windows NT Server domain authenticates the WfWg client, it's easy to share the Windows NT server's resources. To share files, start File Manager on the client. From the Disk menu, choose Connect Network Drive to open the Connect Network Drive dialog. Browse network shares to find the share that you want to connect to, and then double-click the entry to map the drive to the selected drive letter (see Figure 12.22).

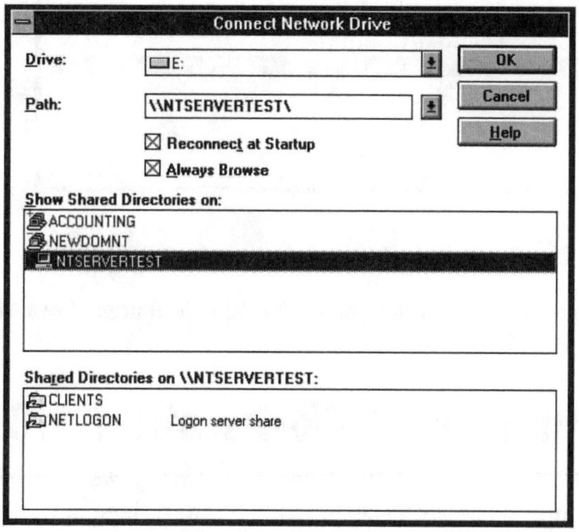

FIG. 12.22

Mapping a Windows NT Server share to a WfWg logical drive.

To connect to printer resources, open Print Manager from the Main program group. From the Printer menu choose Connect Network Printer; from the Connect Network Printer dialog, select the Windows NT server that shares a printer; and double-click the share name of the printer you want to use (see Figure 12.23).

Troubleshooting Network Resource Problems

If you have problems connecting to your Windows NT server resources, following are a number of potential areas for troubleshooting:

- If your client is having trouble connecting to Windows NT Server, you may see a Network Name Not Found message, which means that your client can't find the Windows NT server to which you're trying to connect. If you're using the TCP/IP stack and trying to access Windows NT Server resources in a routed network environment, make sure that you've specified a WINS server address in the client's TCP/IP Configuration dialog.

    ▶ **See** "Implementing Windows Internet Name Service," **p. 342**

- If you can't browse Windows NT network resources with File Manager or Print Manager, make sure that you've installed the most recent network drivers available from Microsoft. Older versions of the network drivers for WfWg cause browsing problems.

Part

II

Ch

12

FIG. 12.23
Using a printer shared
by a Windows NT server.

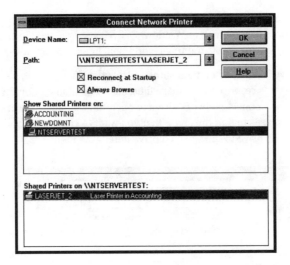

ON THE WEB

You can obtain updated network drivers from Microsoft's Web site at **http://www.microsoft.com**.

Connecting Windows NT Workstation 4.0 Clients

Connecting Windows NT Workstation 4.0 clients to a Windows NT 4.0 server is similar to the process for connecting Windows 95 clients, which is described in Chapter 11, "Configuring Windows 95 Clients for Networking." Connecting a Windows NT workstation to a Windows NT server involves setting up the client's network adapter and protocol(s), and then using Windows NT Workstation 4.0's built-in tools to connect to the server's shared folders and printers. The differences between connecting clients running Windows NT Workstation 3.51 and 4.0 to a Windows NT 4.0 server primarily involve changes to the user interface. The following sections describe how to connect a Windows NT Workstation 4.0 client to a Windows NT Server 4.0 domain.

Installing the Network Software

On a Windows NT workstation, you first need to choose the network protocol you want to use, and then install it. You must choose a protocol based on what the server is running. TCP/IP is the preferred protocol for Windows NT 4.0 networks, so the following steps describe how to install and configure TCP/IP on a client running Windows NT Workstation 4.0:

1. From the Start menu choose Settings and Control Panel, and then double-click the Network tool to open the Network properties sheet.

2. Click the Protocols tab to display the Protocols properties page; then click Add to open the Select Network Protocol dialog.

3. Select the TCP/IP Protocol item and click OK (see Figure 12.24).

FIG. 12.24

Adding the TCP/IP protocol in Windows NT Workstation 4.0.

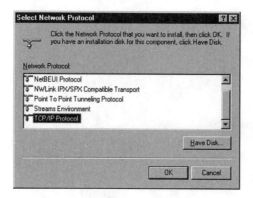

4. A TCP/IP Setup dialog opens, asking whether you want to configure your client's TCP/IP stack for use with DHCP. If you plan to use DHCP, click Yes.

5. A Windows NT Setup dialog opens, prompting you to enter the location of the Windows NT Workstation distribution files. These files are located on the Windows NT Workstation CD-ROM. For example, if your CD-ROM drive is F: and your Windows NT client uses a Pentium processor, type `F:\i386` and click Continue.

6. Windows NT Setup copies the TCP/IP files to your client. When the copy operation is complete, click Close.

7. Windows NT then proceeds to bind the new protocol to your client's network adapter. When the binding process completes, the Microsoft TCP/IP Properties sheet opens (see Figure 12.25). The IP Address page displays by default and gives you the opportunity to enter the IP address, subnet mask, and default gateway for the client. Click the Advanced button to enter additional IP addresses or default gateways for the client's network adapter.

NOTE If you want to access a Windows NT server on a different network segment from your Windows NT 4.0 workstation, you need to enter a default gateway and then enter either a WINS server address or create an LMHOSTS file. You can install the WINS configuration and LMHOSTS file on your Windows NT client by selecting the WINS Address tab of the Microsoft TCP/IP Properties sheet. ▪

8. After you enter all the TCP/IP configuration information, click OK. Windows NT prompts you to restart the system for the changes to take effect. After the system restarts, you must decide whether you want to install the client into the Windows NT domain, or whether to make it a member of a workgroup.

NOTE Domain client users can log on to Windows NT servers in their domains and seamlessly authenticate by a single logon to all resources for which they have permission. Workgroup users log on to their local machines, just as in Windows for Workgroups, and then authenticate explicitly to the needed Windows NT domain resources. If you want the clients to take advantage of all Windows NT features (including centralized security and logon scripts), install Windows NT 4.0 clients into the domain. The next two steps describe this process. ▪

Part

II

Ch

12

FIG. 12.25

Setting Windows NT 4.0
TCP/IP configuration
options.

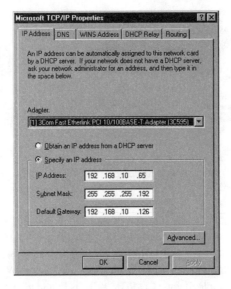

9. To install the workstation into the domain, start Control Panel's Network tool as described in step 1. On the Network property sheet, select the Identification tab. On the Identification page, you see your client's current machine name and the name of the workgroup to which your client belongs.

10. Click the Change button to open the Identification Changes dialog and enter the new domain name you want to join (see Figure 12.26).

FIG. 12.26

Joining the Windows
NT Server domain in
Windows NT Work-
station 4.0.

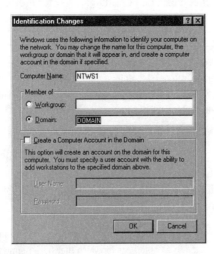

11. You must create for the client a *machine account*, which uniquely identifies your machine to the domain. To do so, you must have Administrator access to the domain. If you're a member of the Domain Administrators group, select the Create a Computer Account in the Domain check box, and then enter your administrator name and password. Then click OK to join the domain. You see a message welcoming you to the domain if the join succeeded.

N O T E If you aren't a member of the Domain Administrators group, a network administrator must create a machine account for the client with the Server Manager utility. The account must exist before you can log on to the domain and is in addition to the user account in the domain. The process for joining the domain is the same as in step 11, except that you don't need to enter an administrative account name at the time you join the domain. ▪

12. After you join the domain, you're asked to restart the workstation to have the changes take effect. The next time the Windows NT logon prompt appears, the Domain text box shows the domain you belong to, plus your workstation name. To log on to the domain, make sure that the domain name appears when you enter your user name and password. If the domain name is missing, type the name in the Domain text box.

Attaching to Domain Resources

After you log on to the domain, you connect to Windows NT Server resources by the same process as Windows 95 or WfWg. Connecting to Windows NT Server 4.0 file and print shares from Windows NT Workstation 4.0 involves the following steps:

1. From the Start menu, choose Programs and Windows NT Explorer to launch Explorer. Double-click the Network Neighborhood icon to display the available servers and their network resources (see Figure 12.27). When you open Network Neighborhood, Explorer displays all the computers in your network domain.

Part II Ch 12

FIG. 12.27
Windows NT Explorer displaying computers on the network.

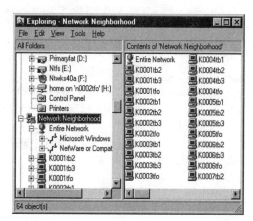

2. Select the name of the server with the share that you want to connect to. The shares for the server appear in Explorer's right pane. Figure 12.28 shows the shared Export, NETLOGON, profiles, and Printers folders of the N0001tfo server share.

FIG. 12.28

Windows NT Explorer displaying server shares in the left pane and share subfolders in the right pane.

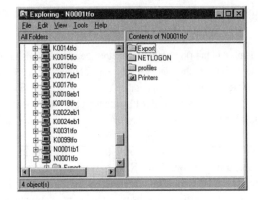

3. From the Tools menu choose Map Network Drive, or click the Map Network Drive button on the toolbar to open the Map Network Drive dialog (see Figure 12.29). (Choose Toolbar from the View menu, if Explorer's toolbar isn't visible.)

FIG. 12.29

Mapping a server file share to a Windows NT Workstation 4.0 logical drive.

4. If you can't connect to the share with your current user name, type the required user name in the Connect As text box. Mark the Reconnect at Logon check box if you want this share connection to be re-established automatically the next time you log on. Click OK to make the connection.

5. To connect to a printer share, from the Start menu choose Settings and Printers to open the Printers window. Double-click the Add Printer icon to start the Add Printer Wizard. Click the Network Printer Server option and then click the Next button to display the Connect to Printer dialog (see Figure 12.30).

6. Browse the available printer resources, and double-click the printer share you want to use. Then click Finish to end the Add Printer Wizard.

FIG. 12.30
Connecting to printers from Windows NT Workstation 4.0.

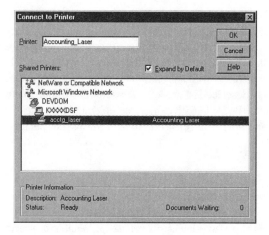

Troubleshooting Connectivity Problems

If you've followed the steps in this section and are still having difficulty connecting your Windows NT 4.0 workstation to Windows NT Server 4.0, the following troubleshooting tips are likely to help you make the connection:

- If you're trying to connect to Windows NT Server shares from Explorer and receive a The Network Path wasn't found message, you have a name resolution problem. If you're using the TCP/IP network protocol, make sure that you have an LMHOSTS or WINS entry for your Windows NT server in your client's TCP/IP Configuration dialog. You can verify that name resolution isn't the problem by issuing the following command from the Start menu's Run command line: **net view\\servername**. This command tells you, regardless of network protocol, whether your client can find the server on the network.

- If you receive access-denied messages to a share or printer resource, make sure that you have the correct permissions to access those resources or files. Windows NT allows user permissions to be placed on shares and printers, as well as files on an NTFS partition. You must have explicit rights, granted by the network administrator, to use these resources.

Previewing the Zero Administration Kit for Windows NT Workstation 4.0 and Windows 95

Cost of PC ownership, which includes hardware, software, training, and support, is a major consideration for larger firms owning thousands or tens of thousands of PCs. There's a remarkable divergence in market research firms' estimates of PC ownership, but even the lowest figures (in the neighborhood of $3,000 per year for Windows 95 clients) exceed what companies want to spend. Oracle, with its diskless Network Computer (NC) designed to run Java applications from a server, gained widespread publicity in 1996. The objective of the NC is to reduce cost of ownership by storing the operating system, system configuration, applications, and user files on the server.

In the fall of 1996, Microsoft and Intel launched a flurry of press releases describing their alternative to the NC, called the Network PC (NetPC). The NetPC, derived from the Simply Interactive PC (SIPC) design that Microsoft first described in April 1996, is a "sealed box" with a fixed disk to store the operating system (Windows 95 or Windows NT) and act as a temporary cache for user files. Along with a preliminary description of the NetPC, the October 1996 announcement vaguely described Microsoft's Zero Administration Windows (ZAW). Intel's Wired for Management (WfM) initiative offers complementary PC client and server management features. Intel and Microsoft released the final NetPC 1.0 specification on April 21, 1997.

ON THE WEB

Version 1.0 of the white paper "Design Guide and System Requirements for the NetPC" is at **http://www.microsoft.com/windows/netpcdg.htm**. You can get details on ZAW from **http://www.microsoft.com/windows/zaw/**. You can download "Wired for Management Baseline Specification" as an Adobe Acrobat file from **http://www.intel.com/managedpc/wired/wfm_spec.htm**.

Microsoft's ZAW involves the following basic elements:

- *Automatic system update and application installation.* The operating system automatically updates itself on booting. The latest patches, service packs, and drivers install automatically from the server or the Internet.

- *Automatic Desktop.* This feature provides users with a choice of productivity and custom applications to be installed automatically from the server.

- *State on the server.* Users' data and configuration files are stored automatically on the server, with an optional local copy. This way, mobile users have access to their data from multiple desktop or portable PCs.

- *Central administration and system lock-down.* Central administrators control server-stored client configuration through user profiles. Users see only menu choices allowed by administrators and can't modify the desktop or gain access to other UI components. Thus, a user's Start menu might include only Programs, Help, and Shut Down choices. Administrators configure the users' Programs submenu to limit applications to those needed by individual users or groups of users, such as Internet Explorer and individual components of Microsoft Office.

Microsoft announced in March 1997 a Zero Administration Kit (ZAK) implementation of ZAW for Windows NT Workstation 4.0. ZAK leverages the existing user profiles and system policies capability of Windows NT 4.0, which are more robust and secure than those of Windows 95. Microsoft also promises a ZAK for Windows 9x.

ON THE WEB

You can get updated on ZAK availability at **http://www.microsoft.com/windows/zak/**.

CAUTION

The Run Only Allowed Windows Application option of System Policy Editor has a security hole when you install Office 97 on workstations. Users can open Msinfo32.exe from the Help menu's About... command of an Office 97 component, and then choose Run from the File menu to open Microsoft System Information's Run Application dialog. This dialog gives users access to Control Panel, the Registry Editor, and other local or network applications. Thus, you should avoid installing Msinfo.exe and Msinfo32.exe on workstations subject to application restrictions.

 ON THE WEB

For further information about the Msinfo.exe and Msinfo32.exe problem, see the Microsoft Knowledge Base article at **http://www.microsoft.com/kb/articles/q156/6/99.htm**.

 When Windows NT 4.0 starts, the Systray.exe program provides the arrow pointing to the taskbar's Start button and displays the Click Here To Start message. To avoid a This operation has been canceled due to restrictions in effect on this computer error message on client startup, be sure to include Systray.exe in the System Policy's list of allowed executables.

Connecting Macintosh Clients

Windows NT Server 4.0 includes Services for Macintosh (SfM), which allows users of Apple Macintosh computers running System 6.0.7 or higher to use folders and printers shared by Windows NT domains. File services for Macintosh, which let Mac users store and retrieve files on the Windows NT server, are provided only from partitions formatted as NTFS.

Adding Services for Macintosh on Windows NT Server

Following are the steps for installing Services for Macintosh on a Windows NT 4.0 server:

1. Insert the Windows NT Server 4.0 CD-ROM in the server's CD-ROM drive.

2. Open the Control Panel and double-click the Network tool.

3. On the Network property sheet, click the Services tab.

4. On the Services page of the Network property sheet, click the Add button to display the Select Network Service dialog. In the Network Service list, scroll to and select the Services for Macintosh item (see Figure 12.31). Click OK to close the dialog and open the Windows NT Setup dialog.

5. Type the path to the installation files for your processor type on the CD-ROM in the text box of the Windows NT Setup dialog. For Intel-based servers, the location is *d*:\i386, where *d*: is the CD-ROM drive letter. Click Continue to copy the files.

Part
II

Ch
12

FIG. 12.31

Starting installation of Services for Macintosh.

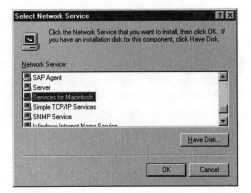

6. After copying is complete, click the Close button of the Network property sheet. Windows NT starts the AppleTalk network protocol and opens the Microsoft AppleTalk Protocol Properties sheet (see Figure 12.32). The default adapter displays the network adapter in your server to which AppleTalk is bound. If you have Macintosh clients connected to the specified network adapter, Windows NT finds and uses the default AppleTalk zone. If not, follow the directions in step 7 to install the Windows NT server as a seed router, and provide the router with your zone information.

7. Selecting the Routing page lets you enable AppleTalk routing (see Figure 12.33). You must enable routing if you have multiple network adapters in your server, each of which is running AppleTalk for individual network segments; there's no other seed router for that segment; and you want to enable AppleTalk communication between the segments.

   For each network interface that appears in the Adapter drop-down list, choose the AppleTalk Phase 2 network number and the default zone. Mark the Use This Router to Seed the Network check box to enable AppleTalk route seeding. Usually, there's one seed router per AppleTalk segment, and all other AppleTalk routers listen for the seed; the seed tells that segment what AppleTalk Phase 2 network address and zone to use.

8. After you complete configuration of AppleTalk network options and click OK, you're prompted to restart your system. Click Yes to shut down and restart.

9. After the server starts up, two new services—File Server for Macintosh and Print Server for Macintosh—are installed. You can verify installation of these services by using the Control Panel's Services tool.

N O T E AppleTalk Phase 2 network addresses are expressed as a range, such as 10–12. Each number in the range supports up to 253 nodes, so a range of 10–12 supports 3×253, or 759 AppleTalk clients. Range values must be unique and can't overlap. Accepted range values are 1 to 62579.

When you assign a range, choose the minimum number of networks you need. If a given segment has only 10 Mac clients, for example, choose a network range of 20–20, which supports up to 253 clients on a single segment. ▪

FIG. 12.32
The General page of the Microsoft AppleTalk Protocol Properties sheet.

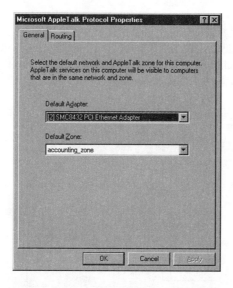

FIG. 12.33
The Routing page of the Microsoft AppleTalk Protocol Properties sheet.

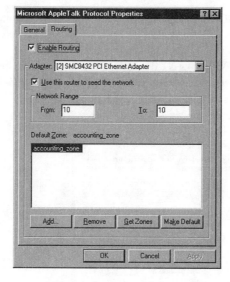

Part
II

Ch
12

Setting Up Macintosh Clients

Clients must run Macintosh System 6.0.7 or higher to access Windows NT Server resources. You don't need to install special software for basic file and printer sharing on the Windows NT network.

From the Macintosh client's Chooser, select AppleShare; any Windows NT Server running Services for Macintosh (SfM) and containing a Mac-accessible volume appears (see Figure 12.34). Click OK and provide a user name and password, which is passed to the Windows NT Server domain account database for authentication. When authenticated, the client can access available volumes based on the user's permissions.

FIG. 12.34
Viewing available
Windows NT servers
running SfM from the
Macintosh Chooser.

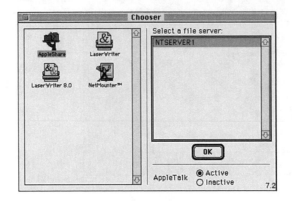

When you log on from a Macintosh client to the Windows NT server running SfM, the Apple User Authentication Module (UAM) handles network security. Microsoft provides a UAM that supports Windows NT 4.0 authentication and encryption. The Microsoft UAM provides greater security and recognizes the Windows NT domain name as a preface to the user logon name (for example, *ntdomain*\joesmith instead of joesmith). This way, a Macintosh client can connect to Windows NT servers that are running SfM and exist in multiple Windows NT domains. Figure 12.35 shows an example of a Macintosh installed with the Microsoft UAM.

FIG. 12.35
The logon screen of a
Macintosh with the
Microsoft UAM installed.

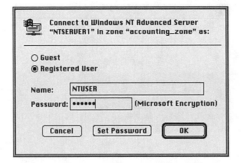

The Microsoft UAM is installed on your Windows NT server drive when you install Services for Macintosh. By default, SfM creates a Macintosh-accessible folder in your system partition named *d*:\Microsoft UAM Volume and a subfolder named AppleShare Folder. Follow these steps to install the Microsoft UAM on your Macintosh clients:

1. From the Macintosh Chooser, select AppleShare. When the Windows NT server running SfM appears, log on by using the default Apple UAM by providing an existing domain user name.

2. Mount the Windows NT server's Microsoft UAM Volume on the Macintosh client. Open the volume's folder to display the AppleShare folder. Open the AppleShare folder and drag the Microsoft UAM file from the Windows NT Server volume to the AppleShare folder on your Macintosh's System Folder. If you don't find an AppleShare folder within the System Folder, drag the whole AppleShare folder from the Windows NT server to the System Folder. Restart the Macintosh client for the changes to take effect.

Accessing Windows NT Server Resources from the Macintosh

After installing Services for Macintosh on your Windows NT 4.0 server, a number of new services, tools, and menu choices have been added to your standard Windows NT utilities. For example, Control Panel has a new MacFile tool, which allows you to view and control the use of SfM on your server. The MacFile tool has four buttons: Users, Volumes, Files, and Attributes (see Figure 12.36).

FIG. 12.36
The opening dialog of Control Panel's MacFile tool.

The following list describes the purpose of the buttons:

- *Users* displays the Macintosh Users on *SERVERNAME* dialog, which lets you view the Macintosh clients connected to a server, disconnect them, or send them a message (see Figure 12.37).

FIG. 12.37
The Macintosh Users on *SERVERNAME* dialog of the MacFile tool.

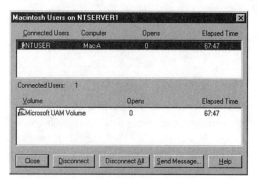

Part
II

Ch

12

■ *Volumes* opens the Macintosh-Accessible Volumes on *SERVERNAME* dialog, which lets you view the current Mac-accessible volumes defined on your server and which clients are connected to the volumes (see Figure 12.38).

FIG. 12.38

The Macintosh-
Accessible Volumes on
SERVERNAME dialog.

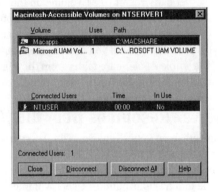

■ *Files* displays the Files Opened by Macintosh Users dialog, showing you which files are open on your server, by whom, and whether the files are locked.

■ *Attributes* opens the MacFile Attributes of *SERVERNAME* dialog (see Figure 12.39), which lets you control parameters of SfM, such as whether the Macintosh clients see a logon message, whether the clients are required to use Microsoft Authentication, and how many sessions a particular user can run.

FIG. 12.39

The MacFile Attributes
of *SERVERNAME* dialog.

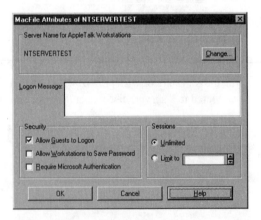

After loading SfM, Server Manager now contains a new MacFile menu choice (see Figure 12.40). From the MacFile menu, you can create new Macintosh-accessible volumes, set permissions, and assign associations. Associations for the Macintosh are similar to File Manager associations in Windows; for instance, .DOC files are associated with the Microsoft Word application. You provide a similar association for Macintosh files stored on your Windows NT server.

FIG. 12.40
Server Manager's
MacFile menu
commands.

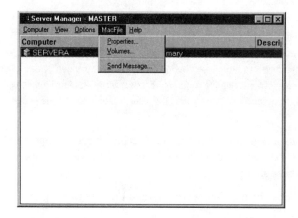

Macintosh files have two "forks": the *data fork* contains the data part of the file, and the *resource fork* contains information about the associated application and the application's icon. To set up Macintosh associations, you must start the familiar File Manager. From the Start menu, choose Run and type the command `winfile`. Next, choose Associate from WinFile's MacFile menu to associate resource fork information with Windows NT file extensions, so that files with extensions have the proper appearance and application association when viewed on the Macintosh client.

To provide printing services to your Mac users, you have two options: connecting a printer to the Windows NT server's parallel or serial port, or connecting an AppleTalk-compliant printer directly to your network.

In the first case (connecting the printer to a port on the Windows NT server running SfM), you can use any printer type. The Print Service for Macintosh converts incoming Macintosh client PostScript jobs to the print language supported by the printer. The Macintosh clients connect to the network printer through the Chooser, as is the case for all Macintosh printing operations. Both Macintosh and PC clients share the same printer(s).

The second case requires an AppleTalk-based, network-attached printer. Such printers are connected to the network via LocalTalk, Ethernet, or Token Ring connections.

N O T E LocalTalk is the native MAC-Layer protocol that came standard for many years in early Macintoshes. You can get ISA bus-based LocalTalk cards for your Intel-based Windows NT server if you need to use LocalTalk to connect clients to your server running SfM. For example, Daystar Digital makes a LocalTalk adapter that's compatible with a Windows NT server. Check the Windows NT 4.0 Hardware Compatibility List for other supported LocalTalk cards. ■

Windows NT Server's SfM provides support for networked AppleTalk printers. Normally, Macintosh clients printing to network-attached Macintosh printers spool the print job on a local Macintosh print spooler, which runs on the client. If you must support printing to networked AppleTalk printers on Windows NT Server 4.0, you must disable print spooling on the Macintosh client.

Part
II

Ch
12

> **CAUTION**
>
> Make sure that you disable spooling on the Macintosh client by running Chooser, selecting the LaserWriter or appropriate printer driver, and turning off background printing. If you don't disable background printing and if more than one client is accessing the Windows NT Server-based AppleTalk printer, print jobs spooled locally will conflict with those spooling on the server. The result will be chaos at the printer.

After you disable background printing, your Macintosh clients share the Windows NT server's print queue with PC clients. To set up a Windows NT Server 4.0 print queue for an AppleTalk printer, follow these steps:

1. From the Start menu, choose Settings and Printers to bring up the Printers window (see Figure 12.41).

FIG. 12.41

Adding a new AppleTalk printer from the Printers window.

2. Double-click the Add Printer icon to start the Add Printer Wizard, select the My Computer button, and click Next.

3. In the next Add Printer Wizard dialog, you see a list of printer ports to use (see Figure 12.42). If you're adding a printer that's connected to your Windows NT server via a parallel or serial port, mark the check box next to the appropriate port, click Next, and skip to step 5.

FIG. 12.42

Selecting a printer port from the Add Printer Wizard.

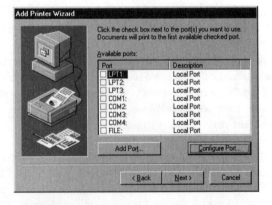

4. If you're adding a network-attached AppleTalk printer, click Add Port to open the Printer Ports dialog. Highlight AppleTalk Printing Devices and click OK. The Available AppleTalk Printing Devices dialog appears (see Figure 12.43), listing all AppleTalk zones available on your Windows NT server. Select the AppleTalk printer you want to use by double-clicking the zone and the printer name; then click OK to close the dialog.

FIG. 12.43

Selecting a network-attached AppleTalk printer.

5. The next Add Printer Wizard dialog (see Figure 12.44) prompts you to specify the make and model of printer you're connecting to and click Next.

FIG. 12.44

Specifying the make and model of your AppleTalk printer.

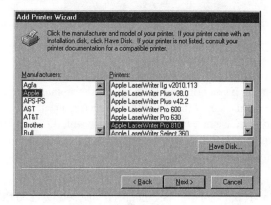

Part
II

Ch
12

6. The next Add Printer Wizard dialog asks you to enter the printer name. Your users will see this descriptive name when they browse printer resources (for example, *8th floor LaserWriter*). Click Next after entering a name.

7. The next dialog lets you set up the printer to be shared by Microsoft Windows clients as well as Macintosh. Unless you plan on supporting these Windows clients on this printer, select the Not Shared button and then click Next.

8. The final dialog asks whether you want to print a test page after the printer is set up. Choose Yes or No and click Finish.

9. The Copying Files – Files Needed dialog appears next, prompting you for the path to the Windows NT Server CD-ROM. On Intel-based systems, enter *d:*\i386, where *d:* is the CD-ROM drive letter.

10. After the appropriate printer drivers are copied from the CD-ROM, the properties sheet appears for your new printer (see Figure 12.45). Here, you can add comments, change configuration, set security on the printer, or modify the printer scheduling properties. Click OK to complete the printer's configuration.

FIG. 12.45

Displaying the Macintosh printer's properties sheet.

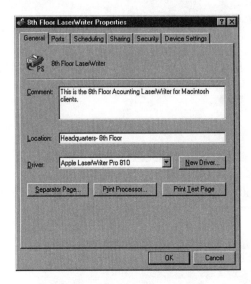

11. The Print Server for Macintosh service is installed with the System account as the Startup user name. If you print to a network printer, you need to change the System account to a domain account that has network access. From the User Manager for Domains utility, create a new user account for use with the Print Server for Macintosh service (you might call the account MacPrintUser).

   ▶ **See** "Managing User Accounts," **p. 447**

12. Use the newly created account to assign permissions to your network-attached AppleTalk printer(s). From the Start menu, choose Settings and then Printers; then highlight your AppleTalk printer in the Printers window. Then choose Properties from the File menu, click the Security tab, and click the Permissions button to assign your new user account access to this printer through the Printer Permissions dialog (see Figure 12.46).

13. From the Printer Permissions dialog, click the Add button; from the Add Users and Groups dialog, click Show Users, and then scroll to the user account defined in step 11.

Assign the user Full Control rights to the printer in the Type of Access drop-down list (see Figure 12.47). Click OK three times to eventually close the property sheet.

FIG. 12.46

Adding user permissions to the AppleTalk printer.

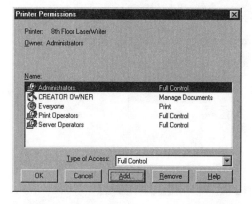

FIG. 12.47

Assigning a user macprintuser Full Control rights to the printer.

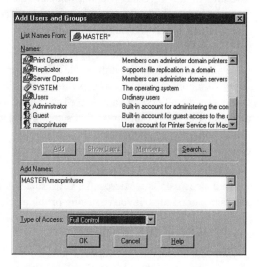

14. You need to assign the new user account to the Print Server for Macintosh service. From the Start menu, choose Settings and Control Panel, and then double-click the Services tool. In the Services dialog, scroll to Print Server for Macintosh, click Startup, click the This Account option, and then type the user account name you created in step 11 in the This Account text box. Enter and confirm the password for the account (see Figure 12.48), and then click OK to complete the change.

If you've installed Macintosh support on a Novell NetWare server, you're certain to find that Windows NT Server's SfM is much easier and more intuitive than Novell's approach.

FIG. 12.48
Modifying the account for the Print Server for Macintosh service.

Troubleshooting Services for Macintosh

If you follow the steps described in the preceding section, you can quickly and painlessly add file and print services for your Macintosh clients. If you have problems after SfM is installed, however, here's a list of common problems you might encounter and their possible solutions:

- Perhaps the most common area of confusion is AppleTalk network numbering and zones. If your Windows NT server isn't the only AppleTalk router on a given segment, make sure that the network configurations you apply to the Windows NT Server adapter correspond with those already defined on your AppleTalk router. For example, if an Ethernet segment contains an AppleTalk router that's configured with AppleTalk network number 10–10 and a zone called Accounting, make sure that your Windows NT server's Ethernet adapter connected to that segment has the same network number and zone.

- Although it's an optional step, installing Microsoft's UAM that's provided with SfM on your Macintosh clients is a good idea. If you're having problems authenticating from your Macintosh client to your Windows NT server, installing the MS-UAM likely will provide a solution to the problem.

- If printer jobs from your Macintosh clients overwrite jobs from PC clients printing to the same printer, make sure that you've disabled Background Printing on all your Macintosh clients that are using the AppleTalk printers defined in Windows NT Server.

- If print jobs get to the Windows NT spooler and stop there, ensure that you've set up the Print Server for Macintosh service with a Startup user account defined in your Windows NT domain. Also make sure that the user account has been granted permission to the printer (see steps 11 through 14 of the earlier section "Accessing Windows NT Server Resources from the Macintosh").

ON THE WEB

For additional troubleshooting help with SfM, check the "Services for Macintosh Troubleshooter" Web page at **http://www.microsoft.com/ntserversupport/content/nt4troubleshoot/sfm/**.

From Here...

This chapter discussed connecting various client computers to a Windows NT Server 4.0 network. Windows 3.1+, which uses the DOS-based Microsoft Network Client that comes with Windows NT Server 4.0 to provide network access to Windows NT Server resources, is limited in networking capability and flexibility. Windows for Workgroups 3.11, which uses Windows-based drivers, provides more networking flexibility to the client, including support for logon scripts and integrated resource-sharing options. Clients running Windows NT Workstation 4.0 provide the greatest networking flexibility and robustness by better integrating with the Windows NT Server 4.0 network.

The chapter closed with a description of the support provided by Windows NT Server 4.0 for Macintosh file and print services, including the steps to install Services for Macintosh on Windows NT 4.0 servers. Also discussed were the configuration options for printer setup on a Windows NT 4.0 server to allow both Mac and PC clients to use AppleTalk-based networked printers.

The following chapters contain information relating to or complementing the contents of this chapter:

- Chapter 11, "Configuring Windows 95 Clients for Networking," describes how to specify the parameters required for clients that use the TCP/IP protocol to connect to Windows 4.0 servers.
- Chapter 13, "Managing User and Group Accounts," describes how to optimize the structure of and manage client accounts on Windows NT 4.0 servers.
- Chapter 18, "Integrating Windows NT with NetWare and UNIX," discusses how to optimize the use of Windows NT Server 4.0 with Novell NetWare and UNIX networks.

Part
II

Ch
12

Administering a Secure Network

13 Managing User and Group Accounts   441

14 Sharing and Securing Network Resources   483

15 Optimizing Network Server Performance   529

16 Troubleshooting Network Problems   559

CHAPTER 13

Managing User and Group Accounts

The fundamental purpose of a network operating system (NOS) is to create a productive environment for users while maintaining a high level of security. This also is the primary goal of all network administrators.

Windows NT Server 4.0 qualifies as an advanced NOS because it not only provides file directory and print services to its users, but also functions as an application server for Microsoft BackOffice and other server-based applications that run as services on Windows NT. The advanced security features of Windows NT Server have the potential to make network administration a very complex and demanding occupation. Fortunately, Microsoft provides a powerful and flexible tool, User Manager for Domains, for managing the users of a Windows NT Server network. User Manager for Domains lets network administrators create and manage individual user accounts and user groups, and manage the security policies that affect the user accounts and groups. ■

User accounts

Add and administer user accounts on a Windows NT Server network.

User groups

Employ user groups to manage the rights and privileges for a large number of users.

Security policies

Manage the security policies for user accounts and user groups.

Administrative Wizards

Use Windows NT Server 4.0's Administrative Wizards to simplify the process of adding new users and user groups.

The *Windows NT Server 4.0 Resource Kit*

Take full advantage of Resource Kit User Administration Utilities.

Defining Account and Group Terminology

User accounts are the foundation on which network security is built; groups define collections of users. The following terms are basic to managing user and group accounts:

■ *User accounts* define all the information necessary for users to connect to the Windows NT network. Each user account includes the user name and password required to log on to the network. An account also defines the user groups to which each user belongs and, most importantly, the rights and permissions to access system resources granted to each user. User accounts contain additional information, such as the user environment profile, a list of logon workstations, and a schedule of logon hours.

■ A *user group* is a management tool that collects user accounts into a named group. You assign rights and permissions to user groups in a manner similar to that for user accounts. You can grant user accounts membership in a user group. When you grant a user account membership in a user group, the account inherits all the rights and privileges of that group. The overall concept of Windows NT's user groups is similar to the group security implemented by database management systems, such as Microsoft SQL Server and Microsoft Access.

■ A *domain* is a network concept that defines a collection of shared resources—such as file and application servers, printers, CD-ROM drives, modems, and other devices—that are centrally managed and advertised to potential users. Only users who've successfully logged on to the domain and been granted access to the resources by means of a set of permissions can use the resources. Individual domains usually are defined by geographic location (such as North America) or by function (such as accounting). Small networks in a single location ordinarily have only one domain.

■ A *global group* is a collection of user accounts within a single domain. A global group can't contain other groups and can include only user accounts from the domain in which the group was created. Global groups can be assigned privileges in domains that trust the domain in which the group was created. This allows global groups to be assigned privileges anywhere on the network. Trusted domains are one of the subjects of Chapter 17, "Distributing Network Services with Domains."

■ A *local group* can be assigned privileges only in the domain in which the local group was created. Unlike a global group, a local group can contain users and global groups. Local groups let you collect groups from several domains and manage them as a single group in the local domain. When privileges are assigned to a local group, all users and global groups in the local group inherit these privileges.

Working with User Manager for Domains

You can employ User Manager for Domains to manage accounts within any domain that users have administrative access to. Individual users have administrative access if they're members of any of the three Windows NT user groups listed in Table 13.1.

Table 13.1 User Groups with Permission to Administer User Accounts and Groups

User Group	Description
Administrators	A local group whose members can perform all user and group management functions.
Domain Admins	A global group that, in most cases, is a member of the Administrators local group. Users in the Domain Admins group are automatically given local Administrator privileges.
Account Operators	A restricted account whose members can manage most properties of user accounts and groups. Members of this group *can't* manage the following Windows NT Server groups: Administrators, Domain Admins, Account Operators, Server Operators, Print Operators, and Backup Operators. Members of this group also can't manage the account of domain administrators and can't alter domain security policies.

The following sections describe how to take full advantage of the User Manager for Domains application.

Starting User Manager for Domains

You can start User Manager for Domains (called *User Manager* from here on for brevity) from the taskbar or from the command line.

To start User Manager from the taskbar's Start menu, choose Programs, Administrative Tools, and User Manager for Domains to open User Manager's window. By default, information for the domain where your user account is defined appears in the window (see Figure 13.1).

FIG. 13.1
Viewing user information for the default domain in User Manager's main window.

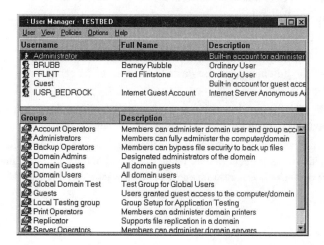

Part
III

Ch
13

N O T E   All Microsoft Networking products—including Windows for Workgroups, Windows NT Workstation, and Windows NT Server—use the Universal Naming Convention (UNC) to indicate a specific server. This requires that the server name be prefaced by two backslashes, as in \\fred. You can display a specific server in User Manager only if the computer maintains its own security database; otherwise, the domain information for your user account is displayed. If the specified server is a primary or backup domain controller, the domain information is displayed instead of that for the specific server. For more information on domains and security databases, see Chapter 17, "Distributing Network Services with Domains." ■

Starting Multiple Instances of User Manager

Unlike applications that are limited to a single instance, such as Windows NT Explorer, User Manager allows multiple simultaneous instances. Multiple instances of User Manager is a valuable time-saving feature for administrators of large networks or multiple domains.

The most effective method for running multiple instances of User Manager is to create program icons for each domain or computer that you administer. Each program icon contains the name of the domain or computer as the command-line argument to the program command line. By creating multiple instances of User Manager in this manner, you can administer each domain simply by double-clicking the program icon.

The easiest method for creating multiple copies of User Manager with assigned domains is to follow these steps:

1. From the Start menu, choose Programs and then Explorer to open an instance of the Windows NT Explorer.

2. Open the Administrative Tools folder by moving to \Winnt\profiles\All Users\Start Menu\Programs, and then double-clicking the Administrative Tools folder.

3. Select the User Manager shortcut icon (see Figure 13.2).

4. From Explorer's Edit menu, choose Copy.

5. Select the destination folder. To create an additional Start menu item in the Administrative Tools folder, don't change folders.

6. From the Edit menu, choose Paste to add a second User Manager shortcut to the selected folder.

7. Right-click the new User Manager shortcut icon. From the pop-up menu, choose Properties to open the User Manager for Domains Properties sheet.

8. Edit the command-line entry in the Target text box by adding a space and the domain name or the computer name to the end of the command line, as in `%SystemRoot%\system32\usrmgr.exe domainname` (see Figure 13.3).

FIG. 13.2

Selecting the User Manager shortcut in the Administrative Tools folder.

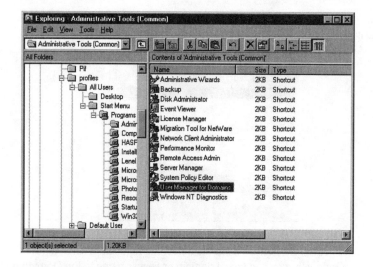

FIG. 13.3

Modifying the properties of the new User Manager shortcut to open to a specified domain.

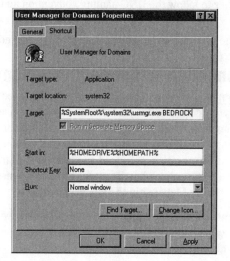

Selecting a New Domain with User Manager

If you choose to manage multiple domains of computers from the same instance of User Manager, changing domains is an easy task. To select a new domain or server, follow these steps:

1. From the User menu, choose Select Domain to open the Select Domain dialog (see Figure 13.4).

FIG. 13.4

Choosing the domain with the Select Domain dialog.

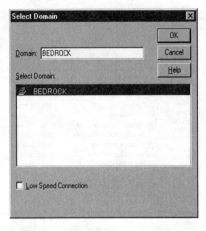

2. Select a new domain from the Select Domain list by clicking the domain name item. Optionally, you can type a domain or server name in the Domain text box. If you enter a server name, remember to follow the UNC naming convention and precede the name with two backslashes.

3. Click OK to display the user and group information for the selected domain or server.

Using a Low-Speed Connection to Connect to a Domain

If you're administering a domain or a server through a low-speed connection such as Switched-56, partial T1, or a modem, you achieve better performance and response if User Manager's Low Speed Connection setting is enabled. When you administer a domain, the lists of user accounts, groups, or computers are displayed. The low bandwidth of some WAN connections impedes the speed at which the lists can be produced and managed. Marking the Select Domain dialog's Low Speed Connection check box improves the management of remote domains by restricting the operation of User Manager in the following ways:

■ The list of user accounts isn't displayed in User Manager's main window, and the User menu's Select Users command is disabled. You can manage all user accounts and create new accounts, but you must specify the name of the account.

■ The list of user groups isn't displayed in User Manager's main window. You can create and manage local groups by making the appropriate choice from the User menu. You *can't* create or manage global groups. You can manage global group memberships indirectly by setting the group memberships through the individual user accounts.

■ All View menu items are disabled.

User Manager remembers the last 20 domains or servers previously administered. The Low Speed Connection setting is set or reset automatically when one of the last 20 domains or computers is selected. The last connection speed setting is applied whether or not the Low Speed Connection check box is marked.

To start User Manager in a low- or high-speed mode, you can include the command-line parameter /l (low speed) or /h (high speed) in the Run dialog, from the command prompt, or in the command-line entry of a User Manager shortcut.

Managing User Accounts

Every user of a Windows NT Server network must have a user account, which consists of all the information that defines a user to the Windows NT network. The user account defines the resources on Windows NT computers and domains that the user can access.

A user account consists of the typical user name and password, as well as how, when, and where a user can attach to the network; what resources the user can access; and what security rights the user has for the accessible resources. The user account also defines the local and global groups of which the user is a member.

> **N O T E** When upgrading an existing Windows NT 3.x server, the user accounts and groups are preserved during the upgrade. For example, a clean Windows NT 4.0 installation doesn't contain the Windows NT 3.x Power Users default group. When upgrading an existing server, this group is preserved and migrated into the new Windows NT Server 4.0 installation. ■

The following sections describe the built-in user accounts, how to add new accounts, and how to modify account properties to take full advantage of Windows NT Server 4.0's support for networked users.

Managing the Built-In User Accounts

When you install Windows NT, two built-in accounts—Administrator and Guest—are established when a domain is created. Unlike named user accounts, the Administrator and Guest accounts can't be deleted. These two accounts are installed on the primary domain controller.

The Administrator Account   The Administrator account is set up by default to allow the installer to manage and configure the Windows NT Server 4.0 software immediately after installation. The user who manages the domain's overall configuration uses the Administrator account. The Administrator account has more control over the domain and its servers than any other user account on the Windows NT network.

During installation of the primary domain controller, the Windows NT Server 4.0 Setup program prompts for the password of the built-in Administrator account. Remember and protect this password. If you forget or lose the Administrator password, the Administrator account is unusable.

> **N O T E** After you install the primary domain controller, it's good practice to create another account that contains administrative-level privileges. After you create this account, use it to manage the domain, and reserve the built-in Administrative account for emergency purposes. ■

Part

III

Ch

13

The Administrator account is added as a member of the following built-in user groups:

- Administrators (local group)
- Domain Admins (global group)
- Domain Users (global group)

The Administrator account can't be removed from these built-in groups. Detailed descriptions of these user groups appear later in the section "Managing User Groups."

N O T E The Administrator account is the most powerful user on the network, having total access to and control over all resources within the domain for which the account is created. To create a user account with the same power as an Administrator, the user account must be included in all three groups that the Administrator is a member of.

One strategy that's often used in large networks is to assign two user accounts to network administrators—one with administrative permissions and one with only user permissions. The administrative account is used only when performing network management, and the user account is utilized at all other times. The objective is to prevent inadvertent changes to network configuration as a result of conventional user activities.

Some Administrator capabilities include managing security policies; establishing domain trust relationships; creating, modifying, and deleting user accounts; creating shared directories and printers; modifying operating system software; and installing and updating devices and partition disks. This is only a small sample of the capabilities available to an administrative account with full Administrator privileges.

The Guest Account The Guest account is at the opposite end of the permissions spectrum from the Administrator account. The Guest account is provided for occasional or one-time users. The built-in Guest account is a part of the Domain Guests built-in group and inherits a very limited set of permissions from that group.

N O T E The Guest account isn't the same as the Internet Guest account, IUSER_*SERVERNAME*, that's created when you install Internet Information Server (IIS). The Internet Guest account allows anonymous logon to the server on which IIS is installed and, by default, includes membership in the Domain Users and Guests groups. If you're using IIS for a private intranet, you can delete the Internet Guest account. Additional information on Internet and intranet accounts is provided in Chapter 20, "Setting Up Internet Information Server 4.0," and Chapter 21, "Administering Intranet and World Wide Web Sites."

Although the Guest account can't be removed from the system, it is disabled by default during installation. This means that you must explicitly enable the account for it to be used. In practice, this account usually is enabled only if some network resources must be accessible by individuals without formal accounts that enable file and other resource sharing. For example, persons who don't need to access server files might be allowed to use the Guest account to use a shared printer.

N O T E The Guest account initially contains an empty password, which allows users from untrusted domains to log on to your domain as Guest and access any resources that are accessible to the Guest account. An administrative account can change the Guest account to add a password, if desired. ■

Adding New User Accounts

Your network isn't useful without users, and it's equally unsecure and unproductive if you use only the two built-in accounts. This means that new user accounts must be added for each network user, with the possible exception of Guest users. Following are the two methods for adding a new user account:

- ■ You can create a new user account from scratch.
- ■ You can copy a new user account from an existing user account and make the appropriate changes to specify information specific to the new user.

Creating a New User Account with User Manager   Add a new user account by choosing New User from User Manager's User menu to open the New User dialog. Fill in the dialog's text boxes, mark the appropriate security check boxes, and click the Add button to create the account. Figure 13.5 shows the New User dialog with text box entries, before security options are selected.

FIG. 13.5

Creating a new account with the New User dialog.

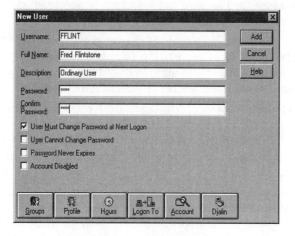

Part

III

Ch

13

The New User dialog contains many controls to which you must assign values:

- ■ *Username.* Each network user must have a unique user name. The user name can contain up to 20 characters. You can use any combination of upper- and lowercase letters, numbers, or punctuation, except for the following characters:

      = + [ ] / \ ; : < > ? * " ' !

N O T E   The user name entered in the New User dialog is used whenever the user logs on to a Windows NT computer or a Windows NT network. The user name is case-sensitive and must be entered with the exact spelling as when the account was created. Establishing a consistent naming policy for all users benefits network administrators and network users.

You can use several common naming conventions, such as the first initial of the first name with the last three letters of the last name (for example, Fred Flintstone would have a user name of ffli). Microsoft uses the first name, followed by as many letters of the last name as are required to create an unique user name, which also is used as the employee's Internet e-mail alias (*firstlast@microsoft.com*). Whatever naming scheme you choose, make sure that it's consistent.

- *Full Name.* Use this optional text box to enter the full descriptive name of the user for which the account is being created—for example, Fred Flintstone. As with the user name, the full name is better if you use a consistent method of full names, such as first name, last name, or last name, first name.

- *Description.* You can use the optional Description text box to further identify the user of this account—for example, a user's department or title.

- *Password and Confirm Password.* The Password text box is used with the Username when users log on from a PC running Windows NT Workstation or Windows 95 with Windows NT Server authentication. You can leave the Password text box empty until users enter their password, but this leaves the network temporarily in a very unsecure state. If you leave the Password text box empty, be sure to select the User Must Change Password at Next Logon check box.

  The Password text box is limited to 14 characters and is case-sensitive. It displays encrypted text as a row of asterisks (*). To make sure that the password is entered correctly, you must fill in the Confirm Password text box with a password identical to what's in the Password text box before you can add the account.

- *User Must Change Password at Next Logon.* If this check box is marked, users must change their password the first time the account is used or the next time they log on to the domain. This check box, marked by default, should be used if users aren't present when their accounts are being created or you can't give them a password directly.

  When you mark the User Must Change Password at Next Logon check box, the initial password must be either blank or something very intuitive to the user, such as the company name or the word *password.* This option allows users to customize their own passwords without administrative assistance. Be sure to verify that users immediately log on and change their password to avoid a potential security breach.

- *User Cannot Change Password.* The User Cannot Change Password option is primarily used when you administer the passwords for user accounts centrally. This option is used primarily if several users share the same account or in very secure networks. This option also is specified for the Internet Guest account, if present.

  Select the User Cannot Change Password option only if users aren't allowed to enter their own password and you assign passwords to users.

■ *Password Never Expires.* When this option is selected, users aren't required to change passwords periodically. Enabling this option isn't a good security practice, however; users should change their passwords on a regular basis, such as quarterly or even monthly. In certain cases—such as a rarely used account like the Administrator—you might want to use this option to avoid forgetting the password.

The Password Never Expires option is also used when security isn't a high priority compared to user convenience. Most users like to keep one password to avoid forgetting a new password. When this option is used, the check box User Must Change Password at Next Logon is cleared.

■ *Account Disabled.* In certain instances, a user account must be disabled. Selecting this check box prevents a user from logging on to the network until the check box is cleared. Some of the reasons for disabling a user account are as follows:

- Creating a template account that's used only to create new accounts by copying (a process explained in the following section)
- Disabling an account temporarily while a person is on vacation or extended leave

Understanding the Additional Account Properties   When adding a new user, a set of six buttons appears at the bottom of the New User dialog (refer to Figure 13.5): Groups, Profile, Hours, Logon To, Account, and Dialin. These buttons let you specify additional properties for user accounts. These properties are explained later in the section "Managing User Account Properties."

Copying a User Account   To ease the task of setting up new user accounts, User Manager lets you copy an existing user account as a template to create a new account. In large networks, you create template accounts that contain all the attributes of a user in a particular department. When a new user account must be created, the appropriate template account is copied and the appropriate account information is changed to reflect the details pertinent to the new user.

N O T E   As noted earlier, template accounts usually are disabled so that users can't access the network or network resources through them. ■

To copy a user account, follow these steps:

1. From User Manager's window, select the user account to be copied.
2. Choose Copy from the User menu to display the Copy of *Username* dialog.
3. Enter the appropriate account information for the new user account (see Figure 13.6).
4. Click the Add button to create the new user account.

Modifying User Accounts

User Manager lets you modify user accounts individually or modify multiple accounts simultaneously.

Part
III

Ch
13

FIG. 13.6

Copying an existing user account to a new user account.

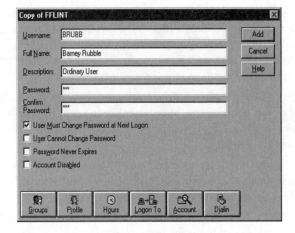

An individual user account can be modified by

- Double-clicking a user account item in the Username list of User Manager's window

- Selecting a user account in User Manager's window, and then either pressing Enter or choosing Properties from the User menu

Either method displays the User Properties sheet (see Figure 13.7), which looks similar to the New User dialog. The only significant difference between the User Properties sheet and the New User dialog is the addition of an Account Locked Out check box, which is used to clear a locked-out account. This check box is disabled unless the account is now locked out because of an excessive number of incorrect logon attempts.

FIG. 13.7

The User Properties sheet for modifying individual user accounts.

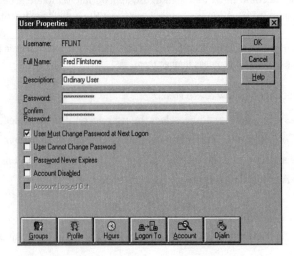

You can modify multiple user accounts simultaneously by any one of the following methods:

■ Select a range of accounts by selecting a starting point in the list of user accounts and dragging the mouse pointer over the accounts to select.

■ Select a range of accounts by clicking a starting point in the list of user accounts and Shift+clicking the last account in the range.

■ Select multiple individual accounts by pressing the Ctrl key and then individually clicking each account to modify.

■ Choose Select Users from the Users menu to open the Select Users dialog (see Figure 13.8). In this dialog, you can select or deselect all users assigned to a particular group within the domain you're administering. Multiple groups can't be simultaneously selected or deselected in this dialog.

FIG. 13.8
Selecting users belonging to a particular group.

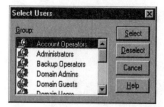

After selecting the user accounts to be modified, press Enter or choose Properties from the Users menu to display the User Properties sheet (see Figure 13.9).

FIG. 13.9
The User Properties sheet for selected user accounts.

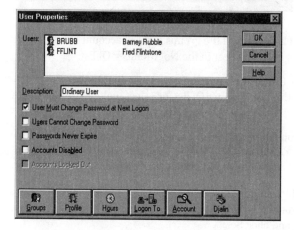

When modifying multiple accounts, only the options common to all the users are displayed. The additional account property buttons located at the bottom of the dialog lets you assign common attributes to all selected user accounts.

Managing User Account Properties

Additional user account properties are accessed and managed through the buttons at the bottom of the New User and Copy of *Username* dialogs and the User Properties sheet: Groups, Profile, Hours, Logon To, Account, and Dialin. These property buttons let you specify additional properties for a user account. The following sections describe the dialogs that appear when you click each button.

Assigning Group Membership to a User Account

You assign group membership to a user account by clicking the Groups button. In the Group Memberships dialog, you can assign and revoke group membership privileges (see Figure 13.10).

FIG. 13.10
Assigning users to groups with the Group Memberships dialog.

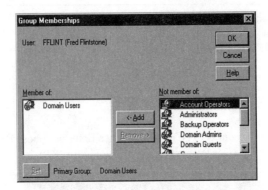

The Member Of list shows all the groups that the account belongs to. All groups to which the account does *not* belong appear in the Not Member Of list.

To assign a user to one or more groups, you can double-click the group to which to add the user account in the Not Member Of list, or select multiple groups in the Not Member Of list and click Add.

To remove a group membership from the user account, double-click the group to be removed from the account in the Member Of list, or select multiple groups in the Member Of list and click Remove.

In the Group Memberships dialog, the Set button applies only to users accessing a Windows NT network through Services for Macintosh. To set the primary group, select a group from the Member Of list and click Set.

▶ **See** "Connecting Macintosh Clients," **p. 425**

N O T E You can't remove from the account's membership list a group that's set as the user
account's primary group. To remove the group from the user account, you must set another
group as the primary group before you can remove the previously selected primary group. ■

Defining and Managing User Profiles

To further define a user profile, use the Profile button to select custom settings for one or more users. Clicking this button displays the User Environment Profile dialog (see Figure 13.11).

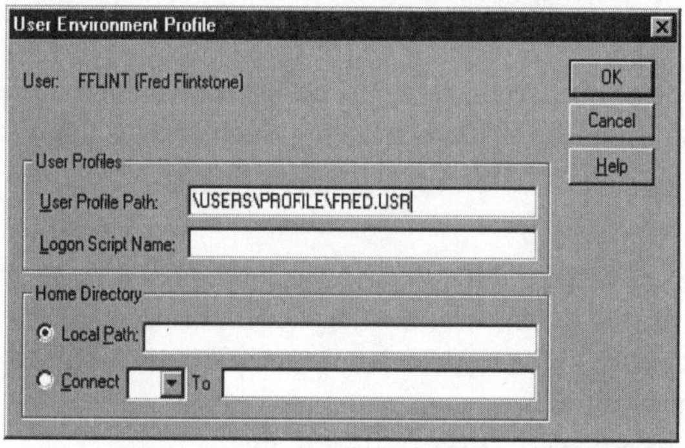

FIG. 13.11
Setting user environment parameters in the User Environment Profile dialog.

User profiles provide power and flexibility for administrators and users when configuring a network environment. User profiles are typically stored in a common folder on a Windows NT server. Windows NT Workstation clients also can have individual user profiles to supplement the user profile stored on the Windows NT server.

▶ **See** "Setting Up User Profiles on the Server," **p. 386**, and "Using System Policies," **p. 388**

N O T E   Windows NT Server 4.0's user profiles apply to Windows 3.1, Windows for Workgroups 3.1+, Windows NT 3.5+ and 4.0, and Windows 95 clients. Windows 95, however, provides its own mechanism for establishing networked user profiles and system policies, which offer several features not included in Windows NT Server 4.0's user profiles. Window NT 4.0 user profiles and system policies form the foundation of Microsoft's Zero Administration Kit for Windows NT 4.0 Workstation.

▶ **See** "Previewing the Zero Administration Kit for Windows NT Workstation 4.0 and Windows 95," **p. 423** ■

User profiles specify the startup information when individual users log on to Windows NT. This information includes the user environment (environment variables, paths, and mapped drives), program groups, and available applications. When a user profile is stored on a central Windows NT server, the user environment is the same regardless of the computer the user logs on from. When the profile is stored on individual Windows NT machines, the environment reflects the settings stored on each machine.

User profiles also can contain mandatory settings that you assign; users aren't allowed to alter these settings. This way, each user has a standard working environment and erroneous changes can't be made to a user profile, such as deleting a Start menu folder or shortcut.

Specifying the User Profile Path   The user profile is specified in the User Profile Path text box, which contains the location of a user profile located on a Windows NT server. If the text box is empty, the profile is stored locally on each machine that the user logs on to.

Part

III

Ch

13

Two types of user profiles are available:

- *Personal user profiles.* Each user is assigned this profile type and can alter the profile. Each user has his own private profile file with the file extension .usr.

- *Mandatory user profiles.* You assign this profile type, and the user can't change it. A mandatory user profile has the file extension .man.

To assign a profile to a user account, type the profile path and file name in the User Profile Path text box. Be sure to follow the UNC naming convention. For example, to store a profile named Profile.usr on the computer BEDROCK in the folder Users, type `\\bedrock\users\profile.usr`.

You can create the profile file ahead of time by using the User Profile Manager. If the specified profile file doesn't exist when the user first logs on, it's created automatically by using the default profile that exists on the workstation the user logs on from. Any changes are saved automatically to the profile file.

▶ **See** "Setting Up User Profiles on the Server," **p. 386**

N O T E   When using mandatory user profiles, the following rules apply:

- Mandatory profiles are added in the same manner, with the exception of the file extension (.man).

- Unlike an individual user account, you must assign a mandatory user account with User Profile Manager. This account must then be placed in the location specified in the profile path. If a profile isn't created, users with mandatory profiles aren't permitted to log on to Windows NT. ◼

Setting a Logon Script Name   *Logon scripts* are optional batch files that are run whenever a user logs on to a Windows NT network. Logon scripts are tailored to the client operating system that's used to log on to the network. All client operating systems for Intel PCs, except OS/2, use the .bat extension for the script file (OS/2 uses the .CMD extension). Windows NT Server 4.0 permits the use of executable logon scripts with an .exe extension, but executable logon scripts are very uncommon.

Logon scripts aren't as flexible as user profiles but can be used instead of user profiles or with user profiles. By default, all logon scripts are stored in the folder *ServerName*\Winnt\system32\Repl\Import\Scripts, where *ServerName* is the UNC server name of the primary domain controller for the domain you're administering. Because all scripts are stored in a central spot, only the name of the script file needs to be entered in the Logon Script Name text box. To use Server Manager to change the location of the Scripts folder, follow these steps:

1. Launch Server Manager from the Start menu's Administrative Tools (Common) choice.

2. Select the server in the opening window, and click the Replication button to open the Replication Properties for *ServerName* dialog.

3. Modify the entry in the Logon Script Path text box to point to your Scripts folder.

If a relative path, such as \Users\Logon.bat, is entered in the Logon Script Name text box for the user account, it's appended to the stored folder path. By using the preceding example, the logon script is run from the folder *ServerName*\Winnt\system32\Repl\Import\Scripts\ Users\Logon.bat.

Logon scripts can be assigned on an individual basis, or the same logon script can be assigned to multiple users. Logon scripts for users of 16-bit Windows must use DOS 8.3 file names.

Specifying a Home Folder By default, a user is placed in the home folder when starting a DOS-command session. The home folder also is used as a repository for user files and can be located on the client's local fixed disk or, more commonly, on a network drive.

N O T E Windows NT 4.0, like Windows 95, has adopted the term *folder* to replace *directory*; thus, this chapter uses the term *home folder*, which is likely to be adopted by most users of Windows 95 client PCs. Microsoft documentation has yet to make a full transition from *directory* to *folder* terminology, however. ▪

To set up a home folder on a local machine, follow these steps:

1. In the User Environment Profile dialog (accessed by clicking the Profile button), select the Local Path option.

2. Type the local path (for example, `c:\user\default`) in the Local Path text box.

In a network environment, where a user can log on from multiple machines, the home folder should be located on a networked drive so that the user can access it from any machine. You can set up shared network drives for users to log on to. To set up a home folder on a networked drive, follow these steps:

1. In the User Environment Profile dialog, select the Connect option.

2. From the drop-down list box, select the drive letter of the client machine to contain the home folder.

3. In the To text box, type a complete path for the home folder by using the UNC naming convention (for example, `\\bedrock\home\fred`). This makes the home folder available to the user on any machine from which he logs on.

If the home folder doesn't exist, Windows NT creates it. Also, the folder is protected so that only the specified user (and administrators) have access to the folder contents.

Managing Profiles for Multiple Users When multiple users are selected in User Manager's window, the User Environment Profile dialog changes to reflect the selection of multiple users within groups (see Figure 13.12). If all the user profiles to be modified are to share the same profile file name, logon script, and home folder, you make the same dialog entries as for individual accounts, as described in the preceding section.

You can streamline the process for creating individual user profiles based on a single profile for multiple users by using the environment variable %USERNAME%. Windows NT Server 4.0 automatically replaces %USERNAME% with the user's logon ID. Assume that each user is to have an

Part
III

Ch
13

individual user profile with the file name derived from the user's first name. For the user names FFLINT, WFLINT, and BRUBBLE, supplying the path \\BEDROCK\Profiles\ %USERNAME%.usr has the same effect as creating three individual user profiles: \\BEDROCK\ Profiles\FFLINT.usr, \\BEDROCK\Profiles\WFLINT.usr, and \\BEDROCK\Profiles\ BRUBBLE.usr. The variable %USERNAME% is expanded and replaced with the actual user name when any of the multiple users specified in the Users list of the User Environment Profile dialog log on to the Windows NT network. The %USERNAME% environmental variable can be used in any of the text boxes of the User Environment Profile dialog.

FIG. 13.12

The User Environment Profile Dialog for multiple user accounts.

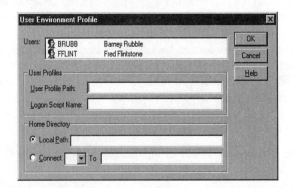

CAUTION

Take care when using the %USERNAME% variable with long file names—the variable name is replaced with the actual user name. This may cause problems when DOS, Windows 3.1+, and Windows NT 3.5 clients log on to the network. DOS, Windows 3.1+ (including Windows for Workgroups 3.1+), and Windows NT 3.5 are limited to 8.3 DOS file names. If your network includes clients other than Windows 95 and Windows NT 3.51+, make sure that the folder and profile names follow the 8.3 naming convention. In particular, the user name must not exceed eight characters.

Managing Logon Hours

When administering a large network, you might want to restrict the hours during which an account has access to the network. For example, certain workers may be able to access network resources only during normal business hours—Monday through Friday from 8 A.M. to 5 P.M.—whereas other users have unrestricted network access. You manage logon hours fora user account by clicking the Hours button at the bottom of the New User and Copy of *Username* dialogs and the User Properties sheet to display the Logon Hours dialog (see Figure 13.13).

FIG. 13.13

Managing user logon time limitations with the Logon Hours dialog.

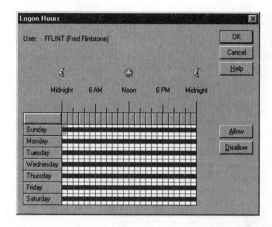

The Logon Hours dialog displays a weekly schedule of times allowed for user logon. The dark areas indicate valid logon times. Logon hours are permitted by selecting the desired hours and clicking Allow. Similarly, restricted hours are specified by selecting the hours and clicking Disallow.

You can use any of the following four methods to select logon times in the Logon Hours dialog:

- Clicking the day of week label—for example, Sunday—selects the entire day.
- Clicking the top of an hour column selects that hour every day of the week.
- Clicking the column square above Sunday selects the entire week.
- Clicking a specific hour selects that hour.

After the logon hours are set, click OK to save the logon hours for that account.

Setting Logon Hours for Multiple Users When managing logon hours for multiple users, select the desired users from User Manager's window and click the Hours button from the User Properties sheet. The Logon Hours dialog changes slightly from the single-user version, as shown in Figure 13.14.

If all the selected users don't have the same logon hours, a message box appears with the warning `The selected users have different Logon Hours settings`. If you continue the operation, all the user logon hours are reset and new logon hours are set in the same manner described earlier for setting the logon hours for an individual user account.

Logging Off Users Who Are Logged On When Logon Hours Expire Although logon hours restrict when users can log on to a Windows NT network, users may be logged on when their logon time expires. The action that occurs in this situation is determined by the Account Policy set up by the domain administrator. (Setting up account policies for terminating after-hour connections is discussed later in the section "Removing Users from the Network When Logon Hours Expire.")

Part
III

Ch
13

FIG. 13.14

Managing logon hours for multiple users.

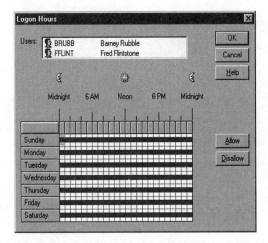

The following two actions can occur when a logged-on user's logon time expires:

- Typically, logged-on users remain logged on, but they're denied the ability to make any new connections or access additional network resources.

- You can choose to forcibly disconnect logged-on users on expiry of their specified logon times. When you choose this option, all logged-on users receive a warning to log off the connected resource before the expiry time. Any users who don't log off before the logoff time are automatically disconnected.

N O T E   The option to forcibly log off applies only to users of client PCs running Windows NT Workstation or Windows 95. All non-Windows NT or Windows 95 computers are *not* disconnected when the logoff time expires. Non-Windows NT/95 computers can't access any new network resources but can continue to use without restriction the resources to which they're then connected. ▪

Restricting Logon Privileges to Assigned Workstations

To restrict which network clients users can log on to, click the Logon To button in the New User and Copy of *Username* dialogs or the User Properties sheet to open the Logon Workstations dialog (see Figure 13.15).

N O T E   The workstations that users are permitted to log on to are restricted to clients running Windows NT Workstation or Windows 95. Users of non-Windows NT or Windows 95 clients aren't affected by these settings. ▪

By default, all new accounts—unless the account is copied and the account that it was copied from has restricted access—can log on from all clients. If client logon access needs to be restricted, follow these steps:

1. Select the User May Log On To These Workstations option.

2. Type up to eight client computer names in the text boxes.

3. Click OK to establish the restriction.

When multiple users are selected in User Manager's window, the Logon Workstations dialog displays information that applies only to all selected users. By selecting the option User May Log On To All Workstations or by restricting client access, all selected users are affected.

FIG. 13.15
Restricting client logon access through the Logon Workstations dialog.

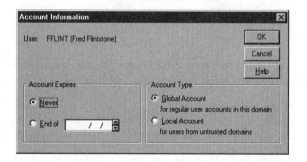

Managing Account Information

To assign specific user account information, click the Account button at the bottom of the New User and Copy of *Username* dialogs or the User Properties sheet to open the Account Information dialog (see Figure 13.16). This dialog lets you determine the expiration date of the account and the type of account.

FIG. 13.16
Altering user accounts through the Account Information dialog.

By default, a user account never expires. In situations where an expiration date is needed (such as when an employee leaves the company or for temporary employees), the account becomes inactive at the end of the day specified in the End Of date edit box.

The Account Type section specifies whether the account is global or local according to the following rules:

Part
III

Ch
13

- Select Global Account if the user account must be recognized by other domains that trust the user logon domain.

- Select Local Account if the user logs on to the domain from an untrusted domain or if user access is to be restricted to the logon domain.

When the Account Information dialog is invoked for multiple users, only the properties common to all accounts are selected. Setting any of the options changes all selected accounts.

Setting User Dial-In Permissions

Windows NT Server 4.0 has eased the burden of granting dial-in permissions to users for Dial-Up Networking (DUN). In previous versions, dial-in permissions had to be assigned from the Remote Access Administration utility. Now you can assign dial-in permissions directly from User Manager by selecting the Dialin button in the New User and Copy of *Username* dialogs or the User Properties sheet. DUN is the subject of Chapter 19, "Managing Remote Access Service."

By default, users do *not* have dial-in permission; it must be granted to each user. Figure 13.17 shows the Dialin Information dialog.

FIG. 13.17

Setting callback properties in the Dialin Information dialog.

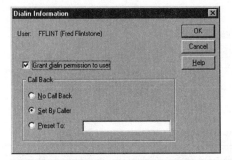

If your network users need dial-in permission, simply mark the Grant Dialin Permission to User check box. Then set the Call Back options: No Call Back, Set By Caller, or Preset To.

If you select Set By Caller, users are prompted to enter an optional number that the server can use to call them back. This option is very valuable for users who travel a great deal, need to access the network for information while on the road, and want to minimize telephone charges.

The Preset To option is limited because the server calls back to a specific number each time a user dials into the network. This option should be used only for strict security purposes where the user, usually a telecommuter, is always at a specific location.

Using the Add User Account Wizard

Wizards are Microsoft's way of automating multistep operations necessary to achieve a specific objective. Wizards, which originated in Microsoft Access and later migrated to all members of the Microsoft Office suite, are intended primarily to aid new users of Microsoft productivity applications.

Windows NT Server 4.0 offers eight Administrative Wizards of varying usefulness. The Add User Account Wizard guides you through the addition of a new user account. To use the wizard properly, however, you must have a fundamental understanding of Windows NT's implementation of user accounts and groups. Thus, the Add User Account Wizard is likely to play a limited or non-existent role in the day-to-day administration of Windows NT 4.0 servers.

To give the Add User Account Wizard a trial run (you must have Domain Administrator privileges), follow these steps:

1. From the Start menu, choose Programs, Administrative Tools, and Administrative Wizards to open the Getting Started with Windows NT Server window (see Figure 13.18).

FIG. 13.18
Selecting the Add User Account Wizard from the Administrative Wizards window.

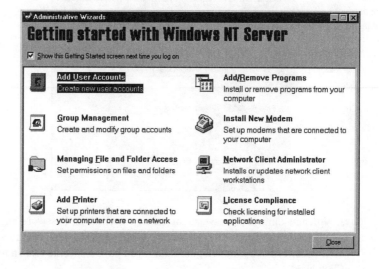

2. Double-click the Add User Accounts icon to open the first dialog of the Add User Account Wizard, which displays the server's domain name (see Figure 13.19). Use the Domain Name drop-down list if you want to add the new user to another domain with which your server has a trust relationship. Click the Next button.

▶ **See** "Implementing Domains and Trusts Between Domains," **p. 618**

FIG. 13.19

Selecting the domain for the new user in the first Add User Account Wizard dialog.

3. Type the full name of the user, the user's logon ID, and an optional user description in the three text boxes (see Figure 13.20). Click Next.

FIG. 13.20

Adding user account information in the second Add User Account Wizard dialog.

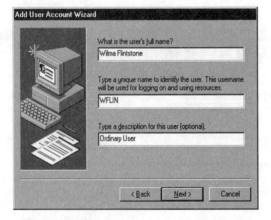

4. Assign and confirm a password for the new user in the Password and Confirm Password text boxes (see Figure 13.21). Use the default option, which requires users to change their password at the next logon, unless you have a specific reason for doing otherwise. Click Next.

5. By default, the new user is added to the Domain Users group. To add the user to another group, select the group in the Available Groups list, and then click Add (see Figure 13.22). To remove a user from an added group, select the entry in the Selected Groups list and click Remove. (The Wizard won't let you remove the user from the Domain Users group.) Click Next.

FIG. 13.21

Specifying a temporary user password in the third Add User Account Wizard dialog.

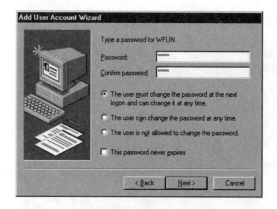

FIG. 13.22

Adding the new user to an additional user group in the fourth Add User Account Wizard dialog.

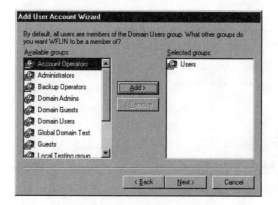

6. Mark the check boxes to set up one or more of the options shown in Figure 13.23. Options not available are disabled. The option to set up a Microsoft Exchange Server account for the user is enabled only if you have Microsoft Exchange Server installed. Click Next.

7. The options specified in step 6 determine the sequence of wizard dialogs. For example, if you selected Home Directory in step 6, the dialog shown in Figure 13.24 appears. Click the On Another Computer option button, specify the user's drive letter mapping in the Connect Drive list for the user's home folder on the server, and type the UNC path to the server share for the home folder in the To text box. (You receive an error message if the share doesn't exist.) Click Next. If you selected more than one option in step 6, additional dialogs open to aid you in setting up those options.

Part
III

Ch
13

FIG. 13.23

Selecting user account options in the fifth Add User Account Wizard dialog.

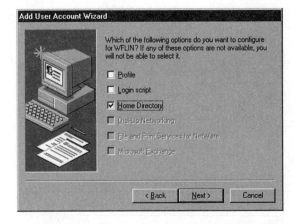

FIG. 13.24

Specifying a home directory and its user share mapping.

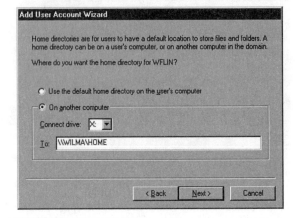

N O T E   You must have previously created the share for the user's home folder and assigned appropriate permissions for the share. Usually, home folders are located in the server's \Users folder. Ordinarily, only Domain Administrators and the user have permissions to the user's home folder. ■

8. To add restrictions to the user's account, select The Following Restrictions option to enable the four check boxes shown in Figure 13.25. If you specify any restrictions, additional dialogs appear to help you define the restrictions. Click Next.

9. When you complete the dialogs for user restrictions (if any), the last dialog that appears indicates that the wizard is about to complete the task (see Figure 13.26). Click the Finish button to create the account.

FIG. 13.25
Specifying user account restrictions, if applicable.

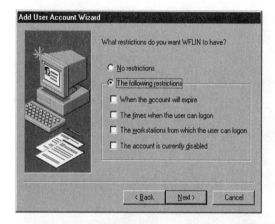

FIG. 13.26
Confirming completion of account information entry in the last Add User Account Wizard dialog.

N O T E The account for the new user isn't created until you click Finish. You can use the Back button to review your prior steps or cancel the account entry at any point in the process by clicking Cancel. ▪

10. A message box confirms the creation of the new user account. Click No to exit the Add User Account Wizard or Yes to add another account.

Administering the Domain Account Policy

The domain account policy determines password and lockout restrictions for all users in the domain. Choose Account from User Manager's Policies menu to open the Account Policy dialog (see Figure 13.27). The following sections describe how to set domain-wide policies for passwords and account lockout.

Part
III

Ch

13

FIG. 13.27

Setting account policies for all domain users with the Account Policy dialog.

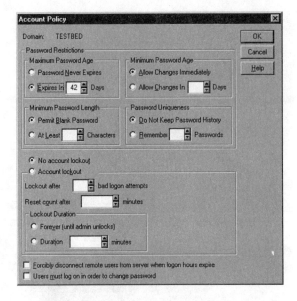

Setting the Account Policy for Passwords

You can define the following types of password restrictions:

- *Maximum Password Age* determines how long account passwords are in effect before they expire. The options are Password Never Expires or Expires In *n* Days (the default).

- *Minimum Password Age* determines how long a user account is forced to retain a new password. The objective is to prevent users from entering a dummy password when their password expires and then immediately changing it back to the old password. The options available are Allow Changes Immediately (the default) or Allow Changes In *n* Days.

- *Minimum Password Length* determines the minimum allowable length for all passwords. The options available are Permit Blank Password (the default) or At Least *n* Characters. To maintain a secure network, require passwords of at least six (preferably eight) characters.

- *Password Uniqueness* tells Windows NT Server whether to keep a history of previously used passwords. The objective is to prevent users from reusing the same password when a password expires. The available options are Do Not Keep Password History (the default) or Remember *n* Passwords. For maximum security, set *n* to 8 or greater.

At the bottom of the Account Policy dialog is a Users Must Log On in Order to Change Password check box. If this option is selected and a user's password expires, the user of the account must ask the account administrator to change the password.

Setting the Account Lockout Policy

The Account Lockout Policy setting determines the actions that are taken if users forget their passwords or illegal attempts are made to access the network, as evidenced by multiple failed attempts to log on. In this event, either of the following actions can be chosen:

- *No Account Lockout.* If this option is selected, any user can try an unlimited number of times to log on to the network.

- *Account Lockout.* If this option is selected, you set up lockout parameters to deter repeated illegal logon attempts. The following sections explain the lockout parameters.

Setting Account Lockout Options   One of the following two options applies to the Account Lockout setting:

- *Lockout After* n *Bad Logon Attempts* locks out the user account after so many failed logon attempts occur. This option forces the account user to wait until the account is unlocked through administrative or automatic intervention.

- *Reset Count After* n *Minutes* automatically resets the number of bad logon attempts to zero after so many minutes of account inactivity since the last bad logon attempt.

Setting Lockout Duration Options   One of the following two options applies to the Lockout Duration setting:

- When *Forever (Until Admin Unlocks)* is selected, the account is locked out indefinitely until you manually reset the account.

- When *Duration* n *Minutes* is selected, the account automatically unlocks after so many minutes of locked time.

Removing Users from the Network When Logon Hours Expire   When users are logged on to a Windows NT network and their logon hours expire, you can either continue to let them access the network resources to which they're already logged on, or forcibly disconnect all users running Windows NT Workstation or Windows 95 from the network. This option is the same as the option described earlier in the section "Logging Off Users Who Are Logged On When Logon Hours Expire," except that all domain users are affected by this option.

If the option Forcibly Disconnect Remote Users from Server When Logon Hours Expire is selected in the Account Policy dialog, remote users whose logon hours expire are prompted to disconnect from the network. If users don't log off, the server will disconnect them automatically.

Managing User Groups

The preceding sections of this chapter make many references to user groups. *User groups* define the rights and privileges that are assigned to the users in those groups. At the bottom of User Manager's window is a scrollable, alphabetically sorted list of the standard (built-in) groups of Windows NT Server 4.0 (see Figure 13.28).

Part

III

Ch

13

FIG. 13.28
Built-in user groups available in User Manager's window.

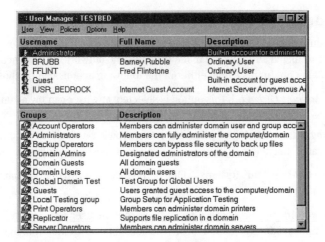

Two types of groups are shown in the Groups list: global and local. A global group is depicted with a world globe in the background; a local group is depicted with a workstation in the background.

User Manager lets you create, modify, and delete groups; assign user accounts to groups; and remove user accounts from groups. The following sections describe the 11 built-in user groups of Windows NT Server 4.0 and explain the management of user groups.

Examining Windows NT Server 4.0's Built-In Groups

The actions that a user account can perform depends on the group memberships assigned to the account, the rights and privileges the account inherits from the group(s), plus specific permissions you assign to the account. Windows NT Server 4.0 has 11 built-in user groups, each with a pre-established set of permissions for use of network resources. Descriptions of a few of these groups, by necessity, appear earlier in this chapter but are repeated here for completeness. Following is a brief description of each built-in user group, in the approximate order of decreasing privilege:

- The *Administrators* group is the most powerful local group in the domain. Administrators are responsible for the overall configuration of the domain and the domain's servers.

- The global *Domain Admins* group is a member of the Administrators group. By default, members of the Domain Admins group are as powerful as the Administrators group. The Domain Admins group can be removed from the Administrators group, if necessary, to restrict the group's authority.

- The local *Users* group provides the capabilities that most users need to perform normal tasks. Members of this group have no rights to administer servers running Windows NT 4.0.

■ The global *Domain Users* group is a member of the local Users group. By default, all new accounts are automatically added to this group, unless you specifically remove this group from the account.

■ The local *Account Operators* group allows its members to utilize User Manager to create new groups and accounts. Members of this group have limited capabilities to administer accounts, servers, and groups in the domain. Group members can't modify or delete accounts or groups belonging to the Administrators, Domain Admins, Account Operators, Backup Operators, Print Operators, or Server Operators Groups, nor can they administer account policies.

■ The local *Backup Operators* group can back up and restore files on the domain's primary and backup controllers. Members of this group also can log on to a server and shut it down, presumably for backup operations.

■ The local *Print Operators* group allows its members to create and manage printer shares in the domain. These members also can log on to a server and shut it down.

■ The local *Server Operators* group allows members to manage the domain's primary and backup controllers. Group members also can manage folder and print shares, as well as administer server functions, such as setting system time for the entire domain.

■ The local *Replicator* group supports the capability to perform folder replication functions. Only accounts needed to log on to the Replicator services of the primary and backup domain controllers should be members of this group.

■ The global *Domain Guests* group is a member of the local Guests group. This group is intended for user accounts with more limited rights than a member of the Domain Users group.

■ The local *Guests* group has very limited capabilities and is used for occasional or one-time users.

N O T E The Power Users group of Windows NT 3.51 isn't included as a built-in group of Windows NT 4.0. When upgrading a Windows NT 3.x server to Windows NT 4.0, the Power Users group is migrated to 4.0. ■

Adding Local Groups

The built-in user groups are adequate for most Windows NT Server 4.0 networks. If you have a large, complex network, you might want to define your own user groups by, for example, organizational function or department. As an example, members of the Finance, Marketing, Sales, and Production departments might have their own groups. Similarly, vice presidents, directors, managers, and supervisors might be assigned to their own groups.

To add a local group to the domain, follow these steps:

1. From User Manager's <u>U</u>ser menu, choose New <u>L</u>ocal Group to display the New Local Group dialog (see Figure 13.29).

Part
III

Ch

13

FIG. 13.29

Adding a new local group with User Manager.

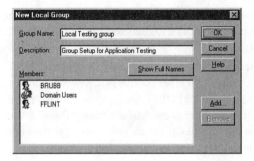

2. In the Group Name text box, type a group name that's no longer than 20 characters. A Group Name is required.

3. Type a group description in the Description text box. Although this is optional, a meaningful description is useful as your network grows and more groups are added.

To add user accounts to the new group, click the Add button to display the Add Users and Groups dialog (see Figure 13.30). To add users to the local account, follow these steps:

1. Select the account entry in the Names list and click the Add button, or double-click the entry in the Names list to add the account to the Add Names list. (A description of each option in the Add Users and Groups dialog follows.)

2. Repeat step 1 for each additional account you want to add to the new group.

3. Click OK to add the accounts to the new group and close the dialog.

FIG. 13.30

Adding new user accounts and global groups to a local group.

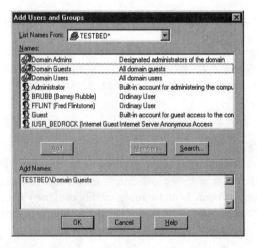

Local groups can include users and global groups from the domain of the local group. Local groups also can include global users and global groups from other domains that are trusted by the local groups' domain.

The purpose of the options in the Add Users and Groups dialog is as follows:

- *List Names From.* This drop-down list lets you select the domain from which to add names or groups. The default setting is the domain for the local group.

- *Names.* This list displays all the users and global groups of the domain being viewed. The items in this list are candidates for inclusion in the new local group.

- *Members.* To view the members of a global group, select the global group from the Names list and click the Members button.

- *Search.* This button is used to find a domain name—a useful feature if your network contains many domains.

Adding Global Groups

The process for adding a new global group is identical to adding a local group, except that rather than choose New Local Group, you choose New Global Group from the User menu to display the New Global Group dialog (see Figure 13.31). Unlike local groups, which can contain global groups and users, a global group can contain only users.

FIG. 13.31

Adding a new global group with User Manager.

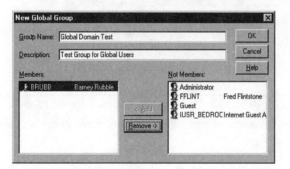

Copying a Group

If a new group needs to be created and will have similar rights and members as another group, it's easier to copy a group than to add a new group and manually set up its attributes. To copy a group, follow these steps:

1. Select a group to copy in User Manager's window.

2. From the User menu, choose Copy.

3. The Add New Local Group or Add New Global Group dialog appears, depending the type of group you selected in step 1.

4. Type a new name and description for the group.

5. Modify the group's membership, as necessary.

6. Click OK to create the new group and close the dialog.

Part
III

Ch

13

Deleting Groups from the Domain

Only user-defined groups may be deleted from the domain. The built-in groups of Windows NT Server 4.0 can't be deleted.

> **CAUTION**
>
> Be careful when deleting groups from a domain. A deleted group can't be restored by an undo process.

Each group you create receives a unique security identifier (SID). If you delete a group and re-create a group with the identical name, the new group receives a different SID and doesn't inherit the original group's attributes.

To delete a group from a domain, follow these steps:

1. Select the group to delete from the Groups list of User Manager's window.

2. From the User menu, choose Delete. A warning message appears (see Figure 13.32).

FIG. 13.32
Warning shown when deleting a group from a domain.

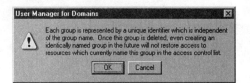

3. Click OK to proceed with the transaction, or click Cancel to abort the operation.

4. If you click OK, a second message asks the operator to confirm the decision. Click Yes to delete the group.

Deciding When to Use Local Groups or Global Groups

Determining when to add a local group or a global group to a domain can often be difficult. Use the following guidelines to determine whether to create a new global or local group:

- Use global groups when user accounts from this domain need to access resources of this domain and others.

- Use local groups when user accounts from this domain or others need to be used in resources of this domain. A local group should also be used when global groups from this domain or others need to be used in resources from this domain.

Providing Users in Trusted Domains Access to Resources in Trusting Domains

Although one domain trusts another domain, the trust relationship doesn't grant users access to resources in the trusting domain. The easiest method for allowing users from other domains access to your resources is to add a global group from the outside domain to a local group in your domain.

User Manager lets you create global groups in other domains if the other domain trusts your domain. You can set up a global group in the external domain, select the user accounts needed from the outside domain, and then assign that global group to a local group in your domain.

▶ **See** "Establishing Trusts," **p. 625**

Using the Group Management Wizard

The Group Management Wizard is a tool for creating new groups and adding users to the new group. You also can use the Group Management Wizard to change the membership of or delete existing groups.

The Group Management Wizard makes entering information into the New Global User or New Local User dialog a multistep process. Thus, it's questionable whether this wizard is of significant benefit to Windows NT network administrators. To decide for yourself whether use of the Group Management Wizard is worthwhile, follow these steps:

1. From the Start menu, choose Programs, Administrative Tools, and Administrative Wizards to open the wizard selection dialog; then double-click the Group Management icon to display the first Group Management Wizard dialog.

2. The wizard lets you create a new group and add members or modify the membership roster of an existing group. To create a new group, accept the default Create a New Group and Add Members option (see Figure 13.33). Click the Next button.

FIG. 13.33
Choosing between creating a new group and working with an existing group in the first Group Management Wizard dialog.

N O T E If you choose to modify an existing group, you select the computer on which the group was created, and then select the group to modify. You can delete the group or, in a succeeding dialog, modify the membership of the group. ▪

3. Type the name of the new group (spaces are allowed in the group name) and an optional description in the two text boxes (see Figure 13.34). Click Next.

FIG. 13.34

Naming and describing a new group in the second Group Management Wizard dialog.

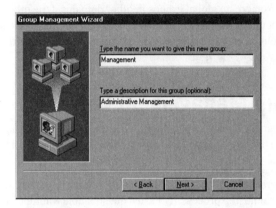

4. If you're working at the server on which the group is to be created, accept the default option, On My Computer (see Figure 13.35); otherwise, select On Another Computer. Click Next.

FIG. 13.35

Specifying the location of the new group in the third Group Management Wizard dialog.

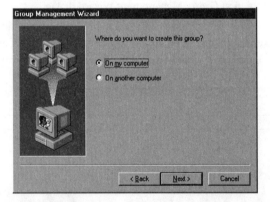

5. If you select a computer that's a domain controller, a message box tells you that the new group will be created on the primary domain controller. Click OK to continue.

6. You can choose between creating a Global Group (the default) and a Local Group (see Figure 13.36). Unless you have a specific reason for creating a Local Group, accept the default and click Next.

FIG. 13.36

Choosing between a new Global Group or Local Group in the fourth Group Management Wizard dialog.

7. All users appear in the Available Members list. Select each user you want to join to the new group and click Add to add the user to Selected Members list (see Figure 13.37). When you've added all the members, click Next.

FIG. 13.37

Adding users to the new group in the fifth Group Management Wizard dialog.

8. The last dialog, in Figure 13.38, confirms the name and domain for the new group. Click Finish to add the new group to the domain.

9. A message confirms addition of the new group. If you've had enough group management wizardry for the moment, click No. If you want to give the Group Management Wizard another try, click Yes.

Part

III

Ch

13

FIG. 13.38
Confirming the addition
of the new group in the
last Group Management
Wizard dialog.

Managing User Rights Policy

Each user's capabilities are determined by the rights and privileges assigned to the user. A
user's *rights* refer to the entire system or domain. User Manager assigns all rights. The rights
assigned to a user directly affect the tasks that user can perform on the network.

> **N O T E**   *Permissions* assigned to a user refer to the specific files, folders, and hardware devices
> accessible to that user. For more information on user permissions, see Chapter 14,
> "Sharing and Securing Network Resources." ■

Determining User Rights

A Windows NT network has two categories of rights: basic and advanced. Table 13.2 lists the
user rights of Windows NT Server 4.0 and the built-in groups that receive these rights.

Table 13.2   Basic Rights for the Built-In Windows NT Groups

User Right	Group Rights Assigned To...
Access this computer from network	Administrators, EVERYONE
Add workstations to domain	Administrators, Backup Operators, Server Operators
Backup files and directories	Administrators, Backup Operators, Server Operators
Change the system time	Administrators, Server Operators
Force shutdown from a remote system	Administrators, Backup Operators, Server Operators
Load and unload device drivers	Administrators

User Right	Group Rights Assigned To...
Log on locally	Account Operators, Administrators, Backup Operators, Print Operators, Server Operators
Manage auditing and security log	Administrators
Restore files and directories	Administrators, Backup Operators, Server Operators
Shut down the system	Account Operators, Administrators, Backup Operators, Server Operators
Take ownership of files or other objects	Administrators
Bypass traverse checking	EVERYONE
Log on as a service	Replicators
Assign user rights	Administrators
Create and manage local groups	Administrators, Users
Create and manage user accounts	Administrators
Create common groups	Administrators
Format computer's hard disk	Administrators
Keep local profile	Administrators, EVERYONE
Lock the computer	Administrators, EVERYONE
Manage auditing of system events	Administrators
Override the lock of the computer	Administrators
Share and stop sharing directories	Administrators
Share and stop sharing printers	Administrators

N O T E The term EVERYONE isn't a group, but a Windows NT convention for indicating that all users in all groups have this right. ■

Part
III

Ch
13

Assigning New User Rights

When you create a new user group, you can customize the rights assigned to the group by adding or deleting them. To add or delete rights from group membership, follow these steps:

1. In User Manager's window, choose User from the Policy menu to display the User Rights Policy dialog (see Figure 13.39).

FIG. 13.39

Assigning user rights to groups and accounts in the User Rights Policy dialog.

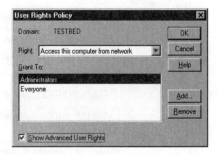

2. The Right drop-down list at the top of the dialog displays rights that you can assign to or remove from Windows NT Server 4.0 groups. By default, only basic rights are listed. To see advanced rights, mark the Show Advanced User Rights check box at the bottom of the dialog, and then select the right you want to examine.

   When you select a user right from the drop-down list, the Grant To list changes to reflect the groups that the right is assigned to.

3. To add new groups to the right, click the Add button to display the Add Users and Groups dialog with a list of users and groups in the domain. Select the groups and users that you want to assign the right to.

   To remove a user right from a group or user, select the right, select the user or group to be removed in the Grant To list, and then click the Remove button.

4. When all your changes are complete, click OK to effect the changes and close the dialog.

Exploring the Resource Kit's User Administration Utilities

The *Windows NT Server Resource Kit, Supplement One* for version 4.0 has 15 User Administration Utilities, nine of which are new with *Supplement One* and two of which are updated from the original *Windows NT Server Resource Kit.* All but one of these programs are command-line executables. Following is a list that briefly describes the most useful of the User Administration Utilities:

■ *Addusers.exe* lets you create a list (dump) of, add, and delete users and groups in comma-separated value (.csv) format. Excel and Access can import and export .csv files. Running `addusers /d users.csv` at the command prompt creates users.csv for the domain, which you can use as a template for creating user and group accounts. Figure 13.40 shows in Excel 97 part of a dump of the OAKLEAF domain. Addusers.exe is updated in *Supplement One.*

■ *Global.exe* and *Local.exe* create lists of members of the global or local group that you specify for a designated domain. Type `global "domain users" domainname >` `dusers.txt` or `local users domainname > lusers.txt` to obtain a text file list of

Domain Users or local users for a particular domain. You must enclose in double quotation marks group names containing spaces. These two utilities are included only in the *Supplement One* CD-ROM.

FIG. 13.40

A partial list of users created by Addusers.exe, displayed in Excel 97 (local and global groups appear after the [User] rows).

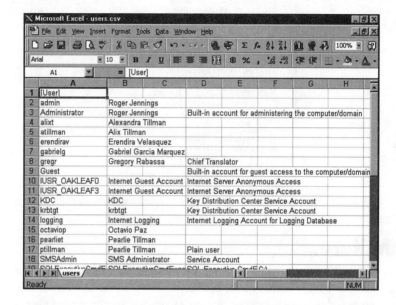

- *Showgrps.exe* and *Showmbrs.exe* list the group membership for a designated user and the members of a designated group, respectively. These two utilities are included only in the *Supplement One* CD-ROM.

- *Srvcheck.exe* creates a list of all non-hidden shares of the server you specify with a list of groups that have rights to the shares. (Redirect the output of Srvcheck.ext to a text file to create a usable list.) Figure 13.41 shows Notepad displaying part of the list of the \\OAKLEAF0 shares created by typing `srvcheck \\oakleaf0 > srvcheck.txt` at the command prompt.

- *Usrstat.exe* creates a list of user accounts in a specified domain with the full name and last logon date and time. Usrstat.exe is new in *Supplement One*.

- *Usrtogrp.exe* uses a specially formatted text file to add specified users to group. The user and group accounts must exist before you can use Usrtogrp.exe.

Part
III

Ch
13

 TIP If you're interested primarily in the Resource Kit's utilities and on-line documentation but not the printed book, purchase only the *Windows NT Server Resource Kit, Supplement One*, which has a list price of $39.99. You save more than $100 compared with buying the *Windows NT Server Resource Kit*, which doesn't include most of the User Administration Utilities of the preceding list. (All prices are in U.S. dollars.)

FIG. 13.41

Part of the list of shares and groups with share permissions created by Srvcheck.exe.

```
srvcheck.txt - Notepad
File  Edit  Search  Help
\\oakleaf0\NETLOGON
     .\Everyone
\\oakleaf0\print$
     BUILTIN/Server Operators
     BUILTIN/Print Operators
     BUILTIN/Administrators
                    OAKLEAF/Administrator
                    OAKLEAF/logging
                    OAKLEAF/Domain Admins
     .\Everyone
\\oakleaf0\Laserjet4P
     BUILTIN/Server Operators
     BUILTIN/Print Operators
     BUILTIN/Administrators
                    OAKLEAF/Administrator
                    OAKLEAF/logging
                    OAKLEAF/Domain Admins
     .\Everyone
\\oakleaf0\Samples
     OAKLEAF\Administrator
     BUILTIN/Administrators
                    OAKLEAF/Administrator
                    OAKLEAF/logging
                    OAKLEAF/Domain Admins
     .\Everyone
```

From Here...

In this chapter, you learned to utilize User Manager for Domains to configure user accounts and groups. The administrator of a Windows NT Server 4.0 network has total control of all users and network resources. You can tailor each user group and user account to meet the operational need of each user, department, or division, commensurate with the required level of security for the network. This chapter also described how to use the Add User Account and Group Management wizards as alternatives to direct manipulation of user accounts and groups with User Manager.

For more information related to the content of this chapter, see the following chapters:

- Chapter 11, "Configuring Windows 95 Clients for Networking," describes how to implement Windows 95's unique networked user logon and system policies.

- Chapter 12, "Connecting Other PC Clients to the Network," describes how to implement Windows NT 4.0 system policies and use the Zero Administration Kit for Windows NT Workstation 4.0.

- Chapter 14, "Sharing and Securing Network Resources," describes user permissions for the common types of networked resources.

- Chapter 17, "Distributing Network Services with Domains," describes how Windows NT Server 4.0 domains are used in wide area networking.

Sharing and Securing Network Resources

The fundamental purpose of any network operating system (NOS) is to give users access to shared network resources such as folders, files, and printers. Just as important as the capability to share these resources is the capability to control which users have access to each resource.

Windows NT Server 4.0 provides all the tools you need to share and secure folders and files. You can control access to folders and files on a very broad level. For example, folder shares of servers that use the FAT file system function like a blunt instrument. Folder shares let you share a FAT folder on the Windows NT server but allow access control only at the group level, and only then to the folder and all subfolders as a group. NTFS folder-access permissions and NTFS file-access permissions, on the other hand, function more like scalpels. They allow you to control access very finely, down to the level of deciding whether one particular user can access one particular file in one particular subfolder.

Choosing between NTFS and FAT

Take full advantage of NTFS's increased security, folder- and file-level access control.

Sharing folders and files

Assign NTFS's explicit folder- and file-sharing permissions to groups and users.

Replicating NTFS folders

Mirror folders on multiple servers to assure shared file accessibility when one server goes down.

Compressing NTFS folders and files

Save room on your NTFS volumes by compressing shared files and folders.

Monitoring shared folder sizes

Use the Resource Kit's Diruse.exe application to keep track of disk space consumption by shared folders.

Sharing network printers

Use the Add Printer Wizard to share printers attached to your Windows NT 4.0 servers and audit their usage.

Windows NT Server 4.0 also provides all the tools you need to share and secure network printers. You can share printers that are physically connected to the computer running Windows NT Server. You also can share printers physically connected to other Microsoft Networking clients on the network, configuring them to appear as shared resources on the Windows NT server. ■

Sharing and Securing Folders and Files

Windows NT Server makes sharing folders and files easy for you. Behind this ease of use lurks the power needed to control which users can access which resources. In the following sections, you learn how to share folders and files and how to control access to them. The extent to which you can secure your folders and files depends on the file system you decide to use.

N O T E Windows NT 4.0, like Windows 95, has adopted the term *folder* to replace *directory*; thus, this chapter uses the term *folder*, which is likely to be adopted by most Windows NT users. (Similarly, this chapter uses the term *subfolder* in place of the term *subdirectory*.) Some Windows NT dialogs and help screens still use the term *directory*. When one of these screen elements is explicitly referred to in the text, this chapter uses the term *directory* to correspond to Microsoft usage and to avoid confusion. ■

Choosing a Windows NT Server File System

During its history, Windows NT has supported the following three file systems:

- The *FAT file system* is marginally faster than the other file systems on small servers but provides none of the data integrity features available with the HPFS and NTFS file systems. Access control is limited to share-level security. Don't consider using the FAT file system on a production server.

- The *High Performance File System (HPFS)*, originally developed by IBM for its OS/2 operating system, is fast and provides good data integrity features, but offers only share-level security. However, NTFS includes all the features of HPFS, so there's no reason to use HPFS. Unlike prior versions of Windows NT, Windows NT 4.0 doesn't support HPFS, although you can access HPFS files and folders running on networked Windows NT 3.x servers.

- The *NT File System (NTFS)* is the native file system designed by Microsoft for Windows NT Server. It's fast, offers excellent security, and provides rock-solid data integrity functions.

Although Microsoft offers you a choice of file systems, don't spend too long thinking about which to pick. Using NTFS provides the best mix of speed, security, and protection for your data. You can compress files and folders stored only on NTFS partitions. Even if you take Microsoft's recommendation to use FAT for your system partition, use NTFS partition(s) for all server shares.

▶ **See** "Handling Files with NTFS," **p. 90**

Understanding Folder Shares

Until a folder is shared, only administrators can access it across the network. Administrators have access to default administrative shares for each logical server drive and all its folders. Administrative shares, discussed later in the section "Using Administrative Shares," are created automatically by Windows NT Server.

Folder shares provide the first level of security by controlling which folders on the server are visible to—and therefore accessible by—logged-on users. As a means of securing access, folder shares have the following drawbacks:

- Sharing a folder automatically shares all files contained in that folder and its subfolders. If you need finer control of which subfolders and files are accessible to which users, you must use folder-access and file-access permissions, which are available only if you're using the NTFS file system.

- A folder share controls access only for those users who log on to the server from a remote workstation. Any user with physical access to the server can log on locally and bypass share-level security.

N O T E Sharing works with all three file systems supported by Windows NT Server—FAT, HPFS (Windows NT Server 3.x only), and NTFS. Shares are the only form of access control available with the FAT and HPFS file systems. This means that any user with physical access to the server can log on locally and bypass security on FAT and HPFS volumes. Windows NT Server 4.0 doesn't support HPFS, so this chapter doesn't discuss HPFS shares. ▪

Creating, Modifying, and Removing Folder Shares   To create a folder share, you must be logged on locally to the computer running Windows NT Server, and your account must be a member of the Administrators, Server Operators, or Power Users group. Follow these steps to create a new folder share:

1. Open Explorer or double-click the My Computer icon to display a list of drives available on your server.

2. Double-click one of the available drives to display a list of folders contained on that drive. If the folder you want to share isn't at the root level, click the + symbol to the left of the parent folder name to display a list of subfolders for that folder.

3. Right-click a folder to display the context-sensitive menu.

4. Choose Sharing to display the Sharing page of the property sheet for that folder (see Figure 14.1).

5. By default, the folder is marked Not Shared. Select the Shared As option button to activate the remaining controls of the dialog so that you can enter information for the share.

6. Type a descriptive name for the share into the Share Name combo box. This is the name by which users access the shared folder. Optionally, type a more complete description of the resource into the Comment text box.

Part
III

Ch

14

FIG. 14.1

Creating a share with the Sharing page of the *Foldername* Properties sheet.

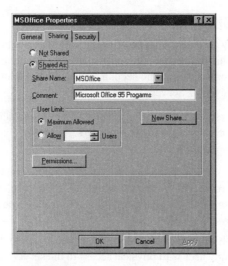

7. Specify User Limit information. By default, the new share is set to Maximum Allowed, which allows any number of users to access the share simultaneously, up to the limit of the number of users for which the server is licensed.

   Select the Allow option button and select a specific number of allowable simultaneous users, if you want to limit the number of users permitted to access this share at any one time. Do this if you're concerned about performance degradation when a large number of users vie for a single resource.

By default, the new share provides Full Control to the group Everyone. This means that any user with an account on the server can add, modify, or delete files contained in this folder. The following section, "Working with Share Permissions," describes how to restrict access to the new share.

> **CAUTION**
>
> Although Windows NT Server 4.0 converts long file and folder names to a form usable by clients running DOS and Windows versions before Windows 95, it doesn't perform a similar conversion for share names. Although Windows NT Server 4.0 allows you to use share names that exceed the MS-DOS 8.3 naming conventions, doing so makes these shares inaccessible to some clients. Windows 95, for example, accommodates share names up to 12 characters long. For better client compatibility, stick with eight-character (or fewer) share names.

To remove a folder share, perform the preceding first four steps to display the Sharing page of the *Foldername* Properties sheet. Select the Not Shared option button and then click the Apply button.

To modify the share, specify a new Share Name, Comment, or User Limit, as described in the preceding steps. You also can create an alias for this shared resource by clicking the New Share button and completing the dialog. An *alias* allows the same shared resource to be accessed by more than one share name.

By clicking the Permissions button, you can determine which users and groups have access to this shared resource, and at what level. The following section describes how to restrict access in this manner.

Working with Share Permissions   Share permissions control which users and groups can access a share, and at what level. You can add, modify, view, or remove the following share permissions for each folder you have shared on the server:

- *No Access* permission restricts all access to the shared folder.

- *Read* permission allows users to view file names and subfolder names within the shared folder. You can change to a subfolder and open a file in the shared folder or in a subfolder in read-only mode, but you can't write to that file or delete it. You can execute program files for which you have only Read permission.

- *Change* permission grants all the rights provided by Read permission and adds the rights to create new files and subfolders, modify the contents of new or existing files, and delete files and subfolders.

- *Full Control* permission grants all the rights provided by Change permission and adds the rights to create and modify NTFS file permissions and folder permissions, as well as take ownership of NTFS files and folders.

Follow these steps to modify, view, and remove share permissions:

1. Perform the first four steps in the preceding section to display the Sharing page of the *Foldername* Properties sheet.

2. Click the Permissions button to display the Access Through Share Permissions dialog (see Figure 14.2). The Name list displays the users and groups authorized to access this share. By default, the group Everyone is assigned the Full Control permission to the share.

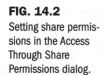

FIG. 14.2

Setting share permissions in the Access Through Share Permissions dialog.

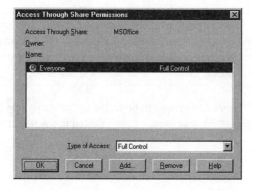

Part
III

Ch
14

3. To modify the share permission for an existing user or group, select that user or group and then select a Type of Access from the drop-down list.

To remove the share permission for an existing user or group, select that user or group and click the Remove button.

4. Click OK to accept the changes and return to the *Foldername* Properties sheet.

Adding a share permission requires a few more steps. Follow steps 1 and 2 in the preceding list to display the Add Through Share Permissions dialog. Then proceed as follows:

1. Click the Add button to display the Add Users and Groups dialog (see Figure 14.3).

FIG. 14.3

Granting share permissions to users and groups in the Add Users and Groups dialog.

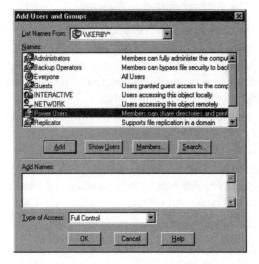

2. Select the domain or computer from which the new users or groups are to be added from the List Names From drop-down list. Member groups of the selected domain or computer are displayed in the Names list.

3. Select a displayed group by clicking its name. (By default, only groups are displayed. To display users, click the Show Users button.)

 To add several users and groups to the share in a single step, select multiple users and groups by using standard Windows selection conventions. Ctrl+click to add additional individual users or groups to the selected list; Shift+click to add a contiguous range of users or groups to the selected list. As you select each user or group to be added, its name appears in the Add Names list.

4. After you select all users and groups to be added to the share, use the Type of Access drop-down list to select the access type to be granted to the selected users and groups.

CAUTION

If you're using share permissions to restrict access to a shared folder, remember to remove the default share permission that grants the group Everyone the Full Control share permission for that folder. Share permissions are cumulative, so any user has *all* share permissions granted to *any* group of which he is a member.

5. Click the Add button and then click OK to add the selected users and groups to the share. The Access Through Share Permissions dialog reappears, with the new users and groups added to the share and their access type displayed.

6. In the Access Through Share Permissions dialog, click OK to return to the *Foldername* Properties sheet. Click OK to accept the changes you've made to the share.

N O T E Share permissions specify the maximum level of access available within the shared folder tree. Any subsequent restrictions you add with NTFS folder permissions and NTFS file permissions (described in the following section) can only further restrict access. They can't grant an access level above that allowed by the share permission. ▪

Using Administrative Shares In addition to the shares you create, Windows NT Server automatically creates several shares for administrative purposes. These administrative shares include at least the following:

- *ADMIN$* points to the location of the shared Windows NT Server folder on the server. For example, if you install Windows NT Server to the C:\Winnt folder on your server, the ADMIN$ share points to this folder.

- *[drive letter]$* points to the root folder of each drive on the server. For example, if your server has three drives, designated C, D, and E, these drives are each represented by an administrative share, named C$, D$, and E$, respectively.

The most common administrative shares are the drive and folder shares. However, administrative shares can also represent a named pipe for remote procedure calls (RPCs), a communication-device queue (only on LAN Manager servers), or a shared printer.

▶ **See** "Calling Remote Procedures," **p. 96**

 T I P If you want to create a share that's not visible to users browsing the network, make the final character of the share name a $. A share so named doesn't appear to a user browsing network resources. To access the share, the user must know the exact share name and must explicitly type it.

Displaying All Shares and Disconnecting Shares A distinctive icon in Windows NT Explorer and the My Computer window indicates shared folders. However, sometimes seeing a comprehensive list of shares displayed in one place is useful. To see a list of all active shares on your server, proceed as follows:

1. From Control Panel, double-click the Server icon to display the Server dialog (see Figure 14.4).

Part

III

Ch

14

FIG. 14.4

The initial dialog of Control Panel's Server tool.

2. Click the Shares button to display the Shared Resources dialog (see Figure 14.5). For each share, this dialog displays the Sharename, Uses (the number of current active sessions for the share), and Path associated with the share name.

3. To disconnect one share, select its name and click the Disconnect button. To disconnect all shares in one step, click the Disconnect All button.

FIG. 14.5

The Shared Resources dialog, displaying share names and number of connected users.

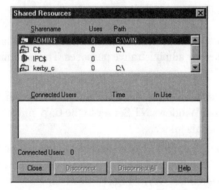

Using the Managing Folder and File Access Wizard

The Managing Folder and File Access Wizard provides a quick and easy way to create and manage folder shares. To use the Managing Folder and File Access Wizard, follow these steps:

1. From the Start menu, choose Programs, Administrative Tools, and Administrative Wizards to display the Administrative Wizards window. Click the Managing File and Folder Access icon to display the first dialog of the Managing Folder and File Access Wizard (see Figure 14.6).

2. Select On My Computer to create or manage shares on the server, or select On Another Computer to manage shares on another computer on the network. In this example, a new share is created on another server. Click Next to display the dialog shown in Figure 14.7.

FIG. 14.6

The opening dialog of the Managing Folder and File Access Wizard.

FIG. 14.7

Selecting the computer where the share is to be created.

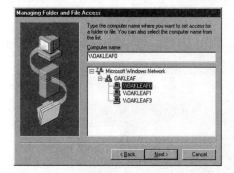

3. Select the computer where you want to create or manage the share and click Next. The Managing Folder and File Access Wizard displays the dialog shown in Figure 14.8. In the example, a new share name is entered into the To Create a New Folder, Type a New Name text box to create a new share named SHARED.

FIG. 14.8

Selecting an existing folder or creating a new folder.

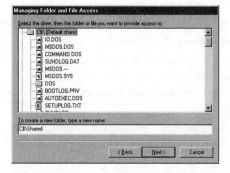

Part
III

Ch
14

4. Click Next to display the Managing Folder and File Access confirmation message shown in Figure 14.9. Click Yes to create the new folder. The Managing Folder and File Access

Wizard displays another message box to confirm that the new folder has been created successfully. Click OK.

FIG. 14.9

Confirming the creation of the new folder for the share.

5. Click Next to display the next Managing Folder and File Access Wizard dialog, which allows you to set permissions for the folder to determine who has access to it, and at what level (see Figure 14.10). By default, the original permissions for the share are retained, and these permissions flow down to affect the files and subfolders contained within this folder.

FIG. 14.10

Assigning permissions to the shared folder.

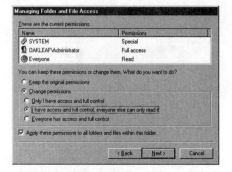

To change these default permissions, click Change Permissions and choose one of the three options presented:

- Only I Have Access and Full Control
- I Have Access and Full Control, Everyone Else Can Only Read It
- Everyone Has Access and Full Control

Mark the Apply These Permissions to All Folders and Files Within this Folder check box if you want the permissions you set here to apply to all subfolders and files contained within this folder. Unmark the check box if you want these permissions to apply only to this folder.

6. Click Next to display a Managing Folder and File Access message box, which lets you specify whether the folder will be shared with network users. Click Yes to allow network users to access the folder.

7. The Managing Folder and File Access Wizard displays the dialog shown in Figure 14.11. You can rename the share, provide a brief description of it, and specify which types of network users can access it. Make any changes necessary and click Next.

FIG. 14.11
Renaming the share, adding a description, and selecting the type of network users who have access to the share.

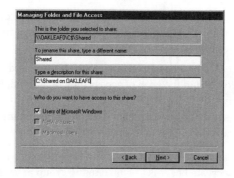

8. The Managing Folder and File Access Wizard displays the summary shown in Figure 14.12. Click Finish to complete creating the share.

9. The final message box lets you exit the Managing Folder and File Access Wizard or continue managing shares. Click No to exit or Yes to manage another share.

FIG. 14.12
The summary displays the choices you've made for the new share.

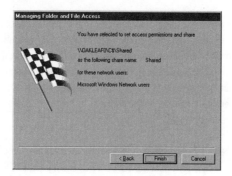

Understanding NTFS Permissions

Share-level access control provides only a limited capability to determine which users can access which files. The FAT file system offers only share-level access control. If you need to control access down to subfolders and individual files, your only choice is to use the NTFS file system. Doing so is no sacrifice at all, because NTFS offers more features, better performance (on all but the smallest volumes), and better security.

In addition to the file name, file size, and date/time stamp, NTFS stores extended attributes with each file and folder entry. One extended attribute, *permissions*, determines which users and groups have access to the shared resource. NTFS has the following types of permissions:

- *File-access permissions* store information about which users and groups are permitted to access a specified file and the level of access they're allowed. For example, the user

Part
III

Ch
14

Admin and the group Programmers might have full read/write access to a particular database file; the group Marketing might have read-only access; and the group Accounting might have no access at all.

■ *Folder-access permissions* store information about which users and groups are permitted to access a specified folder and the level of access they're allowed. For example, the user Webmaster and the group Administrators can have full read/write access to the Web server folder on your server (which contains your private company intranet), the group Everyone can have read-only access, and the user Guest can have no access at all.

By default, users inherit file and folder permissions from the group of which they are members. For example, if a newly created user is assigned to the group *marketing*, he is automatically granted all the group's file- and folder-access permissions. If a user is a member of more than one group, he has *all* permissions owned by *any* group of which he is a member.

Paying careful attention to how you assign group file and folder permissions allows you to reduce or eliminate the time-consuming and error-prone process of assigning permissions on a user-by-user basis.

N O T E   You can use NTFS file and folder permissions only to further restrict share-level permissions established when the original share was created or modified. NTFS permissions can't grant something that was taken away by the share-level permission in effect. For example, if the share-level permission restricts users to read-only access, setting NTFS file or folder permissions to a higher level of access does nothing to increase the users' level of access. Conversely, if the share-level permission allows full access but an NTFS permission further restricts access to read-only, users affected by the NTFS permission are limited to read-only access. ■

Working with NTFS File-Access Permissions   NTFS file-access permissions control which users and groups can access a file, and at what level. Remember that NTFS file-access permissions can further restrict the access level granted by share permissions, but they can't extend access beyond that granted by share-access permissions. You can add, modify, view, or remove the following file-access permissions for each file:

■ *No Access (None)* permission restricts all access to the shared file.

■ *Read (RX)* permission allows you to view the file name and open the file in read-only mode, but you can't write to the file or delete it. Because read (R) permission implies execute (X) permission, if the file is an executable program file, read permission allows you to execute it.

■ *Change (RWXD)* permission grants all the rights provided by Read permission and adds the rights to write (W) and delete (D) the file, create new files and subfolders, modify the contents of new or existing files, and delete files and subfolders.

■ *Full Control (All)* permission grants all the rights provided by Change permission and adds the rights to change NTFS file-access and folder permissions, as well as take ownership of NTFS files and folders.

■ *Special Access* permission allows you to customize the file-access permissions for a particular file. You can specify any combination of read (R), write (W), execute (X), delete (D), change permissions (P), and take ownership (O). For example, you can use Special Access file-access permissions to allow a specified user or group to have read, write, and execute permissions for the file, but not to have delete permission.

Modifying, Viewing, and Removing NTFS File-Access Permissions
Follow these steps to modify, view, and remove NTFS file-access permissions:

1. In Windows NT Explorer, select the file(s) for which permissions are to be added, modified, viewed, or removed.

2. Right-click to display the context-sensitive menu, and choose Properties to display the *Filename* Properties sheet.

3. Click the Security tab to display the Security page (see Figure 14.13).

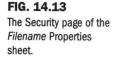

FIG. 14.13
The Security page of the *Filename* Properties sheet.

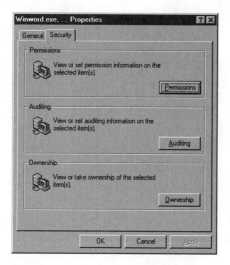

4. Click the Permissions button to display the File Permissions dialog.

5. Select a type of access from the Type of Access drop-down list (see Figure 14.14). You can choose one of the standard types of access—No Access, Read, Change, or Full Control—or you can select Special Access to customize file-access permissions for this file or group of files.

6. If you've selected one of the standard access types, click OK to apply the selected file-access permissions. You then return to the *Filename* Properties sheet. Click OK again to accept the changes and close the *Filename* Properties sheet.

If you select Special Access, the Special Access dialog shown in Figure 14.15 opens. Mark the check boxes to select the types of access to be granted for the selected file(s).

Part
III

Ch

14

The example shows a file for which all permissions except Take Ownership (O) have been granted. This custom set of permissions falls between the standard file-access types Change (RXWD) and Full Control (RXWDPO).

FIG. 14.14

Granting permissions to groups with the File Permissions dialog.

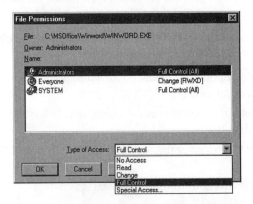

FIG. 14.15

Setting specific permissions for a group in the Special Access dialog.

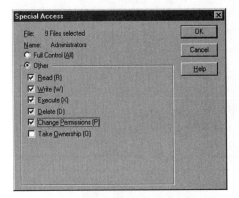

7. After you select the permissions for the file, click OK to accept these settings and return to the File Permissions dialog.

8. In the File Permissions dialog, click OK to apply the selected file-access permissions and return to the *Filename* Properties sheet. Click OK again to accept the changes and exit the *Filename* Properties sheet.

Adding NTFS File-Access Permissions   Follow these steps to add NTFS file-access permissions:

1. Follow steps 1 through 4 from the preceding section to display the File Permissions dialog.

2. Click the Add button to display the Add Users and Groups dialog (see Figure 14.16).

FIG. 14.16

Granting the Power Users group file access in the Add Users and Groups dialog.

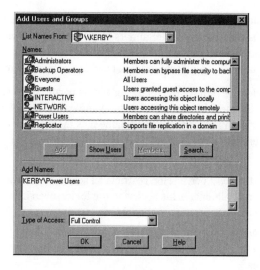

3. Select the domain or computer from which the users and groups are to be added from the List Names From drop-down list. The Names list displays available groups. To display individual users within these groups, click the Show Users button.

4. Select individual users or groups that you want to add file-access permissions for by double-clicking the name in the Names list. Each appears in the Add Names list as you select it.

   You can also select multiple users and groups in the Names list by using standard Windows conventions for making multiple selections. After you finish making selections, click the Add button to transfer all selected names to the Add Names list.

5. Select the access type to be granted to the selected users and groups from the Type of Access drop-down list.

N O T E Only the standard types of access—No Access, Read, Change, and Full Control—are available in the Add Users and Groups dialog. If you need to assign special file-access permissions for the users or groups being added, simply choose any one of the standard permissions here and modify your selection in the File Permissions dialog in the following step. ■

6. Click OK to accept your changes and return to the File Permissions dialog. The newly added users or groups appear in the Names list. If you need to assign Special File Access permissions to the newly added users or groups, do so now by using the steps described in the preceding section and then return to the File Permissions dialog.

7. Click OK to return to the *Filename* Properties sheet. Click OK again to accept the changes and exit the *Filename* Properties sheet.

Part

III

Ch

14

Working with NTFS Folder-Access Permissions   NTFS folder-access permissions control which users and groups can access a folder and its files, and at what level. Remember that NTFS folder-access permissions can further restrict the access level granted by share permissions but can't extend access beyond that granted by share-access permissions.

You can add, modify, view, or remove the following access permissions for each folder. Each named permission affects the folder in question and the files contained within it. The first parenthetical item after each access permission name lists the effect of that permission on the folder; the second parenthetical item lists the effect of that permission on files contained within the folder.

- *No Access (None) (None)* permission restricts all access to the shared folder. Specifying No Access for a user eliminates his access to the folder, even if he is a member of a group or groups that have access to the folder.

- *List (RX) (not specified)* permission allows users to view a list of files and subfolders contained within the folder, and to change to a subfolder, but it doesn't grant permission to access the files.

- *Read (RX) (RX)* permission grants all the rights provided by List permission. It allows users to open a file in read-only mode, but not to write to the file or delete it. Because read (R) permission implies execute (X) permission, if the file is an executable program file, read permission allows you to execute it.

- *Add (WX) (not specified)* permission allows users to create new files and new subfolders within the folder, but doesn't grant permission to access the files, including those newly created.

- *Add & Read (RWX) (RX)* permission combines the rights granted by the Read and Add folder permissions described in the preceding paragraphs.

- *Change (RWXD) (RWXD)* permission grants all rights provided by the Add & Read permission and adds the rights to write to (W) and delete (D) files and subfolders.

- *Full Control (All) (All)* permission grants all the rights provided by the Change permission and adds the rights to change NTFS file-access and folder permissions, as well as take ownership of NTFS files and folders.

- *Special Directory Access* permission lets you customize folder-access permissions. You can specify any combination of read (R), write (W), execute (X), delete (D), change permissions (P), and take ownership (O). For example, you can use Special Directory Access folder-access permissions to allow a specified user or group to have list and read permissions for files within the folder, but not to have execute permission.

- *Special File Access* permission allows you to customize file-access permissions. You can specify any combination of read (R), write (W), execute (X), delete (D), change permissions (P), and take ownership (O). Special file-access permission works in the same way as the Special Directory Access permission described in the preceding paragraph, but affects only specified files contained within the folder rather than the folder itself.

> **N O T E** NTFS folder-access permissions supersede restrictions placed on files by NTFS file-access permissions. For example, if users have the Full Control folder-access permission in a folder that contains a file with file-access permissions set to read (R), they can modify or delete the file. ■

Modifying, Viewing, and Removing NTFS Folder-Access Permissions You can modify, view, and remove NTFS folder-access permissions by following these steps:

1. In Windows NT Explorer, select the folder(s) for which permissions are to be added, modified, viewed, or removed.

2. Right-click to display the context-sensitive menu, and choose Properties to display the *Foldername* Properties sheet.

3. Click the Security tab to display the Security page (refer to Figure 14.13).

4. Click the Permissions button to display the Directory Permissions dialog (see Figure 14.17).

FIG. 14.17

Granting file permissions for two NTFS folders in the Directory Permissions dialog.

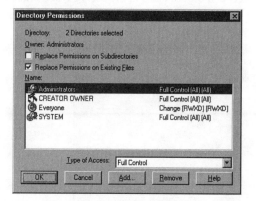

5. Select an access type from the Type of Access drop-down list. You can choose one of the standard types of access—No Access, List, Read, Add, Add & Read, Change, or Full Control. You also can choose Special Directory Access to specify a custom set of access rights for the affected folders, or Special File Access to specify a custom set of access rights for the files contained within those folders.

> **N O T E** The Directory Permissions dialog includes two check boxes—Replace Permissions on Subdirectories and Replace Permissions on Existing Files—that allow you to specify which files and folders within the selected folder tree are affected by the permissions you set. Marking both check boxes causes the permissions you set to affect the selected folder, the files it contains, the subfolders of that folder, and the files contained in these subfolders.

Part
III

Ch
14

continues

continued

Marking only the Replace Permissions on Subdirectories check box causes the permissions you set to affect only the selected folder and its subfolders, but not the files contained within them. Marking only the Replace Permissions on Existing Files check box causes the permissions you set to affect only the selected folder and the files contained within it, but not the subfolders or their files. Clearing both check boxes causes the permissions you set to affect only the selected folder, but not the files contained within it or the subfolders and their files. ▩

6. If you've selected one of the standard access types, click OK to apply the selected folder-access permissions. You then return to the *Foldername* Properties sheet. Click OK again to accept the changes and exit the *Foldername* Properties sheet.

   If you select Special Directory Access, the Special Directory Access dialog opens (see Figure 14.18). Mark the check boxes to select the types of access to be granted for the selected folder or folders. The example shows access being set for two folders for which all permissions except Take Ownership (O) have been granted. This custom set of permissions falls between the standard folder-access types Change (RXWD) and Full Control (RWXDPO).

FIG. 14.18

Granting specific permissions for two NTFS folders in the Special Directory Access dialog.

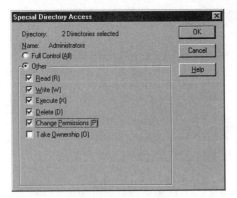

7. After you select the permissions for the folder, click OK to accept these settings and return to the Directory Permissions dialog.

8. In the Directory Permissions dialog, click OK to apply the selected folder-access permissions and return to the *Foldername* Properties sheet. Click OK again to accept the changes and exit the *Foldername* Properties sheet.

9. If you select Special File Access, the Special File Access dialog shown in Figure 14.19 opens. Mark the check boxes to select the types of access to be granted for files contained within the selected folder or folders. The example shows access being set for two folders for which all permissions except Take Ownership (O) have been granted. This custom set of permissions falls between the standard folder-access types Change (RXWD) and Full Control (RWXDPO).

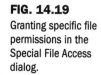

FIG. 14.19
Granting specific file permissions in the Special File Access dialog.

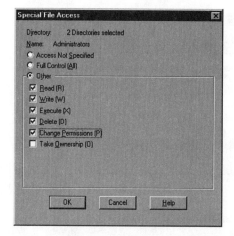

NOTE The Special File Access dialog is almost identical to the Special Directory Access dialog but includes one additional item. Selecting the Access Not Specified option button in the Special File Access dialog prevents files in the affected folder or folders from inheriting folder permissions. ■

10. After you select special file-access permissions for the affected folder or folders, click OK to accept these settings and return to the Directory Permissions dialog.

11. In the Directory Permissions dialog, click OK to apply the permissions and return to the *Foldername* Properties sheet. Click OK again to accept the changes and exit the *Foldername* Properties sheet.

Adding NTFS Folder-Access Permissions Follow these steps to add NTFS folder-access permissions:

1. Follow steps 1 through 4 from the preceding section to display the Directory Permissions dialog.

2. Click the Add button to display the Add Users and Groups dialog (see Figure 14.20).

3. Select the domain or computer from which the users and groups are to be added from the List Names From drop-down list. The Names list displays available groups. Click the Show Users button to display individual users from within these groups.

4. Double-click names in the Names list to select individual users or groups for which you want to add file-access permissions. Each appears in the Add Names list as you select it. (You can also select multiple users and groups in the Names list by using standard Windows conventions for making multiple selections.) After you finish making selections, click the Add button to transfer all selected names to the Add Names list.

5. Select the access type to be granted to the selected users and groups from the Type of Access drop-down list.

Part
III

Ch
14

FIG. 14.20

The Add Users and Groups dialog with the Power Users group added.

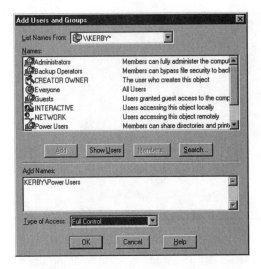

N O T E Only the standard types of access—No Access, List, Read, Add, Add & Read, Change, and Full Control—are available in the Add Users and Groups dialog. If you need to assign Special Directory Access permissions or Special File Access permissions for the users or groups being added, simply choose any one of the standard permissions here and modify your selection in the Directory Permissions dialog in the following step. ■

6. Click OK to accept your changes and return to the Directory Permissions dialog. The newly added users or groups are displayed in the Name list. If you need to assign Special Directory Access permissions or Special File Access permissions to the newly added users or groups, select them now and assign these special access permissions by following the steps in the preceding section.

7. After you properly assign all permissions, return to the Directory Permissions dialog and click OK to return to the *Foldername* Properties sheet. Click OK to accept the changes and exit the *Foldername* Properties sheet.

Replicating Folders

Windows NT Server 4.0 allows you to replicate, or copy, folders to other computers or domains to maintain identical copies of folders and files on more than one computer. The folder from which data is copied is called the *export folder* and is located on the *export server;* the folder to which data is copied is called the *import folder* and is located on the *import computer.* The export and import folders can be located on the same computer or on different computers.

N O T E A server running the Windows NT Server 4.0 replication service can be an export server, an import computer, or both. A client running Windows NT Workstation 4.0 can participate in folder replication, but only as an import computer. ■

Folder replication does more than simply copy data from the export folder source to the import folder destination. The Windows NT Server replication service functions much like an FTP mirror program. It monitors the export folder for changes to existing files and newly created files and subfolders, and replicates these changes and additions to the import folder. The replication service also deletes files in the import folder that have been deleted from the export folder. By doing so, it synchronizes the contents of the two folders.

Folder replication is most commonly used for the following two purposes:

■ *Replicating logon scripts from one domain controller to other domain controllers* allows users of any domain controller to log on locally and reduces server load and network traffic.

■ *Replicating a database from one server to another* allows users who access the database to be distributed among two or more servers in order to share the workload among multiple servers.

You also can use folder replication to keep a frequently updated backup copy of a heavily used database file, which would otherwise be difficult to back up.

Creating a Replication User

Before you can configure the replication service, you must first create a special user for that service as described in Chapter 13, "Managing User and Group Accounts." This new special user must have the following properties:

■ The user must be assigned to the Backup Operators group.

■ The Password Never Expires check box must be marked.

■ The Logon Hours settings must allow this user access at all times.

You won't be able to name the new user Replicator because a group already exists with that name. Choose another similar name, such as Replicate.

Starting the Replication Service

After you create the special user, you must then configure and start the Directory Replicator service before folder replication can occur. To do so, proceed as follows:

1. From Control Panel, double-click the Services tool to display the Services dialog (shown in Figure 14.21 with the Directory Replicator service selected). The Status is shown as blank, indicating that the Directory Replicator service isn't running. Startup is shown as Manual, indicating that this service won't be started unless you do so manually.

2. With the Directory Replicator service selected, click the Startup button to display the Service dialog (see Figure 14.22).

3. In the Startup Type section, select Automatic to indicate that the Directory Replicator service should start automatically each time Windows NT Server is started.

Part
III

Ch
14

FIG. 14.21

Selecting the Directory
Replicator service in the
Services dialog.

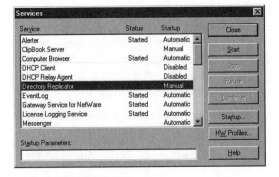

FIG. 14.22

Setting the Startup Type
and Log On As account
in the Service dialog.

4. In the Log On As section, select This Account, and then enter the domain and user
   account name that you created in the preceding section. You can also click the ... button
   to display a list of available accounts to choose from.

   Type the password for this account in the Password and Confirm Password text boxes.

5. Click OK to accept the changes. You're prompted to restart Windows NT Server.

6. After Windows NT Server is restarted, double-click Control Panel's Services tool to
   verify that the Directory Replicator service has been started successfully. You should see
   a display similar to Figure 14.23, with the Directory Replicator service shown with Status
   as Started and Startup as Automatic.

Configuring Folder Replication

After you successfully configure the Directory Replicator service, you must then configure an
export server and an import computer.

FIG. 14.23

Confirming startup of the Directory Replicator in the Services dialog.

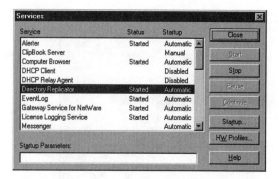

To configure the export server, you must provide the following pieces of information:

- The export folder designates the source folder from which files and subfolders are exported.
- The Export To list designates computers and domains to which files and subfolders are exported. If you designate a domain here, exported data is replicated on all computers in the export-to domain that have replication enabled.

To configure the import computer, you must also provide two pieces of information, as follows:

- The import folder designates the destination folder in which imported files and subfolders are stored.
- The Import From list designates computers and domains from which data to be imported is accepted.

To configure the export server and the import computer, proceed as follows:

1. From Control Panel, double-click the Server tool to display the Server dialog.
2. Click the Replication button to display the Directory Replication dialog (see Figure 14.24).
3. In the export section, select Export Directories to enable exporting. Then designate which folder is to be exported in the From Path text box. Click the Add button to add domains or computers to the To List to designate a target or targets to which files are exported.

N O T E Windows NT Server 4.0 creates default import and export folders when you install it. The default import folder is C:\Winnt\System32\Repl\Import. The default export directory is C:\Winnt\System32\Repl\Export. All folders to be replicated must be subfolders of the ...\Export folder and all replicated folders are created in the ...\Import folder. ■

Part
III

Ch
14

FIG. 14.24

Setting replication paths, lists, and script locations in the Directory Replication dialog.

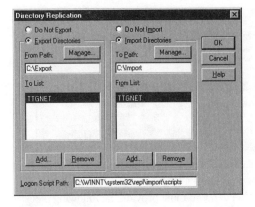

4. Click the Manage button to display the Manage Exported Directories dialog (see Figure 14.25). You can use the controls in this dialog to add and remove exported directories and to add and remove locks on managed directories.

FIG. 14.25

Setting export subdirectory parameters in the Manage Exported Directories dialog.

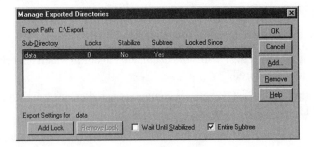

5. If this server will also be an import computer, select the Import Directories option in the import section of the Directory Replicator dialog to enable importing. Then designate which folder is to receive the imported data in the To Path text box. Click the Add button to add domains or computers to the From List to designate computers and domains from which imported data is to be accepted.

6. Click the Manage button in the import section to display the Manage Imported Directories dialog (see Figure 14.26). You can use the controls in this dialog to add and remove imported directories and to add and remove locks on managed directories.

FIG. 14.26
Setting import subdirectory parameters in the Manage Imported Directories dialog.

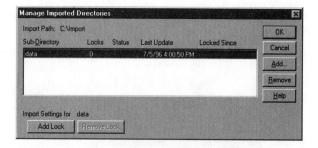

Compressing NTFS Files and Folders

You can save a substantial amount of disk space by compressing files shared from folders on NTFS partitions. Text, word processing, spreadsheet, and some static graphics files (particularly .bmp files) usually achieve better than 40 percent compression. NTFS's file compression/decompression system is similar to that of MS-DOS 6.0's DoubleSpace and MS-DOS 6.22's DriveSpace but is more reliable than either product. The major benefit of NTFS compression is that you can selectively compress individual folders or files; DoubleSpace and DriveSpace require that you compress an entire disk volume.

> **N O T E** The downside of NTFS file compression is a slight reduction in performance due to the overhead of the software compression/decompression process. Thus, compressing your system folders or other folders that store executable files isn't a recommended practice. Also, don't compress folders that store database files, such as SQL Server's .dat device files or Exchange Server message databases. You can't compress files on volumes with cluster sizes in excess of 4K, because compression performance decreases as cluster size increases, and large cluster sizes are used to improve performance, especially with multimedia files. Compressing audio (.wav) and video (.avi or .mov) files usually doesn't result in significant space saving and always degrades performance. ▪

Using Windows NT Explorer's or My Computer's Compression Features

It's most common to use Windows NT Explorer or My Computer to compress entire shared NTFS folders or individual files. To compress a folder and all its files with Explorer, follow these steps:

1. Launch Explorer and choose Options from the View menu. Click the View tab and mark the Display Compressed Files and Folders with Alternate Color check box.
2. Select the folder you want to compress.

Part
III

Ch
14

3. Choose Properties from the File menu to display the General page of the *Foldername* Properties sheet.

4. Mark the Compress check box (see Figure 14.27) and click OK to open the Explorer dialog.

FIG. 14.27

Specifying compression of a NTFS folder, including all its files.

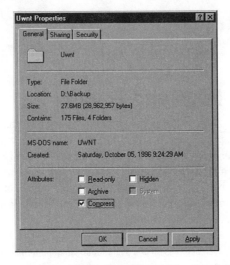

5. Mark the Also Compress Subfolders check box (see Figure 14.28). The Explorer dialog opens whether or not the folder you're compressing has subfolders.

FIG. 14.28

Specifying compression of subfolders, if any, in the folder to be compressed.

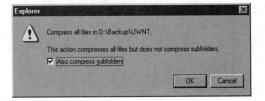

6. Click OK to continue the compression process. The Compress File message box displays the compression status (see Figure 14.29). As mentioned earlier in the section "Compressing NTFS Files and Folders," compression ratios of 40 percent (a 100K file compresses to 60K) are common for text, word processing, worksheet, and similar files.

On completion of the compression process, Explorer displays in blue the file name, size, date, and other text entries for the compressed folder and its files.

To compress an entire volume, follow this procedure:

1. Select the drive letter in Explorer and choose Properties from the File menu to open the volume's Properties sheet.

FIG. 14.29

The message box that reports compression progress and percentage compression.

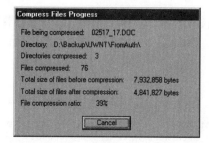

2. Mark the Compress check box of the General page (see Figure 14.30) and click OK.

3. Mark the Also Compress Subfolders check box and click OK.

FIG. 14.30

Specifying compression of an entire volume.

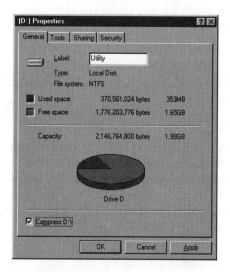

Moving and Copying Compressed Files

Compressed files, including folders, carry a compressed (C) attribute. Following are the general rules that govern whether a compressed file is compressed or decompressed when moved or copied:

■ When you move a compressed file from one NTFS folder to another NTFS folder (including moves between NTFS volumes), the file remains compressed, whether or not the destination drive or folder is compressed.

■ When you copy a compressed file to a NTFS folder, the compression status of the file corresponds to the compression attribute of the folder. That is, copying a compressed file to a decompressed folder results in a decompressed copy; copying a decompressed file to a compressed folder results in a compressed copy.

■ When you move or copy a compressed file to a folder of a FAT volume, the resulting file is decompressed.

Part
III

Ch
14

Using Compact.exe at the Command Prompt

Compact.exe is a command-line utility that you can execute in a batch file to compress or de-compress volumes, folders, and files. Following is the command-line syntax for Compact.exe obtained by redirecting `compact /?` to a text file:

```
COMPACT [/C¦/U] [/S[:dir]] [/A] [/I] [/F] [/Q] [filename [...]]
```

```
/C        Compresses the specified files. Directories will be marked
          so that files added afterward will be compressed.
/U        Uncompresses the specified files. Directories will be marked
          so that files added afterward will not be compressed.
/S        Performs the specified operation on files in the given
          directory and all subdirectories. Default "dir" is the
          current directory.
/A        Displays files with the hidden or system attributes.  These
          files are omitted by default.
/I        Continues performing the specified operation even after errors
          have occurred. By default, COMPACT stops when an error is
          encountered.
/F        Forces the compress operation on all specified files, even
          those which are already compressed. Already-compressed files
          are skipped by default.
/Q        Reports only the most essential information.
filename Specifies a pattern, file, or directory.
```

Multiple command-line parameters must be separated by spaces. If you omit the parameters, Compact.exe displays the compression state of the current folder and the files contained in the folder. Figure 14.31 shows Compact.exe displaying a folder with a single compressed folder (Original Finals) indicated by the C attribute after the compression ratio (1.0:1). Unlike Explorer and My Computer, Compact.exe doesn't ask whether you want to compact subfolders; it automatically compacts all subfolders and their files.

FIG. 14.31

Using Compact.exe at the command line to display compression status of a folder and its subfolders.

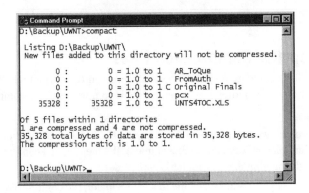

Taking Advantage of the Resource Kit's Diruse.exe Utility

The *Windows NT Server Resource Kit* for version 4.0 provides 12 File Utilities of widely varying usefulness. None of the File Utilities are new or upgraded in *Windows NT Server Resource Kit* for version 4.0, *Supplement One*. The only utility of day-to-day usefulness to Windows NT Server administrators is Diruse.exe, which you can use to report on the amount of server space consumed by folders assigned to individual users or by a particular service, such as Exchange Server. You can set up Diruse.exe to send you an alert in case usage exceeds a specified number of bytes.

Following is the command-line syntax for Diruse.exe, created by redirecting the `diruse /?` command to a text file:

```
DIRUSE [/S¦/V] [/M¦/K¦/B] [/C] [/,] [/Q:# [/L] [/A] [/D] [/O]] [/*] DIRS

/S      Specifies whether subdirectories are included in the output.
/V      Output progress reports while scanning subdirectories.
        Ignored if /S is specified.
/M      Displays disk usage in megabytes.
/K      Displays disk usage in kilobytes.
/B      Displays disk usage in bytes (default).
/C      Use Compressed size instead of apparent size.
/,      Use thousand separator when displaying sizes.
/Q:#    Mark directories that exceed the specified size (#) with a "!".
        (If /M or /K is not specified, then bytes is assumed.)
/L      Output overflows to logfile .\DIRUSE.LOG.
/A      Specifies that an alert is generated if specified sizes
        are exceeded. (The Alerter service must be running.)
/D      Displays only directories that exceed specified sizes.
/O      Specifies that subdirectories are not checked for
        specified size overflow.
/*      Uses the top-level directories residing in the specified DIRS
DIRS    Specifies a list of the paths to check.
```

If you specify the `/Q:#` parameter, you can obtain a return value when executing Diruse.exe and test the value in a batch file. If any folder exceeds the specified size, the return value is 1; otherwise the return value is 0.

 T I P If you run out of space on the drive that contains your Exchange Server database files, recovering empty space in the files by compaction is very difficult. (Exchange Server uses modified Jet database files, which must be compacted to recover the space consumed by deleted records.) Use At.exe to run Diruse.exe periodically to check the amount of space used by Exchange Server databases.

Part

III

Ch

14

Sharing and Securing Network Printers

Beyond sharing folders and files, the most common purpose of most networks is to share print-ers. One justification for early local area networks was their capability to share expensive laser printers among many users. In the past few years, the prices of laser printers have plummeted; it's now economically feasible for many companies to provide sub-$1,000 personal laser print-ers, such as the Hewlett-Packard LaserJet 5L and 5P, to any client that needs one.

Still, in all, the original justification for sharing expensive printers on the network holds true. Ten years ago, you might have been sharing a $3,500 LaserJet that printed eight letter-size pages per minute at 300 dpi. Today, you might instead be sharing a laser printer that prints 20 11-by-17-inch pages per minute at 600 dpi, but that printer still costs $3,500, and budget reali-ties still demand that it be shared. Just as it always did, the network allows you to share scarce and expensive resources, such as high-speed laser printers and color printers.

Windows NT Server makes it easy to share printers on the network. Printers attached directly to the Windows NT server can be shared as a network resource and used by any network client authorized to do so. Network clients running Windows 3.11 for Workgroups, Windows 95, or Windows NT Workstation can also function as printer servers, sharing their attached printers with other network users.

N O T E Any Windows Networking server or client can share an attached printer as a network resource. Windows NT Server also supports sharing of directly network connected Hewlett-Packard network printers, using the HP JetDirect network interface. A *directly network connected printer* is one that contains its own network adapter card and connects directly to the network cable rather than to a network client that provides printer server functions for that printer. Directly network connected printers are also called DLC printers, from the Data Link Control protocol that must be installed to support them. Some network printers use TCP/IP instead of DLC.

You can use directly network connected printers in locations that are too far removed from the network server to be cabled directly to the server, but where you don't want to put a network client computer. High-speed laser printers, color printers, and other output devices designed to be used as shared network resources are often connected directly to the network in this fashion. ■

Configuring Locally Attached Server Printers as Shared Resources

After you physically install the printer to be shared and connect it to the Windows NT server, you can use the Add Printer Wizard to configure it and make it available as a shared printer. To do so, proceed as follows:

1. From the My Computer window, double-click the Printers icon to display available printers. (If you haven't installed any printers yet, only the Add Printer icon appears in the Printers window.)

2. Double-click the Add Printer icon to invoke the Add Printer Wizard (see Figure 14.32). You can select My Computer to add a printer to the local computer, or Network Printer

Server to add a network printer that's physically connected to a different computer. This section describes adding a locally connected printer, so select My Computer and click Next.

FIG. 14.32

Specifying the printer location in the first Add Printer Wizard dialog.

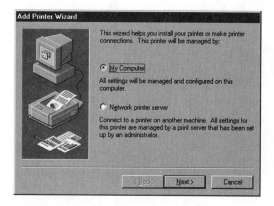

3. The next dialog (see Figure 14.33) lets you specify the port to which the printer is connected, add a port, and modify the properties for a port. Mark the check box that corresponds to the port that your new printer is connected to.

4. If you need to add a port to the Available Ports list, click the Add Port button to display a list of available printer ports (see Figure 14.34). When you add a printer port and accept the change by clicking OK, you return to the preceding Add Printer Wizard dialog, where the newly added printer port appears as an available selection.

FIG. 14.33

Selecting the printer port in the second Add Printer Wizard dialog.

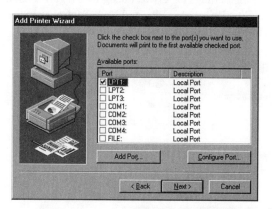

5. In the second Add Printer Wizard dialog, you can click the Configure Port button to display and modify port settings. If the selected port is a parallel port, the Configure LPT Port dialog opens (see Figure 14.35).

Part
III

Ch

14

FIG. 14.34

Adding a new printer port in the Printer Ports dialog.

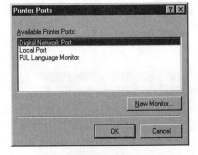

FIG. 14.35

Setting the printer time-out in the Configure LPT Port dialog.

 TIP The only configuration item available for a parallel port is Transmission Retry, which should ordinarily be left at the default setting. If the server to which the printer is connected is very busy, other workstations can have difficulties completing a print job to this shared printer. If so, try increasing the value for Transmission Retry a little at a time until the problem disappears.

If the selected port is a serial port (also called a *COM port*), the Ports dialog opens (see Figure 14.36). Select the COM port that the printer is connected to and click the Settings button to display the Settings for COM*x* dialog (see Figure 14.37). Select the settings for Baud Rate, Data Bits, Parity, Stop Bits, and Flow Control from the drop-down lists that correspond to the settings of the printer being installed.

FIG. 14.36

Choosing between available COM (serial) ports in the Ports dialog.

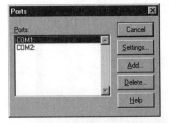

FIG. 14.37

Selecting standard COM port parameters Settings for COMx dialog.

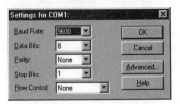

6. Click the Advanced button to display the Advanced Settings for COMx dialog (see Figure 14.38). In this dialog, you can adjust settings for COM Port Number, Base I/O Port Address, and Interrupt Request Line (IRQ). The FIFO Enabled check box, when marked, allows Windows NT to use the buffering provided by 16550 and higher UARTs (Universal Asynchronous Receiver/Transmitter) to improve Windows printing performance. If an advanced UART was detected during Windows installation, this check box is marked by default and should be left marked. If Windows NT didn't detect an advanced UART on this port during installation, the check box is disabled (grayed out).

FIG. 14.38

Specifying the I/O memory address and interrupt level in the Advanced Settings for COMx dialog.

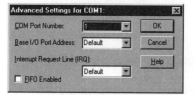

CAUTION

The settings for COM Port Number, Base I/O Port Address, and Interrupt Request Line (IRQ) should almost always be left at their default values. Alter these settings only if you've changed the standard COM port settings for your hardware. Otherwise, Windows NT won't be able to locate the COM port.

---

7. After you finish selecting the printer port, click OK to advance to the Add Printer Wizard printer selection dialog (see Figure 14.39). Select the manufacturer of your printer in the Manufacturers list; then, in the Printers list, select the model of your printer. Click Next.

FIG. 14.39

Selecting the printer manufacturer and model in the third Add Printer Wizard dialog.

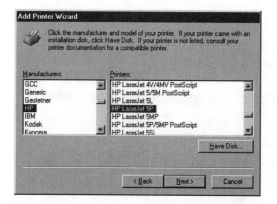

Part
III

Ch

14

N O T E If you have an updated printer driver supplied by the printer manufacturer, click the Have Disk button and follow the prompts to load the updated driver. ∎

8. The fourth Add Printer Wizard dialog (see Figure 14.40) lets you specify whether this printer is shared, to provide a share name for the printer, and to load support for other operating systems that will be printing to this printer. Complete this dialog and click Next. If you've specified that support for operating systems other than Windows NT 4.0 is to be loaded, you're prompted to insert driver disks for those operating systems.

FIG. 14.40

Assigning a share name and specifying types of client PCs in the fourth Add Printer Wizard dialog.

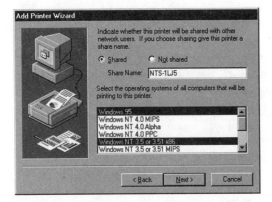

> **CAUTION**
>
> Be careful when you choose a share name for the printer. If this printer will be accessed by clients running MS-DOS or Windows 3.1+, the share name you select must conform to the MS-DOS 8.3 naming conventions; otherwise, the printer won't be visible to these clients. If all your clients are running Windows 95 or Windows NT 4.0, you can select a share name that conforms to Microsoft's long file name conventions.

9. The next Add Printer Wizard dialog lets you print a test page (see Figure 14.41). You should always allow the wizard to print the page to verify that your printer has been installed successfully and is performing as expected. After you print the page and verify that it printed correctly, click the Finish button.

FIG. 14.41

Printing a test page in the fifth Add Printer Wizard dialog.

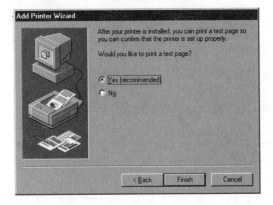

10. The Copying Files – – Files Needed dialog prompts you to insert the Windows NT Server CD-ROM so that the necessary files can be copied from it (see Figure 14.42). Specify the drive and path name for these files, or click the Browse button to browse for the location. Make sure that the CD-ROM disk is inserted in the drive, and click OK to proceed with copying files.

FIG. 14.42

Specifying the location of the required printer driver in the Copying Files –– Files Needed dialog.

11. When all needed files are copied from the Windows NT CD-ROM, the Add Printer Wizard prompts you to insert the distribution media for the other operating systems you've elected to provide printing support for. Insert the media and specify the location of these files as described in step 10.

The Add Printer Wizard now takes you directly to the Printer Properties sheet so you can configure the newly installed printer. This process, used both to configure newly installed printers and to reconfigure already installed printers, is described in the following section.

Configuring Network Printer Servers as Shared Resources

The preceding section described how to configure a printer that's physically attached to the computer running Windows NT Server as a shared printer. The Add Printer Wizard also lets you configure a network printer server as a shared resource on the server. A *network printer server* is a print queue that services a printer that's physically connected to a different computer on the network.

In this section, you learn how to configure a printer queue serviced by a Novell NetWare printer server as a Windows NT Server shared resource. You can use the same procedure to associate a Windows Networking printer queue with a share name on your Windows NT server, letting you present printers connected to Windows Networking clients as a server shared resource.

To install and configure a network printer server as a shared server resource, follow these steps:

1. From the My Computer window, double-click the Printers icon to display available printers.

Part

III

Ch

14

2. Double-click the Add Printer icon in the Printers window to invoke the Add Printer Wizard (see Figure 14.43). You can select My Computer to add a printer to the local computer (as described in the preceding section), or Network Printer Server to add a network printer that's physically connected to a different computer. This section describes adding a network printer server, so select Network Printer Server and click the Next button.

FIG. 14.43

Specifying a networked printer as a shared resource in the first dialog of the Add Printer Wizard.

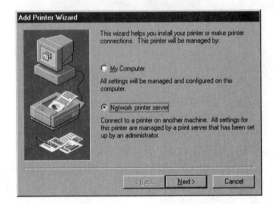

3. The Connect to Printer dialog opens, displaying the available networks and network printer queues visible to Windows NT Server. Double-click the printer server name to display the print queues associated with that printer server (see Figure 14.44). In the example, a Novell NetWare printer server named Theodore is servicing a print queue named \\THEODORE\\LASER_QUE. If more than one print queue exists on that server, double-click the queue you want to select to insert it in the Printer text box. (If only one print queue exists on the printer server, it's inserted into the Printer text box automatically when you select the printer server.) Click OK.

FIG. 14.44

Selecting a printer on a NetWare server from the Connect to Printer dialog.

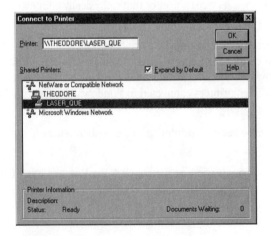

4. If the selected print queue doesn't have a printer driver installed, you're prompted to install an appropriate driver locally on the Windows NT server. Click OK to install the driver locally.

5. The Add Printer Wizard moves next to selecting a printer manufacturer and model (refer to Figure 14.39). Select the manufacturer of your printer in the Manufacturers list, and then select the model of your printer in the Printers list. Click the Next button.

6. The Connect to Printer ‒‒ Copying Files ‒‒ Files Needed dialog prompts you to insert the Windows NT Server CD-ROM so that the necessary files can be copied. Specify the drive and path name for these files, or click the Browse button to browse for the location. Make sure that the CD-ROM disk is inserted in the drive, and click OK to proceed with copying files.

7. When the necessary files are copied, the Printer Properties sheet opens (Figure 14.45 shows a Hewlett-Packard LaserJet 5P printer). The exact contents of this dialog vary, depending on the capabilities of the particular printer you're installing. Configure these settings appropriately, and then click OK.

FIG. 14.45

Setting the printer configuration in the Printer Properties sheet.

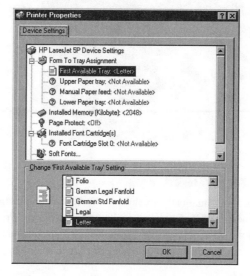

8. The Add Printer Wizard default printer dialog (see Figure 14.46) asks you whether this printer should be set as the default printer. Select the appropriate option and click Next.

9. The final Add Printer Wizard dialog opens (see Figure 14.47). Click Finish to complete installation of your network print queue printer and return to the Printers window.

Part
III

Ch
14

FIG. 14.46
Selecting between default and non-default local printer status in the fourth Add Printer Wizard dialog.

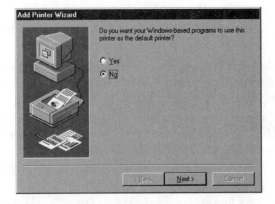

FIG. 14.47
Indication of successful addition of the remote printer in the final Add Printer Wizard dialog.

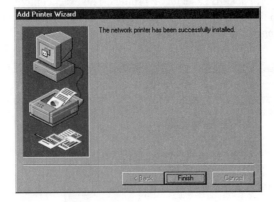

Configuring Printer Properties

The following procedure is automatically invoked as the final step in installing a local printer, described earlier in the section "Configuring Locally Attached Server Printers as Shared Resources." When used in this fashion, the Add Printer Wizard places you at step 3 in the following procedure. You also can use this procedure to reconfigure an existing printer, beginning with step 1:

1. From the My Computer window, double-click the Printers icon to display available printers.

2. Select the printer you want to configure in the Printers window, and right-click to display the context-sensitive menu. Choose Properties to display the General page of the *Printername* Properties sheet (see Figure 14.48).

FIG. 14.48

Specifying printer properties in the General page of the *Printername* Properties sheet.

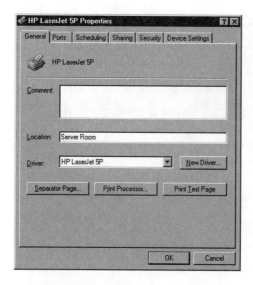

3. On the General page, supply the following information:

   - *Comment* lets you enter a short comment that can be viewed by users of the printer. For example, if the printer is available only during normal business hours, note that in this text box.

   - *Location* lets users view the physical location of the printer to make sure that they know where to pick up their print jobs.

   - *Driver* lets you select from a drop-down list of available drivers for the printer.

   - Click the *New Driver* button to install a new or updated driver for the printer.

   - Click the *Separator Page* button to specify options for separator pages, used to keep print jobs separate.

   - Click the *Print Processor* button to select different methods of processing the incoming byte stream. Use the default WinPrint processor unless you have specific reasons for changing it.

   - Click the *Print Test Page* button to print a test page to verify printer functioning.

4. After you complete the General page, display the Ports page (see Figure 14.49). You can use the Add Port, Delete Port, or Configure Port buttons to modify the port configuration for your printer, as described in the preceding section. The Enable Bidirectional Support check box is marked by default if your printer supports this function; if it doesn't, this selection is grayed out.

Part

III

Ch

14

FIG. 14.49

Selecting a parallel port in the Ports page of the *Printername* Properties sheet.

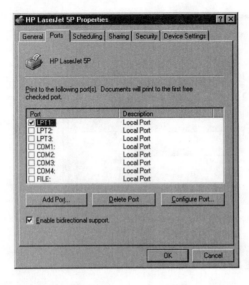

5. After you finish configuring the port, display the Scheduling page (see Figure 14.50). This page lets you specify when the printer is available to users, at what priority print jobs are to be handled, and the various options to control how spooled documents are processed.

FIG. 14.50

Specifying spooler properties in the Scheduling page of the *Printername* Properties sheet.

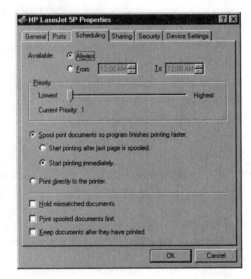

The following options are available from the Scheduling page:

- *Available* defaults to Always, allowing users to access this printer at any hour. You can select the From option and specify From and To times if you want to restrict availability of the printer to specified hours.

- *Priority* lets you specify what priority level Windows NT Server assigns to this printer.

- *Spool Print Documents so Program Finishes Printing Faster* lets you specify that incoming print jobs are written to a temporary file and processed from that file. If you select this option, you can choose between Start Printing After Last Page Is Spooled and Start Printing Immediately. In the first case, Windows NT Server waits until the entire print job has been written to a temporary spool file before it begins printing the document. In the latter case, Windows NT Server begins printing as soon as it has received enough data to complete the first page.

    The latter selection is marked by default, because Start Printing Immediately almost always provides better printing performance. If your network is very heavily loaded, you may need to specify Start Printing After The Last Page Is Spooled to prevent pages from different print jobs from being interleaved, and other printing problems.

- *Print Directly to the Printer* lets you specify that incoming print jobs are sent directly to the printer without first being queued.

CAUTION

Never select Print Directly to the Printer for a shared printer on a Windows NT server. Doing so can cause pages printed directly to the printer to be interleaved with pages from a print job that are being despooled from the printer queue.

- *Hold Mismatched Documents*, if marked, retains documents in the queue that couldn't be printed successfully because of mismatched pages.

- *Print Spooled Documents First*, if marked, gives preference to printing documents contained in the spool before printing other documents.

- *Keep Documents After They Have Printed*, if marked, retains documents in the print queue even after they print successfully. Windows NT Server ordinarily removes documents from the print spool after they're printed. Marking this check box results in all documents being retained in the spool, which causes a rapid growth in disk space consumed for spooled documents. Mark this check box only as a part of diagnosing printing problems.

6. After you finish setting scheduling options, display the Sharing page (see Figure 14.51). The upper section of this page lets you specify that the printer be Not Shared or Shared. If it's set as Shared, you can modify the share name in the Share Name text box.

FIG. 14.51

Specifying a share name and alternate drivers, if required, in the Sharing page of the *Printername* Properties sheet.

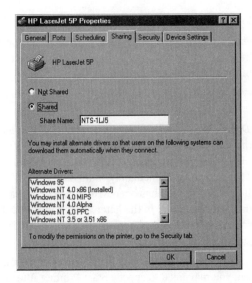

The bottom section of the Sharing page lets you specify alternate drivers that allow users of other operating systems to use the shared printer. In Figure 14.51, the Alternate Drivers list shows that support is installed only for Windows NT 4.0 running on the x86 processor family. You can install support for additional operating systems by selecting them in this list. Later, when you finally accept changes to all pages of the *Printername* Properties sheet by clicking OK, you're prompted to insert the disks containing the printer drivers needed.

7. After you finish setting sharing options, display the Security page, which has three sections, each of which is accessed by clicking that section's button (see Figure 14.52). The Permissions button lets you specify which groups are permitted to access the printer. The Auditing button lets you specify by user and by group which actions are recorded to an audit log. The Ownership button lets you specify which user or group owns the printer.

8. Click the Permissions button to display the Printer Permissions dialog (see Figure 14.53). The Name list displays the name of each group that's now authorized to access the printer on the left, with that group's level of access specified on the right. You can add a selected group by clicking the Add button and responding to the prompts. You can remove a selected group by clicking the Remove button.

To change the access level associated with a selected group or groups, select the type of access to be allowed from the Type of Access drop-down list. You can assign one of the following types of access:

- *No Access* allows the group so assigned no access whatsoever to the printer.
- *Print* allows the group so assigned to print documents, but not to manage the printer or modify its properties. You should assign this access level to ordinary users of the printer.

FIG. 14.52

The Security page of the *Printername* Properties sheet.

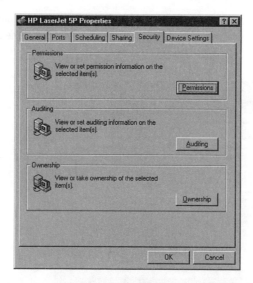

FIG. 14.53

Setting printer permissions for user groups in the Printer Permissions dialog.

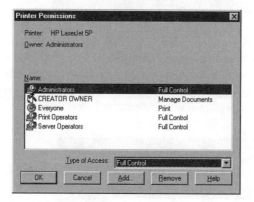

- *Manage Documents* allows the group so assigned to print documents and manage the printer. Manage documents is normally assigned to the creator/owner of the printer.

- *Full Control* allows the group so assigned to print documents, manage the printer, and modify its properties. Full control should normally be assigned to the groups Administrators, Print Operators, and Server Operators.

After you set permissions as necessary, click OK to return to the Security page of the *Printername* Properties sheet.

9. In the Security page of the *Printername* Properties sheet, click the Auditing button to display the Printer Auditing dialog. By default, no auditing is assigned for the printer. To add auditing for specified users and groups, click the Add button to display the Add

Part

III

Ch

14

Users and Groups dialog (see Figure 14.54). To add users and groups to the Add Names list, either double-click the user or group name, or select the name and click the Add button.

FIG. 14.54

Selecting groups for printer auditing in the Add Users and Groups dialog.

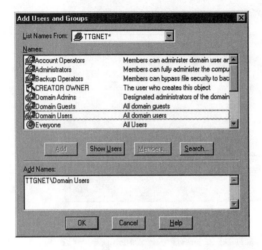

After you finish adding users and groups, click OK to return to the Printer Auditing dialog. Figure 14.55 shows Domain Users added for auditing, as well as auditing configured to report only Print Failure for the selected group. After you specify the desired level of auditing for each selected group, click OK to accept the changes and return to the Security page of the *Printername* Properties sheet.

FIG. 14.55

The Printer Auditing dialog with the Domain Users group added for auditing.

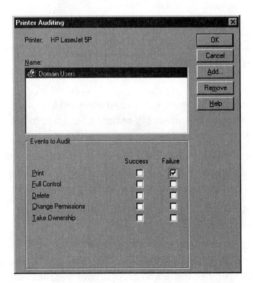

CAUTION

Be careful about assigning auditing for printers. If you assign too many auditing triggers to too many groups, the audit log file soon grows out of control. Not only does it occupy disk space that can otherwise be used for storing user data, but the large number of audit entries makes it impossible to notice the really important ones. If you decide to use auditing at all, limit it to logging attempts at unauthorized activities or with problems that occur during normal operations.

10. In the Security page of the *Printername* Properties sheet, click the Ownership button to display the Owner dialog (see Figure 14.56). You can take ownership of this printer by clicking the Take Ownership button, or close the dialog by clicking Close. In either case, you return to the Security page of the *Printername* Properties sheet.

FIG. 14.56

Taking ownership of the printer in the Owner dialog.

11. In the *Printername* Properties sheet, display the Device Settings page. The appearance of this page varies, depending on the characteristics of the printer for which you're setting properties. After you configure the device settings to your satisfaction, click OK to save the property settings for all pages.

From Here...

This chapter covered how to share the three primary server resources: folders, files, and printers. Although Windows NT Server 4.0's new Managing Folder and File Access Wizard provides a step-by-step approach to sharing files and folders, most network administrators are likely to use the Windows NT Explorer's file or folder property sheets to manage server shares.

The chapter also described how to use the Add Printer Wizard to share a printer connected to an LPT or COM port of the server, as well as how to create a Windows NT shared resource (print queue) from a printer connected to a NetWare server. The chapter concluded with a description of how to change properties of a printer previously set up as a shared Windows NT resource.

The following chapters provide additional information on topics discussed in this chapter:

- Chapter 11, "Configuring Windows 95 Clients for Networking," shows you how to set up PCs running Windows 95 to take maximum advantage of Windows NT 4.0 networks, including the use of printers shared by Windows NT servers.

Part

III

Ch

14

- Chapter 12, "Connecting Other PC Clients to the Network," provides the details on setting up Windows 3.1+, Windows for Workgroups 3.1+, Windows NT Workstation 4.0, and Macintosh clients to communicate with Windows NT 4.0 servers and use printers shared by Windows NT servers.

- Chapter 13, "Managing User and Group Accounts," describes how to use Windows NT Server 4.0's User Manager for Domains, take advantage of the new Add User Accounts and Group Management wizards, and utilize the built-in user groups of Windows NT.

CHAPTER 15

Optimizing Network Server Performance

Take advantage of the new Performance Monitor

You can use Performance Monitor to view the characteristics of a Windows NT 4.0 server.

Customize Performance Monitor views

You can generate custom charts, alerts, logs, and reports from the data gathered by Performance Monitor.

Enhance network performance

You can tune a Windows NT 4.0 server for use primarily as a network file server or an application server with Control Panel's Network tool.

Get the most out of the Resource Kit

Take full advantage of *Windows NT Server Resource Kit's* performance-tuning enhancements.

Although it's relatively easy to set up a Windows NT 4.0 server and connect printers and workstations to form a network, it's not as easy to tune your network for maximum performance. Windows NT Server 4.0 is not only a file server but also an application server, so you must monitor many performance parameters to ensure that your network doesn't grind to a halt.

Fortunately, Microsoft now includes a very powerful tool, Performance Monitor (PerfMon), with Windows NT Server 4.0. PerfMon, which originated in Microsoft Systems Management Server 1.0, lets you view the workings of virtually every component of your Windows NT 4.0 server and network. Performance Monitor also is included with Windows NT Workstation 4.0.

This chapter is divided into three principal sections. The first section, "Using Performance Monitor," helps you understand how PerfMon works and how to use the options available to network administrators. The second major section, "Optimizing Windows NT 4.0 File and Print Servers," illustrates how to use PerfMon to monitor specific characteristics of your network and computers and provides tips to obtain better network performance. The third section, "Optimizing Windows NT 4.0 as an Application Server," suggests techniques for maximizing the performance of Windows NT Server when running Windows NT services, such as SQL Server and Exchange Server. A brief section at the end of this chapter describes elements of the *Windows NT Server Resource Kit* that aid in tuning Windows NT Server 4.0 for maximum performance. ■

Using Performance Monitor

Task Manager's Performance page gives you a quick overview of current consumption of your Windows NT server's resources. PerfMon displays much more detailed operating characteristics, such as histories of system memory consumption and processor usage, of a computer running Windows NT. The data gathered can be displayed as charts, used to generate alerts, and saved in files for later analysis.

To start PerfMon, choose Programs, Administrative Tools, and then Performance Monitor from the Start menu. The Performance Monitor program window opens (see Figure 15.1). By default, no objects are monitored at startup.

FIG. 15.1

Performance Monitor's opening window displaying % Processor Time.

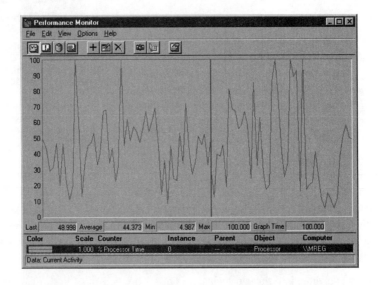

N O T E   Figure 15.1 shows the Processor object being monitored. Later, the section "Creating a New Chart" shows you how to monitor any of the standard objects of Windows NT Server 4.0. ■

Using Objects and Counters in Performance Monitor

PerfMon uses *counters* to record the behavior of objects in the system. In Windows NT, an *object* is a standard entity for identifying and using a system resource. Examples of objects are individual processes, shared memory, and physical devices. Like programming objects, Windows NT objects usually have data (properties) and behavior (methods); most counters record the rate (or a related unit) at which a particular method executes. For example, a counter displays the number of fixed-disk read operations (methods) per second.

PerfMon provides a specific set of counters to provide statistical information for each object type. Table 15.1 lists the most important objects of Windows NT (memory, the paging file, the physical disk, and the processor), the counters associated with each object, and the significance of each counter.

Table 15.1   Important System Objects and Counters of Windows NT 4.0

Counter	Description	Significance
Memory		
Available Bytes	Amount of virtual memory now available	When the value falls below a threshold, Windows NT gradually takes memory from running applications to maintain a certain minimum of available virtual memory.
Pages/Sec	Number of pages that had to be written to or read from disk and placed in physical memory	This counter indicates whether more physical memory is needed in your system. A value greater than 5 for a single disk could indicate a memory bottleneck.
Page Faults/Sec	Number of page faults in the processor	This value indicates that the data needed wasn't immediately available on the specified working set in memory.
Paging File		
% Usage	Amount of the paging file (Pagefile.sys) in use	This counter indicates whether you should increase the size of Pagefile.sys. If this value is near 100 percent, increase the size of the paging file.
% Usage Peak	Peak usage of system paging	This value also indicates whether the paging file is of the appropriate size. If this value nears the maximum age-file size, increase the size of the paging file.

continues

Table 15.1 Continued

Counter	Description	Significance
Physical Disk		
Avg. Disk Bytes/Transfer	Average number of bytes transferred to or from disk during read/write operations	Low values of this counter indicate that applications are accessing the disk inefficiently. If this value is greater than 20K, the disk drive is performing well.
Avg. Disk Sec/Transfer	Amount of time a disk takes to fulfill requests	A high value can indicate that the disk controller is continually retrying the disk because of read or write failures. A high value is greater than 0.3 second.
Disk Queue Length	Number of disk requests outstanding at the time performance data is collected	This value relates to the number of spindles that make up the physical disk. A single disk has one spindle. RAID drives have multiple spindles but appear as a single drive. A typical value is up to two times the number of spindles making up the physical disk.
% Disk Time	Percentage of time that disk is in use	If this value consistently is above 85 percent active, consider moving some files to an additional server or upgrading the disk drive.
Processor		
% Processor Time	Percentage of elapsed time that processor is busy executing a non-idle thread	This counter indicates how busy a processor is. If this value is very high, the system may benefit from a processor upgrade or multiple processors.
Interrupts/Sec	Rate of service requests from I/O devices	This indicates the number of requests processed from device drivers. If this value increases without corresponding increases in system activity, it could indicate a hardware problem on the system.

You can monitor multiple instances of some of the objects listed in Table 15.1. For example, you can view the performance of each processor in a multiprocessor system and can monitor each Physical Disk object in a system with multiple fixed-disk drives.

N O T E Multiple instances of an object can be opened, even if multiple physical devices don't exist in the system. For example, multiple Processor objects can be monitored on a single-processor system; in this case, each instance of the processor displays the same data. ∎

One of PerfMon's most important capabilities is its ability to monitor the performance of Windows NT objects on remote machines. For example, from a client running Windows NT Workstation 4.0, a system administrator can monitor the performance of objects on all Windows NT servers in a domain. This feature is very useful for detecting load-balancing problems in the network.

You monitor behavior of a remote computer's objects by following these steps:

1. If PerfMon isn't displaying a chart, choose Chart from the View menu.
2. Choose Add to Chart from the Edit menu to open the Add to Chart dialog (see Figure 15.2).

FIG. 15.2
Adding a chart to PerfMon with the Add to Chart dialog.

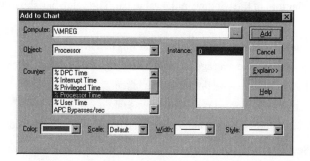

3. In the Add to Chart dialog's Computer text box, type the name of the Windows NT computer to monitor. Alternatively, click the button to the right of the text box to display the Select Computer dialog, which displays a list of all computers on the network (see Figure 15.3).

FIG. 15.3
Using PerfMon's Select Computer dialog to select other computers on the network.

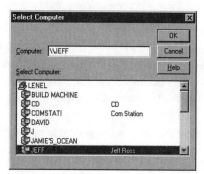

If you use the Select Computer dialog, double-click the name of the domain or workgroup to display a list of servers and workstations in that entity. Select the name of the server or workstation to monitor, and then click OK to close the dialog.

4. In the Add to Chart dialog, a new chart is added to PerfMon by selecting an object from the Object drop-down list, selecting a counter for the object from the Counter list, and then clicking the Add button. Figure 15.2 shows the Processor object and % Processor Time counter selected.

5. Click Cancel to close the Add to Chart dialog. The line chart begins to display % Processor Time (refer to Figure 15.1).

Charting Performance Characteristics

Performance Monitor typically creates line charts, but histograms or bar charts are alternatives for certain types of data. When using charts, PerfMon displays the collected statistical data near the bottom of the window in the value bar. The value bar shows the following information:

- *Last* shows the most recent reading that was taken.
- *Average* displays the average of all data readings taken since the chart was created.
- *Min* shows the lowest reading that was taken.
- *Max* displays the highest reading that was taken.
- *Graph Time* shows the amount of time that one chart on-screen covers.

Creating a New Chart   Creating a new chart requires that you select a computer, object, and counter to monitor. The following example shows how to create a new chart with the Processor object and % Processor Time counter. Monitoring the percentage of processor time consumed indicates whether the server's CPU is overworked. Such a condition indicates that the server needs a faster processor or that some of the work performed by this server should be distributed to another server.

To create a new line chart for monitoring % Processor Time, follow these steps:

1. Choose Chart from the View menu or click the View a Chart button on the toolbar. (If a chart already exists, you can clear it by choosing New Chart from the File menu.)

2. Add to the chart a new line representing the object being monitored by choosing Add to Chart from the Edit menu or by clicking the Add Counter button in the toolbar. The Add to Chart dialog appears. (You must complete the rest of the steps before the new line appears in PerfMon.)

3. In the Computer text box, type the name of the system to monitor, or click the button to the right of the text box to open the Select Computer dialog, which shows all computers on the network (refer to Figure 15.3).

4. In the Add to Chart dialog, select the object you want to monitor from the Object drop-down list. (For this example, choose the Processor object.) When you select an object, the Counter list fills with the appropriate counters for that object.

5. Select the counter that you want to monitor from the Counter list. In this example, select the % Processor Time counter.

TIP You can click the Explain button to see a explanation of what the selected counter represents.

6. If the computer has more than one CPU, the Instance list box fills with an instance for each CPU. Select the instance to monitor. In this example, select 0 for the first CPU.

7. You can choose the Color of the object, the Scale factor, the line Width, and the line Style. These options enable you to identify more distinctly each counter when the same chart is monitoring more than one counter.

8. Click the Add button to add the new performance characteristic to be monitored to the chart.

9. You can add more performance characteristics to the chart by repeating steps 3 through 8.

10. After you add all the objects that you want to monitor, click the Cancel button to return to the Performance Monitor window. PerfMon now begins monitoring the chosen objects.

NOTE To obtain the most realistic readings from your system, make sure that tasks such as screen savers are disabled. Depending on the object being monitored, an active screen saver distorts the readings. ■

Editing a Chart   When your chart is running, you can edit any counters being monitored. As shown earlier in Figure 15.1, a legend of all monitored counters appears at the bottom of PerfMon's window. To edit any counter, select the counter to be edited from PerfMon's legend at the bottom of the window. Then from the Edit menu choose Edit Chart Line, or double-click the counter in PerfMon's legend to open the Edit Chart Line dialog (see Figure 15.4).

FIG. 15.4
Using the Edit Chart
Line dialog to modify a
counter.

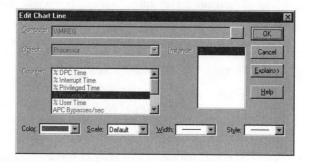

The Edit Chart Line dialog resembles the Add to Chart dialog but doesn't allow for Computer, Object, Counter, or Instance changes. The only changes you can make are to the Color, Scale, Width, and Style of the line representing the object being edited. Make the appropriate changes and click OK.

Deleting Monitored Objects from a Chart Deleting objects from the chart often becomes necessary during the course of monitoring system performance. You may need to delete an object due to inconclusive results obtained from it, or simply to clear a chart that's monitoring many performance characteristics. To delete any counter being monitored, select it on PerfMon's legend and press the Delete key.

Customizing the Chart Options You can modify the presentation of PerfMon charts by using the options in the Chart Options dialog (see Figure 15.5). To open the dialog, choose Chart from the Options menu. Table 15.2 describes all the available chart options.

FIG. 15.5

Customizing the presentation of PerfMon charts with the Chart Options dialog.

Table 15.2 Options for Modifying Charts

Option	Description
Legend	When this default option is selected, the legends for each chart line appear at the bottom of PerfMon.
Value Bar	When this default option is selected, the value bar shows the values of Last, Average, Min, Max, and Graph Time.
Gallery	The Gallery setting determines how the data is displayed. The options are Graph, which is the default and most useful method, or Histogram, which displays data as a bar graph.
Update Time	The default Periodic Update setting, the most commonly used method, tells PerfMon to read new data at the time interval specified in the Interval (Seconds) text box, which defaults to one second. Manual Update tells PerfMon to update on user request.
Vertical Grid	This option displays grid lines on the vertical axis.
Horizontal Grid	This option displays grid lines on the horizontal axis.
Vertical Labels	This default option displays labels for the vertical (y) axis.
Vertical Maximum	This option specifies the maximum value for the vertical axis. This value should be changed to reflect the counter being monitored. For example, set Vertical Maximum to 100 (the default value) when using a percentage counter.

Using Performance Monitor to Set Alerts

One useful feature of PerfMon is the capability to define alerts, which can be sent to any station on the network when a monitored counter reaches a critical value. An *alert* is a method of monitoring any counter and performing a specified action when the counter exceeds or falls below a predetermined threshold value. You can choose to log the alert, send a notification message to a user on the network, or run an application.

You can view the alerts defined by Performance Monitor by either choosing <u>A</u>lert from the <u>V</u>iew menu or clicking the View the Alerts button of Performance Monitor's toolbar. Figure 15.6 shows alerts generated at five-second intervals for % Processor Time counter values in excess of 5 percent.

FIG. 15.6

Viewing alerts in PerfMon's alert view.

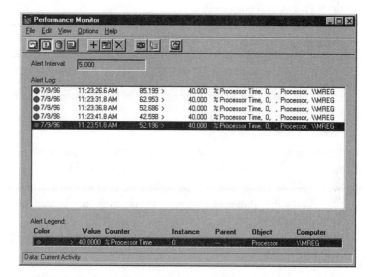

Adding an Alert You add alerts to PerfMon by performing steps similar to the steps used for adding charts to PerfMon. Creating a new alert removes any existing charts that PerfMon is displaying. To add a new alert to the view, follow these steps:

1. Choose <u>A</u>lert from the <u>V</u>iew menu, or click the Alert toolbar button.

2. Choose <u>A</u>dd to Alert from the <u>E</u>dit menu, or click the Add button, to open the Add to Alert dialog (see Figure 15.7).

3. Type the name of the system to monitor in the Computer text box, or click the ... button to open the Select Computer dialog, which shows all computers on the network (refer to Figure 15.3).

4. From the Object drop-down list, select the object that you want to monitor. For this example, choose the Processor object.

FIG. 15.7

Adding alerts with the Add to Alert dialog.

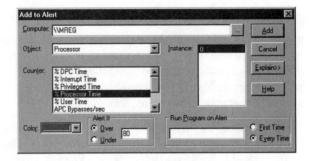

5. Select the counter that you want to monitor from the Counter list box. In this case, select the % Processor Time counter.

 TIP To see an explanation of what the selected counter represents, click the Explain button.

6. If the computer has more than one CPU, the Instance list box fills with an instance for each CPU. Select the instance to monitor. In this example, select instance 0 for the first CPU.

7. Select a Color for the alert.

8. Enter the alert threshold in the Alert If section, and specify whether the alert is to run if the value is Under the threshold or Over the threshold.

9. When the alert triggers and if an application is supposed to run, specify the application name in the Run Program on Alert text box. Indicate whether the alert is to be run the First Time the alert triggers or Every Time the alert triggers.

10. When the options are set, click the Add button to add the alert to PerfMon.

Customizing Alerts   As with charts, you can customize alerts with various options. Choosing Alert from the Options menu opens the Alert Options dialog (see Figure 15.8). Table 15.3 describes the available alert options.

FIG. 15.8

Setting alert options with the Alert Options dialog.

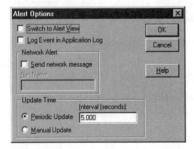

Table 15.3 Actions that Can Be Performed When an Alert Is Triggered

Alert Option	Description
Switch to Alert View	PerfMon switches to alert view when an alert is triggered.
Log Event in Application Log	PerfMon generates an entry in the Application Log when the alert is triggered. You can view the Application Log from Event Monitor.
Send Network Message	PerfMon sends a network message to the machine specified in the Net Name text box. Don't enter double backslashes (\\) before the machine name.
Update Time	Two options are available here. The most used is Periodic Update, which tells PerfMon to read new data at a time interval specified in seconds in the Interval (Seconds) text box. Manual Update tells PerfMon to update on user request.

PerfMon uses NetBIOS as the transport protocol for network messages. If your alerts are sending network messages, you must ensure that NetBIOS is available as a transport protocol and that the NetBIOS service is running. The NetBIOS messenger service must be running for alerts to send network messages to the intended recipients.

You can determine whether the NetBIOS messenger service is started by using Control Panel's Services tool. The service name Messenger appears in the list box of all services, along with the current status of the service. If this service doesn't appear, you must install the NetBIOS Interface protocol from the Services page of Control Panel's Network tool.

The following two methods start the Messenger service:

■ From the Command prompt, type **net start messenger**.

■ In Control Panel, double-click the Services tool. Then select the Messenger service from the list box displaying all services and click the Start button. You can change the startup properties of the service to have it start automatically when the computer boots.

After the Messenger service starts, make sure that the alert recipient is added by typing **net name *machinename* add** at the command prompt, where *machinename* is the name you typed in the Net Name text box in the Alert Options dialog.

N O T E   Several independent software vendors (ISVs) offer extended monitoring and alerting options for Windows NT Server 4.0. As an example, some third-party products can direct alerts to a pager. ■

Using Performance Monitor Log Files

You use log files to provide a history of how your network is operating. You can set up PerfMon to keep a log for the results of running charts and of alerts that occur.

Maintaining log files can ease the burden of network administrators as the network grows and performance begins to degrade. You can examine log files to determine the source and location of bottlenecks and devise plans for correcting the problems.

Recording Data to a Log File To record data to a log file, follow these steps:

1. Select the log view by choosing Log from the View menu or by clicking the View Output Log File Status toolbar button. PerfMon displays a new log view window (see Figure 15.9).

FIG. 15.9

Displaying current log activity in log view.

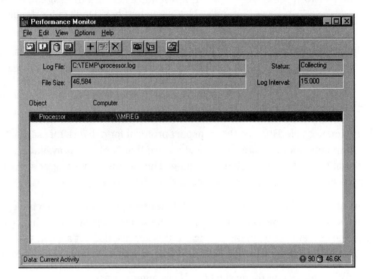

2. From the File menu, choose New Log Settings to clear existing log settings.
3. A new log file is added by choosing Add to Log from the Edit menu or by clicking the Add toolbar button. The Add To Log dialog appears (see Figure 15.10).

FIG. 15.10

Adding objects to be logged through the Add To Log dialog.

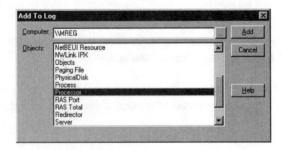

4. Type the name of the system to monitor in the Computer text box, or click the ... button to open the Select Computer dialog (refer to Figure 15.3).

5. From the Objects list box, select the object that you want to monitor. For this example, choose Processor. Unlike in chart view, when an object is selected, all instances of the object are logged.

6. After you select the object you want to log, click the Add button to add the object to the log.

7. To log multiple objects, repeat steps 5 and 6 for each object. Then click Cancel to close the dialog.

8. Now that the objects to log are selected, the log file needs to be set through the Log Options dialog (see Figure 15.11), which you can open by choosing Log from the Options menu.

FIG. 15.11

Setting log options in the Log Options dialog.

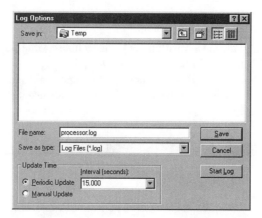

9. Enter a new log file name, or select an existing log file to overwrite from the Log Options dialog.

10. In the Update Time section, either select Periodic Update and set a time interval in seconds, or select Manual Update for user intervention. These selections determine when data is written to the log file.

11. Click the Start Log button to start logging data. PerfMon's window changes to the log view.

To stop data logging, open the Log Options dialog and click the Stop Log button.

Viewing Recorded Data   Logged data, unlike chart data, doesn't appear in PerfMon's window. You can open for viewing only log files that aren't currently opened (in the process of logging). If the log you want to view is in use, you must first stop the log by choosing Log from the View menu. Then choose Log from the Options menu to open the Log Options dialog and click Stop Log.

To view the log data, follow these steps:

1. From the Options menu, choose Data From to open the Data From dialog (see Figure 15.12).

2. Select the Log File option.

3. Type the path and name of the log file to view in the text box, or click the ... button to find the log file.

4. Click OK to close the Data From dialog.

5. To specify a time frame to view within the log file, choose Time Window from the Edit menu to open the Input Log File Timeframe dialog (see Figure 15.13). The bar above the Bookmarks section indicates the time line for logging events in the file. The Bookmarks section lists events when data was logged. The default is the entire time span for the log file.

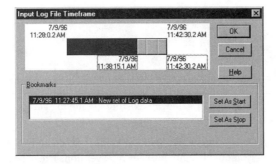

6. To set a new start time, select a bookmark and click the Set As Start button.

7. To set a new end time, select a bookmark and click the Set As Stop button.

8. Click OK to close the Input Log File Timeframe dialog and display the logged data.

To resume viewing current activity, you must open the Data From dialog and select the Current Activity option.

Optimizing Windows NT 4.0 File and Print Servers

Microsoft's developers made an appreciable improvement in Windows NT Server 4.0's file and print services compared with Windows NT 3.5x, especially for high-speed networks with 100BaseT NICs. However, various hardware and software bottlenecks can still reduce the performance of Windows NT 4.0 file and print servers. The following sections describe the process of optimizing a Windows NT Server 4.0 used primarily for file and print sharing.

▶ **See** "Faster File Sharing on High-Speed LANs," **p. 28**

▶ **See** "Printing Enhancements," **p. 29**

Minimizing Disk Bottlenecks

Fixed-disk drives contribute more than their share of performance problems. You use PerfMon's Physical Disk object to check for drive bottlenecks.

Unlike the other objects in PerfMon, the disk subsystem must be initialized before disk activity can be monitored. To activate the monitoring of the disk subsystem, follow these steps:

1. From the Start menu, choose Programs and Command Prompt to open the Command Prompt window.

2. On the command line, type `diskperf -y`.

3. Exit the command line by typing `exit` or by closing the Command Prompt window.

4. Shut down and restart Windows NT.

If performing these steps doesn't start the DiskPerf driver, the Physical Disk's counters don't work. Failure to start DiskPerf becomes evident when a chart is selected for the physical disk and the graph doesn't indicate activity during disk operations.

One of the most obvious counters of the Physical Disk object is the % Disk Time counter, which is equivalent to monitoring the computer's disk activity indicator. When % Disk Time approaches 80 percent or higher, the server has a disk-usage problem and is said to be *disk-bound*.

Another useful counter is Disk Queue Length, which counts the number of processes waiting to use the physical disk. When more than two processes are regularly waiting to access the disk, the server is disk-bound.

Hardware Solutions for Reducing Disk Bottlenecks   Buying SCSI-2 or, better yet, Ultra Wide SCSI-3 fixed-disk drives with fast seek times is the most straightforward solution for increasing data throughput. Many disk drives are available with 4M/sec (4M per second) sustained data transfer rates or greater and 9 ms seek times or less. For example, 4.3G Seagate ST15150W Wide SCSI-2 Barracuda drives can provide a sustained data rate in the range of 6M/sec, which is several times more data than you can transport over 10BaseT media. A large read cache on high-speed drives also improves performance, and enabling a drive's write cache provides a performance boost, but at the expense of data security. The primary advantage of high-speed drives in relatively low-speed networks is that the system devotes less time to reading and writing data, which is only a part of the processor and network workload.

▶ **See** "Specifying Disk Subsystems," **p. 163**

▶ **See** "RAID 5," **p. 225**

 T I P   If your Avg. Disk Sec/Transfer rate is significantly below that calculated for your drive/controller combination, you might have a SCSI termination problem that results in multiple reads or writes as a result of data errors. Active termination is a requirement for high-speed SCSI drives. If the last device on your SCSI chain uses passive termination, it's likely to reduce the effective data rate. If you mix Wide and conventional (narrow) SCSI devices on a host adapter that supports both cable types, such as the Adaptec AHA-2940UW, be sure to follow the manufacturer's recommendation for mixed-SCSI device address settings. Using the wrong addresses for low-speed devices can slow high-speed devices dramatically.

SCSI host controllers represent another potential hardware bottleneck. Attaching a high-performance drive to a legacy SCSI controller (such as an 8-bit SCSI controller) doesn't make economic sense. PCI bus-mastering controllers, such as the Adaptec AHA-2940UW and AHA-3940UW, provide synchronous data access at burst rates of up to 40M/sec and 80M/sec, respectively. You can attach up to 15 devices to a Wide SCSI-2 bus. Replacing Windows NT Server 4.0's software RAID implementation with a controller that implements hardware RAID also improves disk subsystem performance.

▶ **See** "Implementing RAID in Hardware," **p. 233**

Some SCSI host adapters can perform asynchronous I/O, which allows drives to perform operations in parallel. If your host adapter can perform asynchronous I/O, you can use stripe sets to maximize the server's performance. A *stripe set* allows data to be distributed across several drives, making disk operations very fast because the physical drives work in parallel.

N O T E   When buying a SCSI host adapter, make sure that it supports asynchronous I/O. Most host adapters don't support this feature, nor do any IDE drives. ▪

The cost of high-performance fixed-disk drives declined rapidly in 1996 and is expected to drop further in 1997 and 1998 as larger drives that use magneto-resistive heads and embedded servo positioning tracks become common. PCI bus-mastering host controllers range in street price from about $350 to $500, and low-cost hardware RAID controllers priced between $750 and $1,000 became available in late 1996.

CAUTION

If you plan to change SCSI host adapters, make a full, known-good backup (or two) before doing so. Low-level and high-level drive formats aren't identical for all SCSI host adapters. Changing from one SCSI adapter to another may require you to reformat all your disk drives.

ON THE WEB

Adaptec Corp.'s ThreadMark 2.0 is a benchmarking application that measures multithreaded fixed-disk performance on computers running Windows NT 4.0 or Windows 95. Adaptec designed ThreadMark 2.0 to indicate how well a disk subsystem handles bursts of very high I/O activity. ThreadMark 2.0 provides comprehensive performance reports for EIDE and SCSI drives. You can download a free copy of ThreadMark 2.0 from **http://www.adaptec.com/threadmark/**.

Software Solutions for Reducing Disk Bottlenecks   If your Windows NT 4.0 server is used as a print server in addition to a file server, an option is to increase priority of the thread that handles file services and reduce the priority of the thread that handles print services. Boosting the priority of the file-server thread causes file requests to be handled more quickly, at the expense of print services.

By default, the print-server thread is set to 2 and the file-server thread is 1. The larger the number, the higher the priority assigned to the thread. To change the priority of the file-server thread with Registry Editor, follow these steps:

N O T E   The following example uses Regedt32.exe, but you also can use Regedit.exe to change the priority. Chapter 9, "Understanding the Windows NT Registry," covers the use of Regedt32.exe and Regedit.exe. ■

1. From the Start menu, choose Run to open the Run dialog.

2. In the text box, type **regedt32** and click OK to launch Registry Editor (see Figure 15.14).

FIG. 15.14

Using Registry Editor to change Windows NT system values.

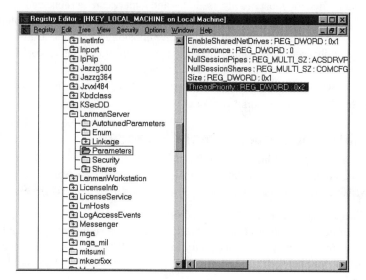

3. Select the HKEY_LOCAL_MACHINE view.

4. Expand the SYSTEM\CurrentControlSet\Services\LanmanServer\Parameters key.

5. Select the ThreadPriority entry.

N O T E   Not all systems have a ThreadPriority entry. If your system doesn't have this entry, it can be added through the Edit menu. Set the initial value to 2. ■

6. Change the value from 1 to 2 to increase the file-server thread priority, and then close Registry Editor.

N O T E   Server threads run at foreground process priority by default. Other threads in the system service (such as the XACTSRV thread, which is used for processing print requests) run at foreground process priority, plus 1. Thus, a file server that's also a print server may suffer from server-thread starvation because the server threads are running at a lower priority than the print threads. Increasing the ThreadPriority value to 2 places a server thread in the same priority class as a print thread. The maximum value for ThreadPriority is 31. Don't increase the ThreadPriority value above 2; a value greater than 2 can cause other undesired system side effects. ■

If your network consists of multiple Windows NT servers, you can use a technique called *load balancing*, which distributes the workload across multiple servers. Load balancing lets all the servers operate at a similar capacity, rather than heavily tax certain servers and underutilize other servers.

Before you load balance a system, evaluate each server to determine where the most activity occurs. Then the most heavily used files and folders can be replicated across other servers to balance the network load. *Replicating* is a method of duplicating the content of folders, files, or even entire disks onto another disk drive on another machine. (Although this technique is primarily used for providing an online path to information in case of a system crash of a primary server, it can be used for load balancing also.) Users that need to view information can be sent to the replicated data, thus reducing the traffic to the primary server.

▶ **See** "Replicating Folders," **p. 502**

Eliminating Unneeded Network Protocols

One advantage of Windows NT is its support for all commonly used network protocols. Although multiprotocol capability is a major selling point, a server doesn't benefit by having all available protocols loaded if some protocols aren't used or aren't necessary.

When a network runs multiple protocols, the performance of the network suffers. For example, if your network includes NetWare file servers, you're running the NWLink protocol with IPX/SPX support. It may not be necessary to run NetBEUI or TCP/IP in this instance. Alternatively, if your network must run TCP/IP, you should consider changing the NetWare servers to use TCP/IP.

The number of bindings that a network contains also affects network performance. By changing the binding order, you can obtain significant gains in network performance. For example, NetBIOS is the binding interface for the Windows NT file server. The problem is that NetBIOS has binding interfaces to three protocols—NetBEUI, TCP/IP, and NWLink—presenting the server software with multiple choices when trying to satisfy a network request.

 T I P If your primary network protocol is TCP/IP, you might be tempted to remove the Windows Network's NetBEUI protocol to improve performance. Removing NetBEUI is likely to cause network browsing problems for Windows 95 clients, especially clients that use Dial-Up Networking (DUN or Remote Access Service, RAS).

Changing the Binding Order of Multiple Protocols

 If you can't reduce the number of network protocols in use, you can alter the binding order to satisfy the most network requests on the first attempt. To view and alter the order of network bindings, follow these steps:

1. From the Start menu, choose Settings and then Control Panel.

2. Double-click Control Panel's Network tool to open the Network property sheet.

3. Click the Bindings tab to display the Bindings properties page. Select the All Protocols entry from the combo box, if it's not already selected.

4. In the list box, you can change the order of the protocol bindings for each service. Double-click the entry for the service for which you want to change the binding priority to display the underlying bindings for the service (see Figure 15.15).

FIG. 15.15
Using the Bindings page of the Network property sheet to rearrange network protocol bindings.

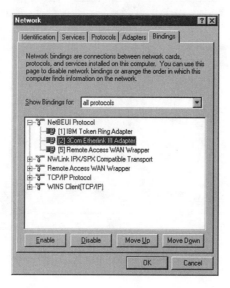

5. If most users use TCP/IP, for example, select this binding and click the Move Up button until TCP/IP is at the top of the list. (The Move Up and Move Down buttons are disabled until you select a protocol for a particular service.)

6. Click OK to accept the changes or Cancel to abort the changes.

7. If you click OK and have made changes, Windows NT re-creates the bindings and asks that you shut down and restart the server. On restart, the new binding priorities are effective.

Overcoming Network Media Limitations

You also can use Performance Monitor to view network characteristics that affect file server performance. Select the Server object and view the Bytes Total/sec counter (see Figure 15.16); compare this number to the rated media speed of your network, such as 4 Mbps or 16 Mbps Token Ring or 10 Mbps Ethernet. If the number of Bytes Total/sec is near the throughput limit of your network, your network is overworked. As an example, the maximum practical throughput of a conventional (shared, hub-based) 10BaseT network is about 300,000 bytes per second; 100BaseT delivers 3M/sec. In this case, you must separate the network into multiple segments to ease the burden. Fortunately, Windows NT Server 4.0 lets you install multiple network cards for segmenting. A more costly alternative is to replace the shared Ethernet system with switched Ethernet.

▶ **See** "Enterprise Hubs, Collapsed Backbones, Ethernet Switches, and Virtual LANs," **p. 150**

FIG. 15.16

Monitoring the network performance of a Windows NT server.

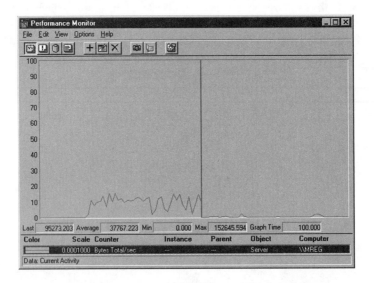

Some additional tips for improving the network performance of your Windows NT Server are as follows:

- If you're using 100BaseT, change the server NIC(s) from the conventional PCI bus-master variety to a model with an on-board processor, such as Intel's EtherExpress PRO/100 Smart Adapter, which has an i960 processor and 2M of RAM. The on-board processor reduces CPU loading.

    ▶ **See** "Network Interface Cards," **p. 141**

- If your server uses WINS (Windows Internet Name Service) and TCP/IP, you can reduce the number of system broadcasts by binding the NetBIOS Interface to TCP/IP.

- If your network contains Windows for Workgroups (WfWg) clients and you use TCP/IP, be sure to update the WfWg clients with the version of WfWg included on the Windows NT Server 4.0 CD-ROM. The new WfWg TCP/IP driver increases the server's performance.

Reducing File Fragmentation

It's a common misconception that Windows NT Server's NTFS eliminates problems with file fragmentation. *Fragmentation*—defined as files stored in multiple, non-contiguous clusters—slows file read and write operations, especially with large files.

Although Windows 95 includes a built-in defragmentation utility, Disk Defragmenter, Windows NT 4.0 doesn't provide such an application. Commercial products are available to help correct and reduce the amount of disk fragmentation for your Windows NT systems. Symantec's Norton Utilities for Windows NT contains a utility similar to the Windows 95 Disk Defragmenter.

One unique product available is Diskeeper for Windows NT from Executive Software (**http://www.execsoft.com**). Diskeeper is a Windows NT service that runs constantly in the background and controls disk fragmentation as it occurs. By having Diskeeper work in real time, you never have to take the server offline to perform defragmentation, and your drive is optimized for the fastest disk access possible.

N O T E When purchasing any third-party accessory software for Windows NT 4.0, make sure that the supplier warrants that the product is designed for Windows NT 4.0. Changes between Windows NT versions 3.x and 4.0 affect many applications that use Windows NT's lower-level services. ∎

Optimizing Windows NT 4.0 as an Application Server

Windows NT gained its initial reputation as a high-performance application server primarily by running client/server relational database management systems (RDBMSes), such as Microsoft SQL Server. The Microsoft BackOffice Server suite adds Exchange Server, Systems Management Server (SMS), and SNA (Systems Network Architecture) Server as server-based applications. Other firms, such as Oracle and IBM, offer server-based RDBMSes and messaging systems that run under Windows NT Server 4.0.

By running on the same system, several client/server applications that service large numbers of users can tax the capabilities of even the highest-performance computer platforms. When dealing with application servers, the most obvious place to look for bottlenecks is the CPU and memory systems.

Examining an Application Server's CPU Usage

Performance Monitor is a valuable tool for detecting overuse of a server's CPU(s). Select the Processor object and watch the % Processor Time counter during periods of the heaviest network traffic. By examining the % Processor Time counter, you can determine CPU loading and how often your CPU is being "maxed out." When % Processor Time reaches 85 percent or more on a regular basis, you should consider upgrading your processor to a higher speed (if supported by your server's motherboard) or add an additional processor (if you have a multiprocessing system). If your server does double duty—acting as a file server and an application server—consider adding a new server to take over application services. If you're running more than one member of BackOffice Server on the computer, install an additional server for heavily used services, such as SQL Server or Exchange Server.

 TIP Multithreaded server applications take much better advantage of multiprocessor systems than file servers. If you intend to add an application server, invest in a system that can support up to four CPUs, even if you install only one processor initially. An application server should be equipped with a minimum of 64M of RAM. Use the largest single-inline memory modules (SIMMs) or dual-inline memory modules (DIMMs) that the motherboard supports to maximize the amount of RAM that you can install in the future. Depending on the usage of your server-based applications, adding RAM may be more cost-effective than increasing the number of CPUs. Memory usage is the subject of the next section, "Examining Memory Usage in an Application Server."

Another area of concern is the number of Interrupts/Sec with which the processor must contend. The number of interrupts per second is not a CPU problem, but the values of the Interrupts/Sec and % Interrupt Time counters can point out potential server hardware problems. A typical Windows NT server handles about 100 to 150 interrupts per second on the average. If the Interrupts/Sec counter shows 600 or more interrupts per second, the problem is likely a faulty or failing hardware component, often an adapter card.

You can detect poorly written device drivers by viewing the value of the System object's Context Switches/Sec counter. If the rate of context switching is more than 500 per second, it's possible that a device driver has built-in critical sections that take too long to process. (A *critical section* is a Win32 synchronization object that ensures that only one thread can execute a particular block of code at a time.)

A less obvious problem is screen savers running on the server. A screen saver is a relatively small task that runs after a period of inactivity, but some screen savers can be CPU killers. Examples of killer screen savers are Windows NT's Bezier Curves and 3-D Pipes, whose 3-D graphics cause a CPU burden. Windows NT 4.0 has a simple built-in screen saver that's operational before an operator logs on at the server console. You remotely monitor most servers, which usually are in a relatively inaccessible location, so turning the monitor off when it's not in use is the most effective screen saver.

Examining Memory Usage in an Application Server

One of the most effective methods for achieving better system performance is through the addition of more physical (DRAM or dynamic RAM) memory. Within reasonable limits, the performance of Windows NT Server 4.0's operating system and the server-based applications improves with the addition of more memory. Application servers generally start at 128M of RAM, and servers with 512M of RAM or more aren't uncommon. Just adding more RAM, however, isn't the entire solution to optimizing application server performance; you must correctly use the available memory.

▶ **See** "The Windows NT Executive," **p. 86**

Experience shows that no matter how much memory exists in a Windows NT Server system, the operating system and server-based applications always find ways to use additional RAM. Windows NT Server uses most memory as a disk cache.

You use the Memory object's counters in Performance Monitor to check memory usage. The number of Committed Bytes should be less than half physical memory available, leaving the other half or more of RAM for disk caching. The number of Available Bytes should be at least 1M—preferably much more. If PerfMon displays less than the preceding values, you need more RAM.

Examining Virtual Memory   Virtual memory supplements RAM with disk files that emulate RAM, a process called *swapping* or *paging*. Virtual memory is defined as the amount of physical memory (RAM) available in the system *plus* a preallocated amount of memory on the system's fixed disk. Windows NT allocates the disk-based component of virtual memory in Pagefile.sys, which by default resides in the root folder of the disk drive on which you install Windows NT.

Pagefile.sys is unique because Windows NT creates the file as a series of contiguous clusters during installation. This structure lets the operating system issue a special set of disk I/O calls to read and write from Pagefile.sys, rather than use the conventional file system for disk I/O. The disk I/O calls to Pagefile.sys are much faster than Windows NT's normal disk operations but are much slower than memory I/O operations. To achieve maximum system performance, your objective is to minimize paging.

N O T E   The amount of paging performed is directly related to the how virtual memory is used. Windows NT reserves about 4M of RAM for its own use and allocates up to half the remaining RAM as a disk cache, so running large server applications is likely to involve paging operations. Check the Memory object's Pages/sec counter during periods of maximum activity of your server-based applications, such as SQL Server and Exchange Server. The Pages/sec counter's value should be 5 or less. If the number of Pages/sec is greater than 5, the server is performing too many paging operations, and you need to increase the amount of server RAM. ■

Virtual memory operations become very slow if the amount of virtual memory needed by Windows NT and running applications exceeds the amount of space allocated to Pagefile.sys. When this situation occurs, Windows NT dynamically expands the size of Pagefile.sys. The expansion process is slowed as Windows NT searches the disk for free disk space. Additional disk space is not in the contiguous-sector block of the original Pagefile.sys, a condition that slows read and write operations.

Maximizing Network Throughput   For application servers, network throughput is extremely important. The following steps help maximize network throughput:

1. From the Start menu, choose Settings and Control Panel.

2. Double-click Control Panel's Network tool to open the Network property sheet.

3. Click the Services tab to make the Services page active, and select Server from the Network Services list (see Figure 15.17).

4. Click the Properties button to open the Server dialog (see Figure 15.18).

FIG. 15.17

Configuring the server network software for better system performance.

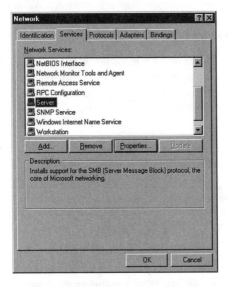

5. Select the Maximize Throughput for Network Applications option.

6. If you don't have LAN Manager 2.x clients on the network, clear the default mark in the Make Browser Broadcasts to LAN Manager 2.x Clients check box.

7. Click OK to accept the changes, or click Cancel if you haven't made changes. If you have made changes, you must shut down and restart Windows NT to make the change effective.

To control the amount of virtual memory allocated to Pagefile.sys, follow these steps:

1. From the Start menu, choose Settings and then Control Panel.

2. Double-click Control Panel's System tool to open the System Properties sheet.

3. Click the Performance tab to display the Performance properties page, and click the Virtual Memory button to open the Virtual Memory dialog (see Figure 15.19).

4. To change the amount of disk space consumed by Pagefile.sys, alter the settings in the dialog.

5. Click OK if you've made changes or Cancel if you haven't made changes. You must shut down and restart the server if you make changes to Pagefile.sys.

FIG. 15.18

Maximizing network throughput for Windows NT server applications.

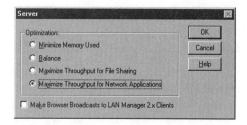

FIG. 15.19

Altering the amount disk space used for virtual memory.

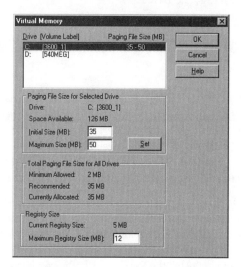

N O T E   When Windows NT allocates memory for Pagefile.sys, it tries to allocate contiguous space on the fixed disk equal to the size specified for virtual memory. If contiguous space equal to the specified size isn't available, the largest amount of contiguous space available is allocated and the remaining amount is allocated from the closest available clusters on the disk. When contiguous space is allocated, Windows NT is much faster at swapping memory to and from disk. Whenever increasing the size of your virtual memory, you should defragment your hard disk to maximize the possibility of allocating contiguous disk space for Pagefile.sys. ■

Viewing Virtual Memory with Performance Monitor   The Commit Limit counter of PerfMon's Memory object shows the amount of memory in Pagefile.sys plus the amount of RAM that can be swapped to disk. In a system with 32M of RAM and a 57M Pagefile.sys file, the Commit Limit is 82.5M. When the number of Committed Bytes exceeds the Commit Limit, Windows NT tries to expand Pagefile.sys. To view the amount of memory that can't be paged from RAM, view the Pool Non-Paged Bytes counter.

There are four recommendations to reduce the amount of page swapping:

- Add more RAM to the system.
- Remove unneeded services to lower operating system memory consumption.
- Remove unneeded device drivers.
- Install a faster fixed disk to reduce paging response time.

Two Windows NT Server 4.0 services consume large amounts of memory: DHCP (Dynamic Host Configuration Protocol) and WINS (Windows Internet Name Service). If you need these services, you might find it a wiser choice to place DHCP and WINS on another server, such as a file server, rather than on the application server. DHCP and WINS are two of the subjects of Chapter 10, "Using TCP/IP, WINS, and DHCP."

Taking Advantage of Resource Kit Optimization Utilities

The *Windows NT Workstation Resource Kit* for version 4.0 devotes six chapters and more than 200 pages to the use of Performance Monitor and debottlenecking processors, disk drives, and cache memory. The CD-ROM of the *Windows NT Server Resource Kit, Supplement One* for version 4.0 provides 27 applications and help files designed to assist network administrators to optimize the performance of Windows NT Server 4.0. Following is a list of the CD-ROM's components that are likely to be the most useful in tuning your Windows NT 4.0 server:

- *Performance Data Log Service* (PerfLog) is a Windows application that creates a tab- or comma-separated file of performance data from the local or remote PC that you can import to Microsoft Excel or Access for analysis. You must manually install the Pdlcnfig.exe and Pdlsvc.exe files for PerfLog from the \i386\Perftools\Logtools folder or the CD-ROM. When you install the Resource Kit, the configuration help files, Pdlcnfig.hlp and Pdlcnfig.cnt, are copied into the \Ntreskit folder. You use Pdlcnfig.exe to specify the logging frequency and the counters to include in the log file (see Figure 15.20).

- *Process Explode* (Pview.exe) is a Windows application that displays in a single dialog a wealth of information about individual processes, such as SQL Server, running on your server (see Figure 15.21). You can view, but not change, the priority and security of the process's threads.

- *Process Viewer* (Pviewer.exe) lets you view details about processes on local and remote PCs running Windows NT (see Figure 15.22) and displays memory consumption and allocation for individual threads of the process (see Figure 15.23).

FIG. 15.20

Adding counters to the PerfLog service to create a 15-second interval performance log in tab- or comma-separated format.

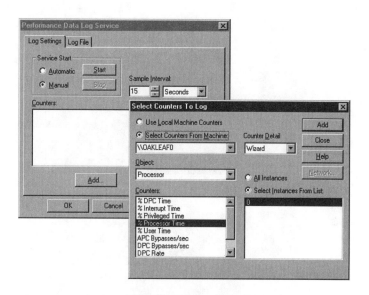

FIG. 15.21

The Process Explode dialog for SQL Server 6.5.

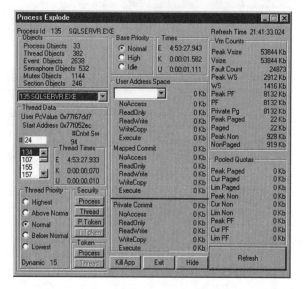

- *Data Logging Service* files (Monitor.exe and Datalog.exe) provide the capability to create performance-monitoring logs on remote computers by an unattended service. Monitor.exe is a command-line executable for configuring Datalog.exe's settings file. You use the At.exe command-line application to run Monitor.exe on remote computers at scheduled intervals.

FIG. 15.22

Process Viewer displaying process details for Excel 97.

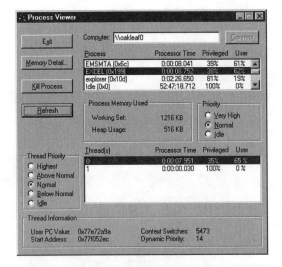

FIG. 15.23

Process Viewer's Memory Details dialog displaying User Address Space of Oleaut32.dll's usage and Virtual Memory Counts for thread 0 of the Excel process.

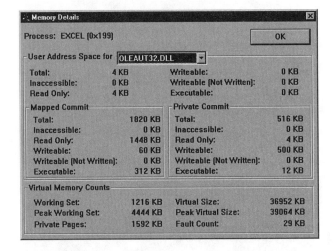

■ *Performance Counter Help* (Counters.hlp) is a help file that provides a detailed description of each built-in counter of Windows NT Server 4.0 (see Figure 15.24) and a description of the calculation method used by each counter type (see Figure 15.25).

■ *Response Probe* (Probe.exe) is a command-line utility that lets you simulate server and network workload. You can create scripts for the server or on clients running Windows NT 4.0 to generate a known level of activity to determine baseline counter values. Figure 15.26 shows the command line required to execute the Diskmax.scr probe script file that runs a disk performance test for 60 seconds, and the Command Prompt output for the script. Figure 15.27 shows the data file written by Probe.exe for the Diskmax.scr script into the default-named file, diskmax.OUT.

FIG. 15.24

Performance Counter Help file's topic for the Logical Disk (fixed-disk partition) counters.

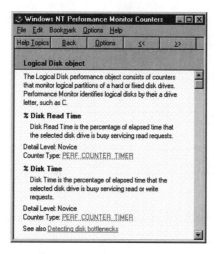

FIG. 15.25

The calculation method employed by the PERF_COUNTER_TIMER type for the % Disk Time counter.

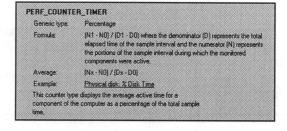

FIG. 15.26

Running Probe.exe's example Diskmax.scr script from the command line.

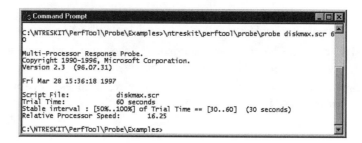

> **N O T E** Contrary to the instructions in the Diskmax.txt and Creatfil.txt files, the dummy Workfile.dat file must be located in the same folder with the script files—in this case, \Ntreskit\Perftool\ Probe\Examples, not \Ntreskit\Perftool\Probe. You receive debugger errors from Probe.exe if Workfile.dat, which contains all zeros, isn't in the proper folder. ■

FIG. 15.27

The response file written by Probe.exe for the Diskmax.scr script.

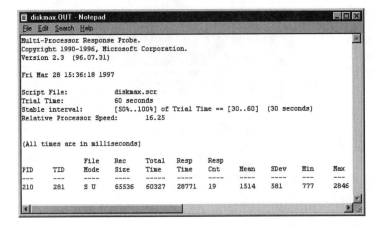

```
diskmax.OUT - Notepad                                                    _ □ X
File  Edit  Search  Help
Multi-Processor Response Probe.
Copyright 1990-1996, Microsoft Corporation.
Version 2.3  (96.07.31)

Fri Mar 28 15:36:18 1997

Script File:           diskmax.scr
Trial Time:            60 seconds
Stable interval:       [50%..100%] of Trial Time == [30..60]  (30 seconds)
Relative Processor Speed:    16.25


(All times are in milliseconds)

          File   Rec    Total  Resp   Resp
PID   TID  Mode   Size   Time   Time   Cnt    Mean   SDev   Min    Max
---   ---  ----   ----   -----  ----   ----   ----   ----   ---    ---
210   281  S U    65536  60327  28771  19     1514   581    777    2846
```

From Here...

This chapter shows that Performance Monitor is an extremely valuable tool for tracking network and server performance characteristics. By analyzing the data obtained from PerfMon combined with the knowledge of how the servers in your network are being used, all the tools are available to achieve optimum network performance. You can expand your performance-tuning capabilities with measurement and logging utilities included with the *Windows NT Server Resource Kit.*

The following chapters provide additional information useful when optimizing Windows NT Server 4.0's performance:

- Chapter 3, "Understanding the Windows NT Operating System," briefly describes the Virtual Memory Manager that's responsible for allocating memory resources.
- Chapter 4, "Choosing Network Protocols," shows you how to add and delete the network protocols supported by Windows NT Server 4.0.
- Chapter 5, "Purchasing Networking Hardware," includes advice on determining server hardware and RAM requirements.

CHAPTER 16

Troubleshooting Network Problems

Troubleshooting network problems is by no means an easy task. Network problems can arise in numerous areas: bad wiring causes problems at the physical layer, a failed network card results in trouble at the data-link layer, and routing errors arise at the network layer. Worse yet, the network operating system or applications may cause problems at the transport, session, presentation, or application layer.

As this litany of potential woes indicates, it's important to have a good understanding of the OSI model (one of the subjects of Chapter 4, "Choosing Network Protocols") when you troubleshoot network problems. Finding a network problem often involves deciding which OSI layer is *not* the culprit. You need good troubleshooting tools and intimate familiarity with the networking protocols in use before you can be an effective network troubleshooter.

This chapter concentrates on solving the most common networking problems associated with Windows NT Server 4.0. Fortunately, Windows NT Server provides several tools (such as Control Panel) and utilities (such as Network Monitor) for configuring and troubleshooting network problems. ■

Protocol-related problems

Solve NetBEUI and NetBIOS-over-IPX broadcast problems and handle basic WINS name resolution issues on TCP/IP networks.

Protocol analyzers

Use hardware or software protocol analyzers to trace network problems to their source.

Windows NT Server's diagnostic tools

Take full advantage of Event Viewer, Network Monitor, Performance Monitor, and command-line tools built into Windows NT Server 4.0.

Tools in the *Windows NT Server Resource Kit*

The Resource Kit's graphical Browser and Domain Monitors and command-line tools, such as Browstat.exe, aid the troubleshooting process.

Connectivity problems

Resolve default gateway, domain trust, browsing, and complex WINS/DNS problems.

Relating Network Protocols and Troubleshooting Issues

Windows NT and its predecessor, LAN Manager, rely on NetBIOS protocols—including Server Message Blocks (SMBs), named pipes, and mailslots—for all native file and print services, plus many of Windows NT Server's application services. Most NetBIOS-based protocol stacks, such as Windows NT's NetBEUI Frame (NBF), rely on broadcasting network packets to every client and server on the network.

Each NetBIOS device on the Windows NT network has a *NetBIOS name*, which uniquely identifies the device and contains information about the NetBIOS-related services the device provides. *Broadcasting* is the means by which a NetBIOS device advertises its NetBIOS name and capabilities to other network devices. Broadcasting is also how a NetBIOS device can locate another device or capability on the network.

Broadcasting is ideal for services that require real-time distribution to multiple clients, such as real-time stock-market data. Broadcasting is well suited to small networks because it reduces network response time. Reduced packet overhead is responsible for NetBEUI's excellent performance on small networks. On larger networks, broadcasting creates a substantial amount of network traffic and adds to the difficulty of identifying a network device that's causing a problem. Much of your network troubleshooting time—if you have a large network—is likely to be devoted to overcoming problems related to excessive broadcasts.

NetBEUI Broadcasting

All NetBEUI traffic is broadcast-based. If you install only the NetBEUI protocol on your Windows NT server, the server responds only to broadcast requests from other NetBEUI devices. NetBEUI isn't routable; if you have two Ethernet segments separated by a router (see Figure 16.1), NetBEUI broadcasts aren't forwarded across the router. The only way to overcome this limitation is to enable bridging on the router, so that both segments appear as one physical segment. In this case, the router bridges the traffic between the two segments by using MAC (Media Access Control) layer addresses. Bridging eliminates the advantages of a segmented network. As you can imagine, maintaining a bridged network in a large LAN installation quickly becomes unmanageable, especially if you also must maintain routed protocols, such as TCP/IP, on the same segments.

▶ **See** "NetBEUI and NetBEUI Frame," **p. 107**

If you must troubleshoot problems with a broadcast-based protocol, most of the tools for a directed protocol, such as TCP/IP, are ineffective. This is because many conventional network analysis tools rely on analyzing the interaction of source-destination network addresses to determine the flow of communication and where a connection is failing. Broadcast-based systems simply flood packets to every network device, whether or not the device is involved in the connection.

FIG. 16.1
NetBEUI broadcast blocking on a routed network.

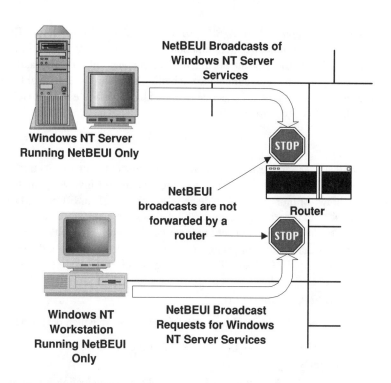

The best way to troubleshoot problems on a broadcast network is to connect a protocol analyzer to the network, and then filter MAC addresses to determine who transmitted what to whom. Protocol analyzers are one of the subjects of the later section "Using Windows NT Server 4.0's Primary Troubleshooting Tools."

N O T E The best way to troubleshoot broadcast-based network problems with a protocol analyzer is to filter out all traffic except those devices you're interested in. For example, with Microsoft's Network Monitor, you can filter on a given source and destination MAC address pair if you know those devices are having network problems. ■

IPX/SPX

Windows NT 4.0's IPX/SPX support is similar to that for NetBEUI, except that IPX implements the OSI network layer, whereas NetBEUI doesn't. The addition of the network layer makes IPX routable. Windows NT's NWLink stack supports the IPX protocol with the NetBIOS session layer. This means that you can run your NT network by using only IPX for file, print, and application services, if you choose. If you use IPX/SPX in addition to other Windows NT networking protocols, Chapter 18, "Integrating Windows NT with NetWare and UNIX," describes how to use the components of Microsoft Services for NetWare.

▶ **See** "NWLink (IPX/SPX)," **p. 111**

In this case, although the IPX/SPX protocol is routable, NetBIOS-over-IPX is broadcast-based. NetBIOS service announcement functions, such as browsing, aren't forwarded across subnets in a routed network. This means that devices running only NWLink and separated by a router normally can't browse or connect to each other's resources. You must have a mechanism on your dedicated routers, such as that provided by Cisco Systems' IPX Helper feature, to forward broadcasts to the desired destination.

TCP/IP

TCP/IP is a directed protocol that eliminates most of the broadcast traffic associated with NetBEUI and IPX protocols. A directed protocol usually involves point-to-point communication between two or more networked devices. Integration of NetBIOS and TCP/IP, which Microsoft calls *NetBT* (or, more commonly, *NBT*), follows two established Request For Comments (RFCs), defined by the Internet Engineering Task Force (IETF) as RFCs 1001 and 1002. From these RFCs, Microsoft built an entire suite of services to facilitate the use of TCP/IP with NetBIOS. Chapter 10, "Using TCP/IP, WINS, and DHCP," covers Windows NT 4.0's implementation of TCP/IP in detail.

▶ **See** "TCP/IP," **p. 108**

The RFCs for NBT specify three TCP/IP service ports, which perform the following functions:

- *NetBIOS Name* uses UDP (User Datagram Protocol) port 137 for name-resolution requests.
- *NetBIOS Datagram* uses UDP port 138 for authentication, name registration, and browsing services.
- *NetBIOS Session* uses TCP (Transport Control Protocol) port 139 for Server Message Blocks (SMBs) that perform file transfers and print jobs.

By using these three ports, Windows NT provides all its native services over TCP/IP. Windows NT also supports more traditional TCP/IP services, such as FTP and Telnet.

For a list of all the TCP/IP services Windows NT supports, view the \Winnt\system32\drivers\ etc\Services file. This file, like its UNIX counterpart, contains service names and port numbers for most TCP/IP services. Services is a simple text file, so you can view it with a text editor such as Notepad.

Windows Internet Name Service (WINS)   Use of TCP/IP requires traditional NetBIOS functions such as network browsing, name lookups, and user messaging to be mapped to the network addresses used by TCP/IP. Microsoft developed the Windows Internet Name Service (WINS) as its method for mapping IP addresses to NetBIOS machine names. The function of WINS is similar to the Domain Name Service (DNS) provided by most UNIX-based systems, but WINS provides additional NetBIOS-related services, including the capability to associate different NetBIOS functions for a given machine name to a single IP address and to register Windows NT domain names to an IP address that represents a domain controller in the specified domain.

▶ **See** "Implementing Windows Internet Name Service," **p. 342**

Machines running Windows NT Server and Workstation with the TCP/IP protocol stack use WINS to register their NetBIOS names and IP addresses. WINS registration occurs dynamically when the device starts up, or statically to guarantee that a certain machine name is registered to a certain IP address. WINS also registers Windows users based on the IP address of the machine from which each user logs on. This feature is used by services that must determine the IP address for a given user. For instance, the `net send` command queries WINS to find the IP address for the message destined for a specified user name.

After all servers and clients are registered with WINS, subsequent NetBIOS-related operations such as browsing, messaging, authentication, and file and print services use the WINS database, located on a Windows NT server, to perform name resolution between NetBIOS names and IP addresses. Using the WINS database eliminates the need for broadcast name resolution, thus decreasing network traffic and easing troubleshooting tasks.

If you're familiar with the LMHOSTS file used by LAN Manager, you can consider WINS to be a centralized version of LMHOSTS. WINS provides centralized NetBIOS name resolution without having to maintain individual LMHOSTS files on each Windows computer. Windows NT automatically uses the LMHOSTS file, if needed.

▶ **See** "LMHOSTS File," **p. 327**

The WINS database is a Jet (Access) database, Wins.mdb, and uses a Jet system database with the default name, System.mdb, both of which are located in the \Winnt\system32\wins folder. Figure 16.2 shows an example view of a WINS database that includes entries for workstations, users, and domains. Assuming that you've installed WINS, follow these steps to view the WINS database on your server:

1. From the Start menu, choose Programs, Administrative Tools, and WINS Manager to open the WINS Manager window.

2. From the Mappings menu choose Show Database to display the Show Database [Local] dialog.

Wins.mdb grows in size as old records are marked as deleted and new records are added, a characteristic of all Jet databases. The initial size of the database is about 2M. When the size of the database exceeds about 10M, stop the WINS service and use the Run dialog to execute `jetpack wins.mdb winspack.mdb` from the \Winnt\system32\wins folder, which compacts the WINS database. (The Winspack.mdb file is a temporary database file to which Wins.mdb is compacted; Winspack.mdb replaces Wins.mdb and is deleted if the compaction is successful.) Periodically compacting the WINS database improves performance.

The hexadecimal value (indicated by the suffix h) in square brackets ([ ]) after each name shown in Figure 16.2 indicates the type of service the entry provides. This value is called the *16th Byte* of the name. Table 16.1 defines each device name type and 16th Byte value you're likely to encounter.

FIG. 16.2

A WINS database viewed in WINS Manager's Show Database dialog.

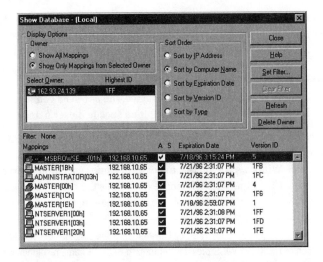

Table 16.1   WINS 16th Byte Values for Domain, User, and Machine Names

Device Name and 16th Byte Value	Usage
Domain Names	
<domain_name>[1Dh]	The name of the Domain Master Browser.
<domain_name>[1Eh]	The name used by browsers to elect a Master Browser.
<domain_name>[00h]	The name registered by the Workstation service on the domain controller to receive browser broadcasts from LAN Manager servers.
<domain_name>[1Bh]	The name registered by all domain controllers in a domain.
<domain_name>[1Ch]	The name registered by all domain controllers, which can contain up to 25 IP addresses of other domain controllers. This group is used to provide a client with a list of domain controllers that can authenticate its logon request.
User Names	
<user_name>[03h]	The name that registers logged-on users for net send operations.
Machine Names	
<computer_name>[00h]	The name registered by the Workstation or Redirector service on this computer.
<computer_name>[03h]	The name registered by the Messenger Service on this computer, which is used to issue a net send command to a machine name.

Device Name and 16th Byte Value	Usage
Machine Names	
`<computer_name>[+++nnh]`	The name used by the Network Monitor agent when it's installed on this computer (*nn* indicates any hexadecimal value).
`<computer_name>[1Fh]`	The name registered by the NetDDE service on this computer.
`<computer_name>[20h]`	The name registered by the Server service on this computer.

Part
III
Ch
16

TIP In Windows NT 4.0, you can now specify your own 16th Byte value (in addition to those shown in Table 16.1) by using the Internet Group type Static Mapping. Each Internet Group type you define can contain up to 25 IP addresses. For example, you might create an Internet Group of printers called PRINTERS, with a 16th byte of [EFh]. An application could then query WINS for a list of all [EFh] type printers and perform some operation based on the list WINS returns.

When you're troubleshooting WINS problems, it's important to keep in mind the different 16th Byte values (also called *types*). If the WINS database becomes corrupted, certain machine functions might be disabled because a 16th Byte entry for the service is missing or has the wrong value. Later, the section "Understanding WINS and DNS Name Resolution" provides assistance in troubleshooting WINS name-resolution problems.

TIP Be sure to back up your Wins.mdb file periodically. Jet database files aren't immune from corruption. WINS attempts to recover a corrupted Wins.mdb file from data stored in .log files, but full recovery isn't always successful. Choose Backup Database from WINS Manager's Mappings menu to create a backup for your Wins.mdb file.

You can also enable automatic backup of the WINS database each time the WINS service is stopped. In WINS Manager, choose Configuration from the Server menu, click Advanced, and mark the Backup on Termination check box.

NetBIOS Node Types Part of RFCs 1001 and 1002 calls for defining NetBIOS over TCP/IP devices based on the method(s) by which they access NetBIOS services. (The methods are called *nodes*.) For example, if a Windows NT server doesn't use WINS, all name-resolution requests are via IP broadcasts. In most cases, the broadcast is a name-resolution packet sent to IP broadcast address 255.255.255.255. If the server is configured to use WINS, the server issues a directed request to the WINS database, and then follows with an IP broadcast if the requested name isn't registered with WINS, called *h-node resolution*. The four sequences of name resolution are as follows:

- *b-node* uses only broadcasts to resolve NetBIOS names.

- *p-node* uses only point-to-point communication (for example, directed packets) to resolve NetBIOS names.

- *h-node* uses p-node operation first to resolve names, and then b-node, if needed.

- *m-node* uses b-node operation first to resolve names, and then p-node, if needed.

By default, a Windows host configured with a static IP address and specifying a particular WINS server is an h-node device. If you want to force another node type, you can use DHCP (Dynamic Host Configuration Protocol) to automatically assign client IP addresses and specify the node type.

▶ **See** "Implementing Dynamic Host Configuration Protocol," **p. 332**

Using Protocol Analyzers

Protocol analyzers are invaluable tools for discovering problems on a network or simply understanding the flow of packets between servers and clients. The advantage of a dedicated (hardware) protocol analyzer is its capability to capture problems from the OSI physical layer up to the application layer. If you have a Token Ring segment that's *beaconing*—that is, generating an excessive number of beacon tokens because of some problem on the ring—you can see what device is responsible. If your network is experiencing intermittent loss of connectivity, a protocol analyzer might show you that a specific server or client workstation is generating a large number of malformed packets, in which case you can remove and repair the offending device. It's particularly important that the hardware or software protocol analyzers you use recognize the unique nature of Windows NT-specific operations such as DHCP, WINS, and SMBs.

Hardware Protocol Analyzers

The best known hardware-based protocol analyzer is Network General's Expert Sniffer. The Sniffer usually comes bundled with a portable PC and includes a specialized network interface card that's designed to capture and decode packets. Network General also supplies PCMCIA cards and software for use in specific notebook PCs, which let you build your own Sniffer. Network General also produces the Distributed Sniffer, a specialized box that lets you plug into and capture packets on multiple segments simultaneously. Devices such as the Expert Sniffer not only let you capture and decode packets, but also provide help with diagnosing problems by analyzing the data and suggesting possible causes for detected problems.

ON THE WEB

Further information on Network General's Sniffer product line is available from **http://www.ngc.com/ product_info/product_info.html**.

Software Protocol Analyzers

Software-only protocol analyzers cost less than hardware devices but provide less functionality. Examples of popular software-based analyzers are Novell's LANalyzer for Windows and

Microsoft's Network Monitor, which is part of Microsoft Systems Management Server (SMS) and is now included with Windows NT Server 4.0. Both applications provide the capability to decode network packets and support various types of pre- and post-packet filtering for several protocols. Network Monitor (NetMon) is ideal for troubleshooting Windows NT networking problems because it's designed to identify the NetBIOS elements specific to Windows NT networks. NetMon is the subject of the later section "Using Network Monitor."

ON THE WEB

See **http://corp.novell.com/market/apr96/mm000109.htm** for more information on Novell's LANalyzer for Windows.

Part
III
Ch
16

Protocol Analyzer Connection

All protocol analyzers, whether they're hardware- or software-based, must be connected to each segment you want to monitor. You need an analyzer agent on each segment of a routed network to capture packets for analysis. The agent is necessary because routers don't forward some packets that may be of interest, such as broadcast packets. Figure 16.3 shows a two-segment network with hardware and software protocol analyzers.

FIG. 16.3
A two-segment network with a hardware and software protocol analyzer.

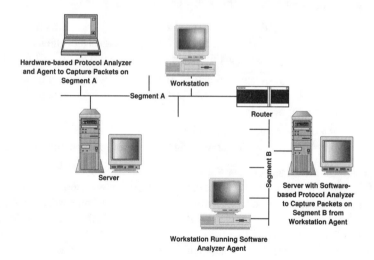

NOTE If you use a software agent such as Novell's LANalyzer, you must make sure that the server is using a network interface card that supports *promiscuous mode*. In normal operating mode, a NIC captures a packet on the wire only long enough to test whether the destination MAC address is its own. If not, it sends the packet back onto the wire. In promiscuous mode, a NIC captures each packet—whether or not the packet is meant for its address—and passes it to the analyzer agent. Modern NICs support promiscuous mode, but if you have an older NIC, such as the original IBM 4/16 Token Ring card, you must upgrade it.

continues

continued

Promiscuous mode operation, however, can induce at least 30 percent more load on the CPU in the PC where the NIC is installed. As a result, Windows NT 4.0's Network Monitor agent now supports Microsoft's NDIS 4.0 specification. This means that any NIC—even those that don't support promiscuous mode—can capture packets to NetMon, as long as the NIC is using NDIS 4.0 drivers. ■

Using Windows NT Server 4.0's Primary Troubleshooting Tools

Windows NT provides a variety of built-in tools for troubleshooting network problems. Using Windows NT tools is important because traditional network troubleshooting tools don't always support the NetBIOS implementation of network protocols that Windows NT requires.

Using Event Viewer

Make Event Viewer's System log your first step in the diagnosis process. You launch Event Viewer by choosing Programs, Administrative Tools (Common), and Event Viewer from the Start menu. Event Viewer's three classes of errors are as follows:

- ■ *Error* (octagonal red stop sign), also called a *stop event*, which indicates a significant problem, such as failure of the server's network card or the inability of a network service to load. A stop event isn't the same as a *stop error*; stop errors are fatal, low-level errors.

- ■ *Warning* (black exclamation point in a yellow circle), which indicates a problem of less severity than a stop event, such as failure of a connection to a backup domain controller or a master browser.

- ■ *Information* (white "i" in a blue circle), which describes successful completion of important events, such as starting SQL Server or Exchange Server.

Look for network-related errors, including BROWSER, WINS, and NetBT errors and warnings. Figure 16.4 shows Event Viewer displaying stop events for Remote Access Service and dependent services caused by a modem hardware failure, and a warning from the BROWSER service. Double-clicking the BROWSER warning opens the Event Detail dialog shown in Figure 16.5, which indicates that the OAKLEAF0 primary domain controller (PDC) can't communicate with the OAKLEAF3 backup domain controller (BDC), which also is a browse master.

All versions of the *Windows NT Resource Kit* include a Windows NT Messages help file, Ntmsgs.hlp, that you can access through the Documentation for Windows NT 4.0 Resource Kit help file. Expand the Other Resource Kit Documentation chapter and click Windows NT Messages to launch Ntmsgs.hlp. Alternatively, double-click the Ntmsgs.hlp file in your \Ntreskit folder. Double-click the Event Log topic, and then click System Log to display the Topics Found dialog for System log events. Scroll to the entry for the Event ID (see Figure 16.6), and double-click the entry to display the help topic for the event (see Figure 16.7). The help topic for the BROWSER warning (ID 8021) isn't very informative, especially if you're the network administrator. Fortunately, the User Action element of most other event help topics contain more useful troubleshooting information.

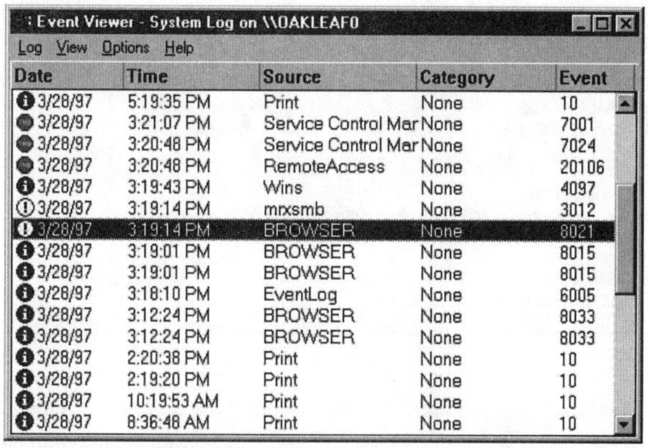

FIG. 16.4

Event Viewer's System log showing stop events for Remote Access Service and a browse master failure warning.

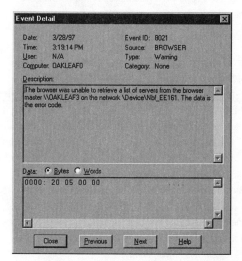

FIG. 16.5

The Event Detail dialog for the BROWSER warning of Figure 16.4.

FIG. 16.6

Ntmsgs.hlp's Topic List for the System log with the topic for the event of Figure 16.5 selected.

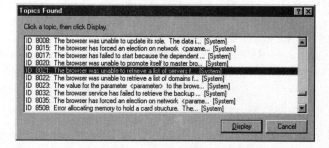

FIG. 16.7
The help topic for Event ID 8021.

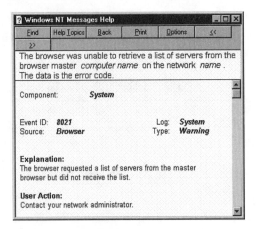

> **N O T E** The Jet (Access) database file, Ntevntlg.mdb, that the Resource Kit installs in your \Ntreskit folder isn't very useful. This 2.7M file includes many more events than Ntmsgs.hlp but only includes EventID, Message, EventSource, and EventType fields. There's no explanation of the message, nor is there a suggestion for user action. ■

Using Network Monitor

The Network Monitor tool that comes with Windows NT Server 4.0 is very handy for troubleshooting Windows NT-related network problems. Because it's software-based, you can use it to view packets going to and from your Windows NT server. The Network Monitor Agent Service comes with Windows NT 4.0 Server and Workstation, and must be installed and running before you can use NetMon. You need only one device running the NetMon agent per routed segment, and that device can be running on Windows NT 4.0, Server or Workstation version.

> **N O T E** The version of NetMon that's included with Windows NT Server 4.0 is limited in its capabilities, compared with the version that now ships with Microsoft Systems Management Server (SMS) 1.2. Specifically, for security reasons, Windows NT Server 4.0 doesn't let you connect to remote NetMon agents running on Windows NT systems across a routed network. You must run the SMS version of NetMon to gain this functionality. ■

Installing NetMon and Its Agent Service   You have two options when installing NetMon components on Windows NT Server 4.0: you can install just the Network Monitor agent, or install both the NetMon GUI tool and the agent. You choose the agent-only install if you have the SMS version of NetMon and want to enable monitoring across a routed network. In this case, the agent-only option is installed on one Windows NT Workstation or Server per segment.

To install the Network Monitor Tools and the Agent Service, follow these steps:

1. From Control Panel, double-click Network to open the Network property sheet, and then click the Services tab.

2. Click Add to open the Select Network Service dialog (see Figure 16.8).

3. In the Network Service list, select Network Monitor Tools and Agent; then click Have Disk to open the Insert Disk dialog.

4. Enter the path to your Windows NT Server distribution CD-ROM and the appropriate subfolder for your processor. For instance, if your CD-ROM drive is E on an Intel-based server, type **e:\i386** and click OK.

5. After Windows NT finishes copying files, you return to the Network property sheet. Click Close to cause Windows NT Server to reconfigure network bindings and request a system restart. You must restart the server for the changes to take effect.

6. By default, the Network Monitor Agent Service is installed for manual startup. To start the Agent Service, type **net start "Network Monitor Agent"** at the command prompt; or from Control Panel's Services tool, select Network Monitor Agent and click Start.

Part

III

Ch

16

FIG. 16.8

Installing the Network Monitor Tools and Agent.

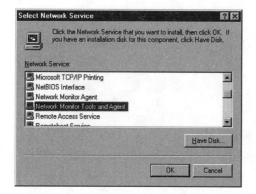

Putting Windows NT 4.0's Network Monitor to Use   If you're using the NetMon version that comes with Windows NT Server 4.0, you can trace packets flowing to and from the server on which you've installed NetMon. To use NetMon, follow these steps:

1. From the Start menu, choose Programs, Administrative Tools, and Network Monitor to launch NetMon (see Figure 16.9).

2. Choose Networks from the Capture menu to open the Select Capture Network dialog (see Figure 16.10). You must connect to the Network Monitor agent bound to your server NIC before using NetMon. If you have more than one NIC in the server, you can bind to one or the other to trace packets.

3. Select the desired adapter to connect, if you have more than one NIC, and click OK to close the dialog.

4. Choose Start from the Capture menu to open the Capture window and begin capturing packets (see Figure 16.11).

   By default, the Capture window is broken into four panes: Total Statistics, Session Statistics, Station Statistics, and Graph. You can toggle which panes you want to see by clicking the four pane toggle buttons of the toolbar. Alternatively, you can mark or unmark the appropriate checked item of the Window menu.

FIG. 16.9
Network Monitor's
window on initial
startup.

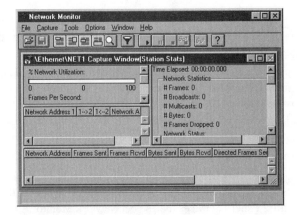

FIG. 16.10
Connecting to the
Network Monitor agent.

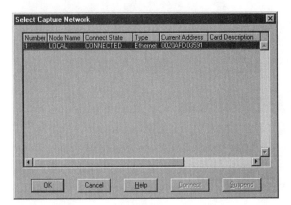

FIG. 16.11
Capturing packets with
NetMon.

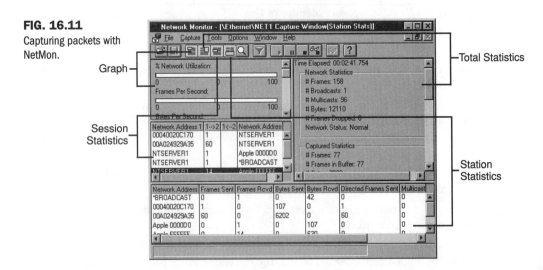

5. After you finish capturing, from the Capture menu choose Stop or Stop and View. If you choose Stop and View, the Capture Summary window appears (see Figure 16.12). This window displays summary information about each packet you've captured, including the frame number, the time since the start of the capture (in seconds and milliseconds), and source and destination MAC addresses or device names, protocol used, and a description of the packet.

FIG. 16.12

Viewing all packets captured in the Capture Summary window.

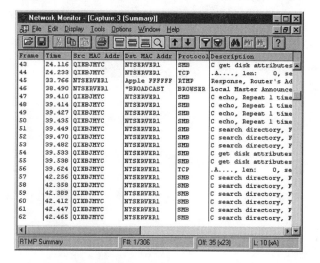

N O T E NetMon keeps a database of names that correspond to a given MAC address. You can view the entries in this database by choosing Addresses from the Capture window's Capture menu or from the Capture Summary window's Display menu.

In Figure 16.13, the address database contains some default entries for broadcasts on Ethernet, Token Ring, and FDDI, as well as a special MAC address used by NetBIOS. Also, a Windows NT server called NTSERVER1 and a Windows 3.1 client called QIEBJMYC have been discovered and automatically added to the database. In the Address Database dialog, you can click Save to save these entries to the default address database, Default.adr. ■

6. Choose Filter from the Capture Summary window's Display menu to open the Display Filter dialog (see Figure 16.14), which lets you create filters for the captured packets. You can filter by protocol, by station address, or by a protocol property. For example, double-click the Protocol == Any entry to enable all protocols and open the Expression dialog. (Whether or not you filter on protocol, address, or property, the Expression dialog appears, to let you define the parameters of your filter.)

If you want to set up a filter so that only IP packets appear, click Disable All in the Expression dialog; then from the Disabled Protocols list, scroll down to select IP:. Click Enable to display only IP packets (see Figure 16.15). Click OK twice to close the dialogs and engage the filter.

FIG. 16.13
Viewing NetMon's
address database.

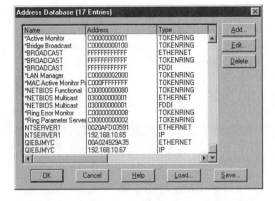

FIG. 16.14
The default filter
expressions of the
Display Filter dialog.

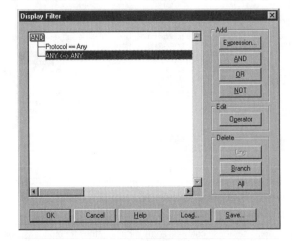

FIG. 16.15
Setting up a display
filter to show only IP
packets.

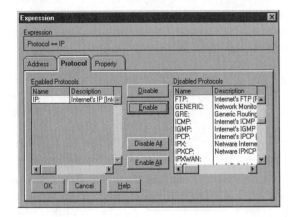

7. Double-click a packet item in NetMon's list to display additional information about the packet. The Capture Summary window opens with three panes that provide summary, detail, and hexadecimal information about the selected packet (see Figure 16.16).

FIG. 16.16

Viewing detailed information on a captured packet.

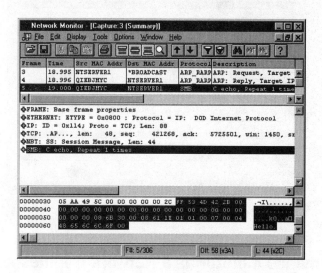

Part

III

Ch

16

8. Click the middle (detail) pane to examine the packet at each protocol layer. Each OSI layer is represented by an entry, including Physical (Frame), MAC (Ethernet, Token Ring, and so on), Network (IP, IPX, AppleTalk, and so on), Transport (TCP), and Session (NBT).

A plus symbol to the left of each layer item indicates that more detail is available under that heading. Double-click one such entry to display detailed information for that portion of the frame. Figure 16.17 shows an expanded IP layer entry that displays all the fields of the IP header, including source and destination IP addresses for that packet, and the packet's size. The content of the selected location of the packet appears in hexadecimal format in the pane at the bottom of the Capture Detail window.

NetMon is useful in troubleshooting various network-related problems, such as name resolution by a WINS server. You can use NetMon to capture packets coming into the WINS server to determine whether a client's name-resolution requests reach the server, and whether the server responds to the requests. By using NetMon's trace capability, you can verify that the client makes a WINS request to the server and the server returns a packet indicating that the name wasn't found. You then use WINS Manager to determine whether the name exists in the server's WINS database or whether the WINS database is corrupted.

FIG. 16.17
Viewing packet detail
within the IP header.

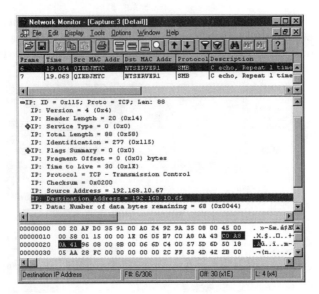

Using Performance Monitor as a Network Troubleshooting Tool

Windows NT's Performance Monitor (PerfMon) is a valuable tool for monitoring the operation
of Windows NT servers and workstations, including their network components. PerfMon lets
you monitor network interfaces on a server to determine bandwidth usage, rates of errors and
broadcasts, and protocol-specific counters. Figure 16.18 shows PerfMon's Add to Chart dialog,
listing some of the counters available for the Network Segment object.

▶ **See** "Using Performance Monitor," **p. 530**

FIG. 16.18
PerfMon's Network
Segment counters.

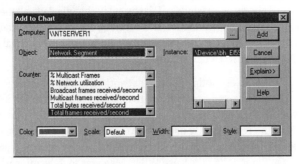

The % Network Utilization counter gives a running snapshot of current network usage on the
segment you're monitoring. This counter is a valuable tool for performing a quick analysis of
a segment in which you suspect problems are occurring. You can launch PerfMon and do a
quick check without having to install a protocol analyzer or software agent.

Installing the SNMP Service   You need to install the SNMP (Simple Network Management Protocol) service to obtain all the available TCP/IP or IPX statistics for your network interface. Without SNMP, PerfMon can't see some of the network objects. To install the SNMP service, follow these steps:

1. From Control Panel, double-click the Network tool to open the Network property sheet, and then click the Services tab.

2. Click Add to open the Select Network Service dialog.

3. In the Network Service list, select SNMP Service (see Figure 16.19), and then click Have Disk to open the Insert Disk dialog.

Part

III

Ch

16

FIG. 16.19

Installing the SNMP service from the Select Network Service dialog.

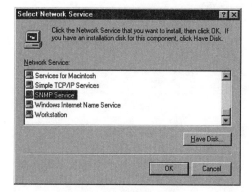

4. Enter the path to your Windows NT Server distribution CD-ROM and the appropriate subfolder for your processor. For instance, if your CD is drive E on an Intel-based server, type `e:\i386` and click OK to copy the SNMP service files.

5. The Microsoft SNMP Properties sheet appears, letting you customize the SNMP agent on your system (see Figure 16.20).

Following is a brief description of each page of the Microsoft SNMP Properties sheet:

- The default Agent page lets you enter contact and location information, as well as specify the services provided by the server. The service selections—Physical, Applications, Datalink/Subnetwork, Internet, and End-to-End—let you specify which SNMP statistics this server should collect. The selection is based on the services that the server provides. For example, marking the Datalink/Subnetwork check box provides MAC-layer statistics on the server's network interfaces. The Internet check box provides information on the network-layer protocol, such as IP or IPX, and is useful if you're running routing services on your server.

- The Traps page lets you select a community name to be used by all trap messages and specify a trap destination, using either IP or IPX protocol (see Figure 16.21). *Traps* are SNMP messages that get sent from your server whenever a significant event occurs. A significant event can be a NIC that has been disconnected or is reconnected, or a user-initiated server shutdown. Traps are sent to an SNMP management console running at the trap destination you specify.

FIG. 16.20
Setting SNMP Agent configuration options.

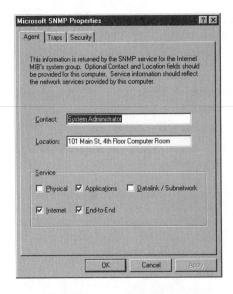

FIG. 16.21
Setting the trap properties for the SNMP service.

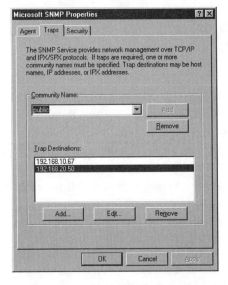

- The Security page lets you set up SNMP security for the service (see Figure 16.22). Options include whether the service should send a trap each time an SNMP manager authenticates with the service, the accepted community names for use by SNMP managers, and whether any SNMP device can communicate with the service or only specified IP or IPX hosts.

FIG. 16.22

Setting Security properties for the SNMP service.

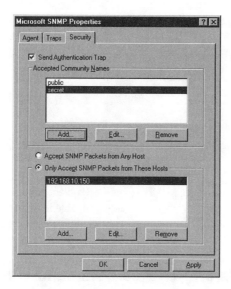

6. After you complete the setup of the SNMP agent for your server, click OK to close the Microsoft SNMP Properties sheet and click Close in the Network property sheet. You're required to restart your system for the changes to take effect.

As part of the installation of the SNMP service, Microsoft provides a number of Management Information Bases (MIBs), which contain the various attributes that the SNMP service tracks. SNMP managers monitor the MIB attributes of servers, routers, and other SNMP-compliant network devices.

If you're familiar with the SNMP MIB specification, Windows NT provides two trees in the private MIB section. 1.3.6.1.4.1.77 is the LAN Manager tree that provides information on shares, sessions, and users. 1.3.6.1.4.1.311 is the Microsoft tree that provides statistics on WINS and DHCP. A *tree* in the MIB, as represented by the Object ID (OID) 1.3.6.1.4.1.77, is really an "address" where an SNMP manager that's connected to Windows NT Server's SNMP service can attach to find SNMP information about a specific attribute on the server. Under each tree are *leaf objects* corresponding to individual characteristics for that device. For ex-ample, under the 1.3.6.1.4.1.311 tree for WINS and DHCP, an SNMP Manager can find what entries are contained in the WINS database on that server, or who the WINS service's replica-tion partners are.

Using PerfMon with TCP/IP Networks After installing the SNMP service on your Windows NT server, you can use PerfMon to gather IP- or IPX-related statistics about your system. The most useful application of PerfMon as a network troubleshooting tool is tracking protocol-related information over time with PerfMon's logging function. By using the IP object in PerfMon, for example, you can track datagram errors, packets received, or packets discarded over time (see Figure 16.23).

FIG. 16.23
PerfMon's Add to Chart
dialog showing IP-
related counters.

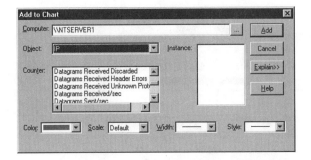

PerfMon also includes counters for ICMP, TCP, and UDP objects that provide similar information to IP. Tracking these counters over time provides valuable information about network
performance on your Windows NT server, especially when you must troubleshoot TCP/IP or
IPX network problems.

Using Windows NT's Network-Related Command-Line Tools

Windows NT 4.0 and its *Windows NT Server Resource Kit* provide many useful command-line
tools for troubleshooting network problems. The following sections describe the most important tools included with Windows NT Server 4.0. Later, the section "Using the *Windows NT
Server Resource Kit* Network Utilities" describes additional command-line utilities provided in
the *Windows NT Server Resource Kit*.

You can use the command-line tools that come with Windows NT 4.0 to help solve many basic
networking problems. Most of the tools are for TCP/IP and are likely to be familiar to UNIX
users.

Address Resolution Protocol   The arp (Address Resolution Protocol) command lets you view
the current contents of the ARP cache on a server or workstation. arp -a displays the contents
of the ARP cache; arp -d and arp -s let you manually remove and add entries to the ARP
cache. With ping, you can use arp to determine whether a device is communicating on the
network. If you ping a device in question, you should see a corresponding entry in the ARP
cache of either the device you're pinging, or that of the default gateway if the device isn't on
your local subnet (see Figure 16.24).

Hostname   The hostname command returns the name of the system on which the command
is executed. The name returned is the name specified in the DNS setup section of the TCP/IP
configuration of the system, rather than the NetBIOS name.

Ipconfig   The ipconfig command returns all the current TCP/IP, DNS, and WINS information for the system. Use ipconfig /all to display all the information, and just ipconfig to
obtain abbreviated information (see Figure 16.25).

The ipconfig command is also a quick way to get the MAC address of the NIC installed in the
device. If you're using DHCP, you can also use ipconfig to renew a DHCP address reservation, or release an address on a DHCP client by using the /renew and /release parameters.

FIG. 16.24

Using the arp command to view the ARP cache.

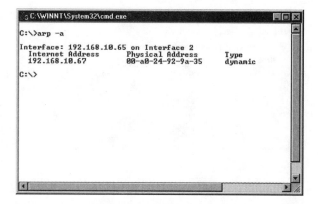

FIG. 16.25

Viewing the output of the ipconfig command.

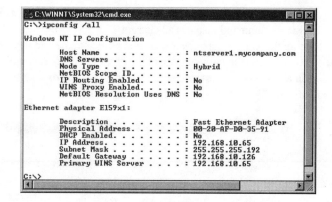

Nbtstat The nbtstat command is one of the most useful Windows NT networking tools because it provides various information about NetBIOS names and their addresses. For example, if you know the NetBIOS name of a workstation and want to know its IP address, follow these steps:

1. Type **net view \\machinename** at the command prompt, where *machinename* is the NetBIOS name of the device. You receive a list of shares available on that machine, or the message There are no entries in the list.

2. Type **nbtstat -c** to display the name and IP address of the machine specified in step 1. You don't need to specify the machine name because the result of the preceding name resolution is cached in the NetBIOS Name Cache, which you can view with the -c parameter.

You also can use the nbtstat -A *ip_address* command to determine what machine is registered to a given IP address (see Figure 16.26). Note that this command requires an *uppercase* A parameter. When you issue this command, the server or workstation sends a name request to the IP address of the primary WINS server specified in the issuing device's TCP/IP WINS configuration page. The returned information is the contents of the WINS database for *ip_address*. This command is useful if you're trying to troubleshoot WINS problems.

FIG. 16.26

Viewing the output of the nbtstat –A command.

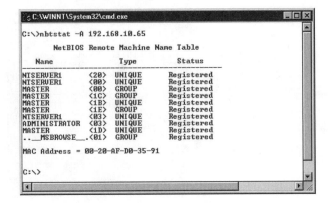

Netstat The netstat command performs many of the same functions as its UNIX counterpart. The netstat -a command displays all current TCP and UDP connections from the issuing device to other devices on the network, as well as the source and destination service ports, and—in the case of TCP—the current state of the connection (for instance, Established or Time-Wait). You also can use netstat -r to post a listing of the routing table on a given machine (see Figure 16.27).

FIG. 16.27

Using netstat -r to view the routing table of a Windows NT server.

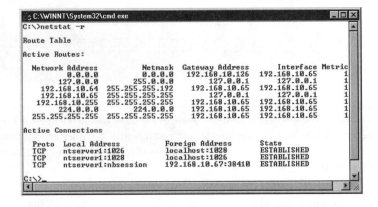

The netstat -e command gives you statistics on your network interface. When combined with an interval parameter—for example, netstat -e 10—the following information is updated every 10 seconds:

Interface Statistics	Received	Sent
Bytes	184763	125248
Unicast Packets	304	437
Non-unicast Packets	1419	1419
Discards	0	0
Errors	0	0
Unknown Protocols	313	

The preceding information is useful if you're troubleshooting suspected network problems and want to determine whether the network interface is generating errors.

Ping   The `ping` command is widely used for testing connectivity. This command sends an ICMP echo packet to the host or IP address you specify on the command line. For example, `ping 200.200.1.1` sends an echo packet to IP address 200.200.1.1. If `ping` is successful, you see a series of replies similar to the following:

```
Reply from 200.200.1.1: bytes=32 time=10ms TTL=32
Reply from 200.200.1.1: bytes=32 time=10ms TTL=32
Reply from 200.200.1.1: bytes=32 time=10ms TTL=32
Reply from 200.200.1.1: bytes=32 time=10ms TTL=32
```

If `ping` fails, you receive the following message:

```
Request timed out.
```

You can test whether a server's TCP/IP subsystem is working correctly with the `ping` `127.0.0.1` command, also known as the *loopback address*. This is the *localhost* address, or the default hostname for that machine; this address and hostname is installed by default when you install Windows NT's TCP/IP stack. A successful ping indicates that this virtual address is alive and that your TCP/IP stack is functioning correctly.

Route   The `route` utility lists a server's TCP/IP routing table and can add or delete static routes. You also can add persistent (static) routes that are maintained through shutdown and startup. To view the current routing table, type **route print**.

You can use the `-p` parameter to create a persistent route. The following example shows how to add a static route to a remote network and make it persistent:

```
route -p add 192.168.20.0 MASK 255.255.255.0 200.200.1.255 1
```

The trailing 1 indicates that the remote network is one router *hop* (one pass through a router) away. The example routes to the remote network 192.168.20.0 by using the gateway/router address of 200.200.1.255. The remote network has a subnet mask of 255.255.255.0.

N O T E   Persistent routes are stored in the HKEY_LOCAL_MACHINE\System\CurrentControlSet\ Services\Tcpip\Parameters\PersistentRoutes entry of the Registry. ■

Tracert   The `tracert` command lets you trace the path to a destination IP address, identifying all the intermediate hops between the source and destination. You can use `tracert`—a very powerful tool for determining how packets are traversing your network—to troubleshoot routing loops or down routers, as well as to discover timeout problems across the network.

The `tracert` command uses ICMP to find the path to the end station you specify. The following example, `tracert EndStation`, traces a path to a client called EndStation at IP address 172.16.12.1:

```
Tracing route to EndStation [172.16.12.1]
over a maximum of 30 hops:
  1   181 ms   130 ms   130 ms  172.16.4.254
  2   160 ms   131 ms   120 ms  routera.mycompany.com [172.16.5.254]
  3   151 ms   120 ms   120 ms  routerb.mycompany.com [172.16.6.254]
  4   160 ms   140 ms   140 ms  172.16.8.254
  5   161 ms   140 ms   140 ms  routerc.mycompany.com [172.16.9.254]
  6   170 ms   141 ms   130 ms  EndStation [172.16.12.1]
Trace complete.
```

In this example, the path to the EndStation client is six hops from the device where the command is initiated. The first hop is to the default gateway (172.16.4.254) on the subnet where the command was issued. Along the way, tracert does a DNS *reverse-address lookup* of each hop (unless you specify the -d parameter) to resolve IP addresses of intermediate hops to host names. If your router interfaces aren't configured in DNS, all you see are the addresses in lines 1 and 4 of the example.

N O T E   A DNS reverse lookup is exactly as it sounds. Rather than resolve a known host name to an IP address, a reverse lookup resolves a known IP address to a host name. ∎

In the following example, the EndStation client is unreachable from the source. The trace stops after the third hop, which could mean that either the end station is down, or the destination subnet isn't accessible from the source. The latter problem can be due to router problems or to an intermediate route filter of some type. The best way to approach solving these kinds of problems is to determine what part of the path *does* work, and narrow the possible suspects as you go. A good troubleshooting technique with tracert is to connect to the last successful step along the path—in this case, routerb.mycompany.com—and determine whether you can get to the destination from there. If not, your problem is likely to be in a destination device or an intermediate router. You might need to run another trace from routerb to determine whether intermediate hops to the destination are failing.

```
Tracing route to 172.16.80.1
over a maximum of 30 hops
  1   140 ms   120 ms   130 ms  172.16.4.254
  2   131 ms   120 ms   120 ms  routera.mycompany.com [172.16.5.254]
  3  routerb.mycompany.com [172.16.6.254]  reports: Destination host unreachable.
Trace complete.
```

Using the *Windows NT Server Resource Kit* Network Utilities

The *Windows NT Server Resource Kit* includes several useful tools for troubleshooting network problems. Many are easy-to-use GUI-based tools, but others are cryptic, not very well documented, and require trial-and-error experimentation to use correctly. Microsoft provides product support (including bug fixes) for the Resource Kit utilities but doesn't respond to requests for enhancements. You also can send questions by e-mail to **rkinput@microsoft.com**; someone at Microsoft might get back to you, if only to tell you that the information you need is available somewhere else.

Following are descriptions of the most useful Resource Kit utilities for network troubleshooting.

Browser Monitor

Browmon.exe is the graphical Browser Monitor. BrowMon is very useful when you need to troubleshoot browser problems. You can check the contents of the Master Browser on each subnet in question to determine whether your missing device is actually contained in the browser list for that segment. To use BrowMon, follow these steps:

1. Launch BrowMon by choosing Programs, Resource Kit 4.0, Diagnostics, and Browser Monitor from the Start menu. When you start BrowMon for the first time, choose Add Domain from the Domain menu and specify your domain name to start the monitoring service. Figure 16.28 shows BrowMon displaying the two browser transports used on the OAKLEAF domain, NBF and NetBT, with an Intel EtherExpress Pro NIC. OAKLEAF0 is the master browser for the OAKLEAF domain.

FIG. 16.28

BrowMon's display for the OAKLEAF domain running NBF and NetBT browser transports.

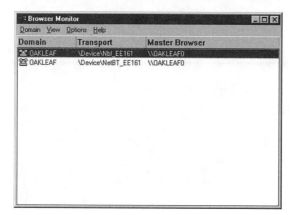

2. Double-click the entry for the browser transport to open the Browser Status dialog (see Figure 16.29), which displays the servers in the browse list and the domains to which the servers belong. (OAKLEAF has no trusted domains.)

3. Double-click an entry in the browse list to display the Browser Info dialog, which shows the statistics for the browser. Figure 16.30 shows the statistics of the OAKLEAF0 browse master and PDC shortly after a reboot.

Error messages that appear when you repeat steps 2 and 3 for each transport in use provide useful but terse guidance to the source of browsing problems.

FIG. 16.29

The Browser Status dialog, displaying the browse list for the OAKLEAF domain.

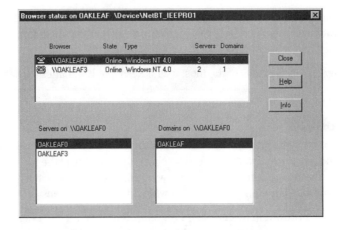

FIG. 16.30

The Browser Info dialog, displaying statistics for the OAKLEAFO browse master.

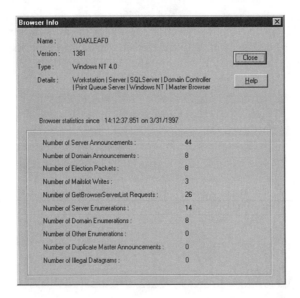

N O T E   When you run BrowMon, you see only browser information for the local network segment. If you want to know what's contained on the Domain Master Browser (almost always the Primary Domain Controller, or PDC), you must run BrowMon from a machine on the same network segment as the PDC. ■

Browser Status

Browstat.exe is the Browser Status command-line utility that's useful for retrieving general browser information, such as statistics and domain information. You can also use BrowStat to force a browser election, force a master browser to stop, and find out whether you have any Windows for Workgroups workstations acting as Master Browsers on a network segment.

The syntax for Browstat.exe, obtained by typing **browstat** at the command prompt, is as follows:

```
Usage: BROWSTAT Command [Options ¦ /HELP]
Where Command is one of:

   ELECT     ( EL) - Force election on remote domain
   GETBLIST  ( GB) - Get backup list for domain
   GETMASTER ( GM) - Get remote Master Browser name (using NetBIOS)
   GETPDC    ( GP) - Get PDC name (using NetBIOS)
   LISTWFW   (WFW) - List WFW servers that are actually running browser
   STATS     (STS) - Dump browser statistics
   STATUS    (STA) - Display status about a domain
   TICKLE    (TIC) - Force remote master to stop
   VIEW      ( VW) - Remote NetServerEnum to a server or domain on transport

In server (or domain) list displays, the following flags are used:
    W=Workstation, S=Server, SQL=SQLServer, PDC=PrimaryDomainController,
    BDC=BackupDomainController, TS=TimeSource, AFP=AFPServer, NV=Novell,
    MBC=MemberServer, PQ=PrintServer, DL=DialinServer, XN=Xenix,
    NT=Windows NT, WFW=WindowsForWorkgroups, MFPN=MS Netware,
    SS=StandardServer, PBR=PotentialBrowser, BBR=BackupBrowser,
    MBR=MasterBrowser, DMB=DomainMasterBrowser, OSF=OSFServer,
    VMS=VMSServer, W95=Windows95, DFS=DistributedFileSystem
```

The *Options* parameter depends on the *Command* you issue; add the /HELP switch for the *Command* to display applicable options. Figure 16.31 shows the result of typing **browstat sta** at the command line.

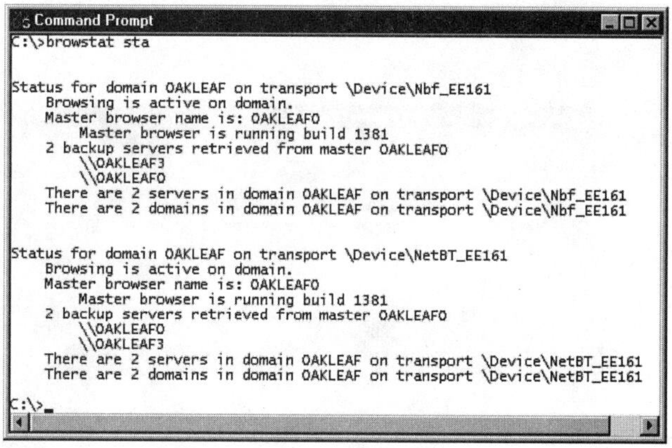

FIG. 16.31
Browstat.exe's return of browser status (run on OAKLEAFO).

```
Command Prompt                                                    _ □ ×
C:\>browstat sta

Status for domain OAKLEAF on transport \Device\Nbf_EE161
    Browsing is active on domain.
    Master browser name is: OAKLEAFO
        Master browser is running build 1381
    2 backup servers retrieved from master OAKLEAFO
        \\OAKLEAF3
        \\OAKLEAFO
    There are 2 servers in domain OAKLEAF on transport \Device\Nbf_EE161
    There are 2 domains in domain OAKLEAF on transport \Device\Nbf_EE161

Status for domain OAKLEAF on transport \Device\NetBT_EE161
    Browsing is active on domain.
    Master browser name is: OAKLEAFO
        Master browser is running build 1381
    2 backup servers retrieved from master OAKLEAFO
        \\OAKLEAFO
        \\OAKLEAF3
    There are 2 servers in domain OAKLEAF on transport \Device\NetBT_EE161
    There are 2 domains in domain OAKLEAF on transport \Device\NetBT_EE161

C:\>_
```

N O T E   The Windows NT 3.51 version of BrowStat is incompatible with Windows NT 4.0. ▪

Domain Monitor

Dommon.exe, the Domain Monitor utility, displays the current status of a given domain's Domain Controller, including whether its Security Accounts Manager (SAM) databases are synchronized. DomMon also shows the current trust status of any domains with which the current domain has a trust relationship. Like BrowMon, you specify the domain to monitor when first using DomMon and add other trusting domains by choosing Add Domain from the Domain menu.

N O T E   The Windows NT 3.51 version of DomMon is incompatible with Windows NT 4.0. ■

Figure 16.32 shows DomMon's opening window for the single OAKLEAF domain. Double-clicking a domain item opens the Domain Controller Status dialog, which displays the status of domain controllers in the domain (see Figure 16.33).

FIG. 16.32
Domain Monitor's window for a domain with no trust relationships.

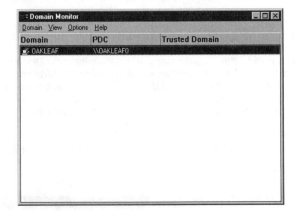

FIG. 16.33
The Domain Controller Status dialog for the OAKLEAF domain.

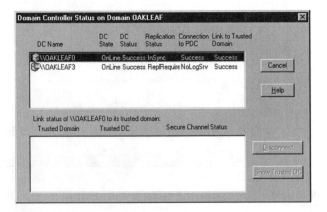

DomMon is useful for troubleshooting problems with trust relationships, because it lets you see which remote domain controller the current domain uses for the trust. From this point, you can verify connectivity between the two servers as part of your troubleshooting process.

GetMac

Getmac.exe is a simple utility that returns the MAC address of the machine on which it's run. GetMac is useful if you're having problems with ARP and need to know MAC addresses. It returns the MAC address of each network protocol loaded on your machine, similar to the following:

```
E:\ getmac
Transport Address    Transport Name
-----------------    --------------
20-4C-4F-4F-50-20    \Device\NetBT_NDISLoop1
00-00-00-00-00-00    \Device\NetBT_NdisWan5
20-4C-4F-4F-50-20    \Device\Nbf_NDISLoop1
20-4C-4F-4F-50-20    \Device\NwlnkNb
```

N O T E The Windows NT 3.51 version of GetMac works with Windows NT 4.0. ▓

Net Watch

Netwatch.exe is a GUI-based utility, similar to Windows 95's Net Watcher, that lets you monitor user connections to shares on servers and clients. As Figure 16.34 shows, you also can see what files a user has open on a given share.

FIG. 16.34

Using the Net Watch utility to view users (OAKLEAF1) logged on to the shares of OAKLEAF0.

N O T E The Windows NT 3.51 version of Net Watch works with Windows NT 4.0. ▓

Windows NT doesn't have the NetWare 3.x concept of user logon connections into each server; Windows NT attaches to domain resources as needed. This utility, however, tells you who's connected to which share on a given server or client, and which files they have open.

▶ **See** "Using Net Watcher Remotely," **p. 394**

NSLookup

Nslookup.exe serves the same function as its UNIX equivalent. You can use NSLookup to query DNS servers to determine the IP address of a specified host name, or the host name of a specified IP address. The nslookup command sends the request to the address and subdomains defined on the DNS page of Windows NT's TCP/IP Properties sheet (see Figure 16.35).

FIG. 16.35

Setting DNS Configuration options in the Microsoft TCP/IP Properties sheet.

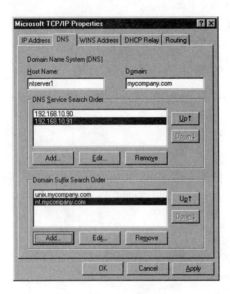

nslookup takes no parameters. When you enter the command, you're placed at the > prompt, where you enter the name or address you want to resolve (see Figure 16.36).

FIG. 16.36

Using nslookup to resolve DNS names and addresses.

N O T E The Windows NT 3.51 version of Nslookup.exe works with Windows NT 4.0. ■

SMBTrace

The Smbtrace.exe command-line utility is similar to the UNIX `etherfind` command, except that SMBTrace tracks Server Message Block packets only. SMBTrace is a real-time packet tracer that shows the SMB packets flowing to and from your system, which is useful for understanding the flow of SMB packets during file transfers and print jobs.

N O T E The Windows NT 3.51 version of Smbtrace.exe works with Windows NT 4.0. ■

By default, `smbtrace` captures incoming packets only. The `/slow` parameter captures both incoming and outgoing packets, and the `/rdr` parameter captures only outgoing packets. You can change the amount of information `smbtrace` displays with each packet by using the `/verbosity:n` parameter, where *n* is a number between 1 and 5, 5 being most verbose.

WNTIPcfg

The Windows NT IP configuration tool, Wntipcfg.exe, lists all the TCP/IP configuration information for the system on which WNTIPcfg runs. WNTIPcfg provides the same information as `ipconfig -a` in a graphical format. The Windows NT 3.51 version of WNTIPcfg is incompatible with Windows NT 4.0.

Taking Advantage of Other Troubleshooting Resources

In addition to the tools described in the preceding sections, the following resources also include network troubleshooting advice and tools:

- Microsoft Knowledge Base (**http://www.microsoft.com/kb/**) is an online repository of known problems and their fixes.

- The Microsoft Technet CD is a monthly subscription that combines fixes, driver updates, and the Knowledge Base, as well as other useful information.

- The Windows NT Resource Center, run by BHS Software of Beverly Hills (**http://www.bhs.com**), is perhaps the most popular Web site for Windows NT-related files, information, and problem resolution. Check out the BHS Tech Center if you have a networking problem that you can't resolve.

- Internet newsgroups, such as **comp.os.ms-windows.nt.admin.networking** and **comp.os.ms-windows.nt.misc**, also are good sources of troubleshooting information.

You can find useful Windows NT-related information in many other places on the Internet. Just choose your favorite search engine and search on **"Windows NT"**.

Part
III

Ch
16

Solving Windows NT Server Network Problems

Windows NT Server is similar to other operating systems when you're troubleshooting basic network problems. *Troubleshooting* identifies the problem; *solving* means correcting the problem. If there are connectivity problems, you check the cabling, the network interface card, and the network protocol configuration. Windows NT, however, includes a number of additional network-related components (such as browsing, trusts, and WINS) that can compound basic network problems. An understanding of some of the common problems related to Windows NT's special networking features helps you become a more accomplished network administrator.

Understanding and Solving Connectivity Problems

Connectivity problems manifest themselves in different ways. In Windows NT, a connectivity problem can cause trust relationships to fail or cause drive mappings to time out.

You were introduced to a number of tools in the preceding sections for testing connectivity. In the following sections, the utilities are applied to help solve connectivity problems that arise in Windows NT environments.

Solving Basic Connectivity Issues   Utilities such as ping allow you to test connectivity from point A to point B. The ping utility may succeed, but success verifies only that TCP/IP is working. If you must verify Windows NT Server's file, print, and application service availability, you must be able to verify connectivity at the NetBIOS level.

The net view command is the NetBIOS equivalent of ping. A net view *servername* command might result in the following message:

```
System error 53 has occurred.
The network path was not found.
```

This message usually means that either the *servername* system is down, or the device's name can't be resolved. You may find the case where ping succeeds but net view fails. An example of such a situation is when a NetBIOS device, such as a server, has found a name conflict on startup. While the server was shut down, WINS may have registered another name at the server's IP address, or the same server name may have been registered at a different network address. You can use the nbtstat -n command to determine whether there's a conflict. In either case, the network subsystem might start, but the NetBIOS services don't. You can check for this situation by searching the system log with the Event Viewer application on the device in question.

If you receive system error 53 and have verified that the system's NetBIOS subsystem isn't in conflict, you likely have a name-resolution problem. In this case, verify on a TCP/IP network that you have an entry in WINS or an LMHosts file to resolve the name in question.

Identifying Router Problems   If you suspect your connectivity problems are related to routing—that is, you've verified that both source and destination are up and can access devices on their local segment—use tracert to determine where in the path you have a problem.

Identifying Default Gateway Problems   If you're in a networked environment where each segment has multiple, redundant routes to reach a specified destination, you should be aware of an idiosyncrasy in Windows NT's TCP/IP stack. Windows NT Server 4.0's Advanced IP Addressing dialog provides the capability to specify multiple default gateways to reach remote segments (see Figure 16.37). If the first gateway in the list fails, however, any subsequent User Datagram Protocol (UDP) packets fail to search the list for the next gateway. When the first TCP packet finds the primary gateway down, the packet goes down the list to the next gateway and makes it the active gateway. Thus, subsequent UDP packets use the new gateway to reach their destination. You may never notice use of an alternative gateway unless the primary gateway is down when you're first powering up a system.

Part
III

Ch
16

FIG. 16.37
Setting multiple default gateways with the Advanced IP Addressing dialog.

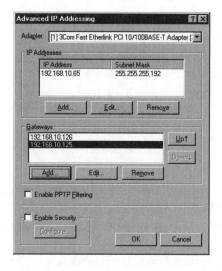

> **N O T E**   To open the Advanced IP Addressing dialog, launch Control Panel's Network tool, select the Protocols page, double-click the TCP/IP Protocol item to open the Microsoft TCP/IP Properties sheet, and then click the Advanced button. ■

The Netlogon service, which is responsible for domain authentication, uses UDP to authenticate a client and user to a domain. As a result, when a server that's a Backup Domain Controller (BDC) starts up with its primary default gateway down, the BDC can't contact other servers not on the same physical network segment—that is, across a router. The result is the following message:

```
A Domain Controller could not be contacted
```

In this case, until the first TCP packet goes out, the BDC can't authenticate—and therefore synchronize—to the domain. Although this is a specialized problem of redundant routing, it's significant, especially on the workstation side.

Browsing

Browsing is a feature unique to Windows NT and its predecessor, LAN Manager. Browsing is solely a function of NetBIOS and slightly parallels Novell's SAP service announcements. Troubleshooting browsing problems, especially in a NetBEUI or IPX-NetBIOS environment, is downright difficult. You're limited to the BrowMon and BrowStat tools (discussed earlier in this chapter). Troubleshooting browsing problems is a bit better in the TCP/IP environment, where browsing is broken up by logical subnets and browser advertisements are broadcast-based, thus not forwarded by the routers.

The best way to troubleshoot browsing is first to understand the browsing process. A domain environment has three types of browsers, as follows:

- *Domain Master Browser.* By default, the Primary Domain Controller (PDC) is the Domain Master Browser for a particular domain.

- *Master Browser.* Each network segment contains at least one Master Browser. In the case where you have only one segment, the PDC is also the Master Browser.

- *Backup Browser.* Each network segment has at least one backup browser, which is responsible for holding elections to pick a new Master Browser if the Master Browser goes away.

Following is a step-by-step description of the election process to determine a new Master Browser:

1. When a client or server starts up, it sends a broadcast browser announcement that identifies the device's presence.

2. The Master Browser on the segment responds by adding the client or server to its browse list and sends back a list of the backup browsers.

3. When a client or server wants to browse the network, it sends a `NetServerEnum` request to the master or backup browsers to retrieve the browse list.

4. Every 12 minutes, each client or server that isn't a browser reannounces itself to the Master Browser. If a client or server doesn't reannounce for three consecutive 12-minute intervals, it's dropped from the Master Browser's list.

5. Every 15 minutes, the backup browser contacts the Master Browser to update its browse list. If the Master Browser doesn't respond, the backup browser holds an election.

6. The Master Browser also must contact the Domain Master Browser, which contains the entire browse list for the domain, including devices announced by other master browsers. Every 15 minutes, the Master Browser contacts the Domain Master Browser, provides its current browse list, and receives the current full domain browse list.

7. Master browsers also announce their domain every 15 minutes. If you have multiple domains on a segment, each domain populates the other domains' Master Browser lists so that users can browse multiple domains. In a TCP/IP environment, browsers use WINS to determine the identity of the domain master browsers, which are indicated by the 16th Byte type: `<domain_name>[1Bh]`.

8. If at any time during the preceding steps the Master Browser goes down, the backup browser forces an election. Alternatively, a client can force an election if it discovers the Master Browser failure before the backup browser does.

   The election proceeds with a predefined preference method. NetBIOS systems have an order of preference for browsability: Windows NT Server, followed by Windows NT Workstation, Windows for Workgroups, and Windows 95. If there's a tie among recipients, other criteria, such as how long the system has been up and the name of the system, can be used to break the tie.

Browser operations use NetBIOS mailslots to perform tasks such as announcements, elections, and updates. Windows NT Server's mailslots are second class. First-class mailslots provide guaranteed delivery; second-class mailslots are connectionless, so message delivery isn't guaranteed.

If you're having browser problems, the first thing to check with BrowMon is the contents of the Master Browser on your network segment. If the computer in question isn't in the list, a possible cause is a Windows for Workgroups client on the segment that has the MaintainServerList parameter of its SYSTEM.INI [386Enh] section set to something other than No.

Another possible problem is that the browser service on a Windows NT server or workstation isn't running. You can check this with Windows NT's Control Panel's Services tool, or issue the net start command to see which services are running.

Finally, you can prevent a Windows NT workstation or server from announcing itself to the Master Browser by issuing the following command:

```
net config server /hidden:yes
```

If the /hidden parameter is set, you don't see the server on the browser, but you can connect to the server by using its UNC name.

Routing

By default, Windows NT Server doesn't support dynamic routing—that is, if you have two NICs in a server, you can't send routing updates between the two NICs. You can set up routing between the two cards by selecting the Enable IP Forwarding check box in the Routing page of the Microsoft TCP/IP Properties sheet (see Figure 16.38), accessed from Control Panel's Network tool.

Microsoft includes with Windows NT Server 4.0 support for dynamic routing with the RIP for NWLink IPX/SPX service and RIP for Internet Protocol Service. Unless you run these services, you must configure routing with the static route command described earlier in this chapter. Most problems with routing in Windows NT relate to this static routing concept. Specifically, if you're trying to communicate from a segment connected to a NIC in a Windows NT server to another segment connected to a second NIC also installed in that server, you need a static route.

Part

III

Ch

16

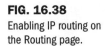

FIG. 16.38
Enabling IP routing on
the Routing page.

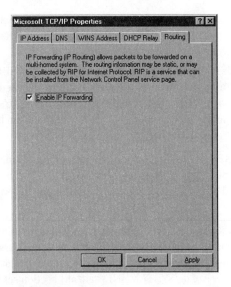

In the example shown in Figure 16.39, if you're trying to communicate from Client A on Network B to Server B on Network C, Windows NT Server C needs a static route to tell traffic how to get to Network C. The persistent route statement is

```
route -p add 172.16.42.0 MASK 255.255.255.0 172.16.40.2 1
```

where 172.16.42.0 is the destination network Client A is trying to get to, and 172.16.40.2 is the router interface on the far end of Network A that forwards the packet to the correct network.

Troubleshooting Trusts

Trust relationships allow resources and user accounts to be shared between domains. The major network problems that arise as a result of trusts occur in TCP/IP WANs. Domain controllers use WINS to determine names and IP addresses of trusted domain controllers in remote domains. If there are problems with WINS, trust relationships break down.

If you're replicating your WINS databases so that all domain controllers in each domain can resolve each other, establishing and maintaining a trust relationship should be easy. Domain controllers, by default, register their domain names in WINS by using the [1Ch] 16th Byte type. However, if this replication has failed or has become corrupted, you can statically map domains in WINS so that each side of the trust can resolve the other—in effect, statically adding the [1Ch] entries. Figure 16.40 shows an example of static mapping of trust domains in the Static Mappings dialog of WINS Manager. To access the WINS Manager, choose Programs, Administrative Tools, and WINS Manager from the Start menu. When you click Add Mappings in the Static Mappings dialog, you see a place to type your static entries, and a number of choices for entry type (see Figure 16.41).

FIG. 16.39
An example of a configuration that requires a static route.

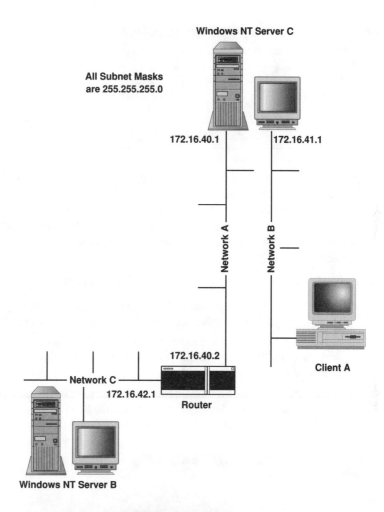

Windows NT Server C

All Subnet Masks
are 255.255.255.0

172.16.40.1   172.16.41.1

Network A

Network B

Client A

172.16.40.2

Network C

172.16.42.1

Router

Windows NT Server B

FIG. 16.40
Displaying WINS static mappings with WINS Manager.

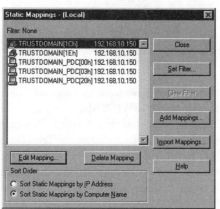

Static Mappings - (Local)

Filter: None

TRUSTDOMAIN[1Ch]   192.168.10.150
TRUSTDOMAIN[1Eh]   192.168.10.150
TRUSTDOMAIN_PDC[00h] 192.168.10.150
TRUSTDOMAIN_PDC[03h] 192.168.10.150
TRUSTDOMAIN_PDC[20h] 192.168.10.150

Close

Set Filter...

Clear Filter

Add Mappings...

Import Mappings...

Edit Mapping...   Delete Mapping

Help

Sort Order
○ Sort Static Mappings by IP Address
◉ Sort Static Mappings by Computer Name

FIG. 16.41

Setting static mapping options in the Add Static Mappings dialog.

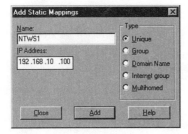

If you're establishing a trust relationship but dynamic registrations in WINS don't seem to be functioning correctly, you can statically map both the remote domain and its domain controllers in your WINS database. Doing so guarantees that your domain controller always has the correct information on how to reach the remote domain, even if the remote domain's WINS database is corrupted and doesn't provide the proper dynamic registrations to other domain controllers.

To statically map a remote domain in your WINS database, follow these steps:

1. From the WINS Manager utility, choose Static Mappings from the Mappings menu. Click Add Mappings to display the Add Static Mappings dialog (refer to Figure 16.41).

2. Select the Group option and enter the name of your trusted domain in the Name text box. Enter the IP address of the trusted domain's PDC in the IP Address text box and click Add to add the address.

3. Repeat step 2 to create a Domain Name type entry for the Remote Domain Name. A scrollable list appears that lets you enter multiple IP addresses (see Figure 16.42). To this list, add the IP addresses of all the Domain Controllers in the Remote Domain.

FIG. 16.42

Adding a Domain Name type static mapping from the Add Static Mappings dialog.

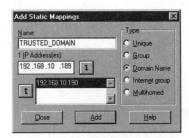

You can verify that your static entries have been entered into the WINS database by choosing Show Database from the Mappings menu in WINS Manager. Figure 16.43 shows the contents of a WINS database after adding the static domain mappings. This example shows a remote domain called TrustDomain, which contains a server called TrustDomain_PDC. The [1Eh] value indicates the Group entry for the remote domain. The [1Ch] value indicates the Internet Group entry, and the three Unique type values ([00h], [03h], and [20h]) are for the PDC itself. If you have a two-way trust between domains, create these static WINS mappings so that they point to each domain on either side of the trust.

FIG. 16.43
Creating a static
mapping set for a
remote domain.

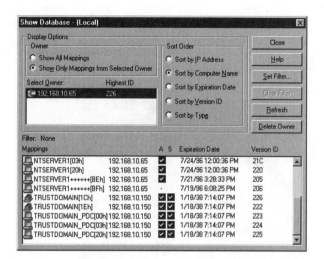

Understanding WINS and DNS Name Resolution

As noted at the beginning of this chapter, name resolution is the source of many networking
problems with Windows NT Server. This is especially true if you're using the TCP/IP stack,
because you may also have to contend with DNS as a potential name service for NetBIOS
name lookups. Windows NT Server offers the following places where you can store names for
resolution in a TCP/IP environment:

- WINS
- LMHOSTS
- HOSTS
- DNS

Depending on the network function being performed, the path that name resolution follows
varies. When you issue a `net view` command to a *servername*, for example, Windows NT first
determines the node type of the device (h-node, p-node, m-node, or b-node). Based on the
determination, NetBIOS name resolution follows these steps:

1. Regardless of node type, Windows NT checks the contents of the local NetBIOS name
   cache, which you can view by using `nbtstat -c`. If the name is in the cache, name
   resolution is complete.

2. If the name isn't in the name cache, this step depends on node type. For h-node and
   p-node systems, the WINS server defined in the TCP/IP configuration is queried. For
   m-node and b-node, a name-resolution broadcast request is sent on the local segment.

3. If either WINS lookup or broadcast lookup fails, h-node broadcasts on the local segment
   for name resolution, whereas m-node queries WINS.

4. If each of the preceding steps fails for the specified node type, this step depends on the device's configuration. In the WINS Address page of the Microsoft TCP/IP Properties sheet, you can choose to use DNS for NetBIOS name lookup or use an LMHOSTS file (see Figure 16.44).

FIG. 16.44
Setting advanced configuration options for name resolution.

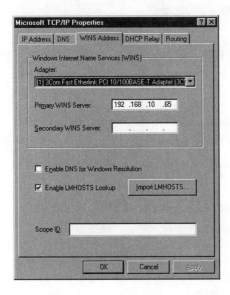

If you've elected to use an LMHOSTS file, all node types consult LMHOSTS for name resolution.

If you're not using LMHOSTS (or if LMHOSTS fails) and you've checked to use DNS for NetBIOS Name Lookup, all node types proceed to use the local Hosts file that's located in the \Winnt\system32\drivers\etc folder. If you haven't selected to use DNS, the name-resolution sequence fails, and you see the message The Network Path was Not Found.

If you've elected to use DNS and the local Hosts file fails, Windows NT queries the DNS servers you've configured in your TCP/IP DNS configuration for your NetBIOS name. If this fails, name resolution fails and again you see the message The Network Path was Not Found.

The process Windows NT uses for name resolution when performing non-NetBIOS operations varies. For Winsock-based (Winsock is the Windows Sockets standard) operations such as ping, Telnet, FTP, or any other function or service that doesn't require name resolution of NetBIOS resources, Windows NT uses the following steps:

1. Regardless of node type, the local Hosts file is checked.

2. If hosts fails, the device queries DNS according to its TCP/IP configuration.

3. If DNS fails, name resolution uses WINS as a last resort. If WINS resolution fails, you receive a failed name lookup message. For example, if you ping a host name and name resolution fails, you receive the message Bad IP Address.

Solving name-resolution problems requires an understanding of the process, and then trouble-shooting each step of the process. A good tool for determining where the flow stops is a proto-col analyzer, which also tells you whether significant delays in name resolution are occurring. Such delays can have the effect of breaking an application that depends on the timeliness of name resolution. If you can detect delays with a protocol analyzer, you can move name entries to guarantee that they occur more quickly.

For example, a DNS lookup for a given host may take more time than the calling application allows. In that case, you might move that hostname address mapping into the local \Winnt\ system32\drivers\etc\hosts file for faster resolution. Alternatively, if WINS is taking too long to resolve a name or you experience delays in reaching a WINS server, you can increase the timeout of the NetBIOS name cache on your server. By default, name-resolution responses from WINS are cached in the name cache for 10 minutes. If your environment is fairly stable—that is, Windows NT devices don't change addresses often—you can increase the value of the name cache timeout. NetBIOS name resolution looks to the name cache first, so you go to WINS less often for name resolution.

 T I P You can increase the timeout value for the NetBIOS name cache by editing the Registry on your Windows NT server. The Cache Timeout value is stored in HKEY_LOCAL_MACHINE\System\ CurrentControlSet\Services\NetBT\Parameters\CacheTimeout. The value in this key is in milliseconds and defaults to 600000 (600 seconds). You can change the value from 60000 to about 4 million milliseconds. Change the value in small increments either direction, depending on your network environment. Too small a value results in excessive requests to WINS. If you set the value too large, devices whose addresses have changed might never be found.

From Here...

This chapter discussed how the different network protocols that Windows NT supports for file, print, and application services affect network troubleshooting. NetBEUI and IPX are broadcast-based protocols that require a bridged network or special router forwarding and aren't very scalable. Windows NT's NetBIOS-over-TCP/IP support, also called NetBT, uses a centralized name service (WINS) to avoid the need to broadcast between subnets. Using TCP/IP and NetBT simplifies network troubleshooting.

The chapter also described the utilities that come with Windows NT 4.0 for interrogating and checking network-related services, such as `ping`, `nbtstat`, and `tracert`, and network diagnostic programs included in the *Windows NT Server Resource Kit*.

The chapter concluded with a discussion of common Windows NT-specific network problems, such as browsing and name resolution, and how you can use the tools and utilities to aid troubleshooting network problems.

The following chapters contain information related to network troubleshooting:

- Chapter 4, "Choosing Network Protocols," explains how to select one or more of the three principal networking protocols supported by Windows NT, based on your network configuration.

- Chapter 15, "Optimizing Network Server Performance," describes the Windows NT Server 4.0 Performance Monitor and explains tuning methodology to help you maintain optimum network throughput as your network usage grows.

- Chapter 18, "Integrating Windows NT with NetWare and UNIX," shows you how to set up and administer Windows NT Server within a Novell NetWare or a UNIX networking environment.

- Chapter 25, "Administering Clients with Systems Management Server 1.2," covers the basics of planning, administration, and management for Microsoft SMS 1.2.

Wide Area Networking and the Internet

17 Distributing Network Services with Domains   605

18 Integrating Windows NT with NetWare and UNIX   635

19 Managing Remote Access Service   687

20 Setting Up Internet Information Server 4.0   723

21 Administering Intranet and World Wide Web Sites   765

CHAPTER 17

Distributing Network Services with Domains

One primary strength of Windows NT Server is its domain facility for providing access to and control of network resources wherever needed. Windows NT Server provides file, print, and application services to a variety of clients in various environments. Access to these services doesn't need to be limited by geography or network bandwidth. More importantly, control and administration of these services can be distributed to fit either a centralized or decentralized support model. Windows NT Server uses domains to provide unified access to and administration of resources in large, distributed networks.

This chapter emphasizes the value domains bring to your Windows NT network environment, and how to take best advantage of domains in LANs and WANs. ▪

Domain-based security

Windows NT organizes servers, printers, workstations, users, and groups into one or more domains.

Domain controllers

You can designate Windows NT servers as Primary or Backup Domain Controllers and promote a backup to a Primary Domain Controller when necessary.

Domain reorganization

Moving a domain controller to another domain or renaming a domain involves a substantial effort.

Trusts between domains

Windows NT Server offers you the choice of single, single- or multiple-master, complete-trust, and hybrid domain trust topologies.

Network performance optimization

Choosing the right domain architecture for your network depends on the number of servers and clients, administration methods, and the type of network connections between domains.

Understanding Domain Architecture and Security

In the simplest terms, a Windows NT *domain* is a logical grouping of servers, workstations, users, groups, and printers within a physical network. The architecture of Windows NT domains is quite complex, involving security issues, different types of user groups, and trust relationships. For this introductory discussion, you can consider a domain to be a group of *resources* (Windows NT objects) that are bound by a common membership into a single administrative unit. The purpose of domains is to permit distributed network management by segmenting the resources of large networks into sets of manageable sizes.

N O T E The complexity of Windows NT's domain structure has been the most serious shortcoming of Windows NT Server in enterprise-wide computing. Windows NT 5.0, expected by mid-1998, will implement the Distributed File System (Dfs), Distributed (Kerberos) Security (DS), and the Active Directory Service, which is based on the Internet-standard Lightweight Directory Access Protocol (LDAP). Substituting a distributed LDAP directory database and Kerberos security for Windows NT's domain-based security system will make Windows NT Server 5.0 competitive with Novell NetWare 4.1x's NetWare Directory Services (NDS) for very large networks. Chapter 27, "Distributing File and Directory Services," describes these forthcoming enhancements. ■

If you've used Windows 95 or Windows for Workgroups in a network environment, you're familiar with the concept of small groupings of users who need access to common resources, such as files and printers. These resources reside either on members' PCs or on a central peer-to-peer file server. Domains are extensions of workgroups, designed to support larger sets of users who may be located at geographically distant sites. Figure 17.1 illustrates the concept of a domain named SalesCo, which consists of two servers (HQ and Regional), plus client PCs for UserA through UserF. The Regional server for the Sales user group and the HQ server for the Accounting user group are connected by a telecommunications link. The HQ server, a Primary Domain Controller (PDC), is the administrative site for the domain. The Regional server is a Backup Domain Controller (BDC). The relationships between PDCs and BDCs is the subject of the later section "Understanding the Roles of Domain Controllers."

Windows NT Server authenticates users when they log on to a server in a domain. *Authentication* is the process by which users gain access to the resources for which they have rights. Unlike earlier network operating systems, such as Novell NetWare 3.x, users log on once to the domain, rather than log on to each server they want to access. Likewise, administrators can assign rights to a Domain User or Domain Group, and these rights are applied universally to any domain resource users want to access.

N O T E Windows NT Server's single-logon approach extends to server-based applications, such as the members of Microsoft's BackOffice suite. If you install BackOffice applications with Windows NT Server's integrated security feature, users aren't required to separately log on to SQL Server, Exchange Server, Systems Management Server, or SNA Server. All BackOffice products use Windows NT's built-in security model to authenticate users to these BackOffice services. ■

FIG. 17.1

A domain containing servers, printers, client PCs, users, and groups.

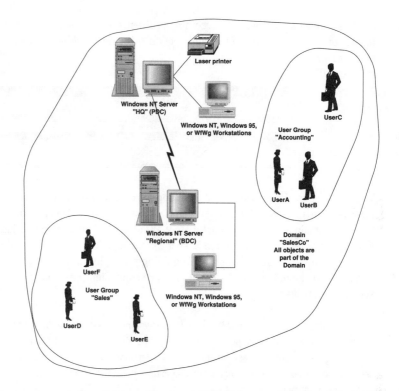

Laser printer

Windows NT Server "HQ" (PDC)

Windows NT, Windows 95, or WfWg Workstations

UserC

User Group "Accounting"

UserA   UserB

Windows NT Server "Regional" (BDC)

Domain "SalesCo" All objects are part of the Domain

UserF

User Group "Sales"

Windows NT, Windows 95, or WfWg Workstations

UserD

UserE

Understanding Windows NT Security Identifiers

Beyond the concept of grouping user, machine, and server resources into logical domains, Windows NT provides a mechanism to secure a resource's right to the domain. That is, when a server or client joins a domain, or when a user or user group is created within a domain, Windows NT Server provides a mechanism to guarantee that the new resource is uniquely associated with the domain. From a security standpoint, this mechanism also assures that a user or machine that isn't properly identified to the domain can't access resources in the domain. Windows NT uses a SID (security identifier), in addition to a name, to identify each domain resource, group, or user. The SID is generated at the time of creation of the resource and is unique. You can't duplicate a SID, because it is based on a variety of CPU information at the moment of its creation.

When you establish a new domain by installing Windows NT Server as the Primary Domain Controller (which is the default for your first Windows NT Server installation), the domain receives its own SID. As you add servers, clients, groups, and users to the domain, their unique SIDs include a reference to the original domain SID. If you move a client PC from one domain to another, the client's SID references the wrong domain and can't use the resources of the new domain. Figure 17.2 illustrates this situation with Server Manager; NTWORKSTATION1's SID doesn't refer to Primary Domain Controller SERVERA's SID, so NTWORKSTATION1 appears with its icon grayed. Overcoming problems with SIDs that reference the wrong domain is one of the subjects of the later section "Moving Machines Between Domains and Renaming Domains."

FIG. 17.2

Server Manager displaying invalid domain client PCs.

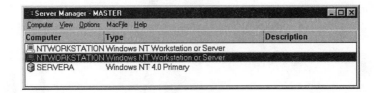

The advantages of a secure logical grouping of resources become apparent when you must manage large groups of users and machines. Network security is paramount in Windows NT Server's domain architecture. Fortunately, Windows NT Server's administrative tools, such as User Manager for Domains and Server Manager, shield you from most (but not all) of the complexity of SIDs. One of Microsoft's guiding principles in the design of Windows NT is that features to make network administration more convenient must not compromise network security in any way.

N O T E Users of clients running Windows for Workgroups 3.1+, Windows 95, and Windows NT can create independent peer-to-peer workgroups within a Windows NT domain. Workgroup members share files, printers, and other resources independently of Windows NT's domain security services. Most Windows NT network administrators discourage the establishment of peer-to-peer workgroups because of their lack of security. ■

Understanding the Roles of Domain Controllers

Windows NT Server supports the following two types of domain controllers, both of which are network servers:

- *Primary Domain Controller (PDC)*. Only one PDC server can exist within a domain.
- *Backup Domain Controller (BDC)*. You can have any number of BDCs in a domain. The number of BDCs in a domain depends on the number of users in a domain and the structure of your network.

Setting Up a Primary Domain Controller   The PDC is by default the first server you install in a new Windows NT network. When you install a new Windows NT server in an existing network and choose to create a new domain, the Setup program scans your network for a domain controller with the domain name you specified. If no PDC for the domain name is found, the server becomes the PDC.

> **CAUTION**
>
> When installing a new server in an existing domain, make sure that the server has network access to the existing PDC. You can install a BDC only if you have a functioning network connection to the PDC. If you

install the unconnected server as a second PDC with the same domain name and later connect the original PDC to the network, you have two PDCs in the same domain with different domain SIDs. No clients or servers can authenticate to the domain. In this situation, you must reinstall Windows NT Server 4.0 on the new server while the PDC is connected to the network. If you reinstall Windows NT Server 4.0 as a BDC, the PDC replicates user and group information to the new BDC.

The PDC's role is critical to Windows NT networking. The PDC is the keeper of all user, group, and machine account information for the domain. This information is stored in the SAM (Security Accounts Manager) database, which resides in files in the \Winnt\system32\config folder on the PDC's fixed disk. As of Windows NT 4.0, the official name for the SAM is *directory database*. The PDC is responsible for maintaining the master version of the domain SAM. When you change user passwords, add or remove user and group accounts, or add or remove machines in the domain, the PDC's SAM records these changes.

Part
IV

Ch
17

N O T E You can use the Getsid.exe command-line application included in the *Windows NT Server Resource Kit* to determine the SID for a specified user account. Getsid.exe is useful for troubleshooting user authentication problems. You can't, however, change the user account SID with Getsid.exe. Use the `getsid` command as follows:

`getsid \\`*servername*` `*accountname*` \\`*servername*` `*accountname*

`getsid` requires two account names because part of its function is to compare the SIDs of each to determine whether they're the same. Figure 17.3 shows an example of the output of `getsid`. ■

FIG. 17.3
Comparing and displaying SID information with getsid.

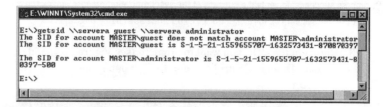

Configuring Backup Domain Controllers If the PDC is the only domain controller in your domain, it's responsible for maintaining the domain SAM and performing routine domain tasks, such as authenticating user logon requests and maintaining user accounts. If you have a large number of users in a domain, routine domain management tasks can occupy a substantial percentage of server resources, slowing normal file, printer, and application server operations.

If servers and clients are connected to a remote PDC by a low-speed network connection, such as Switched-56 or ISDN lines, authentication by the PDC can become very slow. To avoid problems that arise from overload or remote PDCs, Windows NT supports the concept of Backup Domain Controllers (BDCs). A BDC is a Windows NT server installed into a domain after the PDC is installed. The BDC's function is to offload some of the routine domain-related tasks from the PDC and provide redundancy in case the PDC becomes unavailable. The BDC contains a copy of the domain SAM, which is replicated (copied) from the PDC on a periodic basis.

The BDC has a local copy of the SAM, so the BDC also can authenticate users. If you have a geographically dispersed network, you assign a BDC to serve remote users. If users want to change their passwords or an administrator wants to create a new user group, the BDC handles the change, and then passes the new password or user account to the PDC during the synchronization process. If the PDC is shut down or otherwise unavailable, you aren't allowed to make changes, such as user passwords or new accounts, to the domain SAM. Even if the PDC isn't available, you can continue to authenticate existing users and access resources on the BDC and other servers in the domain.

Promoting a Backup Domain Controller to a Primary Domain Controller   When the PDC fails or is unavailable for an extended period of time, or if you want to change PDC machines, you can promote any BDC in the domain to the PDC. The promoted PDC takes over the role of maintaining the master copy of the SAM database, and the old PDC becomes a BDC just as any other. To promote a BDC to a PDC, follow these steps:

1. Launch Server Manager by choosing Programs and then Administrative Tools from the Start menu.

2. If the PDC is operational, highlight the BDC you want to promote and choose Synchronize with Primary Domain Controller from the Computer menu to assure that the BDC's SAM copy and PDC's SAM are identical. Click OK to acknowledge both messages you receive during the synchronization process.

N O T E   Although Windows NT 4.0 performs this step automatically during the promotion process, it's a good idea to synchronize the BDC with the PDC to verify that the synchronization process succeeds. To verify the success of the synchronization process, check the NETLOGON 5711 event in the System Log for a ... completed successfully message. ▪

3. Highlight the BDC you want to promote (see Figure 17.4) and choose Promote to Primary Domain Controller from the Computer menu.

FIG. 17.4

Selecting a BDC to promote to a PDC.

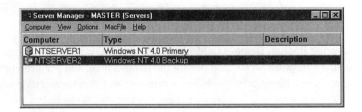

4. If the current PDC is operating, you're prompted to acknowledge that you're promoting a BDC in place of the PDC. Click Yes if you want to promote the BDC. If the current PDC isn't operating (the icon is grayed in Server Manager), you're warned that the PDC can't be contacted, and that promoting the BDC will conflict with the original PDC, if it becomes operational. Click Yes if you're willing to accept this condition.

CAUTION

When you promote a BDC to PDC, the NetLogon service is stopped, and all connections to those two servers are broken temporarily. If either server is a RAS server, remote connections are broken as well. Any users attached to the servers lose their connections to the BDC (and to the PDC, if it's running). If you must perform a BDC promotion, make sure that you warn your users before doing so. From Server Manager, highlight the BDC you're promoting, choose Send Message from the Computer menu, type a warning message in the Send Message dialog, and click OK to send the message. Windows 3.1+ and Windows 95 clients must be running the WinPopup application, and Windows NT clients must have the Messenger service running to receive network messages.

5. You see a series of messages indicating that the NetLogon service is stopping and restarting on each of the two servers. When the promotion completes, the previous BDC indicates that it's now a Primary Domain Controller, and the prior PDC becomes a Backup Domain Controller (see Figure 17.5).

Part
IV

Ch
17

FIG. 17.5
The BDC of Figure 17.4 promoted to a PDC.

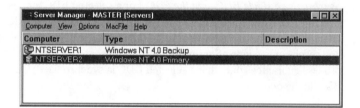

Using Non-Domain Servers   You can choose to add servers to your network that aren't domain controllers. To do so, select the Server option during installation of Windows NT Server 4.0 on the machine. Non-domain servers use Windows NT Workstation security, one of the subjects of the later section "Adding Windows NT Clients to the Domain." You install non-domain servers primarily for the following reasons:

■ The server is used for heavy-duty applications, such as a database or messaging server, and you want to devote all the server's resources to application serving, not domain administrative duties.

■ It's certain (or likely) that the server will be installed in a domain other than the domain in which it's originally set up.

Understanding the Domain Synchronization Process

To spread the load of authentication across BDCs that may reside anywhere on your network, including WANs with slow or unreliable links, Windows NT performs a periodic domain synchronization process. By default, every five minutes a Backup Domain Controller sets up a connection with the PDC, sends all SAM changes that originated on the BDC during the interval, and receives changed information from the PDC's SAM.

The PDC keeps track of the *revision level* (the current version) of the SAM for each BDC in the domain; thus, the PDC sends only the incremental changes needed to keep the SAMs synchronized. If the BDC loses communication with the PDC for an extended period, the PDC performs a full synchronization by copying the BDC's changes to the PDC's SAM and sending a complete copy of the PCD's SAM to the BDC. This process ensures that the BDC's database is complete and up-to-date.

Manually Synchronizing Domain SAMs   If you make a large number of changes to the domain SAM or make changes that must take effect immediately (such as unlocking a user's account), you can perform a full or partial manual synchronization with Server Manager. Server Manager's Computer menu offers the following synchronization options:

- *Synchronize the entire domain.* For a PDC selected in Server Manager's Computer list, choose Synchronize the Entire Domain to cause the PDC to contact each BDC and, depending on the BDC's revision level, send the appropriate records to ensure that the BDC has a complete copy of the current SAM database. A full synchronization is called a *push process.*

- *Synchronize a single BDC with the PDC.* For a selected BDC, choose Synchronize with Primary Domain Controller to force that BDC to contact the PDC and request all changes since the last synchronization (a *pull process*). Figure 17.6 shows the message you receive when using Server Manager to synchronize a BDC with a PDC. This pull process guarantees only that a selected BDC is synchronized; it doesn't affect any other BDC in the domain.

FIG. 17.6

The message you receive when using Server Manager to synchronize a BDC with a PDC.

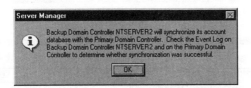

> **N O T E**   As a rule, it's best to synchronize the entire domain from the PDC. Doing so ensures that all changes are pushed to the entire domain. Only changes get pushed, not the entire SAM, so in most cases (less than a 100 changes), network traffic due to domain synchronization is insignificant. ▨

Changing Automatic Synchronization Intervals   If you're concerned that a large number of SAM changes might affect network performance, you can change Registry values on each BDC to control the replication frequency and the percentage of system resources assigned to perform synchronization.

▶ **See** "The Danger of Changing Registry Values," **p. 294**

You add the following new values to the \HKEY_LOCAL_MACHINE\SYSTEM\Current ControlSet\Services\NetLogon\Parameters key of a BDC or PDC to control how much data is sent from the BDC to the PDC and how often SAM replication from the PDC is performed:

■ ReplicationGovernor is a BDC value that governs how much data and for how long a BDC communicates with the PDC while synchronizing. The value uses the REG_DWORD data type and is expressed as a percentage. If the ReplicationGovernor value is missing, the default is 100 (percent). A value of 100 specifies that the buffer the BDC allocates for SAM changes is 128K (the maximum) and the call to the PDC for synchronization occupies 100 percent of the available time to complete the transfer. With a 128K buffer, the BDC can hold about 4,000 SAM changes. If you want to limit the size of the SAM buffers (and, thus, the time a synchronization requires to complete), you can adjust the ReplicationGovernor value for each BDC. For example, on a slow link where few domain changes occur, you might be able to tune the ReplicationGovernor value down to 50. If the value is too low, however, the BDC may never be able to complete the synchronization process.

■ Pulse is a PDC value that governs how often the PDC automatically sends SAM changes to the BDCs. Pulse is a value of type REG_DWORD (see Figure 17.7) for the PDC only and defaults to 300 seconds (five minutes). You can change the value to suit the frequency of SAM updates that occur on your network. Any changes made to the SAM between pulse intervals are sent to BDCs with out-of-date revision levels.

Part
IV

Ch
17

FIG. 17.7
Adding a Pulse value to the PDC's NetLogon\Parameters key with the Registry Editor.

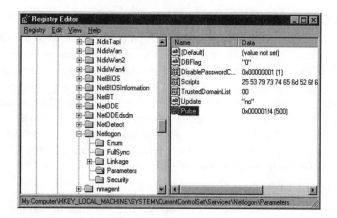

■ PulseConcurrency is a PDC value of type REG_DWORD that specifies how many BDCs a PDC can contact concurrently for updates. This entry defaults to 20 concurrent updates sent to the BDCs. (If you have less than 20 BDCs, you don't need to add this value.) The maximum value is 500. The higher the number, the less time it takes to synchronize the entire domain, because the PDC sends more concurrent synchronizations. High numbers put a much greater load on the PDC and prevent it from performing other tasks during the synchronization process, such as user authentication or user account maintenance.

Adding Backup Domain Controllers to a New Domain

Even in a small, self-contained domain, you should have at least one BDC to accommodate user logons in case the PDC fails. If you're building a large domain, you must determine the number of BDCs needed to accommodate all your users. Microsoft recommends a maximum of 2,000 users per BDC, but your network architecture is more likely to determine this number. For instance, if you have a branch office that connects to the rest of your network with a slow link, it makes sense to place a BDC in the remote office for local authentication as well as file and printer sharing. Fortunately, it's a relatively simple matter to add BDCs as required to handle the authentication load. Later, the section "Deciding on the Right Domain Design" provides recommendations for distributing BDCs within one or more domains.

 If you're building a number of BDCs to be placed on remote networks with slow links, starting the BDC with a local network connection to the PDC is a good idea. The initial SAM replication occurs quickly and completely over the LAN. You then move the BDCs (as quickly as possible) to your remote network locations and resynchronize the BDC SAMs to the PDC during the startup operation. This process ensures that only incremental changes to the SAM occur over the WAN link.

Adding Windows NT Clients to the Domain

After you install the PDC and one or more initial BDCs, you add the network clients to your domain. When a Windows client is added to the domain, Windows NT Server creates a domain *machine account* for the client. The machine account is a unique SID assigned to the client name to identify the client to the PDC and BDC(s) so that users logging on to the client can access domain resources. Before a client running Windows NT Workstation 4.0 is installed to a domain, it's part of its own workgroup. Figure 17.8 shows the NTWS1 client installed to the workgroup WORKGROUP. NTWS1 maintains its own local SAM database of user and group accounts, which you can view with User Manager (see Figure 17.9) by choosing Programs and Administrative Tools from the Start menu.

▶ **See** "Connecting Windows NT Workstation 4.0 Clients," **p. 418**

When you join a PC client running Windows NT Workstation to the domain, the client's local SAM database is "hooked" into the domain SAM database of the BDC or PDC. The Domain Administrators global group automatically is made a member of the client's Administrators local group so that Domain Administrator members have access to the client's resources. When you log on to the client, the local SAM authenticates the logon name and password for access to the client's resources. Next, the logon name and password is passed to the BDC or PDC for domain authentication and access to domain resources. This process, called *workstation security*, permits logging on to the client without the need to join the domain.

FIG. 17.8
A Windows NT 4.0 client installed as a member of a workgroup.

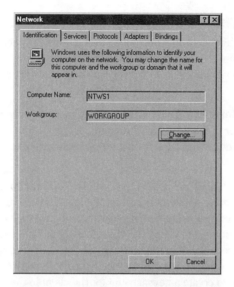

FIG. 17.9
Viewing the local SAM database of a Windows NT 4.0 client with User Manager.

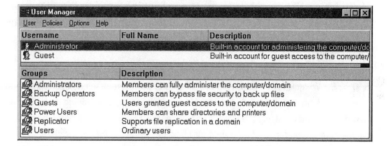

Part
IV

Ch
17

N O T E Windows NT Workstation is the only Microsoft client that uses the concept of machine accounts. Windows 3.1+ and Windows 95 clients don't create machine accounts in a Windows NT domain. When you want to authenticate to resources in a domain from these clients, you're simply using your domain user ID for authentication. The machine account provides an additional level of security for Windows NT Workstation—that is, a valid machine account enables an administrator to restrict access to domain resources based on a user authenticating from a specific domain workstation.

Also, workstations with machine accounts can be administered from Server Manager. From Server Manager, you can view a workstation's shares, files in use, or where to send alerts generated by that workstation. ▇

Moving Machines Between Domains and Renaming Domains

The unique SID of the machine account contributes to Windows NT security, but the SID creates problems when you want to move devices into and out of domains, or to rename a domain. The following sections describe the issues involved with reconfiguring clients and servers for use in different domains.

Moving Clients Between Domains   You may find a need to move a client from one domain to another. For example, a user in the Accounting domain may be relocating to the Sales domain. Moving a client to the new domain means changing that client's domain SID to match that of the new domain.

When you move a client running Windows NT Workstation to a new domain, you connect to the new domain by changing the domain's name in the Identification page of Control Panel's Network property sheet. If you log on to the client as a member of the Domain Administrators group, you can change the domain to which the client is assigned and receive a new SID for its machine account when you connect it to the new domain. To let users change domains on their own, a member of Domain Administrators must choose Add Computer to Domain from Server Manager's Computer menu to create a new account for the client in the other domain.

If you have a Windows NT Workstation client in DomainA that you want to move temporarily to DomainB, you must re-create a machine account for that machine when reconnecting it to DomainA. The DomainA SID originally assigned to the client can't be re-created on re-entering DomainA.

N O T E   Windows 3.1+ and Windows 95 clients don't use machine accounts, so moving a client from one domain to the other is simply a matter of providing that client a user ID in the new domain and changing the client's domain name. You change the domain name of Windows 95 clients in the Login frame of the Client for Microsoft Networks Properties sheet, which you access by selecting Client for Microsoft Networks in the Configuration sheet of Control Panel's Network tool. Change the domain name in the Workgroup text box of the Identification page of the Network tool, unless the client participates in a peer-to-peer workgroup. ■

Moving a Domain Controller to Another Domain   Moving a domain controller from one domain to another isn't a step to be taken lightly. If you want to rename a domain, all domain controllers must be renamed. You can change the domain name of a PDC or BDC to a new, unique domain name (as described in the next section), but changing the domain name doesn't change the domain SID. Thus, you can't move a PDC or BDC to a new domain simply by changing its domain name; a truly new domain requires a new SID, which requires reinstallation of Windows NT Server 4.0. After you reinstall Windows NT Server 4.0, you also must reinstall as upgrades other applications running on the server, such as Exchange Server or SQL Server.

N O T E   The need to reinstall server applications when moving a PDC or BDC to a new domain is one reason for running BackOffice and other server-based applications on a non-domain (plain) Windows NT 4.0 server. Moving a plain server to a new domain follows the same process as moving a client running Windows NT Workstation 4.0. The plain server receives a new machine account SID, but the new SID is transparent to clients that access the server-based applications.

▶ **See** "Choosing the Type of Domain Controller," **p. 191** ■

If you *must* move a server that's now functioning as the PDC from DomainA to existing DomainB, follow these general steps:

1. Verify that the Domain Administrators group has full access to all drives, folders, and files on the PDC to be moved. The Domain Administrators group exists in all domains.

2. Promote a BDC in DomainA to PDC. The PDC to be moved becomes a BDC.

3. Perform an independent full backup of the PDC in DomainA, including the Registry. You can restore the full backup in case you reconsider moving the PDC and want to reinstall it as a BDC in DomainA.

4. Perform a *new* Windows NT Server 4.0 installation on the old PDC into DomainB as a BDC, if the domain exists, or as a PDC if the domain is new. Run Winnt32.exe from the Windows NT Server 4.0 CD-ROM and install a *new* version of Windows NT Server 4.0 to a different folder, such as \winnt41, in an existing partition with sufficient free space for the installation.

N O T E The word *new* is emphasized here because a repair/upgrade installation doesn't alter the existing domain SAM database. If you don't choose a new installation during the Setup process, the server retains the original domain SID without regard to a change of domain names. ■

5. Start the newly installed BDC. The BDC synchronizes with DomainB's PDC on startup; after synchronization is complete, you can promote the new BDC to PDC.

6. Reinstall as upgrades any server-based applications on the new BDC or PDC.

7. Remove and re-create all file, folder, and printer shares by using the local copy of Explorer on the server, or a local or remote copy of Server Manager.

When you move a Primary Domain Controller from one domain to another, all references to user and group accounts that existed in DomainA (such as file and folder permissions for NTFS volumes) are lost. File and folder permissions for the server in the new domain appear as Account Unknown. Groups and users in the new domain are identified with the new domain's SID as a prefix to the group and user SID.

Renaming a Domain   As noted in the preceding section, the original DomainA SID remains as the DomainB SID when you rename a PDC from DomainA to DomainB. Renaming a domain requires you to change the domain names of all devices installed in the renamed domain. Changing the domain name of every device, including BDCs and clients, may be a huge task if you've installed Windows NT to many servers and clients across a dispersed network. If DomainA participates in trust relationships with other domains, renaming the domain breaks the trust relationships, and you must re-create them. (Windows NT trust relationships are the subject of the next section.)

Part
IV

Ch

17

If you *must* change a domain name, follow these steps:

1. First, in Server Manager, highlight the PDC and select Synchronize Entire Domain from the Computer menu.

2. Beginning with the PDC, start Control Panel's Network tool. On the Identification page of the Network property sheet, click the Change button to open the Identification Changes dialog (see Figure 17.10).

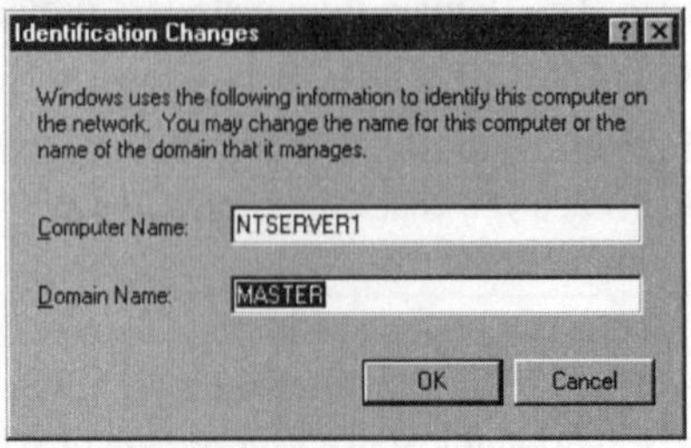

FIG. 17.10

Renaming a domain on the PDC in the Identification Changes dialog.

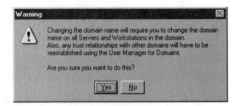

3. Type the new domain name in the Domain Name text box and click OK. The warning shown in Figure 17.11 appears. Click Yes to confirm the name change. You're required to restart your server after the change is confirmed.

FIG. 17.11

The warning you receive before changing your PDC's domain name.

4. Repeat steps 1 through 3 to rename the rest of your domain controllers.

5. Rename all your Windows NT Workstation machine accounts for the new domain name.

See the earlier section "Moving Clients Between Domains" for instructions on how to change domain names for clients running Windows NT Workstation.

Implementing Domains and Trusts Between Domains

The objective of Windows NT Server's domains and trusts is to provide users with a single logon to authenticate them to Windows NT Server resources, no matter where these resources are physically and logically located. An understanding of the authentication process is necessary to take maximum advantage of Windows NT Server 4.0's domain and trust architecture. Familiarity with the authentication process also is necessary to optimize the logical topology of your network to balance logon speed with the performance of applications running on your Windows NT 4.0 servers.

N O T E This book uses the term *logon* to include the authentication process. Technically, authentication precedes logon, because users can't log on to the network until they're authenticated. Unless otherwise indicated in the text, *logon* includes both authentication and logon operations. ▪

Distributing Authentication Services

One principal role a PDC and BDC(s) provide in a domain is authentication of Windows NT client and server machines and all users, including users of Windows 3.1+ and Windows 95 clients. Domain controllers verify that a particular user or machine running Windows NT has valid access to the domain.

The authentication process is provided by the NetLogon service, which runs on Windows NT servers and clients that run Windows NT Workstation. The NetLogon service provides a secure channel for messages associated with authentication and domain synchronization. A *secure channel* is a connection between the NetLogon services on two machines that's established and maintained internally by Windows NT's security subsystem, using its own set of user names and passwords. Administrators have no access to this connection.

Authenticating Windows NT Clients When a client running Windows NT Workstation is powered up, it goes through a series of steps to authenticate to the domain in which it is installed. The authentication process depends, in part, on the network protocol in use. TCP/IP, the recommended protocol for new Windows NT networks, takes the following steps to authenticate a Windows NT client when the Windows Internet Name Service (WINS) is installed:

1. The Windows NT client—installed as a p-node or h-node type WINS client—stores its domain name locally and queries the WINS server database first for all domain name entries of 16th Byte type <1C> for the client's domain.

   ▶ **See** "Implementing Windows Internet Name Service," **p. 342**
   ▶ **See** "NetBIOS Node Types," **p. 565**

2. The WINS server responds with a list of up to 25 domain controllers in its 1C listing for the client's domain. This list is dynamic and represents the last 25 domain controllers for the client's domain that have registered with the WINS server, regardless of the domain controller's location on the network.

3. The client sends a NetLogon mailslot packet to each domain controller in the WINS list. The packet, in effect, asks, "Can you authenticate me to the domain?" For h-node type clients, after the mailslot packet is sent to each 1C type server, a broadcast packet is sent out on the local segment, asking the same question.

4. All domain controllers receiving the request packet respond, if able, and the first affirmative response to arrive at the workstation handles the authentication request. A domain controller that resides on the same physical network segment as the requesting client is likely to respond the fastest.

After the machine is authenticated to the domain by the fastest-responding domain controller, users that log on to that machine use the responding domain controller's domain SAM database to verify their identities by means of user names and passwords.

Part
IV

Ch
17

> **TIP** To view which server a client uses for authentication, inspect the value of the HKEY_LOCAL_MACHINE\
> SOFTWARE\Microsoft\WindowsNT\CurrentVersion\Winlogon\CacheLastController Registry entry.

The process a client uses to choose an authentication domain controller is based on the fact that the controller responding most quickly to the request provides the authentication service to the client. There's no simple means to specify particular domain controllers to provide authentication to a set of workstations. If you have domain controllers across a slow link, there's a finite (but very low) probability that one of those domain controllers might respond first to client requests and provide authentication services across that slow link. This situation is undesirable if the link is very slow. The goal is to prevent unwanted responses from remote domain controllers. In a routed TCP/IP environment, where WINS provides the list of candidate domain controllers, the challenge is to remove the remote domain controller from the 1C list for that domain. You can restrict candidate domain controllers by creating a static mapping in WINS of a domain name type with a list of only those domain controllers that you want to respond for authentication services.

In the case of a network that's broadcast-based, such as NetBEUI or NWLink, you can control where the broadcasts go by using bridge filters and limiting broadcast forwarding between network segments. Any domain controllers that reside on the same physical network segment as a client, however, always receive the broadcast request for authentication.

Optimizing the Placement of Domain Controllers Deciding where to place your domain controllers depends on the network protocol you're using and the topology of your network. In a heavily segmented, routed TCP/IP environment, putting all your domain controllers and other servers in a centralized server farm makes sense. A *server farm* consists of one or more network segments wherein all servers reside (see Figure 17.12). Each workstation segment has an equal opportunity to access both authentication and file and print services provided by the server farm.

In a less-segmented (flat), bridged, or broadcast-based environment such as that illustrated by Figure 17.13, it's more efficient to place one or more domain controllers, plus associated file and print services, on the same client segment. In this configuration, the domain controllers and other servers can quickly service large numbers of workstations, regardless of the network protocol used.

If you're designing a domain to support remote offices that access your corporate network over slow links, such as ISDN or Switched-56 lines, install a BDC in each remote office (see Figure 17.14), especially if the office has more than one or two users that need to access domain resources. The BDC also provides file and printer sharing services for the remote office.

Most traffic on Windows NT networks isn't authentication, domain synchronization, or name and browser requests, which occur relatively infrequently. File and print services provided to users probably account for 80 percent or more of network usage. Where the extra traffic related to authentication and synchronization becomes a problem is in remote offices with low-bandwidth links. Twenty percent more traffic can mean the difference between a reliable connection to the corporate LAN and many dropped packets.

FIG. 17.12
Domain controller placement in a highly segmented network.

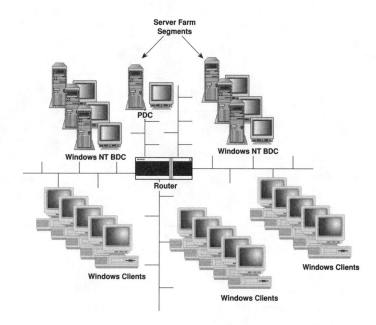

FIG. 17.13
Domain controller placement in a flat network.

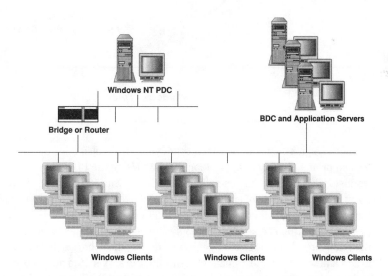

Understanding Memory Requirements for and Loads on Domain Controllers Microsoft recommends the following amounts of RAM for PDCs running Windows NT Server 4.0:

- For up to 8,000 user accounts, at least 32M of RAM is needed.
- From 8,000 to 20,000 users, 64M of RAM is the minimum.
- Beyond 20,000 users and up to about 40,000 users, 148M to 182M of RAM is required.

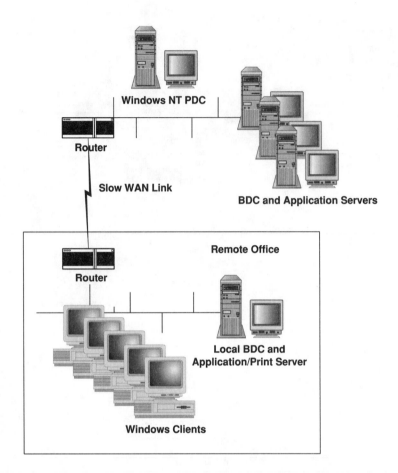

FIG. 17.14

Installation of Backup Domain Controllers in remote offices.

Memory requirements increase if most of your BDCs also must perform other tasks, such as file and printer sharing or application serving. Using the PDC and BDC(s) for ordinary network services is common in smaller networks serving 100 or fewer users. As the number of users increases, bursts of authentication and domain synchronization activity temporarily affect the performance of other services provided by PDCs and BDCs. Users may notice a significant performance drop in client/server applications, such as database front ends to SQL Server or the Exchange client for Exchange Server, during these bursts. Fortunately, it's relatively easy to add a new BDC to the domain to distribute the server load and to back up the existing BDC, in the event you must promote the existing BDC to a PDC. If you have multiple BDCs, consider demoting the BDC running server-based applications to a plain, non-domain server.

N O T E   You can use relatively low-cost configurations for added BDCs, because a second BDC doesn't need to have RAID drives or other high-end server features. (RAID for backing up a backup is overkill.) You can assign BDCs relatively low-priority tasks, such as printer sharing and fax server duties. Similarly, a low-end BDC is an ideal server for CD-ROM jukeboxes, because the data rate of even 8X CD-ROM drives (about 1,200 kbps) is low compared with fixed-disk drives and the network's capacity. ■

Understanding Trust Relationships

If you support a large organization with multiple departments or divisions that want to manage their own resources, use Windows NT Server's trust relationships. A *trust relationship* connects two or more domains and lets users in one domain access resources in another domain. A single logon provides user access to domains with the appropriate trust relationship.

> **N O T E** There's also a trust relationship between a client and the domain, and between domain controllers and the domain. When this trust relationship becomes corrupted—usually by problems with the domain SAM database—you're likely to receive a message indicating that the trust relationship between a client or a server and the domain has failed. Trust relationships between domain resources and their domain are different from the domain-to-domain trusts that are the subject of this section. ▨

You often see domain diagrams depicting one- or two-way trust relationships (with arrows pointing in one or two directions, respectively, between domains, as in Figure 17.15).

Part
IV

Ch
17

Domains are described as either *trusted by* or *trusting* another domain. Resources in the trusting domain (also known as the *resource domain*) are accessed by user accounts residing in the trusted domain (also called the *account domain*). Figure 17.16 shows the one-way trust relationship between a trusted and a trusting domain.

T I P With trusts, it's difficult to remember which domain is trusted and which is trusting. A good mnemonic is to picture the diagram of a one-way trust, indicated by an arrow pointing from one domain to the other. The trusting domain is at the base of the arrow and the trusted domain at the arrowhead.

A two-way trust between two domains, indicated by a two-headed arrow, allows users and groups in either domain to access resources in the other domain. In this case, the two domains are both trusted and trusting.

A trust lets an administrator in the resource domain assign, for example, file permissions to users or groups in the account domain from a file utility such as Explorer. A trust provides only the connectivity between two domains. You must explicitly grant access to resources in the trusting domain for users in the trusted (account) domain, in the same manner that you grant access for users in their own domain.

Trusts allow you to distribute management of resources between multiple domains. For example, your IS department may want to manage creation of all user accounts and certain centralized server resources in the IS-MASTER domain, while providing users and administrators in the Accounting department the ability to manage resources in their own domain, called Accounting. A one-way trust relationship—with Accounting as the trusting domain and IS-MASTER as the trusted domain—accomplishes this objective. The accounting users log on to the IS-MASTER domain but are permitted to access and manage resources in Accounting by means of the trust relationship.

FIG. 17.15

A diagrammatic view of one- and two-way trusts.

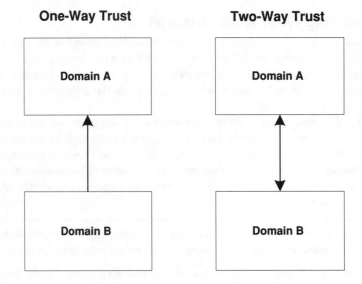

One-Way Trust

Domain A

Domain B

Two-Way Trust

Domain A

Domain B

FIG. 17.16

A one-way relationship between trusted and trusting domains.

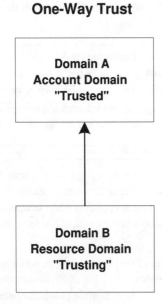

One-Way Trust

Domain A
Account Domain
"Trusted"

Domain B
Resource Domain
"Trusting"

N O T E In most account-resource domain relationships, a Windows NT client's machine account is installed to the resource domain, not the account domain. This approach allows all workstation resources to be managed in the resource domain, whereas the user accounts that log on to the workstations are managed in the account domain. Managing the account domain is simpler because it contains only user and group accounts, plus the domain's servers. ■

Establishing Trusts   Establishing trusts is a relatively simple process. By using the User Manager for Domains utility, you can create one- and two-way trusts between domains. As administrator, you need to have access to a Windows NT Server domain controller in each domain that's part of the trust in order to establish the trust relationship. Follow these steps to create a one-way trust relationship between the account and resource domains:

1. From the account (trusted) domain, launch User Manager for Domains by choosing Programs and Administrative Tools from the Start menu.

2. Choose Trust Relationships from the Policies menu.

3. In the Trust Relationships dialog, click the Add button next to the Trusting Domains list to open the Add Trusting Domain dialog.

4. Enter the name of your resource domain in the Trusting Domain text box; then provide and confirm a password in the Initial Password and Confirm Password text boxes (see Figure 17.17). This password must be supplied when you configure the resource domain's trust relationship to the account domain. Click OK to confirm the trusting domain.

FIG. 17.17

Adding a trusting domain from the account domain with User Manager for Domains.

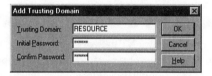

5. Repeat steps 1 and 2 on a Windows NT server in the resource domain. Then, from the Trust Relationships dialog, click the Add button next to the Trusted Domain list. Enter the name of the account domain here, and enter the password you specified in step 4 in the Password text box to establish the trust (see Figure 17.18). Click OK to confirm the trust.

FIG. 17.18

Adding a trusted domain from the resource domain with User Manager for Domains.

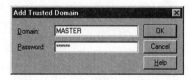

Windows NT Server then tries to contact the trusted domain to establish the trust. If the trust fails, refer to Chapter 16, "Troubleshooting Network Problems," for a discussion of trouble-shooting trust problems.

▶ **See** "Troubleshooting Trusts," **p. 596**

If you're creating a two-way trust, repeat steps 1 through 5. However, starting on the resource domain, define the account domain as the trusting domain. Then from the resource domain, add the account domain to the resource domain's trusted domain list.

> **N O T E** You can use the Domain Monitor utility of the *Windows NT Server Resource Kit* to monitor the status of your trust relationships.
>
> ▶ **See** "Domain Monitor," **p. 587** ▦

When the trust is established, you have access to users and groups in the account domain from any domain utility you run in the resource domain, such as Explorer, User Manager for Domains, or Print Manager.

Working Within the Limitations of Trusts   As useful as trusts are, they have limitations. In Windows NT Server 3.51, a single domain could be trusted by only up to 128 trusting domains. In Windows NT Server 4.0, this number is much larger but still limited.

There's also the issue of trying to manage large numbers of trusts. If you're supporting a large environment with many one- or two-way trusts between domains, the complexities associated with setting up and maintaining a large number of trust relationships aren't trivial. Obviously, you must balance the benefits of providing resources anywhere to anyone against the complexity of the domain design required to provide these resources.

Understanding Windows NT's Domain Models

When you begin the design of your Windows NT network environment, you can choose from four standard domain models to use for your organization, as well as hybrids of the standard models. Before you decide on a specific model, carefully analyze how the model matches the business methods of your organization. When you've installed a large network infrastructure, changing your domain design requires a major effort. Thus, careful up-front planning is a must.

> **N O T E** If you must change your domain structure, it's much easier to build trust relationships between domains than take them away. In the latter case, you're likely to be forced to reinstall user accounts and groups, and reassign permissions to resources when you move account information from a resource domain into an account domain, as in the case of moving from a two-way trust environment to a one-way trust model. ▦

The Single Domain Model

The Single Domain model is the simplest. As its name implies, it involves only a single domain, which holds all account information and resources (see Figure 17.19). The Single Domain model doesn't use trust relationships because there's only one domain.

The Single Domain model is best suited for an organization with centralized administration, a homogeneous user population, and less than 5,000 users. Beyond 5,000 users, it makes sense to start breaking up domains into resource and account domains.

FIG. 17.19

The simple Single Domain model.

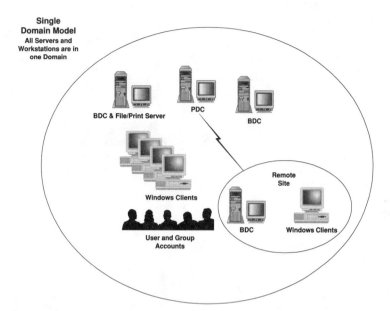

Single Domain Model
All Servers and Workstations are in one Domain

BDC & File/Print Server

PDC

BDC

Windows Clients

User and Group Accounts

Remote Site

BDC

Windows Clients

Part
IV
Ch
17

The Single Master Model

The Single Master model (see Figure 17.20) uses a single master account domain to provide user and group access to multiple resource domains. This model is best suited to an organization with centralized corporate support and a number of departmental or regional groups that want to manage their own resources.

Users log on to the single account domain, so you need to provide account domain BDCs in close proximity to resource domains, especially if the resource domains are spread out across your network and across slow links. In the case where you have remote offices across slow links, and those offices are part of the resource domains, you must have a resource domain server and a BDC from the account domain in the remote office. If you don't have a local account domain BDC, users must authenticate across the slow link to the closest account domain BDC.

N O T E In any one-way trust model, users logging on to the account domain from clients in the resource domain are *pass-through authenticated* to the account domain. That is, the BDC or PDC that authenticates a resource domain workstation passes via the trust relationship a user logon to a BDC or PDC in the account domain. ▪

FIG. 17.20
The Single Master model, with multiple resource domains.

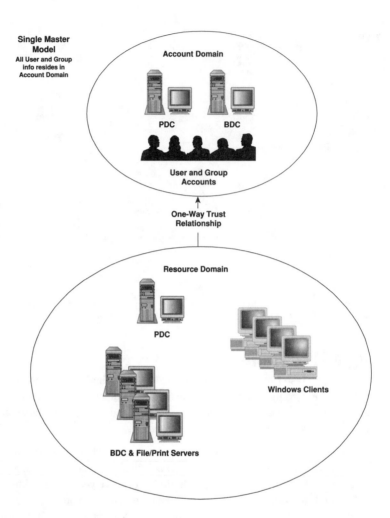

Single Master
Model
All User and Group info resides in Account Domain

Account Domain

PDC   BDC

User and Group
Accounts

One-Way Trust
Relationship

Resource Domain

PDC

Windows Clients

BDC & File/Print Servers

The Multiple Master Model

The Multiple Master model is similar to the Single Master but seeks to provide load-balancing of the Master account domain by providing for multiple account domains, which are two-way trusted with each other (see Figure 17.21). Users in one account domain can access resources of another account domain if the users have been granted permissions in the other account domain.

The Multiple Master is a good choice for large organizations, and organizations where either a centralized or decentralized support structure is used. The Multiple Master model lets you distribute responsibility for each account domain to a separate support organization, with each support organization administering its own set of resource domains.

FIG. 17.21
The Multiple Master model, with multiple account domains.

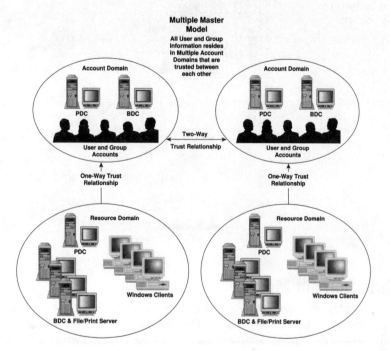

Multiple Master Model
All User and Group Information resides in Multiple Account Domains that are trusted between each other

Account Domain

PDC   BDC

User and Group Accounts

Two-Way Trust Relationship

One-Way Trust Relationship

Resource Domain

PDC

Windows Clients

BDC & File/Print Server

Account Domain

PDC   BDC

User and Group Accounts

One-Way Trust Relationship

Resource Domain

PDC

Windows Clients

BDC & File/Print Server

Part
IV
Ch
17

The Complete Trust Model

A Complete Trust between multiple domains is one where all domains are two-way trusted with every other (see Figure 17.22). In the Complete Trust model, all users and groups potentially can access resources in every other domain. This model is best suited to a fully distributed support organization. The Complete Trust model also assumes that you have some level of trust in administrators from each domain, because they potentially have administrator access to all accounts and all resources in every domain.

Another advantage to the Complete Trust model is that users from one domain can log on to a workstation in any other domain and access their resources as though they were at their home workstation. This is valuable for organizations where employees frequently travel from office to office.

A disadvantage of the Complete Trust model, however, is that for each additional domain you add, you need to establish a two-way trust with every other domain. As you increase the number of two-way domains, the number of two-way trusts you manage quickly grows to unmanageable proportions.

FIG. 17.22

The Complete Trust model implemented by a network of trusts.

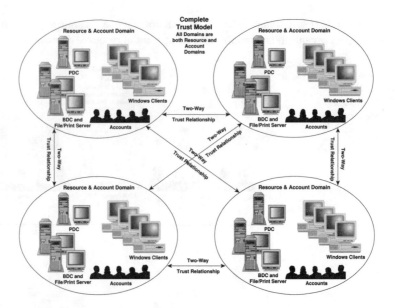

Hybrid Domain Models

In addition to the preceding four models, you can combine two or more of the standard models to create a hybrid model that best fits your organization. For example, you might like the concept of the Multiple Master domain model, but you don't want the Master Account Domains to trust each other. Instead, you want to create a number of Single Master Domains, each with its own resource domains. You also want to give a subset of users in your organization, such as network administrators, access to all domains everywhere, as in the Complete Trust.

You can build a new Master Account Domain, called Shared, for users requiring cross-resource access (see Figure 17.23). In this case, all your existing resource domains also are trusting to the cross-resource domain. Users requiring cross-resource access log on to the Shared domain and are granted access to as many resource domains as needed.

Many other options exist for domain models. The only caveat is that one-way trust relationships aren't transitive—that is, if DomainA resources are trusting DomainB users and DomainB resources are trusting DomainC users, there's no relationship between DomainA resources and DomainC users (see Figure 17.24).

Deciding on the Right Domain Design

The right domain design for your organization depends on the following factors:

- The size of your user base
- The nature of your network topology, including LANs, WANs, and remote offices

- Your support organization—centralized or decentralized
- The needs of your users

FIG. 17.23

An example of a hybrid domain model.

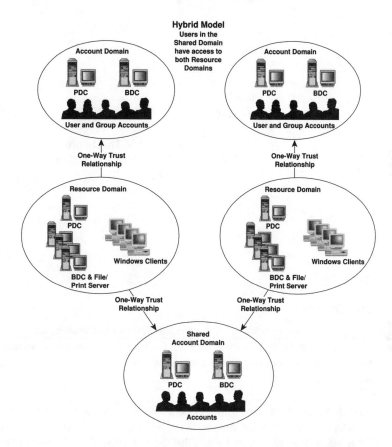

In the real world, it's the "soft" needs, such as requirements of your end users and the role your support organization plays, that drives the domain design. You can develop creative strategies to accommodate limited bandwidth or large numbers of users, but if the environment can't be supported or doesn't provide the flexibility end users want or need, you may as well not even install the infrastructure. Given the nature of Windows NT domain designs and the difficulty of changing established domain models, it's important to choose the right domain model from the beginning.

NOTE The Domain Planner application, which was included with the *Windows NT Resource Kit* for version 3.5, isn't included on the CD-ROM of the *Windows NT Server Resource Kit* for version 4.0. ■

Part
IV

Ch

17

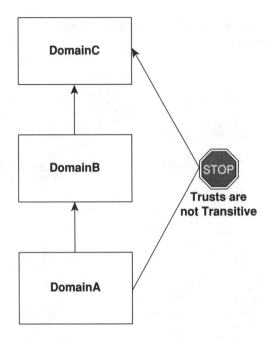

FIG. 17.24
An example of one-way
trusts that lack a
transitive relationship.

ON THE WEB

The "Enterprise Planning Guide," available from **http://www.microsoft.com/ntserver/info/entplan.htm**, and the "Domain Planning for Your Enterprise" white paper, available from **http://www.microsoft.com/ntserver/info/domainplanwp.htm**, are useful documents to aid the domain planning process.

If you have a decentralized but centrally coordinated support team with users whose needs are flexible, the Multiple Master model is the best choice, followed by the Complete Trust model. Some network administrators argue that the Complete Trust "leaves the barn door wide open," but if your support organization is disciplined and communicates well between support units, the complete trust model provides the maximum flexibility.

If your organization has centralized support but end users demand the flexibility to do what they want with their resources, either the Single Master or the Multiple Master model is a good choice. In a large organization with 5,000 or 10,000 users, make sure that you have a well-defined group in charge of user accounts and resource access. Otherwise, maintaining such a large SAM quickly becomes an overwhelming task.

Implementing Resource Sharing

After you install your domains and the trusts are in place, you must assign user and group accounts access to resources in your resource domains. As noted earlier in this chapter, creating a trust relationship in and of itself doesn't provide users with immediate access to resources. You must explicitly permit users or groups from the Account Domain access to the Resource Domain by using tools such as User Manager for Domains and Windows NT Explorer. Generally, the best way to do this is by assigning permissions by groups. Chapter 13, "Managing User and Group Accounts," and Chapter 14, "Sharing and Securing Network Resources," discuss creating global groups and sharing resources with groups, respectively.

Browsing Multiple-Domain Resources

Windows NT, like its LAN Manager predecessor, uses *browsing* to enable network clients to view network resources by using Network Neighborhood or the Windows for Workgroups 3.11 browser. Chapter 16, "Troubleshooting Network Problems," describes the hierarchy of network browsers and how browsers announce the availability of network resources. Each domain includes a single domain master browser, which collects all browse announcements from other computers in the domain, including all Windows NT servers and those peer-to-peer workgroup PCs that share resources, to create a *browse list*. The domain master browser is the PDC for the domain, and BDCs automatically become backup browsers. An additional backup browser is created automatically when 32 computers (clients and servers) are added to the domain. If the domain includes multiple TCP/IP subnet(work)s, the master browser of each subnet announces to the domain master browser.

Part
IV

Ch
17

▶ **See** "Browsing," **p. 594**

After the initial startup of a new master browser, domain master browsers send a `DomainAnnouncement` datagram every 15 minutes. If the domain master browser doesn't send this datagram for three successive announcement periods, the inaccessible domain is removed from the browse lists of other domains. Thus, it's possible that resources of an inaccessible domain might remain in the browse list for up to 45 minutes after failure.

N O T E Windows NT's Browser service relies on datagram broadcasts between browsers. Broadcasts ordinarily don't pass through TCP/IP routers unless the router supports NetBT (NetBIOS over TCP/IP) Name Service (Internet Engineering Task Force RFC 1001 and RFC 1002) on UDP (User Datagram Protocol) port 137. (Windows NT dedicates UDP port 137 to NetBIOS name service broadcasts.) WINS is the best choice for enabling browse datagrams to be transmitted across routers to specified computers. In this case, all servers and clients using TCP/IP must be WINS-enabled. You can enable WINS client services on Windows NT Workstation 3.5x and 4.0, Windows 95, Windows for Workgroups 3.11b with 32-bit TCP/IP drivers installed, and even the Microsoft Network Client 3.0 for MS-DOS. Using an LMHOSTS file limits browsing to a single domain.

▶ **See** "Implementing Windows Internet Name Service," **p. 342** ■

From Here...

This chapter explained the concept of Windows NT domains, a logical grouping of servers, client workstation, users, and groups. The chapter also described the role of Primary and Backup Domain Controllers, and discussed how BDCs can help take the load off the PDC for authentication services. The BDC synchronizes with the PDC to keep the domain SAM database up-to-date on all domain controllers. The difficulties of moving and renaming domains was a major topic of this chapter.

The balance of the chapter dealt with trust relationships and domain models, including the differences between trusted account domains and trusting resource domains, and one- and two-way trusts. Suggestions for criteria to apply when deciding on a Domain Model also were provided. The chapter concluded with a brief description of how to implement resource sharing after you establish a trust relationship between domains and domain browsing.

For more information about the topics covered in this chapter, see the following:

- Chapter 10, "Using TCP/IP, WINS, and DHCP," shows you how to plan for and implement TCP/IP networking, including use of the Windows Internet Name Service and Dynamic Host Configuration Protocol.

- Chapter 13, "Managing User and Group Accounts," describes how to use Windows NT Server 4.0's User Manager for Domains, take advantage of the new Add User Accounts and Group Management Wizards, and use the built-in user groups of Windows NT.

- Chapter 14, "Sharing and Securing Network Resources," explains Windows NT Server's security system for shared file, folder, and printer resources and how to use the new Managing File and Folder Access Wizard and the Add Printer Wizard to simplify sharing Windows NT Server 4.0's resources.

- Chapter 16, "Troubleshooting Network Problems," provides solutions for typical problems encountered when running multiple network protocols, and how to use the command-line tools included with Windows NT 4.0 and the *Windows NT Server Resource Kit* to isolate browsing problems.

CHAPTER 18

Integrating Windows NT with NetWare and UNIX

Network managers in the real world seldom have the luxury of working in a homogeneous network operating system (NOS) environment. If your organization runs Windows NT Server as its only NOS, consider yourself lucky. On the other hand, if, like many system administrators, you must contend with an installed base of mixed NetWare 3.1x and 4.x servers, a UNIX host here and there, and perhaps a System Network Architecture (SNA) host lurking in the glass house, then read on. ■

Gateway Services for NetWare

GSNW allows Windows clients to access shared files on a NetWare server and to print to NetWare printers.

File and Print Services for NetWare

FPNW lets Windows NT Server emulate a NetWare 3.12 server to support existing Novell clients.

Directory Service Manager for NetWare

DSMN exports NetWare user account information into Windows NT Directory Services and maintains all Windows NT Server and NetWare server user account information in a common database.

Domain Name Service (DNS) Server

DNS Server is the Windows NT version of a UNIX service that resolves unknown IP addresses from known host names.

LAN Manager for UNIX

LMU is a third-party product that adds the protocol support needed to allow UNIX hosts to participate in Microsoft Networking with the SMB protocol.

Spanning Multiple Network Protocols

Windows NT Server 4.0 uses a protocol-independent networking architecture, which allows it to interoperate with a wide range of NOSes and protocols. With its support for standard network application interfaces, Windows NT Server easily accommodates simultaneous interoperability with Novell NetWare, UNIX, and IBM SNA networks.

NetWare historically has dominated the NOS market and now holds about two-thirds of both the number of servers installed and the number of workstations using it. Although Windows NT Server is closing this gap quickly, many network managers will find it necessary to support both NOSes on a temporary basis as their organizations transition to Windows NT Server. Others will need to provide such support on a more or less permanent basis in organizations that plan for both NOSes to coexist on a long-term basis. Fortunately, Windows NT Server provides excellent tools for both migration and long-term coexistence.

UNIX is a fact of life in most medium and large organizations, and again Windows NT Server provides many of the tools you need to allow UNIX workstations and hosts to coexist with Windows NT Server. Microsoft has also recognized the continuing importance of mainframe connectivity to the enterprise and has accordingly provided SNA connectivity tools and services with Windows NT Server.

Until recently, the fundamental problem with integrating Microsoft, Novell, and UNIX networks has been that each used a different and incompatible transport protocol. Microsoft networks historically have used NetBEUI, whereas Novell networks depend on IPX/SPX, and UNIX networks use TCP/IP. As observed in Chapter 4, "Choosing Network Protocols," each network and transport protocol is fast and reliable, and each has advantages and drawbacks:

- *NetBEUI* requires minimal setup and is easy to administer. Because NetBEUI packets contain no network layer header information, however, they can only be bridged and can't be routed, making NetBEUI usable only for LANs. Microsoft is de-emphasizing NetBEUI for enterprise networking, relegating it to peer networking only.

  ▶ **See** "NetBEUI and NetBEUI Frame," **p. 107**

- *IPX/SPX* was originally designed for local area networking. Like NetBEUI, IPX/SPX is easy to set up and administer. Unlike NetBEUI, however, IPX/SPX can be routed. Because IPX/SPX was originally designed as a LAN protocol rather than a WAN protocol, it lacks subnetting support, variable packet lengths, and other technical features that make it a less-than-ideal choice as a foundation on which to build an internetwork, at least when considered in isolation. Still, because it combines the ease of use of NetBEUI with much of the flexibility and power of TCP/IP, IPX/SPX can be a good choice as the shared network and transport protocol for a heterogeneous network, particularly one that heavily depends on Novell NetWare servers. Microsoft refers to its IPX/SPX implementation as NWLink.

  ▶ **See** "NWLink (IPX/SPX)," **p. 111**

■ *TCP/IP* was designed from the ground up for internetworking. As the *lingua franca* of the Internet, TCP/IP provides in abundance all the tools needed to build an inter-network. The sole drawback to TCP/IP is that it can be extremely complex to administer, both on the server side and on the client side. If your environment includes UNIX hosts or workstations, or if you want to set up a corporate intranet or connect to the Internet, you must run TCP/IP.

▶ **See** "TCP/IP," **p. 108**

The Novell-centric view is that everyone should speak IPX/SPX. Although Novell has made some half-hearted, expensive, and poorly received attempts to provide native TCP/IP support—for example, NetWare/IP—the Novell world continues to revolve around IPX/SPX. Similarly, in the UNIX universe, you either speak TCP/IP, or no one listens to you. Many net-works, particularly those growing from smaller peer-based environments, depend on NetBEUI, so this protocol, too, needs to be accommodated.

N O T E   Windows NT Server 4.0 may install one, two, or all three main transport protocols by default, depending on your network environment. If peer-based Microsoft Networking clients, such as Windows for Workgroups, are active on the network when Setup is run, Setup detects the presence of NetBEUI frames and installs NetBEUI transport. If a NetWare server is active on the network, Setup detects IPX frames and installs NWLink IPX/SPX compatible transport. If neither condition is true, Setup installs only TCP/IP transport by default.

Regardless of which transport protocols Setup installs, you can choose to run any combination of the available transport protocols. If your network includes NetWare servers, you should leave NWLink installed, or install it manually if Setup didn't do so. If your network includes older peer-based Microsoft Networking clients, you should leave NetBEUI transport installed, or install it manually if Setup didn't do so. If your network includes UNIX hosts, spans multiple sites, or connects to the Internet, make sure that TCP/IP transport is installed when you install Windows NT Server. ▪

Fortunately, Microsoft has realized the importance of all three protocols to those who need to build heterogeneous networks and has provided support for each protocol in Windows NT Server 4.0. You can simultaneously run one, any two, or all three of these protocols to provide the fundamental network and transport layer support you need to build your network. This broad network and transport layer support provides the foundation for linking heterogeneous networking components.

Integrating Windows NT Server with Novell NetWare

The almost seamless integration of Windows NT Server 4.0 with NetWare is one of the major reasons for the phenomenal growth of Windows NT Server sales. In less than three years, Windows NT Server has grown from an also-ran product, which barely appeared in sales charts, to a major competitor to NetWare. Windows NT Server, in contrast to NetWare, pro-vides a superior application server platform. The Microsoft BackOffice suite (the subject of

Part
IV

Ch
18

the chapters in Part V, "Windows NT Server and Microsoft BackOffice") provides a solid foundation for developing client/server applications, and competing client/server application development tools from other vendors increasingly are being ported to the Windows NT Server environment.

All these applications can be accessed natively by Microsoft clients, as well as by NetWare clients, by using either the Novell NETx network shell or the VLM (Virtual Loadable Module) requester. The IPX/SPX protocol (NWLink) provided with Windows NT Server (see Figure 18.1) lets NetWare clients communicate with a server application by using Novell NetBIOS, Winsock, and remote procedure calls (RPCs).

FIG. 18.1

Connecting Windows NT and NetWare servers to a NetWare client with NWLink.

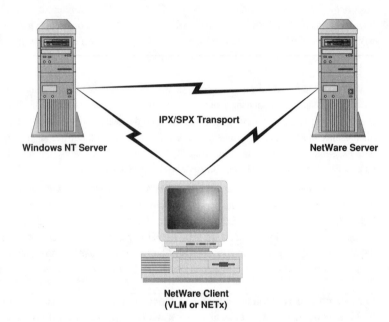

Windows NT Server

IPX/SPX Transport

NetWare Server

NetWare Client
(VLM or NETx)

Although Windows NT Server's support for diverse network and transport layer protocols has eliminated one problem, still remaining is the issue of what core protocol is used for communication between servers and workstations. Microsoft uses the Server Message Block (SMB) protocol for this purpose, whereas NetWare uses NetWare Core Protocol (NCP). If NetWare clients are to be able to access Windows NT servers and Windows NT clients are to be able to access NetWare servers, something must be done to translate between these two fundamental but incompatible protocols. Microsoft provides the following two utilities to bridge this gap:

- *Gateway Service for NetWare* (*GSNW*) lets clients running Microsoft client software access shared files on a NetWare server and to print to NetWare printers. GSNW translates the upper layer SMB calls to and from NetWare NCP calls. GSNW is included with Windows NT Server 4.0.

- *File and Print Services for NetWare* (*FPNW*) allows Windows NT Server to emulate a NetWare 3.12 server. Novell clients can access shared files and printers in the same way that they would access shared resources on any NetWare 3.12 server. FPNW avoids the translation between SMB and NCP by simply dealing with NetWare clients directly as NCP devices.

▶ **See** "File and Printer Sharing for NetWare Networks," **p. 378**

With a market share that now stands at about 60 percent and declining, Novell has little motivation to provide tools to make it even easier for Windows NT Server to coexist with or replace NetWare. On the other hand, with market share now at about 10 percent and growing explosively, Microsoft Windows NT Server has everything to gain from making readily available such tools to ease coexistence and migration. Fortunately, Microsoft, recognizing its second-place position in the networking business, has taken responsibility for bridging the core protocol gap by providing a set of tools designed to facilitate integration of Windows NT Server with NetWare servers.

Accessing Novell NetWare Servers with Microsoft Clients

Clients running Microsoft Networking client software can access shared files and printers on a Novell NetWare server in one of the following ways:

- Use a client operating system, such as Windows NT Workstation or Windows 95, that provides built-in support for Microsoft Networking and NetWare. As supplied, these clients provide full access to NetWare 3.1x servers. They allow you to access NetWare 4.x servers through bindery emulation mode but don't provide NDS support. You can update your Windows 95 clients to provide full NDS support by installing the Service for NetWare Directory Services, available in Windows 95 Service Pack 1.

ON THE WEB

You can download Windows 95 Service Pack 1 from **http://www.microsoft.com/windows95/ default.asp**. You also can download the Microsoft Service for NetWare Directory Services separately as the file msnds.exe from the same location.

- Add a Novell NetWare client protocol stack to a client to provide full access to NetWare services. The Novell NetWare client coexists with the Microsoft Networking client and supports full NDS access on NetWare 4.x servers.

ON THE WEB

You can download the 32-bit client for Windows 95 from **ftp://ftp.novell.com/pub/updates/nwos/ nc32w952** and for DOS/Windows 3.1+ from **ftp://ftp.novell.com/pub/updates/nwos/cl32dw211**.

- Install Gateway Service for NetWare (GSNW) to let clients running only Microsoft Networking client software access NetWare server resources via gateway services provided by Windows NT Server.

The method you use for a particular client depends on both the operating system that client is running and the level of NetWare connectivity you need to provide to that client.

Part

IV

Ch

18

Using a Client Operating System with Built-In NetWare Support   Windows 95 and Windows NT 4.0's Workstation and Server versions include the Windows NT Multiple Provider Router (MPR) API, which isn't to be confused with the Multi-Protocol Routing Service described later in this chapter. The MPR API provides a consistent application interface to the local file system, remote Windows network servers, and NetWare servers.

Any workstation running either 32-bit operating system has access internally to all services needed to use NetWare resources without the need for a separate NetWare-specific protocol stack. NDS isn't supported, although any of these clients can access a NetWare 4.x server running in bindery emulation mode. Installing NetWare support for a Windows 95 client is described fully in Chapter 11, "Configuring Windows 95 Clients for Networking." Installing NetWare support for Windows NT Workstation is described in Chapter 12, "Connecting Other PC Clients to the Network."

Adding a Novell Protocol Stack   If your clients' operating system doesn't include native NetWare support or you require extended access to NetWare 4.1 services, you have no alternative but to install Novell NetWare client software on that client. Novell supplies full-function NetWare client software for numerous workstation operating systems, including DOS, Windows 3.x, Windows 95, Windows NT, OS/2, UNIX, and the Macintosh.

Installing Novell client software has these primary drawbacks:

- Additional effort is required to configure each workstation initially.
- Additional ongoing maintenance is required to support a more complex client environment.
- Additional conventional or base memory is needed for the second protocol stack.

N O T E   These problems are likely to disappear in the long run as Microsoft improves NetWare support in its client operating systems. Both Microsoft and Novell are now shipping 32-bit NetWare clients for Windows 95 that provide NDS support.

Adding NetWare client support to coexist with an existing Microsoft Networking client is relatively straightforward, but doing so successfully requires that you first understand the fundamentals of how a Novell NetWare client accesses a NetWare server.

Novell clients require an IPX driver to provide network and transport layer services, and a shell to provide network redirection. Novell clients can use one of two methods for meeting each requirement:

- The original Novell client software used a monolithic IPX driver with the NETx shell. Novell's WSGEN program generates a monolithic IPX driver, IPX.COM, for each client. The resulting IPX.COM file is specific to the individual client because it's hard-coded for the address and IRQ of the NIC, and so forth. The monolithic IPX.COM drivers are a nightmare to administer; each change to a client configuration requires that the IPX.COM for that client be created anew. More important from an interoperability aspect, IPX.COM supports only a single IPX protocol stack.

- The NetWare shell was originally provided in versions specific to the version of DOS used. NET2.COM, for example, was used with MS-DOS 2.x, NET3.COM was used with MS-DOS 3.x, and so forth. With the advent of MS-DOS 5.0, Novell shipped a version called NETx, which could be used with any version of DOS. Variants of NETx called EMSNETx and XMSNETx were also provided to take advantage of expanded and extended memory, respectively.

With the advent of NetWare 4.0, Novell altered its client software support. The NETx shell was replaced by the Virtual Loadable Module (VLM) requester. More important from an interoperability standpoint, the monolithic IPX.COM was replaced by the Novell Open Datalink Interface (ODI), which breaks down the services formerly provided by IPX.COM into separate layers:

- The link support layer is loaded first by running the program LSL.COM provided by Novell. The link support layer provides a standardized low-level hardware interface and handles routing of frames to the correct protocol service.

- Loaded next is the Multiple Link Interface Driver (MLID), which is specific to the model of network interface card used. For example, if you use a 3Com 3C509 Ethernet card, run the MLID 3C5X9.COM. If instead you're using a Novell NE2000 Ethernet card, run NE2000.COM. The MLID provides an interface to the link support layer running below it and to the protocol stack(s) running above it.

- The last ODI layer loaded is the protocol support layer, which provides services for one or more network protocols. For example, IPX services are provided by the program IPXODI.COM, which is often the only protocol support to be found on NetWare clients. However, LSL and the MLID can simultaneously load and service additional protocols—for example, TCPIP.EXE.

Clients that use ODI to provide protocol support can use either the NETx shell or the VLM requesters to provide redirection services. Although the VLM requester provides superior services and reduced memory usage, many NetWare clients continue to use the NETx shell. In some cases, this is due to incompatibilities between the VLM requester and a few older network applications. In others, it's simply a matter of inertia. Clients that run the monolithic IPX.COM are limited to using NETx because the monolithic drivers don't support the VLM requester.

Whether you choose to install NETx NetWare shell or the VLM NetWare requester, ensure that your NICs are using Novell ODI drivers. The older monolithic drivers are no longer supported by Novell, are much harder to maintain, and—most importantly—don't let you run other protocols. As mentioned earlier, Windows NT Server is protocol independent. Windows NT Server is bundled with the NWLink protocol, so many NetWare system managers will be happy to learn that they don't have to install a second protocol stack on their clients. Other NetWare administrators may opt to load the Microsoft TCP/IP protocol stack supplied on the Windows NT Server 4.0 CD-ROM, giving their clients simultaneous access to NetWare, Windows NT, UNIX, and the Internet.

Part
IV

Ch
18

Microsoft Networking software uses a methodology similar to but incompatible with ODI to communicate with NICs. This method, called the Network Device Interface Specification (NDIS), offers functionality similar to ODI. Fortunately, both Microsoft and Novell provide *shim drivers* (or *shims*) that allow interoperability between ODI and NDIS. Microsoft PC-client software uses the NetWare ODI driver, automatically installing the NDIS-to-ODI shim.

Using Gateway Service for NetWare The Gateway Service for NetWare (see Figure 18.2) is bundled with Windows NT Server 4.0. Running as a service on Windows NT Server 4.0, GSNW lets one or more Microsoft Networking clients access NetWare resources. Used with Client Service for NetWare and the NWLink protocol, GSNW allows Windows NT Server clients to access shared files on a NetWare server and to print to NetWare printers. Microsoft Networking clients don't need to run the IPX/SPX protocol because the GSNW translates the upper layer SMB calls to and from NetWare NCP calls.

FIG. 18.2
Microsoft Networking clients accessing shared resources on a Novell NetWare server with the Gateway Service for NetWare.

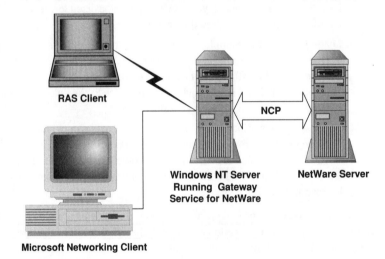

RAS Client

NCP

Windows NT Server Running Gateway Service for NetWare

NetWare Server

Microsoft Networking Client

N O T E An added benefit of using GSNW is that it can be deployed with Remote Access Service to allow remote Microsoft Networking clients to access NetWare file and print services transparently. For more information on Remote Access Service, see Chapter 19, "Managing Remote Access Service." ▨

Before implementing GSNW, the Windows NT Server administrator and the NetWare administrator should consider the following issues:

■ *Performance.* The GSNW uses a single NetWare connection through which all requests are routed to the NetWare server from GSNW clients. This can be an advantage because additional NetWare user licenses beyond the single license needed by GSNW don't need to be purchased for each user logging on to a NetWare server from GSNW. The down side of GSNW is that traffic from all GSNW users is routed through a single NetWare connection, so performance can degrade noticeably under a heavy load.

■ *Shared rights.* GSNW uses a single connection to the NetWare server, so all GSNW clients use the same NetWare account. This means that all GSNW clients have identical trustee rights and other permissions, which are determined by the settings for that one account. All GSNW users are assigned to the NetWare group NTGATEWAY.

■ *Logon scripts.* Microsoft networking clients don't execute NetWare logon scripts.

■ *Backup.* The backup software bundled with NetWare doesn't back up GSNW clients.

■ *Account management.* Whether a particular Windows NT client is granted access to GSNW, as well as global restrictions placed on GSNW users that have been granted access, are determined by the Windows NT Server system administrator.

Configuring a NetWare Server to Use GSNW   Little needs to be done on the NetWare server to prepare it for use with GSNW, but Supervisor access on the NetWare server is required to use the Novell SYSCON utility to make these changes. To prepare the NetWare server, follow these steps:

1. Log on to the NetWare 3.1x server as supervisor (or supervisor equivalent) and run SYSCON.EXE (see Figure 18.3).

FIG. 18.3
Using Novell's
SYSCON.EXE to prepare
the NetWare 3.1x server
for GSNW.

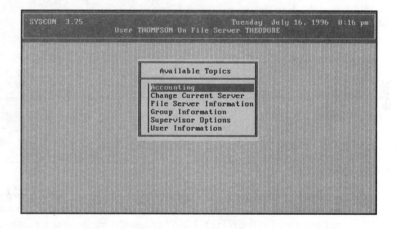

2. Create a new NetWare group with the mandatory name NTGATEWAY (see Figure 18.4). Grant this group the file, directory, and printer rights that you want available to all users of the shared gateway.

3. Create a new NetWare user with the same name and password as that used to log on to the Windows NT Server running GSNW (see Figure 18.5). This user is granted NetWare Supervisor Equivalent rights. This account is used by the system manager for maintenance and can also be used by the Migration Tool for NetWare, which re-quires full access to the NetWare server. With this account, logging on to the NetWare server from the computer running Windows NT Server allows you to run NetWare utilities, in addition to using NetWare files and printers.

FIG. 18.4

Creating the NetWare group NTGATEWAY and granting all file, directory, and printer rights to be shared.

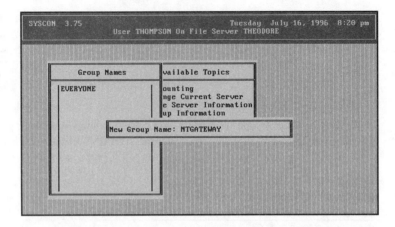

FIG. 18.5

Creating a supervisor equivalent user for system maintenance and to run NetWare utilities.

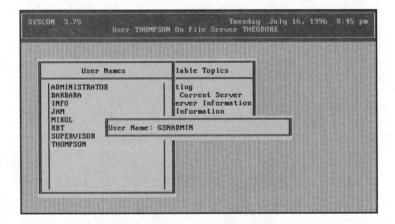

4. Create one or more new NetWare user accounts (see Figure 18.6) to be used by GSNW users, and assign each account to the NTGATEWAY group. Each account inherits the rights granted to the NTGATEWAY group and can also be assigned additional file and directory access rights of its own.

Installing GSNW   After you make the necessary changes to your NetWare server, you need to install GSNW on your Windows NT Server as follows:

1. In Control Panel, double-click the Network tool to display the Network property sheet. Click the Services tab to display installed network services (see Figure 18.7).

2. Click Add to display the Select Network Service dialog (see Figure 18.8).

3. Select Gateway (and Client) Services for NetWare and click OK to display the Windows NT Setup dialog (see Figure 18.9).

4. In the text box, type the drive and path name where the GSNW distribution files are located, and then click Continue to begin copying files. Windows NT Setup displays the progress of the file copying operation.

FIG. 18.6
Creating NetWare user accounts for shared access to the NetWare server, and assigning them to the NTGATEWAY group.

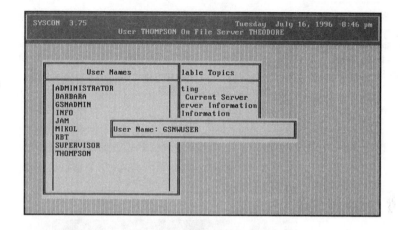

FIG. 18.7
Displaying installed network services in the Network property sheet.

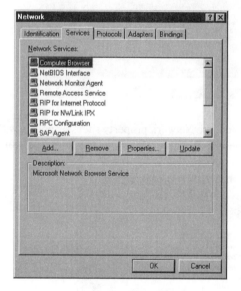

Part
IV

Ch
18

N O T E At this point, the NWLink IPX/SPX Protocol Configuration dialog may appear if you have more than one NIC installed in your server, or if Windows NT can't automatically configure the protocol. If so, specify which NIC is to be used to link to the NetWare server. Windows NT Server normally detects the correct frame type needed by this NIC to communicate with the NetWare server and installs it as a default, showing the Frame Type as Auto Detected. If for some reason you need to change the frame type, choose one from the Frame Type list box. Other tunable parameters are stored in the Registry and can be changed by clicking the Advanced button.

▶ **See** "Using the Registry Editor," **p. 310**

There's usually no reason to alter these settings. Make sure that you have good reason before you attempt to do so. ■

FIG. 18.8

Selecting Gateway (and Client) Services for NetWare in the Select Network Service dialog.

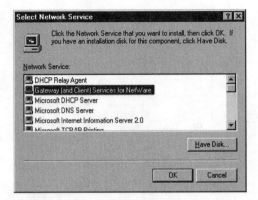

FIG. 18.9

Specifying the location of the GSNW distribution files in the Windows NT Setup dialog.

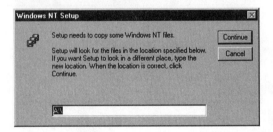

5. After all files are copied, the Network property sheet reappears with Gateway Service for NetWare visible as an installed network service (see Figure 18.10).

FIG. 18.10

The Network property sheet, displaying GSNW as an installed network service.

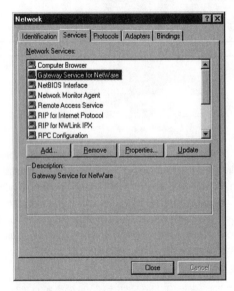

6. Click Close to complete the installation of GSNW. Windows NT Server then configures, stores, and reviews the affected bindings.

When the bindings review is complete, the Network Settings Change dialog tells you that you must restart Windows NT Server before the changes take effect.

Choosing a Preferred NetWare Server If more than one NetWare server exists on your network when GSNW is first run, the Select Preferred Server for NetWare dialog displays to prompt you to choose one of these servers as the default server to which GSNW should connect. You can either choose one of the servers as the default preferred server for that logon account, or choose none. Based on your selection, the preferred server is determined as follows:

- If you specify a server, that server remains your preferred server until you explicitly change it. Because the server that you first attach to performs the logon validation that's then used to determine user access to server resources, specifying a server is normally preferable.

- If you specify no preferred server, GSNW locates the *nearest* NetWare server each time you log on. Understand that *nearest* means the NetWare server that responds the fastest at the moment you log on, so if you choose the None option, you can't predict to which server you'll connect.

Enabling the Gateway and Activating Shares After you create the necessary group and user accounts on the NetWare server and install GSNW, you need to enable GSNW. Follow these steps:

1. From Control Panel, double-click the GSNW tool to display the Gateway Service for NetWare dialog (see Figure 18.11).

FIG. 18.11
Setting the preferred server and other options in the Gateway Service for NetWare dialog.

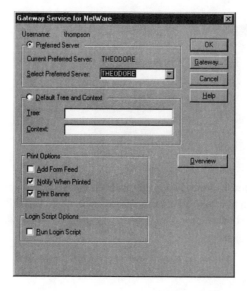

Part
IV

Ch
18

2. Click Gateway to open the Configure Gateway dialog. Mark the Enable Gateway check box, and fill in the Gateway Account, Password, and Confirm Password text boxes (see Figure 18.12).

FIG. 18.12

Enabling the gateway and entering account name and password information in the Configure Gateway dialog.

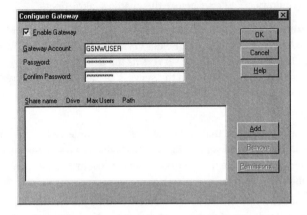

3. Click Add to display the New Share dialog (see Figure 18.13). Enter a share name by which the resource will be known and the network path associated with the share. Optionally, enter a comment to further describe the shared resource. Finally, select a drive letter from the drop-down list to be assigned to the share.

The User Limit section lets you specify the maximum number of users who can access the share concurrently. Either select Unlimited, or select Allow and click the spinner buttons to specify a maximum allowable number of concurrent users.

After you complete all this information, click OK to accept your changes.

FIG. 18.13

Entering a share name, specifying the assoc-iated network path, and designating a drive letter by which the share can be accessed.

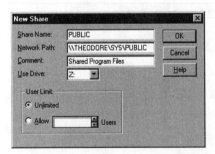

4. The Configure Gateway dialog reappears with the new share visible (see Figure 18.14). Use the Add button to create additional shares as needed, or the Remove button to remove unneeded shares.

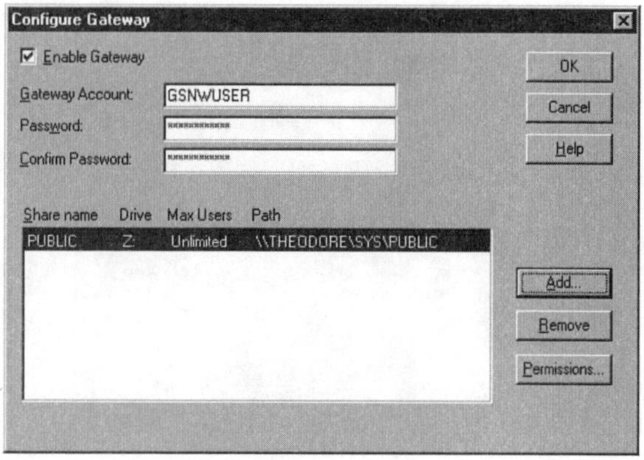

FIG. 18.14
The completed
Configure Gateway
dialog, showing the
newly created share.

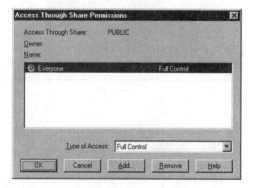

5. To set permissions for the shares you've just created, click Permissions to display the Access Through Share Permissions dialog (see Figure 18.15). Use this dialog to set permissions as described in Chapter 14, "Sharing and Securing Network Resources."

   ▶ **See** "Working with Share Permissions," **p. 487**

FIG. 18.15
Assigning permissions
for the newly created
share in the Access
Through Share
Permissions dialog.

Installing and Configuring a GSNW Print Gateway   Installing a GSNW print gateway lets Microsoft Networking users print to NetWare printers. After GSNW is installed and enabled and a print gateway is configured, a NetWare printer appears on the Windows NT Server computer simply as another shared printer. Access to and control of shared NetWare printers is determined by properties set for the shared printer from within the Printers folder on the Windows NT server. Print jobs sent to the gateway are redirected to the NetWare print queue to which the gateway is mapped.

To install and configure the GSNW print gateway, follow these steps:

1. From the Start menu, choose Settings and then Printers to display the Printers folder. Double-click the Add Printer icon to display the Add Printer Wizard (see Figure 18.16).

   ▶ **See** "Configuring Locally Attached Server Printers as Shared Resources," **p. 512**

FIG. 18.16

Setting up a shared
network printer with the
Add Printer Wizard.

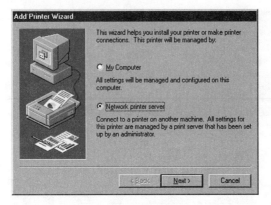

2. Select the Network Printer Server option and click Next to open the Connect to Printer
   dialog (see Figure 18.17).

FIG. 18.17

Displaying available
print queues for a
Windows NT server.

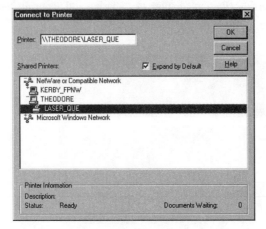

3. In the Shared Printers list, double-click NDS tree names and NetWare 3.1x server names
   to expand the display and list the shared printers available with each server. When
   you've located the printer to be shared, select it and click OK.

4. The Add Printer Wizard next prompts you to specify whether you want this printer to be
   the default printer for Windows applications (see Figure 18.18). Select Yes or No and
   then click Next.

5. The Add Printer Wizard informs you that the printer is installed successfully (see
   Figure 18.19). Click Finish to complete the installation and return to the Printers folder.
   At this point, the shared printer is installed but not yet enabled.

6. To enable the newly created shared printer, right-click its icon to display the context-
   sensitive menu, and choose Properties to display the print queue property sheet.

FIG. 18.18
Specifying that the
printer won't be the
default printer for
Windows applications.

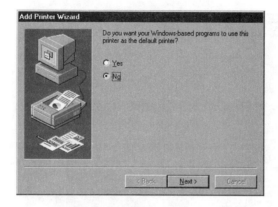

FIG. 18.19
The Add Printer Wizard's
final step in adding a
print queue for a
NetWare printer.

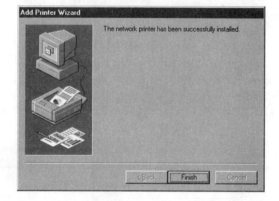

Part

IV

Ch

18

7. Select the Shared option and enter a name for the shared printer (see Figure 18.20). The
   rest of the printer configuration process is described step by step in Chapter 14, "Sharing
   and Securing Network Resources."

   ▶ **See** "Sharing and Securing Network Printers," **p. 512**

8. Choose OK to accept your changes and return to the Printers folder. Close the Printers
   folder. The shared printer is now available for use by authorized GSNW users.

Microsoft Networking clients now see the shared NetWare printer as they would any shared
printer available on the Windows NT server.

Accessing Microsoft Windows NT Servers with NetWare Clients

Many LAN administrators are faced with integrating a new Windows NT server into an
existing network that includes a large installed base of NetWare clients. You may have
scores or hundreds of clients, each already running Novell client software to access the
existing NetWare servers. Visiting each workstation to install and configure new network
client software is expensive, time-consuming, and disruptive. Fortunately, Microsoft offers a
way to avoid this effort and cost by using the existing NetWare client software to access the
new Windows NT server.

FIG. 18.20
Specifying a share name for the printer.

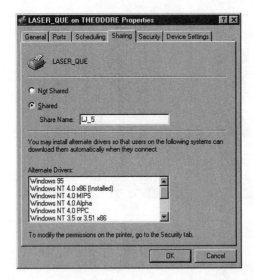

File and Print Services for NetWare (FPNW), shown diagrammatically in Figure 18.21, is an optional utility available from Microsoft that runs on Windows NT Server. Running FPNW causes the Windows NT 4.0 server to appear to Novell clients as a NetWare 3.12 server.

FIG. 18.21
Emulating a NetWare 3.12 server with Windows NT 4.0's File and Print Services for NetWare.

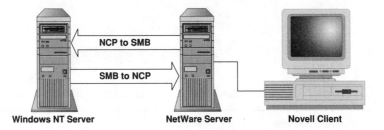

NOTE In version 3.51, FPNW and Directory Service Manager for NetWare (DSMN) were available as separate utilities, each of which was priced at $99 in the United States. With the release of version 4.0, FPNW and DSMN are now bundled as a single product called Microsoft Services for NetWare, which is priced in the U.S. at $149.

The version 3.51-specific versions of these utilities are still available but can't be used with Windows NT Server 4.0. Microsoft Services for NetWare 4.0 includes the 3.51 and 4.0 versions of both software products, and in versions for all processor platforms supported by Windows NT Server 4.0. ∎

Unlike GSNW, the performance of File and Print Services for NetWare is very good and doesn't degrade under a heavy load. Microsoft positions File and Print Services for NetWare as a product that not only eases integration of Windows NT into a NetWare environment, but one that also serves as an excellent transition tool.

N O T E It's easy to confuse the purposes of Gateway Service for NetWare versus File and Print Services for NetWare. They're exactly opposite. Gateway Service for NetWare allows Microsoft clients to access a Novell NetWare server. File and Print Service for NetWare allows Novell clients to access a Windows NT server. ▪

File and Print Services for NetWare uses as its foundation Windows NT Server's NWLink, GSNW, and an enhanced version of the bundled Migration Tool for NetWare. With Directory Service Manager for NetWare, described in a later section, you can centrally manage user accounts for both NetWare and Windows NT servers.

NetWare clients can access a Windows NT server running File and Print Services for NetWare by using either the NetWare NETx shell or the VLM requester. Installing File and Print Services for NetWare creates a new folder named SYSVOL on the server running FPNW. This folder appears to NetWare clients as the SYS: volume for that server, and has a directory structure analogous to a NetWare SYS: volume, including the LOGIN, PUBLIC, MAIL, and SYSTEM directories. Clients can continue to use NetWare-compatible utilities, including ATTACH, LOGIN, LOGOUT, SETPASS, MAP, SLIST, CAPTURE, and ENDCAP to access shared files and printers.

N O T E Although File and Print Services for NetWare allows workstations running Novell client software to access the Windows NT server without using Microsoft client software, you must still provide each such client with a Windows NT Server user access license. ▪

Installing File and Print Services for NetWare To install File and Print Services for NetWare (FPNW), follow these steps:

1. From Control Panel, double-click the Network tool to display the Network property sheet, and then click Add to display the Select Network Service dialog.

2. Click Have Disk to display the Insert Disk dialog. Enter the drive and path where the FPNW distribution files are located, and then click OK to continue.

3. The Select OEM Option dialog appears (see Figure 18.22). You're installing FPNW, so select File and Print Services for NetWare. Click OK to continue. Windows NT Setup copies the distribution files from the diskette.

FIG. 18.22

Installing File and Print Services for NetWare from the distribution CD.

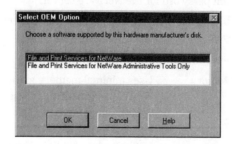

N O T E Choose the File and Print Services for NetWare Administrative Tools Only option to install the utilities needed to manage FPNW remotely from a server that itself won't run FPNW. ▪

4. After all files are copied, the Install File and Print Services for NetWare dialog appears (see Figure 18.23). Use this dialog to specify the location of the NetWare SYS: volume, enter the supervisor account information, and tune server performance. Set the following values:

- *Directory for SYS Volume* is completed with the default value of C:\SYSVOL. Accept this location, or specify an alternate drive and directory name. The location you specify must reside on an NTFS partition if you want to set NTFS file access permissions and NTFS directory access permissions to control access to the volume.

FIG. 18.23

Specifying volume location, supervisor account information, and performance tuning in the Install File and Print Services for NetWare dialog.

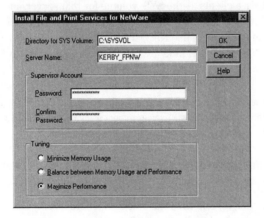

- *Server Name* is completed with the default value of *SERVER_NAME*_FPNW. Accept this name or specify an alternate server name that users will use to access this server. The name you specify can't be the Microsoft computer name for the server.

- *Password* and *Confirm Password* requires that you enter and re-enter the supervisor account password for the NetWare server.

- The options in the Tuning section allow you to determine server performance and resource usage:

Option	Description
Minimize Memory Usage	Uses minimal memory at the expense of slower FPNW performance. This selection is most appropriate for a server that's used primarily for purposes other than sharing files and printers—for example, an application server.

Option	Description
Balance Between Memory Usage and Performance	Provides moderately high server performance with moderate memory usage. This choice is most appropriate for a general-purpose server that will share files and printers as well as run applications.
Maximize Performance	Provides the highest server performance at the expense of increased memory usage. This choice is most appropriate for a server that will be dedicated to sharing files and printers.

5. After you fill in all required values, click OK to accept your changes. The File and Print Services for NetWare dialog appears (see Figure 18.24).

FIG. 18.24

Entering the password for the account to be used to run File and Print Services for NetWare.

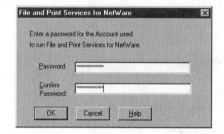

6. Enter and confirm the password to be used to run File and Print Services for NetWare and click OK. Windows NT Setup copies the FPNW distribution files to your server.

7. After all files are copied, the Network property sheet appears (see Figure 18.25), with File and Print Services for NetWare listed as an installed network service.

8. Click Close to complete the installation. Windows NT Server begins Bindings Configuration. After configuring the bindings, it stores and then finally reviews them.

9. After Windows NT Server finishes configuring, storing, and reviewing the bindings, it displays the NWLink IPX/SPX Properties sheet (see Figure 18.26). Enter the Internal Network Number and specify parameters for each NIC. Use the Adapter drop-down list to select each adapter. Leave the frame type set at Auto Frame Type Detection unless you're experiencing problems connecting to the NetWare server.

10. Click the Routing tab (see Figure 18.27). If you want your Windows NT server to act as an IPX/SPX router, mark the Enable RIP Routing check box. After you complete the NWLink IPX/SPX Properties sheet, click OK to continue.

11. If the internal network number you provided in step 10 is invalid, a NWLink IPX/SPX message box appears. When you click OK to return to the NWLink IPX/SPX Properties sheet, Windows NT Server generates a random internal network number for you (see Figure 18.28). Accept this randomly generated number, or enter a correct internal network number of your own. Choose OK to continue.

Part
IV

Ch
18

FIG. 18.25

The Network property sheet, displaying File and Print Services for NetWare as an installed network service.

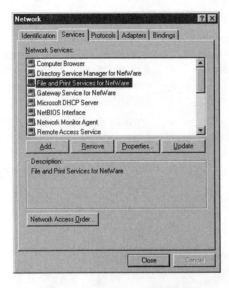

FIG. 18.26

The NWLink IPX/SPX Properties sheet's General page, which lets you specify protocol properties for each adapter.

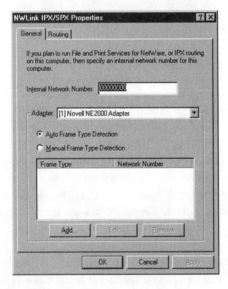

12. Windows NT again configures, stores, and reviews the bindings. The Network Settings Change message box appears to warn you that you must restart Windows NT Server before the changes take effect. After the server restarts, FPNW is available.

FIG. 18.27

Enabling IPX/SPX RIP routing on the Routing page of the NWLink IPX/SPX Properties sheet.

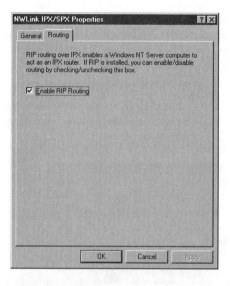

FIG. 18.28

The random internal network number generated by Windows NT Server.

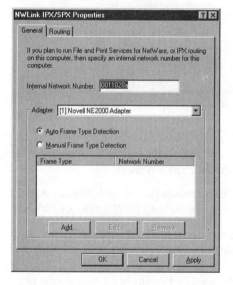

Configuring and Managing File and Print Services for NetWare   After you install File and Print Services for NetWare, you must configure it before Novell NetWare resources are available to users. Follow these steps to configure FPNW:

1. From Control Panel, double-click the FPNW tool to display the File and Print Services for NetWare on *Servername* dialog (see Figure 18.29). The File Server Information section lists various statistics about the associated NetWare file server and the FPNW gateway to that server.

2. The FPNW Server Name text box displays the default name assigned to the FPNW gateway when it was installed. You can assign another name or accept the name as is. If you change the name of the FPNW server, you must stop and restart the FPNW service before the change will take effect.

3. Enter a short description of the FPNW gateway in the Description text box, if needed.

4. The Home Directory Root Path text box displays the NetWare volume assigned to this gateway when it was installed. You can assign another volume or accept the volume displayed.

FIG. 18.29

Statistics and configuration parameters for the FPNW gateway in the File and Print Services for NetWare on *Servername* dialog.

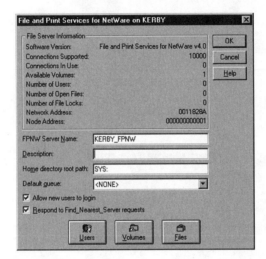

5. The Default Queue drop-down list is initially set to <NONE>. The list displays all NetWare print queues available on the server. Select one of these queues to specify it as the default print queue for FPNW users.

The Users, Volumes, and Files buttons in the File and Print Services for NetWare on *Servername* dialog allow you to manage the FPNW gateway, as follows:

■ Click Users to display the Users on *Servername* dialog (see Figure 18.30). The Connected Users list displays the name, Network Address, Node Address, and Login Time for each user. You can use this list to Disconnect a user, Disconnect All users, or Send Message to a user or users. The Resources list displays the Drives and Opens for each resource. After you finish managing users, click Close to return to the File and Print Services for NetWare on *Servername* dialog.

■ Click Volumes to display the Volumes Usage on *Servername* dialog (see Figure 18.31). The Volume list displays available volumes. For each volume, Users lists the current number of users accessing that volume, Max Users lists the maximum number of concurrent users allowed, and Path lists the Windows NT Server drive and folder associated with the NetWare volume.

FIG. 18.30

Displaying user statistics and managing users with the Users on *Servername* dialog.

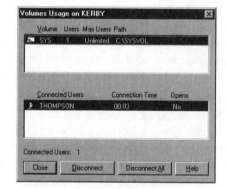

The Connected Users list displays the name of each Connected User, Connection Time, and Opens for the volume highlighted in the Volume list. You can disconnect a selected user by choosing Disconnect, or disconnect all users by choosing Disconnect All. After you finish managing volumes, click Close to return to the File and Print Services for NetWare on *Servername* dialog.

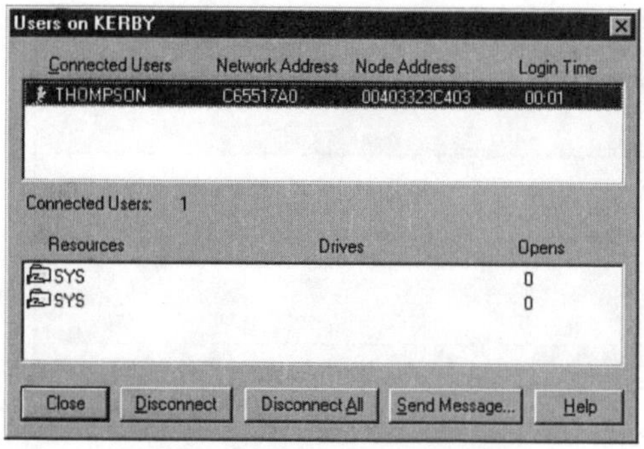

FIG. 18.31

Displaying volume statistics and managing volumes in the Volumes Usage on *Servername* dialog.

■ Click Files to display the Files Opened by Users on *Servername* dialog (see Figure 18.32). The Opened By list displays the name of the user who opened each listed file. For each open file, For displays the permissions associated with that open, Locks displays the number of locks on that file, and Volume and Path display the location of the file. Click Close File to close a selected file, or Close All Files to close all files listed. Click Refresh to update the list of displayed files.

After you finish managing files, click Close to return to the File and Print Services for NetWare on *Servername* dialog.

After you finish configuring and managing the FPNW gateway, click OK to accept the changes and close the File and Print Services for NetWare on *Servername* dialog.

Part

IV

Ch

18

FIG. 18.32
Displaying file statistics and managing files with the Files Opened by Users on *Servername* dialog.

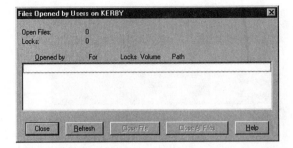

Using Other Windows NT Server Integration Tools for NetWare

In addition to GSNW and the File and Print Service for NetWare, two other tools are available for Windows NT Server to aid integration with Novell NetWare environments. Directory Service Manager for NetWare (DSMN) lets you manage user accounts on Windows NT servers and NetWare servers by using a single integrated database. Multi-Protocol Routing Service allows your Windows NT server to provide software routing to link networks.

Directory Service Manager for NetWare   If, in addition to one or more Windows NT servers, your network includes Novell NetWare 2.x/3.x servers or NetWare 4.x servers running bindery emulation, you might consider buying Directory Service Manager for NetWare. DSMN (see Figure 18.33) is used initially to export NetWare user account information into Windows NT Directory Services and subsequently to maintain all Windows NT Server and NetWare server user account information in a common database.

FIG. 18.33
Directory Service Manager for NetWare connecting NetWare 2.x/3.x servers to a Windows NT 4.0 domain.

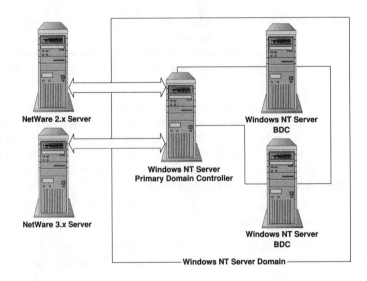

During the initial transfer of NetWare user account information, you have the option of creating a Map File to re-create the NetWare accounts' passwords, assign a single password to all accounts, or set the password to the user name. The Microsoft *Services for NetWare*

Administrator's Guide lists the necessary steps involved to import the NetWare servers user account information. The initial setup process is complicated, so DSMN includes a Trial Run option that creates a log file containing the account information that would be migrated to the Windows NT server.

After you select the user and groups to be propagated to and from the NetWare servers, any changes to those accounts on Windows NT Server are replicated automatically to the NetWare servers. The replication process isn't bidirectional, so all subsequent changes must be made by using DSMN. When the initial migration is complete, the DSMN database doesn't reflect any changes made directly to a NetWare server. Once installed, DSMN provides a single network logon (see Figure 18.34).

FIG. 18.34
Creating a single network logon for NetWare clients across two Windows NT domains.

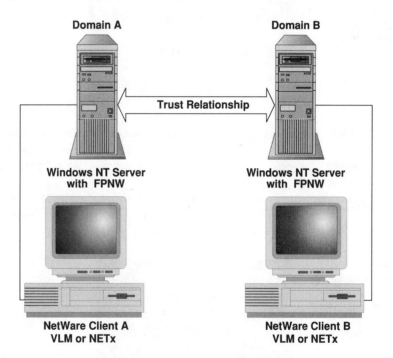

Part
IV

Ch

18

Installing DSMN   To install Directory Service Manager for NetWare, follow these steps:

1. From Control Panel, double-click the Network tool to display the Network property sheet. Click the Services tab.
2. Choose Add to display the Select Network Service dialog. Windows NT Server 4.0 builds a list of available services and displays them in the Network Service list box.

CAUTION

If an older version of Directory Service for NetWare is already installed on the computer, it appears in the Network Service list box. Don't select the older version. Instead, choose Have Disk to install the current version.

3. Click Have Disk to display the Insert Disk dialog. In the text box, type the drive and path name where the DSMN distribution files are located, and then choose OK. The Select OEM Option dialog appears (see Figure 18.35). You're installing the full service, so select Directory Service Manager for NetWare and click OK.

N O T E Choose the Directory Service Manager for NetWare Administrative Tools Only option to install the utilities needed to manage DSMN remotely from a server that won't run DSMN. ▨

FIG. 18.35
Choosing the full Directory Service Manager for NetWare in the Select OEM Option dialog.

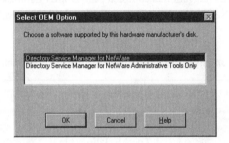

N O T E If you're installing directly from the distribution CD, the DSMN distribution files are located in *d*:\dsmn\nt40*processor*, where *d* is the drive letter assigned to your CD-ROM drive and *processor* is the type of processor installed in your server, such as i386 for Intel computers. ▨

4. After Setup installs the files, the Install Directory Service Manager for NetWare dialog appears (see Figure 18.36). Enter and confirm a password of your choice for the service account, and click OK.

FIG. 18.36
Entering and confirming the password for the account to be used for Directory Service Manager for NetWare (DSMN).

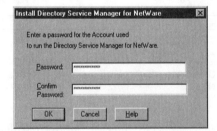

5. Windows NT Server returns to the Network property sheet, displaying DSMN as an installed network service (see Figure 18.37).

6. Click Close to complete the installation. Windows NT Server configures, stores, and reviews bindings. The Network Settings Change dialog notifies you that you must restart the server before the changes take effect.

Configuring and Managing DSMN After you install DSMN, follow these steps to configure and manage it:

N O T E This procedure changes the bindery on your NetWare server. Before you begin, be sure to back up the bindery. To do so, log on to the NetWare server as supervisor or supervisor equivalent from a DOS, Windows 3.1x, or Windows 95 client (you can't run the Novell system utilities from Windows NT). Notify all connected NetWare clients to log off. After they do so, run BINDFIX.EXE. Store the resulting three bindery backup files (NET$OBJ.OLD, NET$PROP.OLD, and NET$VAL.OLD) in a safe place before continuing. ▪

FIG. 18.37

The Network property sheet, displaying DSMN as an installed network service.

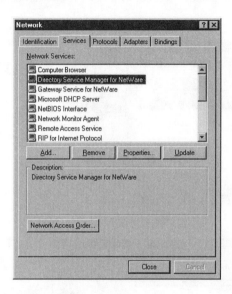

1. From the Start menu, choose Programs, Administrative Tools, and Directory Service Manager for NetWare to run the Synchronization Manager. The title bar displays the domain name you're managing. When first run, the Synchronization Manager displays an empty NetWare Server list box (see Figure 18.38).

FIG. 18.38

The initial status of DSMN's Synchronization Manager.

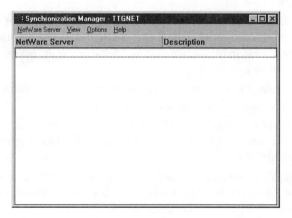

2. From the NetWare Server menu, choose Add Server to Manage to display the Select NetWare Server dialog (see Figure 18.39). The Select NetWare Server list displays available NetWare servers.

3. Select one of the servers listed and click OK to display the Connect to NetWare Server dialog (see Figure 18.40). Enter a user name and a password. This account must be either the supervisor or another account with supervisor equivalent privileges on the NetWare server.

FIG. 18.39

Displaying available NetWare servers in the Select NetWare Server dialog.

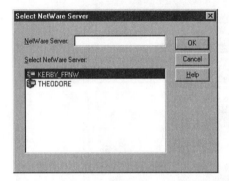

FIG. 18.40

Specifying a user name in the Connect to NetWare Server dialog.

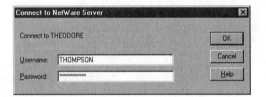

4. Click OK to display the Propagate NetWare Accounts to Windows NT Domain dialog (see Figure 18.41).

5. By default, all NetWare users are placed in the Users to Be Propagated list box, and all NetWare groups are placed in the Groups to Be Propagated list box. Use the Add and Remove buttons to move users and groups between the list boxes. Also specify the following settings:

- *User Must Change Password*, if marked, specifies that when users first log on, they must immediately change their passwords.

- *Add Supervisors to Administrators Group*, if marked, specifies that Novell supervisor and supervisor equivalent users will be added as members of the Windows NT Administrators group.

- *Add File Server Console Operators to Console Operators Group*, if marked, specifies that Novell File Server Console Operators will be added as members of the Windows NT Console Operators group.

- *Use Mapping File*, if selected, specifies that individual user propagation parameters be based on the contents of an ASCII mapping file.

- The *Password* section allows you to specify how passwords will be assigned on the newly created Windows NT accounts. Select an option button to determine password assignments. No Password specifies that the new account won't be assigned a password. Password is Username specifies that the password will be set to the user name for each account. Password Is allows you to specify a single password that will be used for all newly created accounts. Randomly Generated Password Of specifies that each newly created account will have a randomly generated password with the number of characters specified by the Characters spinner box.

FIG. 18.41

The default NetWare users and groups propagated to Windows NT Server by DSMN synchronization.

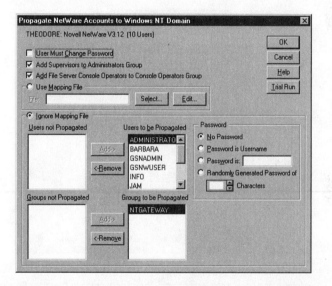

6. After you complete the Propagate NetWare Accounts to Windows NT Domain dialog, click Trial Run to test your settings. If a problem occurs during the trial run, a message box displays the problem and gives you the opportunity to correct it. Fix any problems reported and rerun the trial run until it completes successfully.

7. When the trial run completes successfully, the Synchronization Manager message box tells you so. Click Yes to display the trial run log file (see Figure 18.42).

8. Review the log file to make sure that synchronization will take place as expected. When you're satisfied that everything is correct, close the log file to return to the Propagate NetWare Accounts to Windows NT Domain dialog.

9. Click OK to complete the synchronization. The Synchronization Manager message box notifies you that you should back up your NetWare bindery before proceeding.

10. When you're satisfied that your NetWare bindery is safe, click Yes to display the Set Propagated Accounts on *Servername* dialog (see Figure 18.43).

Part
IV

Ch
18

FIG. 18.42

Displaying the trial run log file in Notepad.

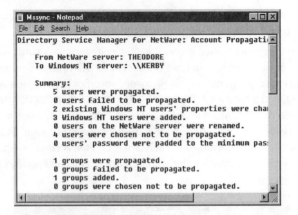

```
Mssync - Notepad
File  Edit  Search  Help

Directory Service Manager for NetWare: Account Propagati

    From NetWare server: THEODORE
    To Windows NT server: \\KERBY

    Summary:
        5 users were propagated.
        0 users failed to be propagated.
        2 existing Windows NT users' properties were char
        3 Windows NT users were added.
        0 users on the NetWare server were renamed.
        4 users were chosen not to be propagated.
        0 users' password were padded to the minimum pas

        1 groups were propagated.
        0 groups failed to be propagated.
        1 groups added.
        0 groups were chosen not to be propagated.
```

FIG. 18.43

Specifying the accounts to be propagated based on group membership.

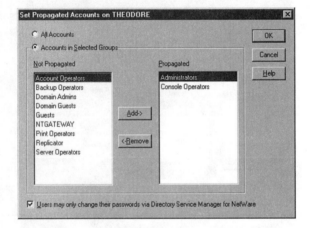

```
Set Propagated Accounts on THEODORE

  ○ All Accounts                                    [ OK ]
  ● Accounts in Selected Groups
                                                   [ Cancel ]
  Not Propagated              Propagated
                                                   [ Help ]
  Account Operators           Administrators
  Backup Operators            Console Operators
  Domain Admins
  Domain Guests
  Guests            [ Add-> ]
  NTGATEWAY
  Print Operators
  Replicator        [ <-Remove ]
  Server Operators

  ☑ Users may only change their passwords via Directory Service Manager for NetWare
```

N O T E By default, the Users May Only Change Their Passwords via Directory Service Manager for NetWare check box is marked. If you want users to be able to change their passwords by using standard Novell utilities, unmark this check box. ■

11. Use the Add and Remove buttons to specify the users to be propagated. After you complete this process, click OK to propagate the accounts and display the Synchronization Manager message box shown in Figure 18.44. Click Yes to remove the users and groups that weren't selected to be propagated from the NetWare server; click No to leave those users and groups on the NetWare server.

12. The Synchronization Manager appears, with the newly propagated NetWare server visible. Select that server and use the NetWare Server menu to manage the server (see Figure 18.45).

Multi-Protocol Routing Service The Multi-Protocol Routing (MPR) Service (see Figure 18.46) allows a Windows NT server to provide a low-cost, software-based LAN-to-LAN routing solution, allowing small companies to avoid buying an expensive hardware router. The

Microsoft MPR Service is analogous to and a direct replacement for the Novell Multi-Protocol Router. MPR is intended primarily for use by small organizations whose only server runs Windows NT Server, as well as by organizations that are replacing NetWare with Windows NT and need a software-based router to replace the Novell MPR.

FIG. 18.44

Synchronization Manager's message that the selected accounts have been propagated.

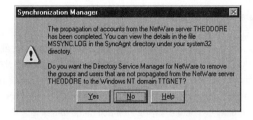

FIG. 18.45

Synchronization Manager displaying the newly propagated NetWare server, allowing you to manage it.

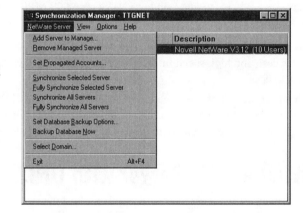

Part **IV**

Ch **18**

FIG. 18.46

The Multi-Protocol Routing Service providing software-based routing between a remote UNIX host and a remote NetWare server.

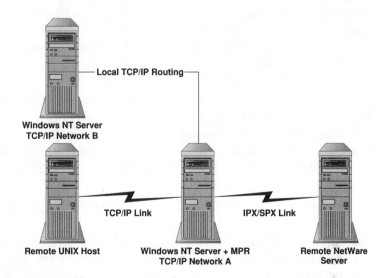

Windows NT Server provides standard software-based routing support for remote users via its Remote Access Service (RAS), as well as for local users running AppleTalk networks. The optional MPR Service extends this software-based routing support to provide enhanced support for IPX/SPX and TCP/IP networks.

N O T E   Like other software-based routing products, MPR Service can be used to link networks into a WAN over dial-up or leased lines. Unlike some commercial products, MPR Service doesn't directly support dial-up links with an asynchronous serial port and modem. Instead, all communications links must be made with NICs or communications support cards that emulate NICs. MPR Service supports a variety of such cards from several manufacturers. These cards can establish links through frame relay, ISDN, x.25, and other telecommunications protocols. Check the latest version of the Windows NT Hardware Compatibility List before buying interface cards to use with MPR Service. ■

Companies of any size are likely to find Windows NT Server 4.0's MPR Service useful in the following ways:

■ Used with an ISDN or frame-relay communications interface, MPR can provide an efficient, low-cost, and high-speed Internet gateway by taking advantage of your existing Windows NT server.

■ Used with one or more high-speed communications interfaces, MPR can provide an inexpensive method to connect branch office networks to the main network without requiring the purchase of expensive dedicated hardware routers for each end.

Integrating Windows NT Server with UNIX

UNIX, in one of its many variants, is commonly found as a host operating system in medium and large companies, often as an application server. Although Windows NT Server is an excellent application server platform that may eventually supplant UNIX for that function in many organizations, you may need to provide client support for UNIX hosts on a temporary basis, if not permanently. If your organization uses UNIX as a client operating system, perhaps on engineering workstations, you might also be faced with providing client support to allow these UNIX workstations to access the Windows NT server.

Integrating UNIX and Windows NT Server means working with TCP/IP. Although Windows NT Server doesn't implement the full TCP/IP protocol suite, it does include both the basic TCP/IP protocol support and most of the TCP/IP utilities you need to allow Windows NT Server and UNIX to interoperate. You can use available third-party products to fill most of the gaps. Windows NT Server 4.0 includes the following core TCP/IP protocols, utilities, and services:

■ *Core protocols.* TCP, IP, UDP, ARP, and ICMP. Remote Access Service (RAS) also provides SLIP and PPP support.

■ *Application interfaces.* Winsock or Windows Sockets (based on the Berkeley Socket API), Remote Procedure Calls (RPCs), NetBIOS, and Network DDE.

■ *Basic Utilities.* `finger`, `ftp`, `lpr`, `rcp`, `rexec`, `rsh`, `telnet`, and `tftp`.

- *Diagnostic tools.* arp, hostname, ipconfig, lpq, nbtstat, netstat, ping, route, and tracert (traceroute).

  ▶ **See** "Using Windows NT's Network-Related Command-Line Tools," **p. 580**

- *Servers.* ftp, lpd, snmp, chargen, daytime, discard, echo, quote, DHCP, and WINS.

The TCP/IP protocol suite evolves continuously. The TCP/IP standards are maintained and published by the Internet Engineering Task Force (IETF). The actual standards documents are called Requests For Comments (RFCs). It's crucial for any TCP/IP implementation to comply with the various RFCs if the implementation is to interoperate with other TCP/IP systems. Table 18.1 lists the RFCs to which the TCP/IP implementation supplied with Windows NT Server 4.0 adheres.

Table 18.1 IETF RFCs Supported by Windows NT Server 4.0

RFC	Title	RFC	Title
0768	User Datagram Protocol	1122	Requirements for Internet Hosts— Communication Layers
0783	TFTP Protocol Revision 2	1123	Requirements for Internet Hosts— Application and Support
0791	Internet Protocol	1134	Point-to-Point Protocol: A Proposal for Multi-Protocol Transmission of Datagrams over Point-to-Point Links
0792	Internet Control Message Protocol	1144	Compressing TCP/IP Headers for Low-Speed Serial Links
0793	Transmission Control Protocol	1157	A Simple Network Management Protocol (SNMP)
0826	Ethernet Address Resolution Protocol: Or Converting Network Protocol Addresses to 48-bit Ethernet Address for Transmission on Ethernet Hardware	1179	Line Printer Daemon Protocol
0854	Telnet Protocol Specification	1188	A Proposed Standard for the Transmission of IP Datagrams over FDDI Networks
0862	Echo Protocol	1191	Path MTU Discovery
0863	Discard Protocol	1201	Transmitting IP Traffic over ARCNET Networks

Part

IV

Ch

18

continues

Table 18.1 Continued

RFC	Title	RFC	Title
0864	Character Generator Protocol	1231	IEEE 802.5 Token Ring MIB
0865	Quote of the Day Protocol	1332	The PPP Internet Protocol Control Protocol (IPCP)
0867	Daytime Protocol	1334	PPP Authentication Protocols
0894	Standard for the Transmission of IP Datagrams over Ethernet Networks	1533	DHCP Options and BOOTP Vendor Extensions
0919	Broadcasting Internet Datagrams	1534	Interoperation Between DHCP and BOOTP
0922	Broadcasting Internet Datagrams in the Presence of Subnets	1541	Dynamic Host Configuration Protocol
0959	File Transfer Protocol	1542	Clarifications and Extensions for the Bootstrap Protocol
1001	Protocol Standard for a NetBIOS Service on a TCP/UDP Transport: Concepts and Methods	1547	Requirements for an Internet Standard Point-to-Point Protocol
1002	Protocol Standard for a NetBIOS Service on a TCP/UDP Transport: Detailed Specifications	1548	The Point-to-Point Protocol (PPP)
1034	Domain Names—Concepts and Facilities	1549	PPP in HDLC Framing
1035	Domain Names—Implementation and Specification	1552	The PPP Internetwork Packet Exchange Control Protocol (IPXCP)
1042	Standard for the Transmission of IP Datagrams over IEEE 802 Networks	1553	Compressing IPX Headers over WAN Media (CIPX)
1055	Nonstandard for Transmission of IP Datagrams over Serial Lines: SLIP	1570	PPP LCP Extensions
1112	Host Extensions for IP Multicasting		

ON THE WEB

You can download the actual RFCs from **http://www.internic.net**.

Using the Microsoft DNS Server

The Microsoft Domain Name Service (DNS) Server is a Windows NT service that resolves unknown IP addresses from known host names. TCP/IP uses numeric addresses to identify hosts, whereas humans find it much more comfortable to use plain English host names for the same purpose. For example, when you point your Web browser to **www.microsoft.com**, DNS resolves this host name to the corresponding IP address, **207.68.156.61**.

DNS isn't the only available method for name resolution in a TCP/IP environment. You can instead use a HOSTS file on each workstation to create static mappings of selected host names to their corresponding IP addresses. You can also use NetBIOS name resolution to resolve IP addresses from NetBIOS (Windows) host names by using either static LMHOSTS files or a dynamic method such as the Windows Internet Name Service (WINS).

Relative to these other methods, DNS has three advantages:

- *DNS is centralized.* Unlike HOSTS files and LMHOSTS files, which must be maintained individually at each client, DNS databases are maintained on a central server.
- *DNS is dynamic.* When it can't resolve a query from its own local database, a DNS server communicates with other DNS servers to resolve the query. The DNS server uses the information it learns in this way to update its own databases. For example, if **www.microsoft.com** is relocated to a server with a different IP address, DNS eventually learns of the change and updates the address in its own database automatically.
- *DNS works in a routed environment.* If your network includes branch office or other remote sites linked by routers, using DNS is the best alternative. DNS was designed to work in the largest internetworking environment of all—the Internet.

Using HOSTS or LMHOSTS files is a viable alternative if you have a very small network in which few changes are made to the IP addresses of hosts, and which will never be connected to the Internet. Using WINS is a viable alternative if your LAN won't be connected to the Internet. WINS is also usable in an internetwork if your routers are RFC 1542 compliant, if your clients are all WINS-enabled, or if you're willing to place a WINS server at each remote site.

You should use DNS if your network is now or will be connected to the Internet, either directly or via a proxy server or firewall. You should also use DNS if you run a routed TCP/IP network, even if that network doesn't connect to the Internet.

Installing the Microsoft DNS Server   To install the Microsoft DNS Server service, follow these steps:

1. From Control Panel, double-click the Network tool to display the Network property sheet. Click the Services tab to display the Services page.
2. Click Add to display the Select Network Service dialog (see Figure 18.47). Select Microsoft DNS Server and click OK to begin installing the service.

Part
IV

Ch
18

FIG. 18.47
The Select Network
Service dialog, allowing
you to choose the
service to be installed.

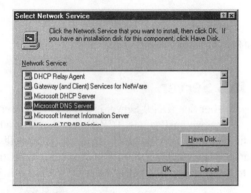

3. The Windows NT Setup dialog prompts you for the location of the Microsoft DNS Server distribution files. Enter the location and click Continue to begin copying the files.

4. Windows NT displays the Network property sheet, shown in Figure 18.48 with Microsoft DNS Server installed. Click Close to complete the installation of the Microsoft DNS Server.

FIG. 18.48
The Services page of
the Network property
sheet, with the
Microsoft DNS Server
installed.

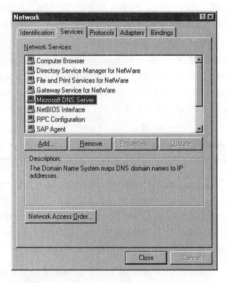

5. Windows NT Server analyzes the changes you've made to your network configuration. It configures, stores, and reviews the bindings, and then displays the Network Settings Change dialog to inform you that you must restart the server before your changes will take effect. Reboot the server to start the Microsoft DNS Server.

Configuring the Microsoft DNS Server   After you install Microsoft DNS Server and restart the server, you must first configure the DNS Server before it can be used. To configure the DNS Server, you must first create zones and then add resource records to the DNS database.

Creating Zones   The first step required to configure the Microsoft DNS Server is to create a zone and a reverse lookup zone for your domain. Follow these steps to create these zones:

1. From the Start menu, choose Programs, Administrative Tools (Common), and DNS Manager to run the DNS Manager (see Figure 18.49).

FIG. 18.49

Configuring and managing the Microsoft DNS Server with the DNS Manager application.

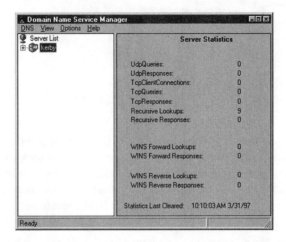

2. In the left pane, click the name of the DNS server that you want to configure to highlight it. Choose New Zone from the DNS menu to start the Creating New Zone Wizard (see Figure 18.50).

FIG. 18.50

Specifying whether this DNS server will be primary or secondary.

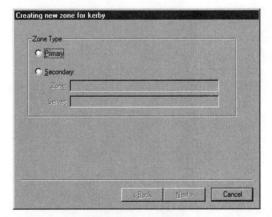

3. Select Primary to configure this DNS server as the primary DNS server for this zone, or select Secondary if you've already configured another DNS server as the primary DNS server for this zone. If you select Secondary, enter values for the primary DNS server in the Zone and Server text boxes. Click Next to display the second screen of the Creating New Zone Wizard (see Figure 18.51).

Part

IV

Ch

18

FIG. 18.51

Entering the name of the DNS zone and the file name where DNS data will be stored.

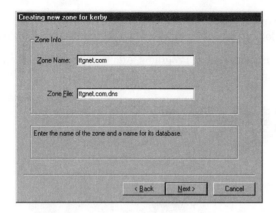

4. Enter the Zone Name. If you're connected to the Internet, use the domain name that InterNIC assigned. If you're running a private TCP/IP network and haven't registered a domain name with InterNIC, use any descriptive name here. By default, DNS Manager fills in the Zone File text box by appending .dns to the zone name you provide. Accept this file name, or enter a new file name. Click Next to continue.

   The Creating New Zone Wizard displays a message to tell you that you've provided all the necessary information. Click Finish to create the new zone and return to the main screen of DNS Manager, which is now updated to include the information you provided, as well as information that the Creating New Zone Wizard generated (see Figure 18.52).

FIG. 18.52

The required 0, 127, and 255 in-addr reverse lookup DNS files generated by the Creating New Zone Wizard.

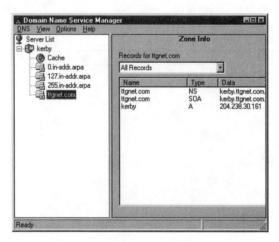

5. Create a reverse lookup zone that corresponds to the zone you just created by repeating steps 1 through 4, but name the zone by using reverse lookup conventions (see Figure 18.53).

FIG. 18.53
Creating a reverse
lookup zone that
corresponds to the
zone just created.

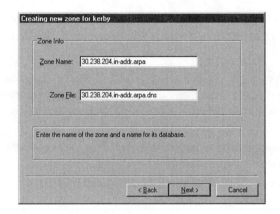

Adding Resource Records   The information in the DNS database is stored in *resource records*.
Broadly speaking, there are two types of resource records:

- *Host DNS resource records* store information about host names and IP addresses. The
  two primary host DNS resource record types are the A record, which maps the host
  name to its associated IP address, and the PTR record, which maps an IP address to its
  associated host name. The A record is used to resolve normal queries, the PTR record to
  resolve reverse lookup queries.

- Optional *non-host resource records* store various supplementary information about the
  DNS environment. For example, the CNAME record is used to create an alias for a host.
  If the host kerby.ttgnet.com, whose IP address is 204.238.30.161, also needs to be known
  as www.ttgnet.com, the administrator can create a CNAME record to map the alias
  www.ttgnet.com to the true host name, kerby.ttgnet.com.

These two types of DNS resource records are added and maintained by using different steps.

Adding Host DNS Resource Records   The Microsoft DNS Server makes it much easier to
create and maintain host DNS resource records than do traditional UNIX-based DNS servers.
Any host on your network that's DHCP- or WINS-enabled registers itself automatically with the
Microsoft DNS Server. Still, you probably need to manually create at least a few host DNS
resource records to register your UNIX hosts, NetWare servers, and other non-Microsoft hosts
with the DNS Server. To add host DNS resource records, follow these steps:

1. From DNS Manager, highlight the zone name for which you want to add a host DNS
   resource record. Choose New Host from the DNS menu to display the New Host dialog
   (see Figure 18.54).

FIG. 18.54
Manually creating a
host DNS resource
record for a non-
Microsoft host in the
New Host dialog.

Part
IV
Ch
18

2. Enter the machine name in the Host Name text box (don't include domain name information in this text box). Type the IP address for this host in the Host IP Address text box.

N O T E The New Host dialog is used to create an A resource record for a host. When creating A resource records, you almost always want to create the corresponding PTR reverse lookup records at the same time. DNS Manager does this for you automatically, as long as two conditions are true:

- You must have already created the reverse lookup zone file described in the preceding section.
- You must have marked the Create Associated PTR Record check box in the New Host dialog. ■

3. If you need to add multiple host resource records, click Add Host to save the record and display an empty New Host dialog. After you finish adding host resource records, click Done to save the final record and return to DNS Manager.

Adding Non-Host DNS Resource Records Non-host resource records aren't strictly necessary for DNS to operate. However, you'll probably want to create at least a few non-host DNS resource records to extend the capabilities of your DNS server and to make it easier to maintain. To add non-host DNS resource records, follow these steps:

1. From DNS Manager, highlight the zone name for which you want to add a host DNS resource record. Choose New Record from the DNS menu to display the New Resource Record dialog (see Figure 18.55).

FIG. 18.55

Creating a non-host DNS resource record in the New Resource Record dialog.

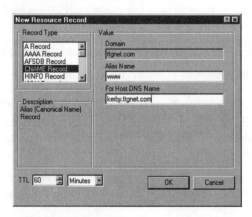

2. Use the Record Type scrolling list to choose a record type. The text boxes in the Value section vary according to the type of record you select. Complete the text boxes as required, and click OK to save the new non-host DNS resource record.

N O T E Configuring any DNS server is non-intuitive, to say the least. Although the Microsoft DNS Server is easier to configure and use than most, space constraints in this book prevent coverage of any but the most essential aspects of DNS server configuration and operation. ▦

Sharing Windows NT Files with UNIX

The Windows NT TCP/IP core protocols and utilities provide only FTP as a means to share files between Windows NT and a UNIX or other TCP/IP host. Windows NT Server implements FTP in both client and server versions. Similarly, virtually every UNIX implementation includes an FTP client and an FTP server. It's common, however, for workstations running operating systems other than UNIX to have only FTP client software.

Although FTP is the primary method for copying files between TCP/IP hosts, problems can occur when transferring files between systems with dissimilar file systems. The FTP protocol has built-in translation schemes that work well for common text and unstructured binary files. However, some systems, such as minicomputers and mainframes, have complex file systems and use file formats that might not successfully transfer between unlike systems.

Although you can use FTP to copy files between UNIX and Windows NT Server hosts, this manual process does nothing to provide a shared file system between the hosts. Clearly, something more is needed if Windows clients are to have real-time access to files stored on a UNIX host. Three methods are available for such access:

- *Network File System (NFS)*, a Sun Microsystems product, is complicated to administer and requires that you buy additional software for your Windows NT server. NFS, however, does provide bidirectional access, allowing UNIX clients to access files stored on a Windows NT server as well as allowing Microsoft clients to access files stored on UNIX hosts.

- *Microsoft LAN Manager for UNIX (LMU)* adds the protocol support needed to allow UNIX hosts to participate in Microsoft Networking by using the SMB protocol. LMU is another complex product to administer and is relatively expensive.

- *SAMBA* is a free product that runs on your UNIX host, allowing it to emulate a Microsoft LAN Manager server. Microsoft clients see a UNIX host running SAMBA as just another Microsoft Networking server and can access files stored on the UNIX file system as though the files were located on an actual Microsoft Networking server. SAMBA is essentially unidirectional, however, and provides only limited batch-mode access via SMBCLIENT for UNIX clients to files that reside on a Windows NT Server volume.

Using Network File System Sun Microsystems, a leading supplier of UNIX workstations and servers, developed the NFS specification and published it in RFC 1094. NFS is now the *de facto* file server protocol implemented on UNIX systems. Since its original inception, NFS has evolved into NFS version 3 as detailed in RFC 1813. The NFS architecture is designed to be independent of the operating system, file system, and transport protocol used. NFS is built on top of the Remote Procedure Call (RPC) API described in RFC 1057. RPC, an interprocess network messaging protocol, allows networking software developers to port NFS to a wide variety of hardware platforms and operating system environments.

NFS, like FTP, is a client/server protocol. Unlike FTP, NFS provides transparent shared access to remote files across a network. A primary design consideration of an NFS server is to have the minimum possible impact on the host machine. In contrast to a NetWare server, an NFS server uses *stateless* protocols. (Stateless means that an NFS server maintains no information about the NFS clients it serves.) The NFS protocol burdens the client with maintaining the connection to the NFS server and requires that the client ensure the integrity of the trans-actions. If, for example, an NFS server crashes, the NFS client must remount the shared files after the server is rebooted.

Microsoft doesn't supply NFS software for Windows NT Server. Several third-party NFS products are available from companies such as Hummingbird Communications, Intergraph, NetManage, and Process Software. These and other NFS products provide NFS services only to the Windows NT host. Windows NT Server clients can't access NFS imported file systems unless NFS software is first installed on the individual clients.

Using Microsoft LAN Manager for UNIX to Add Microsoft Networking Support to UNIX Hosts   LMU allows UNIX hosts to participate in a Microsoft Networking environment. Microsoft licensed LMU to AT&T, which has in turn relicensed LMU to other UNIX vendors. LMU implementations are available for different UNIX flavors, both directly from UNIX vendors (for example, SCO Microsoft LAN Manager for SCO Systems) and from third-party vendors (for example, Unipress Software Microsoft LAN Manager for UNIX).

LMU adds support for the SMB protocol to UNIX hosts. The SMB protocol, developed by Microsoft, IBM, and Intel, is the foundation used for interoperability by all Microsoft Network-ing products. SMB corresponds in function to the NetWare Core Protocol (NCP) used by Novell NetWare. In addition to Windows NT Server, LMU is compatible with Microsoft OS/2 LAN Manager, Microsoft Windows for Workgroups, IBM LAN Server, MS-DOS LAN Manager, DEC PATHWORKS, 3Com 3+Open, and MS-NET.

Installing the SMB protocol on a UNIX host allows interoperability between UNIX and Windows NT Server and its clients. It's possible to install LMU on just one UNIX host, which then shares NFS imported file systems with a Windows NT server and its clients. This process incurs additional overhead for the NFS-to-SMB gateway and slows performance, although doing so may be a cost-effective alternative to buying multiple copies of LMU for lightly accessed UNIX hosts.

Using SAMBA to Allow UNIX Hosts to Emulate Windows NT Server   An alternative to pur-chasing LMU is to install the freely available SMB software SAMBA. Installing the SAMBA suite of programs on your UNIX host allows your Microsoft Networking clients to access UNIX files and printers as though they were resources on a Windows NT server.

ON THE WEB

SAMBA's home page is located at **http://lake.canberra.edu.au/pub/samba/samba.html**.

Originally developed by Andrew Tridgell, SAMBA has since been enhanced and extended with input from "net gurus" all over the world. SAMBA includes the following major components:

- *smbd* is the SMB server itself, which provides the core SMB support needed to handle client connections.
- *smbclient* is the client program run on the UNIX host.
- *smb.conf* is the SAMBA configuration file.
- *nmbd* is the NetBIOS name server, used to allow clients to locate servers.

SAMBA is officially supplied in source code form only, although user-contributed compiled versions (binaries) for most UNIX platforms can be found on the Internet. SAMBA is freely modifiable and may be distributed under the GPL. Make files are available for compiling binaries for a large number of UNIX variants, detailed in Table 18.2. SAMBA source code can be downloaded via anonymous FTP from **nimbus.anu.edu.au**, in the directory /pub/tridge/samba.

Table 18.2   SAMBA-Supported UNIX Implementations

SunOS	HP-UX	SCO
A/UX 3.0	Intergraph	SEQUENT
AIX	ISC SVR3V4 (POSIX mode)	SGI
Apollo Domain/OS sr10.3 (BSD4.3)	Linux	SOLARIS
BSDI	Net BSD	SunOS
Data General UX	NeXT	SVR4
Free BSD	OSF1	ULTRIX

Part
IV

Ch
18

Building Universal Clients for Microsoft Windows NT, Novell NetWare, and UNIX

As this chapter demonstrates, PCs running Microsoft client software can be provided with access to NetWare server resources, but with some limitations. Similarly, workstations running Novell NetWare client software can be provided with access to Windows NT Server resources by running the GSNW or the File and Print Service for NetWare on your Windows NT server. Here again, some restrictions apply, particularly for those who run NetWare 4.x servers.

The explosion of the Internet and of the use of TCP/IP for internetworking also makes TCP/IP client support very desirable. As a result, what many organizations need is a standardized PC client software configuration that simultaneously provides full support for Windows NT Server, NetWare, and UNIX, and does so with a high degree of stability while consuming minimum conventional workstation memory.

As discussed in Chapter 11, "Configuring Windows 95 Clients for Networking," using Windows 95 as your client operating system minimizes or eliminates the problems of dealing with base memory limitations. Windows 95 used with a supported NIC provides protocol support and redirection services with 32-bit drivers. Such drivers eliminate the base memory footprint while providing client services for Microsoft Networking, NetWare, and TCP/IP. Although Windows 95, as shipped, doesn't support NDS on NetWare 4.x servers, both Microsoft and Novell have 32-bit client software that does support NDS available for free downloading via the Internet, MSDL (Microsoft Download service), or NetWire.

Another alternative is to use more than one redirector or shell with multiple protocol stacks on the clients. NetWare and Windows NT Server both support DOS, Windows, Windows for Workgroups, Windows 95, Windows NT, OS/2, and Macintosh clients. Some NetWare system managers have an almost religious aversion to implementing multiple protocol stacks on their client workstations, let alone multiple redirectors.

These NetWare administrators had good reason to be wary in the past. The 640K limitation on base memory inherent to Intel-based PCs running in real mode made for a tight fit. When DOS, the network protocol drivers, and the NetWare shell were loaded, often not enough memory was left to run large applications, let alone enough to consider adding one or more additional protocol stacks and network shells. Modern client operating systems such as MS-DOS 6.x, Windows for Workgroups 3.11, and Windows 95 have dramatically simplified the problem of cramming the network software into base memory and have made running dual protocol stacks and redirectors a realistic alternative.

The quest for such a universal client continues, and a perfect solution doesn't yet exist. If, however, like most LAN administrators, you find that most of your clients are running Windows for Workgroups or Windows 95, it's straightforward to configure either of these client operating systems to provide simultaneous support for Windows NT Server, TCP/IP, and NetWare.

Configuring Windows for Workgroups 3.11 as a Universal Client

Windows for Workgroups 3.11 provides native networking support only for Windows Networking. It can, however, be used as a foundation on which to build a universal network client by using inexpensive or free utilities for TCP/IP and NetWare connectivity. Configuring Windows for Workgroups as a universal client requires the following:

- *Windows Networking support* enabled within Windows for Workgroups
- *NetWare support* provided by installing the ODI drivers and NetWare client software available from Novell, and then enabling NetWare support within Windows for Workgroups
- *TCP/IP support* provided by installing a Winsock-compliant stack, available from Microsoft or third parties
- *Windows Packet Driver support* provided by installing ODIPKT.COM and WINPKT.COM, available via anonymous FTP from **ftp.cica.indiana.edu** in the /pub/pc/win3/winsock directory

Installing Windows Network Support   Chapter 12, "Connecting Other PC Clients to the Network," fully describes how to install Windows Networking support for Windows for Workgroups 3.11.

N O T E   Remember that although Windows for Workgroups provides the client software needed to access your Windows NT Server, you must still purchase a client access license for each computer that does so. ▦

Installing Novell NetWare Support   To add support for NetWare, use the client software provided by Novell. The client software, packaged as several self-extracting archive files named VLMKIT*.EXE, can be downloaded via anonymous FTP from **ftp.novell.com** or via the CompuServe NetWire forum, or can be purchased on disk directly from Novell. The VLM client software is free if your Novell server is version 3.12 or higher and is available at a nominal charge if you use NetWare 3.11 servers.

Installing TCP/IP Support   Adding a TCP/IP protocol stack to Windows for Workgroups is done by installing software written to the Windows Sockets specification, commonly referred to as *Winsock*. Following are some Winsock implementations available from various sources, ranging in cost from free to quite expensive:

- Microsoft distributes a free Winsock implementation for Windows for Workgroups. You can use the version included in the \CLIENTS\TCP32WFW directory on the distribution CD. You also can download the archive TCPIP32B.EXE from the Microsoft Download Service (206-936-6735) or via anonymous FTP at **ftp.microsoft.com**. Earlier versions of this product experienced compatibility and stability problems, but the version on the Windows NT Server distribution CD and the version now posted for download work reliably. Microsoft's Winsock implementation is unique in its support for both DHCP and Microsoft Networking over TCP/IP.

- Various inexpensive shareware Winsock implementations—most notably, Peter Tattam's Trumpet Winsock—can be downloaded via anonymous FTP at **ftp.trumpet.com.au** in the /ftp/pub/winsock directory, as well as from many BBSes. These shareware implementations vary widely in quality, features, and bundled applications. The best of them, like Trumpet, are both inexpensive—at $20 a seat or so—and reliable.

- Many commercial Winsock implementations are available, although this market appears to be rapidly shrinking due both to the availability of inexpensive shareware versions and the bundling of TCP/IP support in Windows 95. Commercial Winsock vendors have tried to fight back by bundling various TCP/IP applications with their products—FTP clients, newsreaders, and so forth—but better applications are available for free on the Internet, and these products remain expensive at $50 to $200 per seat.

Pick one Winsock implementation and use it for all your Windows for Workgroups clients. There's seldom any reason to look further than Microsoft's free Winsock software. Consider Trumpet Winsock and similar products only if you need telephone dialer support. Consider commercial Winsock implementations only if you need specialized features not available with the free or inexpensive products.

Installing Packet Driver Support   The next step is to install packet driver support to enable the ODI NIC drivers and Windows itself to handle packets properly. Two programs are universally used to provide these functions in Windows 3.1x installations: ODIPKT handles the ODI packet interface tasks, and WINPKT handles the Windows packet interface duties.

ODIPKT   ODIPKT is used to provide packet driver support to the Novell ODI NIC drivers. The current version of ODIPKT.COM can be downloaded via anonymous FTP from any Web site or BBS with a Winsock area.

ODIPKT allows a single NIC running ODI to service multiple packet driver protocol stacks, including IPX/SPX and TCP/IP. ODIPKT supports Ethernet, Token Ring, and ARCnet frames.

ODI supports multiple frame types simultaneously on a single physical NIC. Because the frame types typically used with NetWare to transport IPX/SPX packets aren't appropriate to transport TCP/IP packets, it's common to see a single NIC in a NetWare workstation bound to two frame types, such as Ethernet II for TCP/IP, and Novell Ethernet 802.3 or 802.2 for IPX/SPX. One or more frame types are specified for each physical NIC in the NET.CFG file. Each frame type is seen by ODI as a separate logical NIC. The following NET.CFG fragment illustrates a typical configuration:

```
Link Driver NE2000
port 300
int 10
FRAME Ethernet_II
FRAME Ethernet_802.3
```

The first three lines name the link driver and specify that the physical Ethernet card is located at address 300 and interrupt 10. The final two lines bind the Ethernet_II frame type appropriate for UNIX as logical board 0 and the Ethernet_802.3 frame type used for IPX/SPX as logical board 1.

ODIPKT depends on buffers supplied by the ODI link support layer (LSL). Make sure that your NET.CFG specifies enough buffers of a size large enough to support your NIC. For example, 1,514-byte Ethernet frames on a NIC that supports multiple buffers causes your NET.CFG to contain the following:

```
Link Support
        BUFFERS 2 1600
```

This tells LSL to reserve two buffers, each of 1,600 bytes.

ODIPKT.COM is typically loaded by STARTNET.BAT and requires only two command-line arguments—one that specifies the logical board number, and one that specifies the software interrupt, or vector, to be used, which is specified as a decimal number. A typical STARTNET.BAT fragment might look something like the following:

```
lsl
3c5x9
odipkt 0 96
winpkt 0x60
ipxodi
vlm /mx
```

The first line loads the LSL portion of ODI. The second loads the packet driver version of the 3Com 3C509 Multiple Link Interface Driver (MLID). The third loads ODIPKT to support logical board 0 at software interrupt 96 decimal. The fourth line loads WINPKT (described in the following section) and specifies software interrupt 0x60 hexadecimal. (Note that 96 decimal corresponds to 0x60 hexadecimal.) The fifth line loads IPX support for NetWare, and the sixth line loads the NetWare VLM client software into extended memory. ODIPKT must be loaded after LSL.COM and the MLID, but it must be loaded before WINPKT.

WINPKT WINPKT is a shim that provides packet support for Windows. The current version of WINPKT.COM can be downloaded via Internet anonymous FTP from any Web site or BBS with a Winsock area.

WINPKT takes only one command-line argument, which is the software interrupt used by ODIPKT. Make sure that both ODIPKT and WINPKT are using the same software interrupt.

N O T E ODIPKT uses decimal notation; WINPKT uses hexadecimal notation. ■

Using Windows 95 as a Universal Client

Windows 95 is an ideal universal network client. Used with a supported NIC, Windows 95 can provide simultaneous connectivity to Windows NT Server, NetWare, UNIX, and SNA servers, using supplied 32-bit drivers and occupying nearly no conventional memory. The only drawback to using Windows 95 as a client is that, as shipped, the NetWare client software doesn't support NDS. When the first edition of this book was written, beta versions of 32-bit NetWare drivers with NDS support were just becoming available from both Microsoft and Novell. Microsoft and Novell have both now released production versions of their 32-bit clients for Windows 95. For full information on how to configure Windows 95 as a universal network client, see Chapter 11, "Configuring Windows 95 Clients for Networking."

N O T E Although Windows 95 provides client functionality for Windows NT Server, you must purchase a client access license for each computer that uses Windows 95 to access your Windows NT server. ■

Migrating from Novell NetWare to Windows NT Server

Windows NT Server includes a superb set of tools to help it coexist with Novell NetWare servers, but Microsoft wants you to replace your NetWare servers with servers running Windows NT. Having seen other NOSes, including some of their own earlier efforts, fall by the wayside as a result of trying to compete head-on with NetWare, Microsoft wisely has avoided attempting the brute-force method with Windows NT Server 4.0. Instead, Microsoft has cleverly positioned Windows NT Server 4.0 as a product that easily coexists with NetWare.

Few independent analysts question that Windows NT Server 4.0 is an even match for NetWare 4.1. Although Novell continues to trumpet the advantages of its NetWare Directory Services over the domain-based directory services model used by Windows NT Server, the reality is that either method works well for most organizations. Also, the method by which Windows NT

Server provides application server functions is recognized by most observers as being superior both in concept and in execution to the NLM-based method used by Novell.

What has kept other NOSes (some with unquestionable advantages) from replacing NetWare on a wholesale basis is NetWare's installed base. No one seriously questions that NetWare 3.1x is an obsolescent NOS, eclipsed in power and features by Windows NT Server and other modern NOSes, including NetWare 4.x. Yet the fact remains that only recently have new shipments of NetWare 4.x licenses exceeded those of new NetWare 3.12 licenses. The installed NetWare 3.1x base predominates and is expected to continue its dominant role for some time to come. Even NetWare 2.x has a substantial and continuing presence.

The reason for the continuing dominance of earlier versions of NetWare is quite simple. Like an old shoe, NetWare 2.x/3.x is comfortable. For every NetWare 4.x expert available, a dozen technicians and consultants know the earlier versions of NetWare inside and out. For every true Windows NT Server expert, you find perhaps 100 NetWare gurus. Although this situation is starting to change, many network administrators still find comfort in using the old familiar NetWare 2.x/3.1x.

Recognizing this inertia factor, Microsoft has taken an intelligent approach by positioning Windows NT Server as a product that can coexist peacefully in a NetWare shop and do useful things well that NetWare does poorly or not at all. This guerrilla marketing strategy is beginning to pay off, as LAN administrators, bringing up their first Windows NT Server, quickly realize that Windows NT Server was never anything to be afraid of in the first place.

Whether you plan incremental replacement of NetWare servers with Windows NT Server 4.0, wholesale replacement, or simply continuing coexistence, you should become familiar with the Microsoft Migration Tool for NetWare (see Figure 18.56). This tool automates the process of moving files, directories, file attribute and rights, and user and group account information from an existing NetWare server to a Windows NT server.

The Migration Tool for NetWare can be used in several ways. Following are some of the things you can do:

- Migrate the contents of a single NetWare server to a single Windows NT server.
- Migrate the contents of two or more NetWare servers to a single Windows NT server, combining and merging the contents of the NetWare servers during the process.
- Migrate the contents of two or more NetWare servers to two or more Windows NT servers, relocating and distributing the contents of the NetWare servers as you choose among the Windows NT servers.

Using the Migration Tool for NetWare results in no changes whatsoever to the NetWare server and can be done without taking down either the NetWare server or the Windows NT server. All services on both the NetWare server and the Windows NT server continue to be available to users during the migration process.

FIG. 18.56

The Migration Tool for NetWare, which allows you to migrate Novell NetWare users and groups to Windows NT Server.

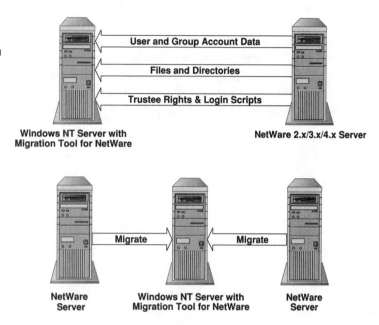

The Migration Tool for NetWare offers the option to do a trial migration, allowing you to test the results of a migration before actually making any changes to either server. Potential conflicts, such as duplicate user names, are highlighted during this trial migration process, allowing you to resolve them before doing the actual migration.

From Here...

If you're integrating Windows NT Server 4.0 into an existing PC network, the odds are that your present network is running Novell NetWare. Thus, the first part of this chapter covered Windows NT's Gateway Services for NetWare, File and Print Services for NetWare, and Directory Services Manager for NetWare. UNIX networks running TCP/IP are commonly used by medium- to large-sized firms, so a substantial part of this chapter was devoted to integrating Windows NT 4.0 with UNIX networks. The chapter closed with detailed recommendations for creating universal Windows 3.1+ and Windows 95 clients for Microsoft Windows NT, NetWare, and UNIX networking, as well as a brief discussion of migrating from NetWare to Windows NT networking.

The following chapters contain information related to the content of this chapter:

- Chapter 4, "Choosing Network Protocols," explains how to select one or more of the three principal networking protocols supported by Windows NT based on your network configuration.

- Chapter 10, "Using TCP/IP, WINS, and DHCP," shows you how to plan for and implement TCP/IP networking, including use of the Windows Internet Name Service and Dynamic Host Configuration Protocol.

Part
IV

Ch
18

■ Chapter 11, "Configuring Windows 95 Clients for Networking," shows you how to set up PCs running Windows 95 to take maximum advantage of Windows NT 4.0 networks, including the use of server-based desktop configurations and policies.

■ Chapter 12, "Connecting Other PC Clients to the Network," provides the details on setting up Windows 3.1+, Windows for Workgroups 3.1+, Windows NT Workstation 4.0, and Macintosh clients to communicate with Windows NT 4.0 servers.

CHAPTER 19

Managing Remote Access Service

Rising sales of laptop and notebook computers for mobile computing, combined with continuing growth in the number of telecommuting workers, makes remote access to computer networks a necessity. Most of today's mobile PC users are limited to Dial-Up Networking (DUN) over a 28.8 kbps modem connection, which can be agonizingly slow. Although 56 kbps modems claim faster downstream delivery, the lack of an international 56 kbps standard worries prospective purchasers. Future implementation of wireless Personal Communication Services (PCS) promises to deliver increased bandwidth without the need for a wired POTS (plain old telephone service) connection. Telecommuters now can take advantage of the increased bandwidth of relatively low-cost ISDN connections. Those lucky enough to participate in trials of cablemodem and xDSL (various high-speed digital telco subscriber line systems) implementations get DUN at T-1's 1.44 Mbps or better, at least in the downstream (receiving) direction.

Installing RAS Dial-Up Networking

Windows NT Server 4.0's Add New Modem feature leads you step by step through the DUN setup process.

Installing and testing RAS clients

Making connections with Windows NT or Windows 95 clients to the RAS server is as simple as establishing an Internet connection.

Monitoring RAS connections

Windows NT Server's Remote Access Admin application lets you monitor and manage RAS servers, as well as remote client connections.

Using PPTP to create virtual private networks

Point-to-Point Tunneling Protocol encrypts your wide area network traffic to assure security.

Taking advantage of Resource Kit RAS utilities

The *Windows NT Server Resource Kit* includes the Raslist.exe and Rasuser.exe command-line utilities and a demonstration version of a third-party graphical Remote Access Manager.

Windows NT Server 4.0's Remote Access Service (RAS) and DUN represents a substantial improvement over the Windows NT 3.51 implementation. Windows NT 4.0 finally supports 32-bit TAPI (Telephony API) 2.0 and the Unimodem driver, both of which originated in Windows 95. TAPI 2.0 brings a client/server architecture to Windows telephony, which makes setting up and administering RAS and DUN a relatively easy task. Even in otherwise NetWare-only environments, Windows NT Server 4.0 is likely to carve a niche as a dedicated RAS server because of its relatively low cost and capability to support up to 255 simultaneous RAS connections.

Windows 95 is likely to remain the client operating system of choice for most mobile PC users because of Windows 95's better support for PC Cards and its battery-saving power-management features. Most telecommuters will continue to use Windows 95 at home because of Plug and Play modem installation, legacy hardware support, and lesser resource requirements than Windows NT Workstation 4.0. The emphasis of this chapter is on conventional analog modem and ISDN connections for RAS; a brief description of new digital technologies for telecommuters appears near the end of this chapter. ■

Touring the New Communications Features of Windows NT Server 4.0

Windows NT Server 4.0 provides the following new telecommunications features, most of which are derived from earlier Windows 95 implementations:

■ *TAPI* is one of Microsoft's recent additions to WOSA, the Windows Open Services Architecture. TAPI 2.0's architecture is based on 32-bit telephony service providers, such as Unimodem, that plug into the TAPI framework. (Windows NT 4.0 now doesn't support the voice features of Windows 95's Unimodem/V upgrade.) Later, the section "Understanding TAPI 2.0" describes the structure and technical features of TAPI 2.0.

N O T E TAPI 2.1, in the beta-testing stage when this book was written, is expected to be included in Windows NT 5.0. TAPI 2.1's new features are more significant to client/server telephony applications, such as call centers, than to RAS. ■

■ *Autodial and Log-on Dial* are client features that let you map an association between a DUN entry and a network address for access to files. As in Windows 95, when you double-click a file icon in Explorer and the file isn't accessible on the network, a pop-up window asks whether you want to connect via DUN.

■ *Restartable file copy* eliminates the frustration of having to start file downloads from scratch after interruption of a RAS connection. Restartable file copy remembers the status of an interrupted file transmission; when you reconnect, RAS sends only the missing part of the file.

- *Idle disconnect* automatically terminates a RAS connection after a specified period of time of no communication activity.

- *PPP Multilink*, combined with *RAS Multilink*, lets you combine (bond) two or more physical communications links to increase RAS throughput when using TCP/IP to connect to the Internet or a private intranet. This feature primarily is useful for supporting multiple simultaneous ISDN connections. If you have a limited number of inbound ISDN lines, remote users can combine two B (bearer) channels for a 112 kbps connection when traffic is light and drop back to a single B channel as more remote users connect.

- *Point-to-Point Tunneling Protocol* (PPTP) lets you connect to your network via the Internet to save long-distance telephone charges. PPTP running on Windows NT Server 4.0 adds virtual private networking (VPN) support for Windows NT Workstation 4.0 clients. PPTP provides a secure connection through encryption of TCP/IP, IPX, and NetBEUI protocols. To take advantage of PPTP, your Internet service provider (ISP) must support PPTP.

With the exception of TAPI 2.0, which benefits Server and Workstation RAS implementations, the new communication features of Windows NT 4.0 primarily are directed to client-side communication. Microsoft's objective is to bring Windows NT Workstation 4.0's communication features up to the ease-of-use level of Windows 95. PPP Multilink and PPTP are Internet-specific technologies that are expected to play a more important role as the use of ISDN increases and more ISPs support PPTP.

Deciding on a Dial-Up Networking Architecture

Before you implement DUN via Windows NT RAS on a production basis, you must decide on the system architecture. Hardware and software requirements depend on the number of inbound lines you intend to support, as well as the method of connection of the hardware to your network. Following are the most common types of RAS architecture:

- *Single or multiple internal modems.* If you have enough ISA slots available on your RAS server and have a built-in PS/2 mouse port, you can install up to a total of four internal modems on COM1, COM2, COM3, and COM4, sharing interrupts IRQ4 (COM1 and COM3) and IRQ3 (COM2 and COM4). Users also can connect to individual modem-equipped client PCs on the network; the Windows 95 Plus! pack adds RAS server capabilities to clients. Figure 19.1 illustrates a Windows NT RAS server with two external modems and a Windows 95 client providing DUN services.

TIP Reliable interrupt sharing by modems depends on the make and model of the modems you install, plus the server's system BIOS and motherboard. (It's seldom practical to install more than two conventional internal modems in a server.) Some Plug and Play modems are difficult to install under Windows NT. Before you buy three or four modems, test two modems sharing IRQ3 or IRQ4 with simultaneous inbound connections. As a rule, you should avoid using internal modems for production RAS servers, because you must reboot the server if an internal modem hangs for any reason.

Part
IV

Ch
19

FIG. 19.1

A small DUN installation with Windows NT and Windows 95 RAS servers communicating with analog modems.

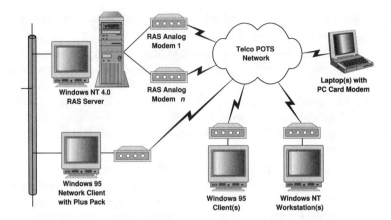

■ *Multiple external modems with multiport serial cards.* Multiport serial cards are the safest choice for providing more than two inbound connections. Relatively low-cost serial cards are available in four-port and eight-port versions. The modem configuration is the same as that shown in Figure 19.1. Some multiport serial cards have built-in microprocessors to minimize server CPU resources devoted to handling multiple connections.

You can use some multiport serial cards to connect to a combination of analog modems and external ISDN devices. Make sure that the supplier includes software that supports Windows NT 4.0 RAS.

 Make sure that the modems you buy support at least the new V.34 standard, which provides 33.6 kbps bandwidth. To take advantage of V.42-bis MNP 5 hardware data compression offered by most V.34 modems, be sure to buy modems for both ends of the connection from the same supplier. Hardware compression, which can increase data transmission rates by a factor of two or more, seldom works properly between modems from different vendors. U.S. Robotics Sportster V.34+ 28.8 kbps modems are used for the examples in this chapter. These modems usually (but not always) provide a 57.6 kbps connection, equivalent to a 1-B ISDN connection with an external ISDN adapter.

N O T E   There originally were three incompatible "standards" for 56 kbps modems: Rockwell Semiconductor Systems' K56Plus, Lucent Technologies' V.flex 2, and U.S. Robotics x2. Rockwell and Lucent joined forces to make their two approach compatible in a K56flex product line. Neither technology is likely to result in a 56 kbps data rate in both directions; upstream data rates are likely to range between 28.8 kbps and about 45 kbps. The International Telecommunications Union (ITU) isn't expected to finalize a global standard until mid-1998. Until there's an ITU standard for 56 kbps modems, adopting the Rockwell/Lucent or U.S. Robotics technology is a chancy proposition, at best. ■

■ *Internal or external ISDN terminal adapters.* External ISDN terminal adapters emulate analog modems, so you simply connect one or two external ISDN adapters to the server's serial port(s). External ISDN adapters provide slower connections because the serial protocol includes stop and start bits, which consume 20 percent of the available bandwidth. Internal ISDN adapters, which don't require stop and start bits, provide connections at the maximum ISDN data rate. Internal ISDN adapters installed in Intel-based servers can use the ISDN miniport driver that originated in Windows NT 3.5. Regardless of the type of ISDN adapter you select, verify that the device supports Windows NT 4.0 RAS before purchasing.

■ *ISDN Ethernet terminal adapters.* Simple ISDN Ethernet terminal adapters have an NT-2 ISDN and a 10BaseT Ethernet connector. You assign a NetBIOS name to the adapter, which emulates a server. Multiple users can share a single ISDN Ethernet adapter (with bridging) for outbound connections to an ISP offering ISDN service. As an example, the Ascend Pipeline-25Fx supports up to four users and has analog connections for a telephone and fax machine. One Ethernet adapter can support two 1-B inbound connections to a single telephone line provisioned as a hunt group.

■ *ISDN Routers.* ISDN routers provide IP and IPX routing in addition to bridging. Some ISDN Ethernet adapters offer IP or IPX routing as an option. The Ascend Pipeline-50, for instance, provides bridging for an unlimited number of users and supports IP and IPX routing, including PPP Multilink. ISDN routers are the best choice for handling high volumes of inbound ISDN traffic. High-end ISDN routers handle multiple BRI lines or a single PRI line, which provides 23 B channels and one D channel. U.S. Robotics' Total Control Enterprise Network Hub supports a combination of analog modems (in groups of four), ISDN adapters, switched-56 lines, and T-1 connections for up to 64 simultaneous connections. Figure 19.2 illustrates an Ethernet router that accommodates ISDN adapters and analog modems.

▶ **See** "Selecting an ISDN Connection," **p. 730**

Part
IV

Ch
19

FIG. 19.2

A combination ISDN and analog Ethernet router for DUN for telecommuters and mobile PC users.

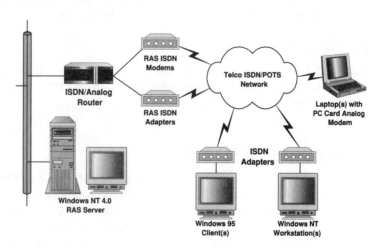

ON THE WEB

Ascend Communications, Inc., which claims to have more than 40 percent of the market for ISDN networking bridges and routers, offers an extensive glossary of ISDN terminology at **http://www. ascend.com/techdocs/glossary.html**. A U.S. Robotics white paper, "The Shape of the ISDN Market: 1996 and Beyond," at **http://www.usr.com/business/3022.html** offers an overview of ISDN technology for Internet and telecommuting applications.

Unless you need to support only a few mobile users or telecommuters, choose a multiple-port serial card and external modems for analog connections. You can add external 28.8/33.6 kbps modems and phone lines as traffic warrants. For ISDN connections, the trend is to ISDN routers because of their rapidly decreasing cost. If you plan to provide users with outbound ISDN connections to your ISP, be sure to install another line to support your telecommuters' inbound calls.

ON THE WEB

Microsoft's Get ISDN program for Windows 95 provides a simplified ordering system for installation of ISDN lines in North America. The details of the program are available at **http://www.microsoft.com/ windows/getisdn/**. Windows 95 clients using internal ISDN modems require the ISDN Accelerator Pack 1.1, which you can download from **http://www.microsoft.com/windows/getisdn/dload.htm**, and compatible version 1.1 drivers for your adapter. The ISDN Accelerator Pack isn't required for external ISDN adapters.

If you plan to support more than occasional use of DUN, you should dedicate a server to RAS. RAS is a more I/O- than CPU-intensive service, so a moderate-performance server will suffice for a few simultaneous connections at 28.8 or 33.6 kbps. Many network managers have resurrected obsolete 80486DX2 servers to establish small RAS systems.

ON THE WEB

Microsoft's "MS Windows NT Server Remote Access Planning" white paper, available at **http:// www.microsoft.com/syspro/technet/boes/winnt/technote/rasplan.htm**, provides hardware recommendations for various RAS scenarios.

Understanding TAPI 2.0

TAPI 2.0 is a 32-bit Windows NT service derived from TAPI version 1.4 introduced by Windows 95. It supports Intel and RISC symmetrical multiprocessing with multithreaded operation and preemptive multitasking. TAPI 2.0 supports Windows 95 32-bit TAPI 1.4 and Windows 3.1+ 16-bit TAPI 1.3 applications and includes additional features for managing communications applications that run in the background. It's designed to support various telephony services, including call-center management and quality of service (QoS) negotiation. The discussion in this chapter is limited to TAPI 2.0's RAS features.

Figure 19.3 illustrates the basic architecture of TAPI 2.0. TAPI.DLL provides core 16-bit telephony services for Windows 95 and Windows 3.1+. In Windows NT 4.0, TAPI.DLL is just a 16-bit thunking layer that converts 16-bit to the 32-bit addresses required by Windows NT 4.0's Tapi32.dll. Tapi32.dll takes advantage of LRPCs (lightweight remote procedure calls) to pass function requests to Tapisrv.exe. Tapisrv.exe runs as a service process in Tapisrv.exe's context, improving performance by eliminating context switching.

FIG. 19.3

The basic components of TAPI 2.0 that support 16-bit and 32-bit telephony services.

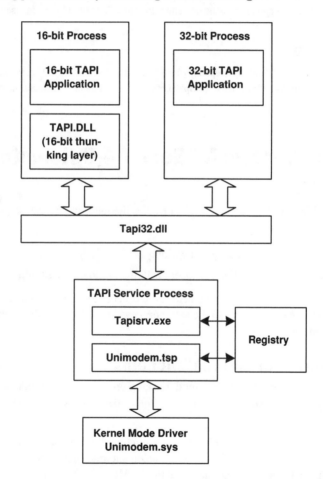

Figure 19.3 also shows the Unimodem TSP (Unimodem.tsp, a DLL) connected to Unimodem.sys, a kernel mode component that provides access to serial ports and internal modems. The Unimodem.tsp and Unimodem.sys components support analog modems and external ISDN adapters that emulate modems. The ISDN miniport driver, which originated in Windows NT 3.5, handles internal ISDN adapters.

Part

IV

Ch

19

Tapi32.dll also supports user interface elements, such as talk/hangup dialogs, designed by third-party TSP suppliers. Many independent software vendors (ISVs) provide fax, call center, and other TAPI services.

N O T E   If you update Windows NT Server 3.5x to Windows NT Server 4.0, installed internal or external modem(s) use the existing Modem.inf file and don't use TAPI 2.0's Unimodem driver. You must remove and reinstall the modem(s) to gain TAPI 2.0 and Unimodem support. ▧

ON THE WEB

A brief technical paper, "Windows Telephony (TAPI) Support in Windows NT 4.0," available at **http:// www.microsoft.com/win32dev/netwrk/tapiwp.htm**, provides additional technical details on TAPI 2.0.

Setting Up Windows NT Server 4.0 Remote Access Service

Setting up Windows NT Server 4.0 RAS involves the following overall steps:

- Install the modem(s)
- Configure RAS for Dial-Up Networking
- Enable dial-in connections for users with the Remote Access Admin application

The following sections describe the RAS setup process for a single analog modem shared by multiple DUN users. Changes to the setup process for multiple modems and ISDN adapters are noted where applicable.

Installing Internal or External Modems

Windows NT Server 4.0 includes a modem setup process similar to that of Windows 95. After you physically install one or more modems, follow these steps to set up the modem(s) for use with RAS:

1. In Control Panel, double-click the Modem tool. If this modem is the first installed on the server, the first Install New Modem dialog automatically appears (see Figure 19.4). If you're installing an additional modem, the Modems Properties sheet appears; click the Add button to display the Install New Modem dialog.

2. Click Next with the Don't Detect My Modem check box cleared to see whether Windows NT can detect your modem.

N O T E   The detection process may fail, even for modems with drivers included on the Windows NT Server 4.0 distribution CD-ROM, resulting in the dialog shown in Figure 19.5. Failure to detect supported modems might be the reason that Microsoft doesn't append "Wizard" to the Install New Modem dialog's caption. If the modem detection process succeeds, skip to step 5. ▧

FIG. 19.4
The first Install New Modem dialog.

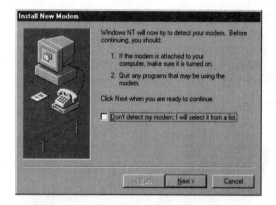

FIG. 19.5
A common response to Windows NT 4.0's attempt to detect a modem.

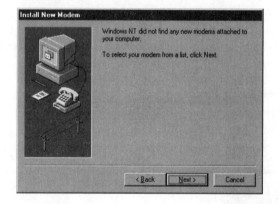

3. Click Next to display the dialog for selecting a modem manually. Select the vendor in the Manufacturers list, and then locate the product in the Models list (see Figure 19.6). If you can't find the model, click Have Disk to use the vendor's driver disk if it includes Windows NT 4.0 drivers. Otherwise, select (Standard Modem Types) in the Manufacturers list and your modem's speed in the Models list. In most cases, the Standard Modem driver works, but it may not implement special features of your modem, such as hardware data compression.

TIP Some external ISDN adapters, such as the Motorola BitSURFR, are supported with drivers included on the Windows NT Server 4.0 distribution CD-ROM. Vendors frequently update drivers for internal and external ISDN adapters, so the versions supplied with Windows NT Server 4.0 may not be the latest. Always check the vendor's Web site for recently updated drivers before installing an ISDN adapter.

FIG. 19.6

Selecting a modem
vendor and product
from Windows NT 4.0's
list of supported
modems.

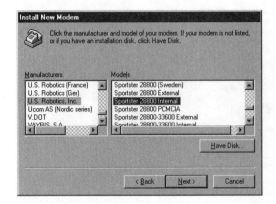

4. Click Next to specify the COM port on which to install the modem. Most modems are
   factory-configured for installation on COM2, so select the default COM2 entry in the list
   (see Figure 19.7). If you've specified a different COM port when configuring the modem,
   click the All Ports button to make a selection.

FIG. 19.7

Specifying the COM port
on which to install the
modem.

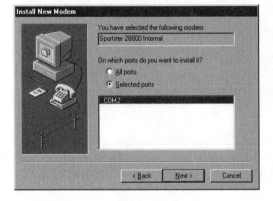

> **N O T E**   You add more COM ports and specify IRQ and base address settings with Control Panel's
> Port tool. ▪

5. Click Next to continue. The Modem Setup message box advises that you must restart
   the system for the modem to become operational. Click OK, but ignore the message;
   Windows NT automatically restarts during the RAS configuration process.

6. The final Install New Modem dialog indicates that modem installation is complete. Click
   Finish to display the Modems Properties sheet (see Figure 19.8), which supports entries
   for as many modems as you can install in the PC or connect to a multiport serial card.

FIG. 19.8
The Modems Properties sheet, with an entry for a single modem.

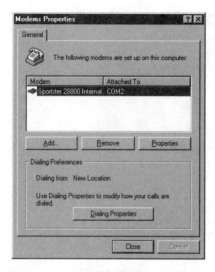

7. Click Properties to display the *Modem_Name* Properties sheet. The General page lets you determine the Speaker Volume (usually off for RAS use) and the Maximum Speed in bps (see Figure 19.9). Accept the default value for the modem (usually 57,600 bps) unless instructed otherwise.

FIG. 19.9
The General page of the selected modem's property sheet.

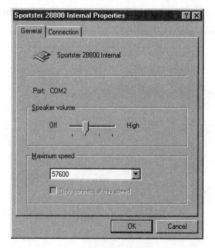

8. Click the Connection tab to display the Connection property page. The standard serial protocol for RAS is 8N1—8 data bits, no parity, and 1 stop bit (see Figure 19.10). Call preferences relate only to dial-out operations. RAS settings override the Disconnect a Call if Idle for More Than… setting specified in this dialog.

FIG. 19.10

The Connection page of the selected modem's property sheet.

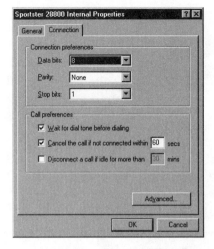

9. Click the Advanced button of the Connection page to display the Advanced Connection Settings dialog. If the modem supports V.42 MNP 2 through MNP 4 error control, the Use Error Control check box is enabled and marked by default. The Compress Data check box also is enabled and checked for modems that support V.42-bis MNP 5 data compression (see Figure 19.11). The default Use Flow Control setting and Hardware (RTS/CTS) option are satisfactory for all RAS connections to clients with modems manufactured in the last five years or so. To create a modem log file for troubleshooting purposes, mark the Record a Log File check box. Click OK to close the dialog, and then click OK to close the specified modem's property sheet and return to the Modems Properties sheet.

FIG. 19.11

The Advanced Connection Settings dialog for a V.34 modem supporting hardware error correction and data compression.

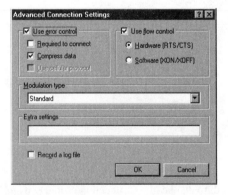

10. Click Dialing Properties to display the Dialing Properties sheet (see Figure 19.12). You need to set up these properties only if you plan to use the server to dial out. (Dialing out to an ISP or other remote server sometimes is useful for troubleshooting modem problems.) Click OK to close the property sheet.

FIG. 19.12

Supplying dial-out information in the Dialing Properties sheet.

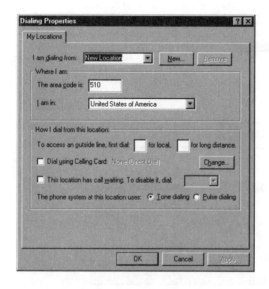

11. Click Close to close the Modems Properties sheet. A Modem Setup message box asks whether you want to configure DUN, the subject of the next section (see Figure 19.13). Click Yes to open the Remote Access Setup dialog.

FIG. 19.13

The message box leading to the configuration process for Dial-Up Networking.

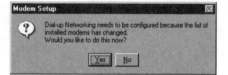

Part
IV

Ch
19

Configuring Dial-Up Networking

Before you can use the first or additional modems, you must configure DUN parameters. Any major changes to a modem's configuration require that you repeat the setup process. To set DUN parameters for a modem or ISDN adapter, follow these steps:

1. In the Remote Access Setup dialog, which lists all modems installed on the server (see Figure 19.14), select the modem to configure and click Configure to open the Configure Port Usage dialog.

N O T E   To open the Remote Access Setup dialog independently of the Install New Modem operation, launch Control Panel's Network tool, click the Services tab, and double-click the Remote Access Service item in the Network Services list. ■

2. In most cases, the default Port Usage option, Receive Calls Only, is satisfactory for a RAS server (see Figure 19.15). If you want to test your modem by dialing out, select the Dial Out and Receive Calls option. Click OK to close the dialog.

FIG. 19.14
The Remote Access Setup dialog with a single modem installed.

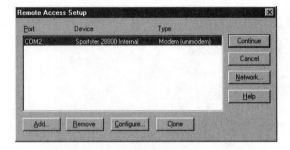

FIG. 19.15
Configuring the usage of the COM port on which the selected modem is installed.

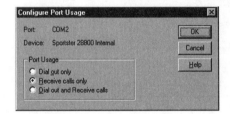

3. Click Network in the Remote Access Setup dialog to open the Network Configuration dialog for the selected modem. By default, RAS supports each of the basic networking protocols (NetBEUI, TCP/IP, and IPX) installed on your server. If you don't use the modem for dial-out, the Dial Out Protocols check boxes are disabled (see Figure 19.16). To provide secure transmission of passwords, accept the default Require Microsoft Encrypted Authentication option if all your clients run Windows and support MS-CHAP (Microsoft Challenge Handshake Authentication Protocol) authentication; otherwise, select Require Encrypted Authentication. You also can specify that data be secured with the RSA Data Security RC4 encryption algorithm by marking the Require Data Encryption check box. If you're installing an ISDN adapter that supports bonding of ISDN B channels, mark the Enable Multilink check box.

4. To configure NetBEUI services, click the Configure button next to the NetBEUI check box to open the RAS Server NetBEUI Configuration dialog. The default option is to allow dial-in clients to connect to the Entire Network (see Figure 19.17). Click OK to close the dialog.

N O T E Remote clients are likely to experience network browsing problems if you install only TCP/IP RAS on a network running WINS and DHCP. Adding NetBEUI (or IPX/SPX, if your remote clients use NetWare) usually solves the browsing problem. In a TCP/IP-only LAN, only the RAS server needs to support the additional protocol. ■

5. To configure TCP/IP services, click the adjacent Configure button to open the RAS Server TCP/IP Configuration dialog. Most RAS clients are configured to obtain a temporary TCP/IP address from the server. If you have DHCP (Dynamic Host Configuration Protocol) installed, select the Use DHCP to Assign Remote TCP/IP Client

Addresses option. If you haven't installed DHCP, select Use Static Address Pool. Specify beginning and ending addresses that provide a sufficient number of addresses to support the maximum number of inbound connections to the server plus a connection for the server itself (see Figure 19.18). The server occupies the first address—131.254.7.10 in Figure 19.18. The rest of the address range, 13.254.7.11 through 131.254.7.20, provides for a maximum of 10 simultaneously connected RAS/DUN clients.

▶ **See** "Implementing Dynamic Host Configuration Protocol," **p. 332**

FIG. 19.16

Setting allowable network protocols, encryption, and multilink options in the Network Configuration dialog.

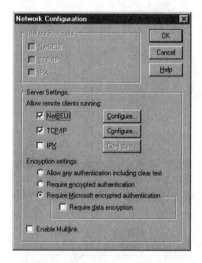

FIG. 19.17

Setting the extent of network access for the NetBEUI protocol.

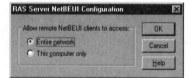

CAUTION

Marking the Allow Remote Clients to Request a Predetermined IP Address check box requires that you specify a fixed TCP/IP address for clients' dial-up adapters. Doing so might prevent the client from connecting to ISPs, such as The Microsoft Network, that assign temporary TCP/IP addresses to connected users.

N O T E The initial version of Windows NT Server 4.0's RAS server failed to release IP addresses from the static pool when clients disconnected. The problem is corrected in Windows NT Service Pack 2 (SP2) and higher. SP3 includes SP2 and hot-fix patches. ■

Part
IV

Ch
19

FIG. 19.18
Setting options for the TCP/IP protocol and assigning a static pool of TCP/IP addresses for RAS clients.

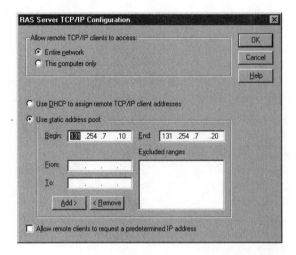

ON THE WEB

For more information on the static pool issue, go to **http://www.microsoft.com/kb/articles/q159/ 3/09.htm**. Service Pack 2 caused some regression problems with RAS dialout, which are corrected in patches that you can obtain from **ftp://ftp.microsoft.com/bussys/winnt/winnt-public/fixes/usa/ NT40/hotfixes-postsp2/ras-fix**. These problems are corrected by installing SP3.

6. Click OK to close the RAS Server TCP/IP Configuration dialog, click OK to close the Network Configuration dialog, and then click Continue in the Remote Access Setup dialog to install bindings for RAS services (see Figure 19.19, top). If you don't have DHCP installed, you receive the Error – Unattended Setup message box shown in Figure 19.19 (middle); click No to continue. When the binding process is complete, the Network Settings Change message box appears (see Figure 19.19, bottom). Click Yes to restart Windows NT Server with RAS operational.

N O T E   If you're installing multiple modems, you can avoid multiple server restarts by setting up all the modems, and then shutting down and restarting Windows NT Server. ■

Granting Client Access with the Remote Access Admin Application

After you set up RAS for DUN, you use the Remote Access Admin application to specify the users who can connect via RAS and control RAS operation. Follow these steps to enable clients to connect to your RAS server:

1. From the Start menu choose Programs, Administrative Tools, and Remote Access Admin to open the Remote Access Admin application, which connects to all RAS servers in your domain. Figure 19.20 shows the OAKLEAF domain with the OAKLEAF0 RAS server set up in the preceding section.

FIG. 19.19

RAS binding progress (top), a message received if DHCP isn't running (middle), and the message indicating the binding process is complete (bottom).

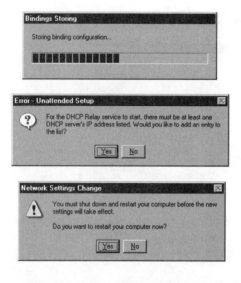

FIG. 19.20

The Remote Access Admin application's window, with a single RAS server in the default domain.

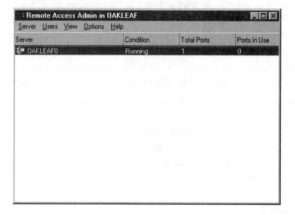

Part
IV
Ch
19

N O T E   If you have running on your RAS server a large number of services, such as the entire BackOffice suite, it might take up to a few minutes after rebooting for RAS to start. ■

2. From the Users menu choose Permissions to open the Remote Access Permissions dialog. Select a user in the Users list, which includes all domain and local users, and mark the check box to grant that user dial-in permission (see Figure 19.21). Alternatively, you can click the Grant All button to grant permission to all users, and then remove the permission from specific users, such as Guest. If you want to enable call-back for security or telco billing purposes, select Set By Caller or Preset To. If you select Set By Caller, a dialog appears when the client logs on, requesting a call-back number. If you select Preset To, type the client's telephone number (with area code) in the text box. You can add parentheses, hyphens, and spaces to make the entry more legible; the dialer ignores punctuation and white space.

FIG. 19.21
Granting dial-in permission to individual Windows NT Server users.

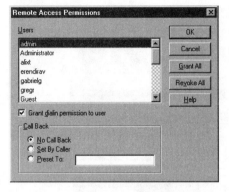

3. Click OK to close the dialog. Before you can test the RAS server, you must set up one or more DUN clients. Setting up Windows 95 and Windows NT clients for DUN is the subject of the following sections.

Installing and Testing Dial-Up Networking on Clients

Setting up DUN for Windows 95 and Windows NT clients, with a few exceptions, is a relatively straightforward process. Windows 95 offers the advantage of supporting Plug and Play for simplified modem installation, plus hot-swapping of modems and other PC Cards for laptops. The following sections assume that the clients have a modem installed and operating, but no entries for DUN.

> **N O T E** You install modems in Windows NT Workstation 4.0 by using the same method as that described earlier for Windows NT Server 4.0 in the "Installing Internal or External Modems" section, except that you specify the Dial-Out Only option in the Configure Port Usage dialog. ▪

Windows 95 Clients

Setting up and testing DUN on Windows 95 clients with a modem installed and tested involves the following steps:

1. From the Start menu choose Programs, Accessories, and Dial-Up Networking to open the Dial-Up Networking window (see Figure 19.22). Double-click the Make New Connection entry to open the first Make New Connection dialog.

2. Type a name for the client connection in the text box and select the modem to use, if more than one modem is installed (see Figure 19.23).

3. To gain a slight improvement in performance, click the Configure button to display the *Modem_Name* Properties sheet, and then display the Connection page (see Figure 19.24). Click Port Settings to open the Advanced Port Settings dialog, and set the Receive Buffer slider to High (see Figure 19.25). Click OK twice to close the dialog and the *Modem_Name* Properties sheet.

FIG. 19.22
Windows 95's Dial-Up Networking window with no DUN connections specified.

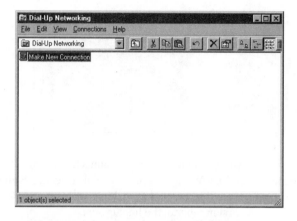

FIG. 19.23
Naming a connection and selecting a modem in the first Make New Connection dialog.

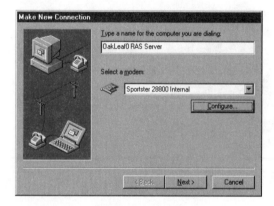

FIG. 19.24
The property sheet for a specific modem.

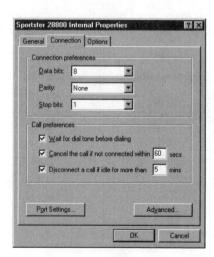

Part

IV

Ch

19

FIG. 19.25
Setting the Receive Buffer to maximum capacity to improve inbound data performance.

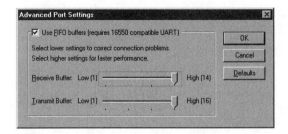

4. Click Next to display the second Make New Connection dialog. Type the area code and telephone number of the RAS server's modem, and select the country code, if necessary (see Figure 19.26). If the RAS server has multiple analog modems or ISDN adapters in a hunt group, use the first number of the hunt group.

FIG. 19.26
Entering the dialing parameters.

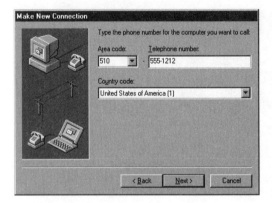

5. Click Next to display the last Make New Connection dialog to confirm the connection name (see Figure 19.27). Click Finish to add the connection to the Dial-Up Networking list.

FIG. 19.27
The last step in the Make New Connection sequence for Windows 95.

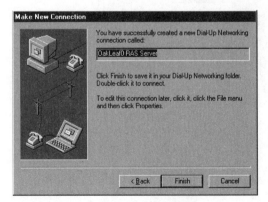

6. Right-click the new entry in the Dial-Up Networking list and choose Properties from the pop-up menu to display the *ConnectionName* Properties sheet. Click the Server Types button to display the Server Types dialog. Accept the default PPP: Windows 95, Windows NT 3.5, Internet entry in the Type of Dial-Up Server drop-down list. Mark all Advanced Options check boxes, and clear the Allowed Network Protocols check box for any protocol not supported by the server (see Figure 19.28).

FIG. 19.28

Setting additional connection properties in the Server Types dialog.

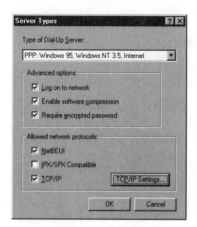

7. Click the TCP/IP Settings button to display the TCP/IP Settings dialog. Make sure that the Server Assigned IP Address and Server Assigned Name Server Address options are selected. (Specifying a TCP/IP address or a name server prevents connection, unless the RAS server is specifically set up to accommodate these client settings.) The Use IP Header Compression and Use Default Gateway on Remote Computer check boxes are marked by default (see Figure 19.29).

Part
IV

Ch
19

FIG. 19.29

Specifying conventional TCP/IP settings for DUN.

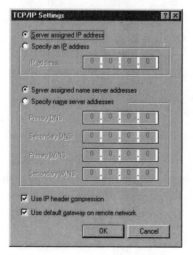

8. Click OK to close the TCP/IP Settings dialog, click OK to close the Server Types dialog, and then click OK again to close the *ConnectionName* Properties sheet.

9. If you must specify special dialing parameters, such as dialing 9 for an outside line, double-click the connection entry in the Dial-Up Networking window to display the Connect To dialog (see Figure 19.30). Click the Dial Properties button to open the Dialing Properties sheet (see Figure 19.31). Make any necessary changes and click OK to return to the Connect To dialog.

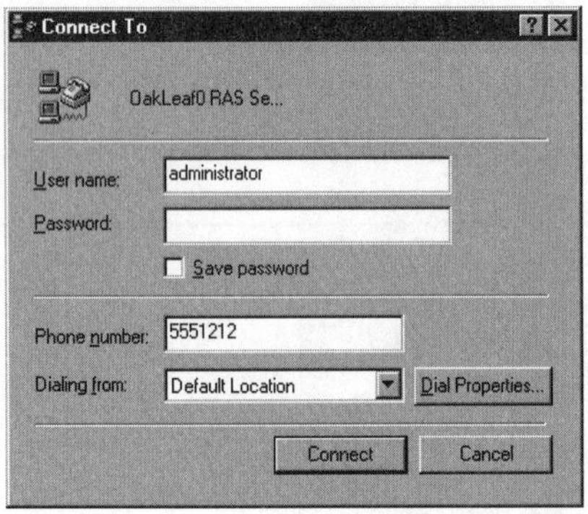

FIG. 19.30

The Connect To dialog with the setting specified in the Make New Connection sequence.

FIG. 19.31

Setting special dialing parameters for the RAS connection.

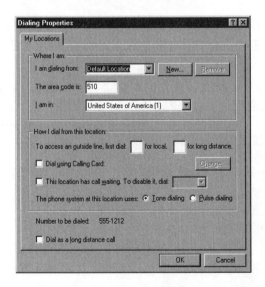

N O T E   If you're setting up a client that's connected to the network, logging off the network is a good idea at this point. Although you can use the same account to maintain a simultaneous network and RAS connection, testing RAS with only a dial-up connection is a more foolproof process. ▪

10. Type your user name, if necessary, and password in the Connect To dialog. The Save Password check box is disabled when the client isn't logged on to the network. Click Connect to start the DUN process. A series of windows displays the connection progress (see Figure 19.32). The first time you make a connection, the standard Windows 95 network logon dialog appears, and you must enter your password for verification.

FIG. 19.32

The sequence of dialogs during the RAS logon process.

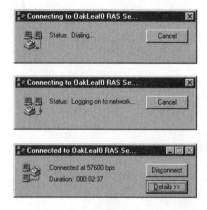

11. Click the Details button of the Connected to *ConnectionName* window to show the protocol(s) in use (see Figure 19.33).

FIG. 19.33

Displaying network protocol(s) in use in the detailed version of the Connected To *ConnectionName* window.

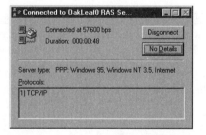

Part
IV

Ch
19

12. Launch Network Neighborhood, and then expand the display of shares for the server to which you're connected (see Figure 19.34).

13. To terminate the connection, click the Disconnect button in the Connected to *ConnectionName* window.

N O T E The notorious could not negotiate a compatible set of protocols Dial-Up Networking message (see Figure 19.35) indicates a problem with your Windows 95 networking protocol(s). If you've selected only NetBEUI as your protocol and the client is connected to the server on the network, two attempts to register the same NetBEUI computer name create the problem. This message also appears on a relatively small percentage of Windows 95 clients that attempt to connect with TCP/IP. Although a client with this problem can't connect to a Windows NT 4.0 RAS server, it likely can connect via TCP/IP to a Windows NT 3.5+ RAS server. The only currently known solution to this problem is to remove all the network protocols on the client, reboot the client, and then reinstall the protocols from scratch with the Windows 95 distribution CD-ROM. ▪

FIG. 19.34

Using Network
Neighborhood to display
DUN shares on the
OAKLEAFO server.

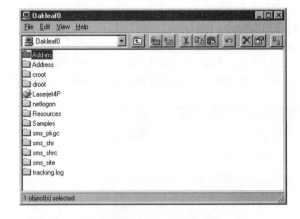

FIG. 19.35

The message that
indicates a problem
with Windows 95's
currently installed
networking protocols.

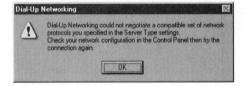

Windows NT Clients

Installation and operation of DUN on a Windows NT 4.0 client varies significantly from Windows 95's approach. The following steps describe how to install the RAS software from the Windows NT 4.0 distribution CD-ROM, and then set up and test Windows NT 4.0 DUN:

1. From the Start menu choose Programs, Accessories, and Dial-Up Networking. The Dial-Up Networking dialog indicates that DUN isn't installed (see Figure 19.36). Click the Install button.

FIG. 19.36

The dialog indicating
that Windows NT 4.0
Dial-Up Networking isn't
installed.

2. The Files Needed dialog vaguely indicates that Some files on (Unknown) are needed (see Figure 19.37) if you didn't specify RAS when you installed Windows NT 4.0. If you previously installed the files, skip to step 3.

FIG. 19.37

The dialog that indicates you need to install RAS files from the distribution CD-ROM or a network installation share.

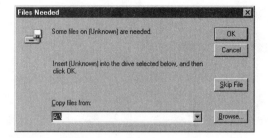

Click Browse and specify the \I386 (or other processor) folder of the distribution CD-ROM. The file needed is Rascfg.dl_ (see Figure 19.38). Click Open to return to the Files Needed dialog (see Figure 19.39). Click OK to install the RAS files.

FIG. 19.38

Specifying the \I386 folder of the distribution CD-ROM for RAS installation.

FIG. 19.39

The Files Needed dialog with the path to the files on the CD-ROM.

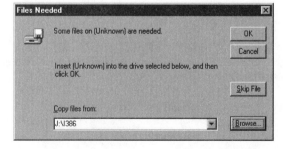

Part
IV

Ch
19

3. The Add RAS Device dialog has a list of RAS Capable Devices (see Figure 19.40). If you have only one modem installed, accept the default; otherwise, select the modem to use with RAS/DUN. Click OK to continue.

4. In the Configure Port Usage dialog, select Dial Out Only unless you want to configure the client as a RAS server (see Figure 19.41). Windows NT Workstation 4.0 supports a single RAS/DUN connection, similar to the RAS server feature installed by the Windows 95 Plus! pack. Click OK to continue.

FIG. 19.40
Selecting a RAS-capable modem.

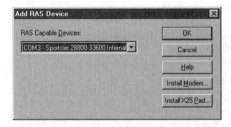

FIG. 19.41
Selecting the RAS operating mode(s) in the Configure Port Usage dialog.

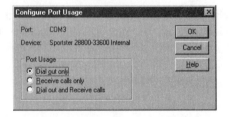

5. The Dial-Up Networking message box indicates that The phonebook is empty (see Figure 19.42). Windows NT 4.0 uses a phonebook model, rather than Windows 95's Dial-Up Connection, for selecting a RAS/DUN connection. Click OK to launch the New Phonebook Entry Wizard.

FIG. 19.42
The message that appears when you haven't added an entry to the DUN phonebook.

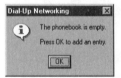

6. Type the name of the RAS connection in the Name the New Phonebook Entry text box (see Figure 19.43). Click Next.

FIG. 19.43
Naming a new RAS connection in the first New Phonebook Entry Wizard dialog.

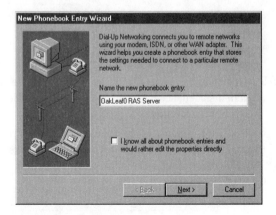

7. The Server dialog offers connection options for the Internet, plain (unencrypted) text passwords, and non-Windows NT RAS servers (see Figure 19.44). None of these options apply when using Windows NT Server 4.0 DUN, so click Next to open the Phone Number dialog.

FIG. 19.44
Choosing options for connecting to the Internet, with unencrypted passwords, and to RAS servers other than Windows NT.

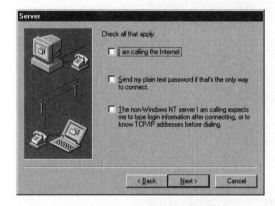

8. You can type the phone number directly in the text box (see Figure 19.45), or mark the Use Telephony Dialing Properties check box to make the extended dialing parameters appear (see Figure 19.46). Select the Country Code and Area Code, and type the Phone Number for the connection.

FIG. 19.45
The default version of the Phone Number dialog.

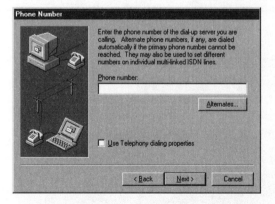

Part
IV

Ch
19

9. If you want to add alternate numbers to dial in case the main number is busy, click Alternates to display the Phone Numbers dialog (see Figure 19.47). To add another number, type it in the New Phone Number text box and click Add. Click OK to close the dialog.

10. In the final New Phonebook Entry Wizard dialog, click Finish to add the entry to the phonebook and open the Dial-Up Networking dialog with the first phonebook entry selected (see Figure 19.48).

11. Click Dial to start the RAS connection. A series of dialogs monitors the connection progress (see Figure 19.49).

FIG. 19.46
The TAPI version of the Phone Number dialog.

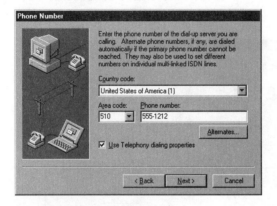

FIG. 19.47
Displaying current RAS server phone numbers.

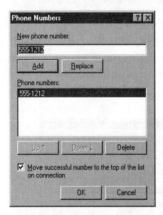

FIG. 19.48
The DUN phonebook entry for dialing a Windows NT 4.0 RAS server.

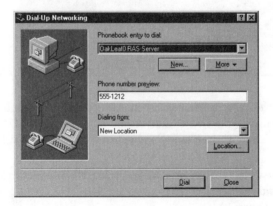

FIG. 19.49

Dialogs that monitor the progress of your DUN connection.

If the client you're testing is directly connected to the network and you use NetBEUI as one of your network and RAS protocols, you receive the error message shown in Figure 19.50. Click Accept to accept a connection via TCP/IP.

FIG. 19.50

The error message that occurs if you're logged on to the network and attempt a RAS connection with the NetBEUI protocol.

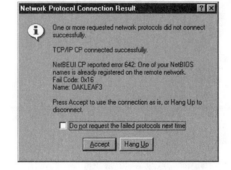

12. When the connection succeeds, the Connection Complete dialog appears (see Figure 19.51). After making the first connection, mark the Do Not Display This Message Again check box, and then click OK.

 You can monitor the status of the connection by right-clicking the DUN icon at the right of the taskbar and choosing Dial-Up Monitor to open the Dial-Up Networking Monitor property sheet (see Figure 19.52). Two of the more interesting statistics of the Status page are the Compression In and Compression Out percentages, which indicate the efficiency of hardware compression.

13. To terminate the connection, right-click the DUN icon of the taskbar and choose Hang Up, and then click Yes when requested to confirm the disconnect.

Part

IV

Ch

19

You also can start DUN by double-clicking the Dial-Up Networking icon in My Computer (see Figure 19.53).

FIG. 19.51

The final step in completing the first DUN connection.

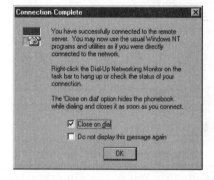

FIG. 19.52

Using the Dial-Up Networking Monitor tool to check the performance of the DUN connection.

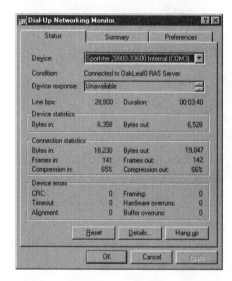

ON THE WEB

Microsoft offers a Knowledge Base (KB) article, "Troubleshooting RAS Client Issues in Windows NT 4.0," which describes common problems encountered with DUN for Windows NT 4.0 clients. The article, available at **http://www.microsoft.com/kb/articles/q162/2/93.htm**, includes links to other Windows NT 4.0 DUN troubleshooting KB articles.

FIG. 19.53
Starting Dial-Up
Networking from My
Computer.

Monitoring Connections with Remote Access Admin

In addition to enabling RAS for users, described earlier in the section "Granting Client Access with the Remote Access Admin Application," Remote Access Admin also lets you supervise RAS connections to the server. To use Remote Access Admin to monitor RAS connections, follow these steps:

1. Launch Remote Access Admin, if necessary. Remote Access Admin's window displays all the servers in the domain set up as remote access servers, and the number of active connections of each (see Figure 19.54).

Part
IV
Ch
19

FIG. 19.54
Remote Access Admin
displaying a single RAS
server with one
connected user.

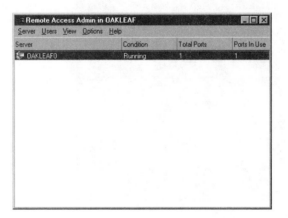

2. Double-click an active server entry in the list to display the Communication Ports dialog. An entry for each COM port of the server set up for RAS appears in the list, along with

the user name and the time the connection started (see Figure 19.55). You can disconnect the user or, if messaging service is enabled on both ends of the connection, send a pop-up message to the user.

FIG. 19.55

Displaying the entry for the RAS server's COM port.

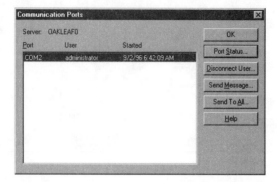

3. Click Port Status to display the Port Status dialog (see Figure 19.56), which is similar to the Status page of the Dial-Up Networking Monitor property sheet for an outbound RAS connection (refer to Figure 19.52). If the server has more than one COM port assigned to RAS, you can select the port from the drop-down Port list.

FIG. 19.56

The Port Status dialog for a TCP/IP RAS connection immediately after user logon.

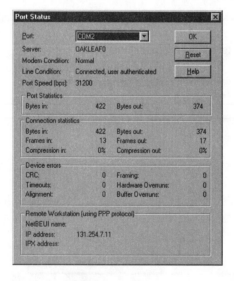

N O T E If you haven't enabled dial-out RAS on the server, the Dial-Up Networking icon doesn't appear in the taskbar. In this case, you launch Dial-Up Networking Monitor from Control Panel's Dial-Up Networking tool. ▪

Using the Point-to-Point Tunneling Protocol

Microsoft's Point-to-Point Tunneling Protocol (PPTP) is an encryption system that provides secure communication between computers over the public Internet. Microsoft has submitted PPTP to the Internet Engineering Task Force (IETF) for incorporation into the IP-Sec (Secure IP) service standard. PPTP uses MS-CHAP for authentication and allows NetBEUI and IPX protocols to "piggyback" on TCP/IP packets.

N O T E When this book was written, PPTP's status was that of a proprietary Microsoft protocol available only in Windows NT 4.0 Server and Workstation. Microsoft promised that PPTP would be available for Windows 95 and Windows 3.1+ by the end of 1996. Microsoft released a beta version of PPTP for Windows 95 in late May 1997. Network TeleSystems has released a beta version of TunnelBuilder PPTP implementation for Windows 3.1, Windows for Workgroups 3.11, and Macintosh. █

ON THE WEB

You can download the beta version of PPTP for Windows 95 from **http://www.microsoft.com/ windows/windows95/info/pptp4w95.htm** and get up-to-date white papers and links to third-party PPTP implementations, including TunnelBuilder, at **http://www.microsoft.com/ntserver/info/ morepptp.htm**.

Using the Internet to provide remote access services for mobile users and telecommuters minimizes time-based telecommunications costs by providing network access through a local call to an ISP. VPNs created with PPTP also can replace costly telco-leased lines. PPTP is especially cost-effective for international connections to remote sites and overseas workers.

Another advantage of PPTP is that it eliminates the banks of modems needed to service multiple simultaneous RAS connections. You create a multihomed server by adding another network card to the server, enabling PPTP on the added card, and connecting the card to a PPTP router. The PPTP router can share existing T-1 or ISDN line(s) to the ISP.

You enable PPTP on Windows NT 4.0 clients and servers by marking the Enable PPTP Filtering check box on the Advanced IP Addressing dialog (see Figure 19.57), which you access from the IP Address page of the TCP/IP Properties sheet. The initial incarnation of PPTP is based on server-to-server connections to create virtual WANs. Windows NT Server 4.0's built-in routing capabilities are useful for isolating PPTP traffic from conventional TCP/IP traffic on the LAN. You also can use PPTP for Dial-Up Networking over POTS or ISDN lines. POTS and ISDN lines are generally regarded as secure channels but aren't immune from physical wiretaps or interception of a wireless segment of the connection. Window NT Server 4.0's Network.wri file in your \Winnt folder provides additional guidelines for Dial-Up Networking with PPTP in the "Dial-Up Networking Notes" section.

Part
IV

Ch
19

FIG. 19.57
Enabling PPTP filtering
for a specified network
adapter.

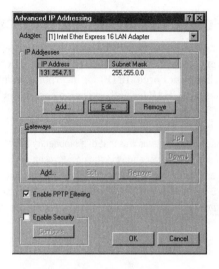

To implement PPTP, all participants in the communication path must have routers equipped to handle PPTP. Networking hardware suppliers, including Ascend, U.S. Robotics, and 3Com, were beta-testing PPTP in the fall of 1996 and should have software upgrades available for their remote-access products by the end of 1996. The extent to which ISPs upgrade their gateways and routers for PPTP depends on the initial demand by Windows NT 4.0 users.

N O T E   If you have separate network interface cards for PPTP and the LAN on your server, clients
may be unable to obtain an IP address from DHCP when dialing in. In this case, you receive
the message The Remote Access Server was unable to acquire an IP Address from the
DHCP Server to be used on the Server Adapter. Incoming users will be unable to
connect using IP. Service Pack 2 and higher corrects this problem. ■

ON THE WEB

For more information on the DHCP address problem, see the KB article at **http://www.microsoft.
com/kb/articles/q158/3/87.htm**. Issues relating to RAS, PPTP, and proxy servers are addressed
by the KB article at **http://www.microsoft.com/kb/articles/q164/0/52.htm**.

Adding Microsoft Routing and Remote Access Service

The Routing and Remote Access Service (Routing and RAS, formerly code-named Steelhead) replaces both the multiprotocol router (MPR) and RAS components of Windows NT Server 4.0.

Routing and RAS adds support for demand-dial routing over temporary (switched) connections, such as a POTS or ISDN line. Routing and RAS makes a connection between the two servers only when required, and then disconnects after handling the traffic. Windows NT 4.0 supports PPTP only between clients and servers; Routing and RAS adds server-to-server PPTP for Windows NT 4.0 servers, so security is maintained when you use demand-dial routing. Microsoft Point-to-Point Compression (MPPC) provides up to a 4:1 increase in speed when using slow WAN links with Routing and RAS. Routing and RAS is covered in more detail in Chapter 26, "Scaling Windows NT Server 4.0 to the Enterprise."

▶ **See** "Using Routing and Remote Access Service," **p. 980**

ON THE WEB

The "Microsoft Routing and Remote Access Service for Windows NT Server 4.0 Reviewers Guide" is available at **http://www.microsoft.com/ntserver/info/Routing&RASabout.htm**. You can download the final release of Routing and RAS from **http://www.microsoft.com/ntserver/info/routing&ras.htm**. Routing and RAS requires installation of Windows NT 4.0 Service Pack 3, which is available at **http://www.microsoft.com/NTserverSupport/Content/ServicePacks/Where.htm**.

Using the Resource Kit's RAS Tools

The *Windows NT Server Resource Kit* for version 4.0 includes the following RAS tools:

- *Raslist.exe* is a command-line utility that lists *RAS announces* (an ungrammatical plural of *RAS announce*) from all LANAs in the format RAS announce received from *NetBIOSName* as the announces occur. Type **raslist** at the command prompt to start the tool; press Ctrl+C to stop the listing.

- *Rasuser.exe* is a command-line utility that lists the logon IDs of all users for whom DUN is enabled in the domain or on a specified server. Type **rasuser** {*domainname* | *servername*} at the command prompt to create a RAS user list.

- *Remote Access Manager* is a demonstration version of a third-party Windows application that lets you display RAS server and port status, disconnect RAS sessions from any port, and enable or disable RAS privileges for any user. The demo version on the CD-ROM (see Figure 19.58) manages a maximum of two ports; you must license the commercial version for production use.

N O T E Remote Access Manager isn't installed by the Resource Kit's Setup program. You must run Setup.exe from the \Apps\Rasmgr folder of the CD-ROM to install Remote Access Manager. ▓

Part
IV

Ch

19

FIG. 19.58

The Resource Kit's Remote Access Manager displaying users in the OAKLEAF domain with and without RAS privileges.

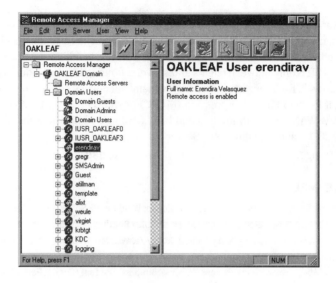

From Here...

This chapter described the architecture of various types of remote access systems, from simple analog modems to high-end RAS routers that combine multiple analog modems and ISDN adapters. Setting up Windows NT Server 4.0 as a RAS server with an internal or external modem, and configuring Windows 95 and Windows NT 4.0 RAS clients also was covered. The chapter concluded with a brief description of PPTP and its use for creating virtual private networks with the Internet as a backbone.

The following chapters include information related to the topics covered in this chapter:

■ Chapter 4, "Choosing Network Protocols," explains how to select one or more of the three principal networking protocols supported by Windows NT based on your network configuration.

■ Chapter 10, "Using TCP/IP, WINS, and DHCP," describes how to set up DHCP services for assigning TCP/IP addresses to DUN clients.

■ Chapter 20, "Setting Up Internet Information Server 4.0," describes the basics of ISDN and includes other useful information relating to telco connections between LANs and ISPs.

Setting Up Internet Information Server 4.0

The Internet's explosive growth in the late 1990s creates an opportunity as well as a challenge for Windows NT network administrators. Organizations that for years have relied on Novell NetWare servers now are adopting Windows NT Server to create private intranets and to connect to the public Internet. The use of the Internet as a marketing tool for a wide range of products and services is increasing at a furious pace. Substituting an Internet connection for 800-number dial-up connections for network access by mobile employees can save a substantial part of a firm's monthly telephone charges.

This chapter introduces you to Microsoft's Internet product line, the linchpin of which is Internet Information Server (IIS) 4.0, a replacement for IIS 2.0 (included with Windows NT Server 4.0) and the IIS 3.0 upgrade to IIS 2.0. This chapter's primary topics are planning for Internet services, connecting to an Internet service provider, how IIS services work, and installing IIS 4.0. IIS HTTP (World Wide Web), FTP (File Transfer Protocol), and Gopher services are fully integrated with Windows NT Server 4.0 and, if installed, Microsoft SQL Server 6.5. Thus, installation and startup of IIS 4.0 is a relatively simple process, especially for a private intranet. Planning and connectivity issues require far more attention than simply starting up IIS; thus, much of this chapter is devoted to these two subjects. ■

Connecting to the Internet

Choose connection methods and an Internet service provider to allow secure inbound access to your intranet and public access to your Web site.

Installing Internet Information Server 4.0

Set up IIS 4.0 and its optional components from the distribution CD-ROM or files downloaded from Microsoft's Web site.

Setting up an Intranet or Internet Web site

Use IIS 4.0's Snap-In for Microsoft Management Console to set options for Web publishing on the Internet or for a private intranet.

Adding file download capabilities

Bring an IIS 4.0 FTP server online to allow users to download files from your site.

Viewing Microsoft's Internet Product Line

Microsoft is pursuing an aggressive strategy to gain the position of premier provider of Internet operating systems, applications, and development tools. Microsoft is betting heavily on the company's ability to succeed in a field that historically has been dominated by UNIX servers and Netscape browsers. Integrating a no-charge copy of Internet Information Server (IIS) 4.0 with Windows NT 4.0 is certain to accelerate the adoption of Windows NT and IIS as the most popular Internet server platform.

Microsoft's Internet-related product offerings, as of mid-1997, include the following browsers, content authoring tools, and servers:

- *Internet Explorer (IE) 3.0*, a browser that includes native support for HTTP, FTP, and Gopher protocols, and provides extensibility through Microsoft's ActiveX technology (IE 4.0 was in the beta-testing stage when this book was written)

- *NetMeeting*, a tool for enabling video and audio conferencing, whiteboarding, and application sharing across the Internet via industry-standard protocols

- *FrontPage 97*, Microsoft's mid-range Web site management tool, which provides WYSIWYG Web page content editing and the server extensions required to deliver the content

- *Visual InterDev*, a comprehensive integrated Web development environment that incorporates language tools and site-management capabilities

- *Internet Information Server 4.0*, the core component of Microsoft's Internet strategy, a suite of services that provide HTTP, FTP, Gopher server capability, plus other Internet and intranet support

- *Index Server*, now a component of IIS that indexes documents in HTML, Word, and other common formats to provide a local search service for users

- *Proxy Server*, which incorporates some firewall features that give your users desktop access to the Internet while maintaining network security

- *Transaction Server*, a combination object request broker (ORB) and transaction monitor that supports a distributed component architecture for Web applications

- *Message Queue Server*, which handles message-based transaction processing, such as credit-card verification, over wide area networks that are subject to slow response times or unscheduled outages

- *Site Server*, which provides a comprehensive Web site environment for creation, deployment, and advanced management of conventional and commerce-enabled Web sites

- *NetShow*, a server application that broadcasts live and on-demand streaming audio and video across the Internet

Microsoft also supplies the following APIs and development tools for programmers of the company's Internet client and server platforms:

- *ActiveX controls* (formerly OLE Controls), for enhancing the appearance and automating the behavior of Web pages

- *Internet Server API* (ISAPI) applications and filters, to extend the server software by creating routines that can be called from those accessing your site to complete database or other processing functions

- *Internet Database Connector* (IDC), an ISAPI extension, to provide easy dynamic access from special Web pages to ODBC data sources

- *ActiveX Data Objects* and the *Advanced Data Connector*, which substitute OLE DB for ODBC to streamline Web-page access to database content

- *ActiveX Scripting*, also called Visual Basic Script (VBScript), for manipulating Web pages with a Visual Basic-like programming language

- *Active Server Pages*, introduced by IIS 3.0, which brings VBScript to Internet Information Server for back-end application development

- *Java and JavaScript support*, by means of ActiveX technology; a fast just-in-time (JIT) compiler to speed execution of Java applets; and a Java development environment, Visual J++

ON THE WEB

What's remarkable about the products described in these two lists is that many of them are available at no charge, except for the cost of downloading time. For a list of products available from the Microsoft Web site, visit the Microsoft Free Product Downloads page at **http://www.microsoft.com/ msdownload/**.

Planning Your Site

It's important to create a comprehensive plan before you start bringing up your site. The plan should include the services you intend to offer and how you plan to provide user access to those services. Following are the issues to resolve before you start the installation of IIS:

- If you want to provide inbound or outbound Internet connectivity, what type of telecommunications link should you use?

- What services are needed? Web services are a given, but you might also want to provide FTP access and, less likely, Gopher service.

- Does the information you offer from the Web site need to be accessible from FTP and Gopher services?

- What types of security should you implement? Security means more than everyone having a password. Decide—down to the folder level, at a minimum—groups that have resource access and groups barred from access.

- Do you want to provide Internet e-mail services from the server running IIS?

Part
IV

Ch

20

■ Who's responsible for creating the design of and content for your site, as well as routine maintenance of the site? Larger organizations usually use independent Web design firms to establish the graphic and navigational features of the site, and use a full-time Web-master to maintain the site.

ON THE WEB

The Microsoft SiteBuilder Workshop at **http://microsoft.com/sitebuilder/** provides a wide range of information and software for developing Web sites, including sections on planning and production as well as site administration.

■ Do you intend to provide custom Web pages created from database information? If your data source is Microsoft SQL Server, you must have the SQL Server Internet Connector license for an Internet server or, if you don't have the required client licenses, for an intranet installation.

■ What type of server audit logging, if any, do you want to use? If you use SQL Server 6.x to store audit logs, you also must have the required server and connection licenses.

ON THE WEB

Microsoft's BackOffice Licensing Guide, accessible from **http://www.microsoft.com/ntserver/info/licensing.htm**, provides details on Microsoft SQL Server licensing policies.

The rest of this chapter helps you determine the answers to the first five of these questions, with emphasis on getting started with IIS 4.0. Chapter 21, "Administering Intranet and World Wide Web Sites," covers logging, database connectivity, and content creation for Web sites.

Connecting to the Internet

The first issue to settle is how you connect to the Internet. Even if you intend to establish only an intranet, you might want to consider using the Internet to provide low-cost inbound access to your Web site for telecommuters and mobile employees. Your company's link to the Internet will be provided by an Internet service provider (ISP). The ISP assigns your site a domain name (*companyname*.com) and an IP address, which is registered with InterNIC, an organization responsible for assuring that all Internet sites have globally unique domain names. The selection of an ISP is a critical step in setting up your Web site.

N O T E If you want to provide public access to your Web site and private dial-up networking via the Internet, you need a firewall to maintain network privacy. A firewall also is necessary to provide security if your Web server is connected to your organization's LAN. Microsoft intends its Proxy Server 2.0 to be a software firewall for providing network users safe access to the Internet; you also can buy third-party software and hardware firewalls. Firewalls are critical components of *extranets*, which enable authenticated business partners to access internal corporate data, such as inventory levels, via the Internet. ■

ON THE WEB

Visit **http://www.microsoft.com/proxy** for more information on Proxy Server.

Choosing an Internet Service Provider

Choosing an ISP used to be easy, because there were very few. As the Internet's popularity has grown, so too has the number of businesses vying for your connectivity dollars. Some ISP names are familiar: MCI, Sprint, GTE, and so forth. Your local telco may have joined the game as well.

Some important points to consider while choosing an ISP include the following:

■ *Price.* Pricing for Internet services is becoming less of an issue. Increasing competition continues to narrow the gap between the low and high ends of the ISP price spectrum.

■ *Connection types offered.* Not all ISPs provide all the different services that you may need, such as Web site hosting. Make sure that you have a complete understanding of what you need and use this as a critical determining factor in selecting the ISP you use.

■ *Capacity.* Be sure to ask what capacity connection your ISP has to the Internet backbone. If the ISP has a single 1.544 kbps T-1 connection and hundreds of users, response time may not be acceptable during times of peak loads. Larger ISPs have at least a T-3 Internet connection.

■ *Fault tolerance.* High-end providers have multiple T-1 or other connections to the Internet backbone. If one circuit fails, another takes over to provide connectivity.

■ *Service.* What kind of service agreement is standard for a particular company? Does the ISP guarantee a minimum bandwidth or minimum downtime? Does the ISP have 24-hours-a-day, 7-days-a-week coverage by support staff?

■ *Reputation.* References are desirable when entering into an agreement for a service on which your business will depend.

■ *Stability.* Small ISPs may offer customized services, but new competition from long-distance carriers and regional telephone companies makes the long-term viability of small ISPs questionable.

■ *Other services.* An ISP should be able to provide domain name services, electronic mail, and Usenet news services, if you need them. Your ISP should also be able to help you secure IP addresses for your internal network and register your domain name.

Part

IV

Ch

20

Understanding Connection Types

Just as important as your choice of an ISP is the technology you use to make the Internet connection to your ISP. Table 20.1 lists the more common telecommunications technologies and their capacities in raw bits per second, approximate number of users supported, approximate monthly cost, and interface type.

Table 20.1 The Different Types of Available Connections to the Internet

Connection Type	Data Rate	Simultaneous Users	Approximate Monthly Cost	Local-Loop Interface
Dial-up	28.8 kbps	1–2	$40–100	2 wire twisted pair
56k	56 kbps	10–20	$300–800	2 or 4 wire twisted pair
ISDN	144 kbps	10–40	$60–250	2 wire twisted pair
Frame Relay	Up to 1.544 Mbps	5–250	$200–1,000	2 or 4 wire twisted pair or fiber
T-1	1.544 Mbps	50–250	$100–3,000	4 wire twisted pair or fiber
T-3	44.736 Mbps	250–4,000	$50,000–150,000	Fiber or coax

Table 20.1 shows that you can approach getting connected to the Internet in many different ways. Your decision must be based primarily on anticipated traffic, which services are available from your ISP, and your local telephone carrier's ability to provide the service to your site. The costs shown are the approximate combined monthly rates of ISP and local carrier charges. These costs don't include hook-up fees or the necessary hardware, such as CSU/DSUs (Channel Service Unit/Data Service Unit) and routers. Of course, the costs in your area may vary, but Table 20.1 should give you a good idea of what expenses to expect.

N O T E Internet access via xDSL and cablemodem connections promise very high bandwidth, at least in the receiving direction, but won't be widely deployed for several years. (*xDSL* is a catch-all term for various Digital Subscriber Line technologies that run on standard telco local-loop wiring.) When your telco or its competitor(s) offer xDSL, you're likely to be required to use the xDSL provider as your ISP. Local cable MSOs (Multiple Service Operators) bundle the cable modem and ISP service as a package and aren't likely to offer Web site hosting services. ■

Selecting a Dial-Up Access Method   The most familiar and popular way to gain access to the Internet is simply a modem and ordinary voice line to dial into an ISP. This method is inexpensive and relatively pain-free for a few users to gain Internet access. Typically, each computer has its own modem and a dedicated POTS (plain old telephone service) line; access is available only to that computer's user. The problem with individual Internet access is the cost of installing dedicated lines and the monthly charge for them.

It's possible, by using Windows NT Remote Access Server or a hardware router, to provide multiuser access with a single POTS line. The performance of this connection type is acceptable for very few simultaneous users. More than about two simultaneous users slows response to an unacceptable level. Although dial-up access may be sufficient for a few internal users occasionally surfing the Net, it's unlikely that external customers would visit your Web site if a 28.8 kbps modem is your primary means of connection.

N O T E Most modem manufacturers tout compatibility with various hardware compression technologies. One manufacturer claims an 8:1 compression ratio, turning its 28.8 kbps modem into a 230.4 kbps speedster. Although this compression is possible with certain types of text data, don't count on throughput being anything near this value for real-life information. Web-site content often is heavily graphical in nature. Graphic files are particularly difficult to compress; in the case of JPEG and GIF files, compression has already taken place, and little or no additional hardware compression is likely. ■

Selecting a 56 kbps Connection   If you plan to host a Web server on your local premises or have several users that need to access the Internet, a dedicated 56 kbps connection is possible. Your carrier may call the 56 kbps connection 56k, DDS, Digital Data Service, Dataphone Digital Service, or some other variation on the same theme. The 56 kbps digital circuits have been around for a long time and were the first commonly available high-speed technology to move information between remote sites. Although 56 kbps communication doesn't seem all that fast by today's standards, users considered it a blistering data rate in the days when 300- and 1,200-baud modems were the standard.

In telecommunications terminology, a 56 kbps circuit is known as a *DS0 circuit*. A DS0 (pronounced "dee-ess-zero") circuit is one of the basic building blocks used by telecommunications companies. A fully digital circuit is being used, so no digital-to-analog conversion is necessary and, accordingly, many problems inherent in analog circuits and modems—primarily noise—are removed from the equation.

The additional bandwidth and reliability don't come free. The cost of a 56 kbps circuit often is an order of magnitude higher than that of a voice circuit. You also need more hardware to set up the link; a router and CSU/DSU is required at each end of the circuit. Figure 20.1 shows the physical configuration of using a 56 kbps circuit to connect your LAN to the Internet through an ISP.

In addition to a router to direct the TCP/IP traffic, you need a CSU/DSU to connect to your carrier's circuit. The CSU is used to terminate the digital circuit in a method acceptable to the phone company. The CSU usually has LEDs on the front of the unit to indicate the status of the link and for loopback testing. The DSU, located between the CSU and your router, is responsible for converting the electrical signal from your router into a signal acceptable by your CSU.

N O T E The disadvantage of using 56 kbps lines lies in their point-to-point operation. Although this obviously isn't a problem if you have a single site, the setup and equipment expenses can become significant if you're connecting multiple sites. If you have several sites to connect, you should investigate frame-relay services. ■

Part
IV

Ch
20

FIG. 20.1

A typical configuration for a dedicated 56 kbps circuit to an ISP that connects to the Internet.

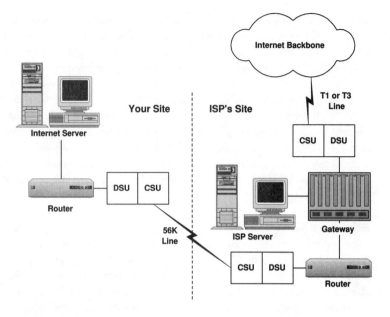

Selecting an ISDN Connection The *Integrated* part of Integrated Services Digital Network refers to ISDN's capability to handle voice and data simultaneously over the same twisted-pair cable that now provides your voice or modem service. ISDN is a switched, point-to-point, connection-based system that's purely digital. ISDN's digital nature allows it to dial, hand-shake, and connect in only a second or two. The average modem can take nearly a minute to perform the same task.

The standard ISDN circuit is called BRI (Basic Rate Interface) service. BRI consists of two 64 kbps data channels and one 16 kbps signal channel. The 64 kbps channels are called B, or *bearer*, channels. (In some locations, the B channels are 56.1 kbps.) The 16 kbps channel, called D, is used for circuit signaling and management. BRI service is also referred to as 2B+D service. The two 64 kbps channels can be used for voice or data in parallel or combination. You can use one channel for data and the other for voice, or both channels for data and voice. You can't make direct use of the standard D channel for data.

N O T E Most ISDN tariffs involve an installation charge, monthly service fee, and time-based usage charges. Usage charges make a continuous connection to the internet uneconomic. Pacific Bell announced in June 1997 an "Always On" D channel for a small monthly surcharge. The D channel moves low-bandwidth traffic, such as e-mail, without the need for a B channel connection. ▪

Through a technique called *bonding*, both B channels can be combined to form a single 128 kbps data connection channel. The most popular type of bonding is called Multi-Link PPP (Point-to-Point Protocol), or MLPPP. Now, no standards for bonding exist, but industry groups are working on a standard. In some cases, you need the same brand of ISDN equipment on each end of the circuit to enable bonding.

Figure 20.2 shows the typical ISDN setup. The service termination point is called the NT-1 (Network Terminator, type 1), which is provided by your carrier or, more commonly, is built into your ISDN equipment. The NT-1 terminates a single twisted-pair cable from the central office (called a *local loop,* or U interface) and converts the data on the local loop to an S/T interface. The T signal connects to an NT-2 network terminator, which is responsible for breaking the signal into its B and D channels and for connecting to non-ISDN devices, such as a voice telephone, through an optional terminal adapter (TA).

FIG. 20.2

The hardware components for an ISDN BRI connection to an ISP.

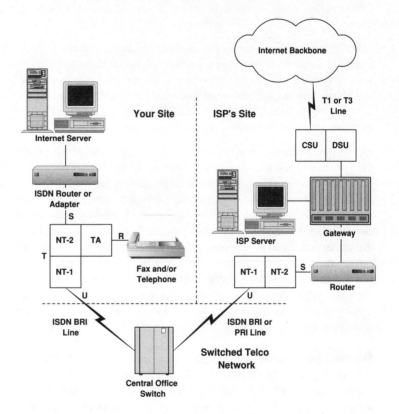

Typical ISDN equipment contains the NT-1, NT-2, and a TA, and is often referred to as an *ISDN adapter.* An ISDN adapter is roughly analogous to the CSU/DSU used by 56 kbps connections. Your terminal equipment, such as your PC or your router, connects to external ISDN adapters, such as Motorola's BitSURFR Pro, with an RS-232 (serial port) connection. The ISDN adapter appears to Windows NT as a very fast modem. Internal ISDN adapters, such as the US Robotics Sportster 128K, also includes the NT-1 and NT-2 components.

N O T E In addition to the R, S/T, and U ISDN interfaces is a V interface at the central office (CO) that connects the Line Termination (LT) function for the local loop to the Exchange Termination (ET) function for connecting the CO to other exchanges. The V interface usually resides in the CO switch.

▶ **See** "Deciding on a Dial-Up Networking Architecture," **p. 689** ■

Part
IV

Ch
20

An alternative to ISDN adapters that emulate analog modems is an ISDN router. All major manufacturers of TCP/IP routers, such as Cisco Systems and Ascend Communications, produce ISDN routers. An ISDN router makes the connection between the U channel and your Ethernet LAN, usually with 10BaseT media. Some ISDN routers support dial-on-demand. If idle for a preset period of time, the line disconnects. When a packet needs to be forwarded over the ISDN link, the router reconnects to the specified ISDN telephone number and forwards the traffic. ISDN connects very quickly, so users notice little or no delay. The cost saving from using a dial-on-demand configuration can be significant if your carrier charges for connect time.

Availability of ISDN service varies considerably. In many areas of the United States, ISDN's popularity has pushed its demand beyond the supply. You may have to wait several months for your carrier to provide you with service. Also, you may have to wait for ISDN service to be available in your area. Many smaller or rural municipalities don't have ISDN service. Carriers in many states realized the benefits of ISDN years ago and, like Pacific Bell in California, have built substantial infrastructure to handle the demand.

ISDN's cost varies just as much as its availability; monthly service charges range from $30 to $180 per month and may depend on usage. ISDN modems range in cost from about $300 to $500. Many carriers charge a substantial installation fee, especially if the customer's premises are a long distance from the central office. If timed usage charges apply and your site generates substantial traffic, ISDN can become more expensive than a dedicated 56 kbps or T-1 circuit. ISDN, however, is well suited for providing Windows NT's Remote Access Service and dial-up networking to mobile users, as well as outbound connections to the Internet.

N O T E   If your Web server is hosted on the ISP's computer rather than on a server at your facility, an ISDN line is likely your most economical choice for managing the site. The speed of ISDN—roughly five times that of a 28.8 kbps modem connection—greatly speeds the process of sending updates to the off-site server.

Selecting Frame Relay Connectivity   Now, frame relay is a hot topic in the wide area networking industry, partly because a mid-1996 decision by the Federal Communications Commission requires carriers to publish tariffs for frame relay services. (Previously, the price of frame relay service was negotiable.) *Frame relay* is a switch-based technology developed by the local telephone companies (telcos). Local exchange carriers (LECs) have developed a network of frame-relay switches. Any point in the frame-relay network can access any of the other frame-relay switches. A company with multiple locations can communicate across the frame-relay network, with each location having to maintain only a single WAN connection.

A frame-relay connection point is called an *access link*. Access links are 56 kbps or T-1 interfaces. The maximum data rate at each access link is called the *port speed* and is equal to or less than the interface link. For example, you may have a 56 kbps access link but only a 32 kbps port speed. Customers with a T-1 access link might have a 128 kbps, 512 kbps, or 1.544 Mbps port speed. The primary advantage of frame relay is that you pay only for the bandwidth you need and the time you use that bandwidth.

N O T E Routes across the frame-relay network are determined by a *permanent virtual circuit* (PVC), which connects frame-relay devices. A single access link can support multiple virtual circuits. ▪

Your guaranteed bandwidth across a frame-relay network is called the *committed information rate (CIR)*. The CIR is always less than the port speed and will be the biggest decision you make when ordering a frame-relay circuit. One highly promoted feature of frame relay is its capability to burst above the CIR. *Bursting* allows network traffic to take advantage of a period of lower activity in the frame-relay network to grab some extra bandwidth. The bursting capacity is available up to the port speed. However, the total bandwidth available within the network is finite, and each PVC is given a percentage based on its CIR.

Because frame relay's popularity has grown, many carriers are finding their networks running at close to maximum throughput. Don't count on operating in burst mode very often. In fact, packets that go above the CIR are eligible to be discarded if the burst bandwidth isn't available at that particular instant. Needless to say, the delays caused by packets being discarded and the protocol recovery mechanism can result in long transmission delays and unhappy users.

One scenario for ISP connection is a T-1 access link with a 512 kbps port speed and a 256 kbps CIR. With this configuration, you always have at least 256 kbps of throughput. Under ideal conditions, the circuit can temporarily burst up to 512 kbps. If you determine that a bigger pipe is needed, you can increase the port speed and the CIR. Figure 20.3 shows an example configuration for a frame-relay installation.

Selecting Connections at T-1 Speeds and Above   Very similar in concept and functionality to 56 kbps lines are T-1 connections, which are used by organizations with large numbers of employees accessing the Internet or large numbers of Internet users accessing their servers. The obvious difference between 56 kbps and T-1 is a 24-fold increase in bandwidth. T-1 circuits have a data rate of 1.544 Mbps in a dedicated, point-to-point configuration.

A T-1 circuit is another major building block for telecommunications networks. Also known as a DS1, a T-1 consists of 24 DS0s. Some carriers offer a variation on T-1, called Fractional T-1 (FT1), which offers speeds from DS0 to DS1 usually in two, four, or six DS0 multiples. Fractional T-1 isn't always financially advantageous. For a slight increase in cost, you may be able to use a full T-1 circuit. Check with your carrier and ISP for price differentials.

Firms with truly huge bandwidth requirements (and very deep pockets) should investigate T-3 services. A T-3 service provides a data rate of 44.736 Mbps. T-3, also known as a DS3 circuit, is equivalent to 28 DS1s. Microsoft uses multiple T-3 circuits to support The Microsoft Network. If you're in the market for T-1 or higher speed circuits, plan on spending some time negotiating with your local carriers and ISP.

Part
IV

Ch
20

FIG. 20.3
Using frame relay to connect several sites to each other and to the Internet.

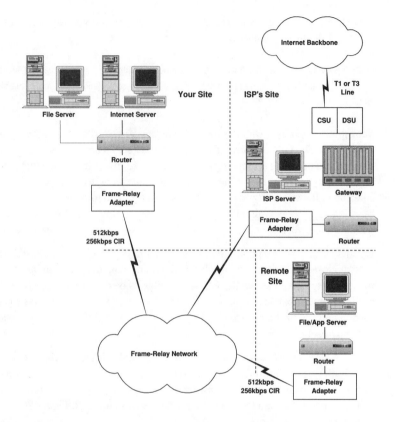

Resolving Names with the Domain Name Service

Names on the Internet are critical to its ease of operation, and the system that ties all the names together is the Internet's Domain Name Service (DNS). DNS is a hierarchical naming system used for Internet navigation and within many organizations that use TCP/IP. Like the Windows Internet Name Service (WINS), DNS maps readable (friendly) names, such as microsoft.com, to numeric IP addresses, such as 207.68.156.49 (the IP address of microsoft.com).

▶ **See** "Using the Microsoft DNS Server," **p. 671**

▶ **See** "Implementing Windows Internet Name Service," **p. 342**

The Internet started as a simple network of a few systems. Each system was responsible for maintaining a HOSTS file, which mapped every system's name to its IP address. The drawbacks of maintaining a static hosts text database become apparent when considering a network of more than a few dozen systems. DNS was developed to overcome these limitations and to provide name services dynamically as the Internet grew and evolved. Although the original designers of DNS had no idea that the Internet would grow to millions of systems internationally, the DNS system has, with a few enhancements along the way, scaled quite well.

The DNS name space is a tree. Domain names are nodes, and systems are leaves on the tree (see Figure 20.4). A fully qualified domain name is constructed by concatenating the domain names to the system name from left to right as you climb the tree. Each component is separated by a dot. The root domain is **.com** for most Web sites, although **.org** (organization), **.gov** (government), **.edu** (educational institution), and country codes (**.ca** for Canada) also are common. The organization name (microsoft, corp, and company) in Figure 20.4 is prepended to the root domain, as in microsoft.com, corp.com, and company.com, forming a fully qualified domain name that corresponds to a particular IP address. Association of a domain name with an IP address is called *name resolution*. Finally, a server type prefix (typically **www**, **ftp**, or **news**) is added, as in **www.microsoft.com**. The **http://** prefix used by Web browsers identifies the hypertext transport protocol for HTML. For e-mail, the prefix typically is the person's e-mail alias, separated from the domain name with an ampersand, as in *anyone*@company.com.

FIG. 20.4
Hierarchical view of the domain name system.

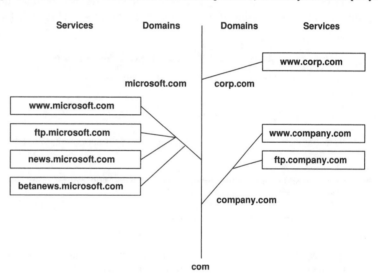

New to Windows NT 4.0 is a native DNS service with a graphical user interface. Previously, you had to buy third-party DNS packages or, more likely, DNS services were provided by UNIX systems on the network. Windows NT Server 4.0's DNS service can integrate with WINS (Windows Internet Name Service). You're likely to be using WINS with DHCP (Dynamic Host Configuration Protocol) to dynamically manage your IP addresses on your internal networks. In this case, DNS handles name resolution at the upper layers and passes the request to WINS for final resolution. This capability is particularly important for those shops that use DNS and DHCP. You need to have WINS or DNS running for intranet users to use friendly Internet-style names, rather than numeric IP addresses, to reach your IIS services.

▶ **See** "Implementing Dynamic Host Configuration Protocol," **p. 332**

Understanding IIS and Its Components

Internet Information Server includes the two basic components you need to create a full-fledged intranet or Internet site: a Web service and an FTP server. Combining these services into IIS 4.0 lets you install, manage, and use them in a suite of applications.

Understanding World Wide Web Service

The World Wide Web server component of IIS is Microsoft's answer to the core technology of today's Internet. Web servers deliver content to Web browsers as text-based documents. The documents contain special formatting called Hypertext Markup Language (HTML) that's derived from the Standardized General Markup Language (SGML). *Tags*—embedded HTML codes enclosed by < and > characters—tell the browser exactly how a document should be displayed to users. Listing 20.1 shows an example of the HTML code for a simple Web page.

Listing 20.1   Simple HTML Example of a Web Page

```
<!doctype html public "-//IETF//DTD HTML//EN">
<HTML>
<HEAD>
<TITLE>HTML Sample pages</TITLE>
</HEAD>
<BODY BACKGROUND="../images/backgrnd.gif" BGCOLOR="FFFFFF">
<TABLE>
<TR>
<TD><IMG SRC="../images/SPACE.gif" ALIGN="top" ALT=" "></TD>
<TD><A HREF="/samples/IMAGES/mh_html.map">
    <IMG SRC="/SAMPLES/images/mh_html.gif" ismap BORDER=0
    ALIGN="top" ALT=" "></A></TD>
</TR>
<TR>
<TD><IMG SRC="../images/SPACE.gif" ALIGN="top" ALT=" "></TD>
<TD><HR> <font size=+3>HTML</font> <font size=+3>S</font>
    <font size=+2>tyle</font> <font size=+3>E</font>
    <font size=+2>xamples</font>
<P>
<font size=2>Below are links to several pages that demonstrate styles
that are built into the HTML language. While looking at these pages,
try using the View Source menu item in your browser to see the HTML
that defines each page. You can copy text from that view to use in
your own Web pages you are authoring.
</font>
</TD>
</TR>
<P>
<TR>
<TD><IMG SRC="../images/space.gif" ALIGN="center" ALT=" "></td>
<td>
<UL>
<IMG SRC="../images/bullet_H.gif" ALIGN="center" ALT=" ">
    <A HREF="/samples/htmlsamp/styles.htm">Very basic HTML styles</A>
```

```
<P><IMG SRC="../images/bullet_H.gif" ALIGN="center" ALT=" ">
   <A HREF="/samples/htmlsamp/styles2.htm">A few additional
   HTML styles</A>
<P><IMG SRC="../images/bullet_H.gif" ALIGN="center" ALT=" ">
   <A HREF="/samples/htmlsamp/tables.htm">Basic HTML tables</A>
</UL></font>
<P>
</td>
</tr>
</TABLE>
</BODY>
</HTML>
```

In addition to plain text that you see in a typical HTML document, there usually are placeholders for graphics and other elements, including video clips, sound clips, and other non-text objects contained in binary (non-text) files. Binary files, such as backgrnd.gif in the preceding HTML example, are stored in files whose relative location from the Web root folder is specified in the tags. The virgule (forward slash, /) is used as the path separator, rather than the DOS backslash (\), because of UNIX's use of /.

Displaying a Web page requires a series of conversations between the Web browser and other components of the Internet or a Windows NT server. The process consists of the following steps:

1. The user types in the Address text box of a browser **http://www.*domainname*.com**, the URL (Uniform Resource Locator) of the Web site to view.

2. The browser looks up the address on the Internet by referencing the DNS server specified by InterNIC for that domain. The address that's returned—say, 198.105.232.5— is then used to connect to the Web server.

3. The browser contacts the specified Web server and requests a document—either the default document specified by the server or a document specified by appending \document.htm[l] to the URL.

4. The server sends the page to the Web browser for display and review, a process called *loading*.

5. When the browser encounters a tag for a binary file, the browser requests transfer of the file's data as a separate and distinct data stream. This process allows the browser to control whether the object is transferred, as well as the timing of the transfer.

Many browsers, including Internet Explorer (IE), let you turn off images altogether, making pages load substantially faster. Figure 20.5 shows The Internet Properties sheet of IE 3.0, in which you can control whether the browser processes still image, sound, or video files by marking or clearing the check boxes in the Multimedia section. Images and other binary types requested by the browser usually are sent with the MIME (Multipurpose Internet Mail Extensions) protocol.

FIG. 20.5

Specifying whether to display multimedia elements of Web pages with IE's The Internet Properties sheet.

NOTE   Image and other binary file loading time is less of an issue with intranets because network speeds generally support much higher throughput than modems or ISDN adapters. Leave the option to load pages/view images selected to display intranet Web pages with graphics. ■

Understanding the File Transfer Protocol Service

File Transfer Protocol offers a means of transferring binary files with tolerance for speed difference between systems, various network traffic, and divergent system platforms. With FTP, users can upload, download, or manage files on your network, on the Internet, or on your intranet server with the support of a proven protocol.

The FTP service is installed on your system when you install IIS, unless you specify otherwise, so you can provide this service to your users. FTP lets you make binary, document, and other types of files available to your users by the following means:

- From within a Web browser
- With a command-line FTP utility
- With a Windows FTP utility

Many Web pages supply links to download graphics, audio, executable, and other types of files to your system. One way Web pages handle file downloads is to provide a link to an FTP address for the file you request. When your browser encounters an FTP address, it uses the FTP protocol to download the file. FTP addresses in Web documents have the following syntax:

```
ftp://ftp.sitename.site extension/[folder/...]filename.ext
```

As an example, **ftp://ftp.intellicenter.com/reality/sitelist.zip** specifies that the file SITELIST.ZIP is found at the IntelliCenter site in the Reality folder. By recognizing the

URL as one that necessitates file transfer, your browser enables downloading the file without leaving the browser environment.

N O T E When you access an URL that refers to an FTP site, your browser indicates that it's signing into the site, sending commands, and—if successful—receiving a file. The browser changes into FTP emulation mode and begins an electronic conversation with the FTP server to retrieve the item you've requested. ▪

The other two options for accessing an FTP site include a command-line, character-based solution and a dedicated Windows FTP utility. When you install Windows 95 or Windows NT, you are automatically provided with a character-based FTP utility. To access a remote site manually with the Ftp.exe utility, follow these steps:

1. From the Start menu choose Run, type **ftp** in the Open text box, and press Enter to run Ftp.exe.

2. Type **open ftp.*domainname*.com** at the prompt and press Enter.

3. Your Internet dialer appears to establish an Internet connection. Click Connect if you're using The Microsoft Network or a similar dialer.

4. When the connection is made to the FTP server, you're prompted for a user name. If the site supports anonymous FTP, type **anonymous**; otherwise, type your user name. Press Enter.

5. Enter your password. Anonymous FTP sites often request your Internet e-mail address as the password. Press Enter.

6. The site responds with a logon confirmation and displays the ftp> prompt (see Figure 20.6). Type any valid FTP command at the prompt. To download a file, type **get** **filename.ext** and press Enter; the file is downloaded to the Desktop folder. Many FTP commands are the same as DOS commands; examples are dir (read the directory/folder) and cd (change directory/folder).

7. When you're through with the session, type **bye**, **quit**, or **disconnect** to log off the FTP server.

FIG. 20.6

Using the command-line version of FTP included with Windows NT and Windows 95.

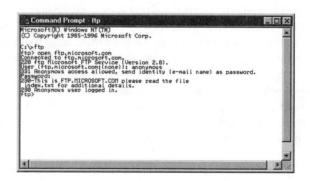

N O T E At a vast majority of FTP sites, you rarely can upload files or other information unless you're a known user to the system. Downloading files is an option that's often left in a more anonymous state, allowing downloads to users who aren't directly known to the system. Anonymous users can download publicly accessible files.

In many cases, if you retrieve sensitive files or other protected information, you must sign into the FTP site with a specific user ID and password, just as you do when you log on to a network. ■

Most Windows FTP utilities, such as WS_FTP (a shareware utility), store configurations for multiple sites. When you start the utility, you're prompted to select the site to which you want to connect. Figure 20.7 shows an example of configuration selection with WS_FTP.

FIG. 20.7
Selecting a configuration for an FTP site in the WS_FTP utility.

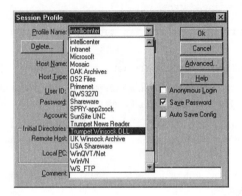

N O T E To log on from a browser to an intranet FTP site with anonymous access, type `ftp://anonymous@servername` in the Address text box. Your browser displays a list of the folders and files in the designated FTP root folder. ■

Understanding Gopher

The Gopher server, installed when you install IIS 2.0 from the Windows NT Server 4.0 distribution CD-ROM, lets you publish conventional text documents for user review. Gopher servers work with ASCII or ANSI documents and provide extensive search and retrieval options. Gopher was created to address the world of the early Internet, where millions of documents in text format were available from hosts at universities, government research institutions, and government contractors. Gopher has fallen victim to the popularity of the Web and Web-based search services, such as Yahoo!, Excite, Lycos, and AltaVista. Microsoft's Index Server gives your users a much easier method of searching for content in text and some types of binary files on your intranet. Gopher requires manual indexing of content, whereas Index Server automatically handles indexing and searching operations.

N O T E Very few users of IIS 2.0+ implemented the Gopher service. The Beta 2 version of IIS 4.0, used to write this chapter, didn't include the Gopher service nor did Microsoft indicate in the Release Notes for IIS 4.0 Beta 2 that Gopher would be provided in the final version. ■

Understanding How IIS Interacts with the Windows NT Domain Model

You set up all access rights with Windows NT Server's User Manager for Domains. Groups and users are the foundation for the security of IIS server processes and their components. If you don't observe the proper security policies when setting up an Internet server connected to your LAN, it's possible for hackers to obtain access to shared directories containing highly confidential information.

▶ **See** "Working with User Manager for Domains," **p. 442**

The Windows NT domain in which your Internet or intranet server resides controls all aspects of who can access your system, how they access it, when they access it, and more. As a result, it's important to understand how to set up your intranet user base, assign rights, and control your users' access privileges. It's equally important to restrict permissions of the account used by visitors to your Internet site.

▶ **See** "Understanding Domain Architecture and Security," **p. 606**

> **CAUTION**
>
> Never grant administrative rights to users you're about to set up for IIS server processes. Be sure to set up separate and distinct accounts for anonymous Web, FTP, and Gopher access, if you support more than a Web publishing service. Although you don't have to predefine these user accounts, you should plan for them and be sure to validate user rights on all services before making the Internet services available to users at any level.
>
> If you use the account with domain administrative privileges for logging on to Internet services, you create a serious security breach. It's only a matter of time before your system is threatened by a user's ability to manipulate the content of the site and possibly destroy the site. Only the network administrator, Webmaster, and designers should have administrative privileges for IIS.
>
> If you use the same account for FTP, Web, and Gopher services, determining where a problem lies is more difficult if you need to track logons, accesses, and other user-specific questions, such as comments and problem reports.

Part
IV

Ch
20

Installing Internet Information Server 4.0

Before you install IIS, make sure that you have enough disk space to store the documents and supporting objects (such as graphics) you intend to bring online. A complete installation of IIS 4.0 requires about 32M, including the sample files; Index Server requires approximately 10M. You can also install a number of other programs and capabilities that are included with IIS 4.0, including the Internet Mail Server, the Internet News Server, the Certificate Server, Site Server Express, the Transaction Sever, and the Script Debugger—all told, more than 60M. Multimedia content consumes extraordinary amounts of disk space. If you aren't sure about the amount of content that you must store, prepare now to move user folders and other files to another server. Alternatively, consider adding another disk drive of 2G or greater capacity to your server.

> **N O T E**   Microsoft recommends that you install IIS on an NTFS partition. This book recommends that all server partitions be formatted as NTFS for heightened security and improved performance. If you've installed Windows NT Server 4.0 in a FAT partition and don't want to convert that partition to NTFS, consider installing the content folders and files to another partition or drive that's formatted with NTFS. It's possible, but not easy, to store additional content on another server in the domain. IIS doesn't recognize server shares mapped to logical drive letters, so you must use UNC in HTML tags if the content is located on a remote server. You'll find life much easier if you keep all your content (publishing) files on the same logical drive. Windows NT's Disk Manager lets you create volume sets of multiple drives that share the same logical drive letter, so you can expand the volume capacity later as capacity requirements increase.

> ▶ **See** "Configuration Considerations: Volume Sets, Extensibility, and Booting," **p. 238** ■

Making an Initial Installation or Upgrading a Prior Version of IIS

When you first install Windows NT Server 4.0 from the standard retail distribution CD-ROM, you're offered a chance to install IIS 2.0 during the latter part of the setup process. IIS 4.0 will install as an upgrade from IIS 2.0 or 3.0, but during a new install of Windows NT, you can skip the IIS 2.0 install and then install IIS 4.0.

> **N O T E**   You must upgrade Windows NT Server 4.0 with Service Pack 3 before installing IIS 4.0. SP3 is included on the IIS 4.0 distribution CD-ROM, but not in the version of IIS 4.0 that you download from the Microsoft Web site.

> ▶ **See** "Installing Service Packs," **p. 206** ■

> **CAUTION**
>
> If you are upgrading from IIS 2.0 or IIS 3.0, back up all files in your \InetPubs or \Inetsrv folder and their subfolders before upgrading IIS 2.0 or 3.0. Also back up your Index Server files. Although upgrades of IIS 2.0 (and ASP) don't alter your Web content and index files or folder structure, there's always the chance that the upgrade of your current IIS installation and the IIS 4.0 setup process might cause unforeseen problems.

To start IIS 4.0 installation, insert the distribution CD-ROM into your server's CD-ROM drive. The CD-ROM uses AutoPlay (new to Windows NT 4.0), so the initial HTML screen should appear automatically; if it doesn't, double-click the icon of the CD-ROM drive in My Computer or Explorer. An instance of Internet Explorer opens with the Welcome to IIS 4.0 page (see Figure 20.8).

> **N O T E**   If you download IIS 4.0 from the Microsoft Web site, the installation process might vary slightly from the following process, which is based on the public Beta 2 version of IIS 4.0. ■

FIG. 20.8

The default Welcome screen opened in Internet Explorer 3.0.

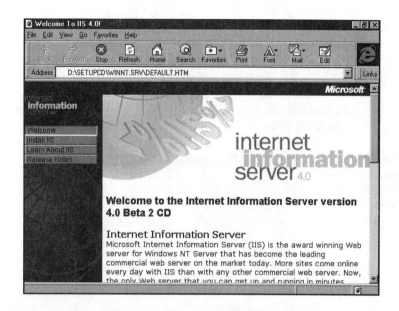

When the Internet Information Server Welcome page opens, follow these steps:

1. Close all running applications; then click the Install IIS button in the left frame to proceed to the second IIS 4.0 setup page and move to the Installing Internet Information Server Version 4.0 section (see Figure 20.9).

FIG. 20.9

Starting the IIS 4.0 installation.

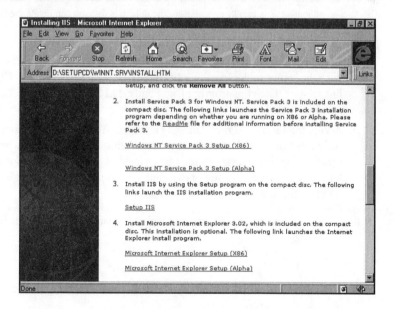

Part

IV

Ch

20

2. If you have a prior version of IIS installed, a dialog appears with three buttons: Add/Remove, Reinstall, and Remove All. Click the Remove All button to delete the prior

installation. Click Yes when asked to confirm removal. If you haven't stopped the
Internet services, you receive message boxes asking whether you want to stop them.
Click Yes in each instance. When you're notified that the services have been removed,
click OK and then return to this HTML page.

3. If you haven't already done so, click the Windows NT Service Pack 3 Setup link to install
SP3 from the IIS 4.0 distribution CD-ROM. Figure 20.10 shows the Welcome dialog that
starts SP3 setup.

FIG. 20.10

The Windows NT Server
4.0 Service Pack 3
installation dialog.

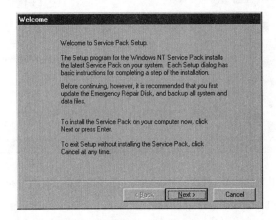

NOTE   You can create an Uninstall folder, which lets you remove the Service Pack at a later date.
Although this is usually unnecessary, the default is Yes; you can delete the Uninstall folder
later when you're sure that the system is stable. ▪

4. After installing the Service Pack, you must reboot your server. When the system comes
back up, return to the Installing IIS HTML page on the CD-ROM. Click the Setup IIS
link to start the Setup program (see Figure 20.11). Click Next to display the License
Agreement dialog.

5. Accept the License Agreement and click Next. You're given the choice of installation
type: Minimum, Typical, or Custom (see Figure 20.12). Minimum installs only basic IIS
functionality. Typical installs the recommended options and the documentation. Custom
lets you choose which components and subcomponents you want installed (see Figure
20.13); after selecting your components, click Next.

NOTE   If you choose to install the Internet Mail Server, it must be installed on an NTFS
partition. ▪

FIG. 20.11

The first dialog of the IIS 4.0 Setup program.

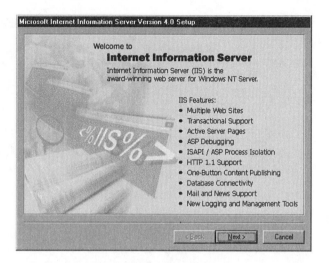

FIG. 20.12

Choosing the type of IIS 4.0 installation.

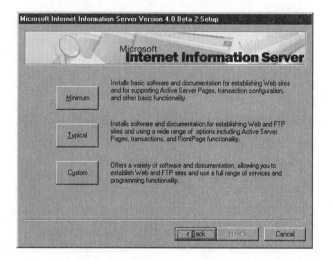

6. The default content (publishing) folder for IIS 4.0 installed from the IIS 4.0 CD-ROM is \InetPub, the same folder used by IIS 2.0 and 3.0. Each service you specify stores its default content in root subfolders: \InetPub\wwwroot and \InetPub\ftproot (see Figure 20.14). You can locate \InetPub and its subfolders on any local volume. Unless you have existing content in another set of folders, accept the default locations. Also, by default any application files will be installed in \Program Files. Click Next to continue with the installation.

7. If you chose to install the Microsoft Transaction Server, you have the chance to specify the destination folder for its files (see Figure 20.15). The default is \Program Files\Mtx. Click Next to continue.

Part
IV

Ch
20

FIG. 20.13
The Select Components dialog for the Custom installation choice.

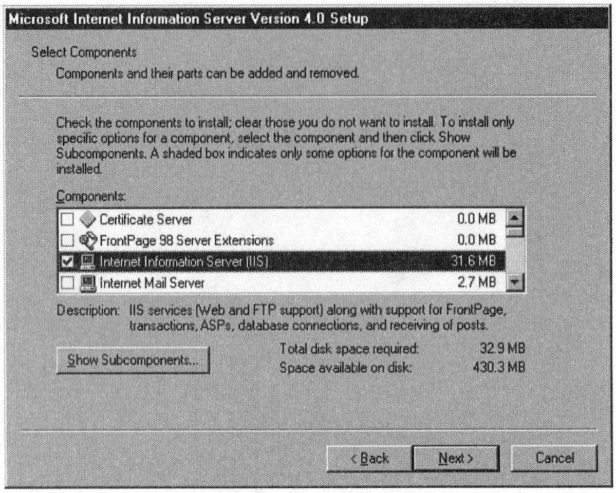

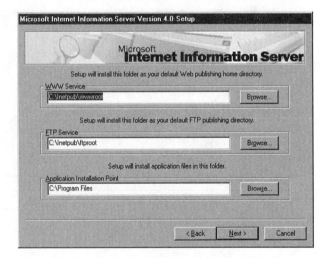

FIG. 20.14
Specifying the location of content files in the publishing directories dialog.

N O T E Microsoft Transaction Server (MTS) 2.0 uses the same core components as MTS 1.1, which was released as an added feature of Windows NT Server 4.0 in late June 1997. MTS 2.0 uses a Microsoft Management Console Snap-In to implement MTS Explorer for administration; MTS 1.1 uses the standard MTS Explorer application released in December 1996 for management.

▶ **See** "Managing the Middle Tier with Transaction Server," **p. 973** ▨

8. If you chose to install Index Server, a dialog opens in which you specify the location of Index Server files. Accept the default C:\Inetpub or specify a different location, and then click Next to start the installation of the IIS 4.0 files.

FIG. 20.15
Specifying the location for the Microsoft Transaction Server files.

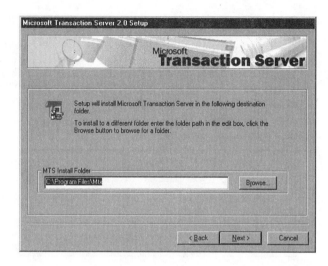

9. When a message appears that IIS 4.0 setup has completed successfully, click Finish to exit the Setup program. Because the installation changes some system settings, you must reboot your server to finish the installation. After the system reboots, you have a new program group, Microsoft Internet Server, which includes Internet Information Server Setup, Internet Service Manager, and Product Documentation, plus other programs and program groups for any other components you installed.

10. If you haven't already done so, you can install Internet Explorer 3.02+ on your server by returning to the Installing IIS page on the CD-ROM.

Using Microsoft Management Console to Administer IIS 4.0

Starting with IIS 4.0, a Snap-In for Microsoft Management Console (MMC) replaces the dedicated Internet Service Manager application. MMC is a universal administrative tool that, starting with Windows NT 5.0, will centralize management tasks for Windows NT Services, including Exchange servers, SQL Server databases, and other services for which Microsoft or third parties provide MMC Snap-Ins. Figure 20.16 shows the components managed by the Iis.msc Snap-In for IIS 4.0.

Also, IIS 4.0 provides a mechanism for remote management of the site. By default, the remote administration capability uses a different IP port for access; therefore, by adding the port number to the server name, a user with administrative privileges can control IIS 4.0 from any browser. In the instance shown in Figure 20.17, the port number is 7826, so the address is http:*servername*:7826.

NOTE You must have administrative privileges to run either version of Internet Service Manager. The HTML version isn't located in the \InetPub\wwwroot subfolders to which, by default, the anonymous Internet or intranet user has access. ▪

Part
IV

Ch
20

FIG. 20.16
Microsoft Management Console displaying the child window for the Iis.msc Snap-In that replaces IIS 2.0's Internet Service Manager.

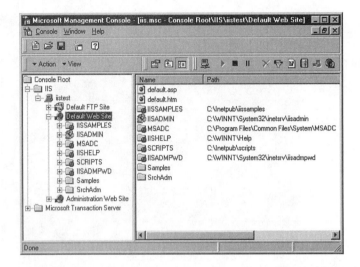

FIG. 20.17
Accessing the management capabilities of IIS 4.0 from a remote browser.

Testing the Default IIS 4.0 Installation

As a quick test of the installation, double-click the Internet Explorer icon on the desktop to start the newly installed browser, which automatically displays a default.htm file. To verify that the IIS demonstration files are installed correctly, type *servername* (such as **iistest**) in the Address text box of the browser to open the InetPub\wwwroot\default.htm page (see Figure 20.18). (Internet Explorer automatically prepends **http://** to *servername*.)

FIG. 20.18

The default home page for the IIS 4.0 demonstration files displayed in Internet Explorer 3.0.

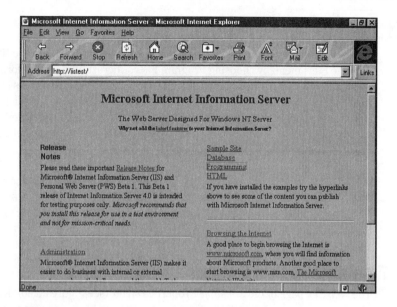

To verify accessibility to your Internet server by networked users, at a remote client type *servername* or http://*servername* in your browser's Address text box. Experiment by navigating to the sample site, Exploration Air, to test the speed of your network connection and IIS 4.0. Exploration Air's home page (see Figure 20.19) includes a Java applet that accesses a Jet (Access) database to produce scrolling headlines as well as graphics and other links.

FIG. 20.19

The home page of the Exploration Air sample Web site displayed in Internet Explorer.

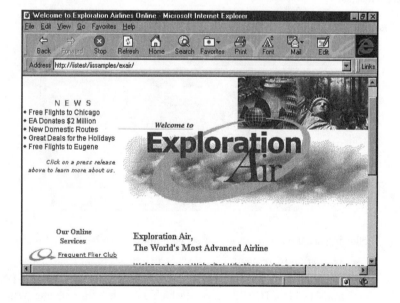

Setting IIS 4.0 Options

To set Web server options and logging parameters, open MMC with the IIS 4.0 Snap-In active from the Start menu by choosing Program Files, Microsoft Internet Information Server (Common), and Internet Service Manager, which launches MMC with the Iis.msc Snap-In file. Expand the IIS entry to display the Default Web Server item; then right-click the server's icon and choose Properties to open the WWW Service Properties sheet. The following sections describe how to set server options and logging parameters for your Web service in the nine pages of the *Sitename* Properties sheet.

N O T E The entry you put in the Description text box in the Web Site Identification section becomes the name for this site throughout MMC. If you change this value to IISTEST, for example, the title bar for all the properties for this Web site changes to IISTEST Properties. For the figures in this chapter, the description is left as Default Web Site. ▪

Configuring Web Site Options

The Web Site page of the *Sitename* Properties sheet (see Figure 20.20) determines Web Site Identification parameters, Connections information, and Logging parameters. The Web Site Identification section lets you set a description, specific IP address or all unassigned addresses, TCP port, and SSL port for the default site on this server.

FIG. 20.20

Setting parameters for the default Web site on the Web Site page of the *Sitename* Properties sheet.

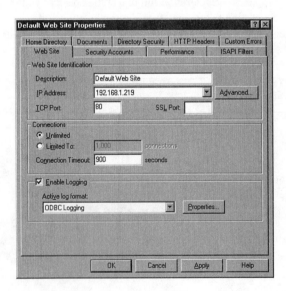

Following are the two methods for serving multiple Web sites on the same machine:

- *Multiple TCP/IP addresses,* each of which has a unique entry in the Domain Name Service (DNS). A Web user points to a site by name; through the DNS, the name is translated to a TCP/IP address, which points to your machine. When the HTTP request arrives at your server, the address you assign to the Web site in the Web Site Identification parameter determines the destination of the request.

■ *Multiple Web sites* assigned to the same TCP/IP address. Through the use of Host Headers, a new feature of IIS 4.0, multiple virtual servers can share the same IP address, although Host Headers aren't supported by all browsers. *Host Headers* are an HTTP 1.1 feature that allows the browser to specify which virtual servers at a particular address to communicate with. Clicking the Advanced button in the Web Site Identification section of the Web Site page gives you access to the parameters for setting up multiple virtual servers on the same machine. The Advanced Multiple Web Site Configuration dialog lets you assign Host Headers to a particular address (see Figure 20.21).

FIG. 20.21

Assigning host headers in the Advanced Multiple Web Site Configuration dialog.

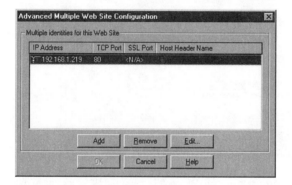

Setting Logging Options

Although logging of your Internet services might appear to be related only to security issues, logging has many other benefits. You should know who is accessing the various services and content offered by your server. User access information helps you recognize the need for additional services, better ways to service users, and emerging trends in usage and server loading.

The log files created by IIS include the IP address for the incoming request, the type of request made, and information about the success or failure of the request. Logs also provide information about access to individual pages. In the case of your Web server, this information is very valuable when determining what content to revise, keep, or remove from the system.

T I P   Always enable logging to spot usage trends and aid in troubleshooting your site. You can set up logging to maintain only a limited history. If you worry about the size of history files, consider setting options to keep only five days or less of history.

You set up system-wide logging options in the Logging section of the Web Site page. If you want to enable logging, mark the Enable Logging check box in the *Sitename* Properties sheet

Part
IV

Ch
20

(refer to Figure 20.20), and then pick one of the three logging options: Microsoft Logging, NCSA Logging, and ODBC Logging. The Microsoft and NCSA logging options are similar; events are logged to a text file with different formats for Microsoft and NCSA log types. Figure 20.22 shows the properties for Microsoft Logging, which creates in *yymmdd*.log files in the \Winnt\System32\LogFiles folder. The *yymmdd* portion of the file name is the year, month, and day of the log file. With NCSA logging, the log file name begins with *nc* rather than *in*.

FIG. 20.22

Setting properties for Microsoft Logging.

N O T E You have the option for both Microsoft Logging and NCSA logging to determine how often you want a new log opened. New files are created at midnight, but midnight is determined by the time zone used by the log format. For NCSA logging, midnight is 12 a.m. local time; for Microsoft logging, midnight is 12 a.m. Greenwich Mean Time (GMT). ■

To use ODBC logging, you must supply the Data Source Name (DSN), table name, user name, and password for the target logging database (see Figure 20.23). The ODBC data source must be an ODBC 3.0 or 3.5 System DNS; File DSNs and User DSNs don't work.

▶ **See** "Logging to an ODBC Data Source," **p. 766**

N O T E IIS 4.0 replaces ODBC 3.0 with the ODBC 3.5 ODBC Data Service Administrator, and updates the Microsoft Access Driver (*.mdb) and SQL Server driver to version 3.5. There are no significant operational changes between the two versions. ■

N O T E The remaining default option values of the Web Site page usually are satisfactory for Web sites with moderate traffic. It's seldom necessary to change the default TCP Port value (80). You might want to decrease the Connection Timeout to less than the default 15 minutes. ■

FIG. 20.23
Setting the options required for ODBC logging.

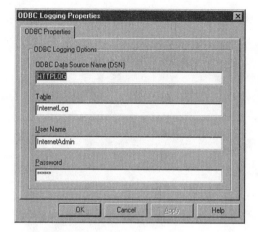

Configuring the Security Accounts

Web browsing is typically an anonymous service, unless your site includes confidential information. You can secure your entire Web site by clearing the Allow Anonymous check box in the Directory Security properties. However, it's more common to assign an anonymous logon account for access to non-confidential information while simultaneously securing other areas for protected access. You must allow anonymous logon if your server is connected to the Internet for public access.

When you install IIS 4.0, a new user is added automatically to your Windows NT user database. The user, given a name of IUSR_ plus the name of your system (IISTEST, in this case), has sufficient rights to access your server's services and browse your server's content. This new user is created with the same basic rights as a user that might be considered "average."

The anonymous user is created as a member of the Domain Users and Guest groups. Of course, the user also belongs to the Everyone group when allowed or disallowed access to a given resource. IIS creates a random password for the anonymous user account. A very important facet of the IUSR_IISTEST account is that it's granted the Log On Locally right.

All users of the Web service must be able to log on locally because the logon request is made to the WWW Server process. That process takes the name provided by the user and logs on through Windows NT's standard security model. By doing so, Windows NT assigns appropriate security rights and permissions to the logon account, providing a solid security model that's fully integrated with the Windows NT domain model.

You determine which users or groups are allowed to administer this Web site in the Security Accounts page (see Figure 20.24). The settings apply to the IIS Snap-In for MMC and to the HTML Internet Service Manager for Web-based IIS administration.

Part
IV
Ch
20

FIG. 20.24

The Security Accounts page of the *Sitename* Properties sheet.

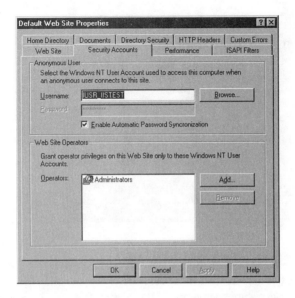

Configuring Performance Options

You set on the Performance page of the *Sitename* Properties sheet the following options related to the performance of your Web site (see Figure 20.25):

- *Performance Tuning* provides a slider to specify the anticipated number of hits on your site per day. IIS uses this information to reserve memory and other resources on the Windows NT server.

- *Enable Bandwith Throttling* is a way to make sure that this Web site doesn't consume all the network bandwidth available to the server.

- *HTTP Keep-Alives Enabled* can reduce network traffic. Normally, an HTTP network connection exists only while data is being transferred. For example, when you navigate to a Web site, you open the default or home page. As soon as that page is transferred, the connection to the Web site closes. If you click a link on that the default page to go to another section of that Web site, a new network connection must be initiated. A certain amount of network overhead is associated with each initiation and disconnect. Most browsers offer HTTP Keep-Alive, which doesn't disconnect from the site until a specified timeout period elapses.

Configuring Folder Security

IIS 4.0 gives you very precise control of Web site security, which can be enforced at every level down to an individual file. Select a folder or file in the hierarchy view in the Microsoft Management Console and click the Properties icon on the toolbar. The IIS Snap-In for MMC provides a Directory Security page at every level in your \InetPubs folder hierarchy. Directory Security properties control the Password Authentication Method, Secure Communications Method, and TCP/IP Access Restrictions for each folder. You set the default security properties for each Web site on your server in the Directory Security page of the *Sitename* Properties sheet (see Figure 20.26).

FIG. 20.25

Setting Web site Performance parameters.

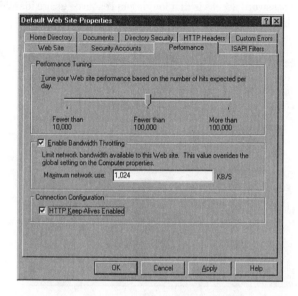

FIG. 20.26

Setting the Directory Security options for the default Web site.

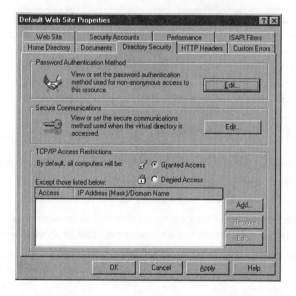

Click the Edit button of the Directory Security page's Password Authentication Method section to open the Authentication Methods dialog. Anonymous access is enabled at every folder level of the selected site by default (see Figure 20.27). In situations where you want every user to log on to the selected site, clear the Allow Anonymous check box to assure that everyone using your Web site provides a user name and password. Intranet users are authenticated by their current credentials—their user name and password for Windows NT Server. Internet users are prompted for a user name and password before being granted access to this site. The advantage of requiring password access is that logging of resource usage identifies the people who are using the system.

FIG. 20.27

Setting authentication options in the Authentication Methods dialog.

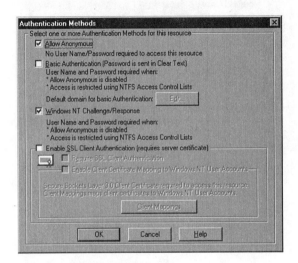

The other important option is the type of authentication to be used. Two different authentication types are used to secure all or part of your site. The mix of browsers used on your intranet dictates your decision of authentication type. As of this writing, the only browser supporting the Windows NT Challenge/Response option is Microsoft Internet Explorer 2.0 or later. If you have a mixed browser community—for example, if you have users with Netscape's Navigator browser—you must also enable Basic (Clear Text) authentication. Otherwise, you block such users from access to your site.

The Windows NT Challenge/Response option works in the following manner:

1. If a user requests a secured Web page but isn't now logged on with sufficient rights, the server fails the request and closes the connection to the browser.

2. The browser is informed of the failure by the server's response.

3. The browser prompts the user for user name and password credentials, passing this information to the server along with another attempt to access the secured resources.

4. The server uses the new credentials to log on to Windows NT and attempts access to the resource. The renewed attempts generally occur up to three times, depending on the browser used.

5. The user ID and password move across the link encrypted, protecting them from being "stolen" in transit by someone with less-than-noble intentions.

With the Basic (Clear Text) option, the User ID and password move across the link encoded but still decipherable by a determined hacker. The browser keeps a channel to the server open as it tries to access the shared resource. If you enable the Basic (Clear Text) option, the Internet Service Manager warns you that you're enabling a less secure method of sending passwords over the network and asks you to confirm your choice (see Figure 20.28).

FIG. 20.28
Internet Service Manager's warning when you enable the Basic (Clear Text) authentication option.

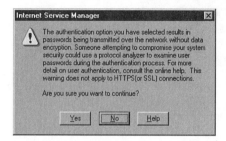

> **N O T E** Most configuration options for the IIS Web and FTP services are largely identical. Thus, this chapter provides limited coverage in the FTP section for completing the basic configuration options. The differences between the standard configuration with the Web server options and the FTP service are covered in the sections devoted to FTP services. ■

Marking the Enable SSL Client Authentication check box (refer to Figure 20.27) enables two check boxes that let you determine the level of encryption available with the Secure Sockets Layer (SSL). You must install IIS 4.0's Certificate Server service and create a self-signed X.509-standard certificate created by the Microsoft Base Cryptographic Provider or a cryptographic service provider from another certificate authority. When you install the Certificate Server, a wizard guides you through the process of creating an X.509 certificate.

ON THE WEB

You can read an overview of the Secure Sockets Layer security mechanism at **http://www.microsoft.com/iis/learnaboutiis/whatisiis/winnt351/tour/ssl.htm**.

Finally, you can grant or restrict access to this entity (directory or file) by TCP/IP address in the TCP/IP Address Restrictions section of the Directory Security page of the *Sitename* Properties sheet (refer to Figure 20.26). This section lets you exclude computers with specific IP addresses or specify the IP address of each computer allowed access to the selected site. Alternatively, you can use a subnet mask to let a group of computers within a subnet access the site.

Another alternative is to indicate that everyone has access to the system except for those IP addresses in the list. In cases where you have a confirmed attempt or attempts to compromise your system, you can remove the offending user's access rights.

To enter an address, click the Add button of the TCP/IP Access Restrictions section to open the Grant Access On or Deny Access On dialog (see Figure 20.29). When you enter the address, you can use "wild cards" by selecting the Group of Computers option and providing the part of the IP address that's constant for the systems addressed. When entering a single computer's address, you can use the DNS Lookup button to resolve a system's name to its TCP/IP address, and then enter the address.

FIG. 20.29
Setting parameters to deny access by network address.

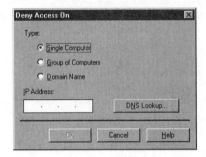

Configuring the Folders

A primary use of the Home Directory page of the *Sitename* Properties sheet is to manage the content you provide to the users of your system. By placing different categories of content in different folder trees, you accomplish the following objectives:

- You place the information in physically different areas, potentially even on a different server.

- You limit the scope of a search engine, such as Microsoft Index Server, incorporated at your site. You usually can limit the scope of the search engine to a particular folder structure. By separating content into different areas, you speed search time for your users.

- You can move static content to a folder tree that may be backed up less frequently, perhaps only on a monthly basis. If you have content that's more dynamic, such as pages for an online magazine or other constantly changing source, keep this content in a folder tree that's backed up daily.

The Home Directory page of the *Sitename* Properties sheet (or the Directory Security page for entities below the home page) determines the permissions allowed for that entity, as well as specifies the default document at that folder level (see Figure 20.30). At the top of the page, you can assign the path type to the folder and the actual path as follows:

- *A Directory Located on this Computer*. The path to the local folder is in normal format.
- *A Share Located on Another Computer*. The path is in UNC format. A user name and password may be required to access that directory on the remote server.
- *A Redirection to a URL*. The path is an alias to a locally accessible URL.

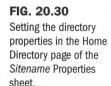

FIG. 20.30
Setting the directory properties in the Home Directory page of the *Sitename* Properties sheet.

Accessing Remote Server Shares   Placing content on a remote server share with the A Share Located on Another Computer option is tricky because when the remote server is accessed, the share is accessed by using the name and password you provide in all cases. If a user name and password you provide doesn't have access to the share, the user can't access the pages the share contains, even if he or she has permissions for the share itself.

The remote server doesn't provide the same level of security that you have when trying to access a secured folder or file physically located on the IIS server. In cases where you have secure information, always put the information on the IIS server, allowing Windows NT's security management to step in, protecting the information. Put public, widely available information on the remote server.

This same approach also applies to virtual server configurations. When you indicate a virtual server, the provided user name and password is used to connect to the remote server. If secure information resides at that remote location, move it to the local system and allow Windows NT to manage the secure access to the information.

Redirecting to Another Page   The A Redirection to a URL option is very useful, especially while changes are being made on your Web site. For example, you can establish the folder and page structure of a new site, but use the Redirection method to point them all to one "under construction" page. As the content for each folder is finished, you can change the path type as appropriate.

Assigning Folder Permissions   The next option in establishing folder properties is to specify the access rights in the Home Directory Properties sheet. To enable viewing content, mark the Read check box. *Read Access* means read-only access; users can't make any changes to the folder. Write Access allows clients to upload files to this directory, or to modify a file. Marking the Log Access check box creates log entries for accesses to this entity, in accordance with the Logging parameters set up for the virtual server as a whole.

Part
IV

Ch
20

To enable a program folder containing executable files that add functionality to your Web pages, mark the Execute check box. Execute access doesn't allow users to scan folder contents; that right is granted by the Directory Browsing Allowed check box. Use Script permission to run scripts, including Active Server Pages and Internet Database Connector scripts, without granting Execute permission for the folder.

> **CAUTION**
>
> Never grant Read access to any of your application or script subfolders. If you do, users may not only browse the folders, seeking programs that "look interesting," but they also can run the programs to see what they do. By providing Execute rights, users can execute applications and scripts but can't perform blind folder listings or copy files from the location. Don't mix scripts and applications with Web pages in a single folder.

Establishing Default Document Names   The Documents page of the Default Web Server Properties sheet lets you enable one or more default documents for a folder. IIS 4.0 establishes Default.htm and Default.asp as default documents; the server returns to the requesting browser the first one it finds in the order listed. Click the Add button to open the Add Default Document dialog to specify additional default document names.

N O T E   If you want to implement a system by following the UNIX standard for default pages, change your default document name from default.htm to index.html, the default starting page on the vast majority of Web servers. Setting the default to the standard makes it easier for an experienced UNIX Webmaster to maintain pages on the server. ■

Setting HTTP Header Options

The HTTP Headers page of the *Sitename* Properties sheet lets you set the following options (see Figure 20.31):

- ■ *Enable Content Expiration* lets you set a freshness value on the content in your site.
- ■ *Custom HTTP Headers* lets you add new types of headers to your pages as defined by Microsoft, third parties, and the World Wide Web Consortium (W3C).
- ■ *Content Rating* lets you help users identify the nature of your Web site's content. The primary purpose of content rating is to identify sites with adults-only content so that parents and schools can exclude access by children and teen-agers. The Recreational Software Advisory Council (RSAC) developed the first content rating system, which is likely to form the basis of an international agreement on this controversial subject.
- ■ MIME Map specifies the Multipurpose Internet Mail Extension (MIME) types you use in HTTP headers.

Setting FTP Server Options

The FTP service options are quite similar to those for the Web service described in the preceding sections. They're accessed in the same way—from MMC, right-click Default FTP Site and then select Properties. The FTP Site page (see Figure 20.32) identifies the FTP server, the TCP/IP address it's attached to, and the port used (by convention, port 21). You specify the maximum number of simultaneous connections as well as the amount of time a connection can remain idle before it's logged off. You also can determine the logging options for the FTP service by a process that's identical to the logging options for Web sites.

FIG. 20.31
Setting HTTP Headers options.

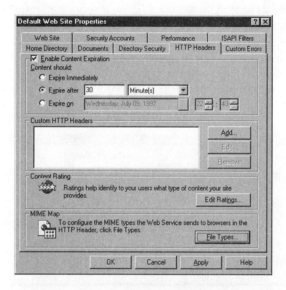

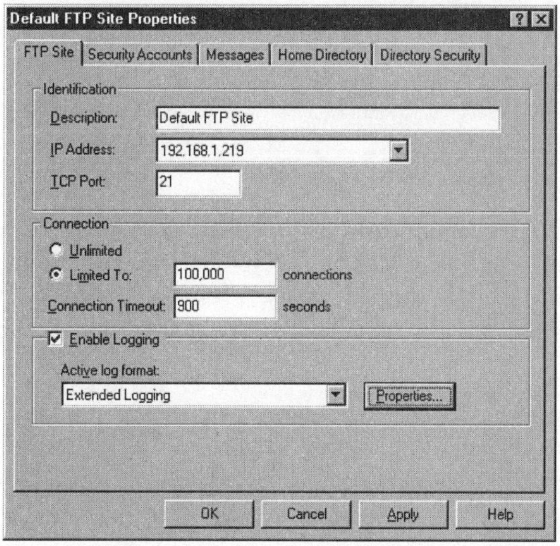

FIG. 20.32
Setting the general options for the Default FTP Site.

T I P   You should adjust the default values for Connection and Connection Timeout shown in Figure 20.32 to more realistic values. For example, you probably want less than 100,000 simultaneous connections, especially if your network or server hardware are strained. Also, the default idle timeout is 15 minutes; you should reduce the time, especially if you severely limit the number of simultaneous connections.

The Security Accounts page of the Default FTP Site Properties sheet (see Figure 20.33) determines whether anonymous FTP connections are allowed and, if so, what user name and password they will use. You can also restrict your FTP server to anonymous connections only; this is useful if all the material you want accessible via FTP can be restricted to certain directories, with their permissions mapped to the anonymous user. This will prevent accesses using cracked or stolen username/password combinations from reading or downloading files outside your public directory.

FIG. 20.33

Setting the Security Accounts options for the FTP site.

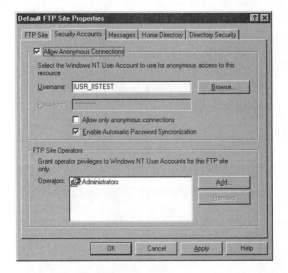

The Messages page (see Figure 20.34) lets you personalize your FTP site with Welcome, Exit, and Maximum connections messages. If you have an index for the content of your FTP site, it's a common practice to suggest that users read the index before proceeding. When you connect to an FTP site with a browser, the Welcome message appears below the FTP Root at *Servername* title.

On the Home Directory page, you can determine virtual directory properties, such as read or write permissions and logging (see Figure 20.35). You can also specify whether a directory listing is presented in UNIX format or MS-DOS format.

FIG. 20.34
Specifying the messages that appear when a user logs on and off an FTP site, and when the maximum number of connections is reached.

FIG. 20.35
Setting the Home Directory options for the FTP site.

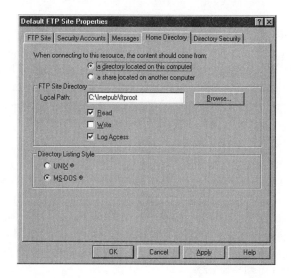

Lastly, the Directory Security page (see Figure 20.36) lets you grant or deny access based on TCP/IP addressing for individual computers or groups of computers.

FIG. 20.36
Setting the Directory
Security options for the
FTP site.

From Here...

Microsoft's IIS 4.0 is intended primarily to be a high-performance Web server for private intranets and the public Internet. This chapter explained how to set up and connect to each service offered by IIS 4.0. World Wide Web and FTP services combine to provide comprehensive sources of information for intranet and Internet users.

The following chapters provide additional information related to the topics discussed in this chapter:

- Chapter 13, "Managing User and Group Accounts," describes how to use Windows NT Server 4.0's User Manager for Domains, take advantage of the new Add User Accounts and Group Management wizards, and use Windows NT's built-in user groups.

- Chapter 14, "Sharing and Securing Network Resources," explains Windows NT Server's security system for shared file and folder resources and how to use the new Managing Folder and File Access Wizard to simplify sharing Windows NT 4.0 server resources.

- Chapter 18, "Integrating Windows NT with NetWare and UNIX," shows you how to set up and administer DNS Server.

- Chapter 21, "Administering Intranet and World Wide Web Sites," describes key elements of maintaining a Web site that reliably distributes the content of HTML-encoded documents, outlines a Webmaster's duties, and briefly describes the integration of popular HTML authoring tools with an intranet or Internet server.

Administering Intranet and World Wide Web Sites

B ringing your intranet or Internet site online after installing and setting up Internet Information Server (IIS) 4.0 is only the first step toward making your new system a success. You must consider many factors in order to achieve the objective of providing accurate and timely information to your site's users. As the site administrator or Webmaster, you need up-to-date details on your site's activity and its demands on your system.

This chapter concentrates on two basic areas: activity logging and distribution of activity reports, and generating Web pages with tools included with IIS or available for no-charge downloading of retail or time-limited demonstration versions from Microsoft's Web site. The chapter also provides a brief overview of new Microsoft tools for Web-site creation and management.

Substitute a database table for IIS 4.0's text logs

Change activity logging on your system to use an Access or SQL Server database with ODBC 3.5 drivers.

Tune your Web site for maximum performance

Display data from IIS 4.0's counters with Performance Monitor.

Generate pages with ASP and VBScript

Add dynamic HTML generation and database capabilities to your Web pages with Active Server Pages, VBScript, and ActiveX Data Objects.

Take advantage of FrontPage 97

Install and use Microsoft Front-Page 97 for Web management and content creation.

N O T E   This chapter uses *IIS* without a version number when discussing features that apply to IIS
2.0, 3.0, and 4.0. *IIS 3.0+* indicates elements that apply to IIS 3.0 and 4.0. ■

Logging to an ODBC Data Source

Chapter 20, "Setting Up Internet Information Server 4.0," describes how to set up logging for
your intranet or Internet server to a text file. As you amass information on the use of your site,
log files in text format become increasingly difficult to analyze. Although you can import text
log files into an Excel worksheet or Access table, appending log records directly to a database
table is a simpler and less error-prone process.

Following are the basic steps to create a logging database and query the IIS log files to find the
information you want:

1. Create a database devoted to logging operations.

2. Add a table with the structure required for IIS logging.

3. Establish an ODBC system data source to connect to the database.

4. Change the logging option for each of your services to the ODBC data source.

5. Write SQL queries that return the information required to analyze use of your site.

The following sections describe these steps in detail or provide references to information in
previous chapters that relate to these steps. Microsoft SQL Server 6.5 and Access 97's Jet 3.5
databases are used as examples, but you can use any client/server or desktop database system
for which you have a 32-bit ODBC 2.5 or higher driver. The examples assume that you have at
least some familiarity with SQL Server 6.x or Microsoft Access.

N O T E   This chapter uses the ODBC 3.5 Data Source Administrator, which is included with IIS 4.0.
There is little difference between the ODBC 3.5 and the ODBC 3.0 Data Source Administrator, which installs from Windows NT 4.0 Service Pack 3 (SP3). In addition to ODBC 3.0, SP3 provides
the FrontPage 97 update, Crystal Reports, and various other additions and fixes for Windows NT Server
4.0. IIS 4.0 installs the server extensions for FrontPage 98.

▶ **See** "Installing Service Packs," **p. 206** ■

Creating the Logging Database

Following are brief recommendations for creating the logging database:

■ For SQL Server databases, create a new device, such as Logging.dat, to contain the
database. Don't install user databases in the Master.dat device. Unless you plan to
accumulate data over long periods of time, a device size of 10M to 25M should suffice.
If you expect a very active Web site, allocate 100M or more to save a week or so of data.
You can use the entire capacity of Logging.dat for your logging database. Be sure to
turn off transaction logging for the database. You can use your SQL Server administrator
account to create the device and database, but adding a new database user account and
a password for the logging operation is a good idea. Chapter 23, "Running Microsoft SQL

Server 6.5," describes how to create new SQL Server devices and databases (with and without transaction logs), and how to add SQL Server user accounts.

■ For Jet 3.5 databases, you must install Access 97 or Visual Basic 5.0 to create the required database and logging table. Alternatively, you can copy the database file from a client PC to the server running IIS 4.0. If you want to implement Jet 3.5 database security, Access 97 is required to provide the System.mdw file that provides security features. Don't turn on Jet security until you confirm that the logging system is operational. Create an Access database, such as Logging.mdb, in a separate subfolder of InetPub. IIS 4.0 installs the 32-bit ODBC driver for Jet 3.5.

Adding the Logging Table

Internet Information Server requires a logging table with a specific structure corresponding to the fields of the text version of the log described in Chapter 20, "Setting Up Internet Information Server 4.0." A single logging file includes records for all IIS services.

Table 21.1 lists the column information for the logging table for SQL Server and Jet data types. The Integer size in the table applies only to the Jet Number data type. Null values are allowed in each column. IIS returns null values in the LogDate field; the LogTime field includes date and time information in string format.

Table 21.1 Table Structure for Logging Table

Column	SQL Data Type	Jet Data Type	Size
ClientHost	Char	Text	255
UserName	Char	Text	255
LogDate	Char	Text	255
LogTime	Char	Text	255
Service	Char	Text	255
Machine	Char	Text	255
ServerIP	Char	Text	255
ProcessingTime	Int	Number	Integer
BytesRecvd	Int	Number	Integer
BytesSent	Int	Number	Integer
ServiceStatus	Int	Number	Integer
Win32Status	Int	Number	Integer
Operation	Int	Number	Integer
Target	Char	Text	255
Parameters	Char	Text	255

Part

IV

Ch

21

TIP Don't create indexes on the table, because they slow appending of new log records by IIS. The improved query performance that indexes deliver doesn't warrant the impact of multiple indexes on your Web site's performance.

Creating a SQL Server Table   Listing 21.1 shows the SQL Server query to create the LogTable table used in the following sections. The four lines of Listing 21.1 beginning with `if exists` delete an existing version of the table before creating the new table.

Listing 21.1   The SQL Server Query to Create the Logging Database

```
/****** Object: Table dbo.LogTable ******/
if exists (select * from sysobjects where id =
   object_id('dbo.LogTable') and sysstat & 0xf = 3)
   drop table dbo.LogTable
GO

CREATE TABLE LogTable (
   ClientHost char (50) NULL ,
   UserName char (50) NULL ,
   LogDate char (12) NULL ,
   LogTime char (21) NULL ,
   Service char (20) NULL ,
   Machine char (20) NULL ,
   ServerIP char (50) NULL ,
   ProcessingTime int NULL ,
   BytesRecvd int NULL ,
   BytesSent int NULL ,
   ServiceStatus int NULL ,
   Win32Status int NULL ,
   Operation char (200) NULL ,
   Target char (200) NULL ,
   Parameters char (200) NULL
)
GO
```

N O T E   The logtemp.sql query that IIS setup installs in \Winnt\System32\Inetsrv is a simplified version of the query in Listing 21.1. The logtemp.sql query creates a table named inetlog with the `varchar`, rather than the fixed-width `char`, data type for text columns. Fixed-width fields provide better performance than variable-width fields, but at the expense of table size. ■

To execute the query of Listing 21.1, follow these steps:

1. Launch SQL Enterprise Manager, if necessary, and select the Logging database in the Server Manager window by expanding the tree for your SQL Server, expanding the Databases tree, and then clicking the Logging item.

2. To open the Query window, choose SQL Query Tool from the Tools menu or click the SQL Query Tool toolbar button. The Query tool opens with the Query page displayed for the selected database.

3. Type the content of Listing 21.1 into the Query page (see Figure 21.1). You can omit the lines preceding CREATE TABLE, if you want. Alternatively, choose Open from the File menu and browse to the logtemp.sql file to use the query supplied with IIS.

FIG. 21.1

Typing the makelog.sql query into SQL Enterprise Manager's Query window.

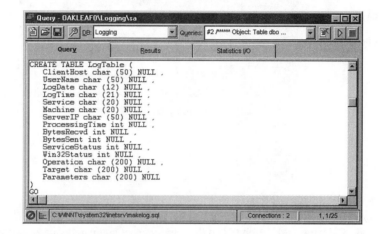

4. From the Query menu choose Execute, or click the Execute Query button (with the VCR play symbol) of the Query toolbar. Assuming that there are no typographical errors, the Results window displays the message This command didn't return data, and it didn't return any rows.

5. Verify the structure of the newly created table by choosing Tables from the Manage menu to open the Manage Tables window. Select LogTable (dbo) from the Table drop-down list (see Figure 21.2).

FIG. 21.2

Verifying the structure of the LogTable table created by executing makelog.sql.

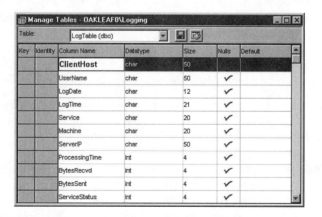

6. Choose Manage from the Logins menu to open the Manage Logins dialog. Select <New User> from the Login Name combo box list, and then type the user name for the logging account, such as **logging**. Type a password for the account in the Password text box.

7. Click the Permit and Default columns for the Logging database to automatically make the Logging database the default for the logging user (see Figure 21.3).

FIG. 21.3

Assigning the Logging database as the default for the logging user.

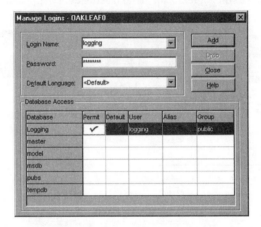

8. Click the Add button to add the logging user, confirm the password when requested, and then click the Close button to close the Manage Logins dialog.

After you verify that the logging of user activity was successful, you can use SQL Server's security system to assure that only authorized persons can access the Logging database.

▶ **See** "Establishing Database Permissions," **p. 865**

N O T E   You can use Access 97 to create a Jet 3.5 LogTable in an .mdb file (as described in the following section), and then use Access's Save As/Export command on the File menu to export the table structure to the SQL Server database. Before exporting the table, you must create an ODBC data source for the SQL Server database, as described later in the section "Creating ODBC Data Sources for SQL Server Databases." ■

Creating a Jet 3.5 Table   Using a Jet 3.5 table eliminates the need to license and administer SQL Server. To create a Jet 3.5 database with a LogTable table, follow these steps:

1. Launch Access 97, preferably with a new System.mdw file, and choose New Database from the File menu to open the New dialog. Click OK to accept the default Blank Database and to open the File New Database dialog.

N O T E   If you've assigned a password to the Access Admin account, the new database you create already has security applied. The System.mdw file that contains account information must also be located on or accessible to the server. If you use a new System.mdw file, the default Admin user has an empty password, eliminating the need for the System.mdw file to open the database. You can create a new System.mdw file with Access 97's Workgroup Administrator application. ■

2. Name the file Logging.mdb, and then click the Create button to close the File New Database dialog and create the database. (The file location isn't important at this point because you can copy Logging.mdb to the server after you create it.)

3. With the Table page of the Database Container active, click the New button to display the New Table dialog. Select Design View in the list and click OK to open the new table in design mode.

4. Assign Field Name, Data Type, and Size values for each column according to Table 21.1. Set the Size value in the General field property page (see Figure 21.4). Accept the default No value for the Required and Indexed field attributes. For text fields, set Allow Zero Length to Yes.

FIG. 21.4

Specifying the field attributes of a Jet 3.5 logging table.

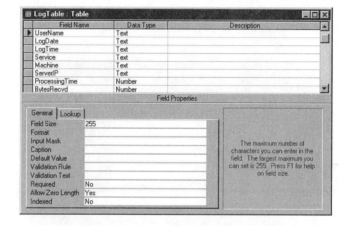

5. Click the Table View toolbar button, and then click Yes when you're asked whether you want to save the table.

6. Type the table name (**Logging**) in the Save As dialog and click OK to continue.

7. When asked whether you want to create a primary key field, click No. Your new table appears in Datasheet view.

8. Close Access and copy Logging.mdb to a logging subfolder of the \InetPub folder on the server. If you created or want to create a secure database, copy System.mdw to the same folder.

Setting Up ODBC 3.x System Data Sources

The ODBC data source is a common source of problems with logging databases, including SQL Server and other client/server or desktop databases having 32-bit ODBC drivers. Thus, it's important to understand the details of setting up ODBC data sources for access by IIS and server applications that run with IIS.

IIS runs as a Windows NT service and starts automatically after Windows NT loads. In most cases, the server runs with no local user logged on. In Windows NT 4.0 and Windows 95,

Part
IV

Ch
21

conventional ODBC data sources are associated with a specific user profile. Thus, a conventional ODBC data source isn't accessible to IIS or IIS server applications until the user who created the data source logs on to Windows NT Server.

To solve this problem, Microsoft added ODBC system data sources for 32-bit ODBC 2.5+. An ODBC system data source is accessible as soon as Windows NT Server (and SQL Server, if used) starts. ODBC system data sources don't depend on a user logging on to the server. You use ODBC system data sources for logging and for most of the dynamic Web pages you create from information stored in databases.

To create an ODBC system database on the server, follow these initial steps:

1. From the server's Control Panel, double-click the ODBC tool to launch the ODBC Data Source Administrator and display the User DSN page. Figure 21.5 shows the MtxSamples user data source name (DSN) set up by the installation of IIS 4.0.

FIG. 21.5

ODBC user data sources displayed by the opening dialog of the ODBC Data Source Administrator.

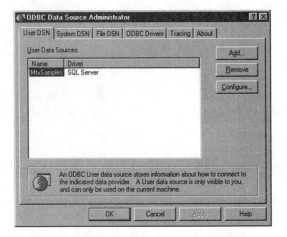

2. Click the System DSN tab to display the System DSN page (see Figure 21.6). The System Data Sources list contains a Microsoft Access data source (CertSrv) for the Certificate Server, plus the LocalServer default ODBC system data source installed for SQL Server and the Web SQL data source for the Internet Data Connector samples.

3. Click the Add button to open the Create New Data Source dialog.

At this point, the steps to create SQL Server and Jet data sources diverge, as described in the next two sections.

Creating ODBC Data Sources for SQL Server Databases   Adding a new ODBC data source with ODBC 3.5 involves the new ODBC Data Source Wizard to guide you through the process. To continue creating an ODBC system database for SQL Server, follow these steps:

1. In the Create New Data Source dialog, select the SQL Server driver in the list (see Figure 21.7). Click Finish.

FIG. 21.6

The System DSN page displaying system data sources for IIS 4.0's Certificate Server, Web page samples, and SQL Server.

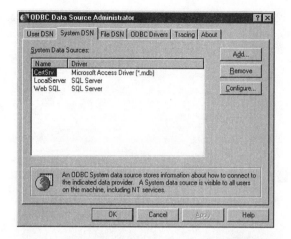

FIG. 21.7

Selecting the SQL Server driver in the Create New Data Source dialog.

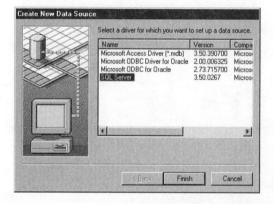

2. In the first Create a New Data Source to SQL Server dialog, type the name of the data source—in this case, **SQLLogging**—in the Name text box and type an optional description of the data source in the Description text box.

3. In the Server combo box, select (local) if SQL Server is installed on the same server as IIS. Otherwise, select the server name on which SQL Server is installed, or type the server name in the text box (see Figure 21.8). Click Next to continue.

4. Select the With SQL Server Authentication option, make sure that the Connect to SQL Server check box is marked, and type the information for the Logging user in the Login ID and Password text boxes (see Figure 21.9). Click Next to continue.

5. Mark the Change the Default Database To check box and select the Logging database in the drop-down list. Accept the default for the remaining three marked check boxes (see Figure 21.10). Click Next to continue.

Part

IV

Ch

21

FIG. 21.8

Specifying the data source name, description, and server for the Logging ODBC data source.

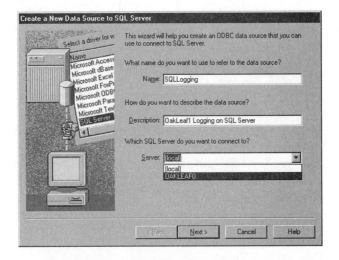

FIG. 21.9

Specifying the login method, login ID, and password for the SQL Server Logging user.

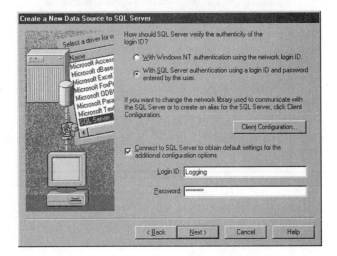

N O T E   The Use the Failover SQL Server check box is enabled only if you have the Enterprise editions of Windows NT Server 4.0 and SQL Server 6.5 installed.

▶ **See** "Clustering for Availability Now and Scalability Later," **p. 970** ■

6. Accept the defaults in the second SQL Server options dialog (see Figure 21.11) and click Next to continue.

FIG. 21.10

Specifying the Logging database and SQL Server options.

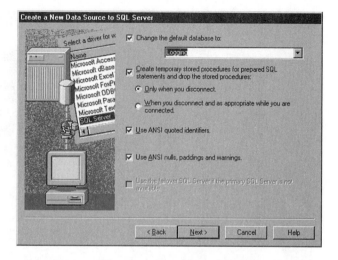

FIG. 21.11

Default values for additional SQL Server options.

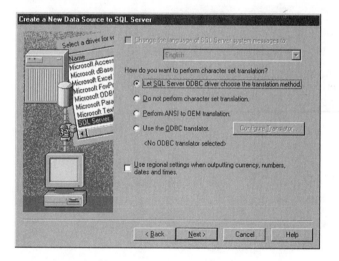

7. Accept the default (unmarked) options for SQL Server and ODBC logging (see Figure 21.12). Click Next to open the ODBC Microsoft SQL Server Setup dialog (see Figure 21.13).

8. Click the Test Data Source button to log on to the database and verify that the SQLLogging data source operates properly. A successful connection displays the SQL Server ODBC Data Source test dialog in Figure 21.14.

9. Click OK to close the dialog and add the new system data source to the System DSN page (see Figure 21.15). Click OK to exit the ODBC Data Source Administrator.

Part

IV

Ch

21

FIG. 21.12

Default values for SQL
Server and ODBC
logging options.

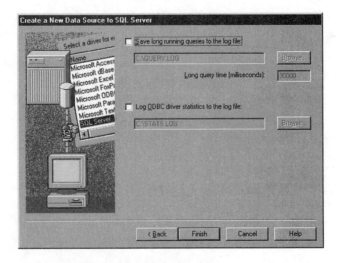

FIG. 21.13

Default values for SQL
Server and ODBC
logging options.

Creating ODBC Data Sources for Jet Databases   The process for creating an ODBC 3.5
system data source for a Jet 3.5 database is similar to that for SQL Server and the ODBC 3.0
Data Source Administrator, but the Access 97 (8.0) ODBC driver presents a different dialog for
specifying the database. To create an ODBC system database for Jet 3.5 tables, start from the
open Create New Data Source dialog and follow these steps:

1. In the Create New Data Source dialog, select the Microsoft Access Driver (*.mdb) item,
    and then click OK to display the ODBC Microsoft Access 97 Setup dialog.

2. Type the DSN—in this case, `JetLogging`—in the Data Source Name text box and
    add an optional description of the data source.

FIG. 21.14
Default values for SQL
Server and ODBC
logging options.

FIG. 21.15
The SQLLogging
data source added
to the System Data
Sources list.

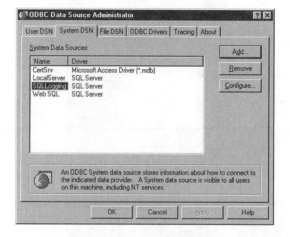

3. Click the Options button to expand the dialog. You don't need to change the defaults for Page Timeout and Buffer Size. Make sure that the Exclusive and Read Only check boxes are cleared (see Figure 21.16).

4. Click Select to open the Select Database dialog. Browse to the \InetPub\Logging folder and select logging.mdb (see Figure 21.17). Click OK to return to the ODBC Microsoft Access 97 Setup dialog.

5. If you want to secure your logging database and have copied System.mdw to the \InetPub\Logging folder, select the Database option in the System Database section of the ODBC Microsoft Access 97 Setup dialog and then click the System Database button to open the Select System Database dialog.

   If you don't plan to secure the database, skip to step 8.

6. Select system.mdw (see Figure 21.18) and click OK to close the dialog.

FIG. 21.16

Entering the DSN and Description in the ODBC Microsoft Access 97 Setup dialog.

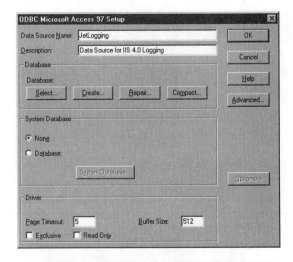

FIG. 21.17

Specifying the logging.mdb file in the Select Database dialog.

FIG. 21.18

Specifying the Access system (workgroup) file in the Select System Database dialog.

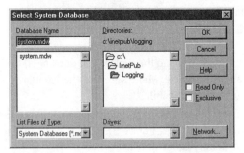

7. Click Advanced in the ODBC Microsoft Access 97 Setup dialog to open the Set Advanced Options dialog. The default admin user appears in the Login Name text box with an empty Password text box. Change the Login Name and Password entries after using Access 97 to secure the database. Optionally, enter the default folder for the file in the Value of DefaultDir text box (see Figure 21.19). Click OK to close the dialog and return to the ODBC Microsoft Access 97 Setup dialog.

FIG. 21.19

The security settings of the Set Advanced Options dialog.

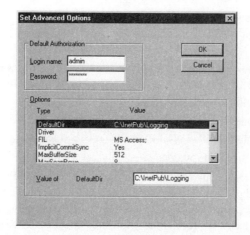

8. The ODBC Microsoft Access 97 Setup dialog displays the specified .mdb and .mdw files (see Figure 21.20). Click OK to close the dialog and add the JetLogging ODBC system data source.

9. On the System DSN page, click Close to exit the ODBC Data Source Administrator.

FIG. 21.20

The completed ODBC Microsoft Access 97 Setup dialog.

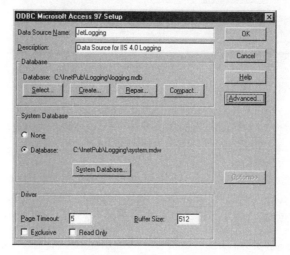

Specifying the ODBC System Data Source for Logging

Now that you've created the table and the ODBC system data source for logging information, change the logging instructions for each service. Follow these steps to implement the changes:

1. From the Start menu choose Programs, Microsoft Internet Information Server, and Internet Service Manager to launch Microsoft Management Console (MMC) with the Internet Service Manager Snap-In active. Expand the IIS folder and the *Servername* folder (Oakleaf1 for this example).

Part

IV

Ch

21

2. Right-click the *Sitename* folder (Default Web Site, for this example) and choose Proper-ties from the pop-up menu to open the *Sitename* Properties sheet with the Web Site page active.

3. Mark the Enable Logging check box and select ODBC Logging from the Active Log Format drop-down list. Click the Properties button to open the ODBC Logging Proper-ties sheet with its default entries.

4. On the ODBC Properties page, type the name of your logging data source (**SQLLogging** or **JetLogging**) in the ODBC Data Source Name (DSN) text box.

5. Type the name of the table you created—in this case, **LogTable**—in the Table text box.

6. If you use the JetLogging data source, clear the User Name and Password text boxes; the user name and password you entered in the ODBC Microsoft Access 97 Setup dialog for the data source provided this information. For the SQLLogging DSN, type the login ID (**Logging**) and password (see Figure 21.21). Click OK twice to close the ODBC Logging Properties sheet and the *Sitename* Properties sheet.

FIG. 21.21

Setting logging options for a SQL Server ODBC system data source in the ODBC Logging Properies sheet.

7. Repeat steps 2 through 6 for the FTP service (Default FTP Service, for this example).

8. Test that your logging database is properly set up by displaying Web pages and downloading files by FTP.

> **N O T E** If users access your server by using the file: protocol, their actions aren't logged. The client handles this type of URL by conventional network file sharing. Be sure to test your logging database with the appropriate URL prefix for each service. ▓

Writing Sample Queries for Reviewing Logs

The log data can quickly become overwhelming unless you write meaningful queries for analysis. Following are some of the questions that queries against the database can answer:

■ What time of day do most people access the server?

■ What pages are most popular?

■ Who is accessing the server (by IP address)?

The sample SQL Server query in Listing 21.2 returns summary information for hits against the server and displays the relative popularity of Web pages. Figure 21.22 shows SQL Enterprise Manager displaying the result set returned by the last three queries of Listing 21.2 against entries created by two brief testing sessions.

Listing 21.2 A Sample Transact-SQL Query that Returns Information on Usage and Web Page Popularity

```
SELECT 'Total hits' = COUNT(*),'Last Access' = MAX(LogTime)
FROM LogTable

SELECT 'Hit summary' = Count(*), 'Date' = SUBSTRING(LogTime,1,8)
FROM LogTable
GROUP BY SUBSTRING(LogTime,1,8)

SELECT 'Time of day' = (SUBSTRING(LogTime,13,2) + ' ' +
SUBSTRING(LogTime,18,2)), 'Hits' = COUNT(SUBSTRING(LogTime,10,2))
FROM LogTable
GROUP BY (SUBSTRING(LogTime,13,2) + ' ' + SUBSTRING(LogTime,18,2))

SELECT 'Page' = SUBSTRING(Target,1,40), 'Hits' = COUNT(Target)
FROM LogTable
WHERE    (CHARINDEX('HTM',target) > 0)
GROUP BY Target
ORDER BY 'Hits' DESC
```

FIG. 21.22

The result set of Listing 21.2's last three queries displayed by SQL Enterprise Manager's Query tool.

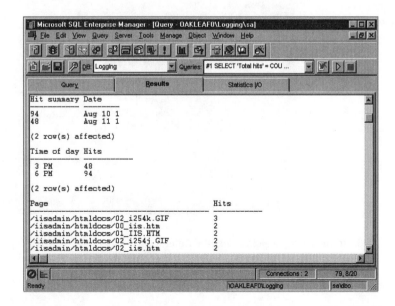

Part IV

Ch 21

You can create queries similar to those shown in Listing 21.2 for FTP services. If you log to a Jet database, you can use Access 97's graphical query-by-design tool to create analytical queries. Access 97's built-in graphing capability also is useful for analyzing use of your site.

Using SQL Server Web Assistant to Distribute Activity Reports

If you want to distribute usage information for your site, SQL Server 6.5's Web Assistant automates the process. Web Assistant automatically creates formatted Web pages containing query result sets formatted as tables. A single page can display the result set from one or more queries. You also can specify the frequency at which the page is updated by a SQL Server 6.5 scheduled task. If you use a scheduled task, you can add a DELETE query after the SELECT queries to maintain records only for a specified period in the logging table. You must have system administrator privileges to use Web Assistant.

The following steps use SQL Server Web Assistant to create a Web page, WWWPages.htm, that displays the result of the last query in Listing 21.2:

1. From the Start menu, choose Programs, Microsoft SQL Server 6.5, and then SQL Server Web Assistant to open Web Assistant's first dialog.

2. In the Login dialog, type the SQL Server Name, Login ID (**logging**, for this example), and Password (see Figure 21.23). Alternatively, you can use SQL Server's integrated security feature to log on to SQL Server by marking the check box labeled Use Windows NT Security to Log In Instead of Entering a Login ID and/or a Password. Click the Next button to continue.

FIG. 21.23
Entering required information in the Login dialog of SQL Server Web Assistant.

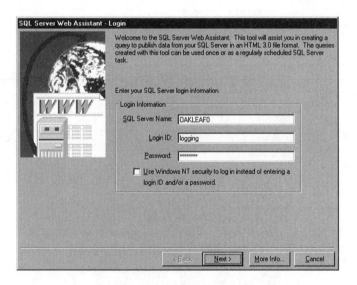

3. In the Query dialog, select the Enter a Query as Free-Form Text option to open the Type Your Query text box. Select your logging database (Logging for this example) in the Which Database Do You Want to Query? drop-down list.

4. Type one or more consecutive SELECT queries in the text box. Figure 21.24 shows the last query of Listing 21.2 pasted into the Type Your Query text box. You can enter multiple SELECT queries; the result of each SELECT query appears in a separate table on the Web page. Click Next to continue.

FIG. 21.24
Specifying the query to create the content for the Web page.

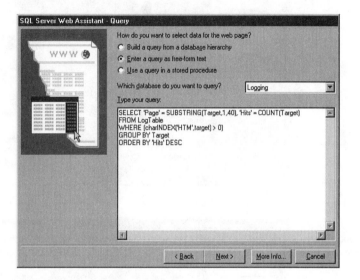

 TIP It's a good idea to copy and paste a previously tested query into the Type Your Query text box to avoid typographical or syntax errors.

5. In the Scheduling dialog, select the frequency at which you want to update the log by choosing On a Regular Basis from the drop-down list and specifying the update interval in the Every text box and interval drop-down list (see Figure 21.25). Intervals include Hour(s), Day(s), and Week(s).

Alternatively, you can choose Now in the When Do You Want to Create Your Web Page? drop-down list to generate a Web page immediately. If you specify Now, you create only a single instance of the page. (Running a scheduled task immediately is described later in this section.) Click Next to continue.

6. In the File Options dialog, type the full path to the file and the name of the file in the top text box. The file must be located in the \InetPub\wwwroot folder or subfolder. If you want to restrict access to the activity report page, specify a subfolder with the appropriate Windows NT group permissions.

7. Select the option button labeled The Following Information. Type the title of the page, which appears in your browser's title bar, and the title for your query result, which appears at the top of the page, in the two associated text boxes (see Figure 21.26). Alternatively, you can specify a pre-existing template file to display the result. Click Next to continue.

Part
IV

Ch
21

FIG. 21.25
Specifying the
refresh interval
for the Web page.

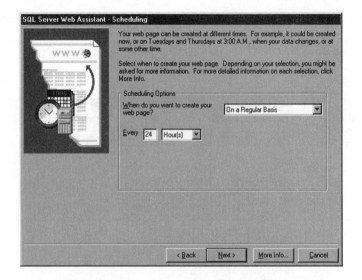

FIG. 21.26
Specifying file options
for the Web page.

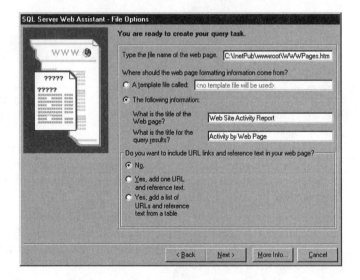

The File Options dialog lets you add URLs and descriptions as either a single line or rows of a table.
Additional URLs are useful for linking to other pages, if your report offers multiple pages.

8. In the Formatting dialog, select how you want the text to appear (see Figure 21.27). In most cases, the options labeled Insert an Update Date/Time Stamp at the Top of the Page and Include Column or View Column Names with the Query Results are adequate for the report. Click Finish to display the Finished dialog and then click Close to terminate Web Assistant.

FIG. 21.27

Setting query text and page formatting options.

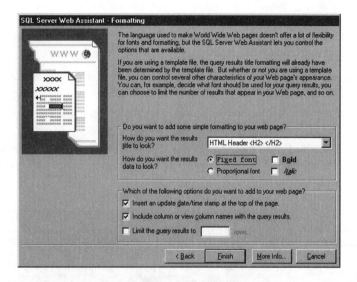

If you specified Now in step 5, you can check your Web page by opening the *Pagename*.htm file with the **file://path/Pagename.htm** URL in the browser on your server, or from a client with the **http://servername/Pagename.htm** URL if the file is in the \InetPub\wwwroot folder. Figure 21.28 shows the page created with the values specified in the preceding steps. If you use a multiple SELECT query, each query result set appears in separate tables separated by a bar.

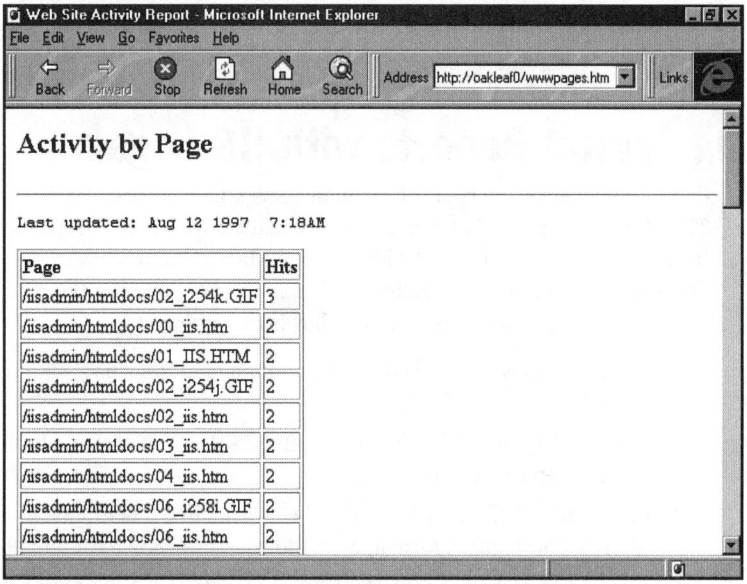

FIG. 21.28

The single-query report page created by using the example values of this section.

If you specified a scheduled task in step 5, Web Assistant creates an encrypted stored procedure in the logging database named Web_*yymmddhhmmsscc*, based on your computer's system time when you created the stored procedure. (The last two digits, *cc*, are hundredths of seconds.) You must take the following steps to run SQL Enterprise Manager's Managed Scheduled Tasks tool to generate a test copy of your Web activity report:

1. From the Start menu, choose Programs, Microsoft SQL Server, and SQL Enterprise Manager.

2. In the Server Manager window, expand the server item; then expand the Databases item and select the logging database.

3. From the Server menu, choose Scheduled Tasks to open the Manage Scheduled Tasks window. Select the Web_*yymmddhhmmsscc* entry for the activity report you just created (see Figure 21.29).

FIG. 21.29

Selecting the task to execute immediately in the Manage Scheduled Tasks window of SQL Enterprise Manager.

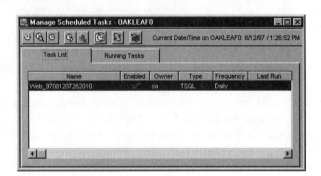

4. Click the Run Task toolbar button (with the clock and the small green arrow), or choose Run Task from the File menu. Click Yes in the confirmation message box to run the task and create the page.

Using Crystal Reports with IIS Logs

Crystal Reports for Internet Information Server 4.5 is a special version of Seagate Software's 32-bit Crystal Reports that creates fully formatted Web activity reports. Other special Crystal Reports versions are included with Systems Management Server (SMS) 1.1+, Visual Basic 5.0 Professional and Enterprise Editions, Visual C++ 4.0+, and the *Windows NT Resource Kit*. Crystal Reports for IIS 4.5 consists of the following components:

■ *Crystal Reports Engine* is the basic component for sorting, summarizing, and grouping log data.

■ *Crystal Web Application Interface* connects the Web server—in this case, IIS—to the Crystal Reports Engine.

■ *Crystal Web Activity DLL* enables the Crystal Reports Engine to read reports in Microsoft's standard format, NCSA format, or from ODBC-enable logging databases.

■ *Crystal Web Publishing Interface* creates formatted Web pages for distribution of activity reports over your intranet or the Internet.

ON THE WEB

You can read additional information on the capabilities of the full version of Crystal Reports 5.0 at **http://www.img.seagatesoftware.com/creports/default.htm**.

N O T E   Crystal Reports won't run unless your server has a connected printer or access to a networked printer. ▨

Installing Crystal Reports for IIS

Crystal Reports isn't installed by the IIS 3.0 or SP3 Setup program. The installation file (Crystal.exe) for Intel servers is located in the \iis30\crystal\i386 folder of the SP3 CD-ROM. A full installation of Crystal Reports requires approximately 16M of disk space. To install Crystal Reports, follow these steps:

1. Double-click Crystal.exe to expand the installation files and start Setup.
2. Click Yes to accept the license agreement and display the Select Components dialog (see Figure 21.30).

FIG. 21.30
Selecting the task to execute immediately in the Manage Scheduled Tasks window of SQL Enterprise Manager.

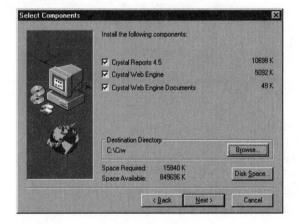

3. Accept the defaults to install the three components of Crystal Reports. Unless you specify otherwise, Setup stores the application files in C:\Crw. Click Next to complete Setup.
4. Click Yes in the message box to restart IIS and display the Setup Complete dialog. Mark the two check boxes to display the Readme.txt file in Notepad and start Crystal Reports. Click Finish to continue.
5. Complete the Crystal Reports Registration Express dialog and click OK, or click Cancel to skip the registration process.
6. Review the Readme.txt file then close Notepad to expose Crystal Reports' main window.

Part
IV

Ch
21

Testing Crystal Reports

Setup installs a collection of sample reports (*.rpt) and a Default.asp Active Server Pages (ASP) page in your \Crw\Logrpts folder. To view a sample report, follow these steps:

1. Launch Internet Explorer (IE) 3.02+ and type **http://servername/logrpts** in the Address text box to open Default.asp (see Figure 21.31).

FIG. 21.31

Crystal Reports' Default.asp page for choosing a sample report.

2. Select one of the report types in the list box and click Generate Crystal Report to process the report. (You don't need to change the remaining default values.) Figure 21.32 shows the Activity by Day of Week graph that appears at the top of the actbywkstd.rpt sample report.

3. Scroll down to view the tabular report data (see Figure 21.33). Links to reports for each day of the week let you drill down to a page showing more detailed data.

4. If the Crystal Reports main window isn't open, from the Start menu choose Crystal Reports 4.5 twice to launch the Crystal Reports designer application.

5. From the File menu choose Open to open the File Open dialog. Double-click a *.rpt file in the \Crw\Logrpts folder to close the dialog and open the report in Preview mode (see Figure 21.34).

6. Click the Design tab to open the report in Design mode (see Figure 21.35). You can use Crystal Reports' designer tools to create a new report or alter the design of an existing report.

7. Close Crystal Reports and IE.

FIG. 21.32
The graph of a Web
page generated by
Crystal Reports.

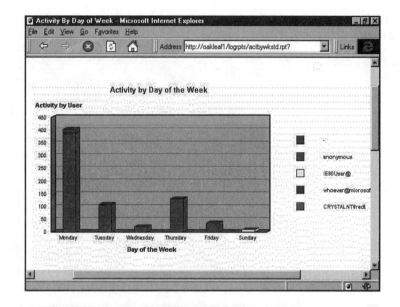

FIG. 21.33
Tabular activity data
for the graph shown
in Figure 21.32.

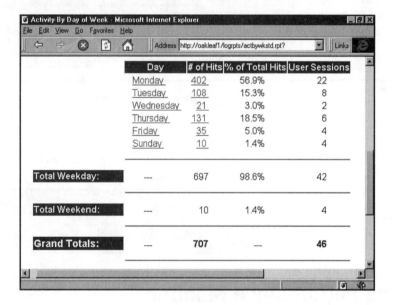

TIP You can create a new report by choosing New from the File menu to launch the Create New Report
dialog and select one of the standard report templates. It's easier, however, to modify an existing report
by changing the log file source to a text log in the \Winnt\System32\Logging folder or to a table in a
SQL Server or Jet database.

FIG. 21.34
Opening an existing report in Crystal Reports' Preview mode.

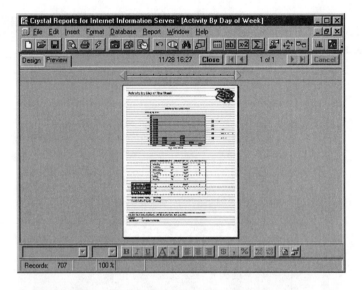

FIG. 21.35
Modifying the design of an existing report.

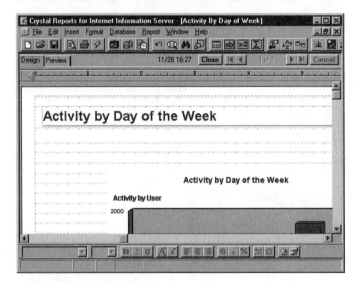

Using Performance Monitor

As the use of your intranet or Internet server grows, it's useful to determine the extent to which user activity taxes your server's resources. Installing IIS 4.0 adds to Windows NT Server's Performance Monitor (PerfMon) the counters shown in Table 21.2 for the HTTP service. Another set of global counters for Internet Information Server also track cache and bandwidth throttling for all IIS services, including FTP. In Table 21.2, the accumulation of totals begins at system startup.

▶ **See** "Using Performance Monitor," **p. 530**

Table 21.2   Counters Added by IIS 4.0 to Performance Monitor's HTTP Service Object

Counter	Purpose
Bytes Received/sec	The instantaneous rate of incoming bytes from all users
Bytes Sent/sec Rate	The instantaneous rate of outgoing bytes sent to all users
Bytes Total/sec Rate	The total of Bytes Received/sec and Bytes Sent/sec
CGI Requests	The accumulated number of Common Gateway Interface (CGI) requests from the Web service
CGI Requests/sec	The instantaneous rate of CGI requests from all users
Connection Attempts	The accumulated number of connections, successful or not
Connection Attempts/sec	The instantaneous rate of requests for Web pages
Connections in Error	The accumulated number of failed connections
Current Anonymous Users	The instantaneous number of users logged on via the Internet
Current CGI Requests	The instantaneous number of CGI operations being processed
Current Connections	The sum of Current Anonymous Users and Current NonAnonymous Users
Current ISAPI Extension Requests	The instantaneous number of ISAPI operations being processed
Current NonAnonymous Users	The instantaneous number of users logged on via an intranet
Delete Requests	The accumulated number of DELETE method requests received by the Web service
Delete Requests/sec	The instantaneous rate of DELETE requests received by the Web service
Files Received Total	The accumulated number of files users have uploaded
Files Sent Total	The accumulated number of files users have downloaded
Files Total	The sum of Files Received Total and Files Sent Total
Files/sec	The instantaneous rate at which the Web service sends and receives files
Get Requests	The accumulated number of GET requests the Web service receives
Get Requests/sec	The instantaneous rate at which the Web service receives GET requests

Part

IV

Ch

21

continues

Table 21.2   Continued

Counter	Purpose
Gopher Plus Requests	The accumulated number of Gopher Plus requests
Head Requests	The accumulated number of queries to determine whether a user needs to refresh a Web document
Head Requests/sec	The instantaneous rate at which the Web service receives HEAD requests
ISAPI Extension Requests	The accumulated number of requests for ISAPI services, such as the Internet Data Connector
ISAPI Extension Requests/sec	The instantaneous rate of requests for ISAPI services
Logon Attempts	The accumulated number of logons, successful or unsuccessful
Logon Attempts/sec	The instantaneous rate of logons, successful or unsuccessful
Maximum Anonymous Users	The peak number of Internet users
Maximum CGI Requests	The peak number of CGI operations
Maximum Connections	The peak number of Internet and intranet users (Maximum Anonymous Users plus Maximum NonAnonymous Users)
Maximum ISAPI Extension Requests	The peak number of operations that use ISAPI
Maximum NonAnonymous Users	The peak number of intranet users
Not Found Errors	The accumulated number of requests that resulted in returning an HTTP 404 error code to the requester
Not Found Errors/sec	The instantaneous rate of requests that resulted in returning an HTTP 404 error code to the requester
Other Request Methods	The accumulated number of requests other than GET, POST, or HEAD
Other Request Methods/sec	The instantaneous rate of requests other than GET, POST, or HEAD
Post Requests	The accumulated number of POST operations
Post Requests/sec	The instantaneous rate of POST operations
Put Requests	The accumulated number of PUT operations
Put Requests/sec	The instantaneous rate of PUT operations
Total Anonymous Users	The accumulated number of Internet users

Counter	Purpose
Total Method Requests	The accumulated number of GET, POST, PUT, DELETE, TRACE, HEAD, and other method operations
Total Method Requests/sec	The instantaneous rate of GET, POST, PUT, DELETE, TRACE, HEAD, and other method operations
Total NonAnonymous Users	The accumulated number of intranet users
Trace Requests	The accumulated number of TRACE operations

 TIP In IIS 4.0, you now can track performance counters by Web site, as well as for the entire service. Select the Web site in the Instance parameter of Performance Monitor.

PerfMon's graph views let you display any of the counters in Table 21.2, but most of the counters deserve only occasional checking. Figure 21.36 shows a PerfMon configuration that displays the most important instantaneous and accumulated values for a Web and FTP site. Table 21.3 lists the counters and scaling factors used to create the graph in Figure 21.36. Scaling factors aren't the defaults; to maintain a readable scale, for example, you must scale the Bytes/sec values by 0.001 to display K/sec. If your site traffic is heavy, change the scaling factors to suit the full-scale values you expect.

FIG. 21.36
Monitoring IIS 4.0 activity.

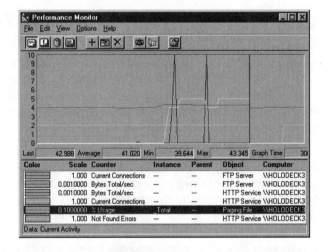

Table 21.3 Performance Monitor Key Indicators

Counter	Scaling Factor	Counter Object
FTP Current Connections	1.0	FTP Service
HTTP Current Connections	1.0	HTTP Service

continues

Part
IV

Ch
21

Table 21.3 Continued		
Counter	Scaling Factor	Counter Object
FTP Total Bytes/Sec	0.001	FTP Service
HTTP Total Bytes/Sec	0.001	HTTP Service
% Usage, Page File	0.1	Paging File
Not Found Errors	1.0	HTTP Service

Figure 21.36 shows, in relative terms, the activity on your server at a glance. You can see very quickly the number of connections and other important parameters. If you observe the % Usage of the page file growing steadily, check the types of access being completed. If you have an ISAPI application running, the application might have a memory-management problem.

An increasing % Usage of the paging file over time indicates that more virtual memory (the paging file) is being consumed. Typically, additional resources are required to handle the load as more users connect to the server. If the % Usage of your page file is more than 80 percent, increase the size of the file. If % Usage continues to rise and you're certain you don't have a resource problem with a CGI executable or an ISAPI extension, consider adding more memory to the system.

Activating Web Pages with ASP, ADO, and OLE DB

Internet Information Server 3.0 added the first release of Active Server Pages to IIS 2.0. IIS 3.0 provided a sample ASP Web site, Adventure Works, to demonstrate how ASP works. IIS 4.0's sample site, Exploration Air (ExAir), is considerably more sophisticated than Adventure Works. ExAir uses transaction-enabled Web pages. *Transaction-enabled* Web pages use Microsoft Transaction Server (MTS, also called MTx) components for operations such as Web-site registration, booking reservations, and making purchases.

ExAir's pages take full advantage of the ActiveX Data Object (ADO) and OLE DB technologies that Microsoft released in mid-1997. According to Microsoft, ADO and OLE DB are intended to replace current database access methods, including ODBC, ODBCDirect, and the Remote Data Object (RDO) of Visual Basic 5.0's Enterprise Edition.

▶ **See** "Managing the Middle Tier with Transaction Server," **p. 973**

N O T E   The ExAir sample site wasn't completed in the Beta 2 version of IIS 4.0 used to write this chapter. The locations and names of the site's files, as well as the appearance of the pages, might vary in the released version of IIS 4.0. ▪

The ExAir Sample Active Server Pages

Active Server Pages consist of a combination of HTML code, VBScript, and JScript (Microsoft's version of JavaScript) that generates .htm files for delivery to requesting clients. ASP's primary advantage is browser independence. Browsers that don't support VBScript, such as Netscape Navigator and Communicator, can display and interact with .htm files generated by .asp files that contain VBScript, because the VBScript code runs on the server.

N O T E The official name of JavaScript became ECMAScript in late June 1997. In 1996, Microsoft turned over for standardization most of its ActiveX technologies to the Open Group, a well-established industry association. Netscape chose the obscure European Computer Manufacturers Association (ECMA) as the standards body for JavaScript. ECMAScript is defined by the ECMA-262 standard. Microsoft announced on June 30, 1997, that version 3.0 of JScript meets the ECMA-262 standard. IIS 4.0 supports JScript 3.0. ■

To examine the ExAir sample .asp files and the HTML files they generate, follow these steps:

1. Launch IE 3.02+ and type **http://servername** in the Address text box to open the Welcome to IIS 4.0 page, the Default.asp file of the \IntetPub\wwwroot folder.

2. Click the Samples button to open the IIS Samples page (Samples3.asp in the …\IISSamples\Default folder).

3. Click the link to the Exploration Air samples to open the home page for Exploration Air (…\IISSamples\ExAir\Default.asp). The scrolling News list is created by a Java applet (`CoolHeadLines.class`) called by Default.asp.

N O T E If you want to make the ExAir site fully operational, you must create the required SQL Server database and tables, and then add a File DSN for the ODBC 3.5 data source used by the ExAir pages. The Readme.txt file in the …\IISSamples\Default folder explains how to perform these operations. You don't need to connect to SQL Server to gain a basic understanding of ASP. ■

4. Choose Source from IE's View menu to launch Notepad with the HTML source code generated by Default.asp. The file name in the title bar appears as Exair(1).htm (see Figure 21.37). Scroll to the bottom of Exair(1).htm to verify that, with the exception of the code to run the Java `CoolHeadLines` applet shown in Figure 21.37, the content of Exair(1).htm is standard HTML (no VBScript or JScript).

5. From the Start menu choose Programs, Accessories, and Notepad to launch another instance of Notepad. Open the …\IISSamples\ExAir\Default.asp file. Compare the parameter list for the `CoolHeadLines` Java applet (see Figure 21.38) with that of Exair(1).htm. Default.asp contains the line `<% ListParams %>`, which specifies a call to the VBScript `ListParams` subprocedure. The `<%= GetPrefixValues() %>` line supplies the return value of the GetPrefixValues function. `<%...%>` flags identify script subprocedure and function calls, as well as script code.

6. Scroll to the `<!--END HTML-->` line near the bottom of the Default.asp file. The VBScript code for `ListParams`, which generates the text and link parameters for the `CoolHeadLines` applet, begins at `<% Sub ListParams`, followed by the `GetPrefixValues` function (see Figure 21.39).

Part
IV

Ch
21

FIG. 21.37

HTML code in Exair(1).htm generated by the Default.asp file of the ExAir sample application.

```
exair(1).htm - Notepad                                              _ □ ×
File  Edit  Search  Help
<!--BEGIN TOP TABLE HOLDING PRESS RELEASE JAVA APPLET AND EXPLORATION AIR LOG▲
<CENTER>
<TABLE WIDTH=100% CELLPADDING=0 CELLSPACING=0 BORDER=0>
        <TR>
                <!-- JAVA APPLET TO VIEW LATEST HEADLINES-->
                <TD WIDTH=175 ALIGN=RIGHT>
                <FONT FACE="VERDANA, ARIAL, HELVETICA" COLOR=#228B22 SIZE="3"
                <BR>
                <APPLET
                CODE=CoolHeadLines.class
                NAME=CoolHeadLines
                CODEBASE=Applets
                WIDTH=170
                HEIGHT=76 >

                <PARAM NAME=BackColor VALUE="255 255 255">
                <PARAM NAME=TextColor VALUE="0 0 0">
                <PARAM NAME=HiliteTextColor VALUE="60 179 113">
                <PARAM NAME=ScrollDelay VALUE=10>
                <PARAM NAME=MessageDelay VALUE=4>
                <PARAM NAME=URLPrefix VALUE=http://oakleaf1/iissamples/exair>

                <PARAM NAME=Text0 VALUE="EA Named Airline of the Year">
<PARAM NAME=URL0 VALUE="pr/970129a.asp">
<PARAM NAME=Text1 VALUE="We Match Blue Yonder">
<PARAM NAME=URL1 VALUE="pr/970122a.asp">
<PARAM NAME=Text2 VALUE="Free Flights to Chicago">
<PARAM NAME=URL2 VALUE="pr/970301a.asp">
```

FIG. 21.38

Calls to the VBScript ListParams subprocedure and GetPrefixValues function embedded in Default.asp.

```
default.asp - Notepad                                               _ □ ×
File  Edit  Search  Help
<!--BEGIN TOP TABLE HOLDING PRESS RELEASE JAVA APPLET AND EXPLORATION AIR LOG▲
<CENTER>
<TABLE WIDTH=100% CELLPADDING=0 CELLSPACING=0 BORDER=0>
        <TR>
                <!-- JAVA APPLET TO VIEW LATEST HEADLINES-->
                <TD WIDTH=175 ALIGN=RIGHT>
                <FONT FACE="VERDANA, ARIAL, HELVETICA" COLOR=#228B22 SIZE="3"
                <BR>
                <APPLET
                CODE=CoolHeadLines.class
                NAME=CoolHeadLines
                CODEBASE=Applets
                WIDTH=170
                HEIGHT=76 >

                <PARAM NAME=BackColor VALUE="255 255 255">
                <PARAM NAME=TextColor VALUE="0 0 0">
                <PARAM NAME=HiliteTextColor VALUE="60 179 113">
                <PARAM NAME=ScrollDelay VALUE=10>
                <PARAM NAME=MessageDelay VALUE=4>
                <PARAM NAME=URLPrefix VALUE=<%= GetPrefixValue() %>>

                <% ListParams %>

        </APPLET>
                <BR>
                <BR>
                <FONT FACE="VERDANA, ARIAL, HELVETICA" COLOR=#0000FF SIZE=2>
```

N O T E ListParams creates in Exair(1).htm the code for CoolHeadLine's Text# and URL# parameters, which begins with <PARAM NAME = Text0... and <PARAM NAME = URL0.... ■

7. Close both instances of Notepad to return to IE.

FIG. 21.39

Calls to the VBScript
ListParams
subprocedure and
GetPrefixValues
function embedded in
Default.asp.

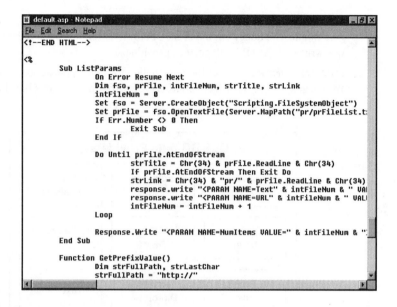

```
default.asp - Notepad
File  Edit  Search  Help
<!--END HTML-->

<%
        Sub ListParams
                On Error Resume Next
                Dim fso, prFile, intFileNum, strTitle, strLink
                intFileNum = 0
                Set fso = Server.CreateObject("Scripting.FileSystemObject")
                Set prFile = fso.OpenTextFile(Server.MapPath("pr/prFileList.t:
                If Err.Number <> 0 Then
                        Exit Sub
                End If

                Do Until prFile.AtEndOfStream
                        strTitle = Chr(34) & prFile.ReadLine & Chr(34)
                        If prFile.AtEndOfStream Then Exit Do
                        strLink = Chr(34) & "pr/" & prFile.ReadLine & Chr(34)
                        response.write "<PARAM NAME=Text" & intFileNum & " VAl
                        response.write "<PARAM NAME=URL" & intFileNum & " VAL|
                        intFileNum = intFileNum + 1
                Loop

                Response.Write "<PARAM NAME=NumItems VALUE=" & intFileNum & ":
        End Sub

        Function GetPrefixValue()
                Dim strFullPath, strLastChar
                strFullPath = "http://"
```

The advantage of the use of server-side scripting in ExAir's Default.asp page is the ability to update the list of press releases without changing the code for the page. The ListParams subprocedure reads a simple text file that contains the text for the caption, followed by the relative location of the press release page on the server. The public relations staff needs to change only the text file when issuing a new press release.

ActiveX Data Objects and OLE DB

Internet Information Server 2.0 used the Internet Database Connector (IDC) to create dynamically updated Web pages from database content. IDC uses a combination of HTML templates (.htx files) and SQL queries (.idc files) to generate the HTML file that appears in the intranet or Internet user's browser. In IIS 3.0+, VBScripted ASP, with ADO and OLE DB, replaces IDC. ADO, an automation "wrapper" for OLE DB, is far more flexible than the .htx/.idc combination. Unlike the Jet database engine, ODBCDirect, and RDO, which interact only with Visual Basic for Applications (VBA) code, you can invoke ADO methods directly from VBScript and VBA statements.

OLE DB promises the ability to work with any type of tabular data, not just relational databases, text files, and Excel worksheets. Figure 21.40 shows the relationship between the three basic OLE DB components, which perform the following functions:

■ *Data providers* for each type of tabular data. When this book was written, Microsoft had released only the Active Directory Service Interface and ODBC data providers. Microsoft promises native OLE DB data providers for SQL Server and Jet databases, plus the Exchange Server message store.

▶ **See** "Activating Directory Services," **p. 997**

Part

IV

Ch

21

■ Optional *service providers* for performing operations such as query execution and report generation. The query engine of SQL Server 7.0 (code-named Sphinx when this book was written) is an OLE DB service provider.

■ *Data consumers* that deliver the information to client applications. ADO enables ASP Web pages, Visual Basic 5.0, and Microsoft Office applications to act as OLE DB data consumers.

FIG. 21.40

Communication between OLE DB data providers, service providers, and data consumers.

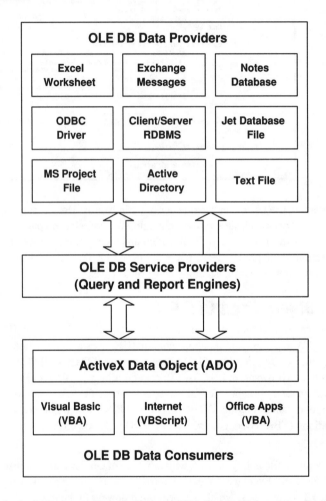

The ExAir site includes several pages that use ADO, but ExAir's most prevalent method of connecting to SQL Server tables is via MTS. For example, the Login.asp page invokes the Member.CheckPassword method of the MTS ExAir.Member component of the ExAir package that IIS 4.0 Setup installs (see Figure 21.41). You can view all the methods of the ExAir.Member component by expanding the Microsoft Transaction Server hierarchy in the MMC Snap-In of the Internet Service Manager (see Figure 21.42). MTS components often use ADO to connect to the database.

FIG. 21.41
VBScript code that invokes the CheckPassword method of the ExAir.Member MTS component.

```
login.asp - Notepad
File  Edit  Search  Help
<%
   Sub CheckPassword
      On Error Resume Next
      Dim Member, intPassResult
      Set Member = Server.CreateObject("ExAir.Member")
      If Err.Number <> 0 Then
         m_strMainPrompt = err.number & err.description & " An error occurred wh
         Exit Sub
      End If
      intPassResult = Member.CheckPassword(Application("DSN"), m_lngAccountID,
      If Err.Number <> 0 Then
         m_strMainPrompt = "An error occurred while checking the database. Pleas
         Exit Sub
      End If
      If intPassResult = 1 Then
         Session("AccountID") = m_lngAccountID
         Response.Redirect("default.asp")
         Response.End
      ElseIf intPassResult = 0 Then
         m_strMainPrompt = "You did not provide the correct password for this ac
      End If
   End Sub

         Function IsWholeNum(input)
            On Error Resume Next
            m_lngAccountID = CLng(input)
            If Err.Number <> 0 Then
                  IsWholeNum = False
```

FIG. 21.42
Microsoft Management Console displaying the CheckPassword method of the ExAir.Member MTS component.

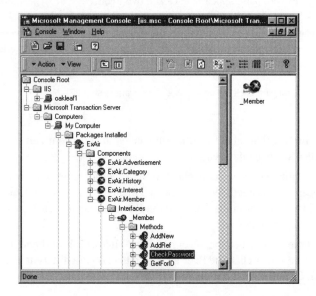

N O T E Microsoft introduced Remote Data Services (RDS, formerly the Advanced Data Control framework) in mid-1997. RDS enables Web pages to connect directly to databases. Because only IE 3.02+ supports RDS, RDS primarily is of use on intranets where everyone uses the Microsoft browser. ■

Managing the Content of Your Web Site with Microsoft FrontPage 97

Windows NT Server 4.0 includes a copy of Microsoft FrontPage 1.1 for IIS 4.0 with a single client license that runs only on Windows NT Server 4.0. Service Pack 2+ updates version 1.1 to FrontPage 97; you must have a prior version of FrontPage installed to perform the FrontPage 97 upgrade. FrontPage has two components: a server-side FrontPage Explorer for maintaining the organization of your Web pages and a client-side WYSIWYG Web page editor for creating HTML files. FrontPage's ease of use makes it a logical tool to create the initial set of custom pages for your Web site.

N O T E The Beta 2 version of IIS 4.0 used to write this chapter included server-side support for FrontPage 98 but didn't include the FrontPage 98 client application. The sections that follow use FrontPage 97 with IIS 3.0, not IIS 4.0. ■

Installing FrontPage 97 and the IIS 3.0 Server Extensions

To install FrontPage 97 from the Windows NT Server Service Pack 3 CD-ROM onto your Web server, follow these steps:

1. Insert the SP3 CD-ROM into the server drive. If you have AutoPlay enabled, the Ntsp3.htm Web page appears; click the two FrontPage 97 hyperlinks in succession to start Setup. (Select the Open It option in the Internet Explorer dialog, click OK, and then click Yes when the Authenticode message appears.) Otherwise, navigate to the \Frontpg\i386 folder of the SP3 CD-ROM and double-click Setup.exe to start the client installation process.

N O T E If IIS is running, click Yes when asked if you want to stop IIS. ■

2. Click the Next button of the first setup dialog to enter your name and company name, and click Yes to confirm your registration data.

3. Click Continue to have Setup check your server for an existing copy of FrontPage 1.1 and open the Installed Servers Detected dialog, which displays Microsoft Internet Information Server in the list. With the IIS item selected, click Next to open the Destination Path dialog.

4. Accept the default location, \Program Files\Microsoft FrontPage, where you installed FrontPage 1.1, or click the Browse button to choose a different location (see Figure 21.43). Click the Next button.

FIG. 21.43

Specifying the location of the FrontPage 97 administrative files.

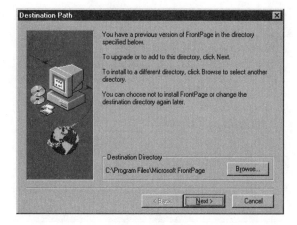

5. In the Setup Type dialog, you can select the Typical option to install the FrontPage Personal Web Server and the standard server extensions. To save disk space, select the Custom option (see Figure 21.44) and click Next to display the Select Components dialog.

FIG. 21.44

Choosing between Typical and Custom installation options for FrontPage 97.

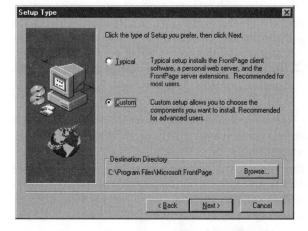

6. You need only select the Client Software because Setup automatically installs the IIS Server Extensions. Clear the Personal Web Server check box (see Figure 21.45), and then click Next.

7. Confirm that the Client Software and Server Extensions appear in the Current Settings list of the Start Copying Files dialog, and then click Next to copy the update files.

Part
IV

Ch
21

FIG. 21.45
Selecting only the Client
Software for an IIS
installation.

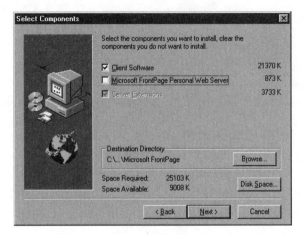

8. When InstallShield completes copying files, click Finish to close the last installation
   dialog and start the FrontPage 97 Server Administrator. The Server Administrator
   installs the FrontPage extensions on Port 80.

9. Click OK in the Server Administrator message box, regarding the need for users with
   basic authentication to have Log on Locally privileges.

10. If you installed the server extensions on a FAT partition, click OK to acknowledge the
    warning message about potential security problems.

At this point, Setup automatically opens the FrontPage Explorer, the Web navigational tool of
FrontPage 97.

Experimenting with FrontPage Explorer and Editor

Organizing Web sites and generating Web content is beyond the scope of this book. You can
gain an understanding of the capabilities of the FrontPage Explorer by using it to map the
sample .htm files supplied with IIS 3.0 and those added by any other Web applications you've
installed. FrontPage automatically organizes groups of Web pages into a hierarchy based on
their contained hyperlinks to other pages at your site, as well links to other sites. FrontPage
calls each group of pages a *Web*. The FrontPage Editor lets you edit existing Web pages and
create new pages in a graphical context.

To create a view of the sample IIS 3.0 Web pages in FrontPage Explorer and run the FrontPage
Editor, follow these steps:

1. Select the With the Import Wizard option in the Create a New FrontPage Web section of
   the Getting Started with FrontPage 97 dialog (see Figure 21.46). Click OK to open the
   Import Web Wizard dialog.

2. Accept your server's host name in the WebServer or FileLocation combo box and type a
   name for the Web in the Name of New FrontPage text box (see Figure 21.47). Click OK
   to open the wizard's Choose Directory dialog.

FIG. 21.46

FrontPage Explorer's first Import Web Wizard dialog.

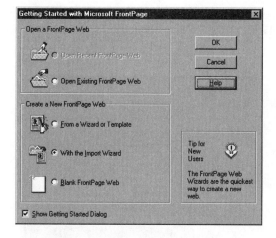

FIG. 21.47

Specifying a name for your FrontPage Web.

3. Browse to or type the source folder for the Web (\InetPub\wwwroot\samples for this example) in the Source Directory text box. Mark the Include Subdirectories check box (see Figure 21.48). Click Next to open the Wizard's Edit File list.

FIG. 21.48

Specifying the source folder for the Web.

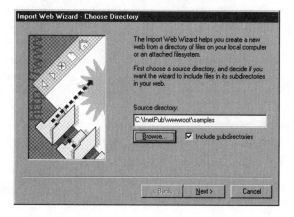

Part
IV

Ch

21

4. Remove references to any pages you don't want to include in your Web by selecting the pages and clicking the Exclude button (see Figure 21.49). Click Next to open the Finish dialog.

FIG. 21.49
The Wizard's Edit File List for removing page references from the FrontPage Web.

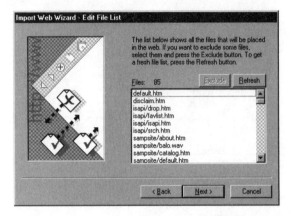

5. Click Finish to display the Web in FrontPage Explorer. A list of pages appears in the Outline View pane, and a map of the hyperlink relationships of the pages appears in the Link View pane.

6. Scroll the Outline View list to display the Internet Database Connector Examples item. Double-click the item to show the linked files (see Figure 21.50).

FIG. 21.50
FrontPage Explorer's view of the OakLeaf Web with IIS 3.0's sample pages.

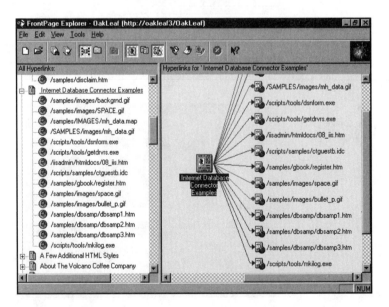

7. Double-click the Internet Database Connector Examples icon in the Link View pane to open the FrontPage Editor in page view (see Figure 21.51).

FIG. 21.51

FrontPage Editor displaying a Web page from the IIS 3.0 sample site.

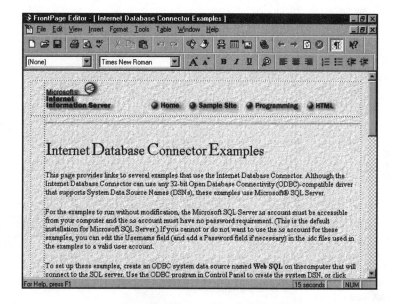

8. From the editor's window, choose HTML from the View menu to display the HTML code for the page in the View or Edit HTML window (see Figure 21.52). The editor color-codes the text in a manner similar to the VBA code editor of Visual Basic 5.0 and Office applications. Unlike FrontPage 1.1, you can edit the HTML code in FrontPage 97's editor.

9. Click Cancel to close the View or Edit HTML dialog and close the FrontPage Editor without saving changes.

FrontPage 97 provides a set of templates and wizards that you can use to learn the basics of Web-content generation, as well as to provide a starting point for the design of production pages. The list of templates shown in Figure 21.53 appears when you choose New and then FrontPage Web from FrontPage Explorer's File menu. Select the Learning FrontPage template if you want to try the tutorial included in the FrontPage help file.

NOTE Site Server 2.0's Site Analyst application provides a more comprehensive site mapping, link management, and reporting capability than FrontPage 97. Site Server 2.0 is a member of the Microsoft BackOffice family; the license cost for the standard edition is $1,499. Site Server 2.0 includes Usage Analyst for Web site traffic reporting and, as a promotion, a copy of Visual InterDev, an advanced Web site development tool that's optimized for creating database-driven sites. The Enterprise Edition of Site Server 2.0, priced at $4,999 for the first server, adds electronic commerce features.

▶ **See** "Upgrading to Site Server 2.0," **p. 47** ■

Part
IV

Ch
21

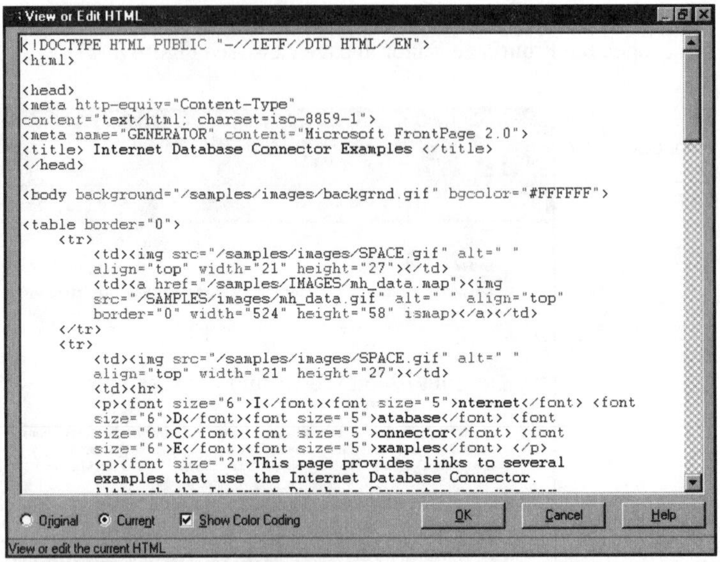

FIG. 21.52

Displaying HTML code in FrontPage Editor's View or Edit HTML window.

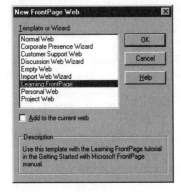

FIG. 21.53

A list of the templates and wizards included with FrontPage 97.

ON THE WEB

For more information on Microsoft SiteServer 2.0, visit **http://www.microsoft.com/backoffice/siteserver/**. You can download a 90-day trial version of the standard version of SiteServer 2.0 from **http://backoffice.microsoft.com/downtrial/server.asp** or the Enterprise Edition from **http://backoffice.microsoft.com/downtrial/site-e.asp**. Visual InterDev isn't included with the trial versions.

From Here...

This chapter provided an introduction to the techniques employed by professional Webmasters to establish and distribute activity logging data with SQL Server 6.5 and its Web Assistant add-in. The Active Server Pages examples demonstrated how to generate browser-independent

HTML pages from .asp files that include VBScript or JScript. The chapter closed with instructions on how to install and use Microsoft FrontPage 97 with IIS 3.0+.

For content related to the subjects discussed in this chapter, see the following chapters:

- Chapter 19, "Managing Remote Access Service," explains how to configure Windows NT Server 4.0's RAS component to support dial-in access to Web pages by mobile users.

- Chapter 20, "Setting Up Internet Information Server 4.0," covers the initial installation and configuration of the latest version of Internet Information Server and its services.

- Chapter 23, "Running Microsoft SQL Server 6.5," describes how to install and set up SQL Server 6.5 and establish database security applicable to Web sites.

Windows NT Server and Microsoft BackOffice

22 Taking Advantage of BackOffice Integration   811

23 Running Microsoft SQL Server 6.5   833

24 Messaging with Microsoft Exchange Server 5.0   871

25 Administering Clients with Systems Management Server 1.2   929

CHAPTER 22

Taking Advantage of BackOffice Integration

Microsoft has acquired about 90 percent of the market for Windows productivity application suites with Microsoft Office. The success of the bundled Office applications led the company to take a similar approach to market its server-based products. Microsoft announced the BackOffice "Integrated Information System" on September 21, 1994, with the release of Windows NT 3.5.

Press reports credit Steve Ballmer, Microsoft's executive vice president, as the originator of the BackOffice name. Although an ebullient Ballmer decreed 1995 to be the "Year of BackOffice," he missed the mark by about a year; BackOffice didn't gain real marketing momentum until 1996. The 1997 growth rate of BackOffice sales is substantially greater than Microsoft's overall income growth, which averages about 40 percent per year. Thus, Ballmer is likely to make good on his 1994 projection that Back-Office products will contribute 25 percent or more of Microsoft's 1999 income.

The Microsoft BackOffice Family

Microsoft BackOffice has expanded from a basic server bundle to an entire family of server-side components.

New Internet-related server components

Microsoft Site Server, Site Server Enterprise Edition, and Commercial Internet System have joined the BackOffice Family.

BackOffice server licensing

The decision to license BackOffice Server or individual BackOffice Family components depends on the size of your network and the location of your server(s).

Windows NT Server 4.0's License Tool and License Manager

The licensing tools included with Windows NT Server 4.0 keep track of your per-seat or per-server licenses and warn you of violations of your license agreements.

N O T E Microsoft is trying to leverage its success with Office and BackOffice bundles in the programming tools market. Microsoft released on March 19, 1997, Professional and Enterprise editions of Visual Studio 97, which combines Visual Basic 5.0, Visual C++ 5.0, Visual FoxPro 5.0, Visual J++ 1.1, Visual InterDev 1.0, and a subset of the Microsoft Developer Network (MSDN) Library CD-ROM. The Enterprise Edition adds Visual Source Safe 5.0, and limited-license Developer editions of Microsoft Transaction Server 1.0 and SQL Server 6.5. ■

ON THE WEB

Detailed information on Visual Studio 97 and its components is available at **http:// www.microsoft.com/vstudio/**.

Since 1994, Microsoft has offered BackOffice as a "full package product," also called an SKU (stock-keeping unit), but BackOffice is better categorized as a concept. The BackOffice bundle, in version 2.5 and called *BackOffice Server* when this book was written, has limited utility in production environments due to its single-server licensing restriction. The BackOffice concept uses Windows NT Server's built-in domain architecture, security system, and application server capabilities to support various integrated back-end services. Full integration of each component with Windows NT Server, including providing a single-user logon for all services, is what has made the BackOffice concept a commercial success.

In late 1996, Microsoft formalized the BackOffice concept as the *BackOffice Family*, which encompasses all its server-side components that run as services on Windows NT Server 4.0. Many new Family members, such as Microsoft Site Server, Proxy Server, and the Microsoft Commercial Internet System (MCIS), are the result of the company's "embrace and extend the Internet" program that Bill Gates announced on December 7, 1995. Other new BackOffice Family components, such as Microsoft Transaction Server (MTS, formerly Viper) and Microsoft Messaging Queue (MSMQ, originally Falcon), are directed toward making BackOffice a primary contender in the enterprise computing market. MTS and MSMQ are included in the Enterprise Edition of Windows NT Server 4.0.

N O T E MTS and MSMQ are middleware products. *Middleware* is a term traditionally used to describe software that interconnects server-side applications running on computers with different operating systems. Later, the "Enterprise Middleware" section briefly describes MTS and MSMQ. ■

Aiming at a Moving BackOffice Server Target

The Microsoft BackOffice Server 2.5 retail SKU, released in November 1996, is a suite consisting of the following bundled components:

■ *Windows NT Server 4.0*, replacing version 3.51 in BackOffice 2.0

■ *Internet Information Server 2.0*, included with Windows NT Server 4.0, replacing version 1.0 in BackOffice 2.0, plus a single-user version of Microsoft FrontPage 1.1, also included with Windows NT Server 4.0

■ *Index Server 1.1*, new in BackOffice Server 2.5 and considered part of Windows NT Server 4.0, for providing search services on the content of Web sites and intranets

■ *FrontPage 1.1* server extensions and a limited FrontPage 1.1 client license (part of Windows NT Server 4.0)

■ *Proxy Server 1.0*, also new in BackOffice Server 2.5, for connecting intranets to the Internet, providing control of users' outbound access to Internet sites and caching frequently requested content to improve performance

■ *SQL Server 6.5*, a client/server relational database management system (RDBMS), which is required for installation of Systems Management Server

■ *Exchange Server 4.0*, the first version (despite the 4.0 version number) of the belated client/server replacement for Microsoft Mail Server 3.5

■ *Systems Management Server (SMS) 1.2* for managing Windows clients, distributing software, and tracking client software, replacing version 1.1 in BackOffice 2.0

■ *SNA Server 3.0*, to provide connectivity to IBM mainframes and AS/400 series minicomputers via IBM's System Network Architecture, replacing version 2.11 in BackOffice 2.0

The preceding list demonstrates that BackOffice Server, as a retail product, is in a constant state of flux. The current version of Internet Information Server is 4.0 and version 5.0 of Exchange Server appeared in March 1997. FrontPage 97 replaced FrontPage 1.1 in late 1996.

Synchronizing the release of updated BackOffice Server components for a specific product version number and SKU appears to be a difficult, if not impossible, task. Component synchronization problems plagued users of early versions of Microsoft Office; release problems finally appear to be overcome in Office 97. Most users don't want to wait for simultaneous upgrades to every BackOffice component before being able to take advantage of the features offered by a new release of Systems Management Server or SNA Server. Complex business issues, such as incremental upgrade pricing for server and client licenses, impede administration of sites that use the BackOffice Server bundle.

N O T E IIS 4.0 is the subject of Chapter 20, "Setting Up Internet Information Server 4.0," and Chapter 21, "Administering Intranet and World Wide Web Sites." SQL Server 6.5 is covered in Chapter 23, "Running Microsoft SQL Server 6.5." Chapter 24, "Messaging with Microsoft Exchange Server 5.0," shows you how to install Exchange Server, and Chapter 25, "Administering Clients with Systems Management Server 1.2," describes how to use SMS 1.2 with Windows NT.

SNA Server is a specialized server application and is beyond the scope of this book, which is limited to conventional PCs. ■

The frequent changes to BackOffice components and Microsoft's Byzantine upgrade licensing policies make buying a Microsoft "software insurance policy" (described later in the section "The Annuity Model for BackOffice Upgrades") a wise investment for most BackOffice users.

Filling Out the BackOffice Family

Additional server-side components not included on the BackOffice Server 2.5 distribution CD-ROMs fall into two categories: Internet/intranet-related and enterprise-level middleware. You can download time-limited demonstration or unrestricted versions of most of these products from the Microsoft Web site.

Internet and Intranet Servers

In addition to the standard BackOffice components of the earlier list, the following Internet-related Windows NT Server 4.0 services and related client applications were released or in various stages of development and testing when this book was written:

- *Commerce Server* for establishing electronic storefronts on the Web, a component of Site Server Enterprise Edition. Commerce Server is the replacement for Merchant Server, which Microsoft ported to Windows NT from eShop's original UNIX version, acquired by Microsoft in 1996 (**http://www.microsoft.com/commerce/**).

- *Microsoft Commercial Internet System 1.0,* a Windows NT Server-based platform for Internet service providers and commercial Web sites, much of the technology of which is based on that of The Microsoft Network (**http://www.microsoft.com/isp/isp-mcis1.htm**).

- *NetMeeting 2.0*, released in late April 1997, is a downloadable client component of Internet Information Server 3.0+ for multipoint audio, video, and data conferencing (**http://www.microsoft.com/netmeeting/**).

- *NetShow 2.0* uses Microsoft DirectX and ActiveMovie to render on-demand (unicast) or live (broadcast) audio and video content on 32-bit Windows clients (**http://www.microsoft.com/netshow/about.htm**).

- *Media Server* (code-named Cougar, formerly Tiger) is designed to broadcast with NetShow real-time streaming video and audio content over intranets and the Internet. Media Server's origins are in Microsoft's now-abandoned Interactive TV project. Media Server is scalable, so you can add slave servers (formerly Tiger Cubs) to increase the number of simultaneous content streams.

- *Routing and Remote Access Service* (Routing and RAS, formerly Steelhead) is an updated IP and IPX/SPX routing service for Windows NT Server. Windows NT Server 4.0 now includes limited routing capability in its Multiprotocol Router (MPR) service. Routing and RAS replaces Windows NT Server 4.0's Router Information Protocol (RIP), Service Advertising Protocol (SAP), and Remote Access Service (RAS) components to provide services similar to Novell's MPR for IntranetWare. Routing and RAS, which provides TCP/IP and IPX/SPX routing via RIP, RIP II, and Open Shortest Path First (OSPF), is one of the subjects of Chapter 26, "Scaling Windows NT Server 4.0 to the Enterprise."

Microsoft Commercial Internet System is the most ambitious of the company's Internet-related projects. Microsoft's BackOffice Live site uses MCIS for demonstration purposes. MCIS includes the following server-side components:

- *Address Book* supplements MCIS Mail with a "white pages" listing of users, which also serves as a directory for setting up NetMeeting conferences. Address Book supports both LDAP (Lightweight Directory Access Protocol) and HTTP interfaces. LDAP is one of the subjects of Chapter 27, "Distributing File and Directory Services."

- *Chat* enables IRC (Internet Relay Chat) one-to-one, one-to-many, and many-to-many conversations among users and user communities.

- *Content Replication* automatically copies file-based content between servers, often to servers beyond a firewall. The primary uses for Content Replication are production server content staging and server mirroring.

- *Internet Locator* maintains a dynamic list of currently online users with their IP addresses. Internet Locator updates the list as users connect and disconnect from the site or service, providing the directory service for Chat and NetMeeting.

- *MCIS Mail* is a SNMP/POP3 Internet mail server that supports MIME-formatted attachments, user mailbox management, routing capabilities, and user authentication for privacy.

- *MCIS News* supports Internet-standard NNTP (Network News Transfer Protocol) with secure password protection and offers moderated newsgroup capability.

- *Membership* authenticates users, authorizes access to specific site areas, and triggers billing events to be processed by a third-party member billing system.

- *Personalization* customizes the appearance and navigation of site content according to a set of preferences set by users.

MCIS also includes Merchant Server so that commercial Internet sites, such as those run by cable-TV MSOs (Multiple Service Operators), can offer pay-per-view and other revenue-supplementing services to subscribers. Microsoft limits sale of the MCIS package to telecommunications carriers, Internet service providers (ISPs), cable network operators, and Internet content providers (ICPs).

ON THE WEB

Microsoft's BackOffice Live site is at **http://backoffice.microsoft.com**. You can link to pages that describe each of MCIS's server components at **http://backoffice.microsoft.com/product/cis/system.asp** and can download 120-day evaluation copies of each component from **http://backoffice.microsoft.com/downtrial/default.asp**.

Enterprise Middleware

Middleware, defined near the beginning of this chapter, is a key element of enterprise-scale computing. Traditionally, Windows middleware has been the province of third-party vendors providing mainframe or UNIX database connectivity through Microsoft's Open Database Connectivity (ODBC) API. Beginning in 1996, Microsoft has devoted substantial resources to developing its own middleware framework for Windows NT Server. The three most important of these frameworks are as follows:

■ *Microsoft Transaction Server (MTS) 1.0* is a combination of an object request broker (ORB) and transaction-processing manager (TPM). ORBs handle deployment and management of middle-tier components, commonly called *business rules,* that link user services (client applications) to data services, such as relational or object database management systems. TPMs manage updates to single or multiple (distributed) databases to assure that critical data, such as banking transactions, remains consistent at all times.

■ *Microsoft Messaging Queue*, in the beta-testing stage when this book was written, is intended to ensure the consistency of transactions over unreliable WANs. If a WAN connection fails, transaction messages remain in the queue until the connection is restored, whereupon the transactions complete. A typical application for message queuing is obtaining credit-card authorizations or debiting user accounts by using a dial-up or T-1 connection to a credit-card network.

■ *Cedar,* the code-name for an extension to MTS 1.0, provides MTS with the ability to work with "legacy" mainframe transaction monitors, such as IBM's Customer Information and Control System (CICS). Cedar uses SNA Server 3.0 to provide the Windows NT Server 4.0 link to mainframes running IBM's System Network Architecture.

MTS and MSMQ are covered in Chapter 26, "Scaling Windows NT Server 4.0 to the Enterprise."

Licensing BackOffice Components

Microsoft sells Windows NT Server 4.0 and other BackOffice components through authorized Microsoft resellers, which include virtually all major software distributors. Large firms qualify to buy directly from Microsoft. Microsoft and its resellers offer quantity discounts, as well as discounted competitive upgrades for current users of NetWare and Banyan VINES. Academic licenses are available at about 60 percent of the commercial price. Microsoft commercial pricing examples shown in the following sections were effective for U.S. purchasers in mid-1997 and may vary depending on the reseller you choose and your negotiation skills.

 For a referral to an authorized Microsoft reseller, call Microsoft at (800) 426-9400.

Per-Seat vs. Per-Server Licensing

Before the introduction of BackOffice, Microsoft priced Windows NT Advanced Server 3.1 and Microsoft SQL Server 4.21 by the number of client connections. Both server products offered "Enterprise" versions that allowed connection of an unlimited number of clients, without the requirement to buy individual client licenses. With the introduction of BackOffice 1.0, however, Microsoft adopted a per-seat licensing system with a per-server option available for some components. The difference between per-seat and per-server licensing is as follows:

- *Per-seat* licensing requires that each client connected to the network have a Client Access License for Windows NT, if the client uses Windows NT's networking services. Each client also must have a Client Access License for each BackOffice service it uses. A per-seat client may connect simultaneously to any number of Windows NT servers with a single Client Access License. There's no built-in server connection limit; the network administrator is responsible for assuring licensing compliance.

- *Per-server* licensing requires that the number of Client Access Licenses must equal the number of PCs simultaneously using Windows NT's networking or BackOffice services. The license is associated with a single server. If one PC is simultaneously connected to two Windows NT servers, two Windows NT Client Access Licenses are consumed. When the Windows NT server's connection limit is reached, no more connections are possible. Per-server licensing often is called *license pooling* or *multiplexing*. Per-server licensing isn't available for Systems Management Server.

Per-seat licensing is the most common choice for larger organizations running multiple Windows NT servers. Per-seat licensing also is the easiest to administer; you count the number of client PCs and buy that many Client Access Licenses for Windows NT Server and each BackOffice server application you run.

Per-server licensing is advantageous under the following circumstances:

- You use Windows NT Server 4.0 only as a remote access server to provide mobile personnel with network services. In this case, you need to purchase only Client Access Licenses for the maximum number of simultaneous inbound connections you support.

- You use Windows NT Server 4.0 and Internet Information Server 3.0+ as an Internet server, with periodic LAN connection by the Webmaster or others for updates and maintenance. You need Windows NT Client Access Licenses for a Windows NT intranet server for clients that use Windows NT networking to connect to the server.

ON THE WEB

See **http://www.microsoft.com/ntserver/info/licensing.htm** for specific details on Internet licensing.

- You're making a test installation that involves sequential evaluation of BackOffice components by various sets of users. You have the one-time option of installing Windows NT Server and the other BackOffice components (except Systems Management Server) in per-server mode, and then changing the licensing method to per-seat. You can't change from per-seat to per-server mode.

N O T E You don't need a Client Access License to remotely administer another computer with Performance Monitor, Server Manager, or User Manager for Domains. Local logon to the server through the built-in Workstation service doesn't require a Client Access License. ▪

These scenarios assume that you use NetWare or another network operating system for file and printer sharing. If you use Windows NT Server only for hosting SQL Server, Exchange Server, SNA Server, or a combination of the three, and use another network operating system for communication with the service, the Windows NT server is called an *application server* and doesn't require Windows NT Client Access Licenses. You must have a Client Access License, either per-seat or per-server, for each service you run.

N O T E   A Client Access License isn't software, it's a document. Windows for Workgroups, Windows 95, and Windows NT Workstation each include the required client software to connect to Windows NT Server. The distribution CD-ROMs for BackOffice components include the required client software for the service. ■

BackOffice Server 2.5 and Client Access Licenses

BackOffice Server 2.5 and BackOffice Client Access Licenses are sold as separate full-package products (SKUs) at a substantial discount (in the range of 30 percent to 40 percent) from the combined prices of the individual components. The full value of the discount, however, is attained only if each of your clients uses every component of BackOffice Server 2.5. For most organizations, the BackOffice Server bundle discount is illusory.

Like Microsoft Office, all the BackOffice Server components are licensed to run only on a single machine and are restricted to per-seat licensing. Similarly, the BackOffice client software is licensed for installation on one PC. You aren't permitted to pool BackOffice client licenses among client PCs on your network.

Microsoft recommends BackOffice Server 2.5 for the following types of customers:

- Small businesses
- Branch offices within organizations running BackOffice components at a central location
- Sites that run Exchange Server and any other BackOffice component
- Sites that use Systems Management Server with SQL Server
- Sites that use Internet Information Server, SQL Server, and Proxy Server
- Client-server development

The WAN-connected branch office scenario is the most likely to show a potential savings by implementing BackOffice. Small businesses seldom have need for SNA Server and aren't likely to devote the administrative resources necessary to implement Systems Management Server. For client/server development, the Microsoft Developer Network (MSDN) offers a yearly Enterprise Subscription (formerly Level 2) that includes quarterly releases of BackOffice (the BackOffice Test Platform) with licenses for five simultaneous connections. The subscription includes special Premium Shipments for BackOffice upgrades between the quarterly releases. The $1,499 for the Enterprise Subscription represents a substantial discount from the ERP (estimated retail price) for BackOffice with five Client Access Licenses.

ON THE WEB

More information on MSDN subscriptions is available from **http://www.microsoft.com/msdn/subscribe/**.

Buying BackOffice to achieve savings resulting from the use of only two BackOffice services on a single server is a marginal proposition, at best. The value of your time spent analyzing such potential savings is unlikely to be recovered by the actual reduction in licensing cost.

Windows NT 4.0 License Packages and Cost

Windows NT Server 4.0 is available in 5- and 10-user versions. Table 22.1 lists the theoretical licensing costs for typical numbers of clients connected to a single Windows NT Server 4.0 installation. Volume discounts available through Microsoft Open Licensing Pack (MOLP) purchases aren't applied to the amounts shown in Table 22.1. Total and per-client costs for 50 or more clients are approximate.

ON THE WEB

Further licensing and pricing details are available at **http://www.microsoft.com/ntserver/info/pricing.htm**.

Table 22.1   Approximate Licensing Cost and Cost per Client for Typical Windows NT Server 4.0 Installations

	Number of Clients					
License	5	10	25	50	100	250
Server	$809	$1,129	$809	$1,129	$809	$1,129
Clients	Incl	Incl	659	1,318	3,130	7,198
Total	809	1,129	1,468	2,447	3,939	9,037
Per Client	162	113	59	49	39	36

N O T E   There's no explanation for the $320 cost difference between the five- and 10-client versions of Windows NT Server 4.0. This difference represents a cost of $64 each for the additional five clients. Single-quantity client licenses are priced at $39.95, about $120 less than the incremental licensing of five clients. There's also no obvious explanation for Microsoft's fascination with the number nine as the terminal digit for pricing its BackOffice components. The $39.95 price for a single Client Access License suggests that consumer product price-pointing may have crept into the process. ■

SQL Server 6.5 Licensing

Microsoft SQL Server 6.5 is available in 5-, 10-, and 25-user versions. Table 22.2 lists Microsoft's published costs (March 1997) for typical numbers of clients connected to a single SQL Server. Microsoft Open Licensing Pack (MOLP) purchases and volume discounts apply for 50 clients or more. Microsoft also offers SQL Workstation that runs on Windows NT Workstation and provides only a single connection.

ON THE WEB

For the latest information on SQL Server 6.5 licensing, check **http://www.microsoft.com/sql/price.htm**.

Table 22.2   Licensing Cost for SQL Server 6.5

License	Number of Clients					
	5	**10**	**25**	**50**	**100**	**250**
Bundled Client Licenses						
Server	$1,399	$1,999	$3,999	$7,999	$15,999	$24,999
Clients	Incl	Incl	Incl	Incl	Incl	Incl
Total	1,399	1,999	3,999	7,999	15,999	24,999
Per Client	280	200	160	160	160	100
Separately Purchased Client Licenses*						
Server	$1,399	$1,999	$1,399	$1,999	$1,999	$1,999
Clients	Incl	Incl	2,369	4,738	11,485	28,428
Total	1,399	1,999	3,999	6,737	13,844	30,427
Per Client	280	200	151	135	126	122

*Figures shown for the 100-client, separately purchased client licenses are for 110, not 100 clients. Microsoft provides no explanation for the discrepancy in prices between the two purchasing methods for quantities of 25 or more clients.

N O T E   The $2,999 Internet Connector License Pack for SQL Server is required if Microsoft Internet Information Server or any other Web server is populated from SQL Server data. Population includes the use of the Internet Database Connector, Active Server Pages, or the SQL Server Web Assistant with SQL Server. ■

Exchange Server 5.0 Licensing

Microsoft Exchange Server 5.0, like SQL Server 6.5, comes in 5-, 10-, and 25-user versions. Table 22.3 lists Microsoft's published costs (March 1997) for typical numbers of clients connected to a single Exchange server. Microsoft Open Licensing Pack (MOLP) purchases and volume discounts apply for 50 clients or more.

ON THE WEB

For pricing details on all versions of Exchange server, check out **http://www.microsoft.com/exchange/erp.htm**.

Table 22.3   Approximate Total Licensing Cost and Cost per Client for Microsoft Exchange Server 5.0

License			Number of Clients			
	5	10	25	50	105	250
Server	$999	$1,329	$2,129	$1,329	$999	$1,329
Clients	N/A	N/A	N/A	2,298	5,745	13,788
Total	999	1,329	2,129	3,627	6,744	15,117
Per Client	200	133	85	72	64	60

N O T E   Microsoft offers the Exchange Connector for $499 per server and the X.400 Connector for $999 per server. You must license the Connector for each Exchange server in your system. An alternative to individual Connector licenses is the Enterprise Edition of Exchange Server ($3,589 with 25 Client Access Licenses or $4,859 with 50 CALs), which includes both the Exchange and X.400 Connectors. The Internet Mail connector of version 4.0 isn't required for Exchange Server 5.0. ■

Systems Management Server 1.2 Licensing

Systems Management Server isn't priced with bundled client licenses. Table 22.4 lists Microsoft's published costs (March 1997) for typical numbers of clients connected to a single SMS 1.2 installation. SMS is the only BackOffice component that requires per-seat licensing. Microsoft Open Licensing Pack (MOLP) purchases and volume discounts apply for 50 clients or more.

Table 22.4   Approximate Total Licensing Cost and Cost per Client for Systems Management Server 1.2

License			Number of Clients			
	5	10	25	50	100	250
Server	$923	$923	$923	$923	$923	$923
Clients	Incl	275	1,100	2,475	5,225	13,475
Total	923	1,198	2,023	3,398	6,148	14,398
Per Client	185	120	81	68	61	58

N O T E At least one SQL Server 6.5 license is required for use of Systems Management Server. Client Access Licenses for the SQL Server installation used with SMS aren't required unless SQL Server is accessed by clients for other purposes. Access to SQL Server for administration of SMS doesn't require a SQL Server Client Access License. ∎

SNA Server 3.0 Licensing

SNA Server 3.0, like Systems Management Server 1.2, now is priced with bundled client licenses, in contrast to prior versions whose server prices didn't include licenses. Table 22.5 lists Microsoft's published costs (March 1997) for typical numbers of clients connected to a single SNA Server 3.0 installation through an application that accesses SNA services, such as Attachmate Extra or WallData Rumba. Microsoft Open Licensing Pack (MOLP) purchases and volume discounts apply for 50 clients or more. An SNA Workstation version, similar in concept to SQL Workstation, also is available. SNA Server requires a mainframe or IBM AS/400 System Network Architecture connection; installing and using SNA Server is beyond the scope of this book.

ON THE WEB

Get SNA Server licensing pricing details from **http://www.microsoft.com/sna/howbuy.htm**.

Table 22.5 Approximate Total Licensing Cost and Cost per Client for SNA Server 3.0

	Number of Clients					
License	5	10	25	50	105	245
Server	$1,359	$1,359	$$2,519	$2,519	$2,519	$2,519
Clients	Incl	339	Incl	2,737	4,796	14,388
Total	1,359	1,059	2,519	5,256	7,315	16,907
Per Client	147	106	101	105	70	70

Licensing Costs for All BackOffice Components

Table 22.6 summarizes and averages the data of Tables 22.1 through 22.5 to provide an example of the total cost for all BackOffice components installed on a single Windows NT server for various numbers of client licenses. As mentioned earlier, running all BackOffice services on a single Windows NT server for more than about 10 or 20 clients is likely to be impractical. For example, a single-server configuration doesn't provide for a Backup Domain Controller, which is necessary for installations with more than 10 or 20 users. Adding Windows NT Server 4.0 licenses at the 25-, 50-, 100-, and 250-client level, however, adds less than 10 percent to total cost per client.

Table 22.6 Approximate Total Licensing Cost and Cost per Client for All BackOffice Components

Component	Number of Clients					
	5	10	25	50	100	250
Windows NT Server 4.0	$809	$1,129	$1,468	$2,447	$3,939	$9,037
SQL Server 6.5	1,399	1,999	3,999	6,737	13,844	30,427
Exchange Server 5.0	999	1,329	2,129	3,627	6,744	15,117
SMS 1.2	923	1,198	2,023	3,398	6,148	14,398
SNA Server 3.0	1,359	1,059	2,519	5,256	7,315	16,907
Total	5,489	6,714	12,138	21,465	37,990	85,886
Per Client	1,098	671	486	429	380	344

When this book was written, it was difficult to confirm pricing information for BackOffice Server 2.5. Table 22.7 shows Microsoft's prices for BackOffice 2.5 from the current Microsoft U.S. Estimated Price List as of April 1, 1997. Licensing costs shown in Table 22.7 are for comparative purposes only; most network administrators consider use of BackOffice Server 2.5 impractical with more than 25 clients.

ON THE WEB

You can find the Microsoft U.S. Estimated Price List at **http://www.microsoft.com/partnering/handbook.htm**.

Table 22.7 Approximate Total Licensing Cost and Cost per Client for BackOffice 2.5

License	Number of Clients					
	5	10	25	50	100	250
Server	$2,499	$2,499	$2,499	$2,499	$2,499	$2,499
Clients	1,309	2,618	5,488	10,976	20,985	44,408
Total	3,808	5,117	7,987	13,475	23,394	46,907
Per Client	762	512	319	270	234	188

The Annuity Model for BackOffice Upgrades

Press reports from a Microsoft briefing for security analysts quoted Bill Gates as saying that the BackOffice software market is "an annuity business." Much of Microsoft's income derives from license fees for the more-or-less yearly updates of the Microsoft Office and BackOffice Family full-package product. Updates to BackOffice occur more frequently because of the lack of synchronization among component upgrades, as discussed earlier in the section "Aiming at a Moving BackOffice Target." The costs of updating servers and clients can be considerable. For example, updating from Windows NT Server 3.51 to 4.0 costs $539 for a 10-user license, and updating 20 clients carries a price tag of $339, both about 50 percent of the original license fees.

Microsoft defines the following types of server-side product upgrades:

- *Major upgrades* are defined as an increment to the integer value of the product version. The upgrade from Windows NT 3.51 to 4.0 is an example of a major upgrade. Major upgrades require upgrading client and server software.

- *Minor upgrades* are defined as an increment to the first decimal digit of the version number. The upgrade of SQL Server from version 6.0 to 6.5 and Systems Management Server from 1.1 to 1.2 are examples of minor upgrades. Minor upgrades also require upgrading client and server software, but Microsoft says that the price for a minor upgrade "will typically be half of the charge for a major upgrade."

- *Step-ups* (sometimes called *updates*) are defined as an increment to the second decimal digit of the version number. The step-up from Windows NT Server 3.5 to 3.51 is an example. Step-ups replace the server software but not the client software.

N O T E   Service packs, which ordinarily correct bugs or provide minor changes to client or server software, are free when downloaded from Microsoft's FTP site or Web server. ■

One problem facing network and system administrators at large firms is the ability to forecast the cost of upgrading clients and servers accurately. Not only is it difficult to predict when Microsoft will release a new upgrade or step-up, but pricing is likely to be unpredictable, too. Thus, Microsoft has gone into the "software insurance" business with a fixed-price annuity, called *maintenance*, for server-side upgrades.

Microsoft offers maintenance for its BackOffice Family of server products under the Microsoft Select or Microsoft Open License programs. Maintenance is a fixed-fee, two-year agreement, which automatically updates all your BackOffice components and Client Access Licenses when Microsoft updates or steps up a product. According to Microsoft, the cost of the program is about 15 percent per year of the total ERPs for your existing license count. One of the more interesting features of the annuity is that you don't have to "be current" to enroll. In Microsoft's terms, you can "get current" and "remain current" for two years for an amount that might be less than the cost of a single major upgrade, depending on how many BackOffice components you license.

T I P If you have a large Windows NT Server 3.51 installation that you plan to upgrade to version 4.0, make sure that you investigate a maintenance agreement before placing an order for the upgrade. A maintenance agreement that includes the current upgrade can reduce two-year upgrade costs substantially. If you're running Systems Management Server, you'll want to make the minor upgrade to version 1.2.

Using Windows NT Server 4.0's License Manager

Most Systems Management Server users were disappointed to learn that version 1.2 still doesn't include a license metering feature. Microsoft includes a relatively simple License Manager application in Windows NT Server 4.0, which performs rudimentary license metering for applications that operate in per-server licensing mode. Control Panel's License tool also is involved in license management.

Control Panel's License Tool

Windows NT Server 4.0's License Management service introduced the term *enterprise server* to define a master Primary Domain Controller (PDC) to which other PDCs in the domain and trusting domains replicate license information. An enterprise server can be a PDC or a plain server. In a single-domain environment, the PDC is the master server for license management purposes. You define the enterprise server or master server with Control Panel's License tool. The License tool also lets you specify the license mode for each service on the computer, the number of per-server licenses, and replication frequency and time. Only the License Manager can administer per-seat licenses.

To use Control Panel's License tool, follow these steps:

1. From Control Panel, double-click the License tool to open the Choose Licensing Mode dialog. Select the server component you want to manage from the Product list. Figure 22.1 shows Windows NT Server selected for the per-server licensing mode.

FIG. 22.1

Control Panel's Choose Licensing Mode dialog.

2. Click the Add Licenses button to add per-server licenses for the selected component in the New Client Access License dialog. Use the spinner buttons or type a new number in the Quantity box (see Figure 22.2). The For License Mode option buttons and the Comment text box are disabled. Click OK to close the dialog.

FIG. 22.2

Adding per-server licenses for Windows NT Server 4.0.

> **N O T E**   You can use the Remove Licenses button of the Choose Licensing Mode dialog to reduce the number of per-server licenses for a component, if necessary, to reflect actual license purchases. ■

3. If you add licenses, the Per Server Licensing dialog appears (see Figure 22.3). Mark the check box to indicate that you agree with the terms of the licensing agreement, and then click OK.

FIG. 22.3

Confirming agreement with the licensing terms for per-server mode.

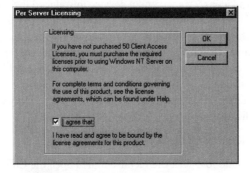

4. Click Replication in the Choose Licensing Mode dialog to open the Replication Configuration dialog to specify an enterprise server, if necessary, and to set the replication frequency or time for the local server. If you don't specify an enterprise server, the PDC for the server's domain is the master server for licensing purposes (see Figure 22.4). Click OK to close the dialog.

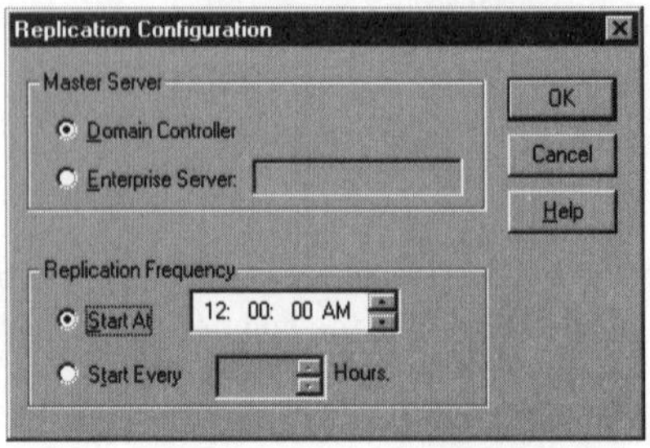

FIG. 22.4

Establishing the master server and a replication frequency in the Replication Configuration dialog.

5. Click OK to close the Choose Licensing Mode dialog.

N O T E   With the exception of specifying the replication options, you can use License Manager to perform all the functions of the License tool. Also, the License tool lets you set the number of per-seat licenses. ▓

License Manager

License Manager is Microsoft's aid to keeping you honest in the licensing department. Unlike some other network operating system and server application suppliers, Microsoft trusts its customers to purchase the required number of server Client Access Licenses for their organizations. License Manager lets you set the number of Client Access Licenses for BackOffice components operating in per-seat (not per-server) mode. Also, you can monitor and administer per-seat and per-server licenses for any server in the domain or in a trusting domain.

To use License Manager, follow these steps:

1. From the Start menu choose Programs, Administrative Tools, and License Manager to open License Manager's window. If you haven't entered per-seat license information, the Purchase History page is empty.

2. Click the Products View tab to display a summary of product licensing. In Figure 22.5, the Windows NT Server item displays the total number of per-server licenses for two servers (OAKLEAF0 and OAKLEAF3). The entry for Systems Management Server displays a warning that three client seats have been allocated, but no per-seat licenses have been purchased. The three allocated seats are the server on which SMS is installed (OAKLEAF0), a Windows 95 client (OAKLEAF1), and a Windows NT 4.0 BDC (OAKLEAF3).

FIG. 22.5

The Products View page of License Manager for a system installed from the BackOffice Test Platform distribution CD-ROM but with per-server licensing.

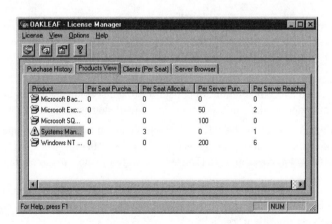

3. To monitor clients with unlicensed usage of per-seat server applications, click the Clients (Per Seat) tab. Figure 22.6 displays the three PCs (two of which are servers) that show unlicensed usage of SMS.

FIG. 22.6
The Clients (Per Seat) page, displaying unlicensed usage of SMS by two servers (OAK00001 and OAK00003) and a client (OAK00002).

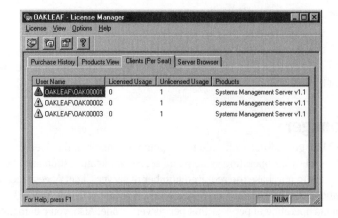

4. To monitor or administer the number of per-seat licenses, or to change from per-server to per-seat licensing, click the Server Browser tab and expand the list to display each server and its services (see Figure 22.7).

FIG. 22.7
Displaying BackOffice components in License Manager's Server Browser page.

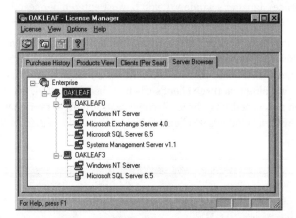

5. To change a component from per-server to per-seat licensing, double-click the component to display the Choose Licensing Mode dialog (see Figure 22.8).

6. Select Per Seat and click OK. A License Violation message box appears, offering you the opportunity to cancel your choice (see Figure 22.9, top). Click No to receive another confirmation message (see Figure 22.9, bottom); click Yes to change the licensing mode.

N O T E   The License Violation message that appears after selecting per-seat licensing doesn't conform to Microsoft's stated policy that you can change from per-server to per-seat licensing without violating your license. ■

FIG. 22.8

The Choose Licensing
Mode dialog.

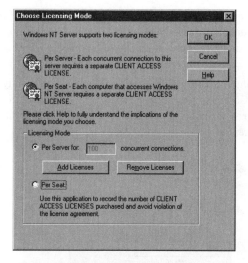

FIG. 22.9

Doubly confirming that
you want to change
licensing mode from
per-server to per-seat.

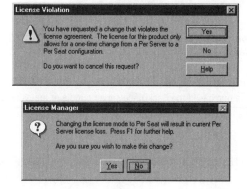

7. Click OK in the Choose Licensing Mode dialog to continue with the mode change. Mark
   the I Agree That check box of the Per Seat Licensing dialog (see Figure 22.10), and then
   click OK to effect the mode change. All per-server license entries for the product are
   deleted.

FIG. 22.10

The final dialog in the
licensing mode change
process.

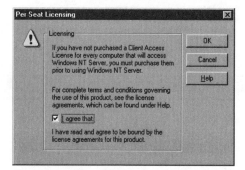

8. From the License menu choose New License to display the New Client Access License dialog. Unlike the dialog displayed by Control Panel's License tool, the Per Seat option is set (but disabled), and the Comment text box is enabled.

9. Select the component to which to add Client Access Licenses in the Product drop-down list box, set the number of licenses in the Quantity box, and then type a description of the transaction in the Comment text box (see Figure 22.11). Click OK to add the new licenses, mark the I Agree That check box of the Per Seat Licensing dialog, and click OK to add the per-seat licenses.

FIG. 22.11

Adding new per-seat licenses for a BackOffice component.

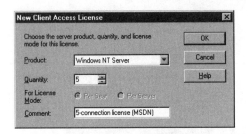

10. Repeat steps 5 through 9 for each component except SMS. For SMS, you need to add Client Access Licenses with only steps 8 and 9.

N O T E You don't necessarily need to change the mode of all your BackOffice servers to per-seat mode unless you've purchased the BackOffice server bundle or are using the BackOffice Test Platform from MSDN. An alternative in these two cases is to specify the number of client licenses for the BackOffice product. ▨

11. Click the Purchase History tab to verify your transactions (see Figure 22.12).

FIG. 22.12

The Purchase History page, displaying changes to per-seat licensing mode.

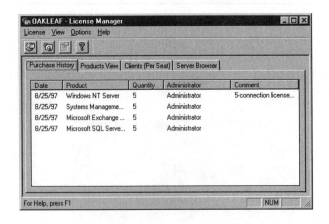

12. Click the Products View tab to verify that per-server licenses no longer appear (see Figure 22.13). Close License Manager.

License violations appear as Stop events in Event Viewer's Application Log window (see Figure 22.14). Double-clicking the event item displays an Event Detail dialog (see Figure 22.15).

FIG. 22.13

The Products View, confirming that prior per-server licenses have been eliminated.

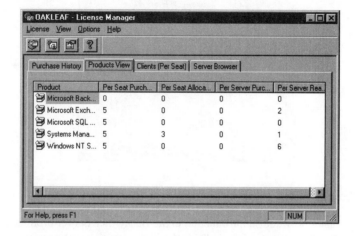

FIG. 22.14

Out-of-license events generated by License Manager.

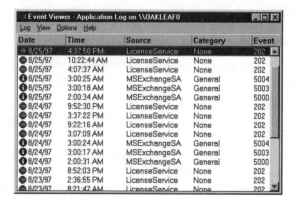

FIG. 22.15

The Event Detail dialog, displaying an out-of-license event for Systems Management Server.

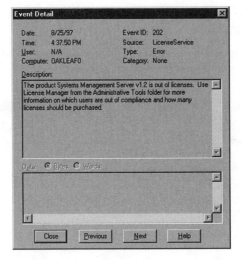

From Here...

This chapter provided an introduction to the BackOffice Server product, and the licensing requirements and costs of the individual components that make up the most commonly used members Microsoft's BackOffice family. Using Control Panel's License tool and License Manager to assure compliance with Microsoft's licensing terms for server licenses and Client Access Licenses also was covered.

For additional information on the three most commonly used services of BackOffice, see the following chapters:

- Chapter 23, "Running Microsoft SQL Server 6.5," describes the basic features of Microsoft's most recent update to SQL Server, which includes new database replication features and a SQL Web Page Wizard.

- Chapter 24, "Messaging with Microsoft Exchange Server 5.0," introduces you to installation and management of Microsoft's new client/server replacement for file-oriented Microsoft Mail 3+ and Internet-oriented upgrade to Exchange Server 4.0.

- Chapter 25, "Administering Clients with Systems Management Server 1.2," covers the basics of planning, administration, and management for Microsoft SMS 1.2.

CHAPTER 23

Running Microsoft SQL Server 6.5

Unlike the other members of the BackOffice Server suite, Microsoft SQL Server is a mature product with a long development history. Sybase Corp. released in 1987 the first version of SQL Server, a client/server relational database management system (RDBMS). In 1988, Sybase, Microsoft, and Ashton-Tate (the developer of dBASE) codeveloped a version of SQL Server for OS/2, the operating system of Microsoft's LAN Manager and IBM's LAN Server. Ashton-Tate, which later was acquired by Borland International, dropped out of the triumvirate, and Microsoft alone marketed the OS/2 version as Microsoft SQL Server. Sybase SQL Server for UNIX minicomputers and Microsoft SQL Server for PC-based systems remained almost indistinguishable through the last OS/2 version, 4.21.

Microsoft and Sybase went their separate ways in 1993, primarily as a result of Microsoft's port of SQL Server 4.21 to Windows NT as version 4.21a. In 1995, Microsoft introduced SQL Server 6.0 and, in April 1996, released the current 6.5 version. SQL Server 6.0 and 6.5 are optimized for Windows NT and include a comprehensive graphical management tool, SQL Enterprise Manager, for administering SQL Server databases. Like other members of the BackOffice family, SQL Server runs as a service and uses

Installing SQL Server 6.5

SQL Server 6.5 is fully integrated with Windows NT Server 4.0, so installation is a simple and fast process.

Installing SQL Server utilities on a client PC

You can administer multiple SQL Server 6.5 installations from Windows NT Workstation 4.0 or Windows 95 clients.

Using SQL Enterprise Manager to create database objects

SQL Enterprise Manager makes it easy to add new database devices, databases, tables, and indexes.

Using Access 97's Upsizing Wizard to import tables

The Upsizing Wizard automatically creates SQL Server 6.5 tables, indexes, defaults, and triggers from your Access 97 databases.

Setting up database security

Using integrated security lets you provide single-logon SQL Server 6.5 access to user groups or individual users.

Windows NT's security system to control access to SQL Server objects, such as databases, tables, views, and stored procedures.

This chapter assumes basic familiarity with the terminology of client/server RDBMSes and their table objects, such as columns (fields), indexes, key fields, foreign keys, and constraints, as well as basic SQL syntax. The primary emphasis of the chapter is on installing SQL Server 6.5, installing and using SQL Enterprise Manager, and establishing basic database security. ■

Positioning SQL Server in the RDBMS Market

Microsoft's version of SQL Server traditionally has been relegated to the *departmental* database category, whereas UNIX RDBMSes (such as Oracle, Sybase, and Informix) and mainframe products (primarily IBM's DB2) have *enterprise* status. The generally accepted definitions of these two categories is as follows:

■ *Enterprise RDBMSes* support large-scale transaction-processing applications, such as airline reservation systems running on mainframe and very large UNIX "boxes" (minicomputers). Enterprise RDBMSes often involve database sizes in the terabyte (1,000G) range. Licensing costs for enterprise RDBMSes start in the $100,000 category and often are in the million-dollar class. Users pay substantial amounts for yearly software maintenance.

■ *Departmental RDBMSes* are dedicated to specific applications (such as inventory control or manufacturing requirements planning) or functions (such as finance or marketing). Departmental RDBMSes support database sizes between about 100G and a terabyte. They can serve the needs of most smaller firms with sales of under $25 million or so.

N O T E   Microsoft's aggressive pricing of SQL Server has brought the average licensing costs for departmental RDBMSes into the $10,000 and less range. Smaller firms now can start with a single SQL Server 6.5 installation and 10 client PCs with an up-front cost of less than $2,000 for licenses. ■

Microsoft's goal is to reposition SQL Server from its current departmental niche to enterprise status while maintaining its rock-bottom price point. Microsoft is about halfway to its target with SQL Server 6.5. In the meantime, Microsoft is counting heavily on small- to medium-sized firms to increase SQL Server's market share. Integration of SQL Server 6.5 with Internet Information Server 2.0 through the Internet Database Connector, SQL Server's Web Assistant, and easy connectivity to SQL Server with the members of Microsoft Office and Visual Basic also contribute to SQL Server's acceptance for a broad range of database applications.

▶ **See** "Using SQL Server Web Assistant to Distribute Activity Reports," **p. 782**

N O T E   Microsoft RDBMS competitors also are jumping on the Windows NT bandwagon. Oracle7, Video Server, Enterprise Manager, Personal Oracle7, and Personal Oracle Lite all run on Windows NT 4.0 Server. Oracle released in June 1997 its Universal Server combined with Oracle Fail Safe technology for two-node Windows NT 4.0 clusters in June. Informix offers Windows NT 4.0

versions its new Universal Server and FastStart data warehousing systems. Most of the other major players in the client/server RDBMS market offer downsized Windows NT versions of their UNIX-based products, often called *workgroup servers*. ■

Data warehousing and *data marts* are two of today's hot database topics. Data warehousing involves extracting data stored in various formats within enterprise RDBMSes, as well as legacy network and hierarchical databases (typified by IBM's VSAM), into separate databases that provide fast response to user queries. The objective is to separate ad hoc decision-support activities (queries) from transaction-processing operations and format the data into a consistent relational structure. *Rollups* of mainframe transaction databases are the traditional method of providing this separation. Rollups create a second database that summarizes daily, weekly, or monthly transactions. A data warehouse stores the rolled-up data for an entire corporation in a separate set of relational databases, usually on a UNIX box.

Several suppliers of RDBMSes are designed specifically for data warehousing; Red Brick Systems was one of the first firms to enter the data warehouse RDBMS business. Oracle offers its Oracle Express Server for data warehousing. The size of a data warehouse easily can grow into the terabyte range.

Data marts are smaller-scale versions of data warehouses devoted to a single department or function, such as sales, finance, or marketing. Properly designed data marts can be combined to create a distributed data warehouse. Microsoft is only beginning to stick its toe in the data mart water. SQL Server 6.5 has added ROLLUP and CUBE statements to Transact-SQL (SQL Server's flavor of SQL) for summarizing (aggregating) data. Microsoft recommends SQL Server for use with data marts less than 200G in size having fewer than 5,000 simultaneous users. These limits, although insufficient for major-scale data warehouses, are adequate for most of today's data marts.

ON THE WEB

Microsoft announced in September 1996 its "Alliance for Data Warehousing" program to gain increased acceptance for SQL Server 6.5 as a data mart or small data warehouse RDBMS. You can obtain the latest information on the use of SQL Server in data warehousing applications from **http://www.microsoft.com/sql/dwoverview.htm**.

Installing SQL Server 6.5

One primary advantage of SQL Server over its competitors is the ease of installation and startup. You can install SQL Server 6.5 in less than 30 minutes. Before you install SQL Server 6.5 for the first time or as an upgrade to an earlier version, be sure to do the following:

- Read the Readme.txt file on the distribution CD-ROM for your server's processor, typically in the \Sql65\I386 folder. This file contains late-breaking information on SQL Server 6.5 that isn't in the Books Online documentation. The file also contains details on disk space requirements for installation and actions you must take when upgrading from prior versions.

■ Provide sufficient free disk space for the installation. Although a new installation requires about 80M of free space, you should have at least 110M free on the logical drive to which you install SQL Server, so you can install a master database device of 50M or larger. You can use other local logical drives to accommodate user databases and transaction logs.

N O T E Less free space is required when upgrading SQL Server 4.21a or 6.0 to version 6.5. You must have free space available in your Master.dat device. Check the Readme.txt file for the exact disk and device free space requirements for upgrading. ■

■ Set up your local tape backup drive, if you haven't already done so. If you're using third-party network backup software, make sure that the tape drive is accessible from the Windows NT server on which you're installing SQL Server. (SQL Server's built-in tape backup function won't back up to a remote tape drive.)

▶ **See** "Using the Windows NT Server 4.0 Backup Application," **p. 278**

ON THE WEB

If you don't have SQL Server 6.5, you can download a 33M evaluation copy, good for 120 days from date of installation, from **http://www.microsoft.com/sql/eval.htm**.

Installing Files from the Distribution CD-ROM

To install SQL Server 6.5 from the distribution CD-ROM, follow these steps:

1. Run Setup.exe from the SQL Server 6.5 folder for your processor type, usually \Sql65\I386, to start the Setup program.

2. When the Welcome dialog appears, click Continue to open the Enter Name and Organization dialog.

3. Complete the Name, Company, and, optionally, the Product ID text boxes (see Figure 23.1), and then click Continue to open the Verify Name and Company dialog.

FIG. 23.1
Entering user and organization names.

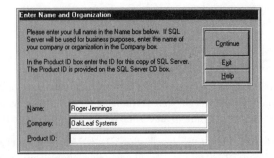

4. Confirm your entries and click Continue to open the Microsoft SQL Server 6.5 – Options dialog. If this is a new installation, select Install SQL Server and Utilities (see Figure

23.2). Otherwise, select Upgrade SQL Server. Click Continue to open the Choose Licensing Mode dialog.

FIG. 23.2

Specifying a new installation of SQL Server 6.5 and its utility applications.

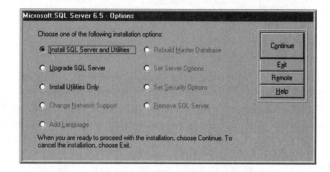

5. Select the Licensing Mode for your installation (see Figure 23.3). The default is Per Server, which you can change later to Per Seat. Click Add Licenses to open the New Client Access License dialog.

▶ **See** "Per-Seat vs. Per-Server Licensing," **p. 816**

FIG. 23.3

Setting the licensing mode for SQL Server.

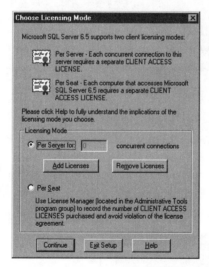

6. Type the number of Client Access Licenses you own in the Quantity box, or use the spinner buttons to set the number of licenses (see Figure 23.4). If you selected Per Seat in step 5, you can enter a note in the Comment text box that appears when you use Windows NT 4.0's License Manager application. Click OK to display the Per Server (or Per Seat) Licensing dialog.

▶ **See** "Using Windows NT Server 4.0's License Manager," **p. 825**

FIG. 23.4

Setting the initial number of Client Access Licenses.

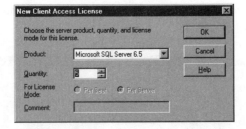

> **N O T E** If you're installing from the BackOffice Test Platform CD-ROM of the Microsoft Developer Network Enterprise Subscription, you're entitled to five simultaneous connections to SQL Server. ■

7. Mark the I Agree That check box (see Figure 23.5) and click OK to add the Client Access Licenses. Click Continue in the Choose Licensing Mode dialog to open the SQL Server Installation Path dialog. (You might need to reconfirm the number of Client Access Licenses at this point.)

FIG. 23.5

Confirming that you've purchased the number of Client Access Licenses you added.

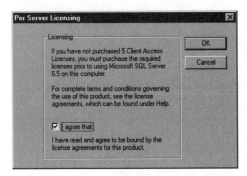

8. Select the local volume on which to install SQL Server and accept the default installation folder, unless you have a reason for doing otherwise (see Figure 23.6). Click Continue to open the MASTER Device Creation dialog.

FIG. 23.6

Specifying the local disk volume and the installation folder for SQL Server.

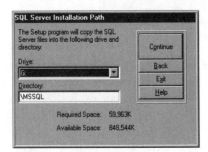

9. You can place the master device on a different volume or in a different folder, if you want. It's recommended that you specify a size of at least 50M for the master device (Master.dat file) of a production SQL Server installation (see Figure 23.7). Click Continue to open the SQL Server Books Online dialog.

FIG. 23.7

Setting the volume and folder for the master device.

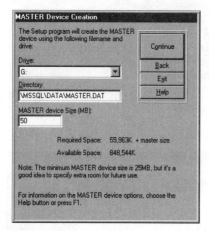

10. Microsoft provides SQL Server's documentation in a searchable Books Online format, similar to a help file. Unless you have another SQL Server installation with Books Online installed, select the Install on Hard Disk option (see Figure 23.8). Click Continue to display the Installation Options dialog.

FIG. 23.8

Options for installing the SQL Server 6.5 online documentation.

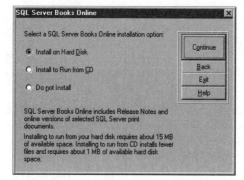

11. Mark the Auto Start SQL Server at Boot Time and Auto Start SQL Executive at Boot Time check boxes (see Figure 23.9). Autostarting SQL Server is especially important if you use it for logging Internet Information Server 2.0 activity.

▶ **See** "Logging to an ODBC Data Source," **p. 766**

12. The default character set (code page) for SQL Server 6.5 is the ISO character set. If you want to change the code page, click the Sets button in the Installation Options dialog to

open the Select Character Set dialog (see Figure 23.10). Choose the code page to use from the Select Character Set list and click OK.

FIG. 23.9

Setting options to start SQL Server and SQL Executive during Windows NT's boot process.

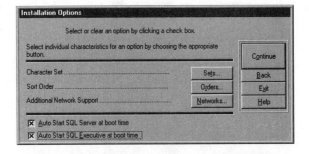

FIG. 23.10

Selecting a character set for your databases.

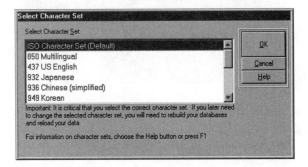

CAUTION

Make sure that you understand the ramifications of using a code page other than the default ISO character set. If you later must change the character set, you must re-create all your databases from backups. The ISO character set has been the standard for SQL Server since version 4.21a.

---

13. The default sort order for SQL Server 6.5 is dictionary order, case-insensitive. Early versions of SQL Server used case-sensitive sort order. If you must change the sort order, click the Orders button in the Installation Options dialog to open the Select Sort Order dialog (see Figure 23.11). The same warning that applies to changing code pages also applies to sort order changes. Select the sort order you want and click OK.

14. The default network protocol for SQL Server is named pipes, which is sufficient for most Windows NT Server installations. To change or add network protocols, click the Networks button in the Installation Options dialog to open the Select Network Protocols dialog. You can add multiple protocols by marking the protocol name in the Install/Uninstall Networks list (see Figure 23.12). After making your selection, click OK.

15. Click Continue in the Installation Options dialog to open the SQL Executive Log On Account dialog.

FIG. 23.11
Selecting a sort order.

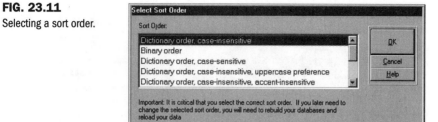

FIG. 23.12
Changing or specifying additional network protocols.

16. SQL Executive, a service for automating execution of SQL Server processes, needs a logon account to start during the boot process. The default is the domain Administrator account (see Figure 23.13), which must previously have been granted Log On as a Service rights. If you don't want to assign a user account for SQL Executive at this point, select Install to Log On as a Local System Account. Click Continue to begin copying files.

FIG. 23.13
Specifying the user account for the SQL Executive service.

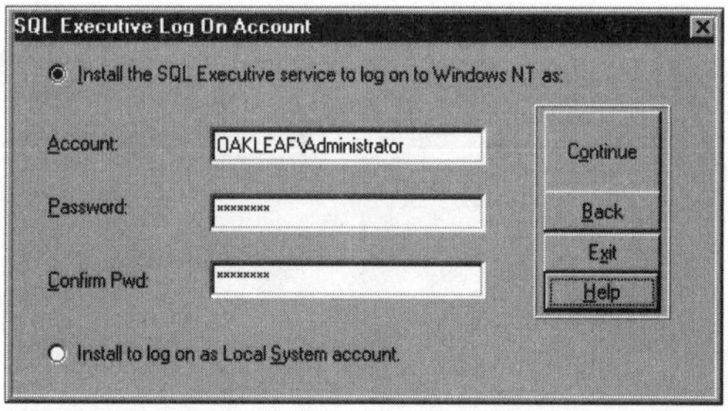

17. Setup copies files to the destination folder you selected earlier in this process, and then creates the master database and other devices and objects. When Setup completes, you see the Microsoft Server SQL 6.5 – Completed dialog. Click Exit to Windows NT.

The Setup process adds a SQL Server 6.5 program group menu to the Programs menu with the choices shown in Figure 23.14. At this point, SQL Server is installed, but neither SQL Server nor SQL Executive is running.

FIG. 23.14
Microsoft SQL Server
6.5's program group
menu choices.

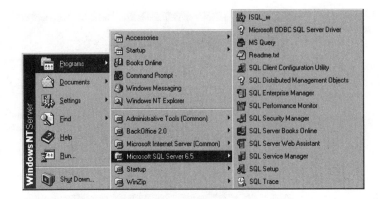

Starting SQL Server and SQL Executive

Before you can configure SQL Enterprise manager for your newly installed SQL Server system, you must start SQL Server 6.5. To start SQL Server and SQL Executive after installation without rebooting Windows NT, do the following:

1. From the Start menu choose Programs, Microsoft SQL Server 6.5, and SQL Service Manager to open the SQL Service Manager window.

2. The Server drop-down list box displays the name of the local SQL Server. Select MSSQLServer from the Services drop-down list and double-click Start/Continue to start SQL Server 6.5 (see Figure 23.15, left).

3. Select SQLExecutive from the Services list and double-click Start/Continue to start SQL Executive (see Figure 23.15, right).

FIG. 23.15
Starting SQL Server 6.5
and SQL Executive with
the SQL Service
Manager.

N O T E You don't need to start SQL Executive to use SQL Enterprise Manager, but it's a good idea to start the service at this point to verify that the service is operable. ■

Installing Service Packs

SQL Server Service Pack 2, released December 23, 1996, was the latest patch for SQL Server 6.5 when this book was written. Service Pack 2, which is cumulative (includes the fixes of Service Pack 1), fixes problems with 32-bit ODBC, replication components, and server components. Fixlist.txt, included with 65sp2x86.exe (for Intel servers), describes the problems corrected by Service Packs 1 and 2.

ON THE WEB

You can download the latest Service Pack from **http://www.microsoft.com/sql/ServicePak.htm**.

To determine whether your SQL Server 6.5 installation has a Service Pack installed, issue a SELECT @@version command from ISQL or ISQL/w, which returns a result similar to the following:

```
Microsoft SQL Server  6.50 - 6.50.240 (Intel X86)
Dec 17 1996 15:50:46
Copyright (c) 1988-1996 Microsoft Corporation
```

Table 23.1 lists the build numbers as displayed by the SELECT @@version command. @@version is one of a number of built-in global variables of SQL Server's Transact-SQL language.

Table 23.1   Build Numbers Corresponding to SQL Server 6.5 Service Pack Status

Build	Version Description
6.50.201	SQL Server 6.5 original release
6.50.213	SQL Server 6.5 with Service Pack 1
6.50.240	SQL Server 6.5 with Service Pack 2

Using SQL Enterprise Manager

SQL Enterprise Manager, called *Starfighter* during its development, is a graphical management tool for SQL Server 6.x. SQL Enterprise Manager replaces the SQL Administrator and SQL Object Manager of SQL Server 4.21a. With very few exceptions, SQL Enterprise Manager lets you perform any administrative operation on SQL Server 6.5 that can be performed by a Transact-SQL script (query). You can run SQL Enterprise Manager locally on the server or from a Windows 95 or Windows NT client. Only ISQL/w, the graphical query manager, is available for 16-bit Windows clients. Most servers are located in restricted-access areas, so managing SQL Server 6.5 from a 32-bit client is the most common practice.

Installing SQL Enterprise Manager on a 32-Bit Client

To install SQL Enterprise Manager on a client running Windows 95 or Windows NT Workstation, follow these steps:

1. Run SQL Server 6.5's Setup.exe from the distribution CD-ROM, either from the client's CD-ROM drive or from a shared CD-ROM drive. The Setup program automatically recognizes that it's running on a client.

2. After Setup starts, click Continue to open the Install/Remove Client Utilities dialog (see Figure 23.16). With the Install Client Utilities option selected, click Continue to open the Install Client Utilities dialog.

FIG. 23.16
Starting installation of the SQL Server utilities on a client PC.

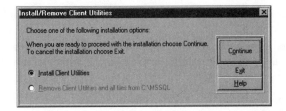

3. Specify the local Drive and Directory in which to install the utilities, and then specify the applications you want in the Utilities to Be Installed section (see Figure 23.17). In most cases, ISQL/w, SQL Enterprise Manager, and SQL Security Manager suffice for remote administration. Click Continue to install the client files.

FIG. 23.17
Selecting the SQL Server client utilities to install.

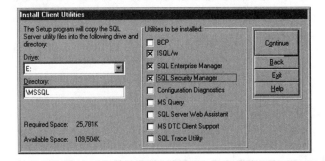

4. After Setup copies the files to your local drive, the Microsoft SQL Server 6.5 – Completed dialog appears. Setup makes changes to the path, so you must reboot the client to make full use of all the utilities.

The examples in this chapter use SQL Enterprise Manager and SQL Security Manager running on a Windows 95 client.

Registering Servers

Before you can use SQL Enterprise Manager with your newly installed server and any other SQL Server 6.x server(s) previously installed, you must register the server(s) with SQL Enterprise Manager by following these steps:

1. From the Start menu choose Programs, Microsoft SQL Server 6.5 Utilities, and SQL Enterprise Manager. Click OK to close the Tip of the Day dialog, if it appears.

2. If you're running SQL Enterprise Manager for the first time, the Register Server dialog appears automatically. Otherwise, choose Register Server from the Server menu to open the Register Server dialog.

3. In the Server combo box, enter the name of the Windows NT server on which the SQL Server you want to register resides. If you installed SQL Server for integrated or mixed security (Trusted Connection), accept the default Use Trusted Connection option (see Figure 23.18). Otherwise, select Use Standard Security and type your administrator account (usually **sa**, the default account) in the Login ID text box and your password (empty if you haven't yet set a password for the sa account) in the Password text box.

FIG. 23.18

Registering a SQL Server 6.5 server with SQL Enterprise Manager.

4. If you want to create a server group for management purposes and add the new server to the group, click the Groups button to display the Manage Server Groups dialog. Type the group name in the Name text box, and then select whether you want a Top Level Group or a Sub-Group of the default SQL 6.5 group (see Figure 23.19). Click Add, and then click Close to return to the Register Server dialog.

FIG. 23.19

Creating a subgroup of the SQL Server 6.5 server group.

5. Click the Register button, and then click Close to return to the SQL Enterprise Manager with your new server added to the Server Manager window.

6. Click the + icon next to the entry for your new server to display the SQL Server objects and object collections installed during the Setup process (see Figure 23.20).

FIG. 23.20

Server Manager's window, with the server and Database Devices entries expanded.

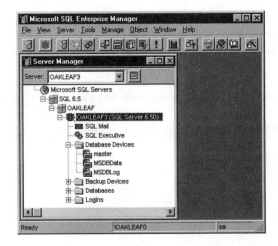

7. Repeat steps 2, 3, and 5 to register any additional servers in your domain or trusting domain(s).

8. To view or change the configuration of a server, right-click the server entry and choose Configuration from the pop-up menu to open the Server Configuration/Options property sheet (see Figure 23.21). Use the Configuration page to establish default values and to tune SQL Server parameters for optimum performance. If you plan to use SQL Server replication and this server will act as a publishing or distribution server, set the memory value to a minimum of 8,192 pages (see Figure 23.22). Click OK to close the property sheet.

FIG. 23.21

The Server Options page of the Server Configuration/Options property sheet.

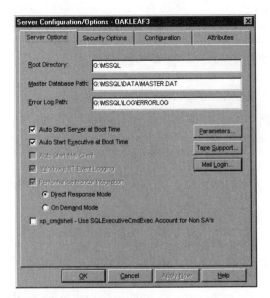

FIG. 23.22

The Configuration page, displaying default values and tuning parameters for SQL Server 6.5.

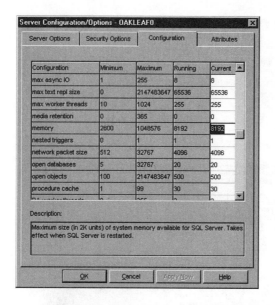

Configuration	Minimum	Maximum	Running	Current
max async IO	1	255	8	8
max text repl size	0	2147483647	65536	65536
max worker threads	10	1024	255	255
media retention	0	365	0	0
memory	2800	1048576	8192	8192
nested triggers	0	1	1	1
network packet size	512	32767	4096	4096
open databases	5	32767	20	20
open objects	100	2147483647	500	500
procedure cache	1	99	30	30

Description:

Maximum size (in 2K units) of system memory available for SQL Server. Takes effect when SQL Server is restarted.

Part V

Ch 23

N O T E You can configure SQL Mail and SQL Executive by right-clicking the entries in the Server Manager window and choosing Configure to display a Configuration dialog or property sheet. ▪

Specifying and Testing Backup Tape Devices

Setup installs only the *diskdump* backup device, which backs up to disk files only. To enable and test your Windows NT Server backup tape drive for use with SQL Server 6.5's backup feature, follow these steps:

1. Right-click the Backup Devices item in the Server Manager window and choose New Backup Device from the pop-up menu to open the New Backup Device dialog.

2. Type a description of the drive in the Name text box and select Tape Backup Device. Accept the default \\.\TAPE0 entry in the Location text box; TAPE0 is the device name Windows NT assigns to the first tape drive of a server (see Figure 23.23). If you use a separate tape drive to back up SQL Server, type the device designator (such as \\.\TAPE1) in the Location text box. Mark the Skip Headers check box if you don't want to assign an ANSI header number to the backup tape. Click Create to add the new backup device.

3. Expand the Backup Devices entry in the Server Manager window to verify that the new tape backup device is recognized (see Figure 23.24).

4. Insert an inactive backup tape in your tape drive and use Windows NT's Backup tool to erase the tape. You must run the Backup tool from the server, unless you have third-party backup software.

FIG. 23.23

Adding a tape
backup device to
SQL Server 6.5.

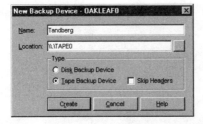

FIG. 23.24

The new tape backup
device added to Server
Manager's Backup
Devices list.

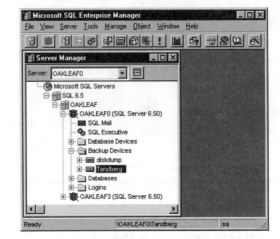

5. Right-click your tape backup device entry in Server Manager's window and select Restore from the pop-up menu. In the Database Backup/Restore dialog, click the Backup tab, if necessary. Select the pubs demonstration database from the Database Backup drop-down list and your tape backup device from the Backup Devices list. Mark the Initialize Device check box and accept the No Expiration Date option (see Figure 23.25). Click Backup Now to open the Backup Volume Labels dialog.

6. Accept the default volume label, or type a six-character Volume number in the Backup Volume Labels dialog (see Figure 23.26). Then click OK to back up the database.

7. A Backup Progress dialog confirms the backup operation, and then a message box indicates that backup is complete. Click OK to return to the Database Backup/Restore dialog.

8. Click the Restore tab and select pubs from the Database drop-down list. After the drive searches the tape and finds the pubs database backup, the Restore page looks like Figure 23.27. Click the Restore Now button to restore the database. A Restore Progress dialog and message box confirm success of the restore operation. Click OK twice to close the message box and the Database Backup/Restore dialog.

FIG. 23.25
Setting backup
parameters for a test
backup of the pubs
sample database.

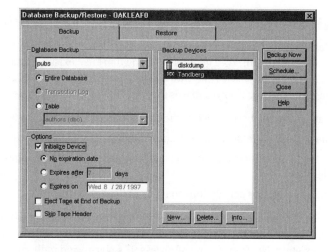

FIG. 23.26
Assigning an ANSI
volume label to the
backup tape.

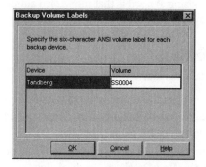

FIG. 23.27
The Restore page,
displaying the param-
eters for restoring the
pubs database from
the backup tape.

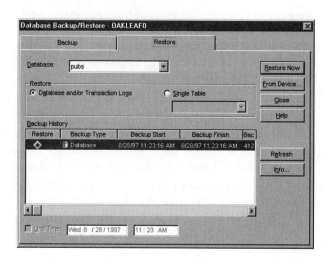

Creating and Managing Database Devices

Setup installs default database devices (master, MSDBData, and MSDBLog) and databases (msdb, pubs, and tempdb). As a general rule, you don't use existing database devices for user databases. A *database device* is a file with a .dat extension in which SQL Server stores databases or log data. Adding user databases involves the following basic steps:

1. Create a new database device of the appropriate size for the database.

2. If the database is to be used for transaction processing, also create a log device.

3. Add the table(s) that comprise the database and, if applicable, import existing data to the tables.

4. Assign appropriate permissions to users of the database.

The following sections describe how to use SQL Enterprise Manager to create a new database device and database, and then use Access 97's Upsizing Wizard to create and populate the tables with existing data from a copy of Access 97's Northwind.mdb sample database. The advantage of using Access 97's Upsizing Wizard is that the wizard automatically creates the tables, indexes, and triggers to maintain referential integrity automatically.

Creating a New Database Device

To create a new SQL Server 6.5 database device, follow these steps:

1. In SQL Enterprise Manager, select the server in the Manage Servers window. Choose Database Devices from the Manage menu to open the Devices window and display the default database devices created by the Setup program.

2. Click the New Device button (at the left on the second toolbar), or choose New Device from the File menu to open the New Database Device dialog.

3. Type the name of the device in the Name text box—in this example, **Northwind**. As you type the name, the default path and file name appear in the Location text box. Select the logical drive on which to create Northwind.dat from the Location drop-down list. This is an example database, so don't mark the Default Device check box.

4. Type the initial size of the device in the Size text box, or use the slider to set the size (see Figure 23.28). For Northwind data and the temporary files created during the export process, 8M is more than adequate. Click Create Now to create the device file.

5. Click OK when a message box tells you that the device is created. Your new device appears in the Devices window. The brown bar (the darker area in Figure 23.29) indicates that the entire device is available to contain the database.

6. From the Manage menu choose Databases to open the Databases window, which displays the default databases installed by Setup.

7. Click the New Database button (at the left on the second toolbar), or choose New Database from the File menu to open the New Database dialog.

FIG. 23.28
Setting the location and size of a new database device.

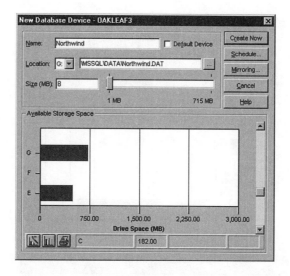

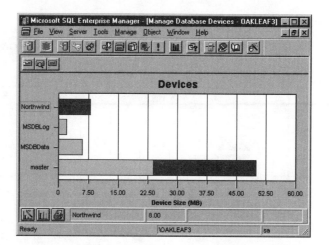

FIG. 23.29
The new database device added to the Devices window.

8. Type the name of the database—**nwind** for this example—in the Name text box and select Northwind in the Data Device drop-down list. (Traditionally, SQL Server databases use lowercase names.) Don't mark the Create for Load check box, which is used when loading a database from a backup. For the moment, you also don't want to specify a log device. By default, the size of the database is equal to the size of the database device; set the database size to 5M (see Figure 23.30).

9. Click the Create Now button to create the database. The new nwind database appears in the Databases window (see Figure 23.31).

FIG. 23.30
Setting the properties of a new database.

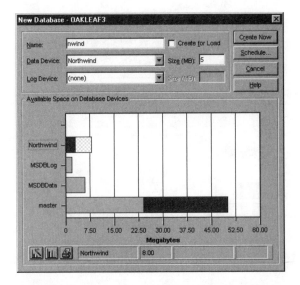

FIG. 23.31
A new database, nwind, added to the database device.

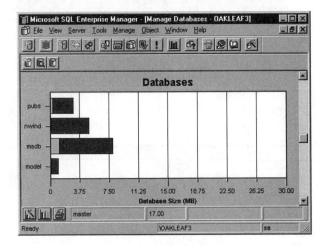

Importing Table Structures and Data

You must have Access 97 and the Access 97 Upsizing Wizard on the server or a client PC to import the data from a copy of Northwind.mdb into the SQL Server database. Use Access 97's Add-In Manager to add the Upsizing Wizard to Access's Tools, Add-Ins menu. Compact Northwind.mdb into another database, such as Upsize Northwind.mdb, before starting the upsizing process.

ON THE WEB

You can download a free copy of the Upsizing Wizard from **http://www.microsoft.com/accessdev/accinfo/aut97dat.htm**.

To upsize the copy of Northwind.mdb to SQL Server, follow these steps:

1. Launch Access 97 (if necessary), open the Upsize Northwind database, and from the Tools menu choose Add-ins and Upsize to SQL Server to start the Upsizing Wizard (see Figure 23.32).

Part
V

Ch
23

FIG. 23.32

Selecting use of the newly created database in the first dialog of the Access Upsizing Wizard.

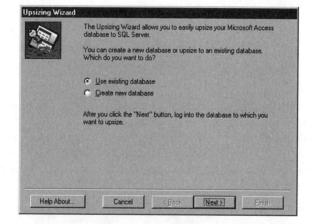

2. With the Use Existing Database option selected, click Next to display the Select Data Source dialog, and click the New button to open the Create New Data Source dialog.

3. Select the System Data Source option to make the data source available to all users of the machine on which you create the data source (see Figure 23.33). Click Next to open a second Create New Data Source dialog.

FIG. 23.33

Selecting a system data source that's available to all users of the client or server.

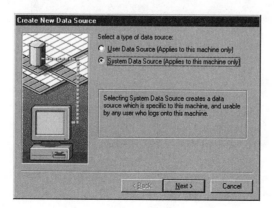

4. Select SQL Server from the list (see Figure 23.34) and click Next to open the ODBC SQL Server Setup dialog.

FIG. 23.34

Selecting the SQL Server ODBC 3.0 driver for a new ODBC data source.

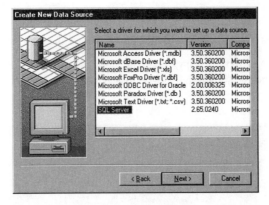

5. Click the Options button to expand the ODBC SQL Server Setup dialog. Type the name of the ODBC data source in the Data Source Name text box, provide an optional description of the data source, enter the name of the SQL Server in the Server combo box, fill in the Database Name text box, and make sure that the Convert OEM to ANSI Characters check box is unmarked (see Figure 23.35). Click OK to return to the SQL Data Sources dialog.

FIG. 23.35

Setting the property values of the new ODBC data source.

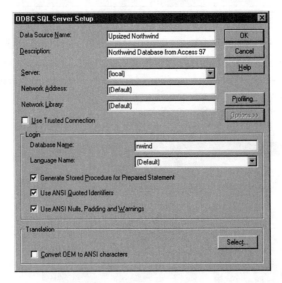

6. Select the new data source in Select Data Source list (see Figure 23.36) and click OK to open the SQL Server Login dialog.

FIG. 23.36

Selecting the new ODBC data source for the upsizing operation.

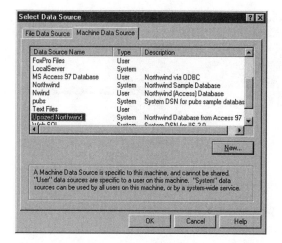

7. Type your SQL Server login ID—usually **sa** with no password, at this point. Click the Options button to expand the dialog and verify the database name (see Figure 23.37). Click OK to open the next Upsizing Wizard dialog.

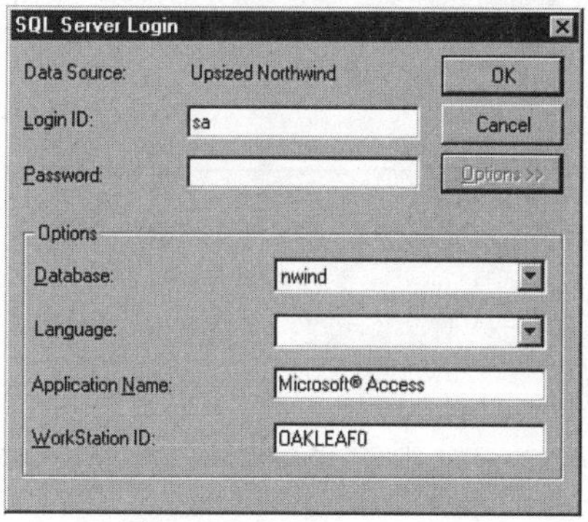

FIG. 23.37

Entering the login ID and password for the data source.

8. Click the >> button to copy all the entries from the Available Tables list to the Export to SQL Server list (see Figure 23.38). Click Next to continue.

9. Mark the Indexes, Validation Rules, Defaults, and Table Relationships check boxes; then select Use Triggers to maintain referential integrity. If you choose Use DRI (Declarative Referential Integrity), you lose cascading deletions.

10. Select Yes, Let Wizard Decide whether to add timestamp fields to tables, and mark the Attach Newly Created SQL Server Tables (to your Access database) and Save Password and User ID with Linked Tables check boxes (see Figure 23.39). Click Next and then Finish if you want the option of having the Wizard prepare an Access upsizing report; otherwise, click Finish at this point.

FIG. 23.38
Selecting all the tables in the Access database for export to SQL Server.

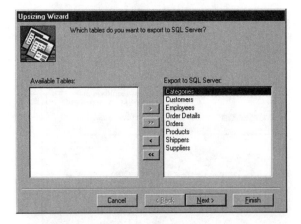

FIG. 23.39
Specifying parameters for the upsizing operation.

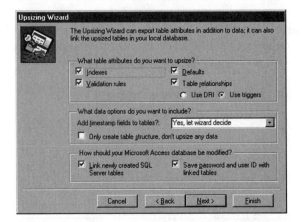

11. The wizard provides a progress bar that reports the wizard's steps. When upsizing is complete, the attached tables appear as shown in Figure 23.40. Tables attached by ODBC are identified by an arrow and a globe icon; the Access source tables are renamed to *TableName*_local. Click OK to terminate the wizard.

You can test the performance of the attached tables by opening any of the Access forms in the database, such as the Customer Orders form.

N O T E If you don't have Access 97 or the Upsizing Wizard, you can use the pubs demonstration database in the examples of the sections that follow. Choose one of the primary pubs tables, such as authors. The pubs database doesn't include demonstration triggers. ■

FIG. 23.40

New references to SQL Server tables attached by the upsized Northwind ODBC data source.

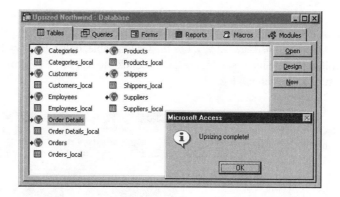

Working with SQL Tables, Indexes, Tasks, and Triggers

Importing table structures and data from an existing Access database provides tables that you can use to gain familiarity with the table-related features of SQL Enterprise Manager. To work with the tables you imported in the preceding section, follow these steps:

1. Select your new database, nwind, in the Server Manager window; then choose Tables from the Manage menu to open the Manage Tables window. The default <new> entry in the Table list lets you add a new table to the database and specify the properties of each column.

2. Select one of the imported tables, such as Orders, from the Table list. The properties of each column (field) of the table appears in the list (see Figure 23.41).

FIG. 23.41

Properties of the first 12 columns (fields) of the Northwind Orders table.

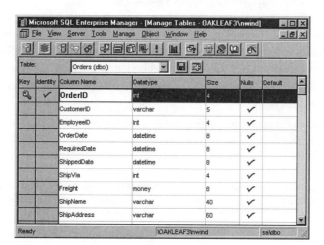

3. Click the Advanced Features button (with the + icon) of the second toolbar to open a set of properties pages that show Primary Key/Identity, Foreign Keys, Unique Constraints, and Check Constraints, if any. For the Orders table, only a Primary Key and Identity Column are defined (see Figure 23.42). Click the Advanced Features button again to return to the column list.

FIG. 23.42

Displaying Primary Key/ Identity properties with the Advanced Features option of the Manage Tables window.

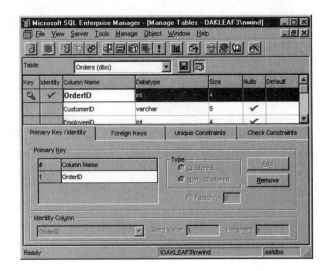

4. To add an index to a column, such as RequiredDate, choose Indexes from the Manage menu to open the Manage Indexes dialog.

5. Select (New Index) in the in the Index combo box, and then type an index name, such as **RequiredDate**, replacing (New Index). Select the RequiredDate column in the Available Columns in Table list and click Add to move the column to the Columns in Index (Key) list (see Figure 23.43). Click the Build button to start the indexing process.

6. In the Index Build message box, click the Schedule As Task button to open the Schedule Index Build dialog.

7. You have the option of running the task Immediately, One Time, or as a Recurring task (see Figure 23.44). For this example, select Immediately and click OK. Click OK when the Run Task message box appears.

 T I P If you have large-scale, low-priority tasks that might affect the performance of your database while in use, scheduling the task for the middle of the night or on a weekend is a good strategy.

8. To view the Task History dialog described in the Run Task message box, choose Scheduled Tasks from the Server menu to open the Task List page of the Manage Scheduled Tasks window (see Figure 23.45). This page displays all scheduled tasks, regardless of status.

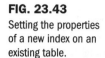

FIG. 23.43
Setting the properties
of a new index on an
existing table.

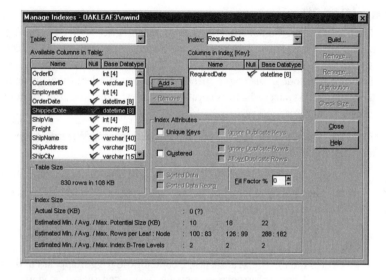

FIG. 23.44
Selecting scheduling
options for the indexing
task.

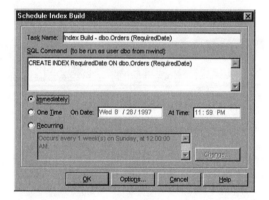

FIG. 23.45
Viewing scheduled
tasks on the Task List
page of the Manage
Scheduled Tasks
window.

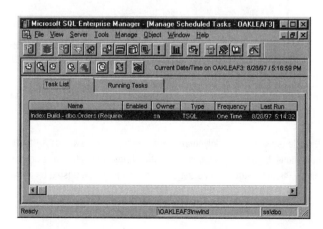

Viewing Triggers

The traditional method of enforcing referential integrity of SQL Server databases is by the use of triggers in transaction-processing operations. *Triggers* are stored procedures that execute when a client application requests an INSERT, UPDATE, or DELETE operation on a table. The Transact-SQL code of the trigger performs one or more tests, usually on one or more related tables. If the test succeeds, the operation executes; otherwise, the trigger cancels the operation and posts an error message.

To view a typical pair of triggers that the Access Upsizing Wizard creates to maintain referential integrity, follow these steps:

1. With the nwind database selected in Server Manager's window, choose Triggers from the Manage menu to open the Manage Triggers window. You edit existing triggers or create new triggers in this window.

2. Select the Orders table from the Table drop-down list.

3. Click the icon to open the Trigger list and select Orders_ITrig (INSERT trigger on the Orders table). The Transact-SQL code for the trigger appears in the window (see Figure 23.46). A CREATE TRIGGER *name* ON *tablename* FOR INSERT AS statement specifies an INSERT trigger.

FIG. 23.46
Part of the Transact-SQL code for an INSERT trigger.

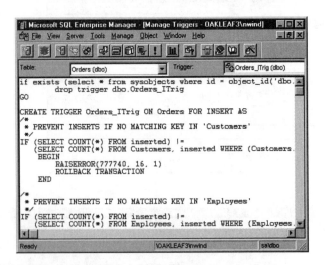

4. Open the Trigger list and select Order_UTrig (UPDATE trigger on the Orders table). A CREATE TRIGGER *name* ON *tablename* FOR UPDATE AS statement specifies an UPDATE trigger.

> **N O T E**   A single table supports only three triggers, one each for INSERT, UPDATE, and DELETE operations. Triggers are self-contained stored procedures that don't accept or return parameter values. The only output from a trigger is an error message posted by a RAISERROR statement. ∎

Viewing Standard Stored Procedures

Many functions performed by SQL Enterprise Manager use *stored procedures*, which are precompiled queries that accept and return parameter values. The master database holds stored procedures that can be executed against any database on the server. Stored procedures specific to a database are stored with the tables of the database. Traditionally, SQL Server names stored procedures with an sp_ prefix, as in sp_addserver.

To view example stored procedures in the master database, proceed as follows:

1. Select the master database in the Server Manager window, and then choose Stored Procedures from the Manage menu to open the Manage Stored Procedures window.

2. Select one of the stored procedures in the Procedure drop-down list, such as sp_addserver, to display its Transact-SQL code (see Figure 23.47).

FIG. 23.47
Part of the Transact-SQL code for the sp_addserver stored procedure.

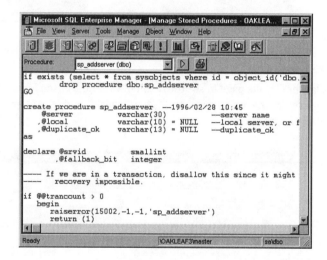

Parameters of stored procedures are identified by an "at" (@) prefix, as in @server, followed by the SQL data type and size (if applicable), such as varchar(30). You also can create local variables with the declare @varname datatype statement.

Executing Queries

SQL Enterprise Manager includes the equivalent of the ISQL/w graphical query tool. You can write your own queries or execute Transact-SQL scripts (queries) stored as .sql files. To execute a query, follow these steps:

1. Choose SQL Query Tool from the Tools menu to open the Query window.

2. Select the database from the DB list.

3. Type the query in the Queries page (see Figure 23.48).

FIG. 23.48

A SELECT query against the nwind database.

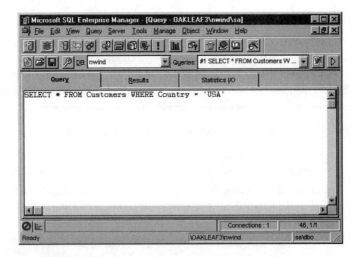

4. Choose <u>E</u>xecute from the Query menu, or click the green arrow button at the right of the second toolbar.

5. Display the Results page to see the result of your query (see Figure 23.49). SELECT queries return the query result set; INSERT, UPDATE, and DELETE queries return the number of rows affected.

FIG. 23.49

The result set of the query shown in Figure 23.48.

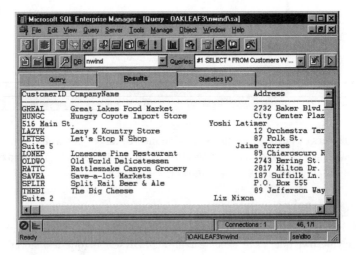

Setting Up Transaction Logging

Transaction logs provide a history of all changes made to the tables of the database by INSERT, UPDATE, and DELETE operations. The purpose of a transaction log is to provide the means to rebuild a database to its state immediately before a catastrophic failure that requires restoring data from the last backup. The basic backup and restore sequence with a transaction log is as follows:

1. Immediately after making a full backup of the database, the transaction log is deleted (dumped).

2. In the event of a failure of the database file, the database is restored from the last backup.

3. The transaction log is executed against the database to bring the content of the database tables to their state immediately before the failure.

You establish transaction logging by specifying a log device for the database when you create the new database. Transaction logging is enabled by default, and the transaction log shares space with the data in the database. A transaction log in the same database or stored on the same physical device provides no protection against failure of the drive that stores the file for the database device. You can't change the log device after the database is created.

To determine the log device for a database, double-click the database entry in Server Manager to display the Database page of the Edit Database property sheet. The nwind database, created earlier in the "Importing Table Structures and Data" section, stores its log with the data (see Figure 23.50). In this case, there's no advantage to maintaining a transaction log, so you can click Truncate to recover the log space used. To prevent further log entries, display the Options page and mark the Truncate Log on Checkpoint check box (see Figure 23.51). Click OK to close the property sheet.

FIG. 23.50

The Database page of the Edit Database property sheet for the nwind database.

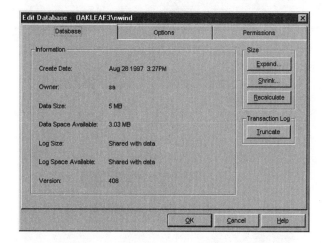

To create a database with a transaction log, follow these steps:

1. In the Manage Devices window, create a new database device of the appropriate size. (Refer to the earlier section "Creating and Managing Database Devices.")

2. Create another database device for the transaction log on a different local fixed-disk drive.

FIG. 23.51

Preventing transaction logging with the Truncate Log on Checkpoint option.

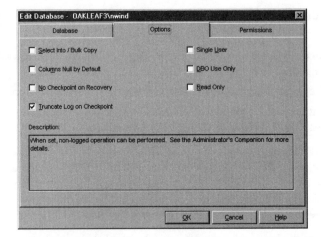

3. Create a new database, selecting the database device in the Data Device combo list and the database device for the transaction log in the Log Device combo list (see Figure 23.52).

4. Click Create Now to create the database and the transaction log.

FIG. 23.52

Specifying a transaction log device for a new database.

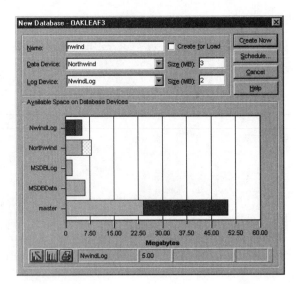

Establishing Database Permissions

SQL Server offers the three following types of user login security:

- *Standard security* requires SQL Server users to specify a login ID and a password to gain access to the server. You set up individual SQL Server accounts for each server user in the Manage Logins window of SQL Enterprise Manager.

- *Integrated security* uses Windows NT security to authenticate SQL Server users with their Windows NT login IDs and passwords. Integrated security is limited to clients that connect with the default named pipes protocol. You use SQL Security Manager to assign group logins to the server.

- *Mixed security* lets SQL Server installations that are set up to accept multiple network protocols take advantage of integrated security for clients by using named pipes. Users of clients connecting by a protocol other than named pipes must supply a login ID and password.

Integrated security is the most common choice for SQL Server 6.5 with clients running Windows 95 or Windows NT Workstation. Regardless of the security type you choose, the default system administrator account, sa, has all permissions for all databases and is the default owner (dbo, database owner) for all SQL Server objects.

> **N O T E**   In the examples of this chapter, the sa account uses the default empty password. SQL Server's sa account and Microsoft Access's default Admin account have similar authority. Be sure to assign a password to the sa account before using SQL Server for production applications. To change the sa password in SQL Enterprise Manager, choose Logins from the Manage menu, select sa in the Login Name list, type a password in the Password text box, and click the Modify button. ■

Using SQL Security Manager to Assign Group Accounts

You can assign all users in a specified group access to one or more SQL Server databases with the SQL Security Manager. Ordinarily, you employ User Manager for Domains to create a specific Windows NT group for access to each database, and then add to the group the users who need database access. In the following example, the Domain Users group is used for simplicity.

▶ **See** "Using the Group Management Wizard," **p. 475**

To set up a SQL Server user group from Domain Users, follow these steps:

1. From the Start menu choose Programs, Microsoft SQL Server 6.5 Utilities, and SQL Security Manager to launch SQL Security Manager.

2. In the Connect Server dialog, type the name of the server, your login ID, and password, if necessary. Click Connect to connect to the server.

3. To view administrators with sa (system administrator) status, choose Sa Privilege from the View menu. Double-click the group names to expand the list and display login IDs with sa privileges (see Figure 23.53).

Part
V

Ch
23

FIG. 23.53

Displaying users with system administrator (sa) privileges.

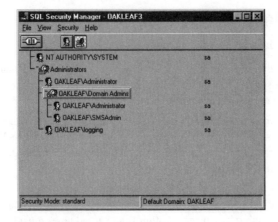

4. From the <u>V</u>iew menu choose <u>U</u>ser Privilege. The no accounts have been granted user authority message appears.

5. Choose <u>G</u>rant New from the <u>S</u>ecurity menu to open the Grant User Privilege dialog.

6. Select the Groups on Default Domain option and select the database user group in the Grant Privilege list.

7. Mark the Add Login IDs for Group Members and Add Users to Database check boxes. Select the database for the group from the drop-down list (see Figure 23.54). Click the Grant button to add the users.

FIG. 23.54

Adding Domain Users as the Domain$Users group of SQL Server.

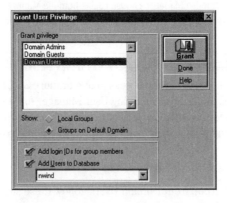

N O T E   SQL Server doesn't permit spaces in names of objects, including names of groups. SQL Server automatically replaces spaces in group names with dollar signs ($). ■

As the users are added, the number of Login IDs, Users, and Groups appear in the Adding SQL Server Login IDs/Users dialog (see Figure 23.55).

8. If errors occur during the login process, click Error Detail to expand the dialog and check the source of the errors (see Figure 23.56).

FIG. 23.55
A summary of users and groups added to the Domain$Users group.

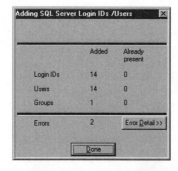

FIG. 23.56
Displaying errors during the addition of SQL Server users.

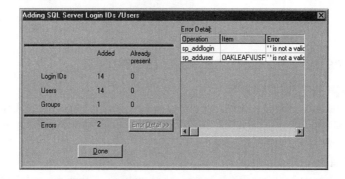

9. Click Done to close the dialog and display the added user accounts (see Figure 23.57).

FIG. 23.57
The new user accounts displayed in the SQL Security Manager window.

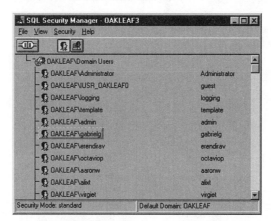

10. Double-click one of the user accounts to display the Account Detail dialog. If you want to add another database for the user, select the database in the Available Databases list and click Add User. Select the default database for the user in the Databases Currently Defined In list and click the Set Default button (see Figure 23.58).

FIG. 23.58

The Account Detail dialog for a newly added user.

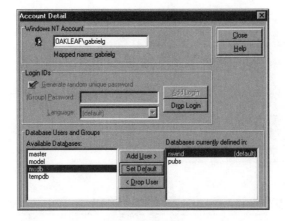

Viewing Logins and Setting Permissions in SQL Enterprise Manager

SQL Enterprise Manager includes complete facilities for managing SQL Server user accounts (logins) and database permissions for each account. To view the logins you added from the Windows NT Domain Users group in the preceding section and set specific user permissions for database objects, follow these steps:

1. Close and relaunch SQL Enterprise Manager, and then expand the Logins item of Server Manager's window for the server to which the users were added. Each user login, with default users added by SQL Server, appears as shown in Figure 23.59.

FIG. 23.59

Logins added to the OAKLEAF3 server from the Domain$Users group.

2. Double-click the user item to display the Manage Logins dialog for the user (see Figure 23.60). You can add or remove permissions for databases by clicking cells of the Permit

column, and set one default database by clicking a cell in the Default column. Click Close to close the dialog.

FIG. 23.60
Displaying the details of the users account in the Manage Logins dialog.

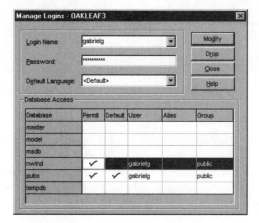

3. Double-click the database in Server Manager to display the Edit Database dialog, and then display the Permissions page. By default, users in the Domain$Users group don't have permissions to modify the database. If you want to grant the group permission to create a view, click the button in the Create View column (see Figure 23.61). When you click OK, the permission is granted to all members of the group.

FIG. 23.61
Adding Create View permission for the Domain$Users group.

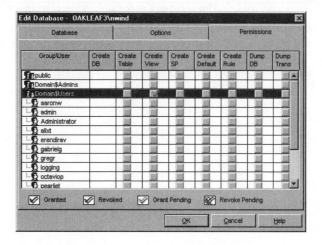

To drop a user group from a database, select the database item in Server Manger, and then choose Groups from the Manage menu to open the Manage Groups dialog. Select the group you want to drop in the Group drop-down list (see Figure 23.62), and then click the Drop button. Confirm in the message box that you want to drop the group.

FIG. 23.62

Selecting a user group to drop in the Manage Groups dialog.

From Here...

This chapter covered the basic operations involved in installing SQL Server 6.5 under Windows NT Server 4.0. Instructions for installing the SQL Server 6.5 Utilities on clients running Windows 95 and Windows NT Workstation 4.0 also were given. The chapter provided examples of creating new database devices, databases, and importing table structures and data to SQL Server databases. The chapter closed with a brief description of SQL Server's integrated security features.

The following chapters contain material related to this chapter's content:

- Chapter 13, "Managing User and Group Accounts," describes how to use Windows NT Server 4.0's User Manager for Domains, take advantage of the new Add User Accounts and Group Management wizards, and utilize the built-in user groups of Windows NT.

- Chapter 21, "Administering Intranet and World Wide Web Sites," describes how to use a SQL Server 6.5 database for logging the activity on your intranet or Internet site.

- Chapter 25, "Administering Clients with Systems Management Server 1.2," covers the basics of planning, administration, and management for Microsoft SMS 1.2, which uses SQL Server 6.5 to store all its client management information.

CHAPTER 24

Messaging with Microsoft Exchange Server 5.0

Exchange Server is often thought of as the electronic mail (e-mail) component of Microsoft BackOffice. There's no question that Exchange Server is an outstanding e-mail product. But Exchange Server offers more than just e-mail. It's a general-purpose messaging and information delivery product that facilitates the exchange of information among groups of people and the development of groupware applications.

This chapter explores Exchange Server's capabilities and shows how to install and manage an Exchange Server site. You learn about Exchange Server's features and investigate some of the benefits it can provide your organization. Exchange Server is a rich product with a great deal of functionality. You can start by using Exchange Server for e-mail, but to fully exploit its capacity, you must fully understand its information-sharing capabilities and be able to leverage its programmable forms. ■

Exchange Server 5.0 components

Understand the relationship of the multiple components that make up Exchange Server 5.0.

Exchange Server 5.0 features

Find out what this product can provide for your organization. Learn about Exchange Server's advanced features that go well beyond basic e-mail.

Client capabilities

Explore the features of Outlook, the integrated personal information manager and e-mail client that's included with Office 97, the Exchange client, and Schedule+.

Install, tune, and configure Exchange Server

Run the Setup program to install Exchange Server, use Performance Optimizer, and customize your Exchange Server site.

Understanding Exchange Server

Microsoft Exchange Server is a collection of software applications, some client-based and some server-based, that cooperate to provide information-sharing facilities to groups of people and entire organizations. On the server, it comprises standard and optional components. The standard server components include the following:

- *User Directory* contains information to facilitate e-mail delivery and other general information that can be customized to fit an organization's needs.
- *Information Store* houses public and private folders containing messages and other information types.
- *Message Transfer Agent (MTA)* exchanges information in the system with other Exchange servers and works with components called *connectors*, which exchange mail with *foreign messaging systems* (a term frequently used to describe other e-mail systems, including PC-based systems and those run on larger mini-computers or mainframes).
- *System Attendant* is a multipurpose component that lets you monitor Exchange Server activities, generates e-mail addresses for new users, and provides a range of status checking, logging, and maintenance services.

The optional server components include the following:

- *Directory Synchronization* synchronizes directory information between Exchange Server and mail systems that use the Microsoft Mail 3.x directory synchronization protocol.
- *Key Management* enables the use of digital signatures and message encryption (encoding a message for protection and authentication).
- *X.400 Connector* works with the MTA to transfer messages among Exchange servers and connects to other X.400-compatible messaging systems.
- *Internet Connector* allows Exchange Server users to trade messages with Internet users.
- *Microsoft Mail Connector* allows the interchange of messages with Microsoft Mail users.
- *Schedule+ Free/Busy Connector* allows users of Schedule+, the Microsoft group scheduling application, to exchange times when users are busy and available with earlier versions of Schedule+.

These components work together as a cohesive unit. Most users aren't aware that the server-based services providing Exchange Server's functionality aren't a single program. Figure 24.1 shows the relationship of the components in an Exchange Server system and loosely represents the interaction among components; it doesn't try to provide a comprehensive picture of all component intercommunication.

A number of client components also work together to provide comprehensive messaging services for desktop computer users. The client components include the following:

- *Exchange Client* is the primary component that helps users manage their mailboxes, compose and send e-mail, and use custom forms to exchange special types of information.

- *Schedule+ Client* displays user and group schedules, assists with scheduling resources such as conference rooms or special equipment, and assists with project and task management.

- *Exchange Forms Designer* lets organizations create custom forms that facilitate the capturing, routing, and sharing of special types of information, such as help desk requests and responses.

FIG. 24.1
Microsoft Exchange components.

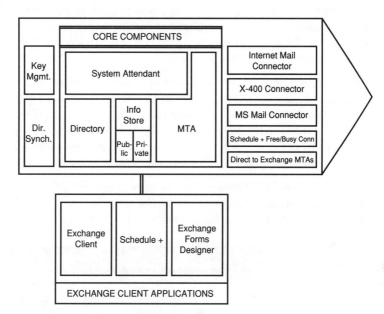

All these components, both client and server, are explored in more detail in the pages ahead. The important point here is the cooperation among components to manage and deliver information. In this respect, Exchange Server is similar to other BackOffice applications, especially Systems Management Server (SMS), which also uses a collection of components to deliver *packages* (usually new application software such as Microsoft Excel) to desktop computers. The client components of Exchange Server are richer and more comprehensive, however, and the type of information being managed is different.

Exchange Server is one of Microsoft BackOffice's newest components. With Internet Information Server and other recently introduced Internet products, such as Proxy Server, Exchange Server rounds out the collection of BackOffice components to form a remarkably powerful and flexible product. In its latest release, Exchange Server has gained many Internet integration features and groupware enhancements for an even greater capability to provide many types of information to many types of clients.

Surveying Exchange Server's Features

A complete exposition of the features of Exchange Server is beyond the scope of this book. To give you a taste of what you can do with Exchange Server, a few examples of Exchange

Server capabilities are presented in the following sections, including features new to Exchange Server 5.0.

Using Exchange for Electronic Mail

Most users first use Exchange Server to send and receive e-mail, manage their e-mail mailboxes, and use the address book to look up other e-mail users. E-mail messages created with the Exchange Client can contain rich text, including bullets, colored text, different fonts, and other formatting. You can assign different priorities to your messages and ask Exchange Server to provide delivery receipts and read receipts to notify you that your messages have been delivered or read by their recipients.

You can address e-mail to individual users or to *distribution lists* that specify a group of recipients. You can chose distribution lists from the address book on the server or create them as personal distribution lists. You can *carbon copy (CC)* additional recipients who should receive the message and *blind carbon copy (BCC)* other recipients without the people listed in the message's To: or CC: line being aware. You can send messages to other users in your organization or anywhere in the world with the appropriate connectors.

Figure 24.2 shows the Exchange Client's user interface. The left pane of the Viewer window shows a personal mailbox, access to an Administrator's mailbox, a local copy of sample applications provided with Exchange Server, and shared public folders.

FIG. 24.2

Reading an e-mail message stored in the Exchange Client's Inbox.

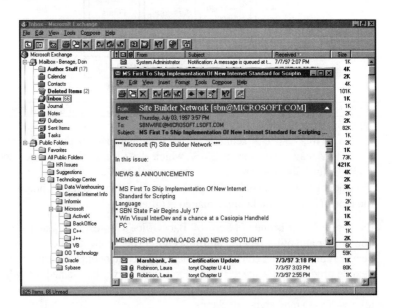

Exchange Server is an enhanced replacement for Microsoft Mail 3.x. For existing Microsoft Mail users, it's possible to use both products side by side during a migration period, as you gradually move users to Exchange Server.

Sharing Information with Public Folders

As the organization and the administrative team become more familiar with Exchange Server, they can exploit the capability to share information in public folders in order to share information among users in a variety of creative ways (see Figure 24.3). Two straightforward examples to implement are *bulletin boards* and *discussion databases*. By creating a public folder and setting its properties, you can control the form of the folder contents, who is authorized to access and modify the information, and how it's viewed.

FIG. 24.3
An Exchange Client viewing a shared public folder.

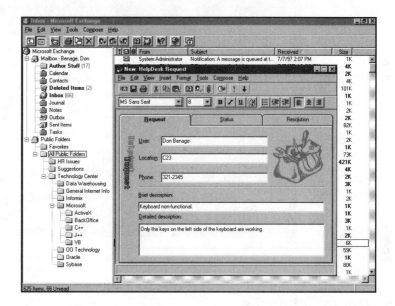

You also can create *replicas* of the public folder, providing multiple copies of the folder to balance the access load among servers. And you can reduce network bandwidth use by placing replicas in proximity to user groups. Exchange Server automatically merges the changes made to various replicas at regularly scheduled intervals that you control, keeping their contents synchronized.

Using Custom Forms to Build Applications

Developers and advanced users, especially those with some experience in using Visual Basic, can take advantage of the *electronic forms* capability to implement powerful and creative applications. These forms can use *controls*, the mechanisms that computer users are accustomed to manipulating in dialogs (see Figure 24.4). The controls may be buttons, simple text boxes, drop-down list boxes, or check boxes; or they may be more elaborate controls, such as a fuel gauge or calendar control. Completed forms can be posted in a public folder, routed to a distribution list, or sent to a specific server for a particular action—updating a database, for example.

Using these forms and a little imagination can yield significant information management capabilities. An example included with Exchange Server, although admittedly somewhat frivolous, hints at the possibilities. It's a chess application that uses a form designed to resemble a chess board. It can be used to make chess moves and send them back and forth between users. The chess application shows how highly customized these forms can be and the automatic routing that can be designated.

FIG. 24.4
A custom form being created with the Exchange Forms Designer.

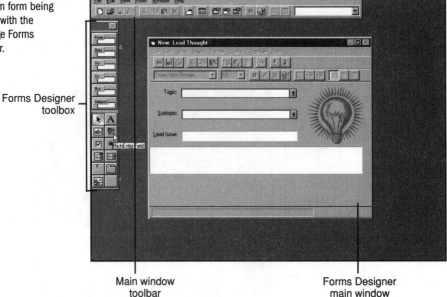

Forms Designer toolbox

Main window toolbar

Forms Designer main window

Using Group Scheduling

The Schedule+ group scheduling program has been available since 1993. Older versions have been included in Windows for Workgroups and have been available separately. Now, Microsoft has enhanced it and bundled it with the Exchange Client.

Schedule+ lets users enter their own appointments on their personal calendar (see Figure 24.5). They can set permissions to give other users access to their schedule with varying degrees of authority. As users enter their appointments, they can mark them as private so that other users know only that they're busy, not the nature of the appointment. Users also can enter recurring appointments—the second Thursday of every month, for example.

With the Planner tab, you can schedule a meeting or event involving a group of people and even consult schedules for resources such as conference rooms or projection equipment. You can use the Planner to ensure that all mandatory attendees are available for the scheduled time, automatically compose a meeting request e-mail for the event, and track responses to the request. You also can enter information about projects and tasks for which you're responsible, drag and drop them onto your daily calendar to schedule them, and track partial completion of lengthy projects.

FIG. 24.5

The Schedule+ user interface.

Events button

Right-click for Tab Gallery

Drag left or right

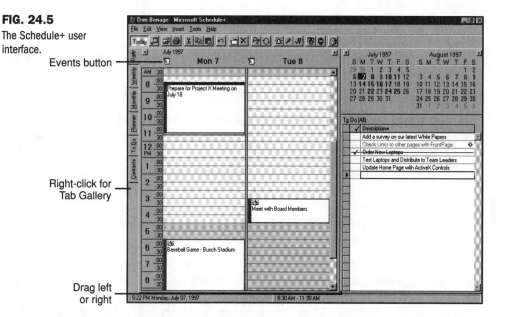

Integrating Exchange with Other Systems

The use of electronic messaging as a component of a custom application is growing. The messaging infrastructure frequently extends beyond the high-speed LAN or WAN to include users who connect to the network from remote locations or who interact with the organization only by e-mail through a public service provider or the Internet. The capability to create applications that use messaging as a transport mechanism extends the reach of the organization's information systems.

It's possible, for example, to create a sales support system that allows traveling or remote sales people to e-mail a request for information on a product or its availability at the end of one day and receive an answer via e-mail early the next morning. SQL Server supports integration with e-mail through the SQL Mail feature. Using the messaging system to route information for validation and approval also can be an integral part of a custom application.

Exploring New Features in Exchange Server 5.0

Exchange Server 5.0 supports many new features. In particular, integration with the World Wide Web (WWW) and other Internet technologies plays an important part in the additions made to this version. There's also support for a growing number of standards and protocols.

The primary new features of Exchange Server 5.0 follow:

- Web browsers can now send and receive mail, access public folders, and use other information that has been published on an Exchange server.

- Post Office Protocol 3 (POP3) client support lets users access their mailbox by using popular Internet mail client software from Microsoft, Netscape, and others.

Part
V

Ch
24

- An Internet News service provides the capability to support Usenet newsgroups with your Exchange server.

- Support for the Lightweight Directory Access Protocol (LDAP) is provided for accessing the directory information in Exchange Server.

  ▶ **See** "Directory Service Providers," **p. 998**

- A new connector for cc:Mail lets Exchange Server postoffices exchange mail with cc:Mail postoffices. The connector can be used as part of a migration strategy or simply to allow the two systems to interoperate.

- New Source Extractors have been added for Novell GroupWise and Collabra Share. By using these extractors, you can easily migrate user accounts, mailboxes, and other information from these systems.

- Schedule+ client software for the Macintosh has been added to the Exchange Server support for that platform.

In addition to the preceding list of features, Exchange Server 5.0 has received overall tuning and bug-fixing attention as you would expect with any new release. Finally, although it's not a feature of Exchange Server itself, Microsoft has added an important new Exchange Server client component to Microsoft Office. This new client, called *Outlook*, includes e-mail, scheduling, browsing for resources, journalizing daily activities, and many other capabilities into a single, integrated package.

Understanding Exchange Server's Server Components

The server-based components of Exchange Server are primarily implemented as Windows NT services. *Services* are special types of applications that run unattended, with no input from users. You can start, stop, pause, or tell a service to continue by using Control Panel's Services tool or Windows NT's Server Manager. You can configure most services by using an administration tool that comes with the product being used.

Some services have accompanying databases—for example, Microsoft Exchange Directory and Microsoft Exchange Information Store. These databases contain the information managed by the services. As you see in upcoming sections, these databases can be shared, distributed databases in multiserver Exchange sites. Entries are also made in the Registry for each service. All Exchange Server services can be configured by using the Exchange Administrator program.

Understanding Exchange Administrator

Exchange Administrator can run on Windows NT Server or Workstation. In Exchange Server 5.0, Exchange Administrator isn't available for Windows 3.1+, Windows for Workgroups, or Windows 95. (A Windows 95 version may be available in the future.) With the appropriate permissions, you can use this tool to configure and manage all the Exchange servers at the site you're now logged on to and view the servers at other sites (see Figure 24.6).

FIG. 24.6
Exchange Administrator showing two sites: GAS-STL-EXHIBIT and GAS-NY-EXHIBIT.

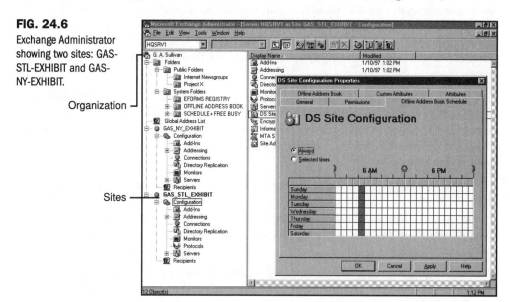

After you install Exchange Server, you use Exchange Administrator to configure the server components, create mailboxes (or import mailboxes from another mail system), and perform other setup and configuration tasks. By monitoring utilities in this program, you also can observe the status of Exchange servers and watch for potential problems. Upcoming sections provide detailed procedures for starting and using Exchange Administrator; the rest of this section provides an overview of the display and the way in which this utility is used.

Like several other tools and utilities provided by Microsoft, the Exchange Administrator window is divided into two panes. The left pane displays a hierarchy of containers. A *container* represents a *directory*, which is made up of all the objects in the Exchange Server organization. The right pane displays the contents of the currently selected container in the left pane. For example, if the Recipients object is selected in the left pane, the mailboxes (and other recipient objects, such as distribution lists) that can be used as the target of a message appear in the right pane.

Examining the Directory

The *directory* is composed of two principal parts: the directory service and a corresponding database. The directory database, which is also called the *Exchange database (EDB)*, is one of the two primary databases managed by Exchange Server (the Information Store is the other). It's located in the file Dir.edb. The directory stores information about Exchange Server users and the components of the system itself. The Exchange Server directory is based on the X.500 specification established by the International Standards Organization (ISO).

The Directory Service (DS) is one of the core components of Exchange Server and must be running for Exchange Server to function. Some optional components, such as connectors, can be temporarily shut down without affecting the overall operation of Exchange Server. The DS is responsible for maintaining Dir.edb's integrity, participating in directory replication, and providing directory information to Exchange clients and the Administrator program. Other services, such as the MTA and the System Attendant, use the configuration and routing information stored in the directory.

Information in the directory is used to build the *Global Address List (GAL)*, part of the address book used by clients. (The Personal Address Book for a user, stored in a file with a .pab extension, is also a component of the address book.) Information from the directory also is used to create the Offline Address Book, which is rebuilt at scheduled intervals based on the GAL or some subset of the directory.

When you start Exchange Administrator, the left pane of the window displays the directory for the server you're viewing. If you select an object, the directory information for that object appears in the right pane. The directory stores different information for different object types. You can use user-definable properties for recipient objects to customize the directory to better suit your organization's needs.

You can set up one Exchange server or many, depending on your organization's size and geographic layout. If you use multiple servers, changes made to the directory on one Exchange server are *replicated*, or copied, to the other Exchange servers in that site. Replication within a site, also called *intrasite replication*, happens automatically. Replication with other sites (*intersite replication*) can be configured to occur automatically on a schedule you establish and control.

Exchange Server can participate in Microsoft Mail 3.x directory synchronization protocol. If your organization uses Microsoft Mail and wants to run both systems side by side, you can install an optional component called the *Directory Synchronization Agent*. Synchronization with Microsoft Mail 3.x directories isn't automatic and requires one server to be configured as the *master server*, whereas others are configured as *requester servers*. An Exchange Server can be a server or a requester in a Microsoft Mail 3.x directory synchronization scenario. The native Exchange Server directory synchronization uses a different architecture known as *multi-master*, in which any server can initiate the replication of directory information.

Understanding the Message Transfer Agent

In a system designed for managing messages, the MTA is a critical component. You can think of it as a postal worker who delivers the mail. The MTA works with the MTAs on other Exchange servers to move messages from one postoffice to another. It also interacts with any connectors installed on your server to route messages addressed to recipients on foreign mail systems somewhere outside your organization.

The MTA uses information from the directory to find a recipient's address, and then consults a routing table to determine whether the recipient is on the same system, in the same site, at another site within the organization, or on a foreign mail system. By defining *address spaces*, you establish the addresses that the MTA recognizes and provide the information needed to create routing tables for each server. Messages addressed to recipients on the same server are treated as special cases and delivered directly by the information store.

Understanding the Information Store

The second primary database that the Exchange Server manages (in addition to the directory database, Dir.edb) is the *information store*, which is the repository for all public folders and messages stored on the server. It's divided into two separate files. The first file, Priv.edb, is the private information store that contains users' messages. The second file, Pub.edb, contains public folders. These files are limited to 16G (gigabytes) each, per server. The information store uses a transaction log, much like SQL Server, to maintain the integrity of information and ensure recoverability in the event of a system failure.

N O T E The Enterprise Edition of Exchange Server (code-named Osmium when this book was written) increases the allowable size of Priv.edb and Pub.edb to 16T (terabytes) and provides for failover clustering with the Microsoft Cluster Server (MSCS) included with Windows NT Server 4.0 Enterprise Edition.

▶ **See** "Clustering for Availability Now and Scalability Later," **p. 970** ▪

Like the directory, the information store also includes an active, server-based process, the *information store service*. This service cooperates with the other services in Exchange Server— the directory, the MTA, and the system attendant—to provide its features to users. In addition to interfacing with other services, the information store service is responsible for the following tasks:

- It's responsible for delivering messages to recipients that share the same *home server*. For messages sent to recipients on the same Exchange server, the information store directly handles the delivery without involving the MTA. If the recipients aren't on the same server, it passes the message to the MTA, which may in turn pass the message to MTAs on other servers or one or more connectors.

- It updates the transaction log and the information store with new information. As information is inserted and deleted, this service also performs defragmentation of the database files to provide contiguous disk space for individual messages, a well-known performance improvement feature. It doesn't, however, compact the disk space used by the database files as messages are deleted. You can use a command-line utility, Edbutil.exe, to reclaim unused space in the database files left by deleted messages and defragmentation.

The information store implements a feature called *single-instance storage*. As much as possible, a message addressed to multiple recipients is stored only once, and each recipient receives a pointer to the message rather than a copy of the message itself. This also is done with *attachments* (operating system files included in a message). To take maximum advantage of single-instance storage, you should group users who exchange many messages together on the same home server.

Understanding the System Attendant

The *System Attendant* is another Windows NT service that performs routine maintenance chores on an Exchange Server. You might think of the System Attendant as the postoffice manager, checking on other services and ensuring the accuracy of message delivery. The System Attendant is responsible for the following tasks:

- As new recipients are added to a server, System Attendant generates the e-mail addresses used to address messages to those recipients. By default, Exchange Server generates three types of addresses: Microsoft Mail, SMTP (Internet), and X.400. If you've installed connectors to other e-mail systems, the system attendant generates an appropriate address for those systems as well.

- System Attendant creates routing tables (and usually regenerates them once a day) that tell Exchange Server where to deliver messages with particular address types. For example, if the Internet Connector is installed on another server in your site, the routing table for your home server indicates that outgoing messages with an SMTP address type should be routed to the server with the connector first and then on to the Internet.

- System Attendant provides a number of monitoring and diagnostic services. For example, the system attendant gathers information on the performance of other services and provides it to monitoring tools. It also checks the links between servers, verifies the accuracy of directory replication information, and repairs inconsistent information.

Understanding Recipients

Any potential target of a message or custom form is called a *recipient*. This target includes not only user mailboxes and distribution lists, but also public folders. An e-mail address defined in the Exchange Server directory but referencing a user's mailbox on another system is called a *custom recipient*. Such a mailbox might be at another company, an organization such as a university, or an online service such as CompuServe, America Online, or The Microsoft Network.

The directory has a *recipients container* that holds the definitions and properties of all the various types of recipients for the Exchange Server system. If you have the necessary access privileges, you can expand the recipients container in Exchange Administrator and view the recipients defined on a particular system. As a normal user of Exchange Server, you can use the address book, which usually contains a Global Address List, a comprehensive list of all recipients. The contents of the address book are controlled by the administrators of the Exchange Server system.

In addition to individual custom recipients defined by an Exchange administrator, the address book may contain lists of recipients from other mail systems that are participating in a directory-synchronization process. Directory synchronization, frequently referred to as *dir synch*, automatically updates the directory information on one system with any changes made to the directory on another, and vice versa. This situation is common in organizations with an e-mail system running on a mainframe or minicomputer and another PC-based e-mail system. It also can be useful during a migration period, so that users on a new system can continue to exchange messages with users on the old system.

Understanding Mailboxes

Several components play a role in the storage of a user's messages. Each Exchange Server user has a designated mailbox, which is located on the user's home server in a private information store. All incoming messages are first transferred into the user's mailbox. Users may create a personal folder file (with a .pst extension) on their computer's disk drive or on their private directory on a server, if they have such a directory. Incoming messages are still stored temporarily in the private store on the home server and then transferred to the personal folder file when the user connects to the server.

Users also can create an offline folder file (with an .ost extension), which is a convenient alternative to a personal folder file for remote users. Public folders and personal folders that the user wants to have available offline are copied into the offline folder file and can be synchronized (or updated) regularly when the user is connected to the network. The information is then available later when the user is disconnected from the network.

Part
V

Ch

24

> **CAUTION**
>
> Personal files can be password protected. It's a good idea to protect personal files, especially if they contain sensitive information. This is even more important for laptop users because the risk of loss or theft is greater. Users should be cautioned, however, that if they forget their password, a new folder file must be created and the information in their old files is lost. This is different from their mailboxes on the server. If the user forgets the password for his mailbox, it can be reset (but not viewed) by an administrator.

A *schedule file* (with an .scd extension) contains the user's schedule information. This file, like the personal folder file, is stored on the user's own computer or a private area on a file server. A corresponding hidden file on the user's home server contains a copy of the user's schedule information to allow other users to view the schedule if they have access permissions. Another hidden file also contains free and busy information, thus letting other users see when someone might be available, even if they aren't allowed to view the actual contents of the schedule. It's also possible to deny access to free/busy information.

In addition to the elements just described for storing messages and schedule information, several elements enable identifying users and addressing messages. Exchange Server administrators define the contents of the address book, which is kept on servers. In addition to the Global Address List, administrators can define custom address lists. An Offline Address Book also is designated. By default, the Offline Address Book contains the entire Recipients container from the local site. Remote users can download a copy of the Offline Address Book to their local hard disk so that they can address messages when they're not connected to the network.

Users also have a *Personal Address Book* (stored in a file with a .pab extension), which can contain user-defined custom addresses and distribution lists. For convenience, users also can add any addresses from other lists to their Personal Address Book to make them easier to find quickly. Finally, one or more profiles can be created to specify the services Exchange Client uses and the user's preferences.

Using a Personal Folder File

Users can create personal folders to organize their own messages. When creating a profile, users can indicate whether new messages should be delivered to their mailbox (on the server) or delivered directly to the Inbox in their personal folder files whenever they launch the Exchange Client. If messages are delivered to their mailbox, users can still file individual messages in personal folders that they've created.

Users also can use Inbox Assistant to create rules that automatically file messages in folders. For example, you can define a rule that places messages from your manager in a folder called Manager, or any messages marked high-priority in a folder called Urgent. You also can create folders within folders, forming a hierarchical storage system. Folders can have names with spaces and other special characters. Folders appear in the left pane of the client program's window. Folders are opened and closed with the plus/minus controls to the left of the folder in question.

Using the Offline Folder File

The *offline folder file* is a powerful and easy-to-use mechanism that lets remote e-mail users or users who travel with laptop computers manage their access to information when they aren't connected to the network. First, users simply designate which mailbox folders on the server and which public folders should be available offline. Then they select an option to synchronize offline folders with the online versions on the server(s). When that process is completed, they can disconnect from the network and continue to work as though they were connected, working with copies of the folders they designated on their own computer. When they reconnect again, they simply resynchronize, and all changes—those made by the user to the offline folders and those made by other users to the online versions—are updated in all folders.

Using Public Folders

Public folders are one of the richest elements of Exchange Server. You can create public folders to serve many different purposes. You can design public folders to hold certain types of information and to display information in different views. Views can be assigned by an administrator and shared among many users. Each user also can define personal views for his own use.

Public folders are stored on servers in the public information store. As users read the messages in a public folder, the read status is tracked per user. In other words, Exchange Server tracks who has read a message and who hasn't. Users running the Exchange Client program who are viewing the public folder see the names of messages that they haven't read appear in boldface type and messages that they've read in normal type. Another user viewing the same folder would see his own read status reflected through the use of boldface and normal type.

Exchange Server supports the capability to *replicate* public folders from one server to one or more additional servers. Although it's possible to have all users connect to a single server for a public folder, it may be wise to have multiple copies of heavily used public folders to distribute the workload among several servers. If your network includes more than one geographic location with slower network links between them, you also may want to replicate public folder information during off-peak hours and let users connect to a local replica, thereby reducing bandwidth use during peak periods.

Public folders use a multiple-master architecture. When information in a public folder changes, it's replicated to all other servers that have been designated to contain a replica of that folder. Changes are replicated through e-mail messages. Exchange administrators can control when replication occurs and set limits on the size of messages that may be transmitted to control the impact of replication on the network.

Any and all of the replicas can be changed at any time. Therefore, at any given instant, the replicas of an active public folder aren't be identical. They're very similar, of course, with only the recently updated information being different. If changes are made to two replicated copies of the same piece of information on different servers, the administrator of the public folder is notified with a message indicating that a conflict must be resolved. Exchange Server doesn't discard any information in this situation.

Understanding Distribution Lists

Part
V

Ch
24

If a group of recipients is frequently used as a target for the same messages, you can create a distribution list that contains each recipient in the group. This list allows users to address messages to a single recipient, which represents the entire list with a single entry. The distribution list can contain individual mailbox names, custom recipients from other systems, public folders, or even other distribution lists. Take care to avoid nesting distribution lists too deeply, to avoid inadvertently sending multiple copies of a message to some recipients. Distribution lists can be defined by administrators and stored on the server. Individual users also can create their own distribution lists and keep them in their Personal Address Books.

Using Connectors

Exchange Server's Enterprise Edition includes enhanced gateways, called *connectors*, which replace some of Microsoft's existing gateway products. Exchange Server maintains compatibility with the existing DOS-based gateways, however. The new connectors are implemented as Windows NT-based services: Internet Mail Connection, the Microsoft Mail (PC) Connector, the Microsoft Mail (AppleTalk) Connector, the Schedule+ Free/Busy Connector, and the X.400 Connector. There's also a *Site Connector*, which is the easiest and most efficient way to connect one Exchange Server site to another. You can also use the Internet Mail Connector or the X.400 Connector to connect sites on your own private network, if you want.

Use of the Internet has exploded in the last few years. In addition to its original purpose of sharing research and information among universities, government agencies, and other organizations, the Internet has become a widely used method for exchanging e-mail messages. Messages are exchanged on the Internet by using SMTP (Simple Mail Transfer Protocol), which defines the form of messages and the requirements for Internet hosts. The Internet Mail Connection can send messages, receive messages, or both.

Messages that contain only text are easily transmitted over the Internet. Messages increasingly contain elements in binary format, however, such as special formatting instructions or attachments. Some of the components that make up the Internet weren't designed to transmit binary files. For these messages to pass through the Internet without being corrupted, they must be modified. The Internet Mail Connector supports two mechanisms for handling this issue: Multipurpose Internet Mail Extensions (MIME) and UUEncode/UUDecode. The Internet Mail Connector can automatically convert outgoing messages by using the method you specify and convert incoming messages of either type.

Connectors are available for both older versions of Microsoft Mail so that existing users can coexist and exchange messages during a migration period, removing the need to upgrade all users at once. In addition to the connectors, migration tools are available that allow administrators to import and export directory information from one system to the other and to move users' mailboxes and existing folders and messages from the old system to Exchange Server. Also, an Exchange server can act as the directory server for the Microsoft Mail 3.x directory-synchronization process, enabling the use of an Exchange Server system as a backbone connecting several older Microsoft Mail postoffices.

An X.400 connector is also available for Exchange Server. This connector has been designed to communicate with other messaging systems that adhere to the X.400 standard as defined by the International Telecommunications Union (ITU). The ITU, an organization of the United Nations, was formerly called the International Telegraph and Telephone Consultative Committee (CCITT). This body has published versions of the X.400 recommendations in 1984, 1988, and 1992. Exchange Server can exchange messages with systems that have implemented the 1984 and 1988 recommendations.

If your organization already has an existing X.400 messaging system in place, the Exchange Server MTA can exchange messages with the MTAs on other X.400 systems. Also, Exchange servers can act as an X.400 backbone themselves by functioning as relay MTAs, which may eliminate the need for a public X.400 network provider. The X.400 Connector can be configured to use TCP/IP, TPO/X.25, and TP4/CLNP.

The X.400 recommendations specify various components of a message, called *body parts*. These components may be the text of a message, an attachment of some type, or other elements. A message also includes *header* information describing the sender, the recipient(s), and other information. Exchange Server supports *P1 envelopes* as described in the recommendations. It also supports P2 and P22 content if the message complies with the 1984 or 1988 recommendations, respectively. Message components that don't comply with the recommendations or simply don't fit the categories now defined are *encapsulated* by using the Transport Neutral Encapsulation Format (TNEF). And in situations where X.400 communications are used between Exchange Server sites, the native format used internally by the information store known as MDBEF is used to increase efficiency. This format is never used when communicating with other X.400 systems.

Finally, a Schedule+ Free/Busy Connector allows Exchange Server to exchange information with older Schedule+ users. Old Schedule+ clients can't view a user's schedule with the new Schedule+ (version 7.0), but they at least can see when the user is busy and available and send a meeting request. This feature is another important part of a temporary coexistence and migration strategy.

Understanding Client Components

An understanding of Exchange's Client components is vital to a successful Exchange Server installation, because you must make the appropriate client applications available to Exchange users. The primary client components are Outlook, the Exchange Client, Schedule+, and the Microsoft Forms Designer. The following sections explore these components in more detail and give you an overview of the features available. Exchange Server 5.0 provides client software for the following operating systems:

- MS-DOS
- Windows 3.1
- Windows for Workgroups
- Windows NT Workstation
- Windows NT Server
- Windows 95

The Windows NT client software is available for four CPU architectures (Intel, Alpha, MIPS, and PowerPC), although MIPS and PowerPC support is being discontinued due to poor market acceptance of those platforms.

Part
V
Ch
24

Examining Microsoft Outlook

Microsoft Office 97 includes a new, integrated information management tool called Outlook. It offers some of the same features as the Exchange Client and Schedule+ but adds significant personal information management capabilities. The original Exchange Client and Schedule+ are still available for those customers who prefer them. Outlook is available only for 32-bit Windows platforms (Windows 95 and Windows NT). Here is a sample of the features provided by this powerful new application:

- Provides an elegant e-mail client with various views available (see Figure 24.7). Also, you can define custom views and flag messages for later action.
- Displays your personal schedule in a daily, weekly, or monthly format (see Figure 24.8).
- Uses an icon bar for easy movement from one display to another. The icon bar is visible at the left of the screen in all the Outlook figures.
- Displays a Journal page that shows when you completed selected tasks, sent or received e-mail from selected individuals, or other important activities that you want to track (see Figure 24.9).
- Stores detailed information on contacts, including addresses, phone numbers, birthdays, and notes.
- Stores a To Do list that can be sorted by project, priority, or other criteria.
- Lets you enter ad hoc notes (similar to Post-It notes), as shown in Figure 24.10.
- Allows you to browse for information on your computer (see Figure 24.11).
- Provides access to public folders on an Exchange Server (see Figure 24.12).

FIG. 24.7

The standard e-mail view with the Office Assistant shown by default when starting Outlook.

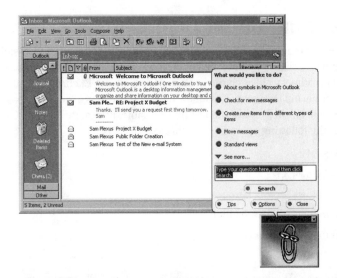

FIG. 24.8

The weekly schedule display provided by Outlook.

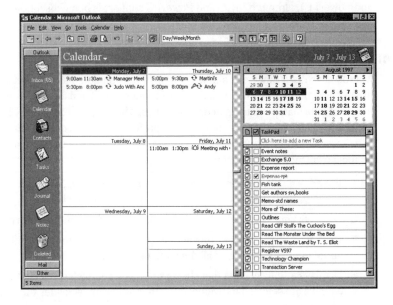

FIG. 24.9
Tracking your activities in Outlook's Journal page.

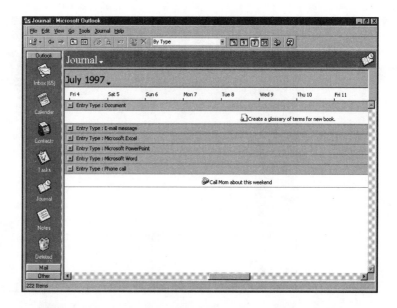

FIG. 24.10
Some sample notes.

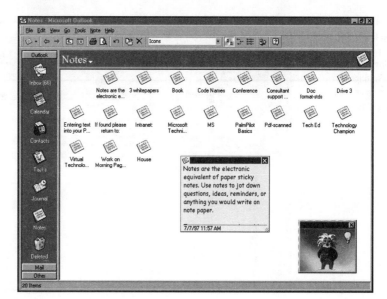

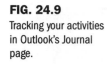

FIG. 24.11

Filing and locating information stored on your computer.

FIG. 24.12

A public folder devoted to object-oriented technology, in which a number of ongoing discussions are visible in the right pane.

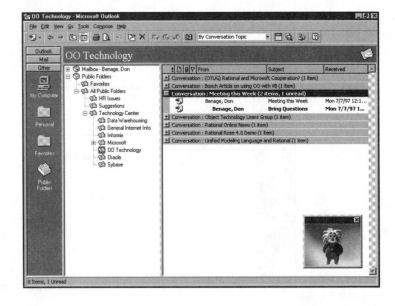

Outlook is a powerful blend of personal information management and activity tracking. It can be used as a task planner with the capability to delegate work and track progress on assigned tasks. For many people, this tool is the best all around for electronic mail and daily personal management.

Understanding the Exchange Client and Schedule+

The original client component included with Exchange was called simply the Exchange Client. This program provides a powerful, easy-to-use e-mail application that also supports information sharing among workgroup members or an entire organization. The Exchange Client contains many advanced features, including

■ Support for profiles to allow multiple users to share the same computer, or one user to use more than one messaging system (see Figure 24.13).

FIG. 24.13

The process of editing a user profile on the Windows 95 Exchange Client.

■ A toolbar to make it easy and fast to activate frequently used commands.

■ A graphical display that incorporates color, animated icons, and hierarchical folder controls to simplify message management.

■ Support for drag-and-drop operations. For example, you can drag an icon representing a message from your Inbox to a personal folder you created to file the message in your own personal filing system. You also can drag files from programs like File Manager or Windows 95 Explorer directly into the body of a message to include that file as an attachment.

■ The Inbox Assistant, an automated agent that filters messages based on criteria you define and stores them in your personal folders. Click the Add Rule button to bring up the Edit Rule dialog (see Figure 24.14). The Inbox Assistant has other features to streamline message management as well.

■ Support for remote e-mail users. Previous versions of Microsoft Mail required a separate client application to take full advantage of remote features. The standard client now supports remote features, such as downloading message headers first and then selectively downloading only those messages you need most or those that are small enough for practical download over a modem connection (see Figure 24.15).

■ Support for rich text such as boldface, italic, different fonts, and colors in messages.

■ Support for OLE objects to be included in messages. These objects can appear as an icon, be represented by a Windows metafile, or appear as a native OLE object of the appropriate type.

■ The capability to use Microsoft Word as your e-mail editor.

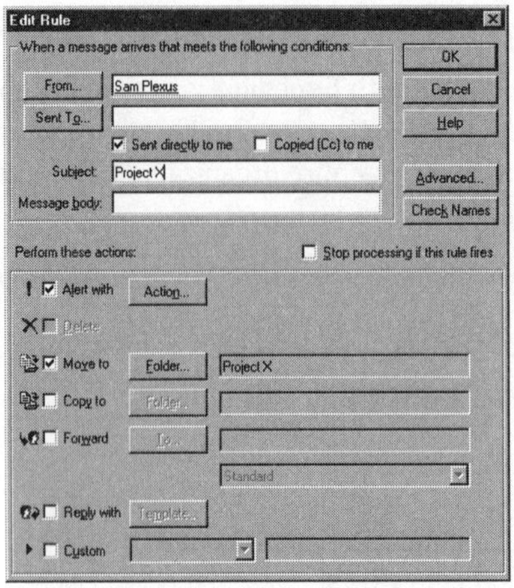

FIG. 24.14

Using the Edit Rule dialog to define a message filter for the Inbox Assistant.

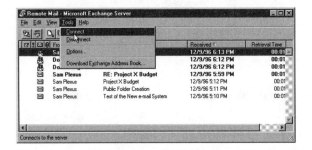

FIG. 24.15

The Remote Mail window being used to selectively download certain messages.

Exchange Server includes an updated version of Schedule+, the group scheduling program. The new version contains many enhancements, including features common in Personal Information Managers (PIMs). Here is a sample of the features provided by Schedule+:

- Displays your personal schedule in a daily, weekly, or monthly format (see Figure 24.16). You can create custom views for your schedule by selecting options.

- Uses a tabbed display window for easy movement from one display to another. You can add tabs to those shown by default to access other views of particular interest.

- Displays a Planner page that shows a user's free and busy times (see Figure 24.17). One or more recipients can be selected and their free/busy times overlaid on the display in different colors to simplify the process of finding a time when several people are available. Schedules can also be created for resources such as conference rooms and special equipment.

- Stores detailed information on a user's contacts, including addresses, phone numbers, birthdays, and notes.

- Stores a To Do list that can be sorted by project, priority, or other criteria (see Figure 24.18). The list includes columns for estimated effort, percentage complete, duration, and others.

FIG. 24.16
Schedule+ displaying a weekly schedule.

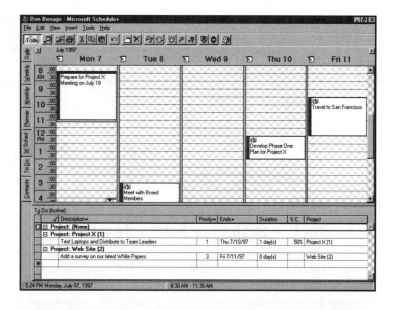

FIG. 24.17
Scheduling a meeting with Schedule+'s Planner page.

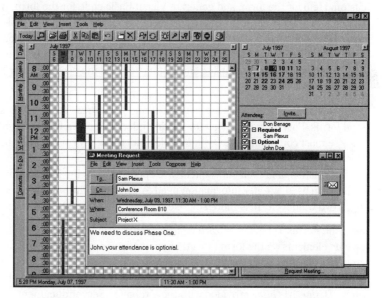

The Schedule+ tool works with e-mail to schedule meetings. A meeting request created in the Planner window generates e-mail messages to each invited recipient and tracks yes and no replies in a list window showing checks and X's to indicate the various responses. It's also possible to integrate Schedule+ with the Microsoft Project application for advanced project management capabilities. The Microsoft Office Developer's Kit has information on programmatic interfaces to Microsoft Project and other useful information on developing integrated applications.

FIG. 24.18

A sample To Do list, with various projects and prioritized tasks for a particular user.

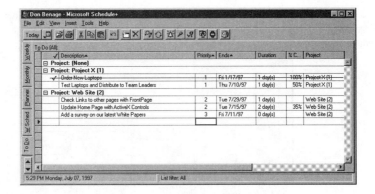

Understanding the Exchange Forms Designer

Exchange Forms Designer isn't a client application in the same sense that Schedule+ and Exchange Client are. It's a development tool that lets administrators or advanced users create custom forms. With the Forms Designer, you can lay out the appearance of the form; add the elements you want to appear on the form, including text, graphics, and other controls; create custom Help for the form; and generate Visual Basic code for the form. A set of templates is included to make it easier to create common types of forms. For example, you can use a template for a send form as the basis for forms used to send information from one user to other recipients. There's even a Form Template Wizard that guides users through the process of selecting an appropriate template and setting some of the properties for the form to match the needs expressed.

The two basic types of forms are *send forms* and *post forms*. You've just learned the purpose of send forms. Post forms are used for posting information in a folder for subsequent viewing. They're most commonly used with a public folder. Each form can contain one or two windows. One-window forms are used when the same window can be used to enter and send (or post) the information, and then subsequently to open and view the information. If the characteristics of the form used to enter information need to vary from the window used for subsequent viewing, a two-window form is more suitable.

After the Forms Template Wizard generates the basic form, you can set properties for the various elements on the form to further customize its appearance and behavior. You can set properties for the entire form, for a particular window, or for individual fields. You also can add controls and Visual Basic code to create forms with highly customized behavior. See the *Application Designer's Guide* provided with the Exchange Server documentation for more information on creating custom forms with the Exchange Forms Designer.

Understanding Organizations, Sites, and Domains

The word *organization* has a special meaning in the context of an Exchange Server discussion. The traditional definition of an *organization* is a collection of people and resources, such as a corporate entity or educational institution, with some common purpose or goal. An Exchange

Server organization is the largest entity describing a collection of servers and related clients that share a directory of objects and addresses. In some cases, either definition is applicable and some ambiguity doesn't affect the meaning of the sentence.

Organizations are divided into sites. A *site* is a collection of servers that share common configuration elements and are connected to each other with high-speed communications links. Usually a site is geographically located on a single LAN, although with (expensive) high-speed WAN links, a logical site could actually extend over a large geographic area. The connectivity and exchange of information among servers on the same site is easy to configure. The servers in a site automatically synchronize directory information (mailboxes, distribution lists, custom recipients, and configuration information for various objects in the system). To connect two sites, you must configure an explicit connector and define processes to share directory information.

Windows NT domains provide the security context that all Exchange Server objects depend on. Windows NT security is the basis for all assigned permissions and the audit and monitoring features offered by Exchange Server. It's not necessary to create a one-to-one mapping between sites and domains. You could, for example, use a single Windows NT domain for your entire organization and still decide to use multiple logical sites (perhaps one per department) for your Exchange Server system. Conversely, a single Exchange Server site might span multiple Windows NT domains. Remember that domains are designed to provide security for shared resources on the network. Exchange Server sites are designed to facilitate the transmission and sharing of information. The two structures may or may not coincide.

Part
V

Ch
24

Organizing Your Enterprise

Although you can certainly use Exchange Server to handle messaging for a small- to medium-sized organization or department, it has been designed with the power and features to handle the needs of the largest organizations. You can add processors and other equipment to a single server (assuming that the computer you've selected supports these additions), and Windows NT and Exchange Server take advantage of the additional capability provided by these additions. You also can increase the power of your Exchange Server system by adding more computers. The architecture of an Exchange Server system allows you to implement services on a collection of machines that work together cooperatively to deliver the facilities provided by the system as a whole.

Careful planning is required for your Exchange Server system to work reliably and deliver the full functionality that it can. If you're implementing more than one or two Exchange servers, you should take the time to study the *Concepts and Planning Guide* provided with Exchange Server. It provides a wealth of planning information that's beyond the scope of this book and can help you with designing medium to very large Exchange Server systems. The following sections provide some basic guidelines to aid your planning process and help make your implementation successful.

Planning Your Site

A good first step when approaching any computer system implementation is to do some research and characterize the intended user community. What are the different tasks performed by these people? What information is required to perform those tasks? Is there information that would be helpful but isn't currently available? Create a table that lists groups of users and the applications they need. Review the features of Exchange Server and look for capabilities that closely match the needs of users. E-mail is a natural starting point with the product, but you also should explore the groupware capabilities provided by shared public folders with or without the use of custom forms.

Evaluate the physical network that supports your Exchange Server system. Get a copy of any existing diagrams that document the network in use, or create such a diagram if none exist. Pay particular attention to slow links between locations, especially if there's a high degree of interaction between the people at those locations. Gather and review statistics on the current network bandwidth use and try to characterize the network's peak and off-peak periods.

When considering the question of how many servers and how many users per server, be conservative in your estimates. It's useful to estimate the approximate number of messages per day that users will send. Talk to a sample of people in each area of your organization. If they aren't sure, ask for a rough estimate—5, 50, 500? What kinds of messages will be sent? Will they frequently include large attachments or primarily be just text? This load-evaluation process, if done carefully and thoroughly, can help tremendously when estimating the number of servers required to meet the needs of your organization. Some rules of thumb that can help you decide are provided in the *Installation Manual* and the *Concepts and Planning Guide* provided with Exchange Server.

You should establish some conventions for naming entities in the Exchange Server system. Every element of the system has a display name and a directory name. In general, you can't change the directory name after the object is defined. The display name is used in the Exchange Administrator program's window, and the directory name is used in entries made into the Windows NT event log and various other log files that can be created. The scheme you define should make it easy to decide on a new name, and it should provide the capability to create unique names throughout the organization without having to always check for a conflict.

Reviewing Geographic Considerations

An important part of the planning process, as pointed out in the preceding discussion, is the identification of slow links between user groups. These links are the potential bottlenecks in the flow of information, and you must take steps to avoid such an eventuality. By using the replication features provided with the product, you can mitigate slow links by locating *replicas*, or copies, of important information in the same local LAN segment with each user group. A single copy of updated information is sent to and from the replica as changes are made. Rather than many users each attach to a folder on the side of a slow link, they can attach to the replica on their own LAN segment.

Using these capabilities can dramatically reduce the burden placed on networking equipment by increased network bandwidth use. By providing users with a local copy of information, you can realize enormous bandwidth savings. If you need to manage further the use of a slow link, you can schedule the updates made between replicas for off-peak hours when the effects of transmitting the information have less impact on other network applications.

As you plan your system, you also should consider backup contingencies for system components that may fail. For example, the Dynamic Remote Access Service (RAS) Connector may be a useful backup alternative to another connector in use over a WAN link. If the WAN link fails and the standard connector can't be used, the Dynamic RAS Connector can provide a useful—perhaps slower—backup connection that gets the information transferred.

▶ **See** "Using Routing and Remote Access Service," **p. 980**

Considering Functional Considerations

In addition to the geographic concerns, you need to consider functional concerns. For example, you should consider redundancy for the components that deliver any critical functionality. The system's design should reflect whether a groupware application created with Exchange Server is required for a department to do its job. In such an environment, it's less desirable to place all users on one large server. Using a small number of large computers to build your system has its advantages and disadvantages. Using smaller computers in larger numbers may provide a better opportunity to distribute the workload and yield some built-in redundancy so that a single component failure won't put everyone out of commission.

Part
V

Ch
24

Sizing Your Server

Before actually setting up your first server, a little more planning is important to ensure that the machine you've selected is appropriate for an Exchange server. Exchange Server places fairly heavy demands on the equipment if you have a large number of users that actively use Exchange Server features. The decisions you make and any limits you set can have a profound impact on Exchange Server's performance and usability.

You've already learned how Exchange servers are grouped in sites and how a collection of sites comprises an organization. You also learned how to undertake a planning process to evaluate user needs and plan for services to meet those needs. The information that you gather and determine during that planning process is an important component of the next step—sizing your server. As you make specific hardware plans for your server(s), your choices must reflect the needs of your user community. The following are some questions you should answer before deciding on a particular server:

- How many users will have mailboxes on this server?
- How active will they be in their use of Exchange Server?
- Will the average user send three messages a day or 50?
- How many messages will be addressed to multiple users on the same server?
- Will messages frequently include the use of special formatting or attachments?

- Does your organization use multimedia data types, including audio and video files?
- Will your organization use electronic forms to build groupware applications?
- Will your organization use public folders for bulletin boards or other shared information applications?

As mentioned earlier, Exchange Server can place significant demands on the server equipment. If you're setting up a single server for a small group of users (fewer than 20) and their use of the system will be light, the guidelines provided here are less important. In most organizations, however, the use of electronic messaging and related technologies grows dramatically as users discover the system's features and capabilities.

Exchange Server offers features that are particularly attractive in environments where it's difficult to meet with colleagues due to hectic schedules, travel demands, or other factors that make face-to-face meetings an infrequent alternative. If collaboration on documents, presentations, or other items that can be included as message attachments is common, your plans also should allow for larger messages with attachments, even if this feature isn't widely used in your current environment. This affects the size of all information stores (server-based and client-based) and the network bandwidth use.

In large organizations with many servers, the decision on what hardware to buy is somewhat complicated by the fact that you may address the needs of your organization with a small number of servers with many users, or a large number of servers with fewer users. If you want to put 500 or more users on a single server, a computer with four Pentium processors, 256M of RAM, and 8G of disk space wouldn't be an unreasonable choice. With fewer than 100 users, a single processor, 64M of RAM, and 2G of disk space may be adequate. Even a relatively small organization may weigh the alternatives between one large server with all services including connectors, or reducing the size of the main server and moving one or more connectors to other computers.

By increasing the number of computers used, you increase the amount of work you must perform to install and configure equipment and software, but you reduce the number of users affected by a single machine failure. You also allow more flexibility in locating servers on the same physical LAN segment with the users whose mailboxes are on that server. This is an excellent way to reduce bandwidth use on large networks with routers or hubs that limit the scope of packet transmissions.

If you opt for fewer large servers, you benefit from an overall reduction in network traffic because many messages are addressed to users on the same server, and there is less replication of directory and public folder information. Installing fewer large servers also leverages Exchange Server's *single instance storage* feature, which stores only a single instance of a message addressed to multiple users on the same server. Upgrading in a large-server environment is generally easier and simplifies replication of directory information and public folders. Large servers place increased demands on the network adapters used in the servers, as these NICs become potential bottlenecks with a large number of users simultaneously accessing the same machine. The increased size of the information stores also affects the time required to perform backup and recovery operations. Many users will be affected by a large-server outage, so you should strongly consider using fault-tolerant devices and an uninterruptible power supply (UPS).

▶ **See** "Providing Power Protection," **p. 166**

Of course, there's no single correct answer to these questions because they depend to some degree on the qualities and culture of the organization in question. Some general guidelines can narrow the possibilities and streamline your selection process, however. Specific minimum requirements are provided on the product box and may change slightly as new versions are released in the future. The information provided here applies to the standard edition of Exchange Server 5.0. If you're using the Enterprise Edition, you should double-check the product package to make sure that there haven't been any significant changes.

Microsoft recommends the following server hardware:

Part
V
Ch
24

- ▪ Use at least a 90 MHz Pentium processor or a RISC processor with equivalent processing power.
- ▪ To improve throughput, use multiple disk drives configured as a RAID 1 stripe set.

    ▶ **See** "RAID 1," **p. 220**

- ▪ In addition to the disk space used by Windows NT Server, you need room for the Information Stores (public and private) and the Directory Service.
- ▪ You also need to provide for a large Windows NT Server paging file, especially if the server has a large amount of RAM. The recommended allowance for a paging file is 100M plus an amount equal to the quantity of physical RAM.

N O T E You can create a RAID 1 stripe set by using the Disk Administrator utility provided with Windows NT Server. Disk Administrator allows Windows NT to spread information across multiple hard disks, thereby improving the speed of information storage and retrieval.

▶ **See** "Creating Windows NT Server Stripe and Mirror Sets," **p. 239** ▪

Regarding disk space, you should generally be deciding how many gigabytes rather than how many megabytes, and remember that buying too much is difficult. The maximum space that Exchange Server can use is 16G per server, which is significantly less than Windows NT Server's theoretical limit.

A good strategy to adopt when choosing a server is to select a machine that you can upgrade later if additional power is needed. Most manufacturers offer models that have slots for additional adapters and support multiple disk controller cards and drives. Some models even let you add additional processors or connect a separate disk subsystem to add a large amount of disk storage capacity. Selecting a machine with a high degree of expandability can make it easier to respond to growth by avoiding the need to build a new server and move user mailboxes.

Running Exchange Setup

You're now ready to install your server. In the following sections, you learn how to use Setup to install files and set up the server-based services that make up Exchange Server. You also learn how to use Performance Optimizer, a utility much like the wizards included in many Microsoft products. Performance Optimizer asks you a series of questions, analyzes the server, verifies or changes the location of files, and tunes various performance parameters to make best use of your equipment.

Running the Setup Program

To install Exchange Server, you must first install Windows NT Server. If you intend to install the Internet Connector on this server, you also must configure the server to use the TCP/IP protocol before installation. You should know what type of Windows NT domain model you're using and understand the implications of domain security. Also, you should create a service account for use by the server-based services in Exchange Server. If you're using a master domain model, the service account should be created in the master domain.

For the installation to be successful, you need information from the planning process outlined earlier in the section "Organizing Your Enterprise." Specifically, you need the following:

■ Information about the naming conventions you've established for your organization, sites, and servers. You also need the actual name for this site and this server.

■ The name and password for a Windows NT account that's a member of the local Administrators group on this server. By default, the global Domain Admins group is added to the local Administrators group when a server is added to a domain.

■ The name and password for the service account that you intend to use.

You also should make sure that no "messaging-aware" applications are running. These applications can open dynamic link libraries (DLLs) that need to be upgraded or replaced and prevent the Setup program from successfully completing. An example of such an application is the Schedule+ Reminder utility, which runs in the background and pops up to remind you of appointments. Although these applications are more commonly run on clients than servers, it's best to make sure that you won't have a problem of this type. The simplest way to ensure that this doesn't happen is to check the Startup group for any such applications and temporarily remove any that you find. Then log off and back on to the server. You may also want to temporarily stop any services that use messaging protocols such as MAPI (for example, a groupware service of some type).

To install Microsoft Exchange Server, follow this procedure:

1. Log on to Windows NT Server with an account having Administrator privileges.

2. Insert the Exchange Server CD into the CD-ROM drive. Some Exchange Server packages—the Enterprise Edition, for example—contain multiple CDs; be sure to use the server CD.

3. Use Explorer to find the directory that corresponds to the type of CPU architecture your computer has (Intel X86, Alpha, MIPS, or PowerPC). Launch Setup.exe. Click OK in the Welcome dialog to open the Microsoft Exchange Server Setup dialog (see Figure 24.19).

FIG. 24.19

The Microsoft Exchange Server Setup dialog displaying the different installation options.

4. If you want to use a different disk drive or directory from the one selected by default, click Change Directory. Enter the location you prefer.

5. Click the button corresponding to the type of installation you want to perform—Typical, Complete/Custom, or Minimum. If you choose Typical or Minimum, skip to step 7.

6. If you chose Complete/Custom, the Microsoft Exchange Server Setup – Complete/Custom dialog appears (see Figure 24.20). In this dialog, you can select exactly those elements you want to install. You also can change the disk drive or directory if you don't find enough disk space on the previously selected drive. Select Microsoft Exchange Server and Microsoft Exchange Administrator and review the Space Required and Space Available fields. When you're satisfied that you've made the appropriate selections, click Continue.

FIG. 24.20

Selecting the elements to install in the Microsoft Exchange Server Setup Complete/Custom dialog.

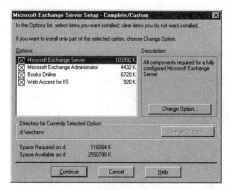

7. In the Choose Licensing Mode dialog, select the type of licensing you want to use, Per Server or Per Seat, and select the I Agree option. If you selected Per Server, be sure to enter the number of client access licenses you've purchased in the Per Server dialog. Click Continue to open the Organization and Site dialog (see Figure 24.21).

8. Click the appropriate option. If you're joining an existing site, enter the site name in the text box; if you're creating a new site, enter your Organization Name and Site Name. Click OK.

Part
V
Ch
24

FIG. 24.21

Using the Organization and Site dialog to join an existing site or create a new site.

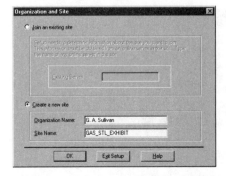

9. In the verification dialog, double-check the entries you made and then click OK if no corrections are needed. The Site Service Account dialog appears (see Figure 24.22). If you're joining an existing site, the same service account that's in use on other servers is used for this one as well.

FIG. 24.22

Using the Site Services Account dialog to indicate the account that should be used by all server-based services for Exchange Server.

10. Click Browse to select the service account and to open the Add User or Group dialog (see Figure 24.23).

FIG. 24.23

Specifying the service account for Exchange Server.

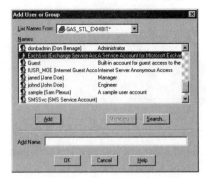

11. Select the account to use from the list of accounts in your domain. If you're using a master domain model, select the master domain from the List Names From drop-down list, and then select the account from the Names list. Click OK to return to the Site Services Account dialog.

12. Enter the Account Password and click OK.

13. A message box may appear, indicating that additional rights have been granted to the service account (for example, the Log On as a Service right). Click OK. If you already granted the service account the Log On as a Service right, this message doesn't appear.

14. Click OK to complete the installation. Setup copies the files required for the options you specified and installs the services. When this process is complete, a dialog appears, asking whether you want to run Performance Optimizer (see Figure 24.24).

FIG. 24.24
The dialog that indicates that Exchange Server setup has successfully completed and offers to run Performance Optimizer.

15. You can run Performance Optimizer now or at a later time. If you want to run Performance Optimizer now, click Run Optimizer and proceed to the next section for instructions on completing this process. Otherwise, skip to the section "Configuring Your Site with Exchange Administrator" to continue.

N O T E Always run Performance Optimizer before placing an Exchange server into production use. Performance Optimizer performs important tuning and optimizations that can greatly affect your server's performance. If you plan to add other elements to your server before using it, wait to run Optimizer after you install all elements (such as connectors). ■

 Setup installs approximately 45M of files that may not be needed on all servers. The online documentation takes up about 30M of space and is located in the file \Exchsrvr\Bin\Exchdoc.hlp by default. The sample applications, including the Getting Started public folder, require approximately 16M and are located in the \Exchsrvr\Sampapps\Clients\Sampapps.pst file. You may want to delete these files from some servers in a multiserver site to conserve space.

Using Performance Optimizer

For the first time, Microsoft has included a utility specifically designed to optimize the performance of a server-based application. Although the Setup programs for other BackOffice components can adjust Registry parameters based on the type of installation you specify, and some components dynamically tune parameters, Performance Optimizer is the first stand-alone utility designed for this purpose.

Performance Optimizer is different from the very useful, general-purpose Performance Monitor provided with Windows NT. Performance Optimizer measures a few specific server elements, such as disk drive speeds, and changes Exchange Server's configuration. Used only for

Exchange Server, it measures only the most important server elements. Performance Monitor provides a vast amount of performance measurement information on virtually every aspect of server (and Windows NT Workstation) operation. It doesn't make changes directly to the server's configuration, however.

▶ **See** "Using Performance Monitor," **p. 530**

You should run Performance Optimizer at the following times:

- Immediately following the successful completion of the Setup program.

- Anytime you change the hardware configuration of your server, especially if you add memory or additional disk storage components, because Performance Optimizer analyzes these elements most carefully.

- Anytime you change the software configuration of a server. If, for example, you add a connector or make significant changes to the size of the Information Store by adding large public folders or importing lots of mailboxes during a migration, you should rerun Performance Optimizer.

- If you want to move files to a different physical disk, even if you haven't added new components.

- During performance-tuning operations. You can use Performance Optimizer with other Exchange Server components, such as server monitors, link monitors, and the Windows NT Performance Monitor, to do comprehensive performance analysis and tuning.

Before you can run Performance Optimizer, you must stop all services before it can continue. If you are running Performance Optimizer on a production server with active users, wait until off-peak hours, when a temporary outage affects the smallest number of users. To run Performance Optimizer, follow these steps:

1. If you're continuing with Performance Optimizer immediately after running Setup, skip to step 2. Otherwise, launch Performance Optimizer from the Exchange Server program group. The Welcome dialog appears (see Figure 24.25).

FIG. 24.25
The Welcome dialog for the Performance Optimizer.

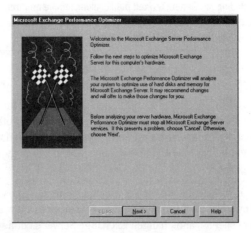

2. If it's acceptable to stop all services now and continue with the optimization process, click Next. A dialog appears with a number of questions for you to answer (see Figure 24.26).

FIG. 24.26
Performance Optimizer requesting information from you that it can't automatically detect.

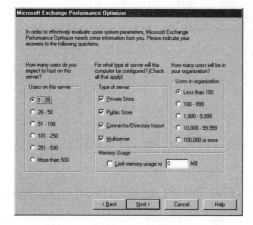

3. Answer the questions regarding the number of users on this server, in your entire organization, and the type of server you're optimizing. Click Next.

4. After running some tests, Performance Optimizer suggests the most desirable locations for various files (see Figure 24.27). To override Performance Optimizer's choices, manually enter a path for any elements you want. Click Next.

FIG. 24.27
The recommended file locations based on the results of disk-speed tests.

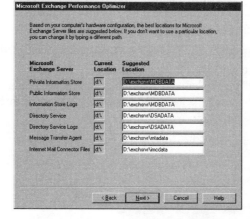

5. A final dialog indicates that you've successfully optimized your server (see Figure 24.28). When you click Finish, the Exchange Server services start with the new operating parameters in effect.

FIG. 24.28

The dialog indicating that Performance Optimizer has successfully completed.

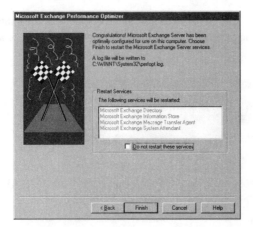

Configuring Your Site with Exchange Administrator

After running Setup and Performance Optimizer, you should take some important steps to finish configuring your server. The steps that you should complete before adding user mailboxes to the server are described first. Other steps are items that may change over the course of time and that you can revisit at regular intervals to see whether changing conditions warrant any new settings.

Before doing any other work, start Exchange Administrator. You can run this utility on computers running Windows NT Workstation or on the Exchange server; you can't run it on computers running Windows 3.1, Windows for Workgroups, or Windows 95. Install Exchange Administrator on at least two different computers running Windows NT to make sure that it's available in case of an emergency or one of the machines is down.

To use Exchange Administrator, you must be logged on to an account with appropriate access rights. By default, the account that was logged on during setup and the service account used by Exchange Server services are both granted administrative privileges. You can grant privileges to other accounts by using Exchange Administrator. Make sure that you're logged on to an appropriate account before you proceed.

To run Exchange Administrator, follow these steps:

1. From the Start menu choose Programs, Microsoft Exchange (Common), and Microsoft Exchange Administrator to open the Connect to Server dialog (see Figure 24.29).

FIG. 24.29

Choosing the server you want to administer in the Connect to Server dialog.

2. Enter the server's name, or click Browse to browse your organization or a particular site. In the Server Browser dialog, select the server you want to administer and then click OK to return to the Connect to Server dialog (see Figure 24.30).

FIG. 24.30

The Server Browser dialog displaying your organization, sites, and servers.

3. Mark the Set as Default check box if you will use this server most frequently.

4. Click OK to open the Microsoft Exchange Administrator window (see Figure 24.31).

FIG. 24.31

Exchange Administrator showing the directory hierarchy in the left pane and the selected element in the right pane.

N O T E   If the account you're using has appropriate access permissions, you also can administer servers on remote sites that are connected LAN/WAN protocols that support remote procedure calls (RPCs). Some connection types are suitable for transferring e-mail messages but don't support RPCs. Exchange Administrator must be installed on a computer that supports RPCs for administrative operations to be performed. ▓

The Exchange Administrator window has two panes. The left pane displays the directory for your entire organization in a hierarchical fashion, starting with the topmost organization elements, sites and their elements, and then servers. Most of the individual objects in the left pane can contain other objects and are therefore called *containers*. The left pane is referred to as the *container area*. The right pane displays the contents of the currently selected container and is referred to as the *contents area*.

Exchange Administrator lets you modify servers and objects in a site only after you connect to a server in that site. When you connect to a particular server, Exchange Administrator lets you modify other servers and objects in the same site as the server to which you connected. Other

Part

V

Ch

24

sites appear dimmed, and the information about these sites and objects is read-only. If you have appropriate rights and want to administer another site that's connected over a network link with RPC support, you can connect to any server in that site. After connecting to one server at startup, you can connect to additional servers by choosing Connect to Server from the File menu.

You can configure most objects in the directory by setting object properties. The next few sections describe important options and properties that you should set before using Exchange Server.

Granting Administrative Permissions to Other Windows NT Accounts

When you installed Exchange Server and created your site, the account that you were logged on to was granted the role of Permissions Admin for the site container. This role gives that account rights to perform administrative functions, including the capability to change permissions for various objects in the site. The first time you want to grant administrative permissions, you should log on to the installing account. Thereafter, any account that has been granted the Permissions Admin role for an object—the site object, for example—can grant other accounts permissions or perform other administrative tasks.

Various roles are available (for example, Permissions Admin, View Only Admin, and User), depending on the object selected. Also, you can create a custom role by selecting various rights on an ad hoc basis. As with other BackOffice components, it's good practice to avoid giving a large group of people extensive administrative permissions. You should certainly have at least two administrators to back up each other in case of emergency; in a large site or organization, it may be appropriate to delegate the administration of individual sites and servers to various individuals, with two "master" administrators. In general, however, people should be granted only the permissions they actually need.

Remember that permissions are inherited *downstream*—that is, if an account is granted permissions on a container, the account has the same permissions on every object in that container. Therefore, objects that are lower in the hierarchy sometimes display a set of inherited permissions that are read-only and a set of permissions for the currently selected object. To change the inherited permissions, you must select the container object. For example, to grant permissions for an entire site, select the site container. If you want to grant permissions for some, but not all, servers in a site, set permissions on the server objects individually.

To grant administrative permissions to additional accounts, make sure that you've logged on to the account you used to install Exchange Server (or an account that has subsequently been granted Permissions Admin capabilities), and then follow these steps:

1. Start Exchange Administrator, if necessary, and connect to a server in the site you want to administer.

2. Choose Options from the Tools menu to open the Options properties sheet. Click the Permissions tab.

3. On the Permissions page, mark the Show Permissions Page for All Objects and the Display Rights for Roles on Permissions Page check boxes, to see exactly which rights correspond to a given role. Click OK.

4. Select the object for which you want to grant permissions in the Exchange Administrator window. From the File menu choose Properties to display the property sheet for the object.

5. Click the Permissions tab (see Figure 24.32).

FIG. 24.32

Setting permissions for the GAS_STL_EXHIBIT site object.

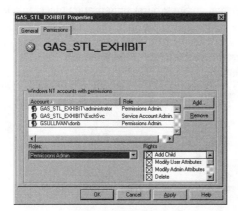

Depending on the object's level, you may see a read-only box labeled Windows NT Accounts with Inherited Permissions. You can't change this information except by opening the property sheet for the appropriate container object from which these permissions are inherited.

6. In the Windows NT Accounts with Permissions section, select existing accounts and then change their role with the drop-down list or delete them with the Remove button.

7. Click Add to grant permissions to a new account. In the Windows NT Add Users and Groups dialog, select the users and groups that you want to grant a specific role and click OK.

8. Select the users one at a time and select the roles they should have from the drop-down list. You can scroll the Roles list to see exactly what permissions correspond to a particular role. The Help button supplies an explanation of the various rights if you want more detailed information. Click OK when you're finished.

Configuring Information Store Options

Several options affect the behavior of the information stores on the servers in your site. By selecting the Information Store Site Configuration object, you can configure all information stores on all servers in your site. You can change the display name of this object by using the procedure described next. Even if the name has been changed, you should be able to recognize the object by its icon. If you can't find the object through the following procedure, consult other administrators in this site for assistance in finding the new display name.

To view the Information Store Site Configuration Properties sheet, follow these steps:

1. Start Exchange Administrator, if necessary, and connect to a server in the site you want to administer.

2. In the window's container area (the left pane), find the site you want to administer. Click the plus sign next to the site name to expand the display if it's not already open. Select the Configuration container. In the contents area (the right pane), you should see the Information Store Site Configuration object.

3. Double-click the Information Store Site Configuration object to open its property sheet (see Figure 24.33).

FIG. 24.33
Using the Information Store Site Configuration Properties sheet to configure options for the information stores on all servers in the site.

Setting Top-Level Folder Permissions An important option to configure is the container that will contain public folders and the list of recipients who can create top-level folders. It's generally a good idea to limit the number of people who can create top-level folders. These folders appear at the highest level of the public folder hierarchy. Anyone who creates a new top-level folder can specify who has the capability to create other folders within that top-level folder. Having too many folders at the top level can make finding a folder difficult and can limit the effective use of public folders. A small group of people is more likely to maintain a sensible structure that lends itself to appropriate usage.

By default, all users can create top-level folders. As soon as you make an entry in the Top Level Folder Creation page of the Information Store Site Configuration Properties sheet, this default is cleared. Only those users listed in the Allowed list can then create top-level folders. Users not listed or those listed in the Not Allowed list are denied. You don't need to list explicitly everyone who should be denied this capability in the Not Allowed list. This list is provided so that if you enter one or more distribution lists in the Allowed list, you can explicitly override individual members of the distribution list.

To set permissions for creating top-level folders, follow these steps:

1. Open the Information Store Site Configuration Properties sheet.

2. On the Top Level Folder Creation page (see Figure 24.34), specify recipients who will be allowed this right in the Allowed to Create Top Level Folders list. Select the All option if you want everyone except those explicitly listed in the Not Allowed list to be able to create top-level folders. Alternatively, select the List option and specify users who can create top-level folders. To specify a distribution list, click the Modify button and select recipients from the Global Address List or any other recipients container.

FIG. 24.34

The Top Level Folder Creation page, listing those recipients allowed to create top-level folders and those who are explicitly denied the capability to do so.

3. Specify any recipients who shouldn't be allowed to create top-level folders, even if they're a member of an allowed distribution list. You also can explicitly deny some recipients if you selected the All option in step 2.

4. Click OK to register your changes.

Setting Properties for Storage Warnings   In the Information Store Site Configuration Properties sheet, you can set options for storage warnings. In most sites, it's appropriate to set some limits on the amount of information that can be kept in mailboxes and public folders. You can set these limits by using the Advanced page of the property sheet for mailboxes and public folders. It's inevitable that sooner or later some limits will be exceeded. Exchange Server can automatically send warnings to mailbox owners or public folder contacts apprising them of the condition. You can specify the schedule for sending these warnings.

To set properties for storage warnings, follow these steps:

1. Open the Information Store Site Configuration Properties sheet.

2. On the Storage Warnings page (see Figure 24.35), select an option to specify the frequency for sending storage warnings:

   • Select Never if you don't want to send any warnings.

   • Always sends warnings every 15 minutes.

   • Selected Times causes storage warnings to be sent based on the schedule you indicate in the grid in step 3.

Part
V

Ch
24

FIG. 24.35

Configuring storage-limit warnings for recipients in the Storage Warnings page.

3. Select specific times for each day of the week that storage warnings should be sent. By default, the grid shows one-hour intervals. Select the 15 Minute option to cause the grid display to show 15-minute intervals if you want to have somewhat finer control over when warnings are sent.

4. Click OK to register your changes.

Setting Up Site Addressing

Clearly, some of the most important elements of a messaging system are components that generate and manage e-mail addresses and calculate the appropriate routes to use when transferring messages. Exchange Server automatically sets up default e-mail addresses and uses these defaults to generate new e-mail addresses as recipients are added to the system. Although the default values may be correct, it's prudent to check the site-addressing parameters before you add recipients so that they have correct address information from the start. You can regenerate e-mail addresses for recipients based on changed address defaults at a later time, if necessary. You also can regenerate routing tables as needed. Regenerating routing tables is particularly important when new elements that affect routing, such as a new connector, are added to a site.

To review and modify site addressing properties, follow these steps:

1. Start Exchange Administrator, if necessary, and connect to a server in the site you want to administer.

2. In the window's container area (the left pane), find the site you want to administer. Click the plus sign next to the site name to expand the display if it's not already open. Select the Configuration container. In the contents area (the right pane), you should see the Site Addressing object.

3. Double-click the Site Addressing object to open its property sheet.

4. On the General page (see Figure 24.36), specify the server that will calculate the routing table for the site. This routing table then is replicated to all other servers in the site. Select the server you want to use in the Routing Calculation Server drop-down list.

FIG. 24.36

Specifying the server generating the routing table on the General page of the Site Addressing Properties sheet.

5. You also can mark a check box to indicate that this Exchange Server site should Share Address Space with Other X.400 Systems. This feature is especially useful when there's a migration period, or when coexistence with another non-Microsoft X.400-based system is needed.

6. The Site Addressing page shows the partial e-mail addresses generated from the organization and site names you specified during installation (see Figure 24.37). If these names contain special characters that aren't permitted in an address or you need to make other changes, select an address type and click Edit. Change the partial address and click OK.

FIG. 24.37

Displaying partial e-mail addresses for generating new recipient addresses.

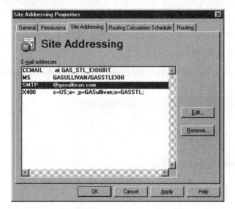

7. The Routing Calculation Schedule page (see Figure 24.38) works in much the same way as the storage warnings page does. Simply select an option for Never, Always, or Selected Times:

- If you choose Selected Times, indicate on the schedule grid when this calculation should occur.

Part

V

Ch

24

- The Always option causes routing information to begin recalculation again as soon as it completes, adding a significant load to the routing calculation server you set on the General page. This level of recalculation is overkill for most sites.

- The Never option lets you manually start the routing recalculation whenever you make changes that necessitate the task. (Routing recalculation is done on the Routing page.)

FIG. 24.38

Specifying when new routing tables should be built on a regular basis on the Routing Calculation Schedule page.

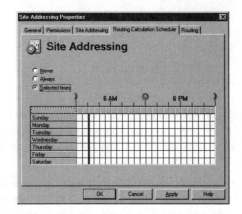

8. The Routing page show the routing table for a site (see Figure 24.39). The routing table is built with information from the Address Space property pages of any connectors or gateways installed in your site and those from connected sites. Select an entry and click Details to see the route, including various hops, that a message would take to reach a destination with a particular address type. To manually force a rebuild of the routing table, click Recalculate Routing.

9. Click OK when you've finished making changes to the Site Addressing Properties sheet.

FIG. 24.39

The Routing page of the Site Addressing Properties sheet showing the routing table for a site.

Configuring Your Servers with Exchange Administrator

You've learned how to set properties that apply globally to services throughout a site. Now you learn how to set properties for a specific server. In some cases, the properties are the same as the site properties you already set and simply provide a more granular level of control by letting you set the properties on individual servers to different values. Also, some properties must be set on a server-by-server basis and can't be specified on a site level.

First, you learn how to set the properties of the server object itself, and then to change the properties of the various services running on that server—the Directory Service, the Information Stores (public and private), the System Attendant, and the MTA.

Most of the time, you don't need to change the server object's properties. You can use the Database Paths page of the server object's property sheet to specify where Exchange Server's various files should be located. This activity is best performed with Performance Optimizer, however, which does actual speed testing to determine the best location for each element and then moves it to the appropriate place. The most likely change you might make to a server object's properties is to change logging levels or add a service to the list of monitored services. Both items can play a role in diagnosing problems with a particular server.

Part
V

Ch
24

To view or modify the properties for the server object for a particular server, follow these steps:

1. Start Exchange Administrator, if necessary, and connect to a server in the site you want to administer.
2. In the window's container area (the left pane), find the site you want to administer. Click the plus sign next to the site name to expand the display if it isn't already open. Click the plus sign next to the Configuration object to expand its display. You should see the Servers object. Click the plus sign next to the Servers object to expand its display.
3. Select the server object you want to view or modify. From the File menu choose Properties to open the property sheet (see Figure 24.40).

N O T E   Double-clicking the server object doesn't open the property sheet for the server. You must choose Properties from the File menu. ■

4. To change the location of the various databases used by Exchange Server, click the Database Paths tab. As mentioned earlier, using Performance Optimizer to change these items is usually better, but you may need to move one or more of these items manually. Select the item you want to move and click Modify. A dialog appears that you can use to select the location for the object in question.
5. Click OK when you're satisfied with your selection.

N O T E   You can change the database paths for a server only by logging on to that server directly. You can't change the paths for a server you've connected to over the network. ■

FIG. 24.40

Setting server-specific properties for the server named HQSRV2.

6. A more common change that's made by using these pages is a change in the logging levels. If you're troubleshooting some difficulty with this server, you can select elements of the server that you want to watch closely and increase the logging level for that element. To change the logging levels for a server component, click the Diagnostics Logging tab (see Figure 24.41).

FIG. 24.41

Selecting an appropriate logging level for various components on the server from the Diagnostics Logging page.

7. Select the service for which you want to change logging levels. In the right list box, you see various categories of events associated with this service and the current levels. Select one or more of the categories you want to change and then select the appropriate option at the bottom of the dialog to set the new logging level. Click Apply to register your changes.

8. By default, the Directory Service, Information Store, and MTA are monitored on the Services page (see Figure 24.42). To add any other services, select them in the Installed Services list and click Add. You also can select services in the Monitored Services box and click Remove to remove them.

FIG. 24.42

Selecting Exchange
Server services to
be monitored.

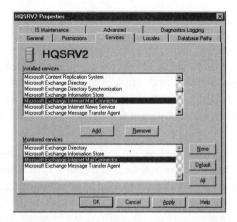

9. Click the Advanced tab (see Figure 24.43). Under normal circumstances, the directory contains an entry for every mailbox and public folder contained in the private and public information stores. No entry for any recipient object is missing a corresponding place in the information stores. In other words, they're consistent and agree with one another. If you ever need to restore the directory or an information store from a backup, the two may disagree with one another. Click the Adjust button to correct any inconsistencies.

10. Click OK to save your changes.

FIG. 24.43

Resolving inconsis-
tencies between the
Directory Service and
the Information Store
on the Advanced page.

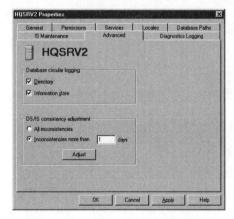

Setting Up Recipients

Clearly, one of the most important tasks you need to perform as an Exchange Server administrator is setting up recipients. This includes not only standard mailboxes for users on this system, but also distribution lists, custom recipients from other messaging systems, and public folders.

Before you actually create new recipients, you should review two items to make sure that they're set properly. These settings simplify the process, and ensuring that they're correct now helps avoid having to individually correct every newly created recipient later. You've already learned how to check the partial e-mail addresses used to generate e-mail addresses for new recipients. The Site Addressing object for this task is located in the Configuration container for the site. Although you can use the property sheet for this object to change this later and regenerate new e-mail addresses for all your recipients, it's best to get it right before defining new recipients. See "Setting Up Site Addressing" earlier in this chapter.

You also should check the Auto-Naming options, which let you define the manner in which default display names and aliases are created for new recipients. These options aren't properties of a site or a server, but rather are defined for use by an administrator using Exchange Administrator on a particular computer. Any new recipients created through Exchange Administrator on that computer reflect the options that have been set. You can change the options at any time to reflect new defaults.

To define Auto-Naming options, follow these steps:

1. Start Exchange Administrator, if necessary, and connect to a server in the site you want to administer.

2. Choose Options from the Tools menu to open the Options dialog (see Figure 24.44).

FIG. 24.44

Setting Auto-Naming defaults and Permissions options for Exchange Administrator running on the local computer.

3. Set options for Display Name Generation and Alias Name Generation. The options represent various alternatives with examples of each one. Select the option corresponding to the method you desire. If you want, you can create a custom entry by using the special character strings described in the bottom panel of the dialog.

4. Click OK to register your changes.

You're now ready to create new recipients. You can do so in various ways, all which lead to the same result. You can create a new recipient by using the following tools:

- Exchange Administrator
- Windows NT User Manager, which creates a new mailbox for a user at the same time you create a new Windows NT user ID

  ▶ **See** "Working with User Manager for Domains," **p. 442**

- Various extraction, importing, and migration tools that are available to facilitate the creation of large numbers of users in a single operation

In the following sections, you learn how to use Exchange Administrator to create a mailbox for use by e-mail administrators and how to create a mailbox at the same time a user account is created with User Manager for Domains. You also learn how to extract a list of Windows NT users from a domain controller to create accounts for multiple users at once and how to create a template mailbox with address and phone information that can be copied as new recipients are created. Other extraction and migration tools are available, and Microsoft continues to work on new migration tools for additional foreign messaging systems. These tools are not covered in this book, but you can find more information on them in the *Microsoft Exchange Server Migration Guide*, part of the documentation available for Exchange Server.

Part
V

Ch
24

Creating an Administrator's Mailbox

You may want to create a separate Administrator's mailbox to use as a dead-letter recipient and as a target for help requests. The Windows NT accounts for several administrators can be granted permissions to use the mailbox. By using the Inbox Assistant or the Delivery Options property page described later, you can create a rule to forward messages directed at this mailbox to the personal mailbox of the administrator now "on call." If administrators don't want their personal mailbox cluttered with e-mail administrator requests, they can simply create a profile for the Administrator's mailbox and open it directly.

N O T E The property that allows users to act as administrators for Exchange Server isn't the mailbox they're assigned to, but the Windows NT account used to log on. For many administrative tasks, users don't even need the use of a mailbox. Permissions to objects in the directory hierarchy are assigned to Windows NT accounts rather than mailboxes. ▮

To create an administrator's mailbox and grant permissions for several Windows NT accounts to share it, follow these steps:

1. Start Exchange Administrator, if necessary, and connect to a server in the site you want to administer.
2. Select the recipients container in which you want to create the mailbox. You might use the site's default recipients container, for example, or the recipients container for a particular server.
3. Choose New Mailbox from the File menu to open the property sheet for a new mailbox (see Figure 24.45).

FIG. 24.45

The property sheet that allows you to set up a new mailbox for one or more users.

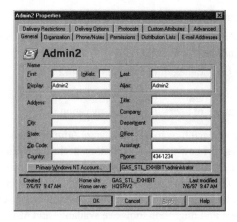

4. Enter appropriate information in the Name section. If this mailbox is shared, you may want to skip the First, Initials, and Last text boxes and simply enter a title (such as Administrator) in the Display and Alias text boxes. The Display name is used for Exchange Administrator's directory listing and the address book seen by users; the Alias name is used to create e-mail addresses for this mailbox.

5. Click the Primary Windows NT Account button and select an account to use this mailbox. For an administrator's mailbox, you may want to have the Administrator account from the Windows NT domain or the master domain be the primary account for this mailbox. You can still give permissions to other accounts to use it on a regular basis, but you'll have the Administrator account as a backup.

6. All other settings on the General page are optional. Fill them in as appropriate and then click the Organization tab (see Figure 24.46).

FIG. 24.46

Indicating the manager and direct reports of the user of this mailbox on the Organization page.

7. The Organization page is less useful for shared generic mailboxes. You may want to indicate the manager responsible for e-mail administrators as a group. Click the Phone/Notes tab (see Figure 24.47).

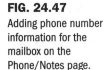

FIG. 24.47

Adding phone number information for the mailbox on the Phone/Notes page.

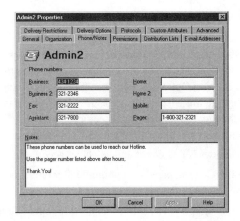

8. For a shared mailbox, you can indicate a shared hotline or pager number that's passed to the person now on call. This page, as well as the General, Organization, Distribution Lists, and E-mail Addresses pages, is visible in the Address Book on every client workstation. This is therefore a convenient way to distribute any phone numbers associated with e-mail administrators. Click the Permissions tab.

9. As you learned earlier in the section "Granting Administrative Permissions to Other Windows NT Accounts," you can grant permissions to any object in the directory. The Permissions property page functions in the same manner as other permissions pages. Click the Add button and add the Windows NT accounts of administrators who will share this account.

10. One additional option you may want to set is on the Delivery Options page. Rather than use the Inbox Assistant to forward messages to the on-call administrator, you can set another mailbox as an alternate recipient. Mark the Deliver Messages to Both Recipient and Alternate Recipient check box to keep a record of all messages received in this mailbox. If someone is the primary person on call for long periods of time, this may be a more efficient means of forwarding mail than the Inbox Assistant.

    You may add this recipient to any appropriate distribution lists, but you should avoid using this as a personal mailbox. Each administrator should still have his own private mailbox and use this only for e-mail administration tasks.

11. The mailbox is now ready. Click OK to create the mailbox.

Creating User Mailboxes with Exchange Administrator

To create a mailbox for a standard user, follow these steps:

1. Start Exchange Administrator, if necessary, and connect to a server in the site you want to administer.

2. Select the recipients container in which you want to create the mailbox. You might use the site's default recipients container, for example, or the recipients container for a particular server.

Part

V

Ch

24

3. From the File menu choose New Mailbox. The property sheet for a new mailbox appears.

4. Enter appropriate information in the Name section. Fill in the First, Initials, and Last text boxes; the Display and Alias text boxes are generated according to the rules you specified in the Auto-Naming Options dialog (see "Setting Up Recipients" earlier in this chapter). You can override the Display name or the Alias name if you want. The Display name is used for Exchange Administrator's directory listing and the Address Book seen by users; the Alias name is used to create e-mail addresses for this mailbox.

5. Click the Primary Windows NT Account and select an account to use this mailbox.

6. All other settings on the General page are optional. Fill them in as appropriate and click the Organization tab.

7. You can indicate the manager and any other people who report directly to the owner of this mailbox. Click the Phone/Notes tab.

8. Enter phone numbers and any notes that you want for the user of this mailbox. The Phone/Notes page, as well as the General, Organization, Distribution List Membership, and E-mail Addresses pages, is visible in the Address Book on every client workstation. This is, therefore, a convenient way to distribute any phone numbers associated with users. Click the Distribution Lists tab (see Figure 24.48).

FIG. 24.48

Adding a mailbox to one or more distribution lists and displaying any lists of which you're now a member on the Distribution Lists page.

9. Add this recipient to any appropriate distribution lists. Click Modify to open a dialog for this purpose. You can select predefined distribution lists from any recipients container and then return to the property sheet. Click the Advanced tab of the property sheet (see Figure 24.49).

 TIP To suppress a mailbox from displaying in the Address Book, make it "hidden" by marking the Hide from Address Book check box on the Advanced page of the recipient's property sheet. This technique is especially useful if service accounts or administrator accounts have associated mailboxes that most users shouldn't use.

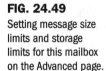

FIG. 24.49

Setting message size limits and storage limits for this mailbox on the Advanced page.

10. In the Message Sizes section, specify the maximum size of incoming or outgoing messages allowed for users of this mailbox. You also can set storage limits for this mailbox.

N O T E To set message size limits and storage limits for all mailboxes on a server, use the MTA's General property page and the Private Information Store's General property page, as described earlier in the section "Configuring Your Servers with Exchange Administrator." ■

11. The mailbox is now ready. Click OK to create the mailbox.

Creating Mailboxes with User Manager for Domains

When you installed Exchange Server, the User Manager for Domains utility provided with Windows NT was updated to provide new capabilities. You can create mailboxes for new users at the same time their Windows NT account is created. If you want to do this as a default option, you can launch User Manager and choose Options from the Exchange menu. Mark the check box labeled Always Create an Exchange Mailbox When Creating Windows NT Accounts.

After you enable this option, you can create a mailbox as you create a new user by following these steps:

1. Start User Manager for Domains. Notice that an Exchange menu is added to the program's menu bar. If this menu isn't visible, you need to log on to an Exchange Server machine or install Exchange Administrator on the computer you're using.

2. Choose New User from the User menu. Enter appropriate account information in the New User dialog. Click Add. The Connect to Server dialog appears.

3. Enter the name of the Exchange server that should contain this new mailbox. You can easily move mailboxes by using the Advanced property page for a recipient in Exchange Administrator (or choose Move Mailbox from the Tools menu) if you later need to move it.

Part
V

Ch
24

4. A property sheet appears. Fill in this sheet exactly as you would when using Exchange Administrator as described earlier in the section "Creating Mailboxes with Exchange Administrator."

Creating a Recipient Template for Use with Directory Import

If you're adding Exchange Server to an existing Windows NT domain or to another type of network that's supported with migration tools, you can automate the process of creating user accounts. You can extract the list of users defined on the network and use that list as the basis for a directory import process. The Exchange Server directory contains more detailed information than is provided on most networks, so you may want to use a recipient template to complete some of the information shared by a group of users. For example, if a large group of users shares the same address information or a common phone number (for a main switchboard), you can create a mailbox with only common fields completed among the group. Then during the import process described in the next section, you can specify this mailbox as the recipient template.

Create the mailbox following the standard procedures outlined earlier in the section "Creating Mailboxes with Exchange Administrator." You need to complete the mandatory fields (Display and Alias) required by Exchange Server, but they're not be applied to new mailboxes when this mailbox is used as a template. Then complete those fields that are shared by many users, such as the street address, city, state, and so on. Then proceed with the next section.

Using Directory Import to Create Mailboxes

As previously mentioned, Microsoft has created a variety of migration tools to facilitate the process of implementing Exchange Server, and new migration tools may be added in the future. By using these tools, you can extract the list of users that are defined for a network and use it to create new mailboxes. This section describes how to extract a list of users from a Windows NT domain and then use it as the basis for creating new mailboxes.

To extract a list of users from a Windows NT domain, follow these steps:

1. Start Exchange Administrator, if necessary, and connect to a server in the site you want to administer.

2. From the Tools menu choose Extract Windows NT Account List to open the Windows NT User Extraction dialog (see Figure 24.50).

FIG. 24.50

Extracting domain user accounts with the Windows NT User Extraction dialog.

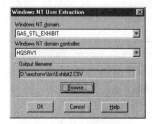

3. From the Windows NT Domain drop-down list, select the name of the domain from which you want to extract user accounts. Select the Primary Domain Controller or a Backup Domain Controller in the Windows NT Domain Controller drop-down list.

4. Enter a fully qualified path name for the file you want to create, or click Browse and use the resulting dialog to select a directory and create a file name.

5. Click OK. A dialog appears that reports progress during the extraction. If you have a relatively small domain, this dialog may appear only momentarily.

6. The NT User Extractor Complete dialog appears, providing an error status report, if any, on the extraction process. Click OK.

The file that results, with a default .csv extension, is a text file that you can read and modify with any text editor. The function and syntax of the various components are relatively obvious. The identifier `~Server` is replaced on import with the name of the server where the import operation is being performed and becomes the default home server for the newly created mailboxes. If you want to use a different home server, you can replace `~Server` with the name of an Exchange server in your site before importing the list.

To do a directory import operation for automatically creating new mailboxes, follow these steps:

1. Start Exchange Administrator, if necessary, and connect to a server in the site you want to administer.

2. From the Tools menu choose Directory Import. The Directory Import dialog appears (see Figure 24.51).

Part
V

Ch
24

FIG. 24.51

Specifying the extraction file to import, a recipients template, and the recipients container for the new mail-boxes in the Directory Import dialog.

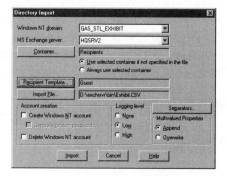

3. Click Import File and browse for the file you just created or any other appropriate import file you want to use. Click OK to return to the Directory Import dialog.

4. Select the recipients container in which you want to create the new mailboxes. If you're using a recipients template as described earlier in the section "Creating a Recipient Template for Use with Directory Import," click Recipient Template and select the mailbox you want to use as a template from the Global Address List or other recipients container.

5. You shouldn't use the options in the Account Creation section in the context described here. It's possible, however, to create a .csv file from another database, or even manually, and use it to create mailboxes and corresponding Windows NT accounts at the same time. In such a situation, mark the Create Windows NT Account check box.

6. Click Import. A dialog appears that reports progress during the import operation. If you have a relatively small list of users, this dialog may appear only momentarily.

7. The Directory Import Complete dialog appears, providing an error status report, if any, on the extraction process. Click OK.

The new mailboxes now appear in Exchange Administrator's window, in the contents area for the container in which they were created. They also are added to the Global Address List and now can be added to any distribution lists in which they should be included.

Creating Distribution Lists

When a group of recipients is frequently the target of the same information, the group can be put into a distribution list. The group then can be addressed with a single recipient name, rather than each individual recipient be included in the To: or CC: line of a message. Like custom recipients, distribution lists can be created in the directory by an administrator, or personal distribution lists can be added to users' Personal Address Books.

To create a distribution list, follow these steps:

1. Start Exchange Administrator, if necessary, and connect to a server in the site you want to administer.

2. Select the recipients container in which you want to create the distribution list. You might use the site's default recipients container, for example, or the recipients container for a particular server.

3. From the File menu choose New Distribution List to open a property sheet for the new distribution list (see Figure 24.52).

FIG. 24.52

The property sheet for a distribution list.

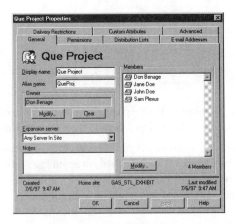

4. Enter a Display Name and Alias Name for the distribution list. These required names serve the same function for distribution lists as they do for mailboxes.

5. In the Owner section, click Modify to select a recipient to act as the owner of this address list.

 TIP The owner of a distribution list can modify the members of the address list by using the Exchange Client program. Exchange administrators can modify the member list by using Exchange Administrator as you're doing now.

6. In the Members section, click Modify to select the members of this distribution list. The Distribution List dialog appears (see Figure 24.53).

FIG. 24.53
Selecting list recipients in the Distribution List dialog.

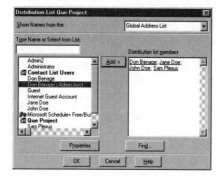

7. Select names in the list box on the left and click Add to move them into the Distribution List Members list on the right. You can select any recipient and click Properties if you want to check a recipient for further identification, and you can use the Find button to search for recipients matching certain criteria in the specified address book.

8. The other pages on the property sheet are similar to normal mailboxes, with a few differences. In particular, the Advanced page lets you specify Distribution List options you may want to consider.

9. The Distribution Lists page lets you make this distribution list a member of another dis-tribution list, thereby *nesting* the lists. At times, nesting is appropriate. For example, you might have a distribution list for each department and include all of them in a dis-tribution list for the entire organization. You should avoid nesting too deeply, however, or you may cause some recipients to receive multiple copies of messages.

10. When you've finished entering information into the property pages, click OK to create the distribution list.

From Here...

This chapter provided only a brief overview of Exchange Server's client/server messaging capabilities. A full exposition of the features of Exchange requires a book in itself. Step-by-step procedures were provided for installing Exchange Server, using Exchange Administrator to configure your server, installing the Exchange client programs, and adding Exchange mailboxes for new user accounts. The chapter closed with a short section on using Directory Import to automatically create many mailboxes in one operation. For more information relating to topics covered in this chapter, refer to these chapters:

- Chapter 13, "Managing User and Group Accounts," describes how to use Windows NT Server 4.0's User Manager for Domains, take advantage of the new Add User Accounts and Group Management wizards, and utilize the built-in user groups of Windows NT.

- Chapter 17, "Distributing Network Services with Domains," covers Windows NT Server's trusted domains and other distributed networking features that allow a single-user logon for multiple network servers and server-based applications, such as Exchange, running on LANs and WANs.

- Chapter 19, "Managing Remote Access Service," explains how to configure Windows NT Server 4.0's RAS component to support dial-in access by mobile users to Exchange mail.

Administering Clients with Systems Management Server 1.2

This chapter describes the fundamentals of Microsoft Systems Management Server 1.2, including its key components and how these components are integrated in LAN and WAN environments. This basic understanding is necessary for IS staff planning to implement SMS, because it's a complex product with extensive capabilities. When you achieve a basic understanding of SMS, you can plan the customization of SMS to suit your network environment.

The key factors in a successful SMS system design and rollout are an understanding of how SMS operates and a thorough knowledge of your LAN and WAN topology. Some functions performed by SMS are bandwidth-critical, so where you place SMS servers and how you define their functions has a significant impact on the network performance. If you're planning on an enterprise-wide SMS rollout, as you read this chapter you gain insight into how each component of SMS fits into your overall network strategy and how SMS affects your network operations.

The features and capabilities of SMS 1.2

SMS offers software distribution and inventory, hardware inventory, remote client control, and customized reports.

System requirements for SMS

SMS requires 32M of dedicated RAM and prior installation of Microsoft SQL Server.

Installing SMS on a Windows NT server

You install the Primary (Central) Site first, and then install Secondary Sites to distribute the SMS workload.

Designing SMS queries

SMS queries let you find networked PCs having particular hardware configurations or software installed.

Installing SMS software on client PCs

SMS modifies Windows NT Server logon scripts to automatically install SMS client software the next time each user logs on.

ON THE WEB

Detailed recommendations for configuring SMS installations are available from Microsoft's SMS home page at **http://www.microsoft.com/SMSmgmt/**. ■

Introducing Systems Management Server

Organizations spend large amounts of money on upgrading, maintaining, and supporting the hardware and software for desktop computing. The PC support group typically is forced to revisit priorities in order to resolve end-user issues and, at the same time, design, deploy, and maintain new enterprise-wide applications and infrastructure. At the same time, PC support often must deal with budget restrictions and staff reductions as a result of downsizing, out-sourcing, or re-engineering.

Some of the major issues that PC support staff face are

- Quick end-user support and problem resolution
- Support of multiple offices in a LAN and WAN environment
- Support for multiple platforms and desktop operating systems
- Installing or upgrading many PCs with new or updated software in a very short period
- Support for multiple networking protocols
- Maintaining the hardware and software inventory for all desktop PCs

Microsoft Systems Management Server version 1.2, released August 19, 1996, is the third major release of this application to address these issues. Following are the most important new features of SMS 1.2:

- Remote control of Windows NT 3.51 or 4.0 Workstation and Server. You can log on to Windows NT machines remotely. (Version 1.1 added Windows 95 remote control capabilities.)
- Inventory collection runs as a service on Windows NT machines. A user doesn't need to be logged on to collect software and hardware inventory details.
- Improved performance loading Management Information Format (MIF) files into the central SMS database.
- Program Group Control (PGC) provided for Windows 95 and Office 95.
- Simple Network Management Protocol (SNMP) trap receiving and forwarding, so you can specify SMS and Windows NT events to be forwarded to network management applications, such as HP OpenView. You also can receive traps from routers, hubs, and other active network components.

  ▶ **See** "Installing the SNMP Service," **p. 577**

Systems Management Server provides centralized management of the networked PCs. Centralized management includes identification, control, maintenance, and software upgrades of all PCs on the LAN or WAN. The following sections describe the primary features of SMS 1.1 and above, its server requirements, and its support for network operating systems and protocols.

Remote Control and Troubleshooting

Remote control and troubleshooting (also called *helpdesk*) functions let you view a client PC's display and control the client's keyboard and mouse. The helpdesk feature lets you run the PC without being physically present at the client's location. You also can conduct a text chat session with users, remotely execute programs, copy files, or even reboot the client operating system. End-user support requests are addressed from a central location, thereby saving valuable time and resources.

N O T E SMS 1.1 was limited to remote control of MS-DOS, Windows 3.x, Windows for Workgroups 3.1+, and Windows 95 clients. SMS 1.2 lets you remotely control machines running Windows NT 3.51 and 4.0. ■

Hardware and Software Inventory

Part
V

Ch
25

The capability to take an inventory of hardware and software installed on client PCs (an important part of *asset management*) is one of the features most requested by IS technical support staff. This SMS feature is installed automatically when the SMS client components are installed on client machines. The inventory agent identifies the hardware and low-level software on each desktop PC and reports the results back to the server. A similar feature included with SMS, the Audit package, also allows complete software audits. Asset management is used with SMS's software distribution and installation features, as well as its software metering capabilities.

Software Distribution and Installation

SMS's software distribution and installation feature sets up applications on individual PCs and servers at local and remote sites. You can initiate the delivery of a predefined software package to targeted systems by using drag-and-drop methods. You also can define targeted groups of machines to create customized distribution and installation procedures.

A package can be any type of file, including an executable, so SMS can be used to run a program automatically without installing it on the targeted machine. For example, you can package an antivirus program to run every day at midnight. With the asset management feature of SMS, you can identify and deliver a package only if a specified criterion is met by the destination client, if desired.

Network Protocol Analysis

Systems Management Server includes an extended version of Windows NT Server 4.0's Network Monitor tool. By using this tool, you can watch for network congestion caused by excess activity, or diagnose problems caused by low-level networking problems. SMS's Network Monitor lets you remotely capture, filter, decode, analyze, edit, and replay network protocol packets, including TCP/IP, IPX/SPX, NetBIOS, AppleTalk, NCP, and SMB packets. You also can set up dedicated network monitoring workstations and even monitor remote segments by running a remote capture agent in a session of a client running Windows NT Workstation. The primary differences between the SMS and Windows NT Server 4.0 versions of Network Monitor is that the SMS version can connect to remote Network Monitor agents across routed networks and can monitor activity involving computers other than the one on which it's running.

▶ **See** "Using Network Monitor," **p. 570**

Remote Performance Monitoring

When using SMS's primary administration tool, you can directly initiate Performance Monitor when looking at the details of a Windows NT workstation or server.

▶ **See** "Using Performance Monitor," **p. 530**

Customized Data Analysis, Transfer, and Reporting

Systems Management Server relies on a SQL Server database named SMS to store data gathered by SMS. This database contains 84 user tables. The Identification_SPEC table contains one record for each PC for which you install the SMS client; other related tables store information on each PC's hardware and installed software.

You can design custom reports by using Microsoft Access, Visual Basic, or any other ODBC-compliant application development tool that can query the SMS database. For example, you can create an Access or Visual Basic front end to extract PC inventory data from the SMS database and to generate a new table compatible with the asset management features of an accounting application.

N O T E   SMS includes the SMS Database View Generator (Smsview.exe) program, which generates SQL Server views on the SMS database. Views are much easier to use for generating reports than directly accessing SMS tables with SQL Server. ■

Differences Between SMS and Network Management Applications

Microsoft doesn't position SMS as an enterprise network management application. Network management software such as HP OpenView or Computer Asz   ciates CA-Unicenter TNG typically discover and then maintain the internetwork devices such as hubs and routers. A network management tool can use SNMP to turn on and off ports of hubs and routers. SMS, on the other hand, discovers and maintains only the end-node devices, primarily PC clients. This distinction is important between these two types of products because they complement one another, and both are necessary for large-scale network management.

▶ **See** "Considering Network Management Needs," **p. 69**

N O T E Microsoft and Computer Associates announced in 1996 an agreement to collaborate on an enterprise network management system based on CA-Unicenter TNG and Microsoft's Internet technologies, such as Internet Explorer, ActiveX controls, the HyperMedia Management Schema (HMMS), and HyperMedia Management Protocol (HMMP) for network management. HMMS is designed to make network management information available via Web browsers. Subsequently, the Desktop Management Task Force (DMTF) Common Information Model (CIM) replaced HMMS.

On March 19, 1997, Microsoft and Hewlett-Packard issued a joint press release describing HP's plans to market SMS "as part of an OpenView IT/Administration package." According to the press release, "Microsoft will distribute, with the next major release of Microsoft Systems Management Server, HP OpenView IT/Administration and IT/Operations agents." HP promises to deliver the Windows NT version of OpenView IT/Operations by the end of 1997. ▦

ON THE WEB

You can read the entire Microsoft-HP joint press release at **http://www.microsoft.com/corpinfo/press/1997/Mar97/mshpjtpr.htm**.

Server Requirements

A server running SMS 1.2 must meet the following minimum specifications:

- Windows NT Server 3.5+ or 4.0
- SQL Server for Windows NT 4.21+
- An Intel-based system with a 486/66 or faster processor, or a RISC system supported by Windows NT
- 32M of memory dedicated to SMS
- A fixed disk with at least 100M free and an NTFS partition for installing SMS (SMS won't install on a FAT partition)
- CD-ROM drive
- Network adapter card
- All requirements for running Windows NT Server 3.5+ or 4.0

N O T E Systems Management Server processes may be divided among multiple servers to reduce the requirements on a single server in large installations. The preceding minimum requirements are for a relatively small SMS installation. A Pentium PC is strongly recommended, and 64M of memory should be available, as a minimum, if SQL Server is to be run on the same server. Considerably more disk space should be allocated for package creation and distribution. ▦

Part
V

Ch
25

Supported Networks

Systems Management Server is supported on the following local area networks:

- Windows NT Server
- Microsoft LAN Manager 2.1+
- Novell NetWare 3.1+ (requires installation of Gateway Service for NetWare)
  - ▶ **See** "Using Gateway Service for NetWare," **p. 642**
- IBM LAN Server 3.x and 4.0

Wide Area Network Options

Systems Management Server supports the following WAN and remote access connection protocols:

- TCP/IP
- IPX/SPX
- Asynchronous dial-up
- ISDN
- X.25
- LU 6.2 (requires Microsoft SNA Server)

Clients Supported

SMS 1.2 supports the following clients:

- MS-DOS 5.0+
- Windows 3.1+
- Windows for Workgroups 3.11
- Windows 95
- Windows NT 3.x and 4.0 (remote control with SMS 1.2 requires Windows NT 3.51 or 4.0)
- Apple Macintosh System 7.x
- IBM OS/2 version 2.x, or OS/2 Warp

Planning for Systems Management Server

Planning is required to use SMS effectively. The planning requirement for SMS is similar in scope to that for Microsoft Exchange Server installations, described in Chapter 24, "Messaging with Microsoft Exchange Server 5.0." The following sections describe the topology of SMS sites and the SMS components you install at the sites.

ON THE WEB

Microsoft has published the "Systems Management Server (version 1.2) Concepts and Planning" guide, which also is included on the SMS 1.2 installation CD-ROM, at **http://www.microsoft.com/ smsmgmt/planguide.htm**. Various technical white papers on the use of SMS 1.2 are available from **http://www.microsoft.com/smsmgmt/whitepaper.htm**.

Enterprise Site Topology

Figure 25.1 illustrates an enterprise-wide, multiple-server SMS configuration with a number of roles for the SMS servers installed at each location. In this figure, the Chicago, New York City, and London servers are connected directly in a WAN environment. Each site has multiple clients connected via a LAN. The Milan site is supported by the London office.

FIG. 25.1

A typical enterprise topology of SMS sites.

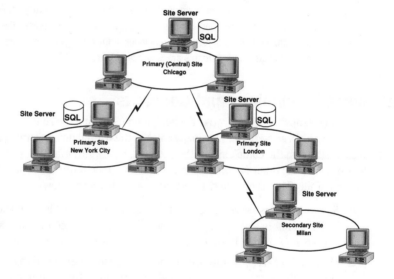

Part
V
Ch
25

For the purposes of SMS, a *site* is a group of servers and clients in a LAN or WAN environment that typically are located in a single geographical area. In Figure 25.1, Chicago, New York City, London, and Milan are all sites.

A *Primary Site* is one with a local SQL Server database. A Primary Site with a SQL Server connection to the SMS database is responsible for collecting all information from the nodes in that site. Chicago, New York City, and London are all Primary Sites.

A site without a local SQL Server installation, such as Milan, is called a *Secondary Site* and is supported by a Primary Site. All the information collected in a Secondary Site by SMS agents is reported to the Primary Site; therefore, bandwidth availability between primary and secondary sites is a major design consideration.

The SMS enterprise design also includes the concept of *parent* and *child* relationships. A parent site is one that has a Primary or Secondary Site as a child site. In Figure 25.1, Chicago and London are parent sites, and New York City, London, and Milan are child sites. A Primary Site can be a parent site if a Secondary Site is below it. A Primary Site can also be a child site. A Secondary Site, such as Milan, is always a child site.

SMS's hierarchical design has major advantages over a simple collection of Primary Sites. One key advantage is that all the reports can be sent to a central administration office to achieve centralized enterprise management. This site is called a *Central Site* and must be a Primary Site with access to SQL Server. All the sites in the SMS hierarchical structure report to the Central Site. A second advantage of a hierarchical design is that adding sites to an existing environment becomes a simple task, because a site can easily be added as a child in the hierarchy tree of the SMS installation.

N O T E Primary Sites most commonly are used where a site has local network administrators. Having their own primary server lets administrators use SMS to manage their site and any subsites but not control other sites beyond the boundaries of their designated responsibilities. Locations without designated administrators are Secondary Sites. ▓

Component Terminology and Concepts

After you establish your enterprise design, you must define the role of the SMS servers in these sites. SMS servers can play many roles in the overall design strategy. The selection of roles depends on the complexity of the network, bandwidth availability of the LAN and WAN, the workload, and other factors. You must first understand the SMS role of each possible server at a site. The terminology for SMS server roles is as follows:

- *Site Server.* This server is central to SMS. Each site must have at least one Site Server, which monitors and manages the site. The Site Server coordinates all the other servers, collects information from them, and provides instructions to them.

- *Distribution Server.* A software distribution environment needs a server that's responsible for distributing new or updated software to all the desired nodes. This is the responsibility of the Distribution Server. This server can run NetWare, Windows NT Server, IBM LAN Server, or Microsoft LAN Manager. The Distribution Server provides a copy of the software to one client machine, to a group of client machines, or to all client machines to which it connects. The Distribution Server can be (and often is) the Site Server.

- *Logon Server.* This server must be a domain controller, responsible for validating user logons. During execution of the SMS component of the logon script, the client puts the inventory details on the Logon Server. If the Logon Server is the Primary Site server, this information is placed in local SQL Server tables. If the Logon Server is a separate server, it acts as an agent and delivers all the information to the Site Server. The Logon Server also makes instructions available for clients to receive packages or to share applications.

■ *SQL Server.* As mentioned in previous sections, SMS requires SQL Server to provide the database component. The overall system is more efficient if all the servers have access to their own SQL Server installation to minimize reporting activity and network bandwidth. If you can't justify a SQL Server license at every site, you can use multiple Secondary Sites that report to the Primary Site. In the latter case, you must carefully analyze bandwidth usage.

■ *Helper Server.* Helper Servers are used to offload some of the processing from the Site Server. If you have a large environment and many clients, you can transfer some functions, such as the scheduler, despooler, inventory processor, and sender functions, from the Site Server to a Helper Server. The Helper Server lets you balance the load among machines running SMS to achieve better performance.

In smaller environments, a single server can be responsible for all the preceding roles. Installing SQL Server on the same machine as SMS (and dedicating it to SMS) usually provides better performance by avoiding LAN traffic constraints. In larger environments, however, multiple servers play specific roles to provide efficient and timely transfer of information and files to and from clients.

Installing Systems Management Server

Part **V**

Ch **25**

Systems Management Server must be installed on a Windows NT Primary or Backup Domain Controller (PDC or BDC) and, if a Primary Site, must have access to SQL Server locally or over a network. The first SMS installation must be a Primary Site and usually is the Central Site; after you install the Primary Site, you can install other primary and secondary sites that report to the Central Site.

▶ **See** "Understanding the Roles of Domain Controllers," **p. 608**

ON THE WEB

Microsoft provides a Reviewer's Guide for SMS 1.2 at **http://www.microsoft.com/SMSmgmt/revgd/**. This guide provides detailed installation instructions and user guidelines for evaluating SMS 1.2.

Creating a Service Account

Before you install SMS on any Windows NT server, you must create the user account for the SMS services. You create this account, typically called SMSAdmin, with User Manager for Domains as follows:

1. Open User Manager for Domains, and then choose New <u>U</u>ser from the <u>U</u>ser menu to open the New User dialog.

   ▶ **See** "Working with User Manager for Domains," **p. 442**

2. Type **SMSAdmin** as the Username, and then specify a Full Name, Description, and Password. (The password must not be the same as the value of Username.)

3. Clear the User Must Change Password at Next Logon check box, and mark the User Cannot Change Password and Password Never Expires check boxes (see Figure 25.2).

FIG. 25.2

Specifying the properties of the SMSAdmin account.

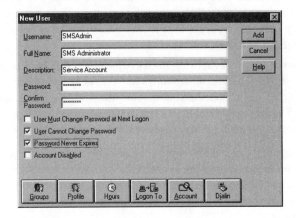

4. Click the Groups button to open the Group Memberships dialog, select Domain Admins in the Not Member Of list, and click Add. Select Domain Admins in the Member Of list, and then click Set to make Domain Admins the Primary Group (see Figure 25.3). Click OK twice to close the Group Memberships and New User dialogs.

FIG. 25.3

Adding the SMSAdmin account to the Domain Admins group.

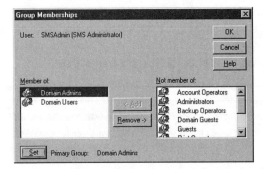

5. Select SMSAdmin in the Username list of User Manager for Domains' main window. From the Policies menu choose User Rights to open the User Rights Policy dialog. Mark the Show Advanced User Rights check box and select SMSAdmin in the Grant To list. Select Log On as a Service from the Right drop-down list, and click Add (see Figure 25.4). Click OK to close the dialog.

6. Exit User Manager for Domains.

FIG. 25.4
Adding the Log On as
a Service right to the
SMSAdmin account.

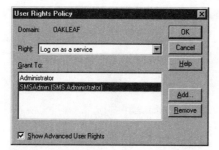

Setting Up SQL Server

You must specify that SQL Server (MSSQLServer) and SQL Executive start as a service during
Windows NT Server's boot process. Use Control Panel's Services tool to verify that the Startup
property of these two services is set to Automatic, and both services are started before installation of SMS. Chapter 23, "Running Microsoft SQL Server 6.5," covers installing and using SQL
Server 6.5.

If you intend to run SQL Server and SMS on the same Windows NT server, SMS creates the
SQL devices and databases automatically. If you run SQL Server on a separate Windows NT
server, you must manually create the SMSData and SMSLog devices with SQL Enterprise
manager. The default sizes of the SMSData and SMSLog devices are 45M and 8M, respectively.

▶ **See** "Creating and Managing Database Devices," **p. 850**

Installing Systems Management Server on the Primary Site Server

Systems Management Server installation takes 15 to 20 minutes. You must install SMS to an
NTFS partition. To install SMS, follow these steps:

1. Run SETUP.BAT from the \Smssetup folder of the distribution CD-ROM. This batch file
   determines which platform (x86, Alpha, or MIPS) to install and starts the Setup program.

2. Click Continue in the first message box, complete the Registration dialog entries, and
   click Continue to display the Installation Options dialog (see Figure 25.5). Click the
   Install Primary Site button.

3. Mark the I Agree That check box of the Licensing dialog and click OK. SMS offers only
   per-seat, not per-server, client licensing.

   ▶ **See** "Per-Seat vs. Per-Server Licensing," **p. 816**

4. Click Continue to bypass the dialog that describes the prerequisites for installing SMS.

5. In the Installation Directory dialog, accept the default or change the location of the folder
   to store the SMS files (see Figure 25.6). The drive must be formatted as NTFS. Click
   Continue.

FIG. 25.5

The Installation Options dialog for SMS.

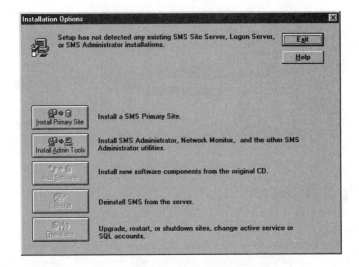

FIG. 25.6

Specifying the folder for installation of SMS's primary components.

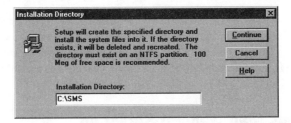

6. In the Setup Install Options dialog, click Continue to install the default Systems Management Server components (see Figure 25.7). Alternatively, you can specify installation options for other platforms by clicking the Custom button.

FIG. 25.7

The default installation options for SMS.

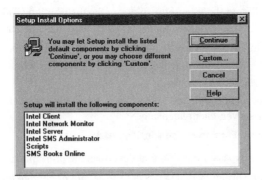

7. In the SQL Database Configuration dialog, type the password and confirmation password for the default sa (system administrator) account. The rest of the entries are completed for you with default values (see Figure 25.8). If you use a SQL Server installation on another machine, type the name of the server in the SQL Server Name text box. You can change the path, device file name, and size of the local SQL Server devices by clicking the Device Creation button to open the SQL Device Creation dialog (see Figure 25.9). Click Continue in the SQL Database Configuration dialog.

FIG. 25.8

Specifying the SQL Server name, logon account, password, database name, and devices.

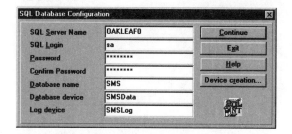

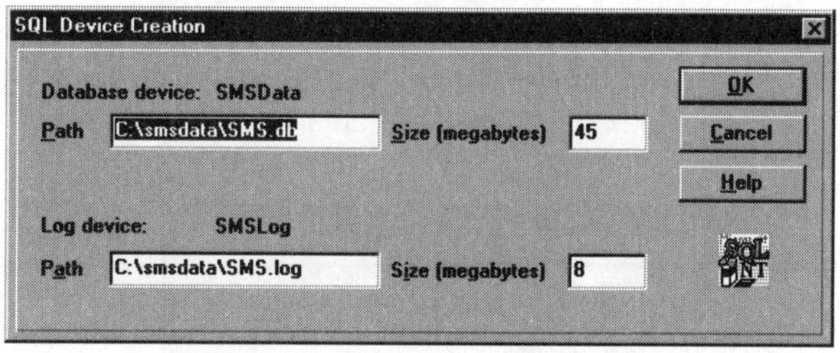

FIG. 25.9

Altering the location or size of the local SQL Server devices created for SMS.

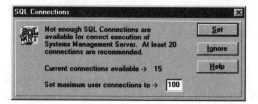

Part
V

Ch
25

8. If you haven't set a sufficient number of SQL Server connections (minimum of 20), the SQL Connections dialog appears. Enter a reasonable number of connections to service your users and SMS (see Figure 25.10). Click Set to continue.

FIG. 25.10

The message box that appears if you have fewer than 20 connections specified for the SQL Server installation used with SMS.

9. In the Primary Site Configuration Information dialog, type a three-character Site Code and a descriptive Site Name. Accept the default values for Site Server and Site Server Domain. For a conventional installation with Windows Networking or TCP/IP, mark the

Automatically Detect All Logon Servers check box. Type **SMSAdmin** in the Username text box and the password you assigned to SMSAdmin (see Figure 25.11). Click Continue.

FIG. 25.11

Specifying the configuration information for a Primary Site.

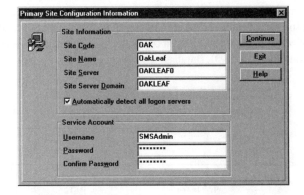

The Setup program copies files, completes the database installation, and starts the SMS services. A Setup Progress dialog (see Figure 25.12) displays the status of the installation, which usually takes about 10 to 15 minutes. When the SMS setup process is complete, click OK in the Setup Success message box to have the Setup program create a Start menu SMS program group. It isn't necessary to restart the server after installing SMS.

FIG. 25.12

The Setup Progress dialog near the end of the SMS installation process.

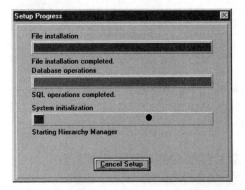

If you plan to install other Primary Sites, the process is basically the same as that described in the preceding steps. You must assign a unique code to each site. You also might want to use different database sizes, depending on the number of clients served at each Primary Site. The steps that let you group SMS sites into a hierarchy are detailed near the end of this chapter in the section "Building Sites for Enterprise Networks."

Using SMS Administrator

The Microsoft SMS Administrator application is SMS's primary management tool. To run SMS Administrator, follow these steps:

1. From the Start menu choose Programs, Systems Management Server, and SMS Administrator.

2. The Microsoft SMS Administrator Login dialog displays the SQL Server name, database, and logon ID that you last used (see Figure 25.13). Type the password for the SQL Server sa account and click OK.

FIG. 25.13

Specifying the parameters required to start SMS Administrator.

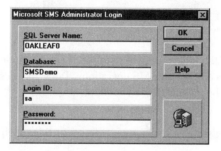

Part
V

Ch
25

N O T E If you haven't used SMS Administrator before, you also must provide the other details in the Microsoft SMS Administrator dialog. In the most common initial configuration, the database is named SMS, the server is the current machine's name, and the sa (system administrator) account is the initial logon ID. The sa account password for a new SQL Server installation is empty until you change it. ▪

3. The Open SMS Window dialog is intended for new users of SMS Administrator. (To prevent future appearances of this dialog, clear the Show this Dialog at Startup check box.) As you select the various window types, a description of the window appears (see Figure 25.14 and Table 25.1). Spend a few minutes reading the description for each window. For example, select Sites and click OK to display SMS Administrator with the Sites window active.

N O T E The SQLDemo database shown in Figure 25.13 is used in the following SMS Administrator examples. The SQL Server query (Sms.sql) and database (SmsDemo.dat) is included on the SMS Server 1.2 distribution CD-ROM. ▪

ON THE WEB

If you don't have SMS Server 1.2, you can save Sms.sql as a text file and download Smsdemo.dat from **http://www.microsoft.com/SMSmgmt/demodata.htm**. Installation instructions for SMSDemo are found at **http://www.microsoft.com/SMSmgmt/revgd/sms02e.htm**.

FIG. 25.14

Selecting the SMS window to display.

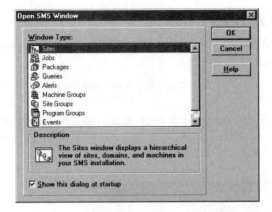

The SMS Administrator application is deceptively simple. It has 11 windows that you use to perform administrative duties or monitor SMS operations. Table 25.1 describes each window. The following sections describe the use of each window.

Table 25.1   SMS Administrator's Window Names and Descriptions

Window	Description
Sites	Displays a hierarchical view of sites, domains, and machines in your SMS installation
Jobs	Lets you create and administer jobs at your SMS installation
Packages	Manages software packages that SMS can inventory or install on any workstation
Queries	Manages stored queries used to locate assets and workstations
Alerts	Manages alerts used to monitor and act on change in your SMS system
Machine Groups	Lets you group servers and workstations together for administrative purposes
Site Groups	Lets you group sites together for administrative purposes
Program Groups	Lets you manage the contents of shared SMS program groups
Events	Lets you monitor the status and actions of other components in your SMS system
SQL Server Messages	Displays messages from SQL Server caused by SMS Administrator

Sites Window

The Sites window displays all the SMS sites in a hierarchical list. The right pane displays the next level of the hierarchy selected in the list. Figure 25.15 shows the site hierarchy from the SMSDemo database; the Canada and USA Primary Sites are expanded to show the first level of detail, their child sites, and the domains to which the sites belong.

FIG. 25.15

The Sites window of SMS Administrator displaying a partial expansion of the SMSDemo site hierarchy.

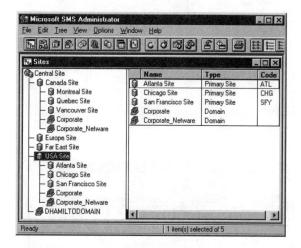

N O T E Secondary Sites are created by using the SMS Administrator on a Primary Site, selecting the server in the Sites window, and choosing New Item from the File menu. After you provide details for the server to be used, the Secondary Server is set up automatically. Setting up the Secondary Server usually takes 3 to 12 hours, depending on network speeds. ∎

Double-clicking an entry in the Sites list expands the hierarchy for the site. For example, Figure 25.16 shows in the right pane the client PCs of the Engineering domain of the San Francisco site. The right pane displays the NetBIOS Name of the computer, the SMSID (an SMS identification code), the most recent LogOn Name, the SystemType (client platform), and the SystemRole (workstation or server).

Double-clicking a client item in the right pane displays the Personal Computer Properties child window for the client (see Figure 25.17). You select the properties to view or actions to take in the Properties list. Most information in the Attribute and Value list is derived from performing SMS's PC inventory function. Table 25.2 lists the properties and actions available in the Personal Computer Properties window.

FIG. 25.16

The fully expanded hierarchy of the San Francisco site.

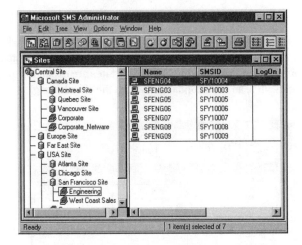

FIG. 25.17

Displaying network attributes and values in the Personal Computer Properties window.

Table 25.2 Properties and Actions Available in the Personal Computer Properties Window

Property/Action	Description
Identification	Displays the NetBIOS name, SMS Name, System Role and Type, and other identifying features of clients and server
Workstation Status	Displays the date and time of the Last Hardware Scan, Last Software Scan, Files Not Installed, and other status parameters
Processor	Displays the processor type and speed, and indicates whether the processor includes a floating-point coprocessor

Property/Action	Description
Operating System	Displays the DOS version (if applicable) and the Windows version running on the client
Network	Displays various information on the current network connection maintained by the client
Netcard	Displays the code for the network interface card ($EPRO for Intel EtherExpress 16 Pro)
Disk	Displays the type and size of each removable disk drive and each partition of fixed disk drive(s)
PC Memory	Displays the amount of RAM and the paging file size, if applicable
Serial Port	Displays serial port parameters for COM1 through COM4
Parallel Port	Displays parallel port parameters for installed parallel port adapters
Video	Displays the type of graphics adapter installed, the name of the manufacturer, and the adapter's BIOS date
Mouse	Displays information about the installed mouse driver
PC BIOS	Displays the BIOS Manufacturer, Category, and Release Date
IRQ Table	Displays the address and use of interrupts 0 through 15
Environment	Displays the content of each environment variable in the DOS environment
Help Desk	Lets you start the Remote Control, Remote Boot, Remote Chat, and related features
Diagnostics	Opens the Diagnostics window, which lets you query the current status of the machine's CMOS memory, hardware, and network connection
Network Monitor	Lets you start Network Monitor for the machine
User Information	Provides the full user name and logon ID of the machine's current or last user

Part

V

Ch

25

N O T E   In the case of the demonstration system used in these examples, you can display only properties that are stored in the SQLDemo database. Actions such as obtaining Diagnostics information or performing the Help Desk (remote control) function require the SMS client software to be installed on the client PC and an active network connection to the client. ■

Packages Window

A *package* is the very basic element for software distribution and software installation. It's used by a prescribed job, which delivers the package to a client. A package contains the information about the software, including the files in the software, configuration information, and identification information. When a package is prepared, you can install it on the client, install it on a server to be used as a shared application, or maintain inventory on the package. SMS has three general package properties: Workstation, Sharing, and Inventory.

Workstation Packages Workstation packages are used to install or run software on a workstation (the targeted client machine), so you must specify the commands and files needed by the package. The client uses a Package Command Manager (PCM) to initiate the installation or execution of the package.

PCM is installed and set up automatically when SMS is first set up on the client PC. PCM periodically checks with an SMS logon server to determine whether any packages are to be installed. If so, PCM pulls the package from the distribution server and follows the installation instructions. PCM allows the installation of the software on the workstation in two ways:

- It lets the end user decide when to install the package. PCM automatically notifies users of pending package installations. You also can specify a deadline so that the package is installed even if the user refuses to install the package during the prescribed period of time.

- It installs the package unattended overnight, if you set the job to become mandatory during the night. This process requires that the end user leave the client PC turned on.

Sharing Packages This method of software distribution is good for large sites with several servers. When sharing packages, the sharing software is installed on the distribution servers and users run the software from one of those servers. This method has several advantages, especially when used with SMS Program Group Control features:

- *Fault tolerance.* Another server can make the application available to the end user even if the file server that the end user normally utilizes isn't available.

- *Load balancing.* The distribution server used to provide the application is chosen at random from those now available, so all servers should get an equal load.

- *Metering.* Windows NT's ability to limit the number of users accessing a share can be used to limit the number of end users accessing the application.

- *Consistent end-user interface.* SMS provides users with program groups tailored to their requirements, regardless of the computers used to log on.

The Program Group Control functionality of SMS is responsible for checking the SMS logon server's applications database to see whether users who logged on have access to any server applications. This process occurs when users log on from any computer on the network. When validated, the Program Control Group builds and displays program groups and application icons.

When users launch an application, the Program Control Group checks with the SMS logon server application database to see which distribution servers have the application. It then connects the users to an available server.

The load-balancing and fault-tolerance features derive from the fact that the Program Control Group connects to any available application distribution server. As a result, you can install applications on several servers to allow multiple servicing points (load balancing) and ensure that users always have access to their network application (fault tolerance).

Inventory Packages The Inventory package defines the rules that SMS uses to identify, inventory, and collect applications and files on the local workstation. The packages you define for inventory are saved in the SMS database and appear in the Personal Computer Properties window of SMS Administrator for machines with that package.

Package Definition File A Package Definition File (PDF) is a text file containing predefined Workstations, Sharing, and Inventory property values for a package. To create a new package, you can choose Import from the File menu to open Package Properties dialog and use one of SMS's predefined PDFs to specify the properties for that package. SMS includes PDFs for some of the more popular applications, such as Microsoft Excel and Microsoft Word; other software publishers also create PDFs.

Figure 25.18 shows the creation of a new package for installation of Word 6.0c. Clicking the Sharing button lets you specify the location of the package and the share name (see Figure 25.19).

Part
V

Ch
25

FIG. 25.18
Creating a new package from a PDF file included with SMS.

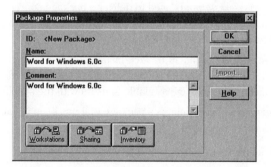

FIG. 25.19
Setting up the package source and specifying a server share name.

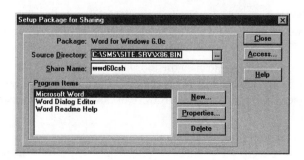

Jobs Window

After a package is created, it can be delivered to a targeted machine or set of machines with a job. The Jobs window displays these jobs (see Figure 25.20).

FIG. 25.20

Four System Jobs and one Share Package pending in SMS's Jobs window.

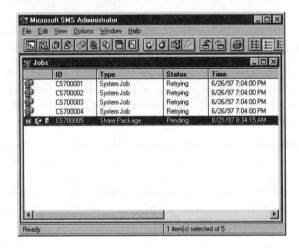

There are four types of jobs in SMS. SMS automatically creates one job type, *System Job*, to deal with configuration issues. Following are the three types of jobs that you can create:

- *Run Command on Workstation* is used to deliver a package source directory with the package command to the targeted workstation. The user runs the commands by choosing a package in the Package Command Manager.

- *Shared Package on Server* is an automated installation of a network application. The job sends the package source directory to a distribution server. Needed directories are shared, thus making the package available to users with the specified permissions.

- *Remove Package from Server* deletes a package that has been installed on one or more distribution servers.

To create a new job, follow these steps:

1. From the File menu choose Open, and select Jobs from the Open SMS Window dialog.

2. From the File menu choose New to open the Job Properties dialog. Type a brief description of the job in the Comment text box, and choose the Job Type from the drop-down list (see Figure 25.21).

3. Click the Details button to open the Job Details dialog. Select the Package for the job from the drop-down list and specify the Job Target, Send Phase, and Distribute Phase details (see Figure 25.22). Click OK twice to close the Job Details and Job Properties dialogs.

FIG. 25.21

Creating a new Share Package job.

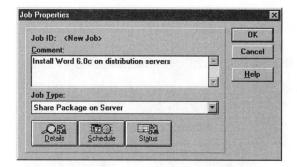

FIG. 25.22

Specifying the details for the new Share Package job.

Queries Window

In a large SMS installation, you need a flexible tool to let you easily search the database to find machines that match your required criteria. For example, you might want to find machines with the necessary disk space for a Windows 95 installation, Intel-based machines that run DOS, or machines that have been upgraded with a particular application.

Systems Management Server's Queries window lets you run queries to find clients meeting specific criteria and to see the appropriate details. The workstation information is collected by the inventory agent when the SMS client logs onto the network. The inventory information is saved in a set of SQL Server tables. The Queries window lets you select queries that, when run, execute SQL SELECT queries against these tables. The window also automates the process of writing the SQL statements for these queries.

After the server and client software are installed, it's a good idea to run the query tool to get a report on the status of the machines in the network so you can plan your software distribution accordingly. You must first create and then execute a query. Follow these steps to create and execute a query:

Part
V

Ch
25

1. In SMS Administrator, choose Open from the File menu, and then open the Queries window. SMS includes a variety of useful predefined queries (see Figure 25.23).

FIG. 25.23

The Queries window displaying the default queries included with SMS.

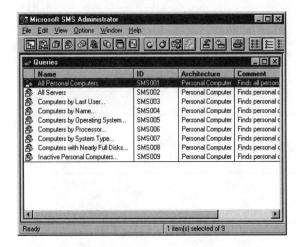

2. From the File menu choose New to open the Query Properties dialog.

3. In the Query Name text box, type `Windows NT Computers` and click Add OR to open the Query Expression Properties dialog.

4. In the Operating Systems section, select the Operating System Name attribute, select Is in the Operator list, and select Microsoft Windows NT in the Value list. Click OK to close the dialog and return to the Query Properties dialog (see Figure 25.24).

FIG. 25.24

A new query displayed in the Query Properties dialog.

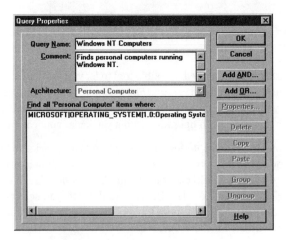

5. Click OK to close the Query Properties dialog and add the query to the list in the Queries window.

6. From the File menu choose Execute Query to open the Execute Query dialog. Select the Windows NT Computers query from the Query drop-down list, accept the default Identification in the Query Result Format list, and optionally mark the Limit to Sites and Include Subsites check boxes (see Figure 25.25).

FIG. 25.25

Selecting the query, query format, and sites to inventory.

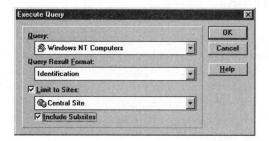

7. Click OK to execute the query. The query result set appears as shown in Figure 25.26 for the SMSDemo database.

FIG. 25.26

The query result set for the Windows NT Computers query against the SMSDemo database.

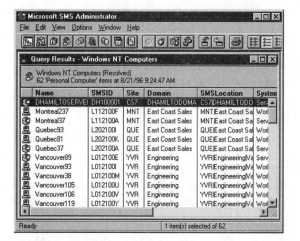

Part
V

Ch
25

These steps create and execute a simple query that has only one criterion. By using additional Add AND or Add OR functions, however, you can add more operators to define more query details. For example, you can add an AND operator with the System Role of the machine and choose Server. Such a query detects only Windows NT servers.

Alerts Window

Systems Management Server lets you create alerts that are triggered by criteria you define. For example, you can define a rule to alert you when a server disk is 70 percent full. An alert can be sent to one or more system administrators. Alerts also can be sent by e-mail, you can set up the system to page the system administrator, or specify other actions.

Machine Groups Window

Systems Management Server lets you group machines together so that you can perform administrative tasks for a group systematically. Suppose that you want to upgrade all high-end workstations in the western region to Windows 95. First, you create a new group simply by using the File menu's New command. Then you can run a query for all the machines in the western region, have an Intel Pentium chip, and have at least 16M of RAM. When the result is delivered, you simply drag and drop all these machines in the group that you created. Now you can perform your upgrade to this group. Grouping machines can provide a simpler administrative system, particularly if you have a large network.

Site Groups Window

SMS lets you group different sites together for easier manageability. For example, if Los Angeles and San Francisco are two of the sites in the western region, you can put them together in one group.

Program Groups Window

This tool lets you put program shortcuts in a program group to be delivered to targeted workstations. As a result, you can control the user's desktop contents and provide desktop consistency wherever the user logs on.

Events Window

This window lets you monitor Windows NT events generated by SMS. Figure 25.27 shows the Events window with events triggered by operations on the SMSDemo database. You double-click the event item to display the Event Detail dialog (see Figure 25.28).

Installing and Configuring the SMS Client Software

One of the better features of SMS is its capability to automatically install the required SMS client software on PCs. If you have only a small number of clients, you can install the software manually. Installing the SMS client software on a large number of clients is a major project, so automating the process can save many hours.

Manual Client Software Installation

When SMS is installed, the SMS_SHR share is created, which includes the RUNSMS.BAT batch file. This is the only file you need to run to install the SMS client software on Windows

3.1x, Windows for Workgroups 3.1x, Windows 95, and Windows NT machines. Running this file from the workstation automatically installs the required components onto the client and then inventories the machine's hardware and software. The inventory of the client is performed during installation, which takes 30 to 60 seconds.

FIG. 25.27
The Events window, displaying Windows NT events generated while using the SMSDemo database.

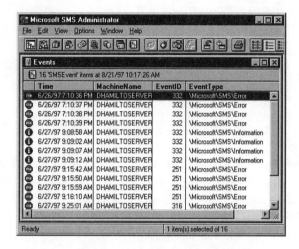

FIG. 25.28
Displaying detailed information about a selected event.

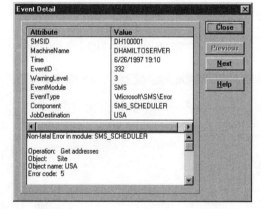

Automatic Installation

To install the client software automatically, you must update the system logon script. To add the SMS logon script to the users' domain logon scripts from within SMS, follow these steps:

1. In SMS Administrator, open the Sites window and select the Site Server in the left pane.

2. From the File menu choose Properties to open the Site Properties dialog (see Figure 25.29).

3. Click Clients to open the Clients dialog, which displays the Current Properties for clients.

FIG. 25.29
Site characteristics displayed in the Site Properties dialog.

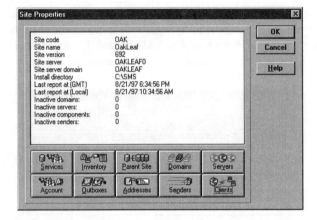

4. Click the Proposed Properties option button to enable the dialog's settings.

5. Mark the Automatically Configure Workstation Logon Scripts check box; you can specify that the client execute the SMS commands at the start or the end of the script (see Figure 25.30).

6. Click OK twice to close both dialogs.

7. Click Yes when asked whether you want to update the site.

These steps enable SMS to update the Windows NT server's logon scripts for each user and to amend the NetWare system logon scripts, if applicable, on all servers within the site being managed. The next time the client logs on, the script installs the SMS client software.

FIG. 25.30
Specifying the addition of the SMS client installation to client logon scripts.

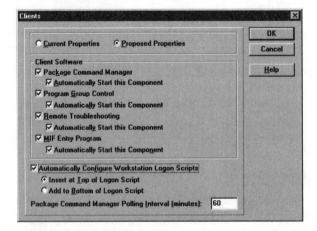

N O T E For SMS to add the SMS components to the logon scripts automatically, it's necessary to let SMS find all the domain logon servers so that the appropriate files can be copied into place. This may not be desirable if some of the logon servers are available only via slow WAN links. In this case, don't automatically set up the logon scripts. Instead, manually add the call to the SMS logon script for the domain logon scripts, and manually set up the NETLOGON shares. ▩

Client Inventory Management

As explained earlier in the section "Hardware and Software Inventory," inventory management is one of SMS's primary functions. When the client software is installed, the Inventory Agent reads the client's CMOS (EEPROM) chip and runs an abbreviated version of the Microsoft Diagnostics program to collect the hardware information. The client application then scans the local fixed disk to collect information about the software installed. After the initial collection, the Inventory Agent runs periodically, based on a frequency you specify.

Each time Inventory Agent runs, it collects the hardware and software information and reports it to the SMS logon server. The logon server doesn't need to be a Windows NT server; other servers, such as NetWare 3.1+, can be used to collect this information.

The site server then collects the information from the logon server(s). The site server determines whether there have been any updates on the workstation and updates its Microsoft SQL database with the new information. This information also is sent up the SMS hierarchy.

Information about software installed on client computers can be collected in two ways: by using an audit package or by using the inventory agent that runs during the execution of the SMS logon script components. The differences between the two methods are as follows:

- ▩ The *audit package* uses a set of rules in a rule file to compare the installed applications with given parameters. Microsoft provides a number of these rules for common applications, especially Microsoft applications. You can edit this file to add or delete applications. The rule file is compiled and provided with an auditing program provided by Microsoft in an audit package. Audit packages can be sent to users whenever appropriate and can be executed when convenient for users.

- ▩ The inventory agent uses parameters much like those for a rule file, but you define them when setting the inventory details for a package. This information is saved in the SMS database with the other package details. The inventory agent uses this information to compare the file on the disk against the parameters you provide. When the inventory agent finds a match, the information is included in the inventory details returned to the logon server. The inventory agent always executes automatically, so it may run at an inconvenient time for users. Therefore, the inventory agent should be used to inventory only a small number of critical software packages, such as the operating system.

Figure 25.31 shows the client's Package Command Manager with a pending Audit Software package created from the Audit.pdf file included with SMS. When users click the Execute button, the result of the audit is staged for transfer to the Primary Site.

Remote Control

To perform Remote Control or Help Desk functions on a targeted machine, the Remote Control Agent must be running on the client. For you or the helpdesk personnel to support a machine, access rights must be granted by the machine's user. For security reasons, some machines might be made inaccessible to support personnel.

FIG. 25.31
A pending Audit job displayed in the client's Package Command Manager.

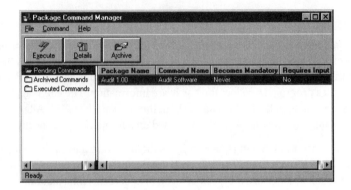

> **N O T E** You must restart the client PC after installing the SMS client software to enable the Remote Control Agent. ▦

To enable Help Desk support, follow these steps for each client PC:

1. From the Start menu choose Programs, SMS Client, and Remote Control to start the Remote Control Agent.

2. From the Start menu choose Programs, SMS Client, and Help Desk Options to open the Help Desk Options dialog (shown with the default options in Figure 25.32).

3. Clear or mark the options you want for the client.

4. If you make changes to the options, click Save As Default and Save As Current, and then click Exit.

With the options shown enabled in Figure 25.32, the user is notified when someone takes control of the machine remotely. If the machine is always to be supported remotely, it's a good idea to add the Remote Control Program to the user's Startup program menu.

To remotely control a client PC from the SMS Administrator application, follow these steps:

1. From the File menu choose Open, and select the Sites window. Expand the Sites list as needed to display the entry for the client in the right pane.

2. Double-click the client item to open the Personal Computer Properties window.

3. Scroll to and click the Help Desk icon. SMS tries to connect to the client's Remote Control Agent with each supported protocol until a connection is established. When the connection is established, buttons are enabled for those services permitted by the client (see Figure 25.33).

4. Click Remote Control to open an image of the client's display (see Figure 25.34). Depending on the relative resolution of the server and client displays, you see all or part of the client screen, surrounded by a yellow and black border.

FIG. 25.32

The client's Help Desk Options for the Remote Control Agent.

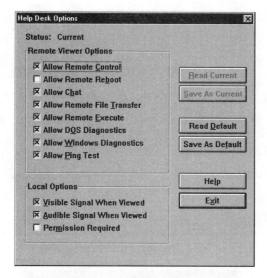

FIG. 25.33

Making a connection from SMS to the client's Remote Control Agent.

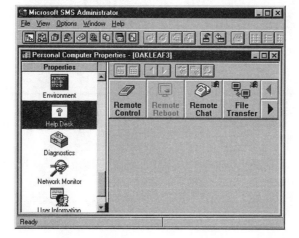

5. Click the button with the hand icon at the upper right of the display to open a small Area window that you can use to position the server viewport for the client display.

6. Click the Alt button to enable server control key keystrokes to be sent to the client. Click the Alt button again to disable sending control key keystrokes.

In addition to Help Desk, a number of tools are available from the Diagnostics tool in the Properties pane. When you click one of the Diagnostics buttons, the server interrogates the client. Figure 25.35 illustrates the result of a Ping Test on a client.

FIG. 25.34
Part of a remotely controlled client's 800×600 screen displayed on a server with 640×480 resolution.

FIG. 25.35
Running a real-time Ping Test diagnostic on a client.

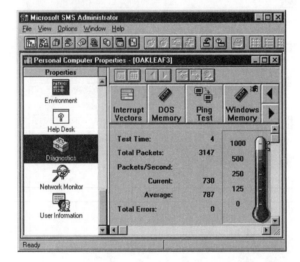

Network Monitor

The Network Monitor tool captures frames from a remote computer by running the Network Monitor Agent (see Figure 25.36). The capability to capture frames from any client is what distinguishes SMS's Network Monitor from that which comes with Windows NT 4.0. Clicking Start Network Monitor opens Network Monitor with the client selected (see Figure 25.37). After you capture the data, you can highlight certain data or filter the data based on your desired criteria.

▶ **See** "Using Network Monitor," **p. 570**

FIG. 25.36
Starting Network
Monitor for a remote
client.

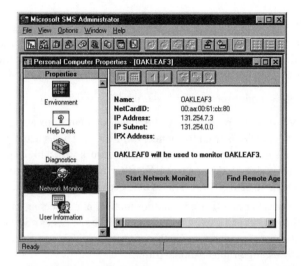

FIG. 25.37
Network Monitor, dis-
playing the result of a
Ping Test of the client.

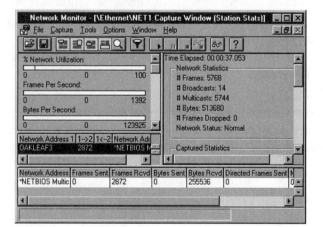

Part
V

Ch
25

Building Sites for Enterprise Networks

After you create your Central Site and set up the central server, you can begin creating child sites and add them to the SMS hierarchy. The hierarchical structure provides flexible system administration for the entire network. For example, you can provide decentralized Help Desk capabilities by designating some of the child sites as Primary Sites. The inventory data contin- ues to be sent up the hierarchy to the Central Site server for overall administration and asset management. The Secondary Sites, which don't have local databases, are managed by the Primary Sites.

Communication Between Sites with Senders

A *Sender* is a service that SMS uses to transmit instructions and data from one site to another. The use of Senders is an important factor in enterprise design, because the available bandwidth may vary depending on the connection, which in turn affects overall system performance.

Three types of SMS Senders are available—LAN, RAS, and SNA:

- If your SMS servers are located in a LAN environment (typically Ethernet or Token Ring), a LAN Sender is used to connect the servers. This is usually the case for multiple servers in a server room, or a campus-wide network with a high-speed backbone. The LAN Sender is also used whenever a NetBIOS-compatible protocol is used, such as TCP/IP, DECnet, or IPX/SPX. This is true even over wide area network connections.

- Remote Access Service (RAS) is another method of connecting the servers together (RAS is the subject of Chapter 19, "Managing Remote Access Service"). RAS can use X.25, conventional modems, or ISDN connections. X.25 connections are common and particularly useful for international traffic.

- The Microsoft SNA Sender is used to connect servers in an IBM environment.

Remote control via connections other than LANs or T-1 lines is likely to be unsatisfactory. Remote control requires that the client's screen graphics be sent over the connection to your display. Sufficient bandwidth is required so that the normal network traffic isn't affected when Help Desk is operating.

Distributing packages such as Microsoft Office or Windows 95 requires enough bandwidth to complete the installation in a reasonable period. Although SMS allows job scheduling so that packages can be delivered during the time when the network is least used, it's unrealistic to assume that an efficient installation can be performed over a RAS connection, even if using ISDN.

Coexistence with NetWare Environments

If you're running Novell NetWare 3.x servers in your environment, you can add Microsoft SMS to the network and use all its features without any changes to the NetWare server or the client. The NetWare server can be used as a logon server or a distribution server. You need to add only a few lines to the user's logon script to run the installation program. You must install Gateway Services for NetWare to take full advantage of SMS in a heterogeneous networking environment.

▶ **See** "Using Gateway Service for NetWare," **p. 642**

The best way to manage NetWare servers and workstations is to group them together so that they're managed as one unit. NetWare 3.x doesn't support a domain concept and therefore doesn't offer a single logon account. Because most NetWare 3.x servers don't share the same user account database, an SMS account with supervisory rights must be created in each server that needs to participate in the SMS hierarchy. The account allows SMS to communicate with the NetWare server and to install a software package for distribution, or retrieve the inventory data from the NetWare server.

From Here...

This chapter showed how Systems Management Server provides a number of capabilities that reduce the cost of ownership of PCs by providing an efficient method of supporting PC users. SMS is a feature-rich and reasonably complicated network application that requires an understanding of a number of MIS-related issues such as LAN and WAN connections, network bandwidth, and organization structure. With proper planning (which includes setting up a pilot project before rollout), SMS enhances the system administrator and end-user environments.

The following chapters contain information related to the topics covered in this chapter:

- Chapter 17, "Distributing Network Services with Domains," covers Windows NT Server's trusted domains and other distributed networking features that allow a single-user logon for multiple network servers and server-based applications running on LANs and WANs.

- Chapter 18, "Integrating Windows NT with NetWare and UNIX," shows you how to set up and administer Windows NT Server within a Novell NetWare or UNIX networking environment.

- Chapter 19, "Managing Remote Access Service," explains how to configure Windows NT Server 4.0's RAS component to support dial-in access to shared network resources by mobile users.

Part
V

Ch
25

The Trail to Windows NT 5.0

26   Scaling Windows NT Server 4.0 to the Enterprise   967

27   Distributing File and Directory Services   987

CHAPTER 26

Scaling Windows NT Server 4.0 to the Enterprise

Windows NT Server's success in the network operating system market primarily is the result of its relatively low license cost, ease of installation and management, and prowess as an application server. These features make Windows NT Server especially attractive to small businesses that can't afford (or won't pay for) the network support expertise required for NetWare 4.x or UNIX installations. Computer Intelligence, a market research firm, reported in June 1997 that 71 percent of Windows NT Server installations are in small businesses with fewer than 100 employees.

Many information systems (IS) managers today view Windows NT Server as a workgroup- or department-level product suitable for supporting, at most, a few hundred client PCs. The IS perception is that Windows NT, unlike UNIX, isn't a scalable operating system. In this context, scalability means the ability to install additional processors, disk drive subsystems, and memory to meet increasing server workload. Windows NT Server 4.0 and BackOffice 2.5 applications, which are designed to take advantage of Windows NT's symmetrical multiprocessing (SMP) features, demonstrate significant improvements in

Upgrading to the Enterprise Edition

The Enterprise Edition of Windows NT Server 4.0 and BackOffice Server 2.5 is targeted at the market for high-end UNIX systems.

Clustering for high availability

Microsoft's first version of its Cluster Server provides automatic failover to a working server when a clustered node goes offline.

Distributing transactions

Microsoft Transaction Server and Message Queue Server coordinate transactions that are distributed over multiple databases, servers, and platforms.

Routing and Remote Access Service

Routing and Remote Access Service (RAS) lets you implement a WAN over a switched telephone network by automatically establishing and terminating connections on demand.

Reducing total cost of ownership

Microsoft's pawns in the fight against the forthcoming Network PC include the 32-bit Windows Network PC and Windows Terminals based on the Hydra technology.

workload capacity as you add up to a total of four CPUs, called a 4-way processor configuration. In contrast, most high-end UNIX flavors support 8-way, 16-way, 32-way, and even 64-way configurations.

Third-party server vendors, such as NCR and Sequent, have demonstrated 16-way and larger systems running modified versions of Windows NT Server 4.0. Mainstream Windows NT servers, however, remain in the 4-way or smaller category. According to the Aberdeen Group, a computer research and consulting firm, about 90 percent of all servers sold have four or fewer processors. Like Windows 95, Microsoft targets the off-the-shelf version of Windows NT Server 4.0 to the high-volume market, primarily composed of PC packagers and value-added resellers (VARs) who preinstall Windows NT Server 4.0 on their purpose-built server product lines.

ON THE WEB

You can read the Aberdeen Group's analysis "Debunking the NT/SMP Scalability Myth" at **http://www. microsoft.com/ntserver/info/aberdeen.htm**.

Not content to compete only with Novell's NetWare and low-end UNIX variants, Microsoft wants a piece of the remaining 10 percent of the market (in unit sales), which now is dominated by high-end UNIX servers and mainframes. Microsoft's first step in this direction is the Enterprise Edition of Windows NT Server 4.0, named *Windows NT Server/E* or, in some Microsoft publications, simply *NT/E*. This chapter describes the features that distinguish Windows NT Server/E from the standard edition, which is the subject of the preceding chapters of this book. ■

Understanding Microsoft's Incremental Approach to Scalability

Scalability Day, held on May 20, 1997, in New York City, was Microsoft's first large-scale attempt to remove Windows NT's scalability onus by demonstrating giant servers running enhanced versions of Windows NT Server, SQL Server, and Exchange Server. With minor exceptions, the systems that demonstrated a billion transactions per day and a terabyte (T) database used beta versions of products, such as SQL Server 7.0, that weren't available in mid-1997 and probably won't appear as retail products until some time in 1998.

Microsoft chose Scalability Day for the formal announcement of Windows NT Server/E, scheduled for release as a retail product in fall 1997. Windows NT Server/E, an upgrade to Windows NT Server 4.0 (and called *Granite* during beta testing), adds the following features to the operating system:

- *Microsoft Cluster Server* (MSCS, formerly code-named *Wolfpack*) improves server availability with failover clustering. Failover enables two servers to share a single set of RAID drives. Clustering for scalability via load sharing isn't expected until sometime in 1998, probably with the release of Windows NT Server 5.0 Enterprise Edition.

■ *Microsoft Transaction Server* (MTS, formerly *Viper*) is a combination object request broker (ORB) and transaction processor (TP) for creating multiple-tier client/server database applications. Microsoft released MTS 1.0 in December 1996. In late June 1997, Microsoft licensed MTS 1.1 as a no-charge upgrade to Windows NT Server 4.0.

■ *Microsoft Message Queue Server* (MSMQ, formerly *Falcon*) provides reliable, prioritized delivery of data over unreliable wide area networks. MSMQ also requires installation of SQL Server 6.5. The primary initial applications for MSMQ involve communication with mainframes.

■ *Microsoft Routing and Remote Access Service* (Routing and RAS, formerly *Steelhead*) replaces the multiprotocol router (MPR) and RAS components of Windows NT Server 4.0. Routing and RAS isn't likely to replace high-end Cisco hardware routers and Cabletron switches, but the RAS enhancements make this new add-on worthwhile for sites with large numbers of dial-in users.

■ *Increased SMP scalability* lets the Enterprise Edition gain an 8-way processor configuration and "superserver" status. The extent to which Windows NT Server/E takes advantage of more than four CPUs remains to be demonstrated in real-world applications.

■ *4G RAM Tuning (4GT)* lets Windows NT Server/E allocate 3G of RAM to applications in a 4G system by reducing the amount of RAM dedicated to the kernel from 2G to 1G. 4GT improves the performance of large database servers in applications such as data warehousing.

ON THE WEB

Microsoft's initial description of the new features of Windows NT Server/E is available at **http://www. microsoft.com/ntserver/info/ntseetb.htm**.

Part

VI

Ch

26

MTS and Routing and RAS are released products; you can download a time-limited trial version of MTS and an unrestricted version of Routing and RAS from Microsoft's Web site. Microsoft released in late June 1997 MTS version 2.0 as a component of beta 2 of Internet Information Server 4.0. Beta 2 of MSMQ was released on the Microsoft Developer Network Level III (Enterprise Subscription) CD-ROMs in June 1997, along with beta 2 of MSCS. Four sections later in this chapter discuss MSCS, MTS, MSMQ, and Routing and RAS in greater detail.

Microsoft's tentative estimated retail price for a single-server license for Windows NT Server /E is $3,999, including 25 client licenses. Existing client licenses for Windows NT Server 4.0 are valid for use with Enterprise Edition servers. Windows NT Server 4.0 with 25 clients costs $1,468, making the premium for the Enterprise Edition about $2,500 per server. Microsoft recommends that you update only those servers that can gain the most benefit from Enterprise Edition's features, especially failover clustering. Complicating the licensing issue for Windows NT Server/E is the prospect of another round of upgrade surcharges for Windows NT 5.0 and its Enterprise Edition, with a possible (but improbable) increase in client license fees.

▶ **See** "Windows NT 4.0 License Packages and Cost," **p. 819**

N O T E   Microsoft recommends a minimum of a 90MHz Pentium processor and 64M of RAM to run
Windows NT Server/E. You're wasting your money on the Enterprise upgrade if you don't
have a system with two or more 200MHz or faster Pentium Pro or Pentium II processors and 256M or
more of RAM. Microsoft supports MSMQ only on servers that appear in a forthcoming Cluster Server
hardware validation list. Such servers are likely to be each vendor's newest, fastest, and thus most
expensive products. ■

Clustering for Availability Now and Scalability Later

A clustered system consists of a collection of subsystems—individual server PCs (called *nodes*)
and sets of external disk drives—that appear to networked clients as a single server. Clustered
systems are designed to provide either of the following objectives:

■ *High availability* to assure that failure of a single component, such as a server PC or a
disk drive, doesn't prevent access by clients to the cluster's resources. High availability is
achieved by redundant servers connected to each other and to disk drive subsystems.
Thus, high-availability clusters usually involve only two nodes. If one server PC fails,
another takes over its duties; thus, the term *failover clustering* often is applied to high-
availability systems. Conventional RAID 1 and higher disk arrays handle disk drives
failures by mirroring, striping with parity, and related types of data redundancy.

  ▶ **See** "Understanding RAID Levels," **p. 216**

■ *Improved scalability* to distribute processor workload over multiple server nodes. A well-
designed scalable cluster (also called a *performance cluster*) provides more efficient use
of a large number of CPUs than conventional symmetrical multiprocessing (SMP) with
shared memory. For instance, a four-node cluster of 4-way nodes is likely to outperform
a single 16-way node because of memory-access bottlenecks. Interconnecting performance cluster nodes requires a high-speed I/O system and special cabling. If a cluster
node fails, the other nodes share its load until the failed node is repaired or replaced.
Most performance clusters also provide high-availability features.

MSCS 1.0 uses failover methodology for high availability, which is much simpler than implementing performance clusters. Microsoft's 1997 market research for MSCS indicates that more
than 80 percent of potential users are more interested in availability through failover clusters
than in performance clusters. There are two common architectures for high-availability clusters:

■ *Shared-nothing,* in which each node owns a specific set of resources, such as a disk
subsystem with replicated data. If one node fails, a standby node with its own disk
subsystem takes over. The data on the standby disk drives is current only as of the last
replication operation. Shared-nothing systems are expensive and don't take full advantage of RAID 1 through 5's fail-safe data storage.

■ *Shared-disk,* in which two nodes share a common external disk subsystem via an independent SCSI controller in each server PC. A connection either directly between the two nodes or over the network provides a continuous indication of the health of each node by means of a *heartbeat* signal. Shared-disk failover clusters can be assembled with off-the-shelf hardware and can be upgraded to performance clusters later. The key to success of a shared-disk cluster is a RAID subsystem that meets the RAID Advisory Board's standards for Failure Resistant Disk System Plus or better.

▶ **See** "The RAID Advisory Board," **p. 217**

▶ **See** "Summarizing RAID Recommendations," **p. 253**

MSCS uses the shared-disk approach illustrated in Figure 26.1. Each server node has its own SCSI host controller that connects to an external shared disk subsystem, in addition to an unshared local drive to store the operating system. The two SCSI host controllers must use different SCSI bus addresses; one controller must be assigned an address other than 7, the default host controller address. Each shared drive must be formatted with a single NTFS partition with volumes configured into a RAID array before you install MSCS. An additional shared physical drive must be added to store MSCS configuration and administration files. In most cases, the shared disk subsystem and local unshared drive(s) are Ultra-Wide SCSI, although it's possible to use Extended Integrated Device Electronics (EIDE) or, preferably, Ultra DMA/33 (also called Ultra ATA) drives to hold the system and the Windows NT paging file. Ultra DMA/33 drives give about the same performance as high-end Ultra-Wide SCSI drives at about one-third the cost. Cost of individual system drives, however, isn't a major factor in the overall cost of a validated cluster system.

FIG. 26.1

Hardware components and interconnects required to implement Microsoft Cluster Server 1.0 in a failover system.

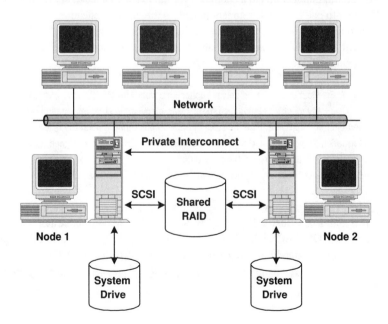

N O T E   One major incentive for adopting failover clustering is the ability to upgrade a node's operating system without shutting down the cluster. You can specify the active node, thus enabling Service Packs, server application upgrades, and the like to be installed on the system drive of the inactive node. When the upgraded node is installed and tested, you activate it and deactivate the other node for the upgrade. ■

MSCS requires a private network interconnect, which consists of two dedicated network interface cards (NICs) and a cross-connect cable between the two nodes, in addition to the NICs that connect the nodes to the external network hub or switch. The external network backs up the private network interconnect. 100BaseT NICs are the obvious choice for these multihomed nodes, but Microsoft says a 10BaseT interconnect is adequate. The MSCS Resource Monitor periodically checks the LooksAlive or IsAlive functions to determine whether all node resources are operable. In the event that a resource fails the IsAlive test, the Failover Manager takes appropriate action to substitute a live resource of the appropriate type.

ON THE WEB

Microsoft's "Windows NT Server Clustering Frequently Asked Questions" sheet is available at **http://www.microsoft.com/ntserver/info/clusteringfaqs.htm**.

MSCS can recover from a server failure in a minute or so, depending on the number and nature of services in use. In the case of a Web server, users connected to the site would notice a delay in retrieving a page because Web services are stateless. Clients with conventional (stateful) connections to a client/server database on a failed server node receive an error when trying to use the dead connection. Unless the client application is designed to automatically try reconnecting to the database, users must reconnect manually. It's relatively easy to modify client applications to automatically attempt reconnection to the database running on the operating server node.

N O T E   Most well-behaved server applications work with MSCS. *Well-behaved* applications, by Microsoft's definition, store their own recoverable state information on the disk array, so the operable node can determine the state of applications running when the failed node died. Internet Information Server 3.0+ and SQL Server 6.5 Enterprise Edition are designed for failover clustering. An upgrade to Exchange Server 5.0 for clustering and a much larger (16T) message store is scheduled for release in early 1998 as a component of the BackOffice Enterprise Edition. ■

MSCS includes a graphic Cluster Administrator that simplifies setting up and administering the two nodes of a cluster. Figure 26.2 shows the Cluster Administrator's window for a cluster named WOLFPACK. Like MTS's Transaction Explorer, the Cluster Administrator is likely to migrate to a Snap-In for Microsoft Management Console (MMC).

▶ **See** "Using Microsoft Management Console to Administer IIS 4.0," **p. 747**

FIG. 26.2

The beta 2 version of MSCS's Cluster Administrator application.

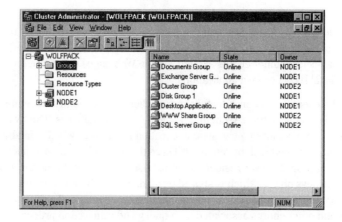

Several third parties provide failover clustering solutions that don't rely on MSCS; for example, Compaq offers its Recovery Server Option for ProLiant and ProSignia servers running Windows NT Server 3.5 but not 4.0. Oracle uses its own clustering layer for the Oracle Parallel Server product line. Compaq and its Tandem subsidiary, DEC, IBM, HP, and a number of other PC server vendors have announced their intention to provide prepackaged clusters based on MSCS that meet Microsoft's validation requirements. Although it's possible to assemble your own cluster from off-the-shelf components, Microsoft won't provide support for MSCS running on unvalidated hardware.

Microsoft promises that future versions of MSCS will add the scalability features of performance clusters. Phase 2 of the Microsoft's clustering strategy, expected to arrive in 1998, is designed to support four-node clusters. Larger performance clusters (16 nodes or more) are scheduled for Phase 3 of the MSCS program, probably for arrival in 1999.

Part
VI

Ch
26

Managing the Middle Tier with Transaction Server

Three-tier client/server architecture is a hot topic among today's database developers. The following elements most commonly make up this relatively new design model:

- *Data services* are provided by a relational database management system (RDBMS), such as Microsoft SQL Server, Oracle, or Informix. Data services provide the basic storage, retrieval, and update functions but, in the three-tier model, don't interact directly with client applications. This base layer provides basic transaction processing management, usually through server-resident stored procedures and triggers.

- *Business services* comprise a middle tier that provides communication between client applications and data services. Business services, which often enforce complex business rules, are created from custom-programmed objects (business objects, line-of-business objects, or LOBjects) that may reside on the application server for the RDBMS or on server(s) dedicated to business services only. If multiple, intercommunicating business objects span client-to-data services, the architecture is called *n-tier*.

■ *Client services* provide the user interface to display or update data in response to user queries. The capability of intermediate business objects to verify data updates and pre-process queries reduces client application complexity. Moving code to the middle tier makes for thinner clients and lets simple Web pages substitute for custom-designed C++, Visual Basic, or Java applications.

Three-tier client/server architecture makes client applications independent of changes to changes in data structures (schema) of client/server databases. The two-tier model requires distribution of an entirely new client application to all users when a database field or table is added, deleted, modified, or renamed. Three-tier also offers client applications the capability to use a set of robust, server-resident generic business objects. In the three-tier structure, only a single business object, which is shared by all database clients, must be updated. All clients can share a common set of business objects for database logon and authentication, data-entry validation, and other chores associated with query and transaction processing.

Brokering Business Objects

One primary problem with distributing business objects over multiple servers is providing a method for a client application to find a particular object on the network. Another problem is to manage the creation or allocation of instances of objects to individual client sessions. (Each client needs its own instance of an object for the duration of its usually brief activity directly involving the RDBMS.) A middleware component called an *Object Request Broker (ORB)* handles these two problems. Although Microsoft calls MTS a "Transaction Server," it's MTS's ORB features that have the greatest appeal to three-tier developers writing business objects in C++, Visual Basic, and Java.

MTS provides the Windows NT Server process within which to run ActiveX Components. (ActiveX Components also are known as *ActiveX DLLs* or *in-process Automation servers*.) MTS also lets you combine one or more ActiveX Components into a single MTS package that shares a common set of security features to authenticate users and their permissions to use the objects in the package. MTS uses the Distributed Component Object Model (DCOM) to communicate with 32-bit Windows clients and RDBMSes running as services on Windows NT Server 4.0+. 16-bit Windows clients use an early version of DCOM called NetworkOLE. Figure 26.3 illustrates the architecture of MTS-based systems, showing Web browser and conventional 32-bit and 16-bit clients communicating through MTS to mainframe, UNIX, and SQL Server databases.

▶ **See** "Distributed Component Object Model (DCOM)," **p. 39**

You use MTS Explorer with MTS 1.0 to deploy packages of ActiveX Components. Figure 26.4 shows a package called Remote Order Entry, which contains a single ActiveX Component, RemoteServer, created with Visual Basic 5.0. RemoteServer has a single method, AddNewOrder; MTS supplies the additional seven methods shown in Figure 26.3 to manage instances of the RemoteServer component. Package security uses *roles* to determine the permissions of groups or individual users for a package. The Accounting Supervisor role has a single user account, and the Order Entry Clerks role is assigned to a Windows NT Server group.

FIG. 26.3

Software components for implementing MTS-based systems for various client and data services.

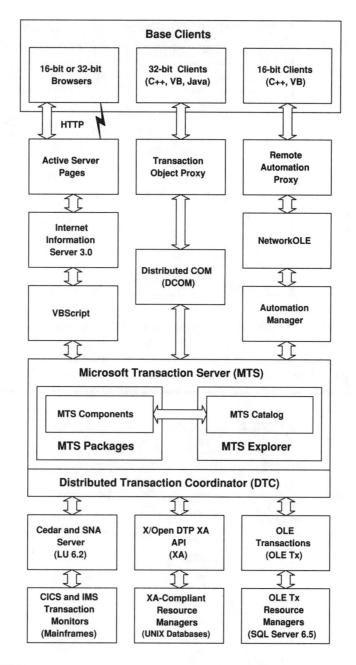

ON THE WEB

You can read an MTS technical white paper and download MTS 1.1 at **http://www.microsoft.com/ transaction/default.asp**.

FIG. 26.4

MTS Explorer displaying methods of the RemoteServer ActiveX Component, seven of which are supplied by MTS.

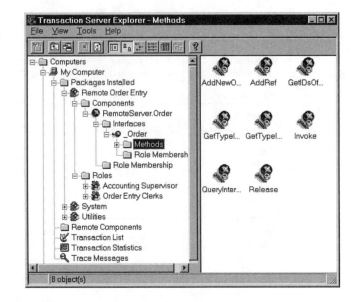

Beta 2 of IIS 4.0 includes MTS 1.1, which uses an MMC Snap-In (Mtxexp.msc) for administration. (MTx was Microsoft's original abbreviation for MTS.) Figure 26.5 shows beta 2 of MMC with Mtxexp.msc active, displaying the components of the Exploration Air (ExAir) example package included with IIS 4.0. Microsoft is actively promoting the IIS 4.0/MTS 1.1 combination for electronic commerce and other Web-based applications that involve transactions.

FIG. 26.5

The Microsoft Management Console's MTS Explorer snap-in, displaying ActiveX Components included with the ExAir sample Web site.

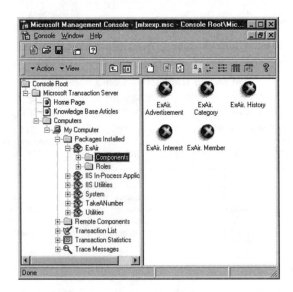

Spanning Transactions over Multiple Components and Databases

Database transactions involve simultaneous, related updates to two or more tables in one or more databases. A transaction that spans more than one database is called a *distributed transaction*. Transactions must meet the *ACID test* of atomicity, consistency, isolation, and durability:

■ *Atomicity* requires all updates to database tables as the result of a specific transaction to be committed (made durable) or aborted and rolled back (recovered) to values existing immediately before execution. Atomicity is an "all-or-nothing" approach to changing the state of the participating database(s). If a multirow update to a table fails halfway through the operation, for instance, all updated rows roll back to their original state.

■ *Consistency* requires all operations to produce data entities that preserve consistency constraints for each table participating in the update. If a consistency violation occurs at any stage of the process, the entire transaction is rolled back.

■ *Isolation* requires that until an entire transaction is committed, its intermediate results (including the work of nested transactions) should not be visible to other concurrent transactions operating on the same tables.

■ *Durability* requires that committed table updates survive network, communication, process, or system failures, including fixed-disk crashes. Transaction logging is the most common method of handling disk failures. In the event of a failure, you restore the last backup and apply the transaction log to the restored database.

The two-phase commit process assures that distributed transactions pass the ACID test. Transaction monitors (TMs)—such as MTS for Windows NT, Tuxedo for UNIX, and CICS for IBM mainframes—supervise the two-phase commit process. In the preparation phase, the transaction monitor enlists a resource manager for each database to set up the pending table updates. SQL Server 6.5's DTC is the resource manager for SQL Server databases. When all resource managers report that preparation is complete, the transaction monitor issues the commit instruction to all the resource managers. Figure 26.6 illustrates a complex distributed transaction involving multiple databases, such as might occur when you purchase a book from an online store.

Part
VI

Ch

26

When preparation of all resource managers is complete, the transaction's fate still remains in doubt because other concurrent transactions may have altered the state of the databases or a resource manager may be inaccessible. If all resource managers report that their individual commit succeeded, the entire transaction is made durable. Otherwise, each resource manager rolls back its part of the transaction. It may take operator intervention to resolve the outcome of transactions that remain in doubt for an extended period, usually as a result of network, communication link, or server failure. MTS Explorer includes a facility for terminating in-doubt transactions.

N O T E Cedar, a Microsoft add-on to SNA Server, was in the beta-test stage when this book was written. Cedar provides an LU 6.2 connection from MTS to IBM's IMS and CICS transaction managers running on mainframes. ■

FIG. 26.6

A distributed transaction for an order placed with a hypothetical online book store.

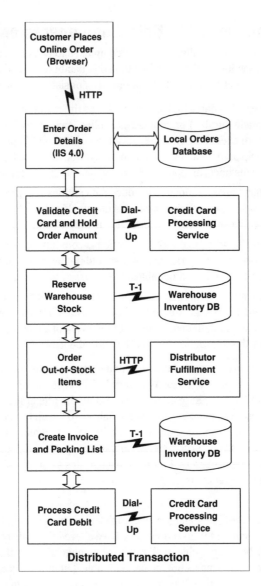

ON THE WEB

Microsoft demonstrated at Scalability Day a 45-server system (five of which were devoted to MTS) that claimed to handle one billion simulated Automated Teller Machine (ATM) transactions per day. You can read the details at **http://www.microsoft.com/backoffice/scalability/billion.htm**.

Using Messages to Enable Wide-Area Transactions

The distributed transaction illustrated in Figure 26.6 involves intersystem connections that are classified as *reliable* and *unreliable*. Synchronous communication between IIS 4.0 and MTS, on the same server or on a LAN, is considered a reliable connection. Dial-up connections to a credit-card processing service are classified as unreliable because the credit service's incoming lines might be busy or their server might be offline. WANs using T-1 lines or satellite links usually are classified as unreliable because the remote server may be unavailable.

Conducting transactions over unreliable channels requires a different approach than that for low-latency LANs. Messages, rather than direct DCOM connections, mitigate latency problems with distant resource managers by using asynchronous communication. Messages requesting resource manager participation in a transaction go into a message queue at the origin, a process similar to preparing and sending e-mail messages. Each message has a priority level recognized by the resource manager. A message queuing service, such as IBM's MQSeries for mainframes, makes repeated attempts to send the message (if necessary), makes sure that the message is set only once, and handles confirmation and return message(s).

Microsoft Message Queue Server, which was in beta testing when this book was written, is a message-queuing service for Windows NT Server 4.0+. MSMQ integrates directly with MTS, but other applications also can use MSMQ services independently of MTS. Figure 26.7 shows the MSMQ Explorer, which is similar to the MTS Explorer described earlier. (MSMQ Explorer undoubtedly will become an MMC Snap-In.) MSMQ's primary competitor is IBM's MQSeries, which is available for a wide variety of platforms, including Windows NT.

FIG. 26.7
Microsoft Message Queue Explorer displaying messages in a MSMQ journal.

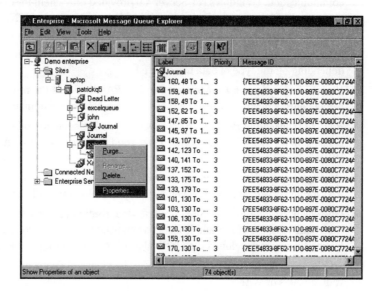

ON THE WEB

You can download an overview of MSMQ in Word 95 .doc format at **http://www.microsoft.com/ntserver/info/msmqover.htm**.

N O T E The Standard Edition of MSMQ for Windows NT Server 4.0 has limited connectivity options. Windows NT Server/E includes the MSMQ Enterprise Edition, which has no limit on concurrent users and adds cluster support, intelligent routing functions, and ability to link to IBM MQseries messaging systems via optional third-party gateways. ▦

Using Routing and Remote Access Service

Microsoft released version 1.0 of Routing and Remote Access Service in June 1997 as a no-charge add-on to Windows NT Server 4.0. Routing and RAS adds the following new features to the Remote Access Service provided with Windows NT Server 4.0:

▦ *Demand Dial Routing* initiates a dial-up connection when needed, eliminating costly continuous connections. *RAS Idle Disconnect* terminates the connection after a preset interval of no activity. Routing and RAS supports up to 48 simultaneous Demand Dial Routing connections.

▦ *Server-to-Server PPTP* enhances the Point-to-Point Tunneling Protocol support in Windows NT 4.0 by enabling remote servers to connect by using secure, encrypted communication. (Windows NT Server 4.0 provided only client-to-server PPTP.) Server-to-Server PPTP lets you substitute a Virtual Private Network (VPN) on the Internet for more expensive WAN links.

▦ *Microsoft Point-to-Point Compression (MPPC)* provides compression of up to about 4:1, depending on the type of data transmitted.

▦ *Remote Authentication Dial-In User Service (RADIUS)* lets Routing and RAS users enable remote authentication by using either Windows NT Server domains or a RADIUS server.

▦ *Routing Information Protocol (RIP)* is widely used in small to mid-sized networks because of its ease of use and reasonably good performance. Routing and RAS supports RIP versions 1 and 2.

▦ *Routing Information Protocol and Service Advertising Protocol for IPX* enable Routing and RAS for all servers in mixed Novell NetWare and Windows NT networks.

▦ *Open Shortest Path First (OSPF)* is a link state routing protocol that's more sophisticated than both versions of RIP and is faster when used in large networks. Microsoft and Bay Networks jointly developed the OSPF algorithms for Routing and RAS.

▦ *DHCP Relay Agent* for IP makes Dynamic Host Control Protocol assignments across routed LANs or WANs.

▶ **See** "Implementing Dynamic Host Configuration Protocol," **p. 332**

Routing and RAS can replace low-end hardware routers in a small network, but its enhanced RAS features, including demand-dialing to remote servers in the case of a T-1 line failure, are useful with networks of any size. Even if you support RAS only for dial-in users, the Routing and RAS Admin application (see Figure 26.8) simplifies RAS administration.

FIG. 26.8

The Routing and RAS Admin window after installing the default MyRemoteRouter for demand-dial operation.

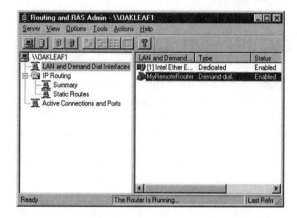

ON THE WEB

A "Microsoft Routing and Remote Access Service for Windows NT Server 4.0 Reviewers Guide" and the downloadable Routing and RAS update to Windows NT Server 4.0 is at **http://www.microsoft.com/ntserver/info/routing&ras.htm**. The Routing and RAS upgrade requires Windows NT 4.0 Service Pack 3, and you must remove your existing Remote Access Service and DHCP Relay Agent before completing the installation of Routing and RAS.

Part
VI

Ch
26

Upgrading BackOffice Members for the Enterprise Edition

The Enterprise Edition of BackOffice 2.5, which is expected to be released at about the same time or shortly after Windows NT Server/E, provides the following upgrades:

- The Enterprise Edition of SQL Server 6.5 includes modifications to accommodate Windows NT Server/E's eight-processor SMP and the changes needed for failover clustering with MSCS. SQL Server 7.0 (code-named *Sphinx*) is needed for the multiterabyte (T) databases Microsoft and its partners demonstrated at Scalability Day.

- The Enterprise Edition of Exchange Server 5.0 increases the size limit of folders from 16G to 16T, supports failover clustering, and adds a few other Internet-related messaging features. Microsoft demonstrated at Scalability Day an Exchange Server system with 50,000 simulated users, 1.8 million messages per day, and a 50G message store. The system included two DEC Alpha servers running the beta version of Exchange Server 5.0 Enterprise Edition, one DEC Celebris (Intel) server, and 20 DEC Celebris GL workstations.

Microsoft didn't announce at Scalability Day its plans for upgrading Systems Management Server and SNA Server. It's likely that both of these BackOffice Family members will be updated for the Enterprise Edition. By the time Microsoft releases BackOffice/E, the final version of Cedar should be available to make the LU 6.2 connection to CICS and IMS for distributed transaction processing.

Reducing Client PC Management Costs

The Network Computer (NC), championed by Oracle's Larry Ellison, has received extensive press coverage, establishing a new record for the number of articles on a projectorware system. The objective of the NC, aside from increasing the revenue of Oracle Corporation, is to reduce the cost of ownership of clients. *Total cost of ownership (TCO)* is the sum of the cost of the hardware and licenses for software, plus support costs, including allocation of network operating expenses, over the life of the client. Despite the lack of a hardware implementation to test, Ellison and other NC proponents have claimed TCO savings in the range of 25 percent to 50 percent, compared with PCs running 32-bit Windows.

N O T E   The term *projectorware* stems from a reporter's question: "On what platform does the NC run best?" The answer: "On the overhead projector." ■

The initial design for the NC forbade local storage, relying on the network to download the Java-based operating system and productivity applications. All user-generated documents were to be stored on a central server, presumably making possible the target NC price point of $500 (less monitor). Such a design obviously doesn't satisfy the needs of mobile PC users, so the restriction against local operating system and data storage has been relaxed, and target NC pricing continues to creep toward $1,000. The first and likely major application for diskless NCs is replacing the conventional "dumb terminals" that communicate with mainframes and multi-user UNIX boxes.

The Network PC

Initially, Microsoft ignored the NC apparition but subsequently caved in with a specification for the Network PC (NetPC), based on the erstwhile Simply Interactive PC (SIPC) design announced at the April 1996 Windows Hardware Engineering Conference (WinHEC). The NetPC is a sealed-case version of a conventional Intel-based PC running 32-bit Windows, preferably Windows NT Workstation 4.0. Compaq, Dell, HP, Intel, and Microsoft released on April 21, 1997, the first "Network PC Design Guidelines" document. The essence of the NetPC design is a client with no "user-serviceable components inside," a network connection, a fixed-disk drive for storing the operating system or caching networked files (including Web pages), but no floppy or CD-ROM drive. (A NetPC must be capable of booting from the network.) The target price for a NetPC is less than $1,000 without a monitor. Compaq, Dell, HP, IBM, Mitsubishi, and others announced in June 1997 a variety of NetPCs at PC Expo in New York City.

NOTE The SIPC design envisioned a sealed case with expansion devices connected via the Universal Serial Bus (USB) and IEEE-1394 High Performance Serial Bus (better known by Apple Computer's trademark, FireWire). Both USB and FireWire connectors were required for the Entertainment PC '97 specification, due for imposition by Microsoft on July 1, 1997. Most motherboards manufactured after September 1996 include one or more USB connectors, but Microsoft didn't complete its work on the Win32 Driver Model (WDM) support for both of these buses in time to meet the July 1, 1997, deadline. (Windows 95 OEM Service Release 2 supports USB devices, but not IEEE-1394 devices.) WDM support for these buses isn't expected until the release of Windows 9x (code-named *Memphis*) and Windows NT 5.0 some time in "the first half of 1998," according to Microsoft. ▩

ON THE WEB

You can download the latest version of the "Network PC Design Guidelines" in Word 6.0 format from **http://www.microsoft.com/hwdev/netpc.htm**. When this book was written, the current edition was version 1.0a, published on May 23, 1997.

Zero Administration Windows

The key to gaining a low TCO with the NetPC is minimizing administrative costs. The sealed-case design with no removable-media drives eliminates problems that arise when users install virus-ridden game software from diskettes but doesn't deal with the issue of downloading similar software from the Internet. Microsoft hopes to reduce TCO primarily by restricting users' Start menu choices, and automating software updates and upgrades from a central server.

Despite its oxymoronic name, Microsoft's Zero-Administration Windows (ZAW) initiative automates operating system updates and application installation, provides stateless desktops and persistent central data storage, lets you quickly replace failed desktop PCs, and gives you tools for central administration and desktop system lockdown. As of mid-1997, Microsoft had announced its Zero Administration Kit (ZAK) for Windows NT 4.0 and Windows 95, but only the Windows NT Workstation 4.0 version of ZAK was available for download.

ON THE WEB

More information on ZAW and ZAK is available at **http://www.microsoft.com/windows/zaw/**. You can download the ZAK for Windows NT Workstation 4.0 from **http://www.microsoft.com/windows/zak/zakreqs.htm**. ZAK requires Service Pack 3 on the server.

Hydra and the Windows NT Terminal

Microsoft announced on May 12, 1997, a joint development agreement with Citrix Systems to provide support in Windows NT Server 4.0 and 5.0 for Windows terminals (WinTerms). A WinTerm is the ultimate thin client, which launches and runs Windows NT applications from the server. Citrix developed the original WinFrame server based on Windows NT and claims

Part
VI

Ch

26

an installed base, as of mid-1997, of 500,000 concurrent WinFrame connections. Microsoft named its WinTerm project *Hydra*, which consists of the following three components:

- *Hydra Server* (Hydra Multiclient Core) hosts multiple, simultaneous client sessions on Windows NT Server 4.0+, including Citrix ICA-based WinFrame clients by means of an ICA plug-in available directly from Citrix.

- *Hydra Client* runs 32-bit Windows on low-cost WinTerm devices, conventional PCs, UNIX workstations, X-terminals, and NCs. Hydra Client also accommodates existing 16-bit DOS and Windows 3.1x PCs.

- *Hydra Remote Protocol* connects a Hydra Client to the network and the Hydra Server. The protocol is based on Microsoft T.Share protocol used by NetMeeting, which in turn is based on the T.120 multichannel conferencing protocol.

Hydra doesn't require downloading of applications or operating systems from the server. Instead, the Hydra Client stores in ROM (or non-volatile RAM) the low-level software necessary to boot the client, establish a connection to the server, and display the user interface. The operating system and all user applications run on the server, so Hydra Clients don't require fixed-disk drives. Thus, the Hydra Client is even thinner than the original NC design; Hydra Clients don't perform any local processing, so they require very little RAM. Like the NC, Hydra is a candidate to replace the millions of dumb terminals used for mundane data-entry applications, such as airline and hotel reservation systems.

ON THE WEB

You can read the preliminary details on Hydra and download the white paper "Hydra: The Advantages of a Managed Windows-based Environment with the Low Cost of a Terminal" at **http://www. microsoft.com/windows/innovation/hydra.htm**.

From Here...

This chapter described the features added by the Enterprise Edition of Windows NT Server 4.0, including failover clustering, distributed transaction processing, and messaging systems. The chapter also briefly described new Routing and Remote Access Service, Enterprise upgrades to SQL Server 6.5 and Exchange Server 5.0, and Microsoft's approaches to reducing the total cost of ownership of Windows clients to compete with forthcoming Network Computers.

The following chapters include information related to the topics of this chapter:

- Chapter 10, "Using TCP/IP, WINS, and DHCP," shows you how to plan for and implement TCP/IP networking, including use of the Windows Internet Name Service and Dynamic Host Configuration Protocol.

■ Chapter 19, "Managing Remote Access Service," explains how to configure Windows NT Server 4.0's RAS component to support dial-in access to network resources shared by mobile users.

■ Chapter 23, "Running Microsoft SQL Server 6.5," describes the basic features of Microsoft's most recent update to SQL Server that includes the Distributed Transaction Controller.

■ Chapter 24, "Messaging with Microsoft Exchange Server 5.0," introduces you to installation and management of Microsoft Exchange Server 5.0.

Part
VI

Ch
26

CHAPTER 27

Distributing File and Directory Services

Distributed computing is an all-encompassing term that distinguishes PC-based networking from traditional centralized mainframe architecture. Distributed systems replace mainframes or large multiuser UNIX systems with multiple low-cost servers placed in close proximity to groups of networked clients. The primary objectives of distributed architecture are hardware and software cost reduction, decentralization of information system (IS) administration, and faster response to user requirements for new and improved custom applications. A continuing controversy in IS management circles is whether today's implementation of distributed computing has achieved—or can ever achieve—its stated objectives.

A major problem with distributed computing is the burden of administering the multiplicity of servers, hubs, routers, switches, and other components that make up a typical PC-based network. As networks become more complex, the cost of training users to navigate through a maze of servers to find a particular resource, such as a file share or remote printer, increases dramatically. Microsoft proposes two new technologies to aid in solving network navigation problems: the Distributed File System (Dfs) and the Active Directory Service Interfaces (ADSI), both of which are released (version 1.0) products.

Distributed File System

The Distributed File System for Windows NT Server 4.0 lets you organize shares on multiple servers into one or more hierarchical tree structures.

Active Directory Service Interfaces

Microsoft's new Active Directory Service Interfaces now supports Windows NT, NetWare Bindery, NetWare Directory Services, and the Internet's Lightweight Directory Access Protocol.

Kerberos security

Microsoft's Distributed Security Service Interfaces enable multiple Security Service Providers, including a provider for Internet-standard Kerberos 5.0.

Directory Service applications

The COM interface to the Active Directory Service lets developers write directory-enabled management applications in VBScript, JavaScript, Visual Basic, and C++.

This chapter introduces Dfs and ADSI, plus ADSI's Kerberos security and administrative components. All the elements described in this chapter are destined for inclusion in Windows NT Server 5.0. ■

Distributing Server Shares with Dfs

Large organizations devote substantial resources to planning a transition from centralized to distributed computing. Smaller firms, which comprise the bulk of the market for Windows NT Server 4.0, often start with a single server and expand the network on an *ad hoc* basis, as dictated by growth in the number of users and the services deployed. Departments or divisions manage their own servers, often with little regard to establishing uniform folder structures and share naming conventions. Adding new servers to accommodate increased network load and requirements for additional storage capacity requires relocating shares. Users are dismayed when shares mapped to logical drive letters disappear without notice. It's seldom practical to completely restructure all existing server shares to provide users with a cogent hierarchical view of a complex network. Lack of structured shares often causes users to run out of logical drive letters for mapping.

Dfs is a simple, low-cost approach to bringing order from the chaos of random server installations and share structures. Dfs gives you, in Microsoft's words, "a logical view of physical storage," letting shares on multiple Windows NT servers "appear as one giant hard drive." Most network administrators probably won't use the single giant hard drive option but will use Dfs to set up a limited number of hierarchical shares that deliver specific categories of information or groups of users.

ON THE WEB

You can read the "Microsoft Distributed File System for Microsoft Windows NT Server 4.0 Administrator's Guide" at **http://www.microsoft.com/ntserver/dfs/dfsdocdl.htm** and release notes for version 1.0 at **http://www.microsoft.com/ntserver/dfs/readme.doc**. Both documents are included in the freely downloadable version of Dfs 1.0 at **http://www.microsoft.com/ntserver/dfs/dfsdl.htm**.

Understanding Dfs Roots and Leaves

Dfs lets you establish a hierarchical (tree) share structure based on Dfs root volumes and leaf folders. Only Windows NT Server 4.0+ supports Dfs root volumes, and you must install Dfs version 1.0 on each server that hosts a Dfs root volume. You can install only one Dfs root volume per server, which must be created on a pre-existing share. Leaf folders may be located on almost any server, including NetWare and NFS servers, accessible to the Windows NT server hosting the Dfs root volume. (Dfs doesn't support Banyan volumes.) A Dfs root can contain only leaf folders, but leaf folders can point to other Dfs root volumes, making possible a multilevel hierarchical structure. Leaf folders that point to other Dfs root shares are called *junction points*.

One of the most interesting features of Dfs is its capability to provide alternative Dfs paths to shares. If you specify two or more servers as the source of a leaf folder, Dfs provides load sharing and lets users access the share in case they can't connect to the primary server.

Installing Dfs on Servers

Installing Dfs is a relatively simple and straightforward process. Follow these steps to set up a Dfs share point and a Dfs root volume on an Windows NT server:

1. Download Dfs-v40-i386.exe (462K) from **http://www.microsoft.com/ntserver/dfs/ dfsdl.htm** to a temporary folder.

2. Create a share for the Dfs root volume on each Windows NT server that hosts Dfs. Choose a share name appropriate to the folders shared by the server. In this example, the share name is Books on the OakLeaf1 server.

3. Log on as a member of the Administrators group and execute Dfs-v40-i386.exe on the Windows NT server from which you will install Dfs on other servers and Windows 95 clients. Launching the downloaded executable file opens the Microsoft Dfs for Windows NT Server – Web Download window (see Figure 27.1).

N O T E Only members of the Administrators group can install and administer Dfs on a Windows NT 4.0 server. ▪

FIG. 27.1
The first window of the Dfs setup program.

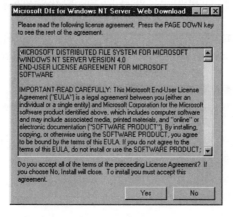

Part
VI

Ch
27

4. Click Yes to open the main setup dialog, which explains what setup does and doesn't do (see Figure 27.2).

5. Click Continue to install the Dfs files in your \Winnt\System32\Dfs folder.

6. When installation is complete, click the Exit button of the message box (see Figure 27.3) to display the Readme.doc file in WordPad.

7. Close WordPad after reviewing Readme.doc and reboot Windows NT Server when requested.

FIG. 27.2

The main dialog of the Dfs setup program.

FIG. 27.3

The message box that leads to display of the Readme.doc file.

8. Launch Control Panel's Network tool and click the Services tab.

9. Click the Add button to open the Select Network Service dialog.

10. Click the Have Disk button to open the Insert Disk dialog. Type the location of the ...\Dfs folder, usually `c:\winnt\system32\dfs`, in the text box (see Figure 27.4).

FIG. 27.4

Specifying the location of the Dfs network service files.

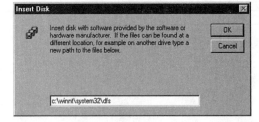

11. Click OK to open the Select OEM Option dialog with the Distributed File System option selected (see Figure 27.5).

12. Click OK to open the Configure Dfs dialog. Mark the Host a Dfs on Share check box and select the share you created in step 2 for the Dfs root from the drop-down list (see Figure 27.6).

13. Click OK to close the Configure Dfs dialog and return to the Services page of the Network tool. Distributed File System appears in the Network Services list (see Figure 27.7).

FIG. 27.5
The Select OEM Option dialog for Dfs.

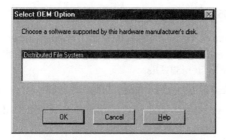

FIG. 27.6
Selecting the server share for a Dfs root volume.

FIG. 27.7
Distributed File System added to the Network Services list.

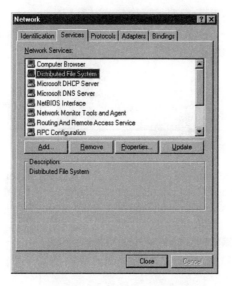

14. Click Close to rebuild the network bindings. When prompted to reboot your server to make the Dfs service active, click Yes.

N O T E If you want to install Dfs on other Windows NT servers or Windows 95 clients, share your \Winnt\System32\Dfs folder with Administrators-only permissions. ▓

Installing the Windows 95 Dfs Client

The retail versions of Windows NT 4.0 Server and Workstation support client-side Dfs, but Windows 95 doesn't. If your Windows 95 clients don't have the .cab files on the local drive, you need the Windows 95 CD-ROM to complete the setup operation.

To install Dfs for Windows 95, follow these steps:

1. If you want users to be able to install the Dfs client, create a share for \Winnt\ System32\Dfs\Win95 with appropriate user permissions. Otherwise, use an administrative share of \Winnt\System32\Dfs.

2. Map a temporary logical drive letter to the ...\Dfs or ...\Dfs\Win95 share.

3. Launch Control Panel's Network tool, which opens with the default Configuration page active.

4. Click the Add button to open the Select Network Component Type dialog.

5. Select Service in the list box and click the Add button to open the Select Network Service dialog.

6. Click the Have Disk button to open the Install from Disk dialog, and then click the Browse button to open the Open dialog. Select the newly mapped drive in the Drives list (see Figure 27.8).

FIG. 27.8

Selecting the server share for installation of the Windows 95 Dfs client service.

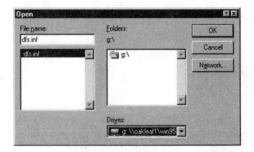

7. With Dfs.inf in the File Name text box, click OK to close the Open dialog. Click OK again to close the Install from Disk dialog and open the Select Network Service dialog with the DFS Services for Microsoft Network Client in the Models list (see Figure 27.9).

FIG. 27.9

DFS Services for Microsoft Network in the Select Network Service dialog.

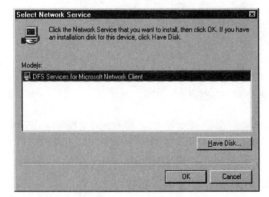

8. Click OK to close the Select Network Service dialog and add Dfs to the Windows 95 client's network components list (see Figure 27.10).

FIG. 27.10

DFS Services for Microsoft Network added to the network components list of a Windows 95 client.

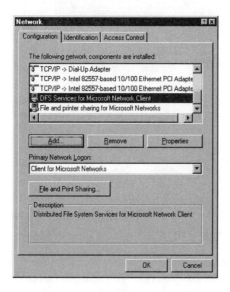

9. Click OK to close the Network tool. Windows 95 rebuilds the network bindings and asks you to reboot the client.

When Windows 95 reopens, you can connect to the Dfs root share with Network Neighborhood or assign a logical drive letter to the share.

Administering Dfs

You construct your Dfs tree with the newly installed Dfs Administrator on each of your Windows NT servers. You must be a member of the Administrators group to use Dfs Administrator.

N O T E Users don't need permissions for the Dfs root volume share on the server unless users need access to files in this share. Dfs doesn't change permissions for Dfs leaf shares; user permissions are based on those assigned for the source share to which the Dfs leaf share points. ■

To use Dfs Administrator to add leaf folders to the Dfs root volume, follow these steps:

1. From the Start menu choose Programs, Administrative Tools (Common), and Dfs Administrator to open the Dfs Administrator window. The Dfs root volume you created earlier in the "Installing Dfs on Servers" section is selected (see Figure 27.11).

2. Click the Add Dfs Volume (leftmost) button of the toolbar to open the Add to Dfs dialog. Type the Dfs path for the first leaf of the Books volume—**Que** for this example—in the When a User References this Path text box.

FIG. 27.11

Dfs Administrator with only the Dfs root volume for the server.

N O T E   The Add Dfs Volume tooltip caption is misleading. In this case, the button opens a dialog to add a Dfs leaf share, not a Dfs root volume. ▦

3. Click the lower Browse button to open the Browse for Folder dialog to select the server share for the \Oakleaf1\Books\Que Dfs path—in this case, \Oakleaf0\Public Documents\Que Corporation (see Figure 27.12).

FIG. 27.12

Selecting a server share to be added as a leaf to the Dfs volume in the Browse for Folder dialog.

4. Click OK to close the Browse for Folder dialog and add the conventional UNC path to the Send the User to this Network Path text box (see Figure 27.13).

FIG. 27.13

The UNC path to the server share for the Dfs leaf.

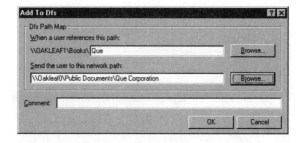

5. Add a descriptive comment for the Dfs leaf, if you want, and click OK to add the new leaf share to Dfs Administrator's list (see Figure 27.14).

FIG. 27.14

A Dfs leaf share added to the Dfs volume.

6. Repeat steps 2 through 5 for each leaf you want to add to the Dfs root volume. The leaf can point to any share on any accessible server.

To add an alternate server for a leaf share, follow these steps:

1. Right-click the selected Dfs leaf in Dfs Administrator's list, and choose Properties from the pop-up menu to open the *LeafName* Properties sheet (see Figure 27.15).

2. Click the Add button. A message box appears, warning you that Dfs doesn't replicate content between alternate shares. Click OK to open the Add Server dialog.

3. Click the Browse button of the Add Server dialog to open the Browse for Folder dialog and select the alternate server share for the selected Dfs leaf share.

4. Click OK to close the Browse for Folder dialog and add the selected share as the alternate (see Figure 27.16).

5. Click OK to add the alternate share and close the Add Server dialog; then click OK again to close the *LeafName* Properties sheet. When you create an alternate share, 2 Servers replaces the Server entry in Dfs Administrator's list (see Figure 27.17).

Part
VI
Ch
27

FIG. 27.15
The properties sheet for a selected Dfs leaf share.

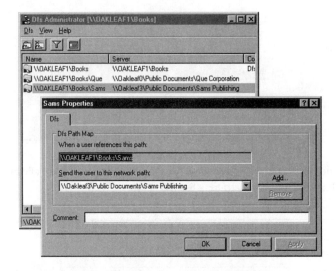

FIG. 27.16
Adding an alternate share to a Dfs leaf share in the Add Server dialog.

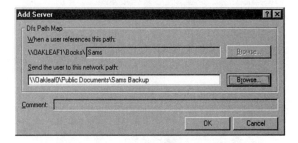

FIG. 27.17
The Dfs leaf share with an alternate server share.

As noted in step 2, Dfs doesn't provide replication services to assure that the contents of the primary and alternate shares are identical. Thus, Dfs leaf shares with alternates should, in most cases, store read-only files. You can use Server Manager's Directory Replication service or a third-party replication tool to maintain synchronization between alternate folders.

▶ **See** "Replicating Folders," **p. 502**

Activating Directory Services

Windows NT Server 4.0 lacks an enterprise-class directory service, such as Novell's NetWare Directory Services (NDS) or Banyan's StreetTalk. Directory services provide a global view of available network resources organized by function ("yellow pages"), regardless of a resource's physical location on a LAN or WAN. Global directory services also provide unified group designations, searchable user lists ("white pages"), and a single-user login regardless of user location or network operating system. Windows NT Server's domain architecture delivers single- user login to multiple domains and services, but doesn't offer many of the features that make NDS attractive to large firms.

Microsoft distributed a preview version of its Active Directory Service Interfaces (ADSI) for BackOffice at the Microsoft Professional Developer Conference (PDC) in November 1996. The PDC presentations and ADSI applications were included on the Microsoft Developer Network (MSDN) CD-ROMs distributed in January 1997. Microsoft subsequently released version 1.0 of the ADSI Software Developer Kit in April 1997. ADSI, a set of COM interfaces, stems from the previously announced Open Directory Services Interface (ODSI, a Windows Open Services API) and OLE Directory Services (OLE DS). ODSI and OLE DS directory namespaces are analogous to Microsoft's ODBC and OLE DB for databases and other tabular data. Microsoft has described ODSI as "ODBC for directories" because of the architectural similarity of the two technologies.

ON THE WEB

ADSI market bulletins, white papers, and a downloadable version of ADSI 1.0 are available at **http://www.microsoft.com/ntserver/info/adsi.htm**. You can read or download PDC white papers and presentations from **http://www.microsoft.com/pdc/**.

Figure 27.18 shows the tiers that comprise ADSI and directory-enabled applications. Using the ODBC analogy, directories correspond to databases, Directory Service Providers (DSPs) take the place of ODBC drivers, and the Active Directory COM implementation mimics the ODBC Driver Manager. You can write directory-enabled applications with scripting languages, such as VBScript or JavaScript, as well as conventional Windows programming tools, such as Visual Basic 5.0 or Visual C++. WScript and CScript are the Windows and command-line versions, respectively, of the new Windows Scripting Host (WSH) application that lets you write VBScript or JavaScript applications to replace conventional batch files. WSH will become a component of Windows NT 5.0.

Part
VI

Ch
27

FIG. 27.18
The tiered structure of the Active Directory Services Interfaces.

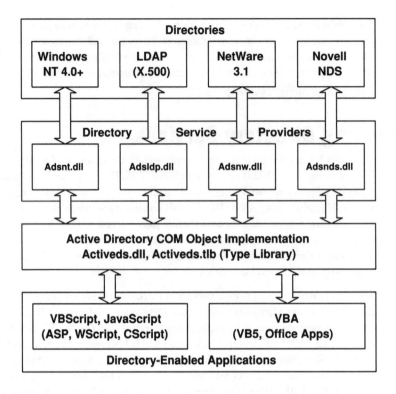

Directories

| Windows NT 4.0+ | LDAP (X.500) | NetWare 3.1 | Novell NDS |

Directory   Service   Providers

| Adsnt.dll | Adsldp.dll | Adsnw.dll | Adsnds.dll |

Active Directory COM Object Implementation
Activeds.dll, Activeds.tlb (Type Library)

| VBScript, JavaScript (ASP, WScript, CScript) | VBA (VB5, Office Apps) |

Directory-Enabled Applications

> **N O T E**   The downloadable version of ADSI 1.0, Ads.exe, includes only the four Directory Service Providers, the Active Directory DLLs, and other supporting DLLs. To use ADSI 1.0 with Windows NT Server 4.0, you must write your own directory-enabled applications. Ads.exe doesn't include any sample applications. ▓

ON THE WEB

The Windows Scripting Host for Windows 95 and Windows NT 4.0 is available for download from **http:/ /www.microsoft.com/management/wsh.htm**. The white paper "Windows Scripting Host: A Universal Scripting Host for Scripting Languages" also is available from this page.

Directory Service Providers

Microsoft supplies the Internet-standard Lightweight Directory Access Protocol (LDAP) Directory Service Provider (DSP) based on Exchange Server's X.500 directory technology, plus DSPs for Windows NT, NetWare 3.1, and NetWare Directory Services (NDS) for version 4.x. X.500 is a complex naming system that depends on a set of Directory Service Agents (DSAs) that operate only in Open Systems Interconnection (OSI) networking. The LDAP subset of the X.500 protocol is Microsoft's primary choice for its global directory services because LDAP is an Internet standard that communicates with TCP/IP. DSPs for other directory services, such as Banyan StreetTalk and IBM/Lotus Notes, were under development when this book was written.

ON THE WEB

Extensive information on LDAP and its relationship to X.500 is the FAQ and Web bibliography available at **http://www.leland.stanford.edu/group/networking/directory/x500ldapfaq.html**. Microsoft offers a LDAP market bulletin at **http://www.microsoft.com/ntserver/info/ldapmb.htm** and links to Internet Engineering Task Force (IETF) papers on LDAP version 3 at **http://www.microsoft.com/ntserver/info/ldapv3.htm**.

The PDC preview of ADSI includes a Directory feature, which uses the Windows NT and LDAP service providers to display users, groups, and servers in an Explorer-like format. Directory, which you access from a desktop icon, is an alternative for Network Neighborhood, My Computer, or Explorer. Figure 27.19 shows the Windows NT view of the Oakleaf domain, whereas Figure 27.20 shows the same resources for the Oakleaf X.500 Organization Unit (OU) with their LADP Common Name (CN). It's likely that Windows NT 5.0 will include Directory or a similar hierarchical tool to simplify directory browsing. Double-clicking an entry for a user or group opens the browser-based administrative tool described in the "ADSI Management" section at the end of this chapter.

FIG. 27.19

Directory's view of Oakleaf domain users, groups, and resources displayed by the Windows NT DSP.

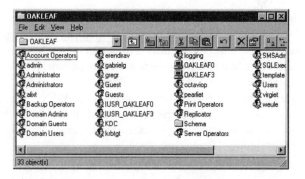

FIG. 27.20

The users, groups, and resources of Figure 27.19 displayed by ADSI's LDAP provider.

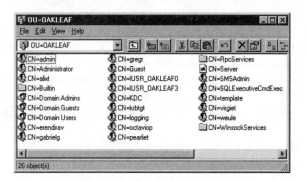

Part

VI

Ch

27

Directory Search and Replication

Global directories can grow to huge proportions, making location of specific users or resources difficult without an efficient search mechanism. ODSI uses OLE DB to provide directory query services that enable creation of a much more sophisticated version of the 32-bit Windows Find feature to locate network users and resources. OLE DB has the advantage of operability with non-relational, hierarchical data structures typical of directory services. OLE DB is the foundation of Microsoft's ActiveX Data Objects (ADO) technology that provides database connectivity to Internet Information Server 3.0+ Active Server Pages.

▶ **See** "Activating Web Pages with ASP, ADO, and OLE DB," **p. 794**

Directories serving tens or hundreds of thousands of users require a replication process that's more sophisticated than Windows NT's domain controller approach. Directories that use the master/slave model require that all changes be made to a single directory master copy, and then propagated from the master to a host of slave copies. ADSI uses multimaster replication to distribute directory updates throughout the network. To avoid problems with synchronizing the system clocks in WANs, ADSI substitutes Update Sequence Numbers (USNs) for timestamps, which SQL Server uses to resolve concurrency conflicts, to assure that the latest version of directory updates propagate correctly via direct LAN connections and store-and-forward messaging systems.

Distributed Security

ADSI is intended to replace Windows NT's Security Accounts Manager (SAM) database with a globally distributed LDAP database for domain management. ADSI supports both Kerberos 5.0 and NT LM security; you select the security provider for server login by expanding the login dialog with an Advanced button and choosing a security provider from a drop-down list. Distributed Security Service Interfaces (DSSI) use Kerberos on the LAN; Secure Sockets Layer 3.0 and CryptoAPI 2.0 provide security over Internet-based WANs. The architecture of DSSI, with a middle tier of Security Service Providers, parallels that of ADSI. ADSI and distributed security eliminate the need for complex transitive trust relationships between multiple-master or complete-trust Windows NT domains.

▶ **See** "Understanding Windows NT's Domain Models," **p. 626**

The Kerberos authentication protocol, developed at the Massachusetts Institute of Technology, uses a Key Distribution Center (KDC) to define interactions between clients and the network for security services. The user obtains a Kerberos ticket, which is cached on the client PC, which defines the resources for which the user has permissions. The Internet-standard Kerberos implementation is defined in Internet RFC 1510. Windows NT adds KDC as the authentication service to existing domain controllers. The Kerberos equivalent of a Windows NT domain is called a *realm*. Kerberos is more efficient than Windows NT's NT LM security system for authenticating users to Windows NT services, such as SQL Server or Exchange.

ON THE WEB

You can download a security white paper that explains the benefits of Kerberos authentication at
http://www.microsoft.com/msdn/sdk/techinfo/secwp.doc.

ADSI Management

ADSI also lets you automate a wide variety of directory operations, such as adding and deleting users. The initial release of ADSI, which primarily is for independent software vendors (ISVs) and developers, requires you to roll your own Visual Basic, Visual C++, or scripted applications. At the PDC, Microsoft previewed a Web-based ADSI management application, called DS Web, that lets you add, delete, and update Active Directory entries over an intranet or the Internet (see Figure 27.21). DS Web is a complex set of Active Server Pages, accessed from the Directory tool described in the earlier "ADSI Management" section, that run under Internet Information Server 3.0+. It's likely that Windows NT 5.0 will include a Web-based ADSI administrative application, similar to DS Web, as well as an ADSI Snap-In for the Microsoft Management Console (MMC).

▶ **See** "Using Microsoft Management Console to Administer IIS 4.0," **p. 747**

FIG. 27.21

Editing a directory entry for a user with the DS Web application included on the CD-ROM distributed at the November 1996 PDC.

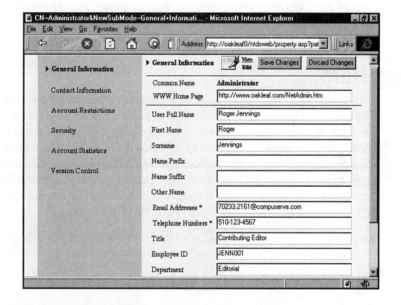

N O T E Microsoft described at the PDC a Web-Based Enterprise Management (WBEM) initiative that provides a hierarchical framework for managing physical and logical managed objects by means of Web pages. A *managed object* can be a device (a disk or tape drive, router, or an adapter card in a PC) or a construct (a file system, folder, or file). WBEM is a cooperative project involving Microsoft, BMC Software, Compaq, Cisco, Intel, and more than 70 other firms. WBEM is based on *schemas* that conform to the Common Information Model (CIM) and are published by the HyperMedia Management Protocol (HMMP). Object classes, properties, and methods are the key elements of schemas; classes also can have events, associations, and references. The schema is extensible to accommodate new and derived classes.

Part

VI

Ch

27

continues

continued

> WBEM was in the definition stage in mid-1997, and Microsoft hasn't divulged the extent of Windows NT 5.0's support for WBEM. Classes are the foundation of the successor to the Object File System (NTOFS) promised for Cairo (the original code name for Windows NT 4.0+). According to Jim Allchin, Microsoft senior vice president, Windows NT 5.0's file system will offer "native properties." Native ADSI properties are implemented through the FileSystem managed object class. It's also likely that future versions of Systems Management Server and Microsoft Management Console will take advantage of WBEM schema. ▓

ON THE WEB

Detailed information on WBEM is available at **http://www.microsoft.com/management/wbem/default.htm**. You can get more information on HMMP from **http://wbem.freerange.com/** and see a demonstration of WBEM in action at **http://wbem.freerange.com/wbem/activex/console_p.htm**. (Click the flashing exclamation points to proceed through the demo.)

From Here...

This chapter described enterprise-scale additions to Windows NT Server 4.0 released by Microsoft in 1997 and expected to be included in Windows NT Server 5.0. Dfs, which you can use today to reorganize your server shares into a hierarchical tree structure, is a simple but useful tool that makes life much easier for network users. The Active Directory Service Interfaces promise to integrate the NetWare Bindery, NDS, Windows NT, and LDAP directory services within a common framework. The released version of ADSI 1.0 is designed primarily for software developers, but you can expect Microsoft and ISVs to deliver various ADSI applications before the general availability of Windows NT Server 5.0.

Glossary

10BaseT The most common network cabling method for Ethernet, which handles traffic at a speed of 10 Mbps. 10BaseT uses a pair of unshielded twisted conductors to connect between a network interface card (NIC) and an Ethernet hub. 10Base2 (thin Ethernet, or *thinnet*) uses coaxial cable connections between computers and doesn't require a hub. 100BaseT is a newer medium that supports up to 100 Mbps. See *Ethernet, hub,* and *NIC.*

Access Control List (ACL) Part of Windows NT's security description that controls access to a Windows NT object, such as a file. The owner of an object can change access control entries in the list to grant or revoke permissions (access rights) for the object.

access token A Windows NT object that identifies a logged-on (authenticated) user. The access token contains the user's security ID (SID), the groups to which the user belongs, and other security information. See *SID.*

Active Data Objects (ADO) A set of data-access interfaces optimized for use in Internet and intranet applications. ADO is an object-based wrapper for OLE DB. ADO is included in Internet Information Server 3.0 and Microsoft's Visual InterDev development toolset, which is part of Visual Studio. See *OLE DB.*

Active Directory Service (ADS or ADSI, Active Directory Service Interface) Microsoft's answer to Novell's NetWare Directory Services (NDS), a uniform method of locating network resources, regardless of their location in the network topology. ADS (Interface) uses LDAP, an Internet standard, as the directory services middleware. See *LDAP* and *X.500*.

Active Group A standards organization, under the auspices of The Open Group, created by Microsoft to manage ongoing development, management, and licensing of ActiveX technologies.

ON THE WEB

The Active Group maintains a Web site at **http://www.activex.org/**.

Active Platform A set of Microsoft client (Active Client) and server (Active Server) development technologies based on ActiveX components, primarily devoted to Internet and intranet applications.

Active Server Pages (ASP) The technology introduced in Internet Information Server 3.0 that enables server-side scripting with Visual Basic Script (VBScript) or JavaScript to create Web pages dynamically in response to user requests.

ActiveX A family of Microsoft object technologies, formerly called *OLE (Object Linking and Embedding)*, based on the Common Object Model (COM), serving as one of the foundations of Microsoft's Internet products. See *COM* and *DCOM*.

ActiveX Automation The latest of three consecutive names Microsoft has assigned to OLE Automation objects in less than two years. See *Automation*.

ActiveX control An insertable COM object (component) that usually provides user interface components and can fire events. ActiveX controls are lightweight versions of OLE Controls, which have considerably more overhead and are becoming obsolete. ActiveX and OLE controls both use the .ocx extension.

address The numerical value, usually in hexadecimal format, of a particular location in your computer's RAM.

address space Memory allocated to an application by the operating system. See *virtual address space*.

alert In Windows NT, a message sent between two simultaneously executing threads that results in an asynchronous procedure call (APC) executed by the receiving thread. Also means a message indicating abnormal operation of a Windows NT process.

anonymous FTP A method of connecting to a remote computer by using the File Transfer Protocol as an anonymous or guest user for file transfer operations. See *FTP*.

ANSI An acronym for the *American National Standards Institute*. In the Windows context, ANSI refers to the ANSI character set. Windows 95 and Windows NT include both ANSI (suffix A) and Unicode (suffix W) versions of Windows API functions. See *ASCII* and *Unicode*.

Apartment Model   A Windows NT or Windows 95 threading model having a message queue that assigns threads, managed by COM or DCOM, to multiple operations. See *COM*, *DCOM*, and *thread*.

API   An acronym for *application program interface*. Generically, a method by which a program can obtain access to or modify the operating system. See also *DLL*.

applet   An application that runs within another application, such as a Java applet running within a Web browser. Also, a Windows application that's supplied as a component of another Windows application, rather than as a retail product. The Notepad and Wordpad applications supplied with Windows NT are examples of applets.

application server   A networked server enhanced for sharing applications, rather than or in addition to files. Windows NT Server gained its initial commercial acceptance as an application server for SQL Server, Microsoft Office, and other services and applications. See *file server*.

ARP   An acronym for *Address Resolution Protocol*, a TCP/IP protocol that resolves IP addresses to Media Access Control (MAC) addresses. See *MAC*.

ASCII   An acronym for *American Standard Code for Information Interchange*. A set of standard numerical values for printable, control, and special characters used by PCs and most other computers. Other commonly used codes for character sets are ANSI (used by Windows 3.1+), Unicode (used by Windows 95 and Windows NT), and EBCDIC (Extended Binary-Coded Decimal Interchange Code, used by IBM for mainframe computers). See *Unicode*.

asymmetric multiprocessing   A multiprocessing technique in which individual processors are dedicated to particular tasks, such as running the operating system or performing user requests. See *SMP*.

asynchronous   A process that can occur at any time, regardless of the status of the operating system or applications that are running. An example is Windows NT's asynchronous procedure call (APC).

asynchronous I/O   Input/output operations in which an application issues an I/O request to a device, and then continues operation while the device transfers data. Asynchronous I/O greatly speeds fixed-disk file operations. *See synchronous I/O*.

Asynchronous Transfer Mode (ATM)   A high-speed networking and telecommunications protocol that uses small, fixed-size (53-byte) packets. ATM primarily is used for wide-area networking (WAN) and network backbones, rather than as a local-area networking (LAN) protocol.

auditing   Windows NT's capability to record and report security-related events, such as accessing, creating, or deleting files.

authentication   The process of verifying (validating) a user's logon ID and password, usually used to provide access to network resources.

Automation   An ActiveX (OLE) term that refers to a means of manipulating another application's objects by the use of a programming language, most commonly Visual Basic for Applications (VBA). Microsoft renamed Automation to ActiveX Automation in early 1997.

Automation controller   An ActiveX-compliant Windows application with an application programming (macro) language, such as VBA, that can reference and manipulate objects exposed by ActiveX components and Automation servers. *Automation controller* replaces the term *OLE Automation client.*

Automation server   Technically, any OLE 2-compliant Windows application that supports OLE Automation operations by exposing a set of objects for manipulation by OLE Automation client applications. In ActiveX terminology, ActiveX components are Automation servers.

Autoplay   A feature of Windows 95's and Windows NT 4.0's CD-ROM file system (CDFS) that automatically executes a program on the CD-ROM when inserted into the CD-ROM drive.

back up   To create a file (backup file) that duplicates data stored in one or more files on a client or server computer.

bandwidth   The rate at which a communication channel can transmit data, usually expressed in Mbps (megabits per second) for networking and digital data and MHz (megahertz) for analog transmission. Depending on the modulation method, 1MHz of analog bandwidth can transmit several Mbps of digital information.

batch   A group of statements processed as an entity. Execution of DOS batch files (such as AUTOEXEC.BAT) and SQL statements are examples of a *batch process.*

BDC   An acronym for *Backup Domain Controller*, a Windows NT server that provides an alternative source of authentication for network users. Account and group information from a Primary Domain Controller (PDC) is replicated periodically to each BDC in the domain. See *PDC* .

binary file   A file whose content doesn't consist of lines of text. Executable (.exe), dynamic link library (.dll), and most database files are stored in binary format.

binding   In ActiveX and OLE, a term for the act of connecting a component (server object) to a controller (OLE client).

bit   The smallest piece of information processed by a computer. A bit, derived from the contraction of BInary digiT (or Binary digIT) has two states—on (1) or off (0). Eight bits make up a *byte*; 16 bits combined is called a *word.*

BLOB   An acronym for *Binary Large Object*, a term that describes long strings of data handled by database management systems. The most common use of BLOBs is for storing image, audio, and video data.

blue screen   The screen displayed when Windows NT 4.0 crashes and cannot recover, usually as the result of a serious fault at the HAL or kernel level. Also known as BSOD, the "Blue Screen of Death."

Boolean   A type of arithmetic in which all digits are bits—that is, the numbers may have only two states: on (true or 1) or off (false or 0). Widely used in set theory and computer programming, Boolean, named after mathematician George Boole, also is used to describe a data type that may have only two states: true or false.

BOOTP An abbreviation for TCP/IP's Bootstrap Protocol (RFCs 951 and 1542) used by DHCP. See *DHCP*.

bps An acronym for *bits per second*. Mbps is one million bits per second; kbps is one thousand bits per second. See *bit*.

Bps An acronym for *bytes per second*, the equivalent of 8 bits per second. MBps (also M/sec) is one million bytes per second; kBps (also K/sec) is one thousand bytes per second. See *byte*.

break To cause an interruption in program operation. Ctrl+C is the standard DOS break-key combination but seldom halts operation of a Windows application. Esc is more commonly used in Windows to cause an operation to terminate before completion.

BRI An acronym for *Basic Rate Interface*, the standard ISDN service for business and residential Internet connections. BRI has two 56 kbps B (bearer) channels and one 16 kbps D (data) channel, providing a maximum bandwidth of 112 kbps. See *ISDN* and *PRI*.

bridge An active network device used to divide a network into mutually isolated segments while maintaining the whole as a single network. Bridges operate at the data-link layer of the OSI Reference Model. See *OSI*.

browser An application or component of an operating system (for instance, Windows 9x) that displays text (usually encoded with HTML), graphics, audio, or video content originating at a World Wide Web site. See *HTML*.

browsing The process of viewing network resources available to users, usually with My Computer, Explorer, or Network Neighborhood.

buffer An area in memory of a designated size (number of bytes or characters) reserved, typically, to hold a portion of a file or the value of a variable.

business rules A set of rules for entering data in a database that are specific to an enterprise's methods of conducting its operations. Business rules are in addition to rules for maintaining the domain and referential integrity of tables in a database. Business rules most commonly are implemented in a three-tier client/server database environment. See *three-tier*.

byte The basic measure of memory and storage capacity of a computer (8 bits), usually abbreviated B. This book uses K (kilobyte) and M (megabyte) abbreviations. A byte traditionally contains one character of data; Windows NT 4.0's Unicode requires 2 bytes to define a character.

cache A block of memory reserved for temporary storage. Caches usually store data from disk files in memory to make access to the data faster. By default, Windows NT caches all disk read and write operations.

cache manager A component of Windows NT's I/O system that uses the virtual memory (VM) manager to create temporary storage in the paging file to speed disk I/O operations. See *VM*.

CDFS   The 32-bit *CD-ROM file system* shared by Windows NT and Windows 95.

Cedar   The code name for Microsoft's extensions to Microsoft Transaction Server (MTS, formerly Viper) that provide interaction with IBM's mainframe transaction processing monitors, such as CICS (Customer Information and Control System). See *MTS*.

CGI   An acronym for *Common Gateway Interface*, a server-side programming system for initiating software services, such as database access for Web servers. CGI services run as separate processes under UNIX and Windows NT Server. See *ISAPI*.

channel   A dedicated communication connection between a transmitting and receiving device. *Channel* is also used to identify an I/O port in mainframe and mini-computers.

CISC   *Complex instruction set computer*, a microprocessor whose internal instructions often involve many individual execution steps and thus many clock cycles. The Intel 80x86 processors are the most common CISC devices. See *RISC*.

class   An object-oriented programming term that describes a group of one or more instances of objects having identical properties and behavior. See *instance* and *instantiate.*

class identifier   See *CLSID.*

client   The device or application that receives data from or manipulates a server device or application. The data may be in the form of a file received from a network file server, or an object created from an ActiveX component or OLE server. See *Automation controller.*

CLSID   An identification tag that's associated with an ActiveX or OLE object created by a specific component or server. CLSID values appear in the Registry and must be unique for each type of object that the server can create. See *Registry.*

clustering   A server architecture that emulates multiprocessing by interconnecting two or more individual computers to share the application processing load. Microsoft's forthcoming clustering technology for Windows NT carries the code name *Wolfpack.* (Novell's clustering technology is code-named *Wolf Mountain.*) A number of third parties offer proprietary clustering hardware and software for Windows NT Server 4.0.

collection   A group of objects of the same class that are contained within another object. Collections are named as the plural of their object class.

COM   An acronym for *Component Object Model*, the name of Microsoft's design strategy to implement OLE 2+ and ActiveX. Distributed COM (DCOM) allows networked and cross-platform implementation of ActiveX and OLE 2+ operations and Automation. See *Automation* and *DCOM.*

Component Object Model   See *COM.*

concurrency   The condition when more than one user has access to a specific set of records or files at the same time. *Concurrency* also describes a database management system's capability to handle simultaneous queries against a single set of tables.

concurrent application   An application capable of simultaneous execution in multiple address spaces. Windows NT uses threads of execution to support concurrent applications.

console   A character-based interface to an operating system. Windows NT uses the Command Prompt tool as the console.

container   An object or application that can create or manipulate compound documents. For example, Internet Explorer is a container for ActiveX objects.

context switching   The process of saving an executing thread or process and transferring control to another thread or process. Windows NT 4.0's context switching, one of the major bottlenecks in COM operations, is substantially faster than in Windows NT 3.x.

control object   In Windows NT, objects that control system tasks, such as asynchronous and deferred procedure calls.

cookie   A file created by a Web server on a user's PC to identify the user and, optionally, to cache his ID and password for logon purposes or store information on customization of a Web site to conform to a user's preferences.

CORBA (Common Object Request Broker Architecture)   A specification of the Object Management Group for the definition of object interfaces. CORBA is the primary competitor to Microsoft's COM and DCOM object architecture. See *COM* and *DCOM*.

custom control   A control object not native to the application, such as an ActiveX control or a Visual Basic Extension control (VBX).

data integrity   The maintenance of rules that prevent inadvertent or intentional modifications to the content of a database that would be harmful to its accuracy or reliability. See *domain integrity*.

database device   A file in which databases and related information, such as transaction logs, are stored. Database devices usually have physical names, such as a file name (Master.dat for SQL Server), and a logical name, such as `master`.

DCE (Distributed Computing Environment)   The Open Software Foundation (OSF) specification for a set of distributed computing services. Microsoft's Remote Procedure Call (RPC) protocols are DCE-compliant. See *OSF* and *remote procedure call*.

DCOM   An acronym for *Distributed Common Object Model*. DCOM allows communication and manipulation of objects over a network connection. Windows NT 4.0 is the first Microsoft operating system to support DCOM (formerly called NetworkOLE). See *COM*.

DDE   An acronym for *dynamic data exchange,* an early Interprocess Communication (IPC) method used by Windows and OS/2 to transfer data between different applications. Automation (ActiveX Automation, formerly OLE Automation) provides a more robust IPC method.

default   A value assigned or an option chosen when no value is specified by users or assigned by a program statement.

demand lock   Precludes more shared locks from being set on a data resource. Successive requests for shared locks must wait for the demand lock to be cleared.

device   A computer system component that can send or receive data, such as a keyboard, display, printer, disk drive, or modem. Windows NT uses device drivers to create device objects that connect applications to devices.

Dfs   An acronym for Microsoft's *Distributed File System*, a server component that enables files resident in shares on a number of servers to be united in a single name space. Dfs and Distributed Security will be integrated into Windows NT 5.0 Server. See *Kerberos*.

DHCP   An acronym for *Dynamic Host Configuration Protocol*, an Internet standard protocol that allows IP addresses to be pooled and assigned as needed to clients. Windows NT 4.0 includes DHCP Manager, a graphical DHCP configuration tool. See *IP* and *IP address*.

dialog   A pop-up modal child window, also called a *dialog box*, that requests information from users. Dialogs include message boxes, input boxes, and user-defined dialogs for activities such as choosing files to open.

directory services   A class of middleware used to locate a network address based on partial name, address, or other address attribute. Microsoft Active Directory Services (ADS or ADSI), which is destined for inclusion in Windows NT 5.0, is an example of a directory service. See *Active Directory Service*.

disk mirroring   Creating on two or more physical disk drives exact duplicates of a disk volume to make files accessible in case one drive of the mirror set fails. Disk mirroring is called RAID 1. See *RAID*.

disk striping   Distributing the data for a single logical disk volume across two or more physical disk drives. Simple disk striping (RAID 0) provides faster I/O operation but no data protection. Disk striping with parity (RAID 5) provides faster I/O and protection from failure of a physical disk in a stripe set. See *RAID*.

dispatcher   A Windows NT operating system component that schedules the execution of application threads.

distributed database   A database, usually of the client/server type, that's located on more than one database server, often at widely separated locations. Synchronization of data contained in distributed databases is most commonly accomplished by the two-phase commit or replication methods. See *replication* and *two-phase commit*.

distributed processing   The physical or logical location of software components and data on multiple networked servers to enhance application performance or ensure data integrity.

DLC   An acronym for *Data Link Control*, a Windows NT protocol used to communicate with mainframes and networked laser printers.

DLL   An acronym for *dynamic link library*, a file containing a collection of Windows functions designed to perform a specific class of operations. Most DLLs carry the .dll extension, but some Windows DLLs, such as Gdi32.exe, use the .exe extension. Functions within DLLs are called (invoked) by applications as necessary to perform the desired operation.

DNS   An acronym for *Domain Name Service*, the primary method of associating numeric Internet Protocol (IP) addresses with friendly names, such as **microsoft.com**. Windows NT 4.0 includes a graphical DNS management tool.

domain   In Windows NT, a group of workstations and servers that share a common Security Accounts Manager (SAM) database and allow a user to log on to any resource in the domain with a single user ID and password. On the Internet, a name assigned to specific sites (**microsoft.com**) or classifications of sites (**.com**, **.org**, **.gov**, and the like). The **.com**, **.org**, and **.gov** extensions are called *top-level domains*.

domain integrity   The process of assuring that values added to fields of a table comply with a set of rules for reasonableness and other constraints. See *business rules* and *three-tier*.

Domain Name Service   See *DNS*.

DSN   An acronym for *Data Source Name*, the name used by ODBC to connect to a specified ODBC-enabled database.

DSOM   An acronym for *Distributed System Object Model*, IBM's distributed object technology, which originated with OS/2 2.0 and IBM's UNIX operating system flavor, AIX. DSOM is the network version of the System Object Model (SOM) but uses a separate object model. DSOM competes with Microsoft's DCOM, and SOM is related to COM. See *COM* and *DCOM*.

dynamic data exchange   See *DDE*.

dynamic link library   See *DLL*.

environment   A combination of the computer hardware, operating system, and user interface. A complete statement of an environment follows: a Pentium PCI-bus computer with 64M of RAM, a Wide and Fast SCSI host adapter, SVGA display adapter, sound card, and two-button mouse, using the Windows NT Server 4.0 operating system.

environmental subsystem   In Windows NT, the four sets of APIs that support Win32, MS-DOS, POSIX, and OS/2 applications.

Ethernet   A networking medium developed at the Xerox Palo Alto Research Center (PARC) in the 1970s; was improved by Xerox, Intel, and DEC; and is now the most popular cabling method for LANs. The IEEE 802.3 specification for Ethernet is the most common implementation.

exception   An error, such as division by zero, detected by hardware or by the operating system. Fatal exceptions halt execution of an application and, in a few circumstances, kill the operating system.

executive   In Windows NT, the components of the operating system that run in the kernel (ring 0) and handle interprocess communication, interrupt requests, and object security. Graphics operations have been moved from user mode to kernel mode in Windows NT 4.0 to speed performance. See *kernel mode* and *user mode*.

failover   A fault-tolerant clustering architecture in which two servers share a common set of fault-tolerant fixed disk drives. If one server fails, the other transparently assumes all server processing operations. See *clustering* and *fault tolerance*.

Falcon   The code name for Microsoft Message Queue (MMQ). See *MMQ*.

FAT   An acronym for *file allocation table*, the disk file system used by MS-DOS, Windows 95, and (optionally) Windows NT. Windows NT is compatible with the 16-bit FAT system but not the optional 32-bit FAT (FAT32) for Windows 95 that Microsoft announced in mid-1996. See *HPFS* and *NTFS*.

fault tolerance   A computer system's capability to maintain operability, despite failure of a major hardware component such as a power supply, microprocessor, or fixed-disk drive. Fault tolerance requires redundant hardware and modifications to the operating system. Windows NT Server includes fault tolerance for a failed disk drive by disk mirroring (RAID 1) or disk striping with parity (RAID 5). Clustering provides fault tolerance for individual computers. See *clustering* and *RAID*.

FC-AL   An acronym for *Fibre Channel-Arbitrated Loop*, a high-speed interconnection method for computer peripherals (primarily fixed disk drives and RAID subsystems) that uses fiber-optic media to achieve high performance and freedom from electrical interference.

FDDI   An acronym for *Fiber Distributed Data Interface*, an ANSI standard for high-speed (100 Mbps) network data communication that uses fiber-optic technology. FDDI commonly is used as a network backbone and uses a loop (Token Ring) architecture.

fiber   A lightweight thread, introduced in Windows NT 4.0, that makes it easier for developers to optimize scheduling within multithreaded applications. See *thread*.

file server   A network server used primarily for sharing files rather than applications. Servers running Novell NetWare usually are classified as file servers. See *application server*.

firewall   A security mechanism for providing Internet access to network clients while preventing access to the internal network by unauthorized Internet users (hackers). Firewalls are implemented by dedicated hardware or proxy servers. See *proxy server*.

FireWire   Apple's trademark for the IEEE-1394 High-Performance Serial Bus. See *IEEE-1394*.

flash ROM   Rewritable read-only memory used to store the system BIOS of motherboards and to create "solid-state disks." Flash ROM, also called *non-volatile RAM (NVRAM)*, retains data when powered down.

front end   When used with database management systems, an application, a window, or a set of windows by which the user may access and view database records, as well as add to or edit them.

FTP   An acronym for *File Transfer Protocol*, the standard protocol for downloading or uploading files from one computer to another on the Internet. Internet Information Server includes an FTP server.

gateway   A hardware device or software program used to translate between incompatible protocols. A gateway can function at any one layer of the OSI Reference Model or at several layers simultaneously. For example, a gateway is used to translate between mail systems, such as SNMP and MHS. (Internet terminology uses the term *gateway* in place of *router*.)

global   Pertaining to an entire entity, such as a Windows NT domain or a collection of trusted/trusting domains. Windows NT distinguishes global groups from local groups; local groups have permissions only for objects on the server in which the local group exists.

Gopher   An early Internet protocol and application, developed at the University of Minnesota, that searches for, retrieves, and displays documents on servers. (The U of M's mascot is the gopher.) The World Wide Web has replaced Gopher for all but the most die-hard UNIX users.

group   A collection of network or database users with common permissions for particular objects, such as shared files or database tables. See also *permissions*.

GUID   See *CLSID*.

H.263   An ITU standard for low-speed (typically 28.8 kbps) video encoding, primarily for videoconferencing over the Internet and switched telephone networks. See *ITU*.

H.320, H.323, and H.324   A set of related ITU protocols for audio, video, and data conferencing over higher-speed connections, such as ISDN. See *ITU*.

HAL   An acronym for *hardware abstraction layer*, a Windows NT DLL that links specific computer hardware implementations with the Windows NT kernel. Windows NT 4.0 includes HALs for 80x86, Alpha, MIPS, and PowerPC hardware platforms.

handle   An unsigned long (32-bit) integer assigned by Windows NT or Windows 95 to uniquely identify an instance (occurrence) of an object or a component of an object, such as a file or a window.

hive   A collection of built-in, top-level Registry keys used by Windows NT and Windows 95. See *key* and *Registry*.

host   Any computer on a network that uses the Internet Protocol (IP). See *IP* and *IP address*.

HPFS   An acronym for the *High-Performance File System* used by OS/2 and (optionally) Windows NT 3.x. Windows NT 4.0 doesn't support HPFS but can connect via a network to files on HPFS volumes of Windows NT 3.x PCs.

HTML   An abbreviation for *Hypertext Markup Language*, a variant of SGML (Standardized General Markup Language), a page-description language for creating files that can be formatted and displayed by Web browsers.

HTTP   An abbreviation for *Hypertext Transfer Protocol*, the basic communication protocol used by the World Wide Web. See *S-HTTP*.

HTTPS   See *S-HTTP*.

hub A concentrator that joins multiple clients by means of a single link to the rest of the LAN. A hub has several ports to which clients are connected directly, and one or more ports that can be used to connect the hub to the backbone or to other active network components. A hub functions as a multiport repeater; signals received on any port are immediately retransmitted to all other ports of the hub. Hubs function at the physical layer of the OSI Reference Model.

IDC An acronym for *Internet Database Connector*, which provides database connectivity between Internet Information Server and ODBC-compliant databases through the use of .idc (query) and .htx (template) files.

idle In Windows, the condition or state in which both Windows and the application have processed all pending messages in the queue from user- or hardware-initiated events and is waiting for the next event to occur. In Windows NT multiprocessing, one idle thread exists for each processor.

IEEE An acronym for the *Institute of Electrical and Electronic Engineers*, a professional organization that develops standards for electrical and electronic definitions, test methods, symbols, units, and safety. Networking is the province of the IEEE 803 working committees.

IEEE-1394 The common designation for IEEE 1394-1995, the High Performance Serial Bus, better known by the Apple Computer trademark *FireWire*. IEEE-1394 now is used primarily for interconnecting consumer audio-video equipment, such as Digital Video (DV) camcorders. IEEE-1394, which now supports 100 Mbps and 200 Mbps transport, is one of the buses supported by the new Windows Driver Model. See *WDM*.

IETF An acronym for the *Internet Engineering Task Force*, an international group of network designers, operators, vendors, and researchers dedicated to the evolution of Internet architecture and improving the Internet's operation.

ON THE WEB

IETF operates under the auspices of the Internet Society, which operates an informative Web site at **http://www.info.isoc.org/**.

IIS An acronym for Microsoft's *Internet Information Server*, of which version 3.0 was current and version 4.0 was in beta testing when this book was written.

impersonation In Windows NT, the capability of a thread in one process to assume the security identity of another process. Impersonation is employed by a named pipe to acquire and use the security ID of the service requester.

in-process A term applied to Automation servers, also called *Automation DLLs*, that operate within the same process space (memory allocation) of the Automation controller manipulating the server. In-process servers commonly are called *InProc servers*. See *out-of-process*.

installable file system In Windows NT, the capability to load a file system (such as NTFS, CDFS, FAT, or HPFS) dynamically, depending on the format of the file to be opened.

instance   A term used by Windows to describe the temporal existence of a loaded object or application, or one or more of an application's windows.

instantiate   The process of creating an instance of an object in memory.

interface   A noun describing a connection between two dissimilar devices or COM objects, such as Automation clients and servers. A common phrase is *user interface*, meaning the "connection" between the display-keyboard combination and the user. Use of *interface* as a verb is jargon.

interrupt   An asynchronous message, usually issued by an I/O device, requesting the service of an operating system's or device driver's interrupt handler.

intranet   A private network that uses Internet protocols and common Internet applications (such as Web browsers) to emulate the public Internet. Intranets on LANs and high-speed WANs provide increased privacy and improved performance compared with today's Internet.

invoke   To cause execution of a block of code, particularly a procedure or subprocedure. *Invoke* also is used to indicate application of a method to an object.

I/O manager   A component of the Windows NT executive that handles all input/output (I/O) requests.

IP   An acronym for *Internet Protocol*, the basic network transmission protocol of the Internet.

IP address   The 32-bit hexadecimal address of a host, gateway, or router on an IP network. For convenience, IP addresses are specified as the decimal value of the four address bytes, separated by periods, as in 124.33.15.1. Addresses are classified as types A, B, and C, depending on the subnet mask applied. See *subnet mask*.

IPX/SPX   An acronym for *Internetwork Packet Exchange/Sequenced Packet Exchange*, the transport protocol of Novell NetWare, supported by Windows NT's NWLink service. See *NWLink*.

ISAM   An acronym for *Indexed Sequential Access Method*, an indexing mechanism for expediting access to desired rows of data in a database file. Microsoft Jet databases (.mdb) and other desktop databases, such as dBASE, use ISAM. See *Jet*.

ISAPI   An acronym for *Internet Server Application Program Interface*, which substitutes Windows DLLs for CGI executable applications used by Web servers. ISAPI provides more efficient and faster execution of specialized functions, such as IDC database access, than CGI scripts and applications. See *CGI* and *IDC*.

ISDN   An acronym for *Integrated Services Digital Network*, a switched telephone service that provides mid-band digital communication capabilities used for Internet connections and for remote access to LANs, as well as voice communication. Windows NT 4.0 has built-in support for ISDN modems, more properly called *network terminators*. See *BRI* and *PRI*.

ISO An acronym for the *International Standards Organization*, a branch of the United Nations headquartered in Geneva, Switzerland. ISO is involved in setting worldwide standards, except those established by the International Electro-Technical Committee (IEC) and the International Telecommunication Union (ITC). Many IEEE and ANSI standards have ISO counterparts.

ITU An acronym for the *International Telecommunication Union*, a United Nations-chartered organization that has taken over the standards and regulatory activities of the CCITT (Consultative Committee for International Telephone and Telegraph). ITU publishes many standards and recommendations for the broadcast industry, such as ITU-R BT.603 (formerly CCIR-603) for digitizing analog TV signals.

Java A simplified, proprietary derivative of the C++ programming language developed by SunSoft, a subsidiary of Sun Microsystems, Inc.

JavaScript A scripting language derived by Netscape Communications, Inc. from its original LiveScript language. JavaScript competes with Visual Basic Script (VBScript) for client-side programming of Web pages. Microsoft's version of JavaScript is called *JScript*.

Java Beans SunSofts' object model, based on CORBA, that competes with Microsoft's ActiveX COM-based components.

JDBC An abbreviation for *Java Database Connectivity*, which provides data access interfaces for use with the Java language. JDBC is based on Microsoft's ODBC (Open Database Connectivity API). See *ODBC*.

Jet Microsoft's desktop database engine (now at version 3.5) used by Microsoft's development tools, such as Visual Basic, and productivity applications, including Access, Word, and Excel. Exchange Server and Windows NT 4.0's DNS use a modified version of Jet. Jet originally was an acronym for *Joint Engine Technology*; an earlier version was called the Red database.

JScript See *JavaScript*.

Kerberos The name for the security services for the OSF's Distributed Computing Environment (DCE). Microsoft's Distributed File Services (Dfs) use Kerberos for distributed security as an alternative to Windows NT's security system. For the Internet, Kerberos uses public key encryption; intranets ordinarily use private keys. See *Dfs*.

kernel mode The mode in which the Windows NT system runs, providing the operating system with access to system memory and other hardware devices.

key A collection of one or more Registry values (properties) that relate to a single object. See *hive*.

LAN An acronym for *local area network*. A LAN is a system comprising multiple computers physically interconnected through network adapter cards and cabling.

launch To start a Windows application.

LDAP An acronym for *Lightweight Directory Access Protocol*, an Internet standard protocol (RFC 1777) for providing clients, applications, and servers access to directory services. LDAP was derived from the ITU's X.500 protocol. See *X.500*.

local area network See *LAN*.

locale The environment for an operating system or application, usually based on a specific language or a dialect of a language. Windows NT uses the National Language Support (NLS) API to provide localization.

logical The manifestation of physical devices in software, including operating systems. For example, a logical disk drive may consist of part of the space on a single disk drive or, by using Windows NT's capability of spanning drives, space on multiple disk drives.

logon The process by which Windows NT detects a user's attempt to gain access to the operating system. Successful completion of the logon process authenticates the user.

LRPC An acronym for *lightweight remote procedure call,* used for communication between ActiveX controllers (OLE clients) and ActiveX components (OLE servers) residing on a single computer. See *remote procedure call*.

MAC An acronym for *Media Access Control*, the globally unique hardware address of an Ethernet network interface card.

map To translate a physical memory address to a virtual memory (VM) address, or vice versa. See *VM*.

MAPI Acronym for the Windows *Messaging API* originally created by Microsoft for use with Microsoft Mail, which implements Simple MAPI. Microsoft Exchange Client and Server implements MAPI 1.0 (also called *Extended MAPI*).

Marble Microsoft's code name for a set of electronic commerce applications specifically designed to facilitate electronic banking operations.

method One characteristic of an object and a classification of keywords in VBA. Methods are the procedures that apply to an object. Methods applicable to a class of objects are inherited by other objects of the same class and may be modified to suit the requirements of the object.

MIB An acronym for *Management Information Base*, a set of attributes for active network components, including servers, used by SNMP. Windows NT provides MIBs for server shares, sessions, and users, plus DHCP and WINS data. See *SNMP*.

middleware A layer of software between applications, the operating system, and the network transport that facilitates cooperative processing across various networked resources. Microsoft middleware includes directory services (Active Directory), message-passing mechanisms (MMQ), distributed transaction processing monitors (MTS), object request brokers (MTS), remote procedure call (RPC) services, and database gateways (ODS). See *MMQ, MTS,* and *remote procedure call*.

MIME   An acronym for *Multipurpose Internet Mail Extensions*, which add to Internet mail the capability for handling attachments with special file formats (such as Microsoft Word .doc and compressed .zip files), voice mail, video mail, faxes, and the like.

mirroring   See *disk mirroring*.

MISF   An acronym for *Microsoft Internet Security Framework*, a set of high-level security services that rely on CryptoAPI 2.0 functions to provide certificate- and password-based authentication. MISF also incorporates secure channel communication by using SSL (Secure Sockets Layer) 2.0 and 3.0, plus PCT (Personal Communications Technology) and SET (Secure Electronic Transactions) for credit-card purchases, and the Microsoft Certificate Server for issuing authentication certificates.

MMC   An acronym for *Microsoft Management Console*, a framework for creating management applications for Windows NT 4+ and Windows 9x. Formerly code-named Slate, MMC uses Microsoft and third-party Snap-in components to perform the actual management functions. Future versions of Systems Management Server are expected to be delivered in the form of Snap-ins for MMC.

MMQ   An acronym for *Microsoft Message Queue*, previously code-named Falcon, a message-based middleware product that assures completion of transactions over unreliable networks or in case a participating network node temporarily fails.

MPPP   An acronym for *Multilink Point-to-Point Protocol*, which joins multiple (usually two) B channels (64 kbps) of an ISDN connection to transfer data at 128 kbps or faster.

MTS   An acronym for *Microsoft Transaction Server*, which combines a transaction-processing (TP) monitor and an object-request broker (ORB) for COM objects. MTS was known as Viper during its development cycle.

multiprocessing   The capability of a computer with two or more CPUs to allocate tasks (threads) to a specific CPU. See *SMP*.

multitasking   The capability of a computer with a single CPU to simulate the processing of more than one task at a time. Multitasking is effective when one (or more) of the applications spends most of its time in an idle state, waiting for a user-initiated event such as a keystroke or mouse click.

multithreaded   An application that contains more than one thread of execution; a task or set of tasks that executes semi-independently of other task(s).

multiuser   Concurrent use of a single computer by more than one user, usually through the use of remote terminals. UNIX is inherently a multiuser operating system. *Multiuser* is often used as a term to describe an application that allows multiple users to view and update a single shared file, such as a Microsoft Access .mdb file.

named pipes   A method of interprocess communication, originally developed for OS/2, that provides a secure channel for network communication.

NBF   An abbreviation for *NetBEUI Frame*, the transport packet structure used by NetBEUI.

NCBS   An acronym for *Network Control Block Session*, a NetBIOS connection that uses the NetBEUI Frame protocol. Clients issue an NCB CALL and the destination server returns an NCB LISTEN to establish the session.

NDIS   An acronym for Microsoft's *Network Driver Interface Specification* for writing device drivers for network interface cards (NICs) that work with Windows 3.x, Windows 95, and Windows NT.

NetBEUI   An acronym for *NetBIOS Extended User Interface*, the transport protocol of Microsoft Networking. NetBEUI isn't a routable network, so its popularity is declining in comparison with TCP/IP.

NetBIOS   An acronym for *Network Basic Input/Output System*, the original network API for MS-DOS and the foundation for NetBEUI.

NFS   An acronym for *Network File System*, a file format and set of drivers created by Sun Microsystems Incorporated that allows DOS/Windows and UNIX applications to share files on disk drives running under UNIX. NFS relies on remote procedure calls (RPCs) for communication between clients and servers.

NIC   An acronym for *network interface card*, a plug-in adapter card that provides the physical connection to the network. The most common NICs support 10BaseT network media; 100BaseT NICs, which are 10 times faster, are gaining acceptance in Windows NT networks.

NNTP   An acronym for *Network News Transport Protocol*, the standard (RFC 977) for Internet exchange of Usenet messages.

node   A computer connected to a network; often called a host. On a LAN, a device (not necessarily a computer) that's connected to the network and can communicate with other network devices.

NT   An acronym for *New Technology* used by Windows NT. Windows NT is a registered trademark of Microsoft Corporation, so the full name of the operating system, *Windows NT*, is used in this book.

NTFS   An acronym for *New Technology File System*, Windows NT's replacement for the DOS FAT (File Allocation Table) and OS/2's HPFS (High-Performance File System). NTFS offers many advantages over other file systems, including improved security and the ability to reconstruct files in case of hardware failures. Windows 3.1+ and Windows 95 can access files stored on NTFS volumes via a network connection but can't open NTFS files directly.

NWLink   Microsoft's implementation of the Novell NetWare IPX/SPX protocol for Windows NT Server and Workstation. See *IPX/SPX*.

object   In programming, an element that combines data (properties) and behavior (methods) in a single code container. Objects inherit their properties and methods from the classes above them in the hierarchy and can modify the properties and methods to suit their own purposes.

object manager A Windows NT executive component that manages operating system resources. In Windows NT, all system resources are objects.

object permissions Permissions granted by the network administrator for users to access shared Windows NT objects. Object permissions also may be granted to users through group membership.

ODBC An abbreviation for the Microsoft *Open Database Connectivity* API, a set of functions that provide access to client/server RDBMSes, desktop database files, text files, and Excel worksheet files through ODBC drivers. Windows NT 4.0 and Windows 95 currently use 32-bit ODBC 3.0. ODBC most commonly is used to connect to client/server databases, such as Microsoft SQL Server.

OLAP An abbreviation for *Online Analytical Processing*, a class of applications that use or emulate multidimensional databases (data warehouses) for decision support.

OLE An acronym for *Object Linking and Embedding*, Microsoft's COM-based method for embedding a document or creating a link to a document file (such as a Microsoft Excel spreadsheet) within another document (such as a Microsoft Word file).

OLE Automation See *Automation*.

OLE Control See *ActiveX control*.

OLE DB A new set of COM data-access interfaces intended to provide access to both SQL and non-SQL data sources. OLE DB now uses ODBC to connect to conventional relational (SQL) databases. Ultimately, OLE DB data providers will replace ODBC. See *Active Data Objects*.

OLE DLL A synonym for an in-process Automation server implemented as a Windows DLL. See *in-process*.

OLTP See *transaction*.

OpenDoc A standard originally proposed by Apple Computer, Borland International, Lotus Development, Novell, and other Microsoft competitors to supplant or replace COM, DCOM, and OLE. Apple Computer announced in March 1997 the abandonment of further development work on OpenDoc.

OMG An acronym for the *Object Management Group*, a consortium of vendors opposed to Microsoft's COM and DCOM specifications and aligned to define and promote the CORBA object specifications. See *COM*, *CORBA*, and *DCOM*.

Open Group The parent organization for various standards organizations such as The Active Group, OSF, and X/Open. See *Active Group*, *OSF*, and *X/Open*.

ORB An acronym for *Object Request Broker*, middleware that manages the location and binding of objects involved in multitier client/server applications.

OSF An acronym for the *Open Software Foundation*, a vendor consortium for defining software interoperability specifications. OSF now is part of The Open Group.

OSI An acronym for *Open System Interconnection,* the model for standard levels of networking functions and the services performed at each level. The seven-level OSI standard is defined by the International Standards Organization (ISO).

out-of-process An (OLE or ActiveX) Automation server in the form of an executable (.exe) file that operates in its own process space (memory allocation). Out-of-process servers use LRPCs (lightweight remote procedure calls) to communicate with the Automation client. The term *OutOfProc* often is used as shorthand for *out-of-process.*

page A block of contiguous virtual memory (VM) addresses that Windows NT moves between physical RAM and a disk (paging) file as needed to support network operations and applications. Paging is used when physical RAM can't store the required data. See *VM.*

page fault An event that occurs when a thread refers to an invalid (out-of-date) VM page. The VM manager must refresh the page from the page file. See *VM.*

paged pool System memory that can be paged to Windows NT's Pagefile.sys paging file. The non-paged pool (approximately 4M for Windows NT 4.0) must reside in RAM and can't be paged to disk.

PCT An acronym for *Private Communication Technology,* one of several proposals designed to provide secure transactions over the Internet.

PDC An acronym for *Primary Domain Controller,* the Windows NT server in a domain that's responsible for maintaining user and group accounts for a domain. Primary and Backup Domain Controllers authenticate domain users during the logon process. See *BDC* and *logon.*

Perl An acronym for *Practical Extraction Report Language,* an interpreted scripting language used for writing CGI scripts. Perl primarily is used in UNIX environments, but many Windows NT Server 4.0 Web servers also use Perl for CGI scripting. See *CGI.*

permissions Authority given by the system administrator, database administrator, or database owner to perform operations over a network or on data objects in a database.

PKCS An acronym for *Public Key Certificate Standard,* which defines a form for requesting a certificate of authentication, a standard syntax for attaching signatures to a block of data, and public key encryption algorithms.

POP3 An acronym for *Post Office Protocol 3,* an Internet messaging protocol supported by Exchange Server 5.0. POP3 is based on the SMTP standard for Internet mail. See *SMTP.*

port A connection to an external hardware device, such as a modem (serial port) or a printer (printer). In Windows NT, a communications channel object for local procedure calls.

PPP An acronym for *Point-to-Point Protocol,* the most common Internet protocol for connection to TCP/IP networks via conventional and ISDN modems. See *SLIP.*

PPTP An acronym for *Point-to-Point Tunneling Protocol,* a Microsoft-sponsored protocol included with Windows NT 4.0 that uses encryption to assure privacy of communication over the Internet. See *VPN.*

preemptive multitasking The multitasking process used by Windows NT and Windows 95 in which the operating system assures that all active threads have the opportunity to execute. Preemptive multitasking prevents a single thread from monopolizing a processor.

PRI An acronym for *Primary Rate Interface*, an ISDN service for high-speed communication. PRI has twenty-three 64 kbps B (bearer) channels and one 64 kbps D (data) channel, which may be used as independent channels or bonded to provide bandwidths higher than 64 kbps. See *BRI* and *ISDN*.

property One of the two principal characteristics of objects (the other is *methods*). Properties define the manifestation of the object—for example, its appearance. You can define properties for an object or for the class to which the particular object belongs, in which case the properties are said to be *inherited*. See *method*.

property sheet A dialog used to set the value(s) of properties of an object, such as an ActiveX control or an operating system component. For example, Control Panel's Network tool is a property sheet. The tabbed elements of a property sheet are called *property pages*.

protected subsystem A process that operates in a block of virtual memory that's not shared with other processes. Windows NT's protected subsystems prevent an errant process from killing the entire operating system.

protocol A description of the method by which networked computers communicate. Windows NT allows the simultaneous use of multiple network protocols, including TCP/IP, NetBEUI, and IPX/SPX.

protocol stack Network protocol software that implements a specific protocol, such as TCP/IP.

proxy server An intermediary server that creates a secure subnet for connecting networked client computers to the World Wide Web without allowing unauthorized outside access. Microsoft Proxy Server also provides caching of popular or important Web pages to provide enhanced performance.

QoS An acronym for *Quality of Service*, a method for allocating a specific amount of bandwidth on a network to support time-sensitive transmissions, such as audio and video content. ATM provides QoS guarantees; other protocols, such as RSVP, are intended to implement QoS on non-ATM networks. See *Asynchronous Transfer Mode* and *RSVP*.

query A request to retrieve data from a database with the SQL SELECT instruction or to manipulate data stored in tables.

RAID An acronym for *redundant array of inexpensive disks*, a method of connecting multiple disk drives to a single controller card to achieve faster data throughput, data storage redundancy for fault tolerance, or both. See *disk mirroring, disk striping*, and *fault tolerance*.

raising exceptions A process by which the operating system transfers control to a block of software (exception handler) when an error or unexpected condition occurs. Windows NT's exception handler adds items to the event log.

RDBMS   An abbreviation for *relational database management system*. An RDBMS is an application that can create, organize, and edit databases; display data through user-selected views; and, in some cases, print formatted reports.

redirector   Software that intercepts requests for remotely provided services, such as files in server shares, and sends the request to the appropriate computer on the network.

Registry   A database that contains information required for the operation of Windows NT and Windows 95, plus applications installed under Windows NT and Windows 95. The Windows Registry takes the place of Windows 3.1+'s REG.DAT, WIN.INI, and SYSTEM.INI files, plus *PROFILE*.INI files installed by Windows 3.1 applications. The Registry also includes user information, such as user IDs, encrypted passwords, and permissions. Windows NT and Windows 95 include RegEdit.exe for editing the Registry. The Windows NT and Windows 95 Registries vary in structure and thus are incompatible.

relational database   See *RDBMS*.

Remote Automation Object   An out-of-process (OLE) Automation server, usually called an RAO, that resides on a server and is accessible to RAO-compliant applications that connect to the server. RAOs comprise the middle tier of three-tier client/server database applications. See *business rules* and *three-tier*.

remote procedure call (RPC)   An interprocess communication method that allows an application to run specific parts of the application on more than one computer in a distributed computing environment. Windows NT 4.0's DCOM uses RPCs for network communication between COM objects.

replication   The process of duplicating server shares and database objects (usually tables) in more than one location, including a method of periodically rationalizing (synchronizing) updates to the objects. Database replication is an alternative to the two-phase commit process. Microsoft SQL Server 6+ supports replication of databases across multiple Windows NT servers. Updating Windows NT Backup Domain Controllers (BDCs) from a Primary Domain Controller (PDC) occurs by replication of the Security Accounts Manager (SAM) database.

RFC   An acronym for *Request For Comments*, the method by which proposed Internet standards are submitted to the IETF and numbered when accepted. See *IETF*.

RISC   An acronym for *reduced instruction set computer*, a processor that uses a simplified set of internal operating instructions to speed execution. RISC processors supported by Windows NT 4.0 are Alpha, MIPS, and PowerPC. See *CISC*.

rollback   A method used in transaction processing to cancel a proposed transaction that modifies one or more tables and to undo changes, if any, made by the transaction before a `COMMIT` or `COMMIT TRANSACTION` SQL statement.

router   An active network component that connects one network to another network. Routers operate at the network layer of the OSI and work with packets that include logical addressing information.

RSA   An acronym for *Rivest, Shamir, and Adleman*, the developers of a public key cryptography system for Internet security.

RSVP   An abbreviation for *Resource Reservation Protocol*, a proposed Internet standard supported by Microsoft and Intel for providing a guaranteed bandwidth (Quality of Service) for transmitting time-sensitive information on the Internet. See *QoS*.

RTP/RTCP   An acronym for *Real-Time Protocol and Real-Time Control Protocol*, respectively, which define a packet format for sending time-sensitive information, such as audio and video content, on the Internet.

SAM   An acronym for *Security Accounts Manager*, a Windows NT subsystem that maintains a database of user account names and passwords for authentication.

scalable   The property of a multiprocessing computer that defines the extent to which addition of more processors increases aggregate computing capability. Windows NT Server 4.0 is generally considered to be scalable to eight Intel processors.

SEPP   See *SET*.

server   A computer on a LAN that provides services or resources to client computers by sharing its resources. Servers may be dedicated, in which case they share their resources but don't use the resources themselves, except in performing administrative tasks. Servers in client/server databases are ordinarily dedicated to making database resources available to client computers. You also can use a server to run applications for users, in which case it's called an *application server*. Peer-to-peer or workgroup servers, such as those created by using PCs running Windows NT Workstation to share disk folders, comprise another server class.

SET   An acronym for *Secure Electronic Transactions*. A protocol developed by MasterCard and VISA for securing electronic credit-card payments over the Internet. SET incorporates many features of the competing Secure Electronic Payment Process (SEPP) and Secure Transaction Technology (STT) proposals, which ultimately were combined and merged into SET.

shared application memory   Memory that's allocated between processes involved in a lightweight remote procedure call (LRPC). See also *LRPC*.

S-HTTP   An abbreviation for *Secure Hypertext Transport Protocol*, often called HTTPS, which encrypts Web documents rather than all transmissions in a session. See *SSL*.

SID   An acronym for *security ID*, a numeric value that identifies a logged-on user who has been authenticated by Windows NT or a user group.

SLIP   An acronym for *Serial Line Interface Protocol*, the first common method of connecting via a modem to TCP/IP networks, now less widely used. See *PPP*.

SMB   An acronym for *Server Message Block*, a networking protocol used by NetBEUI to implement Microsoft Networking.

SMP   An abbreviation for *symmetric multiprocessing*, implemented in Windows NT, which distributes tasks among CPUs by using a load-sharing methodology. Applications must be multithreaded to take advantage of SMP. See *asymmetric multiprocessing*.

SMTP An acronym for *Simple Mail Transfer Protocol*, the standard protocol for exchanging e-mail messages over the Internet.

SNA An acronym for IBM's *Systems Network Architecture*, a communications framework for networked mainframe systems used by Microsoft SNA Server and many other mainframe-oriented Windows applications.

SNMP An acronym for *Simple Network Management Protocol*, an Internet standard that defines methods for remotely managing active network components such as hubs, routers, and bridges.

spindle A synonym for a physical drive, usually in RAID arrays. See *RAID*.

SQL An acronym, pronounced either as "sequel" or "seekel," for *Structured Query Language*, a language developed by IBM for processing data contained in mainframe computer databases. (*Sequel* is the name of a language, similar to SQL, developed by IBM but no longer in use.) SQL has now been institutionalized by the creation of an ANSI standard for the language.

SSL An acronym for *Secure Sockets Layer*, a standard for providing encrypted and authenticated service over the Internet by using RSA public-key encryption for handling electronic commerce payments. See *RSA*.

stack See *protocol stack*.

Steelhead Microsoft's code name for Internet and intranet routing technology to be added to Windows NT Server. Steelhead uses Windows Sockets to handle routing with TCP/IP, IPX, X.25, leased telco lines, ADSL, ATM, and other networking protocols and transports. Microsoft says Steelhead will support Internet-standard Open Shortest Path First (OSPF) routing and include Quality of Service (QoS) features.

stripe set See *disk striping* and *fault tolerance*.

Structured Query Language See *SQL*.

STT See *SET*.

subnet mask A local bit mask (set of flags) that specifies which bits of the IP address specify a particular IP network or a host within a subnetwork. An IP address of 128.66.12.1 with a subnet mask of 255.255.255.0 specifies host 1 on subnet 128.66.12.0. The subnet mask determines the maximum number of hosts on a subnetwork.

synchronous I/O An input/output method in which the process that issues an I/O request waits for the requested process to complete before returning control to the application or operating system. See *asynchronous I/O*.

system administrator The individual(s) responsible for the administrative functions for all applications on a LAN or users of a UNIX cluster or network, usually including supervision of all databases on servers attached to the LAN. If the system administrator's responsibility is limited to databases, the term *database administrator* (DBA) is ordinarily assigned.

T.120   A set of ITU-standard protocols for transport-independent, multipoint data conferencing. See *ITU*.

T-1   The most common moderate-speed telecommunications connection between LANs to create a WAN. Dedicated T-1 lines in North America provide 1.544 Mbps of bandwidth, also called DS1 (Digital Signal Level 1). T-1 lines also are the most common method of connecting servers to the Internet. T-3 (DS3) lines provide a 44.736 Mbps circuit for Web sites with heavy traffic.

TCP/IP   An acronym for *Transport Control Protocol/Internet Protocol*, the networking protocol of the Internet, UNIX networks, and the preferred protocol for Windows NT networks. TCP/IP is a routable protocol that supports subnetworks. See *IP*.

TDI   An acronym for *Transport Driver Interface*, used by Windows NT to implement multiple network protocols by using various network interface cards.

telco   An acronym for a local telephone company, which usually refers to the Regional Bell Operating Carriers (RBOCs or "Baby Bells").

Telnet   A terminal emulation protocol and software that lets a user log on and operate another computer over the Internet. Windows NT 4.0 includes a Telnet application.

thread   Part of a process, such as an executing application, that can run as an object or an entity. Threads of execution are the basis of Windows NT's symmetrical multiprocessing capability. See *multiprocessing* and *SMP*.

three-tier   The architecture of a database application, usually involving a client/server RDBMS, where the front-end application is separated from the back-end RDBMS by a middle tier application. The middle tier usually is implemented as a remote Automation server, which implements the database connection, enforces business rules, and handles transfer of data to and from databases of the RDBMS. See *business rules* and *Remote Automation Object*.

time stamp   The date and time data attributes applied to a disk file when created or edited.

Token Ring   A network medium developed by IBM in which each computer in the ring passes a token, which carries network messages, to the adjacent computer. Token Ring provides each computer on the ring with guaranteed capability to transmit at regular intervals; Ethernet doesn't provide such a guarantee. Token Ring is specified by the IEEE-802.5 standard. See *Ethernet*.

transaction   A group of processing steps that are treated as a single activity to perform a desired result, also called TP (transaction processing) or OLTP (online transaction processing). A transaction might entail all the steps necessary to modify the values in or add records to each table involved when a new invoice is created. RDBMSes that can process transactions usually include the capability to cancel a transaction by a rollback instruction or to cause it to become a permanent part of the tables with the COMMIT or COMMIT TRANSACTION statement.

trap   Windows NT's method of intercepting an event (such as an interrupt request or an unexpected result) that occurs during execution of a thread.

trust In Windows NT domain terminology, a relationship between domain controllers in which users who are members of the trusted domain can access services on another trusting domain without the need to log on to the trusting domain.

two-phase commit A process applicable to updates to multiple (distributed) databases that prevents a transaction from completing until all the distributed databases acknowledge that the transaction can be completed. The replication process has supplanted two-phase commit in most of today's distributed client/server RDBMSes. See *replication*.

UNC An acronym for *Unified Naming Convention*, the method of identifying the location of files on a remote server. UNC names begin with \\. Windows NT and Windows 95 support UNC; 32-bit Windows applications must support UNC to qualify for application of Microsoft's "Designed for Windows NT" logo. All Microsoft Office 95 and later applications support UNC.

Unicode A replacement for the 7-bit or 8-bit ASCII and ANSI representations of characters with a 16-bit model that allows a wider variety of characters to be used. Unicode is especially useful for representing the written characters of Asian languages. Windows NT and Windows 95 support Unicode.

UNIX Registered trademark of a multiuser operating system, now administered by the Open Systems Foundation (OSF). Extensions and modifications of UNIX include DEC Ultrix, SCO UNIX, IBM AIX, and similar products.

UPS An acronym for *uninterruptible power supply*, a device used to power a computer in case of a primary power outage.

user mode The processor mode used by Windows NT to run applications launched by users. Threads running in user mode are restricted to calling system services. See *kernel mode*.

UTP An acronym for *unshielded twisted pair*, the type of cabling used to implement 10BaseT and 100BaseT network media.

vaporware A derisive term that describes software that's promised but not yet (or ever) delivered.

VBA An acronym for *Visual Basic for Applications*, the official name of which is "Visual Basic, Applications Edition." VBA is Microsoft's common application programming (macro) language for Access, Excel, Project, and the Visual Basic programming environment.

VBScript An abbreviation for *Visual Basic, Scripting Edition*, also abbreviated *VBS*. VBScript is a subset of VBA designed for client- and server-side programming of Web pages.

VDM An acronym for *virtual DOS machine*, a Windows NT protected subsystem for running DOS applications in a console window.

virtual address space The range of unique virtual memory addresses allocated to the threads of a single Windows NT process. See *VM*.

Virtual Machine   Software required by the Java language to execute Java bytecode on a computer, sometime abbreviated VM. The Virtual Machine interprets the Java bytecode for compatibility with the instruction set of the computer's processor or operating system. Specific Virtual Machines are required for Intel, PowerPC, and other RISC processors, as well as Windows and UNIX.

virtual memory   See *VM*.

Visual Basic for Applications   See *VBA*.

Visual Basic Script   See *VBScript*.

VM   An acronym for *virtual memory*, a method of mapping a combination of RAM and images of RAM stored in a paging file to provide an address space larger than that available from the RAM installed in the computer.

VM manager   The Windows NT executive service that loads memory images stored in a paging file on demand, as well as saves memory images in the paging file when the memory no longer is needed by a thread.

VPN   An acronym for *Virtual Private Network*, a means of establishing secure communication channels on the Internet by using various forms of encryption. See *PPTP*.

WAN   An acronym for *wide area network*. A WAN is a system for connecting multiple computers in different geographical locations by switched telephone network or leased data lines; by optical or other long-distance cabling; or by infrared, radio, or satellite links.

WDM   An acronym for *Windows Driver Model*, a 32-bit architecture for creating device drivers that run under both Windows NT and Windows 9x. Microsoft hadn't issued the WDM specification when Windows NT 4.0 was released.

Win32   An API for running 32-bit Windows applications under Windows NT and Windows 95. The Win32 APIs of Windows NT and Windows 95 vary. To use Microsoft's "Designed for Windows NT" logo, applications must run under Windows NT 4.0 and Windows 95.

Win32S   A subset of the Win32 API designed to add limited 32-bit capabilities to Windows 3.1+. Very few applications have been written to the Win32S API, which appears to have become obsolete.

Windows 9x   The latest official name of what was to be Windows 97, the successor to Windows 95, but now is likely to be Windows 98.

WINS   An acronym for *Windows Internet Name Service*, a proprietary Microsoft application that maps easily remembered Windows machine names to the corresponding IP addresses.

Winsock   An abbreviation for *Windows Sockets*, a networking API for implementing Windows applications that use TCP/IP, such as FTP and Telnet.

Wolfpack   See *clustering*.

working set The set of active virtual memory pages for a process stored in RAM at a given instant.

workstation A client computer on a LAN or WAN that's used to run applications and connected to a server from which it obtains data shared with other computers. *Workstation* is also used to describe a high-priced PC that uses a high-performance microprocessor and proprietary architecture to create what some call an "open" system.

WOSA An acronym for *Windows Open Services Architecture*, the foundation for such APIs as ODBC, MAPI, and TAPI. Microsoft also develops special vertical-market WOSA APIs for banking, financial, and other industries.

WOW An acronym for *Windows on Win32*, a subsystem of Windows NT that allows 16-bit Windows applications to run in protected memory spaces called *virtual DOS machines*. See *VDM*.

WSM An acronym for *Windows Scripting Model*, a feature of Windows NT 5.0 and Windows 9x that enables VBScript to be used for command-line operations and in batch files. See *VBScript*.

X.500 The ITU Directory Access Protocol (LDAP), which defines object classes for a directory and a method for accessing names from a directory. The X.500 protocol provides directory browsing, directory administration, schema management, and authentication. LDAP is a subset of X.500. See *LDAP*.

X.509 Certificate An ITU protocol for an encrypted certificate for vendor authentication that identifies an unique name and provides an associated public key.

X/Open A consortium of computer and software suppliers, operating under the auspices of The Open Group, that establish computing standards intended to assure interoperability of software and hardware components. See *Open Group*.

Index

Symbols

100BaseT Fast Ethernet (media-access models), 128-129
100BaseFX for single-mode and multimode cabling, 129
100BaseT4 for Category 3 UTP cabling, 129
100BaseTX for Category 5 UTP cabling, 129

100VG-AnyLAN (media-access models), 129

10Base2 (Ethernet coax cable), 135

10BaseT, 1003

32-bit clients, installing SQL Enterprise Manager, 843-844

4GT (4G RAM Tuning), 50, 969

56 kbps Internet connections, 729

8mm tape (helical scan backup tapes), 277

A

Aberdeen Group Web site, 29

access, Registry keys (restricting), 313-315

Access Control page (Windows 95 network support), 362-363
share-level access control, 362
user-level access control, 363

Access Through Share Permissions dialog, 487

access tokens, 1003

Account Lockout Policy setting, domain account policies (user accounts), 469

Account Operators user group, 443

accounts
terminology, 442
user, 447-453
Add User Account Wizard, 463-467
adding new, 449-451
built-in, 447-449
domain account policy, 467-469
modifying, 451-453
properties, 454-462
User Manager for Domains, 442-447
low-speed connections, 446-447
multiple instances, starting, 444
selecting new domains,
445-446
starting, 443-444

ACLs (Access Control Lists), 85, 1003

Active Directory Service Interfaces, see ADSI

Active Group, 1004

active network components (network cabling systems), 141-155
bridges, 147-149
collapsed backbones, 151
enterprise hubs, 151
Ethernet switches, 151-154
gateways, 149-150
hubs, 145-147
NICs (network interface cards), 141-144
recommendations, 154-155
repeaters, 144-145
routers, 148-150
virtual LANs, 154

Active Platform, 1004

Active Server Pages, see ASP

ActiveX, 1004
Automation, 1004
controls, 725, 1004
data objects, 725
scripting, 725

ActiveX Data Objects, see ADO

activity reports
Crystal Reports (Internet Information Server 4.0), 786-789
SQL Server Web Assistant distribution (ODBC), 782-786

adapters, network, settings (installations), 194

Add & Read permission (NTFS folder-access permissions), 498

Add permission (NTFS folder-access permissions), 498

Add Printer Wizard, 24

Add User Account Wizard, 23, 463-467

Add Users and Groups dialog, 488, 496-497, 501-502

Add/Remove Programs Wizard, 25

adding
alerts (Performance Monitor), 537
BDCs to new domains, 614
logging tables (ODBC), 767-771
Jet 3.5 tables, 770-771
SQL Server tables, 768
new user accounts, 449-451
account properties, 451-455
copying accounts, 451
creating the account, 449
resource records (DNS UNIX intergration), 675
Windows NT clients (to domains), 614-615

Address Book (BackOffice), 815

Address Resolution Protocol, see ARP

address space, 1004

addresses, 1004
resolving (TCP/IP), 325-326

Addusers.exe (Windows NT Resource Kit), 480

administration (network installations), 69-71

administrative shares, 489

administrative wizards (server usability), 23-25
Add Printer Wizard, 24
Add User Account Wizard, 23
Add/Remove Programs Wizard, 25
Group Management Wizard, 24
Install New Modem Wizard, 25
License Wizard, 25
Managing File and Folder Access Wizard, 24
Network Client Administrator Wizard, 25

Administrator (SMS), 943-954
windows
Alerts, 954
Events, 954
Jobs, 950
Machine Groups, 954
Packages, 948-949
Program Groups, 954
Queries, 951-953
Site Groups, 954
Sites, 945-947

Administrator Account (built-in user accounts), 447-448

Administrator passwords, setting (installations), 191

administrators, creating mailboxes (Exchange Administrator), 919-921

Administrators user group, 443

ADO (ActiveX Data Objects), 37, 1003
Internet Information Server 4.0 (activating Web pages), 797-799

ADS (Active Directory Service), 997

ADSI (Active Directory Service Interfaces), 997
directories
search and replication, 1000
service providers, 998-999
distributed security, 1000
management, 1001-1002
Web site, 997
Windows NT Server 5.0, 52

alerts, 1004
Performance Monitor, 537-539
adding, 537
customizing, 538-539

Alerts window (SMS Administrator), 954

Alpha AXP, 86

American National Standards Institute, see ANSI

analyzers (protocol), 566-568
connections, 567-568
hardware, 566
software, 566-567

Annuity Model (BackOffice upgrades), 824-825

anonymous FTP, 1004

ANSI (American National Standards Institute), 1004

Apartment Model, 1005

APIs, 1005
version 4.0 additions (network performance features), 29

Apple Macintosh, *see* Macintosh

AppleTalk, 112
client support, 116

applets, 1005

application layer (OSI model), 105

application servers, 1005
Windows NT Server 4.0
optimization, 549-554
CPU usage, 550-551
memory usage, 551-558

application-level encryption (data communication security), 61

applications
building custom forms
(Exchange Server 5.0), 875-876
NTBACKUP (backup application), 278-289
choosing options, 284-287
preparing/labeling media, 281
restoring data, 287-289
selecting elements to backup, 282-284
tape drive setup, 279-281
SMS (Systems Management Server) analysis (network management differences), 932-933

ARCnet (media-access methods), 124

ARP (Address Resolution Protocol), 325, 1005
command-line tools, 580
TCP/IP, 326

arrays
RAID (multiple), 230
sizing, 228-229

Ascend Communications Web site, 692

ASCII, 1005

ASP (Active Server Pages), 37, 1004
Internet Information Server 4.0, activating Web pages, 794-797

assigned workstation restrictions (user account properties), 460-461

asymmetric multiprocessing, 1005

asynchronous, 1005

asynchronous cache memory, 160

asynchronous I/O, 1005

ATM (Asynchronous Transfer Mode), 106, 129, 131, 1005

attributes, Master File Table (NTFS), 93-94

audit logs, viewing
Registry security, 315-317

auditing, 1005

authentication services, 1005
distributing, 619-622
Windows NT clients, 619

Autodial, 688

AUTOEXEC.BAT (Windows 3.1 configuration file), 292

automatic client setup (Windows 95 networking), 353

automatic rebuild (RAID product features), 231

automatic server reconnections (Windows 95 networking), 353

automatic synchronization intervals, changing (domain security), 612-613

automating installations, 212-213

Automation (ActiveX), 1005-1006

Automation server, 1006

Autoplay, 1006

B

BackOffice Licensing Guide Web site, 726

BackOffice Live Web site, 815

BackOffice Server 2.5, 812-813
enterprise middleware, 815-816
Cedar, 816
Microsoft Messaging Queue, 816
MTS (Microsoft Transaction Server), 816
Internet and intranet servers, 814-815
licensing components, 816-825
client access licenses, 818-819
cost summary, 822-823
Exchange Server 5.0, 820-821
per-seat vs. per-server, 816-818
SNA Server 3.0, 822
SQL Server 6.5, 820
Systems Management Server 1.2, 821-822
Windows NT 4.0 license packages, 819
SQL Server 6.5, 834-835
assigning group account (Security Manager), 865-867
creating database devices, 850-851
database permissions, 865-869

executing queries,
861-862
importing table
structures, 852-856
indexes, 857-858
installing, 835-843
licensing, 820
setting permissions,
868-869
SQL Enterprise
Manager, 843-848
transaction logs,
862-864
viewing logins
(Enterprise Manager),
868-869
viewing standard stored
procedures, 861
viewing triggers, 860
upgrading
Annuity Model, 824-825
members (scalability),
981-982

**Backup, changing Registry
values, 295**

Backup Browser, 594

**Backup Domain
Controllers,** *see* **BDCs**

**BackupExec Version 6.11
Web site, 287**

backups, 258-275, 1006
archive bits, 258-259
copy backups, 260
daily copy backups, 262
differential backups,
261-262
enterprise backup
systems, 273
hardware, 275-278
tape drives, 275-277
WORM drives, 278
writable optical drives,
277-278
HSM (Hierarchical Storage
Management), 272
incremental backups,
260-261

installing Windows NT
Server, 181-182
master boot records,
201-205
DiskProbe
(Dskprobe.exe),
202-205
DiskSave, 202
matching media to disk
size, 267
normal backups, 259
NTBACKUP (backup
application), 278-289
choosing options,
284-287
preparing/labeling
media, 281
restoring data, 287-289
selecting elements to
backup, 282-284
tape drive setup,
279-281
open files, 266
organizing disk storage,
264-265
Registry, 308-310
restore plans, 274-275
rotation methods, 267-272
daily full backups with
two-set rotation,
269-271
grandfather-father-son
rotation, 270-271
Tower of Hanoi
rotation, 271-272
weekly backups with
daily differentials, 267
weekly backups
with daily
incrementals, 269
security (network
installations), 59
software trends, 289-290
storing data off site, 273
tape drives, specifying and
testing (SQL Enterprise
Manager), 847-848
type selection, 262-264
verifying integrity, 265-266

bandwidth, 1006

Basic Rate Interface,
see **BRI, 1007**

batches, 1006

**BDCs (Backup Domain
Controllers), 175, 191,
1006**
domain security, 609-610
promoting to PDCs,
610-611

binary files, 1006

binding, 1006

**bindings (network)
confirming installations,
197**

**Bitmap attribute (NTFS
Master File Table), 94**

**bitmaps (NTFS Master File
Table), 94**

bits, 1006

BLOBs, 1006

blue screens, 1006

Boolean, 1006

**boot disks, creating,
183-184**

**BOOTP (Bootstrap
Protocol), 1007**

**bps (bits per second),
1007**

**Bps (bytes per second),
1007**

breaks, 1007

**BRI (Basic Rate Interface),
38, 1007**

bridges, 1007
active network
components, 147-149

**Browser Monitor
(Browmon.exe),**
*Windows NT Server
Resource Kit* **utilities,
585-586**

Browser Status (Browstat.exe), *Windows NT Server Resource Kit* **utilities, 586-587**

browsers, 1007
multiple domain resources, 633
troubleshooting networks, 594-595
Windows 95 client issues, 396-397

budgets
allocating funds (network installations), 79-80
network installations, 72-74

buffers, 1007

built-in user accounts, 447-449
administrator account, 447-448
guest account, 448-449

built-in user groups, 470-471

bus topologies (network cabling systems), 133

buses
choosing types (server hardware), 162
NIC types, 142

business objectives (network installations), 56-57

business objects, brokering (Transaction Server middle-tier management), 974-976

business rules, 1007

byte striping (RAID level 3), 230

bytes, 1007

C

cabling
active network components, 141-155
bridges, 147-149
collapsed backbones, 151
enterprise hubs, 151
Ethernet switches, 151-154
gateways, 149-150
hubs, 145-147
NICs (network interface cards), 141-144
recommendations, 154-155
repeaters, 144-145
routers, 148-149
virtual LANs, 154
expandability (maintenance), 141
network systems, 132-141
cable types, 135-139
topologies, 133-135
structured systems, 139-140
system recommendations, 140
types, 135-139
coaxial, 135
fiber-optic cable, 139
STP cable (shielded twisted-pair), 136-139
UTP cable (unshielded twisted-pair), 137-139

cache, 1007

Cache Manager, 88

caching
cache memory, sizing (processors), 159
RAID level 5, 226-227

Carrier Sense Multiple Access with Collision Detection, *see* **CSMA/CD**

CD-R (CD-Recordable) drives, 278

CD-ROM, SQL Server 6.5 files (installing), 836-841

CD-ROM drives (detecting hardware), 179-183

CDDI (Copper Distributed Data Interface), 131-135

Certificate Request dialog, 36

Change permission
NTFS file-access permissions, 494
NTFS folder-access permissions, 498

channels, 1008

characteristics, charting (Performance Monitor), 534-536

charts (Performance Monitor)
creating, 534
customizing options, 536
deleting objects, 536-537
editing, 535

Chat (BackOffice), 815

CISC (Complex Instruction Set Computing), 86

Class A IP addresses, 109

Class B IP addresses, 109

Class C IP addresses, 109

Client for Microsoft Networks Properties sheet, 363-364

Client for NetWare Networks Properties sheet, 364-365

clients
32-bit, installing SQL Enterprise Manager, 843-844
automatic reconnections (Windows 95 networking), 353

BackOffice access
licenses, 818-819
client-side server features,
25-27
remote server
administration, 26
System Policy Editor, 26
user profiles, 26
Windows 95 RPL
(Remote Program
Load), 27
Exchange Server 5.0
components, 887-894
Exchange Client,
891-893
Exchange Forms
Designer, 894
Microsoft Outlook,
887-890
Schedule+, 891-893
granting access
(Remote Access Admin
application), 702-704
leasing IP addresses,
DHCP (Dynamic Host
Configuration Protocol),
333-334
Macintosh, 425-436
adding services,
425-426
setup, 427-429
troubleshooting
connections, 436
Windows NT Server
resource access,
429-435
Microsoft (NetWare server
access), 639-651
moving (between
domains), 616
multiple (Windows 95
networking), 352
NetWare (Windows NT
server access), 651-659
network protocol support,
113-116
Macintosh support, 116
MS-DOS support,
115-116
OS/2 support, 116

UNIX workstations, 116
Windows 3.1, 115
Windows 95, 114-115
Windows for
Workgroups 3.1x, 115
Windows NT
workstations, 114
non-WINS (static
mappings), 345
protected subsystem
servers, 89-90
reducing costs
(scalability), 982-984
SMS (Systems
Management Server)
support, 934
SMS software, 954-960
automatic installation,
955-957
help-desk functions,
957-959
inventory management,
957
manual installation,
954-955
Network Monitor, 960
remote control
functions, 957-959
testing (DHCP server
configurations), 340
testing DUN, 704-716
Windows 95 clients,
704-709
Windows NT clients,
710-716
universal, 679-683
Windows 95
configurations, 683
Windows for
Workgroups 3.11
configurations,
680-683
viewing leases and
reservations (DHCP
server configurations),
340-341
Windows 95
browsing issues,
396-397
configuring, 363-366

installing/removing,
358-361
remote management,
390-396
Windows for Workgroups
3.11, 410-418
configuration file
changes, 414-415
initialization file
changes, 414-415
installing 32-bit
TCP/IP, 410-414
troubleshooting,
417-418
Windows NT Server 4.0
resource connections,
416-417
Windows NT Workstation
4.0, 418-425
attaching to domain
resources, 421-422
authenticating, 619
installing network
software, 418-421
troubleshooting
connections, 423
ZAK preview, 423-425

clone NICs, 143

**clustered systems
(scalability), 970-973**
middle-tier management
(Transaction Server),
973-978
Routing and RAS, 980-981
wide-area transactions,
979-980

**CNEs (Novell Certified
NetWare Engineers), 79**

**coaxial cable (network
cabling systems), 135**
Ethernet 10Base2
coax, 135
Ethernet coax, 135
RG-62 coax, 136

**collapsed backbones
(active network
components), 151**

COM (Component Object Model), 105

command-line tools (troubleshooting networks), 580-585
arp (Address Resolution Protocol) command, 580
hostname command, 580
ipconfig command, 580
nbtstat command, 581
netstat command, 582-583
ping command, 583
route utility, 583
tracert command, 583-584

Commerce Server
BackOffice, 814
Site Server 2.0, 49

commercial TCP/IP implementations, 111

communications features, 688-689
Autodial, 688
DUN (Dial-Up Networking), 689-692
installing, 704-716
testing on clients, 704-716
idle disconnect, 689
Log-on Dial, 688
PPP Multilink, 689
PPTP (Point-to-Point Tunneling Protocol), 689, 719-720
RAS (Remote Access Service), 694-704
configuring DUN (Dial-Up Networking), 699-702
installing modems, 694-699
Remote Access Admin application (client access), 702-704
Resource Kit tools, 721
Remote Access Admin application (monitoring connections), 717-718

Routing, 720-721
TAPI 2.0 (Telephony API), 688, 692-694

Compact.exe utility (NTFS file compression), 510

Complete Trust model, 629

Complex Instruction Set Computing, *see* **CISC**

Component Object Model, *see* **COM**

component terminology (SMS planning), 936-937

compression (NTFS files), 507-509
Compact.exe utility, 510
Diruse.exe utility (Resource Kit), 511
moving and copying, 509
Windows NT Explorer compression features, 507-509
Windows NT My Computer compression features, 507-509

Computer Technology Review Web site, 217

conductor size UTP cable, 137-138

CONFIG.SYS files
Registry interaction, 317-318
Windows 3.1 configuration file, 292

configuration files, Windows for Workgroups 3.11, changing, 414-415

configurations
Registry, 292-296
backing up, 308-310
changing values, 294-295
hives, 297-299, 301
information types, 292

.INI and CONFIG.SYS files, 317-318
keys, 299, 301
organization settings, 294
Registry Editor, 293-294, 310-311
remote editing, 311-312
Resource Kit, 318-319
security, 313-317
value entries, 300-301
Windows 3.1 configuration files, 292-293
Windows 95 differences, 296
Windows NT Diagnostics Utility, 307-308
server, DHCP (Dynamic Host Configuration Protocol), 334-342
Windows 3.1 clients
configuration file changes, 406-408
initialization file changes, 406-408
MS-DOS network drivers, 408
troubleshooting connection problems, 410
Windows NT file and printer resources, 408-409

configuring
Directory Service Manager for NetWare (Windows NT Server integration), 662-666
displays (installations), 199-202
DNS (Domain Name Service), UNIX integration, 672
fixed-disk drives, 205-206
folder replication, 504-506

FPNW (File and Print
Services for NetWare),
657-659
global options (DHCP
server configurations),
335-337
Internet Information
Server 4.0 interaction
folder security, 754-760
folders, 758-760
performance
options, 754
security accounts, 753
network installations
(minimum
configurations), 79
scope options (DHCP
server configurations),
337-338
servers (Exchange
Administrator), 915-917
SMS client software,
954-960
TCP/IP, 328-331
Windows 95 network
clients, 363-366
for Microsoft Networks,
363-366
for NetWare Networks,
364-365
setting Primary
Network Logon, 366
Windows 95 network
protocols, 366-376
NetBEUI, 367-368
NWLink, 369-371
TCP/IP, 371-377
WINS (Windows Internet
Name Service), 344-350
database maintenance,
348-349
static mapping for non-
WINS clients, 345
viewing name
mappings, 346

connections
Internet, 726-735
56 kbps connections, 729
connection types,
727-733

dial-up access, 728
DNS (Domain Name
Service), 734-735
frame relay
connectivity, 732-733
ISDN connections,
730-732
ISPs (Internet service
providers), 727
multiple server protocol
support, 118
T-1 connections, 733
Macintosh clients, 425-436
adding services,
425-426
setup, 427-429
troubleshooting, 436
Windows NT Server
resource access,
429-435
monitoring (Remote
Access Admin
application), 717-718
network, 192-198
adapter settings, 194
confirming network
bindings, 197
describing, 192
Internet Information
Server, 192-193
network adapters, 193
protocols (choosing),
193-194
services (choosing),
193-194
outside (network
installations), 68-69
protocol analyzers, 567-568
simultaneous (Windows 95
networking), 352
Windows 3.1 clients,
400-418
configuration file
changes, 406-408,
414-415
creating installation
disks, 400-402
initialization file
changes, 406-408,
414-415

installing, 402-405
installing 32-bit
TCP/IP, 410-414
MS-DOS network
drivers, 408
troubleshooting, 410,
417-418
Windows NT file and
printer resources,
408-409
Windows NT Server 4.0
resource connections,
416-417
Windows NT Workstation
4.0 clients, 418-425
attaching to domain
resources, 421-422
installing network
software, 418-421
troubleshooting, 423
ZAK preview, 423-425

**connectors (Exchange
Server 5.0), 885-886**

**Console subkey
(HKEY_CURRENT_USER
hive), 306**

consultants
CNEs (Novell Certified
NetWare Engineers), 79
MCSEs (Microsoft
Certified System
Engineers), 79
network installations, 77-81

**content, Web sites,
managing (FrontPage
97), 800-806**

Content Replication
BackOffice, 815
Site Server 2.0, 48

**Control Panel subkey
(HKEY_CURRENT_USER
hive), 307**

controllers
disk subsystems, 166
domains
choosing types
(Windows NT Server
installation), 191

installing Windows NT Server as, 181
moving (security), 616-617
optimizing placement, 620
domain security, 608-611
BDCs (Backup Domain Controllers), 609-610
non-domain servers, 611
PDCs (Primary Domain Controllers), 608-609
conventional memory use (Windows 95 networking), 354
copying
backups, 260
compressed files (NTFS), 509
new user accounts, 451
user groups, 473
costs (licensing)
BackOffice cost summary, 822-823
Exchange Server 5.0, 820-821
SNA Server 3.0, 822
SQL Server 6.5, 820
Systems Management Server 1.2, 821-822
Windows NT Server 4.0 packages, 819
counters
HTTP Service Object (Performance Monitor), 791-793
Performance Monitor, 531-534
CPUs
application server usage (Performance Monitor), 550-551
server hardware, 157-169
Intel, 159
multiprocessor systems, 160
RISC-based servers, 158-159
sizing cache memory, 159

Create New Key dialog, 36
creating
administrator mailboxes (Exchange Administrator), 919-921
boot disks, 183-184
distribution lists (recipients), 926-927
emergency repair disks (installations), 200-201
installation disks (Windows 3.1 clients), 400-402
logging databases (ODBC), 766-767
mailboxes (Directory Import), 924-926
mirror standard volumes (RAID 1 mirror sets), 247
new charts (Performance Monitor), 534
new user accounts, 449
recipient templates (Directory Import), 924
replication users (folders), 503
scopes (DHCP server configurations), 334
service accounts (SMS installations), 937-938
standard volumes (RAID 1 mirror sets), 244-247
user mailboxes
Exchange Administrator, 921-923
User Manager for Domains, 923-924
zones (DNS UNIX intergration), 673-674
Crystal Reports (Internet Information Server 4.0), 786-789
installing, 787
testing, 788-789
CSMA/CD (Carrier Sense Multiple Access with Collision Detection), 126
custom forms, building applications (Exchange Server 5.0), 875-876

customizing
alerts (Performance Monitor), 538-539
chart options (Performance Monitor), 536

D

daily copy backups, 262
daily full backups with two-set rotation (rotation methods), 269-271
DAO (Data Access Objects), 37
DAT (Digital Audio Tape), helical scan tapes, 277
data
caching (RAID level 5), 226-227
compression (NTFS), 91
frames, 103
recording (log files), 540-541
restoring (backups), 274-275
storing off site (backups), 273
Data Access Objects, see DAO
Data attribute (NTFS Master File Table), 94
data communication security (network installations), 59-62
application-level encryption, 61
firewalls, 62
packet-level encryption, 62
Data Link Control, see DLC
Data Logging Service files (Windows NT Workstation Resource Kit), 555
data types (Registry value entries), 300-301

data-link layer (OSI model), 103

databases
creating devices (SQL Server 6.5), 850-851
DHCP (server configurations), 341-342
maintaining (WINS), 348-349
ODBC data sources, logging onto, 766-786

date and time, setting (installations), 198

DCE (Distributed Computing Environment), 96, 105

DCOM (Distributed Component Object Model), 39-41

default installations, Internet Information Server 4.0 (testing), 748-749

deleting objects, from charts (Performance Monitor), 536-537

departmental servers, 156

describing network connections, 192

design (domains), 630-632

detecting hardware, 175-180
CD-ROM drives, 179-183
fixed-disk drives, 177-179
Legacy SCSI host adapter drivers, 176
network adapters, 179-180

device drivers, 88

Dfs (Distributed File System), 51
distributing server shares, 988-997
Dfs Administrator, 993-997

installing, 989-991
roots and leaves, 988-997
Windows 95 Dfs client (installing), 991-993

Dfs Administrator, 993-997

DHCP (Dynamic Host Configuration Protocol), 110
TCP/IP, 327-328, 332-342
configuring global options, 335-337
configuring scope options, 337-338
creating a scope, 334
leasing IP addresses to clients, 333-334
maintaining databases, 341-342
server configurations, 334-342
testing clients, 340
viewing client leases and reservations, 340-341

Diagnostics Utility (Registry), 307-308

dial-in permissions (user account properties), 462

dial-up Internet access, 728

dial-up networking (Windows 95 networking), 353

dialog
Access Through Share Permissions, 487
Add Users and Groups, 488, 496-497, 501-502
Certificate Request, 36
Create New Key, 36
Directory Permissions, 499
File Permissions, 495-496
Server, 489
Shared Resources, 490
Special Access, 495-496

Special Directory Access, 500
Special File Access, 500-501

differential backups, 261-262

Digital Audio Tape, see DAT

Digital Linear Tape, see DLT

directory database (Exchange Server 5.0), 879-880

Directory Import
creating mailboxes, 924-926
creating recipient templates, 924

Directory Permissions dialog, 499

Directory Replicator, replicating folders, 503-504

directory search and replication (ADSI), 1000

Directory Service (Exchange Server 5.0), 879-880

Directory Service Manager for NetWare (Windows NT Server integration), 660
configuring, 662-666
installing, 661-662

directory service providers (ADSI), 998-999

Directory Services Manager for NetWare, see DSMN

Directory Synchronization (Exchange Server 5.0), 872

Diruse.exe utility, NTFS file compression (Resource Kit), 511

disconnecting shares,
489-490

Disk Administrator,
changing Registry
values, 295

disk controllers
(disk subsystems), 166

disk storage (backups),
264-265

disk subsystems
disaster tolerant disk
system criteria, 255
failure resistant criteria, 254
failure resistant plus
criteria, 254-255
server hardware, 163-166
disk controllers, 166
SCSI (Small Computer
System Interface), 163,
165-166

Diskeeper for Windows NT
Web site, 549

DiskMap output (code
listing), 205-206

DiskProbe, 211

DiskProbe (Dskprobe.exe)
(MBR backups),
202-205

DiskSave, 211

DiskSave
(DISKSAVE.EXE) MBR
backups, 202

displays, configuring
(installations), 199-202

Distributed Computing
Environment, see DCE

distributed security
(ADSI), 1000

distribution software, SMS
(Systems Management
Server), 931

distribution lists
creating (recipients),
926-927
Exchange Server 5.0, 885

distribution servers
(SMS terminology), 936

DLC (Data Link Control),
111

DLT (Digital Linear Tape)
tape drives, 276

DNS (Domain Name
Service), 30
graphical TCP/IP tool, 30
name resolution
(troubleshooting
networks), 599-601
resolving IP addresses
(TCP/IP configurations),
374-376
resolving names, 734-735
TCP/IP, 327
integrating WINS, 349
UNIX integration, 671-677
adding resource
records, 675
configuring, 672
creating zones, 673-674
installing, 671-672

domain account policy
(user accounts),
467-469
Account Lockout Policy
setting, 469
setting for passwords, 468

Domain Admins user
group, 443

domain controllers
(optimizing placement),
620

Domain Master
Browser, 594

Domain Model (Internet
Information Server 4.0
interaction), 741

Domain Monitor
(Dommon.exe), *Windows
NT Server Resource Kit
utilities*, 587-588

Domain Name Service,
see DNS

Domain Planner
application, 631

domains, 442
controllers
choosing types
(Windows NT Server
installation), 191
installing Windows NT
Server as, 181
designs, 630-632
Exchange Server 5.0
components, 894-895
implementing
between domains,
618-626
memory requirements,
621-622
trusts between
domains, 618-626
models, 626-630
Complete Trust, 629
hybrid models, 630
Multiple Master,
628-629
Single Domain, 626
Single Master, 627
multiple resources,
browsing, 633
names (TCP/IP), 324
resource sharing, 632-633
resources, attaching to
(Windows NT
Workstation 4.0 clients),
421-422
security, 606-618
adding BDCs to new
domains, 614
adding Windows NT
clients to domains,
614-615
domain controllers,
608-611
identifiers, 607-608
moving clients between
domains, 616
moving domain
controllers, 616-617
renaming domains,
617-618

synchronization process, 611-613
trust relationships, 623-626
trusted (user access), 474-475
User Manager for Domains, 442-447
low-speed connections, 446-447
multiple instances, starting, 444
selecting new domains, 445-446
starting, 443-444

dotted decimal notation (IP addresses), 324

drive configuration disks (RAID server stripe sets), 242-244

drivers
device, 88
Legacy SCSI host adapters, detecting hardware, 176
network, 88
MS-DOS, 408

drives, selecting for backup (NTBACKUP), 282-284

DSMN (Directory Services Manager for NetWare), 31

DUN (Dial-Up Networking), 689
configuring, 699-702
installing, 704-716
Windows 95, 704-709
Windows NT, 710-716
Remote Access Admin application, granting client access, 702-704
testing on clients, 704-716
Windows 95, 704-709
Windows NT, 710-716

duplexing (RAID level 1), 221

Dynamic Host Configuration Protocol, see DHCP

E

e-mail (Exchange Server 5.0), 874

editing
charts (Performance Monitor), 535
Registries, 311-312
opening remote Registries, 312
Windows 95 from Windows NT, 312
Windows NT from Windows 95, 312-319
Windows NT from Windows NT, 312

editors
Registry Editor, 293-295

emergency repair disks
creating (installations), 200-201
installations, 191-192
RAID server stripe sets, 242-244

encryption (application-level)
data communication security, 61
packet-level encryption, 62

End-User License Agreement, see EULA

enterprise backup systems, 273

Enterprise Edition, 49-51
4GT (4G RAM Tuning), 50
Microsoft Routing and Remote Access Service, 50
MSCS (Microsoft Cluster Server), 50
MSMQ (Microsoft Message Queue Server), 50
MTS (Microsoft Transaction Server), 50

enterprise hubs (active network components), 151

Enterprise Manager (SQL Server 6.5), 843-848
backup tape drives (specifying and testing), 847-848
installing on 32-bit clients, 843-844
registering servers, 844-847
setting permissions, 868-869
viewing logins, 868-869

enterprise middleware (BackOffice), 815-816
Cedar, 816
Microsoft Messaging Queue, 816
MTS (Microsoft Transaction Server), 816

Enterprise Network sites, building (SMS), 961-963

Enterprise Planning Guide Web site, 632

enterprise servers, 156

enterprise site topology (SMS planning), 935-936

Environment subkey (HKEY_CURRENT_USER hive), 307

eShop technology (Site Server 2.0), 47

Ethernet
10Base2 coaxial cable, 135
coaxial cable, 135
full-duplex vs. half-duplex, 143
high-speed variants
ATM (Asynchronous Transfer Mode, 131
CDDI (Copper Distributed Data Interface), 131-135
FDDI (Fiber Distributed Data Interface), 130
media-access methods, 128-131

ISDN terminal
adapters, 691
media-access
methods, 126
recommendations,
131-132
switches (active network
components), 151-154
**EULA (End-User License
Agreement), 187**
Event Viewer
changing Registry
values, 295
remote server
administration
utilities, 26
troubleshooting networks,
568-570
**Events window (SMS
Administrator), 954**
**Exchange Administrator
(Exchange Server 5.0),
878-879, 906-914**
granting administrative
permissions, 908-909
Information Store
(configuring), 909-912
recipient setup, 917-927
server configurations,
915-917
site addressing, 912-914
**Exchange Client
(Exchange Server 5.0),
872, 891-893**
**Exchange Forms Designer
(Exchange Server 5.0),
873, 894**
Exchange Server 4.0, 813
**Exchange Server 5.0,
872-873, 878-886,
895-897**
client components, 887-894
Exchange Client,
891-893
Exchange Forms
Designer, 894

Microsoft Outlook,
887-890
Schedule+, 891-893
connectors, 885-886
custom forms (building
applications), 875-876
Directory Service and
database, 879-880
distribution lists, 885
domains, 894-895
e-mail uses, 874
Exchange Administrator,
878-879, 906-914
granting administrative
permissions, 908-909
Information Store
(configuring), 909-912
recipient setup, 917-927
server configurations,
915-917
site addressing, 912-914
Information Store, 881
license packages, 820-821
mailboxes, 883
MTA (Message Transfer
Agent), 880-881
new features, 877-878
offline folder files, 884
organizations (sites),
894-895
personal folder files, 884
public folders, 875, 884-885
recipients, 882
Schedule+ group
scheduling, 876
server size, 897-899
Setup program, 900-905
Performance Optimizer,
903-908
site planning, 896
functional
considerations, 897
geographic
considerations,
896-897
System Attendant, 882
system intergration, 877
**Executive Software Web
site, 549**

**existing operating systems,
installing from, 185**
**expanded directory
services (network
performance features), 29**
**Exploration Air
Web site, 749**
**Extended Attributes
attribute (NTFS
Master File Table), 94**
**External Data
Representation,** *see* **XDR**
external modems
installing (RAS), 694-699
multiple, 690

F

FAT file system, 484
**FATs (file allocation
tables), 91**
fault tolerance, 91
network installation
requirements, 63-66
**FDDI (Fiber Distributed
Data Interface), 130**
**FDE (Full Duplex
Ethernet), media-access
models, 128**
**fiber-optic cable (network
cabling systems), 139**
**fibers (network
performance
features), 29**
**File and Print Services for
NetWare,** *see* **FPNW**
**File Permissions dialog,
495-496**
**file servers (Performance
Monitor), 543-549**
application server uses,
549-554
disk bottlenecks, 543-546
network media limitations,
548-549

protocol binding order,
547-548
reducing file
fragmentation, 549
unneeded protocols,
546-547
**file sharing (Windows 95
networking), 376-379**
Microsoft Networks,
377-378
NetWare Networks,
378-379
file systems
choosing, 484
FAT file system, 484
High Performance File
System (HPFS), 484
NT File System
(NTFS), 484
**File Transfer Protocol,
see FTP**
**file-access permissions,
493-497**
adding, 496-497
modifying, 495-496
removing, 495-496
**Filename attribute (NTFS
Master File Table), 93**
files
backups, 258-275
archive bits, 258-259
copy, 260
daily copy, 262
differential, 261-262
enterprise backup
systems, 273
hardware, 275-278
HSM (Hierarchical
Storage
Management), 272
incremental, 260-261
matching media to disk
size, 267
normal, 259
NTBACKUP (backup
application), 278-289
open files, 266
organizing disk storage,
264-265

restore plans, 274-275
rotation methods,
267-272
storing data off site, 273
type selection, 262-264
verifying integrity,
265-266
long file-name support
(Windows 95
networking), 353
naming (share names), 486
NTFS, compressing,
507-511
Registry, backing up,
308-310
selecting for backup,
NTBACKUP, 282-284
sharing, high-speed
LANs, 28
**firewalls (data
communication
security), 62**
fixed-disk drives
backups, 264-265
bottlenecks, 543-546
hardware solutions, 543
software solutions,
545-546
detecting, 186-187
hardware, 177-179
disaster-tolerant
disk system criteria
(RAID), 255
failure-resistant
disk system criteria
(RAID), 254
failure-resistant disk
system plus criteria
(RAID), 254-255
RAID (redundant array of
inexpensive disks),
216-229
array sizing, 228-229
implementation
specifications, 229-236
level 0, 217-219
level 1, 220-222
level 2, 222-223
level 3, 223-224
level 4, 224

level 5, 225-227
mirror sets, 239-251
RAB (RAID Advisory
Board), 217
recommendations,
253-255
recovering software
sets, 251-253
restoring mirror
sets, 252
restoring stripe sets
with parity, 252-253
server stripe sets,
239-251
software
implementations,
236-239
stacked, 227-228
recovering from failures,
210-212
multiple drive partition
table corruption, 212
RAID subsystem
recovery, 212
stripe set recovery, 212
system drive boot
failures, 211
volume set recovery,
212
saving configuration data
(installations), 205-206
setup, 188-189
formatting, 188
Install Folder
specifications, 188-189
partitions, 188
folder shares, 485-490
creating, 485-486
Managing Folder and File
Access Wizard, 490-493
modifying, 487
removing, 486
**folder-access permissions,
494, 498-502**
adding, 501-502
modifying, 499-501
removing, 499-501
**Foldername Properties
sheet (Windows
Explorer), 22**

folders
configuring (Internet Information Server 4.0), 758-760
accessing remote server shares, 759
assigning permissions, 759-760
redirecting to another page, 759-764
naming (share names), 486
NTFS, compressing, 507-511
offline files (Exchange Server 5.0), 884
personal files (Exchange Server 5.0), 884
public
Exchange Server 5.0, 884-885
sharing data (Exchange Server 5.0), 875
replicating, 502-506
configurations, 504-506
creating replication users, 503
starting the Directory Replicator, 503-504
security, configuring (Internet Information Server 4.0), 754-760
selecting for backup (NTBACKUP), 282-284
share permissions, 487-489
adding, 488-489
modifying, 487-488
removing, 487-488

formatting
fixed-disk drives, 188
mirror standard volumes (RAID 1 mirror sets), 247
standard volumes (RAID 1 mirror sets), 244-247

forms, custom, building applications (Exchange Server 5.0), 875-876

FPNW (File and Print Services for NetWare), 30, 638
configuring, 657-659
installing, 653-656

FQDN (Fully Qualified Domain Name), 324

fragmentation, file, reducing (Performance Monitor), 549

frame relay Internet connectivity, 732-733

frames, 103

FrontPage Web site, 38

FrontPage 97, 724
client license, 813
managing site content, 800-806
FrontPage Editor, 802-806
FrontPage Explorer, 802-806
installing, 800-802
server extensions, 813

FTP (File Transfer Protocol)
anonymous, 1004
server options (Internet Information Server 4.0), 738-740, 760-763

Full Control permission
NTFS file-access permissions, 494
NTFS folder-access permissions, 498

full-duplex Ethernet (NICs), 143

Fully Qualified Domain Name, 324

future growth (network installations), 71-72

G

Gateway Service for NetWare, see GSNW

gateways
active network components, 149-150
default gateway problems (connectivity issues), 593
print, installing/configuring (GSNW), 649-651
TCP/IP (Windows 95 configurations), 373-374

Get ISDN Web site, 692

GetMac (Getmac.exe) *Windows NT Server Resource Kit* utilities, 589

Getsid.exe command-line application, 609

gigabit Ethernet (media-access models), 130

global groups, 442

global options, configuring (DHCP server configurations), 335-337

global user groups, adding, 473

Global.exe (*Windows NT Resource Kit*), 480

Gopher server (Internet Information Server 4.0), 740

grandfather-father-son rotation (backup rotation methods), 270-271

Granite Digital Web site, 166

group accounts (terminology), 442

Group Management Wizard, 24
user groups, 475-477

group membership (assigning to user accounts), 454

groups
scheduling, Schedule+ (Exchange Server 5.0), 876
user, 469-475
adding global groups, 473
adding local groups, 471-473
built-in, 470-471
copying groups, 473
Group Management Wizard, 475-477
trusted domain resource access, 474-475
User Rights Policy, 478-480

growth planning (network installations), 71-72

GSNW (Gateway Service for NetWare), 30, 638
Microsoft client server access, 642
choosing preferred NetWare servers, 647
configuring NetWare servers, 643
installing, 644-647
print gateways (installing/configuring), 649-651

Guest Account (built-in user accounts), 448-449

H

HAL (hardware abstraction layer), 87

half-duplex Ethernet (NICs), 143

hardware
allocating funds (network installations), 79-80

backups, 275-278
tape drives, 275-277
WORM drives, 278
writable optical drives, 277-278
detecting, 175-180
CD-ROM drives, 179-183
fixed-disk drives, 177-179, 186-187
Legacy SCSI host adapter drivers, 176
network adapters, 179-180
disk bottleneck solutions, 543
inventory, SMS (Systems Management Server), 931
network installation issues, 67-68
protocol analyzers, 566
RAID implementations, 233
adding dedicated RAID 5 controller cards, 234-235
external RAID enclosures, 235-236
mirroring with current SCSI host adapters, 234
obtaining as a server option, 233
upgrading existing servers, 233-234
servers, 155-169
choosing components, 157-169
departmental servers, 156
enterprise servers, 156
HCL conformance, 156
local service, 157
maintenance, 157
warranties, 157
workgroup servers, 156
SMS (Systems Management Server), minimum requirements, 933

hardware abstraction layer, 87

hardware addresses, *see* **machine addresses, 323**

Hardware Compatibility List, *see* **HCL**

Hardware Device Modules, 162

hardware key (HKEY_LOCAL_MACHINE hive), 305

HCL (Hardware Compatibility List), 89, 144
server hardware conformance, 156
Web site, 89, 156

HCL terminology (Web site), 175

HDMs (Hardware Device Modules), intelligent I/O subsystems, 162

helical scan tape drives (backups), 277
8mm, 277
DAT (Digital Audio Tape), 277

Help Desk functions, SMS client software, 931
installing, 957-959

helper servers (SMS terminology), 937

Hierarchical Storage Management, 272

hierarchies (Registry)
hives, 297-299, 301
keys, 299, 301
value entries, 300-301

High Performance File System (HPFS), 484

high-speed Ethernet variants (media-access models), 128-131
100BaseT Fast Ethernet, 128-129

100VG-AnyLAN, 129
ATM (Asynchronous Transfer Mode, 131
CDDI (Copper Distributed Data Interface), 131-135
FDDI (Fiber Distributed Data Interface), 130
FDE (Full Duplex Ethernet), 128
gigabit Ethernet, 130

hives (Registry), 297-299, 301
    HKEY_CLASSES_ROOT, 297, 305-306
    HKEY_CURRENT_CONFIG, 297, 305
    HKEY_CURRENT_USER, 297, 306-307
    HKEY_LOCAL_MACHINE, 297, 301-305
    HKEY_USERS, 297, 307

HKEY_CLASSES_ROOT hive (Registry), 297, 305-306

HKEY_CURRENT_CONFIG hive (Registry), 297, 305

HKEY_CURRENT_USER hive (Registry), 297, 306-307

HKEY_LOCAL_MACHINE hive (Registry), 297, 301-305
    hardware key, 305
    SAM (Security Account Manager) key, 301
    security key, 302
    software key, 302
    system key, 302-305

HKEY_USERS hive (Registry), 297, 307

home folders (user profiles), 457

host DNS resource records (adding), 675

host names (TCP/IP), 324

hostname command (command-line tools), 580

HOSTS file (TCP/IP), 327

hot spare disks (RAID product features), 231

hot swappable disks (RAID product features), 231

HPFS (High Performance File System), 484

HSM (Hierarchical Storage Management), 272

HTTP, Service Object counters (Performance Monitor), 791-793

HTTP headers (Internet Information Server 4.0), 760-764

hubs (active network components), 145-147
    enterprise, 151
    managing, 146-147
    stackable, 146
    stand-alone, 145

hybrid domain models, 630

Hydra Server (scalability), 983-984

I

IBM LAN Server, 107

IDC (Internet Database Connector), 37, 45, 725

Identification Page (Windows 95 network support), 361-362

identifiers (domain security), 607-608

identifying, hardware (Windows NT Server 4.0 installations), 180

idle disconnect, 689

IDP (Internet Datagram Protocol), 111

IEEE (Institute for Electrical and Electronic Engineers), 124

IETF (Internet Engineering Task Force), 108

IETF RFC support (UNIX integration), 669-670

implementation schedules (network installations), 69

implementation specifications (RAID), 229-236
    automatic rebuild, 231
    disk drive issues, 231-232
    hot spare disks, 231
    hot swappable disks, 231
    multiple-level independent RAID, 232-233
    power supplies, 232
    user needs, 229-230

importing table structures (SQL Server 6.5), 852-856

incremental backups, 260-261

Index Allocation attribute (NTFS Master File Table), 94

Index Root attribute (NTFS Master File Table), 94

Index Server 1.1, 724, 813

indexes (SQL Server 6.5 database structures), 857-858

industry standards (future growth planning), 72

Information Store (Exchange Server 5.0), 872
    configuring options, 909-912
    Exchange Server 5.0, 881

.INI files (Registry), 317-318

initialization files
Windows 3.1 (client installation changes), 406-408
Windows for Workgroups 3.11 (changing), 414-415

Install Folder specifications (fixed-disk drives), 188-189

Install New Modem Wizard, 25

installation disks (Windows 3.1 clients), 400-402

installing
Crystal Reports (Internet Information Server 4.0), 787
Dfs (Distributed File System), 989-991
Dfs Administrator, 993-997
Windows 95 Dfs client, 991-993
Directory Service Manager for NetWare (Windows NT Server integration), 661-662
DNS (Domain Name Service) (UNIX integration), 671-672
DUN (Dial-Up Networking), 704-716
Windows 95, 704-709
Windows NT, 710-716
FPNW (File and Print Services for NetWare), 653-656
FrontPage 97, managing site content, 800-802
GSNW (Gateway Service for NetWare), 644-647
Internet Information Server 4.0 interaction, 741-749
default installation tests, 748-749
initial installations vs. upgrades, 742-747

modems (RAS), 694-699
MS-DOS clients, 402-405
Network Monitor, 570-575
network software (Windows NT Workstation 4.0 connections), 418-421
networks, 56-74, 79-80
allocating remaining funds, 79-80
budgets, 72-74
determining user needs, 57-59
determining workgroup needs, 57-59
existing infrastructures, 66-68
fault-tolerance requirements, 63-66
future growth, 71-72
implementation schedules, 69
management needs, 69-71
meeting business objectives, 56-57
minimum configurations, 79
outside connections, 68-69
outside help, 77-79
project-management software, 75-77
protocol-related planning issues, 66
security, 59-63
training users, 74
vendors, 80-81
SMS (Systems Management Server), 937-942
creating server accounts, 937-938
on Primary Site Servers, 939-942
SQL Server setup, 939
SMS client software, 954-960
automatic installation, 955-957

client inventory management, 957
help desk functions, 957-959
manual installation, 954-955
Network Monitor, 960
remote control functions, 957-959
software, SMS (Systems Management Server), 931
SQL Enterprise Manager (on 32-bit clients), 843-844
SQL Server 6.5, 835-843
distribution CD-ROM, 836-841
Service Packs, 842-843
SQL Executive (starting), 842
starting SQL Server, 842
TCP/IP, 328-331
Windows 3.1 clients, 402-405
Windows 95 network support, 354-363, 380-386
Access Control page, 362-363
Identification page, 361-362
installing/removing clients, 358-361
NICs (network interface cards), 354-358
Windows NT Server 4.0, 174-181
automating installation, 212-213
backups on existing computer, 181-182
choosing domain controller types, 191
confirming basic system information, 187
creating RAID subsystems, 201
creating setup boot disks, 183-184

detecting mass-storage
devices, 186-187
display configurations,
199-202
domain controller
installations, 181
emergency repair disks,
191-192,
200-201
fine tuning, 192
fixed-disk configuration
data (saving), 205-206
fixed-disk drive setup,
188-189
from existing operating
systems, 185
from network servers,
184-185
hardware setup, 175-181
Internet Information
Server (installing), 198
master boot record
backups, 201-205
names and
identification, 180
naming components, 190
network connections,
192-198
observing the copying
process, 189-190
Pentium floating-point
division bug, 191
recovering from fixed-
disk failures, 210-212
repairing existing
installations, 186,
209-210
restarting the server,
201
Service Packs, 206-208
setting Administrator
passwords, 191
setting time and date,
198
upgrading from
previous versions,
174-181, 187
user preparation, 206
**Institute for Electrical
and Electronic
Engineers, 124**

**integrated security
(SQL Server 6.5), 865**
**Integrated Services Digital
Network, see ISDN**
integrating
Windows NT Server with
NetWare, 637-668
Directory Service
Manager for NetWare,
660
Microsoft client server
access, 639-651
Multi-Protocol Routing
service, 666-668
NetWare client server
access, 651-659
Windows NT Server with
UNIX, 668-679
DNS (Domain Name
Service) Server,
671-677
file sharing, 677-680
IETF RFC support,
669-670
**integration (Exchange
Server 5.0), 877**
Intel processors, 159
**intelligent I/O subsystems
(server hardware), 162**
**interfaces, user
(Windows 95), 21**
internal modems
installing (RAS), 694-699
single vs. multiple
(DUN), 689
**internal security Web
site, 59**
Internet, 43-49
BackOffice servers,
814-815
connecting to, 726-735
56 kbps connections,
729
connection types,
727-733
dial-up access, 728
DNS (Domain Name
Service), 734-735

frame relay
connectivity, 732-733
ISDN connections,
730-732
ISPs (Internet service
providers), 727
T-1 connections, 733
connections (multiple
server protocol
support), 118
DCOM (Distributed
Component Object
Model), 39-41
FrontPage, 38
Internet Information
Server 2.0, 36, 44-46
managing, 46-47
Internet Information
Server 3.0, 37
intranets, 44-46
see also LANs and
WANs, 44-46
Microsoft products,
724-725
planning sites, 725-726
PPTP (Point-to-Point
Tunneling Protocol), 38
RAS Multilink Channel
Aggregation, 38-54
Site Server 2.0, 47-49
Commerce Server, 49
eShop technology, 47
Intersé market
focus 3, 48
Microsoft Wallet, 49
NetCarta
WebMapper, 48
Usage Analyst
Enterprise Edition, 49
TAPI 2.x (Telephony
API), 41
**Internet Connector
(Exchange Server
5.0), 872**
**Internet Database
Connector, 37,45,725**
**Internet Datagram
Protocol, 111**
**Internet Deployment
Guide Web site, 46**

Internet Engineering Task Force, 108

Internet Explorer (IE) 3.0, 724

Internet Information Server 2.0, 36, 44-46
installing, 192-193, 198
managing, 46-47
Web site, 36

Internet Information Server 3.0, 37

Internet Information Server 4.0, 724, 736-740
activating Web pages
ADO (ActiveX Data Objects), 797-799
ASP (Active Server Pages), 794-797
OLE DB, 797-799
BackOffice Server 2.5, 812-813
Enterprise middleware, 815-816
Internet and intranet servers, 814-815
licensing components, 816-825
configuring
folder security, 754-758
folders, 758-760
performance options, 754
security accounts, 753
Crystal Reports, 786-789
installing, 787
testing, 788-789
domain model interaction, 741
FrontPage 97, managing content, 800-806
FTP (File Transfer Protocol) service, 738-740
Gopher server, 740
installing, 741-749
default installation tests, 748-749

initial installations vs. upgrades, 742-747
MMC (Microsoft Management Console), 747
Performance Monitor, 790-794
HTTP Service Object counters, 791-793
setting options, 750-760
FTP server, 760-763
HTTP header, 760-764
logging, 751-752
Web site, 750-751
World Wide Web service, 736-738

Internet Locator (BackOffice), 815

Internet Server API, 37, 725

Internet Service Providers, 727

Internet Services Application Programming Interface, 37, 725

Internetwork Packet Exchange/Sequenced Packet Exchange, see IPX/SPX

InterNIC Web site, 322, 324

interoperability (network plans), 118-120

Intersé market focus 3 (Site Server 2.0), 48

intranets, 44-46
BackOffice servers, 814-815
DCOM (Distributed Component Object Model), 39-41
FrontPage, 38
Internet Information Server 2.0, 36
Internet Information Server 3.0, 37
local server protocol support, 117-118

PPTP (Point-to-Point Tunneling Protocol), 38
RAS Multilink Channel Aggregation, 38-54
TAPI 2.x (Telephony API), 41
see also LANs and WANs

inventory
client management (SMS client software installing), 957
hardware, SMS (Systems Management Server), 931
packages, SMS Administrator Packages window, 949
software, SMS (Systems Management Server), 931

IOM (Input/Output Manager), 87

IP addresses
allocating (TCP/IP configurations), 371
leasing to clients, DHCP (Dynamic Host Configuration Protocol), 333
resolving with DNS, TCP/IP, 374-376
TCP/IP, 109
dotted decimal notation, 324

ipconfig command, 580

IPX/SPX
network protocols, 561-562
NWLink, 107

ISAPI (Internet Server API), 37, 725

ISDN (Integrated Services Digital Network)
Internet connections, 730-732
modems, 112
routers, 691
terminal adapters, 690
Ethernet, 691

ISDN Accelerator Pack
1.1 Web site, 692
ISO (International
Standards
Organization), 102
ISPs (Internet Service
Providers), 727

J

Java, 725
JavaScript, 725
Jet 3.5 tables, creating
(ODBC logging tables),
770-771
Jet databases, data
sources, creating,
776-779
Jetpack.exe (DHCP
databases), 341-342
Jobs window (SMS
Administrator), 950
jumpers (configurable
NICs), 143

K

Kerberos 5.0 security
(Windows NT
Server 5.0), 52
kernels, 87
Key Management
(Exchange Server
5.0), 872
KeyboardLayout subkey
(HKEY_CURRENT_USER
hive), 307
keys
    HKEY_LOCAL_MACHINE
    hive
        hardware, 305
        SAM (Security Account
        Manager), 301
        security 302

software, 302
system, 302-305
Registry, 299, 301
subkeys, 299

L

labeling media
(NTBACKUP), 281
LANalyzer for Windows
Web site, 567
LANs (local area
networks)
    data communication
    security, 60
    faster file sharing, 28
    virtual (active network
    components), 154
    see also intranets
large fixed-disk support
(NTFS), 90
leaves, Dfs (Distributed
File System), 988-989
License Manager
(Windows NT
Server 4.0), 825-831
    Control Panel License tool,
    825-827
License tool (License
Manager), 825-827
License Wizard, 25
licensing (BackOffice
components), 816-825
    client access licenses,
    818-819
    cost summary, 822-823
    Exchange Server 5.0,
    820-821
    per-seat vs. per-server,
    816-818
    SNA Server 3.0, 822
    SQL Server 6.5, 820
    Systems Management
    Server 1.2, 821-822
    Windows NT 4.0 license
    packages, 819
line printer daemon, 110

List permission (NTFS
folder-access
permissions), 498
listings
    DiskMap output
    (code listing), 205-206
    HTML Web page example,
    736-737
    sample Transact-SQL
    query (reviewing ODBC
    logs), 781
    SQL Server query (logging
    databases), 768
LLC (Logical Link
Control), 103
LMHOSTS file
(TCP/IP), 327
local broadcasts
(TCP/IP), 326
local groups, 442
local intranet servers
(protocol support),
117-118
local service
(server hardware
conformance), 157
local user groups, adding,
471-473
localization (NTFS), 92
log files (Performance
Monitor), 539-543
    recording data, 540-541
    viewing recorded data,
    541-542
Log-on Dial, 688
logging databases (ODBC),
creating, 766-767
logging off users, 459-460
logging options (Internet
Information Server 4.0),
751-752
logging specifications
(ODBC data sources),
779-780

logging tables (ODBC), adding, 767-771
Jet 3.5 tables, 770-771
SQL Server tables, 768

Logical Link Control, 103

login servers (SMS terminology), 936

logon hours, user account properties, 458-460

logon script names (user profiles), 456

logons
ODBC data sources, 766-786
adding logging tables, 767-771
creating logging databases, 766-767
single network (Windows 95 networking), 353

logs, reviewing (ODBC sample queries), 780-782

long file-name support (Windows 95 networking), 353

low-level parameters (TCP/IP), 374

LPC (Local Procedure Call), 87

LPD (line printer daemon), 110

M

MAC (Media Access Control), 103, 560

machine addresses (TCP/IP), 323

Machine Groups window (SMS Administrator), 954

Macintosh
clients, 425-436
adding services, 425-426

setup, 427-429
troubleshooting connections, 436
Windows NT Server resource access, 429-435
network protocol support, 116

magneto optical drives (backups), 278

mailboxes
administrator, creating (Exchange Administrator), 919-921
creating (Directory Import), 924-926
Exchange Server 5.0, 883
user, creating
Exchange Administrator, 921-923
User Manager for Domains, 923-924

mainframes (multiple server protocol support), 118

maintenance
disaster-tolerant disk system criteria, 255
failure-resistant disk system criteria, 254
failure-resistant disk system plus criteria, 254-255
network cabling systems (recommendations), 141
networks, 568-584, 591-601
browsing, 594-595
command-line tools, 580-585
connectivity problems, 592-593
DNS name resolution, 599-601
Event Viewer, 568-570
Network Monitor, 570-575
Performance Monitor, 576-580
routing, 595-596

trust relationships, 596-602
Windows NT Server Resource Kit utilities, 584-591
WINS name resolution, 599-601
preventative (server hardware power protection), 166-169
server hardware conformance, 157

Managing Folder and File Access Wizard, 24, 490-493

"Managing Windows NT Domains" Web site, 59

mass-storage devices, detecting, 186-187

master boot records
backing up (installations), 201-205
saving (RAID stripe and mirror sets), 251

Master Browser, 594

Master File Table (NTFS), 92-94

MAU (multistation access unit), 125

McAfee VirusScan (data security), 60

MCIS Mail (BackOffice), 815

MCIS News (BackOffice), 815

MCSE (Microsoft Certified System Engineer), 79

Media Access Control, 103, 560

Media Server (BackOffice), 814

media-access methods, 124-132
ARCnet, 124
Ethernet, 126

high-speed Ethernet
variants, 128-131
100BaseT Fast
Ethernet, 128-129
100VG-AnyLAN, 129
ATM (Asynchronous
Transfer Mode), 131
CDDI (Copper
Distributed Data
Interface), 131-135
FDDI (Fiber
Distributed Data
Interface), 130
FDE (Full Duplex
Ethernet), 128
gigabit Ethernet, 130
recommendations, 131-132
Token Ring, 124-126

**Membership
(BackOffice), 815**

memory
application server usage
(Performance Monitor),
551-558
cache (sizing), 159
conventional, minimizing
use (Windows 95
networking), 354
domain requirements,
621-622
server hardware, 157-169

**Message Queue
Server, 724**
see also MSMQ

**MIB (Management
Information Base),
network installations, 70**

Microsoft
Internet products, 724-725
Networks (file/printer
sharing), 377-378

**Microsoft Cluster Server,
50, 968**

**Microsoft Commercial
Internet System 1.0
(BackOffice), 814**

**Microsoft Exchange
Server,** *see* **Exchange
Server 5.0**

**Microsoft Free Product
Downloads Web
site, 725**

**Microsoft Index Server
Web site, 37**

**Microsoft Knowledge Base
Web site, 591**

**Microsoft LAN
Manager, 107**
UNIX file sharing, 678

**Microsoft Mail
Connector (Exchange
Server 5.0), 872**

**Microsoft Management
Console,** *see* **MMC**

**Microsoft Message Queue
Server, 50, 969**

**Microsoft Messaging
Queue (Enterprise
middleware)
(BackOffice), 816**

Microsoft NetShow 2.0, 44

**Microsoft Outlook
(Exchange Server client
components), 887-890**

Microsoft Project, 75

**Microsoft Proxy Server
Web site, 37**

**Microsoft Routing
and Remote Access
Service, 50**

**Microsoft Service for
NetWare Directory
Services Web site, 360**

**Microsoft Service Pack 1
Web site, 361**

**Microsoft Services for
NetWare Web site, 31**

**Microsoft SiteBuilder
Workshop Web site, 726**

**Microsoft SiteServer 2.0
Web site, 806**

**Microsoft Transaction
Server, see MTS**

**Microsoft U.S. Estimated
Price List Web site, 823**

**Microsoft Wallet (Site
Server 2.0), 49**

**Microsoft-HP joint press
release Web site, 933**

**minimum configurations
(network installations), 79**

MIPS, 86

mirror sets
RAID (restoring), 252
RAID implementations,
239-251
level 1, 244-247

mirroring
RAID hardware
implementations (with
current SCSI host
adapters), 234
RAID level 1, 220, 230

**mixed security (SQL
Server 6.5), 865**

**MMC (Microsoft
Management Console), 46**
Internet Information Server
4.0 interaction, 747
Windows NT Server 5.0, 52

**models (domains),
626-630**
Complete Trust model, 629
hybrid models, 630
Multiple Master model,
628-629
Single Domain model, 626
Single Master model, 627

modems
external (multiple), 690
internal (single vs.
multiple (DUN)), 689
ISDN (Integrated Services
Digital Network), 112

modifying (user accounts),
451-453

**modularity (future growth
planning), 72**

moving
clients (between
domains), 616
compressed files
(NTFS), 509
domain controllers,
616-617

**MPR (Multi-Protocol
Router) (TCP/IP), 31**

MS-DOS
clients, installing, 402-405
network drivers, 408
network protocol support,
115-116

**MSCS (Microsoft Cluster
Server), 50, 968**

**MSDN subscriptions
Web site, 819**

Msinfo.exe Web site, 425

**Msinfo32.exe Web
site, 425**

**MSMQ (Microsoft Message
Queue Server), 50, 969**

**MSOs (Multiple Service
Operators), 815**

**MTA (Message Transfer
Agent), Exchange Server
5.0, 872, 880-881**

**MTS (Microsoft
Transaction Server),
50, 969**
Enterprise middleware
(BackOffice), 816

**Multi-Protocol Routing
service (Windows NT
Server integration),
666-668**

**multiple arrays
(RAID), 230**

**multiple client support
(Windows 95
networking), 352**

**multiple data streams
(NTFS), 91**

**multiple drive partition
table corruption,
recovering from, 212**

**Multiple Master model,
628-629**

multiple protocols
spanning, 636-637
Windows 95 networking
support, 352

**multiple resources,
domains (browsing), 633**

**multiple servers (protocol
support), 116-118**
interconnected Windows
NT servers, 117
Internet connections, 118
local intranet servers,
117-118
mainframes, 118
Novell NetWare
servers, 117
UNIX servers, 117

**multiple user profiles,
457-458**

**multiple-level independent
RAID (product features),
232-233**

**multiport serial cards
(DUN), 690**

**multiprocessor
systems, 160**

**multistation access
unit, 125**

N

**name mappings, viewing
(WINS), 346**

name-brand NICs, 143

names, resolving
DNS (Domain Name
Service), 734-735
TCP/IP, 325-326

naming
components (Windows
NT Server 4.0
installations), 190
hardware (Windows
NT Server 4.0
installations), 180
Registry value entries, 300

**National Software Testing
Laboratories, 28**

**nbtstat command-line
tool, 581**

**NDAs (non-disclosure
agreements), 44**

**NDIS (Network Device
Interface Specification),
105-106**

**NDS (NetWare Directory
Services), 30-31**

**Net Watch (Netwatch.exe),
*Windows NT Server
Resource Kit* utilities, 589**

**Net Watcher (remote client
management), 391,
394-396**

NetBEUI
broadcasting (network
protocols), 560-561
configuring (Windows 95
network protocols),
367-368
Windows 3.1 support, 115

**NetBEUI (NetBIOS
Extended User
Interface), 107-108**

**NetBEUI Frame
(workstation
support), 114**

**NetBEUI Frame protocol,
107-108**

NetBIOS
datagram, 562
name, 562
names (TCP/IP), 325
node types (TCP/IP),
565-566

registering/resolving
names (WINS), 342-343
session, 562
**NetCarta WebMapper
(Site Server 2.0), 48**
**NetMeeting 2.0
(BackOffice), 724, 814**
**NetShow 2.0 (BackOffice),
724, 814**
**netstat command-line tool,
582-583**
NetWare, 29-31
coexistence with
enterprise network sites
(SMS), 962-963
DSMN (Directory
Services Manager for
NetWare), 31
choosing preferred
servers, 647
FPNW (File and
Print Services for
NetWare), 30
GSNW (Gateway Service
for NetWare), 30
integrating with Windows
NT Server, 637-668
Directory Service
Manager for
NetWare, 660
Microsoft client server
access, 639-651
Multi-Protocol Routing
service, 666-668
NetWare client server
access, 651-659
multiple server protocol
support, 117
networks (file/printer
sharing), 378-379
protocol stacks (Microsoft
client server access),
640-642
universal clients, 679-683
Windows for
Workgroups 3.11
configurations, 681

Windows NT Server
migration, 683-685
**NetWare Directory
Services, 30-31**
network adapters
detecting hardware,
179-180
installing, 193
**Network Client
Administrator Wizard, 25**
**Network Device Interface
Specification, 105-106**
**Network General's
Sniffer product line
Web site, 566**
**network interface cards,
see NICs**
**network layer (OSI
model), 103**
Network Monitor
SMS client software
installing, 960
troubleshooting networks,
33-36, 570-575
installing, 570-575
Web site, 567
**Network Node Manager
Web site, 71**
**Network PC (NetPC),
reducing client PC costs
(scalability), 982-983**
**Network PC Design
Guidelines Web site, 983**
**Network property sheet
(Windows 95 network)**
Access Control page,
362-363
Identification page,
361-362
networks
cabling systems, 132-141
active network
components, 141-155

cable types, 135-139
expandability, 141
maintenance, 141
topologies, 133-135
connections, 192-198
adapter settings, 194
confirming network
bindings, 197
describing, 192
Internet Information
Server, 192-193
network adapters, 193
protocols (choosing),
193-194
services (choosing),
193-194
DCOM (Distributed
Component Object
Model), 39-41
DUN (Dial-Up
Networking), 689
FrontPage, 38
installing, 56-74, 79-80
allocating remaining
funds, 79-80
budgets, 72-74
determining user
needs, 57-59
determining workgroup
needs, 57-59
existing infrastructures,
66-68
fault-tolerance
requirements, 63-66
future growth, 71-72
hardware-related
planning issues, 67-68
implementation
schedules, 69
management needs,
69-71
meeting business
objectives, 56-57
minimum
configurations, 79
outside connections,
68-69
outside help, 77-79

project-management
  software, 75-77
security, 59-63
software-related
  planning issues, 66
training users, 74
vendors, 80-81
Internet, 43-49
  Internet Information
    Server 2.0, 44-47
  intranets, 44-46
  Site Server 2.0, 47-49
Internet Information
  Server 2.0, 36
Internet Information
  Server 3.0, 37
Macintosh clients, 425-436
  adding services,
    425-426
  setup, 427-429
  troubleshooting
    connections, 436
  Windows NT Server
    resource access,
    429-435
maximizing throughput
  (application servers),
  552-553
NetWare, 29-31
  DSMN (Directory
    Services Manager
    for NetWare), 31
  FPNW (File and Print
    Services for
    NetWare), 30
  GSNW (Gateway
    Service for
    NetWare), 30
performance features,
  27-29
  expanded directory
    services, 29
  faster LAN file
    sharing, 28
  fibers, 29
  new APIs, 29
  printing
    enhancements, 29
PPTP (Point-to-Point
  Tunneling Protocol), 38

protocols, 106-116, 560-566
  analyzers, 566-568
  AppleTalk, 112
  choosing, 120
  DLC (Data Link
    Control), 111
  interoperability, 118-120
  IPX/SPX, 561-562
  Macintosh client
    support, 116
  MS-DOS client support,
    115-116
  multiple server support,
    116-118
  NetBEUI (NetBIOS
    Extended User
    Interface), 107-108
  NetBEUI broadcasting,
    560-561
  NetBEUI Frame,
    107-108
  NWLink (IPX/SPX), 111
  OS/2 client support, 116
  OSI (Open Systems
    Interconnection)
    model, 102-106
  RAS (Remote Access
    Service), 112
  SMS (Systems
    Management Server)
    analysis, 931-932
  spanning multiple,
    636-637
  streams, 113
  TCP/IP, 108-111,
    562-566
  UNIX workstation
    support, 116
  Windows 3.1, 115
  Windows 95 support,
    114-115
  Windows for
    Workgroups 3.1x
    support, 115
  Windows NT
    workstations, 114
RAS Multilink Channel
  Aggregation, 38
resource kits, 42
scalability, 27-29

SMP (symmetrical
  multiprocessing),
  28-29
securing printers, 512-527
server hardware, 155-169
  choosing components,
    157-169
  departmental
    servers, 156
  enterprise servers, 156
  HCL conformance, 156
  local service, 157
  maintenance, 157
  warranties, 157
  workgroup servers, 156
servers, installing from,
  184-185
sharing printers, 512-527
  locally attached server
    printers, 512-517
  network printer servers,
    517-519
  printer property
    configurations,
    520-527
SMS (Systems
  Management Server)
  support, 934
structured cabling
  systems, 139-140
  recommendations, 140
TAPI 2.x (Telephony
  API), 41
TCP/IP, 29-31
  graphical DNS tool, 30
  MPR (Multi-Protocol
    Router), 31
troubleshooting, 568-584,
  591-601
  browsing, 594-595
  command-line tools,
    580-585
  connectivity problems,
    592-593
  DNS name resolution,
    599-601
  Event Viewer, 568-570
  Network Monitor,
    570-575

Performance Monitor,
576-580
routing, 595-596
trust relationships,
596-598
*Windows NT Server
Resource Kit* utilities,
584-591
WINS name resolution,
599-601
troubleshooting tools,
31-35
Network Monitor tool,
33-36
Windows NT
Diagnostics tool, 32
Windows 3.1 clients,
400-410
configuration file
changes, 406-408
creating installation
disks, 400-402
initialization file
changes, 406-408
installing, 402-405
MS-DOS network
drivers, 408
troubleshooting
connection
problems, 410
Windows NT file and
printer resources,
408-409
Windows 95, 352-354
client browsing issues,
396-397
configuring clients,
363-366
configuring network
protocols, 366-376
file/printer sharing,
376-379
installing from network,
380-386
installing support,
354-363
remote client
management, 390-396

system policies, 388-391
user profiles, 386-387
Windows for Workgroups
3.11 clients, 410-418
configuration file
changes, 414-415
initialization file
changes, 414-415
installing 32-bit
TCP/IP, 410-414
troubleshooting,
417-418
Windows NT Server 4.0
resource connections,
416-417
Windows NT operating
system, 98-99
Windows NT Workstation
4.0 clients, 418-425
attaching to domain
resources, 421-422
installing network
software, 418-421
troubleshooting
connections, 423
ZAK previews, 423-425
new features, 20-41
client-side features, 25-27
remote server
administration, 26
System Policy Editor, 26
user profiles, 26
Windows 95 RPL
(Remote Program
Load), 27
DCOM (Distributed
Component Object
Model), 39-41
FrontPage, 38
Internet Information
Server 2.0, 36
Internet Information
Server 3.0, 37
NetWare, 29-31
DSMN (Directory
Services Manager for
NetWare), 31
FPNW (File and Print

Services for
NetWare), 30
GSNW (Gateway
Service for
NetWare), 30
network performance
features, 27-29
expanded directory
services, 29
faster LAN file
sharing, 28
fibers, 29
new APIs, 29
printing
enhancements, 29
PPTP (Point-to-Point
Tunneling Protocol), 38
RAS Multilink Channel
Aggregation, 38-54
resource kits, 42
scalability, 27-29
SMP (symmetrical
multiprocessing),
28-29
server usability, 21-25
administrative wizards,
23-25
Task Manager, 23
Windows 95 user
interface, 21
Windows Explorer,
21-23
TAPI 2.x (Telephony
API), 41
TCP/IP, 29-31
graphical DNS tool, 30
MPR (Multi-Protocol
Router), 31
troubleshooting tools,
31-35
Network Monitor tool,
33-36
Windows NT
Diagnostics tool, 32
**NFS (Network File
System), UNIX file
sharing, 677**

NICs (network interface cards), 124, 141-144
bus types, 142
full-duplex vs. half-duplex
Ethernet, 143
jumper-configurable, 143
name brands vs.
clones, 143
server, 143-144
software-configurable, 143
Windows 95 network
support, 354-356
changing settings,
356-358

NLMs (NetWare Loadable Modules), 84

No Access permission
NTFS file-access
permissions, 494
NTFS folder-access
permissions, 498

non-disclosure agreements, 44

non-domain servers (domain security), 611

non-host DNS resource records (adding), 676-677

normal backups, 259

Novell NetWare,
see NetWare

NSLookup (Nslookup.exe),
Windows NT Server
Resource Kit **utilities,**
590

NT File System (NTFS), 484

NTBACKUP (backup application), 278-289
choosing options, 284-287
preparing/labeling
media, 281
restoring data, 287-289
selecting elements to
backup, 282-284
tape drive setup, 279-281

Ntcomp.exe (Web site), 176

NTFS, 484
file compression, 507-509
Compact.exe utility, 510
Diruse.exe utility
(Resource Kit), 511
moving and
copying, 509
Windows NT Explorer
compression features,
507-509
Windows NT My
Computer
compression features,
507-509
Windows NT operating
system, 90-95
Master File Table, 92-94
recoverability, 94-95

NTFS permissions, 493-502
file-access permissions,
494-497
adding, 496-497
modifying, 495-496
removing, 495-496
folder-access permissions,
498-502
adding, 501-502
modifying, 499-501
removing, 499-501

NSTL (National Software Testing Laboratories), 28

NWLink (IPX/SPX), 111
configuring (Windows 95
network protocols),
369-371
workstation support, 114

O

objects (Performance Monitor), 531-534

ODBC (Open Database Connectivity) data sources, 37
distributing activity reports
(SQL Server Web
Assistant), 782-786
logging onto, 766-780
adding logging tables,
767-771
creating logging
databases, 766-767
logging specifications,
779-780
setting up, 771-779
creating Jet database
data sources, 776-779
creating SQL Server
data sources, 772
writing sample queries,
reviewing logs, 780-782

ODIPKT (universal client packet driver support), 682

offline folder files (Exchange Server 5.0), 884

OLE DB, Internet Information Server 4.0 (activating Web pages), 797-799

OM (Object Manager), 87

Open Database Connectivity, *see* **ODBC**

open files, backing up, 266

Open Software Foundation, 105

opening (remote Registries), 312

OpenNT Web site, 85

operating system, 84-90
networking processes,
98-99
NTFS, 90-95
Master File Table, 92-94
recoverability, 94-95
protected subsystem
servers, 89-90

RPCs (remote procedure calls), 96-98
Windows NT Executive, 86-89
  Cache Manager, 88
  device drivers, 88
  HAL (hardware abstraction layer), 87
  IOM (Input/Output Manager), 87
  kernel, 87
  LPC (Local Procedure Call), 87-89
  network drivers, 88
  OM (Object Manager), 87-89
  PM (Process Manager), 87-89
  SRM (Security Reference Monitor), 87-89
  VMM (Virtual Memory Manager), 87-89

operating systems, existing, installing from, 185

options (Internet Information Server 4.0 interaction), 750-760
  FTP server, 760-763
  HTTP header, 760-764
  logging, 751-752
  Web site, 750-751

organizations (Exchange Server 5.0 components), 894-895

OS-Specific Module, 162

OS/2
  network protocol support, 116
  subsystem, 90

OSFT (Open Software Foundation), 105

OSI (Open Systems Interconnection) model (network protocols), 102-106

application layer, 105
data-link layer, 103
network layer, 103
physical layer, 102
presentation layer, 104-105
session layer, 104
transport layer, 104
Windows NT comparisons, 105-106

OSM (OS-Specific Module), intelligent I/O subsystems, 162

OSR 2 Web site, 385

Outlook (Microsoft) (Exchange Server client components), 887-890

outside consultants
  CNEs (Novell Certified NetWare Engineers), 79
  MCSE (Microsoft Certified System Engineer), 79
  network installations, 77-81

overall performance (RAID level 1), 222

overcapcity, building in (future growth planning), 72

P

package definition file (SMS Administrator Packages window), 949

Packages window (SMS Administrator), 948-949
  inventory packages, 949
  package definition file, 949
  sharing packages, 948

packet drivers, universal clients (Windows for Workgroups 3.11 configuration), 681-686

packet-level encryption (data communication security), 62

pair count UTP cable, 137-138

parameters, low-level (TCP/IP), 374

partition tables, saving (RAID stripe and mirror sets), 251

partitions (fixed-disk drives), 188

passwords
  Administrator (installations), 191
  setting domain account policies (user accounts), 468

PDCs (Primary Domain Controllers), 175, 191
  domain security, 608-609
  promoting BDCs to PDCs, 610-611

peer-to-peer networking (Windows 95 networking), 353

Pentium floating-point division bug (installation issues), 191

per-seat licensing (BackOffice), 816-818

per-server licensing (BackOffice), 816-818

PerfMon, see Performance Monitor

performance
  network features, 27-29
    expanded directory services, 29
    faster LAN file sharing, 28
    fibers, 29
    new APIs, 29
    printing enhancements, 29
  remote analysis, SMS (Systems Management Server) analysis, 932

Performance Counter Help (Counters.hlp) (*Windows NT Workstation Resource Kit*), 556

Performance Data Log Server (PerfLog) (*Windows NT Workstation Resource Kit*), 554

Performance Monitor, 530-542
alerts, 537-539
adding, 537
customizing, 538-539
application server uses, 549-554
examining CPU usage, 550-551
examining memory usage, 551-558
changing Registry values, 295
charting characteristics, 534-536
creating new charts, 534
customizing options, 536
deleting objects from charts, 536-537
editing charts, 535
file and print servers, 543-549
disk bottlenecks, 543-546
network media limitations, 548-549
protocol binding order, 547-548
reducing file fragmentation, 549
unneeded protocols, 546-547
Internet Information Server 4.0, 790-794
HTTP Service Object counters, 791-793
log files, 539-543

recording data, 540-541
viewing recorded data, 541-542
objects and counters, 531-534
troubleshooting networks, 576-580
installing SNMP service, 577
TCP/IP networks, 579-580

Performance Optimizer (Exchange Server setup), 903-905

performance options, configuring (Internet Information Server 4.0), 754

personal folder files (Exchange Server 5.0), 884

Personalization System (Site Server 2.0), 48

PERT (Program Evaluation and Review Technique), 75

physical layer, OSI (Open Systems Interconnection) model, 102

physical security (network installations), 59

ping command-line tool, 583

pipeline burst cache memory, 160

PM (Process Manager), 87

PolEdit.exe application, 26

POSIX.1 subsystem, 90

Posting Acceptor (Site Server 2.0), 48

power protection (server hardware), 166-169

power supplies (RAID product features), 232

PowerPC, 86

PPP Multilink, 689

PPTP (Point-to-Point Tunneling Protocol), 38, 112, 689, 719-720

presentation layer, OSI (Open Systems Interconnection) model, 104-105

Primary Domain Controllers, *see* PDCs

Primary Network Logon (configuring network clients), 366

Primary Site Servers, installing SMS, 939-942

print gateways, installing/ configuring, GSNW (Gateway Service for NetWare), 649-651

print servers (Performance Monitor), 543-549
disk bottlenecks, 543-546
network media limitations, 548-549
protocol binding order, 547-548
reducing file fragmentation, 549
unneeded protocols, 546-547

printers
securing, 512-527
sharing, 376-379, 512-527
locally attached server printers, 512-517
Microsoft Networks, 377-378
NetWare Networks, 378-379
network printer servers, 517-519
printer property configurations, 520-527

Windows NT resources
(Windows 3.1 clients),
408-409
**Printers subkey
(HKEY_CURRENT_USER
hive), 307**
printing
enhancements, 29
TCP/IP support, 110-111
**Process Explode
(Pview.exe) (*Windows
NT Workstation
Resource Kit*), 554**
**Process Viewer
(Pviewer.exe) (*Windows
NT Workstation
Resource Kit*), 554**
processors
application server usage
(Performance Monitor),
550-551
server hardware, 157-169
Intel, 159
multiprocessor
systems, 160
RISC-based servers,
158-159
sizing cache
memory, 159
profiles
paths (user profiles), 455
user
client-side server
features, 26
defining, 455-458
**Program Evaluation and
Review Technique, 75**
**Program Groups
window (SMS
Administrator), 954**
properties
printer, configuring,
520-527
user accounts, 454-462
account information,
461-462

assigned workstation
restrictions, 460-461
assigning group
membership, 454
defining user profiles,
455-458
logon hours, 458-460
user dial-in
permissions, 462
**protected subsystem
servers, 89-90**
protocols
AppleTalk (client
support), 116
choosing (network
connections), 193-194
client stacks (Microsoft
client server access),
640-642
FTP (File Transfer
Protocol), Internet
Information Server 4.0,
738-740
multiple
binding order
(Performance
Monitor), 547-548
Windows 95
networking, 352
NetBEUI (Windows 95
configurations), 367-368
network, 106-116, 560-566
analyzers, 566-568
AppleTalk, 112
choosing, 120
DLC (Data Link
Control), 111
interoperability, 118-120
IPX/SPX, 561-566
Macintosh client
support, 116
MS-DOS client support,
115-116
multiple server support,
116-118
NetBEUI (NetBIOS
Extended User
Interface), 107-108

NetBEUI broadcasting,
560-566
NetBEUI Frame,
107-108
NWLink (IPX/SPX), 111
OS/2 client support, 116
OSI (Open Systems
Interconnection)
model, 102-106
RAS (Remote Access
Service), 112
SMS (Systems
Management Server)
analysis, 931-932
spanning multiple, 636
streams, 113
TCP/IP, 108-111
UNIX workstation
support, 116
Windows 3.1, 115
Windows 95 support,
114-115
Windows for
Workgroups 3.1x
support, 115
Windows NT
workstations, 114
network installation
issues, 66
NWLink (Windows 95
configurations), 369-371
PPTP (Point-to-Point
Tunneling Protocol),
38, 112, 719-720
SNMP (Simple
Network Management
Protocol), 36
TCP/IP, 29-31, 322-328
allocating IP
addresses, 371
ARP (Address
Resolution
Protocol), 326
binding to clients/
services, 374
configuring, 328-331
DHCP (Dynamic Host
Configuration

Protocol), 327-328, 332-342
DNS (Domain Name Service), 327
domain names, 324
dotted decimal notation, 324
graphical DNS tool, 30
host names, 324
HOSTS file, 327
installing, 328-331
IP addresses, 324
LMHOSTS file, 327
local broadcasts, 326
low-level parameters, 374
machine addresses, 323
MPR (Multi-Protocol Router), 31
NetBIOS names, 325
resolving IP addresses with DNS, 374-376
resolving names and addresses, 325-326
Windows 95 configurations, 371-377
WINS (Windows Internet Name Service), 30, 328, 342-349
unneeded (Performance Monitor), 546-547
Windows 95 networking, configuring, 366-376
proxy agents, 70
Proxy Server 1.0, 724, 813
public folders
Exchange Server 5.0, 884-885
sharing data (Exchange Server 5.0), 875
Pulse (PDC values), 613
PulseConcurrency (PDC value), 613

Q

QIC (Quarter-Inch Cartridge) tape drives, 275
quality grades (UTP cable), 138-139
Quarter-Inch Cartridge tape drives, 275
queries
executing (SQL Server 6.5 database structures), 861-862
writing (ODBC log review), 780-782
Queries window (SMS Administrator), 951-953
Quota Server (Web site), 177
QuotaAdvisor (Web site), 177

R

RAB (RAID Advisory Board) Web site, 217
RAID (redundant array of inexpensive disks), 64, 91, 216-229
array sizing, 228-229
external enclosures, 235-236
hardware
implementations, 233
adding dedicated RAID 5 controller cards, 234-235
external RAID enclosures, 235-236
mirroring with current SCSI host adapters, 234
obtaining as a server option, 233
upgrading existing servers, 233-234

implementation specifications, 229-236
automatic rebuild, 231
disk drive issues, 231-232
hot spare disks, 231
hot swappable disks, 231
multiple-level independent RAID, 232-233
power supplies, 232
user needs, 229-230
level 0, 217-219
level 1, 220-222
overall performance, 222
read performance, 221
recovering software sets, 251-253
write performance, 222-225
level 2, 222-223
level 3, 223-224
level 4, 224
level 5, 225-227
adding dedicated controller cards, 234-235
data caching, 226-227
read performance, 226
recovering software sets, 251-253
transaction processing, 226
write performance, 226
levels, 216-229
mirror sets, 239-251
level 1, 244-247
restoring, 252
RAB (RAID Advisory Board), 217
recommendations, 253-255
disaster-tolerant disk system criteria, 255
failure-resistant disk system criteria, 254
failure-resistant disk system plus criteria, 254-255

server stripe sets, 239-251
  drive configuration
    disks, 242-244
  emergency repair disks,
    242-244
  level 0, 239-242
software implementations,
  236-239
  extensibility, 238-239
  server options, 237-238
  volume sets, 238-239
stacked, 227-228
stripe sets
  level 5 with parity,
    248-251
  saving master boot
    records, 251
  saving partition
    tables, 251
stripes sets, restoring with
  parity, 252-253
subsystem recovery (fixed-
  disk failures), 212
subsystems, creating
  (installations), 201

**RAM (memory),
server hardware
requirements, 160**

**RAS (Remote Access
Service), 112, 694-704**
  BackOffice, 814
  configuring DUN (Dial-Up
    Networking), 699-702
  installing modems, 694-699
  PPTP (Point-to-Point
    Tunneling Protocol),
    719-720
  Remote Access Admin
    application
    granting client access,
      702-704
    monitoring
      connections, 717-718
  Resource Kit tools, 721
  Routing, 720-721

**RAS Multilink Channel
Aggregation, 38-54**

Raslist.exe, 721

Rasuser.exe, 721

**RDBMSes (relational
database management
systems), 28**
  SQL Server 6.5, 834-835
    assigning group
      accounts (Security
      Manager), 865-867
    creating database
      devices, 850-851
    database permissions,
      865-869
    executing queries,
      861-862
    importing table
      structures, 852-856
    indexes, 857-858
    installing, 835-843
    setting permissions,
      868-869
    SQL Enterprise
      Manager, 843-848
    transaction logs,
      862-864
    viewing logins
      (Enterprise Manager),
      868-869
    viewing standard stored
      procedures, 861
    viewing triggers, 860

read performance
  RAID level 1, 221
  RAID level 5, 226

Read permission
  NTFS file-access
    permissions, 494
  NTFS folder-access
    permissions, 498

**Real-Time Operating
System, 162**

recipients
  creating
    administrator
      mailboxes, 919-921
    Directory Import
      mailboxes, 924-926

    distribution lists,
      926-927
    recipient templates
      (Directory
      Imports), 924
    user mailboxes, 921-923
    User Manager for
      Domains mailboxes,
      923-924
  Exchange Server 5.0, 882
  setting up (Exchange
    Administrator), 917-927
  templates, creating
    (Directory Import), 924

**recording data (log files),
540-541**

**recoverability (NTFS),
91, 94-95**

**redundant array of
inexpensive disks,
see RAID**

**REG.DAT (Windows 3.1
configuration file), 292**

**REG_BINARY data type
(value entries), 300**

**REG_DWORD data type
(value entries), 300**

**REG_EXPAND_SZ data
type (value entries), 300**

**REG_MULTI_SZ data type
(value entries), 300**

**REG_SZ data type
(value entries), 300**

**Regedt32.exe (Registry
Editor), 297**

Registry, 292-296
  backing up, 308-310
  changing values, 294-295
  configuration files
    (.INI and CONFIG.SYS),
    317-318
  hives, 297-299, 301
    HKEY_CLASSES_ROOT,
      297, 305-306
    HKEY_CURRENT_CONFIG,
      297, 305

HKEY_CURRENT_USER, 297, 306-307
HKEY_LOCAL_MACHINE, 297, 301-305
HKEY_USERS, 297, 307
information types, 292
keys, 299, 301
  HKEY_CURRENT_USER key, 26
  HKEY_LOCAL_MACHINE, 26
subkeys, 299
organization settings, 294
Registry Editor, 293-294, 310-311
  changing values, 294-295
remote editing, 311-312
  opening remote Registries, 312
  Windows 95 from Windows NT, 312
  Windows NT from Windows 95, 312-319
  Windows NT from Windows NT, 312
Resource Kit (entry help file), 318-319
security, 313-317
  restricting access, 313-315
  viewing audit logs, 315-317
value entries, 300-301
Windows 3.1 configuration files, 292-293
Windows 95 differences, 296
Windows NT Diagnostics Utility, 307-308
Registry Editor (remote client management), 391, 393
relational database management systems, see RDBMSes
Remote Access Admin application (monitoring connections), 717-718

Remote Access Manager, 721
Remote Access Service, see RAS
remote control, SMS (Systems Management Server), 931
remote control functions (SMS client software installing), 957-959
remote editing (Registries), 311-312
  opening remote Registries, 312
  Windows 95 from Windows NT, 312
  Windows NT from Windows 95, 312-319
  Windows NT from Windows NT, 312
remote management
  network installations, 69-71
  Windows 95 clients, 390-396
    Net Watcher, 394-396
    Registry Editor, 393
    System Monitor, 394
    System Policy Editor, 392
Remote Monitoring, 146
remote performance analysis (SMS analysis), 932
remote procedure calls, see RPCs
remote server administration utilities (client-side server features), 26
removing network clients (Windows 95), 358-361
renaming domains (security), 617-618
repairing
  existing installations, 186
  installations, 209-210

repeaters (active network components), 144-145
replicating folders, 502-506
  configurations, 504-506
  creating replication users, 503
  starting the Directory Replicator, 503-504
ReplicationGovernor (BDC values), 613
resellers (network configuration advice), 77
Resource Kit (optimization utilities), 554-557
  Data Logging Service files, 555
  Performance Counter Help (Counters.hlp), 556
  Performance Data Log Server (PerfLog), 554
  Process Explode (Pview.exe), 554
  Process Viewer (Pviewer.exe), 554
  Response Probe (Probe.exe), 556
resources
  adding records (DNS UNIX integration), 675
  domains, sharing, 632-633
  managing (network installations), 75-77
Response Probe (Probe.exe), *Windows NT Workstation Resource Kit*, 556
restarting servers (installations), 201
restoring data
  backups, 274-275
  NTBACKUP, 287-289
reviewing logs (ODBC sample queries), 780-782
RFCs (Request For Comments), 108

RG-62 coaxial cable, 136

ring topologies (network cabling systems), 134

RISC-based servers (choosing processors), 158

RMON (Remote Monitoring), 146

roots, Dfs (Distributed File System), 988-989

rotation methods (backups), 267-272
  daily full backups with two-set rotation, 269-271
  grandfather-father-son rotation, 270-271
  Tower of Hanoi rotation, 271-272
  weekly backups with daily differentials, 267
  weekly backups with daily incrementals, 269

route command-line tool, 583

routers
  active network components, 148-149
  connectivity issues, 592
  ISDN, 691

Routing (RAS), 720-721
  scalability, 980-981
  troubleshooting networks, 595-596

RPCs (Remote Procedure Calls), 104
  Windows NT operating system, 96-98

RTOS (Real-Time Operating System), intelligent I/O subsystems, 162

S

SAM (Security Account Manager) key, HKEY_LOCAL_MACHINE hive, 301

SAMBA
  UNIX file sharing, 678-683
  Web site, 679

sample queries, writing (ODBC log review), 780-782

sample Transact-SQL query, reviewing ODBC logs (code listing), 781

SAMs (manual domain synchronization), 612

scalability, 968-970
  clustered systems, 970-973
  Hydra Server, 983-984
  middle-tier management (Transaction Server), 973-978
  network features, 27-29
    SMP (symmetrical multiprocessing), 28-29
  reducing client PC costs, 982-984
    Network PC (NetPC), 982-983
  upgrading BackOffice members, 981-982
  wide-area transactions
    message enabling, 979-980
    Routing and RAS, 980-981
  Windows NT Terminal, 983-984
  Zero Administration Windows, 983

SCAM (SCSI Configured AutoMagically), 165

Schedule+
  Exchange Server client components, 891-893

group scheduling (Exchange Server 5.0), 876

Schedule+ Client (Exchange Server 5.0), 873

Schedule+ Free/Busy Connector (Exchange Server 5.0), 872

schedules, managing (network installations), 75-77

scope options, configuring (DHCP server configurations), 337-338

scopes, creating (DHCP server), 334

scripting support (Windows 95 networking), 353

SCSI (Small Computer System Interface) disk subsystems, 163
  bus termination, 165-166

SCSI Configured AutoMagically, 165

Seagate Software Web site, 287

sector striping (RAID level 5), 230

security
  administrative shares, 489
  backups, 258-275
    archive bits, 258-259
    copy backups, 260
    daily copy backups, 262
    differential backups, 261-262
    enterprise backup systems, 273
    hardware, 275-278
    HSM (Hierarchical Storage Management), 272

incremental backups,
260-261
matching media to disk
size, 267
normal backups, 259
NTBACKUP (backup
application), 278-289
open files, 266
organizing disk storage,
264-265
restore plans, 274-275
rotation methods,
267-272
storing data off site, 273
type selection, 262-264
verifying integrity,
265-266
domains, 606-618
adding BDCs to new
domains, 614
adding Windows NT
clients to domains,
614-615
domain controllers,
608-611
identifiers, 607-608
moving clients between
domain, 616
moving domain
controllers, 616-617
renaming domains,
617-618
synchronization
process, 611-613
folder, configuring
(Internet Information
Server 4.0), 754-758
folder shares, 485-490
creating, 485-486
Managing Folder and
File Access Wizard,
490-493
modifying, 487
removing, 486
Internet Information
Server 2.0, SSL (Secure
Sockets Layer), 36

network installations, 59-63
data communication
security, 60-62
physical security, 59
network printers, 512-527
NTFS permissions, 91,
493-502
file-access permissions,
494-497
folder-access
permissions, 498-502
passwords, Administrator
(installations), 191
Registry, 313-317
restricting access,
313-315
viewing audit logs,
315-317
share permissions, 487-489
adding, 488-489
modifying, 487-488
removing, 487-488
shares
disconnecting, 489-490
displaying, 489-490
SQL Server 6.5 database
structures, 865-869
assigning group
account (Security
Manager), 865-867
setting permissions,
868-869
viewing logins
(Enterprise Manager),
868-869

**security accounts,
configuring (Internet
Information Server
4.0), 753**

**Security Descriptor
attribute (NTFS
Master File Table), 93**

**security key
(HKEY_LOCAL_MACHINE
hive), 302**

**Senders, Enterprise
Network site
communication
(SMS), 962**

**Serial Line Internet
Protocol, 112**

**server, network, installing
from, 184-185**

Server dialog, 489

**Server Manager
(remote server
administration
utilities), 26**

**Server Message Blocks,
560**

**server stripe sets (RAID
implementations),
239-251**
drive configuration disks,
242-244
emergency repair disks,
242-244
level 0, 239-242

servers, 592-601
administrative wizards,
23-25
Add Printer Wizard, 24
Add User Account
Wizard, 23
Add/Remove Programs
Wizard, 25
Group Management
Wizard, 24
Install New Modem
Wizard, 25
License Wizard, 25
Managing File and
Folder Access
Wizard, 24
Network Client
Administrator
Wizard, 25
automatic reconnections
(Windows 95
networking), 353
browsing problems,
594-595
command-line
troubleshooting tools,
580-585
arp (Address
Resolution Protocol)
command, 580

hostname
  command, 580
  ipconfig command, 580
  nbtstat command, 581
  netstat command,
    582-583
  ping command, 583
  route utility, 583
  tracert command,
    583-584
configuration
  DHCP (Dynamic Host
    Configuration
    Protocol), 334
  Exchange
    Administrator, 915-917
connectivity problems,
  592-593
  default gateway
    problems, 593
  router problems, 592
distributing shares (Dfs),
  988-997
  Dfs Administrator,
    993-997
  installing, 989-991
  roots and leaves,
    988-989
  Windows 95 Dfs client
    (installing), 991-993
DNS name resolution,
  599-601
Exchange Server 5.0,
  872-873, 878-886, 895-897
  client components,
    887-894
  connectors, 885-886
  custom forms (building
    applications), 875-876
  Directory Service and
    database, 879-880
  distribution lists, 885
  domains, 894-895
  e-mail uses, 874
  Exchange
    Administrator, 878-879

functional
  considerations
  (site planning), 897
geographic
  considerations (site
  planning), 896-897
Information Store, 881
mailboxes, 883
MTA (Message
  Transfer Agent),
  880-881
new features, 877-878
offline folder files, 884
organizations, 894-895
personal folder
  files, 884
public folders, 875,
  884-885
recipients, 882
Schedule+ group
  scheduling, 876
server size, 897-899
Setup program, 900-905
site planning, 896
sites, 894-895
System Attendant, 882
system integration, 877
hardware, 155-169
  choosing components,
    157-169
  departmental
    servers, 156
  enterprise servers, 156
  HCL conformance, 156
  local service, 157
  maintenance, 157
  warranties, 157
  workgroup servers, 156
Internet sites, planning,
  725-726
Microsoft Proxy Server, 37
multiple (protocol
  support), 116-118
  interconnected
    Windows NT
    servers, 117

Internet
  connections, 118
  local intranet servers,
    117-118
  mainframes, 118
  Novell NetWare
    servers, 117
  UNIX servers, 117
NICs, 143-144
Performance Monitor,
  530-542, 576-580
  alerts, 537-539
  application server uses,
    549-554
  charting characteristics,
    534-536
  installing SNMP
    service, 577
  objects and counters,
    531-534
  server optimization,
    543-549
  TCP/IP networks,
    579-580
protected subsystem, 89-90
registering (SQL
  Enterprise Manager),
  844-847
routing problems, 595-596
security (network
  installations), 59
SMS (Systems
  Management Server),
  930-937
  application differences,
    932-933
  client support, 934
  component
    terminology, 936-937
  Enterprise Network
    sites, 961-963
  enterprise site topology,
    935-937
  hardware inventory, 931
  installing, 937-942
  network protocol
    analysis, 931-932
  remote control and
    troubleshooting, 931

remote performance
analysis, 932
server requirements,
933
SMS Administrator,
943-954
SMS client software
installation, 954-960
software distribution,
931
software installation,
931
software inventory, 931
supported networks, 934
WAN options, 934
software RAID options,
237-238
Task Manager, 23
trust relationships
problems, 596-602
usability, 21-25
Windows 95 user
interface, 21
Windows Explorer, 21-23
Foldername Properties
sheet, 22
*Windows NT Server
Resource Kit* utilities,
584-591
Browser Monitor
(Browmon.exe),
585-586
Browser Status
(Browstat.exe),
586-587
Domain Monitor
(Dommon.exe),
587-588
GetMac (Getmac.exe),
589
Net Watch
(Netwatch.exe), 589
NSLookup
(Nslookup.exe), 590
SMBTrace
(Smbtrace.exe), 591
WNTIPcfg
(Wntipcfg.exe), 591
WINS name resolution,
599-601

**service accounts, creating
(SMS installations),
937-938**
Service Packs
installing, 206-208
SQL Server 6.5, 842-843
Web site, 208, 843
**services, choosing
(installations), 193-194**
**session layer
(OSI model), 104**
**SET (Secure Electronic
Transaction), 49**
setup
creating boot disks,
183-184
ODBC data sources,
771-779
creating Jet database
data sources, 776-779
creating SQL Server
data sources, 772
**Setup program (Exchange
Server 5.0), 900-905**
**SGML (Standardized
General Markup
Language), 736**
share names, 486
**share permissions,
487-489**
adding, 488-489
modifying, 487-488
removing, 487-488
**share-level access
control (Access Control
page), 362**
**Shared Resources dialog,
490**
shares
administrative shares, 489
disconnecting, 489-490
displaying, 489-490
folder shares, 485-490
creating, 485-486
Managing Folder and
File Access Wizard,
490-493

modifying, 487
removing, 486
server, distributing (Dfs),
988-997
share permissions, 487-489
adding, 488-489
modifying, 487-488
removing, 487-488
sharing
data, public folders
(Exchange Server
5.0), 875
domain resources, 632-633
files, 376-379
high-speed LANs, 28
Microsoft Networks,
377-378
NetWare Networks,
378-379
network printers, 512-527
locally attached server
printers, 512-517
network printer servers,
517-519
printer property
configurations,
520-527
packages (SMS
Administrator Packages
window), 948
printers, 376-379
Microsoft Networks,
377-378
NetWare Networks,
378-379
Windows NT files
(with UNIX), 677-680
**sheath material
(UTP cable), 138**
**Showgrps.exe (Windows
NT Resource Kit), 481**
SIDs (Security IDs), 87
domain security, 607-608
**Simple Network
Management Protocol,
see SNMP**

simultaneous connections (Windows 95 networking), 352

Single Domain model, 626

Single Master model, 627

single network logons (Windows 95 networking), 353

site addressing, setting up (Exchange Administrator), 912-914

Site Analyst and Usage Analyst (Site Server 2.0), 48

Site Groups window (SMS Administrator), 954

Site Server 2.0, 724
Enterprise Edition Web site, 49
upgrading to, 47-49
  Commerce Server, 49
  eShop technology, 47
  Intersé market focus 3, 48
  Microsoft Wallet, 49
  NetCarta WebMapper, 48
  Usage Analyst Enterprise Edition, 49

site servers (SMS terminology), 936

SiteBuilder Workshop Web site, 43

sites
Exchange Server 5.0
components, 894-895
  functional considerations (site planning), 897
  geographic considerations (site planning), 896-897
  planning, 896
Web
  Aberdeen Group, 29
  ADSI, 997
  Ascend Communications, 692

BackOffice Licensing Guide, 726
BackOffice Live, 815
BackupExec Version 6.11, 287
Computer Technology Review, 217
Diskeeper for Windows NT, 549
Enterprise Planning Guide, 632
Executive Software, 549
Exploration Air, 749
FrontPage, 38
Get ISDN, 692
Granite Digital, 166
HCL (Hardware Compatibility List), 89, 156, 175
internal security, 59
Internet Deployment Guide, 46
Internet Information Server 2.0, 36
InterNIC, 322, 324
ISDN Accelerator Pack 1.1, 692
LANalyzer for Windows, 567
"Managing Windows NT Domains," 59
Microsoft Free Product Downloads, 725
Microsoft Index Server, 37
Microsoft Knowledge Base, 591
Microsoft Proxy Server, 37
Microsoft Service Pack 1, 361
Microsoft Services for NetWare, 31
Microsoft SiteBuilder Workshop, 726
Microsoft SiteServer 2.0, 806
Microsoft U.S. Estimated Price List, 823
Microsoft-HP joint

press release, 933
MSDN subscriptions, 819
Msinfo.exe, 425
Msinfo32.exe, 425
NDIS, 106
Network General's Sniffer product line, 566
Network Monitor, 567
Network Node Manager, 71
Network PC Design Guidelines, 983
Ntcomp.exe, 176
OpenNT, 85
OSR 2, 385
planning, 725-726
Quota Server, 177
QuotaAdvisor, 177
RAB (RAID Advisory Board), 217
SAMBA, 679
Seagate Software, 287
Service Packs, 208, 843
Site Server 2.0 Enterprise Edition, 49
SiteBuilder Workshop, 43
SQL Server 6.5, 820, 836
TAPI 2.1 Software Developer Kit, 41
ThreadMark 2.0, 545
Upsizing Wizard, 853
Visual Studio 97, 812
Windows 95 browsing, 108
Windows 95 Service Pack 1, 639
Windows Hardware Quality Labs, 258
Windows NT Resource Center, 591
workgroup browsing issues, 397
ZAK (Zero Administration Kit), 388
ZAW, 388

Sites window (SMS Administrator), 945-947

sizing (Exchange Server 5.0), 897-899

SLIP (Serial Line Internet Protocol), 112

SMBs (Server Message Blocks), 560

SMBTrace (Smbtrace.exe), *Windows NT Server Resource Kit utilities*, 591

SMP (symmetrical multiprocessing), scalability, 28-29

SMS (Systems Management Server), 36, 71, 813, 930-934
  application differences, 932-933
  client support, 934
  Enterprise Network sites, 961-963
    NetWare environments, 962-963
    Sender communication, 962
  installing, 937-942
    creating service accounts, 937-938
    on Primary Site Servers, 939-942
    SQL Server setup, 939
  inventory
    hardware, 931
    software, 931
  license packages, 821-822
  network protocol analysis, 931-932
  planning, 934-937
    component terminology, 936-937
    enterprise site topology, 935-936
  remote control and troubleshooting, 931

remote performance analysis, 932
server requirements, 933
SMS Administrator, 943-954
  Alerts window, 954
  Events window, 954
  Jobs window, 950
  Machine Groups window, 954
  Packages window, 948-949
  Program Groups window, 954
  Queries window, 951-953
  Site Groups window, 954
  Sites window, 945-947
SMS client software, 954-960
  automatic installation, 955-957
  client inventory management, 957
  help desk functions, 957-959
  manual installation, 954-955
  Network Monitor, 960
  remote control functions, 957-959
software
  distribution, 931
  installing, 931
  supported networks, 934
  WAN options, 934

SNA Server 3.0, 111, 118, 813
  license packages, 822

SNMP (Simple Network Management Protocol), 36, 146
  installing (Performance Monitor), 577

software
  allocating funds (network installations), 79-80

backups (new trends), 289-290
configurable NICs, 143
disk bottleneck solutions, 545-546
distribution, SMS (Systems Management Server), 931
installing, SMS (Systems Management Server), 931
inventory, SMS (Systems Management Server), 931
network installation issues, 66
project-management (network installations), 75-77
protocol analyzers, 566-567
RAID implementations, 236-239
  extensibility, 238-239
  server options, 237-238
  volume sets, 238-239
RAID sets, recovering, 251-253
SMS (Systems Management Server), minimum requirements, 933

software key (HKEY_LOCAL_MACHINE hive), 302

Software subkey (HKEY_CURRENT_USER hive), 307

spanning transactions, multiple components (Transaction Server middle-tier management), 977-978

Special Access dialog, 495-496

Special Access permission (NTFS file-access permissions), 495

Special Directory Access dialog, 500

Special Directory Access permission (NTFS folder-access permissions), 498

Special File Access dialog, 500-501

Special File Access permission (NTFS folder-access permissions), 498

SQL Server 6.5, 813, 834-835
  data sources, creating, 772
  database devices
    creating, 850-851
    executing queries, 861-862
    importing table structures, 852-856
    indexes, 857-858
    transaction logs, 862-864
    viewing standard stored procedures, 861
    viewing triggers, 860
  database permissions, 865-869
  installing, 835-843
    setup, 939
  license packages, 820
  SQL Enterprise Manager, 843-848
    backup tape drives, 847-848
    installing on 32-bit clients, 843-844
    registering servers, 844-847
    setting permissions, 868-869
    viewing logins, 868-869
  SQL Security Manager, assigning group accounts, 865-867
  tables, creating (ODBC logging tables), 768
  Web Assistant, distributing

ODBC activity reports, 782-786
Web site, 820, 836

SRM (Security Reference Monitor), 87

Srvcheck.exe (*Windows NT Resource Kit*), 481

SSL (Secure Sockets Layer), 36

stackable hubs, 146

stacked RAID, 227-228, 230, 232

stand-alone hubs, 145

standard security (SQL Server 6.5), 865

standard stored procedures, viewing (SQL Server 6.5 database structures), 861

standard volumes, creating (RAID 1 mirror sets), 244-247

Standardized General Markup Language, see SGML

star topologies (network cabling systems), 133

starting
  SQL Executive, 842
  SQL Server 6.5, 842
  User Manager for Domains, 443-444
    low-speed connections, 446-447
    multiple instances, 444
    selecting new domains, 445-446

static mappings (non-WINS clients), 345

storage
  data, off site (backups), 273

fixed-disk drives (backups), 264-265
tape drives, matching to disk size, 267

STP cable (shielded twisted-pair), network cabling systems, 136-137

streams (network protocols), 113

stripe sets
  RAID implementations
    level 5 with parity, 248-251
    restoring with parity, 252-253
    saving master boot records, 251
    saving partition tables, 251
  RAID level 0, 230
  recovery (fixed-disk failures), 212

structured cabling systems (network cabling systems), 139-140

subkeys (Registry), 299

symmetrical multiprocessing, 28-29

synchronization process (domain security), 611-613
  changing automatic intervals, 612-613
  manual SAM synchronization, 612

synchronous cache memory, 160

System Attendant (Exchange Server 5.0), 872, 882

system drive boot failures, recovering from, 211

system key (HKEY_LOCAL_MACHINE hive), 302-305

System Monitor (remote client management), 391, 394

System Network Architecture, *see* **SNA Server 3.0**

system policies, Windows 95 network, 388-391

System Policy Editor, 388, 390
  client-side server features, 26
  remote client management, 390, 392

SYSTEM.INI (Windows 3.1 configuration file), 292

Systems Management Server 1.2, 36
  license packages, 821-822

Systems Management Server, *see* **SMS**

T

T-1 Internet connections, 733

table structures, importing (SQL Server 6.5), 852-856

tape drives
  backups, 275-277
    DLT (Digital Linear Tape), 276
    helical scan tapes, 277
    QIC (Quarter-Inch Cartridge) drives, 275
  matching to disk size, 267
  NTBACKUP setup, 279-281

TAPI 2.0 (Telephony API), 688, 692-694

TAPI 2.1 Software Developer Kit Web site, 41

TAPI 2.x (Telephony API), 41

Task Manager (server usability), 23

TCP/IP, 29-31, 108-111, 322-328
  32-bit, installing (Windows for Workgroups 3.11), 410-414
  ARP (Address Resolution Protocol), 326
  binding to clients/services, 374
  commercial implementations, 111
  configuring, 328-331
    Windows 95 network protocols, 371-377
  DHCP (Dynamic Host Configuration Protocol), 327-328, 332-342
    leasing IP addresses to clients, 333-334
    server configurations, 334-342
  DNS (Domain Name Service), 327
    integrating WINS, 349
  domain names, 324-328
  dotted decimal notation, 324-328
  graphical DNS tool, 30
  host names, 324-328
  HOSTS file, 327
  installing, 328-331
  IP addresses, 109, 324-328
    resolving with DNS, 374-376
  LMHOSTS file, 327
  local broadcasts, 326
  low-level parameters, 374
  machine addresses, 323-328
  MPR (Multi-Protocol Router), 31
  NetBIOS names, 325-328

  network protocols, 562-566
    NetBIOS node types, 565-566
    WINS (Windows Internet Name Service), 562-566
  Performance Monitor, 579-580
  printing, 110-111
  resolving names and addresses, 325-326
  universal clients (Windows for Workgroups 3.11 configuration), 681
  Windows 3.1 support, 115
  Windows for Workgroups 3.1x support, 115
  WINS (Windows Internet Name Service), 30, 328, 342-349
    configuring, 344-350
    integrating DNS, 349
    NetBIOS names (registering/resolving), 342-343
  workstation support, 114

TDI (Transport Driver Interface), 105

Telephony API, *see* **TAPI**

templates, recipient, creating (Directory Import), 924

term redirector, 88

terminal adapters (ISDN), 690
  Ethernet, 691

testing
  backup tape drives (SQL Enterprise Manager), 847-848
  clients (DHCP server configurations), 340
  Crystal Reports 4.5 (Internet Information Server), 788-789
  default installations (Internet Information Server 4.0), 748-749

DUN (Dial-Up Networking), on clients, 704-716

ThreadMark 2.0 Web site, 545

throughput, maximizing (application servers), 552-553

time and date, setting (installations), 198

Token Ring (media-access methods), 124-126

tools (troubleshooting), 31-35
  Network Monitor tool, 33-36
  Windows NT Diagnostics tool, 32

topologies (network cabling systems), 133-135

Tower of Hanoi rotation (backup rotation methods), 271-272

tracert command (command-line tools), 583-584

training users (network installations), 74

Transaction Server, 724
  middle-tier management, 973-978
    brokering business objects, 974-976
  spanning transations (multiple components), 977-978
  wide-area transactions, 979-980

transactions
  logs (SQL Server 6.5 database structures), 862-864
  NTFS recoverability, 94-95
  processing (RAID level 5), 226

Transmission Control Protocol/Internet Protocol, see TCP/IP

Transport Driver Interface, 105

transport layer, OSI (Open Systems Interconnection) model, 104

triggers, viewing (SQL Server 6.5 database structures), 860

troubleshooting
  connection problems (Windows 3.1 client installations), 410
  Macintosh client connections, 436
  networks, 568-584, 591-601
    browsing, 594-595
    command-line tools, 580-585
    connectivity problems, 592-593
    DNS name resolution, 599-601
    Event Viewer, 568-570
    Network Monitor, 570-575
    Performance Monitor, 576-580
    routing, 595-596
    trust relationships, 596-602
    Windows NT Server Resource Kit utilities, 584-591
    WINS name resolution, 599-601
  tools, 31-35
    Network Monitor tool, 33-36
    Windows NT Diagnostics tool, 32
  Windows for Workgroups 3.11 resource (connections), 417-418
  Windows NT Workstation 4.0 client connections, 423

trust relationships
  domain implementation, 623-626
  troubleshooting networks, 596-598

trusted domains (user access), 474-475

trusts, implementing (between domains), 618-626

tutorials (resource kits), 42

U

U.S. Department of Defense C2 security standard, 85

UDP (User Datagram Protocol), 562

UNC (Universal Naming Convention), 444

uninterruptible power supply, see UPS

universal clients, 679-683
  Windows 95 configurations, 683
  Windows for Workgroups 3.11 configurations, 680-683

UNIX
  integrating with Windows NT Server, 668-679
    DNS (Domain Name Service) Server, 671-677
    file sharing, 677-680
    IETF RFC support, 669-670
  multiple server protocol support, 117
  universal clients, 679-683
  workstations (network protocol support), 116

unshielded twisted-pair, see UTP cable

upgrading
BackOffice Server 2.5
(Annuity Model), 824-825
Internet Information
Server 4.0, 742-747
previous Windows
versions, 174-175, 187
RAID (existing servers),
233-234
to Site Server 2.0, 47-49
Commerce Server, 49
eShop technology, 47
Intersé market
focus 3, 48
Microsoft Wallet, 49
NetCarta
WebMapper, 48
Usage Analyst
Enterprise Edition, 49

**UPS (uninterruptible
power supply), 166**
hardware protection,
166-169

**Upsizing Wizard Web
site, 853**

**Usage Analyst Enterprise
Edition (Site Server
2.0), 49**

user accounts, 447-453
Add User Account Wizard,
463-467
adding new, 449-451
account properties,
451-455
copying accounts, 451
creating the account,
449
built-in, 447-449
administrator account,
447-448
guest account, 448-449
domain account policy,
467-469
Account Lockout Policy
setting, 469
setting for passwords,
468

modifying, 451-453
properties, 454-462
account information,
461-462
assigned workstation
restrictions, 460-461
assigning group
membership, 454
defining user profiles,
455-458
logon hours, 458-460
user dial-in
permissions, 462
terminology, 442

**User Directory (Exchange
Server 5.0), 872**

**user groups, 442,
469-475**
adding global groups, 473
adding local groups,
471-473
built-in, 470-471
copying groups, 473
Group Management
Wizard, 475-477
trusted domain resource
access, 474-475
User Rights Policy,
478-480
assigning new user
rights, 479-480

User Manager
changing Registry
values, 295
remote server
administration
utilities, 26

**User Manager for
Domains, 442-447**
low-speed connections,
446-447
selecting new domains,
445-446
starting, 443-444
multiple instances, 444

**user profiles, defining
(user accounts),
455-458**

**User Rights Policy,
478-480**
assigning new user rights,
479-480

**user-level access
control (Access Control
page), 363**

users
administration utilities
(*Windows NT Resource
Kit*), 480-481
creating mailboxes
Exchange
Administrator, 921-923
User Manager for
Domains, 923-924
determining needs
(network installations),
57-59
preparing installations, 206
profiles (client-side server
features), 26
replication, creating, 503
server profiles, 386-387
training (network
installations), 74
Windows 95 interface, 21

**Usrstat.exe (*Windows NT
Resource Kit*), 481**

**Usrtogrp.exe (*Windows
NT Resource Kit*), 481**

utilities
Compact.exe (NTFS file
compression), 510
Diagnostics (Registry),
307-308
Diruse.exe, NTFS file
compression (Resource
Kit), 511
remote server
administration (client-
side server features), 26
route (command-line
tools), 583

utiltities (Windows NT Workstation Resource Kit), 554-557
Data Logging Service files, 555
Performance Counter Help (Counters.hlp), 556
Performance Data Log Server (PerfLog), 554
Process Explode (Pview.exe), 554
Process Viewer (Pviewer.exe), 554
Response Probe (Probe.exe), 556

UTP cable (unshielded twisted-pair), 125
network cabling systems, 137-139
conductor size UTP cable, 137-138
pair count UTP cable, 137-138
quality grades, 138-139
sheath material, 138

V

values, 300-301
data types, 300-301
names, 300
Registry, changing, 294-295

vendors
network configuration advice, 77
network installations, 80-81

viewing
client leases and reservations (DHCP server configurations), 340-341
name mappings (WINS), 346
recorded data (log files), 541-542
virtual memory (Performance Monitor), 553-554

virtual DOS machines, 89

virtual LANs (active network components), 154

virtual memory
application server memory usage, 551
viewing (with Performance Monitor), 553-554

viruses (data communication security), 60

Visual InterDev, 724
Site Server 2.0, 48

Visual Studio 97
Web site, 812

VMM (Virtual Memory Manager), 87

Volume Information attribute (NTFS Master File Table), 94

volume sets
mirror standard, creating (RAID 1 mirror sets), 247
recovery (fixed-disk failures), 212
software RAID configurations, 238-239
standard, creating (RAID 1 mirror sets), 244-247

W

WANs (wide area networks)
SMS (Systems Management Server) support, 934
data communication security, 60
see also intranets

warranties (server hardware conformance), 157

WDM (Win32 Driver Model), Windows NT Server 5.0, 52

Web pages, activating
ADO (ActiveX Data Objects), 797-799
ASP (Active Server Pages), 794-797
OLE DB, 797-799

Web Publishing Wizard (Site Server 2.0), 48

Web sites
Aberdeen Group, 29
ADSI, 997
Ascend Communications, 692
BackOffice Licensing Guide, 726
BackOffice Live, 815
BackupExec Version 6.11, 287
Computer Technology Review, 217
content, managing (FrontPage 97), 800-806
Diskeeper for Windows NT, 549
Enterprise Planning Guide, 632
Executive Software, 549
Exploration Air, 749
FrontPage, 38
Get ISDN, 692
Granite Digital, 166
HCL (Hardware Compatibility List), 89, 156, 175
internal security, 59
Internet Deployment Guide, 46
Internet Information Server 2.0, 36
Internet Information Server 4.0 options, 750-751
InterNIC, 322, 324
ISDN Accelerator Pack 1.1, 692

LANalyzer for
Windows, 567
"Managing Windows NT
Domains," 59
Microsoft Free Product
Downloads, 725
Microsoft Index Server, 37
Microsoft Knowledge
Base, 591
Microsoft Proxy Server, 37
Microsoft Service for
NetWare Directory
Services, 360
Microsoft Service
Pack 1, 361
Microsoft Services for
NetWare, 31
Microsoft SiteBuilder
Workshop, 726
Microsoft SiteServer
2.0, 806
Microsoft U.S. Estimated
Price List, 823
Microsoft-HP joint press
release, 933
MSDN subscriptions, 819
Msinfo.exe, 425
Msinfo32.exe, 425
NDIS, 106
Network General's Sniffer
product line, 566
Network Monitor, 567
Network Node
Manager, 71
Network PC Design
Guidelines, 983
Ntcomp.exe, 176
OpenNT, 85
OSR 2, 385
planning, 725-726
Quota Server, 177
QuotaAdvisor, 177
RAB (RAID Advisory
Board), 217
SAMBA, 679
Seagate Software, 287
Service Packs, 208, 843
Site Server 2.0 Enterprise

Edition, 49
SiteBuilder Workshop, 43
SQL Server 6.5, 820, 836
TAPI 2.1 Software
Developer Kit, 41
ThreadMark 2.0, 545
Upsizing Wizard, 853
Visual Studio 97, 812
Windows 95 browsing, 108
Windows 95 Service
Pack 1, 639
Windows Hardware
Quality Labs, 258
Windows NT Resource
Center, 591
workgroup browsing
issues, 397
ZAK (Zero Administration
Kit), 388
ZAW, 388

**weekly backups with daily
differentials (rotation
methods), 267**

**weekly backups with daily
incrementals (rotation
methods), 269**

**wide-area transactions,
979-980**

**WIN.INI (Windows 3.1
configuration file), 292**

Win32 Driver Model, 52

**windows (SMS
Administrator)**
Alerts, 954
Events, 954
Jobs, 950
Machine Groups, 954
Packages, 948-949
Program Groups, 954
Queries, 951-953
Site Groups, 954
Sites, 945-947

Windows 3.1
clients, 400-418
configuration file
changes, 406-408,
414-415

creating installation
disks, 400-402
initialization file
changes, 406-408,
414-415
installing, 402-405
installing 32-bit
TCP/IP, 410-414
MS-DOS network
drivers, 408
troubleshooting,
410, 417-418
Windows NT file and
printer resources,
408-409
Windows NT Server 4.0
resource connections,
416-417
configuration files, 292-293
network protocol
support, 115

Windows 95
browsing (Web site), 108
clients, testing DUN,
704-709
Dfs clients (installing),
991-993
networks, 352-354
client browsing issues,
396-397
configuring clients,
363-366
configuring network
protocols, 366-376
file/printer sharing,
376-379
installing from, 380-386
installing support,
354-363
protocol support,
114-115
remote client
management, 390-396
system policies, 388-391
user profiles, 386-391
Registry differences, 296

RPL (Remote Program Load), client-side server features, 27
Service Pack 1 Web site, 639
universal client configurations, 683
user interface, 21
Windows Explorer (server usability), 21-23
Foldername Properties sheet, 22
Windows for Workgroups 3.11 (universal client configurations), 680-683
Windows for Workgroups 3.1x (network protocol support), 115
Windows Hardware Quality Labs Web site, 258
Windows Internet Name Service, *see* WINS, 328
Windows NT Diagnostics tool (troubleshooting), 32
Windows NT Executive, 86-89
Cache Manager, 88
device drivers, 88
HAL (hardware abstraction layer), 87
IOM (Input/Output Manager), 87
kernel, 87
LPC (Local Procedure Call), 87-89
network drivers, 88
OM (Object Manager), 87-89
PM (Process Manager), 87-89
SRM (Security Reference Monitor), 87-89
VMM (Virtual Memory Manager), 87-89

Windows NT Explorer (file compression features), 507-509
Windows NT My Computer (file compression features), 507-509
Windows NT operating system, 84-90
networking processes, 98-99
NTFS, 90-95
Master File Table, 92-94
recoverability, 94-95
protected subsystem servers, 89-90
RPCs (remote procedure calls), 96-98
Windows NT Executive, 86-89
Cache Manager, 88
device drivers, 88
HAL (hardware abstraction layer), 87
IOM (Input/Output Manager), 87
kernel, 87
LPC (Local Procedure Call), 87-89
network drivers, 88
OM (Object Manager), 87-89
PM (Process Manager), 87-89
SRM (Security Reference Monitor), 87-89
VMM (Virtual Memory Manager), 87-89
Windows NT Resource Center Web site, 591
***Windows NT Resource Kit* (user administration utilities), 480-481**
Windows NT Server 4.0
application server uses, 549-554
CPU usage, 550-551
memory usage, 551-558

clients
adding to domains, 614-615
authenticating, 619
testing DUN, 710-716
domain models, 626-630
Complete Trust, 629
hybrid models, 630
Multiple Master, 628-629
Single Domain, 626
Single Master, 627
installing, 182-206
automating installation, 212-213
backups on existing computer, 181-182
choosing domain controller types, 191
confirming basic system information, 187
creating RAID subsystems, 201
creating setup boot disks, 183-184
detecting mass-storage devices, 186-187
display configurations, 199-202
domain controller installations, 181
emergency repair disks, 191-192, 200-201
fine tuning, 192
fixed-disk configuration data (saving), 205-206
fixed-disk drive setup, 188-189
from existing operating systems, 185
from network servers, 184-185
hardware setup, 175-181
Internet Information Server, installing, 198
master boot record backups, 201-205

names and
identification, 180
naming components,
190
network connections,
192-198
observing the copying
process, 189-190
Pentium floating-point
division bug, 191
recovering from fixed-
disk failures, 210-212
repairing existing
installations, 186,
209-210
restarting the
server, 201
Service Packs, 206-208
setting administrator
passwords, 191
setting time and
date, 198
upgrading from
previous versions, 187
upgrading from
previous Windows
versions, 174-181
user preparation, 206
integrating with Novell
NetWare, 637-668
Directory Service
Manager for
NetWare, 660
Microsoft client server
access, 639-651
Multi-Protocol Routing
service, 666-668
NetWare client server
access, 651-659
integrating with UNIX,
668-679
DNS (Domain Name
Service) Server,
671-677
file sharing, 677-680
IETF RFC support,
669-670
License Manager, 825-831
Control Panel License
tool, 825-827

license packages, 819
Macintosh clients
(accessing resources),
429-435
NetWare migration,
683-685
universal clients, 679-683
Windows for
Workgroups 3.11
configurations, 680
Windows for Workgroups
3.11 (resource
connections), 416-417
**Windows NT Server 4.0
Enterprise Edition,
49-51**
4GT (4G RAM Tuning), 50
Microsoft Routing and
Remote Access
Service, 50
MSCS (Microsoft Cluster
Server), 50
MSMQ (Microsoft
Message Queue
Server), 50
MTS (Microsoft
Transaction Server), 50
**Windows NT Server 5.0,
51-53**
ADSI (Active Directory
Services), 52
Dfs (Distributed File
System), 51
Kerberos 5.0 security, 52
MMC (Microsoft
Management
Console), 52
WDM (Win32 Driver
Model), 52
WSH (Windows Scripting
Host), 52
*Windows NT Server
Resource Kit,* 42
RAS tools, 721
troubleshooting networks,
584-591
Browser Monitor
(Browmon.exe),
585-586

Browser Status
(Browstat.exe),
586-587
Domain Monitor
(Dommon.exe),
587-588
GetMac (Getmac.exe),
589
Net Watch
(Netwatch.exe), 589
NSLookup
(Nslookup.exe), 590
SMBTrace
(Smbtrace.exe), 591
WNTIPcfg (Wntipcfg.exe),
591, *see also* Resource Kit
**Windows NT Terminal
(scalability), 983-984**
**Windows NT Workstation
4.0**
clients, 418-425
attaching to domain
resources, 421-422
installing network
software, 418-421
troubleshooting
connections, 423
ZAK previews, 423-425
*Windows NT Workstation
Resource Kit,* 42
optimization utilities,
554-557
Data Logging Service
files, 555
Performance Counter
Help (Counters.hlp),
556
Performance Data Log
Server (PerfLog), 554
Process Explode
(Pview.exe), 554
Process Viewer
(Pviewer.exe), 554
Response Probe
(Probe.exe), 556, *see
also* Resource Kit
Windows on Win32, 90

Windows Scripting Host, 52

WinHEC (Windows Hardware Engineering Conference), 64

WINPKT (universal client packet driver support), 683

WINS (Windows Internet Name Service)
name resolution (troubleshooting networks), 599-601
protocol, 30
TCP/IP, 328, 342-349, 562
  configuring, 344-350
  integrating DNS, 349
  NetBIOS names (registering/resolving), 342-343
  Windows 95 TCP/IP configurations, 372

wizards
Add User Account Wizard, 463-467
administrative, 23-25
  Add Printer Wizard, 24
  Add User Account Wizard, 23
  Add/Remove Programs Wizard, 25
  Group Management Wizard, 24
  Install New Modem Wizard, 25
  License Wizard, 25
  Network Client Administrator Wizard, 25
  Managing Folder and File Access Wizard, 24, 490-493

WNTIPcfg (Wntipcfg.exe), *Windows NT Server Resource Kit* **utilities, 591**

workgroups
browsing issues Web site, 397

determining needs (network installations), 57-59
servers, 156

workstations
assigned restrictions (user account properties), 460-461
network protocol support, 114

WORM (write once, read many) drives (backups), 278

WOW (Windows on Win32), 90

writable optical drives (backups), 277-278
CD-R (CD-Recordable) drives, 278
magneto-optical drives, 278

write performance
RAID level 1, 222-225
RAID level 5, 226

WSH (Windows Scripting Host), Windows NT Server 5.0, 52

WWW (World Wide Web), Internet Information Server 4.0, 736-738

X-Z

X.400 Connector (Exchange Server 5.0), 872

XDR (External Data Representation), 104

Xerox Network System, 111

XNS (Xerox Network System), 111

ZAK (Zero Administration Kit), 26
previewing (Windows NT Workstation 4.0 client connections), 423-425
Web site, 388

ZAW Web site, 388

Zero Administration Kit, *see* **ZAK**

Zero Administration Windows (scalability), 983

zones, creating (DNS UNIX integration), 673-674

Check out Que® Books on the World Wide Web
http://www.quecorp.com

As the biggest software release in computer history, Windows 95 continues to redefine the computer industry. Click here for the latest info on our Windows 95 books

Make computing quick and easy with these products designed exclusively for new and casual users

Examine the latest releases in word processing, spreadsheets, operating systems, and suites

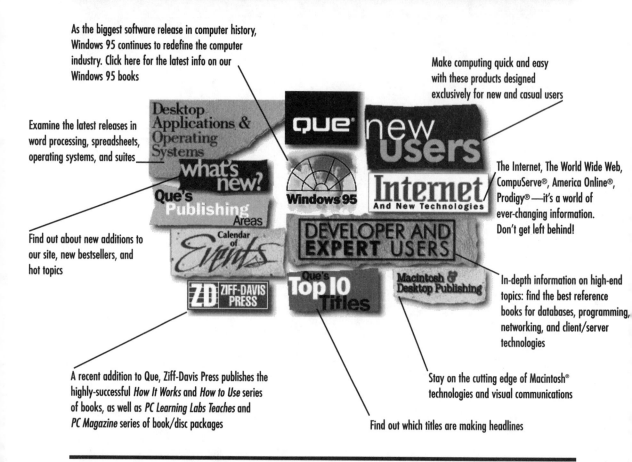

The Internet, The World Wide Web, CompuServe®, America Online®, Prodigy®—it's a world of ever-changing information. Don't get left behind!

Find out about new additions to our site, new bestsellers, and hot topics

In-depth information on high-end topics: find the best reference books for databases, programming, networking, and client/server technologies

A recent addition to Que, Ziff-Davis Press publishes the highly-successful *How It Works* and *How to Use* series of books, as well as *PC Learning Labs Teaches* and *PC Magazine* series of book/disc packages

Stay on the cutting edge of Macintosh® technologies and visual communications

Find out which titles are making headlines

With 6 separate publishing groups, Que develops products for many specific market segments and areas of computer technology. Explore our Web Site and you'll find information on best-selling titles, newly published titles, upcoming products, authors, and much more.

- Stay informed on the latest industry trends and products available

- Visit our online bookstore for the latest information and editions

- Download software from Que's library of the best shareware and freeware

Complete and Return this Card
for a *FREE* Computer Book Catalog

Thank you for purchasing this book! You have purchased a superior computer book written expressly for your needs. To continue to provide the kind of up-to-date, pertinent coverage you've come to expect from us, we need to hear from you. Please take a minute to complete and return this self-addressed, postage-paid form. In return, we'll send you a free catalog of all our computer books on topics ranging from word processing to programming and the internet.

☐ Mrs. ☐ Ms. ☐ Dr. ☐

me (first) ☐☐☐☐☐☐☐☐☐☐☐☐☐ (M.I.) ☐ (last) ☐☐☐☐☐☐☐☐☐☐☐☐☐☐☐☐☐

dress ☐☐☐☐☐☐☐☐☐☐☐☐☐☐☐☐☐☐☐☐☐☐☐☐☐☐☐☐☐☐

☐☐☐☐☐☐☐☐☐☐☐☐☐☐☐☐☐☐☐☐☐☐☐☐☐☐☐☐☐☐

y ☐☐☐☐☐☐☐☐☐☐☐☐☐☐☐☐☐☐☐ State ☐☐ Zip ☐☐☐☐☐ ☐☐☐☐

one ☐☐☐ ☐☐☐ ☐☐☐☐ Fax ☐☐☐ ☐☐☐ ☐☐☐☐

mpany Name ☐☐☐☐☐☐☐☐☐☐☐☐☐☐☐☐☐☐☐☐☐☐☐☐☐☐☐☐

mail address ☐☐☐☐☐☐☐☐☐☐☐☐☐☐☐☐☐☐☐☐☐☐☐☐☐☐☐☐

Please check at least (3) influencing factors for purchasing this book.

nt or back cover information on book .... ☐
ecial approach to the content .... ☐
mpleteness of content .... ☐
thor's reputation .... ☐
blisher's reputation .... ☐
ok cover design or layout .... ☐
lex or table of contents of book .... ☐
ce of book .... ☐
ecial effects, graphics, illustrations .... ☐
er (Please specify): _____ ☐

How did you first learn about this book?

w in Macmillan Computer Publishing catalog .... ☐
commended by store personnel .... ☐
w the book on bookshelf at store .... ☐
commended by a friend .... ☐
ceived advertisement in the mail .... ☐
w an advertisement in: _____ ☐
ad book review in: _____ ☐
er (Please specify): _____ ☐

How many computer books have you purchased in the last six months?

is book only .... ☐   3 to 5 books .... ☐
ooks .... ☐   More than 5 .... ☐

4. Where did you purchase this book?

Bookstore .... ☐
Computer Store .... ☐
Consumer Electronics Store .... ☐
Department Store .... ☐
Office Club .... ☐
Warehouse Club .... ☐
Mail Order .... ☐
Direct from Publisher .... ☐
Internet site .... ☐
Other (Please specify): _____ ☐

5. How long have you been using a computer?

☐ Less than 6 months   ☐ 6 months to a year
☐ 1 to 3 years   ☐ More than 3 years

6. What is your level of experience with personal computers and with the subject of this book?

	With PCs	With subject of book
New	☐	☐
Casual	☐	☐
Accomplished	☐	☐
Expert	☐	☐

Source Code ISBN: 0-7897-1388-8

7. Which of the following best describes your job title?

Administrative Assistant .... ☐
Coordinator .... ☐
Manager/Supervisor .... ☐
Director .... ☐
Vice President .... ☐
President/CEO/COO .... ☐
Lawyer/Doctor/Medical Professional .... ☐
Teacher/Educator/Trainer .... ☐
Engineer/Technician .... ☐
Consultant .... ☐
Not employed/Student/Retired .... ☐
Other (Please specify): _____ ☐

8. Which of the following best describes the area of the company your job title falls under?

Accounting .... ☐
Engineering .... ☐
Manufacturing .... ☐
Operations .... ☐
Marketing .... ☐
Sales .... ☐
Other (Please specify): _____ ☐

9. What is your age?

Under 20 .... [
21-29 .... [
30-39 .... [
40-49 .... [
50-59 .... [
60-over .... [

10. Are you:

Male .... [
Female .... [

11. Which computer publications do you read regularly? (Please list)

_____
_____
_____
_____
_____
_____
_____
_____
_____
_____

Comments: _____
_____
_____

Fold here and scotch-tape to ma

MACMILLAN CO...

A VIACO...

Technical

Support:

If you need assistance with the information in this book or with a CD/DI...
accompanying the book, please access the Knowledge Base on our Web
site at **http://www.superlibrary.com/general/support**. Our most
Frequently Asked Questions are answered there. If you do not find the
answer to your questions on our Web site, you may contact Macmillan
Technical Support **(317) 581-3833** or e-mail us at **support@mcp.com**.